THE OXFORD EDITION OF THE
WORKS OF JOHN WESLEY

Editor in chief FRANK BAKER

*The Directors of the Oxford Edition of Wesley's Works
gratefully acknowledge the financial support of
John D. Earle of Asheville, North Carolina,
Mrs. and the late Dr. W. M. Elliott of Forest City, North Carolina,
and the late Mr. and Mrs. Oscar J. Mooneyham of Forest City, North Carolina
in the preparation of this volume*

THE WORKS OF
JOHN WESLEY

VOLUME 25

═══

LETTERS
I
1721–1739

EDITED BY

FRANK BAKER

Professor of English Church History
Duke University
Durham, North Carolina

CLARENDON PRESS   OXFORD

1980

Oxford University Press, Walton Street, Oxford OX2 6DP

OXFORD LONDON GLASGOW
NEW YORK TORONTO MELBOURNE WELLINGTON
KUALA LUMPUR SINGAPORE HONG KONG TOKYO
DELHI BOMBAY CALCUTTA MADRAS KARACHI
NAIROBI DAR ES SALAAM CAPE TOWN

Published in the United States by
Oxford University Press, New York

© *Oxford University Press 1980*

British Library Cataloguing in Publication Data
Wesley, John
    The works of John Wesley
    Vol. 25: Letters I, 1721–1739. – (The Oxford edition
    of the works of John Wesley)
    1. Methodist Church – Doctrinal and controversial
    works
    I. Baker, Frank, b. 1910   II. Series
    230′.7   BX8331.2   78-40741

ISBN 978-0-687-46216-2

The monogram used on the case and half-title is
adapted by Richard P. Heitzenrater from one of
John Wesley's personal seals

Printed in the United States of America

THE OXFORD EDITION OF
WESLEY'S WORKS

THIS edition of the works of John Wesley reflects the quickened interest in the heritage of Christian thought that has characterized both ecumenical churchmanship and dominant theological perspectives during the last half-century. A fully critical presentation of Wesley's writings had long been a desideratum in order to furnish documentary sources illustrating his contribution to both catholic and evangelical Christianity.

Several scholars, notably Professor Albert C. Outler, Professor Franz Hildebrandt, Dean Merrimon Cuninggim, and Dean Robert E. Cushman, discussed the possibility of such an edition. Under the leadership of Dean Cushman, a Board of Directors was formed in 1960 comprising the deans of four sponsoring theological schools of Methodist-related universities in the United States—Drew, Duke, Emory, and Southern Methodist. They appointed an Editorial Committee to formulate plans, and enlisted an international and interdenominational team of scholars for the 'Wesley Works Editorial Project'. The Delegates of the Oxford University Press agreed to undertake publication.

The works were divided into units of cognate material, with a separate editor (or joint editors) responsible for each unit. Dr. Frank Baker was appointed textual editor for the whole project, with responsibility for supplying each unit editor with a collated critical text for his consideration and use. The text seeks to represent Wesley's thought in its fullest and most deliberate expression, in so far as this can be determined from the available evidence. Substantive variant readings in any British edition published during Wesley's lifetime are shown in appendices to the units, preceded by a summary of the problems faced and the solutions reached in the complex task of securing and presenting Wesley's text. The aim throughout is to enable Wesley to be read with maximum ease and understanding, and with minimal intrusion by the editors.

It was decided that the edition should include all Wesley's original or mainly original prose works, together with one volume devoted to his *Collection of Hymns for the use of the People called*

Methodists, and another to his extensive work as editor and publisher of extracts from the writings of others. An essential feature of the project is a bibliography outlining the historical settings of over 450 items published by Wesley and his brother Charles, sometimes jointly, sometimes separately. The bibliography also offers full analytical data for identifying each of the 2,000 editions of these 450 items which were published during the lifetime of John Wesley, and notes the location of copies. An index is supplied for each unit, and a general index for the whole edition.

Dean Robert E. Cushman of Duke University undertook general administration and promotion of the project until 1971, when he was succeeded in the chairmanship by Dean Joseph D. Quillian, Jr., of Southern Methodist University, these two universities having furnished the major support and guidance for the enterprise. During the decade 1961–70 literery planning was undertaken by the Editorial Committee, chaired by Dean Quillian. International conferences were convened in 1966 and 1970, bringing together all available unit editors with the committee, who thus completed their task of achieving a common mind upon editorial principles and procedure. Throughout this decade Dr. Eric W. Baker of London, England, serving as a General Editor along with Dean William R. Cannon and Dean Cushman, assisted the Directors in British negotiations, as well as at the conferences. In 1969 the Directors appointed Dr. Frank Baker, early attached to the project as biliographer, and later as textual editor, as their Editor-in-Chief also. In 1971 they appointed a new Editorial Board to assist him in co-ordinating the preparation of the various units for publication.

Other sponsoring bodies were successively added to the original four: The United Methodist Board of Higher Education and Ministry, The Commission on Archives and History of The United Methodist Church, and Boston University School of Theology. For the continuing support of the sponsoring institutions the Directors express their profound thanks. They gratefully acknowledge also the encouragemant and financial support that have come from the Historical Societies and Commission on Archives and History of many Annual Conferences, as well as the patronage of The World Methodist Council, The British Methodist Church, private individuals, and foundations.

On June 9, 1976, The Wesley Works Editorial Project was incorporated in the State of North Carolina, U.S.A., as a non-profit corporation. In 1977 by-laws were approved governing the appointment and duties of the Directors, their Officers, and their Executive Committee.

THE BOARD OF DIRECTORS

The Board of Directors

President: Joseph D. Quillian, Jr., Dean of Perkins School of Theology, Southern Methodist University, Dallas, Texas

Vice-President: Robert E. Cushman, The Divinity School, Duke University, Durham, North Carolina

Secretary: Gerald O. McCulloh, Nashville, Tennessee

Treasurer: Thomas A. Langford, Dean of The Divinity School, Duke University, Durham, North Carolina

Editor-in-Chief: Frank Baker, The Divinity School, Duke University, Durham, North Carolina

Assistant Editor-in-Chief: Richard P. Heitzenrater, Perkins School of Theology, Southern Methodist University, Dallas, Texas

William R. Cannon, Bishop of The United Methodist Church, Atlanta, Georgia

Rupert E. Davies, Warden of John Wesley's Chapel, Bristol, England

Joe Hale, General Secretary of the World Methodist Council, Lake Junaluska, North Carolina

James E. Kirby, Jr., Dean of The Theological School of Drew University, Madison, New Jersey

Dwight E. Loder, Bishop of The United Methodist Church, Columbus, Ohio

Richard Nesmith, Dean of Boston University School of Theology, Boston, Massachusetts

John H. Ness, Jr., Executive Secretary of The Commission on Archives and History of The United Methodist Church, Lake Junaluska, North Carolina

Elizabeth Perkins Prothro, Wichita Falls, Texas

Donald H. Treese, Associate General Secretary of the Division of the Ordained Ministry, The United Methodist Board of Higher Education and Ministry, Nashville, Tennessee

Jim L. Waits, Dean of Candler School of Theology, Emory University, Atlanta, Georgia

PREFACE AND ACKNOWLEDGEMENTS

ALTHOUGH many of the letters of John Wesley are of value as literature, especially as crisp statements of his views or desires, with little attempt at embellishment, their major importance is as a revelation of him as a man, and of the people and events of his day, especially those linked with the Methodist movement. They furnish us, in fact, with a portrait through seventy years both more revealing in detail and fuller in coverage than any other source. Together with the diary (which gives the factual background) they offer many intimate glimpses of the man during his early years which are available nowhere else: of his strong family ties, of his leaning upon his mother for theological and spiritual as well as moral guidance, of his bedazzlement by Mary Pendarves (later Mrs. Delany), of the noble experiment of the Holy Club at Oxford, of the struggle between spiritual ideals and worldly reality during his brief ministry in Georgia, and of the birth of the Methodist societies in London and Bristol. All these are covered in this first volume of seven.

Because this important formative period of his life is comparatively little known, much fuller use has been made in this volume than in later volumes of the letters which he received—about 240 in each category, some given fully, some by extracts, quotations, or summaries. Most are presented from contemporary holographs, and most of the in-letters here given fully appear thus for the first time.

An appendix to each volume will list Wesley's total known correspondence for the period covered, incorporating clues to letters which have disappeared, the location of the texts of many in-letters not included in the volume, and brief extracts and abstracts of many of Wesley's letters otherwise unknown. The appendix to this volume lists some 2,150 letters, furnishing quotations from many not inserted in the main text. More than one-third of Wesley's out-letters printed in the combined main text and appendix are not to be found in Telford's edition of Wesley's letters.

A lengthy introduction describes the British postal system of Wesley's day, his own techniques and idiosyncrasies in letter-writing, and the magnitude, variety, and importance of his correspondence. Footnotes identify his correspondents, trace his quotations from many sources, and elucidate the more important or puzzling allusions for his out-letters, though not his in-letters. At the end of each letter the source is noted, as well as details about the address, seal, postmarks, postal inscriptions, and endorsements.

My major indebtedness is to the many librarians and individual owners of holographs who have made it possible for me to secure xeroxes of literally thousands of letters—though hundreds are still untraced to their owners, whose co-operation is earnestly sought, so that future volumes may contain even larger percentages of 'new' letters and more authentic texts of others. Easily the greatest collection in the world is that in the Methodist Archives, formerly in London, now in The John Rylands University Library of Manchester; upon this collection I have been privileged to work for over thirty years under many different administrators, and my debt is especially great to the Revd. Drs. Frank H. Cumbers and John C. Bowmer and their assistants. In this first volume the more important additional collections represented are those in the following centres: in Bristol, Wesley College; in London, Lambeth Palace, the Moravian Archives, the P.R.O., the S.P.C.K., the S.P.G., and Wesley's Chapel; in Oxford, Lincoln College; in Melbourne, Australia, the Public Library, and Queen's College; in Herrnhut, DDR, the Archiv der Brüder-Unität; in the U.S.A., The University of Georgia, Athens, Georgia, Garrett-Evangelical Theological Seminary, Evanston, Illinois, and Drew University, Madison, New Jersey. To the officers of these institutions, and to other individuals and institutions named in the sources and footnotes, I am deeply grateful.

That I have been able to spend so much time in research and writing is largely owing to the understanding and enthusiasm of successive Deans of Duke Divinity School, Professors Robert E. Cushman and Thomas A. Langford. I am grateful to Professor Albert C. Outler and his fellow-workers Wanda Smith and Kate Warnick for sharing the fruits of their researches in identifying many of Wesley's quotations. My wife Nellie and my daughters Margaret and Enid have undertaken many chores to build up lists and indexes invaluable not only for studying Wesley's letters but his other writings. To the magnificent holdings of the Duke University Library, to the University Librarian, Mrs. Connie R. Dunlap, to the Divinity School Librarian, Professor Donn Michael Farris, and to their wonderfully co-operative staff, I am constantly indebted.

In the preparation of this particular volume my thanks go to many. For their warm encouragement in reading the introduction to this unit, and for making perceptive suggestions, to the official reader appointed by the Press, Dr. John Walsh of Jesus College, Oxford, and my colleagues at Duke, Professors Benjamin Boyce, Robert E. Cushman, and McMurry S. Richey—to the latter also for exercising an eagle eye and literary judgment in perusing the text of the complete volume. I am especially grateful to Professor Richard P. Heitzenrater, who not only read the text, but gave me the invaluable assistance of his masterly knowledge of Wesley's early diaries, and who (together with another helpful colleague, Dr. Oliver A. Beckerlegge) has alone joined me in achieving some familiarity with Byrom's shorthand, used by Wesley. Other friends and colleagues have helped greatly in the areas of their own special competence: Professors William F. Stinespring (Hebrew), William H. Willis (Greek), Francis Newton (Latin), Charles R. Young (Medieval Studies), Mrs. Ruth S. Phelps (German), and the Revd. B. Maurice Ritchie (Tauler). To the staff of the Oxford University Press I am grateful for friendly guidance along the thorny paths of publication.

F.B.

CONTENTS

Signs, Special Usages, Abbreviations   xv

Some Major Events in John Wesley's Life   xxi

INTRODUCTION

I.   Wesley as seen in his Letters   1

II.   An Age of Correspondence   11

III. Wesley as a Correspondent   28

IV.   The Anatomy of a Letter   45

V.   Wesley's Correspondents and Correspondence   79

VI.   On Editing Wesley's Letters   107

VII. The Letters as Literature   129

LETTERS FROM AND TO JOHN WESLEY
1721–1739   141

Appendix: Wesley's Correspondence   705

Index of Wesley's Correspondents   761

ILLUSTRATIONS

1.   John Wesley to Joseph Benson (Jan. 8, 1774)   58–9

2.   The Folding of Wesley's Letters (Nov. 29, 1775)   68–9

3.   Redirection (May 14, 1768)   77

SIGNS, SPECIAL USAGES
ABBREVIATIONS

[ ]   Entries within square brackets indicate editorial insertions or substitutions in the original text, or (with a query) doubtful readings.

⟨ ⟩   Entries within angle brackets indicate conjectural readings where the original text is defective.

. . .   Three points are used to indicate a passage omitted by the writer from the original, for which Wesley generally used a dash.

[. . .]   Three points within square brackets indicate a passage omitted from the original text by the present editor. (N.B. The distinguishing brackets are not used in the introduction, footnotes, appendix, etc.)

[[ ]]   Entries within double brackets are supplied by the editor from shorthand or cipher, from an abstract or similar document in the third person, or reconstructed from secondary evidence.

(( ))   Entries within double parentheses have been struck through for erasure.

/   A solidus or slant line indicates the division between two lines of text.

^{a}, ^{b}, ^{c},   Small superscript letters indicate footnotes supplied by Wesley.

^{1}, ^{2}, ^{3} Small superscript figures indicate footnotes supplied by the editor.

Cf.   'Cf.' before a scriptural or other citation indicates that Wesley was quoting with more than minimal inexactness, yet nevertheless displaying the passage as a quotation.

See   'See' indicates an undoubted allusion, or a quotation which was not displayed as such by Wesley, and which is more than minimally inexact.

Wesley's publications. Where a work by Wesley was first published separately its title is italicized; where it first appeared within a different work such as a collected volume the title is given within quotation marks. References such as '*Bibliog*, No. 3' are to the forthcoming Bibliography in this edition, which has a different numbering system from Richard Green's *Wesley Bibliography*, although cross-references in the new bibliography are given to Green's numbers.

Book-titles in Wesley's text are italicized if accurate, given with roman capitals (following Wesley's normal usage) if inaccurate, and if comprising only one generic word (such as 'Sermons' for a volume entitled *Discourses*) are given in lower case unless that word forms a major part of the original title, when it is italicized.

Abbreviations. The following are used in addition to many common and obvious ones such as c[irca], cont[inued], ed[itio]n, espec[ially], intro[duction], MS[S], n[ote], orig[inal], para[graph], st[anza].

A.M.	Wesley, *Arminian Magazine* (1778–97), cont. as *M[ethodist] M[agazine]* (1798–1821), and *W[esleyan M[ethodist] M[agazine]* (1822–1913).
A.M. Supp, 1797	*A Collection of Letters on Religious Subjects, from various ministers and others, to the Rev. John Wesley. Being a Supplement to the Methodist Magazine*, London, Whitfield, 1797.
Asp	John Wesley's transcript of selections from his correspondence with Mrs. Pendarves, 1730–4 (in MA).
Atmore	Atmore, Charles, *The Methodist Memorial; being an Impartial Sketch of the Lives and Characters of the Preachers*, Bristol, Edwards, 1801.
A.V.	Authorized Version of the Bible, 1611 ('King James Version').
B.C.P.	The Book of Common Prayer, London, 1662.
Benham	Benham, Daniel, *Memoirs of James Hutton*, London, Hamilton, Adams, 1856.
Benson	Benson, Joseph (ed.), *The Works of the Rev. John Wesley*, 17 vols., London, Conference Office, Jones, Cordeux, 1809–13, espec. Vol. 16, comprising Wesley's letters.
Bibliog	Bibliography of the publications of John and Charles Wesley, in preparation by Frank Baker to form Vols. 32–3 of this edition.
BL	The British Library, London (formerly British Museum).
Bristol Wesley	Wesley College, Bristol, England (manuscript collections).
Clarke	Clarke, Adam, *Memoirs of the Wesley Family*, 4th edn., revised, corrected, and considerably enlarged, 2 vols., London, Tegg, 1860.
Coulter & Saye	Coulter, E. Merton, and Albert B. Saye, eds., *A List of the Early Settlers of Georgia*, Athens, University of Georgia Press, 1949.
Curnock	Curnock, Nehemiah (ed.), *The Journal of the Rev. John Wesley. A.M., . . . enlarged from Original Manuscripts*, 8 vols., London, Epworth Press, 1938.
CWJ	Wesley, Charles, *Journal*, ed. Thomas Jackson, 2 vols., London, Wesleyan Methodist Book Room, n.d.
Delany	Llanover, Lady (ed.), *The Autobiography and Correspondence of Mary Granville, Mrs. Delany*, 6 vols., London, Bentley, 1861–2.
D.N.B.	*The Dictionary of National Biography*, ed. Sir Leslie Stephen and Sir Sidney Lee, 22 vols., Oxford, Oxford University Press, 1921–2.
Drew	Drew University, Madison, New Jersey, U.S.A.
Duke	Duke University, Durham, North Carolina, U.S.A.
Egmont *Diary*	Egmont, Earl of, *Diary of Viscount Percival, afterwards First Earl of Egmont*, 3 vols., London, Historical Manuscripts Commission, 1920–3.

Egmont *Journal*	McPherson, Robert G. (ed.), *The Journal of the Earl of Egmont: abstract of the Trustees' Proceedings for Establishing the Colony of Georgia*, 1732–1738, Athens, Georgia, University of Georgia Press, 1962.
Egmont Papers	Papers of the First Earl of Egmont, University of Georgia, Athens, Georgia, U.S.A.
Emory	Emory University, Atlanta, Georgia, U.S.A.
end	endorsement/endorsed by (only the more important are noted).
Foster	Foster, Joseph, *Alumni Oxonienses*, 8 vols., 1887–91.
Garrett	Garrett-Evangelical Theological Seminary, Evanston, Illinois, U.S.A.
Gent's Mag	*The Gentleman's Magazine*, London, Jeffries, etc., 1731–1907.
Green	Green, V. H. H., *The Young Mr. Wesley*, London, Arnold, 1961.
Hall MS	Fragment of MS in hand of JW giving account of his brother-in-law, the Revd. Westley Hall (in MA); cf. Curnock, VIII. 147–52.
Hampson	Hampson, John *Memoirs of the late Rev. John Wesley, A.M.*, 3 vols., Sunderland, Graham, 1791.
Hearne	*Remarks and Collections of Thomas Hearne*, Vols. VIII (1722–5), IX (1725–8), X (1728–31), XI (1731–5), Oxford, Oxford Historical Society, Vols. 50, 65, 67, 72 (1907, 1914, 1915, 1918).
Heitzenrater	Heitzenrater, Richard P., 'John Wesley and the Oxford Methodists, 1725–35', Ph.D. dissertation, Duke University, 1972.
Herrnhut	Archiv der Brüder-Unität, Herrnhut, DDR.
Homilies	*Certain Sermons or Homilies appointed by the King's Majesty* (1547), usually referred to as The Book of Homilies.
Jackson	Jackson, Thomas (ed.), *The Works of the Rev. John Wesley*, 3rd edn., 14 vols., London, Mason, 1829–31.
Jones	Jones, George Fenwick (ed.), *Henry Newman's Salzburger Letterbooks*, Athens, Georgia, University of Georgia Press, 1966.
JWJ	John Wesley, *Journal*, ed. by W. Reginald Ward to form Vols. 18–24 of this edition; cf. Curnock.
Kempis	*De Imitatio Christi*, published by John Wesley as *The Christian's Pattern*, London, Rivington, 1735 (*Bibliog*, No. 4).
Law, *Serious Call*	Law, William, *A Serious Call to a Devout and Holy Life* (1728), 5th edn., London, Innys, 1750.
Lawton	Lawton, George, research files of Wesley's usage of words, lying behind his volume, *John Wesley's English* (London,

Allen & Unwin, 1962) and his articles on Wesley's use of slang and proverbs in W.H.S., kindly made available to the editor.

LB A letter-book into which Wesley transcribed copies of letters from his family, 1724–9 (in MA).

Loeb The Loeb Classical Library, London, Heinemann; Cambridge, Massachusetts, Harvard University Press.

Lond Mag *The London Magazine: or Gentleman's Monthly Intelligencer*, London, Ackers, etc., 1732–85.

MA Methodist Archives, The John Rylands University Library of Manchester.

M.M. *Methodist Magazine* (1798–1821), continuing *A.M.*

Moore Moore, Henry, *Life of the Rev. John Wesley*, London, Kershaw, 2 vols., 1824–5.

MorA The Moravian Archives, Muswell Hill, London.

Morgan MSS Wesley's correspondence with Richard Morgan, 1732–4, transcribed by Charles Wesley (at Drew).

Musgrave Musgrave, Sir William, *Obituary prior to 1800*, Vols. 44–9 of the *Publications* of the Harleian Society, 1899–1901.

O.E.D. *The Oxford English Dictionary upon Historical Principles*, Oxford, Clarendon Press, 1933.

Poet. Wks. John and Charles Wesley, *The Poetical Works*, 13 vols., ed. G. Osborn, Wesleyan-Methodist Conference Office, 1868–72.

Priestley Priestley, Joseph, *Original Letters by the Rev. John Wesley and his Friends*, Birmingham, Pearson, 1791.

P.R.O. The Public Record Office, London.

Sel John Wesley's transcript of selections from his correspondence with Ann Granville, 1730–1 (in MA).

Simmonds list a passenger list for the ship *Simmonds* on which Wesley sailed to Georgia, 1735–6 (at Bristol Wesley); imperfect transcript in Clarke II. 175–7.

S.M.U. Perkins School of Theology, Southern Methodist University, Dallas, Texas, U.S.A.

S.P.C.K. The Society for Promoting Christian Knowledge, London: Archives, espec. 'Henry Newman's Miscellaneous Letters', 'Abstracts of Letters Received and Read to the Society', and 'Minutes'.

S.P.G. The Society for the Propagation of the Gospel, London: Archives.

State Papers: Col *Calendar of State Papers: Colonial Series, America and West Indies*, XLII (1735–6), XLIII (1737), XLIV (1738), London, Her Majesty's Stationery Office, 1953, 1963, 1969.

Stev George J. Stevenson, *Memorials of the Wesley Family*, London, Partridge, [1876].

Taylor, *Works*   Taylor, Jeremy, *Works*, ed. Reginald Heber, revised Charles Page Eden, 10 vols., London, Longman, etc., New Edn., 1862, espec. Vol. III, *The Rule and Exercises of Holy Living and Dying.*

Telford   Telford, John (ed.), *The Letters of the Rev. John Wesley*, 8 vols., London, Epworth Press, 1931.

Tyerm (*JW*)   Tyerman, Luke, *The Life and Times of John Wesley*, London, Hodder and Stoughton, 3 vols., 1870–1.

Tyerm (*OM*)   Tyerman, Luke, *The Oxford Methodists*, London, Hodder and Stoughton, 1873.

Tyerm (*SW*)   Tyerman, Luke, *The Life and Times of the Rev. Samuel Wesley*, London, Simpkin, Marshall, 1866.

Tyerm (*Wd*)   Tyerman, Luke, *The Life of the Rev. George Whitefield*, 2 vols., 2nd edn., London, Hodder and Stoughton, 1890.

V.C.H.   The Victoria History of the Counties of England (in progress).

Venn   Venn, John and J. A., *Alumni Cantabrigienses*, 10 vols., 1922–54.

Weis   Weis, Frederick Lewis, *The Colonial Clergy of Maryland, Delaware, and Georgia*, Lancaster, Mass., 1950; cf. similar vols. on New England (1936), the Middle and Southern Colonies (1938), Virginia, North Carolina, and South Carolina (1955).

Wes Ch   Wesley's Chapel, City Road, London.

Wesley, *Works*   Wesley, John, *Works*, 32 vols., Bristol, Pine, 1771–4.

Whitefield, *Journals*   Whitefield, George, *Journals*, London, Banner of Truth Trust, 1960.

Whitefield, *Works*   Whitefield, George, *Works*, 7 vols., London, Dilly, 1771–2.

Whitehead   Whitehead, John, *The Life of the Rev. John Wesley*, 2 vols., London, Couchman, 1793–6.

W.H.S.   *The Proceedings of the Wesley Historical Society*, Burnley and London, 1898–.

W.H.S. Pub.   Occasional publications of the W.H.S.

W.M.C.   The World Methodist Council, Lake Junaluska, North Carolina, U.S.A.

W.M.M.   *Wesleyan Methodist Magazine* (1822–1913), continuing A.M. and *M.M.*

(Cf. also the abbreviations used in the Appendix only, pp. 705–60 below.)

Postmarks.   See especially 'B/ris/tol', described p. 612.

Seals.   The numbers within parentheses after the occasional descriptions refer to the forthcoming table of seals in Vol. 31.

SOME MAJOR EVENTS IN
JOHN WESLEY'S LIFE

1703 June 17 born at Epworth, fifteenth child of Samuel and Susanna Wesley

1709 Feb. 9 saved from the burning rectory at Epworth

1711 May 12 nominated for Charterhouse School by the Duke of Buckingham

1714 Jan. 28 entered the Charterhouse, London, as a gown-boy

1720 June 24 entered Christ Church, Oxford

1724 Summer? graduated B.A.

1725 Apr. 5 began to keep a diary

1725 Sept. 19 ordained deacon by Dr. John Potter, Bishop of Oxford

1726 Mar. 17 elected fellow of Lincoln College, Oxford

1727 Feb. 14 graduated M.A.

1728 Sept. 22 ordained priest by Dr. Potter

1729 Nov. 22 returned from serving as his father's curate to become a resident tutor at Lincoln College

1735 Apr. 5 the Revd. Samuel Wesley, Sen., died at Epworth, aged 72

1735 Oct. 14 embarked for Georgia; first entry in first published *Journal* extract

1736 Feb. 6 first set foot on American soil

1737 Apr. 18 corrected proofs for *A Collection of Psalms and Hymns*, Charleston, South Carolina

1737 Dec. 22–Feb.1, 1738, returned to England

1738 May 1 with Peter Böhler formed Fetter Lane Society, London

1738 May 24 felt his heart 'strangely warmed'

1738 June 13–Sept. 16, visited the Moravians at Herrnhut

1739 Apr. 2 following Whitefield's example, began field-preaching in Bristol

1739 June 3 preached in the shell of the New Room, Bristol

1739 Nov. 6 the Revd. Samuel Wesley, Jun., died, aged 49

1739 Nov. 11 preached in the ruins of the Foundery, London

1742 Feb. 15 first 'classes' established in Bristol

1742 July 30 Mrs. Susanna Wesley died at the Foundery, London, aged 73

1743 Feb. 23 wrote *The Nature, Design, and General Rules of the United Societies*

1743 May 29 conducted first Methodist communion service in leased West Street Chapel, London

1744   June 25–30 held first Methodist Conference in London
1746   Nov. 6   published first volume of *Sermons on Several Occasions*
1747   Aug. 9–27 paid first visit to Ireland
1748   June 24   opened new Kingswood School
1751   Feb. 17 or 18 married Mary Vazeille, a widow
1756   May 14   published *Explanatory Notes upon the New Testament* ('1755')
1769   Aug.4   sent two itinerant Methodist preachers to serve in America
1778   Jan.   began his monthly *Arminian Magazine*
1778   Nov. 1   opened the New Chapel in City Road, London
1780   May 1   published *A Collection of Hymns for the Use of the People called Methodists*
1781   Oct. 8   Mrs. John Wesley died, aged 71
1784   Feb. 28   executed a deed poll legally incorporating the Methodist Conference
1784   Sept. 1–2 ordained preachers for the United States of America
1784   Sept. 9   wrote preface to *The Sunday Service of the Methodists in North America*
1788   Mar. 29   the Revd. Charles Wesley died, aged 79
1791   Feb. 24   made the last entry in his diary
1791   Mar. 2   the Revd. John Wesley died in his home, London, aged 87, and was buried Mar. 9

INTRODUCTION

I. WESLEY AS SEEN IN HIS LETTERS

JOHN WESLEY'S life is documented as fully as that of any man of his age, perhaps of any age. For a full thirteen years of his young manhood and for his last decade we possess a diary which covers not only the events of almost every day, but of almost every hour. For the forty intervening years, and overlapping at both ends, we can turn to a published journal of his activities. In manuscript we have commonplace books, memoranda on various subjects and events, financial accounts. We have four hundred works which he published. These documents tell us in detail what Wesley did for most of his eighty-seven years, and what he thought. Strangely enough, however, only rarely do they reveal what he felt. Contrary to popular belief, John Wesley did not wear his heart—even his warmed heart —on his sleeve. He was never effusive, never given to ecstatic writing—a reticent, private man compelled by inner impulses to occupy the centre of the stage in what he was convinced was a divinely directed drama. True, his emotions frequently surfaced in his writings as his spiritual energies were directed at some national shame, some piercing human need, but very rarely in recording events in his personal life. Only in his diary for a few years from 1734 do we find a code of symbols denoting how he actually *felt* each hour,[1] though a vestige of this was continued throughout his life in the exclamation mark singling our incidents in his diary (or letters selected for preservation) which had proved greatly moving. The careful reader of his *Journals* is able to read between the lines and discover the private behind the public John Wesley. The fullest personal revelation, however, undoubtedly comes in his letters. Here he expresses emotion more frequently and more fully. Here only can we meet the John Wesley known personally to his friends and followers, when he was writing to and for one person alone, whom instinctively he visualized, and to whom he wrote, as it were, face to face. His letters form the proving-ground for all the theories about him which we derive from his published writings, the source of many new insights. In this introduction we are able to touch on

[1] Heitzenrater, pp. 252-7.

only a few of the aspects of the John Wesley who is revealed by his letters.

Even from the outset Wesley's letters reveal him as a probing, logic-chopping thinker. In correspondence with his mother in his early formative years he almost instinctively developed a theological position which formed part of the core of his later teaching:

> What then shall I say of predestination? An everlasting purpose of God to deliver some from damnation does, I suppose, exclude all from that deliverance who are not chosen . . . How is this consistent with either the divine justice or mercy? . . . Is it merciful to ordain a creature to everlasting misery? Is it just to punish man for crimes which he could not but commit?[1]

As he matured, doctrinal definitions and expositions appeared frequently in his letters, to preachers, laymen, and women alike, sometimes in language echoing what he had already proclaimed in sermon or treatise, often fresh-minted and crisp:

> By perfection I mean the humble, gentle, patient love of God and man ruling all the tempers, words, and actions, the whole heart and the whole life. I do not include an impossibility of falling from it, either in part or in whole.[2]

> Nothing is sin, strictly speaking, but a voluntary transgression of a known law of God. Therefore every voluntary breach of the law of love is sin—and nothing else, if we speak properly.[3]

> The plerophory (or full assurance) of faith is such a divine testimony that we are reconciled to God as excludes all doubt and fear concerning it. This refers only to what is present. The plerophory (or full assurance) of hope is a divine testimony that we shall endure to the end; or, more directly, that we shall enjoy God in glory. This is by no means essential to, or inseparable from, perfect love.[4]

We see him as a perfectionist, of course, not only in his frequently-repeated exhortation, 'Go on to perfection', but in his careful attention to the administrative details of the Methodist societies.[5] It was largely this which led to his irascibility with inefficient subordinates, which in turn led them occasionally to complain about his autocracy. 'All our preachers', he maintained, 'should be as punctual as the sun, never standing still, or moving out of their course.'[6] 'I hate delay,' he wrote, 'The King's business requires haste!'[7] If preachers did not measure up to his own high standards he did not disguise his impatience: 'I am surprised at what you say of the total neglect of discipline in the Armagh Circuit. Was Thomas

---

[1] July 19, 1725, to his mother.   [2] Jan. 27, 1767, to Charles Wesley.
[3] June 16, 1772, to Mrs. Bennis.   [4] Oct. 6, 1778, to Elizabeth Ritchie.
[5] e.g. his letter to Heath, p. 92 below.
[6] Nov. 2, 1763, to Lady Frances Gardiner.   [7] Sept. 3, 1763.

Halliday dead or asleep? He stands in the *Minutes* as the Assistant.
Has another taken his place?"[1] When a major principle of his
organization was challenged, such as the autonomy of the preachers
in Conference (under his supervision, of course), he dug his heels
in firmly. He told the trustees at Dewsbury, edging towards a
congregational polity: 'The question between us is, "By whom shall
the preachers sent from time to time to Dewsbury be judged?"
You say, "By the trustees." I say, "By their peers, the preachers
met in Conference." You say, "Give this up, and we will receive
them." I say, "I cannot, I dare not, give up this." Therefore, if you
will not receive them on these terms, you renounce connexion with,
Your affectionate brother, J. Wesley.'[2] Allied to this granite efficiency
was a puritanical streak. To Joseph Cownley he wrote: 'The great
hindrance of your spiritual health in time past was, want of seriousness. You used to laugh and cause laughter . . . "Be serious." Let
this be your motto.'[3] Yet an impatient letter could quickly be followed
by an apology, as when he confessed to a preacher: 'I wrote to
Molly Dale on Saturday in haste; but today I have wrote her my
cooler thoughts.'[4]

The truth should be faced, that Wesley (like most of us) was a
bundle of contradictions, though apparently inconsistent beliefs or
behaviour achieved a form of consistency in constituting equally a
following of the will of God as he saw it from moment to moment.
This did not necessarily mean that he was subject to will-o'-the-
wisp whims, but that he had an alert, flexible mind, and was coura-
geous enough, and humble enough, to venture upon experiments,
and then to cast them aside if initial success turned to failure. He
was eager for spiritual advance: 'What a shame it is that we should
so long have neglected the little towns round Dublin, and that we
have not a society within ten miles of it!'[5] He strove to maintain a
balance, however, between the venturesome pioneer and the cautious consolidator: 'I doubt not you will be useful in Dundee Circuit,
provided you, (1), strive to strike out into new places . . . and (2),
constantly visit *all the society* in course from house to house.'[6] And
he warned that pioneering called for patience, not hit-and-run
tactics: 'To preach once in a place and no more very seldom does
much good; it only alarms the devil and his children, and makes

[1] Feb. 25, 1778, to John Bredin.   [2] July 30, 1788.
[3] Sept. 17, 1755.   [4] Feb. 14, 1768.
[5] June 21, 1784, to Arthur Keene.   [6] Oct. 3, 1784.

them more upon their guard against a fresh assault.'[1] Nevertheless, as he told another preacher, 'When no good can be done, I would leave the old, and try new places!'[2] His mind was sufficiently open to admit that some of his teaching had been erroneous. About Christian perfection he wrote to his brother Charles: 'Can one who has attained it, fall? Formerly I thought not; but *you* (with T. Walsh and Jo. Jones) convinced me of my mistake.'[3] Similarly he confessed to Sarah Crosby: 'I am more and more inclined to think that we have been a little mistaken in this matter, that there are none living so established in grace but that they may possibly fall.'[4]

Contrary to popular opinion, it seems clear that Wesley's self-analysis was correct: 'I am very rarely led by impressions, but generally by reason and by Scripture. I see abundantly more than I *feel*.'[5] He was basically an honest inquirer rather than an enthusiast, in spite of his brother Charles's repeated charges of credulity: 'When my brother has told me ten times, "You are credulous," I have asked, "Show me the instances." He could not do it. No, nor any man else. Indeed, jealousy and suspiciousness I defy and abhor as I do hell-fire. But I believe nothing, great or small, without such kind of proof as the nature of the thing allows.'[6] Similarly he wrote to the Revd. Thomas Stedman: 'With regard to the accounts of demoniacs and apparitions which I have occasionally published I observe, I am as certain of the facts as I am of the war between the Turks and Austrians. I do not retail them from books (like honest Richard Baxter), nor take them at third or fourth hand, but have them all either from the testimony of my own eyes and ears, or at first hand from eye- and ear-witnesses.'[7] This was always his approach to the supernatural, as to other strange phenomena. He kept an open mind, neither believing nor disbelieving until the evidence was in, even though he was indeed always eager for fresh instances of the uncanny. An early letter described in detail an account of levitation, and speculated on an appearance of the devil and a haunted house—yet at the same time offered a pedigree authenticating the narrative of the levitation, and affirmed about the haunted house: 'I design to go thither the first opportunity, and see if it be true; which I shall hardly believe till I am an eye- or ear-

[1] Nov. 30, 1786.
[2] Dec. 3, 1780.
[3] Feb. 12, 1767.
[4] Nov. 7, 1784.
[5] Feb. 24, 1786, to Elizabeth Ritchie.
[6] Mar. 20, 1762, to Samuel Furly.
[7] Sept. 1, 1774.

witness of it.'[1] He corresponded with his brother about 'music heard before or at the death of those that die in the Lord', offering the opinion that this was not 'the inward voice of God', but 'rather the effect of an angel affecting the auditory nerve, as an apparition does the optic nerve or retina'.[2] He was deeply interested in the afterlife and in communication with the dead, affirming that since her death he had 'found a wonderful union of spirit with Fanny Cooper', and had 'sometimes suddenly looked on one side or the other side, not knowing whether I should not see her'.[3] This deep interest clothed itself in the words of the scientific observer, with true intellectual curiosity, who nevertheless regarded the Bible as an integral element in the factual evidence:

But what is the essential part of heaven? Undoubtedly it is to see God, to know God, to love God. We shall then know both his nature, and his works of creation, of providence, and of redemption. Even in paradise, in the intermediate state between death and the resurrection, we shall learn more concerning these in an hour than we could in an age during our stay in the body. We cannot tell, indeed, *how* we shall then exist, or what kind of organs we shall have. The soul will not be encumbered with flesh and blood; but probably it will have some sort of ethereal vehicle, even before God clothes us 'with our nobler house Of empyrean light'.[4]

Wesley's eager inquiry into natural and supernatural wonders throughout his life was for him quite deliberately (to use the title borrowed from John Ray for his oft-revised scientific compendium) *A Survey of the Wisdom of God in the Creation*.[5] Like his prayers for weather conducive to his evangelistic enterprise,[6] this was based upon a conviction that God was even now at work in the world: 'It is a great step toward Christian resignation to be throughly convinced of that great truth, that there is no such thing as chance in the world; that fortune is only another name for Providence. Only it is *covered* Providence. An event the cause of which does not *appear* we commonly say "comes by chance". Oh no! It is guided by an unerring hand; it is the result of infinite wisdom and goodness.'[7] He remained eager to discover and describe to his friends examples of God's moving in his mysterious ways—a trait which made Alexander Knox somewhat uncomfortable.[8]

---

[1] Dec. 18, 1724; cf. Sept. 25, 1723.   [2] Oct. 20, 31, 1753.
[3] Feb. 17, 1780; cf. Mar. 3, 1769.   [4] Apr. 17, 1776.
[5] See *Bibliog*, No. 259, and Vol. 17 of this edn.
[6] e.g. Apr. 11, 1785 to Charles Wesley.   [7] Jan. 2, 1781, to Ann Bolton.
[8] Of Wesley's letters Knox wrote: 'In those prompt effusions all Mr. Wesley's peculiarities are in fullest display: his confident conclusions from scanty or fallacious

Because he was thus conscious of living under the shadow of the eternal the humility which Wesley had rigorously pursued during his early years became as natural to him as breathing, and he attempted to analyse himself, his strengths and his weaknesses, with utter honesty. To 'John Smith' he wrote in 1746: 'To this day I have abundantly more temptation to *lukewarmness* than to *impetuosity*, to be a saunterer *inter sylvas academicas* ['in academic glades'], a philosophical *sluggard*, than an itinerant *preacher*. And, in fact, what I now do is so exceedingly little compared with what I am convinced I ought to do, that I am often ashamed before God, and know not how to lift up mine eyes to the height of heaven.' 'Smith' replied that this was 'over-done humility', but Wesley insisted: 'I do not spend *all* my time so profitably as I might, nor all my strength; at least not all I might have if it were not for my own *lukewarmness* and remissness, if I wrestled with God in constant and fervent prayer.'[1] In 1765 he wrote: 'When I was young I was *sure* of everything. In a few years, having been mistaken a thousand times, I was not half so sure of most things as before. At present I am hardly sure of anything but what God has revealed to men.'[2] To be humble for Wesley was to recognize human limitations in the presence of God: 'The knowledge of ourselves is true humility; and without this we cannot be freed from vanity, a desire of praise being inseparably connected with every degree of pride. Continual watchfulness is absolutely necessary to hinder this from stealing in upon us.[3]

Allied with this humility was a childlike simplicity in Wesley's acceptance of life. This was true of his approach to money, as he told his sister Patty: 'Money never stays with *me*. It would burn me if it did. I throw it out of my hands as soon as possible, lest it should find a way into my heart.'[4] He encouraged this guileless behaviour

premises; his unwarrantable value for sudden revolutions of the mind; his proneness to attribute to the Spirit of God what might more reasonably be resolved into natural emotions or illusive impressions. These and suchlike evidences of his intellectual frailty are poured forth without reserve; in strange union, however, with observations on persons and things replete with acuteness and sagacity.' ('Remarks on the Life and Character of John Wesley', in Robert Southey, *Life of Wesley*, New edn. 2 vols., ed. C. C. Southey, London, 1864, II. 295.)

[1] June 25, § 1; Aug. 11, 1746, § 3; Mar. 25, 1747, § 4.
[2] Jan. 4, 1765 (*Lond Mag*, 1765, p. 28).
[3] May 30, 1776, to Miss March.
[4] Oct. 6, 1768. Cf. his letter to Mrs. Charles Wesley, July 25, 1788: 'My wife used to tell me, "My dear, you are too generous. You don't know the value of money." I could not wholly deny the charge.'

in his followers, writing to Hannah Ball: 'I was glad . . . that you was not ashamed to declare what God had done for your soul . . . Even this kind of simplicity, the speaking artlessly, as little children, just what we feel in our hearts, without any reasoning what people will think or say, is of great use to the soul.'[1] For this he commended Ann Bolton: 'You seem not only to retain simplicity of spirit (the great thing), but likewise of sentiment and language.'[2] This was what others saw in his own life, reproduced faithfully in his letters, as Alexander Knox testified: 'He wrote as he spoke. Their unstudied simplicity must give this impression; and I myself, who so often heard him speak, can attest to its justness . . . He . . . literally *talks* upon paper.'[3]

Wesley's letters to many correspondents display a frankness remarkable in a public man, though with others he deliberately sought to hold himself in check, as he admitted to Sarah Crosby: 'I speak of myself very little to anyone, were it only for fear of hurting *them*. I have found exceeding few that could bear it. So I am constrained to repress my natural openness. I find scarce any temptation from any *thing* in the world. My danger is from *persons*.'[4] To Dorothy Furly he wrote: 'I am so immeasurably apt to pour out all my soul into any that loves me.'[5] He tried to describe his mental processes in writing to a correspondent with whom such inhibitions were banished: 'When I speak or write to you, I have *you* before my eyes, but, generally speaking, I do not think of myself at all. I do not think whether I am wise or foolish, knowing or ignorant; but I see *you* aiming at glory and immortality, and say just what I hope may direct your goings in the way, and prevent your being weary or faint in your mind.'[6]

One characteristic which comes through in Wesley's letters as nowhere else is his personal warmth. He loved people. He wrote once to his wife, 'Without a companion in travel I am like a bird without a wing.'[7] In the age of reason words like 'affectionate' and 'love' occur on almost every page of his letters, to men and women

---

[1] Sept. 1, 1773. [2] Aug. 8, 1773. [3] Knox, op. cit., II. 296.
[4] May 11, 1780. [5] Jan. 18, 1761.
[6] July 6, 1770, to Miss March. This approach also he urged upon his correspondents: 'When we write to a friend, to one we can trust, it is good for us to *think aloud*. What would be prudence in conversing with others has no place here. The more openness you use, the more comfort you will find; especially in the case of strong temptations.' (June 15, 1766, to Mrs. Woodhouse. Cf. his words to Eliza Bennis, July 25, 1767: 'You have only to *think aloud*, just to open the window in your breast.')
[7] Apr. 22, 1757.

alike. To Alexander Knox he wrote: 'The longer I know you, the more I love you. I am not soon tired of my friends. My brother laughs at me, and says, "Nay, it signifies nothing to tell you anything; for whomsoever you once love you will love on through thick and thin."'[1] Knox himself realized this, realized also that Wesley was especially drawn to women:

It is certain that Mr. Wesley had a predilection for the female character; partly because he had a mind ever alive to amiability, and partly from his generally finding in females a quicker and fuller responsiveness to his own ideas of interior piety and affectionate devotion. To his female correspondents, therefore, . . . he writes with peculiar effluence of thought and frankness of communication. He in fact unbosoms himself, on every topic which occurs to him, as to kindred spirits, in whose sympathies he confided, and from whose re-communications he hoped for additional light.[2]

For at least one correspondent this warmth was kindled even before he met her. To Ann Loxdale he wrote—and we turn in relief from Knox's turgid 'literary' language: 'I cannot tell that I ever before felt so close an attachment to a person whom I had never seen. Surely it is the will of our gracious Lord that there should be a still closer union between you and, Yours in tender affection, J. Wesley.'[3] John Wesley was indeed built for friendship. Sadly, however, he believed it necessary to wear a mask in public, and thus was frequently misjudged both by his contemporaries and by posterity. He explained his predicament to Sarah Crosby:

'I used to wonder', said one, 'that you was *so little affected*, at things that would make *me* run mad. But now I see it is God's doing. If you *felt* these things as many do, you would be quite incapable of the work to which you are called.' Consider this well. I am called to a peculiar work. And perhaps the very temper and behaviour which you blame is one great means whereby I am capacitated for carrying on that work. I do not 'lessen my authority' . . . over two hundred preachers and twenty thousand men and women by any tenderness of speech or behaviour . . . God exceedingly confirms my authority thereby . . . The wants I feel within are to God and my own soul; and to others only so far as I *choose to tell them.*[4]

Wesley was not the unconcerned manipulator of people whom many thought they discerned, but a man who was suppressing his feelings lest they run away with him, and thus undermine the effectiveness of his mission. All the more did he need at least a few confidants with whom prudence could be cast aside. We cannot recapture his

---

[1] Nov. 18, 1780. [2] Knox, op. cit., II. 295.

[3] Dec. 16, 1781. [4] Sept. 12, 1766.

private conversations with these close friends, but at least we can hear him talking to them in his letters, as when he tried whimsically to encourage a little thaw in Miss March, a pious gentlewoman with whom he had been corresponding for fifteen years: 'Very possibly, if I should live seven years longer, we should be acquainted with each other. I verily think your reserve wears off, though only by an hair's breadth at a time. Quicken your pace . . . Am I not concerned in everything which concerns you?'[1]

And yet . . . We must not swing to the other extreme of envisaging Wesley as the victim of dangerously suppressed emotions, or a person who was in the third heaven one moment and in the depths of despair the next. For most of his life he sailed along calmly on an even keel. He thus analysed himself to one of his confidants: 'I do not remember to have heard or read anything like my own experience. Almost ever since I can remember I have been led in a peculiar way. I go on in an even line, being very little raised at one time or depressed at another.'[2] The marriage of this calm temperament to an acquired belief in special providence issued in the remarkable serenity which suffuses his letters. In a letter written when he was 74 he seemed to ascribe this to his opportunities for solitude (while travelling like a broken-winged bird!), though he certainly knew that there was more to it than that:

> You do not at all understand my manner of life. Though I am always in haste, I am never in a hurry; because I never undertake any more work than I can go through with perfect calmness of spirit. It is true I travel four or five thousand miles in a year. But I generally travel alone in my carriage, and consequently am as retired ten hours in a day as if I was in a wilderness. On other days I never spend less than three hours (frequently ten or twelve) in the day alone. So there are few persons in the kingdom who spend so many hours secluded from all company. Yet I find time to visit the sick and the poor; and I must do it, if I believe the Bible . . . When I was at Oxford, and lived almost like a hermit, I saw not how any busy man could be saved. I scarce thought it possible for a man to retain the Christian spirit amidst the noise and bustle of the world. God taught me better by my own experience. I had ten times more business in America (that is, at intervals) than ever I had in my life. But it was no hindrance to silence of spirit.[3]

This serenity did not arise from ease or seclusion, but from his acceptance of life, and of people, as they were. To Samuel Furly's critical comments he replied: 'Sammy, beware of the impetuosity

---

[1] June 9, 1775.   [2] Feb. 24, 1786, to Elizabeth Ritchie.
[3] Dec. 10, 1777, to Miss March.

of your temper! It may easily lead you awry . . . Don't expect
propriety of speech from uneducated persons. The longer I live, the
larger allowances I make for human infirmities. I exact more from
myself, and less from others. Go thou and do likewise!'[1] To Furly's
sister Dorothy he expounded another of his multifarious rules: 'It is
a rule with me to take nothing ill that is well meant; therefore you
have no need ever to be afraid of my putting an ill construction on
anything you say.'[2]

In his approach to both people and events Wesley was an almost
incurable optimist, reminding Mary Bosanquet, 'You know I am
not much given to suspect the worst. I am more inclined to hope
than fear.'[3] Yet he claimed that this was at least in part caused by
self-discipline rather than temperament, announcing still another
rule: 'My constant rule is to believe everyone honest till I *prove* him
otherwise. But were I to give way to my natural temper I should
believe everyone a knave till I *proved* him honest. And that would
turn me into a man-hater, and make life itself a burden.'[4] Contentment with life as it was came also through trusting in God: 'By the
grace of God I never fret, I repine at nothing, I am discontented at
nothing. And to hear persons at my ear fretting and murmuring at
everything is like tearing the flesh off my bones. I see God sitting
upon his throne and ruling all things well.'[5] Even a few months
before his death he wrote cheerfully of his ailments: 'In August
last my strength failed almost at once, and my sight in great measure
went from me. But all is well: I can still write almost as easily as
ever, and I can read in a clear light. And I think, if I could not
read or write at all, I could still say something for God.'[6]

Throughout his life Wesley's vitality was remarkable, and this
seemed if anything to increase during his last quarter of a century.
To his brother Charles he wrote in 1766: 'I find rather an increase
than a decrease of zeal for the whole work of God, and every part of
it. I am φερόμενος,[7] I know not how, that I can't stand still.'[8] Frequently he compared his health in these later years with that of his
youth: 'It pleases God that my health and strength are just the
same now that they were forty years ago. But there is a difference in
one point: I was then frequently weary, my body sunk under my
work. Whereas now, from one week or month to another, I do not

---

[1] Jan. 25, 1762. [2] Sept. 25, 1757. [3] Jan. 2, 1770.
[4] Nov. 17, 1780. [5] Aug. 31, 1755. [6] June 6, 1790.
[7] 'borne along', like Paul's vessel, Acts 27: 15, 17. [8] June 27, 1766.

know what weariness means.'[1] Not that he was free from ailments, of course, but he observed: 'My disorders are seldom of long continuance; they pass off in a few days, and usually leave me considerably better than I was before.'[2] The pearl (or cataract) which afflicted one eye in 1788 was accepted with wry humour: to Henry Moore he wrote: 'Lately I have been threatened with blindness. But still you and I have two good eyes between us. Let us use them while the day is!'[3] In his eighty-sixth year he realized that old age was at last catching up with him, telling R. C. Brackenbury: 'My body seems to have nearly done its work, and to be almost worn out. Last month my strength was entirely gone, and I could have sat stock still from morning to night. But, blessed be God, I crept about a little and made shift to preach once a day.'[4] He wrote to Freeborn Garrettson in America: 'Time has shaken me by the hand, and death is not far behind.'[5] Yet still he planned ahead, writing to Mrs. Armstrong in Dublin: 'My sight is no worse than it was some months since, and my strength ⟨is cons⟩iderably increased. It is not impossible I may live ⟨till spr⟩ing; and if so, I am likely to see Ireland once more.'[6] In September, 1790, he was perceptibly weaker, but as late as Jan. 6, 1791, he wrote, 'I hope I shall not live to be useless', and one of his last letters, if not the very last, written less than a week before his death, voiced a rousing challenge to William Wilberforce: 'Go on, in the name of God, and in the power of his might, till even American slavery (the vilest that ever saw the sun) shall vanish away before it.'[7]

II. AN AGE OF CORRESPONDENCE

The writing of letters is an ancient art (or craft), not unknown in the Old Testament, and comprising over one-third of the New. That it was an art would doubtless be claimed by Cicero and Pliny, yet the world of scholarship has been immeasurably enriched by the Egyptian business correspondence unearthed at Tel-el-Amarna, making no pretensions to literary excellence. Indeed the craft of true letter-writing implies not only the concealment of art, but its forsaking. Communication by letters is a kind of private conversation

---

[1] Feb. 26, 1786; cf. July 13, 1782; July 23, 1784; Feb. 2, 1785.
[2] Oct. 30, 1782.   [3] Apr. 6, 1788; cf. May 28, 1788.
[4] Sept. 15, 1789.   [5] Feb. 3, 1790.
[6] Aug. 4, 1790.   [7] Feb. 24, 1791.

across the barriers of space and time, demanding that each writer should think of the other, not of a possible public audience. By means of his letter the writer should therefore appear in spiritual image before his reader, warts and all. In this Wesley, as we have seen, succeeded admirably.[1] Even Horace Walpole, in spite of keeping one eye on posterity most of the time, maintained that he had 'no patience with people that don't write just as they talk', letters being 'nothing but extempore conversations on paper'—and the evidence shows that in fact he *did* write as he talked.[2] Any artifice beyond what is common to his conversation when the writer is 'on form', therefore, would push the letter over the hairline that separates this skilled craft from the art of 'epistolary literature'—which, in spite of its ugly name, does have its uses.

The debate continues, however, and neither the definition of a letter given above, nor any other, is assured of universal acceptance. What is certain, however, is that the letter is one of the most enduring literary forms, as well as the most intimate and revealing. For that reason many great literary figures (notably Walpole) live most fully in their letters, whether because of the fascination exerted by the personality thus displayed, because of their disclosure of the social scene and the human elements in the making of history, or simply because they deliberately chose this medium for their most polished literary efforts. Although there is no evidence that either Walpole or John Wesley ever read the volume, their own correspondence aptly illustrates the advice of *The Compleat Letter Writer; or, New and Polite English Secretary:*

> . . . This sort of writing should be like conversation . . . But, though lofty phrases are here improper, the style should not be low and mean; and to avoid it let an easy complaisance, an open sincerity, and unaffected good nature, appear in all you say; for a fine letter does not consist in saying fine things, but in expressing ordinary ones with elegance and propriety, so as to please while it informs, and charm even in giving advice.[3]

The full flowering of letter-writing as a literary form came during Wesley's lifetime, but as a personal means of expression and of communication it had formed the subject of 'How to' handbooks from Elizabethan times. *The Enimie of Idleness* (1568), *A Panoplie of Epistles* (1576), *The English Secretarie* (1586), and *The Merchants*

---

[1] See p. 7 above.
[2] W. S. Lewis, *Selected Letters of Horace Walpole*, New Haven, Yale University Press, 1973, pp. xv–xviii.
[3] *The Complete Letter-Writer*, 3rd edn., London, 1746, p. 46.

Avizo (1589?) were followed by dozens of similar works during the seventeenth and eighteenth centuries.[1] Some of these ran through scores of editions, as did *The Young Secretary's Guide* from 1687 to 1764.[2] Increasingly they developed into collections of sample letters for all occasions, of which the best was Samuel Richardson's *Familiar Letters*, from the preparation of which—and in the same form—developed his first experimental novel, *Pamela* (1740).[3]

The eighteenth century. The largest output of letters during the eighteenth century was probably that of Voltaire (1694–1788), whose published correspondence comprises twenty thousand letters to and from some seventeen hundred correspondents, necessitating almost a hundred volumes, together with nine devoted to appendixes and indexes.[4] The correspondence of England's greatest letter-writer, Horace Walpole (1717–97), is about half as voluminous, with something over four thousand letters to about two hundred correspondents.[5] Walpole is generally acknowledged to be supreme in quality, though some have followed Macaulay in sniping at him (apparently without sufficient cause) for superficiality and lack of true humanity. His letters constitute a fascinating social chronicle of sixty years—anecdotal, gossipy, whimsical, witty, though occasionally unkind. He stands head and shoulders above the rest.

Nevertheless eighteenth-century England produced other giants, though none approaching Walpole's stature: Alexander Pope (1688–1744), who in 1737 published the first collection of literary letters; Lady Mary Wortley Montagu (1689–1762), the 'elegant language' of whose *Letters* (1763) failed to convince Wesley that the Turks were socially and spiritually to be preferred to Christians;[6] Thomas Gray (1716–71), a writer of solid conversational correspondence on a higher intellectual plane than that of Walpole; Philip Dormer Stanhope, Earl of Chesterfield (1694–1773), whose letters to his

[1] K. G. Hornbeak, *The Complete Letter-Writer in English, 1568–1800*, Northampton, Mass., 1934, pp. 128–45.   [2] Ibid., pp. 77–85.

[3] Ibid., pp. 100–16; see Samuel Richardson, *Familiar Letters on Important Occasions*, with an introduction by Brian W. Downs, New York, Dodd, Mead & Company, 1928, pp. ix–xxvi.

[4] Ed. Theodore Besterman, 1953–65; cf. *Editing Eighteenth Century Texts*, ed. D. I. B. Smith, University of Toronto Press, 1968, pp. 7–24.

[5] George Sampson, *Concise Cambridge History of English Literature*, Cambridge University Press, 1941, p. 539; *New Cambridge Bibliography of English Literature*, II. 1591; 39 of the projected 50 volumes had been completed between 1937 and 1974, including some 3,300 letters by Walpole and 6,500 from his correspondents.

[6] Sermon 63, 'The General Spread of the Gospel', § 4.

son (1774) frankly depicted an age in which impeccable manners were more important than virtuous conduct; and William Cowper (1731–1800), with his 'divine chit-chat'. Scores of other names could be added, some of them more recent discoveries, including a number of Wesley's own correspondents, Philip Doddridge (1702–51), Samuel Johnson (1709–84), Mary Delany (1700–88), and Alexander Knox (1751–1831). Nor is it too much to claim that John Wesley himself (1703–91) merits a place among the literary figures of his day, for his letters almost equally with his *Journal*—letters comparable in numbers to those of Walpole, but encompassing a longer period, and written to eight times as many correspondents; letters completely different in tone and style, briefer and pithier, offering not entertainment but improvement, yet with their own interest and charm despite their earnest purpose, perhaps occasionally because of it.

Writing materials. Like most of its literary kind, *The Complete Letter-Writer* gave much attention to style, and not a few hints on grammar, spelling, and even the use of capitals—but said nothing about the physical aspects of letter-writing. In this it has been followed by most literary historians and editors, apparently upon the assumption that the reader will assimilate such antiquarian trivia by osmosis. Unfortunately experience proves that this is not the case: not only booksellers' catalogues, but even the index cards of learned museums and libraries occasionally furnish the information (quite nonsensical when relating to the letters of Wesley or his contemporaries): 'The envelope is missing.' The envelope, of course, was not invented until after Wesley's death, just as many other writing materials which we take for granted are comparatively recent innovations.

Yet the absence from the eighteenth century of commonplace artifacts of the twentieth leaves a void which the imagination is unable to fill unless furnished with the contemporary facts of literary life—as is exemplified by the reference to Wesley's envelopes. It is therefore important to recount (or in the case of some readers to recapitulate) the actual conditions under which these letters were written—not only their personal and social and historical setting, but their background of writing customs and habits and everyday artifacts, especially those which have now been completely replaced. At times this reconstruction of Wesley's background is extremely difficult, especially as scholarly studies, even of the more ancient artifacts connected with letter-writing, such as paper, and seals, have concentrated upon the centuries before his. Nor is it only to recover with some accuracy the historical texture of literary life in Wesley's day that a study of contemporary writing materials and processes should be undertaken. Frequently such details enable us to interpret an obscure passage, to restore a missing phrase, to piece together a mutilated document, to demonstrate or disprove authenticity, or to clarify the reasons for certain occurrences. In those days as in these, postal history frequently exercised a direct impact on personal history, on social history, and even on national history.

Paper is, of course, a very ancient product, yet in Wesley's day some of the varieties to which we have become accustomed were not available. Although China clay had been discovered in 1733 it was not much used to make 'art paper' until early in the nineteenth century.[1] Similarly 'wove' paper, though rediscovered during the eighteenth century, was slow in being adopted, and came into general use only after Wesley's death.[2] All Wesley's publications, and all his letters, were produced on handmade 'laid' paper, prepared by dipping a rectangular mould or sieve into a porridge made of rotted rags soaked in water. The thicker crossed wires of the mould were called 'chains', and with the thinner wires fastened at narrow intervals between them formed a grid of translucent indentations in the pulp 'laid' on them. Usually added to these chain-lines and wire-lines impressed in the paper were watermarks distinctive of the manufacturer and of the paper size, and occasionally the date. These were made by wire fashioned into letters, figures, or other patterns which were sewn into the mould with very fine wire. The watermarks frequently furnish important evidence (as do the chain-lines and wire-lines) about the conjugacy of parts of a letter which have become separated, accidentally or deliberately (both causes having been at work); in turn the proof that one half belongs to the other may determine the identity of the recipient, or whether we are dealing with two letters sent at the same time on the same sheet. Occasionally watermarks furnish confirmation of the approximate date of an undated letter.[3]

[1] Dard Hunter, *Papermaking*, 2nd edn., London, Alciades Books, 1947, p. 490.

[2] Ibid., p. 495; cf. Philip Gaskell, *A New Introduction to Bibliography*, Oxford, Clarendon Press, 1974, pp. 65–6.

[3] See letters of Mar. 15, 1748; Oct. 20, 1788; Aug. 29, 1789. Unfortunately the standard works on watermarks, filling two shelves in the North Library of the British Library, prove of only minor assistance. Charles-Moïse Briquet, *Les Filigranes*, stops

Weight, quality, and even size of this hand-made paper were all subject to at least minor variations, even in the same batch. Wesley normally used a medium weight, similar to that used for most of his publications. Although he hated to waste money, he did secure good quality paper, which has lasted well. Described as 'white', there is little doubt that even without the mellowing of age it was in fact a pale cream. From about 1770 paper with a green tint begins to appear among his letters, greatly increasing in frequency during the 1780s until it accounts for 5 per cent of the paper which he used, including an occasional sheet of a quite deep green.[1]

The first point to be noted about the size of the paper used by Wesley is that very rarely was it a full sheet folded to make four folio pages, even in his journal-letters, though this was the normal practice in this genre for his brother Charles.[2] Instead Wesley used what were technically half-sheets, which he then folded in two for his almost uniformly four-page letters. From the evidence of the edges, this writing-paper was apparently purchased already cut to half the manufacturer's size, and we shall therefore speak of 'sheets' rather than half-sheets, and the resulting leaves when folded as 'half-sheets' rather than quarter-sheets. Wesley normally avoided both small octavo pages (arising from dividing a crown sheet into four) and large quarto pages (from half a crown sheet), though his letters do contain examples of both.[3] Instead he regularly used one of the intermediate foolscap sizes, ranging anywhere from 33·5 × 21·5 cm to 30·5 × 19·8 cm. The variations in size are innumerable; rarely are sheets exactly square, so that rarely do they measure exactly the same.

short in 1600, and Wesley's holographs include a host of watermarks not to be found in either W. A. Churchill, *Watermarks* (1935), or Edward Heawood, *Watermarks* (1957), both of which concentrate on the seventeenth and eighteenth centuries. Even though Mr. Heawood himself and other filigranologists have followed up the latter volume, much more work needs to be done in the field.

[1] This, like some other statistics here given, is based on a detailed comparison of 500 holograph letters in the Methodist Archives, Manchester, which form a representative cross-section of his whole correspondence. Other statements from time to time will be based on 500 letters from various sources comprising his letters to fourteen selected correspondents. (See p. 27 below.)

[2] One extant example, however, is the lengthy letter to the Revd. Samuel Walker, Sept. 3, 1756, though this is a copy prepared by an amanuensis for signature by Wesley; cf. also those of Dec. 6, 1726, to his brother Samuel (a draft), and of Mar. 19, 1727, to his mother (possibly a draft or a copy).

[3] e.g. for small 8vo those to Charles Wesley, May 25, 1764, and Apr. 11, 1785, measuring 23·5 × 18·5 cm, and for quarto that to the Revd. John Newton, May 14, 1785, measuring 37·7 × 23·3 cm.

Although metal pens were known to antiquity, and the principle of the fountain pen was understood in the seventeenth century and was experimentally in use during Wesley's day, in practice the quill-pen held its own well into the nineteenth century. (The very word 'pen', of course, derives from the Latin *penna*, a feather.) Wesley employed no other. Although those from other birds were in use, it seems likely that he accepted the normal goose-quills. The lower barrel of the quill wore so rapidly that it needed frequent 'mending', i.e. sharpening to a point and slitting so that the ink was channelled down the nib. It was this disadvantage which led to their displacement by the more durable steel pen. Although the complete feather was often used, many, perhaps most pens, utilized the lower part of the barrel only, into which was inserted a penholder. The attested 'last pen Mr. Wesley wrote with' is of this kind, as apparently (from the evidence of the compartments in his travelling writing-case) were most of those which he used.[1] Some of the vagaries of the quill-pen are revealed in Wesley's letters, such as their liability suddenly to run out of ink, and to lose their point rapidly.[2] It was handy, however, to be able to switch from his usual fine nib to a very broad one in order to write a Hebrew phrase, as he did in his letter of September 23, 1723.

Writing ink has also been in use for several thousands of years. Early inks depended upon lamp-black suspended in water and gum. In medieval times it was discovered that a more durable ink resulted from the use of galls (oak-apples) and ferrous sulphate (then known as 'copperas' or 'vitriol'). Mixed and stirred for two or three weeks, the iron salt combined with the gallic or tannic acid to make a purplish-black compound, though this black iron ink eventually faded to brown. To secure a denser black, carbon could be added.[3] The attempts to achieve a permanent black ink are reflected in Wesley's letters. A few letters from every period of his life have

[1] Both the pen and the writing-case are displayed in Wesley's House, City Road, London. The pen is $\frac{1}{4}$ in. in diameter and $4\frac{3}{16}$ in. long. The cut for the nib begins $\frac{7}{8}$ in. from the tip, and the central cut is $\frac{7}{16}$ in. deep. The point is stained with black ink up to and beyond the end of the central cut. For pens in general use see L. C. Hector, *The Handwriting of English Documents*, 2nd edn. London, Edward Arnold, 1966, pp. 18–19.

[2] In signing a letter of March 21, 1790, Wesley began with a faint 'J', redipped his pen, and completed the signature over the 'J'. Beginning a letter to a nobleman on Jan. 25, 1783, after two lines he found the writing too coarse, so changed his worn pen (or possibly sharpened the nib), continuing in a much finer hand.

[3] See C. Ainsworth Mitchell and T. C. Hepworth, *Inks: Their Composition and Manufacture*, London, Griffin, 1904, espec. pp. 8–13, 35–46, 87–8, 92–104.

matured to a pale brown or bright orange-brown, though this is more frequent in his earlier years. By 1750 a medium brown, in varying shades, is more typical, and this remains true for about twenty years. From that point onwards we see a gradual darkening of his ink to sepia, through added black pigmentation. This increases from about 5 per cent of his letters during the years 1770–4 to about 75 per cent during the years 1785–9. About 10 per cent of the letters from these closing years, indeed, are written in pure black ink, apparently because of the use of a quite different formula.[1] Wesley told one of his correspondents: 'You must write with better ink if you would have anyone read.'[2] Wesley's own travelling inkhorn is preserved in Wesley's House, London, and this is coated with black powder attesting to the type of ink in use. He seems never to have used red ink for his letters (though it was available), and never to have used pencils, though they also were available, and he occasionally did use them to annotate passages in books.

The use of somewhat uncertain pens led naturally to the danger of blots, or of smears caused by touching ink which had not dried. Blotting-paper had been known in England for over two hundred years, but did not come into general use until soon after Wesley's death. He apparently used the normal contemporary method of letting ink dry naturally, or of spreading upon it fine white sand from a shaker.[3] On the whole his letters are remarkably free from blots, because he tried to keep a fine pen always ready at hand, but occasionally, especially in his old age, they did occur.[4]

[1] The search for black ink is reflected in an article in Wesley's *Arminian Magazine* for 1794, which complained about the difficulty of procuring anything except 'a pale, dirty, yellow liquid', which proved almost illegible, so that the author carefully described how to make one's own by means of logwood chips, best blue galls in powdered form, pomegranate peel, ferrous sulphate, sal ammoniac, and gum arabic (p. 271).

[2] Oct. 28, 1789, to Thomas Taylor.

[3] Hunter, op. cit., p. 476. Cf. three consecutive entries in Wesley's accounts for Feb., 1726–7:

For an Inkhorn, Sandglass, Sand and Cotton	0 – 1 – 10
For paper books and Sermon paper	0 – 6 – 0
For a pencil	0 – 0 – 3

[4] After completing a letter to Henry Moore on Feb. 6, 1791, for instance, he dropped a huge blob of ink near the top of the letter, which splashed eight other large blots in addition to some tiny splatterings. On Aug. 2, 1777, Wesley folded his letter over a blot before it had dried, leading to a symmetrical black frog pattern inside the folds. In one instance (Feb. 11, 1789, to Walter Churchey), he seems deliberately to have smeared a date written in error, in order to make a correction, and in that of July 8, 1777, to Joseph Benson, the error is struck through as well as smeared. Occasionally the ink shows through the paper, and sometimes a photographic image has transferred itself to the

Seals were present, in one form or another, on all Wesley's letters. In an age before envelopes, seals fulfilled two functions, securing the privacy and safety of the folded letter, and proclaiming its authenticity. That the latter use was important to Wesley is illustrated by the fact that when translating a passage from Bengel for his *Explanatory Notes upon the New Testament* (1755), about Christ being 'the express image of God' (Heb. 1:3), he added the comment: '*the express image*, or "stamp"—Whatever the Father isis exhibited in the Son, as a seal in the stamp on wax.'[1]

When the letter had been folded (in the manner described later),[2] a dab of wax was usually applied under the flap, which was then pressed down so that the two paper surfaces stuck together. An alternative was the ready-made wafer. Sometimes mechanical pressure was applied to wax or wafer by means of a hand embosser, which left a series of patterned indentations on the outside. In addition, or possibly as the only measure, heated wax was dropped across the edge of the flap and the adjoining paper, and the writer's personal seal was impressed over the junction. This in itself might serve as an adhesive to seal the letter, difficult to replace if tampered with after it had hardened, and the design of the seal would inform the recipient of the identity of its sender. Even during the last decade of Wesley's life impressions are found on his letters from no fewer than fifteen different seals, as well as thirteen different embossed stamps—a fact which prompts many questions. Unfortunately for our purposes the study of seals (sigillography) has been chiefly confined to ancient and medieval examples, but its importance to eighteenth-century correspondence should not be overlooked.

Several kinds of furnishings connected with Wesley's writing of letters are preserved in his former home in London. The major item is his magnificent walnut bureau, with its many shelves (including two extending ones for use as candle-rests), pigeon-holes, and even secret compartments. It was in this bureau that he preserved his correspondence, rifled by his wife when she became jealous of his

sheet resting upon it, apparently after the ink itself had dried; cf. the letter of Sept. 16, 1785, to Alexander Suter, where there is both a mirror-image opposite the right fold, and another opposite the central fold, clearly arising from two different patterns of folding for lengthy periods.

[1] Wesley explained to a correspondent that being 'sealed by the Spirit' (Eph. 1 : 13) implies 'the receiving the whole image of God . . . as the wax receives the whole impression of the seal when it is strongly and properly applied' (Oct. 4, 1771).

[2] See pp. 68–70 below.

many female correspondents. There is a straddle-chair stuffed with horse-hair, supposedly given to Wesley by a cockfight bookmaker; this has a sloping back fitted with an adjustable writing board and recesses for pen and ink. And there is his portable writing-case, a miniature roll-top desk with handles at each side for carrying it, and fitted with several drawers. It measures 12 in. $\times$ 9$\frac{1}{2}$ in. $\times$ 6$\frac{1}{4}$ in. Pulling out the drawer at the front (for paper already folded) raises the roll-top to reveal three bottles in sockets, two for ink and the central one (with a pierced brass lid) for sand. By bringing the hinged lid forward to rest on the drawer a sloping writing surface is formed from the two leaves, almost 12 in. square, and covered with green felt. Raising the upper leaf reveals a pen tray beneath the inkrack, and beneath the tray two tiny drawers 5 $\times$ $\frac{3}{4}$ $\times$ $\frac{3}{8}$ in., just large enough to hold new quills the size of Wesley's last pen, the holders themselves presumably resting in the tray above.[1]

The postal service. Although postal systems operated in the ancient world, the beginnings of reasonably efficient services for the letters of the general public date from the seventeenth century. England was probably the pioneer, with the appointment by Charles I in 1635 of Thomas Witherings, his 'Postmaster-General for Foreign Parts', to take in hand the organization also of a scheme 'for settling . . . packet posts betwixt London and all parts of His Majesties dominions for the carrying and recarrying of his subject's letters.'[2] Postboys on horseback carried the mail along six post roads fanning out from London: to Plymouth, to Bath and Bristol, to Chester and Holyhead *en route* to Ireland, to Edinburgh, to Yarmouth, and to Dover. These were based upon the Elizabethan post roads, which in their turn can sometimes be traced back to the network set up by the Romans fifteen centuries earlier. From these post roads 'byposts'[3] went to neighbouring towns, usually by means of letter-carriers on foot. The charges were 2*d.* for a distance of not more than 80 miles, 4*d.* up to 140, and 6*d.* over 140, 8*d.* to Scotland, and 9*d.* to Ireland.[4] Little more was done for two centuries than to introduce improvements and modifications of this system, as in 1660 (confirming actions

---

[1] See Max W. Woodward, *One at London*, London, Epworth Press, 1966, pp. 80, 84, 86, 92, and the illustrated guide, *Wesley's House and Chapel*.

[2] Howard Robinson, *The British Post Office*, Princeton University Press 1948, p. 29.

[3] The term 'bypost' or 'by-post' was more commonly used for the carriage of 'way-letters' passing between two towns on the same post road (see p. 22).

[4] Robinson, op. cit., pp. 23–69; cf. F. George Kay, *The Royal Mail*, London, Rockliff, 1951, pp. 23–7.

taken by Cromwell's Parliament in 1657), when the foreign and domestic services were united in a General Post Office, and changes were made in the rates.[1] Letters were left at the nearest post town, to be picked up personally or to be delivered in some other way negotiated with the local postmaster, sometimes by the payment of an additional charge,[2] though in 1774 the delivery fee was successfully challenged as illegal.[3] The admirable Penny Post was set up in 1680 as a venture in private enterprise to serve London, Westminster, and the surrounding area. For a uniform prepaid charge of one penny anything up to a pound in weight which was taken to one of hundreds of convenient receiving houses was delivered to the inscribed address, and insured throughout its speedy transit. After the government had sued the initiator, William Dockwra, for breaching its monopoly, the scheme was taken over in 1682 by the Post Office itself. The Revolution of 1688 led to a greater use of the postal system, but little change in its methods of operation, except by a gradual extension of regular services between other towns both on and off the post roads, and the adoption of another bright idea from another duly prosecuted private individual (who had set up a halfpenny foot-post), namely that of using bellmen to collect letters, or to announce their arrival at the local post office.[4]

By the Act of 1711 the postal service was both improved and co-ordinated with the embryo services for Scotland and Ireland. At the same time the rates in England and Wales were increased, a single letter costing 3*d.* for the first 80 miles, and 4*d.* beyond, while from London to Edinburgh or Dublin it cost 6*d.* 'Country letters' (those passing through London) continued to be charged twice, once for carriage to London, and a second time when the London clerks sorted them for the roads leading to their final destination. The original charge (or 'tax') inscribed by the receiving postmaster was then erased and a new combined one added, often preceded by the phrase, 'In All'.[5] The 1711 Act governed the British postal system, with minor modifications, throughout the major part of Wesley's

---

[1] Robinson, op. cit., pp. 37–58.
[2] Cf. Kay, op. cit., pp. 42–3, and A. D. Smith, *The Development of Rates of Postage*, London, Allen, 1917, pp. 13–14.
[3] Herbert Joyce, *The History of the Post Office*, London, Bentley, 1893, pp. 197–203.
[4] Robinson, op. cit., pp. 77–89; cf. Kay, op. cit., p. 43, and George Brummell, *The Local Posts of London, 1680–1800*, Bournemouth, Alcock, 1938, espec. pp. 15–18, 40–4.
[5] R. M. Willcocks, *England's Postal History*, printed by Woods of Perth, Scotland, for the author, 1975, pp. 32–3, and John G. Hendy, *The History of the Early Postmarks of the British Isles*, London, L. Upcott, Gill, 1905, pp. 11–12.

life.[1] Although prepayment of postage had been permitted by the 1660 Act, and was compulsory under the London Penny Post, it was by no means usual, and charges continued to be collected from the recipients of letters until the nineteenth century. Wesley told one of his correspondents, for instance, 'I shall never think much of paying postage of a letter from *you*.'[2]

Many of the gaps in the provincial services were filled by the labours of Ralph Allen of Bath, to whom was farmed out in 1720 the delivery of letters which did not pass through London, namely the byposts (carrying letters between intermediate points on one post road) and the crossposts (carrying letters across country from one post road to another). Allen extended the system greatly, and by careful supervision secured much more efficiency, so that his contract was periodically renewed until his death in 1764, and he became of far more importance in postal history than any of the Postmasters-General during this period.[3] In 1765 a new Act encouraged local services by reducing the charge for letters carried short distances—for one post stage it became 1*d*., and for two stages, 2*d*. At the same time the Act allowed any town to establish its own Penny Post Office similar to that in London, which Dublin and Edinburgh speedily did.[4]

Massive reforms were instituted by John Palmer through the Act of 1784, which arose at least in part from William Pitt's financial difficulties, so that a greatly improved service was counterbalanced by higher rates. Single letters were now charged 2*d*. instead of 1*d*. for the first stage, 3*d*. instead of 2*d*. for two stages, and 4*d*. instead of 3*d*. up to 80 miles; between 80 and 150 miles now cost 5*d*., beyond 150 miles 6*d*. instead of 4*d*., and from London to Edinburgh 7*d*. instead of 6*d*. Rates in Scotland itself were also raised—the Irish Post Office had been separated from that in Great Britain the previous year.[5] Palmer's various innovations greatly improved the revenue of the Post Office, and greatly increased the speed of delivery; although he himself was shortly dismissed, his improvements remained.[6]

Slowness of delivery had for a century been a frequent complaint,

[1] Robinson, op. cit., pp. 90–8; Smith, op. cit.
[2] Jan. 14, 1764. For prepayment see Willcocks, op. cit., pp. 20–1.
[3] Robinson, op. cit., pp. 99–111. Cf. Benjamin Boyce, *The Benevolent Man*, Cambridge, Mass., Harvard University Press, 1967.
[4] Robinson, op. cit., pp. 111–12.   [5] Ibid., pp. 136–7.
[6] Ibid., pp. 141–52.

in spite of the blare of the posthorn, the clatter of hooves, and the traditional cry of 'Haste, post, haste!'.[1] Post-riders did not average more than four miles an hour, and sometimes considerably less.[2] This was largely because of the terrible conditions even of the post roads. Ogilby's survey, printed in 1675, had helped to define the problem, and hundreds of turnpike Acts had brought about some piecemeal improvement, gaining greater impetus during the middle years of the eighteenth century, especially after the General Turnpike Act of 1773 had simplified the legal procedure.[3] John Wesley's letters, however, bear testimony to the frequent delays, even in this period, especially when he used the crossposts, or was in a distant part of the kingdom, witness the frustration revealed in a letter to his wife (in London) from Athlone, July 10, 1756: 'Two or three of your letters . . . I have just received all together, together with eight or ten letters from various parts dated in March. Where they have been stuck these four months I cannot imagine.' A decade later he was still unhappy, writing from Kilkenny, July 5, 1765, to Miss Peggy Dale, 'I send Miss Lewen's letter by Portpatrick, to try which comes soonest.' That to Miss Lewen has not survived, but the evidence of the postmarks on that to Peggy Dale shows that it passed through the Dublin post office on July 9, moved through the London office on July 15, and would take another two or three days to reach her at Newcastle. A letter written to Thomas Rankin in Redruth on the same day bears exactly the same postmarks, although this had been directed by Wesley (fruitlessly), 'per Manchester', altered by him to read, 'per Gloucester'. A letter written in England, July 25, 1775, to Ann Bolton, added a P.S.: 'I did not receive yours of May 8th till yesterday.' Even in 1782 Wesley felt it necessary to warn a correspondent expecting a speedy reply in an emergency: 'You do not consider the slowness of the byposts. A letter could not be wrote on the receipt of yours so as to reach Skillington by Wednesday, January the 1st.'[4] Happily he was able to mingle some wry humour with his complaints, writing from Londonderry: 'The Irish posts are not the quickest in the world, though I have known one travel full two miles in an hour. And they are not the most certain. Letters fail here more frequently than they do in England.'[5]

Problems were compounded, of course, for letters dispatched

[1] George Walker, *Haste, Post, Haste!*, London, Harrap, 1938, pp. 29, 119, 132–4.
[2] Robinson, op. cit., p. 59.   [3] Ibid., pp. 126–7.
[4] Dec. 31, 1782.   [5] June 5, 1787.

overseas, especially trans-Atlantic mail, where, to the obvious dangers of storms, war, and piracy on the high seas, were added long delays while ships waited for a favourable wind, and throughout Wesley's lifetime a very poor postal system in America.[1] In 1775 Wesley wrote to his 'General Assistant' in America, Thomas Rankin: 'That letters travel very slow from us to America is a great inconvenience. But it is a still greater that they travel so uncertainly, sometimes reaching you too late, sometimes not at all.'[2] During 'the troubles in America', of course, and especially after the closing of all the ports except New York to British ships, it was even more difficult, though the British Navy still kept some lanes open, so that on October 20, 1775, Wesley wrote to Rankin, 'I was glad to receive yours by Captain Crawford.'

The gradual improvement of the British roads made possible the greatest accelerator of all, the mail coach, introduced in 1784 by John Palmer, first on trial runs between London and Bristol, and then extended to other post roads, even to the slowest of them all, the Great North Road.[3] By 1787 the mail covered the four hundred miles from London to Edinburgh in sixty hours each way, instead of the round trip of 167 hours in 1757, and over two hundred in 1750. Prior to 1784 those writing from London to other major cities on a Monday could not expect an answer until Friday. Henceforth the answer might arrive on Wednesday.[4] This increased speed may well have been a minor factor associated with the rise in the numbers of extant letters from Wesley after 1784, when he reached the age of 81 and might be expected to reduce his activities.[5]

Franking privileges were retained by the Post Office for its own employers. Members of Parliament and other officers of state were granted free carriage of letters which contained their signature and the words 'Free' or 'Frank'. The letters thus franked came to be more numerous than those that paid postage,[6] and abuses led to an enormous loss of revenue, so that in 1764 the practice had for the first time become subject to legislation, with carefully defined

[1] See Howard Robinson, *Carrying British Mails Overseas*, New York University Press, 1964, and Frank Staff, *The Transaslantic Mail*, New York, Harrap, n.d.

[2] May 19, 1775.

[3] Robinson, *British Post Office*, pp. 126–40.

[4] Ibid., p. 139; cf. Charles R. Clear, *John Palmer*, London, Blandford, 1955, pp. 16–25.

[5] There is no sudden surge during 1784–6, however, and the increase in Wesley's extant letters peaks in the years 1788–9.

[6] Robinson, *British Post Office*, p. 116.

restrictions—but with only minimal effect upon ingrained customs. A similar relatively fruitless attempt at regulation was made in 1784, and in many subsequent years; parliamentary franking was finally abolished in 1840. Mere rules hardly touched an institution which had come to be regarded as a rightful perquisite of office, which could legitimately be extended to one's friends by giving them covers already signed. Franks, indeed, became a kind of public commodity, and Wesley's old tutor, Henry Sherman, writing to him on January 10, 1728, closed, 'Pray let me hear from you. I have accordingly sent you a frank.' Consciences were aroused very little by this custom, or even by the frequent counterfeiting of signatures, although Wesley firmly warned the Methodists against this 'illegal fraud'.[1] Wesley happily accepted franked sheets from his friends in Parliament, although these reveal a gradually increasing strictness in the operation of the system, so that 'Free, James Erskine' in the lower left corner of the address panel gradually gave way to a complete address written in the hand of the M.P., as well as the authorization, 'ffree, W. Strahan'.[2] He even sought to bypass the heavy cost of sending frequent batches of proofs for his *Explanatory Notes upon the New Testament* by returning them to London c/o William Belchier, M.P.[3] And he was naturally irritated when his London helper divided a franked double letter into two before redirecting it to Wesley in Bristol: 'Does not John Atlay know that he should always send me a franked letter as it is? The Duke of Beaufort's, for instance. Half the letter costs something; the whole would cost nothing.'[4]

Postmarks were introduced in 1661 by the first Postmaster-General after the Restoration, Henry Bishop, in order to prevent the dilatory handling of the mail by the letter-carriers. In the two halves of a circle divided horizontally were printed the day and the

---

[1] Ibid., pp. 50-1, 114-19, 153; cf. George Brummell, *A Short Account of the Franking System in the Post Office*, 1652-1840, Bournemouth, 1936, and Willcocks, op. cit., pp. 54-62. At his Conference in 1758 Wesley reported, 'Counterfeit franks are commonly used in Ireland', and asked, 'Ought any of us to use them? Can a Member of Parliament empower other persons to frank letters for them?' As usual he also supplied the answer: 'By no means. It is an illegal fraud, against which therefore we must warn all our societies.' (Manuscript Minutes, W.H.S. Pub. No. 1, supplemented in *Proceedings*, Vol. IV, Pt. 5 (1904), pp. 70-1.)

[2] Letters dated June 18, 1745, Apr. 4, 1783; cf. Mar. 30, 1751; July 16, 1755; June 5, 1758; Dec. 9, 1760; July 29, 1771; July 10, 1772.

[3] Apr. 9, 1755.

[4] Mar. 12, 1779. For double letters see below, pp. 64-8.

month. With variations in composition, lettering, and size these 'Bishop marks' remained in use until 1787, when they were displaced by concentric circles showing the day, month, and year. The Bishop mark seems to have been used in the head office in London only, to mark the day when the letter was either received, transferred, or delivered, except that Edinburgh and Dublin used a similar mark with the month shown above (as had been true in London until 1713). Under Ralph Allen's leadership (largely as a safeguard against fraud), most provincial cities developed their own distinctive postmarks to use at least on outgoing letters, again with variations in design or size from time to time. Other stamps or inscriptions were occasionally added to the letter to denote various elements in its status, such as 'In All', 'Pd' or 'Post Paid', 'Penny Post Not Paid', 'Free', inspectors' marks (usually a crown, frequently authorizing some added charge), and 'Ship Letter' (with the name of the port of dispatch).[1] The postal charges to be collected at its destination were usually marked on the cover by hand, frequently in stylized figures somewhat difficult to identify, so that a '3' might well be mistaken for a '7'.

Postmarks and postal inscriptions may furnish important evidence about the history of a letter, and it is very unfortunate that in hundreds of instances the cover has become separated from the letter, so that speculation must replace hard evidence upon many points. Postmarks are especially useful, of course, in determining the date of a mutilated or undated letter; from their size and type they may even furnish clues to the year or the letter's place of origin. One minor example from the hundreds in the following volumes may suffice. On the basis of internal evidence John Telford's edition of Wesley's *Letters*[2] dated a letter to William Church as '[London, Aug. 3, 1779]'—a sound deduction as far as it went. The mutilated letter itself, however, probably cut from the foot of another letter, reveals the Bishop mark, '29/IY', proving (along with the other evidence) that the letter was dispatched (and therefore probably written) on July 29, 1779.

Personal letter-carriers. In view of both the cost and the uncer-

---

[1] Robinson, *British Post Office*, pp. 58, 106–8. For more detailed studies see R. C. Alcock and F. C. Holland, *The Postmarks of Great Britain and Ireland*, Cheltenham, Alcock, 1940, espec. pp. 17–25, 57–63, 76, 87, 92, 106, 125–6, 131–6, 152–3, 193–4, 412, 450. See also R. M. Willcocks, op. cit., pp. 46–53, 102–16, and the same author's *The Postal History of Great Britain and Ireland*, London, Vale Stamps, 1972.

[2] Telford, VI. 351.

tainty of the postal system many letters were delivered by friendly travellers. Thus in a postscript Wesley wrote to James Hutton, 'Pray give our brother Böhler the enclosed, to be delivered with his own hand.'[1] In writing to Mrs. Savage, Wesley closed, 'Be free with Sister Brisco, who brings this.'[2] No fewer than 30 per cent of the extant letters to Wesley's wife which retain their covers thus by-passed the regular mail, and of all Wesley's letters probably one in ten was carried by personal courier—a layman on business, a gentle-woman making a visit, a preacher on his rounds. Many such letters were written to people within the same town, or a short distance away. Nevertheless most travelled quite long distances, from Georgia or Germany to London, from London to Jersey, from London to Londonderry. Letters to or from London, the hub of British communications, were perhaps the simplest to negotiate, and Wesley could frequently find helpful travellers going to other major centres such as Bristol and Dublin. Half of these hand-delivered letters were addressed with the name of the recipient alone ('To the Revd. Mr. C. Wesley' etc.), and the other half added the town ('To Mr. Alexander Knox in Londonderry' etc.). A few of the latter contained more elaborate directions, as if prepared for the regular postal service and handed to a messenger at the last moment—although in fact much detail in addresses was neither necessary nor practicable in Wesley's day, and none of the forty-four letters known to have been posted to Alexander Knox bore any fuller address than that given above.[3] Like the postal system, however, this private letter-

---

[1] Apr. 28, 1738. 'The enclosed' was in fact a letter written to Charles Wesley on the same sheet; cf. double letters, p.p. 64-8.

[2] Aug. 31, 1771.

[3] On p. 16 above statistics were given from a miscellaneous cross-section of 500 letters. This present summary (like others to follow) is based upon an examination of 500 different letters, compiled to represent the major categories of Wesley's correspondents through most of his writing life. This was done by taking all the holograph letters available in xerox written to fourteen people, preachers, laymen, women, Wesley's family, with one correspondent in Ireland, one in America, one in Canada, covering the years 1738-90 in something like the proportions of the total correspondence. (It would have been quite simple to choose a different five hundred, of course, or a thousand, but it is doubtful whether there would have been any major variation in the findings.) It may be of value to list these persons: Joseph Benson, preacher, 1751-90 (59 letters); Ebenezer Blackwell of London, banker, 1739-62 (30); Mary Bishop, schoolmistress in Bath and Keynsham, 1769-84 (37); William Black, pioneer preacher in Nova Scotia, 1783-90 (6); Ann Bolton, a gentlewoman of Witney, Oxfordshire, 1768-88 (60); James Hutton, bookseller of London, 1737-72 (29); Alexander Knox, theological writer of Londonderry, Ireland, 1775-90 (50); George Merryweather, merchant, of Yarm, 1758-70 (15); Thomas Rankin, preacher, and from 1773 to 1777 Wesley's General Assistant

carrier system occasionally broke down. One of the most important letters in Wesley's personal life, rejecting John Bennet's claims to Wesley's already espoused wife, Grace Murray, was committed to the hands of William Shent, the Methodist barber of Leeds, and—for whatever reason—never delivered, so that a month later Bennet married her.[1]

III. WESLEY AS A CORRESPONDENT

Like the physical aspects of letter-writing, the habits and idiosyncrasies of letter-writers have drawn far less attention than the content of their letters. Yet the one illuminates the other. Some information on this subject may be gleaned from extraneous sources, but for a maximum understanding it is essential to study a large number of original manuscripts. Only in this way can we visualize the processes by which the written letter became a major element in the complex and awe-inspiring ministry of John Wesley. A careful examination may also enable us to make valid deductions about his normal procedures, which in turn may throw light on the many problems of interpretation which arise.

A voluminous correspondence. Wesley's correspondence was enormous. This edition will publish some 3,500 out-letters, about one-third more than those in Telford's edition, yet still only a fraction of his actual output. Nevertheless it is, we believe, a representative fraction, both in its content and in its distribution among the years. For the first decade, 1721–30, we publish (using 'round' figures) only 30 letters, for the second and third decades, taking us to 1750, about 200 each. By this time Methodism was completely developed as a system, though it was not yet fully launched upon its vast expansion. For the following decade, 1751–60, there are about 300 letters, a figure which expands during 1761–70 to 500. By this time Wesley was approaching seventy, but instead of a gradual diminution in his writing of letters there was a doubling during the follow-

---

in America, 1762–80 (19); Ann Tindall, Methodist poetess of Scarborough, 1774–90 (36); John Valton, preacher, 1769–90 (26); the Revd. Charles Wesley, 1738–88 (77); Mrs. John Wesley, 1751–78 (27); Thomas Wride, preacher, 1771–89 (29). Of these 500 letters 95 lacked the address section, and of the 405 remaining 41 display no evidence of passing through the postal system. (N.B. For various reasons xeroxes of some holographs to these correspondents were not available during the time of this study, so that the above figures do not always represent the totals available for the eventual text.)

[1] Sept. 7, 1749.

ing decade to 1,000, and between 1781 and 1790 this phenomenal increase continued, to reach 1,300. Over 2,000 letters are extant which he wrote after reaching the age of seventy—more than for all the preceding years added together. Undoubtedly this was in part because a larger proportion of his later letters were preserved by eager devotees, and because improved postal services had led to a general increase in letter-writing. The major factor governing this great increase during his later years, however, was surely the demands made upon Wesley's pastoral concern by a rapidly growing Methodist community, combined with his amazing vigour—for even during these years when his physical strength was ebbing he continued to undertake undiminished itineraries throughout the British Isles, and even ventured on two trips to Holland. This view seems to be confirmed by statistics compiled from his diaries (and other sources) of letters which he wrote but which have not survived, which show comparable survival rates for both his earlier and later years.[1]

The number of Wesley's correspondents grew in similar manner over the seven decades of his letter-writing life. For the present edition his named correspondents at present number about sixteen hundred, and many more remain anonymous, pseudonymous, or still unidentified. That his correspondents in fact reached several times this number is implied by his whole style of life, as well as by the facts that some known correspondents are not represented by any extant letters,[2] and that for fewer than 25 per cent of these correspondents do we have both in-letters and out-letters, while 50 per cent are represented only by letters from Wesley to them—in half of these instances by one letter only. (These, of course, are the letters which have been preserved and are known to the editor, and can offer no reliable guide to the numbers of original correspondents or letters.) With such a large percentage of 'one-shot' letters

---

[1] During the years for which his early diary is extant (1725–41) some 1,650 letters are recorded, of which about 325 are extant in one form or another—20 per cent. During the last nine years for which his diary is available (1782–91) he wrote a minimum of 4,700 (counting all references to 'letters' as two only), of which 1,200 are available in one form or another—25 per cent. If 'writ letters' is interpreted as writing an average of three per session instead of two (which is still probably an underestimate for the much briefer letters of Wesley's later years, especially during writing sessions which sometimes lasted two or three hours), the total figure becomes 6,600, of which those extant form 18 per cent.

[2] e.g. his letter of June 18, 1757: 'I have heard from both Mrs. Gaussen and Miss Bosanquet.' No correspondence with Mrs. Gaussen is known, and none with Mary Bosanquet before 1761.

extant, however, it seems highly probable that more such will turn up, and thus the list of his known correspondents be extended.

It is nevertheless of some value to study statistics derived from the total correspondence so far known. It begins very modestly with one extant letter to him in 1717, when he was fourteen, followed by 24 correspondents during the decade 1721–30,[1] which multiplied to 122 during 1731–40, increased to 152 during 1741–50, and then declined to 139 in 1751–60. The following decade, 1761–70, when Wesley was in his 60s, it increased to 208, and each of the following decades reveals increases of a hundred in the number of Wesley's correspondents, to 306 by 1780 and 406 by 1790. Even during his last two months of letter-writing in 1791 he corresponded with 27 people, more than all noted for his first decade, just as more letters from him are extant for January and February, 1791, than during his first decade, 31 against 28.[2]

A religious duty. For many people writing letters is mere drudgery, for others creative joy, for most a mixture of both. John Wesley belonged to the last group, though the arduous religious chore was relieved by only occasional moments of personal pleasure. Even at the beginning of the Methodist movement, on Nov. 16, 1738, he wrote to Benjamin Ingham and James Hutton—trying to satisfy two correspondents with one letter—'I have four- or five-and-thirty other letters to write, so can say no more.' The rapid growth of Methodism, combining with his own inner urge to maintain personal oversight of its multitudinous ramifications and their attendant problems, necessarily entailed a steady increase in the number of letters which he received, from scores to hundreds every year, and even to many hundreds. Nor was this eased by two of his declared principles: 'I generally write to all that desire it, though not often in many words',[3] and, 'It is a rule with me to answer every letter I receive.'[4] An incidental remark made by him in 1781 was probably close to the truth: 'I have had, for many years, and have at this day,

---

[1] The figures given are for correspondences which were active during any year of each decade, so that one with letters in 1758, 1769–72 would be counted in three decades.

[2] Obviously one would not expect the number of correspondents to increase at the same rate as the actual letters written to them by an active correspondent, nor do they, but the general curve of increase is similar, though not so steep. Taking the first decade in each case as the norm (and using approximations), during the seven decades Wesley's correspondents increased in the ratio 1 : 5 : 6 : 6 : 8 : 12 : 16, while his actual letters increased in the ratio 1 : 6 : 6 : 10 : 17 : 31 : 43.

[3] Feb. 16, 1787, to John King.

[4] Apr. 5, 1781; cf. July 13, 1783.

a greater number of pious correspondents than any person in England, or perhaps in Europe.'[1] The five thousand extant letters to or from Wesley represent only the tip of the iceberg. The contemporaries of his later years realized something of the enormous pressures thus put upon him, and Henry Moore remarked: 'Mr. Wesley had many correspondents; and it often surprised his friends that he could answer one-fourth of the letters he received.'[2]

The English weather was an influential factor in Wesley's letter-writing, because it tended to govern his travelling. Only during the summer were most of the country roads reasonably passable, so that his major itineraries were undertaken between April and October, including his alternating biennial tours in Ireland and Scotland—though in fact spring was far from ideal for his Scottish itinerary.[3] He found that he could read in a coach or a chaise, and even on horseback, but writing was almost impossible.[4] During his journeys, therefore, he informed his correspondents where and when letters might reach him.[5] Thus at the post towns scattered along the post roads he would collect batches of letters, occasionally answering immediately any that were urgent, but adding the bulk to the bundles of those already awaiting replies. In some parts of the country even this was not practicable, so that after spending most of June and July, 1745, in Cornwall and Wales, and then touring Wiltshire and Somersetshire, he wrote from Bristol: 'I now had leisure to look over the letters I had received this summer.'[6] There were many weeks during his summer itineraries when he seems neither to have received nor to have written any letters.[7] Summer, therefore, except for the few weeks spent every two years in Dublin, and occasional week-ends in other large centres, was not his basic time for correspondence, though he did dispatch letters from a remarkable number

---

[1] *A. M.*, 1781, Preface, Jan. 1, 1781, § 4. [2] Moore, II. 152.

[3] See Wesley F. Swift, *Methodism in Scotland*, London, Epworth Press, 1947, p. 19.

[4] e.g. diary, Sept. 8–9, 1740, *en route* from Bristol to London, when he read for a total of 14½ hours.

[5] e.g. July 23, 1768, to Jane Hilton: 'You may direct your next to me in Haverfordwest, Crosspost'. He left instructions for redirecting his letters with his helpers in London and Dublin: 'Letters directed to the Foundery will find me wherever I am' (May 10, 1755; cf. Aug. 6, 1769); 'When I am in Ireland, you have only to direct to Dublin, and the letter will find me' (Mar. 18, 1769).

[6] JWJ, Aug. 12, 1745.

[7] There are no extant letters for Aug. 13 to Sept. 6, 1776, which he spent mostly in Cornwall. On Sept. 16 he wrote from Bristol to Hetty Roe: 'As I did not receive yours of August the 28th before my return from Cornwall, I was beginning to grow a little apprehensive lest your love was growing cold.'

of places—not only from Yorkshire, Lancashire, and the Midlands, but from Cornwall, Wales, and many parts of Scotland and Ireland. This becomes more marked during his later years, with the improvement in the postal services, as well as the phenomenal increase in his own correspondence.

Almost every year, however, he spent about four months in the London area, from November to February, as well as a week or so during the summer to catch up with events.[1] During this one-third of the year he penned roughly one-half of his total letters for the year, sometimes considerably more, sometimes slightly less. The Bristol–Kingswood area was his next most important headquarters, where he usually spent two or three periods a year, of varying lengths, amounting to almost two months in all, though here the proportion of letters sent to time spent is not so stable or so remarkable.[2]

Even during his itineraries Wesley tried to keep on top of his correspondence by setting aside a few hours on most non-travelling days for this task, preferably in the morning.[3] He also attacked large accumulations during periodical bursts of literary spring-cleaning when he could secure appropriate conditions in his own studies in London, Bristol, Dublin, or some other of his preaching-houses, or a private room in a friendly and spacious home. Because he took his writing seriously he always sought the best working conditions possible. He was careful about posture, guarding others (and surely himself) against leaning on their stomachs, or writing for too long at a time.[4]

During his middle years the occasions when he could spend an hour upon a letter became rare indeed, but nevertheless he did manage to secure a few large blocks of time during which he could develop a close-knit argument on important subjects with influential people, witness his correspondence with 'John Smith', a thoughtful but critical clergyman who sought to understand Wesley's theological and ecclesiastical principles. Each of the six letters written to him by Wesley from 1745 to 1748 occupies the space (and presumably

[1] 'In the beginning of October I generally move towards London, in the neighbourhood of which I usually spend the winter.' (Aug. 14, 1782.) This simply confirms the evidence of his journeys recorded in *Journal* and letters, best displayed in 'An Itinerary in which are traced the Rev. John Wesley's Journeys from October 14, 1735, to October 24, 1790', prepared by Richard Green for W.H.S. VI, 1907–8.
[2] These figures are based on spot checks for every fifth year from 1750 to 1790.
[3] See, for example, his diary for July 4, 12, 21, 23, 27, 30, 1739, and his letter to Philothea Briggs, Jan. 25, 1771: 'Whatever you write, you should write in the forenoons.'
[4] Jan. 25, 1771; Jan. 18, 1782.

occupied the time) devoted to seven or eight of his run-of-the-mill letters of that period—or about twice as many of those written forty years later. Wesley explained that for such an important correspondence he would rather write late than write inadequately, and that his letter of Sept. 28, 1745, 'was the longer delayed because I could not persuade myself to write at all till I had leisure to write fully'. To Richard Tompson, with whom he was conducting a doctrinal controversy a decade later, he wrote:

I am a very slow, you seem to be a very swift writer . . . My time is so taken up, from day to day, and from week to week, that I can spare very little from my stated employments; so that I can neither write so largely nor so accurately as I might otherwise do. All, therefore, which you can expect from me is (not a close-wrought chain of connected arguments, but) a short sketch of what I should deduce more at large if I had more leisure.[1]

Thirty years later the greatly increased pressure compelled him to try to work letter-writing sessions into nearly every day, sometimes three or four sessions a day. The time devoted to each letter was (in general) reduced, and long letters became exceptional. He came to feel very distressed about this, confessing to Mary Cooke (who married Adam Clarke): 'Considering that I am usually obliged to write in haste, I often doubt whether my correspondence is worth having.'[2] Some idea of the burden of these chores during his eighties may be gathered from the diary entries for two days chosen almost at random. The first is for January 14, 1789, the second of two days spent with 'old friends at Newington', in the London area:

5.30 prayed, letters; 8 tea, conversed, prayer; 9 on business, letters, journal; 1 dinner, conversed; 2.30 letters; 5 tea, conversed; 6 letters; 8 supper, conversed, prayer; 9.30

The second was during the sessions of the annual Conference in Leeds, July 31, 1789:

4 sleep; 5 prayed, letters; 6 Conf[erence], letters, Conf.; 12 letters; 2 dinner; 3 letters; 5 tea, conversed, prayer; 6 Mark 13:32![3] letters; 8 supper, conversed, prayer; 9.30

(Perhaps it should be pointed out that *none* of at least eighteen letters written on these two days appears to have survived—a fair

[1] Feb. 5, 1756.
[2] Mar. 31, 1787. Cf. a letter to Lady Maxwell: 'I have often wondered that you were not weary of so useless a correspondent' (July 4, 1787.)
[3] The text of the 'official' sermon which he preached at the Conference.

indication of the fractional nature of the extant letters, even for Wesley's later years.)[1]

With a few correspondents, however, Wesley did spend more time, not only because they sought spiritual improvement, but because he was actually enjoying himself, simply allowing his pen to flow along almost effortlessly as he imagined himself talking to them, just as he innocently relaxed like a contented child in the company of congenial, cultivated, and devout young women—who predominated among these favoured correspondents. To Jenny Hilton he wrote: 'There would be little cross in writing letters if I found it as pleasant to write to others as it is to write to *you*.'[2] In a similar vein he wrote to Ally Eden, at the same time expounding his strict economy of effort in correspondence:

> If either young or old were to write to me on trifles, there would be room to blame them. Indeed, I should blame them myself, and soon put a stop to such unprofitable correspondence. But Nancy Bolton and you and two or three more who write to me, though they are young, are not triflers. Neither do they write on subjects of a trifling nature, but on those of the greatest importance. Let my dear Ally Eden continue to do this, whoever praises or blames. You give me much pleasure thereby, and sometimes reap profit to yourself.[3]

Opening a correspondence. As might be expected, Wesley rarely initiated a correspondence. One clue to this is to be found in an incidental phrase in a printed letter addressed to the subscribers to his *Explanatory Notes upon the Old Testament*, which was being issued in weekly numbers and proving a heavy burden to him: 'All my time is swallowed up, and I can hardly catch a few hours to answer the letters that are sent me.'[4] The vast majority of his own letters were such, 'answers to the letters . . . sent' him, asking help or advice of some kind. When the origins of fifty fairly large series of correspondence are checked, it is seen that in only twenty-four is there any indication of the initiator, and in only five does it appear to have been Wesley; the others seem to have been begun by Wesley's correspondents. In opening a correspondence with Elizabeth Ritchie he points out that this is quite contrary to his normal practice:

My dear Betsy,
    It is not common for me to write to anyone first; I only answer those that write to me. But I willingly make an exception with regard to *you*; for it is not

---

[1] Nor is the diary necessarily a complete record of the letters sent. For September, 1787, a check of extant letters shows one dated Sept. 7 and two dated Sept. 30, though no letter-writing is noted in the diary for those dates.

[2] Mar. 1, 1769. [3] May 2, 1771. [4] June 20, 1766.

[a common] concern that I feel for you. You are just rising into life; and I would fain have you not almost but altogether a Christian.[1]

Other exceptions, of course, were his preachers. As the one who called them into the itinerant work it was clearly up to him to make the first approach, and a typical instance is probably his letter to Zechariah Yewdall, just launching into his first circuit:

Wherever you are, be ready to acknowledge what God has done for your soul, and earnestly exhort all the believers to expect full salvation. You would do well to read every morning a chapter in the New Testament, with the *Notes*, and to spend the greatest part of the morning in reading, meditation, and prayer. In the afternoon you might visit the society from house to house, in the manner laid down in the *Minutes* of the Conference. The more labour, the more blessing![2]

There is also some evidence that in addition to occasional letters to them Wesley made a practice of writing each winter to all his preachers, or at least to all his 'Assistants'—those preachers in administrative control of the circuits.[3]

Frequency of writing. The same pattern continued throughout Wesley's correspondence. In general he responded to the writer's letter, rather than venturing upon many new points of his own, apart from the almost universal closing paragraph or sentence of spiritual exhortation. Normally he did not reply immediately unless he sensed an emergency. To John Fletcher's widow he wrote: 'When I receive letters from other persons, I let them lie, perhaps a week or two, before I answer them. But it is otherwise when I hear from *you*. I then think much of losing a day, for fear I should

[1] May 8, 1774. He did make overtures to other people from time to time, however, though not always successfully, as he told Samuel Bardsley: 'I wrote to Mr. Powys, as I promised, but I never had any answer' (Jan. 28, 1770.)

[2] Oct. 9, 1779. Similar models of compact advice are to be seen in his first responses to the opening letters of those asking help of various kinds, witness those to Alexander Knox (June 6, 1755, a health regime), the spiritual exhortation to Penelope Newman (June 3, 1763), and the critique on Ann Tindall's verse of July 6, 1774.

[3] This statement is based on a study of Wesley's letters to the twelve preachers with names beginning between B and H to whom he addressed from four to thirty letters. To these men he wrote 175 letters during a combined total of 89 connexional years, i.e. from July of one to June of the following. During these 89 years extant winter letters were sent by Wesley in no fewer than 74, although in four cases these were from Bristol rather than London. Even making allowances for the fact that Wesley wrote more letters during the winter months, this shows a very high proportion dispatched to preachers at this period of the year. The statistics seem especially significant in the case of Samuel Bardsley: of 29 extant letters written to him during 19 years, in only two of those years is there no London letter during January to March, and in eleven years this is the only known letter.

give a moment's pain to one of the most faithful friends I have in the world.'[1] Probably nearer the norm was his correspondence with Mrs. Eliza Bennis of Limerick, Waterford, and then Philadelphia, as revealed by extracts published in 1809 by her son.[2] These show a pattern of four or five letters each per year from 1763 to 1776, though there are a few gaps where letters were apparently not preserved, certainly not utilized. In all except one instance (when Wesley was returning some of her manuscript journals), his letters were always replies to hers, and although her letters were sometimes written months after receiving his last, Wesley's own always recur at regular intervals of about two or three weeks after hers. We are able to visualize his putting the letter at the bottom of a growing pile after reading it, to await its turn for a reply—unless, indeed (which is quite possible), he was maintaining in these later years as well as in his earlier ones a written scheme of correspondence with various people.

Wesley let it be known that he did not welcome letters too frequently, and that there should be something important to answer when letters were sent to him. Thus Mrs. Bennis, after receiving his letter of April 1, 1773, delayed until August 25 before writing: 'The want of anything particular this some time past has prevented my troubling you, or intruding on your more precious time. But the desire of receiving a line from you has obliged me to break through.' With most correspondents letters were no more frequent than one a month, so that Wesley himself wrote to them about every two months. Wesley informed a preacher in Ireland, 'You should not write seldomer than once in two or three months.'[3] When Ann Tindall delayed in writing beyond this, he chided her: 'I really think it would be a pardonable fault if you wrote once in two months instead of once in six.'[4] Wesley's letters to Alexander Knox followed a similar two-monthly pattern, but they tailed off considerably during some years, and there are none from Wesley dated 1786 or 1788. On Sept. 3, 1781, however, Wesley wrote apologizing to

---

[1] Jan. 13, 1786. What little evidence is available supports Wesley's statement; on July 12, 1782, he answered her letter of the 5th, and on Sept. 15, 1785, he was able to announce the publication of her lengthy letter to him about Fletcher's death, written to him Aug. 18.

[2] *Christian Correspondence: being a Collection of Letters written by the late Rev. John Wesley and several Methodist Preachers in connection with him to the late Mrs. Eliza Bennis, with her answers*, Philadelphia, Graves, 1809. [3] Dec. 14, 1761.

[4] Jan. 19, 1776.

Knox for a slight delay beyond his normal waiting period: 'Almost ever since I received yours I have been in perpetual motion, travelling from Yorkshire to London, from London to Bristol, and thence through the West of England. Otherwise I should not have delayed writing so long, lest you should imagine I was regardless of you.'[1] The implication seems to be that in a complete series any lengthy gaps were due more to the lack of overtures from his correspondent than to Wesley's abnormally delayed responses.

With a few people Wesley exchanged letters more rapidly, at least for a period of several months or years at a time. He told Thomas Olivers in London, 'Certainly you should write to me a little oftener—once a month at the least.'[2] To Nancy Bolton, Wesley wrote anywhere from eight to ten letters a year between 1768 and 1791, answering hers about two or three weeks after he had received them, though occasionally sooner. The same pattern is seen in his correspondence with Elizabeth Ritchie, 1774–88, during which period he wrote nine or ten letters a year, usually replying to hers after two or three weeks.

It is quite clear that Wesley greatly preferred a rhythmic exchange of letters, whether every two weeks, every month, or at longer intervals, though occasionally letters did cross in the post, or the correspondence was disrupted in some other way. He wrote to his wife, far less methodical than he: 'I can easily remove that difficulty of your not knowing which of your letters I answer, by writing just letter for letter. Then there can be no mistake. There could never have been any if I had not wrote two or three letters to your one.'[3] In an emergency, of course, he tried to reply immediately. To Mary Bishop he wrote about a problem which had arisen in Bath: 'I have laid your letter so carefully by that I cannot find it. But as I am going into Norfolk early in the morning I will not stay till I come back before I write.'[4] Unusual circumstances occasionally broke the rhythm from time to time both for others and for Wesley himself. During the early months of 1761 Mary Bosanquet was experiencing something like sanctification, as well as being involved with a spiritual revival in the local Methodist society. Within two

---

[1] Knox seems to have preserved all his letters from Wesley carefully, a total of fifty, all bound in a volume except one, which is loose. No letters from Knox to Wesley have been preserved, but the evidence of Wesley's travels implies that he had received Knox's letter in late July or early August; the answer, therefore, was only a week or so beyond the period when it would be expected.

[2] July 10, 1756.   [3] May 21, 1756.   [4] Oct. 31, 1773.

months she wrote ten letters, a kind of running commentary upon these events. None of Wesley's replies survive, but it is highly unlikely that he matched her letters one for one, though hints are given of two which have disappeared.[1] Similarly Wesley himself wrote three letters within the space of nine days to Samuel Tooth, the contractor who was building the New Chapel in City Road, London,[2] and in 1788 wrote three letters in eleven days to Henry Moore.[3]

Drafts and copies. Like most careful writers, Wesley usually prepared drafts for his more important letters, and also kept fair copies for reference. Occasionally these drafts have survived, including those for three letters written in his climactic year of 1738, two to William Law, and one to his brother Samuel.[4] In the case of his letter to Mary Bishop, attempting to elucidate the doctrine of the atonement, Wesley retained the draft, and the actual letter itself has also survived.[5]

A draft, of course, might also serve as a reference copy, and in the absence of any corrections it is not always certain whether a holograph letter did not originally function as a draft. The absence of an address, and of Wesley's characteristic folding and sealing, will in most instances announce immediately that the document is not the letter itself, as dispatched to the recipient. Many of these copies retained by Wesley remain when the letter itself has disappeared, and their evidence (like that of a draft) is almost as valuable as that of the letter itself as far as literary content is concerned, though they tell us nothing of the letter's postal history, and are occasionally inaccurate.[6] Both John and Charles Wesley made copies of letters and other documents prepared by the other—indeed several of John Wesley's sermons have been preserved only through Charles Wesley's copies. Frequently, perhaps usually, copies were made by amanuenses, such as one endorsed by Wesley, 'To G. Wh[itefield], March 16, 1739', and a controversial letter to Francis Okeley of Oct. 4, 1758. One letter to Mrs. Mary Parker of Fakenham, dated Jan. 21, 1784, gave a lengthy rebuttal of her reasons for denying Methodist

---

[1] Her letters were dated February, Mar. 7, 19, Apr. 1, 6 (two), 17 (two), May 1 and 5; his were probably written *c.* Feb. 2 and Apr. 11.

[2] Sept. 27, Oct. 1, 5, 1778.   [3] May 6, 11, 17.

[4] May 14, 20, Oct. 30.   [5] Feb. 7, 1778.

[6] For instance, the draft preserved by Wesley as a reference copy of his letter of May 14, 1738, to William Law, does not contain one criticism added to the letter as sent (see p. 542 below).

preachers access to the pulpit in her private chapel; of this the original is extant, as also a contemporary copy in two different hands. The copy of an ultimatum to his wife, however, written July 15, 1759, was (not unexpectedly) prepared by Wesley himself. The preparation of such copies was an important part of contemporary letter-writing, and it was doubtless for this purpose mainly that Wesley secured secretarial assistance for a day spent in answering the 'abundance of letters' which awaited him at Bath in 1787.[1] It was from such copies that he occasionally published his own letters in his *Journal* or in the *Arminian Magazine*.[2]

Wesley sometimes duplicated the same or a very similar letter to different persons. Such was one about the beginnings of the Methodist campaign in Kingswood, which he published in the *Journal* as having been written to 'Mr. D[unscombe?]'. Within a few days a copy was written to Howell Harris, and another a little later to 'Mr. Thomas Price'.[3] The most important examples of this time-saving practice are the duplicate letters pleading that Britain should not become involved in war against the Americans, one of which Wesley wrote on June 14, 1775, to Lord Dartmouth, Secretary of State for the Colonies, and the other on June 15 to Lord North, the First Lord of the Treasury—letters which are identical except for a few minor variants. On at least one occasion he seems to have signed handwritten copies of no fewer than sixty-two letters sent to all his Assistants about various aspects of Methodist discipline: the manuscripts of at least three survive, and another was printed from a different original in 1821.[4] Similarly he seems to have employed amanuenses to prepare copies of a letter to his preachers seeking Methodist support for his abridgement of John Goodwin's treatise on justification,[5] of which the copy sent to Thomas Rankin has survived—addressed, dated (Nov. 2, 1764), and signed by Wesley himself.

Frequently Wesley followed a simpler path, making multiple copies by the relatively inexpensive method of printing, signing

[1] JWJ, Sept. 15, 1787.

[2] e.g. that of Sept. 15, 1762, to the Revd. Samuel Furly, which appeared in the *A.M.* for Dec., 1781 (IV. 670-1).

[3] JWJ; see p. 701 below.

[4] See Nov. 12, 1779. Three of the Assistants were Thomas Carlill of Tiverton, William Church of Glamorgan, and John Mason of Taunton; to the identity of the other there is no clue.

[5] *Bibliog*, No. 266.

them, and distributing them through the mail—a very different practice, of course, from actual publication.[1] One example is that of Oct. 15, 1766, seeking the co-operation of evangelical clergy, for which Wesley reproduced one written to Lord Dartmouth on April 19, 1764. He utilized the same expedient for circulating letters seeking help in securing financial stability for Methodism. If that of Nov. 24, 1767, is any guide, Wesley himself addressed copies to the few people known personally to him in each circuit, and then instructed his Assistant to distribute them to the remainder of the likely prospects. Thus his letter to Robert Costerdine: 'I have wrote to T. Colbeck, Jam. Greenwood . . . The rest in your circuit I leave to you . . . When you receive the printed letters, seal, superscribe, and deliver them in my name to whom you please.'[2]

Interruptions. With a correspondence so voluminous it is scarcely surprising that Wesley sometimes failed in his good intentions. 'Ten times, I believe', he told one correspondent, 'I have been going to answer your last, and have been as often hindered.'[3] Occasionally he began a letter, was interrupted, and never finished it.[4] Sometimes he would head a sheet with the place of writing, probably utilizing a few moments insufficient to complete a letter, but when eventually he took it up again found it necessary to alter the heading.[5]

Letters sometimes took two or even more sessions to complete. On Jan. 10, 1775, Wesley began writing to Ann Bolton early in the morning, but broke off after the first paragraph because he was setting out on a preaching tour. He finished it the following day, witness the postscript: 'I began this at London, but could not end it till I came to Luton.'[6] This letter was delayed still further in the mail.

---

[1] They remain private, quite unlike 'open letters' on sale to the public, even when (as was apparently the case with *A Plain Account of the People called Methodists*, *Bibliog*, No. 159, printed in Vol. 9 of this edition) they originated as personal letters to individuals.

[2] Cf. similar letters dated Nov. 20, 1769, and Dec. 12, 1772, and those in later years appealing for the New Chapel, City Road, London, or for that in Dewsbury, which (as Wesley told Henry Moore, Sept. 5, 1789) 'should be printed and sent to every Assistant'.

[3] Nov. 5, 1762; cf. July 11, 1763.

[4] As on Oct. 28, 1758, when he broke off in the middle of the second sentence of a letter. Those of Dec. 28, 1784, and July 4, 1789, he abandoned after the opening sentences, striking through those passages a few days later and using the same sheets to write complete letters; on the first he wrote the letter of Dec. 30, 1784, to Ann Tindall, on the second that of July 7, 1789, to Mr. Hall. Cf. a sheet addressed to Nancy Holman and later used for a letter to Joseph Benson, dated Dec. 21, 1779.

[5] See a letter dated 'Witney, Oct. 16, 1783', and re-dated, 'London, Oct. 17, 1783'.

[6] The break is confirmed and pinpointed by the different pen, ink, and handwriting.

Postmarks enable us to trace the individual misadventures of many letters. One to Samuel Furly, for example, written from Mount-mellick on June 19, 1769, was not postmarked by the London post office until July 12, and still had to travel north to Yorkshire. It is quite possible, of course, that on this occasion as on others the delay was Wesley's fault rather than that of the postal service. Another letter to Ann Bolton, for instance, was written Feb. 17, 1774, but bore the following conclusion: 'March 2, 1774. I found the above (which I thought had been finished and sent) among my papers this morning. I hope you did not think you was forgotten by, My dear Nancy, Your affectionate brother, J. Wesley.'[1] Far worse was the fate of a letter to Mr. York of Stourport, which Wesley discovered in his bureau over three weeks later—after the visit to Stourport to which it referred.[2] Sometimes a letter seems to have remained unanswered because Wesley did not quite know what to do with it.[3] Personal emergencies might intervene for him as well as for his correspondents. Thus to his letter of Nov. 20, 1755, to the Revd. Samuel Walker, Wesley added the postscript: 'All but the last paragraph of this I had wrote three weeks ago, but the dangerous illness of my wife prevented my finishing it sooner.'[4] A few letters Wesley held back permanently because of second thoughts or the advice of friends. This happened to his loyal address to George I, written March 5, 1744, upon the urgent request of some Methodists, but abandoned when his brother Charles argued: 'It would consti-tute us a sect; at least it would *seem to allow* that we are a body distinct from the national Church, whereas we are only a sound part of that Church.'[5]

Corrections and revisions. To Nancy Bolton Wesley confessed, 'I often write in haste',[6] and this was especially true of his personal letters, which are riddled with minor corrections and revisions—as well as undiscovered errors. Of seventy-six holographs of his letters

---

[1] Similarly on Nov. 20, 1766, he wrote a letter to Christopher Hopper, but discovered it still unsent on Nov. 27, whereupon he added another message, beginning, 'It is well my letter was overlooked till I came home. So one will do for two.' Still later he added a further postscript revising the second message before he sent the letter on its way.

[2] Feb. 6, 1791, with the postscript dated (apparently) Feb. 28, 'This morning I found this in my bureau.' That the letter was in fact dispatched is shown by the postmark and the postal-charge inscription.

[3] Oct. 20, 1768.

[4] As the cover was in fact postmarked Nov. 22 it is clear that what Wesley had finished earlier was a draft of this important letter.

[5] CWJ, Mar. 6, 1744. [6] Jan. 29, 1773.

to his brother Charles, stretching from 1738 to 1788, no fewer than sixty-eight show alterations of one kind or another, including both the earliest and the latest. Some of these are afterthoughts, such as the addition of the sentence, 'I never saw it till it was printed.'[1] Most (like the last) are written over the line, and indicated by a caret, implying that they were added during a later perusal of the letter, possibly whilst preparing a reference copy—a good argument for such a practice! Occasionally the revision was certainly made during the process of writing, as where the manuscript reads, 'to "Take thou authority . . . " '[2] or 'be at the he chief'.[3] Usually they are careless errors caused by haste, such as writing 'horse' for 'house',[4] but sometimes stylistic, even the changing of the position of quotation marks.[5] Easily the largest group of errors, however—and a clear indication of how his thoughts frequently ran ahead of his pen—consisted of the omission of a word or words. No fewer than thirty-five of the seventy-six letters contain such corrections, one having three, including two in one line,[6] and another no fewer than five.[7] The same is true of the series to Alexander Knox and Ann Tindall, of which once more about half contain corrected errors of omission, and occasionally such errors uncorrected.[8] Indeed, so universal (and so multitudinous) are the alterations in Wesley's extant manuscripts, whether of letters or works intended for publication, that there seems little point in indicating them in the text unless in very exceptional circumstances.

Wesley's handwriting. There is a slight family resemblance between the hands of John Wesley, his brother Charles, and several of his sisters; some of Wesley's preachers—whether by chance or design is not always certain—used a similar hand. Yet his remains distinctive, and once recognized is difficult to confuse with that of anyone else.[9] Wesley's first extant letter (Nov. 3, 1721) is in a fully rounded, forward sloping, somewhat feminine hand, with each letter formed separately ('script'). By the time of his second extant letter (Sept. 23, 1723) this had become somewhat firmer, and was much more so

---

[1] Feb. 22, 1774.   [2] June 23, 1739.
[3] Feb. 28, 1766, changing 'be at the he[lm]', the last word unfinished, to 'be the chief'.
[4] Sept. 28, 1760.   [5] June 23, 1739.
[6] June 8, 1789.   [7] Nov. 3, 1775.
[8] e.g. Aug. 5, 1782, to Ann Tindall, with one corrected and one not.
[9] For fuller details on Wesley's calligraphy see an article by the editor in W.H.S. XXV. 97–9. Michael Fenwick is said deliberately to have mimicked Wesley in many ways (see Atmore, p. 123), and evidence of his success can be seen in his letter of Aug. 26, 1790, to Samuel Bardsley (in MA).

by his third (Nov. 1, 1724), when he began to forsake script for a cursive hand, and the edge was taken from its almost too precise beauty. This was explained in the letter itself: 'I should have writ before now had I not an unlucky cut across my thumb, which almost jointed it, but is now pretty well cured. I hope you will excuse my writing so ill, which I can't easily help, as being obliged to get done as soon as I can.' In the following letter (Dec. 18, 1724), script again appeared alongside cursive, as it did also in 1725. The speed of the cursive hand, however, answered the needs of Wesley's proliferating correspondence, and script was gradually discarded —or almost discarded. His handwriting continued to present something of the general appearance of script, and even into old age he used the script epsilon and sigma as well as the cursive 'e' and 's', and made breaks after other letters within words. Age, of course, including varying periods of semi-blindness and shaking hands, brought near ruin to his calligraphy, proving a trial both to himself and to his readers, and bequeathing to future generations many errors caused by the inability of compositors and scholars alike to interpret some of his later scrawls.

What about the character evidenced by this handwriting? One of these days the writer of these lines hopes to offer some graphologist (probably through an intermediary) a specimen of Wesley's handwriting which does not immediately give him away by its subject-matter—if indeed such can be found. Forty years ago a gentleman with forty years' practical experience as a graphologist did offer such an opinion, claiming that his slight knowledge of Wesley's history and teaching (as a non-Methodist) had not been allowed to influence him. His delineation, though somewhat lengthy, is worth preserving, and every claim could indeed be illustrated from independent documentary evidence:

The handwriting of the Rev. John Wesley reveals a refined and sensitive nature; one who feels intensely any unkindness or slight; but who appreciates most gratefully any token of affection or esteem.

The mind is cultured, expressing grace and refinement; there is considerable business ability, mental dexterity, clearness of ideas, and application to detail.

The character is straightforward, candid, honest, and conscientious. There is real affection, a gentle spirit, true humility, and an unusual degree of kindness.

His habits are methodical and precise; he cannot endure disorder or confusion of any kind.

Artistic taste and a poetic temperament are clearly revealed. He has an imaginative mind; is versatile, having a knowledge of and interest in many subjects. His ideas follow each other in logical sequence; he can express his thoughts fluently, in words both pleasing and graceful.

The handwriting discloses his innate economy, his scrupulous neatness in dress, and in his domestic arrangements.

Discouragement affects his spirit; he suffers silently, more than his outward behaviour reveals; he is a patient man, persevering without wavering.

He is quick to criticism; he sees at once the weak point in the argument of an opponent; he has a facility for making comparisons, and illustrating ideas.

Throughout, his handwriting reveals a purity of heart and mind, elevation of thought, and deep spirituality.[1]

Amanuenses and secretaries. Wesley frequently used an amanuensis to prepare a copy of a letter. Occasionally the letter dispatched was itself in the hand of an amanuensis, such as one of Sept. 21, 1739, to Charles Wesley, in which only a covering note and the address were written by John. This was in effect a journal-letter, apparently copied at Wesley's request from his written journal. A similar case is an account of Methodist activities in Kingswood, of which duplicates appear to have been made.[2] Other types of letters are also found in the hands of scribes, probably because Wesley had prepared a draft, which was retained as the reference copy, while a companion was asked to write out a fair copy to send to the recipient. Instances of such letters are reported by Dr. John Whitehead as written by Benjamin Ingham,[3] and those to 'John Smith'. Wesley's letter to 'John Smith' dated Dec. 30, 1745, referring back to the previous letter, states, 'I find my transcriber has made a violent mistake, writing 13,000 instead of 1,300.'[4] (Which implies that although Wesley usually proof-read letters and thus discovered at least some of his own errors, he did not always proof-read fair copies of important letters dispatched on his behalf.) Similarly on Jan. 4, 1768, in sending Richard Libby a copy of his printed circular of Nov. 20, 1767, a covering note was added in the hand of a scribe, to which John Wesley appended his signature. Transcriptions of letters copied by an amanuensis and authorized by Wesley's signature continued to appear until his closing years.[5] Occasionally Wesley wrote the letter and his amanuensis the address, as well as folding the sheet (quite differently from Wesley's normal practice).[6]

[1] Mr. W. A. Brewster, Lancing, in *The Methodist Recorder*, Dec. 16, 1937. There is no indication about which manuscripts he had studied.

[2] Dec. 6, 1739.

[3] Feb. 24, 26, 1737, to Oglethorpe and Bray's Associates.   [4] § [8].

[5] e.g. Nov. 29, 1782; Mar. 13, 1787; Mar. 13, 1788.   [6] Nov. 11, 1786.

During his eighties, however, another factor began to operate, when there seems to have been no intention of preserving a copy. Because of failing eyesight or some other physical infirmity he dictated a letter to a companion, simply adding his own signature. Such were the letters written during Wesley's last month, to Thomas Roberts on February 8, 1791, to John Gaulter on the 10th, to Francis Wrigley on the 18th, to Walter Churchey on the 22nd. The marvel is that he continued to address at least some of these letters, and even from his deathbed to write out a few completely, including his famous letter to William Wilberforce, attacking slavery, on February 24, 1791.

In addition to utilizing the services of amanuenses who copied verbatim what he had written, or who wrote at his dictation, Wesley also employed what might be called confidential secretaries, who were charged to pass on messages on his behalf. These, of course, signed their own names, but made it quite clear that they were acting for him, not for themselves. Dr. Thomas Coke wrote letters of this kind, such as one to Robert Dodsley, Feb. 24, 1781 : 'Sir, Mr. Wesley is desirous of employing two or three booksellers in different parts of the town to sell his publications, allowing the 25 per cent profit, the usual allowance to booksellers . . .' Many others performed this function from time to time: Peter Jaco (Feb. 18, 1777), Thomas Tennant (Nov. 12, 1783, and Feb. 12, 1785), John Atlay (Feb. 23, 1784), Henry Moore (Dec. 24, 1784), John Broadbent (Jan. 24, 1787), Joseph Bradford (June 14, 1788), and probably many others, including a layman, Arthur Keene (see July 31, 1785). Andrew Blair wrote such a letter on Wesley's behalf on April 28, 1790, and Wesley added a note in his own handwriting. The process was reversed in a letter written by Wesley on Feb. 6, 1791, to which a postscript on his behalf was added by James Rogers. Wherever such letters are discovered, containing a specific message explicitly written on behalf of Wesley, they have been included among his own correspondence.

IV. THE ANATOMY OF A LETTER

John Wesley had his own idiosyncrasies, not only in his general approach to writing letters, but in handling the specific elements of which a letter was composed. If we are to understand the significance,

not only of what was said, but of how it was said, we need to establish norms for all the bones and sinews which constitute the anatomy
of a letter. Because these norms are also of major importance in
helping the reader to assess the authenticity and finer points of the
letters which he may wish to study with special care, as also in
evaluating conjectures about such matters as their context, dates,
and recipients, we make no apology for dealing with this complex
and generally neglected subject at some length and in some detail.

Place and date of writing. Wesley was much more regular than
many of his correspondents (including his brother Charles) in
furnishing settings in time and space for his letters, and he displays
some marked preferences in the method of their presentation. Both
pieces of information were present in 95 per cent of his letters,
usually on separate lines.[1] In fewer than 7 per cent (scattered throughout the years with no discernible rationale) were these details given
on one line rather than two. In only 3 per cent were they given at
the end rather than at the beginning of the letter (most of the
exceptions appearing during Wesley's early years), and in only six
out of 500 letters did the place appear after the date.

Very rarely indeed did Wesley supply any more than the name of
the town from which he was writing, except that occasionally he did
locate the smaller places by reference to the larger, as in 'Kighley,
near Leeds' (Apr. 29, 1755), or 'Ennis, near Limerick' (July 12,
1760), though much more frequent is the less specific 'near Leeds',
'near Oxford', and especially 'near London', apparently indicating
that he was staying with friends in Lewisham, Newington, or some
other retreat—though the names of these two places do themselves
occur. Occasionally Wesley identified the specific building: in his
early years he sometimes used 'Christ Church' or 'Lincoln College'
instead of 'Oxford' (or 'Oxon.'), and in his later years 'City Road',
instead of London, and 'Whitefriar Street' instead of Dublin, or
some similar indication of the Methodist preaching-house from
which he wrote. An almost unique heading is, 'Tetsworth, 42 miles
from London', but this is explained by the fact that he had just
left his newly wedded wife, and was counting the miles between
them, asking her, 'Do I write too soon?'[2]

Almost invariably Wesley wrote his dates in the form, 'Dec. 26.
1771', abbreviating the months from August to February, and writing

---

[1] Statistics based on the 500 letters noted on p. 27.
[2] Mar. 27, 1751.

the others in full.[1] In 3 per cent of his letters he reversed the order, writing '3 July. 1751.' (He seems always to have used periods rather than commas in his headings, and spread them about much more liberally than we shall do henceforth in quoting from him, even writing such headings as 'Dublin. 15. March. 1747/8'; all such idiosyncrasies are normalized in the text.) In only 0·5 per cent did he use an ordinal instead of a cardinal number for his dates, and on one occasion at least he employed the form, 'July ye 17th, 1785'— though on only one of three letters extant for that date.

From one only out of five hundred letters did Wesley omit the date completely, giving only the place of writing,[2] and in one other he omitted the year.[3] He was usually very careful in giving a date precisely, in the form which would prevent future problems in letters retained for reference. Until 1752, when the calendar was reformed, confusion was rife, because in the Old Style ('O.S.') the legal year in England began on March 25 and ended on March 24, although common usage accepted the Julian calendar, which reckoned the year as beginning on January 1. The only certain way to avoid ambiguity about dates between January 1 and March 24 was to list both years of which they formed a part in the different styles, and this Wesley did in twenty-two out of the thirty holograph letters available,[4] giving the dates as 'Janu. 8, 1745/6' etc. In the other eight instances (occurring in 1736, 1740, 1748, 1750, and 1751), he showed his own strong preference by accepting the common usage, the New Style ('N.S.'), made standard in 1752.[5]

Only very rarely did Wesley add the day of the week, but three instances occur in the five hundred selected letters, including one which adds an even rarer feature, the time of day: 'Friday, April 1, 1774, 5 o'clock'.[6]

Like most people, he occasionally misdated his letters, especially

[1] His normal abbreviations were: 'Aug.', 'Sept.', 'Oct.', 'Nov.', 'Dec.', 'Janu.' and 'Feb.', but cf. 'Apr. 23, 1745', 'Septr. 1, 1777', and 'Jan. 8, 1774'—even though a letter to James Hutton of the same date has 'Janu. 8, 1774'.

[2] Jan. 28–9, 1770.

[3] Nov. 24, 1738.

[4] Not including transcripts of any kind, even by Wesley himself.

[5] The reforms of 1752 also incorporated the suggestions of Pope Gregory XIII for various measures correcting the defective computations of the Julian calendar, the most radical being that of omitting several dates—in England, almost the last to adopt the system, Sept. 3–13, 1752. (Cf. JWJ, Sept. 14, 1752.)

[6] Cf. July 31, 1742; Sept. 29, 1773. For another instance of the unusual pinpointing see a letter to Charles Wesley: 'Bristol, March 17, 1788, between four and five'.

at the beginning of a new year or a new month.[1] Other more peculiar errors occur, by no means so simple to explain. In a sheet combining letters to both Miss Gibbes and her younger sister Agnes, Wesley dated one (correctly), '25th April, 1783', and the other, 'April 25, 1785'.[2]

Salutations. Occasionally Wesley launched right into a letter without a salutation, but this happened in fewer than one in twenty letters, and those almost always to his friends. Following the normal convention of an opening salutation he employed a hierarchy of terms (without any following punctuation mark) which we may arrange in ascending order of intimacy: Sir/Madam; Dear sir/ Dear madam; My dear Mr.—/Mrs.—/Miss X; My dear brother/ sister; Dear James/Jane, etc.; Dear Jemmy/Jenny, etc. The frequent variations in his mode of address between 'brother' or 'sister' and a personal name, however, implies that the difference in warmth was not as greatly marked as it might be with us, and perhaps was almost imperceptible to those who could mentally hear the affectionate tone in which 'My dear brother' was spoken. This was even true of 'Dear sir', which Wesley consistently used to address some of his friends. Nor did he apparently feel any nuance of greater intimacy in 'My dear Nancy' than in 'Dear Nancy', using them interchangeably, though the latter is easily his preferred term in addressing his favourite correspondent outside his immediate family, Ann Bolton. Similarly he mixed up 'Dear Alleck' (twenty-nine times) with 'My dear Alleck' (twenty times) in his correspondence with Alexander Knox. Wesley also frequently incorporated into his letters a closing salutation, usually a repetition of the opening one, omitting this feature in about one of five instances. When the closing salutation was different from that at the beginning it tended to be slightly less formal.[3]

---

[1] Thus a letter to his brother Charles was headed 'Janu. 5, 1762', when in fact it was 1763, and one to R. C. Brackenbury written in 1784 was dated 'Janu. 4, 1783'. Similarly he headed a letter, 'York, June 10, 1774', when he should have written 'July 10', and in another instance discovered his error in time, smearing out 'Aug.' before writing 'Sept. 10, 1785'. In each case the place of writing clinches the actual date, and in one instance this is confirmed by the postmark which is available.

[2] The final '5' in the year may have been caused by the influence of the final '5' in the month. For an unexplained post-dating see two letters to Charles Wesley, both dated Oct. 19, 1775, but written from two different places, at which he was apparently present respectively two days and one day earlier, and a letter dated Dec. 17, 1787, which is shown by the postmark to have been dispatched two days earlier.

[3] Thus in his thirty-six letters to Ann Tindall he usually began, 'My dear sister', but

Even with members of his own family Wesley employed formality, remembering childhood rules about speaking politely to everyone, and prefixing a sibling's name with 'brother' or 'sister'.[1] His father was uniformly addressed as 'Dear sir', his mother as 'Dear mother', and both his brothers as 'Dear brother' to the end of their days, with no hint of a personal name. He relaxed a little with his sisters, perhaps because there were so many of them. The evidence is scanty, however, letters to only two having survived. One only is extant from the dozens which were written to his oldest sister, and it begins, 'Dear Emly',[2] but Martha continued to be addressed as 'Dear sister' until at least 1756, the first occurrence of 'Dear Patty' being in 1761. With his wife it was very different. The one letter written before their marriage both opened and closed with the slightly formal, 'My dear sister', but most of the remainder began, 'My dear Molly', varied with, 'My dear love', or occasionally 'My dear soul', 'My dear life', or simply 'My dear'.

Allied to the measure of formality seen in his family letters was Wesley's sensitivity to age and rank or position. Members of the nobility were always saluted formally, as 'My Lord',[3] and 'My Lady', or 'My dear Lady'.[4] A person in the professions or the upper classes was addressed as 'Dear sir', and his wife as 'Dear madam', which would probably continue even after they had become friends instead of acquaintances.[5] Merchants and artisans seem usually to have been greeted as 'Dear brother', or (as throughout fifteen letters to George Merryweather, Methodist stalwart of Yarm) 'My dear brother'.

His fellow clergy Wesley addressed as 'Reverend and dear sir', 'Reverend sir', or 'Dear sir', with the apparent implication that the longer the title the more formal the tone. Only with close friends did he unbend further, to 'My dear brother'. Even the intimate colleagues of his Oxford days, such as Benjamin Ingham and George

ended, 'Dear Nancy' (twenty-three times) or 'My dear Nancy' (six times), though in two fairly late instances he both began and ended, 'Dear Nancy'.

[1] See Mrs. Susanna Wesley to John Wesley, July 24, 1732.

[2] June 30, 1743.

[3] See the Earl of Dartmouth, June 14, 1775, and Lord North, June 15, 1775.

[4] See the Countess of Huntingdon, Jan. 8, 1764; Sept. 15, 1776, etc.; D'arcy, Lady Maxwell, June 22, 1766, etc. Here one does detect added warmth in the prefixed 'My'.

[5] As in the case of Ebenezer Blackwell, the banker, although with Mrs. Hutton of Dean's Yard, Westminster, he actually began with two letters to his former critic as 'Madam' before unbending to 'Dear madam' (Aug. 22, 1744; Jan. 18, 1746; June 19, 1746).

Whitefield, were thus addressed, not by their personal names.[1] In the sixteen extant letters to John Fletcher only once did Wesley forsake 'Dear sir' for 'My dear brother',[2] and Dr. Thomas Coke was always, 'Dear sir', as was James Creighton. In 1785 Wesley addressed young Peard Dickinson, however, as 'My dear brother', then twice in 1787 as 'Dear sir', returning to 'My dear brother' for the ten extant closing letters of their correspondence.

Always, of course, there was with Wesley the hope, and indeed the likelihood, of deepening friendship, for he undoubtedly possessed great charm. This would be followed by the confident use of diminutive personal names, especially with those young enough to be his children, such as Peard Dickinson (1758–1802). Similarly with the Revd. Samuel Furly (*c.* 1736–95) he quickly moved from 'Dear sir' to 'My dear brother', and then to 'Dear Sammy'.[3] With Furly's sister Dorothy, however, he seems only to have progressed from 'Dear Miss Furly' to 'My dear sister'—if we may trust Joseph Benson, who is our sole source for the twenty-three letters to her.[4] Wesley was not always successful in achieving *rapport*. He failed in the case of Miss Mary Bishop. All thirty-seven of his extant holograph letters began and usually ended, 'My dear Miss Bishop' or 'My dear sister', except for one occasion when at the end he tried out 'My dear Molly'—an experiment which was not repeated and so was apparently not welcomed; their relationship remained cordial, but a trifle formal.[5]

With the Methodist preachers Wesley seems normally to have begun a correspondence with 'My dear brother', then quickly to have broken through to a diminutive Christian name, especially as befitted a father-in-God to his 'sons in the gospel'.[6] In some in-

---

[1] But James Hervey was greeted as 'My dear friend' (Nov. 21, 1738), and then 'My dear brother' (Mar. 20, Aug. 8, Oct. 25, 1739), though during and after his controversy with Wesley in 1756 this became 'Dear sir' (Oct. 15, 1756; Nov. 29, 1758).

[2] Oct. 1, 1773.

[3] Mar. 30, Sept. 21, 1754, etc., and Sept. 15, 1755.

[4] In this matter, however, Benson is hardly to be trusted, for in his edition of Wesley's letters he consistently (and surely deliberately) altered Wesley's use of personal names in his salutations to women, as in the case of Ann Bolton, where every instance of 'Dear Nancy' found in the extant holographs was transformed into the innocuous 'My dear sister'.

[5] Similarly he confessed: 'After an acquaintanceship of four-and-thirty years, I myself cannot have freedom with Miss Johnson.' (June 17, 1774.)

[6] It is an interesting fact that although he lived to a great age, and was loved by many young men and women (and in his turn loved them), he never seems to have addressed them as 'Dear boy' or 'Dear son', 'Dear daughter' or 'Dear girl', but almost always by

stances, as with Joseph Benson, no shortened form was used, but this was probably due less to a lack of warmth than to the fact that 'Joe' or 'Joey' were not then in common use.[1] Nor does the lack even of the usual Christian name in the salutation necessarily imply coldness or lack of respect, but was probably a connotation of seniority or status: John Valton remained 'My dear brother' to Wesley throughout twenty-one years and twenty-six extant letters (having joined the itinerary ranks from commerce when he was about 35), and Robert Carr Brackenbury, the squire of Raithby Hall, who served as an itinerant preacher during Wesley's last decade, was always addressed as 'Dear sir', though any implied lack of cordiality is belied by Wesley's frequent subscription, 'Your very affectionate friend and brother'.

Occasionally, of course, Wesley had to deal with critical and even offensive letters. To one very stiff letter he replied, 'My dear brother, or to speak civilly, Sir,' and ended, 'Your affectionate brother, or if you choose it rather, Your humble servant'.[2]

All this emphasizes the fact that Wesley lived in a formal age, was himself a formal person, and carefully practised the formalities, though in such a manner that we can detect subtle graduations and nuances which should carefully be observed, and their importance noted though not exaggerated, bearing in mind always that Wesley's shades of meaning were not necessarily those which we have inherited or invented. Even apart from the value of his salutations in illuminating his character and the setting of his letters, however, his norms for their use may prove of great importance in establishing or confirming, as well as in refuting, the identity of many undocumented recipients.

The body of the letter. Sandwiched between somewhat formal yet often very revealing opening and closing courtesies came the letter itself. Throughout most of his life Wesley felt no need to embroider a simple message, nor to use up all the paper available to him.[3] Sometimes the letter proper was far shorter than the formalities, or than the address. Most of these shorter ones were, of course, simple directions or challenges to his followers. To one preacher he wrote:

their given names or diminutives of them, though on at least one occasion he did write, 'My dear maiden' (Jan. 18, 1790).

[1] Joseph Cownley was also addressed as 'Joseph', as were others bearing the same name, including Pescod, Pilmore, Sutcliffe, and Taylor.　　　[2] Apr. 27, 1748.

[3] To one of his inquirers he wrote: 'Indeed my time seldom allows me to write long letters. But we can tell our minds without a multitude of words.' (Nov. 6, 1756.)

'Are you out of your wits? Why are you not at Bristol?'[1] To another the message was, 'You shall be in Oxfordshire.'[2] The complaints of a Sunday School superintendent Wesley countered with, 'John White, whoever is wrong, you are not right.'[3] The shortest letter of all consisted of three words to James Chubb, another Methodist layman. We reproduce it completely:

Aug. 13, 1774

My dear brother

All is well. I am,

Yours affectionately
J. Wesley

One of the longest personal letters—as opposed to controversial or apologetic letters prepared for publication—was that to his wife, written Dec. 9, 1774, covering over seven pages.[4] There were very few such. Wesley believed strongly in economy of time and expense, and both these principles were reinforced by his characteristic desire for simplicity and brevity. Only very rarely indeed, therefore, did he venture beyond the four small pages which should be sufficient for any normal letter written in a neat, compact hand, and (by writing a little smaller) for most longer ones also.

There seems little doubt that Wesley planned each letter in advance, even when he did not prepare a draft, deciding whether it was going to occupy one page, two pages, or three.[5] For each approximate length he had a different procedure, from which he rarely varied. His basic letter covered one of the four small pages made by folding his half-sheet in two. We will call this page 1, as if this were a 4-page folder. The letter always began on this page. The address was written on p. 3, inscribed on a central panel, writing from the foot to the head of the paper, and from the centre of the page towards the outer edge.[6] At least half of Wesley's letters were in exactly this form, the first extant being that of Mar. 31, 1737, to the Georgia Trustees.

A planned two-page letter usually followed the same procedure (at least until the 1750s), with the address on p. 3, and the overflow

---

[1] Sept. 15, 1773, to Francis Wolfe.   [2] June 1, 1784, to Simon Day.
[3] [July, 1784].
[4] The letters to 'John Smith', defending his teaching and practice, must similarly have used two half-sheets of paper folded to make eight pages.
[5] To Nancy Bolton he wrote, Nov. 28, 1772: 'I designed to have wrote but one page. But I know not how, when I am talking with *you*, I can hardly break off.'
[6] See illus. facing p. 58.

from the letter on p. 1 written vertically from head to foot of p. 4, again from the inside fold to the outer edge. Postscripts to a one-page letter were added in this same way. The first extant two-page letter of this kind was that sent to his mother, Jan. 13, 1735.[1] In the rare instances when a last-minute addition was needed, this was probably added vertically on p. 2.[2]

With a planned three-page letter Wesley wrote the address on p. 4, began his letter on p. 1, and continued to p. 2 and then to p. 3, writing horizontally all the time except for the address, which was written from foot to head, and again from the centre of the page towards the outer edge. If three full pages proved insufficient he usually continued on the margins and on the head and foot of p. 4, which would later be folded over and hidden from view.[3] Occasionally a letter planned to occupy three pages was finished on two, leaving p. 3 blank, and it appears that in the 1750s Wesley began to write what he had envisaged as two-page letters in this alternative format, and continued to use both methods interchangeably for the remainder of his life.[4]

Wesley was neat and methodical in all his ways, and this reveals itself clearly in his letters. Every page was set out carefully, with a square left margin, and lines so straight and equidistant from each other that one might wonder whether he used a ruled guide.[5] Even when Wesley was well into his eighties, and his legibility was declining

---

[1] His first extant letter, Nov. 3, 1721, followed a different format, as probably did others during his youth.

[2] Cf. Mar. 27, 1751, to his wife, and Feb. 12, 1767, to his brother Charles.

[3] See below, pp. 68–70, for folding the sheet. See for examples Apr. 29, May 7, May 28, and June 7, 1739, to James Hutton.

[4] A handful of different combinations occur from time to time, but only about one in a hundred letters does not follow the patterns here described as Wesley's normal routine, a fact which occasionally proves of value in resolving various problems connected with the many imperfect letters. Thus it can be stated almost categorically that any supposed photograph or xerox of a Wesley letter with a signed page of text on the right and the address on the left is not genuine, but has been artificially contrived in some way; see, for instance, one so prepared by John Wesley himself because p. 1 was already used by John Atlay, Aug. 13, 1775. (But for one prepared by Wesley three can be cited prepared by later collectors of his letters.)

[5] The watermarks did not offer a built-in guide, for Wesley's chosen format meant that he was writing across the grain of the wire-lines. Only an adjustable guide would have been practicable, for the gap between his lines did in fact vary from letter to letter, though rarely within individual letters: the governing factor was the number of lines per full page, and this depended upon the size of the handwriting, which in turn depended upon Wesley's preconception of the length of the letter. The letter to Benson, Sept. 17, 1788, p. 2, has 19 lines, and in that to Mrs. Wesley, Dec. 9, 1774, pp. 5, 6 have 32; in this letter Wesley allowed himself eight pages, but towards the end realized that

seriously, the almost mathematical precision of his lines continued. Even the letter written from his deathbed to William Wilberforce at first glance seems to vary only slightly from the norm, though in fact the margin wavers somewhat, and every one of the seventeen lines forsakes the absolute horizontal at one point or another. Both eyes and hand, after eighty-seven years, were failing badly, but the inner spirit almost achieved his accustomed neatness.

Wesley's eye was not only accurate in setting out the lines of his page, but artistic in seeking a harmonious balance between its various elements. If he planned a very brief letter he would begin lower on the page, as well as spacing his lines further apart.[1] Each feature was usually begun on a separate line from the others: on the right the place of writing, followed on a fresh line by the date; below that on the left the salutation, again with a line to itself; then the letter proper, its opening line indented. The closing courtesies occupied two or more separate lines according to the amount of space left; the signature was given a line to itself.

The preparation of a draft facilitated neatness in the fair copy dispatched to Wesley's correspondents. When this practice was all but abandoned except for especially important letters, Wesley could never be quite sure whether he was correctly estimating the length and therefore the disposition of the various elements of the letter. Frequently he did find himself cramped for space. Only in extremely rare instances, however, did he vary the size of his writing or the space separating the lines on any individual page, except for the insertion of corrections or afterthoughts.[2] Instead he utilized other expedients to reduce infelicitous overcrowding. One was the running-together of some of the closing courtesies.[3] Another was what we may term the internal paragraph.

he was writing too large a hand (25 lines to p. 2, 27 to p. 3, so that on p. 4 he wrote 30, on pp. 5 and 6, 32, on p. 7, 31—and even then needed to squeeze the ending on to the flap of the address page).

[1] One example is the letter to James Chubb quoted above, written on imaginary lines distant from each other 24, 19, 15, and 16 mm, with the first 23 mm from the head and the last 29 mm from the foot of the scrap of paper, which has apparently been cut down at the foot. A more normal example is a letter of Feb. 24, 1764, to Thomas Hanson, whose thirteen lines are separated by an average 12 mm, with 17 mm between the salutation and the first paragraph, and also between the first and second paragraphs, while from the head of the page to the address line is 16 mm, and from the signature to the foot of the page 31 mm.

[2] In a letter of Dec. 14, 1776, however, he did squeeze together the two lines of courtesies and his signature.

[3] See below, pp. 58-62.

Like many of his contemporaries, in Wesley's first two extant letters he indicated no paragraphs at all, but by the end of 1724 he was familiar with the technique of paragraphing. In 1738 he occasionally introduced a new idea by a less drastic method than that of beginning a fresh line: he left a space of about 1 in. after the previous period instead of the normal ⅛ in.[1] For two decades this device, which we propose to call an internal paragraph, seems to have remained experimental, but came into frequent use for the remainder of Wesley's life. It proved most valuable to save space when the closing sentence of a paragraph ended only two or three words into a new line, but he also used it when only a small portion of the line was left.[2] This in turn enabled him to manipulate his paper to secure his favourite one-page letters, though he used it also in longer letters, which might thus be prevented from spilling over on to the address page.[3]

Normally Wesley carried his writing very close to the edge of the paper for his right margin, while leaving between ¼ in. and ½ in. for the left margin—sometimes more, sometimes less, depending on the planned length of the letter. Rarely did he follow the compositor's practice of 'justifying' his lines by adding space between words or letters, though to a limited extent he followed the reverse practice of squeezing them together to fit them into his line, and also abbreviated words which he normally wrote out fully, such as 'employᵗ' or 'judgmᵗ'.[4] He seems to have sought a page which approached the printed page as nearly as possible without any appearance of

---

[1] Cf. June 28, 1738, to his mother—the peroration; Nov. 26, 1738, to James Hutton —an internal division within a lengthy paragraph; June 7, 1739, also to Hutton—a clear change of subject.

[2] e.g. a one-page letter to Samuel Furly, July 28, 1758, where the first internal paragraph separates four words at the beginning of the line from four at the end, and the second separates six at the beginning from two at the end. In some instances the space remaining allowed room for only one word at the end of the line, as in letters to Joseph Benson, Oct. 5, 1770, and Jan. 21, 1771.

[3] In seventy-three letters to Charles Wesley, for instance, he used forty-five internal paragraphs, almost equally divided between one-page letters and pp. 1–3 of longer letters. The three internal paragraphs in his letter of Oct. 5, 1770, probably saved writing down the margin or using the flap on p. 4. For an example in the closing courtesies see his letter of Nov. 29, 1775, to Sarah Crosby, facing p. 68.

A similar device was apparently used to distinguish the verse-endings in his presentation of Scripture in continuous paragraphs, though this is so spotty that it may have been a simple extension of compositorial justifying. (See early editions of his *Explanatory Notes* on the New Testament (1755) and the Old Testament (1765).)

[4] e.g. letters of May 1, 1758; Dec. 22, 1768; Dec. 14, 1776; for some compression of the last line see illus., facing p. 58.

artificiality, so that he remained content with a jagged right margin, but was prepared to perform some squeezing at the end of a one-page letter. There seems little doubt that many of his abbreviations were designed with this in mind, for he often used them interchangeably with their full forms, such as 'and' and the ampersand '&'; 'which', 'wch', and even 'wᶜ'; 'that' and 'yᵗ'; 'the' and 'yᵉ'; 'shou'd' and 'shᵈ', etc. Sometimes they occur in the same letter, though not always with the shorter form near the end of a line, which would offer confirmation that his chief motive was justifying the line or saving space.[1] Occasionally he would lengthen the cross-stroke of an 'f' or a 't' more than normally at the end of a line, however,[2] or slant the last line downwards as well as compressing the words together,[3] or place a stroke over a vowel to indicate a missing final consonant.[4] Perhaps the most revealing measure to achieve something like an even right margin, however, was the division of words at the end of the line, for which he normally used a hyphen, but occasionally a colon. In general he followed accepted practice, with 'hurt-full', 'with:out', 'Hind-marsh', etc.[5] His concern to justify his lines, however, led to some divisions which would be frowned upon by the purist: 'refor-mation',[6] 'persecut-ed',[7] 'un:derstand',[8] 'trans-late', but 'translati-on',[9] 'conside-rable'.[10] One letter alone furnishes the following: 'unim-portant', 're:wards', 'Taberna-cle', 'congre:gations', 'ex:pected', 'Mon:day', and 'Chap:pel'.[11] There is little question that a tidy page mattered to Wesley!

Even margins were deliberately forsaken for two purposes, one connected with the ideal of securing a pleasing layout, the other not. Short prose quotations Wesley ran into the text, with double quotation marks (the closing ones often *over* the last word rather than after it); verse quotations, however, even of one line, he normally indented, again (and this time unnecessarily) enclosed within double quotation marks. The other occasion for a deliberate intrusion into the margin over two or three lines occurred only in longer letters, on p. 3, i.e. on the reverse of the position that he expected

[1] Wesley's 59 holograph letters to Joseph Benson furnish ample illustrations for most of the points made in this section. For interchangeable word-forms see May 27, 1769; Jan. 21, 1771; June 21, 1774; July 31, 1776. Cf. that to Sarah Crosby, Nov. 29, 1775, lines 10, 11, 15 ('the', 'yᵉ'), and also 6 ('shᵈ') and 19 ('wch') (illus., p. 68).

[2] e.g. Nov. 7, 1768; Dec. 4, 1768; Nov. 30, 1770.

[3] Nov. 19, 1769.   [4] Mar. 16, 1771.

[5] Dec. 4, 1768; Jan. 2, 1769; Aug. 7, 1769; cf. Nov. 29, 1775, lines 5–6 (illus., p. 68).

[6] Dec. 24, 1776.   [7] Jan. 11, 1777.   [8] Mar. 5, 1777.

[9] Oct. 22, 1777.   [10] Dec. 8, 1777.   [11] Nov. 30, 1770.

the seal to occupy; the cutting or tearing of the paper around the seal, or even breaking the seal itself, would often damage the adjacent writing, so that Wesley usually took precautions (not always successfully) against this danger.

A full study of Wesley's stylistic practices would most readily be possible from his letters, for these account for by far the largest body of his extant holograph material. In this introduction a small attempt is being made to note a few of his literary idiosyncrasies, which in general apply not only to the letters themselves but to manuscripts for publication, nearly all of which have disappeared. As we have seen, the body of a letter approximated very closely in his mind to a page intended to appear in print. Both exhibited his strong belief in setting out the material methodically, his tendency towards antiquarianism tempered by a readiness to adapt to changing conventions of literary presentation wherever nothing crucial was lost, so that his later manuscripts, like his later publications, are much freer from archaic spellings, the regular capitalization of all nouns, and the underlinings for italicization of proper nouns— indeed this latter feature, the universal convention for his early printers, is almost completely absent from his manuscript letters. Nor is his underlining for emphasis as prolific as some published versions have implied.[1] (In accordance with the policy for this edition as a whole, we do not here reproduce archaisms which do not affect Wesley's meaning or pronunciation, nor (in general) idiosyncrasies of styling).

A handful of other stylistic features of Wesley's letters should be noted briefly, and may be illustrated from one page of one letter, that to Joseph Benson, Jan. 8, 1774.[2] He made lavish use of the apostrophe in verbal forms such as 'conquer's',[3] as well as 'conquer'd'; frequently he omitted the silent 'e' altogether, as in 'seemd';[4] he used the comma as a rhetorical rather than a grammatical device, often in place of the word 'that'.[5] He always capitalized

---

[1] It is necessary to distinguish between Wesley's own sparse underlinings and those of his correspondents, which can falsify the nuances of what Wesley was himself saying. Almost half the letter to his wife dated May 22, 1752, for instance, is underlined, but only the closing two phrases were so distinguished by Wesley himself, the remainder having been done by his wife. Similarly in the letter of Nov. 3, 1775, to his brother Charles, one phrase was underlined by John, the remainder by Charles, and in that of Oct. 28, 1785, all fifteen instances of underlining were made with Charles's broad nib. In this edition only Wesley's own underlinings will be reproduced in the text, though others will usually be shown in footnotes as indicating the reactions of the correspondent.

[2] Facing p. 58.   [3] Line 19.   [4] Line 17.   [5] Lines 8, 12, 20.

each letter in 'GOD', and continued to capitalize what he deemed other specially important words, including the technical terms of Methodism,[1] such as 'Conference' and 'Society'. Occasionally (as noted above) he underlined for emphasis, but very rarely for other purposes, such as distinguishing the titles of publications.[2] He frequently abbreviated words or used the ampersand for some purpose (or possibly whim) unconnected with the urgent saving of space.[3]

Whether the letter were short or long, Wesley normally closed on a pastoral note, with a challenge, a promise, a blessing, a prayer or a request for prayer, frequently in scriptural language. These closing sentences were often memorable, such as his words to Benson: 'Beware you be not swallowed up in books. An ounce of love is worth a pound of knowledge.'[4] Compare those to Thomas Wride: 'Be zealous, serious, active! Then you will save your own soul and them that hear you!'[5] A letter to Ann Tindall he ended: 'O be all in earnest! Life is short!'[6] To his brother Charles: 'I must and will save as many souls as I can while I live, without being careful about what may *possibly be* when I die.'[7] Sometimes he sought to infuse confidence into the wavering: 'But you cannot, shall not, depart hence, till your eyes have seen his salvation.'[8] Or in a closing paragraph he would call for complete dedication: 'As long as you are seeking and expecting to love God with all your heart, so long your souls will live.'[9] Sometimes the closing message would be embodied in verse:

All the promises are sure
To persevering prayer.[10]

Frequently these pastoral challenges were followed by a blessing, as in a letter to Charles Wesley: 'It is not safe to live or die without love. Peace be with you all! Adieu.'[11] One of his favourite closing phrases was, 'Peace be with all your spirits', and another, 'Peace be with you and yours', though many changes were rung upon this basic theme.

Closing courtesies. As noted earlier, even one so far from enslaved

[1] Lines 7, 9, 14, 15, 16, 18, 19, 21.   [2] Lines 7, 9 ('Minutes'), 19, 20.
[3] Lines 7, 19.   [4] Nov. 7, 1768.   [5] Sept. 7, 1771.
[6] Feb. 20, 1786.   [7] Sept. 19, 1785.   [8] Apr. 7, 1768, to Ann Bolton.
[9] June 24, 1770, to George Merryweather.
[10] Oct. 13, 1784, to John Valton, quoting Charles Wesley, *Hymns and Sacred Poems*, 1749.
[11] Aug. 10, 1775.

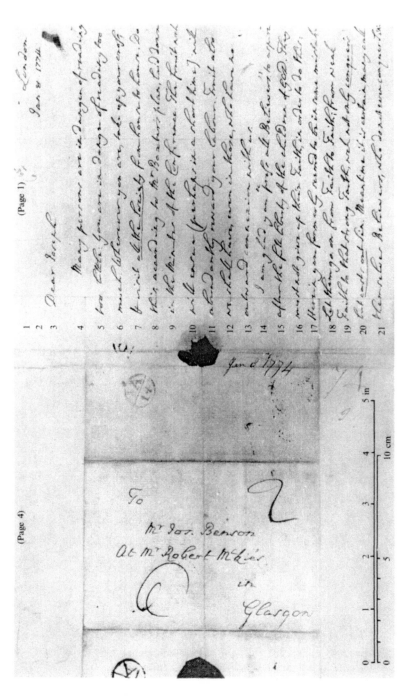

JOHN WESLEY TO JOSEPH BENSON
Jan. 8, 1774 (recto)

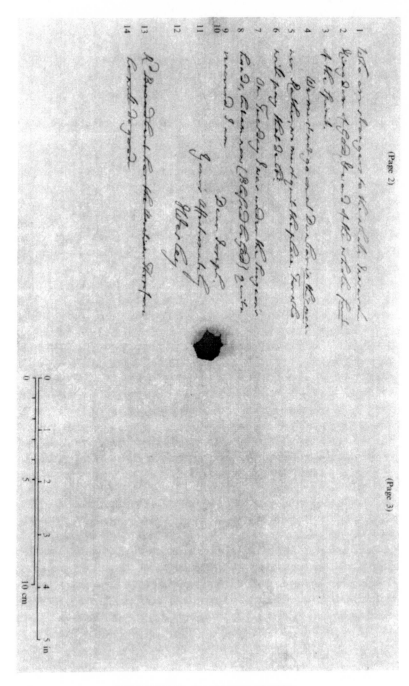

JOHN WESLEY TO JOSEPH BENSON
Jan. 8, 1774 (verso)

by custom as John Wesley nevertheless remained class-conscious in a strongly class-conscious age. *The Complete Letter-Writer* and similar manuals prescribed different rules for writing to one's social superiors, equals, and inferiors. Wesley does not seem to have followed the convention that 'letters should be wrote on quarto fine gilt post to superiors', nor that of enclosing such gilt-edged letters loose inside a separate sheet folded and sealed as a cover.[1] He did, however, when closing a letter to strangers of high social standing, follow the accepted pattern: 'When the subject of your letter is finished, conclude it with the same address as at first, as *Sir, Madam;* or, *May it please your Grace, Lordship, Ladyship*, etc., etc.'[2] Thus to the Lord Mayor and Corporation of Bristol he began, 'Gentlemen', and ended, 'Gentlemen, Your obliged and obedient servant, John Wesley'.[3] This shows the three elements which were expected in all closing courtesies: the address (usually repeated from the opening salutation), the 'compliments' or 'services' (normally introduced by the phrase, 'I am' or 'I remain'), and the signature. Only in rare instances did Wesley not end a letter in this manner, and then only to family or close friends. His variations upon the formula, however, are remarkable, and in themselves constitute a useful guide both to his general relationships with the recipient, and to sensitive changes in that relationship.

Some letters to titled persons remained formal throughout the correspondence. With others we can observe cordiality developing, without Wesley being either obsequious or unmannerly. Even with his close friends among the nobility, however, he maintained a framework of formality in his correspondence, although the body of the letter and the closing courtesies witness to the warm relationship which had developed. His twenty-five extant letters to Lady D'Arcy Maxwell (apparently only a minority of those actually written) always begin, 'My dear Lady', and always end, 'My dear Lady, your affectionate servant', with the frequent addition of 'ever' or 'most' or 'very' before 'affectionate', but (if we may follow the evidence of the eight holograph controls) no variation in the closing 'servant'.[4] Yet the letters themselves are genuinely and warmly affectionate, and occasionally forthright in their challenge.

[1] *The Complete Letter-Writer*, 10th edn., 1765, pp. 36, 38–9; cf. *The New Art of Letter-Writing*, 3rd edn., London, 1763, p. 17.
[2] *Complete Art*, p. 38; cf. *New Art*, p. 18.   [3] Dec. 20, 1764.
[4] Telford follows Jackson and Benson in printing 'Friend' in the letter of June 4, 1767, but the holograph clearly reads 'Servant'.

As noted earlier, Wesley used a very formal address to strangers (and even friends) in the professions and the merchant class. The formal salutation of 'Dear sir' was almost automatically repeated in a formal closing, introducing Wesley's 'services', which furnished the thermometer registering the degree of warmth in the relationship. All the letters to Ebenezer Blackwell, using the formula 'My dear sir' at beginning and end, followed with, 'Your affectionate servant' (occasionally adding 'ever', 'most', 'very') or 'Your affectionate brother and servant', and once, 'Your affectionate friend and servant in Christ'; in only two out of thirty letters did 'servant' not appear, when Wesley closed, 'Yours most affectionately'. Yet these formalities are so cordial that by themselves they are almost sufficient to refute the suggestion that a letter ending with a cold, 'Your obedient servant' was in fact written to Blackwell.[1]

The vast majority of Wesley's letters, however, were written to those whom he addressed as 'My dear brother', 'My dear sister', or by their Christian names. Usually this address was repeated in the conclusion, frequently with a little more intimacy, 'My dear sister' becoming 'My dear Nancy', etc. His basic 'compliment' after this closing salutation was, 'Your affectionate brother', to which 'Yours affectionately' ran a close second. Popular variants were, 'Your affectionate friend and brother' (with 'ever' and 'very' sometimes added), and occasionally a reversal of pronoun and adverb to 'Affectionately yours' or 'Very affectionately yours'.[2] No fewer than fifty different forms occur, however, in five hundred letters, including many examples of 'Ever yours', and single instances of 'Your affectionate / J. Wesley' and 'Yours in tender affection'.[3]

Most of these phrases were introduced with the words, 'I am', though not always on the separate line which strict etiquette demanded. Occasionally Wesley introduced variants here also, such as, 'and am',[4] 'I always am',[5] 'You know I am',[6] or 'Everywhere I am'.[7] Sometimes greetings intervened between the introductory formula and the salutation: 'I am, with tender love to all the family, My dear Alleck, Yours affectionately, J. Wesley'.[8] With friends Wesley

---

[1] Mar. 17, 1760.
[2] Dec. 5, 1776, to Alexander Knox; Feb. 26, 1778.
[3] Aug. 20, 1776, to Alexander Knox; June 8, 1785.
[4] Dec. 26, 1769, etc., to Joseph Benson.
[5] Oct, 26, 1776, to Ann Tindall.   [6] July 27, 1773, to Ann Bolton.
[7] May 28, 1776, to Ann Bolton.
[8] Feb. 10, 1783, to Alexander Knox.

frequently omitted the formula completely, running his letter over into the address and closing 'services': 'Write quite freely to, Dear Joseph, Your affectionate brother, J. Wesley';[1] 'O lose no time! Buy up every opportunity of doing good; and give more and more joy to, My dear friend, Yours affectionately, J. Wesley';[2] 'Be of good courage! Strengthen yourself in the Lord, and you will see good days, and will send better news to, Dear Tommy, Your affectionate friend and brother, J. Wesley'.[3] To his closest female friend, Ann Bolton, such endings occurred in over half of his letters, even after the formal opening, 'My dear sister': 'Continue to love and pray for, My dear Nancy, Yours most affectionately, J. Wesley';[4] 'Write without any reserve to, My dear Nancy, Yours invariably, J. Wesley';[5] 'Still love and pray for, My dear Nancy, Your ever affectionate brother, J. Wesley'.[6]

Other variations appeared in letters to close members of his family. Almost invariably he ended letters to his brother Charles with 'Adieu!' (usually in Byrom's shorthand—ζ), although occasionally he added or substituted Ἔρρωσο or Ἔρρωσθε,[7] both meaning 'Farewell', a word which is occasionally found also in English, and at least once in shorthand—ᴡ[8] Once he closed, 'So adieu!'[9] Wesley occasionally used 'Adieu' to other very close friends: 'Aspasia', 'Selima', James Hutton, Ann Bolton, Joseph Benson, Alexander Knox, and his wife. The closing courtesies to his wife form a microcosm of their stormy relationship: 'Ever yours'; 'Dear Molly, adieu!'; 'My dear soul, adieu!'; 'My dear, adieu!'; 'Your affectionate husband, lover, and friend'; 'Your much injured, yet still affectionate husband'; 'Your affectionate husband' (with 'affectionate' struck through, apparently by Mrs. Wesley); 'Your still affectionate husband'; and (the final letter), 'I bid you farewell, John Wesley'.[10]

Not only was this closing letter to his wife signed in full: so were all the last fifteen out of the twenty-three complete extant holographs to her—basically all those which did not end with 'Adieu!',

---

[1] Jan. 21, 1771, to Joseph Benson.   [2] Dec. 26, 1776, to Mary Bishop.
[3] Dec. 4, 1773, to Thomas Rankin.   [4] Sept. 27, 1777.
[5] May 18, 1779,   [6] Jan. 2, 1781.
[7] From the Textus Receptus margin of Acts 23:30; see June 21, 1767 and June 14, 1768; Mar. 25, 1772.   [8] Feb. 22, 1774.
[9] Aug. 3, 1771.
[10] Mar. 11, Apr. 2, 7, 1751; July 10, 1756; Apr. 24, 1757; Apr. 9, 1759; Mar. 23, 1760; Dec. 9, 1774; Oct. 2, 1778.

which in Wesley's practice seems to have rendered a signature superfluous.[1] Wesley's more formal letters in general ended with his full signature, including those to the nobility and gentry. Letters to everyone else normally closed, 'J. Wesley' (though with no period after the 'J'), or occasionally with no signature at all in his more informal correspondence. The occasional letter of rebuke, however, might transform the usual 'J. Wesley' into 'John Wesley'.[2] In a mere handful of instances did Wesley employ his initials alone.[3]

Postscripts. The *Complete Letter-Writer* advised: 'When you write to your superiors, never make a postscript; and (if possible) avoid it in letters to your equals, especially complimentary postscripts to any of the person's family or relations to whom you write, as it shows disrespect in your neglecting such persons in the body of your letter.'[4] John Wesley, like many before and since, found this too much a counsel of perfection. In our sample five hundred letters no fewer than ninety-two carry a postscript of some kind. Most are brief, but a few cover two or three themes, one of them five points (as if in response to a letter or message received later),[5] and the longest comprised an additional page written a day after a two-page letter had been completed.[6] A few give mailing directions, or information about Wesley's projected itineraries. Some seem to have been added in order by isolation to emphasize a pastoral or practical point, such as the appeals to James Hutton to despatch Wesley's publications[7] or to John Valton to spread the *Arminian Magazine*.[8] There are several deeply affectionate appeals to Ann Bolton: 'Write soon; or come. Write and come!';[9] 'Write soon, and write freely.';[10] 'If possible, you should ride every day.'[11] One of the most interesting is that to Thomas Rankin, in charge of American Methodism, who had apparently given up one bad habit (in Wesley's opinion) only to embrace another, and whom Wesley wished at the

[1] In one strange instance Wesley closed a letter to Ann Bolton, 'My dear Nancy, Your affectionate brother, J. Wesley', and then added on the left, as a postscript, 'My dear Nancy, Adieu!' (Jan. 12, 1769).

[2] Witness the letter to Thomas Wride, Aug. 29, 1774.

[3] See July 12, 1758, to Ebenezer Blackwell, and Aug. 13, 1775, to Thomas Rankin, where he was short of space. Strangely enough, however, three of the nine extant letters to Mary Cooke were signed 'JW' (Sept. 24, Oct. 30, 1785, and Dec. 12, 1786); three ended 'Adieu!', and the other three, 'J. Wesley'. Initials also appear in drafts, and occasionally in letters prepared by amanuenses.   [4] Op. cit., p. 38.

[5] Sept. 8, 1761, to Charles Wesley.   [6] July 9, 10, 1766, to Charles Wesley.
[7] Nov. 16, 1738; May 16, June 7, 10, 1739.   [8] Dec. 31, 1780.
[9] Nov. 7, 1771.   [10] Nov. 26, 1775.   [11] May 28, 1776.

very least to dissuade from infecting others: 'If you love me, Tommy, grant me two things: (1). Never take snuff more, nor let any of our preachers. (2). Let no ⟨one⟩ ever *see you smoke*.'[1]

A few postscripts related to events which had clearly come to Wesley's attention after the letter had been completed, as when he told James Hutton, 'I had wrote before I received yours,'[2] or one to his wife (added after his letter to her had been folded): 'It is believed John Fenwick cannot live twelve hours.'[3] Almost half of them, however, seem to have been sheer afterthoughts, indications that Wesley had probably prepared no draft in advance, but was reading through his letter to see that all the major points in his correspondent's letter had been covered, and all his own messages conveyed. To James Hutton he began one postscript quite frankly, 'I forgot . . .'.[4] Writing to Ebenezer Blackwell he added postscripts: 'I suppose my brother will be with you almost as soon as this',[5] and, 'I thank you for sending me the letters.'[6] To William Black in Halifax, Nova Scotia, he added as an afterthought: 'My brother is alive and tolerably well.'[7] After signing a letter discussing with Joseph Benson the editing of some of John Fletcher's manuscripts he added; 'But hold! Does not Mrs. Fletcher consider this impression as *her* property?'[8] Some were afterthoughts confessing that the original letter had been delayed or mislaid.[9] One that later he wished to retract was written to his wife: 'If any letter comes to you directed to the Revd. Mr. John Wesley, open it: it is for yourself.'[10]

The smaller postscripts Wesley usually added at the bottom left of his page, opposite the signature, but the longer ones almost always formed a continuation of the letter proper, following the signature. Occasionally they were written, or partially written, down the margin.[11] Frequently, however, the postscript was divorced from the main letter by being written down p. 2 or 4 of a one-page letter, and has sometimes been overlooked.[12] On one occasion Wesley broke the seal of a letter to add a second postscript (distinguishable by different ink and slightly different hand), noting on the cover: 'I opened this to insert the postscript.'[13]

---

[1] July 28, 1775.   [2] Jan. 10, 1772.   [3] June 10, 1774.
[4] Apr. 9, 1739.   [5] Mar. 15, 1748.   [6] Aug. 15, 1761
[7] May 11, 1784.   [8] Sept. 17, 1788.   [9] See above, pp. 40-1.
[10] Mar. 27, 1751—but he may have been warning hert o expect a franked letter (see under date).
[11] e.g. Apr. 7, 1751, to his wife; July 5, 28, 1765, to Thomas Rankin.
[12] Nov. 20, 27, 1766; Sept. 26, 1774.   [13] July 31, 1785.

Enclosures and double letters. Almost one in ten of Wesley's post-scripts were added for the purpose of saving time and money by persuading his correspondents to convey a message to someone else. Thus to Thomas Rankin he wrote: 'Pray give my love to brother Mallon of Mary Week society. I thank him for his letter, and exhort him to stand fast in the liberty wherewith Christ has made him free.'[1] To John Valton he wrote: 'Pray send my love to Geo. Brown, and tell him I have his letter.'[2] Occasionally this message was conveyed in a separate letter folded within the one sent through the mail. In writing to his wife from Ireland he added in a postscript, 'Pray put the enclosed into the post directly.'[3] In this instance the enclosure was almost certainly for someone in London, and the saving between the London Penny Post and an additional letter from Ireland was considerable. The same principle operated in reverse when Wesley wrote from London to R. C. Brackenbury in Jersey, saying, 'I enclose a few lines to Miss Bisson, for whom I feel an affectionate concern.'[4] An additional motive was at work when Wesley enclosed in a letter to Mrs. Eliza Bennis in Limerick another letter which he had written to a preacher, saying: 'I enclose James Perfect's letter . . . on purpose that you may talk with him. He has both an honest heart, and a good understanding; but you entirely mistake his doctrine.'[5] Very rarely some more bulky 'enclosure' accompanied a letter, such as the book which Wesley sent to Dr. Wrangel.[6]

In nine cases out of ten, however, Wesley's use of the term 'enclose' did not imply what it seems to imply. Rather than 'enclose' he should have written 'incorporate'. He was availing himself of a device which was very neat, but which has led to many problems for scholars who have not understood his methods of correspondence: on one sheet he wrote two letters to two different people. This was relatively simple, of course, in writing to members of the same household, such as the two Miss Gibbes. Indeed, of the ten extant letters to Miss Agnes Gibbes the first four were written on p. 3 of four-page letters addressed to her older sister, in such a

---

[1] Jan. 13, 1765.   [2] Jan. 16, 1783.
[3] Apr. 22, 1757; cf. Sept. 20, 1789, where also the presence of the complete letter shows that Wesley's reference was in this instance to a physically enclosed separate letter.
[4] Oct. 20, 1787.
[5] Mar. 1, 1774; cf. hers to him, Apr. 12, 1774. In the event Perfect was 'on the circuit', so that she was not able to deliver Wesley's letter personally, but left it for him.
[6] Jan. 30, 1770.

format that they could have been separated without the elder Miss Gibbes losing anything except the address on p. 4.[1] Similarly at least two of Wesley's letters to his brother's recently bereaved widow and her daughter Sally were written on the same sheets, even though they were later separated, so that they now appear to be four distinct letters.[2] Wesley also wrote such double letters to married couples, each of whom had formerly been his correspondents, such as Joseph Benson and his wife,[3] John Pawson and his wife,[4] the Revd. John Fletcher and his wife, the former Mary Bosanquet,[5] and the Revd. Levi and Mrs. Heath, the first President of Cokesbury School.[6] Although he usually addressed the man, as was to be expected in that era, on at least one occasion he wrote a double letter to a woman, Mrs. Ann Smith, his housekeeper at the New Room, Bristol, with an appended letter for John Whitehead, the preacher with whom she was contemplating marriage.[7]

An early extant example of a double letter is that sent from Cologne on June 28, 1738, addressed to his brother Charles in London, which begins: 'You will send my mother, wherever she is, her letter, by the first opportunity.' 'Her letter' was written on pp. 1-2, which Charles therefore cut off and dispatched to his mother, presumably under a separate cover containing a letter from himself. Dozens of other examples might be cited, spread over every decade to within a few months of Wesley's death. Some, to close partners, have remained unseparated on the one sheet.[8] Most have become separated, as Wesley usually intended that they should be, and have sometimes found their way into different collections. In numerous instances one half only is known, crying aloud for an explanation, such as the half of a double letter written from Ireland, on April 16, 1773, bearing on one side the address of Mrs. Kathy Lambe in Edinburgh, and on the other the heading, 'To Mollie Lowrie' and a complete letter beginning, 'My dear sister'. These were undoubtedly pp. 3 and 4 of a letter on p. 1 of which (or possibly on pp. 1-2) Wesley had written his main letter to Mrs. Kathy Lambe, which has disappeared: a heading such as, 'To Molly Lowrie', always carries with it a strong implication that this is in fact a subsidiary message intended by Wesley to be cut off and delivered by the

---

[1] Apr. 25, May 19, June 10, Aug. 16, 1783; the following six were written to Miss Agnes independently of her sister's chaperonage.

[2] Apr. 14, 21, 1788.   [3] May 21, 1781.   [4] Nov. 26, 1785.

[5] Apr. 2, 3, 1785.   [6] Oct. 20, 1788.   [7] June 16, 1769.

[8] Cf. that to Charles Wesley, in Wesley's letter to James Hutton, Apr. 28, 1738.

recipient of the complete double letter. In some instances the other half alone is extant, a one-page letter with no address on the verso, indistinguishable from other such half-letters separated from their address sheets except for some internal clue, such as that in a letter of May 12, 1785, written from Ireland to Charles Wesley: 'To save tenpence postage I will write a few lines to Patty in your letter.' To one of his preachers Wesley wrote: 'To save her postage I write a line or two in yours to poor sister Bastable.'[1]

Four of the eight extant letters written by Wesley to Thomas Rankin in America are such double letters. In these some new features of this method of postal thrift are demonstrated. The letter of March 1, 1775, is really three letters in one: the covering letter from Wesley to Rankin, closing, 'I add a line to all the preachers' (p. 1); the challenging pastoral letter to the American preachers in general (p. 2); and a letter to Rankin from Charles Wesley (p. 3, completed in the margin); the address is on p. 4. That of June 13, 1775, from Ireland, was a single letter readied for dispatch, but held back for a reason which Wesley's travelling companion Joseph Bradford explained in a letter added on p. 4, dated June 22: 'In a few hours after Mr. Wesley at [had] wrought your letter he was taken ill of a fever, and have continued so to this houer . . . What the event will be God only knows. I fear he his about to finish his course.' That of July 28, 1775, contains the address on p. 4, a letter to Rankin on p. 1, which ends halfway down p. 2, and is followed by a signed letter 'To Mr. [James] Dempster', and another on p. 3 'To John King'—two of Wesley's preachers in America. The other was written on Aug. 13, 1775, but appeared abnormally on pp. 2–3, because Wesley was using a sheet on which p. 1 had already been commandeered for a letter the previous day, written by John Atlay, the address being in Wesley's hand on p. 4.

According to the 1711 Act any number of letters on a single sheet of paper should be charged at the rate for a single letter, and only the addition of a true enclosure warranted charging the double rate, and an increase above one ounce the quadruple rate. An interpretative Act of 1719, aimed at merchants, sought to extend the double rate to single sheets containing bills of exchange or letters written thereon to different people, which resulted in some opening of

---

[1] Oct. 12, 1778. In this instance not only is the main letter on p. 1, but the address on p. 2, both pp. 3 and 4 presumably being given over to a long letter to the lady whom Wesley tried to serve in her poverty.

letters by the Post Office to detect double letters and small enclosures. The whole situation remained somewhat murky, however, and the new interpretation did not seem to be widely understood, accepted, or enforced.[1] Certainly Wesley sent such letters without announcing them as double letters under the 1719 Act, and just as certainly they were usually charged as single letters, as were the four in this category sent to the two Miss Gibbes as late as 1783. It is possible that the interpretation as well as the scale of charges became stricter by the Act of 1784. At any rate on Dec. 2, 1788, Wesley wrote to Henry Moore, his senior lay itinerant preacher in London, 'You will seal, and put Mr. Asbury's letter into the post.' This one-page letter was addressed on the verso to Moore, and bore a note for the attention of the postal authorities in the bottom left corner: 'Double Letter. In his absence [i.e. Moore's] to Mr. Whitfield' (the London Book Steward). The postmaster nevertheless scrawled '3' on the cover (the single rate), though this was later struck through, and the charge altered to sixpence.

Many other examples remain of Wesley's writing to two recipients, or of his joining with another writer to send a letter to a third. Probably scores more rest incognito because the tell-tale address half is missing. Sufficient has probably been said, however, to make it quite clear that this important feature of eighteenth-century correspondence may help to explain some literary puzzles. We close this section by describing the background of a letter to be presented in a later volume. On April 21, 1787, John Wesley wrote to John King, a preacher in the Bradford (Wiltshire) circuit, beginning: 'Adam Clark[e] is doubtless an extraordinary young man, and capable of doing much good. . . . He may have work enough to do if he adds the Isle of Alderney to those of Guernsey and Jersey. If you have a desire to go and labour with him, you may, after the Conference.' Three weeks later, on May 15, Adam Clarke himself—the future Bible commentator, of course—returned to Wiltshire from the Channel Islands. This had been his first circuit, and he had come a-courting his future wife, Mary Cooke. He found the letter still lying about awaiting the return of his friend John King from his preaching rounds to the circuit headquarters, having been informed that King would not be back before he must leave on his borrowed horse. Seeing King's name on the cover, recognizing Wesley's handwriting, and thinking of his own frustrated attempt

[1] Joyce, op. cit., pp. 139, 177-9; Robinson, *British Post Office*, pp. 96-8, 123-5.

to get in touch with King, he toyed with the letter, squeezed the sides, and through the partially opened fold saw his own name. That settled it. There might be 'something essential' in the letter concerning himself, and John King was an understanding personal friend who in similar circumstances would do just what he was about to do. He opened the letter, added his own apologetic message within, explaining the situation, and hinting at the reasons for his presence in the area, which he still wished to keep secret from all except his friend King. Such an incident helps us to visualize the long postal delays, the absence of preachers (or of Wesley himself) on itineraries while letters awaited them, and the physical conformation of a letter which enabled words to be glimpsed without unsealing the letter.

Folding the sheet. It seems possible, even probable, that foolscap sheets of writing paper could be purchased already folded in half to make four equal pages, and many people, probably most, undoubtedly began their folding of a sheet from the centre.[1] Wesley's portable writing-case would hold only such paper, not the flat foolscap sheet. Yet the evidence is overwhelming that Wesley did use a flat sheet for his letters, and when folding it deliberately made his first fold about 1 in. to the right of the centre, apparently in order to achieve a neater and stronger cover.[2]

The process can best be visualized with the aid of the illustrations facing pp. 68–9 (a typical letter with the message on p. 1 only, and the address on p. 3), together with a sheet of paper about 12 in. × 8 in., on which the salient features of the letter should be inserted.[3]

---

[1] In a series of over a hundred letters from Lady Huntingdon to John and Charles Wesley, 1741–66, in the Methodist Archives, all are on paper folded in various ways (none like Wesley's), but always beginning with a central fold. The same is true for most of those sent to Wesley by his correspondents, including his parents and other members of his family. The one exception is his brother Charles, who used the same method as John in his first extant letter, Jan. 20, 1728, though he was by no means as consistent in its use as John. (There is also at least one instance of their father's using the method, Jan. 27, 1730, in a letter to his two sons at Oxford, though all his previous letters used the normal central fold.) The same central fold seems customary for letters available in the display cabinets at the British Library and elsewhere. The well-known postal historian, R. Martin Willcocks, to whom I am greatly indebted for generous help in interpreting stamps and inscriptions on postal covers, agrees that in the thousands which he has handled he cannot remember any not beginning with a central fold.

[2] Wesley's holograph letters have usually been preserved folded centrally, but the original folds remain, and are occasionally more marked than those in the centre. The hundreds of instances where Wesley's first fold breaks into his writing furnish abundant proof that the writing came before the folding. (See illus. facing pp. 58 and 68.)

[3] The black saucepan appearing in the photocopy (where the seal has torn away the

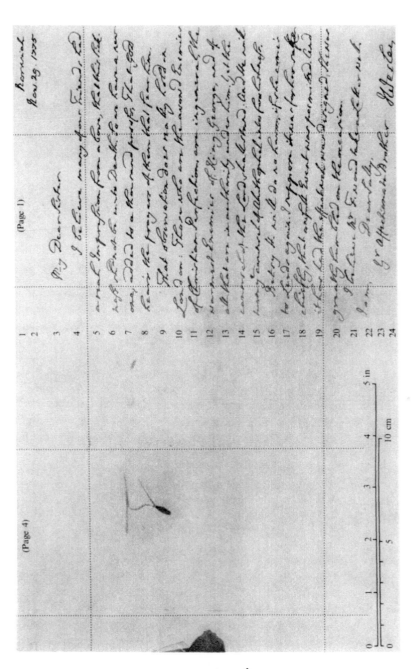

THE FOLDING OF WESLEY'S LETTERS
Nov. 29, 1775 (recto)

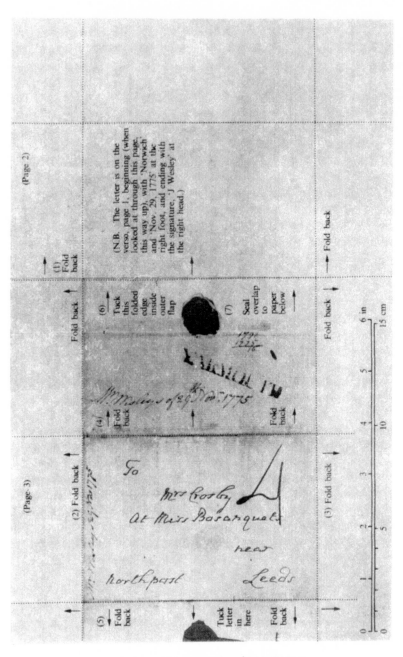

THE FOLDING OF WESLEY'S LETTERS
Nov. 29, 1775 (verso)

First we place the open sheet in front of us, with the message uppermost and to our right, and the blank p. 4 to our left (p. 68). (1) We fold p. 1 over to our left, thus concealing the message. By making the first fold about 1 in. to the right of the centre, as Wesley did, we leave a 2 in. column of p. 4 uncovered. Turning this folded sheet over from head to foot we now have a narrow leaf underneath (pp. 2, 1) and a wide leaf above (pp. 4, 3), with the address to our left on the uppermost p. 3. (For this and the remaining steps see p. 69). With folds (2) and (3) we turn under the head and foot of the folded sheet, about $1\frac{1}{2}$ in. each. We are left with a rectangle about 7 in. $\times 4\frac{3}{4}$ in. Fold (4) is made perpendicular to (2) and (3), beginning about $\frac{1}{2}$ in. to the right of the centre, turning under a rectangle of about 3 in. $\times 4\frac{3}{4}$ in., and leaving at the left a rectangle of about 4 in. $\times 4\frac{3}{4}$ in. Fold (5) turns the overlapping portion at the left over the rectangle beneath, making both rectangles of equal size. Thus folded, the letter is turned anti-clockwise through 90°, in which position we write the address.[1] (6) The rectangular panel beneath is then tucked into the winged flap, which because of Wesley's peculiar method of folding contains only one thickness of paper instead of the two which arise from beginning with a central fold. (7) If we follow Wesley's normal practice we then place a small dab of sealing-wax as an adhesive between the inner surface of the flap and the folded rectangle tucked into it. The process of folding and sealing is completed by dropping more of the hot wax in a large circle spreading across the junction of the edge of the flap and the paper beneath; upon this we impress our personal seal.[2]

When folded Wesley's letters displayed many variations in size— all smaller than most modern envelopes—but the same basic system of folding. This he followed uniformly throughout his life except for the early 1720s (for which very few holograph letters are available), when he fashioned a much smaller and squarer address panel, and

edge of the paper) will prove valuable in registering the back and front of the sheet correctly.

[1] Sometimes Wesley added the address after securing and sealing, but we believe that he usually did it just before making the fifth fold, and there is clear evidence that in at least some instances he wrote the address even before he began the message itself (see below, p. 73).

[2] Thus the postboy would carry a kind of flattened tube, whose edges could indeed be pressed open, as in the incident narrated above (pp. 67–8). In the case of the typical one-page letter, however, nothing would then be visible within—a good reason for folding p. 3 inward. With a longer letter, however, addressed on p. 4, such as that to Joseph Benson (between pp. 58–9), portions of the message on p. 1 could thus be read.

occasionally slightly different patterns of folding and sealing. For all practical purposes the only major variant during his last sixty years and more was the rare use of a quarto rather than a foolscap sheet, either folded into four octavo pages or with the letter written on one side and the address on the other. For these also he still employed the same method of folding, though with the four narrower pages the first fold was almost in the centre of p. 1, and the address was written perpendicular to the chain-lines in the paper rather than parallel to them.[1] The single quarto sheet Wesley folded in his normal manner, but tucked into the flap an outer margin instead of the folded centre of the letter.[2]

Seals. The last decisive act was the affixing of a seal. It was through rifling his pockets and reading a letter to Sarah Ryan which Wesley had 'finished but had not sealed' that his wife flew into a rage and left him.[3] Almost all Wesley's letters were sealed in one way or another, usually with red sealing-wax, but occasionally with black. Unfortunately, in only 20 per cent is any identifiable portion of the seal left intact. Most recipients (including the members of the Wesley family) broke the seal in two, or tore the letter open with no attempt to protect the brittle wax. This was true of most of his correspondents, with the major exception of Ann Bolton, who frequently cut round the seal with scissors so as to preserve it intact; almost half the extant letters to her thus retain an unbroken and distinct impression of Wesley's seal.[4] In our cross-section of five hundred only one letter seems clearly to have used no seal of any kind,[5] though in at least a dozen instances an adhesive wafer was used instead, and in one only the internal dab of wax. In over 50 per cent of the extant holographs the only traces of a seal are such things as a hole in the paper where the seal originally adhered, or some tiny fragments of wax, and in 6 per cent the letter lacks the address half where such evidence is most likely to appear, though it seems highly likely that a seal was indeed present. Strangely enough,

[1] See Apr. 11, 1785, to Charles Wesley.
[2] See Jan. 13, 1763, to Jenny Lee; May 31, 1771, to Betsy Perronet; Apr. 5, 1775, to Patty Chapman, and probably that of June 1, 1790, to Henry Moore. These need to be distinguished, of course, from the quarto sheets which have become separated from the other half of a double letter.
[3] Jan. 20, 27, 1758.
[4] Others such as Thomas Rankin occasionally did the same, and one or two cut out the seal and mounted it elsewhere on the letter, as did Lady D'Arcy Maxwell for his letter of June 22, 1766, securing it on the blank p. 3, with the appended note, 'J W, Mr.'.
[5] June 26, 1777, delivered by personal letter-carrier to Mary Bishop.

with all Wesley's use of tapers lit at fire or stove in order to melt
the sealing-wax there remain few traces of accidental burns—just
one in five hundred, that of Mar. 12, 1759, in which a large hole
was burnt, so that he added another seal just to the side.

The first purpose of the seal was to secure the folded letter, and
in some instances Wesley assisted this process by pinprick punctures
to key the warm wax to the paper before it hardened.[1] Instead of
wax he frequently used a ready-made wafer, a thin disc, $\frac{3}{4}$ in. in
diameter, made of flour, gum, and colouring matter, which needed
only moistening and pressure. (*The Complete Letter-Writer* maintained that these should never be used in letters to superiors, but
only to equals or inferiors.[2]) With both wax and wafer he sometimes
used embossing stamps to ensure good adhesion. No fewer than
eighteen different types of embossing stamps have been noted on his
letters, usually consisting of from two to five pressure points within
concentric circles, but occasionally in more elaborate designs, within
borders—a cross, a lion rampant, and what might be a crown over
three cockle-shells and crossed swords, with an indecipherable
legend, the second element of which appears to be 'CORI'.

The seal proper, impressed on the warm wax over the junction
on the outside of the cover, although serving as an adhesive to
secure privacy, was historically employed for authentication of a
document as coming from the owner of the seal. This may well have
been true with many of the seals which Wesley himself used, but it
is a remarkable fact that impressions exist on his letters from over
forty different seal-dies. This is all the more strange when it is
remembered that these impressions represent only 20 per cent of
the extant holographs, roughly about four hundred letters, so that
there may well have been several more, in addition to multiplied uses
of those with which we are already familiar.[3]

Seal-dies (or matrices) could be important items of jewellery,
beautifully carved from agate, or they might be fashioned from
metal.[4] The essential feature was the recessed design with which the
hot wax was impressed just before it hardened. The very large
number of seals used by Wesley prompts many questions which

---

[1] e.g. July 24, 1725; Feb. 15, 1735; Mar. 11, 1785.   [2] Op. cit., p. 39.

[3] These will be listed in an appendix in Vol. VII, and where possible that used will
be indicated at the end of each letter.

[4] For a general introduction see Hilary Jenkinson, *Guide to Seals in the Public Record
Office*, London, H.M.S.O., 1968, and for much greater detail see A. B. Tonnolly,
Catalogue of British Seal-Dies in the British Museum, London, British Museum, 1952.

may eventually be answered (or more probably answered in part) by further research. Did he have all or any of these seals (to give them their common misnomer) made for him personally, or did he purchase them from a jeweller's stock? Did he keep different seals at his different headquarters around the country? Did he carry favourites around with him? What led him to change his seals so frequently, in view of the fact that they were almost indestructible? What part did chance or whimsy play in the use of different seals during the same period? How many were borrowed from other people, such as that of Adam Clarke, used on Sept. 23–4, 1789?

What we may affirm with certainty, however, is that he did use seals of many different kinds, with mottoes, monograms, busts, birds, animals, coats of arms. Seals displaying a cross were in use by both John and Charles Wesley in 1738, but for some months following his return from Germany he used one showing a crucifix and the legend, 'Der ist mein' ('He is mine'). During the following decade he came to favour a dove bearing an olive twig, with the legend, 'Nuntia pacis' ('the messenger of peace'). One such seal within an oval frame was used in the late 1740s, another within an octagonal frame in the 1750s, and still another within an oval frame (this time with the spelling 'Nuncia') in the 1760s; still another, in a round frame, has been noted in 1784. Perhaps linked with this favourite motif were seals showing two birds billing, one with the legend 'l'Amitié' (friendship), two similar ones in 1773, single birds in 1748 and 1766, and one with the legend 'l'Amour' (love) in 1766.[1] The two most frequently-used seals during Wesley's later years, however, were his own monogram, 'JW' (adapted by Richard Heitzenrater to become the symbol of this edition of his works), which also carries the legend, 'Believe, Love, Obey' (1774–85), and a tiny sunflower looking up to the sun, bearing the motto, 'Tibi Soli' ('for thee alone', 1774–89).

The 'Tibi Soli' seal-die is extant in his Bristol headquarters, and three others are associated with him. One shows a crown over a cross, and the legend, 'Be thou faithful unto death', which he certainly used on Dec. 13, 1783. A fob-seal of agate in a gold setting preserved in Wesley's House, London, depicts him in profile. A reversible metal fob-seal, showing on one side a profile of Wesley and on the other his monogram, also boasts a pedigree, though no

---

[1] Cf. 'La Paix' (peace) in 1786, a dove with a twig, 1788, and what may be a dove, 1757.

actual use of the last two seals by Wesley himself has so far been noted.[1] In view of his large collection of seals it is perhaps strange to witness Wesley writing to Ann Bolton, when she seemed to be dying: 'O Nancy, I want sadly to see you: I am afraid you should steal away into paradise. A thought comes into my mind, which I will tell you freely. If you go first, I think you must leave me your seal for a token: I need not say, to remember you by, for I shall never forget you.'[2]

The address. We have seen that Wesley almost uniformly used four pages for his letters, and that if the beginning were termed p. 1, then the address would normally be written on p. 3, unless the message covered two or three pages, when it would appear on p. 4. *The Complete Letter-Writer*[3] assumed that the address would be written after the letter was folded and sealed, and this would indeed seem the natural procedure, removing any guess-work about the actual position of the rectangular panel formed on the outside of the letter by the process of folding.[4] Nevertheless it is clear that Wesley himself sometimes wrote the address first, witness especially the instances when a sheet with the address already written was left unfinished, and the sheet later used for a letter to a different recipient.[5] Wesley seems always to have followed the practice prescribed by *The Complete Letter-Writer*, beginning his address with the word 'To' in the upper left-hand corner, and frequently by writing the recipient's town of abode in slightly larger characters.[6] After the

[1] For the pedigree see W.H.S. XXVIII. 23. The present owner is Dr. Paul Sangster of Kent College, Canterbury, England, who was most helpful in furthering my researches. Another seal with a verbal pedigree going back to the late nineteenth century is now in Wesley Theological Seminary, Washington, D.C.; this bears the motto, 'Le temps nous joindra' ('time will join us').

[2] June 7, 1768.

[3] Op. cit., p. 39.

[4] Cf. Wesley's instructions to Robert Costerdine about a signed circular: 'Seal, superscribe, and deliver them in my name.' (Nov. 24, 1767.)

[5] See June 26, 1777 to Mary Bishop (first addressed to Mr. Wathen), and Dec. 21, 1779, to Joseph Benson (originally addressed to Nancy Holman). Cf. the address on p. 3, which separates parts of the letter to Mary Cooke, Sept. 24, 1785, and also implies that the address was already written. On the other hand see the letter to Ann Tindall, Dec. 30, 1784, written on a sheet which already contained the beginnings of a letter, but no address.

[6] Op. cit., p. 39. Not one of the 500 selected letters bearing addresses omits the 'To', but the evidence about the prominent name of the town is very mixed, many examples revealing no trend, except that larger writing does not seem to occur with long names such as Newcastle upon Tyne, and those that do occur are usually not much larger than the remainder of the address, and tend to become less frequent in Wesley's later years. See illustrations, facing pp. 58, 69.

line with 'To' followed another with the recipient's title and name
in the centre (sometimes with an identifying occupation), another
with the local address (if needed), usually another with the word 'in'
(or occasionally 'at'), and then the town or county, sometimes two
spaces below the previous line, and gaining prominence by this
separation if not by its larger size.[1]

Wesley was always very careful about courteous formality on the
covers of his letters. Jane Hilton pleaded with him to drop the 'Miss'
on the outside when writing to her, as he had speedily done within.
He replied: 'You lay me under a difficulty. When I speak to you
alone I can't use ceremony. I love you too well. But in superscribing
a letter I would be as *civil* to you as if I did not love you at all. Yet
I know not how to deny you anything.' This letter, therefore, like
the others which reached her every month until her marriage seven
months later, was addressed, 'To / Jenny Hilton'—possibly unique
in this open formality.[2]

'Civil' in Wesley's day and in his own usage implied positive
politeness rather than a negative disguised rudeness. It can be seen
also in his desire to use the appropriate title on the cover, demonstrated especially in his many letters to clergy, before whose names he
seems always to have inserted 'The Revd. Mr.'. This included his
brother Charles.[3] Even some of his lay itinerant preachers, normally
addressed as 'Mr. Jos. Benson', 'Mr. Tho. Rankin', etc., were
accorded the additional clerical courtesy after he had ordained them
for service in Scotland. Thus a letter to Alexander Suter, ordained
by Wesley in 1787, was addressed on Nov. 24 of that year, 'To the
Revd. Mr. Al. Suter in Aberdeen', but when his return to England
rendered that distinction both unnecessary and likely to arouse
prejudice among his colleagues, Wesley's superscription once more
became, 'To Mr. Suter, At the Preaching house in Plymouth Dock',
or 'To Mr. Suter, At the Preaching house in Penzance, Cornwall'.[4]

The lay itinerant preachers had no settled abode, and were usually
addressed at one of Wesley's 'preaching-houses' in their circuit, or
to the care of the steward or leading layman in the town where
Wesley (with his fairly detailed familiarity with the itinerant plans

---

[1] See illus. facing p. 77.   [2] July 23, 1768.

[3] The only exceptions were two letters written from Europe, addressed in French,
'Monsieur Charles Wesley', June 28 and July 7, 1738.

[4] May 4, 21, 1789; Oct. 3, 1789. He used similar courtesy in addressing the American
preachers after 1784: 'The Revd. Mr. Whatcoat' (July 17, 1788) and 'The Revd. Mr.
Fr. Garretson' (Jan. 24, 1789), etc.

for all the circuits) expected them to be when the letter arrived. Thus the six sent during the winter of 1764-5 to Thomas Rankin in the Cornwall circuit were directed to him at four different addresses: 'At Mr. John Nance's, in St. Ives', 'At Mr. Joseph Andrew's, in Redruth', 'At Mr. Wood's, Shopkeeper, In Port Isaac, near Camelford' (in each case with 'Cornwall' on the bottom line), and 'At Mrs. Blackmore's, Shopkee[pe]r, in Plymouth Dock'.[1]

In larger centres the name alone might not be sufficient to identify the recipient (or his agent or lodgings), so that Wesley (like his contemporaries) added some descriptive phrase, such as may be seen in his letters to Miss Bishop: 'To Miss Bishop, In the Vineyards, Bath', or 'near Lady Huntingdon's Chapel, in Bath', or 'To Miss Bishop, Schoolmistress, in Bath', which from 1781 became, 'To Miss Bishop, at the Boarding School in Keynsham, near Bristol'. In many instances this was unnecessary, and Wesley's favourite Irish correspondent was addressed uniformly, 'To Mr. Alexander Knox in Londonderry', except that the first letter used the phrase 'at Londonderry', and seven out of thirty-six did not give a separate line to the word 'in', combining it with Knox's name.

If Wesley were away from London when writing he might feel it necessary to give some postal directions in the bottom left-hand corner, indicating the route which he thought the letter should take.[2] Some he labelled, 'North post', thus requesting that they should be carried to London to catch that post, which at least some did;[3] or 'Cross post' (in later years '+ post'), recommending that they should not be sent to London first.[4] Similarly he specified 'per Glo[uce]ster' for various letters, including one from Bristol to Brecon;[5] or 'per Portpatrick' for many letters both to and from Ireland; or 'per London' for one from Portarlington in Ireland to Philadelphia.[6]

Wesley developed very strong habits in adding these addresses, almost always writing towards the outer margin of the folded sheet, though in three instances out of four hundred letters retaining their

[1] Sept. 21, Nov. 6, 1764; Jan. 26, Feb. 9, 1765; cf. Jan. 13, Mar. 9, 1765.
[2] These amounted to some 6 per cent or 7 per cent of all the addressed letters which were not delivered personally.
[3] e.g. from Worcester to Newcastle, July 8, 1777, and from Oxford to Scarborough, Aug. 10, 1779.
[4] e.g. from Rochdale to Bath, Apr. 17, 1776, and from Oxford to Londonderry, Oct. 22, 1777. From the lack of Bishop marks these two in fact did not pass through London, but others marked 'Cross post' did, such as Newcastle to Evesham, June 7, 1768, and Leeds to Witney, July 12, 1768.
[5] Oct. 5, 1770.   [6] Apr. 21, 1775.

addresses in Wesley's hand these were written from the outer margin inwards.[1] The panels upon which the addresses were written varied in size, though normally they were about $4\frac{1}{2}$ in. × 3 in. (115 × 76 mm.) In the emergency caused by a very long letter, however, Wesley completed it on the tuck-in flaps, which were therefore made much larger, thus reducing the panel left on p. 4 to $3\frac{1}{4}$ in. × $2\frac{7}{8}$ in. (83 × 73 mm).[2]

Postmarks and charges. The story of the letter after it left the writer's hands is reflected in the postal markings and other inscriptions which it carries. We have already spoken about the varieties and importance of postmarks,[3] and full details of these will be given at the end of each letter, together with an explanation of their significance when this seems necessary. The date stamps were normally impressed on the back of the folded and sealed cover. The postmasters at the receiving offices also made their own hand-written notes on the address panel, indicating the charges to be collected, which varied according to the number of sheets in the letter and its place of destination. A letter travelling within the area covered by the London Penny Post was usually prepaid, and this was indicated by a triangular 'Penny Post Paid' stamp on the back, to which was added in later years a circular stamp showing the time and the office where it was posted.[4] During Wesley's lifetime, however, prepayment was very rare for letters travelling outside London, and in these cases an indication of the fact was made on the cover either in writing or by the addition of a printed stamp—'PD' within a circle until 1765, 'Post Paid' within a circle from 1766 to 1791, with more elaborate stamps being introduced from 1787 onwards. Very few of these survive on Wesley's letters, however, and even as late as July 17, 1788, his letter to Richard Whatcoat in America was inscribed by hand in the lower left corner, 'Post pd. to New York'. The vast majority of Wesley's unmutilated letters do bear postmasters' inscriptions, but almost all of them simply point out the charges to be paid when the letter was collected or delivered. Sometimes these are small and neat, more often large and scrawling, frequently with erasures and revised charges substituted, usually on the address panel itself, though occasionally

---

[1] Aug. 23, 1739, to Ebenezer Blackwell; Sept. 15, 1776, to Ann Bolton; and Sept. 5, 1785, to John Valton.

[2] May 7, 1739, to James Hutton.

[3] See pp. 25-6 above.

[4] See letters to Mrs. Hutton, Aug. 22, 1744, and James Hutton, Dec. 26, 1771.

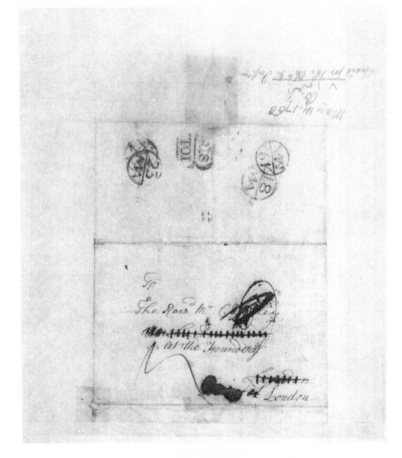

REDIRECTION
John Wesley to Charles Wesley, May 14, 1768

postal inscriptions are found on the back also. This information frequently proves of value in documenting the history of the letter, and an attempt will be made to record the inscriptions in addition to the postmarks wherever they occur. Their absence, of course, from a letter with the integral address half, shows that the letter was either not dispatched, or was delivered by personal messenger.

Many letters needed redirecting when they reached their original address. This seems frequently to have been done without charge in the London area, but Wesley's stewards at the Foundery would also pay the additional penny to have letters for Charles Wesley redirected to his home in Chesterfield Street.[1] Occasionally a letter was redirected several times, and its travels may be followed by means of the postmarks and the added inscriptions. Thus one written by John to Charles from Edinburgh, May 14, 1768, was first stamped on the back with a Bishop mark in Edinburgh, dated 'MY/14', and the charge of sixpence was noted on the address panel, for collection in London.[2] Reaching the London office on May 18, the London Bishop mark was added. By that time, however, Charles was apparently on a brief visit to his wife in Bristol—she was nursing their latest child, John James ('Jacky'), who died in July. The London postal charge was apparently paid, and struck through when the letter was redirected to Bristol the following day, at the same time acquiring another Bishop mark, and probably a further charge of fourpence. When it arrived in Bristol (almost certainly on May 21), Charles Wesley was on his way back to London. It was accordingly redirected to London, receiving the distinctive Bristol stamp, a large 'B' with 'RIS' and 'TOL' enclosed within the loops. At this stage a further fourpence might possibly have been demanded, but perhaps the postmaster was touched by the sad story, and let it go without further charge, although this is conjectural. Once more it arrived at the London office, was postmarked '23/MA', the fourpence was paid, and Charles Wesley, having read the letter, docketed it, 'May 14, 1768, B[rother], for the Church [in shorthand]', and at a later time, 'Afraid for the Ch[urc]h and Perf[ectio]n'.

Many of Wesley's correspondents docketed his letters with notes about the date on which they were written, and occasionally

[1] e.g. June 27, 1781, May 2, 1783, Apr. 11, 1784, Mar. 2, 1788; the first and the last of these examples have the original charge struck through, apparently an indication that this was paid before the Penny Post Paid stamp was added.

[2] See illus. facing p. 77.

summarized their contents, just as Wesley himself did for the letters which he received.[1] These often confirm or even supply the dates in those instances when the letter itself is for any reason deficient or defective.[2] Even more valuable are the replies which are sometimes copied out on a blank page.[3] Some of his correspondents numbered the letters which they received from him—a valuable indication of the actual frequency of writing, as also about any missing letters.[4] All such inscriptions will here be recorded in full.

Like some series numberings, however, many inscriptions were added considerably later. Some were made by booksellers, auctioneers, or collectors—and not always in pencil. Perhaps the most interesting and valuable are editorial annotations made by those who were preparing Wesley's letters for publication. Almost all of the numerous examples in this category are from the pen of Wesley's correspondent from 1768, Joseph Benson, who as a respected Methodist and scholar and connexional editor later edited the first comparatively complete edition of Wesley's *Works*, including one volume devoted mainly to his letters.[5] In many instances Benson's published version constitutes our earliest source. It is therefore the more important to be able to see his editorial practice in actual operation with the holograph letters themselves. He prepared them in a similar manner to that which he had probably witnessed in Wesley himself, striking passages through, altering words, improving grammar and sense, adding link words (all in ink, of course), before handing the heavily amended document to the printer.[6]

[1] Both brothers did this from their early years, e.g. Wesley's letter to his brother Charles, docketed, 'B. Utph, July 7, 1738', and again later, 'B. from Utph, Panegyric on Germany'.

[2] e.g. Wesley dated a letter to his brother, 'Janu. 5, 1762', but Charles docketed it correctly, 'B. festinans lente! Jan. 5, 1763'.

[3] e.g. the letter to Samuel Lloyd, June 19, 1751, which contains Lloyd's reply of June 25, and that to Charles Wesley, Sept. 13, 1785, on which Charles copied his reply of Sept. 19; sometimes Charles copied his replies in shorthand, as in the case of that (Aug. 7) to John's letter of July 31, 1775.

[4] Unfortunately most of the extant numberings were not added by the recipients themselves, but at a later stage, so that their value as evidence of the original correspondence is sadly diminished. One example of a recipient's numbering is in the early letters to Mary Cooke, before she married Adam Clarke, though of the eighteen recorded letters (Sept. 10, 1785, to Dec. 21, 1787) only eight appear to be extant in any form. In the case of Mrs. Eliza Bennis the few extant holographs bear two numberings, one being her own, the other that of her son, who combined Wesley's originals to her with her copies of letters to him (similarly numbered) to publish selections from her correspondence.

[5] See below, pp. 112–13.   [6] See below, pp. 119–20, 121; cf. illus. facing pp. 58, 59.

V. WESLEY'S CORRESPONDENTS AND CORRESPONDENCE

John Wesley probably had his finger on the pulse of British life as closely as any man, and more closely than most. Among his many hundreds of correspondents were numbered the great of the land: the king and his ministers of state, the lords of the church and the higher clergy, the nobility and titled gentry; they included also the poor and destitute, and not a few criminals both high and low; they were scattered around several European countries and in the rapidly expanding eastern settlements of the New World; above all, however, they comprised any who were eager to foster personal religion, and especially the preachers and leaders of his Methodist societies, developed and nurtured for this express purpose. Deservedly of great interest are his letters offering advice, encouragement, and challenge to Lord North,[1] William Pitt,[2] or William Wilberforce,[3] even though their replies are not known. Yet a letter is never complete in itself; we need to know who and what prompted it, what response it evoked. To understand Wesley's letters we must know something about his correspondents and his correspondence. Sometimes, indeed, the only evidence for missing letters comes from his correspondents, as in the case of Dr. Samuel Johnson, from whom we have two to Wesley but none from him.[4] Without Wesley's in-letters his out-letters put us in the position of someone listening to one end of a telephone conversation upon a subject with which we may be unfamiliar—the more frustrating because the man at our end of the line is normally much the more taciturn of the two, answering lengthy sentences with a brief comment, reacting rather than initiating.

Correspondence in and out. Ideally we would wish to have complete series of both sides of several correspondences over long periods, so that we could study in documented detail the development of relationships and the maturing of ideas over a generation or more, for at least a few truly representative figures. Such we have in the case of Horace Walpole. Not with Wesley, however. Only a few series can be regarded as anywhere near complete, and these for

---

[1] June 15, 1775.

[2] Sept. 6, 1784; June 22, 1790.

[3] July 30, 1790; Feb. 24, 1791.

[4] Feb. 6, 1776, and May 3, 1779, the latter a letter of introduction for Boswell. There is no question that Johnson and Wesley both respected and were influenced by each other. (See Richard E. Brantley, 'Johnson's Wesleyan Connection', *Eighteenth-Century Studies*, X. 143–68 (Winter, 1976/7).)

limited periods only. One is Wesley's correspondence with a learned and sympathetic (though highly critical) clergyman who employed the pseudonym 'John Smith', whose identity remains unknown. Between May, 1745, and Mar. 22, 1748, they exchanged twelve lengthy letters dealing with the beliefs and practices of Wesley and the Methodists. (This correspondence was transcribed by Wesley's trusted friend, the Revd. John Jones.) A fairly complete series of about fifty letters between Wesley and the young Bible scholar Adam Clarke has also survived, stretching over the years 1784–91, including sixteen by Clarke himself—usually two or three times longer than Wesley's. In a few other instances we possess publications by Wesley's opponents making controversial capital out of briefer and less substantial correspondences, such as those by a Baptist, the Revd. Gilbert Boyce (1750), by an Irish Presbyterian, the Revd. James Clark (1756), and by a backsliding Methodist, John Atlay (1788).

Several notable series are available apart from these, but no long one which is even relatively complete from both sides. The longest correspondence of all, that with his brother Charles, covering the years 1724–88, comprises (at present) 113 from John to Charles and 79 from Charles to John, but there are huge gaps where letters undoubtedly passed between them, alike in their youth, their middle years, and their old age, nor do most of the letters so far known connect with one preceding or following. The next largest series consists of 93 to Miss Ann Bolton of Witney, covering the years 1768–91. In this instance also Wesley seems to have preserved those he received, as she did his. After his death, however, her letters were fed to a bonfire behind his home in City Road, London,[1] though fortunately he had already printed extracts from 25 of them in his *Arminian Magazine*. The series of fifty letters to Alexander Knox (1775–90) appears to be complete, but not a single example remains of Knox's letters to Wesley.

The letters which Wesley received were often turned to important advantage in his societies, on regular 'letter-days', when selections would be read emphasizing conversions, spiritual experience, and the progress of the work of evangelism in various parts of the world, a practice which may have been adopted from the Moravians. At a noonday gathering on Saturday, Aug. 9, 1740, for instance, he

[1] James Everett, *Adam Clarke Portrayed*, London, Hamilton, Adams, 1843, I. 345-6.

recorded: 'Instead of the letters I had lately received I read a few of those formerly received from our poor brethren who have since then denied the work of God, and vilely cast away their shield.'[1] Monthly letter-days in London, Bristol, and Newcastle were scheduled at the early Conferences,[2] and the practice seems to have continued through most of Wesley's life. His *Journal* for Dec. 26, 1769, recorded the immediate results of British Methodism's greatest missionary venture, the sending of preachers to America a few months earlier: 'I read the letters from our preachers in America, informing us that God had begun a glorious work there; that both in New York and Philadelphia multitudes flock to hear, and behave with the deepest seriousness; and that the society in each place already contains above a hundred members.'[3]

The major source of holograph letters to Wesley is the Methodist Archives, in which have gradually accumulated most of those which Wesley himself set out to preserve, and which escaped the spring-cleaning enthusiasm at his death. As is demonstrated by his endorsements on wrappers and individual letters, it was his practice to gather them together in labelled bundles: 'L[ette]rs rec[eive]d in Georgia from Engl[an]d';[4] 'Savannah L[ette]rs';[5] 'L[ette]rs writ at Sav[anna]h and a[fte]r my return';[6] 'L[etter]rs of June, July, Aug., Sept., 1740';[7] 'L[ette]rs to be answered',[8] etc. Frequently he burned letters after reading them,[9] though not always—even when his correspondents asked him to do so.[10] Others he weeded out at intervals.[11] Most of them were destroyed once he had transcribed extracts from them,[12] or published them in his *Journal* or elsewhere.[13] The

---

[1] *Journal* and diary for that date.

[2] See *Minutes* of the Conferences, 1744–7, Vol. 10 of this edition.

[3] JWJ, Dec. 26, 1769; cf. Sept. 3, 1745; Apr. 27, 1748; July 17, 1750; Apr. 18, 1758; Aug. 4, 1760; Sept. 19, 1773.   [4] Nov. 18, 1735, from James Vernon.

[5] Mar. 16, 1736, from General Oglethorpe.

[6] Oct. 9, 1736, from the Revd. Thomas Broughton.

[7] Sept. 2, 1740, from the Revd. Henry Piers.

[8] Dec. 25, 1740, from John Brownfield.   [9] July 10, 1756, to his wife.

[10] e.g. Jan. 1, 1734, from his mother, and May 24, 1788, from his niece Sally.

[11] 'I employed all my leisure hours this week in revising my letters and papers. Abundance of them I committed to the flames. Perhaps some of the rest may see the light when I am gone.' (JWJ, Jan. 21, 1765; cf. Jan. 3, 1740, and Aug. 12, 1745, an occasion which led to the publication of a batch of letters in his *Journal*.)

[12] 'I do transcribe what I choose to keep, and burn the originals.' (May 11, 1780, to Sarah Crosby.)

[13] Ibid., but cf. Aug. 16, 1756, to the Revd. Samuel Walker, and Sept. 15, 1762, to the Revd. Samuel Furly, letters preserved even after he had published them in the *A.M.*

few score which survived were almost always those which he had endorsed with a cross to indicate their importance either in content or as representative samples from a writer of whom he wished to preserve at least one souvenir.

He was rightly concerned about what would happen to his 'papers and letters' after his death, wondering in 1772 whether he should bequeath them to the Revd. John Fletcher.[1] In the end he outlived both Fletcher and his brother Charles, and by his last will (Feb. 20, 1789) stated: 'I give all my manuscripts to Thomas Coke, Doctor Whitehead, and Henry Moore, to be burned or published as they see good.'[2] Unfortunately Whitehead was at loggerheads with the other two literary executors, and all three were to some extent frustrated by the precipitate action of one of the senior preachers in destroying material.[3]

These holographs are supplemented by the in-letters which he himself published, together with those which survive in letter-books, biographies, magazines, and the like, bringing the total at present available to about 1,300, many of them much lengthier than Wesley's own compact missives, which number some 3,500. When to holographs and copies are added clues from diaries, biographies, and other letters, however, it is possible to furnish specific documentation (though not texts) of some ten thousand letters which passed between him and about sixteen hundred correspondents.[4]

Classes of correspondents to 1739. It is helpful to divide Wesley's life into two basic stages, that preparatory to the flowering of Methodism, and that in which he guided its affairs. Although many features of his Methodist societies were foreshadowed by events in Oxford, Georgia, and Germany, the full flowering did not come until 1739, when he ventured upon many practices which set Methodism off from the Church of England as a religious group with a distinct ethos of its own. During this first period, 1717–39, we can document some 1,373 out-letters and 490 in-letters for Wesley, a total of 1,863, of which 226 out-letters and 303 in-letters are extant in one form or another, a total of 529, or about 28 per cent of the whole. Almost three-quarters of these may be described as to family and friends.

---

[1] Apr. 26, 1772.   [2] Somerset House, London.
[3] See above, p. 80 and n.
[4] For details of the brief presentation of this massive correspondence see below, p. 123, and the appendix to this volume. For the reproduction of select letters see pp. 128–9.

Family ties were very important to Wesley, and his diaries furnish a strong illustration of this, including the documentation of letters which are no longer extant. From 1724 until Samuel Wesley's death in 1735 at least 120 letters passed between John and his father. He was even closer to his mother, although letters passed between them at similar intervals, an accumulation of about 160 between 1723 and 1739. Perhaps more remarkable is his correspondence with his older brother Samuel, who died in 1739 after John had recorded writing to him 115 times from June 17, 1724. The Revd. Samuel Wesley, Jun., had apparently written a similar number of letters in reply, although only forty-five are documented.[1] A similar devotion is shown in varying degrees in John's letters to his sisters. Between 1724 and 1739 he wrote forty to Emily; only two to Suky, the next oldest, unhappily married to Richard Ellison, who seems to have made things difficult for her; seventeen to Molly, who died in 1734; seven to Hetty (1725–32); nine to Nancy—widely scattered; fifty-four to Patty (Martha), who married the Revd. Westley Hall; and thirty-nine to the youngest, Kezia (1729–39). To Charles during the same period John records writing thirty-eight letters, although certainly more passed. In spite of the deficiencies in the records and the low survival rate of the actual letters, it can readily be seen that there existed very close ties, not only of duty, but of affection, between Wesley and his parents, and between him and his brothers and sisters, especially Samuel, Emily (ten years his senior), Martha (three years younger), and baby Kezia, six years younger.

Allied with these letters during this preparatory period were a host of letters to a close circle of friends, especially those arising from his career at Oxford. He maintained friendships with other Fellows, with his own students and their families, and especially with the committed few who were nicknamed Methodists. Through his Oxford friends he was introduced to a circle of young women, mainly the sisters of Oxford men, and especially to a group living in three Cotswold villages, with whom he corresponded frequently during the intervals between idyllic holidays in the area. To his various Oxford correspondents during the period 1726–39 he wrote some 333 letters, to the Cotswold group (1725–34), 178, a total of 511, or over 37 per cent of his total correspondence for the whole period under study.

For these two groups, family and friends, during his young

[1] In his diary Wesley recorded in-letters far less frequently than out-letters.

manhood, Wesley maintained careful records of letters sent and received, preserved samples of actual letters received from them, and notebooks containing summaries of their correspondence, not all of which, unfortunately, have survived. His family letter-book furnishes a valuable supplement to those actual letters which have been preserved, and the selections from his correspondence with 'Aspasia' (the young widow, Mary Pendarves, formerly Granville, and later Mrs. Delany, who has herself become known to the literary world for her letters), and 'Selima' (her sister Anne) furnish glimpses of an aspect of his character that would otherwise be extremely difficult to reconstruct. One acute loss is the letter-book containing extracts from his correspondence with 'Varanese'—Sally Kirkham, who probably meant much more to him than either. Their correspondence began in 1725, the year of his ordination, only a few months before she married the Revd. John Chapone, and continued until 1736, during which time she was apparently a happy wife and mother, yet sharing tender feelings of platonic love with Wesley, who wrote at least forty-three letters to her.

The remaining quarter of Wesley's correspondence before 1740 was meagre by comparison: some 150 letters written to individuals and organizations connected with his Georgia ministry of 1736-7; about 164 linked with the beginnings of experimental Methodism in Britain (1738-9); about 50 connected with his publishing activities, notably 41 to Charles Rivington (1731-6); and about 20 linked with the Moravians and his visit to Germany in 1738. This latter period of 1738-9, however, is very fruitful with hints of what was to come: a handful of letters replying to written and printed attacks upon the new movement,[1] letters to the nobility and titled gentry,[2] to civic authority,[3] to sympathetic evangelicals both in the Anglican fold,[4] among the Nonconformists,[5] and in other countries.[6] From 1725 onwards he clearly set out to prove himself 'a faithful minister of our blessed Jesus',[7] committed to saving souls,[8] and by 1739 was

---

[1] By the Revd. Arthur Bedford, Mrs. Anne Dutton, 'Mr. Hooker' (Dr. William Webster) of the *Weekly Miscellany*, Dr. Henry Stebbing, and the Revd. Josiah Tucker.

[2] Lord Perceval, later the Earl of Egmont, Lady Cox, Sir John and later Sir Erasmus Phillips.

[3] The Mayor of Bristol.   [4] The Revd. Griffith Jones.

[5] Dr. Philip Doddridge.

[6] Dr. Ralph Erskine in Scotland, Howell Harris and Thomas Price in Wales, Dr. Timothy Cutler in Boston, Massachusetts, Dr. Koker in Holland, Messrs. Gottschalk, Marschall, Moschere, Steinmetz, and the Moravians, in Germany.

[7] Feb. 15, 1733.   [8] Jan. 24, 1727.

beginning to look upon all the world as his parish,[1] and in this task was already seeking help from the enthusiastic layman as well as the sympathetic cleric. The fifty years which followed saw the unfolding of this enterprise, together with the inevitable curtailing of the time devoted to family and friends.

Major correspondents from 1740. A statistical survey of Wesley's correspondents for the last fifty years of his writing life is less conclusive than for the first twenty, even though the letters available are multiplied eight times, because it must be based upon the accidents of preservation rather than upon Wesley's own fairly complete records. Nevertheless some general indications may be given from a study of those who are represented by (say) a total of twenty letters or more in either direction. This is true of 48 correspondents, 26 men and 22 women, with similar proportions for the numbers of Wesley letters to those correspondents—882 and 687, a total of 1,569, about 45 per cent of Wesley's extant letters to all correspondents. (It should perhaps be pointed out that the proportion of women in Wesley's total correspondence, including the many to whom no extant letters are available, is much smaller—only 300 out of 1,400.)

The majority of Wesley's favoured letter-receiving and letter-saving men were from the ranks of his itinerant preachers—sixteen out of the twenty-six. Naming these in order of the beginnings of the extant correspondence, they consist of John Bennet (1744–53), who left the ranks to become an Independent minister, after marrying Wesley's espoused wife, Grace Murray;[2] Christopher Hopper (1750–88); Thomas Rankin, his General Assistant in America (1761–86); John Valton (1764–90); Thomas Wride (1765–90); Robert Costerdine (1767–85); Joseph Benson (1768–90); John Mason (1768–90); John Bredin (1772–89); Thomas Rutherford (1774–90); Samuel Bradburn, 'The Methodist Demosthenes' (1775–89); Zechariah Yewdall (1779–89); Henry Moore, one of Wesley's literary executors (1783–91); and Adam Clarke, the young biblical scholar (1785–91). Four were evangelical clergy: Wesley's brother Charles (1728–88); his former pupil, George Whitefield (1735–69); Samuel Furly (1754–73), whom Wesley took under his tutorial wing while Furly was still a student at Cambridge; and the

---

[1] Mar. 24, 1739.

[2] See Frank Baker, 'John Wesley's First Marriage', *London Quarterly Review*, 192 (Oct., 1967), pp. 305-15.

saintly John Fletcher (1755–85); all except Furly were closely involved in Methodist activities. Two of the six laymen were preachers: Howell Harris (1739–61), one of the two chief leaders of the Welsh revival, and Robert Carr Brackenbury (1779–90), a Lincolnshire squire who served Wesley for a time as an itinerant. The other four were men of intelligence and substance, with strong Methodist sympathies but differing degrees of involvement in the societies: Ebenezer Blackwell of London, a banker (1739–66); Walter Churchey of Brecon (1770–91), an attorney and also a versifier, whose *Poems* Wesley somewhat reluctantly published; Alexander Knox of Londonderry (1775–90), a descendant of John Knox, who achieved some fame as a theological writer, and whose spiritual life Wesley strove to enrich; and Arthur Keene of Dublin (1778–90), described simply as 'gentleman' by Wesley in his will, which appointed Keene one of the trustees for Kingswood School. (It is worth noting that only one of these laymen lived in England, two in Wales, and three in Ireland—the latter in particular a significant indication of the importance of Ireland to Methodism.)

Most of the women with whom Wesley corresponded were either single, widowed, or separated from their husbands, and this is strongly borne out by the list of major female correspondents. Usually his correspondence with those who were single dried up after they married, whether through motives of prudence or courtesy. Again we list them in order of the beginnings of the extant correspondence: Lady Huntingdon, founder of The Countess of Huntingdon's Connexion (1741–79); Mary Vazeille, whom Wesley married on the rebound from the loss of Grace Murray, but who became psychotically jealous of his relationships with the devout women of Methodism, so that eventually they separated (1750–78); Dorothy Furly, sister of the Revd. Samuel Furly, who married a Methodist preacher, John Downes (1756–83); Mrs. Sarah Ryan, separated from her third husband, whom Wesley regarded highly, and appointed one of his housekeepers, but who became a focal point of Mrs. Wesley's jealousy (1756–66); Mrs. Sarah Crosby, deserted by her husband, who became Wesley's first woman preacher (1757–89); Mary Bosanquet, also a preacher, and a close associate of Sarah Ryan and Sarah Crosby, who eventually married the Revd. John Fletcher (1761–88); Mrs. Eliza Bennis, a Methodist class-leader who emigrated with her husband from Ireland to Philadelphia (1763–76); the widowed Lady D'Arcy Maxwell, one of the most devout and influential Methodist leaders in Edinburgh (1764–88); Mrs. Elizabeth Woodhouse of Owston near Wesley's native Epworth, a staunch Methodist leader in spite of her unsympathetic husband (1764–88); Margaret Dale, who in 1773 married Edward Avison of Newcastle, but died four years later (1765–72); Jane Hilton, a young Methodist of Beverley, Yorkshire, whose correspondence with Wesley continued vigorously even after her marriage in 1769 to William Barton (1766–88); Hannah Ball, the Sunday School pioneer of High Wycombe (1768–89); Ann Bolton of Witney, whom Wesley termed the 'sister of my choice'[1] (1768–91); Philothea Briggs, granddaughter of the Revd. Vincent Perronet of Shoreham, and daughter of William Briggs, Wesley's first Book Steward, and from 1781 wife of Thomas Thompson, the first Methodist Member of Parliament (1769–75); Mary Bishop, proprietor of private schools in Bath and then Keynsham near Bristol (1769–84); Sarah Wesley, his brother Charles's sole surviving daughter (1772–90); Elizabeth Ritchie, who faithfully attended Wesley on his deathbed, and later became Mrs. Mortimer (1774–88); Ann Tindall of Scarborough, whose poems Wesley published in his *Arminian Magazine* (1774–90); Hester Ann Roe of Macclesfield, who married Wesley's preacher, James Rogers (1776–89); Ann Loxdale, who in 1811 married Dr. Thomas Coke as his second wife (1768–91); and Mary Cooke of Trowbridge, another budding poetess, who in 1788 married Adam Clarke (1785–91).

The number of these favoured women correspondents, in a masculine world, serves to emphasize the way in which Wesley was sensitive to the feminine mystique, appreciated female achievements, and encouraged the leadership of women in his societies. Clearly they were not all fashioned from the same mould, just as they were the product of different parts of the British Isles (though mainly English), and came from different social backgrounds (though chiefly from the comfortable, respectable middle to upper class). They shared some important characteristics, however, which drew and retained Wesley's interest: they evinced a strong dedication to personal spirituality, and were usually strongly allied to the Methodist societies; they engaged as far as their health allowed in practical religious service; they were thoughtful and intelligent. Most of them were also teachable and somewhat deferential, perhaps partly because they were younger—and towards the end of the list,

[1] Sept. 27, 1777.

considerably younger—than Wesley himself. It should be said, however, that although Wesley in his seventies and eighties undoubtedly warmed to the company and correspondence of attractive young female disciples, he would brush them off if they proved to be empty-headed hero-worshippers.

These men, these women, therefore, represent the hundreds of others to whom Wesley devoted most of many hours of correspondence almost every week from the beginnings of organized Methodism in 1739 until within a week or two of his death on March 2, 1791. With many other similar persons he maintained a similarly extensive correspondence, though fewer examples, and in some cases none, have survived. There were other hundreds, however, men in public office, editors of periodicals, critics, local clergy, people in urgent distress, to whom he wrote only one or a handful of letters in response to some passing stimulus, and probably never again. With these the occasion or the theme sometimes holds greater significance than the intermediary individual, even though Wesley's letters to men such as Lord North, William Pitt, and William Wilberforce may be also of national importance. In dealing with public affairs as with private concerns, however, Wesley's letters retain their characteristic Methodist overtones.

Occasions. The occasions which brought Wesley into touch with his correspondents were varied, but his annual itineraries around the British Isles proved a source of much correspondence of different kinds. The needs and dangers of the Methodist societies furnished the context of many letters, as did concern for the national welfare as a whole. His constant theme was the well-being of man as a child of God, which involved the fostering of a cultured mind in a healthy body, with happy and disciplined social relationships, and a vigorous personal experience of religion.

As Methodist societies proliferated through England and Wales, to which in 1747 were added Ireland, and in 1751 Scotland, careful planning was needed if Wesley was to keep in touch with them personally, and a multiplication of letters connected with his annual itineraries. The societies *en route*, and especially his preachers and hosts, must be kept informed of his projected route. To John Bennet he wrote on Mar. 12, 1751: 'I expect to leave London on the 27th instant; to be at Wednesbury the 31st, and at Alpraham on Thursday, April 4; whence I think (at present) to go on to Manchester. The Saturday following I am to be at Whiteheaven. The Wednesday and Thursday in Easter week I can spend wherever you think proper. I propose taking Leeds in my return fron Newcastle.' Ten years later he wrote from Newcastle: '⟨My⟩ work in the country cannot be finished before ⟨the l⟩atter end of August, as the circuit is now larger by ⟨two?⟩ hundred miles than when I was in the north two ⟨years⟩ ago.'[1] Four years later still he wrote to his Assistant in Cornwall, Thomas Rankin: 'You see my plan on the other side. Tell me of any alteration or addition which you think proper, and fix your Quarterly Meetings as you please; only let full notice be given.' This was part of a double letter, the other half being detachable so that Rankin could circulate it to the different societies:

My dear brethren,
   I shall have little time to spare this autumn; yet I will endeavour (with God's leave) to spend a few days in Cornwall. I hope to be at Tiverton on Tuesday, September 3; on Wednesday, 4th, at Bideford; on Thursday evening, 5th, at Millhouse; on Friday at Port Isaac; on Saturday the 7th at St. Cuthbert's; on Sunday morning and afternoon at St. Agnes; on Monday, 9th, St. Just; Tuesday, 10th, St. Ives; Friday, 13th, St. Just; Saturday, 21st, Bristol.[2]

This may be compared with his Cornish itinerary eight years later, sent to the Circuit Steward, Captain Richard Williams of Redruth, because the Assistant was on his way to the Conference in London:

On Monday, August 16th (if God permit) I shall be at Launceston; on Tue. 17 at Camelford (noon), Port Isaac six in the evening; Wed. 18, St. Cuthbert; Thur. 19, St. Just; Fri. 20, St. Ives; Sun. 22, Redruth; five in the evening, Gwennap; Mon. 23, St. Austell; Tue. 24, The Dock; Thur. 26, Cullompton. I preach at six in the evenings . . . Pray send the plan of my journeys to all the preachers.[3]

Every year brought new societies to visit, though Wesley had the courage to drop a few, so that in 1786 he wrote: 'I have now so many places to visit that the summer hardly gives me time for my work.'[4] Letters outlining his itineraries consumed much thought, but he made liberal use of amanuenses and secretaries (as in the last two instances). In his later years he also resorted to circulating printed itineraries to those affected.

   Sometimes Wesley stayed overnight at inns, but more often at the proliferating preaching-houses: 'I always lodge in our own houses',

---

[1] June 14, 1761. (The angle brackets denote the conjectural restoration of mutilated manuscripts; see p. 125 below.)
[2] Both were dated Limerick, June 9, 1765.
[3] July 31, 1773.
[4] Feb. 22, 1786, to Mrs. Middleton.

he told one preacher.[1] Often, however, he was welcomed to private homes, sometimes on the spur of the moment, sometimes by prior arrangement. This entailed the courtesy of an exchange of letters before the visit or after, and sometimes both. We can trace this pattern developing in 1739, when he accepted a pressing invitation to visit the newly-formed society at Wells, though not to stay overnight, sending a message to that effect from Bristol the previous day.[2] Similarly his visits to Oxford and Bengeworth near Evesham in early October were heralded by letters to Mr. Bedder of Oxford and Benjamin Seward of Bengeworth on Sept. 29.[3] It was just such a visit to Londonderry which eventually led to Wesley's correspondence with his host's son, Alexander Knox, ten years later. After the first unexpected stay in John Knox's home in 1765 Wesley wrote: 'I am much obliged to Mrs. Knox and you for your open and friendly behaviour while I had the pleasure of staying with you; as well as for your helping me forward on my journey.'[4] The same is true of the much briefer correspondence, spreading over some twenty-eight months, with about a letter a month being written, with the two daughters of Sir Philip Gibbes. This began with a typical courtesy letter after his first visit:

I cannot but return my sincere thanks to Lady Gibbes, and to my dear Miss Gibbes and Miss Agnes, for the friendly entertainment I received at Hilton Park, which I shall not easily forget. I have frequently since then reflected with pleasure on those happy moments, and shall rejoice should it ever be in my power to wait upon you again.

I must beg the favour of you to accept of the *Concise History of England*, which fully clears the character of that much injured woman.[5] And I beg Miss Agnes to accept of *Henry, Earl of Moreland*,[6] which I think will speak to her heart. I have ordered both of them to be put up in one parcel, and directed to you at Hilton Park.[7]

On his journeys Wesley usually tried to attend public worship in the local parish church, and encouraged his followers to do the same. By some clergy he was invited to preach; others pointedly preached at him. Where there seemed a possibility of a sympathetic

[1] Oct. 8, 1785, to Thomas Wride.
[2] JWJ, Aug. 9, 1739.
[3] JWJ and diary, Sept. 29–Oct. 3, 1739.
[4] July 20, 1765; cf. JWJ, May 11, 1765.
[5] Mary Queen of Scots, about whom they had doubtless conversed. The *Concise History* was Wesley's own publication in four volumes (*Bibliog*, No. 357).
[6] Again Wesley's own publication, an abridgement of Henry Brooke's novel, *The Fool of Quality* (*Bibliog*, No. 414).
[7] Apr. 7, 1783. He had stayed at Hilton Park Mar. 25–6 (see *Journal*).

response he might offer his services in advance by writing, though not always with the happiest results. During his northern tour in 1780, for instance, Wesley was planning to preach in the new Methodist preaching-house at Sheffield on Sunday morning, July 2, at 8 a.m., and then to accompany his congregation to the parish church, where it was communion Sunday. He therefore wrote to the vicar the previous day:

Revd. sir.
   As I apprehend the service tomorrow morning at the Old Church will be exceeding long, I should be glad to assist you in any part of it.
                            I am, Revd. sir, your affectionate brother and servant,
Rotherham   John Wesley
July 1, 1780

The vicar's reply was clearly not very encouraging, for on the Sunday morning Wesley sent him another note:

Sir
   There is no harm done. If you don't want *me*, I don't want you.
                                              I am your fellow servant,
July 2, 1780   J. Wesley

(The Methodists attended morning worship nevertheless, and Wesley recorded in his *Journal* that there was 'such a number of communicants as was never seen at the Old Church before'.)
   Like most religious leaders, Wesley found himself drawn reluctantly into seeking financial support from his followers. Constantly he pressed the issue of stewardship, as in a letter to the extremely wealthy Sir James Lowther: 'You are not the proprietor of anything—no, not of one shilling in the world. You are only a steward of what Another entrusts you with, to be laid out not according to your will but his.'[1] With the multiplying societies, and the need for buildings to accommodate members who were frequently poor, Wesley realized that Methodism was slipping further and further into debt. In 1767 he organized 'a push toward paying the whole debt', telling his preachers that he would 'state the case in writing to the most substantial men in our society'.[2] For six successive winters he conducted a nation-wide campaign, writing letters to hundreds of people. Some of these appeals were printed, with

---

[1] Oct. 28, 1754.
[2] *Minutes of some late Conversations* (*Bibliog*, No. 269), 1767, Question 18.

Wesley usually adding a personal note, as well as his signature.[1]
Typical of his approach were the letters written in 1768:

> Let me have joy over *you*, my brother, in particular. You *have* a measure
> of 'this world's goods'. You 'see your brother hath need'. *I* have need of your
> help, inasmuch as the burdens of my brethren are my own. Do not 'pass by on
> the other side', but come and help as God has enabled you. Do all you can to
> lighten the labour and strengthen the hands of,
>
> Your affectionate brother
> J. Wesley[2]

In the general administration of Methodism Wesley found himself involved in a multitude of different activities, in all of which he
sought to give careful attention to detail, following out his own
advice, 'Do not make too much haste. Give everything the last
touch.'[3] One illustration of this is his effort to guide on his way to
America the first president whom he had secured for Coke and
Asbury's Cokesbury College, the Revd. Levi Heath, of Stourport:

> Dear sir,
> In your way to London I believe you must spend the first night at Oxford,
> where you may inquire at the preaching-house in New Inn Hall Lane for Mr.
> Harper, who is the Assistant in that circuit. Thence you have four-and-twenty
> miles to High Wycombe, where Mr. Battin will entertain you hospitably, by a
> word of recommendation from Mr. Harper. You have then thirty miles to
> London. At my house near Moorfields I hope you will be at home. And Mr.
> Bradburn there will recommend you to our friends at Reading, Newbury, Bath,
> and Bristol. At Bristol I hope you will find your family well, and probably a
> ship ready to sail. I commend you to the grace of God, and am, dear sir, your
> affectionate friend and brother, J. Wesley[4]

From his early years Wesley had found it necessary to defend
the reputation of Methodism, lest its work be undermined. The open
letter printed in pamphlet form was one of his basic weapons of
defence, as well as of attack, and more than twenty of his publications appear in this format, addressed to individuals. He pursued a

[1] Dec. 1, 1768; cf. Nov. 24, 1767, Nov. 20, 1769, Dec. 12, 1772, and p. 40 above.

[2] Dec. 1, 1768, in the hand of an amanuensis, but signed by Wesley. See an identical
letter, dated Dec. 7, addressed to Mark Middleton. Similarly by writing campaigns and
printed circulars Wesley secured financial support for the American Methodists in
1769 (cf. Frank Baker, *From Wesley to Asbury*, Durham, N.C., Duke University Press,
1976, pp. 70–83), and for the London Methodists from 1776 onwards as they sought to
replace the old Foundery with the New Chapel in City Road (Oct. 18, 1776, etc.),
though not always successfully (see the correspondence with Richard Ireland, Apr. 25,
June 26, 1777).

[3] Feb. 21, 1770.

[4] Aug. 6, 1787; for fuller details see Frank Baker, 'John Wesley and Cokesbury
College's First President', *Methodist History*, Vol. XI, No. 2, pp. 54–9 (Jan., 1973).

similar policy in writing letters to the editors of newspapers, daily, tri-weekly, and weekly, both in London and the provinces. More time than he relished was consumed in this unpleasing task. James Erskine, Lord Grange, an evangelical Member of Parliament, drew Wesley's attention to an attack on Methodism in the *Craftsman*. Wesley replied:

> I have some scruple as to answering that passage in the *Craftsman*, because I am afraid if I were to begin answering reflections of that kind (especially such as advance no new matter of any sort) I should scarce ever make an end.
>
> In one view, indeed, it may appear worthwhile to take notice of a mere trifle, if it be a providential opportunity of opening the eyes of some whom otherwise we could not well reach.
>
> If I should have a leisure hour tomorrow or the day following, I think on this ground I would write a few lines.[1]

Wesley frequently found himself thus trapped into answering attacks on Methodism and his own credibility: on Methodist 'enthusiasm' in the *Bristol Intelligencer*;[2] on his own truthfulness in the *Gentleman's Magazine*;[3] on his honesty in disbursing money collected for charitable purposes, in the *Morning Chronicle*;[4] in the *London Chronicle* he repudiated George Bell and his prophecy that the world would end on Feb. 28, 1763;[5] he replied to shotgun attacks against Methodism in general in the *London Magazine* and *Lloyd's Evening Post*, whence the controversy spread to the *London Chronicle* and the *Westminster Journal*, continuing for four months;[6] an attack on his popular medical handbook, *Primitive Physic*, by Dr. William Hawes, in the *Gazetteer*;[7] and the most wide-spread furore of all, aroused by his *Calm Address to our American Colonies*, concentrated in three Bristol newspapers, but running over into many London newspapers, and echoed by others all around the country.[8] Wesley tried to observe two basic principles: he rarely answered anonymous letters,[9] and he himself always added his own name.[10] Normally he sought to place his reply in the same periodical which had printed the attack, though this was not always possible. In his *Journal*, for instance, he published two letters to the editor of the *Monthly Review* which will be sought in vain in

---

[1] July 6, 1745. Wesley did indeed reply, and later published his letter as a four-page pamphlet (*Bibliog*, No. 104).

[2] Jan. 12, 1750.   [3] Mar. 8, 1756.

[4] Nov. 4, 1759; cf. Feb. 18, 1760, in *Lloyd's Evening Post*.

[5] Feb. 9, 1763.   [6] Nov. 17, 1760, etc.   [7] July 20, 27, 1776.

[8] Nov. 28, 1775, etc.   [9] Oct. 6, 1786.   [10] Feb. 10, 1765.

the columns of that unfriendly magazine, apparently because the editor refused to print them.[1] It was partly to remedy this kind of predicament that in 1778 Wesley began his own *Arminian Magazine*, not as a forum for controversy, but as a vehicle for Arminian apologetic and propaganda.[2] From that time onwards Wesley dabbled very little in newspaper controversies (which in any case had died down), though in 1789 he found it necessary to defend himself in the *Dublin Chronicle* because of charges that he was 'a double-tongued knave, an old crafty hypocrite', undermining the Church of England.[3]

Believing as he did in the social outreach of the Christian community, Wesley dealt faithfully with his many requests for transmitting character references to people whom occasionally he knew only slightly. For a needy person seeking to rehabilitate himself Wesley prepared a letter to be delivered personally to Samuel Lloyd, a well-to-do merchant in Devonshire Square: 'The bearer has behaved extremely well from the very time that he left London. I do not perceive that he is addicted to drinking or any other vice. I am apt to think he would made a good servant.'[4] He gave a similar note to James Kenton, a publisher fallen on hard times, to be presented to a potential benefactor whose identity is not known:

Sir,
     May I take the liberty to request a favour of you? It is, to assist an honest man. I have known Mr. Kenton, the bearer, these forty years. He has lived in affluence, but is now reduced. If it was convenient for you to speak in his favour to any of the Governors of the Charterhouse, you would much oblige,
                                        Dear sir, your affectionate servant,
⟨Car⟩low   John Wesley
⟨26⟩ April, 1789

Wesley saw himself as a servant of the general public as well as of the Methodist societies, and sought worthily to discharge any trust placed in him. Thus when he received £20 from an anonymous donor for the use of those in prison he gave an accounting of its disbursement by means of a letter to *Lloyd's Evening Post*.[5]

One of his most interesting interventions in public affairs was in a letter to William Pitt, the First Lord of the Treasury. Wesley pleaded (as he had earlier and successfully done with Lord North)

---

[1] Sept. 9, Oct. 5, 1756. The *Journal* in which they appeared was in fact not published until 1761, long after the event.

[2] Jan. 15, 1778. [3] June 2, 20, 1789.

[4] Mar. 20, 1755. [5] Feb. 18, 1760.

for Captain Thomas Webb, the Methodist preacher and dispossessed British loyalist, a refugee from America. Having secured Pitt's attention in briefly commending Webb, Wesley devoted the remainder of a very long letter to a discussion of the collection of taxes, suggesting that in the difficult task of increasing the revenue it was probably unnecessary to impose many new taxes, if only Pitt could secure the universal application of the old. He claimed that many people unfairly avoided the land tax, the window tax, the tax on servants, and customs duties, affirming that through smuggling 'in Cornwall alone the King is defrauded of half a million yearly'. Duties on spirits were also avoided, he continued, but here he took another line, urging that the trifling revenue from this source was dearly bought at the cost of the huge waste in grain and the loss of twenty thousand lives a year, urging that distilling should be made a felony.[1]

Wesley advised his preachers, both in England and in America, to stay out of politics, but he certainly did not wish them to be insensitive to national and local affairs, no more than he was himself. His concern about public events sometimes assumed what might be considered a puritanical colouring, as when he urged the Mayor and Corporation of Bristol to follow Nottingham's example by forbidding the erection of a new theatre.[2] Frequently, however, his approach was both unconventional and yet unexceptionable: he wrote to James West, Joint Secretary to the Treasury, offering to secure two hundred Methodist volunteers to give a year's military service in London in the event of the feared invasion;[3] he wrote to the *London Chronicle* heralding the greatly improved conditions in Newgate prison;[4] in a long letter printed in several newspapers, and later enlarged for publication as a pamphlet, he analysed the economic situation, especially the shortage and high price of different kinds of staple foods, and offered some practical remedies.[5] It is scarcely surprising that at the beginning of the 'awful crisis' of the American Revolutionary War he pleaded with Lord Dartmouth to recommend to the king a public call to prayer and fasting.[6] It is a different matter, however, when we discover him canvassing for votes for a specific parliamentary candidate, writing to one of his

[1] Sept. 6, 1784.   [2] Dec. 20, 1764.
[3] Mar. 1, 1756.   [4] Jan. 1, 1761.
[5] Dec. 9, 1772; cf. *Thoughts on the Present Scarcity of Provisions* (*Bibliog*, No. 344).
[6] Dec. 24, 1775.

preachers in Cornwall: 'Mr. Gregor, I am informed, is a lover of his king and country. Therefore I wish you would advise all our brethren that have votes to assist him in the ensuing election. And disperse everywhere the *Word to a Freeholder*.'[1]

Themes. Wesley was in correspondence with a multitude of people in all ranks of society, in Britain and Europe and America, for a few weeks, for many months, or the greater part of his lifetime or theirs. The ties of blood or friendship, the occasions which linked him in correspondence with strangers, found expression in many different kinds of letters, yet to some extent they were all pastoral, all variations upon one all-pervading theme—personal religion, 'the life of God in the soul of man'.[2] To the Revd. Samuel Walker he wrote: 'I have one point in view—to promote, so far as I am able, vital, practical religion; by the grace of God to beget, preserve, and increase the life of God in the souls of men.'[3] When his wife in psychotic jealousy stole much of his correspondence with women, and twisted excerpts from it to support accusations of infidelity, Wesley claimed: 'The subject of our correspondence was heart-religion, the inward kingdom of God. You have both their letters and mine.[4] Produce them just as they are. And if they do not answer for themselves to any competent judges, I will bear the blame for ever.'[5] A closing letter of appeal to an old Irish friend, James Knox of Sligo, emphasized the same subject:

Do you now see that true religion is not a negative or an external thing, but the life of God in the soul of man, the image of God stamped upon the heart? Do you now see that in order to this we are justified freely through the redemption that is in Jesus Christ? Where are the *desires* after this which you once felt, the hunger and thirst after righteousness? And where are the outward marks of a soul groaning after God, and refusing to be comforted with anything less than his love?[6]

---

[1] Oct. 3, 1789, to Alexander Suter; cf. a similar letter to John Mason, Oct. 1, 1789, and another of Dec. 24, 1789: 'As I know the Rev. Mr. Abdy to be both a good man and a good preacher, I wish all that fear God would give him their vote and interest in the present election. John Wesley.' In his *Word to a Freeholder* (*Bibliog*, No. 139), Wesley urged the refusing of gifts at an election, voting 'as if the whole election depended on your single vote', and voting for a man who loved God and the king. Cf. his letter to Bristol Methodists at the approach of the General Election of 1768: 'On no account take money or money's worth . . . Give, not sell, your vote.' (Nov. 7, 1767?)

[2] Wesley took this expression from the title of a book by Henry Scougal (1650–78), which he abridged for publication in 1744; see *Bibliog*, No. 93.

[3] Sept. 3, 1756. The phrase 'vital, practical religion' occurs three times in this lengthy letter.

[4] i.e. copies of the latter.

[5] Dec. 9, 1774, § 5.

[6] May 30, 1765.

Only a few months before his death it was to this that he urged his nephew Samuel:

I fear you want (what you least of all suspect) the greatest thing of all—religion. I do not mean external religion, but the religion of the heart: the religion which Kempis, Pascal, Fenelon enjoyed; the life of God in the soul of man; the walking with God, and having fellowship with the Father and the Son . . . You are called to know and love the God of glory; to live in eternity, to walk in eternity; to live the life which is hid with Christ in God. Hearken to the advice of one that stands on the edge of eternity.[1]

Nevertheless, although (as he frequently said) 'one thing is needful' (Luke 10:42), many other things were highly important, and Wesley's correspondents drew his attention to almost every subject under the sun, though some aspects of the God-guided life were discussed more frequently and stressed more urgently than others.

Wesley's letters often reveal the preacher wrestling to introduce someone to this life of God in his soul, possibly someone of high social standing such as D'Arcy, Lady Maxwell:

Christ has died for *you*; he has bought pardon for *you*. Why should not you receive it *now*? While you have this paper in your hand? Because you have 'not done' thus or thus? . . . O let it all go! None but Christ! None but Christ! . . . Do not wait for this or that *preparation*, for something to *bring* to God! Bring Christ! Rather, let him bring *you*. Bring you home to God! Lord Jesus, take her! Take her and all her sins! Take her, *as she is*! Take her *now*! . . . Let her sink down into the arms of thy love, and cry out, 'My Lord and my God!'[2]

Perhaps even more frequently he urged his faithful followers to seek 'the second blessing', to 'go on to perfection'—a phrase which occurs scores of times, especially in challenging letters to his preachers: 'Never be ashamed of the old Methodist doctrine. Press all believers to go on to perfection. Insist everywhere on the second blessing as receivable in a moment, and receivable now, by simple faith.'[3]

In his letters Wesley displayed the pastor, however, far more than the preacher. An intelligent, as well as concerned, spiritual counsellor, he realized the full significance of this ministry by correspondence, telling one of his inquirers: 'If no other end be answered by your writing, it may be an ease to your own mind. And we know not but God may apply to your heart a word written as well as a word spoken.'[4] In memorable phrases he often summarized the

---

[1] Apr. 29, 1790.   [2] May 25, 1765.
[3] Apr. 3, 1772; cf. Mar. 24, 1757; Oct. 8, 1774; June 4, 1786, etc.
[4] Nov. 6, 1756; cf. Aug. 23, 1763.

Christian way, the Christian hope: 'Keep close to your rule, the
Word of God, and to your guide, the Spirit of God; and never be
afraid of expecting *too much*.'[1] He prescribed for inquirers various
religious exercises: 'It might be of use if you were to read over the
first volume of *Sermons* seriously and with prayer. Indeed, nothing
will avail without prayer. Pray, whether you can or no. When you
are cheerful, when you are heavy, pray; with many or few words, or
none at all; you will surely find an answer of peace. And why not
now?'[2] His pleading advice might be prefaced by a diagnosis of the
spiritual problem:

> From the time you omitted meeting your class or band you grieved the
> Holy Spirit of God . . . I exhort you for my sake (who tenderly love you),
> for God's sake, for the sake of your own soul, begin again without delay. The
> day after you receive this, go and meet a class or a band. Sick or well, go!
> If you cannot speak a word, go; and God will go with you. You sink under the
> sin of omission! My friend, my sister, go! Go whether you can or not.[3]

He discussed their spiritual ailments in careful detail: 'The difference between heaviness and darkness of soul (the wilderness state)
should never be forgotten. Darkness (unless in the case of bodily
disorder) seldom comes upon us but by our own fault. It is not so
with respect to heaviness, which may be occasioned by a thousand
circumstances, such as frequently neither our wisdom can foresee
nor our power prevent.'[4] Mrs. Eliza Bennis complained, 'The inconstancy of my mind is a continual cause of grief to me.'[5] Wesley
replied: 'As thinking is the act of an embodied spirit, playing upon
a set of material keys, it is not strange that the soul can make but ill
music when her instrument is out of tune. This is frequently the
case with *you*; and the trouble and anxiety you then feel are a natural
effect of the disordered machine, which proportionably disorders the
mind.'[6] As with other correspondents, however, he had to return to
the same problem more than once, reassuring her, 'There may be
ten thousand wandering thoughts and forgetful intervals without
any breach of love.'[7]

Too frequently for Wesley's comfort his calling as a faithful pastor
involved administering a rebuke. He wrote to a prosperous merchant:

> The hand of God is over you for good. He is labouring to bring you wholly

[1] June 17, 1761.   [2] Jan. 31, 1764.   [3] Nov. 4, 1790.
[4] Sept. 13, 1774.   [5] Oct. 15, 1771.
[6] Oct. 28, 1771.   [7] June 16, 1772.

to himself, that you may give him all your heart. But how many hindrances are in the way! First, the deceitfulness of riches . . . Is not levity another main hindrance of your growth in grace? Often indulged by jesting and foolish talking? Can anything untune the soul more than this does? Or more unprepare it for a deep sense of things eternal?

I fear another hindrance is a kind of natural fickleness and inconstancy of temper. Perhaps it is peculiarly difficult to you to be long at one stay, to retain any impression for any length of time. How often have I known you deeply moved! But did it not pass away as a morning cloud? O that God may stablish your heart in grace! That you may count all things loss, so you may win Christ!'[1]

Similarly Wesley warned a young lady (later the biographer of Lady Maxwell) who was preening herself as a writer: 'My dear maiden, Beware of pride! Beware of flattery! Suffer none to commend you to your face. Remember, one good temper is of more value in the sight of God than a thousand good verses. All you want is to have the mind that was in Christ, and to walk as Christ walked.'[2] Wesley was sensitive to people's temperaments and true needs, however, and therefore undertook the unpleasant task of chiding with great caution, and urged others to be equally careful. To Thomas Rankin he wrote: 'I am sorry for poor Tommy Rourke . . . He has much more need of comfort than of reproof. His great danger is despair.'[3] He found it far more congenial to offer consolation in distress and sorrow, or practical advice in building a healthy body, a cultured mind, happy human relationships.

Wesley's letters abound in health hints. Typical was his laconic advice to Lady Maxwell: 'I believe medicines will do you little service; you need only proper diet, exact regularity, and constant exercise, with the blessing of God.'[4] The diets he prescribed might be approved today: eating meat in moderation, fruit and vegetables in abundance,[5] and for 'the flux' (diarrhoea) a light diet with milk puddings, toast, and lemonade.[6] He told his niece Sally that like many people she suffered from an unrecognized ailment—'intemperance in sleep'—and went on: 'After all the observations and inquiries I have been able to make for upwards of fifty years, I am fully persuaded that men in general need between six and seven hours' sleep in four-and-twenty, and women in general a little more—namely, between seven and eight . . . I advise you, therefore, from this day ⟨forward⟩ . . . to take exactly so ⟨much⟩ sleep as nature

---

[1] June 19, 1751, to Samuel Lloyd, who copied his contrite reply on the blank page.
[2] Jan. 18, 1790, to Agnes Collinson (later Bulmer).
[3] Apr. 21, 1775.   [4] July 5, 1765.
[5] June 6, 1775; Apr. 24, 1788.   [6] Oct. 18, 1780.

requires, and no more.'[1] Exercise he constantly urged on the sedentary, such as the young candidate for Holy Orders, Samuel Furly: 'You must, absolutely must, find time for exercise. Otherwise you are penny wise and pound foolish. For one fit of sickness will cost you more time than you have saved in several years.'[2]

In addition to suggestions about regimen, however, Wesley did echo his *Primitive Physic* in offering cures for scores of specific ailments: for colic,[3] gall-stones,[4] gout (a Wesley family complaint),[5] hoarseness,[6] the itch,[7] mortification,[8] nettle rash,[9] and scorbutic sores,[10] to name a few. Usually diet, medicine, and exercise were combined in his prescriptions, as in this to Mrs. Christian:

> The gravel may be easily prevented by eating a small crust of bread the size of a walnut every morning, fasting. But your nervous disorders will not be removed without constant exercise. If you can have no other, you should daily ride a wooden horse, which is only a double plank nine or ten feet long, properly placed upon two trestles. This has removed many distempers and saved abundance of lives. I should advise you likewise to use nettle tea (six or eight leaves) instead of foreign tea for a month, and probably you will see a great change.[11]

So concerned was Wesley about public health that he wrote three successive letters to the *Bristol Gazette* lamenting the use of that 'poisonous weed', hops, in the brewing of ale, claiming from his own experience that unhopped ale kept just as well, while he clearly preferred the 'soft, sweetish taste' of the old-fashioned beverage which he had known in his earlier years, before it began to be 'adulterated by bitter herbs'.[12]

Another aspect of Wesley's pastoral concern which shows up frequently in his letters is his enthusiasm as an educator. He served as a private correspondence tutor for several young men and women, offering them advice on methods of study, the reading of specific books, and even a five-year course of study, which he urged them to follow faithfully, because, as he told Joseph Benson: 'When I recommend to anyone a method or scheme of study, I do not barely consider this or that book separately, but in conjunction with the rest,' adding, 'And what I recommend, I *know*: I know both the

---

[1] July 17, 1781.   [2] Mar. 24, 1757.   [3] June 16, 1772.
[4] July 17, 1785.   [5] Sept. 26, 1776.   [6] Dec. 15, 1764.
[7] July 8, 1774; Jan. 27, 1776.   [8] Oct. 5, 1789.
[9] Nov. 5, 1772.   [10] May 17, 1781.
[11] July 17, 1785. On Oct. 13, 1784, he had written to John Valton, 'I suppose nettle tea is the best bracer in the world.'
[12] Sept. 7, 25, Oct. 3, 1789.

style and the sentiments of each author, and how he will confirm
or illustrate what goes before, and prepare for what comes after.'[1]
His guidance for young ladies was a little less rigid, and he wrote to
his niece Sally: 'Might not you read two or three hours in the morning, and one or two in the afternoon? When you are tired with
severer studies, you may relax your mind by history or poetry.'[2] He
was especially concerned that his preachers should develop their
minds. To John Trembath he wrote:

What has exceedingly hurt you . . . is want of reading . . . Hence your talent
in preaching does not increase . . . It is lively, but not deep; there is little
variety; there is no compass of thought. Reading only can supply this, with
meditation and daily prayer . . . O begin! Fix some part of every day for private
exercises . . . Whether you like it or no, read and pray daily. It is for your life;
there is no other way: else you will be a trifler all your days, and a pretty, superficial preacher.[3]

The Revd. Vincent Perronet's curate at Shoreham asked Wesley's
advice on his own studies, and Wesley's compressed reply provides
bibliographical comments on over sixty books and authors which are
as frank and revealing as those in his *Journal*: 'Leland's *View* is
excellent in its kind; so is Grotius . . . Clerc's works are muddling.
The Antiq. Hebraica I have not seen. Seneca's Tragedies and Ovid's
Metamorphoses are worth reading once . . . Terence is worth
studying. It is the finest Latin in the world . . . Aristotle is an
admirable writer.' Wesley's closing comment is typical: 'But you
need not half these books. A few well digested are better than ten
thousand. It would be worth your while to consider the Course of
Female Study in the *Arminian Magazine*.'[4]

Wesley was also approached many times for advice by potential
authors. To a young poetess, Ann Tindall, he wrote: 'It is by writing
that we learn to write. Some of your verses are good, particularly
those you wrote latest.'[5] Subsequently he warned her: 'I am generally
thought a severe critic. Take care, therefore, how you fall into my
hands. I do not at all consider *who* writes, but *what* is written', and
went on to advise her on specific improvements needed in her
poem.[6] Eventually he published some of her verse in the *Arminian*

---

[1] Dec. 22, 1768; cf. Mar. 30, 1754; Feb. 18, 1756.
[2] Sept. 8, 1781. This was a modified version of a letter published in his *A.M.* for
Nov. 1780, entitled, 'A Female Course of Study'.
[3] Aug. 17, 1760. As a spur to other preachers Wesley published this letter in his
A.M. for Aug. 1780.
[4] Jan. 15, 1785. For the course see note 2 above.
[5] Jan. 19, 1776.   [6] Oct. 26, 1776

Magazine, as he did that of other correspondents, such as the Revd. Joshua Gilpin, to whom he wrote: 'You may preach the gospel in verse as well as in prose; and sometimes with more effect.'[1] Other writers, however, he did not encourage, such as John Glover of Norwich, about whose published work Wesley wrote to Duncan Wright, one of his preachers:

> I wish you would go to him . . ., give my love to him, and thanks for the little book he sent me. But what can one say of the book itself? It is well-meant, but exceeding weak. Yet I know not how to tell him so, for fear of grieving him, as he appears to me to be a man of a tender spirit. I would willingly buy a dozen or two of him, if I knew what to do with them. And yet I would not put him upon writing more, because it is not his talent.[2]

Wesley knew perfectly well, however, that 'few authors will thank you for imagining you are able to correct their works'.[3] Reading between the lines of a dozen mildly critical letters one realizes that he suffered greatly when one of his most influential laymen, the Brecon attorney, Walter Churchey, insisted on publishing a huge volume of mediocre verse, which dropped almost stillborn from the press, though Wesley saved him from financial disaster by supervising its publication.[4]

People wrote to Wesley about the perplexities of human relationships in general, and he proved a faithful pastor in seeking to reconcile those who were estranged, such as Jasper Winscom and his son: 'You may say, "Well, what would you advise me to do now?" I advise you to forgive him. I advise you to lay aside your anger (it is high time), and to receive him again (occasionally) into your house. For you need forgiveness yourself: and if you do not forgive, you cannot be forgiven!'[5] The problems with which Wesley found himself confronted most frequently seem to have been those of courtship and marriage. He wrote to one young lady: 'Nothing under heaven is so critical and so dangerous as what is commonly called, "the time of courtship". But God is able, even now, to cause all grace to abound, and to perfect his strength in your weakness.'[6] He laid down one basic rule: parental obedience. He stated that if a preacher 'married a person without the consent of her parents he would thereby exclude himself out of the Methodist connexion'.[7]

---

[1] Sept. 30, 1787.   [2] Oct. 20, 1768.   [3] July 8, 1774.
[4] See *Bibliog*, No. 504, and letters to Churchey, 1788-9.
[5] Oct. 13, 1783; cf. Wesley's letter to the son's wife, Dec. 10, 1785.
[6] May 2, 1771, to Ally Eden.   [7] Apr. 10, 1782.

He was therefore ready to intervene when a local preacher ventured on this slippery ground:

> I was much concerned yesterday when I heard you was likely to marry a woman against the consent of your parents. I have never, in an observation of fifty years, known such a marriage attended with a blessing. I know not how it should, since it is flatly contrary to the fifth commandment. I told my own mother, pressing me to marry, 'I dare not allow you a *positive* voice herein; I dare not marry a person because you *bid* me. But I must allow you a negative voice: I will marry no person if you *forbid*. I know it would be a sin against God.'[1]

On marriage in general he reassured his correspondents: 'Certainly it is possible for persons to be as devoted to God in a married as in a single state.'[2] In that era of match-making he advised what should be weighed in seeking a partner: 'In such a case I should consider: (1), the religion; (2), the natural temper; (3), the understanding and person (in the common sense); and in the fourth and last place, the fortune. This is undoubtedly of some importance, and *caeteris paribus* [other things being equal], might turn the scale. But the other circumstances have a far more direct influence both on our present and future happiness.'[3] He approved, or occasionally disapproved, of their choice of prospective partners: 'I believe J[ohn] D[ownes] is throughly desirous of being wholly devoted to God, and that (if you alter your condition at all) you cannot choose a more proper person.'[4] Sometimes he corresponded with both man and woman about their proposed marriage, occasionally in the same letter.[5]

When Wesley, as a father in God, did frown on a proposed marriage, and the match was broken off, he remained deeply concerned to heal the resulting wounds, even praising the benefits of a single life, upon which he had published a pamphlet.[6] His first extant letter to Ann Bolton began:

> My dear sister, The best and most desirable thing of all is that you should live and die wholly devoted to God, waiting upon him without distraction, . . . an whole burnt sacrifice of love. If you have not steadiness and resolution for this, the next thing to be desired is that you marry a man of faith and love, who has a good temper and a good understanding. The temptation you are now in was perhaps the most dangerous one you ever had in your life. God deliver you from that almost certain destruction which attends the being unequally yoked to an unbeliever![7]

---

[1] Sept. 11, 1781.   [2] July 16, 1763.   [3] June 7, 1767.
[4] July 16, 1763; cf. letter to Thomas Roberts, Dec. 22, 1787.
[5] June 16, 1769.
[6] *Thoughts on a Single Life*, 1765 (*Bibliog*, No. 263).   [7] Feb. 13, 1768.

After an intervening personal conversation he wrote again: 'It was not a small deliverance which you had in escaping the being joined to one who was not what he seemed. If he had acted thus after you were married, it would almost have broke your heart. See how the Lord careth for you! Surely the hairs of your head are all numbered!'[1] Less than ten years later he was again emphasizing the same point:

> God has lately delivered you out of imminent danger, that of being un-equally yoked with an unbeliever. That he is so now will admit of no dispute. And it is not plain that ever he was otherwise . . . And now, instead of praising God for your great deliverance, you are reasoning against him, as [if] it were no deliverance at all! . . . My Nancy, arise and shake yourself from the dust! You have acted wisely and faithfully. God has heard your prayer; and he is well pleased with the sacrifice you have made. Admit no thought to the con-trary.[2]

Far less attention seems to have been devoted (as was the custom of that age) to problems *within* marriage—with which Wesley him-self was even more fully acquainted. But examples are present, and although in general Wesley courteously withdrew from the scene when a female correspondent married, there were exceptions, such as that of Jane Hilton, through whom he continued to assist both partners to build a happy home in Beverley after she became Mrs. Barton.[3] Perhaps unexpectedly, he expressed somewhat liberal views about divorce, even before his own marriage had gone sour, writing to a preacher:

> As to the point in general (though we need not say so much in public, because of accidental ill consequences) nothing under heaven can be clearer than this: (1), that adultery does in that moment dissolve the marriage tie, as much as if the offender had then died; (2), that *divorce* is only an open declaration of that dissolution; (3), that the *method* of divorce now used in England and Ireland is so vile, and clogged with so many diabolical additions, that no honest man would care to meddle with it. I should myself be so far from *seeking* it (in the case of adultery), that I should scruple to *submit to* it.[4]

About remarriage he had no qualms, and after Samuel Bradburn's first wife had died in childbirth happily gave his blessing to the projected second union, replying: 'As soon as I saw you and Sophy Cooke together at Gloucester it came into my mind at once, There is a wife for Bradburn (though I did not tell anybody).'[5]

During his middle and later years a large proportion of Wesley's

---

[1] Apr. 7, 1768. [2] Sept. 15, 1777.
[3] Apr. 9, 1769, etc. [4] Feb. 17, 1753.
[5] June 20, 1786. He replied in similar terms to Sophy Cooke on the same day.

letters were concerned with the well-being of his societies. In large measure the administration of these was delegated to their lay officers, the band-leaders, the class-leaders, the stewards, under the over-sight of the preachers stationed in each circuit, or group of societies.[1] To Miss March he wrote about the small fellowship group under her oversight:

As to your band, there are two sorts of persons with whom you may have to do —the earnest and the slack. The way you are to take with the one is quite different from that . . . with the other. The latter you must *search* and find out why they are slack; exhort them to repent, be zealous, do the first works. The former you have only to encourage, to exhort to push forward to the mark, to bid them grasp the prize so nigh! And do so yourself.[2]

The preachers were of key importance, and Wesley tried to keep in touch with all of them personally, and seems to have made a point of writing to the senior preacher, or 'Assistant' in each circuit, at least annually.[3] As we have seen, by means of his letters he guided his preachers' studies and their matrimonial ventures. He also sent them books and advanced them money.[4] He advised them on their preaching, especially along the lines of a letter to Thomas Rankin: 'Likewise, be temperate in speaking—never too loud, never too long.'[5] While he urged some to work harder, he told others to ease off, warning them: 'We must not offer murder for sacrifice. We are not at liberty to impair our own health in hopes of doing good to others.'[6] He also insisted that they must give careful attention to discipline: 'If a man preach like an angel, he will do little good without exact discipline.'[7] Very occasionally he stepped in with his personal authority to bolster their own in a troublesome situation, somewhat like a headmaster dealing in his study with an unruly pupil long suffered by an almost despairing teacher:

Those who will not conform to the rules of our society are no members of it. Therefore I require John Campbell, John Laird, and Peter Ferguson to take their choice, one way or the other. If they will meet their class weekly, they are with us. If they will not, they put themselves from us. And if the rest of

---

[1] In 1765, when the first annual *Minutes* of the Methodist Conference appeared, there were 26 English circuits, 5 Scots, 1 Welsh, and 8 Irish. At the last Conference which Wesley attended, in 1790, these had increased to 71 English, 8 Scots, 29 Irish, 11 in the West Indies and British North America, and 65 in the U.S.A.

[2] May 13, 1762. [3] See above, p. 35.

[4] Aug. 31, 1775; Sept. 25, 1787.

[5] Nov. 18, 1765; cf. Oct. 13, 1770; July 28, 1775.

[6] Nov. 19, 1781, to R. C. Brackenbury; cf. Feb. 9, 1780; Mar. 26, 1787.

[7] Oct. 13, 1770.

the society cannot or will not bear the expense, our preachers shall trouble Greenock no more.

But show them the reason of the thing, in the *Plain Account of the People called Methodists.*[1] After they have considered this, let them either join with us upon these terms, or be our friends at a distance.[2]

Sometimes such a letter was itself used not only to give instructions to the preacher but to assert authority (as may well have been true in this instance). Wesley wrote to Samuel Bradburn about the recalcitrant senior preacher in the Cork circuit: 'When therefore you have been four weeks at Bandon I desire you to return straight to Cork. And if John Hampson will not then go to Bandon, I will order one that will. Pray show this letter to Mr. Mackrill, whom I beg to assist you in this matter.'[3]

In his later years Wesley's vision of God's task for the Methodists became ecumenical. He realized that it was hardly possible to send any more preachers to America until the 'troubles' were over.[4] But in 1784 he sent vicarious ordination, a revised Book of Common Prayer, and his blessing, in a pastoral letter ending: 'As our American brethren are now totally disentangled both from the state and from the English hierarchy, we dare not entangle them again, either with the one or the other. They are now at full liberty, simply to follow the Scriptures and the primitive church. And we judge it best that they should stand fast in that liberty wherewith God has so strangely made them free.'[5] Constantly, however, he sought to tighten the bonds between Methodists in the United States, in British North America, and in the United Kingdom, and within a month of his death went beyond even this, exhorting Ezekiel Cooper in America: 'See that you never give place to one thought of separating from your brethren in Europe. Lose no opportunity of declaring to all men that the Methodists are one people in all the world.'[6]

The deep concern which Wesley brought to this many-sided

---

[1] See *Bibliog*, No. 156, and Vol. 9 of this edition.

[2] Mar. 3, 1776, to Thomas Rutherford, Assistant of the Edinburgh circuit. The Scots, like the Americans, did not take kindly to control from England.

[3] Oct. 17, 1778. Wesley's letters conveyed similar authority overseas, witness a letter from T. R., recently arrived in Baltimore from England, to Lawrence Coughlan, June 21, 1774: 'I . . . conversed with one of Mr. Wesley's preachers; but as I had no letter from Mr. Wesley he seemed very cold.' (L. Coughlan, *An Account of the Work of God in Newfoundland*, London, Gilbert, 1776, p. 60.)

[4] July 28, 1775.

[5] Sept. 10, 1784.

[6] Feb. 1, 1791.

pastoral care through his letters to hundreds of correspondents is seen in one to his brother Charles:

> O what a thing it is to have *curam animarum* [the care of souls]. You and I are called to this: to save souls from death, to watch over them as those that must give account! If our office implied no more than preaching a few times in a week, I could play with it; so might *you*. But how small a part of our duty . . . is this! God says . . ., 'Do *all thou canst*, be it more or less, to save the souls for whom my Son has died.' . . . I am ashamed of my indolence and inactivity. The good Lord help us both![1]

VI. ON EDITING WESLEY'S LETTERS

Sources. The primary and most satisfying source for a letter is the document written fully in the hand of the author, the 'holograph', signed by him, and delivered into the hands of the intended recipient. For this edition well over two thousand Wesley holographs have been traced and utilized.[2] The great treasure-house for Wesley's manuscripts is the Methodist Archives, recently transferred from London to the John Rylands University Library of Manchester. In 1931 John Telford reported over 330 holographs in that collection, to which have been added other collections which he listed: 162 collected by Edmund S. Lamplough, 44 in the James Everett Collection from Hartley-Victoria College, Manchester, 39 in the collection of J. Russell Colman. Since that time hundreds more have been added, so that there are now over 700 holographs in the Methodist Archives, quite apart from the major collection of secondary sources and of letters to him. About one-third of the extant Wesley correspondence is preserved in the Methodist Archives. In one way or another, however, much has disappeared, quite apart from the many letters acquired for resale during this century.[3] Five other institutions own a hundred or more each: Wesley's Chapel, London; Drew University, Madison, New Jersey; Emory University, Atlanta, Georgia; Wesley College, Bristol; and Southern Methodist University, Dallas, Texas (arranged, as are those which follow, in order of the size of their holdings). Five hold

---

[1] Mar. 25, 1772. [2] For in-letters see pp. 81–2 above.

[3] For example, Charles Wesley's son sold to the Wesleyan Methodist Conference what the indenture of sale describes as twenty-five letters between Wesley and Mrs. Sarah Ryan—those which especially aroused his wife's jealous anger, of which only three pages appear to remain, and imply that the sale involved another of Wesley's letter-books rather than the holograph letters (see copy of indenture, Drew University).

from sixty-seven down to thirty letters: The Upper Room Library Nashville, Tennessee; The British Library, London; The Moravian Archives, London; The World Methodist Council, Lake Junaluska, North Carolina; and Duke University, Durham, North Carolina. Fourteen other collections include ten or more holographs.[1] The remainder are spread thinly among a hundred institutions and as many private owners. To all of these, grateful acknowledgement is made by the printing of their name or symbol after those letters which they are believed still to own at the time of going to press.

Unfortunately many of Wesley's holographs are mutilated. At least one out of five lacks the address half of the original sheet. Occasionally a fragment has been cut or torn off to satisfy the misapplied zeal of autograph hunters, even one with three fragmentary lines of the letter on the reverse.[2] Sometimes names have been inked over or even cut out as a safeguard for someone's reputation.[3] Scores of letters preserved as relics have been framed in such a way that some inscribed portions are invisible, or have been mounted upon cardboard or stiff paper so that it is almost impossible to determine whether the reverse is indeed blank.

Only very rarely have series of letters from Wesley preserved by the recipient remained intact, the most noteworthy example being the fifty written to Alexander Knox of Londonderry, though even in this case six are without the address halves and one letter which escaped binding inside the volume seems to have disappeared. The usual fate of such collections has been to be divided among members of the family through successive generations, from whom some have been bequeathed to public institutions or have come on to the open market, though others have been forgotten, lost, even destroyed. The migrations of many of these holographs may sometimes be followed through several excursions to Sotheby's auction rooms, via dealers' catalogues, into private collections, and back to the

---

[1] John Wesley's Chapel, Bristol; The Pierpont Morgan Library, New York; The Public Record Office, London; The Wesley Historical Society, London; Lincoln College, Oxford; Garrett-Evangelical Theological Seminary, Evanston, Illinois; Wesley Theological Seminary, Washington, D.C.; Dr. Frederick E. Maser, Philadelphia, Pennsylvania; The John Rylands University Library of Manchester; The United Church of Canada, Victoria University, Toronto, Canada; The Wellcome Institute for the History of Medicine, London; The Wesley Historical Society, Belfast; Queen's University, Melbourne, Australia; and the Baltimore Conference of the United Methodist Church, Baltimore, Maryland.

[2] At the Methodist Archives, reading '. . . evil. The other, that Mr. Hall . . . assured me (which indeed did n . . . the demand) that whatever h . . .'.

[3] e.g. Sept. 29, Oct. 12, 1764.

auction room again for another round or more, until finally a resting-place is found in one of our major libraries—much to the relief of the weary researcher! One relatively unimportant letter, for instance, to Peter Garforth, dated Dec. 11, 1773, passed through Sotheby's no fewer than four times between the publication of Telford's edition of Wesley's *Letters* in 1931 (Telford did not know of it) and 1955, when it was purchased by the Epworth Press for resale, and eventually came into the hands of a co-operative Methodist collector in South Africa, Mr. Lewis J. Picton. The editor can sadly produce evidence that hundreds of other Wesley holographs are in private hands or less obvious libraries waiting to be 'discovered', and of course is eager to hear of any such, in order to verify the text or possibly publish the letter for the first time. Meanwhile catalogues may furnish useful abstracts or extracts. In using such material, however, we must remain alert, for even expert cataloguers cannot be expected to be familiar with all the peculiarities of Wesley's hand-writing, especially in his later years.

Forgeries of Wesley letters are almost unknown. One was published in the *Leeds Intelligencer*, however, as long ago as 1758—a deliberate attempt to hoax the public into buying a refutation of Wesley's *Address to the Clergy*. When Wesley challenged it the editor replied that he 'really believed it to be Mr. Wesley's own writing'.[1] One forgery was illustrated as a genuine Wesley letter even in A. M. Broadley's *Chats on Autograph Collecting* (1910), and eventually found its way into a prominent American seminary.[2] Many years ago the editor himself bought one (for a much lower price than that being asked for the supposedly genuine article!), after having demonstrated that it was a very poor forgery, so poor an invention, indeed, that it is not being included in these volumes. With escalating values it seems likely that more (and better crafted) forgeries will appear on the market in the future, but it is hoped that no careful reader of this introduction will be deceived.

Many facsimiles have been sold, bequeathed, and dignified by cataloguing in libraries, as original holographs. Most of them have been nineteenth-century lithographs, although deservedly popular among collectors have been the two artistic reproductions in W. H. Fitchett's *Wesley*[3] and the three presented by George Eayrs in his

[1] See Sept. 13, 1758.
[2] June 14, 1788. The original holograph is in the Methodist Archives.
[3] London, Smith Elder & Co., 1906. The letters are both to Ann Bolton, dated May 13, 1774, and Feb. 26, 1780.

Letters of John Wesley.[1] Perhaps the most deceiving facsimile of all, displayed as the original by owners on both sides of the Atlantic, is that of Wesley's important letter to the Revd. Samuel Walker of Truro, dated Nov. 20, 1755. The genuine holograph (as well as several facsimiles) resides in the Methodist Archives. The facsimile is in faded ink, correctly reproduced on both sides, including the postmark, though it bears no trace of the seal fragments and endorsements which are present in the original, and—the clinching factor —the paper, though of an authentic tint, is trimmed too regularly, and watermarked 'GR/1815/CMD'. In some instances, however, a facsimile is our only evidence that a letter existed, and can serve as excellent evidence of the text.[2]

Bibliographers are familiar with the phenomenon known as a 'ghost', the record of an imaginary book of which no extant copy is known, but to which references occur in contexts which imply genuine existence, and encourage the hope that eventually a 'flesh and blood' original may turn up. This also occurs with letters, and usually for the same predominant reason, a misread date. With Wesley's letters 'Janu.' is often misread as 'June', '1782' as '1784', '1768' as '1788', etc. Other less likely misreadings occur. On one occasion, for instance, the salutation, 'Dear Sammy', noted in a catalogue for a letter dated 'London, Nov. 9, 1742', immediately sent a warning quiver down my suspicious antennae, and sure enough I found that it was to Samuel Bradburn, and in fact dated 1782. It is too much to claim that all 'ghosts' have been exorcized from this present edition, however, and the editor is far from denying the actual existence of all improbable literary entities which make him suspicious. Nevertheless critical awareness and much cross-checking are essential in every instance where a genuine holograph or other Wesley manuscript is not available. And even then caution cannot be dismissed, for an address panel may have been reversed, a section lost along a fold, or two halves of different letters joined together.

As we have seen, Wesley frequently prepared a preliminary draft of his letters, and he or his amanuenses made reference copies.[3] Sometimes copies or extracts from his more important letters

[1] Jan. 13, 1735, to his mother; May 7, 1767, to Lady Maxwell; and June 16, 1787, to Dr. Leslie. Each is in a special folder dated 1916, although the volume itself is dated 1915.

[2] e.g. that to the Revd. Peard Dickinson, July 10 [1787], preserved in Boston Public Library, Massachusetts.

[3] See pp. 38–9 above.

were sent to others of his correspondents. Wesley's contemporaries frequently made their own copies of individual letters, whose trustworthiness can sometimes be checked by comparison with an original.[1] In keeping with his passion for preserving memoranda of key events and relationships, Wesley also made abstracts of his correspondence with family and friends.[2] It was a great age for keeping journals, and a number of these have survived which include copies of letters to and especially from Wesley. Again the major collection of such secondary documents is that in the Methodist Archives.

Sometimes even posthumous copies achieve a high degree of authenticity, such as the facsimiles carefully penned by James Everett in volumes which later came into the possession of Wesley's biographer, Luke Tyerman. (Indeed Everett's copies seem *always* to be preferable to the printed versions of Wesley's earlier editors.) Unfortunately, however, most later transcripts have proved unreliable in minor details, and sometimes in major points—a fact which led to hundreds of errors in Telford's edition of Wesley's *Letters*, and will inevitably bequeath a heritage of errors to this, because in default of a better source we must make the best of a poor one.

Many letters are known only through contemporary printed sources. Fifty come from Wesley's *Journal*, 130 from his *Arminian Magazine*; over 70 were written to periodicals other than the *Arminian Magazine*,[3] and about 50 come from other contemporary publications—a total of almost three hundred. Altogether, therefore, over 2,600 out of the 3,500 letters included in this edition (about 75 per cent) will be presented from contemporary sources, even though from contemporary sources exhibiting varying degrees of authenticity, fullness, and accuracy. There is reason to hope that this proportion may grow even larger as further holographs come to the knowledge of the editor.

The remaining letters have been accumulated from a variety of

[1] Good examples are the correspondence with Richard Morgan of Dublin, prepared by Charles Wesley (at Drew), and John Bennet's own transcripts of his correspondence with Wesley and others (in MA).

[2] See p. 83–4 above.

[3] Not an outstanding reward, perhaps, for scanning a million (by computation) newspaper columns, except that by this means no fewer than twenty-three letters hitherto unknown to Wesley scholars have been discovered, some of them quite important. At least a few others are surely waiting to be found, for the editor has only been able so far to work through what proved by experimentation to be the most likely and accessible sources.

later printed sources, preference having been given to those known
or presumed to have been based on the holographs, such as (in
round numbers) 40 from John Whitehead's *Life of Wesley* (1792–6),
100 from Vol. XIII of Joseph Benson's edition of Wesley's *Works*
(1813), 130 from Thomas Jackson's edition (1829–31 and later), a
similar number (having differing degrees of reliability) from 500
annual volumes of various Methodist magazines, about 200 from
many other sources, notably 1,500 Methodist biographies and over
two thousand local histories of Methodism issued over the last 180
years, and a similar number printed from untraced sources in
Telford's edition of 1931.

Earlier editions. The printing of Wesley's selected correspondence
began quite early in his own lifetime, with Ralph Erskine's *Fraud
and Fals[e]hood discover'd* (Edinburgh, 1743), and *Letters to the
Reverend Mr. John Wesley: against Perfection, as not Attainable in
this Life*, published in London the same year by Anne Dutton. A
number written by or to him appeared in *A Collection of Letters, on
Sacred Subjects*, published in Sheffield, 1761 (republished with
additions in Dublin, 1784), and *Spiritual Letters by Several Eminent
Christians* (Chester, 1767), though the value of these is diminished
by the editorial excisions and the use of initials and dashes, prompted by an almost exclusive interest in 'improving' passages and the
desire to disguise the names of the writers. The first scholarly work
in this genre was published in the year of Wesley's death by Dr.
Joseph Priestley, *Original Letters by the Rev. John Wesley and his
friends, illustrative of his early history* (Birmingham, 1791), which
contained twelve letters by John and seven to him from various
members of the family, in addition to letters among themselves and
an account of the Epworth poltergeist.

The first major collection of Wesley's letters was prepared by his
preacher, friend, and correspondent, Joseph Benson, who printed
400 in Vol. XVI of his edition of Wesley's *Works* (London, 1813)—
the 'second', counting Wesley's own of 1771–4 as the first.[1] Benson
began with those already printed in the *Arminian Magazine*, in the
order of their appearance therein, though in a somewhat hit-and-
run manner, with omissions. Then he turned to those written to
Eliza Bennis, as published by her son in 1809. Thenceforward he
seems to have presented those which were available to him in holo-

---

[1] *The Works of the Rev. John Wesley*, 17 vols., London, Conference Office, Jones,
Cordeux, 1809–13.

graph form, beginning with those to Lady Maxwell (for whom he remains the sole source for 17 out of 26 known). Other major series included 14 to Ann Bolton, 22 to Elizabeth Ritchie, 15 to Hester Ann Roe, 36 to Benson himself, 23 to Dorothy Furly, and 19 to 'a young disciple'. Benson was an editor of his day, disguising names by the use of initials, erasing what he considered unimproving passages, and altering Wesley's vocabulary and grammar. The holographs for many which he reproduced have survived, so that we can actually see the physical traces left by his editorial pen, and thus speculate intelligently about the changes made in the many letters where the originals have disappeared.[1]

In the third edition of Wesley's *Works* (1829–31) the editor, Thomas Jackson, took over Benson's collection and more than doubled it, so that it contained about 900 letters.[2] He began with the early letters and worked his way onward by series arranged chronologically according to their onset. Jackson presented many letters from the holographs—to Wesley's mother, his brother Charles, to Ebenezer Blackwell, Christopher Hopper, Jane Hilton, Mary Bosanquet, Walter Churchey, Zechariah Yewdall, and others, as well as those appearing in recent Methodist magazines. For the most part he repeated Benson's inaccurate datings and text, though he made some corrections, and presented a more authentic text for those which he personally introduced. Through the years new batches were added from manuscript or magazine, so that by the edition of 1872 the total had risen to 955.

The next outstanding publication was that prepared by George Eayrs, *Letters of John Wesley: a selection of important and new letters, with introductory and biographical notes*.[3] In this selection of over 300 letters, sixty-nine were 'new or little known'. The letters were distributed among several chapters devoted to different groups of people and themes, with a good introduction and a running commentary, as well as three facsimiles.[4]

Even before this time, however, thought had been given to a much fuller and annotated edition of Wesley's letters, as a project sponsored by the Wesley Historical Society, founded in 1893. One of its founders, Richard Green, accumulated notes for this in an

[1] Cf. illus. facing pp. 58–9 above.
[2] *The Works of the Rev. John Wesley*, 3rd edn., ed. Thomas Jackson, 14 vols., London, Mason, 1829–31. Letters appear in the last three volumes.
[3] London, Hodder & Stoughton, 1915; see pp. 109–10 above.
[4] Ibid.

interleaved set of Wesley's *Journal*, and transcripts of 'new' letters, so that by the time of his death in 1907 he had increased Jackson's total of 955 to 1,600. Green gave the interleaved volumes to his fellow-worker in the Wesley Historical Society, Thomas E. Brigden, who for some years edited its *Proceedings*. These transcripts came to the Methodist Publishing House, London, where John Telford had been appointed Connexional Editor in 1905.[1]

Telford was surrounded by a group of enthusiastic helpers, all members of the Wesley Historical Society: Nehemiah Curnock, the indefatigable editor of Wesley's *Journal*, into whose hands Green's transcripts seem first to have been placed, and who a few months before his death in 1915 was urging a massive campaign to make the letters as complete as possible;[2] Dr. W. L. Watkinson, a retired Connexional Editor, supporting the project from his high standing as a popular preacher and writer, as well as an ex-President of the Wesleyan Conference, who proved of great help to both Curnock and Telford; Marmaduke Riggall, circuit minister, who tirelessly transcribed documents; Brigden, of course, George Eayrs, and Arthur Wallington, a careful reader at the Publishing House. There was some jockeying for position among these. As early as 1911 Brigden had declined to collaborate with Eayrs in editing a separate volume of selected Wesley letters for Hodder & Stoughton,[3] and in 1915 was himself persuaded to defer publishing such a volume incorporating his own findings until after the complete edition had appeared,[4] only to be upstaged by Eayrs's volume—and characteristically to write a generous review of it.[5] Curnock died in 1915, by which time the number of transcripts had swollen to 2,120.[6] His own successful venture behind him, George Eayrs, unlike the others a United Methodist rather than a Wesleyan Methodist, sought fuller involvement in the official Wesleyan project. After some uneasy sparring he was accepted as an assistant to Telford, and eventually as assistant editor, with some payment involved,[7] but was 'concerned and surprised' at the suggestion that his commissioned introductory

---

[1] The complex story of Telford's edition can best be traced through his papers, preserved in several boxes in the Methodist Archives. See T. E. Brigden to J. A. Sharp, Mar. 25, 1914, therein. Cf. W.H.S. XI. 13, and Telford, I. viii.

[2] Curnock to Telford, Mar. 19, 1915.

[3] Brigden to Telford, Nov. 9, 1911.

[4] Sharp to Brigden, Apr. 9, 1915.

[5] W.H.S. XI. 12–14.

[6] Telford, I. viii.

[7] Eayrs to Telford, May 29, 1919.

chapter on 'Wesley's characteristics as a letter writer' should be switched to the *London Quarterly Review*,[1] a problem which was resolved by his death a few months later. Meanwhile Mr. Wallington was maintaining a chronological inventory of letters and their sources, numbered 1–2,463, with about eighty extra-inserted by him, and more than that number added by Telford, and possibly by his assistant, G. A. Bartlett.[2] Printing specimens for the new edition were prepared in 1926, by which time the proposed four or five volumes had expanded to six.[3] It was eventually published as a set of eight volumes in 1931, the year in which Telford turned eighty and officially retired.

The new 'Standard Edition' contained 2,670 letters, a brief introduction, and many valuable introductory notes to some series and individual letters, as well as many footnotes, an index, and other apparatus. There can be no question that it was not only incomparably fuller than Jackson's edition, but incomparably better. Telford utilized admirably the great manuscript resources of the Methodist Archives as well as the *Proceedings* and personnel of the Wesley Historical Society, and received assistance from collectors in many parts of the world. Unfortunately, however, he was also at the mercy of many poor transcribers whose work he had inherited from others or received through the post. Quite frequently he himself misread the manuscripts which he used, and did not follow out his announced principle of enclosing editorial additions and conjectures within square brackets. Only in the later volumes did he begin to include the addresses on the letters, and very rarely did he note his source. Nevertheless it was a wonderful achievement, and has remarkably served scholars and general readers for over a generation.

Editorial pitfalls. Even when an editor is at least a little younger than Telford, and able to work from many more holograph manuscripts, he still needs care in avoiding the many pitfalls waiting for unwary feet. The major problem is that of misreading the date, and thus placing the letter in its wrong context, and perhaps at the same time conjuring up a 'ghost'. As indicated earlier, Wesley himself occasionally misdated his letters.[4] And his writing, even when firm, is sometimes misleading. He might write '8' with an open loop at

---

[1] Eayrs to Telford, Mar. 20, Apr. 19, 1926.

[2] See this list, in a notebook among Telford's papers in MA; cf. Telford, I. xi.

[3] Brigden to Telford, Nov. 18, 1919; Eayrs to Telford, May 29, 1919; Eayrs to Telford, Apr. 19, 1926.

[4] See pp. 47–8 above.

the top, so that one Wesley scholar 'corrected' the date of a letter
from the actual Oct. 18 to Oct. 10.[1] He might add a tail to his '2',
so that it could easily be mistaken for '3'.[2] Misreadings by scholars
are legion. On one day the editor received letters from two different
librarians listing Wesley letters in their collection: one noted a date
as 1733 when it turned out to be 1777; the other transcribed a letter
as for 1753 when in fact the date was 1788. Nehemiah Curnock's
edition of the *Journal* presents a facsimile of a letter with the implied
dating of 1769 when in fact it is 1789.[3] A huge reference folio of
facsimiles in The British Library, London, gives the date of one of
the Wesley letters in that collection as March 25, 1783, when in
fact it is 1787. These problems are compounded when the holograph is not available. There are a few instances of transcripts by
different people, each bearing different dates, *both* being admitted
into Telford's edition as genuine letters.

Clearly it is essential to examine the date of every holograph very
carefully, and to check the handwriting against that of supposedly
contemporary letters, as well as the internal evidence and (where
available) its postal history. In the absence of the holograph this
scrutiny must be redoubled. Fortunately we can fairly easily be
delivered from the scores of common misreadings of Wesley's
'Janu.' as 'June', for in January he was rarely out of London, and
in June rarely in the city.[4] The evidence of Wesley's known itinerary
can be almost conclusive wherever one is sure that the place has not
been added to a letter conjecturally by an editor (but not within
brackets) solely upon the basis of the (misread) date—of which
Telford's edition contains some examples.[5]

[1] W.H.S. XXXII. 175.

[2] e.g. Mar. 12, 1782, where the '12' is normal but the '82' appears like '83'.

[3] Curnock, V. 343.

[4] Thus four letters were at one time published as being written in London in June,
1788—on the 9th, 11th, 18th, and [30th]. One was corrected by Telford to January,
two left as June, and the fourth (not in Telford's edition) was noted by the present
writer in 1945 as June on the basis of William Toase's printed version of 1874 (W.H.S.
XXV. 51). For only the last is a holograph now available, yet because of the combination
of 'London' with the transcribed 'June' each may confidently be assigned to January of
that year.

[5] e.g. that to Isaac Andrews, where the original has 'Janu. 24, 1776', but no place of
writing, while in Telford (VI. 224) the date is misread as 'June 24', and the place where
he actually was on that June day, Scarborough, is supplied without indicating that it is a
conjecture. Similarly Wesley's letter of Jan. 11, 1775, to William Allwood, taken by
Telford from F. F. Bretherton, *Early Methodism in and around Chester* (1903), p. 280,
where it was headed 'June 11th, 1775', was anchored in its incorrect situation by Telford's insertion (without brackets) of the place where Wesley was on June 11.

Transcribing the text of Wesley's letters also frequently presents problems, especially when manuscripts are mutilated or written in a hand tremulous with age. Parts of words may be torn away by the breaking of the seal, in spite of Wesley's attempts to minimize this.[1] Wear may render words indecipherable in the folds or at the margins, or a strip may be torn away. Letters may become badly damaged by damp, and through loss of their sizing may disintegrate in whole or in part.[2] Wesley's own errors seemed to increase with age, especially the omission of words.[3] At the same time he became less able and less willing to revise his holographs carefully, so that reading some of the letters written during the closing months of his life almost becomes an exercise, not in deciphering what is physically there, but in trying out different hypotheses about the words and phrases penned, and deciding whether the physical evidence will fit the hypothesis; and one must always bear in mind that one element in the hypothesis might need to be an omission in the text, just as an element in the physical evidence might be the straying of a word or phrase from one line into another.

Reconstruction of the text of a mutilated manuscript may sometimes be completed with a fair amount of certainty when only a narrow marginal strip is missing.[4] With more extensive mutilations a previously published text may furnish a useful guide, though it must nevertheless be accepted to that extent as a secondary substitute for the primary source.[5] Sometimes the combination of context, physical evidence, and earlier publication, is still insufficient to remedy accident or vandalism, if names have been snipped out.[6] This is even more true when a whole address panel and an adjoining flap have taken with them into oblivion more than half a page of writing.[7] Once address sheets or panels have become separated

---

[1] e.g. Dec. 14, 1770.

[2] e.g. five of Wesley's letters to Mrs. Jane Armstrong, now at Drew University, one of which seems totally to have disintegrated (Apr. 22, 1789), and another almost so (July 19, 1787), before coming to Drew. Fortunately they had all been published in the *Irish Christian Advocate*, so that the text is not completely lost, although (on the basis of the fairly sound originals) the printed versions of both probably contain misreadings.

[3] See pp. 41-2 above.

[4] e.g. Mar. 27, 1781 (?), to Miss Loxdale, where three or four letters are missing from the beginning of fourteen lines; in only two instances is there any real doubt about the letters to be supplied within ⟨ ⟩, indicating the mutilation of the manuscript.

[5] e.g. that to Samuel Bardsley, Jan. 30, 1780, where the holograph has been torn in two since its publication in the 1825 *M.M.*

[6] e.g. Sept. 29, Oct. 12, 1764.

[7] e.g. the letter to Miss Agnes Gibbes, Aug. 1, 1784.

from the parent letter it is difficult to match them up again, though not quite impossible, especially if they remain in the same collection.[1]

One of the major problems facing the editor in those frequent instances when the address is missing is to identify the recipient. Here the most valuable guide will usually be the salutations, studied against the background of Wesley's known methods of addressing different people.[2] The experienced student will soon progress beyond the all-too-common *naïveté* of assuming that 'Dear sister' implies that Wesley was writing to one of the Wesley girls, or that 'Dear Charles' could only mean his younger brother—actually he was in known correspondence with seven preachers and clergy whose Christian names were Charles, and might well have been in touch with five more. (We have already seen that clergy could probably be ruled out, including his brother Charles.[3]) An index of such Christian names both for male and female correspondents can prove enormously useful, as the editor found the first time he turned to it, discovering after going through 33 names out of 101 that the 'Dear Tommy' of a mutilated letter of Feb. 25, 1764, could be none other than Thomas Hanson. In default of a personal name (as well as supplementary to it) the clues afforded by the manner of address and the subject matter, as well as personal reference, may combine to afford a reasonable certainty about the recipient. A consolidated list of Wesley's known correspondence with every known correspondent can show whether this fills a gap at a normal interval, or whether it is at odds with some more fully documented letter, in which latter instance some other possible recipient must be studied. The handwriting of endorsements may furnish a clue, or even proof, of the recipient, and in the case of one series (to John Mason), the major clue comes from the numbering. The patient use of numerous specially devised research tools and methods will not answer every such question, of course, and too often we are left with a hypothetical name or a sad 'If only . . .!'.

In a number of cases problems are caused by differing versions, which need in some way to be reconciled. If one of the versions is the holograph, of course, the problem is quickly settled: we present the

---

[1] The half-sheet containing the address and a postscript has become detached from the letter to Adam Clarke of Dec. 8, 1787, at Wesley College, Bristol, and is now in Emory University, Atlanta, Georgia.

[2] See above, pp. 48–51.

[3] See above, pp. 49–50.

holograph, and probably note any major variants discovered in the draft, or the copy, or any contemporary printed version, but ignore all else. If we have two or more secondary versions, however, we have to decide which best represents the holograph. Nor is that always easy. With Wesley's letter of Dec. 10, 1734, setting out at length for his father the reasons why he was not prepared to accept the Epworth living, we have five good secondary sources, differing slightly among themselves: Wesley's *Journal*, Priestley's *Letters*, Whitehead's *Wesley*, Coke and Moore's *Wesley*, and a copy in shorthand by Charles Wesley. These must be collated and their relationship to each other decided before any clear determination can be made about their relative dependence upon the original. The same is true (though in a less complex manner) of many other letters, usually the more important ones, many of which Charles copied and Whitehead printed, but whether from the holograph, a draft, or a reference copy it may not always be possible to determine, and certainly not without careful investigation. Occasionally a much later version may prove more reliable than an earlier one, because it is based upon the original rather than upon a draft or a copy, or because it was prepared with much greater care. There is therefore no rule of thumb which can eliminate careful study of differing versions of a letter.

One of the elements which must form an important ingredient of such study, as indeed in the study of the text of any letter not clearly based upon the original holograph, is an evaluation of the sources, whether manuscript or printed. It is simple, for instance, to decide from the manuscript letter if Wesley employed an amanuensis to copy a letter: not only will the handwriting differ from Wesley's, but probably the spelling, the punctuation, and even the paragraphing; and the amanuensis will probably introduce his own errors, or possibly try to correct Wesley's. The typical amanuensis, however, was not likely to correct Wesley's grammar, or to alter his vocabulary. Therefore the normal contemporary copy is usually quite reliable as a guide to the basic text of the letter. Wesley himself, of course, was perfectly prepared to make major alterations when he published either his own letters or even those of his correspondents, and we can learn to recognize his literary idiosyncrasies.[1] Similarly his early editors felt quite free to alter his grammar to that more suited

---

[1] See below, p. 124, for his editing for publication of a letter to the Mayor of Newcastle.

to their own taste, so that where Wesley wrote to him, 'Bishop Newton's book on the prophecies is well wrote',[1] Joseph Benson altered the last word to 'written' when he prepared it for publication in Wesley's *Works*, and so it has remained until this edition.[2] Whenever it can thus be demonstrated that a source emended Wesley's original text (as Benson constantly did), a warning signal should flash for the careful editor. The easy acceptance of any form of editorial malpractice may well imply the acceptance, and the practice, of them all. In seeking the genuine text of a letter, therefore, we may be better served by a scribe (whether contemporary with Wesley or a century later) who painfully reproduced each capital, each misplaced comma, each error, or even by one who made careless errors of his own as well as reproducing Wesley's, than by the sophisticated editor who was determined to clothe Wesley in the literary fashions of his own day, or to emend the text in accordance with his own standards of propriety and importance.

Editorial malpractice. Numerous editors in the past, and even a few in the present, have been guilty of conduct unbecoming of an editor and a gentleman. Wesley himself frequently omitted names from his publications, or faintly disguised them by the use of initials, in order to protect tender reputations. He followed this practice in reproducing some letters in the *Arminian Magazine*. When continued to the third and fourth generation, however, this laudable desire to save others pain degenerates into an exaggerated desire to protect oneself or one's friends from the flimsiest link with anything slightly flawed, a readiness to suppress the uncomfortable truth at all costs.[3] Hundreds of examples could be cited of the heritage of problems caused by such malpractice. In editing the letter of March 2, 1782, to Robert Costerdine, John Telford used the text printed in the *Methodist Magazine* for 1845, where he found

---

[1] Dec. 8, 1777.

[2] There is no question that in Wesley's speech and writing (as in that of his contemporaries) this was no solecism, but normal correct English. Gray's most famous poem was published in 1751 as 'An Elegy wrote in a Country Church Yard' (cf. p. 136 below). Wherever, therefore, 'written' appears in a similar context we may assume that an editorial hand has been at work; and similarly where we find 'wrote' we may assume that we are dealing with a scribe who copied what he found, without emendation. Even Telford (or possibly his sources) was not blameless. He followed his printed sources in changing 'wrote' to 'written' and 'don't' to 'do not', but it was on his own initiative that he changed Wesley's 'you was' to 'you were' (see letters to Benson, Dec. 8, 1777; Mary Bosanquet, Oct. 17, 1773; and Benson again, May 19, 1783).

[3] It is pleasant to note that in reproducing his early *Journal* in his *Works* a generation later (1774), Wesley himself filled out many of the disguising initials.

'a particular account of the behaviour of W. G— toward S. P—'. Assuming that these were two disaffected preachers he extended the initials (unfortunately without using brackets) to William Gill and Stephen Procter. When the original eventually came to light the actual names were found to be W. Goodrich and Sally Phipps, implying a very different context for the letter.[1]

A related form of face-saving has earned the name of 'bowdlering' from Dr. T. Bowdler, whose 1818 edition of Shakespeare omitted 'those words and expressions . . . which cannot with propriety be read aloud in a family'. A strange example comes from Telford's edition, where (one suspects) he was presented with a transcript which had been bowdlerized without his being able to do anything about it, by the omission of five lines describing conflicting reports about Mr. Woodcock having been guilty 'of an immodest thing, said to be done or attempted'. The addition from the holograph is not only of interest in itself, but also because it begins a chain-reaction (as is frequently the case), immediately supplying the background for another hitherto obscure letter.[2]

An extension of this same principle has been the unduly protective attitude which early Methodist editors assumed towards Wesley himself, most of them evincing a strong tendency to suppress anything which might imply that 'Mr. Wesley' was human. Thus when he came to edit Wesley's letters Joseph Benson struck through the opening sentences of one to Sarah Crosby: 'Before you mentioned it, that was my purpose, not to let anyone know of your writing. Therefore I do transcribe what I choose to keep, and burn the original.'[3] A similar motive may have been at work in Benson's constant alterations of Wesley's grammar.[4] Perhaps it is natural to wish your dead hero to look his best, even if it entails the application of cosmetics to his gnarled and faded features.[5] The editors of this edition, however, are clear in their determination that Wesley shall be presented with literary 'warts and all', including

[1] See W.H.S. XXVI. 125-6, where the present editor notes a similar case of Telford extending the initials incorrectly, though on this occasion within brackets.

[2] Mar. 3, 1776, to Mrs. Woodhouse, and Mar. 26, 1776, to Robert Costerdine.

[3] May 11, 1780 (date, place, and recipient's name supplied by Benson on a holograph lacking the address half).

[4] See above, pp. 119-20.

[5] Cf. William Mason's readiness to doctor letters outrageously in order that no one should 'behold Mr. Gray in any light than that of a scholar and a poet'. (See William Henry Irving, *The Providence of Wit in the English Letter Writers*, Durham, North Carolina, Duke University Press, 1955, pp. 231-2.)

colloquialisms, contractions which imply a different spoken expression, and grammatical usages which have now become outdated.

The remaining types of editorial malpractice to be mentioned fall into a different category. One of the most frustrating things for a conscientious editor is to be compelled to rely upon texts which are not only altered in phraseology, obscured by initials, and truncated by excisions, but also wrenched out of their historical context by the compression of two or more letters—or more usually extracts of letters—into one. This was a common practice both in Wesley's day and later, and may often be suspected where it cannot be proved. One example may suffice. In the *Methodist Magazine* for the years 1805–7 the editor presented a series of twelve letters, usually described as 'an original letter of the Rev. John Wesley to Miss B.'. 'Miss B.' was in fact Mary Bishop, to whom thirty-seven holograph letters from Wesley survive. Of the twelve in the magazine only one comprises a single letter, seven contain conflated extracts from two letters, two from three, and two from no fewer than five letters each. Worse still, the range of dates covered in two of these so-called letters is three years! Yet but for the survival of the holographs we should perforce have had to rely upon the editor's avowal that each of these twelve was in fact 'an original letter'. There is little question that some of the texts reappearing in this edition suffer from similar severe limitations.

In view of what has been said above about the importance of Wesley's closing salutations,[1] it will occasion no surprise that the editor of these volumes considers it a serious dereliction of editorial duty to close the text of any letter with a truncated and colourless, 'Yours, etc.'. In reproducing some letters, however, that is the best that can be done, because it was all that was done by former editors, and no better source has been discovered.[2] In this feature Benson gains higher marks than his successors, for he not only reproduced the closing courtesies, but even the signature, in which he was not followed by Jackson and Telford.

It is understandable that the general reader will not enjoy the intrusion of square brackets or angle brackets surrounding groups of letters or words, yet it is the editor's task both to reproduce accurately

---

[1] See above, pp. 58–62.

[2] e.g. the letters to Thomas Roberts, Aug. 13, 1790, and Feb. 8, 1791, where Telford depended upon Luke Tyerman's transcriptions (Tyerm (JW), III. 622, 647), rather than turning to the 1837 *M.M.*, where both the endings were given fully, though in the second case with a misreading of the date as Feb. 18.

what is present in the text, and not to introduce a fuller text than is actually before him without by some method informing the reader —the truth, the whole truth, and nothing but the truth. In a definitive edition to serve twentieth-century scholars anything else would constitute a serious misdemeanour. Endless examples could be cited where the neglect of this has led to historical error, but two have been noted already in another connection.[1] In the present edition all that is humanly possible will be done both to uncover such errors in past transcripts, and to prevent their continuation or initiation.

The Oxford Edition. Readers of this introduction will have realized that the editor has tried to profit from the labours, the experience, the mistakes, of many predecessors. Some elements of what may be expected in this new edition of Wesley's letters have already been touched upon, and the major features will be briefly recapitulated here, along with a statement of the edition's scope and its methods of authentication and presentation.

These volumes set out to reproduce all Wesley's personal letters— to individuals, to groups of people such as his preachers, and to periodicals, upon private or public issues, even if they were reproduced in his *Journal* or on broadsheets for multiple circulation.[2] The major exclusion (which filled well over one of Telford's eight volumes) is published letters, i.e. those which were not only printed but were offered for sale as distinct publications, such as the open letters to his critics.[3] Also normally excluded are letters prefixed to his own publications, which will appear with the publications themselves. Letters represented only by evidence of their composition, by references, by very brief abstracts or extracts, will not be inserted in the main text, but only in an appendix designed to list all his known correspondence, of all kinds, published as well as personal. In this appendix all known letters with specific dates or written by or to specific recipients will be noted in chronological order. The main text will present a selection of Wesley's total correspondence, comprising all his out-letters for which a substantial text is available, and (in smaller type) those of his in-letters (or extracts from them) which illuminate his extant out-letters, or seem of special importance. The editor recognizes—a sad blow to his pursuit of perfection

---

[1] See p. 116 above.

[2] See pp. 39–40 above.

[3] e.g. the open letters to Edmund Gibson, Bishop of London, George Lavington, Bishop of Exeter, the Revd. George Horne, and William Warburton, Bishop of Gloucester, given in Vol. 11; others will appear in Vol. 9.

—that this is the one unit for which an infallible prophecy of incompleteness may be made, for letters hitherto unknown to him will surely continue to surface even after the last volume has added its quota of those coming to hand too late to be included in their chronological setting.

Many different kinds of sources have been employed to prepare this edition,[1] of which the holograph letter is the ideal, and has been secured in about 60 per cent of the letters published in the main text.[2] Failing that, we print any of the following (given in order of preference): the original draft or a reference copy made at the time by Wesley or under his supervision; a facsimile of one of the above; a transcript prepared either during Wesley's lifetime or subsequently by someone known to be trustworthy or demonstrating its own fidelity by reproducing minor details such as capitalization and spelling; an abstract prepared by Wesley—which might need to be supplemented from other sources; some other abstract, preferably contemporary, again supplemented from other sources where possible. If no authentic manuscript is available we use one of the following printed sources, though the actual position in the order of preference depends upon its ascertained relationship to the holograph and the reliability of its originator as demonstrated in other contexts (in some instances these may make a printed source preferable to a Wesley abstract instead of merely supplementary): a printed version published by Wesley; some other published version, preferably in its first appearance and from the holograph, either during Wesley's lifetime or subsequently. As a last resort an inferior transcript may be utilized, or a printed version demonstrably changed in substance by editing. Where the holograph is available other versions may well be ignored, except for the more important variants stemming from Wesley himself. Because the letter as despatched is our primary text, only the more important erasures in preliminary drafts are noted, on the assumption that the final draft is nearest to what we seek.[3] Where only secondary sources are available, the

---

[1] See pp. 107–12 above.

[2] Thus for the letter of Oct. 26, 1745, to the Mayor of Newcastle, we present the actual letter preserved in the Northumberland County Record Office, rather than the version of it printed by Wesley himself in his *Journal*, which omits the closing sentences from two paragraphs and five single words, as well as making several editorial changes—a clear indication as to how Wesley edited his own letters for publication.

[3] Occasionally, however, even these are extensive, e.g. Dec. 5–6, 1726 (to his brother Samuel), and May 14 and 20, 1738 (to William Law).

preferred one will be presented, supplemented by additional passages from other versions, and with the important variants noted.[1] Conjectural emendations even of unreliable sources are enclosed within square brackets.

Any substantive variant readings arising in printed versions supervised by Wesley himself are footnoted in a similar manner to that followed for the other units in this edition, for it seems important to see not only what he originally wrote, but the way in which for various reasons he was moved to revise it for publication. If he had no hand in parallel printed versions, however, the preferred source furnishes the copy-text, and variant readings in inferior sources are noted only if it appears possible that they reflect the holograph.[2]

Where a manuscript is mutilated an attempt is made to restore missing words within angle brackets, ⟨ ⟩, square brackets, [ ], being reserved for the rare editorial insertions within the text. Ellipses indicated by Wesley are reproduced thus, . . . ; passages omitted by the editor are indicated by an ellipsis within the editorial square brackets, [. . .]. Erased passages in drafts have been enclosed within

[1] One actual instance may be presented in summary to illustrate this investigative process. For Wesley's important letter to William Wogan, March 28, 1737, on the art of Christian conversation, the holograph is missing. There are seven sources, five printed, two in manuscript: (1), in James Gatliff's life of Wogan, prefixed to his edition of Wogan's *Essay on the Proper Lessons*, 1818; (2), in *The Pulpit*, Dec. 20, 1827; (3), a transcript by Thomas Marriott, probably a little later; (4), a transcript by James Everett, dated 1833; (5), in the *W.M.M.*, 1842; (6), in the *Wesley Banner*, 1852; (7), in Telford's edition of Wesley's *Letters*, 1931. One version was typed out, and all the variants in each other version, however minute, were entered in this typescript. This careful collation indicated that the first four versions were all based on the same holograph, but independently of each other. Gatliff, the *Pulpit*, and Marriott's transcript all edited the contents to make smoother reading, Marriott more heavily than the *Pulpit*, changing Wesley's 'chearfullest' to 'most cheerful', and omitting the opening paragraph, which is personal and does not touch on the main theme. The last three are clearly derivative: 1842 was based on Marriott, 1852 on Everett, though each introduced its own minor changes; Telford supplemented Marriott's transcript with the opening paragraph printed in 1852. Everett's transcript is unique in reproducing not only the complete text of the holograph, but even the minutiae of Wesley's capitalization, his known idiosyncrasies of punctuation, and some errors both corrected and uncorrected—it is, in fact, a kind of facsimile. Everett's copy, therefore, even though it is later than at least two other sources, furnishes our copy-text, with footnotes indicating variants from (1), (2), and (3) which may preserve some other features of the holograph.

Similarly with Wesley's letters to Philothea Briggs, both Benson and Telford (or his informant) appear to have used the holographs, which Telford prints more fully, Benson in parts more accurately; if the holographs do not turn up, Telford will furnish the copy-text, with variants inserted or footnoted from Benson.

[2] Thus in the example above, variants arising from Gatliff, the *Pulpit*, and Marriott's transcript *might* be footnoted if sufficiently important, but those arising in the other three would *certainly* be ignored.

double parentheses, (( )). During his Oxford days Wesley used an abridged longhand for his private manuscripts, including copies and abstracts of letters. In this v stood for 'the',– for 'and', ɔ for 'for', ū for 'but', ō for 'not', etc. Later both he and Charles largely displaced this by the use of Byrom's shorthand for confidential passages in their correspondence, and occasionally for making copies. All such passages, of course, have been presented in deciphered form—with confidence in the case of the abbreviated longhand, occasionally with much uncertainty in the case of the shorthand, for which reason these latter transcriptions are enclosed within double square brackets, [[ ]], and footnoted.

Assigning a likely date when the source presents insufficient or confusing evidence, or when that evidence has been damaged, is an even trickier business, and calls for the interplay of many different internal clues.[1] In this edition scores of letters have been uprooted from the positions which they occupy in Telford's volumes for compelling reasons which it would be tedious to recount at length, though in a few instances with no absolute certainty that their new conjectural date is any more than probable. Any conjecture, however, whether relatively certain or uncertain, is indicated by the use of square brackets.

The letters furnish us with a valuable key to Wesley's preferred styling practices, as distinct from those of his various editors and printers.[2] These latter gentlemen reduced his lavish use of capitals from the 1770s onwards, when it went out of fashion. In his letters, however, he continued to capitalize common nouns selectively until his death, though by that time he rarely used capitals to impart a minor emphasis to adjectives and verbs. In his earlier years he also frequently capitalized pronouns, especially You and Your, though hardly ever pronouns referring to God; the divine name itself he penned completely in capitals until his dying day. In accordance with the principles adopted for this edition as a whole, however, capitals unfamiliar to the modern eye have usually been eliminated.

In his letters Wesley rarely used the underlining which then as now indicated italics, though this was his normal styling for scriptural quotations in his publications. Titles of books he sometimes placed within quotation marks, sometimes simply capitalized; in both cases we have used italics if Wesley cited accurately, but retained his capitals only if his citation was inaccurate. Underlining

---

[1] See pp. 115-16 above.   [2] See pp. 55-8.

carried out by some other hand than Wesley's is not reproduced, though it may occasionally be footnoted.[1]

Wesley's punctuation has been modernized in a manner similar to that in the other volumes of this edition, mainly by omission, aiming at 'open' or minimal punctuation when the meaning remains clear. Wherever there is any doubt about the original meaning, however, and wherever it seems possible that some significant nuance might be lost by any alteration, the punctuation of the holograph is retained. Indeed, whenever holographs are reproduced, the original punctuation is given much greater weight than in the case of the printed works, though no attempt is made to reproduce idiosyncrasies such as Wesley's verbal forms 'seem's', 'clear's', etc. Thus we have followed Wesley in treating many subordinate clauses as if they were complete sentences, and have retained the comma which he used frequently instead of 'that' to introduce a subordinate clause. We have omitted, however, the quotation marks within which he enclosed direct speech transformed into indirect, except for any portions which remain acceptable as direct speech. Wesley frequently inserted one quotation mark only, normally at the beginning; here we have supplied the missing mark, usually without enclosing it within square brackets. We have not added quotation marks, however, where Wesley has none at all, or does not indicate a quotation by his use of italics.

Wesley's frequent abbreviations have been expanded, including his frequent dropping of the final 'e' in the past tense, and his use of the ampersand. Contractions, however, which afford evidence of his actual pronunciation of words and phrases, have been retained: thus he apparently said as well as wrote ''tis' rather than 'it is', and 'can't' rather than 'cannot', and seemed to prefer these terms in print as well as in longhand.

Thus in reproducing the text, antiquarian minutiae such as the lavish use of capitals and abbreviations are forsaken, even though those same minutiae may have proved of importance in deciding the authenticity of a transcript and the descent of the text. No word has been deleted or added or changed, however (except in spelling), without in some way informing the reader, nor have we felt justified in amending Wesley's grammar by changing such phrases as 'you was' or 'this was wrote'.[2] His spelling is quite another matter, however. We have felt few qualms in clothing his words in the

---

[1] See p. 57 n. 1.   [2] See p. 120 above.

typographical dress which became familiar to him in his later years, and almost equally familiar to us, and therefore makes for smoother reading. Nor does the change from 'chearful' (1740) to 'cheerful' (1770), for example, imply any change in pronunciation, but only in spelling fashions. With a very few exceptions, therefore, throughout this edition we follow the spelling conventions normal for the Oxford University Press.

Wherever present the address is given, but in this one instance reproduced *literatim*, though in continuous form rather than on several separate lines. This is followed by details of the surviving seals, postmarks, postal or other inscriptions, and an indication of the source or sources from which the text has been derived. At their first introduction footnotes identify the recipients and supply information necessary to understand the context of the letter. Footnotes also identify allusions in the text to persons, places, events, and subjects. The selected in-letters are footnoted very lightly indeed, if at all. Information is only duplicated in the case of Wesley's quotations, and cross-references are minimal, awaiting the complete index in the final volume. As a partial immediate aid an alphabetical index is furnished covering those correspondents represented in the main text of each volume. The appendix summarizing Wesley's total correspondence is not indexed.

Almost all that has been said above about discovering and reproducing the text of the holograph applies equally to in-letters and out-letters, except that of the in-letters only a select number are reproduced, and sometimes only select portions of that select number. Little attempt has been made to annotate in-letters, except in indicating their relationship to specific out-letters, supplying translations of Latin and Greek quotations, and elucidating points of special importance for an understanding of Wesley's own letters. The principle of selecting only those in-letters which illuminate out-letters has been applied somewhat more generously in his early family correspondence, especially letters from his father and mother, which enable us to visualize the formative period of his life not covered by his *Journal*. Here we have given weight to the words with which he introduced the series of about six hundred letters (both in and out) which he presented in the *Arminian Magazine* from 1778 until his death: 'It is natural to hope that what has been of use to ourselves may be of use to others also. I may then be excused for beginning this Collection of Letters with some that were of use to me many years ago.' 'Letter I' was that written by his father on Jan. 26, 1725, when he was approaching ordination, for which we are fortunate to possess the original holograph, the copy in Wesley's letter-book, and the version in the magazine. Collation of these three (confirmed in other instances where holograph controls are available) demonstrates that his early letter-books (like his later reference copies) usually transcribed the original accurately, almost *literatim*, and often noted omissions either by summaries or a dash. In the later printed versions, however, he treated his originals with very great freedom, reversing the order of phrases, substituting one word for another, omitting words or passages without warning, and even adding phrases. These later alterations, of course, represent Wesley's editorial point of view, and in that they possess their own significance. In attempting to reproduce the actual text of the holograph received by Wesley, however, we must bypass these wherever possible (which is not always the case), though occasionally the more important of these editorial revisions are reproduced in footnotes. Sometimes (as in the letter from Susanna Wesley of June 8, 1725), it is impossible to be absolutely sure which are additions from the holograph and which Wesley's revisions.

VII. THE LETTERS AS LITERATURE

The redoubtable Sir Leslie Stephen, editor of *The Dictionary of National Biography*, and no friend to Methodism, saw in Wesley a great literary talent 'unluckily' gone to waste in 'obsolete theological speculation'.[1] He paid the highest tribute to Wesley's letters: 'He shows remarkable literary power . . . It would be difficult to find any letters more direct, forcible, and pithy in expression. He goes straight to the mark without one superfluous flourish. He writes as a man confined within the narrowest limits of time and space, whose thoughts are so well in hand that he can say everything needful within those limits. The compression gives emphasis and never causes confusion.'[2] The justice of this and a hundred other tributes to Wesley as 'a master of strong, simple, direct English'[3] must already have been realized by the reader of this introduction.

[1] *History of English Thought in the Eighteenth Century*, 3rd edn., London, John Murray, 1902, II. 423.
[2] Ibid., II. 409.
[3] George Sampson, *The Concise Cambridge History of English Literature*, Cambridge University Press, 1941, p. 552.

Wesley's direct and forceful style did not come by chance. It arose from a happy combination of his classical education, his reading of the Authorized Version of the Bible (coupled with Cranmer's Book of Common Prayer), and his call to communicate the gospel to the poor—nor would any one of these elements have been quite sufficient without the others.

In the Oxford of Wesley's youth the classics of Athens and Rome remained the basis of higher education, and the swing to modern languages and the sciences had barely begun. Rhetoric was not peripheral but central to those studies. During his Oxford years we can sometimes see Wesley consciously striving to emulate his classical examples, especially in his letters to 'Aspasia' and 'Selima'; witness the following neat, yet somewhat contrived, sentence: 'Indeed, a great part of most days (I sigh while I speak it) is torn from you by your barbarously-civil neighbours.'[1] This deliberately structured use of language, with its tropes and figures of speech, gradually became second nature to Wesley, through the art which conceals art, but remained a dominant element in securing controlled tautness in his sentences, together with an ability to write what the Americans term a good 'punch line'. This may be illustrated in a letter to Francis Asbury, written after Wesley had heard that he and Dr. Thomas Coke, the joint 'superintendents' of Methodism in America, were now using the title 'bishop', and building an institution named Cokesbury College:

> You are the elder brother of the American Methodists: I am, under God, the father of the whole family. Therefore I naturally care for you all in a manner no other person can do . . .
>
> But in one point, my dear brother, I am a little afraid both the doctor and you differ from me. I study to be *little*; you study to be *great*. I *creep*; you *strut* along. I found a *school*; you a *college*! Nay, and call it after your own names! O beware! Do not seek to be *something*! Let me be nothing, and '*Christ be all in all*'!
>
> One instance of this, of your *greatness*, has given me great concern. How can you, how dare you, suffer yourself to be called *bishop*? I shudder, I start at the very thought! Men may call *me* a knave or a fool, a rascal, a scoundrel, and I am content: but they shall never by my consent call me bishop! For my sake, for God's sake, for Christ's sake, put a full end to this! Let the Presbyterians do what they please, but let the Methodists know their calling better.[2]

---

[1] Sept. 27, 1730, to Ann Granville.

[2] Sept. 30 (?), 1788; not Sept. 20, as transcribed by Moore, when in fact Wesley was in Bristol, not London. One suspects that most of the italicizing was Moore's gilding of the lily.

The second major influence in the forging of Wesley's style was the Bible, allied with the Book of Common Prayer (whose version of the Psalms he seems to have quoted at least as frequently as that in the Authorized Version of the Bible). Daily Bible reading was the basis of Wesley's devotional life, and even of his education at his mother's knee, from his early youth. When at Oxford he became a Bible scholar, devoting much time to the careful study of the Hebrew and Greek originals, he did not forsake King James's version, but apparently continued to read the daily lessons appointed in the Calendar, which entailed reading through most of the Old Testament and much of the Apocrypha once a year, and the New Testament three times a year. He became steeped in its English as well as its teaching and challenge. He thought and spoke and wrote, perhaps sometimes unconsciously, in the language of the English Bible. Long sections of his letters are little more than a stringing together of scriptural phrases,[1] and at least one brief letter consists solely of a quotation from the Psalms.[2] In general this was from a deliberate design 'always to express Scripture-sense in Scripture-phrase'.[3] He told John Newton, 'The Bible is my standard of *language* as well as sentiment.'[4] A letter to Ann Bolton illustrates both his thought and his practice:

In obedience to that direction, 'In wickedness be ye children, but in understanding be ye men,' I would in every respect both act and speak in the most accurate manner I could. And in speaking for God, particularly in public, we have a farther direction: 'If any man speak, let him speak as the oracles of God.' Now in the oracles of God there is no improper expression. Every word is the very fittest that can be . . . I do not advise either Sammy Wells or Neddy Bolton to use any harder words than are found in St. John's First Epistle.[5]

In order to communicate with the man in the street, however, Wesley moulded his classical and biblical scholarship into 'plain truth for plain people.'[6] He told the Revd. Samuel Furly how in

---

[1] The comparatively short pastoral letter of Aug. 4, 1738, blends quotations fully indicated with those indicated by one quotation mark and those not indicated at all, twenty-three in all, together with many others which were probably not self-conscious quotations or allusions. Those documented range over fourteen books of the Bible.

[2] Aug. 31, 1775, quoting Ps. 37 : 3.

[3] Sept. 28, 1745, to 'John Smith', §§ 6, 7.   [4] Apr. 1, 1766.

[5] Jan. 29, 1773; Wesley quotes 1 Cor. 14 : 20 and 1 Pet. 4 : 11. He constantly directed people to 1 John, 'by which, above all other, even inspired writing, I advise every young preacher to form his style' (JWJ, July 18, 1765).

[6] *Sermons* (1746), Preface, § 3; see Vol. 1 of this edition.

August, 1730, his attempts at evangelism as an Oxford Methodist were foundering on the rock of academic speech: 'When I had been a member of the university about ten years I wrote and talked much as you do now. But when I talked to plain people in the castle or the town I observed they gaped and stared. This quickly obliged me to alter my style, and adopt the language of those I spoke to. And yet there is a dignity in this simplicity, which is not disagreeable to those of the highest rank.'[1]

There is little doubt that through his tireless visits to the homes of ordinary people throughout the British Isles Wesley knew the common people better than any other educated person of his day. His letters, even more than his *Journal*, constantly reveal this in his use of slang and colloquialisms. He commended a preacher who returned quickly to work after losing his little boy of three, rather than 'sit mooning at home'.[2] He told his brother Charles, 'My wife, I find, is on the high ropes still.'[3] Of Thomas Olivers he averred, 'There is good in him, though he is a rough stick of wood',[4] and of James Deaves that he would 'dispute through a stone wall',[5] and that a book by William Romaine was 'such a hotch-potch as I have seldom seen'.[6] In discussing a 'noble proposal' which entailed considerable financial outlay he warned Freeborn Garrettson that the English Methodists 'do not roll in money, like many of the American Methodists'.[7] Such expressions, freely adopted from common currency, formed a vigorous colouring of his normal speech, and his normal speech was faithfully reproduced in his letters, even to the better educated.[8]

Wesley absorbed and utilized both the language and the wisdom of the common man in another way, his use of proverbs, and probably did it the more readily because this also found strong precedent in Scripture. Literally hundreds of proverbs are to be found in his letters, some of them many times over, and many unrecognized as such, shading from colloquialisms on the one hand to consciously literary epigrams and aphorisms on the other.[1] One that struck the present writer, for instance, in leafing through the letters, was the

---

[1] July 15, 1764.   [2] June 16, 1781, to Samuel Bradburn.
[3] Aug. 3, 1771.   [4] Jan. 18, 1762.   [5] Apr. 23, 1789.
[6] July 13, 1771, to Philothea Briggs.   [7] June 26, 1785.
[8] See George Lawton, 'The Slang and Colloquial Expressions in Wesley's *Letters*', W.H.S. XXXII. 5-11, 25-33.
[9] See George Lawton, 'Proverbs and Proverbial Echoes in John Wesley's *Letters*' W.H.S. XXVI. 111-14, 120-34.

expression, 'It is a bad dog that is not worth whistling for',[1] which only after research did he discover was indeed Wesley's adaptation of a proverb. And what about 'blessings in disguise'? The theme occurs in a number of letters, in the form, 'Afflictions, you know, are only blessings in disguise'.[2] Was Wesley alluding to the phrase as he might have found it in *Reflections on a Flower Garden* (1746), by his former colleague, James Hervey,[3] or David Mallet's *Amyntor and Theodora* (1747),[4] or were all three bringing to the literary surface some folk-wisdom buried in folk-speech? Whatever be the truth of this and a thousand similar puzzles which may yet tempt some post-graduate researcher, the important thing is that Wesley did indeed draw deeply from the well of common speech, and in so doing was able to address Mr. and Mrs. Everyman in terms that were direct, picturesque, and pithy, and that therefore hit their mark.

Thus from the 1730s onwards Wesley developed his own style, at first self-consciously, but eventually without thinking about it, simply setting down the words that first flowed into his fertile mind from the three chief literary streams which enriched his thought. In the opening volume of his letters it is possible to trace the gradual transition from the cultured Oxford don, with his measured periods and somewhat stilted style, to the forceful evangelist, even before he came to experience and proclaim man's utter dependence upon God by faith in Christ for redemption, while his gospel still remained one of salvation by the works of holiness; we can see the strong Anglo-Saxon monosyllables from the Bible invigorating those precise polysyllables derived from the Latin; and we see increasingly demonstrated the truth of his claim in 1745 that 'for little less than twenty years' he had been 'diligently labouring' to 'use the most common words, and that in the most obvious sense', though *any* word from the Bible still remained appropriate: 'I cannot call those uncommon words which are the constant language of Holy Writ.'[5]

[1] May 3, 1786.
[2] Apr. 23, 1776; July 12, 1782; and (to describe 'trials') July 24, 1780.
[3]   E'en crosses from his sov'reign hand
         Are blessings in disguise.
Cf. *Oxford Dictionary of Quotations*, 2nd edn., p. 248.
[4]   Are afflictions aught
         But blessings in disguise?
Cf. *Stevenson's Book of Quotations*, London, Cassell, 1934, 16 : 9.
[5] Sept. 28, 1745, to 'John Smith', § 6.

Thus were interwoven into Wesley's spoken and written English the literature of Rome and Jerusalem and the common speech of London, creating a versatile instrument of communication best revealed in its natural, unpolished state in his letters. Writing to a literary parson with a distinctive style of his own, the Revd. John Berridge, Wesley ended: 'I have not time to throw these thoughts into a smoother form; so I give you them just as they occur. May the God whom you serve . . . give a blessing to the rough sincerity of, Dear sir, Your affectionate servant, John Wesley'.[1]

Wesley also became a promoter of this approach to speech and writing in others. His most important and self-conscious discussions of English style appear in his letters to the Revd. Samuel Furly. Furly's new Oxford tutor cast some doubts upon the Cambridge man's basic education, and strove to remedy its deficiencies:

> I doubt you had a dunce for a tutor at Cambridge, and so *set out* wrong. Did he never tell you that of all men living a clergyman should 'talk with the vulgar'? Yea, and *write*, imitating the language of the *common people* throughout, so far as consists with purity and *propriety* of speech! *Easiness*, therefore, is the first, second, and third point. And *stiffness, apparent* exactness, *artificialness* of style the main defect to be avoided, next to solecism and impropriety . . . Dr. Middleton is no standard for a preacher—no, not for a preacher before the university. His diction is stiff, formal, affected, unnatural. The art glares, and therefore shocks a man of true taste. Always to talk or write like him would be as absurd as always to walk in minuet step. O tread natural, tread easy, only not careless. Do not blunder or shamble into impropriety. If you *will* imitate, imitate Mr. Addison or Dr. Swift.[2]

They were able to meet shortly afterwards for a conversation on style, and this Wesley followed up with another letter:

> What is it that constitutes *a good style*? Perspicuity, purity, propriety, strength, and easiness, joined together. Where any one of these is wanting it is not a good style . . .
>
> As for *me*, I never think of my style at all; but just set down the words that come first. Only when I transcribe anything for the press, then I think it my duty to see that every phrase be clear, pure, and proper. Conciseness (which is now, as it were, natural to me) brings *quantum sufficit* [as much as is necessary] of strength. If after all I observe any *stiff* expression, I throw it out, neck and shoulders.
>
> Clearness in particular is necessary for you and me, because we are to instruct people of the lowest understanding. Therefore we, above all, if we *think* with the wise, must yet speak with the vulgar. *We* should constantly use the most common, little, easy words (so they are pure and proper) which our language affords . . . Have this end always in your eye, and you will never designedly use

---

[1] Apr. 18, 1760.   [2] Mar. 6, 1764.

an hard word. Use all the sense, learning, fire you have, forgetting yourself, and remembering only, These are the souls for which Christ died! Heirs of an happy or miserable eternity![1]

Furly, however—and who knows what part inter-university rivalry played in this?—continued (as Wesley thought) tiresomely argumentative. Wesley reiterated his basic advice about seeking a simple, natural style, and answered Furly's objections. He added an observation upon the length of sentences:

That 'poor people understand long sentences better than short' is an entire mistake. I have carefully tried the experiment for thirty years, and I find the very reverse to be true. Long sentences utterly confound their intellects; they know not where they are. If you would be understood by them you should seldom use a word of many syllables or a sentence of many words. Short sentences are likewise infinitely best for the careless and indolent. They strike them through and through. I have seen instances of it an hundred times.[2]

It would be possible to illustrate each of the five points listed by Wesley as the essential ingredients of a good style—perspicuity, purity, propriety, strength, and easiness. Most have in one way or another been touched upon already. Precision in the use of words was important to him, and he was ready to make fine distinctions. When the suggestion was put forward that more preachers should attend the annual Conference he wrote: 'I will only *require* a select number to be present. But I will *permit* any other travelling preacher who desires it to be present with them.'[3] He criticized the careless use of catchwords for party purposes: 'I find no such sin as *legality* in the Bible: the very use of the term speaks an antinomian. I defy all *liberty* but liberty to love and serve God, and fear no *bondage* but bondage to sin.'[4]

In spite of his disclaimer to 'John Smith', he did not completely eschew uncommon non-biblical words, such as 'docity',[5] 'coxcomicality',[6] and 'namby-pambical'—coined by Jonathan Swift, and used to describe one or two of his brother's verses.[7] For one of his correspondents he defined a word supposedly coined a few years earlier by Catharine Talbot, but which he found useful: '*Accommodableness* is only the art of becoming all things to all men, without wounding our own conscience. St. Paul enjoins it in those words,

---

[1] July 15, 1764.   [2] Oct. 11, 1764.   [3] Aug. 15, 1767.
[4] Nov. 30, 1770; cf. Nov. 27, 1770; Feb. 16, 1771.
[5] May 3, 1786.
[6] Nov. 27, 1766—the earliest example cited by *O.E.D.*
[7] Dec. 26, 1761, to Charles Wesley.

"Please all men, for their good, unto edification." Bare rules will hardly teach us to do this. But those that have a single eye may attain it (through the grace of God) by reflection and experience.'[1] He was quite prepared to coin his own words, as when he claimed, 'A lifeless, unconverted, unconverting minister is the murderer-general of his parish.'[2]

All these unusual words are to be found in letters to persons of superior education, of course. The same is true of most of Wesley's quotations. His letters to the clergy frequently contained tags and longer quotations from both Latin and Greek authors: Aristophanes, Cicero, Homer, Horace, Juvenal, Martial, Ovid, Persius, Phaedrus, Plautus, Suetonius, Terence, Virgil, and others. Often these are remarkably apposite, as when he spoke about the installation of one of the new-fangled organs by the Dublin society: 'An organ! *Non defensoribus istis tempus eget*. This will help them just as old Priam helped Troy.'[3] He was very fond of inserting English verse into his letters, especially those to women correspondents, and an incomplete list of those quoted includes Addison, Byrom, Churchill, Congreve, Cowley, Dryden, Gambold, Herbert, Milton, Parnell, Pomfret, Pope, Prior, Shakespeare ('our heathenish poet'),[4] Spenser, and Watts—a few of them, such as Milton, dozens of times. To one of his young friends who nursed poetic ambitions Wesley prescribed as an exercise an imitation of Thomas Gray: 'You may write in four-lined stanzas, such as those of the "Elegy wrote in the Churchyard".'[5]

Wesley frequently found his own poetic gifts of value as he employed rhetorical devices of various kinds. Examples have already been quoted. He drew his metaphors (the most important of the 'tropes') from many realms: an elaborate topographical metaphor appears in, 'I desire to have both heaven and hell ever in my eye, while I stand on this isthmus of life, between these two boundless oceans';[6] and a nautical one in, 'You was in danger of having more sail than ballast, more liveliness of imagination than solid wisdom.'[7] Sometimes he sustained a metaphor through several phases, as in

[1] June 28, 1784. See Rom. 15 : 2 and *O.E.D.*

[2] Mar. 25, 1747, § 12; neither 'unconverting' nor 'murderer-general' is to be found in *O.E.D.*

[3] Apr. 6, 1788. He quotes Virgil, *Aeneid*, ii. 521–2, 'The time does not need such defenders.'

[4] Oct. 26, 1745.

[5] Oct. 16, 1771.

[6] July 10, 1747, § 1.

[7] Sept. 13, 1771.

this answer to the charge that he was opposing 'the most *fundamental principles* and *essentially constituent* parts of our Establishment':

'The most fundamental principles!' No more than the tiles are 'the most fundamental principles' of a house. Useful, doubtless, they are; yet you must take them off if you would repair the rotten timber beneath. 'Essentially constituent parts of our Establishment'! Well, we will not quarrel for a word. Perhaps the doors may be 'essentially constituent' parts of the building we call a church. Yet if it were on fire we might innocently break them open, or even throw them for a time off the hinges. Now this is really the case. The timber is rotten, yea, the main beams of the house. And they want to place that firm beam, salvation by faith, in the room of salvation by works. A fire is kindled in the Church, the house of the living God: the fire of love of the world, ambition, covetousness, envy, anger, malice, bitter zeal—in one word, of ungodliness and unrighteousness! O who will come and help to quench it? Under disadvantages and discouragements of every kind, a little handful of men have made a beginning. And I trust they will not leave off till the building is saved, or they sink in the ruins of it.[1]

Equally picturesque and compelling is his laconic description of some homiletic products: 'I think those sermons may stop bottles.'[2]

It would prove a relatively simple, though exhausting chore, to search out examples of all the tropes, figures of speech, and 'fine turns' listed in *The Art of Rhetoric*.[3] It is probably preferable, however, to draw attention to what eventually developed from these studies, the instinctive art of balancing phrases, whether by setting off against each other contrasting words and phrases, by piling up synonyms, or by other means. He told Mary Bishop, 'You look *inward* too much and *upward* too little.'[4] To Lady Maxwell, wondering whether he should rebuke her, 'Certainly I would not run the hazard did I not regard your happiness more than your favour.'[5] And again: 'I love your spirit; I love your conversation; I love your correspondence: I have often received both profit and pleasure thereby. I frequently find a want of more light; but I want heat more than light.'[6] To George Holder and his wife he wrote: 'It cannot be that the people should grow in grace unless they give themselves to reading. A reading people will always be a knowing people. A people who talk much will know little.'[7] Some of these phrases became favourites, to appear again and again, alone or in combination with others,

---

[1] Apr. 10, 1761, 3. (7).
[2] Oct. 8, 1785, to Thomas Wride.
[3] This was a common textbook title, of which we may cite that published by John Holmes in 1755.
[4] Feb. 16, 1771. [5] Sept. 30, 1788.
[6] May 3, 1777. [7] Nov. 8, 1790; cf. Feb. 11, 1773.

such as, 'God is willing to give always what he gives once.'[1] Perhaps every preacher at one time or another read Wesley's words about recalcitrant Methodists: 'Either *mend* them or *end* them.'[2]

It is not surprising, therefore, to find in Wesley's letters a rich vein of maxims, epigrams, aphorisms, and apophthegms. Only a few nuggets and gems may here be displayed. This gift for the pointed phrase appeared early as a reflection of his classical training: 'Leisure and I have now taken leave of one another.'[3] 'Experience is worth a thousand reasons.'[4] 'Till a man gives offence he will do no good.'[5] 'Elegance of style is not to be weighed against purity of heart.'[6] 'I look upon all the world as my parish.'[7] As the years went by his memorable sayings became more numerous, more pointed, more vigorous, until he came into full stride:

> Among my parishioners in Lincolnshire I tried [to do good] for some years. But I am well assured I did far more good to them by preaching three days on my father's tomb than I did by preaching three years in his pulpit.[8]

> Men who neither preach nor live the gospel are suffered publicly to overturn it from the foundation; and in the room of it to palm upon their congregations a wretched mixture of dead form and maimed morality.[9]

> I do not think (to tell you a secret) that the work will ever be destroyed, Church or no Church.[10]

> Of all gossiping, religious gossiping is the worst. It adds hypocrisy to uncharitableness, and effectually does the work of the devil in the name of the Lord.[11]

> Your lordship did not see good to ordain [John Hoskins]. But your lordship did see good to ordain and send into America other persons, who knew something of Greek and Latin, but knew no more of saving souls than of catching whales.[12]

> I look upon that very common custom to be neither better nor worse than murder. I would no more take a pillow from under the head of a dying person than I would put a pillow upon his mouth.[13]

> One soul is worth all the merchandise in the world; and whoever gets money, do you win souls.[14]

It is hard to believe that such a man could seriously be regarded as deficient in a sense of humour, though such is a common misconcep-

---

[1] Dec. 24, 1768; cf. Sept. 13, 1758; May 13, 1764; to Mrs. Fuller (? Feb., 1783).
[2] Mar. 29, 1768; cf. Nov. 12, 1772; Feb. 25, 1778; Nov. 23, 1786.
[3] Dec. 5, 1726.   [4] Dec. 10, 1734, § 15.   [5] Sept. 30, 1735.
[6] Oct. 15, 1735.   [7] ? Mar. 24, 1739.   [8] Mar. 25, 1747, § 13.
[9] Apr. 10, 1761.   [10] Sept. 8, 1761.   [11] June 20, 1772.
[12] Aug. 10, 1780.   [13] Nov. 26, 1786.   [14] June 14, 1790.

tion, perhaps because most of Wesley's humour was expressed in understatement and in irony. This can be seen from a careful reading of his published works: it is much more evident in his letters. Ironically he referred (as did his brother Charles) to his bitter wife as 'my best friend', and when she was in a good temper remarked, 'Miracles are not ceased.'[1] His dismay at frequent postal delays vented itself in a mild, 'The post-boys in Ireland do not ride Pegasus.'[2] One hopes that Joseph Cownley also possessed a sense of humour when he read, 'A fever is the noblest medicine in the world, if a man does not die in the operation.'[3] And likewise young Sally Wesley, when her uncle wrote: 'I do not advise you to drink any sea water. I am persuaded it was never designed to enter any human body for any purpose but to drown it.'[4] Christopher Hopper certainly enjoyed Wesley's humour, for so much of it is to be found in letters to him, not only quiet whimsicalities, such as a reference to the portraits in the *Arminian Magazine*, 'We must get your goodly countenance by-and-by',[5] but occasional humour of a much more obvious kind: 'Peter Jaco would willingly travel. But how? Can you help us to an horse that will carry him and his wife? What a pity we could not procure a camel or an elephant!'[6]

More important, however, to Wesley as to his readers, is that he was able to make both intelligible and interesting—even at times entertaining—observations upon men and manners, upon man's need and God's bounty, in a way which has rarely been equalled. And what he penned for men and women of his own day has remained remarkably fresh and alive for succeeding generations, in spite of a few archaisms and subtle changes in the nuances of meanings. We present a few pen-pictures. Of Thomas Lee:

> T. Lee is of a shy, backward natural temper, as well as of a slow, cool speech and behaviour. But he is a sincere, upright man, and it will be worth all the pains to have a thorough good understanding with him.[7]

Of Alexander M'Nab, just being stationed in Edinburgh:

> His natural temper, I think, is good: he is open, friendly, and generous. He has also a good understanding, and is not unacquainted with learning, though not deeply versed therein. He has no disagreeable person, a pleasing address, and is a lively as well as a sensible preacher. Now when you add to this that he is quite new and very young, you may judge how he will be admired and caressed! 'Surely such a preacher as this never was in Edinburgh before! . . .

---

[1] Mar. 24, 1761; July 9, 1766.   [2] May 21, 1762.
[3] Sept. 17, 1755.   [4] Sept. 1, 1788.   [5] Oct. 25, 1780.
[6] Oct. 7, 1773.   [7] Dec. 28, 1768.

What an angel of a man!' Now, how will a raw, inexperienced youth be able to encounter this?[1]

Of the Revd. John Fletcher:

He writes as he lives. I cannot say that I know such another clergyman in England or Ireland. He is all fire; but it is the fire of love. His writings, like his constant conversation, breathe nothing else to those who read him with an impartial eye.[2]

Perhaps we may fitly close with one lengthier example of Wesley's style, written when he was sixty, an *apologia pro vita sua* written to the Revd. Henry Venn, one of the lesser leaders of the Evangelical Revival, who was unhappy about a Methodist society continuing to be maintained even in his own parish:

The distance between you and me has increased ever since you came to Huddersfield, and perhaps it has not been lessened by that honest, well-meaning man Mr. Burnett, and by others, who have talked largely of my dogmaticalness, love of power, errors, and irregularities. My dogmaticalness is neither more nor less than a 'custom of coming to the point at once', and telling my mind flat and plain, without any preface or ceremony . . .

The *power* I *have* I never *sought*. It was the undesired, unexpected result of the work God was pleased to work by me. I have a thousand times sought to devolve it on others; but as yet I cannot. I therefore suffer it till I can find any to ease me of my burden.

If anyone will convince me of my *errors* I will heartily thank him. I believe all the Bible, as far as I can understand it, and am ready to be convinced. If I am a heretic, I became such by reading the Bible. All my notions I drew from thence; and with little help from men, unless in the single point of justification by faith. But I impose my notions upon none: I will be bold to say there is no man living farther from it. I make no opinion the term of union with any man: I think, and let think. What I want is holiness of heart and life. They who have this are my brother, sister, and mother . . .

As to *irregularity*, I hope none of those who cause it do then complain of it. Will they throw a man into the dirt, and beat him because he is dirty? Of all men living those clergymen ought not to complain who believe I preach the gospel (as to the substance of it). If they do not ask me to preach in their churches, *they* are accountable for my preaching in the fields.

. . . I desire to have a league offensive and defensive with every soldier of Christ. We have not only one faith, one hope, one Lord, but are directly engaged in one warfare. We are carrying the war into the devil's own quarters, who therefore summons all his hosts to war. Come then, ye that love him, to the help of the Lord, to the help of the Lord against the mighty! I am now wellnigh *miles emeritus, senex, sexagenarius*.[3] Yet I trust to fight a little longer. Come and strengthen the hands, till you supply the place of, Your weak but affectionate brother, John Wesley.[4]

[1] Jan. 24, 1771, to Lady Maxwell.   [2] Feb. 8, 1772.
[3] 'A worn-out, sixty-year-old warrior'.   [4] June 22, 1763.

LETTERS FROM AND TO
JOHN WESLEY
1721-1739

To Ambrose Eyre[1]

Christ Church, Nov. 3, ⟨172⟩1

Sir

I am extremely sorry that an accident should happen, which has given you reason to have an ill opinion of me, but am very much obliged to your civility for putting the most favourable construction 5 on it. I hope this will satisfy you that it was by mistake and not my design that you have twice delivered the exhibition for the first Michaelmas quarter, which indeed was through the mistake of my mercer,[2] who returns it, or rather through the negligence of his correspondent, who forgot to inform him of his having received 10 the money. This made him suspect that it was detained, in which he was confirmed by receiving no answer from London; and at Lady day, when I gave him my tutor's bill for that quarter, he told me he had not received the exhibition for the first, which he supposed was detained because I had been absent the whole eight weeks in one 15 quarter, and which made him advise me to write a receipt for that and the other due at the end of the year. These five pounds if you please shall be deducted at Christmas, or if that does not suit with your conveniency shall be returned as soon as possible. I am, sir, your obliged and humble servant, 20

John Wesley

Address: 'For Mr Eyre, Treasurer of The Charter-house, London'   *Postmark*:
'8 NO'   *Source*: The Charterhouse, London.

[1] John Wesley was a gown-boy at the Charterhouse, London, from 1714 until he went up to Christ Church, Oxford, in June 1720, with an exhibition of £20 a year. It appears that there had been some misunderstanding about the quarterly payment due on Michaelmas day, Sept. 29, 1720, so that on Sept. 29, 1721, the exhibition was paid twice. Wesley's first extant letter was written to explain this mix-up to Ambrose Eyre (1684–1756), the treasurer at Charterhouse, affirming his desire to put the matter right in whatever way was most convenient to Eyre.

[2] A mercer dealt in fabrics, but merchants of various kinds set up as merchant-bankers to facilitate the transfer of money, and it seems that Wesley's financial agent in Oxford was a mercer. (Cf. A. S. Turberville (ed.), *Johnson's England*, Oxford, Clarendon Press, I. 258.)

To Mrs. Susanna Wesley[1]

Ch[rist] Ch[urch], Oxon.
[Sept. 23, 1723]

Dear mother

I suppose my brother told you that Mr. Wigan[2] had resigned his
5 pupils and was retired into the country to one of his livings. I was
lately with Mr. Sherman,[3] who is now my tutor, and who, asking me
what Mr. Wigan had of me for tutorage, told me he would never
take any more of me than he had done, but would rather add something to than take from what little I had. I heard lately from my
10 brother,[4] who then promised me to order Mr. Sherman to let me
have the rent of his room, and this quarter's studentship, by which,
together with my five pounds[5] from the Charterhouse at Michaelmas
day, I hope to be very near out of debt everywhere.

The smallpox and fever are now very common in Oxford; of the
15 latter a very ingenious young gentleman of our college died yesterday, being the fifth day from the beginning of his illness. There is
not any other in the college sick at present, and it is hoped that the
approach of winter will stop the spreading of the distemper.

I am very glad to hear that all at home are well; as I am, I thank
20 God, at present, being seldom troubled with anything but bleeding
at the nose, which I have frequently. A little while ago it bled so
violently while I was walking in the evening a mile or two from
Oxford that it almost choked me; nor did any method I could use

[1] Mrs. Susanna Wesley (1669-1742), though continuing in affectionate touch with
all her children after they left home, felt a special relationship with John, and he with
her. In May 1711, as he approached his eighth birthday, she had resolved to be 'more
particularly careful of the soul of this child' (Moore, I. 112). Eighteen of Wesley's
letters to her survive, and forty of hers to him. Their correspondence frequently covered
theological and ecclesiastical matters, as well as family topics.

[2] Revd. (from 1749 onwards Dr.) George Wigan, who proceeded M.A. at Christ
Church in 1718, and retired from his tutorial duties to serve as rector of Old Swinford,
Worcestershire, where he died in 1776.

[3] Revd. Henry Sherman, about whom little is known except that he graduated from
Christ Church as B.A. in 1714 and M.A. in 1717. Wesley preserved a letter written
from Sherman to him, Jan. 10, 1727/8, and they remained friendly after Sherman left
Oxford for London, where he apparently secured a living. Wesley's diary records
visiting 'Mr. Sherman' there in 1733 and several times in 1738.

[4] Revd. Samuel Wesley, Jun. (1690-1739), who had been at Christ Church 1711-18,
and was now usher of Westminster School, London.

[5] Orig., 'llb'.

at all abate it, till I stripped myself and leapt into the river, which happened luckily not to be far off.

I shall not want the notes of my entrance and examination a great while yet, but shall take care to write time enough for them when I do; they can but be brought by the post at last, if nobody comes this way or to London in the meantime.

I should have been very glad to have heard from my sister Suky[1] or any other of my sisters; nor am I so poor but that I can spare postage now and then for a letter or two.[2]

I heard yesterday one of the most unaccountable stories that I ever heard in my life; and the father of the person who told it me had it from the late Bishop of Raphoe in Ireland,[3] who was concerned in it. It is too long and perhaps too impertinent to repeat now, but the most remarkable thing in it was that an actor in it, who by other circumstances pretty plainly appears to have been the devil, distinguished himself, and was known to his fellows[4] by a name (אֱלָהּ פְּלִאי),[5] which title can only belong to the Great God. I shall conclude with begging yours and my father's blessing on your dutiful son,

John Wesley

Sept. 23, 1723

Pray remember my love to all my sisters, and my service to Mr. Romley[6] and his wife.

Address: 'For Mrs Wesley at Wroote, To be left at ye Posthouse In Bawtry, Nottinghamshire' *Postmark*: '2[4?] SE' *Charges*: stylized '3'[pence] (by Oxford postmaster), and 'In All 7' (added by the London clerk, who also erased the original '3' because the letter was being sent forward to Bawtry) *Source*: MA. Paragraphing added.

[1] Susanna Wesley (? 1695–1764), who married Richard Ellison *c.* 1719.

[2] See Intro., pp. 21–2; it is highly unlikely that this refers to the cost of sending rather than of receiving letters.

[3] William Smyth (1638–98); see letter of Dec. 18, 1724.

[4] Orig., altered by Wesley, 'stiled himself, & was term'd by his Fellows'.

[5] 'God of wonders', though no such phrase is found in the Hebrew Bible. In the promised full account of the incident (Dec. 18, 1724) Wesley implies that he himself suggested this Hebrew transliteration of the name of the one 'whom they all honoured as a king, and termed, as he thought, Awly Pawly'.

[6] Mr. William Romley of Burton, Lincolnshire, whose son John succeeded Samuel Wesley as rector of Epworth. Wesley's *Journal* for Apr. 13, 1759, states: 'I called on Mr. Romley of Burton, one of my former parishioners, a lively, sensible man of eighty-three years old, by whom I was much comforted.'

To the Revd. Samuel Wesley, Jun.[1]

Ch[rist] Ch[urch], Oxon. June 17, 1724

Dear brother

I believe I need not use many arguments to show I am sorry for
your misfortune, though at the same time I am glad you are in a
5 fair way of recovery. If I had heard of it from anyone else, I might
probably have pleased you with some impertinent consolations; but
the way of your relating it is a sufficient proof that they are what you
don't stand in need of. And indeed, if I understand you rightly, you
have more reason to thank God that you did not break both, than to
10 repine because you have broke one leg. You have, undoubtedly,
heard the story of the Dutch seaman, who having broke one of his
legs by a fall from the mainmast, instead of condoling himself,
thanked God that he had not broke his neck.[2]

I scarce know whether your first news vexed me, or your last
15 news pleased me, more; but I can assure you that though I did not
cry for grief at the former, I did for joy at the latter part of your
letter. The two things which I most wished for of almost any in the
world were to see my mother, and Westminster again; and to see
them both together was so far above my expectations that I almost[3]
20 looked upon it as next to an impossibility. I have been so very
frequently disappointed when I had set my heart on any pleasure,
that I will never again depend on any before it comes: however, I
shall be obliged to you if you tell me as near as you can, how soon
my uncle[4] is expected in England, and my mother in London.

[1] Samuel Wesley (1690–1739) was the oldest child of the Revd. Samuel Wesley,
Sen., and his wife Susanna. Educated at Westminster School and Christ Church, Oxford,
he returned to Westminster School as usher. In spite of the thirteen years' difference in
their ages he was very close to John (as also to Charles), and maintained a frequent and
lively correspondence with him. The patronage of Francis Atterbury, Bishop of Roches-
ter and Dean of Westminster, which secured him his position, also brought Wesley into
touch with London literary and political circles. He became the protégé of Harley,
Earl of Oxford, and the friend of Pope and Prior. His own verse had already secured him
some repute, and his *Battle of the Sexes* (frequently quoted by John Wesley in his own
writings) was already in its second English edition and a pirated Irish edition.

[2] See *Spectator*, No. 574, July 30, 1714.

[3] *Westminster Magazine*, 'always'.

[4] Mrs. Wesley's brother, Samuel Annesley (*c*. 1658–1732), factor of the East India
Company in Surat, India, whose return in one of the company's ships had been reported
in the press, so that she came down to London to meet him, only to be confronted by his

I hope my sister is pretty well recovered by this time, and that all at Westminster are in as good health as your loving brother,

John Wesley

Pray give my service to Mrs. Harris,[1] and as many as ask after me.

Since you have a mind to see some of my verses, I have sent you 5 some, which employed me above an hour yesterday, in the afternoon. There is one, and I am afraid but one, good thing in them, that is, they are short.

From the Latin[2]

As o'er fair Cloe's rosy cheek, 10
    Careless, a little vagrant passed,
With artful hand around his neck
    A slender chain the virgin cast.

As Juno near her throne above
    Her spangled bird delights to see; 15
As Venus has her fav'rite dove,
    Cloe shall have her fav'rite flea.

Pleased at his chains, with nimble steps
    He o'er her snowy bosom strayed:
Now on her panting breast he leaps, 20
    Now hides between his little head.

Leaving, at length, his old abode,
    He found, by thirst or fortune led,
Her swelling lips, that brighter glowed
    Than roses in their native bed. 25

Cloe, your artful bands undo,
    Nor for your captive's safety fear;
No artful bands are needful now
    To keep the willing vagrant here.

Whilst on that heav'n 'tis given to stay, 30
    (Who would not wish to be so blest)
No force can draw him once away,
    Till death shall seize his destined breast!

mysterious disappearance. John Wesley passed on to his own nephews the tradition of a missing fortune promised by this rich uncle to the Epworth Wesleys, in spite of a tiff between him and Samuel Wesley, but the tradition was exploded this century by the discovery of his will, cutting them each off with a shilling. (Clarke, I. 381–94; Arnold Wright, *Annesley of Surat*, London, Melrose, 1918, pp. 38, 329–35; cf. letters from Mrs. Wesley, Aug. 19, Sept. 10, Nov. 24, 1724.)

[1] Of this lady nothing is known, nor does she reappear in the correspondence. (Links with the Westminster pupil, Joseph Harris (1719–23), or another 1725 onwards, appear unlikely, as does one with Jephtha Harris, an associate of the Wesleys in 1738—see in-letter of Jan. 2, 1738, and out-letter of Nov. 27, 1738.)

[2] Apparently from some unidentified contemporary Latin verse.

If you will excuse my pen and my haste, I shall be once more

Yours

This is my birthday.

Sources: Westminster Magazine, Apr. 1774, p. 181, prepared by Samuel Badcock from the original; Whitehead, I. 382–4, a lengthy extract, probably from the original. The body of the letter has no paragraphing.

From Mrs. Susanna Wesley[1]

Wroot, Aug. 19, 1724

5   Dear J[acky][2]

I am somewhat uneasy, because I've not heard from you so long, and think you don't do well to stand upon points, and write only letter for letter, since I decline apace, and 'tis more trouble for me to write one than for you to write ten times. Therefore let me hear from you oftener, and inform me of the state
10 of your health, how you go on, and whether you are easier than formerly, and have any reasonable hopes of being out of debt.

We have dismal weather, and can neither get hay, corn, nor firing, which makes us apprehensive of great want. I am most concerned for that good, generous man that lent you £10; and am ashamed to beg a month or two
15 longer, since he was so kind to grant us so much time already. Give my service to him, and thanks, however.

We were strangely amused with your uncle's coming from India, but suppose those fancies are laid aside. I wish there had been anything in it, then perhaps it had been in my power to have provided for you. For if all these things fail, I
20 hope God will not forsake us: we have still his good providence to depend on, which has a thousand expedients to relieve us beyond our view.

Dear J[acky], be not discouraged; do your duty, keep close to your studies, and hope for better days; perhaps, notwithstanding all, we shall pick up a few crumbs for you before the end of the year.
25   Dear son, I beseech Almighty God to bless thee!

S[usanna] W[esley]

Source: LB, pp. 24–5.

[1] John Wesley kept copies of select letters to him from members of his family in a small notebook entitled, 'Letters: 1724, 25, 26 / & 1727, 28–29'. This letter-book ('LB' frequently henceforth) is preserved in the Methodist Archives. The letters are all in the highly compressed longhand with special signs noted in the Introduction, p. 126. The text is always here expanded without comment, and square brackets used only where some doubt exists about the original. In these copies Wesley's dash represents a hyphen, and is so shown here (cf. Feb. 23, 1724/5).

[2] Orig., 'D.J.'; her holograph letters of Feb. 23, 1724/5, Oct. 25, 1732, show that she used 'Jacky' rather than 'John' or 'Jack'; from 1734 onwards she seems to have addressed him as 'Dear son'.

From Mrs. Susanna Wesley

Wroot, Sept. 10 [1724]

Dear J[acky]

'Tis above a week since I received your kind letter,[1] which has greatly revived my spirits; and though I should not have an ill opinion of you though there had really been some neglect on your side, yet I find I am much better 5 pleased to think you do not grudge the pains of writing.

I'm nothing glad that Mr.— has paid himself out of your exhibition . . . Though I cannot hope, I do not despair, of my brother's coming, or at least remembering me where he is; for I am persuaded God will yet order things so that either I or mine shall sometime be the better for that man; though most 10 of my family are of another opinion . . .

The smallpox has been very mortal at Epworth most of this summer. Our family have all had it besides me, and I hope God will preserve me from it, because your father can't yet well [[spare money to bury me]][2] . . .

I heartily wish you were in Orders, and could come and serve one of his 15 churches. Then I should see you often, and could be more helpful to you than 'tis possible to be at this distance . . .

Dear J[acky], I beseech Almighty God to bless thee!

Source: LB, pp. 25–6.

To Mrs. Susanna Wesley

Nov. 1, 1724. Oxon.

Dear Mother   20

We are most of us now very healthy at Oxford, as I hope you are, which may be in some measure owing to the frosty weather we have lately had, preceded by a very cool summer. All kind of fruit is so very cheap that apples may be had almost for fetching, and other things are both as plentiful and as good as has been known in a long 25 time. We have[3] indeed something bad, as well as good; for a great many rogues are about the town, insomuch that it is very unsafe to be out late. A gentleman of my acquaintance, only standing at a coffee-house door about seven in the evening, had no sooner turned about but his cap and wig were snatched off, which he could not 30

[1] A missing letter of about Aug. 26, answering his mother's of Aug. 19.

[2] From cipher, for whose interpretation here as elsewhere I have leaned very heavily upon Prof. Richard P. Heitzenrater.

[3] Orig., 'have ((had))'.

recover, though he pursued the thief a great way. However, I am pretty safe from such gentlemen; for unless they carried me away, carcass and all, they would have but a poor purchase.

The chief piece of news with us is concerning the famous Sheppard's[1] escape from Newgate, which is indeed as surprising as most stories I have heard. It seems he had broke out twice before, besides once out of the condemned hold, which, together with his having got his chains off again when the keeper came in, made them still more apprehensive of him. However, that he might be secure, if art could make him so, he was fettered, manacled, and chained down to the ground by one chain round his waist and another round his neck, in the strongest part of the Castle. Notwithstanding which he found means to force open his chains and fetters, break through the ceiling there, and then, sliding to the leads of an adjoining house, to pass six several locked doors, and get clear off without discovery, all which was done between six and eleven at night. I suppose you have heard that Brigadier Mackintosh[2] was once more taken, but made his escape from a messenger and six dragoons after an obstinate fight.

Three gentlemen of our college were in September last walking in the fields near Oxford about half an hour after six, of whom the foremost was named Barnesley,[3] who, going to cross the path, of a sudden started back and turned as white as ashes; but being asked by the others what ailed him, answered, Nothing. The second man, coming up to the same place, seemed presently more frighted than he, and bawled out that he saw one in white shoot [a]cross the path as swift as an arrow. Mr. Barnesley, hearing that, told him he had seen it just before; and both of them describe it to have been like a man or woman in light grey, but of so thin a substance that they could plainly see through it. They had likewise another accident the same evening, though not quite so remarkable; both which made Barnesley so curious as to write down the day of the month, which

---

[1] John ('Jack') Sheppard (1702–24), a carpenter and locksmith of Spitalfields, London, whose escapes from prison made him a popular celebrity. This last escape, from the most secure part of the prison, known as the 'Castle', took place on Sept. 16, 1724, but he was captured a little over a week later, and publicly executed at Tyburn on Nov. 16. (See *D.N.B.* for details.)

[2] William Mackintosh (1662–1743), a Brigadier-General in the Old Pretender's army, was taken prisoner when the rebellion collapsed at Preston on Nov. 16, 1715, but escaped six months later.

[3] Apparently John Barnesley, son of John of 'St. Luke's' (possibly Luke Street, for there is no such parish), Dublin, who matriculated Oct. 21, 1724, aged 16.

was the 26th of September. We thought no more of it afterwards, till last week, when Barnesley was informed by a letter from his father in Ireland, that his mother died the 26th of September, between six and seven in the evening.

I suppose you have seen the famous Dr. Cheyne's book of *Health and Long Life*,[1] which is, as he says he expected, very much cried down by the physicians—though he says they need not be afraid of his weak endeavours while the world, the flesh, and the devil are on the other side of the question. He refers almost everything to temperance and exercise, and supports most things he says with physical reasons. He entirely condemns eating anything salt or high-seasoned, as also pork, fish, and stall-fed cattle; and recommends for drink two pints of water and one of wine in twenty-four hours, with eight ounces of animal and twelve of vegetable food in the same time. I shall trouble you no more about him here, since you may have probably seen the book itself, which is chiefly directed to studious and sedentary persons.

I should have writ before now had I not had an unlucky cut across my thumb, which almost jointed it, but is now pretty well cured. I hope you will excuse my writing so ill, which I can't easily help, as being obliged to get done as soon as I can; and that you will remember my love to my sisters and brother, and my service to as many as ask after me. I should be exceeding glad to keep a correspondence with my sister Emly,[2] if she were willing; for I believe I have not heard from her since I was at Oxford. I have writ once or twice to my sister Suky,[3] too, but have not had an answer either from her or my sister Hetty,[4] from whom I have more than once desired the Poem

[1] George Cheyne, M.D. (1671–1743), whose *Essay of Health and Long Life* went through many editions, the first appearing earlier this year. Cheyne exercised a strong influence upon Wesley's personal health and upon his healing ministry, by means of both this volume and a later work, *A Natural Method of curing the Diseases of the Body and the Disorders of the Mind depending on the Body* (1742). Cf. *A Letter to the Bishop of London* (11. 344–5 in this edition), JWJ, June 28, 1770, and Intro., pp. 99–100.

[2] Emilia Wesley (1692–*c.* 1771), Wesley's oldest surviving sister, who was unmarried at this time, but married Robert Harper of Epworth, apparently in the late summer of 1735.
N.B. There are many problems in assigning dates to members of the Wesley family. Emilia has traditionally been supposed to have been born in 1691, but the diocesan transcripts of the parish registers note her baptism on Jan. 13, 1692/3, showing that she was almost certainly born a few weeks earlier, in Dec. 1692.

[3] Susanna Wesley (*c.* 1695–1764), who married (*c.* 1719) Richard Ellison, a rich but brutal farmer, whom eventually she left after bearing several children, the first christened John in Feb. 1719/20.

[4] Mehetabel Wesley (*c.* 1697–1750), who on Oct. 13, 1725, married William Wright of

of the Dog.[1] I should be glad to hear how things go at Wroot,[2] which I now reflect on with more pleasure than Epworth; so true it is, at least in me, that the persons, not the place, make[3] home so pleasant. You said something of it in your last letter which I wish could come to pass, but I am afraid I flattered myself too soon.[4] It is well my paper will hold no more,[5] or I don't know when I should have done; but the scantiness of that obliges me to conclude with begging yours and my father's blessing on your dutiful son

                                                                John Wesley

Address: 'For Mrs Wesley at Wroote, To be left at ye Posthouse, In Bawtry, Nottinghamshire'   *Postmark*: '3 NO', and an almost indecipherable town stamp, 'Oxford'   *Charges*: stylized '3' charged by the Oxford postmaster, and erased by a London clerk; 'In All 6' added in error by a London clerk, possibly thinking that the London–Bawtry charge was 3*d*., and incorrectly left unerased when the correct charge of 4*d*. was added as a component of the inscribed 'In All 7'   *End* by JW: 'Nov. 1724. Acc[oun]t of Appari[tion]'   *Source*: MA.

From Mrs. Susanna Wesley

Wroot, Nov. 24 [1724]

Dear J[acky]

I have now three of your letters before me unanswered, and take it very kindly that you would write so often though you heard not from me. Indeed I'm afraid of being chargeable, or I should miss few posts; it being exceeding pleasant

Louth, at Haxey, while her child by an unnamed lover was baptized at Louth on Feb. 18, 1725/6, and buried on Dec. 27 that year. Some of the family took sides with Hetty against her father over this unhappy affair (cf. letter of Dec. 5–6, 1726).

    [1] Probably the poem by Samuel Wesley, Jun., which may well have been addressed to her (*Poems*, 1736, pp. 148–50), entitled 'The Dog', and beginning, 'Thee, sister, gladly would my verse provoke'. John Wesley did secure it, and transcribed it in its incomplete state into his MS 'Miscellany Verses' (in MA), pp. 79–81. Samuel Wesley added eight closing lines before publication.

    [2] Orig., as usually in Wesley's writings at this period, 'Wroote', though his mother's letter of Feb. 23, 1724/5, spells it 'Wroot'. From 1722 until he resigned it in 1734, Samuel Wesley held this adjacent living as well as that of Epworth, in plurality, and members of the family lived sometimes at the one, sometimes the other. A succession of curates helped him with this double task, including John, 1727–9. It will be noted that John's letters to his mother from 1723 to 1725 are addressed to Wroot, but from 1730 onwards to Epworth.   [3] Orig., 'make((s)).

    [4] His living near her by becoming his father's curate; see her letter of Sept. 10, 1724.

    [5] This sentence and 'self too soon' of the preceding sentence are written vertically down the gutter between pp. 1 and 4.

to me in this solitude to read your letters, but I believe they would be pleasing anywhere.

Your disappointment in not seeing us as at Oxon was not of such ill consequence as mine, in not meeting my brother at London. Not but your wonderful curiosities might excite a person of greater faith than mine to travel to your 5 museum on purpose to visit them. 'Tis almost pity that somebody does not cut the wezon[1] of that keeper with Adam's sword, to cure his lying so enormously.

I wish you would save all the money you can conveniently spare, not to spend on a visit, but for a wiser and better purpose—to pay debts, and make yourself easy. I am not without hope of meeting you next summer, if it please God to 10 prolong my worthless life. If then you will be willing and have time allowed you to accompany me to Wroot, I'll bear your charges, and do other ways for you, as God shall enable me . . .

The story of Mr. B[arnesley][2] has afforded me many curious speculations. I do not doubt the fact, but cannot conceive for what reason those apparitions 15 should come unto us. If they were permitted to speak to us, and we had strength to bear such conversation; if they had commission to inform us of anything relating to their invisible world that would be of any use to us in this; if they could instruct us how to avoid any danger, or put us in a way of being wiser and better, there would be sense in it. But to appear for no end that we know of, 20 unless to fright people almost out of their wits, seems altogether unaccountable.

. . . I hope at your leisure you will oblige me with some more verses, on any, but rather on a religious subject . . .

Dear J[acky], I beseech Almighty God to bless thee!

Source: LB, pp. 26–7.

To Mrs. Susanna Wesley

[Dec. 18, 1724] 25
Ch[rist] Ch[urch], Oxon.

Dear mother

I am very glad to hear you are all well at home, as we are here, the smallpox, which raged so much a little while ago, being now almost quite over. Only one gentleman of our college had it, who is 30 now recovered, so that the others who feared it are freed at last from their apprehensions. I have not lately heard from Westminster, but Mr. Sherman, who did, assured me that my brothers[3] and sister there were very well. He has given me one or two books lately, of

[1] i.e. throat, one of many variants of the obsolete 'weasand'.

[2] See Wesley's letter to her, Nov. 1, 1724.

[3] In 1716 Charles Wesley had entered Westminster School, where Samuel was usher; he matriculated at Christ Church, Oxford, June 13, 1726.

which one is *Godfrey of Bulloigne*.[1] We have still very warm weather
at Oxford; and a gentleman, now in the room with me, says that
several of the flowers in his father's garden, who lives in town, are
blown as if it were spring.

5   The story of which I said something in my last[2] was, as I believe
I told you before, transacted a little before King James's abdication.[3]
The Bishop of Raphoe, one of the principal actors in it, was then
pretty old, but never reckoned superstitious or easy to be imposed
upon.[4] From him it came to Mr. Span,[5] Vicar-General of Ireland,
10   and was by him related to Mr. Harrison, a clergyman, in the hearing
of his son,[6] who told it me. The substance of it was this. It was told
to the bishop that a lad in his diocese frequently bragged that he
was carried up into the air by invisible hands; who immediately
sent for him, to find out the truth. The lad in private, though not
15   without menacing, confessed that he was often carried into the air
by he knew not whom, to a fine palace; where he was made to sit
down at table with a great many people, who feasted and made
merry; but that he was afraid they would be angry with him for
telling it. The bishop endeavoured by many arguments to dissuade
20   him from spreading such stories, which he told him could not be
true, and were at best but the effects of a troubled fancy. But the
boy persisted in it, and told his lordship that if he would have a little
patience he would presently be convinced of the truth of his relation;
for by certain symptoms which he said always preceded his trans-
25   portation he was sure it was not far off. This was presently confirmed
in the bishop's presence, the boy being hoisted away out of the

---

[1] Torquato Tasso (1544–95), *Gerusalemme Liberata*, telling the story of the capture
of Jerusalem during the First Crusade, was translated into English verse by Edward
Fairfax as *Godfrey of Bulloigne, or the Recoverie of Jerusalem* (1600). Tasso's work was
also translated into English in 1763 by John Hoole (1727–1803), and in 1780 Wesley
recommended both works as part of his reading course for young ladies (see Intro.,
p. 101).

[2] i.e. Sept. 23, 1723.

[3] James II fled from London on Dec. 11, 1688.

[4] The Bishop of Raphoe at the time was William Smyth (1638–98), who in 1693 was
translated to Kilmore, where he died (James B. Leslie, *Armagh Clergy*, 1911, p. 38).

[5] Benjamin Span (or Spann, *c.* 1657–1718), rector of Templemichael (1693–1718),
rector of Conwall (1694–1715), etc., who was Vicar-General of the diocese of Ardagh
in 1709 (James B. Leslie, *Raphoe Clergy*, 1940, p. 55; Henry Cotton, *Fasti Ecclesiae
Hibernicae*, III. 371).

[6] Robert Harrison, who had matriculated at Christ Church on Oct. 21, 1723, aged
21, and graduated B.A. Mar. 23, 1723/4, and who is mentioned several times in Wesley's
Oxford diary. His father was the Revd. Robert Harrison of Strete, Co. Westmeath,
Ireland.

window, to his no small amazement. The next day about the same
time the boy was let down into the same room, but so bruised and
dispirited that it was a hard matter to get a word from him. After
some time, and repeated threats and promises, he told the bishop
that he was carried to the place he had before spoken of, but that 5
instead of sitting down as he used to do with the company, one or
two were set apart to beat him, while the rest were making merry.
His lordship now believed it was something more than a jest, being
convinced that it was the devil, who for some unknown reason was
permitted to exert an extraordinary power over this lad. He never- 10
theless proceeded to comfort and pray by him; yet even while he
was praying the boy was once more taken from him, nor was he
restored again till after some hours, into the same chamber. He was
not then soon prevailed upon to discover anything; but at last confessed that he was beat by the same persons worse than before; that 15
they threatened him with death if he told again; and that as for the
bishop, a person whom they all honoured as a king and termed, as
he thought, Awly Pawly,[1] said that he might bluster as he would,
and build himself houses, but that he should never live to lie in the
new one he had built already. The bishop on this sent for several of 20
his friends, whom he acquainted [with] the whole matter, and then
desired them, that he might prove the devil a liar, to go with him
immediately to his new house, in which, though not entirely finished,
he said he would, God willing, both sup and lie that very night.
Accordingly provisions and necessaries were sent thither, which were 25
followed by the bishop and his friends; but while they were at
supper a very large stone was whirled with an incredible force
through the window, and passed in the sight of the whole company
close to the bishop to the other side of the room. This the bishop
said was in his opinion the work of the devil, who was willing to 30
keep his word, though it pleased God not to suffer him to accomplish
his design. However, the bishop lay there that night; but it was the
last which he spent in it, for the wars breaking out immediately after,
obliged him to fly his country,[2] and the boy, as far as he could
learn, suffered in the same manner to his death, which soon followed. 35
   This puts me in mind of an odd circumstance, which I know not

---

[1] See letter of Sept. 23, 1723.
[2] James II landed in Ireland to popular acclaim in 1789, besieging Londonderry
April 20–July 30. His army burnt Smyth's palace, and the bishop fled to Wales (Leslie,
Armagh Clergy, p. 38, and Supplement, 1948, p. 12).

yet what to make of. I was last week walking two or three mile[s]
from Oxford, and seeing a fair house stand by itself which I never
observed before, I asked who lived in it, of a countryman; who
informed me that it had long stood empty, by reason of its being so
5 much haunted that no family could ever stay long in it. I design to
go thither the first opportunity, and see if it be true; which I shall
hardly believe till I am an eye- or ear-witness of it. Pray remember
my love to all my sisters. I would have writ to one or two of them
if I had had either room or time; but I am just going to church; for
10 which reason will you will [sic] excuse me for breaking off so
abruptly, and writing so bad. I shall therefore conclude with begging
yours and my father's blessing on your dutiful son,

Dec. 18   John Wesley

Address: 'For Mrs Wesley at Wroote, to be left at ye Post-house in Bawtry,
Nottinghamshire'   *Postmarks*: 'OXFORD'; '[2]o [D]E'   *Charges*: '3',
'In all 7'   *End* by JW: '1724' 'Acct of a Diabolical Transacc̄.'; by a later
hand, 'J. Wesley / Decemr 18.'   *Source*: MA.

From the Revd. Samuel Wesley[1]

Jan. 5, [17]24/5
15   Your brother will receive £5 for you on next Saturday, if Mr. S[herman]
is paid the £10 he lent you; if not, it must go to h[im]. But I promise you,
I shan't forget you are my son, if you do not that I am your loving father,
Sam:Wesley

Source: LB, p. 10.

[1] Revd. Samuel Wesley (1662–1735), rector of Epworth from 1695 until his death.
He achieved a measure of recognition by his writings, especially his massive *Life of* . . .
Jesus Christ (1693) in verse, dedicated to Queen Mary, which apparently resulted in the
offer of the Epworth living. He was one of the major scholars contributing regularly to
the *Athenian Gazette*, on a variety of religious and literary subjects, and engaged in
lengthy controversies with the Dissenters, whom he had left to become a member and
minister of the Church of England. He was a faithful pastor, but his strict discipline and
his strong political views made him unpopular with his parishioners.

From Mrs. Susanna Wesley

Jan. 5, [17]25

Dear J[acky]

(About sending money)[1]

Your brother talks of coming hither at Whitsuntide, perhaps between this
and that something may occur, or it may happen that you may come with him . . .
God bless thee!   5

I wish you a happy new year.

Source: LB, p. 27.

From the Revd. Samuel Wesley

Wroot, Janry. 26, 1724/5

Dear son,

I'm so well pleased with your present behaviour, or at least with your letters,
that I hope I shall have no occasion to remember any more some things that are   10
past. And since you have now for some time bit upon the bridle, I'll take care
hereafter to put a little honey upon it as oft as I'm able. But then it shall be of
my own *mero motu*,[2] as the last 5[1b] was,[3] for I will bear no rivals in my kindness.

I did not forget you with Dr. Morley, but have moved that way as much as   15
possible, though I must confess hitherto with no great prospect or hope of
success.

As for what you mention of entering into Holy Orders, 'tis indeed a great
work, and I am pleased to find you think it so, as well as that you don't admire
a callow clergyman any more than I do. As for the motives you take notice of,   20
my thoughts are: (1), It's no *harm* to desire getting into that office, even as
Eli's sons, 'to eat a piece of bread'; 'for the labourer is worthy of his hire'.
Though, (2), a desire and intention to lead a stricter life, and a belief one should
do so, is a better reason; though this should by all means be begun before,
or else, ten to one, 'twill deceive us afterward. (3), If a man be *unwilling* and   25
undesirous to enter into Orders, 'tis easy to guess whether he can say, so much as
with common honesty, that he believes he's 'moved by the Holy Spirit' to do it.
But, (4), the principal spring and motive, to which all the former should be
only secondary, must certainly be the glory of God, and the service of his
church, in the edification and salvation[4] of our neighbour. And woe to him who   30
with any meaner leading view attempts so sacred a work. For which, (5),
he should take all the care he possibly can, with the advice of wiser and elder
men—especially imploring with all humility, sincerity, and intention of mind, and

---

[1] Wesley summarizes a section which he omits.
[2] Wesley's transcription in his letter-book, 'mere motion'.
[3] See letter of Jan. 5, 1725, referring to the gift of £5.
[4] Wesley's transcription omits 'and salvation'.

with fasting and prayer, the direction and assistance of Almighty God, and his Holy Spirit, to qualify and prepare him for it. The knowledge of the languages is a very considerable help in this matter, which, I thank God, all my three sons have to a very laudable degree, though God knows I had ne'er more than
5 a smattering of any of 'em. But then this must be prosecuted to the thorough understanding the original text of the Scriptures, by constant and long conversing with them. You ask me which is the best commentary on the Bible. I answer, The Bible. For the several paraphrases and translations of it in the Polyglot, compared with the original and with one another, are in my opinion,
10 to an honest, devout, industrious, and humble mind, infinitely preferable to any commentary I ever saw writ upon it, though Grotius is the best (for the most part), especially on the Old Testament.

And now, the providence of God (I hope it was) has engaged me in such a work wherein you may be very assistant to me, I trust promote his glory, and at
15 the same time notably forward your own studies in the method I have just now proposed. For I've some time since designed an edition of the Holy Bible in octavo, in the Hebrew, Chaldee, Seventy,[1] and Vulgar Latin, and have made some progress in it; the whole scheme whereof I han't time at present to give you, of which scarce any soul yet knows unless your brother Sam. What I desire of
20 you on this article is, that you would immediately fall to work: read diligently the Hebrew text in the Polyglot, and collate it exactly with the Vulgar Latin, which is in the second column, writing down all (even the least) variations or differences between 'em. To these I'd have you add the Samaritan text, in the last column but one (don't mind the Latin translation in the very last column),
25 which is the very same with the Hebrew except in some very few places, onl⟨y⟩ differing in the Samaritan character (I think the true Old Hebrew), the alphabet whereof you may learn in a day's time, either from the prolegomena in Walton's Polyglot, or from his grammar. In a twelvemonth's time, sticking close to it in the forenoons, you will get twice through the Pentateuch; for I have done it
30 four times the last year, and am going over it the fifth, collating the Hebrew and the two Greek, the Alexandrian and the Vatican, with what I can get of Symmachus, Theod[otion], etc. Nor shall you lose your reward for't, either in this or tother world. Nor are your brothers like to be idle. But I'd have nothing said of it to anybody, though your brother Sam shall write you shortly about it.
35 In the afternoon read what you will, and be sure to walk an hour if fair in the fields. Get Thirlby's Chrysostom *De Sacerdotio.* Master it; digest it. I took some pains, a year or two since, in drawing up some advices to Mr. Hoole's brother, then to be my curate at Epworth, before his ordination, which mayn't be unuseful to you, wherefore I'll send 'em shortly to your brother Sam for you;
40 but you must return 'em me again, I having no copy—and pray let none but yourself see 'em.[2]

By all this you see I'm not for your going over hastily into Orders. When I'm for your taking 'em, you shall know it, and 'tis not impossible but I may then be with you, if God so long spare the life and health of your affectionate
45 father,   Sam Wesley

    [1] i.e. the Septuagint Greek.
    [2] Published by John Wesley in 1735, after his father's death, as *Advice to a Young Clergyman* (see *Bibliog*, No. 5).

I like your verses on the 65th Psalm, and would not have you bury your talent.

All are well, and send buss.[1]

Work and write while you can. You see time has shaken me by the hand, and death's but a little behind him. My eyes and heart[2] are now almost all I have 5 left, and bless God for them.

End by JW: 'my F. Jan. 26, 1725'   *Source*: Bristol Wesley; cf. LB, pp. 11–13, with the long paragraph on the proposed biblical publication summarized. See also *A.M.* I. 29–30 (1778), probably based upon LB, with many and considerable editorial revisions by Wesley.[3]

From Mrs. Susanna Wesley

Wroot, Feb. 23, 1724[/5]

Dear Jacky

I have received two letters from you, neither of which I've answered. Your father kept the first, it being included in one to him, and since the receipt of 10 the last I have been very ill, and confined to my chamber, but I thank God I'm much better.

Your last brings surprising news indeed about the Pope, whom I doubt the Conclave will not permit long to live. His justice to the young gentleman, in restoring him the estate his bigotted father gave from him to the monks, is 15 really very commendable, but his allowing the Scriptures to the laity, and declaring against his own infallibility, are actions truly Christian. In the latter he has given a mortal wound to the infallibility of that see, and whether he were in the right or whether he was in the wrong the matter is the same, for both horns of the dilemma strikes them. They must resign their more profitable 20 than honest pretence to infallibility. The King of Prussia talks often, but is not to be depended on for action. Emly has answered for herself. Tis strange Mr. Leybourne[4] should send any service to me, but I accept the compliment, and without one wish him health and happiness.[5]

---

[1] i.e. a kiss, or love.   [2] Instead of the word itself Wesley drew a heart.
[3] For the value of these three sources as evidence see Intro., pp. 128–9.
[4] Robert Leybourne (c. 1694–1759), a contemporary of Samuel Wesley, Jun., at Westminster School and Christ Church, who became fellow of Brasenose College, Oxford, in 1717, B.D. and D.D. in 1731. He was rector of St. Dunstan's, Stepney, 1729, and of St. Anne's, Limehouse, from 1730 until his death, when he was buried in Bath Abbey in the grave of his second wife, Rebeccah Towne of St. Mary's, Stratford-at-Bow, Essex, whom he was licensed to marry Jan. 20, 1732/3. For some time it had seemed likely that he would marry Emily Wesley, but 'a near relation' (apparently her brother Samuel) and her mother intervened. See her letter to John Wesley, Apr. 7, 1725. She and John remained very close.
[5] Wesley's transcript in his letter-book summarizes: 'Of news, the Pope, the King of Prussia, and of Mr. L.'.

The alteration of your temper has occasioned me much speculation. I, who am apt to be sanguine, hope it may proceed from the operations of God's Holy Spirit. That by taking off your relish of sensual enjoyments, [it] would prepare and dispose your mind for a more serious and close application to things of
5   a more sublime and spiritual nature. If it be so, happy are you if you cherish those dispositions, and now in good earnest resolve to make religion the business of your life. For after all that is the one thing that strictly speaking is necessary; all things beside are comparatively little to the purposes of life. Dear Jacky, I heartily wish you would now enter upon a serious examination of yourself,
10 that you may know whether you have a reasonable hope of salvation by Jesus Christ,[1] that is, whether you are in a state of faith and repentance or not, which you know are the conditions of the gospel covenant on our part. If you are, the satisfaction of knowing it will abundantly reward your pains. If not, you'll find a more reasonable occasion for tears than can be met with in a
15 tragedy. This matter deserves great consideration in all, but especially those designed for the clergy ought above all things to make their calling and election sure, lest after they have preached to others they themselves should be cast away.
    Now I mention this, it calls to mind your letter to your father about taking Orders. I was much pleased with it, and liked the proposal well. But 'tis an
20 unhappiness almost peculiar to our family, that your father and I seldom think alike. I approve the disposition of your mind, I think this season of Lent the most proper for your preparation for Orders, and I think the sooner you are a deacon the better, because it may be an inducement to greater application in the study of practical divinity, which of all other I humbly conceive is the best study
25 for candidates for Orders. Mr. Wesley differs from me, and would engage you, I believe, in critical learning (though I'm not sure), which though of use accidentally, and by way of concomitance, yet is in no wise preferable to the other. Therefore I earnestly pray God to avert that great evil from you, of engaging in trifling studies to the neglect of such as are absolutely necessary. I dare advise
30 nothing. God Almighty direct, and bless you. Adieu.
    I have much to say, but cannot write more at present. I even long to see you.

Source: Wes Ch; cf. transcript in LB, pp. 23–4.

From the Revd. Samuel Wesley

Wroot, March 17, 1724/5

Son
    I've both yours. I've changed my mind since my last, and now incline to your
35 going this summer into Orders, and would have you turn your thoughts and studies that way. But in the first place, if you love yourself or me, pray heartily! ... I'll struggle hard, but I'll get money for your Orders, and something more ...

---

[1] Wesley's letter-book transcript omits 'by Jesus Christ'.

Mr. Downes has spoke to Dr. Morley[1] about you, who says he'll inquire of your character . . .

Trust in the Lord, and do good, and verily thou shalt be fed!

This, with blessing, from your loving father,

Sam Wesley 5

Source: LB, p. 13.

From Emily Wesley

April 7, 1725

Brother

Yours of March 7[2] I received, and thank you for your care in dispatching so speedily the business I desired you to do. It is the last of that kind I shall trouble you with. No more shall I write or receive letters to and from that 10 person. But lest you should run into a mistake, and think we have quarrelled, like Sam and him, I assure you we are perfect friends. We think, wish, and judge alike; but what avails it, we are both miserable. He has not differed with my mother, but she loves him not, because she esteems him the unlucky cause of a deep melancholy in a beloved child. For his own sake it is that I cease 15 writing, because 'tis now his interest to forget me.

[She urges John to avoid 'engaging his affections' before he is able to marry speedily, and recounts in detail the long story of her own arduous life at Epworth, her acquaintance with Robert Leybourne, their correspondence over several years, her teaching in Lincoln, and her return home after her father secured the 20 additional living at Wroot. She describes how while her mother is alive she thinks it 'barbarous to abandon her', and speaks of Hetty's absence.]

I have quite tired you now. Pray be faithful to me. Let me have one relation I can trust. Never give any hint to anyone of aught I write to you, and continue to love your unhappy but affectionate sister, 25

Emilia Wesley

Source: MA; cf. *W.M.M.*, 1845, pp. 359–62.

From the Revd. Samuel Wesley

Wroot, May 10, 1725

Dear son

Your brother Samuel (with his wife) and Ch[arles] are here. I did what I could that you might have been in Orders this Trinity, but I doubt your 30 brother's journey hither has for the present disconcerted all our measures,

[1] John Morley (*c.* 1669–1731), Rector of Lincoln College.
[2] Apparently discussing her break with Leybourne (see p. 159).

though hereby you'll have more time to prepare yourself for it; which I pray
God you may, as I'm your loving father,

Sam Wesley

Source: LB, p. 13.

To Mrs. Susanna Wesley

May 28,[1] 1725

5 Dear mother

My brother Charles, I remember, about a month or two since,
was bemoaning himself because my brother and I were to go into
the country, and he was to be left behind. But now I hope he has no
reason to complain, since he had the good fortune to go down in my
10 stead.[2] It was indeed very reasonable that he should, since he had
never been at Wroot before, and I have, besides that my father
might probably think it would be a hindrance to my taking Orders,
which he designed I should do on Trinity Sunday.[3] But I believe
that would have been no impediment to my journey, since I might
15 have taken Buckden[4] in Huntingdonshire, where Bishop Reynolds[5]
ordained, in my way, and by that means I might have saved the
two guineas which I am told will be the charge of Letters Dimissory.[6]

I was lately advised to read Thomas á Kempis[7] over, which I had
frequently seen, but never much looked into before. I think he must
20 have been a person of great piety and devotion, but it is my misfortune to differ from him in some of his main points. I can't think

---

[1] Orig., '22', with '8' written over the second '2'.

[2] See letter of Samuel Wesley, May 10, 1725.

[3] Ibid. In 1725 Trinity Sunday was May 23.

[4] Orig., 'taking Bugden' (from the pronunciation). Here the bishops of Lincoln had
a palace, dismantled in the nineteenth century.

[5] Richard Reynolds (1674-1743), Bishop of Lincoln from 1723 to 1743.

[6] A document issued by his bishop to a candidate for orders allowing him to seek
ordination from a bishop in another diocese. Wesley was in fact ordained deacon by
Dr. John Potter, Bishop of Oxford, in Christ Church Cathedral, on Sunday morning,
September 19, 1725.

[7] i.e. the *Imitatio Christi*, of which Thomas á Kempis (*c.* 1380-1471) was the most
likely of the reputed authors. Wesley read the work in the translation of George Stanhope (1660-1728), which was entitled *The Christian's Pattern* (see JWJ, May 24, 1738),
and adapted this title for his own many editions of the work in various forms (see
Bibliog, Nos. 4, 45, etc.).

that when God sent us into the world he had irreversibly decreed that we should be perpetually miserable in it. If it be so, the very endeavour after happiness in this life is a sin, as it is acting in direct contradiction to the very design of our creation.[1] What are become of all the innocent comforts and pleasures of life, if it [is] the intent[2] of our creator that we should never taste them? If our taking up the cross implies our bidding adieu to all joy and satisfaction, how is it reconcilable with what Solomon so expressly affirms of religion, that her ways are ways of pleasantness, and all her paths peace?[3] A fair patrimony indeed which Adam has left his sons, if they are destined to be continually wretched! And though heaven is undoubtedly a sufficient recompense for all the afflictions we may or can suffer here, yet I am afraid that argument would make few converts to Christianity if the yoke were not easy, even in this life, and such a one as gives rest,[4] at least as much as trouble.

Another of his tenets, which is indeed a natural consequence of this, is that all mirth is vain and useless, if not sinful. But why then does the Psalmist so often exhort us to rejoice in the Lord, and tell us that it becomes the just to be joyful?[5] I think one could hardly desire a more express text than that in the 68th Psalm: Let the righteous rejoice, and be glad in the Lord; let them also be merry and joyful.[6] And he seems to carry the matter as much too far on this other side afterwards, where he asserts that nothing is an affliction to a good man,[7] and that he ought to thank God even for sending him misery.[8] This, in my opinion, is contrary to God's design in afflicting us. For though he chasteneth those whom he loveth,[9] yet it is in order to humble them. And surely the method Job took in his adversity was very different from this; and yet in all that he sinned not.[10]

I hope when you are at leisure you will give me your thoughts on that subject, and set me right if I am mistaken. Pray give my service

[1] Orig., 'our ((being)) creat((ed))'.
[2] Orig., '((de[sign]))'.
[3] Prov. 3: 17.
[4] See Matt. 11: 28–30.
[5] See Ps. 33: 1 (B.C.P.): 'Rejoice in the Lord, O ye righteous: for it becometh well the just to be thankful.'
[6] Ps. 68: 3 (B.C.P.).
[7] Orig., '((the R[ighteous]))'.
[8] See possibly Pss. 9: 15, 34: 19, 37: 23–4, 119: 67, 71, 75–7.
[9] Heb. 12: 6.
[10] Job 1: 22.

to any that ask after me, and my love to my sisters, especially my
sister Emly. I suppose my brothers are gone. I am your dutiful son,

John Wesley

End by JW: 'May 1725' and 'of Kempis'   *Source*: MA, probably a draft
preserved as a reference copy, though the tearing away at an early stage of the
major portion of the sheet on which the address might have been written makes
this somewhat uncertain.

From Mrs. Susanna Wesley[1]

Wroot, June 8, 1725

5 Dear J[acky][2]

Whatever satisfaction you may think your brother Charles would find in his
journey, I believe it did in no wise answer his expectation. They were at Mr.
Berry's before they came hither, where he was much mortified with your sister
Wesley's ungentle usage of him, and for want of liberty [[for eating and drink-
10 ing]].[3] The case was somewhat mended here, for I would so far overrule in
my own house as to let h[im] [[fill his belly]],[4] but we were none of us very
easy. She resented my taking notice of h[im], and I her behaviour on the other
side. To say truth, I never heard her once speak well of him all the time they
were here; nor have I used the meanest servant I ever had in my life with less
15 civility than she observed towards him. Not to mention the rest of the children,
who were very unnecessarily provoked, in doing which she was very wrong.

I've Kempis by me, but have not read him lately, and cannot recollect the
passages you mention. But believing you do him justice, I do very positively
aver that he is extremely in the wrong in that impious—I was about to say,
20 blasphemous—suggestion, that God by an irreversible decree hath determined
any man to be miserable in this world. His intentions, as himself, are holy,
just, and good, and all the miseries incident to men here or hereafter proceed
from themselves. The case stands thus. This life is a state of probation, wherein
eternal happiness or misery are proposed to our choice, the one as the reward
25 of a virtuous, the other as a consequence of a vicious life. Man is a compound
being, a strange mixture of spirit and matter; or rather, a creature wherein
those opposite principles are united without mixture, yet each principle after
an incomprehensible manner subject to the influences of the other. The true
happiness of man, under this consideration, consists in a due subordination of

---

[1] In answer to John's of May 28.

[2] In preparing extracts from his contemporary abstract for his *A.M.* (1778), Wesley
altered this to 'Dear Son'.

[3] Wesley has transcribed this passage, like a few others, in cipher. Ursula ('Nutty')
married Samuel Wesley, Jun., about 1715. She was the daughter of the Revd. John
Berry (*c.* 1662–1730) of Barnstaple, Devon, who was apparently vicar of Watton,
Norfolk, from 1691 until his death, though records also show him as rector of Griston,
1694–9, and rector of Threxton, 1698.   [4] In cipher.

the inferior to the superior powers, of the animal to the rational nature, and of both to God. This was his original righteousness and happiness, that was lost in Adam; and to restore man to this happiness by the recovery of his original righteousness was certainly God's design in admitting him to this state of trial in the world, and of our redemption by Jesus Christ! And surely 5 this was a design truly worthy of God! And the greatest instance of mercy that even Omnipotent Goodness could exhibit to us!

As the happiness of man consists in a due subordination of the inferior to the superior powers, so the inversion of this order is the true source of human misery. There is in us all a natural propension towards the body and the world: 10 the beauty, ease, and pleasures of the world strongly charm us; the wealth and honours of the world allure us; and all, under the manage[1] of a subtle, malicious adversary, give a prodigious force to present things. And if the animal life once get the ascendant of our reason, it utterly deprives us of our moral liberty, and by consequence makes us wretched. 15

Therefore for any man to endeavour after happiness in gratifying all his bodily appetites in opposition to his reason is the greatest folly imaginable, because he seeks it where God has not designed he shall ever find [it]. Yet this is the case of most men. They live as mere animals, wholly given up to the interests and pleasures of the body; and all the use of their understanding is 20 to 'make provision for their flesh, to fulfil the lusts thereof', without the least regard to future happiness or misery. 'Tis true our eternal state lies under a vast disadvantage, in that it is future and invisible. And it requires great attention and application of mind, frequent retirement, and intense thinking, to excite our affections and beget such an habitual sense of it as is requisite to 25 enable [us] to walk steadily in the paths of virtue, in opposition to our own corrupt nature and the vicious customs and maxims of the world. Our blessed Lord, who came from heaven to save us from our sins, as well as the punishment of them, as knowing we could not be happy in either world without holiness, did not intend by commanding us to 'take up the cross' that we should 30 bid adieu to all joy and satisfaction,[2] but he opens and extends our views beyond time to eternity. He directs us where to place our joy, that it may be durable[3] as our being; not in gratifying but retrenching our sensual appetites; not in obeying but correcting our irregular passions;[4] bringing every appetite of the body and power of the soul under subjection to his laws, if we would follow 35 him to heaven.[5] And because he knew we could not do this without great contradiction to our corrupt animality, therefore he enjoins us to take up this cross, and to fight under his banner against the flesh, the world, and the devil.[6] And when by the divine grace[7] we are so far conquerors as that we never willingly offend, but still press after greater degrees of Christian perfection, sincerely 40

---

[1] Wesley reproduced this same word, now obsolete, in 1778.

[2] In 1778 Wesley added, 'indefinitely'.

[3] 1778, 'joy, how to seek satisfaction durable'.

[4] 1778, 'which is not to be found in gratifying, but retrenching our sensual appetites; not in obeying the dictates of our irregular passions, but in correcting their exorbitancy'.

[5] LB omits 'if we would follow him to heaven', without indicating the ellipsis.

[6] 1778 only, 'and to fight . . . devil'.

[7] 1778, 'And when by the grace of God's Holy Spirit'.

endeavouring to plant each virtue in our minds that may through Christ render us pleasing to God;[1] we shall then experience the truth of Solomon's assertion, 'The ways of virtue are ways of pleasantness, and all her paths are peace.'

5   I take Kempis to have been an honest, weak man, that had more zeal than knowledge, by his condemning all mirth or pleasure as sinful or useless, in opposition to so many direct and plain texts of Scripture.[2] Would you judge of the lawfulness or unlawfulness of pleasure, of the innocence or malignity of actions? Take this rule.[3] Whatever weakens your reason, impairs the tenderness

10 of your conscience, obscures your sense of God, or takes off your relish of spiritual things; in short, whatever increases the strength and authority of your body over your mind; that thing is sin to you, however innocent it may be in itself. And so on the contrary.

'Tis stupid to say nothing is an affliction to a good man. That's an affliction

15 that God makes an affliction, either to good or bad. Nor do I understand how any man can thank God for present misery. Yet do I very well know what it is to rejoice in the midst of deep affliction: not in the affliction itself, for then it must necessarily cease to be one. But in this we may rejoice, that we are in the hand of a God who never did, nor ever can exert his power in an act of

20 oppression, injustice, or cruelty! In the power of that superior wisdom which disposes all events, and has promised that all things shall work together for good (for the spiritual and eternal good) of those that love him! We may rejoice in hope that Almighty Goodness will not suffer us to be tempted above what we are able, but will with the temptation make a way to escape, that we may

25 be able to bear it.[4] In a word, we may and ought to rejoice that God has assured us he will never leave or forsake us; but if we continue faithful to him he will take care to conduct us safely through all the changes and chances of this mortal life[5] to those blessed regions of joy and immortality where sorrow and sin can never enter!

30 Your brother has brought us a heavy reckoning for you and Charles. God be merciful to us all. Prithee, J[acky], what reception did Mr. L[eybourne] give your sister Wesley? Or did you ever affront her? I have somewhat against that same man, but I hope he is good in the main, and I think humanity and good breeding are not among his wants.

35 Dear J[acky], I earnestly beseech Almighty God to bless you. Adieu!

Sources: LB, pp. 28–32, collated with *A.M.* I. 33–6 (1778), which is apparently based upon the holograph, though probably with some editorial revisions by Wesley. The letter-book version, in abbreviated longhand, with some cipher, alone contains the opening and closing paragraphs, and this forms the basis of the hypothetical holograph. Only passages from the *A.M.* which almost cer-

[1] LB omits, without indication, 'sincerely endeavouring . . . pleasing to God'.
[2] LB omits, indicating the ellipsis by a dash, 'or useless, . . . Scripture'.
[3] LB omits, indicating by a dash, 'of the innocence . . . Take this rule'.
[4] LB omits, indicating by a dash, 'that we may be able to bear it'.
[5] LB seems to abridge the original, reading: 'In a word, we may and ought to rejoice, that we are assured he will never forsake us, but if we continue faithful to him, will conduct us safely through this mortal life'.

tainly derive from the holograph are inserted in the text; those reproduced in the footnotes may either be original or Wesley's revisions; several minor differences have been completely omitted as almost certainly editorial alterations. For a discussion of the problems presented by these sources see Intro., pp. 128-9.

To Mrs. Susanna Wesley[1]

June 18, 1725

Dear mother

I am very much surprised at my sister's[2] behaviour towards my brother Charles, and wish it is not in some measure of his own procuring. She was always, as far as I could perceive, apt to resent 5 an affront, and I am afraid some reflection or other upon her, of which I have formerly heard him make several, has by accident come to her knowledge. If so, I don't at all wonder at anything which might follow. For though I believe she does not want piety, I am not of opinion she abounds in charity, having observed her some- 10 times to retaliate with great bitterness an imagined contempt or slighting expression.

She has always been particularly civil to me, ever since I was fifteen or sixteen years old, nor do I ever remember to have received an ill word from her, even to the time of her last being at Oxford. 15 We had then a pretty deal of talk together, frequently by ourselves, and sometimes about my brother Charles; and I don't know that she once intimated anything to his disadvantage, so that either she must be a very skilful dissembler, or the misunderstanding between them has took its rise very lately. 20

About a fortnight before Easter, upon my visiting Mr. Leybourne,[3] he informed me that my brother had writ to him to provide a lodging. Mr. Leybourne immediately made him a proffer of Dr. Shippen's,[4] then out of town. But a second letter of my brother's in which he accepted the proffer not being answered in three days (Mr. Ley- 25 bourne says, because he did not receive it), a third comes from my

---

[1] Replying to hers of June 8, given above.

[2] Mrs. Samuel (Ursula) Wesley: see p. 164, n. 3 above.

[3] Robert Leybourne; see p. 159 above. In that letter Mrs Wesley spelt his name 'Leybourn'; Emily and John seemed to prefer 'Leyborn', and he also appears as 'Leyborne' and 'Leybourne'.

[4] Robert Shippen (1675-1745), Master of Brasenose College, Leybourne's uncle.

brother, which indeed was a very strange one if he had met with
no other provocation. It began with words to this purpose; that he
well hoped Mr. Leybourne had been wiser than to express his anger
against his humble servant, though but by silence, since he knew it
5 would be to no purpose; and that now he need not fear his troubling
him, for lodgings would be taken for his wife and him elsewhere.
How the matter was made up I don't know, but he was with them
the day after they came to town, and almost every one of the succeeding. We were several times entertained by him, and, I thought, very
10 handsomely, nor was there the least show of dislike on either side.
But what I heard my sister say once, on our parting with Mrs.
Leybourne, made the former proceedings a little clearer: 'Thus
should we have been troubled with that girl's attendance everywhere
if we had gone to lodge at Dr. Shippen's.'[1]
15   You have so well satisfied me as to the tenets of Thomas of
Kempis that I have ventured to trouble you once more on a more
dubious occasion. I have heard one I take to be a person of good
judgment say that she would advise no one very young to read
Dr. Taylor, of Living and Dying.[2] She added that he almost put her
20 out of her senses when she was fifteen or sixteen year[s] old, because
he seemed to exclude all from being in a [way of][3] salvation who did
not come up to his rules, some of which are altogether impracticable.
A fear of being tedious will make me confine myself to one or two
instances in which I am doubtful, though several others might be
25 produced of almost equal consequence.
    In his fourth section of the second chapter, where he treats of
humility, these among others he makes necessary parts of that
virtue:

Love to be little esteemed, and be content to be slighted or undervalued.[4]
30   Take no content in praise when it is ⟨offere⟩d thee.[5]

---

[1] It is possible that the future second wife of Robert Leybourne was at this time a
maid at Dr. Shippen's, but this is pure speculation about an obscure reference. Certainly
the fact that Shippen was Leybourne's uncle constitutes an element in any explanation.
    [2] Jeremy Taylor (1613–67), D.D., Bishop of Down and Connor from 1660, whose
devotional writings made a great impact upon his age, some becoming spiritual classics,
including his *Rule and Exercises of Holy Living* (1650), and the companion *Rule and
Exercises of Holy Dying* (1651). In the preface to his *Journal* Wesley testified that these
works prompted him to keep a diary.
    [3] Added by Susanna Wesley.
    [4] See Taylor, *Works*, III. 70: 'Love to be concealed and little esteemed; be content to
want praise, never being troubled when thou art slighted or undervalued . . .'
    [5] Ibid., p. 71.

Please not thyself when disgraced by supposing thou didst deserve praise, though they understood thee not, or enviously detracted from thee.[1]

We must be sure in some sense or other to think ourselves the worst in every company where we come.[2]

Give God thanks for every weakness, deformity, or imperfection, and accept 5 it as a favour and grace, an instrument to resist pride.[3]

In the ninth section of the fourth chapter he says:

Repentance contains in it all the parts of a holy life, from our return to our death.[4]

A man can have but one proper repentance, viz. when the rite of baptism is 10 verified by God's grace coming upon us and our obedience. If after this change, if we ever fall into the contrary state, there is no place left for any more repentance.[5]

A true penitent must all the days of his life pray for pardon, and never think the work completed till he dies. Whether God has forgiven us or no we 15 know not; therefore still be sorrowful for ever having sinned.[6]

I take the more notice of this last sentence because it seems to contradict his own words in the next section, where he says that by the Lord's Supper all the members are united to one another, and to Christ the Head; the Holy Ghost confers on us the graces we 20 pray for, and our souls receive into them the seeds of an immortal nature.[7] Now surely these graces are not of so little force as that we

---

[1] Ibid., 'Make no suppletories to thyself when thou art disgraced or slighted, by pleasing thyself with supposing thou didst deserve praise, though they understood thee not, or enviously detracted from thee . . .'

[2] Ibid., p. 72.

[3] Ibid., p. 73, slightly varied. Mrs. Wesley added her own comment to the holograph: 'Weakness, deformity, or imperfection of body are not evil in themselves, but accidentally become good or evil according as they affect us and make us good or bad.' (Cf. her reply of July 21 below, p. 173.)

[4] Cf. ibid., p. 206.

[5] See ibid.: 'For we must know that there is but one repentance in a man's whole life, if repentance be taken in the proper and strict evangelical covenant sense, and not after the ordinary understanding of the word; that is, we are but once to change our whole state of life from the power of the devil . . . to the life of grace, to the possession of Jesus, to the kingdom of the gospel; and this is done in the baptism of water, or in the baptism of the Spirit, when the first rite comes to be verified by God's grace coming upon us, and by our obedience to the heavenly calling, we working together with God. After this change if ever we fall into the contrary state, and profess ourselves servants of unrighteousness, God hath made no more covenant of restitution to us; there is no place left for any more repentance, or entire change of condition, or new birth: a man can be regenerated but once. . . But if we be overtaken by infirmity, . . . so we be not in the entire possession of the devil, . . . we are in a recoverable condition . . .'

[6] Ibid., pp. 210–11, abridged.

[7] Ibid., p. 220: 'There all the members of Christ are joined with each other, and all to Christ their head; and we again renew the covenant with God in Jesus Christ, and God seals his part, and we promise for ours, and Christ unites both, and the Holy Ghost

can't perceive whether we have 'em or not; and if we dwell in Christ and Christ in us, which he will not do till we are regenerate, certainly we must be sensible of it. If his opinion be true, I must own I have always been in a great error; for I imagined that when I communi-
5 cated worthily, i.e. with faith, humility, and thankfulness, my preceding sins were *ipso facto* forgiven me—I mean, so forgiven that unless I fell into them again I might be secure of their ever rising in judgment against me, at least in the other world. But if we can never have any certainty of our being in a state of salvation, good
10 reason it is that every moment should be spent, not in joy, but fear and trembling, and then undoubtedly in this life WE ARE of all men most miserable![1]

God deliver us from such a fearful expectation as this! Humility is undoubtedly necessary to salvation, and if all these things are
15 essential to humility, who can be humble, who can be saved? Your blessing and advice will much oblige, and I hope improve, your dutiful son,

John Wesley

Address: 'For Mrs Wesley, At Wroote, To be left at ye Posthouse In Bawtry, Yorkshire'[2]   *Postmarks*: 'OXFORD', '24 [I]U', added at London, showing considerable delay   *Charges*: ((3)) (Oxford), struck through by London clerk, who added 'In all 7'   *End* by Mrs. Wesley: ' + Jacky's Letter, Humility. Answer June 1'; by Henry Moore, 'His mother's indorsement', 'To his mother on Bp. Taylor', and 'An Extract from this letter may be found in my Life of Mr. Wesley, Vol. 1, Page 126. H.M.'   *Source*: MA.

From the Revd. Samuel Wesley

Wroot, July 14, 1725

20 Son

'Tis not, I'm sure, from want of affection that I'm some letters in your debt, but because I could not yet answer yours so as to satisfy myself or you, though I hope still to do it soon enough, that is, in a few weeks.

signs both in the collation of those graces which we then pray for and exercise and receive all at once. There our bodies are nourished with the signs, and our souls with the mystery: our bodies receive into them the seed of an immortal nature, and our souls are joined with him who is the first-fruits of the resurrection, and never can die.'

   [1] See 1 Cor. 15: 19.
   [2] Bawtry was partly in Nottinghamshire (to which it was assigned in the addresses in previous letters to his mother), but chiefly in Yorkshire, as in this and subsequent addresses.

As for T. Kempis, all the world are apt to strain o' one side or t'other. And 'tis no wonder if contemplative men, especially when wrapped in a cowl, and the darkness of the seraphical divinity, and near akin, if I mistake not, to the obscure ages, when they observed how mad the bulk of the world was (as they still will be) for sensual pleasures, should run the matter too far o' the contrary 5 extreme, and attempt to persuade us to have no senses at all, or that God made 'em to very little purpose: an opinion not very improper for those who fancy they can and do believe transubstantiation.

But for all that, mortification is still an indispensable Christian duty. The world's a siren, and we must have a care of her; and if the young man will 10 'rejoice in his youth', yet 'twould not be amiss for him to take care that his joys be moderate and innocent, and in order to this sadly to remember 'that for all these things God will bring him into judgment'. I've only this to add of my friend and old companion T. Kempis: that making a pretty many grains of allowance he may be read to great advantage, and that notwithstanding all his 15 superstition and enthusiasm, 'tis almost impossible to peruse him seriously without admiring and (I think) in some measure imitating his heroic strains of humility, piety, and devotion. But I reckon you have ere this received your mother's, who has leisure to 'bolt the matter to the bran', and can write without pain, which I cannot, though I han't seen her letter. 20

As for your standing at Lincoln, I waited on Dr. Morley (and found him civiller than ever) in a day or two after I had yours. He says the election is talked of to be about, or on, St. Thomas's day; that you are welcome to stand, and that he knows but one that will stand against you, and that him you have no great reason to apprehend. (But for all that, study hard, lest the tortoise should 25 beat you; for which you'll have near a quarter of a year after you're in Orders.) The doctor says he [e'er?] keeps up his correspondence with Mr. Nicols, and I doubt not but Sam. will ply him for you, as I'll set Sir. N. Hickman, Mr. Downes, and Mr. Kirkby upon the doctor.

I'll write to the Bishop of Lincoln again. You shan't want a black coat as soon 30 as I've any WHITE, etc.

You may transcribe any *part* of my letter to Mr. N. Hoole (but not the whole) for your own private use;[1] neither lend it; but any friend may read it in your chamber. I'm not yet in haste for it. Master St. Chrysostom, our Articles and form of ordination. Bear up stoutly against the world, etc. Keep a good, an 35 honest, and a pious heart. Pray hard, and watch hard, and I'm persuaded your quarantin is almost at an end, and all shall be well. However, nothing shall be wanting to make it so that lies in the power of your loving father,

Sam Wesley

I'll write to your brother Sam. next post. Why do you never write to him? 40

Source: Wes Ch. Cf. Wesley's transcription of all except the summarized fourth paragraph in LB, pp. 16–17, and of the second paragraph, edited, in *A.M.* I. 30 (1778).

[1] See p. 158, n. 2, above.

From Mrs. Susanna Wesley[1]

Wroot, July 21 [1725]

Dear J[acky]

Whether Charles have given occasion for her contemptuous usage or no I can't determine; but h[is] time of bondage is now near expired, and if it be'nt
5 h[is] own fault h[is] future life may be easier . . . 'Tis well your sister has ever been civil to you, and would have you also so to her. But never put it in the power of that w[oman] to hurt you; stand upon your guard, and converse with caution; and I wish Mr. L[eybourne] would take the same advice. He has in my opinion done much to oblige those that have not the most grateful sense of his kindness.
10 Though I have a great deal of unpleasant business, am infirm and but slow of understanding, yet 'tis a pleasure to me to correspond with you upon religious subjects; and if it may be of the least advantage to you, I shall greatly rejoice. May what is sown in weakness be raised in power!

I know little or nothing of Dr. Taylor's Holy Living and Dying, having not
15 seen it above twenty years; but I think 'tis generally well esteemed, therefore can't judge of the rules you suppose impracticable. Of humility I'll tell you my thoughts as briefly as I can.

What he calls humility is not the virtue itself, but the accidental effects of it, which may in some instances, and must in others, be separated from it.
20 Humility is the mean between pride, or an overvaluing ourselves, on one side, and a base, abject temper on the other. It consists in an habitual disposition to think meanly of ourselves, which disposition is wrought in us by a true knowledge of God, his supreme, essential glory, his absolute, immense perfection of being! A just sense of our dependence on and past offences against him, together
25 with a consciousness of our present infirmities and frailty.

In proportion to the sense we have of God's infinite majesty and glory, and our own vileness and unworthiness, this disposition will be stronger or weaker. And those who are arrived to a great degree of Christian perfection, that know and are assured by reason and experience that there is none good but God, will
30 be sure to hold him in the highest estimation, and are generally observed to be the most humble and mortified of men. Such persons as these make the glory of God their principal aim in all their actions; and to please him is to them more eligible than to enjoy the esteem of the whole universe.

They will be very well content to be slighted or undervalued,[2] provided
35 their conscience do not reproach them, and the honour of God be unconcerned in the case. But where it is concerned none are more wary in their outward deportment, lest they give occasion of scandal to the profane, or of stumbling to the weak. None are more careful to observe, 'Whatsoever things are lovely, whatsoever things are of good report', and if through surprise or inadvertency
40 they have said or done amiss, such slips commonly make them more watchful and humble ever after.

[1] In answer to John's of June 18.
[2] Here Mrs. Wesley begins to deal point by point with Wesley's quotations from Taylor.

As we should not covet to be little esteemed, because a fair reputation is of excellent service in promoting the glory of God, so neither should we desire the praise of our good actions to terminate in ourselves; for of a right it belongs to him of whose grace it is that we either will or do according to his good pleasure.

If we are in disgrace, either we deserve it or we do not. If we do, his caution 5 is good; if not, he is wrong; for we certainly may, and I believe should be pleased with consciousness of our innocence.

I will not say we must judge of ourselves as he directs, but believe there are some who are much inclined to think themselves not only the worst in a particular company, but worse than any in the world. For being strongly pressed on 10 by thirst after universal righteousness, they behold their own deficiencies with great severity: every mote in their own eye appears a beam, while every beam in their brother's eye seems to them as a mote.

Weakness, deformity, and imperfection of body are not moral evils, and may accidentally become good to us.[1] Yet surely they are not to be desired, for 15 strength and comeliness are valuable blessings, may be of great use, and ought to be enjoyed with thankfulness. If they prove incentives to pride, 'tis our own fault: a humble man will improve all those advantages for God's service, and a ⟨. . .⟩

Source: LB, pp. 32–4. The following four pages are missing, apparently having contained both the remainder of this influential letter (for which see John's reply of July 29), her reply of Aug. 2 (John's answer to which of Aug. 11 is missing), and the beginning of her next important letter of Aug. 18, for which see below. (That the four pages were lost at an early period is implied by John's misdating the Aug. 18 letter as July 18 in his transcription for the *A.M.*)

To Mrs. Susanna Wesley[2]

[July 29, 1725] 20

Dear mother

I must in the first place beg you to excuse my writing so small, since I shall not otherwise have time to make an end before the post goes out—as I am not sure I shall, whether I make haste or no.

The King of Poland has promised what satisfaction shall be 25 thought requisite in the affair of Thorn;[3] so that all Europe seemed now disposed for peace as well as England, though the Spaniards

[1] See her endorsement added to the fifth passage quoted in Wesley's letter, p. 169.
[2] Replying to her letter of July 21, 1725, and apparently answered by hers of Aug. 18.
[3] August II, Elector of Saxony, proved a weak successor to John Sobieski as king of Poland, so that he became a puppet of Russia. One among many turmoils was a religious riot in Thorn involving Jesuit students and Protestants, for which several leading citizens were executed in December 1724. This caused an outcry from the Protestant powers in Europe, including strong criticism from the English minister at Ratisbon.

daily plunder our merchantmen as fast as they can catch them in the West Indies.[1]

You have much obliged me by your thoughts on Dr. Taylor, especially with respect to humility, which is a point he does not
5 seem to me sufficiently to clear. As to absolute humility (if I may venture to make a distinction which I don't remember to have seen in any author), consisting in a mean opinion of ourselves considered simply, or with respect to God alone, I can readily join with his opinion. But I am more uncertain as to comparative, if I may so
10 term it; and think some plausible reasons may be alleged to show it is not in our power, and consequently not a virtue, to think ourselves the worst in every company.

We have so invincible an attachment to truth already perceived that it is impossible for us to disbelieve it. A distinct perception
15 commands our assent, and the will is under a moral necessity of yielding to it. It is not therefore in every case a matter of choice whether we will believe ourselves worse than our neighbour or no, since we may distinctly perceive the truth of this proposition, He is worse than me; and then the judgment is not free. One, for instance,
20 who is in company with a free-thinker or other person signally debauched in faith and practice, can't avoid knowing himself to be the better of the two; those propositions extorting our assent, An atheist is worse than a believer; a man who endeavours to please God is better than he who defies him.

25 If a true knowledge of God be necessary to absolute humility, a true knowledge of our neighbour should be necessary to comparative. But to judge oneself the worst of all men implies a want of such knowledge. No knowledge can be where there is not certain evidence, which we have not, whether we compare ourselves with
30 acquaintances or strangers. In the one case we have only imperfect evidence, unless we can see through the heart and reins;[2] in the other we have none at all. So that the best [that] can be said of us in this particular, allowing the truth of the premises, is that we have been in a pious error—if at least we may yield so great a point to free-
35 thinkers as to own any part of piety to be grounded on a mistake.

Again, this kind of humility can never be well-pleasing to God, since it does not flow from faith, without which it is impossible to

---

[1] In an attempt to recover her lost possessions in the New World, Spain was seeking to monopolize commerce by exercising rigorously the right of search on the high seas.
[2] See Ps. 7: 9, etc.

please him.[1] Faith is a species of belief, and belief is defined, an assent to a proposition upon rational grounds. Without rational grounds there is therefore no belief, and consequently no faith.

That we can never be so certain of the pardon of our sins as to be assured they will never rise up against us I firmly believe. We know 5 that they will infallibly do so if ever we apostatize, and I am not satisfied what evidence there can be of our final perseverance, till we have finished our course. But I am persuaded we may know if we are *now* in a state of salvation, since that is expressly promised in the Holy Scriptures to our sincere endeavours,[2] and we are surely 10 able to judge of our own sincerity.

As I understand faith to be an assent to any truth upon rational grounds,[3] I don't think it possible, without perjury, to swear I believe anything unless I have rational grounds for my persuasion. Now that which contradicts reason can't be said to stand on rational 15 grounds; and such undoubtedly is every proposition which is incompatible with the divine justice or mercy. I can therefore never say I believe such a proposition; since 'tis impossible to assent upon reasonable evidence where it is not in being.

What then shall I say of predestination? An everlasting purpose 20 of God to deliver some from damnation does, I suppose, exclude all from that deliverance who are not chosen. And if it was inevitably decreed from eternity that such a determinate part of mankind should be saved, and none beside them, a vast majority of the world were only born to eternal death, without so much as a possibility of 25 avoiding it. How is this consistent with either the divine justice or mercy? Is it merciful to ordain a creature to everlasting misery? Is it just to punish man for a crime which he could not but commit? How is man, if necessarily determined to one way of acting, a free agent? To lie under either a physical or a moral necessity is entirely 30 repugnant to human liberty. But that God ⟨should be⟩ the author of sin and injustice, which must, I think, be the consequence of main⟨taining⟩ this opinion, is a contradiction to the clearest ideas we have of the divine ⟨natur⟩e and perfections.

I call faith an assent upon rational grounds because I hold divine 35 testimony to be the most reasonable of all evidence whatever. Faith

---

[1] Heb. 11: 6.

[2] See Rom. 8: 16, 1 Cor. 2: 12, etc., quoted in Wesley's sermons on 'The Witness of the Spirit' (Vol. 1 of this edition).

[3] For this definition, from Richard Fiddes, see below, pp. 186, 188.

must necessarily at length be resolved into reason. God is true, therefore what he says is true. *He* hath said this; therefore this is true. When anyone can bring me more reasonable propositions than these, I am ready to assent to them. Till then it will be highly
5 unreasonable to change my opinion.

I used to think that the difficulty of predestination might be solved by supposing that it was indeed decreed from eternity that a remnant should be elected, but that it was in every man's power to be of that remnant. But the words of our Article will not bear
10 that sense.[1] I see no other way but to allow that some may be saved who were not always of the number of the elected. Your sentiments on this point, especially where I am in an error, will much oblige, and I hope improve, your dutiful son,

John Wesley

15 July 29

Address: 'For Mrs Wesley at Wroote. To be left At the Post-house In Bawtry, Yorkshire'   *Postmark*: '31 IY'   *Charges*: ((3)), 'In all 7'. On the back of the cover is an '8', apparently implying that in accordance with some mutual arrangement made with the Wesley household this letter, not having been collected within an agreed period, was being delivered to Epworth at an additional charge of 1*d*.   *End* by JW (?): '1725', and in a later hand, 'J. Wesley, July 29, +'   *Source*: MA.

From the Revd. Samuel Wesley

Wroot, Aug. 2, 1725

Son

. . . If you be but what you write, you and I should be happy: and that would much alleviate my misfortune in her whom I have this day lost—though she's
20 not so well as dead[2] . . . I was at Gainsbro' last week to wait on Sir John Thorold, and shall again, by God's leave, tomorrow, to endeavour to make way for you from that quarter.[3]

As for the gentlemen candidates you write of . . ., does anybody think the devil

---

[1] Article 17 of the Thirty-nine Articles.

[2] Wesley's older sister, Hetty. On April 7 Emily told John, 'We have heard nothing of her for three months'. She apparently returned to Wroot, engaged in another love affair, was betrayed, on the evidence of this letter eloped, on Oct. 13 married (at Haxey) William Wright of Louth, had her infant baptized at Louth on Feb. 18, 1726—only to bury her on Dec. 27 that same year.

[3] The fellowship at Lincoln College which Wesley eventually secured had become vacant on May 3, 1725, by the resignation of John Thorold, son of Sir John Thorold of Gainsborough.

is dead, or so much as asleep, or that he has no agents left? 'Tis a very callow
virtue, sure, that can't bear being laughed at . . . I think our Captain and Master
endured something more for us, before he entered into glory; and unless we . . .
track his steps, in vain do we hope to share that glory with him. Nor shall any
who sincerely endeavour to serve him, either in turning others to righteousness, 5
or keeping them steadfast in it, lose their reward. Nor can you have better
directions (except Timothy and Titus) than Chrysostom *De Sacerdotio*, and
our Form of Ordination—and 'God forbid that I should ever cease to pray
for you'! I hope with more success than I've done for your wretched sister, at
whose elopement this day your mother was a little shocked, but has partly 10
recovered it . . . Naught else but blessing from your loving father,

Sam Wesley

Have a care of giving characters in your letters.

Source: LB, p. 15.

From the Revd. Samuel Wesley

Aug. 12, 1725, Bawtry

Dear son 15
   Two minutes since I had yours to H[etty];[1] and since she's lost to me, as
in my last, . . . I opened it. I'm glad I saw it, and this is my answer.
   I don't know one of my children whom I would not suffer everything for in
this world to make 'em happy. I hope I have given evidence of the same, and
shall still continue to do so, whether or not they are sensible of it. 20
   Your [[once]] sister and [[my]] d[aughter], H[etty],[2] is no exception to this
rule, though I've had little hopes of her—I consider what I write—since she has
been half a year old. (A character of her.)[3] Yet though I knew this, and she was
returned upon me, after I had been twice at the charge of setting her out handsomely (I never reproached her for coming home again, but told her she was 25
welcome to stay), as she has often acknowledged, and would throw the fault on
her mother, whom I could [not] blame for being heartily weary of her.
   But O[h]! too much of this! Gangrene, farewell! And mayst thou never cause
me any pain hereafter . . . Won't my s[on] J[ohn] give me more comfort?
   As for your business at L[incoln College], I think it stands pretty fair . . . 30
Sir John Thorold has writ to his son, Mr. Rainer to his. I hope the doctor is
firm.
   No more yet (I wish I could) from your loving father,

Sam Wesley

Source: LB, p. 14.

   [1] Cf. previous letter.
   [2] Partly in cipher, viz. 'Yr .mb. S - n‿ D, H'.
   [3] Wesley summarizes a section which he omits.

From Mrs. Susanna Wesley[1]

Aug. 18, 1725

⟨. . .⟩ but still insist on that single point in Dr. Taylor, of thinking ourselves the worst in every company; though the necessity of thinking so is not inferred by my definition. But this I perceive much affects you, and you can't well digest
5 it. Therefore you employ your wit in making distinctions and formal arguments; which arguments I shall reply to after I've observed that we differ in our notions of the virtue [of humility] itself. You will have it consist in thinking meanly of ourselves, I in an habitual disposition to think meanly of ourselves; which I take to be more comprehensive, because it extends to all the cases when that
10 virtue can be exercised, either in relation to God, ourselves, or our neighbour, and renders the distinction of absolute and comparative perfectly needless.

We may in many instances think very meanly of ourselves without being humble. Nay, sometimes our very pride will lead us to condemn ourselves, as when we have said or done anything which lessens that esteem of men we
15 earnestly covet. As to what you call absolute humility with respect to God, what greater matter [is][2] there in that . . . had we no more than a mere speculative knowledge of that Awful Being, and only considered him as the Creator and Sovereign Lord of the universe; yet since that first notion of him implies that he is a God of absolute and infinite perfection and glory, we can't contemplate
20 that glory, or conceive h[im] present, without the most exquisite diminution of ourselves before him!

The other part of your definition I can't approve, because I think all those comparisons are rather the effects of pride than humility.

The truth is the proper object of the understanding, and all truths, as such,
25 agree in one common excellence; yet there are some truths which are comparatively of so small value, because of little or no use, that 'tis no matter whether ever we know them or not. Nay, in some instances 'tis better never to know them. Among those I rank the right answer to that question, whether our neighbour or we be worse. Of what importance can this enquiry be to us?
30 Comparisons in this case are very odious, or do most certainly proceed from some bad principle in those that make them. So far should we be from reasoning upon the case, that we must not permit ourselves to entertain such thoughts, but if they ever intrude, should reject them with abhorrence.

Suppose then in some cases the truth of that proposition, My neighbour is
35 worse than me, . . . be ever so evident, yet what does it avail? Since two persons in different respects may be [both] better and worse than each other. As in your own instance. One who in company with a free-thinker, or other person signally debauched in faith and practice (we must suppose he is debauched in neither) can't avoid knowing himself to be the better of the two. He may be so
40 in appearance; but if he trust in his own righteousness, and value himself upon it, he may appear more vile and contemptible in the sight of God than the other, merely on account of his self-idolizing pride. Though the Pharisee might speak

---

[1] Apparently answering John's letter of July 29, even though other letters had meantime passed between them. [2] Orig., 'in'.

very truly with respect to many of his neighbours when he said, 'I am not as other men are,' and probably his outward behaviour was more regular and decent than the poor publican's had been, whom perhaps he despised because he knew he had been a scandalous offender; yet we find the humility of the publican . . . rendered him acceptable to his Maker, while the Pharisee returned 5 unjustified.

If we are not strictly obliged to think ourselves the worst in every company, I am perfectly sure that a man sincerely humble will be afraid of thinking himself the best in any, though it should be his lot (for it can never be his choice) to fall into the company of notorious sinners. 'Who makes them to differ?' or 10 'What hast thou that thou hast not received?' is sufficient, if well adverted to, to humble us, and silence all aspiring thoughts and self-applauses; and may instruct us to ascribe our preservation from enormous offences to the sovereign grace of God, and not to our own natural purity or strength.

There's nothing plainer than that a free-thinker, as a free-thinker, an atheist, 15 as an atheist, is worse in that respect than a believer, as a believer. But if that believer's practice does not correspond with his faith . . . he is worse than an infidel . . .

You are somewhat mistaken in your notion of faith. All faith is an assent, but all assent is not faith. Some truths are self-evident, and we assent to them 20 because they are so. Others, after a regular and formal process of reason, by way of deduction from some self-evident principle, gain our assent; and this is not properly faith but science. Some again we assent to, not because they are self-evident, or because we have attained the knowledge of them in a regular method, by a train of arguments, but because they have been revealed to us, 25 either by God or man, and these are the proper objects of faith.

The true measure of faith is the authority of the revealer, the weight of which always holds proportion with our conviction of his ability and integrity. Divine faith is an assent to whatever God has revealed to us, because he has revealed it. And this is that virtue of faith which is one of the two conditions of our salvation 30 by Jesus Christ . . . But this matter is so fully and accurately explained by Bishop Pearson (under 'I Believe') that I shall say no more of it . . .

I have often wondered that men should be so vain, to amuse themselves with searching into the decrees of God, which no human wit can fathom; and do not rather employ their time and powers in working out their salvation, and making 35 their own calling and election sure. Such studies tend more to confound than inform the understanding, and young people had better let them alone. But since I find you've some scruples concerning our Article of Predestination, I'll tell you my thoughts of the matter, and if they satisfy not, you may desire your father's direction, who is surely better qualified for a casuist than me. 40

The doctrine of predestination, as maintained by the rigid Calvinists, is very shocking, and ought utterly to be abhorred; because it directly charges the most h[oly] God with being the author of sin. And I think you reason very well and justly against it. For 'tis certainly inconsistent with the justice and goodness of God to lay any man under either a physical or moral necessity of committing 45 sin, and then punish him for doing it. 'Far be this from thee, O Lord . . . Shall not the Judge of all the earth do right?'

I do firmly believe that God from eternity hath elected some to everlasting

life. But then I humbly conceive that this election is founded on his foreknow-ledge, according to that in the 8th of Romans: 'Whom he did foreknow, he also did predestinate, to be conformed to the image of his Son . . . Moreover, whom he did predestinate, them he also called . . . And whom he called, them he also
5 justified, and whom he justified, them he also glorified.'

Whom in his eternal prescience God saw would make a right use of their powers, and accept of offered mercy, . . . he did predestinate, adopt for his chil-dren, his peculiar treasure. And that they might be conformed to the image of his Son, he called them to himself, by his external Word, the preaching of the gospel,
10 and internally by his Holy Spirit. Which call they obeying by faith and repen-tance, he justifies them, absolves them from the guilt of all their sins, and acknowledges them as just persons, through the merits and mediation of Jesus Christ. And having thus justified, he receives them to glory—to heaven.

This is the sum of what I believe concerning predestination, which I think
15 is agreeable to the analogy of faith, since it never derogates from God's free grace, nor impairs the liberty of man. Nor can it with more reason be supposed that the prescience of God is the cause that so many finally perish, than that our knowing the sun will rise tomorrow is the cause of its rise.

I am greatly troubled at your [[increasing debts]][1] Your brother writes for
20 your father to get you £60 before you stand for the fellowship . . . Alas!

I shall not cease to pray for you, that God would sanctify all conditions, and deliver you out of present distress.

J[acky], may God Almighty bless thee!

Source: LB, pp. 39–43 (cf. notes on the source of her letter of July 21). The closing paragraphs on predestination were printed by Wesley in *A.M.* 1778, pp. 36–8, slightly revised.

From the Revd. Samuel Wesley

Wroot, Aug. 27, 1725

25 Dear son

Thanks be to God, we are all well (*excepta excipienda*[2]), who I doubt never will be so.

I send the certificate on t'other side,[3] and will be soon with Mr. Downes at Dr. Morley's. Your loving father,

30   Sam Wesley

[1] In cipher.

[2] 'The necessary exception being made', i.e. Hetty.

[3] Stev., p. 123, gives the likely form of this certificate of baptism necessary for Wesley's ordination:

'Wroote, August 21st, 1725
John Wesley, of Lincoln College, Oxford, was twenty-two years old the 17th of June last, having been baptized a few hours after his birth by me
Samuel Wesley, Rector of Epworth.'

There are several discrepancies in this, however, and Stevenson is notoriously unreliable.

You need not show t'other side unless 'tis asked for. Say you are in the twenty-third current.

Source: LB, p. 15.

From the Revd. Samuel Wesley[1]

Bawtry, Sept. 1, 1725

Son!
    I came hither today because I can't be at rest till I make you easier. I could 5
not possibly manufacture any money for you here sooner than next Saturday;
when, I think, I shan't miss on't, and design to wait on Dr. Morley with Mr.
Downes on Monday next, and try if I can prevail with the doctor to return you
eight pounds, which I shall then pay him (to assist you for the charge of the
ordination), and I hope bigger sums afterwards, between this and Christmas, as 10
well as after, though I'm now just struggling myself for life. This eight pounds
you may depend on the next week, or the week after.
    I like your way of thinking and arguing, and yet must say I'm a little afraid
on't. He that believes *without* or *against* reason is half a Papist, or enthusiast:
he that would mete revelation by his own shallow reason is either half a deist 15
or an heretic. O my dear, steer clear between this Scylla and Charybdis, and
God will bless you, and you shall ever be beloved by (as you'll ever be a comfort
to) your affectionate father,

Sam Wesley

    If you have any scruples about any part of revelation, or the scheme of the 20
Church of England, which I think is exactly agreeable to it, I think I can answer
'em.

Address: 'For Mr John Wesley, Comoner of Christ-Church, Oxford'
Postmarks: 'BAWTRY', '3 SE'   *Charges*: '4' (erased), and 'In all 7'   *End
by JW*: 'Sept. 1. 25'   *Source*: MA; cf. LB, p. 17, slightly abridged.

It seems highly likely that he carelessly concocted an earlier version of a similar certificate
written by the rector for the occasion of John's ordination as priest, which Adam Clarke
'transcribed *literatim* into Wesley's diary notebook for 1782-90' (see letter of Sept. 5,
1728):

'Epworth, Augt. 23, 1728
John Wesley, M.A., Fellow of Lincoln Colledge, was twenty-five year old the 17th of
June last, having bin baptiz'd a few hours after his birth, By mee,

Saml. Wesley
Rector of Epworth
(In fact the bishop's transcripts prove that Samuel Wesley was confusing John Wesley
with a former child, John Benjamin, thus hastily baptized. John himself was baptized
July 3, 1703, a week after his birth, and with no second name.)

[1] Apparently answering John's of Aug. 18, to which it offers some clues.

From the Revd. Samuel Wesley

Gainsbro', Sept. 7 [1725]

Dear son J[ohn]

With much ado you see I'm for once as good as my word, and carry Dr. Morley's note to the Bursar . . . I hope to send you more, and believe by the
5 same hand. God fit you for your great work. Fast, watch and pray, believe, love and endure, and be happy. Towards which you shall never want the most ardent prayers of your affectionate father,

Sam Wesley

Source: LB, p. 18.

From the Revd. Samuel Wesley

Wroot, Oct. 19 [1725]

10 Dear son

I had yours of the 20th ult., with the welcome news that you were in Deacon's Orders. I pray God you may so improve in them as to be in due time fit for an higher station.

If you formerly gave any occasion for what's said of you at L[incoln], you
15 must bear it patiently, if not joyfully. But be sure never to return the like treatment . . . I've done what I could; do you the same, and rest the whole with Providence.

The hard words in our creeds are of the same nature with an anathema, whose point is levelled against obstinate heretics. Is not even schism a work of
20 the flesh, and therefore damnable? But is there not a distinction between what is wilful and what may be in some measure involuntary? God knows, and doubt-less will make a difference! We don't so well know it, and therefore must leave that to him, but keep to the rules which he has given us . . .[1]

As to the main of the cause, the best way to deal with our adversaries is to
25 turn the war and their own vaunted arms against them. From balancing the schemes it will appear that there are many irreconcilable absurdities and con-tradictions in theirs, but none such, though indeed some difficulties, in ours . . . To instance but in one of a side . . . They can never prove a contradiction in our Three and One, unless we affirmed 'em to be so in the same respect, which
30 every child knows we do not. We can prove there is One in a Creature's being a Creator, which they assert of our Lord.

If you turn your thoughts and studies this way, you may do God and his

---

[1] Wesley's version in 1778: 'You seem staggered at the severe words in the Athanasian Creed. Consider, their point is levelled against, only against, obstinate heretics. A distinction is undoubtedly to be made between what is wilful, and what is in some measure involuntary. God certainly will make a difference. We don't so well know it. We therefore must leave that to him, and keep to the rule which he has given us.'

Church good service . . . To his blessed protection I commit you, and am your
loving, etc.

S. W.

Source: LB, pp. 18–19. The third and fourth paragraphs were published by
Wesley in *A.M.*, 1778, p. 31, the third paragraph probably being heavily edited
rather than based upon the holograph.

From Mrs. Susanna Wesley

Wroot, Nov. 10th, 1725

Dear Jacky

I believe I've received three letters from you since I wrote to you; but the
dismal situation of our affairs, which has found me full employment at home,
and my unwillingness to burden you, prevented my writing hitherto. But I will
now look over your letters, and reply to each if there be occasion.

Your first of Aug. 4th requires no answer, only there's one passage in it
which I don't well understand. You say Berkeley has convinced you 'that there
is no such thing as matter in the world, if by the real existence of matter is
meant a subsistence exterior to the mind, and distinct from its being perceived'.
What does he mean by imperceptible matter?[1]

Your second bears date Aug. 24th, wherein you are satisfied about humility;
and I wish you had also a better notion of that faith which is proposed to us as
a condition of salvation. I think Pearson's definition of divine or saving faith
is good, and no way defective. For though the same thing may be an object of
faith as revealed, and an object of reason as deducible from rational principles,
yet I insist upon it that the virtue of faith, by which through the merits of our
Redeemer we must be saved, is an assent to the truth of whatever God hath been
pleased to reveal, because he hath revealed it, and not because we understand it.
Thus St. Paul, 'By faith we understand that the world was made'—q.d.,[2]
rejecting the various conjectures of the heathen, and not resting upon the testimony of natural reason, but relying on the authority of God, we give a full
assent to what he hath been pleased to reveal unto us concerning the creation of
the world. Now the reason why this faith is required is plain, because otherwise
we do not give God the glory of his truth, but prefer our weak and fallible
understanding before his eternal word, in that we will believe the one rather
than the other. If you will but read Bishop Beveridge on faith, and repentance,
Vol. 7th, you'll find him a better divine than Fiddes.[3]

I can't recollect what book I recommended to you, but I highly approve your
care to search into the grounds and reasons of our most holy religion, which
you may do if your intention be pure, and yet retain the integrity of faith.
Nay, the more you study on that subject, the more reason you will find to

[1] See Wesley's reply to this letter, Nov. 22.

[2] *quasi dicat*, 'as if he were to say'.

[3] In his LB transcript Wesley summarized this para., 'Of Hylas and Philonous, and
the nature of faith'. See letter of Nov. 22.

depend on the veracity of God; inasmuch as your perceptions of that awful Being will be clearer, and you will more plainly discern the congruity that there is between the ordinances and precepts of the gospel, and right reason; nor is it a hard matter to prove that the whole system of Christianity is grounded thereon.

5   If it be a weak virtue that can't bear being laughed at, I am very sure 'tis a strong and well confirmed virtue that can stand the test of a brisk buffoonery. I doubt there are too many instances of people that, being well inclined, have yet made shipwreck of faith and a good conscience, merely through a false modesty, and because they could not bear the raillery of their companions. Some young
10 persons have a natural excess of bashfulness, others are so tender of what they call honour that they can't endure to be made a jest of. Nay, I've often observed that those very people which will on all occasions take the liberty to play upon their neighbours are of all living the worst able to bear being so used themselves. I would therefore advise young persons in their beginning of a Christian course
15 to shun the company of profane wits as they would the plague, or poverty; and let 'em never contract an intimacy with any but such as have a good sense of religion. And if 'tis their hap to live where few of that character can be found, let them learn the art of living alone; and when once they are masters of that rare secret, and know how to converse with God, and themselves, they'll want
20 no other company. For properly speaking no man wants what he can be happy without.

   I now proceed to answer your last, of Oct. 14th. And in this you desire me to speak on a subject above my comprehension. I do not mean as to the nature of zeal, for that is easily defined; but to assign precisely every instance when
25 it is allowable, or we are required to show that zeal to the world needs a better head and pen than mine. However, I'll offer some hints, which you may correct or improve by your own meditation.

   [The preceding paragraph, and fourteen lengthy ones which follow, were summed up in his transcript in LB by Wesley thus: 'Of the nature, properties,
30 and expressions of zeal'. They occupy almost three-quarters of the letter. A few passages only are given here.]

   [. . .] The habit of this zeal is always necessary, being indeed inseparable from our love to God; but the visible expressions of it must be ever under due restriction, always according to knowledge, and strictly guarded by prudence and
35 Christian charity; for without restriction and such a guard 'tis the most pernicious thing in nature, and has done more mischief in the world than even licentiousness or infidelity [. . .]

   [. . .] Prudence is more especially concerned in the manner of our speaking or acting, either for God or our neighbour. For be our intention never so good, our
40 zeal ever so fervent, unless we perform all after a due manner we shall not compass our design. If we would serve Almighty God, we must do it with that vigour, that cheerful gravity, and becoming reverence, as ⟨the⟩ importance of the work requires. If we are about to instruct the ignor⟨ant let⟩ us proceed with so much seriousness that they may see we are well appriz⟨ed of the⟩
45 truths we teach, and are ourselves under the same impressions we endea⟨vour to⟩ make on their minds. If we would confirm the weak, it should be done witho⟨ut any⟩ reproach, and with that tenderness, and arguments so well adapted to their cas⟨e,⟩ as may serve to convince them that we are really con-

cerned in their safety and happiness. If we reprove the sinner, let us avoid pride and vainglory, and be careful lest we fall into indecent passion, or be guilty of unchristian revilings, and contemptuous language, which would probably prove a greater sin in us than that we are about to reprehend in another. As we should never undertake a matter of this nature without desiring to do good, so we ought by all proper methods to make the person spoken to sensible of that desire; for we gain a great point if we can persuade them that we really bear them goodwill, and have no design to upbraid, much less expose them, but merely to do 'em good.

The second thing mentioned as a guard of our zeal was charity, which I shall briefly speak of, and so conclude.

Love to God, and love to our neighbour, which often in Scripture is called charity, is, or ought to be, the principle and rule of all our thoughts, words, and actions, with respect to either. And whatever we do for God or man that flows not from this principle, and is not squared by this rule, is wrong, as wanting a good foundation, and a right conduct [. . .].

I have not time to discourse on divine charity, but shall only mention a few instances wherein charity must correct our zeal [. . .].

And first, we must never conclude any man so bad as 'tis possible for him to be; nor think because he is guilty of many sins that therefore he must be guilty of all; nay, we should not judge that the most profligate sinner cannot possibly amend [. . .]

Secondly, our charity should strictly confine our zeal within the bounds of truth and soberness. We must not lie for God, nor falsely accuse our brethren; nor in a pretended zeal run into censoriousness and evil-speaking, crimes utterly to be abhorred of all good men.

Thirdly, no pretence of zeal should make us lay aside our humanity, or exercise any act of injustice or cruelty towards our neighbour. Nor must we suffer a bad man to perish for want of our relief [. . .]

Yet after all that can be said, though prudence and charity should correct the irregular motions of our zeal, they must by no means extinguish it. But we must keep that sacred fire alive in our breasts, and carefully lay hold of all opportunities of serving God, nor should we tamely endure to hear his glorious name blasphemed in execrable oaths or impious discourses without expressing a just indignation against such offences. And if we happen to be in presence of those that either are so superlatively wicked or too much superior to admit of reproof, we may find some way to testify our dislike of such conversation, and leave their company.

I've room to add no more but that I send you my love and blessing.

S. W.

Your sisters send their love.

I've just received a letter from you, which I'll answer if I've leisure.

Your brother Wright fetches your sister Hetty from hence the end of this week.

Address: 'For The Revd. Mr John Wesley, Commoner of Christ-Church, Oxon'   *Postmarks*: 'BAWTRY', '15 NO'   *Charges*: ((4)), 'In All 7'
Source: MA; cf. LB, pp. 44–5.

To Mrs. Susanna Wesley

Ch[rist] Church, Nov. 22, 1725

Dear mother

I must beg leave to assure you that before I received yours I was
fully convinced of two things: first that Mr. Berkeley's notion,[1]
5 which at first sight appeared very plausible, as indeed an ingenious
disputant will make almost anything appear, was utterly groundless,
and that he either advanced a palpable falsehood, or said nothing at
all. And secondly that I had been under a mistake in adhering to that
definition of faith which Dr. Fiddes sets down as the only true one.[2]
10 Mr. Berkeley's reasons, on a second reading, I found to be mere
fallacy, though very artfully disguised. From one or two you may
easily judge of what kind his other arguments are. He introduces
Hylas charging Philonous with scepticism for denying the existence
of sensible things, to which Philonous replies that if denying the
15 existence of sensible things constitute a sceptic he will prove those
to be ⟨sceptics⟩ who assert sensible things to be material: for if all
sensible things are material, then if it be proved that nothing material
exists, it will follow that no sensible thing exists; and that nothing
material can exist he undertakes to demonstrate.[3]
20 Matter, says he (by which you must mean something sensible, or
else how came you to know of it?) you define a solid, extended
substance, the existence of which is exterior to the mind, and does

---

[1] See his letter of Aug. 4, quoted in his mother's of Nov. 10: 'that there is no such
thing as matter in the world . . .'. George Berkeley, D.D. (1685–1753), Bishop of Cloyne
from 1734, is famous for his metaphysical teaching, which attacked materialism by
claiming that material objects only exist for us because they are perceived (*esse est
percipi*), and only continue in existence because they are in the mind of God. This theory,
outlined in his *Treatise concerning the Principles of Human Knowledge* (1710), was expounded in more popular form in *Three Dialogues between Hylas and Philonous* (1713).
It was probably the second edition of the latter work, published in 1725, which Wesley
began to read (and also to 'collect', or epitomize) early in August this year.

[2] Richard Fiddes (1671–1725), whose *Body of Divinity*, Part I (1718), earned him
an Oxford D.D., though he was best known for his *Life of Cardinal Wolsey* (1724).
Wesley began reading and 'collecting' Fiddes in July 1725, and first used his definition
of faith, as 'an assent to any truth upon rational grounds', in his letter of July 29.

[3] The summaries of Berkeley's arguments which Wesley gives in this letter are not
quotations from the *Three Dialogues*, but ideas derived from his reading of the work as a
whole, set down without consulting the original, but only his précis of it. Pertinent
passages for some of Wesley's paragraphs may be cited, however. For this cf. Berkeley,
Works (ed. A. A. Luce and T. E. Jessop, London, Nelson), Vol. II (1949), pp. 172–3,
206, and for the succeeding three pp. 216–17, 214–15, 232–3.

in no ways depend on its being perceived. But if it appear that no sensible thing is exterior to the mind, your supposition of a sensible substance independent on it is a plain inconsistency.

Sensible things are those which are perceived by the senses; everything perceived by the senses is immediately perceived (for the senses make no inferences; that is the province of reason); everything immediately perceived is a sensation; no sensation can exist but in a mind: *ergo*, no sensible thing can exist but in a mind. Which was to be proved.

Another of his arguments to the same purpose is this: nothing can exist in fact the very notion of which implies a contradiction; nothing is impossible to conceive unless the notion of it imply a contradiction; but 'tis absolutely impossible to conceive anything existing otherwise than in some mind, because whatever anyone conceives is at that instant in his mind. Wherefore, as matter is supposed to be a substance exterior to all minds, and as 'tis evident nothing can be even conceived exterior to all minds, 'tis equally evident there can be no such thing in being as matter.

Or thus: everything conceived is a conception; every conception is a thought; and every thought is in some mind. Wherefore to say you can conceive a thing which exists in no mind is to say you can conceive what is not conceived at all.

The flaws in his arguments which do not appear at a distance ⟨may be⟩ easily seen on a nearer inspection. He says, artfully enough, in the Preface, ⟨that in⟩ order to give his proofs their full force it will be necessary to place them in as many different lights as possible.[1] By this means the object grows too big for the eye, whereas had he contracted it into a narrower compass the mind might readily have taken it in at one view, and discerned where the failing lay.

How miserably does he play with the words *idea* and *sensation*! Everything immediately perceived is a sensation. Why? Because a sensation is what is immediately perceived by the senses. That is, in plain English, everything immediately perceived is immediately perceived. A most admirable discovery! The glory of which I dare say no one will envy him.

And again. All sensible qualities are ideas, and no idea exists but in some mind. That is, all sensible qualities are objects of the mind in thinking, and no image of an external object painted on a mind exists otherwise than in some mind. And what then?

---

[1] Berkeley, *Works*, II. 169 (the closing sentence).

Fiddes' definition of faith I perceived on reflection to trespass against the very first law of defining, as not being adequate to the thing defined, but which[1] is but a part of the definition. An assent grounded both on testimony and reason takes in science as well as
5 faith, which is on all hands allowed to be distinct from it. I am therefore at length come over entirely to your opinion, that saving faith (including practice) is an assent to what God has revealed, because he has revealed it, and not because the truth of it may be evinced by reason.[2]

10 Affairs in Poland grow worse and worse. Instead of answering the Remonstrances from the Protestant powers the Poles remonstrate themselves against their listing troops, and meddling with what does not concern them. It seems above fifty schools, and near as many churches, have been taken from the Protestants in Poland and Lithu-
15 ania since the treaty of Oliva,[3] so that the guarantees of it would have had reason to interpose though the persecution at Thorn had never happened.[4]

The late Bishop of Chester[5] was buried on Friday last, five days after his death, which was occasioned by the dead palsy and gout in
20 the head and stomach. He was in the sixty-third year of his age. 'Tis said he will be succeeded either by Dr. Foulkes or Dr. Tanner, Chancellor of Norwich, one whom all parties speak well of.[6]

I have only time to beg yours and my father's blessing on your dutiful son,

25   John Wesley

Pray remember me to my sisters, who, I hope, are well. If I know when my sister Emly would be at home, I would write.[7]
Nov. 23.

Address: 'For Mrs Wesley at Wroote, To be left At the Posthouse in Bawtry,

[1] Orig., 'bwch'.
[2] See his mother's letter of Aug. 18, 1725, p. 179, ll. 28–9.
[3] May 3, 1660, by which John Casimir of Poland abandoned his claims to Sweden and gave up his Baltic territories.   [4] See above, p. 173.
[5] Francis Gastrell (1662–1725), saluted by Samuel Wesley, Jun., as 'Gastrell, the learn'd, the pious, and the wise!' (*Poems*, 1736, p. 126). He was also Canon of Christ Church, Oxford, where he died during the night of Nov. 14–15. John Wesley attended his funeral on Friday, Nov. 19.
[6] Peter Foulkes (1676–1747), like Gastrell, educated at Westminster and Christ Church, and a Canon of Christ Church; Thomas Tanner (1674–1735), also a Canon of Christ Church, became Bishop of St. Asaph in 1732. In fact Gastrell was succeeded as Bishop of Chester by Samuel Peploe (1668–1752).
[7] See Mrs. Wesley's reply, Dec. 7.

Yorkshire'   *Postmarks*: 'OXFORD', '26 NO'   *Charges*: ((3)), 'In all 7'
End: '+', 'J. Wesley, Novr 22. 1725.', 'Of Hylas – Philonous'   *Source*: MA.

From the Revd. Samuel Wesley

Wroot, Nov. ult. [30, 1725]

Son J[ohn]!
    You see by the enclosed . . . I'm not unmindful of you; and all I can do for
you, and God knows more than I can honestly do, is to give you credit with
Richard Ellison for £10 next Lady day . . .   5
    Nothing else from your loving father,

Sam. Wesley

Source: LB, p. 19.

From Mrs. Susanna Wesley

Wroot, Dec. 7th [1725]

Dear J[acky]
    (Of Mr. Norris's Sermon on Divine Love.)   10
    Who but an atheist will deny that God, and God alone, is the supreme
efficient cause of all things, the only uncreated good! But can it be inferred from
hence that he hath imparted no degree of goodness to his creatures? . . . We may
full as well argue that because they are not self-existent, therefore they have no
being at all . . .   15
    Your sister Wright went with her husband about three weeks since to their
house in Louth, with Molly to keep her company this winter. Your sister Anne
was married last Thursday at Finningley to John Lambert, and goes this day
home with him. He has hired the red house as we go to church, which they have
made very pretty and comfortable, and we hope they will do well.   20
    Emly sends her love to you, as do all the rest. S[he] goes not hence this
winter, and greatly desires to hear from you.
    I suppose the election at Lincoln College draws near, and your father gives
me small encouragement to hope for your success . . . Our crop at Wroot was
almost destroyed by floods; and of the small remains your sister Nancy has the   25
best part in dowry, besides near, if not quite, £30 for h[ers] and Hetty's clothing,
which I've yet to pay. What then can I do you? Nothing but pray for you;
nothing but lift my helpless eyes and hands to heaven and beseech Almighty
God, to whom all power belongs, to do that for you which I cannot: to appoint
some expedient for your relief, and raise you some friend in this time of distress.   30
And who can tell? Perhaps he may condescend to hear the unworthiest of his
creatures . . . I will not despair, but against hope, believe in hope: for I know

that often man's extremity is God's opportunity, wherein he delights to manifest his mercy to such as call upon him.

Dear J[acky], I send you my love and blessing. Adieu!

Source: LB, pp. 45–6.

To the Revd. Samuel Wesley, Jun.

[Oxford, Mar. 21, 1725/6][1]

5 Dear brother

I should certainly have writ you word of my success on Friday (all Thursday I was detained at Lincoln) but that I thought it more advisable, since I had promised to send some verses in a few days, to do both in the same letter. I am, at the same time, to ask pardon
10 for letting anything prevent my doing the first sooner, and to return you my sincere and hearty thanks, as well for your past kindness, as for the fresh instance of it you now give me in the pains you take to qualify me for the enjoyment of that success, which I owe chiefly, not to say wholly, to your interest. I am the more ready to profess
15 my gratitude now because I may do so with less appearance of design than formerly; of any other design, I hope, than of showing myself sensible of the obligation, and that, in this respect at least, I am not unworthy of it.

I have not yet been able to meet with one or two gentlemen from
20 whom I am in hopes of getting two or three copies of verses. The most tolerable of my own, if any such there were, you probably received already from Mr. Leybourne. Some of those that I had besides I have sent here, and shall be very glad if they are capable of being so corrected as to be of any service to you.[2]

25   HORACE, Lib. I, Ode xix

The cruel queen of fierce desires,
    While youth and wine assistants prove,
Renews my long-neglected fires,
    And melts again my mind to love.

---

[1] John Wesley's diary recorded: 'Was elected Fellow of Lincoln' (Thursday, Mar. 17, 1725/6), 'Writ to my father' (Mar. 18), and 'Writ to my brother' (Mar. 21).
[2] Samuel Wesley was assisting David Lewis (1683?–1760) prepare *Miscellaneous Poems by Several Hands*, which appeared later this year, and contained a large number of his own poems. According to Wesley's diary he began to read Lewis's *Poems* on Aug. 21, 1726. Cf. pp. 192, 196 below.

On blooming Glycera I gaze
　By too resistless force opprest!
With fond delight my eye surveys
　The spotless marble of her breast.

In vain I strive to break my chain;　　　　　5
　In vain I heave with anxious sighs;
Her pleasing coyness feeds my pain,
　And keeps the conquests of her eyes.

Impetuous tides of joy and pain
　By turns my lab'ring bosom tear;　　　　　10
The queen of love, with all her train
　Of hopes and fears, inhabits there.

No more the wand'ring Scythian's might
　From softer themes my lyre shall move;
No more the Parthian's wily flight:　　　　　15
　My lyre shall sing of naught but love.

Haste, grassy altars let us rear;
　Haste, wreathes of fragrant myrtle twine;
With Arab sweets perfume the air,
　And crown the whole with gen'rous wine.　　20

While we the sacred rites prepare,
　The cruel queen of fierce desires
Will pierce, propitious to my prayer,
　Th'obdurate maid with equal fires.

Ode xxii　　　　　25

Integrity needs no defence;
The man who trusts to innocence,
Nor wants the darts Numidians throw,
Nor arrows of the Parthian bow.

Secure o'er Libya's sandy seas,　　　　　30
Or hoary Caucasus he strays;
O'er regions scarcely known to fame,
Washed by Hydaspes' fabled stream.

While void of cares, of naught afraid,
Late in the Sabine woods I strayed;　　　　35
On Sylvia's lips, while pleased I sung,
How love and soft persuasion hung!

A ravenous wolf, intent on food,
Rushed from the covert of the wood;
Yet dared not violate the grove　　　　　40
Secured by innocence and love.

Nor Mauritania's sultry plain
So large a savage does contain;
Nor e'er so huge a monster treads
Warlike Apulia's beechen shades.

5   Place me where no revolving sun
Does o'er his radiant circle run;
Where clouds and damps alone appear,
And poison the unwholesome year:

Place me, in that effulgent day,
10   Beneath the sun's directer ray;
No change from its fixed place shall move
The basis of my lasting love.

Sent to a Gentleman whose Father was lately dead
In Imitation of Quis desiderio sit pudor, *etc.*[1]

15   What shame shall stop our flowing tears?
       What end shall our just sorrow know?
Since fate, relentless to our prayers,
       Has given the long-destructive blow!

Ye Muses, strike the sounding string,
20   In plaintive strains his loss deplore;
And teach an artless voice to sing
       The great, the bounteous, now no more!

For him the wise and good shall mourn,
       While late records his fame declare;
25   And oft as rolling years return,
       Shall pay his tomb a grateful tear.

Ah! what avail their plaints to thee!
Ah! what avails his fame declared!
Thou blam'st, alas! the just decree
30   Whence virtue meets its full reward.

Though sweeter sounds adorned thy tongue
       Than Thracian Orpheus whilom played,
When list'ning to the morning song
       Each tree bowed down its leafy head:

[1] Horace, *Odes*, I. xxiv. This poem (presumably by John Wesley), appeared in
Lewis's *Miscellaneous Poems*, pp. 232-4—probably his first published piece—with
some alterations, including the opening couplet, which read:
       What decent time shall stay our tears?
       What bounds shall our just sorrow know? . . .

Never! ah never from the gloom
  Of unrelenting Pluto's sway,
Could the thin shade again resume
  Its ancient tenement of clay.

Indulgent patience! heav'n-born guest!   5
  Thy healing wings around display:
Thou gently calm'st the stormy breast,
  And driv'st the tyrant grief away.

Corroding care and eating pain
  By just degrees thy influence own;   10
And lovely lasting peace again
  Resumes her long-deserted throne.

Source: Westminster Magazine, Apr., 1774, pp. 182–3 (cf. letter of June 17, 1724).

From the Revd. Samuel Wesley

Wroot, March 21, 1725/6

Dear Mr. Fellow (Elect) of Lincoln

  I've done . . . more than I could for you. On your waiting on Dr. M[orley]   15
with this he'll pay you £12. You are inexpressibly obliged to that generous man.
We are all as well . . . as can be expected . . . Your loving father,

Sam Wesley

Source: LB, p. 19.

From Mrs. Susanna Wesley

Wroot, March 30, 1726

Dear J[acky]   20

  I think myself obliged to return great thanks to Almighty God for giving you
good success at Lincoln. Let whoever he pleased be the instrument, to him, and
him alone, the glory appertains. For as the best concerted measures often prove
ineffectual, so sometimes things that carry little probability in them shall succeed
beyond expectation. And why is this? But because God prospers the one, and   25
(as his Spirit expresses it) 'blows upon the labour of the other'.

  I am much more pleased and thankful because I have observed sometime that
the Holy Jesus (to whom the whole manage of our salvation is committed) seems
to have taken the conduct of your soul into his own hand, in that he has given
you a true notion of saving faith, and, I hope, an experimental knowledge of   30
repentance. Therefore I trust that he will be pleased to direct your intentions,
and assist you in the exercise of the ministerial office, that he will incline your
heart to the love of justice, so that you will not look on the small addition to your

fortunes as given you to make provision for the flesh, but as a talent committed to your charge: to pay your debts in the first place, and the residue to be employed as religion and prudence direct.

(Of Norris's distinction between compla[cenc]e and goodwill.)

5 Many and great are the trials it has pleased God to exercise us with; and though that is not the reason of my not writing so long, yet I must say they have found me sufficient employment to keep my mind from fainting. And your father being displeased at my writing so often, because of the expense it was to you, our pressures disposed me to a more implicit obedience than perhaps I

10 should otherwise have paid him. I would not inform you of anything that might grieve, but Dr. M[orley] advising your coming into the country,' tis not probable any unhappy circumstances or practices of some of our family should remain concealed from you. Dear J[acky], I hope you are a good Christian, and as such do firmly believe that no events happen but by the commission, or rather[1] at

15 least permission of divine Providence. Therefore do not much afflict yourself, let what will befall. God hath promised, 'All things shall work together for good to those that love him.'

(Of my father's getting money for me.)

How or when do you intend to come hither? It will be necessary to let us have

20 timely notice of your intentions. Dear J[acky], all send their love, I my love and blessing.

Source: LB, pp. 46–7.

From the Revd. Samuel Wesley

Wroot, Apr. 1, 1726

Dear Son Jnō

I had both yours since your election.[2] In both you express yourself as became

25 you for what I had willingly, though with greater difficulty than you imagine, done for you. For the last £12 pinched me so hard that I'm forced to beg time of your brother Sam till after harvest to pay him the ten that he lent you, nor shall I have so much as that, I question whether five, to keep my family from May-day till after harvest, and don't expect I shall be able to do anything for

30 Charles when he goes to the university; and what will be my own fate God knows, before this summer be over. *Sed passi graviora*[3]—and wherever I am, my Jacky is Fellow of Lincoln.

Yet all this, and perhaps worse than you know, has not made me forget you. For I wrote to Dr. King, enclosed in one to Sam, desiring leave for you to come

35 for two or three months into the country, where you should be gladly welcome, though with small hopes of obtaining it, because you know what has passed already.

As for advice, keep your best friend fast, and next to him Dr. Morley (to whom

---

[1] Orig., 'o/r'.   [2] Mar. 18, 25?
[3] 'But I have suffered worse things' cf. Virgil, *Aeneid* i. 199).

service). And have a care of your other friends, especially the younger. All at
present from your loving father,

Sam Wesley

Source: MA, compared with LB, p. 20.

To the Revd. Samuel Wesley, Jun.

Lincoln Coll., Oxon, April 4, 1726

Dear brother   5

I should have written long before now, had not a gentleman of
Exeter[1] made me put it off from day to day in hopes of getting some
little poems of his, which he promised to write out for me. Yesterday
I saw them, though not much to my satisfaction, as being all on
very wrong subjects, and run chiefly on the romantic notions of love   10
and gallantry. I have transcribed one which is much shorter than
any of the rest, and am promised by tomorrow night, if that will do
me any service, another of a more serious nature.

I believe I have given Mr. Leybourne, at different times, five or
six short copies of verses; the latest were a translation of part of the   15
second Georgic[2] and an imitation of the 65th Psalm.[3] If he has lost
them, as it is likely he has, in so long a time, I can write them over in
less than an hour, and send them by the post.

My father very unexpectedly, a week ago, sent me in a letter a bill
on Dr. Morley for twelve pounds, which he had paid to the rector's   20
use at Gainsborough.[4] So that now several of my debts are paid, and
the expenses of my treat[5] defrayed, I have above ten pounds remaining; and if I could have leave to stay in the country till my college
allowance commences, this money would abundantly suffice me till
then.   25

As far as I have ever observed, I never knew a college besides ours

---

[1] Henry Pitt (*c.* 1706–33), brother of the better-known poet Christopher Pitt (1699–
1748). Henry Pitt became a fellow of Exeter College in 1724. Wesley dined with him
Apr. 3, 1726 (see diary).

[2] Of Virgil.

[3] In his *Collection of Psalms and Hymns* (1737) Wesley published an adaptation
of Ps. 65 from Watts (pp. 61–2), and in that of 1738 one from the New Version
(pp. 68–70), but it is unlikely that he had either of these in mind.

[4] See above, Mar. 21; cf. letter of Apr. 1. In addition to being Rector of Lincoln
College, Dr. John Morley was rector of Scotton, near Gainsborough.

[5] Probably a meal celebrating his election, paid for by Wesley.

whereof the members were so perfectly satisfied with one another,
and so inoffensive to the other part of the university. All I have
yet seen of the fellows are both well-natured and well-bred, men
admirably disposed as well to preserve peace and good neighbour-
5 hood among themselves as to promote it wherever else they have
any acquaintance.

> By a cool fountain's flow'ry side
>   The fair Celinda lay;
> Her looks increased the summer's pride,
10   Her eyes the blaze of day.
>
> Quick through the air to this retreat
>   A bee industrious flew,
> Prepared to rifle every sweet
>   Under the balmy dew.
>
15 > Drawn by the fragrance of her breath
>   Her rosy lips he found;
> There in full transport sucked in death,
>   And dropped upon the ground.
>
> Enjoy, blest bee, enjoy thy fate,
20 >   Nor at thy fall repine;
> Each God would quit his blissful state
>   To share a death like thine.

The seven former verses of the 46th Psalm[1]

> On God supreme our hope depends,
25 >   Whose omnipresent sight
> Even to the pathless realms extends
>   Of uncreated night.
>
> Plunged in th'abyss of deep distress,
>   To him we raise our cry;
30 > His mercy bids our sorrows cease,
>   And fills our tongue with joy.
>
> Though earth her ancient seat forsake,
>   By pangs convulsive torn;
> Though her self-balanced fabric shake,
35 >   And ruined nature mourn:

---

[1] This poem was inserted in Lewis's *Miscellaneous Poems* (1726), pp. 255–7, with
some variants. Wesley himself used the first four and last two stanzas in his *Collection
of Psalms and Hymns* (1737), p. 4 (*Bibliog*, No. 8).

Though hills be in the ocean lost,
   With all their shaggy load:
No fear shall e'er molest the just,
   Or shake his trust in God.

What though th'ungoverned, wild abyss   5
   His fires tumultuous pours;
What though the wat'ry legion's rise,
   And lash th'affrighted shores;

What though the trembling mountains nod,
   Nor stand the rolling war;   10
Sion, secure, enjoys the flood,
   Loud echoing from afar.

The God most high on Sion's hill
   Has fixed his sure abode:
Nor dare[1] th'impetuous waves assail   15
   The city of our God.

Nations remote, and realms unknown,
   In vain reject his sway;
For lo! Jehovah's voice is shown,
   And earth shall melt away.   20

Let war's devouring surges rise,
   And rage on every side;
The Lord of Hosts our refuge is,
   And Jacob's God our guide.

Mr. Le Hunte[2] and Sherman send their service. I am, your loving 25
brother,

                              John Wesley

    I believe I could put off two or three more receipts if I had them.[3]
Pray, my love to my brother and sister.

    On Friday St. Peter's Church in the Bailey was beaten down by 30
the fall of the steeple.[4] Saturday morning a chandler here murdered

---

    [1] Orig., 'dares'.
    [2] William Le Hunte, born *c*. 1692, and Samuel Wesley's contemporary at Christ
Church, though a year behind him. In 1729 he became vicar of Kidderminster,
Worcestershire, and in 1731 rector of Oxhill, Warwickshire.
    [3] This may have been for those subscribing for copies of Lewis's *Miscellaneous
Poems*.
    [4] Cf. Hearne, IX. 109 for fuller details of the collapse of the decrepit central tower of
this ancient church in New Inn Hall Street. Another church was built on the same site
in 1740, and this was replaced 1872–4.

two men and wounded a third; in the evening a fire broke out at the Mitre, but was stopped in a few hours.

Address: 'To the Rev. Mr. Wesley, In Great Dean's Yard, Westminster'
Source: Priestley, pp. 1–5; cf. a contemporary MS transcript at Duke.

From Mrs. Susanna Wesley

Apr. 9 [1726]

Dear J[acky]
5   . . . I th[ought] to send a servant the 25th of this month, with two horses . . .
Send now a speedy answer, that we may give them a little food extraordinary.
Dear J[acky], I beseech Almighty God to bless Thee!

Source: LB, p. 47. Cf. Wesley's diary, Apr. 12: 'recd a L. from my M dated Apr. 9'; this he answered the same day.

From Mrs. Susanna Wesley

Apr. 16 [1726]

Dear J[acky]
10   . . . Your father has ordered his servant, Alexander Clark, to set out hence on
the 18th instant . . . One thing I suppose needful to admonish you of, that you
do not propose to yourself too much satisfaction in coming hither; for what the
world calls joy lives not within these walls. But if your heart be right, and you
can rejoice in God whether you have or have not anything else to rejoice in; if
15 he be the pleasure of your mind, so that you can feel delight in each perception
of his presence, though encompassed with [[poverty, reproach, and]][1] shame,
then you may spend a few months in Wroot as happily as in any place of the
world . . .
Dear J[acky], God bless thee!

Source: LB, pp. 47–8.

From the Revd. Samuel Wesley

20   Apr. 17 [1726]

Dear son
I hope Sander[2] will be with you by Wednesday noon, with the horses, books,
bags, and this . . . I got your mother to write the enclosed (for you see I can hardly

----

[1] In cipher.   [2] Probably short for Alexander, i.e. Clark (see Apr. 16).

scrawl) because 'twas possible it might come to hand on Tuesday; . . . but my
head was so full of other cares that I forgot on Saturday last to put it into the
posthouse . . . I should be very glad to see you, though but for a day; but much
more for a quarter of a year . . . I think you'll make what haste you can . . .
I design to be at the Crown in Bawtry, Saturday sennight. God bless and send 5
you a prosperous journey to your affectionate father,

Sam Wesley

Source: LB, pp. 20–1.

From Mrs. Susanna Wesley

Sept. 28 [1726]

[Dear Jacky]
(Of my father's mare, left ill at Banbury, and my plain nightgown)   10

Oct. 12 [1726]

[Dear Jacky]
(Of my father's mare, and my nightgown)
I greatly rejoice that your lot is cast among such agreeable companions, nor am
I a little pleased with the hopes of your being [[out of debt]].[1] Would Almighty 15
G[od] n[ow] permit me the satisfaction of being so 'myself, and seeing my
children [[clear]][2] in the world, with what pleasure could I leave it! . . .
Your brother and sister Wright are now in Wroot at John Lambert's. By your
father's permission I went to see her, and was much surprised to find that she
met me without the least emotion of joy or grief. I desired a private conference, 20
which she could not deny, though I found she was not pleased with it. I spoke
what I thought proper for the occasion, but observed she was on the reserve, nor
could I prevail with her to speak freely on anything. To induce her to it I used
as much mildness as I am mistress of, told her I freely forgave all her offences
against me, and spake more than perhaps was required on my part. She heard 25
me with great indifference, made no acknowledgment of my proffered kindness,
but seemed rather not pleased that I supposed she stood in need of my pardon.
I then proposed a reconciliation between her and Mr. Wesley, and asked her if
she would not see him if he were willing to see her. She told me she had no
desire to see him, because she knew he would reproach her with what was past, 30
and that she could not bear. I replied, he would certainly put her in mind of her
faults, which I thought he was obliged to do, as a father and as a clergyman; and
that she was not to call the just rebukes of a parent reproaches, but submit herself to him, which she would certainly do if she were truly penitent. She repeated
her not desiring to see him, and added, she wished for no reconciliation till one 35
of 'em came to die. What effect my discourse had on her I know not, but I'm
sure I returned home strangely mortified, neither pleased with her nor myself.

---

[1] In cipher. This is in reply to Wesley's letter of Oct. 3.   [2] In cipher.

I hoped from Molly's representation of matters to have found her in a different temper from what I did. Therefore I did not say enough to convince her of her duty, and was troubled to find her averse from her father, whom I take to be as well disposed to be reconciled to her as man can be. For he seemed pleased that
5 I went to her, and never restrains any of the children from being with her as much as they will. I verily believe that I could by a few words speaking reconcile him to her, but God forbid those few words should be spoken by me till she is better disposed. What her inward frame of mind is, is best known to the Searcher of hearts, to whose mercy I leave her, beseeching him to give her true repentance,
10 without which I desire to see her face no more.

Charles is greatly to blame in not writing to Sam . . .

Dear J[acky], I pray God to bless thee!

I desire what I've spoken of Hetty may be concealed. I have not spoken so freely of her to our folks, nor is it necessary they should know my thoughts. Let
15 all think as they please.

Source: LB, pp. 48–9; Wesley answered this letter Oct. 20 (see Appendix).

From Mrs. Susanna Wesley[1]

Nov. 29. Tues. [1726]

Dear J[acky]

. . . The mare cost £4. 10s. 9d before we got her home. (Of the money I left at Wroot.) Dear J[acky], I must say unto thee as Naomi to her daughters, 'It
20 grieveth me much for your sake that the hand of the Lord is gone out against me.'

This has withheld me from writing, though I had a great desire to hear from you and poor starving Charles. For it seemed a palpable piece of cruelty to make you pay for a letter unless I could send money too. But [as] I can't fix a time of payment, I now think it better to write, lest you should impute my silence to
25 a worse cause.

. . . Let us know how you like your plaid . . .

I heartily wish your converse with your friend[2] may prove innocent and useful; but old folks are scrupulous, and much given to fear consequences. May God preserve you from sin and danger.
30 Dear J[acky], I pray God bless thee.

Mr. Wesley is this day gone to Mr. Farmery's (late Minister of Blighton's) funeral.

Source: LB, p. 50.

[1] In answer to his of Oct. 20.
[2] Probably Sally Kirkham, now Mrs. Chapone, with whom Wesley was corresponding regularly; cf. p. 210.

To the Revd. Samuel Wesley, Jun.[1]

[Dec. 5–6, 1726]

Dear brother

The very thing I desire of you is this, that you would not content yourself with your own opinion, nor fix your own opinion at all till you have heard my story, as well as theirs who accuse me. 'Tis very 5 hard; I have said all that I can say, I have professed my sincerity and integrity, more perhaps than it became me to profess them; I have asked yours as well as my father's pardon for any real or supposed slight I have put upon you; to you, in particular, I have given all the satisfaction which I could contrive to give in words; 10 and yet am now just as far, if not farther from a reconciliation than I was when I first set out.

Since all probable methods of gaining my cause have failed I will try one way more: I will relate the controverted facts as plainly as I can, without desiring you either to believe me or not. If you do, 15 I shall be glad both for your sake and my own; if not, I have done my part, and can therefore quietly commit my ways to him who in his own good time will make my innocence as clear as the light.

First I shall tell you what I suspect, and next what I know. My suspicion is that on your receiving a letter from me you immediately 20 set yourself to consider what 'tis probable I shall say to your last; and if you hit upon any of my objections, then they are to go for nothing—you have already found out the emptiness of them. You then proceed to read, taking it for granted that if I will not tell a downright lie, which is a question, I will however colour and palliate 25 everything, as far as my wit will serve me to do with any show of truth; that calmness is an infallible mark of disrespect, as warmth is of guilt; and with a few of these either *praecognita* or *praeconcessa*[2] 'tis perfectly easy to demonstrate that I am totally in the wrong.

---

[1] Because of their father's complaints to his oldest son about what he considered John's unfilial advocacy of their sister Hetty, Samuel had become very cold in his letters, apparently making frequent allusions to John's failure to pay the debts incurred by his Oxford education and advancement. The focal point of discord was a sermon which John had preached Aug. 28, 1726, on charity, while he and Charles were spending some weeks at home. The sermon contained a brief allusion to his father's harsh treatment of Hetty, though no names were used. In this letter John seeks to bring these undercurrents to the surface, and to achieve a mutual understanding.

[2] Preconceived convictions or concessions.

Without some proceedings of this kind I cannot imagine or guess how you come to be so displeased at me. Why, after I have over and over desired that my past miscarriages might be forgotten, your language still shows them to be fresh in your memory. To what end, since it does not appear that different expressions would not do as well, [do] you give me in every one of your letters one or more of those taunting sentences? ('It would have been fair enough *ad hominem*,[1] 'I hope 'tis not only *pro forma*[2] that you labour.'). I do believe you are yet my affectionate friend, but very much fear you will not be so long, if everything I say has so strange a construction put upon it.

My father's words, and your reflection upon them, were both perfectly unintelligible to me till I read the Canon he mentions.[3] I should then have been exactly as much at a loss as before but that my brother Charles, accidentally, while we were in the country, repeated to me part of a conversation he had with my father, in their return from my brother Ellison's. The substance of it, as near [as] I remember, was this: 'My father last night was telling me of your disrespect to him. He said you had him at open defiance. I was surprised, and asked him how or when. He said, "Every day. You hear how he contradicts me, and takes your sister's part before my face. Nay, he disputes with me, preach—", and then he stopped short, as if he wanted to recall his word, and talked of other things.' I said I wondered what he meant, till recollecting with my brother that my father, mother, sister Emly, and I had several times been speaking of the treatment we should show ill men; and that my brother having likewise had many disputes with me about it, I told him I had for near a twelvemonth intended writing on Universal Charity, having read over Dr. Clarke[4] and Bishop Atterbury's[5] sermons for that purpose; that I would set about it immediately, and there he should hear at once, and so would be better able to judge of my arguments. I wrote it accordingly, and after my mother's perusal and approbation (she making one alteration in the expression) preached it, on Sunday, August 28.[6] I had the same day the

---

[1] '[an argument] relying on personal abuse'.   [2] 'a mere formality'.

[3] The 53rd; see below, p. 204.

[4] Dr. Samuel Clarke (1675–1729) preached a sermon before Queen Anne on universal charity, from 1 John 4: 21, on Dec. 30, 1705.

[5] Francis Atterbury (1662–1732) preached on the power of charity to cover sin, from 1 Pet. 4: 5, in Bridewell Chapel, London, on Aug. 16, 1694.

[6] This was in the parish church at Wroot, where the Wesley family still lived.

pleasure of observing that my father the same day, when one Will Atkins was mentioned, did not speak so warmly nor largely against him as usual. The next day (29) I went to Epworth, and returned from thence on Thursday (Sept. 1). In the evening my brother desired me to take a walk, and told me what I have above recited. 5 We supped, and walked about a quarter of an hour in the garden, from whence I ran in to find my father. I met him by himself in the hall, and told him, not without tears, that I learned from my brother I had offended him, both by speaking often in contradiction to him, and by not offering myself to write for him; but I now promised to 10 do whatever he pleased. He kissed me, and, I believe, cried too; told me he always believed I was good at bottom (those were his words), and would employ me the next day. The next day I began transcribing some papers for him; and find by my diary I employed the same way part of every day from the 2nd to the 12th inclusive, only 15 excepting Sunday the 11th, in which all the spare time I had was employed in writing what I remembered of my father's sermon. On Thursday of the following week I dined at my sister Lambert's and was her son's godfather,[1] and was detained there by fresh company[2] coming in, till evening. On Friday my father, brother, and I 20 walked over to dinner to Mr. Hoole's;[3] on Saturday morning came over Mr. Harper[4] of Epworth and Mr. Pennington,[5] to take leave of my brother and me. In the rest of the week I wrote and transcribed a sermon against rash judging, which with my father's leave I preached on Sunday. On Monday the 19th we set out for Oxon. 25

Neither did my father while I was with him speak one word to me of that sermon[6] he complains of; nor did it appear, unless by[7] that one word to my brother, that he had then taken offence at all. If he had, he would surely have used some means[8] 'to have satisfaction made[9] where the offence was given'; and not have suffered me again 30

---

[1] The bishop's transcripts of the Wroot parish registers record the baptism on Sept. 15, 1726, of 'John Son of Jno. & Ann Lambert'.

[2] Cf. Wesley's diary, Sept. 15, 1726: 'At my sister's—much company—came home, danced.'

[3] At Haxey, about five miles west by south of Wroot, by road.

[4] Robert Harper, Epworth apothecary, who later married Emilia Wesley.

[5] The Revd. John Pennington (1699-1768), the rector's curate at Epworth (cf. letter of Apr. 22, 1727, p. 216).

[6] Orig., 'My father ((did not)) speak one word to me ((while I stayed in the country,)) of that sermon.'

[7] Orig., ((otherwise than)).

[8] Orig., ((method or other)).

[9] Orig., ((given)).

to occupy[1] that place 'I had once abused', especially[2] till I had 'faithfully promised to forbear all such matter of contention in the church',[3] which I was not likely to do[4] till I was apprised of my fault.

5   The 53rd Canon runs thus:[5]

If any preacher in the pulpit particularly, or namely of purpose, impugn or confute any doctrine delivered by any other preacher in the same church, or in any church near adjoining, . . .[6] because upon such public dissenting and contradicting there may grow much offence and disquietness to the people; the
10 churchwardens, or party grieved, shall forthwith signify the same to the [said] bishop, and not suffer, etc.[7]

Against this I have offended, if I have in the pulpit, particularly or of purpose, impugned any doctrine there delivered before. But this plainly supposes the impugner to know that the doctrine he
15 opposes was preached there before; otherwise he can't possibly be said to impugn it particularly, or on purpose. Now it is not possible he should know it was there delivered unless he either heard it preached himself, or was informed of it by others. The disputed point between my father and me was the particular measure of
20 charity due to wicked men: but neither have I heard him, neither did he himself or any other person inform me, that he ever preached at all in Wroot Church on that subject. So that I am in no wise guilty of breaking the Canon, unless it obliges every preacher to inquire what particular tenets have ever been maintained (for the time is not
25 limited) both in his own and the adjoining churches. If he is to inquire of the former he must inquire of the latter, too, the Canon equally speaking of both. If there be any objection made to the sermon itself, I have it by me, and for the matter of it am not ashamed or afraid to show it anybody.

30 Why you defer your advice till my debts are paid you may probably

---

[1] Orig., 'given. ((So far would he have been from)) suffering me to occupy'.

[2] Orig., 'abused', ((which the Canon so strictly forbids.)) Especially'.

[3] This paragraph contains much rewriting by Wesley, but he is quoting passages from Canon 53.

[4] Orig., 'which ((it was impossible I should)) do'.

[5] Orig., 'The ((words of the)) Canon run thus:'

[6] *Constitutions and Canons Ecclesiastical* (1604), of which Wesley quotes the 53rd almost word for word. The passage which he here omits runs: 'before he hath acquainted the bishop of the diocese therewith, and received order from him what to do in that case'.

[7] The Canon continues: 'the said preacher any more to occupy that place which he hath once abused, except he faithfully promise to forbear all such matter of contention in the church until the bishop hath taken further order therein . . .'

see a reason. I do not. I reckon my fellowship near sixty pounds a year. Between forty and fifty it will infallibly cost to live at college, use what management I can. As for pupils, I am not qualified to take them till one of our tutors goes away; when that will be is very uncertain. What you mean by my debt at Wroot I do not apprehend; if the whole I have at any time received of my father, I know not how much it is, and shall not therefore know (as neither will you) when it is satisfied; if what I have received at the university, I may be ruined for want of advice before I can possibly repay that; if what I received when last in the country, that was nothing at all, for I not only bore my own expenses in travelling, but paid ready money for whatever I brought from thence, and left money behind me, though for several reasons I did not think good to tell my father so much when he blamed[1] me with being so expensive to him in that journey.

My sister Hetty's behaviour has, for aught I have heard, been innocent enough since her marriage. Most of my disputes on charity with my father were on her account, he being inconceivably exasperated against her. 'Tis likely enough he would not see her when at Wroot; he has disowned her long ago, and never spoke of her in my hearing but with the utmost detestation. Both he, my mother, and several of my sisters were persuaded her penitence was but feigned. One great reason for my writing the above-mentioned sermon was to endeavour, as far [as] in me lay, to convince them that even on supposit[ion] that she was impenitent some tenderness was due to her still; which my mother when I read it to her was so well aware of that she told me as soon as I had read it, 'You writ this sermon for Hetty; the rest was brought in for the sake of the last paragraph.'

My sister L[ambert] behaved herself unexceptionably while [we] were in the country; that she had lately altered her conduct, which indeed is highly improbable, I did not hear till now.

I very heartily desire (though I see not how it can be effected, unless you will take my word till my actions disprove it), that you should entertain a just opinion, as of the morals in general, so in particular of the gratitude of your loving brother,

J Wesley

Linc[oln College], Dec. 6 [1726]

Address: 'To Mr Saml Wesley Junr' *End* by JW: 'JW. Dec. 6 1727 / To SW.

[1] Orig., ((twitted)).

+'; a later hand has changed '27' to '26', and another hand has written, '6th Decr. 1727', once more with '7' altered to '6'   *Source*: MA, a draft, with many alterations by Wesley. Most of the words to be deleted are so indicated by underlining, though in our footnotes enclosed within (( )). Wesley's diary shows that he wrote the letter on the 5th and transcribed it (presumably a fair copy for despatch) on the 6th.

From the Revd. Samuel Wesley, Jun.[1]

Dec. 10, 1726

Dear Jack

I thank you for your speedy and large answer. If you are not nearer reconciliation than before I should wonder much. I left some particulars untouched
5 to that end, particularly your supposition if anything you could do could give me either hope or fear. I think I may fairly say, though I have now and then assumed some superiority, I have given you no ground to imagine I look upon myself as unconcerned in your welfare, or as if I were of a species above you. If I had not feared your being guilty I had not mentioned my father's anger; if I had not
10 *hoped* from you I would never have spent a farthing upon you. Don't take this as an upbraiding or grudging what is past. I mentioned it only to show I thought my last was not only just but tender. The expression *pro forma* I don't perfectly remember, but I think it related more especially to your university exercises; and if so it was so far from harshness that it was a kind wish to hope you might
15 improve yourself by them. However I shall not pretend to defend what I have almost forgotten. The other *ad hominem* was severe, I own, yet so fair an occasion might probably have excused even more; though after all, if this is, as I believe it is, the worst of my treatment, I persuade myself on more mature deliberation you will not mightily complain of hardship. An opinion of your
20 imprudence to my father might have drawn more keen expressions, and his word was sufficient to ground an opinion, though not to pass a sentence upon. As to anything concerning myself, as you now assure me you have submitted and asked pardon, I am heartily at this instant writing reconciled to you.

The sentence I sent you about the 53rd Canon was my only *praecognitum*.[2] I
25 reckon myself obliged to you for your frankness in that matter, and freely acknowledge 'tis impossible you should break that law without set purpose and design. Neither do I think your previous dispute amounts to such a purpose. It was indeed an unhappy circumstance, which might have made your silence more advisable. Your reading to my mother was a wrong step, too; you might have
30 had it to say that no one living had seen it; for the authority of her approbation on the one side did not outweigh the suspicion of combination on the other. My father, you say, was seemingly well satisfied that evening. How came he afterwards altered? Did anyone tell him you had such or such intentions? Or was he

---

[1] Replying to John's of Dec. 6, 1726. Wesley's diary shows that he received it on Dec. 17.

[2] 'basic knowledge necessary to arrive at an informed judgment'.

insulted with your declaring authoritatively against him? Some cause or other must have changed him. I find the point of doctrine was not so plain but that doctors differed; and therefore, if you please, I shall be glad to read your sermon as soon as you shall have an opportunity to send it.

By your debt *in foro conscientia[e]*[1] I mean the whole of your education, as far 5 as you may be able to return it to the family. You have had better luck than I if you have not been upbraided with the disproportioned charge of the boys and of the girls. My mother and sisters in all likelihood will need more than we can do. My advice therefore is needless, because you must know as well as I where to place your superfluities.   10

I wish you had spared the paragraph of my father's temper. I have lived longer with him than you, and have been very intimate, and yet almost always pleased him, and am confident I shall do so to the end of my life. So that what you are persuaded is flatly impossible, I affirm upon experience is direct fact. I beg you would not use any more solemn appeals to the Searcher of hearts; I 15 believe you sincere without them; neither is my satisfaction an occasion august enough for so tremendous asseverations. If you are not high-minded, fear.

I wish my mother and sister Em. were heartily reconciled to Hetty. I am resolved to try what I can do both with them and my father; though upon supposition indeed of her being penitent; otherwise I will never plead for 20 innocence and guilt's being treated alike. You own your sermon was aimed at the person, though not the priesthood, of my father. A letter to him had been better much; I think you no more than imprudent in the case.

You are widely mistaken if you think I charge sister Lambert with an alteration for the worse in her conduct. I suppose the very contrary, and therefore 25 wonder there should be any alteration for the worse in her treatment from others —if any such there be.

I hope we are now near an end of our altercation, methinks I see land. I am very well satisfied as to your sentiments towards me, but would always have you remember, I place the whole of my merit to the account of my mother and 30 sisters. Repay them. We join in love to you and Charles. I am, and hope shall be till death, your sincere and affectionate friend and brother,

S. Wesley

Pray send me your receipt for the Michaelmas Charterhouse money. My father has sent me the certificate.   35

Address: 'To the Revd. Mr. Wesley, Fellow of Lincoln Colledge, Oxford
Postmarks: Two circular, different sizes, including one Bishop mark, both indecipherable   *Charge*: '3'   *End*: 'SWy' and 'Dec. 26' (both by John Wesley), and in another hand, '1726'   *Source*: MA.

[1] 'before the tribunal of conscience'.

To Mrs. Susanna Wesley

[Lincoln College, Jan. 24, 1726/7]

[Dear mother]

I am shortly to take my Master's degree.[1] As I shall from that time be less interrupted by business not of my own choosing, I have
5 drawn up for myself a scheme of studies from which I do not intend, for some years at least, to vary.[2] I am perfectly come over to your opinion, that there are many truths it is not worth while to know.[3] Curiosity indeed might be a sufficient plea for our laying out some time upon them, if we had half a dozen centuries of life to come, but
10 methinks it is great ill-husbandry to spend a considerable part of the small pittance now allowed us in what makes us neither a quick nor a sure return.

Two days ago I was reading a dispute between those celebrated masters of controversy, Bishop Atterbury and Bishop Hoadly,[4] but
15 must own I was so injudicious as to break off in the middle. I could not conceive that the dignity of the end was at all proportioned to the difficulty of attaining it. And I thought the labour of twenty or thirty hours, if I was sure of succeeding, which I was not, would be but ill rewarded by that important piece of knowledge, whether
20 Bishop Hoadly had misunderstood Bishop Atterbury or no . . .

About a year and a half ago I stole out of company at eight in the evening with a young gentleman with whom I was intimate.[5] As we

[1] He was examined Feb. 7, disputed for his degree on the 8th, read three lectures (*De Anima Brutorum*, *De Julio Caesare*, and *De Amore Dei*—'The Souls of Animals', 'Julius Caesar', 'The Love of God'), and actually took his degree at 11 a.m., Feb. 14 (see diary, and Moore, I. 144).

[2] He began to follow this scheme Friday, Jan. 27 (diary).

[3] See her letter of Aug. 18, 1725, p. 208, ll. 24-7.

[4] In a funeral sermon for Thomas Bennet (1706), Francis Atterbury (not yet a bishop, but a royal chaplain and Dean of Carlisle) expounded 1 Cor. 15 : 19 ('If in this life only we have hope in Christ, we are of all men most miserable') to imply that virtue often brings suffering in this life, thus arguing for a blessed future life. Benjamin Hoadly (1676-1761), then lecturer of St. Mildred's, Poultry, London, claimed that this misinterpreted Paul's words, and the printed controversy continued through a series of tracts into the following year.

[5] John ('Robin') Griffiths, son of the Revd. John Griffiths of Broadway, Worcestershire, in the Cotswold Hills. He had matriculated at New College, Oxford, on Mar. 24, 1719/20, when he was sixteen, and thus a few months younger than Wesley. He had graduated in 1724, but whether he was still in residence in 1725 or on a visit to Oxford is not known; the two were corresponding regularly at least from May 12, 1725. It was probably through this friendship that Wesley first came in touch with the group of

took a turn in an aisle of St. Mary's Church, in expectation of a young lady's funeral with whom we were both acquainted,[1] I asked him if he really thought himself my friend, and if he did, why he would not do me all the good he could. He began to protest, in which I cut him short by desiring him to oblige me in an instance which he could 5 not deny to be in his own power—to let me have the pleasure of making him a whole Christian, to which I knew he was at least half persuaded already; that he could not do me a greater kindness, as both of us would be fully convinced when we came to follow that young woman. 10

He turned exceedingly serious, and kept something of that disposition ever since. Yesterday was a fortnight he died of a consumption. I saw him three days before he died, and on the Sunday following did him the last good office I could here, by preaching his funeral sermon, which was his desire when living.[2] 15

Source: Whitehead, I. 407-9, dated by Wesley's diary. For other clues to the contents see her reply of Jan. 31.

From Mrs. Susanna Wesley

Jan. 31, 17[26/]27

Dear J[acky]

... Emly can have no time to work the chairs, having given her promise to Mrs. T. to go with her at Lin[coln] at May Day. The small interval between this and that is hardly sufficient to prepare for her removal. I would gladly have kept 20 her here, but it cannot be: our seas run high, and each succeeding wave impairs her health, so that I plainly perceive she has not strength to ride out the storm; but must either make some other port, or shortly leave the world. For which reason I am content to part with her, however pleasing or useful she might otherwise be to me. 25

... I often revolve the state of my family and the wants of my children over in my mind. And though one short reflection on the sins of my youth and the

friends in the Cotswolds who occupied much of his attention during the following years, especially the Kirkhams and the Granvilles. He visited the area over Christmas, 1726, his stay being prolonged because of Robin's death.

[1] The occasion may have been that recorded in Hearne's *Collections* for Friday, July 2, 1725: 'On Wednesday night last was buried at St. Mary's in Oxford the eldest daughter (aged 15 years) of Mr. Carter, a cutler of St. Mary's parish. She died of a consumption Sunday night last.'

[2] The manuscript of this his seventh sermon, composed Jan. 10-12, 1726/7, is still extant. It was from 2 Sam. 12 : 23, 'Now he is dead', and Wesley preached it at Broadway on Sunday, Jan. 15 (see Vol. 4 of this edition). For Wesley's illness at the time cf. letter of Mar. 19, 1727, p. 214, ll. 18-21.

great imperfection of my present state solves all the difficulty of Providence relating to myself, yet when I behold them struggling with misfortunes of various kinds, some without sufficiency of bread, in the most literal sense, all destitute of the conveniences or comforts of life, it puts me upon the expostu-
5 lation of David, 'Lo, I have sinned, and I have done wickedly, but those sheep, what have they done?' Though thus the tenderness of a mother pleads their cause, yet I dare not dispute God's justice, wisdom, or goodness. I know that to allot all men such a sphere of action as all things considered is best for them is the proper exercise of his providence, as it is what none but he can do. We
10 yesterlings do not know whether prosperity or adversity, health or sickness, honour or disgrace, would most conduce to our good . . . What then to desire for myself or children I wot not. One thing I know, that the unsearchable wisdom of God is a good reason why we should not censure those mysterious methods of Providence which we cannot comprehend, but rather vigorously
15 apply ourselves to do our duty in our several stations, leaving all things else to be disposed of by that almighty goodness which was exhibited to us in the redemption of the world by Jesus Christ. Only let us join in this petition to our Incarnate God, that as our day is, so our strength may be! Amen!
(Of my father's borrowing money for brother Charles, detained by brother
20 Sam.)
I have many thoughts of the friendship between V[aranese] and thee, and the more I think of it, the less I approve it. The tree is known by its fruits, but not always by its blossoms; what blooms beautifully sometimes bears bitter fruit . . .
(Against the continuing the acquaintance with V[aranese].)
25 I often muse on the prodigious force of present things, and am grieved to observe with what a strong impetus passion and appetite bear us in pursuit of sensitive enjoyments, contrary to our best informed understandings.
. . . We would freely serve God with what costs us naught, but if he require a costly sacrifice, a right eye, or a right hand, we are ready to say, 'These are
30 hard sayings, Who can bear them?' We are apt to think heaven too dear a purchase if our favourite must be given for it . . .
. . . I am verily persuaded that[1] the reason why so many 'seek to enter into the kingdom of heaven, but are not able', is because there is some Delilah, some one beloved vice,[2] they will not part with; hoping that by a strict observance of
35 other duties that one fault will be dispensed with. But alas! they miserably deceive themselves. The way to heaven is so narrow, the gate we must enter in so strait, that it will not permit a man to pass with one known unmortified sin about him. Therefore let everyone in the beginning of a Christian course seriously weigh what it will cost to finish it. 'For whosoever having put his hand
40 to the plough, looketh back, is not fit for the kingdom of God!'
I am nothing pleased we advised you to have your plaid; though I am that you think it too dear, because I take it to be an indication that you are disposed to thrift, which is a rare qualification in a young man who has his fortune to make. Indeed, such an one can hardly be too wary, or too careful.[3] Not that he should

---

[1] 'I am . . . that' (the beginning of the *A.M.* selection) is not in LB.

[2] LB, 'because there is some beloved vice'.

[3] In LB the paragraph begins: '. . . One who has his fortunes to make can hardly be too careful.'

take thought for the morrow, any farther than is needful for his improvement of today, in a prudent manage of the talents God has committed to his trust. So far I think 'tis his duty; I heartily wish you may be well apprised of this, while life is young.

> Believe me, youth, for I am read in cares,   5
> And bend beneath the weight of more than fifty years.

Believe me, dear son, old age is the worst time we can choose to mend either our lives or our fortunes. If the foundations of solid piety are not laid betimes, in sound principles and virtuous dispositions, and if we neglect, while strength and vigour last, to lay up something ere the infirmities of age overtake us, 'tis a 10 hundred to one odds but we shall die both poor and wicked.

Ah! my dear J[acky], did you with me stand on the verge of life, and see before your eyes a vast expanse, an unlimited duration of being, which you were obliged shortly to enter upon, you can't conceive how all the inadvertencies, mistakes, and sins of youth would rise to your view; and how different the sentiments of 15 sensual pleasures, the desire of sexes, and pernicious friendships of the world would be then,[1] . . . from what they are now, while health is entire, and seems to promise many years of life! . . .

My love and blessing attends you and your brother. Dear J[acky], adieu!

Sources: LB, pp. 51–3, collated with a fuller version of the last four paragraphs edited by Wesley for publication in *A.M.*, 1778, pp. 38–9. In general the earlier version has been followed except where the additions and alterations seem to stem from the holograph rather than from Wesley's zeal for editing. Wesley's diary shows that he received it on Feb. 4.

From Mrs. Susanna Wesley[2]

March 14 [1726/7] 20

Dear J[acky]

. . . I congratulate your good success in taking your Master's degree . . .

I'm greatly pleased with your reflections on the methods of divine providence relating to a family, and am entirely of your mind, that less violent motives would not have prevailed (on me at least) to make us seriously apply ourselves 25 to the study and practice of the virtues you mention.

(Commendation of Sherlock on Providence.)

The relation I have to your friend Theod[osius] made me think it my duty to speak freely on his friendship to V[aranese]; which having done, I have no more to say or do, but only earnestly to pray for him; and to commit the conduct of 30 his soul to that superior wisdom which alone can guide it into the ways of truth and peace. I have a good opinion of the honesty of his intention, and believe he

---

[1] LB, 'and how different your sentiments would be then'.

[2] Apparently a reply to Wesley's letter of Feb. 10, in which he described the exercises for his M.A., even though the degree was not conferred until Feb. 14.

proposes to himself no happiness at present but what appears to him solid, rational, and Christian. But age has less fire and more caution than youth, and may perhaps sometimes be afraid where no fear is. But I hope it is excusable, and that no offence will be taken, where none was intended.

5   (Of Bishop Sprat's Sermon on Zeal.)

. . . I wish I had that funeral sermon you preached; but if that can't be, prithee send me the text, and bring the sermon, if you should come again ere I die.

Dear J[acky], I beseech Almighty God to bless you!

Source: LB, pp. 53–4.

To Mrs. Susanna Wesley[1]

10   Linc[oln College], March 19th, 1726/7

Dear mother

One advantage, at least, my degree has given me: I am now at liberty, and shall be in a great measure for some time, to choose my own employment. And as I believe I know my own deficiencies best,

15 and which of them are most necessary to be supplied, I hope my time will turn to somewhat better account than when it was not so much in my own disposal.

On Saturday next I propose beginning an entirely different life with relation to the management of my expenses from what I have

20 hitherto done.[2] I expect then to receive a sum of money, and intend immediately to call in all my creditors' bills (that they may not grow by lying by, as it sometimes happens), and from that time forward to trust no man of what sort or trade soever so far as to let him trust me.

25   Dear mother, I speak what I know. My being little and weak, whereas had it not been for a strange concurrence of accidents (so called in the language of men) I should very probably have been just the reverse, I can easily account for; I can readily trace the wisdom and mercy of Providence in allotting me these imperfections.

30 (Though what if I could not? Since while I took through a glass I

---

[1] Replying to hers of Mar. 14.

[2] On 'Saturday next', March 25, 1727, the beginning of the legal new year, he did in fact begin a new system of accounts in the volume used for his diary. It seems almost certain that the 'sum of money' which he then expected to receive was in some way connected with his fellowship, though it is difficult to understand 'the complex financial machinery of the college' (see Green, pp. 100–1; cf. pp. 119 n., 320–1).

can only expect to see darkly.)[1] But here the difficulty was likely to lie: Why would Infinite Goodness permit me to contract a habit of sin even before I knew it to be sinful, which has been a thorn in my side almost ever since? 'How can I skill of these thy ways?'[2] So well that I am verily persuaded, had it not been for that sinful habit, I had scarce ever acquired any degree of any virtuous one.[3] Is not this the finger of God? Surely none else could have extracted so much good from evil! Surely it was MERCY not to hear my prayer!

The conversation of one or two persons whom you may have heard me speak of (I hope, never without gratitude) first took off my relish for most other pleasures so far that I despised them in comparison of that. From thence I have since proceeded a step farther, to slight them absolutely. And I am so little at present in love with even company, the most elegant entertainment next books, that unless they have a peculiar turn of thought I am much better pleased without them. I think 'tis the settled temper of my soul that I should prefer, at least for some time, such a retirement as would seclude me from all the world, to the station I am now in. Not that the latter is by any means unpleasant. But I imagine it would be more improving to be in a place where I might confirm or implant in my mind what habits I would without interruption, before the flexibility of youth is over, than to stay where, among many advantages, I lie under the inconvenience of being almost necessarily exposed to much impertinence and vanity.

A school in Yorkshire, forty miles from Doncaster, was proposed to me lately, on which I shall think more when it appears whether I may have it or no.[4] A good salary is annexed to it, so that in a year's time 'tis probable all my debts would be paid, and I should have money beforehand. But what has made me wish for it most is the frightful description, as they call it, some gentlemen who know the place gave me of it yesterday. The town (Skipton in Craven) lies in a little vale, so pent up between two hills that it is scarce

---

[1] See 1 Cor. 13 : 12.

[2] George Herbert, 'Justice', a poem reprinted in Wesley's *Select Parts of Mr. Herbert's Sacred Poems*, 1773 (*Bibliog*, No. 349), pp. 19–20.

[3] It is not clear what specific 'sinful habit' Wesley had in mind. From 1725 he had become extremely sensitive about faults of various kinds, and developed a complex system of recording and tabulating them. See Heitzenrater, espec. pp. 58–9.

[4] Skipton School, founded in 1548, whose headmaster was to be appointed by the Rector and fellows of Lincoln College if the vicar and churchwardens of Skipton were unable to secure a successor within a month of a vacancy arising—which in this instance they were able to do. (See Green, pp. 117–18.)

accessible on any side, so that you can expect little company from
without, and within there is none at all. I should therefore be
entirely at liberty to converse with companions of my own choosing,
whom for that reason I would bring with me; and company equally
5 agreeable, wherever I fixed, could not put me to less expense.

> The sun, that walks his airy way
> To cheer the world, and bring the day,
> The moon that shines with borrowed light,
> The stars that gild the gloomy night [. . .];
10 > All of these, and all I see,
> Should be sung, and sung by me.
> These praise their Maker as they can,
> But want and ask the tongue of man.[1]

The text of that sermon I preached on the Sunday following Mr.
15 Griffith's death was, 'Now he is dead, wherefore should I fast?
Can I bring him back again? I shall go to him, but he shall not
return to me.'[2] I never gave more reason to suspect my doctrine did
not agree with my practice, for a sickness and pain in my stomach,
attended with a violent looseness, which seized me the day he was
20 buried, altered me so much in three days, and made me look so pale
and thin, that those who saw me could not but observe it.

A letter from my sister Emily, my brother tells me, was brought
to my chamber the other day, but wherever the fellow laid it I have
not been able to set eyes upon it from that time to this.

25 I am full of business, but have found a way to write without taking
any time from that: 'tis but rising an hour sooner in a morning and
going into company an hour later in the evening, both which may
be done without any inconvenience.[3] My brother has got the other
side away from me.[4] I am, your affectionate, dutiful son,

30   John Wesley

I return you thanks for your thoughts on zeal, and my sister

---

[1] Cf. Thomas Parnell, 'A Hymn to Contentment'. Wesley included this poem in his
Collection of Moral and Sacred Poems, 1744 (*Bibliog*, No. 78), I. 265–7, where he gives
the original more accurately and fully.

[2] 2 Sam. 12: 23. Cf. letters of Jan. 24 (pp. 208–9) and Mar. 14 (p. 212).

[3] Actually in view of his confessions of 'intemperate sleep' he had resolved to 'rise at
dawn' the previous spring (see Heitzenrater, p. 60), but 7.00 remained his usual hour,
only slowly and painfully to become a habitual 4.00 or 5.00 during the years 1729 and
1730—a process dramatically romanticized in 1782 to a few days' transformation (see his
sermon, 'On Redeeming the Time', No. 93 of this edition).

[4] This apparently means that Charles had asked if he might add a letter on the other
side of the sheet.

Emly for hers on—I know not what—However, I am persuaded they were very good. My love attends my other sisters—I should have said, brother Charles's too; for now he has a line, mor⟨e the g⟩ood.[1]

Source: MA, in a large hand on pp. 1–2 of a full sheet folded to make 4 pp., of which pp. 3–4 are missing. From the size and folding, as well as the note about his brother taking the other side, it seems likely that this was a reference copy, though the large hand, the scarcity of contractions, and the postscript's being written down one margin and up the other, introduce doubts.

From Mrs. Susanna Wesley[2]

April 22 [1727] 5

Dear J[acky]

I have so much to say that I verily believe I shall forget at least one half of it . . . Therefore 'tis the best way to begin with that which seems of most importance.

(Of my cutting off my hair; reasons for it.) 10

Your drawing up for yourself a scheme of studies highly pleases me, for there is nothing like a clear method to save both time and labour in anything. 'Tis a pretty observation of Seneca's, 'Most people pass through the world like straws upon a river, which are carried on by the wind or stream without having any proper action of their own.' Whether it proceed from mere impotence of mind, 15 intemperate love of pleasure, want of courage, or indolence, 'tis certain there are very few that will persevere in a regular course of life; and 'tis as certain that without such a course a man must necessarily spend most of his days in doing nothing, or nothing to the purpose . . . I know very well that if a man . . . will resolutely break through the foolish customs and maxims of that world, . . . he 20 must submit to be often the sport, perhaps the scorn, of the profane and the witty; but

> Slight those that say, amidst their sickly healths,
> Thou liv'st by rule. What does not so, but man?

A little well-timed neglect, or a prudent withdrawing from such company, is the 25 best answer in those cases; and the inward peace that results from a well-ordered life is an ample recompense for all its difficulties.

There is another thing in your last letter that almost equally pleases me, and that is your wise and honest resolution of not being trusted again by anyone. I heartily wish, Dear J[acky], that God may enable you to keep it . . ., and that his 30 merciful providence will ever grant you all things that are necessary for life and godliness, without your being compelled to live the life that I have done; and

[1] This conjectural reading assumes the use of 'v' for 'the'.

[2] Clearly an answer to John's missing letter of Apr. 4, about the contents of which it affords many clues. Wesley's accounts show that it was received Apr. 26.

that you may have such power over yourself as to be able to live cheerfully without such things as his wisdom thinks fit to withhold from you . . .

How you account for your being weak and little I know not; but I believe the true cause of your being so is want of sufficiency of food for ten or twelve years
5 when you were growing, and required more nourishment. If your contracting any ill habit was a means of your acquiring or confirming any good ones, the reason of God's permitting you to contract it is very clear. He often demonstrates the power of his mercy toward us by bringing good out of sin, the greatest evil; and his not hearing our prayers proves sometimes, in the event, the greatest
10 instance of his favour.

I am not sorry that you missed the school. That way of life would not agree with your constitution, and I hope God has better work for you to do . . . I would not have you leave making verses . . . Rather make poetry sometimes your diversion, though never your business.
15   I must own I vehemently suspect your doctrine and practice did not well agree. I know Mr. Griffiths was a favourite on more accounts than one or two. Be that as it will, I am glad you are better; though I verily believe you will never have any good state of health while you keep your hair.

My L[ord] Nottingham has given Mr. Pennington a small living, about £74
20 a year, paid in money, to which he goes the 10th of May . . . 'Tis your father's intention to serve both his cures for a year, which (beside that I think it too much for him) I know would satisfy neither parish. Now I think, if it will be no great prejudice to your affairs, and you can submit to live as we must do in his absence, it will be a charitable thing to come hither and supply his place during that
25 time. I am persuaded that if it be in your power to help us, you will do it . . .

Thus far I had written when Mr. William Hume, who succeeded his father in Laughton living, sent a servant to tell Mr. Wesley that his third brother, Daniel, enters into Holy Orders on Trinity Sunday; and that he desires, since Mr. Pennington is preferred, he would accept of him for a curate. On Thursday
30 next the two young gentlemen are to meet here about it. I shall [not] fail to inform you of what they resolve, as soon as it comes to my knowledge.

Your sister Emly is upon the point of leaving us, and we intend, if God permit, to put M[olly] to a trade at midsummer. So we shall have only P[atty] and K[ezzy] at home.
35   Dear J[acky], I beg of you to leave drinking green tea. It ill agrees with a weak constitution. If you drink sage, be sure you make it of sage well dried . . .

I beg Almighty God to bless and guide you in all your ways.

Dear J[acky], adieu.

I have abundance more to say, had I time.
40   J[acky], do you really think Charles has [[victuals]][1] enough? He writ me a mighty kind letter, with an air of great sincerity; but yet I am sometimes afraid he represented his case rather too well, out of mere goodness, to make me easy.

Source: LB, pp. 54–6.

[1] In cipher.

From Mrs. Susanna Wesley

Wroot, May 14 [1727]

Dear J[acky]

I wrote some [time] since to your brother Charles and you, but have not yet heard whether either of you received my letter. Yours, dated the 7th of April, found me engaged in much business, and if I had not I should have made no 5 great haste to answer it, because you told K[ezzy] you were to be absent from College for some time . . . And now I am about to answer it, I don't know how to do it to your satisfaction; for I've very little to say on zeal more than I've said already. Yet I can deny you nothing that is in my power to grant, though I write to no purpose. (Of zeal.) 10

The difficulty of separating the ideas of things that nearly resemble each other, and whose properties and effects are much the same, has made some think that we have no passion but love, and that what we call hope, joy, fear, etc., are no more than various modes of it. This notion carries some show of reason, though I can't acquiesce in it. I must confess I never yet met such a definition of love 15 as fully satisfied me. 'Tis indeed commonly defined, 'a desire of union with a known or apprehended good'. But this directly makes love and desire the same thing, which I conceive they are not, for this reason: desire is strongest and acts most vigorously when the beloved object is distant, absent, or apprehended unkind or displeased; whereas when the union is attained, delight and joy fills 20 the lover, while desire lies quiescent; which plainly shows that desire of union is an effect of love, not love itself.

What then is love? How shall we define its strange, mysterious essence? It is—I don't know what: a powerful something; source of our joy and grief! Felt by everyone, yet unknown to all! Nor shall we ever comprehend what it is till 25 we are united to our First Principle, and there read its wondrous nature in the clear mirror of Uncreated Love! Till which time it is best to rest satisfied with such apprehensions of its essence as we can collect from our observation of its effects and properties; for other knowledge of it in our present state is too high and wonderful for us, neither can we attain unto it![1] 30

Dear J[acky], suffer now a word of advice. However curious you may be in searching into the natures or distinguishing the properties of the passions or virtues, for your own private satisfaction, be very cautious of giving definitions in public assemblies, for it does not answer the true end of preaching, which is to mend men's lives, not to fill their heads with unprofitable speculations. And 35 after all that can be said, every affection of the soul is better known by experience than any description that can be given of it. An honest man will more easily apprehend what is meant by being zealous for God, and against sin, when he hears what are the properties and effects of zeal, than by the most accurate definitions of its essence.[2] And it is of incomparably greater concern to every 40 individual soul of your auditory to be well instructed how to temper zeal than to have the most accurate definition of its essence . . .

[1] 'Till which time . . . unto it' added from *A.M.*
[2] 'And after all . . . of its essence' added from *A.M.*

I've now received yours dated May 8th, and find by it you have my last. If you are so averse from parting with your hair . . . I've no more to say . . . I wish you health, and, if it please God, a long life . . .

Your being subject to frequent bleedings at the nose is no sign of the fluids 5 being too thick, but . . . of the contrary . . . The cramp is a nervous distemper, and proceeds from some obstruction that prevents the regular circulation of the spirits. 'Tis no wonder you should be afflicted with it, when your father has had it so violently, especially when he was young. One of the best remedies in this case is eight or nine hours of sleep, and moderate exercise, avoiding as much as 10 possible the being abroad after sunset . . . Water does certainly increase the fluids, but whether it corrects their viscidity or no I cannot tell . . .

(A r[ecipe] for viscidity or sharpness in the blood.)

What curate your father will hire I don't know. I think Mr. Hume will be the man. Till Martinmas he designs to serve both cures himself . . . I did once with 15 some degree of earnestness wish you here, but I don't now; rather I am glad that there is no occasion for your coming at all. For 'tis best for me to have as few attachments to the world as possible.

Dear J[acky], the conclusion of your letter is very kind. That you were ever dutiful I very well know, but I know myself enough to rest satisfied with a 20 moderate share of your affection. Indeed it would be unjust of me to desire the love of anyone. Your prayers I want and wish; nor shall I cease while I live to beseech Almighty God to bless you! Adieu!

I congratulate your composure of mind; for sure 'tis a happy temper, and can never make you unfit for good conversation. 'Tis my simple opinion that no man 25 is so well qualified for converse in the world as he that most despises it.

Charles has writ a letter to your father which much pleases him.

Em[ily] is gone to Lincoln.

Sources: LB, pp. 56–9, collated with Wesley's edited version of sections of the holograph in *A.M.*, 1778, pp. 78–9; of this only two major additions are inserted above.

From the Revd. Samuel Wesley, Jun.[1]

[May 15, 1727]

Dear Jack

30 I have sent you your sermon,[2] and like it very well on the whole. What passages seem exceptionable to me are these that follow. 'Tis far from certain the Samaritans were guilty of idolatry; most think it a slander thrown on them by the intemperate zeal of the Jews, who were willing to paint them as black as possible. The very end for which our religion was instituted is charity; it should 35 be more determinate one great end, because you presently name another to

---

[1] Answered by Wesley's of May 23.
[2] On Charity: see letter of May 22, 1727.

which this is only subordinate—the glory of God. This commandment is new in respect of its extent; I much doubt it. Strangers are expressly and frequently entitled to benevolence in the Old Testament; and enemies are directly, not by implication, included. If thou meet thine enemy's ox or his ass going astray, thou shalt surely bring it back to him again. God never yet bid man hate his 5 enemy; that was only one of the many traditions of the Jews which made the Law of God of none effect. The command may be new as to the plainness and frequency of its injunction, the degree and importance of our love, the Person who gave it, and the motives to its practice. We are under more particular obligation to the household of faith, indeed we are not only more bound to love them, but 10 bound also to love them more, in an higher degree and manner than others, which I think you have not inserted. Our Saviour's example is well urged, but methinks it would have been highly proper to have taken off a seeming objection —that even he called the scribes and Pharisees hypocrites and painted sepulchres, and Herod a fox, and so have showed that even such sharpness was not 15 railing. We are not only to forgive but also love our enemies. I am of opinion some degree of love must be before we can possibly forgive, but 'tis of small import which is first, provided they are inseparable, as I believe they will be found. Repentance is not necessary to these, but in order to trust it doubtless is. You have fairly proved that God's enemies are not excluded, no more than 20 our own. That all speaking what is evil of another is not contrary to εὐφημεῖυ[1] is plain from St. Stephen himself, who in his very prayer charged his murderers with sin. I do not well understand what you mean by violent methods in church rulers, and if excommunication, I hold it so far from being contrary to the Gospel that 'tis one of the institutions of it. They ought doubtless to use their 25 utmost caution in that as well as other matters, since 'tis required of a steward that he be found faithful. Severe proceedings are entirely foreign to the duty of a private man. I have several things here to offer. First, I take the endeavours to amend scandalous offenders to be much more especially the duty of governors. (2). Heresy is not the only ground of our withdrawing, nay is not mentioned 30 1 Cor. 5 : 11, but merely immoralities. (3). I don't think it plain either by general precept or particular that we ought always to admonish, over and over, before we avoid. (4). There is a special reason why private and weak Christians ought immediately to shun such persons, and namely lest evil communication should corrupt good manners. Our Saviour was above temptation, and therefore might 35 safely frequent the company of publicans and sinners, but we read not the same of his Apostles; they preached to all, but did not feast but with brethren. A physician may frequent a pest-house, where 'tis madness and presumption for another to go without a call. You had not room to insert these guards. There is but one passage which I think can be well taken as levelled at my father, which 40 is this: 'if Providence has pointed you out for the agents by the near relation between you and the offending person'; wherein I own I see no harm, unless it contain an insinuation that he had not set about that work before, which is so severe that truth itself could not have excused it in the pulpit.

I have received a letter from my sister Hetty since my last to you, wherein she 45 tells me her child is dead, and she has set up a school; by which, though not

---

[1] To speak auspiciously—'of good report', as in Phil. 4: 8.

meeting with so much encouragement as she expected, she hopes to get food at least, and somewhat to put her out of her present condition of a heathen philosopher. Brother Lambert may want money perhaps sufficiently, but I am sure he does not want confidence to ask you to lend it him; I am afraid you have
5   more than one reason for not complying with so unreasonable a request. I fancy my mother's earnestness for having your hair off proceeds from the length of it; for sure if you take away but two or three inches of its old size it would be full as primitive and sacerdotal as a wig.

I have never taken the least notice to my father of your sermon, nor ever
10   design it unless I should come face to face, and then not unless I found it still stuck hard at his heart.

My love to all friends. I must leave some room for a letter to Charles. Your sister sends her love. I am, dear Jack, your affectionate friend and brother,

S. Wesley

15   Monday, May 15,
1727
[The letter to Charles follows, adding after a similar subscription:]
Deans Yard, Westminster
Show the bearer, Taylor, a cousin of Mr. Leybourne's, the university, if you
20   can.

Address: 'To the Revd. Mr. Wesley, Fellow of Lincoln, Oxford'   *Source*:
MA.

To the Revd. Samuel Wesley, Jun.[1]

[May 22, 1727][2]

Dear brother

I return you thanks for your favourable judgment on my sermon,[3] and for the alterations you direct me to make in it; yet in order to be

---

[1] Answering the letter of May 15, 1727.

[2] The (undiscovered) holograph is apparently undated; Priestley hazarded no date; Telford dated it Dec. 5, 1726 (with no indication that this was a conjecture); Sotheby's catalogue conjectures 1739, along with the valuable information that it was postmarked May 23. In fact the postmark, added in London, would be most appropriate for a letter leaving Oxford (where on the evidence of the letter of May 15 Wesley was still in residence) on Monday, May 22, though it may well have been written on May 21 (the diary is missing). Internal clues point to 1727, and the obvious links with the letter of May 15 clinch the matter.

[3] The controversial sermon on Universal Charity, on Luke 9: 55—his fourth listed sermon (see Richard P. Heitzenrater, 'John Wesley's Early Sermons', W.H.S. XXXVII. 110–28). Several references have already been made to this sermon in Wesley's correspondence, as having been preached by Wesley in Wroot on Aug. 28, 1726, arousing his father's wrath and his elder brother's coolness, until John succeeded in discovering

still better informed, I take the liberty to make some objections to some of them, in one or two of which I believe you misunderstood me.

[I.] The reasons why I conceive the Samaritans to have been idolaters are, first, because our Saviour says of them, 'Ye worship ye know not what,'[1] which seems to refer plainly to the object of their worship; and secondly, because the old inhabitants of Samaria, who succeeded the Israelites, were undoubtedly so, and I never heard that they were much amended in after times: 'These nations feared the Lord, and served their graven images, both their children and their children's children.'[a]

II. Were the Jews obliged to love wicked men? And is not our commandment extended to some cases to which theirs did not reach? To the excluding some instances of revenge, which were indulged to them?

We are doubtless to love good men more than others, but to have inserted it where I was only to prove that we were to love them, and not how much, would not, I think, have been to my purpose. Where our Saviour exerts his authority against his opposers I can't think it safe for me to follow him. I would much sooner in those cases act by his precepts than example: the one was certainly designed for me, the other possibly was not. The Author had power to dispense with his own laws, and wisdom to know when it was necessary: I have neither.[2]

No one would blame a man for using such sharpness of speech as St. Stephen does, especially in a prayer made in the article of death, with the same intention as his.[3]

[III.] What you understand as spoken of *rulers* I expressly say of private men: 'As well every ruler as every private man must act in a legal way; and the latter might with equal reason apply the civil sword himself as use violent means' (by which I here mean reviling, studiously and unnecessarily defaming, or handing about ill stories of wicked men) 'to preserve the church.'

---

[a] 2 Kgs. 17: 41.

where the trouble lay. In his letter of Dec. 10, 1726, Samuel Wesley expressed a desire to see the manuscript, and on May 15, 1727, he returned it with his comments. The manuscript has disappeared, but the correspondence enables us partially to reconstruct it; several quotations appear in this letter. Cf. especially the letter of Dec. 6, 1726.

[1] John 4: 22.
[2] This paragraph is transliterated in Sotheby's sale catalogue; the only basic difference is Priestley's printing 'can't' as 'cannot'.
[3] See Acts 7: 60; cf. letter of May 15, p. 219, ll. 22-3 above.

[1.] I believe it to be more especially the duty of governors to try to amend scandalous offenders. 2. That flagrant immorality is a sufficient reason to shun anyone. 3. That to the weak and private Christian it is an unanswerable reason for so doing. 4. That in many cases a private Christian, in some a clergyman, is not obliged to admonish more than once. But this being allowed, still the main argument stands, that the Scripture nowhere authorizes a private person to do more than to shun an heretic, or (which I expressly mention) an obstinate offender. I had not the least thought of any retrospect in them, neither when I wrote or spoke those words: 'If Providence has pointed you out, etc.'[1]

My mother's reason for my cutting off my hair is because she fancies it prejudices my health.[2] As to my looks, it would doubtless mend my complexion to have it off, by letting me get a little more colour; and perhaps it might contribute to my making a more genteel appearance. But these, till ill health is added to them, I cannot persuade myself to be sufficient grounds for losing two or three pounds a year.[3] I am ill enough able to spare them.

Mr. Sherman says there are garrets somewhere in Peckwater[4] to be let for fifty shillings a year; that there are, too, some honest fellows in college who would be willing to chum[5] in one of them; and that could my brother but find one of these garrets, and get acquainted with one of these honest fellows, he might very possibly prevail upon him to join in taking it; and then, if he could but prevail upon someone else to give him seven pounds a year for his own room, he would gain almost six pounds a year clear, if his rent were well paid.[6] He appealed to me whether the proposal was not exceedingly reasonable. But as I could not give him such an answer as he desired, I did not choose to give him any at all.

[1] See Samuel Wesley's strong criticism of the one sentence in the sermon which might appear to have been levelled at his father, if indeed it contained an insinuation of the rector's pastoral neglect (see p. 219, ll. 42–3 above).

[2] See letters of Apr. 22, May 14, May 15.

[3] By wearing his own hair Wesley could save heavy charges for the purchase and care of a wig or wigs to be worn over close-cropped hair, which remained the fashionable practice throughout his life.

[4] The third-floor attics on Peckwater Quadrangle, an enlargement of Christ Church on the NE rebuilt by Dean Aldrich, 1706–11.

[5] The noun 'chum', first recorded in 1684, may have been an abbreviation of 'chamber-fellow' or 'chamber-mate'. This is the first use recorded in *O.E.D.* of the verb derived from it.

[6] Charles Wesley had entered Christ Church in June, 1726, and like the rest of the family continued impoverished.

Leisure and I have now taken leave of one another. I propose to be busy as long as I live, if my health is so long indulged to me.[1] In health and sickness I hope I shall ever continue with the same sincerity, your loving brother,

John Wesley 5

My love and service to my sister.

Address: 'To Mr. Wesley, Great Dean's Yard, Westminster,   *Postmark:* [23 MY]   *Sources:* Priestley, pp. 5–8; description of holograph in Sotheby's sale catalogue, of Dec. 16, 1958, giving postmark and transcripts as noted above.

From the Revd. Samuel Wesley

Wroot, June 6, 1727

Son John

I hope I may still be able to serve both my cures this summer, or if not, die pleasantly in my last dike. Though I believe if I should not hold it out, whereof 10 I've yet no symptom or suspicion, your mother would write you word. If that should happen, I see no great difficulty in bringing your pupil down with you for a quarter of a year or so, wh[en] you may both live (at least) as cheap as at Oxford. I shall be myself at Epworth, as soon as I can get a lodging.

This is all to you at present, but you'll see more than enough to poor Charles 15 o' t'other side from your humble father,

Sam Wesley

Source: LB, p. 21. Wesley does not transcribe any of Charles's part of this double letter. His accounts show that the letter was received on June 10, and the following letter from his father shows that he replied on June 14.

From the Revd. Samuel Wesley

Bawtry, June 21, 1727

Dear lads

This moment I had the satisfaction of yours o' 14 instant.   20

In answer to John:

I had no more reason to doubt of your duty to me than you have had of mine to you. Although I'm sure you can't think it proper there should be two masters in a family. Read! Reflect! You know I can't but love you, if you please, and if you think it worth your while that an old father should love you.   25

[1] These two sentences are transcribed from the holograph in Sotheby's catalogue, adding the word 'now' to Priestley's version.

What should I be if I did not take your offer to come down soon, as I ought? But you could not now get from hence to Wroot, though I can make a shift from Wroot to Epworth per boat, and it can't be worse this summer. However, if you have any prospect of doing good on Freeman (O let none of my lads ever 5 despair!), I beg you for God's sake to take to him again. For how do you know but you may thereby 'save a soul from death, and cover a multitude of sins'? If not of your own, yet of mine, who heartily give you this advice, and beg of you, as you love God or me, that you'd follow it as far as 'tis practicable. Once more, remember what a soul is worth, as you know what price was paid for it.

10 I hope in a fortnight to be able to walk to Epworth. When I'm tired I'll send you word. If you should come, buying a horse would be best (for I've now ground enough to spare for a dozen, and could make him as fat as a bear).

Your mother is well; Em fat, and (quasi) rich at Lincoln; Polly, creeping out of the CAVE this midsummer.

15 I'm weary, yet must still walk further.

Ah Charles

You shall see Wroot again, and your bowers of bliss, as soon as I'm able . . . Your loving father,

S. Wesley

Address: 'For ye Revd Mr Jno Wesley, Fellow of Lincoln College, Oxon'
Postmarks: 'Bawtry', '26 IV' (Wesley's accounts, however, show it as received June 24)   *Charge*: ((4))   *End* by JW: '<u>m</u> f. June 21st, 1727'   *Source*: MA; cf. LB, pp. 21, 65.

From the Revd. Samuel Wesley

20   Wroot, June 26, 1727

Dear son Jno

I don't think I've yet thanked you enough for your kind and dutiful letter of the 14th instant, which I received at Bawtry last Wednesday, and answered there in a hurry. Yet on reflection I see no reason to alter my mind much as to 25 what I then writ; but if you had any prospect of doing good on your pupil, should have been pleased with your attempting it some time longer. If that is passed, or hopeless, there's an end o' that matter.

When you come hither, after having taken care of Charterhouse and your own Rector, your headquarters will I believe be for the most part at Wroot, as mine, 30 if I can, at Epworth, though sometimes making an exchange. The truth is, I am hipped (with an i) by my voyage and journey to Epworth and fro[m] last Sunday; being lamed with having my breeches too full of water, partly with a downfall from a thunder shower, and partly from the wash of the tor[rent?] over the boat. Yet, I thank God, I was able to preach here ith' afternoon, and was as well this 35 morning as ever, ex⟨cept⟩ a little pain and lameness, both which I hope to wash off with an hair of the same dog this evening.

I wish the rain had not reached us on this side Lincoln; but we have it so

continual that we have scarce one bank left, and I can't possibly have one
quarter of oats in all the levels; but, thanks be to God, the field-barley and rye
are good. We can neither go afoot, or horseback, to Epworth, but only by boat
as far as Scawcett[1] Bridge, and then walk over the common, though I hope
'twill be soon better. I would gladly send horses, but don't think I've now any 5
that would perform the journey; for, (1), my filly has scarce recovered [from]
the last, and I question if she ever will. However, I've turned her up to the
wagon, and very seldom ride her; (2) Mettle is almost blind; (3) your favourite
two-eyed-nag they have ta'ne care to swing in the back, and he's never like to
be good for riding [any] more; (4), and Bounce, and your mother's nag, you 10
know.

   Therefore if you can get a pretty strong horse, not over fine, nor old, nor fat,
I think 'twould improve, especially in summer, and be worth your while. I
would send as far as Nottingham to meet you, but would have your studies as
little intermitted as possible, and hope I shall do a month or two longer, as I'm 15
sure I ought to do (at least) all I can both for God's family and my own; and
when I find it sinks me, or perhaps a little before, I'll certainly send you word,
with about a fortnight's notice; and in the meantime sending you my blessing,
as being your loving father,

Sam Wesley 20

Dear Charles
   I must be succinct [. . .]
   Were I a man, your argument should be—Job's horse, or sea-monsters. Were
I you, it should go hard but I'd get one of the Blenheim prizes.—Thomas calls.
—Goodnight t'ye. 25

Wroot, June 26, 1727
   I promise to pay £10 per ann. (at the least) to my son, Charles Wesley, of
Christ Church, Oxon, at every May Day, commencing at May Day next for this
present year.

Sam Wesley, Senr. 30

End by JW: 'F. Jun. 26, 1727'   *Sources*: Charterhouse School, Godalming,
England, collated with the excerpts in LB, p. 65.

From the Revd. Samuel Wesley

Wroot, July 5, 1727

Dear children
   I had yours of the 25th instant, and that before, I think of the 14th. In answer:
though you could neither of you be assisting to me here, as I know you would
both be much so, yet your company would be very acceptable if we can possibly 35

---

[1] Orig., 'Scawsit'.

find any way to get you hither. The main reason of my being willing to delay my son John's coming was his pupil; but his last has satisfied me, that is over. There was another, that I knew he could not then get between Wroot and Epworth either on foot or horseback (nor can he yet) without hazarding his health or life

5 (though I hope 'twill soon be better). Whereas my hide is tough, and I think no carrion can kill me; having walked eight or ten miles on Monday, the breadth of Hatfield Mor[ass?], part of it, and about sixteen yesterday, which was like to be enough for me. But this morning I thank God I was not a penny worse. (Only sixpence I spent, myself and my attendant, in my two days' journey.) The

10 occasion of this pretty-rank-booted walk, for I can't spare one horse from [carrying] coals, was to hire a room for myself, and sometime perhaps for you, if I can get you hither, to lodge in at Epworth; and now I have achieved it. I writ you last that I approve my son John's proposal of buying a horse for the journey, and think, for the reasons there given, that, at the far end, it will cost

15 him less than nothing. All the difficulty is for Charles, for I think you'd be either of you like a bird with one wing without the other. The only way your mother and I can think possible is, if he could go to Banbury, whence, they say, there is a carrier and wagons come to Nottingham, whither we could send an horse for him, as we could to Lincoln, for I see your route is now laid per London.

20 And further I cannot say on this head, but would have you write both from Oxon and London.

I thank Charles heartily for the Horse. He who made those verses need not fear winning the poetical prize in any academy in Europe.

God bless and guide you, and send you both a speedy and happy meeting
25 with your loving father

Sam Wesley

You'll find your mother much altered. I believe what will kill a cat has almost killed her. I've observed of late little convulsions in her mouth, very frequent, which I don't like.

Source: MA, a double letter from both Samuel and Susanna Wesley; cf. LB, p. 66.

From Mrs. Susanna Wesley

30   [July 5, 1727]

Dear Jacky
I had answered your letter, but was prevented by an unusual illness, which I thank God is pretty well over. When I wrote last I thought your father had laid aside his design of sending for you hither, but perceive now he has altered

35 his purpose, and has desired you to come. He does certainly want an assistant, though I believe if you stay a little longer ere you come hither he will want none. How Charles can get to Wroot I can't tell. 'Tis impossible for us to send horses farther than Nottingham, and I suppose he may scruple coming so far with the carrier.

In great haste I send ye both my love and blessing.

S. W.

End by JW: 'm̲ F. Jul̲ 5'   *Source*: MA, a double letter, without address, with that from Samuel Wesley; cf. LB, p. 59. The letter from Samuel replies to John's of June 25, but Mrs. Wesley's opening sentence seems to refer to John's letter of June 14.

From the Revd. Samuel Wesley

Wroot, July 18, 1727

Dear son John!

We received last post your compliments of condolence and congratulation to 5
your mother on the supposition of her near approaching demise, to which your
sister Patty will by no means subscribe, for she says she is not so good a philosopher as you are, and that she can't spare her mother yet, if it please God,
without very great inconveniency.

And, indeed, though she has now and then some very sick fits, yet I hope the 10
sight of you would revive her. However, when you come you will see a new face
of things, my family being now pretty well colonized, and all perfect harmony;
much happier in no small straits than perhaps we ever were before in the
greatest affluence. And you'll find a servant that will make us rich, if God gives
him leave, and us anything for him to work upon. I know not but it may be this 15
prospect, together with my easiness in my family, which keeps my spirits from
sinking, though they tell me I've lost some of my tallow between Wroot and
Epworth. But that I don't value, as long as I've strength still left to perform my
office.

If Charles can get to London I believe Hardsley at the Red Lion, Aldersgate 20
Street, might procure him an horse as reasonable as any to ride along with you to
Lincoln (city), and direct him where to leave it there with the carrier to return,
which will be the cheapest and the safest way; and I'll war'nt you we'll find
means to bring Charles up again. Your own best way, as in my last, will be to
buy an horse for yourself [IF.∴] for the reasons I then told you. I'm weary, but 25
your loving father,

Sam Wesley

Address: 'For the Revd Mr John Wesley, Fellow of Lincoln-College, Oxon. Per
Lond:'   *Postmarks*: 'BAWTRY', '21 IY'   *Charges*: ((4)), 'In all 7'   *End*
by JW: 'Jul̲ 18—27'   *Source*: MA; on the verso is a similarly dated and
signed letter to Charles Wesley, for which see Clarke, I. 303–4. For the letter
to John cf. LB, pp. 66–7.

From the Revd. Samuel Wesley

July 26 [1727]

Son John

I shall be at Lincoln (*Deo volente*) on the 21st instant,[1] and shall stay till Friday morning. If you can get thither by Wednesday or Thursday night, I shall be glad of your company home. And not long after I hope to send Charles a tolerable reason for following you . . . Whenever you come, you'll be fully welcome to your loving father,

Sam Wesley

Source: LB, p. 67.

From Mrs. Susanna Wesley

July 26, 1727

Dear J[acky]

The very ill health I have had this two or three last months makes me much indisposed to write, or I should have answered yours of the 15th instant sooner.

'Tis certainly true that I have had large experience of what the world calls ill[2] fortune; but as I have not made those improvements I ought to have made under the discipline of providence,[3] I humbly [conceive] myself to be unfit for an assistant to another in affliction. But blessed be God you are at present in pretty easy circumstances, which I thankfully acknowledge is a great mercy to me, as well as you. Yet if hereafter you should meet with troubles of various sorts, as 'tis very probable you will in the course of life, the best preparative I know of for suffering is a regular and exact performance of present duty. For this will surely make a man pleasing to God, and put him directly under his protection, so that no evil shall befall him but what he will certainly be the better for.

'Tis incident to all men to regard the past and the future, while the present moments pass unheeded; whereas in truth neither one nor the other is of use to us any farther than they put us upon improving the present time . . .

You did well to correct that fond desire of dying before me, since you do not know what work God may have for you to do ere you leave the world. And besides, as you observed, I ought surely to have the pre-eminence in point of time, and go to rest before you. Whether you could see me die without any motion of grief I know not; perhaps you could. 'Tis what I've often desired of the children, that they would not weep at our parting, and so make death more uncomfortable than it would otherwise be to me. If you, or any other of my children, were like

[1] This is clearly an error. In the absence of Wesley's diary it is difficult to reconstruct the situation.

[2] *A.M.*, 'adverse'.

[3] *A.M.*, 'but I have not made those improvements in piety and virtue, under the discipline of Providence, that I ought to have done; therefore'.

to reap any spiritual advantage by being with me at my exit, I should be glad
to have you with me. But as I have been an unprofitable servant during the
course of a long life, I have no reason to hope for so great an honour, so high a
favour, as to be employed in doing our Lord any service in the article of death.
It were well if you spoke prophetically, and that joy and hope might have the 5
ascendant over my other passions at that important hour. But I dare not presume,
nor do I despair, but leave it to our Almighty Saviour to do with me both in life
and death just what he pleases; for I have no choice.[1]

The family you mention under some affliction I suppose to be that of Varanese. I hope no branch of it has proved so bad as Hetty. If it has, I pray God to 10
comfort the rest of them, for they have trouble enough . . .

I have writ so often to my sister Annesley, and have received no answer, that
I believe she either never got my letters, or has forgotten me. I wish you would
see her . . . and inquire whether my sister Richardson be alive, and how she
lives. 15

Your father, I suppose, is for your coming hither presently. But what becomes
of poor Charles? I'm ill, and can't write to him.

I shall be glad if your coming to Wroot may be to your satisfaction. We are
under some pressures, but will endeavour to make things as easy to you as
possible. 'Tis well you've left [[drinking tea]];[2] for 'tis doubtful whether I shall 20
be able to get you any.

Dear J[acky], God bless thee!

Your sisters Patty and K[ezzy], who are both recovering from a fever that has
brought them very low, send their love to you; and do humbly petition that if
you have any [[old shirts]],[2] you would give 'em to them. 25

Once more, Adieu!

Your letter was not sent till the 15th of August. We have been sick, and I
could not finish it.

Sources: LB, pp. 59–61, collated with Wesley's editing of a selection for *A.M.*,
1778, pp. 79–80. Additions which appear to come from the holograph have been
inserted from this selection, which omits the opening sentence and several of the
closing paragraphs.

From Charles Wesley[3]

Jan. 20, 1727[/8]
Oxon 30

Dear brother

Half an hour ago I received yours, and have laid by my collections to talk with
you awhile. When I can find time to finish my letter I no more know than our
brother S[am] did at beginning one of his, being at least as busy as he can be for

---

[1] The *A.M.* selection ends here.   [2] In cipher.
[3] Replying to John's of Jan. 17, which it quotes.

the life of him. Yesterday I had penned a full and true account of my treatment at and departure from Dean's Yard for Christ Church (where I breathe once again, a free though sharp air), which said account upon second thoughts, judging not altogether so fit for travel, I have thrown by, not designing you shall
5 see it before you do me, if then.

As to your queries—'how those accidents shall be your last', I don't think proper to say. To 'what company was in the York coach' my answer is, a relation of that business is fitter for a private conference. To 'what said B[rother] and S[ister]', ditto. As to 'the surprising particulars' I must beg to be excused. Miss
10 Weston, since broke off with the Cit, has willed her service to be presented you more than once. 'Somebody' for many reasons shall be nobody. Your 'who wonders' I don't understand. Want of money and clothes are great temptations to dullness. I wish the person that says I'm like you had ⟨mo⟩re reasons for so saying. 'The necessity I lay under' is past, now ⟨tha⟩t I'm turned out with some
15 shillings in my pocket. This is the speediest, largest, distinctest, and as matters go now the only answer I can make to 'all and every of your questions'.

'Tis an ill wind that blows nobody good! That same favourable blast, at which my father may say, '*Ego in portu navigo*',[1] has quite overset my patience, which you know is but a slight vessel at best, and at present is sadly at a loss for
20 ballast. 'Settled for life—at least for years! ['] You can't imagine what a violent effort those few words had upon this gentle reader. Bob[2] and I have been ready to knock our heads against every post we have met since that plaguy piece of news: 'twill most certainly have one of two widely different effects upon me; make me a very hard student, or none at all; an excellent economist, or a poor
25 desperate scoundrel; a patient Grizzle like Moll, or a Grumbletonial like Pat. 'Tis in the power of a few Epworth or Wroot guineas and clothes to give things the favourable turn, and make a gentleman of me. Come money, then, and quickly, to rescue me from my melancholy maxim, *ex nihilo nihil fit*—I can possibly save nothing, where there is nothing to save.

30   Nor yet from my dim eyes THY form retires!

(the cold empty starving grate before me makes me add the following disconsolate line:)

                   Nor cheering image of thine absent fires.

                            Hinksey's
35   No longer now on Horrell's airy van,
           With thee shall I admire the subject plain,
           Or where the sight in neighbouring shades is lost
           Or where the lengthened prospect widens most;
           While or the tuneful poet's (something) song,
40   Or truths divine flow easy from thy tongue.[3]

You'll pardon my turning your own words upon you, as likewise my dwelling so long upon so trifling a subject as is that of our separation, for a few years only.

----

[1] 'I have reached port.'   [2] i.e. Kirkham.
[3] From an early poem by John, 'Verses to the Memory of an Unfortunate Lady', given in his manuscript 'Miscellany Verses', pp. 39–43, and published in *A.M.*, 1778, pp. 380–3. The orig. has 'Horrel's' (cf. p. 281), and 'sprightly poet's tuneful song'.

I'm glad, however, at some passages in your letter. I picked up some crumbs of comfort at reading the Christian had got the upper hand of the Turk: if you can but tie up the beast (or at least his tongue) to his good behaviour, and prevent his falling foul on the family in your awful presence, you'll have achieved a nobler enterprise than did Sir Calidore when he chained up the blatant one.[1] He   5 may perchance rebel against me too, if he scapes you, who are confessedly the very pink of courtesy. Though I was resolved to say nothing of Westminster I can't choose telling you my sister triumphs hugely upon your not sending up immediately a receipt for your last quarter as my passport to Oxon. My brother, you must know, expecting it as a reimbursement for what he expended there for 10 me, and in my journey hither, I could wish you would spare it, but if not you needn't fear my giving in to my sister's persuasion, who would willingly have me think you don't care a farthing for me, and is desirous I should care just as much for you. But this trial of my passive valour is at last over. [. . .] She is at London, and I at Oxford! One sister I parted from with great regret, and one person 15 more. Poor Hetty! It grieves me almost to think how kindly she treated me, who am seldom so happy as to meet with bare humanity from others. 'Tis a shocking comparison! 'Twas but a week before I left London that I knew she was at it. Little of that time, you may be sure, did I lose, being with her almost continually. I could almost envy myself the deal of pleasure I had crowded within that 20 small space. In a little neat room she has hired did the goodnatured, ingenious, contented wretch and I talk over a few short days which we both wished had been longer. As yet she lives pretty well, having but herself and honest Will to keep, though I fancy there's another a-coming. Brother and sister are very kind to her, and I ⟨hope⟩ will continue so, for I have cautioned her never to con- 25 tradict my sister, whom she knows. [. . .] I'd like to have forgot, my sister begs you'd write to her: at Mr. Walkden's in Crown Court, Dean Street, near Soho Square. [. . .] Lush: is still at London. I would have you write to him, and direct to Stephen L[ushington], at Will's Coffee House in Scotland [?] Yard. [. . .] Bob's come, and I must resign my pen, though never so much your loving 30 brother,

⟨C⟩

Write as soon as may be. Mem: clothes.

[From Robert Kirkham][2]

My dearest friend

I beg you would excuse my not writing to you before I had any directions. 35 Term no more 'scurvy, lousy knave'; this time I shall forget it. Bett has been delivered of a very great burden and trouble, I believe, since you were at Stanton. Varanese's time is nigh come. You sent your last letter to your brother

---

[1] For Sir Calidore and the Blatant Beast see Spenser, *Faerie Queene*, Bk. VI.

[2] Added to the previous letter. Robert Kirkham (*c.* 1708–67), a student of Merton College, Oxford, son of the Revd. Lionel Kirkham, rector of Stanton, Gloucestershire, whom Robert succeeded after his death in 1736, having earlier served as curate to his uncle, Henry Kirkham, vicar of Stanway, Gloucestershire.

the most lamentable piece of news, save one, that ever I saw, or at least was made sensible of. I now almost wish I had never knew thee, for then I should never have knew the loss of you. The thought of it [is] grievous unto me, the burden of it scarce tolerable. Had I been still kept in the dark I should have entertained
5 some hopes of great pleasure and real happiness, i.e. of your return. But I thank God who has not left me quite desolate, but has sent a comforter unto me, and has blessed me with Charles, who is the greatest consolation to your most sincere friend.

Address: 'To The Revd Mr John Wesley, Curate at Epworth in the Isle of Axholm near Wroot' [in CW's hand; no evidence of posting]   *Source*: MA.

From Mrs. Susanna Wesley

Epworth, Aug. 12, 1728

10 Dear J[acky]
      I had not failed to give you advice of your box sending, but that I have been ill ever since you went hence. Within these few days the fever left me, and now, I thank God, I'm pretty well . . . My sickness, and somewhat worse, has made our work here go on very slowly; and when you return you'll not find the house
15 much better than you left it.
      I am glad you met with so good a reception at London, and that the place of your residence is so pleasing to you. Whatever my circumstances are, or wherever it seems good to Infinite Wisdom to cast my lot, I am greatly delighted to hear that others are more easy in their fortunes, company, or habitation; and have as
20 true a taste of what they enjoy as they have themselves. Were it in my power to make all men happy I should not fail of being so too. Though, blessed be God, as it is I am far from miserable.
      You did well to visit poor Tim; 'tis a little hearty mortal, and I dare say was very glad to see you. If you happen to see him again, pray return his services . . .
25 (R[ecipe]s for Syrup of Mulberries, Mulberry Wine, or Wine and Shrub). If there be anything else in which I can serve you, let me know. I beseech Almighty God to bless thee!

Source: LB, pp. 61–2.

From the Revd. Samuel Wesley

Epworth, Sept. 5, 1728

Dear son
30   Your mother had yours yesterday, as I suppose you have ere this hers, and mine with the certificate.[1] Yours brought the good news of Charles's recovery, which will supersede his country-journey, and help him to regain the time he has lost in his studies.

---

[1] See note to letter of Aug. 27, 1725.

(Of his [[wants]], and [[borrowing money]])[1]

N[ancy?] has been again upon me several weeks, her mistress being sick, but returned to Thorne last Sunday. M[olly] miraculously gets money, even in Wroot, and has given the first-fruits of her earnings to her mother, lending her money, and presenting her with a new cloak of her own buying and making— for which God will bless her. When we get to Epworth she will grow monstrously rich, for she will have more work than she can do, and the people are monstrously civil.

God has given me two fair [e]scapes for life within these few weeks: the first when my old nag fell with me, trailed me by my foot in the stirrup about six yards (when I was alone, all but God and my good angel), trod on my other foot, yet never hurt me.

The other scape was much bigger. On Monday sennight at Burringham Ferry we were driven down with a fierce stream and wind, and fell foul with our broadside against a keel. The second shock threw two of our horses overboard, and filled the boat with water. I was just prepared to swim for life when John Whitelamb's long legs and arms swarmed up into the keel, and lugged me in after him. My mare was swimming a quarter of an hour, but at last we got all safe to land. Help to praise him 'who saves both man and beast'.

I write with pain; therefore nothing else but love and blessing from your affectionate father,

Sam Wesley

Dick's just Dick still; but I hope Suky is not Suky.

Source: LB, pp. 67–8.

From Mrs. Susanna Wesley

Sept. 1728

Dear J[acky]
(Of my brother Charles's coming to Epworth)
If he come, he must not think of returning till after winter.

Source: LB, p. 62.

From Charles Wesley

Jan. 5 [22, 1728/9]

Dear brother
I have been so entirely taken up with my collections that I could not write sooner. At present I am head of the third class, and shall be of the table this term, and then there will be brave living for me!

---

[1] In cipher.

'Tis in your fate surely to have to do with disputants: as soon as one drops his disputatiousness another catches it up: Bob is what I was. No wonder he and I made such rare work on't, if you two make no better. I pity you, for I know him! But as you brew you must bake; e'en[?] make the most of him now you
5   have him.

I'm much of your opinion as to Molly's design upon me, but can't imagine the mother would purvey no better for her daughter, if she wasn't in a desperate condition indeed. To do the old lady justice, she *did* give us opportunities enough, could I have had the grace to ha' laid hold on them; and but for my
10 strange college dullness Molly *might* have made something of me. Lushington would have made a better use of his time, or I'm mistaken, but hints were *lost* upon so dull, stupid a fellow as I was; and as such no doubt I have been since sufficiently laughed at.

After such a slight put upon her 'twould be impudence in me ever to look her
15 in the face again, unless in the playhouse, and I believe I durst venture there, so the music-box was between us, and you on one side of me. I can't imagine, by the by, why you should mistrust her abilities; she's never the less qualified for the stage for being a whore, sure! Warter, an eye-witness, commends her capacity in spite of the villainous words Barford had put into her mouth. After
20 all, I don't take her frailty much to heart, as I can without any regret resolve never to change another word with the pretty creature; which I can the more easily refrain from as my eyes were partly opened by my last saving journey to London, and I trust I shall keep 'em open, and see the clearer by it, all the days of my life. One benefit I'm sure to get by the bargain: from henceforth *peculiarem*
25 *habito nominem*;[1] I shall be far less addicted to gallantry, and doing what sister Nutty with less justice said you did—liking woman merely for being woman.

Since I began this I have picked up another scrap of intelligence about the dear creature at Lincoln's Inn. You must know, living near a seat of the Duke of Richmond, his grace did her the honour of taking a fancy to her when about
30 thirteen years old. From his hands she passed through several others before she came into happy Mr. Thompson's. She had once set up for a milliner! But it would not do, nature and her stars (I think 'tis very gallant in me to lay the blame upon *them*) having designed her for the stage. But enough of her. I'll blot my brain and paper no longer with her.

35 I can't take so long views as to foresee for a whole life, but could manage a month, perhaps, or a year, and shall be glad of your advice how I may make my best use of the following. What I propose myself is to lay in a good stock of Latin and Greek against I'm examined for my degree, which at present termi-nates my prospect. Suppose for Latin I read Tully, Terence, and Horace, for
40 Greek Xenophon? Prose is more serviceable than verse, and I don't know a man fitter for my purpose than he. I expect you should either approve my choice or direct me to a better; and if you'd send a paragraph about what particular seasons are best for what particular studies 'twould save me a great deal of trouble, and cost you but little.

45 Our dean has narrowly missed of preferment of late, and through his own refusal, too. He had the proffer of the bishopric of Peterborough, but would not accept it without the deanery of Windsor annexed. However, he *will* be removed

---

[1] 'I must live with the reputation for being peculiar.'

speedily, the Queen having promised to prefer him for the good of Christ Church. *Amen!*

'Twould be an easy matter for me, as the dean is now at London, and will be till September, to get leave out of town; but how shall I get to Epworth? Answer me that. Or how back again? My standing *here* is so very slippery, no wonder 5 I long to shift my ground. Christ Church is certainly the worst place in the world to begin a reformation in; a man stands a very fair chance of being laughed out of his religion at his first setting out, in a place where 'tis scandalous to have any at all. Was the damning others the only means of saving themselves, they could scarce labour more heartily! I need say no more of 'em; you partly know 10 'em, and are got out of their cursed society. I wish to God I was, and shall be, I'm confident, when he sees it best for me!

I have just got Hutchinson come home, but haven't had time to read him yet, as I design to do with great diligence. I have got Collier's *Essays*, too, and like 'em exceedingly. I'm sorry I can have no assistance from Epworth, but have 15 thence one more reason to rely upon Providence, for I don't yet see the human means of getting clear of debt, which I must inevitably run farther into every day. But I shall say no more of this than needs must; you know my condition, and that's enough.

I here send the programme you asked for. There were but five against it, 20 among whom was our dean, who opposed it with might and main on very slender reasons and to very little purpose. However, to show his dislike, he entered his protest against it by not letting it be put up in our hall, as it was in most of the halls in town besides.

Whereas there is too much reason to believe that some members of the university 25 have of late been in danger of being corrupted by ill-designing persons, who have not only entertained wicked and blasphemous notions contrary to the truth of the Christian religion, but have endeavoured to instil the same ill principles into others, and the more effectually to propagate their infidelity have applied their poison to the unguarded inexperience of less informed minds, where they thought it might operate with the 30 better success . . .; and whereas therefore it is more especially necessary at this time to guard the young of this place against these wicked advocates for pretended human reason against divine revelation, and to enable them the better to defend their religion, and to expose the pride and impiety of those who endeavour to undermine it; Mr. Vice-Chancellor, with the consent of the Heads of Houses and Proctors, has thought fit 35 to recommend it as a matter of the utmost consequence to the several tutors of each college and hall in the university that they discharge their duty by a double diligence in informing their respective pupils in their Christian duty, as in explaining to them the Articles of Religion which they profess and are often called upon to subscribe to, in recommending to them the frequent and careful reading of the Scriptures and such other 40 books as may serve more effectually to promote Christianity, sound principles, and orthodox faith; and farther Mr. Vice-Chancellor with the same consent does hereby forbid the said youth the reading such books as may tend to the weakening their faith, subverting the authority of the Scripture, and introducing deism, profanest [*sic*], and irreligion in their stead. 45

Edwd. Butler, V.C.

Jan. 22

Your last is now come to hand. Lushington is not come to college yet, though there has been a terrible uproar about his *not* coming. He's expected very shortly now, and as soon as he is visible depend upon't I'll solicit your business very *faithfully*!

By what I can pick up from my mother's and your account I find poor Bob hangs upon your hands a small matter, and is likely so to do unless the other
5 string is better than what you mention to me. There's old consultations in my mother's chamber, 'What's to do?' I don't question! But you don't tell me what Bob says to the matter, and how he likes his company and place of abode, which was what I most wanted to know. I prophesy, though, however he may like 'em *now*, he will hanker after Oxford sometime before he gets at it; and without the
10 help of a collation, too. He must be going to Epworth, must he? And now he's in for't let him get out how he can: 'twas an easier matter, he'll find, to sink than to emerge; the business is

revocare pedem superasque evadere *ad auras.*[1]

I have sent him a few lines of comfort by this post.
15 In my pursuit of knowledge I own I have this advantage of you in some things. My brothers were born before me; I start at twenty. But then I'm sure I'm less indebted to nature than you. I'm very *desirous* of knowledge, but can't *bear* the drudgery of coming at it near so well as you could. In reading anything difficult I'm bewildered in a much shorter time than I believe you used to be at
20 your first setting out. My head will by no means keep pace with my heart, and I'm afraid I shan't reconcile it in haste to the extraordinary business of thinking.

I would willingly write a diary of my actions, but don't know how to go about it. What particulars am I to take notice of? Am I to give my thoughts and words, as well as deeds, a place in it? I'm to mark all the good and ill I do; and what
25 besides? Must not I take account of my progress in learning as well as religion? What cipher can I make use of? If you would direct me to the same or a like method with your own, I would gladly follow it, for I'm fully convinced of the usefulness of such an undertaking. I shall be at a stand till I hear from you.

God has thought fit (it may be to increase my wariness) to deny me at present
30 your company and assistance. 'Tis through him strengthening me I trust to maintain my ground till we meet, and neither before or after that time shall I, I hope, relapse into my former state of insensibility. 'Tis through your means, I firmly believe, God will establish what he has begun in me, and there is no one person I would so willingly have to be the instrument of good to me as you.
35 I verily think, dear brother, I shall never quarrel with *you* again till I do with my religion, and that I may never do *that* I am not ashamed to desire your prayers. 'Tis owing in great measure to somebody's (my mother's, most likely) that I am come to think as I do, for I can't tell myself how or when I first awoke out of my lethargy—only that 'twas not long after you went away.
40 Write soon. I am your truly loving brother,

Charles Wesley

Address: 'To the Revd. Mr. John Wesley, to be left at the Post-house in Gains-borough, Lincolnshire' *Postmarks*: 'OXFORD', '26 IA' *Charges*: ((3)), 'In all 7' *End* by JW: 'C. June 5, 1729' [*sic*] *Source*: MA.

[1] 'to recall your step and return to the upper air'; cf. Virgil, *Aeneid*, vi. 128.

From Charles Wesley[1]

[May 5, 1729]

Dear brother

What y⟨ou say ab⟩out coldness has put me upon considering whence mine can proceed, and how it may be remedied. I think I may truly esteem it the natural and just consequence of my past life. One who like m[y]s[elf] has for 5 almost thirteen years been utterly inattentive at public prayers can't expect to find there that warmth he has never known at his first seeking; he must knock oftener than once before 'tis opened to him; and is (I think) in some measure answerable for a heartlessness of which he himself is the cause. Be that how it will, I resolve that my falling short of my duty in one particular shan't discourage 10 me from vigorously prosecuting it in the rest. I look upon this coldness as a trial, and that unless I sink under it 'twill in the end greatly contribute to my advantage. I *must*, I *will*, in spite of nature and the devil, take pains. While my strength lasts I *will* put it to the utmost stretch, for a day's relaxing throws me back to my first setting out. I won't give myself *leisure* to relapse, for I'm 15 assured, if I have no business of my own, the devil will soon find me some. You may show this if you think proper to my mother, for I would gladly have a letter from her upon this subject.

Providence has at present put it in my power to do some good. I have a modest, humble, well-disposed youth lives next me, and have been (I thank 20 God!) somewhat instrumental in keeping him so. He was got into vile hands, and is now broke loose. I assisted in setting him free, and will do my utmost to hinder his getting in with 'em again. He is already content to live without any company but Bob's and mine. He was of opinion that passive goodness was sufficient, and would fain have kept in with his acquaintance and God at the 25 same time; he durst not receive the sacrament but at the usual times for fear of being laughed at. I have persuaded him to neglect censure on a religious account, and thereby greatly encouraged myself to do so; by convincing him of the duty of frequent communicating I have prevailed on both of us to receive once a week. He has got Nelson upon my recommendation, and is resolved to spare no 30 pains in working out his salvation. Ought I not to give God the glory? Ought I not to despise the hard constructions people put upon our acquaintance, even though they should say and think what I am far from judging they do, that he is a cully and I a sharper? Ought I not to seek opportunities of appearing in public with him, if for no other reason, yet because I am averse to it? He is an object 35 worthy your charity and acquaintance; how far he deserves either you'll be better able to judge when we meet. Meantime let me hear what you say to him.

Would to God I could give you a like account of Bob! But I'm afraid, so he can but get to heaven any way, the less pains, he thinks, the better. I'm not uncharitable in my opinion; you can't imagine how wretchedly lazy he is, and 40 how small a share of either learning or piety will content him: four hours a day he *will* spare for study out of his diversions, not so many hours for diversion out of his studies! What an excellent inverter! Nay, to my knowledge he is not so

[1] Replying to John's of Apr. 30 (?).

scrupulous but half this four will serve his turn at most times. What is to be done with him, think ye? He's past my skill; I wish he mayn't be beyond yours too. You might have spared the line to him, for you couldn't think me so mad, sure, as to show it him, unless I had a mind he should plague my heart out to see all
5 the rest. He went from me lately in a furious chafe on my refusing to show him a letter I was so imprudent as to tell him I had received from sister Patty, wherein she let me into some secrets of Epworth economy. What therefore you may have to say to him, or what to me that he may see, write on the first half-sheet; what's between you and I only, on the second.
10 One more word of the commentators, though I'm quite sick of 'em. I must own I don't conceive how what brother Sam says is so little to the purpose as you imagine: 'Wills is an honest man, and one of sound principles, which none could ever say of Dr. Whitby.' Now in my apprehension his meaning is as obvious and apposite as heart can wish! To caution me against understanding
15 what he said of aught but the commentary had been as absurd as though he should have warned me not to think 'honest' meant either Whig or Tory.
I'm so far from expecting but small satisfaction at Stanton that all I fear is meeting too much. Indeed I durst on no account trust myself there without you, for as I take it strong pleasure would be dangerous to one in my unconfirmed
20 condition. They have had the good fortune there to have a couple of aunts die and leave the three girls £200 apiece. There's news for you, you rogue! I'm heartily glad for poor Bett, and not a little for poor Damaris, because I believe it may help her to a husband the sooner. 'Tis well you at last own Sally not infallible, though she is so, I verily believe, for all your suspicions; all the
25 business is, she is *not* changed, but Chapone is Chapone still.
How shall I dispose of Lushington's money now I have got it, as much (I mean, now you have turned over)[1] as I ever shall. You may set your heart at rest about it, for I'm confident your creditor has taken his final leave of Oxford. He has been guilty of such wretched extravagancies lately (his half year at Chester
30 cost him £130) that his mother will never venture him here again, but chain him up at home till she can send him away for good and all; so all your hopes of payment depend solely now upon his honour. He borrowed a shirt and half a guinea of me a little before his departure; the shirt I have recovered, but the money is safe—with yours. Bob contributed his half-crown too, and so—exit
35 Lushington. Will I ever trust a friend again that has no religion? I *did* think our friendship would have lasted for *this* life, but what intimacy can I ever have hereafter with a man of his morals and his gratitude? God be praised he has robbed me of nothing but my money!
I earnestly long for and desire the blessing God is about to send me in you.
40 I am sensible *this* is my day of grace, and that upon my employing the time before our meeting and next parting will in great measure depend my condition for eternity.
An accident (if it may be called so) has lately happened to me, which has made me resolve never upon any account to omit or defer my prayers. Last Saturday,
45 being upon a design to do Lushington a piece of service, I could not come home till eight at night. I then found myself utterly averse to prayers, and spent half an hour in vain in striving to recollect my dissipated thoughts. Upon this I gave

[1] Charles had just turned over the sheet of paper, beginning with the words 'as much'.

out, and passed the whole night in the utmost trouble and discomposure of mind. I rose in the morning two hours later than usual, in utter despair of receiving the sacrament that day, or of recovering myself in less than two or three. In this condition I went immediately to church. On my way a thought came across me, that it might be less sin to receive even without the least 5 immediate preparation (for the whole week till Saturday evening I had spent to my satisfaction) than to turn my back upon the sacrament. I accordingly resolved, if I found myself anything affected with the prayers, to stay and communicate. I *did* find myself affected, and stayed. I not only received the sacrament at that time with greater warmth than usual, but afterwards found my 10 resolutions of pursuing considerably strengthened. This wasn't all. On Sunday night I received a great blessing from God, and have continued since in a better frame of mind than I have yet known. Dear brother, remember and pray for me when you receive this. I am, yours entirely,

Ch. W. 15

Christ Church
Oxon, May 5
I *did* design to write to my sisters this post, but can't. Give my love, pray, and duty to father and mother.

Address: 'For The Revd. Mr Jno Wesley at Epworth, to be left at the Post-House in Ganesborough, Lincolnshire' *Postmarks*: 'OXFORD', '6 MA' *Charges*: ((3)), 'In all 7' *End* by JW: 'C. May 5, 1729' *Source*: MA, with many examples of the abbreviated longhand and symbols for 'and', 'con', 'for', which John Wesley had doubtless passed on in response to Charles's request of Jan. 22, 1729.

From Mrs. Susanna Wesley[1]

Aug. 11, 1729 20

Dear J[acky]
I need not tell you I should be glad to see you, because you know it already; and so I should to see poor Charles too; but what to say to his coming I know not. J[ohn] L[ambert], h[is] w[ife] and ch[ild], we are still like to keep, for we hear no news of a place for h[im]; though I would fain hope it would please God 25 to provide for h[im] some way ere winter, and take off their w[eigh]t, which really grows very heavy.
I wrote with some earnestness to your brother Sam. Wesley, to persuade him to come to Epworth; but I find I can't prevail . . . He will be here toward the end of the month . . . He sent me a pound of Bohea tea and two pounds of 30 chocolate, which were very acceptable; for none could I buy, and I was somewhat ill for want of tea . . .
I think you had better contrive to meet your brother at Lincoln, and then

[1] Replying to his of Aug. 6.

come all together . . . I have a bad arm, and write in much pain, or I have a deal
to say else . . . Perhaps I may live to see you.

May Almighty God bless and preserve you!

Source: LB, p. 62.

From Dr. John Morley[1]

[Oct. 21, 1729]

5   At a meeting of the society, just before I left college, to consider the proper
method to preserve discipline and good government, among several things
agreed on it was, in the opinion of all that were present, judged necessary that
the junior fellows who should be chosen moderators shall in person attend the
duties of their office, if they do not prevail with some of the fellows to officiate
10 for them. We all thought it would be a great hardship on Mr. Fenton to call him
from a perpetual curacy or donative, yet this we must have done had not Mr.
Hutchins been so kind to him and us as to free us from the uneasiness of doing
a hard thing, by engaging to supply his place in the hall for the present year.
Mr. Robinson would as willingly supply yours, but the serving of two cures
15 about fourteen miles distant from Oxford, and ten at least as bad as the worst of
your roads in the Isle, makes it, he says, impossible to discharge the duty constantly. We hope it may be as much for your advantage to reside at college as
where you are, if you take pupils, or can get a curacy in the neighbourhood of
Oxon. Your father may certainly have another curate, though not so much to his
20 satisfaction; yet we are persuaded that this will not move him to hinder your
return to college, since the interest of college and obligation to statute
requires it.

Source: Whitehead, I. 415–16, date noted as Oct. 21, 1729.

To the Revd. Samuel Wesley

Lincoln College, Dec. 19, 1729

Dear Sir

25 As I was looking over the other day Mr. Ditton's Discourse on
the Resurrection of Christ,[2] I found toward the end of it a sort of

---

[1] This letter from the Rector of Lincoln College brought about Wesley's return from
Lincolnshire to Oxford, where he eventually arrived on Nov. 22, soon becoming the
leader of the tiny academic and religious group which was to be nicknamed the
'Methodists'.

[2] Humphrey Ditton (1675–1715), a mathematician, in his *Discourse concerning the
Resurrection of Jesus Christ* (1714) emphasized the importance of 'moral evidence' as
proof. The appendix claimed that thought could not be produced from matter and

essay on the origin of evil. I fancied the shortness of it, if nothing
else, would make you willing to read it, though very probably you
will not find much in it which has not occurred to your thoughts
before:

Since the Supreme Being must needs be infinitely and essentially good, as 5
well as wise and powerful, it has been esteemed no little difficulty to show how
evil came into the world. *Unde malum*[1] has been a mighty question.

There were some who, in order to solve this, supposed two supreme governing
principles, the one a good, the other an evil one. Which latter was independent
on and of equal power with the former, and the author of all that was irregular 10
or bad in the universe. This monstrous scheme the Manichees fell into and much
improved; but were sufficiently confuted by St. Austin, who had reason to be
particularly acquainted with their tenets.

But the plain truth is, the hypothesis requires no more to the confutation of
it than the bare proposing it. Two supreme, independent principles is next door 15
to a contradiction in terms. It is the very same thing, in result and consequence,
as saying two absolute infinites; and he that says two had as good say ten, or
fifty, or any other number whatever. Nay, if there can be two essentially distinct
absolute infinites, there may be an infinity of such absolute infinites: that is as
much as to say, none of them all would be an absolute infinite, or that none of 20
them all would be properly and really infinite. ('For real infinity is strict and
absolute infinity, and only that.')[2] From the nature of liberty and free will we
may deduce a very possible and satisfactory (perhaps the only possible just)
account of the origin of evil.

There are, and necessarily must be, some original, intrinsic arguments and 25
disagreements, fitnesses, and unfitnesses of certain things and circumstances, to
and with each other; which are antecedent to all positive institutions, founded
on the very nature of those things and circumstances, considered in themselves
and in their relation to each other.

As these all fall within the comprehension of an infinite, discerning mind, who 30
is likewise infinite, essential, rectitude and reason; so those on the one side must
necessarily (to speak after the manner of men) be chosen or approved of by him,
as the other disliked and disapproved, and this on the score of the eternal,
intrinsic agreeableness and disagreeableness of them.

Farther, it no way derogated from any one perfection of an Infinite Being to 35
endow other beings which he made with such a power as we call liberty; that is,
to furnish them with such capacities, dispositions, and principles of action that

motion, and treated other themes also, Section XV (pp. 424-7 in the 4th edn., 1727)
being devoted to the origin of evil. Wesley's diary shows that he had read and 'collected'
at least parts of the appendix in October, 1725, referring to it as 'Ditton of matter's
thinking'—probably the same as the extract published in *A.M.* 1786. This extract on the
origin of evil is similarly 'collected', being a précis of the original, with many omissions
and minor alterations, only one sentence deliberately setting out to be an exact quotation.
For extracts from the more substantial work by Archbishop William King on the origin
of evil see letters of Dec. 11, 1730, and Jan. 15, 1731.

[1] 'Whence came evil?'
[2] This sentence Wesley quotes *literatim* from the original.

it should be possible for them either to observe or to deviate from those eternal rules and measures of fitness and agreeableness with respect to certain things and circumstances which were so conformable to the infinite rectitude of his own will, and which infinite reason must necessarily discover. Now evil is a deviation
5 from those measures of eternal, unerring order and reason—not to choose what is worthy to be chosen, and is accordingly chose by such a will as the divine. And to bring this about no more is necessary than the exerting certain acts of that power we call free will. By which power we are enabled to choose or refuse, and to determine ourselves to action accordingly. Therefore, without having re-
10 course to any ill principle, we may fairly account for the origin of evil from the possibility of a various use of our liberty, even as that capacity or possibility itself is ultimately founded on the defectibility and finiteness of a created nature.[a]

I am, dear sir, your dutiful and affectionate son,
15   John Wesley

Source: *A.M.* 1780, pp. 604–6.

From Martha Wesley[1]

Epworth, Jan. 10, 1729[/30]

Dear brother

I received your kind letter with a great deal of satisfaction, and 'twas not for any want of kindness that I have not answered it before now; but I have had so
20 much business that I have not really had time to answer it sooner. [. . .]

I was very agreeably surprised to find several of your thoughts so exactly agree with my own, and had I but your command of words I should say a great deal to you; but I find the same inconvenience in writing to you which I do in speaking. In conversation with most of my acquaintance I have very little
25 occasion for sense or learning, but when I speak or write to you I always find my want of both. However, you must accept the will for the deed. Many of your correspondents may be better able to entertain you agreeably, but none more willing than myself.

I have indeed frequently been disquieted with those thoughts which you say
30 'have often bewildered you. If' (as you say) 'God sees I sincerely desire devotion in prayer, and that I can do no more than desire it, why does not he do the rest?' Why indeed! We cannot certainly know the reason why he does not till the next life. This affliction is so vastly different from any other that 'tis a comfort to me that you share it with me. If God's withholding that grace from a person he sees
35 they earnestly desire were always a mark of his displeasure, sure he would not withhold it from you. We very often, even in this world, see reason to admire the goodness and wisdom of God in denying us what perhaps we once

---

[a] Page[s] 424[–7].

---

[1] Replying to his of Dec. 5–6, 1729, which it quotes.

passionately desired, so 'tis likely in the next we may find reason to admire the
divine goodness and wisdom in denying us even that progress.

Upon that very principle I have accounted for almost all the uneasiness I have
met with, and when I was capable of attending to reason it has always satisfied
me, particularly when I have met with what I thought unkindness from you. I   5
then considered that he who has the hearts of all men entirely in his disposal
certainly knew that had he permitted you to have returned my love with equal
tenderness I should ha' been a loser by it, or, to use your own beautiful expression, I 'should probably have set up my rest, and have been content with using,
not enjoying religion'. [. . .]   10

I have lamented the poor unfortunate young lady you told me of almost ever
since. There's the mischief of being pretty, and living at Court. Had she had
less beauty, and lived at Wroot, she might have been alive and innocent to
this day.

My father has got a curate! John Lambert heard of him when he was survey-   15
ing some miles off. He was a perfect stranger to my father, and my father to him.
I can't tell you exactly what sort of a man he is, because I have not yet found
him out, though he has been a fortnight with us; but by the best judgment I
can make of him I shall be in no danger of running into one extreme you warned
me of, liking him too well. Most of our town people fancy him to be like Mr.   20
Pennington; indeed he's not unlike him in shape, and at least as genteel; but you
will cease to wonder I should not like him very well when I tell you he thinks
as differently from you as light from darkness—or else he is one of those cunning
gentlemen that think fit to dissemble their own sentiments till they have tried
those of others.   25

Dick[1] is (if possible) 'tenfold more the child of Hell' than he used to be. He
took it into his head 'tother night almost to beat out his wife's brains for taking
his man off of him that was going to murder him—at least that made him cry out
he had killed him.

Last Tuesday I received a letter for you (and made a shift notwithstanding my   30
poverty to pay 6d for it), which I have sent you, but could not help making you
pay for a double letter. I thought at first I had known the hand, but I can't say
I do, and 'tis the most incomparable seal I ever set eyes on. Dear brother, pardon
the length and tediousness of my epistle, and believe me to be with the utmost
tenderness, your affectionate friend and sister,   35

M Wesley

I hope you'll let me hear from you again, and let me know how all
Mr. Kirkham's family do.

Address: 'To The Revd Mr John Wesley, Fellow of Lincoln College, Oxford, by
way of London   *Postmark*: '16 IA'   *Charges*: ((IN)) 'in all IN 9'   *End*
by J W: 'SP / Jan. 1730'   *Source*: MA.

[1] i.e. Richard Ellison, husband of Wesley's sister Suky.

To Mrs. Susanna Wesley

Linc[oln College], Feb. 28, 1729/30

Dear mother

Two things in Bishop Taylor I have been often thinking of since I writ last. One of which I like exceedingly, and the other, not that I dislike, is his account of hope, of which he speaks thus: 'Faith believes the revelations, hope expects his promises . . . Faith gives our understanding to God, hope our passions and affections . . . Faith is opposed to infidelity, hope to despair.'[1]

In another place his words are: 'Faith differs from hope in the extension of its object, and the intension of its degree. Faith belongs to all things revealed, hope only to things that are good, future, and concerning ourselves.'[2]

Now, to pass over less material points, doesn't this general objection seem to lie against him, that he makes hope a part or species of faith? And, consequently, contained in it, as is every part in its whole. Whereas had it been so St. Paul[3] would have broken that universally received rule, never to set things in contradistinction to each other, one of which is contained in the other. May we not therefore well infer that whatever hope is, it is certainly distinct from faith, as well as charity, since one who we know understood the rules of speaking contradistinguishes it from both?

As faith is distinguished from other species of assent, from knowledge particularly, by the difference of the evidence it is built on, may we not find the same foundation for distinguishing hope from faith as well as from knowledge? Is not the evidence on which we build it less simple than that of faith? And less demonstrative than the arguments that create knowledge? It seems to have one of its feet fixed on the Word of God, the other on our opinion of our own sincerity, and so to be a persuasion that we shall enjoy the good things of God, grounded on his promises made to sincere Christians, and on an opinion that we are sincere Christians ourselves. Agreeably to this Bishop Taylor himself says in his Rules for Dying; 'We are to be curious of our duty, and confident of the article of remission of

---

[1] Jeremy Taylor, *Holy Living*, IV (see *Works*, III. 145). Wesley has not only abridged the passage, but omitted all the references to the third element in the Pauline triad, charity.

[2] Cf. ibid., III. 150.   [3] Here, as frequently, Wesley writes 'S. Paul'.

sins, and the conclusion of those premisses will be that we shall be full of hopes of a prosperous resurrection.'[1] Everyone therefore who inquires into the grounds of his own hope reasons in this manner:

> If God be true, and I am sincere, then I am to hope;
> But God is true, and I am sincere (There is the pinch);   5
> Therefore, I am to hope.

What I so much like is his account of the pardon of sins, which is the clearest I ever met with:

Pardon of sins in the Gospel is [a] sanctification: 'Christ came to take away our sins by turning every one of us from our iniquities.' (Acts 3 : 26) And there is 10 not in the nature of the thing any expectation of pardon, or sign or signification of it, but so far as the thing itself discovers itself. As we hate sin, and grow in grace, and arrive at the state of holiness, which is also a state of repentance and imperfection, but yet of sincerity of heart and diligent endeavour, in the same degree we are to judge concerning the forgiveness of sins. For indeed that is 15 the evangelical forgiveness, and it signifies our pardon, because it effects it; or rather, it is in the nature of the thing, so that we are to inquire into no hidden records. Forgiveness of sins is not a secret sentence, a word, or a record. But it is a state of change, and effected upon us; and upon ourselves we are to look for it, to read it and understand it.[2]   20

In all this he appears to steer in the middle road exactly: to give assurance of pardon to the penitent, but to no one else.

Yesterday I had the offer of another curacy, to continue a quarter or half a year, which I accepted with all my heart. The salary is thirty pounds a year, the church eight miles from Oxford, seven of 25 which are, winter and summer, the best road in the country. So now I needn't sell my horse, since it is at least as cheap to keep one as to hire one every week.[3]

I have another piece of news to acquaint you with, which as it is more strange will I hope be equally agreeable. A little while ago 30 Bob Kirkham took a fancy into his head that he would lose no more time, and waste no more money. In pursuance of which he first resolved to breakfast no longer on tea; next to drink no more ale in an evening, or however but enough to quench his thirst; then, to read Greek or Latin from prayers in the morning till noon, and from 35 dinner till five at night. And how much may one imagine he executed

---

[1] Taylor, *Holy Dying*, V. v (*Works*, III. 425).   [2] Ibid.
[3] It seems that this appointment fell through, for Wesley's diary shows him preaching on Mar. 8, 22, 29, and May 24 (and three more times during the following year), at Pyrton, 13 miles SE. of Oxford, and on Mar. 1 and 15 at three churches 10 miles NW. of Oxford (Stonesfield, Combe, and Wilcote), though the fees received for these and similar occasional services would have brought in a comparable amount to the curacy.

of these resolutions? Why, he has left off tea, struck off his drinking acquaintance to a man, given the hours above specified to Greek Testament and Hugo Grotius,[1] and spent the evenings either by himself or with my brother and me. I am, dear mother, your dutiful
5 and affectionate son,

John Wesley

I don't despair of spending two days with you before Whitsuntide is over.

Address: 'To Mrs Wesley at Epworth, To be left at ye Posthouse in Gainsborow, Lincolnshire. by London' *Postmarks*: 'OXFORD", '3 MR' *Charges*: ((3)), 'In all 7' *Source*: MA.

To Mrs. Mary Pendarves[2]

Linc[oln College], Aug. 14, 1730

10 M[adam]

It would ill become me to let this (I must not now say trifle, since it has been honoured with some share of your approbation) wait

---

[1] Hugo Grotius (1583-1645), several of whose publications Wesley used at Kingswood School, though the one intended here is probably *De Veritate Religionis Christianiae*; cf. letter of Oct. 22, 1777, to Joseph Benson.

[2] Mary Granville (1700-88) was the niece of George Granville, Lord Lansdowne, and was a familiar figure in court and literary circles. Her uncle used some pressure to secure her marriage in 1718 to the wealthy and elderly Alexander Pendarves, who died in 1725. In 1743 she became the second wife of Patrick Delany, the intimate friend of Jonathan Swift.

Her widowed mother and her sister Ann had lived at Buckland in the Cotswold Hills, where they became friends of the Kirkhams of Stanton, especially of Sally. From Buckland they moved to Gloucester, though retaining their Cotswold friendships. Mary Pendarves, however, spent much of her time in London, whence she wrote to her sister on April 4, 1730: 'I honour *Primitive Christianity*, and desire you will let him know as much when next you see him.' (Delany, I. 250.) She was probably the instigator of the many nicknames used by the literary circle into which Wesley found himself drawn through his friendship with Robin Griffiths, Sally Kirkham being 'Varanese', Ann Granville 'Selima', Mary Pendarves 'Aspasia', and he himself 'Cyrus'—'Primitive Christianity' being another pseudonym appropriately designed by her for this serious but attractive young priest. Although Wesley's diary shows that Sally Kirkham had conversed with him about Mary Pendarves and one of her suitors on Dec. 24, 1726, it seems to have been several years before they actually met. During the summer of 1730 'Aspasia' stayed in the country, heard Wesley preach at Stanton on August 2, commended him upon his sermon, and asked for a copy. His diary summary for that month contains the entry: 'Transcribed a sermon and V's letters for Mrs P.' (See her reply, Aug. 28.)

upon you without endeavouring in some sort to express the sense I have of your goodness to me. This, I acknowledge it was, which seeking something to approve, extorted so favourable a sentence from your judgment. And however that may be hereafter forced to take part against me, this I trust will be ever on my side. 5

While I was transcribing the letters, those last monuments of the goodness of my dear V[aranese],[1] I could not hinder some sighs which between grief and shame would now and then find their way. Not that I was so much pained at seeing my utmost efforts so far surpassed by the slightest touches of another's pen: those which 10 that observation has often called were always tears of joy. But I could not, I ought not to be unmoved when I observe how unworthy I am of that excellent means of improvement; how few features I can even now call my own of that lovely piece which was drawn long ago, every stroke of which bore so true a resemblance to the 15 person by whom (though not for whom) it was drawn, and therefore gloriously showed what I ought to have been, though not what I was.

Yet I trust so unusual a blessing of Providence has not been utterly useless to me. Surely something I have gained by it. To this I owe both the capacity and the occasion of feeling that soft emotion 20 with which I glow even at the moment while I consider myself as conversing with a kindred soul of my V[aranese]; though I own I feel not half that tenderness of gratitude which ought to expand my heart when I have the honour of subscribing myself, yours and M[rs] Gr[anville]'s most o[bliged] and m[ost] o[bedient] servant, 25

J[ohn] W[esley]

Here is one at my elbow that pretends to be not only as much obliged, but as much devoted to your service as I am.[2]

Source: MA, pp. 1–2 of Asp[asia Letters], a notebook in which Wesley entered abstracts of his correspondence with Mrs. Mary Pendarves, 1730–4. Like his

[1] Despite the phraseology, Varanese was still very much alive, though their incipient love affair had been broken off. In spite of her marriage in 1725 to the Revd. John Chapone, however, and in spite of Wesley's mother's frowning upon his continued relationship with her (Nov. 29, 1726, Jan. 31, 1727), letters still passed between them, at least until 1736. For Mrs. Sarah Chapone (1699–1764) see also 'Sappho' in letter of June 17, 1731 (pp. 285–6 below).

[2] This was his brother Charles, nicknamed 'Araspes', a friend of Cyrus the Great. 'Selima' (Ann Granville) was another name appearing in the story of Cyrus as related by Chevalier Ramsay in his work of 1728. Strangely enough 'Aspasia' was the name given to the wife of Cyrus the Younger nearly two centuries after the days of Cyrus the Great (see Heitzenrater, p. 114 n.).

family letter-book, this is in abbreviated longhand, with occasional passages in cipher. All have been expanded without indication unless some element of doubt exists, except in this first example, where square brackets have been used more lavishly than is strictly necessary. Wesley's diary shows that he 'beg[an] l[ette]r to Mrs. P[endarves]' on Aug. 13.

From Mrs. Mary Pendarves

28 August, 1730

Sr,

I think myself extremely obliged to you for the favour of the sermon, and those letters that alone were worthy of the correspondence they maintained. I re-
5 ceived them safe last week, and should sooner have made my acknowledgements for them, but that I have been engaged with so much company since my return from dear delightful Stanton that till this moment I have not had time to express my gratitude for the elegant entertainment I have had, not only from the manu-scripts, but in recollecting and repeating the conversation you and your brother
10 made so agreeable, which I hope will soon be renewed. If you have any affairs that call you to Gloucester, don't forget you have two pupils who are desirous of improving their understanding, and that friendship which has already taught them to be, sir, your most sincere, humble servants.

My companion joins with me in all I have said, as well as in service to Araspes.

[From Mrs. Sarah Chapone][1]

15   This letter was sent round this way, Aspasia not knowing how to direct to Cyrus. I believe she will soon go to the Bath for a few days upon business. If Cyrus designs waiting on her, I think he had best write to her to know when she will be absent from G[loucheste]r. Varanes[e] sent a letter by the carrier about a fortnight ago. If it is received, an information that it is safe would be very
20 agreeable.

I hope to see that beautiful hymn in verse according to a promise I had from Cyrus. I take this to be a plain translation, as near the author's sense as the lan-guage will bear, but that I submit to his better judgment, from whom I expect to see it in as great perfection as in the original.
25   The little religion, and the redundance of ill-natur⟨e,⟩ that abounds in the conversation of mankind, makes me w⟨ell⟩ pleased to spend many hours alone, since it is not often my happy fate to pass them with those who are as gentle in their censures of the mistakes of others as they are severe to themselves, and as they are blind to their own excellencies. Cyrus and Araspes will come into
30 my mind upon this occasion, and upon every other when I am thinking of those persons whose principles are not of this world, and whose hope and expectation shall not perish forever.

Sep: ye 9th.

[1] Added on p. 3 of the previous letter.

Address: [by 'Varanese'] 'To The Revd. Mr. John Westley, Fellow of Lincoln College, Oxon.' [Also by Varanese:] 'Post Paid 3d' [but there are no postmarks or other postal inscriptions]   *End* by JW; 'Aug. 28', and 'Aug. 38, [*sic*] 1730'; in a later hand, ? CW, 'Mrs Delany'   *Source:* MA; cf. Asp, pp. 2–3.

To Mrs. Mary Pendarves[1]

Sept. 12 [1730]

M[adam]

I am greatly ashamed that I can only think how much I am obliged to you. Your last favour leaves me utterly at a loss, and even without hope of making any suitable acknowledgement, at the same time 5 that it convinces me of a mistake, which I should not otherwise have so easily given up; it convinces me it was possible I should enjoy a higher pleasure than even your conversation gave me. If your understanding could not appear in a stronger light than when it brightened the dear hill, the fields, the arbour, I am now forced to confess your 10 temper could: you even then showed but half your goodness.

I spent some very agreeable moments last night in musing on this delightful subject, and thinking to how little disadvantage Aspasia or Selima would have appeared even in that faint light which the moon glimmering through the trees poured on that part of our 15 garden where I was walking! How little would the eye of the mind that surveyed them have missed the absent sun! What darkness could have obscured gentleness, courtesy, humility, could have shaded the image of God! Sure none but that which shall never dare to approach them; none but vice, which shall ever be far away! 20

I could not close this reflection without adding with a sigh, When will they shine on me? When will Providence direct my wandering feet to tread again that flowery path to virtue? My dear V[aranese] informs me you are going yet farther from us, but cannot inform me how soon. If either this or any other ill-natured accident (to speak in 25 the language of men) denies me the happiness of waiting upon you so soon as I sometime hoped I should, 'tis best it should be denied me. Wise is he that disposes of us: I acquiesce in his disposal.

Nothing can excuse me, of all persons in the world, from entirely acquiescing in all his disposals, to whom alone I can ascribe the 30

---

[1] Replying to hers of Aug. 28.

happiness I now enjoy, so far above my most aspiring hopes. To him alone can I ascribe it that I have found any favour in the sight of Selima or Aspasia; that I have before me such a proof of your generous condescension as the thanks of my life will poorly repay; 5 that I once more feel the exquisite pleasure of calling myself, their ever obliged and most obedient servant.

Source: Asp, pp. 3–4; diary, 'beg[an] to Asp[asia]', completed in three sittings.

To Mrs. Mary Pendarves

Oct. 3 [1730]

Madam

Though I am utterly ignorant where you are, whether at Glouces-
10 ter, or Bath, or London, yet I can't bear to be silent any longer while so ill consequences may attend it. I even tremble to think what opinion you must have of me, if my last is not come to your hands: how inexcusable a neglect it is of which you can't but believe me guilty. An imputation of this kind is what of all others I suffer with 15 most regret. A little gratitude and a constant readiness to own my obligations was all the merit I could ever pretend to; and if I lose this too I can never pretend to any share in Aspasia's friendship.

I am sensible nothing but this can atone for those improprieties of behaviour i[nto] which my inexperience in the world so frequently 20 betrays me; which both you and Selima must have so often observed, though still with pity and not contempt. Yet I wished I had no greater faults than these; I wish one of which I was lately guilty may meet with what doubtless it does not deserve, as mild a censure from them. I own I deserve a severer censure for my want of considera- 25 tion in positively recommending to them a book of which I had read but a few pages; the beauties of which I find, upon a closer examina- tion, to be joined with so many imperfections, with so many fallacies and falsehoods and contradictions, as more than balance them, and make it highly unworthy to take up any of their hours who know 30 so well how to employ every moment. The only reparation I can now make for the injury I did them in recommending it is to beg leave to present you with an abridgment of it, which I hope to have finished shortly, in fewer words, at least, if not with fewer mistakes, than would perplex you in the original.[1]

Methinks I would fain ask another favour of you: I am persuaded if it is not fit to be granted you will impute my desiring it not to my want of modesty but of judgment. Indeed sometimes I am 5 inclined to defer speaking of it till I have the pleasure of seeing you again. But I fear I should then be less able to speak than now; I should be more ashamed and confused than I am at a distance. I will therefore defer no longer the begging Aspasia to be like my Varanese in one more instance, in continuing to me the honour and advantage of 10 reading her sentiments when I am not permitted to hear them. I will not offer any reasons for my request. If it be fit to be granted, you do not need them.

The reason why I have not yet made use of that title which you or my Varanese was so good as to assign me[2] is because it seems to 15 imply, what never can be, some sort of equality between us. But this I totally disavow; as there can be no grounds for it in nature, I am startled at an expression that even seems to set me on a level with Selima or Aspasia. No, it will not be! The eternal law is between us! I may pursue, but must not overtake! I cannot leap the bounds. It is 20 not in friendship itself that I should ever be their equal, though it is most certain that so long as the breath of life is in me (if not long after that is lost in common air) I shall continue to be with the tenderest esteem, their most obliged and most faithful servant.

Source: Asp, pp. 5–7.

From Mrs. Mary Pendarves

Gloucester, 12 Octr. 1730 25

Sr
    I am almost afraid to own my having had both your letters,[3] lest I should for-feit that good opinion that I extremely desire Cyrus should always have of Aspasia. I must farther confess that had I not received the second letter I should not have had courage to have wrote. I am but too sensible how unequal I am to 30 the task. Could I, like our inimitable dear Varanese, express my sentiments, with what pleasure should I agree to the obliging request you make! But why should

---

[1] Peter Browne (*c*. 1664–1735), Bishop of Cork, whose *The Procedure, Extent, and limits of Human Understanding* (1728) Wesley glanced at Aug. 30, 1729, but 'read over' in September, 1730. A copy of his abstract still survives, and it was published in his *Survey of the Wisdom of God in the Creation* (see *Bibliog*, No. 259).
[2] 'Cyrus'.   [3] Of Sept. 12, Oct. 3.

I be afraid of your superior understanding, when I know at the same time the delight you take in not only entertaining but improving all those you converse with? Then take me into your protection! Look on me as one surrounded with infirmities and imperfections, who flies to you for assistance against the assaults
5 of vanity and passion. If you are desirous I should think you my friend, let this be the trial of it, not to leave any of my follies unreproved. I shall not scruple to discover to you those many defects which on a longer acquaintance with me your own observation must have pointed out to you; and it is no small argument of the great desire I have of improvement that I will run so great a hazard; for certainly
10 you will value me less when you know how weak I am.

You have no reason to make an apology for recommending the book you mention (which I suppose was the Bishop of Cork's). I have not yet read it, but I shall wait with impatience for the abstract you promise me, which I am sure will very well deserve the time I shall bestow in reading of it. My stay in Gloucester is
15 uncertain; but when we go to town we shall call at Oxford, where we shall not fail of inquiring after Cyrus and Araspes.

[From Ann Granville]

Aspasia is called away before she has finished her letter,[1] and has not said one word for Selima, who thinks of Cyrus and Araspes with that esteem their merit justly claims; desires always to be thought their friend, and wishes she was
20 worthy of it. When we go to Oxford, we don't know at what college to inquire after our agreeable friends.

Source: Asp, pp. 7–8; cf. that in Wesley's abstract of his correspondence with Sel[ima], p. 1, which omits the last sentence.

To Mrs. Mary Pendarves[2]

Oct. 24[–5, 1730]

Madam

My brother and I are both sensible how poor a return our most
25 humble acknowledgments are for the very many instances of goodness which both Mrs. Granville and yourself and M[iss] Granville so lately showed us; which can't but be ever remembered by us, and remembered with the sincerest gratitude. Nothing less than experience

---

[1] She arrived in London on Oct. 15 (Delany, I. 263).

[2] After taking up the invitation in Aspasia's letter of Aug. 28, Wesley and his brother Charles had just returned from a visit on horseback to Gloucester, where they had stayed at Mrs. Granville's overnight on Oct. 20; they met with various adventures, including the running-away of Wesley's horse and their being lost twice on the return journey. (See diary, Vol. 18 of this edn.; for Mrs. Granville see below, pp. 259–60 n.)

could have given us the pleasing conviction that so many favours could be crowded into so short a time. Short indeed! Much too short we should have thought it, but that he who seeth not as man seeth[1] showed by forcing us away so soon that it ought not to have been longer. 5

I am however persuaded the effects of those happy hours will be of longer continuance, and every day give us the strongest reason to wish ardently for their return. What the advantage of being present with you must be may be easily conceived from what you do even when absent. To your good wishes I can't but in a great measure 10 impute it that we should exactly find our way t[hrough] a country in which we were utter strangers, and for some miles without either human creature, or day or moon or stars to direct us. By so many ties of interest as well as gratitude am I obliged, whether present or absent, to be, madam, your most obliged and most 15 obedient servant.

Bobby[2] and my brother join with me in tendering their most humble service to Mrs. Granville and the two excellent sisters.

Source: Asp, p. 9.

From Mrs. Mary Pendarves

Gloucester, 26 Octr. [1730]

Sr 20

We have determined to leave this place on Monday the 9th of November, and hope to see you on Tuesday at Oxford. Perhaps the weather and your inclinations may be so favourable to us that we may meet sooner. (Of hiring a coach)[3]

You are very just to those friends you have lately obliged with your company when you seem assured of their good wishes. The success that attended your 25 journey was certainly owing to yours and Araspes' merit: your guardian angels would not forsake a charge so worthy of their care. Happy should we be could our intercession secure you from accidents.

The pleasure you gave us in your conversation we think of daily with thankfulness, and hope nothing will happen to prevent your making the visit you have 30 promised us in January. My mother charges me with her particular compliments to you and your brother. Selima says she will not be contented with my making a bare compliment for her. If time would permit, I would gladly say more for her as well as for myself; but I have been in a hurry all this day. When shall I be

---

[1] 1 Sam. 16: 7.   [2] Robert Kirkham.
[3] Wesley's diary shows that he met them at Burford on Nov. 9, and travelled in the coach with them to Oxford. Cf. her letter of Nov. 19.

worthy to subscribe myself, what I very sincerely desire to be, Cyrus's friend, and most faithful servant

                                                                    Aspasia

Source: Asp, p. 10.

To Mrs. Mary Pendarves[1]

                                                        Nov. 3 [1730]

5 Madam

I sincerely ask pardon for not having acknowledged the favour of yours sooner. I might have considered that every day I passed by made my omission more inexcusable, as no business of my own could be a sufficient reason for seeming to neglect yours a moment.
10 I ought doubtless to have set aside everything else till I had given you an account of this (of the coach).

I am now more than ever at a loss how to avoid the imputation my brother throws upon me, that I take the obliging things you say as patiently as if I thought they were my due. Indeed I don't think
15 so; I am convinced they are entirely owing, not to mine, but to your goodness. But I don't know how to express my sense of that goodness in such terms as it requires, and therefore commonly hide my want of words in silence, and don't attempt to express it at all. I own it is a fault to pay no part of my debt because I am unable to dis-
20 charge the whole. I hope it is one of those many for which a remedy is designed me in the conversation I enjoyed at Gloucester.

For the sake of those less experienced travellers who have the cold hills beyond Burford to go over, I shall greatly wish that these sharp winds may either stay with us or be quite gone before Monday.
25 To me any weather will be favourable, or any circumstance of life which gives me the least opportunity of approving myself, madam, your ever obliged and most obedient servant.

Source: Asp, p. 11.

                    [1] Replying to her letter of Oct. 28.

From Mrs. Mary Pendarves

New Bond Street, [London], 19 Novr. [1730]

The pleasure you and your brother gave us of your conversation at Burford, the entertainment we had upon the road to Oxford, which neither the dirty way nor rattling wheels could entirely deprive us of, the book to which we owe many agreeable hours, and the great consolation and civility which my mother 5 received from you (which she has not failed to inform us of) after we left her; are favours that ought to be acknowledged with the utmost gratitude. You might reasonably have expected this small return much sooner, but we have been in a perpetual hurry since our arrival. I have not had time even to write to Varanese. You are inclined to think favourably of Selima and Aspasia; therefore 10 I believe you will not easily accuse them of ingratitude. They are sensible of the advantage your friendship will be to them, and desire more than to be worthy of it. Nor is this a small ambition, for you cannot place your esteem but where there is the appearance of some perfection. Your example and instruction may in time make so great an impression on them as that they may challenge your 15 favour as their due. At present they look on it as an obligation.

Our journey ended with as good success, though not altogether so much satisfaction, as it begun. The company in the coach were tolerably entertaining, and very complaisant. We got to town by six o'clock, and were not at all fatigued, nor have we caught any cold since we came. The life of noise and vanity that is 20 commonly led here cannot possibly afford any entertainment for you. When we have an opportunity of conversing with a reasonable friend we wish that Cyrus and Araspes were added to the company. I have been at two operas, and very much delighted. I hope it is not a fault to be transported by music; if it is, I will endeavour to correct it. I am ashamed of sending you so blotted a piece of paper, 25 but I am in haste, and must trust to your partiality to excuse the faults of your most obliged humble servant.

Araspes may assure himself of the good wishes of Selima and Aspasia.

Source: Asp, pp. 12–13.

To Mrs. Mary Pendarves

Nov. [24–]5 [1730]

At[1] last, then, the desire of my heart is given me, and I may say 30 something of what I owe to good Aspasia. This too is your gift, and consequently given in such a manner as doubles it[s] native value. Would I could thank you for it as it requires! That vain wish would

[1] Orig., 'And'.

give me much more pain were I not assured you will believe I feel what I cannot speak. You believe I have not been unmindful of that favour in particular of which I could not speak at all till now, which so far outwent the highest expectations I could form even of Aspasia
5 and Selima. O Aspasia, how unequal am I to the task you so obligingly assign me! How gladly do I fly to you, how earnestly do I hope for your assistance as well as pardon, in those numberless imperfections of my own, of which you would, but can't, long be ignorant! I can't expect that your eyes should always be held, and far, far am
10 I from desiring it. Only this let me desire, let me adjure you to this, that when you can no longer help seeing them, you would not see them with the anger they deserve, but with pity, that you may cure them.

This is friendship indeed! Such offices as this have a right to
15 that lovely name. O that our friendship (since you give me leave to use that dear word) might be built on so firm a foundation! Were it possible for you to find me any way of repaying part of the good I experience from you, then I would not dare to doubt but I should experience it still, but I should still have some place in your thoughts!
20 And why indeed should I doubt, since he who hath hitherto sustained me is the same yesterday and forever! And since so long as I own and depend upon them his wisdom and strength are mine!

> Still shower thine influence from on high,
> Author of friendship's sacred tie!
25 > Shower thy graces, Holy Dove,
> God of peace and God of love![1]

Thus it is that I often pour out my heart by myself, when it is full of Selima and Aspasia and Varanese. Thus I endeavour to steal into their protection, and to interweave my interests with theirs, if
30 haply part of the blessing descending on you may light on my head also. Would they could be so interwove as that when humility, which sitteth by his throne, is sent down to rest upon you, one ray of it might glance upon my heart, to remove the stone from it; to make it duly sensible both of its own many infirmities, and of your gener-
35 ous desire to lessen their number. For want of this I cannot follow you as I would; I must be left behind in the race of virtue. I am

---

[1] Cf. the refrain to *A Wedding Song*, by Samuel Wesley, Jun. (*Poems*, 1736, pp. 193–200), the opening couplet there reading:

> Shower thine influence from on high,
> Author of the nuptial tie.

sick of pride: it quite weighs my spirits down. O pray for me, that I may be healed!

I have the greater dependence on your intercession because you know what you ask. Every line of your last, too, shows the heart of the writer, where with friendship dwells humility. Ours, dear 5 Aspasia, it is to make acknowledgements; upon us lie the obligations of gratitude; 'tis our part, till we have some better return in our power, at least to thank you for the honour and favour of your friendship. As I do Selima for her last instance of it in particular, in which I found a way to make even Mr. Pope more pleasing. If it 10 be a fault to have too harmonious a soul, too exquisite a sense of elegant, generous transports, then indeed I must own there is an obvious fault both in Selima and Aspasia. If not, I fancy one may easily reconcile whatever they think or act to the strictest reason; unless it be your entertaining so favourable a thought of your most 15 obliged and most faithful

C[yrus]

Source: Asp, pp. 13-16. Wesley's diary shows that the letter was begun on Nov. 24.

To the Revd. Samuel Wesley[1]

Lincoln College, Dec. 11, 1730

Dear sir

We all return you our sincere thanks for your timely and neces- 20 sary advice, and should be exceeding glad if it were as easy to follow it as 'tis impossible not to approve it. That doubtless is the very point we have to gain before any other can be managed successfully, to have an habitual, lively sense of our being only instruments in his hand who can do all things either with or without any instrument. 25 But how to fix this sense in us is the great question. Since to man this is impossible, we hope you and all our friends will continue to intercede for us to him with whom all things are possible.[2]

Tomorrow night I expect to be in company with the gentleman

---

[1] For his father's encouraging letters about the progress of the Oxford Methodists see John's long letter to Richard Morgan, Oct. 19, 1732, which gives extracts from those of Sept. 28 and Dec. 1, 1730 (pp. 337-8, 338-9).

[2] See Matt. 19: 26.

who did us the honour to take the first notice of our little society.[1] I have terrible reasons to think he is as slenderly provided with humanity as with sense and learning. However, I must not slip this opportunity, because he is at present in some distress, occasioned by his being obliged to dispute in the Schools on Monday, though he is not furnished with such arguments as he wants. I intend, if he has not procured them before, to help him to some arguments, that I may at least get that prejudice away from him, that we 'are friends to none but what are as queer as' ourselves.

A week or two ago I pleased myself mightily with the hopes of sending you a full and satisfactory solution of your great question, having at last procured the celebrated treatise of Archbishop King, *De Origine Mali*.[2] But on looking farther into it I was strangely disappointed, finding it the least satisfactory account of any given by any author whom I ever read in my life. He contradicts almost every man that ever writ on the subject, and builds an hypothesis on the ruins of theirs which he takes to be entirely new, though if I do not much mistake, part of it is at least two thousand years old. The purport of this is, 'that natural evils flow naturally and necessarily from the essence of matter, so that God himself could not have prevented them, unless by not creating matter at all'. Now this new supposition seems extremely like the old one of the Stoics, who I fancy always affirmed, *totidem verbis*,[3] that 'all natural evils were owing not to God's want of will, but to his want of power to redress them, as necessarily flowing from the nature of matter'.

I breakfasted today with a great admirer of the Septuagint,[4] who was much surprised to hear that anyone should charge them with want of integrity, and seemed to think that charge could not be made out. Nay, he went so far as even to assert that he took this Greek to be more faultless than our present Hebrew copies. I wished I had had one or two of the places you mention, at hand, and I would have given him them to chew upon.

[1] The diary does not identify this critic.

[2] The *magnum opus* of William King (1650–1729), Archbishop of Dublin, published in Latin in 1702, and first translated into English in 1729, as *An Essay on the Origin of Evil*. Cf. letter of Dec. 19, 1729, for the 'great question', and of Jan. 15, 1731, for a summary of King's work.

[3] 'In just so many words'.

[4] Emanuel Langford, of Christ Church, about two years John's junior, and one of his close friends. See Samuel Wesley's reply, Feb. 6, 1730/1, and his dissertation on the Septuagint, which he sent to Langford, who replied Apr. 17, 1730, in Clarke, II. 418–26 (Clarke gives his name as Langley).

One pretty large dissertation I have by me still. I propose to read and transcribe it against I go up to London to the Westminster Great Day,[1] which I am afraid will be as soon as my brother will want it. I am glad the rector[2] is in so fair a way of recovery. I showed Mr. Robinson[3] what related to him this morning, who I found had 5 received from Mrs. Morley a fuller account of the doctor's illness. Before she writ he had got over all remains of his distemper, except a weakness in the fingers of his left hand.

We can't compass Thomas Burgess's[4] liberty yet, though it seems to have a fairer show than formerly. On Sunday they had prayers 10 and a sermon at the Castle;[5] on Christmas Day we hope they will have a dinner, and the Sunday after, a communion, as many of them as are desirous of it and appear prepared for it. I had almost forgot to tell you that on Tuesday sennight Mr. Morgan opened the way for us into Bocardo.[6] I am, dear sir, your dutiful and affectionate 15 son,

John Wesley

Address: 'To The Revd Mr Wesley'   *End* by JW: 'JW to my Father,
Dec. 11, 1730. †'   *Source*: MA.

To Mrs. Mary Granville[1]

Lincoln College, Dec. 12, 1730

Madam

Were it possible for me to repay my part of that debt which I 20 can't but be sensible is still growing upon me, your goodness would

---

[1] The feast and play on Jan. 28; see diary, and letter of Jan. 27, 1731.

[2] Dr. John Morley.

[3] Revd. Michael Robinson, also a Fellow of Lincoln (1723-57) from Lincolnshire.

[4] A prisoner committed to the Castle for assault on July 2, 1730, 'for want of sureties'. The Oxford Methodists raised funds to secure bail and other help for such prisoners (see Heitzenrater, p. 122).

[5] The prison in the old castle on the western outskirts of Oxford, which William Morgan had been visiting for some time before the two Wesley brothers accompanied him on Aug. 24, 1730, and then took it fully under their wing.

[6] The prison over the north gate, primarily for debtors. On Dec. 1 Morgan again led the way, and on Dec. 5 John Wesley visited William Green there, giving him sixpence. Soon this was linked with the Castle in the regular social and religious activities of the Methodists.

[7] Mary, daughter of Sir Martin Westcomb, Consul of Cadiz, who married Bernard Granville, youngest brother of George Granville, Lord Lansdowne. Her husband died

give me a still greater pleasure than I have yet experienced from it. To be the instrument of *some advantage* to a person from whom I have received *so much*, as it would be the truest instance of my gratitude, is the utmost wish I can form. But a view of my own numerous
5 failings checks the vanity of this hope, and tells me that though he in whom I move and speak[1] does not always require wisdom and prudence, yet some degree of purity he does always require in those who would move or speak to his glory. I have therefore little reason to expect that he will direct any motion of mine to that end, espe-
10 cially when the particular end proposed relates to one who is far advanced in the great race which I am but lately entered upon, if indeed I am entered yet. What shall I say to such a one as is almost possessed of the crown, which I dimly see afar off? To another I could recommend those assistances which I find so necessary for
15 myself. I could say that if our ultimate end is the love of God, to which the several particular Christian virtues lead us, so the means leading to these are to communicate every possible time, and whatso-ever we do. To pray without ceasing;[2] not to be content with our solemn devotions, whether public or private, but at all times and in
20 all places to make fervent returns 'by ejaculations' and 'abrupt intercourses of the mind with God'; to thrust 'these between all our other employments',[3] if it be only by a word, a thought, a look, always remembering,

    If I but lift my eyes, my suit is made!
25   Thou canst no more not hear than thou canst die![4]

To account what of frailty remains after this a necessary encum-brance of flesh and blood; such an one as God out of his mercy to us will not yet remove, as seeing it to be useful, though grievous. Yet still to hope that since we seek him 'in a time when he may be
30 found',[5] before the great water-flood hath overwhelmed us, he will in his good time 'quell the raging of this sea, and still the waves thereof when they arise'![6] To you, *who know them so well*, I can but

in 1723, leaving her with two sons, Bernard and Bevil, and two daughters, Mary (largely brought up by her aunt Stanley in London), who became successively Mrs. Pendarves and Mrs. Delany, and Ann, who married John Dewes. Mrs. Granville died in 1747, and was buried in Gloucester.

[1] See Acts 17: 28.   [2] 1 Thess. 5: 17.
[3] See Taylor, *Holy Living*, IV. vii (*Works*, III. 184–5).
[4] George Herbert, 'Prayer' (included in Wesley's *Select Parts of Mr. Herbert's Sacred Poems*, 1773, p. 23).
[5] See Isa. 55: 6.   [6] See Ps. 89: 10 (B.C.P.).

just mention these considerations, which I would press upon another. Yet let me beg you to believe that though I want the power, I have the most sincere desire of approving[1] myself, madam, your most obliged and most obedient humble servant,

John Wesley 5

My brother joins with me in his best respects both to yourself, and those good ladies whom we love to call your family.

Address: 'To Mrs Granville, at Great Brickhill, near Stony Stratford'
Source: Delany, I. 269–71.

To Mrs. Mary Pendarves

Innocents' Day [Dec. 28, 1730]

Had I not been engaged almost every hour in an employment which set Aspasia continually before my eyes,[2] I could by no means 10 have satisfied myself so long without saying anything of my obligations to her; I could not have been easy without repeating my acknowledgments for them, particularly for the last, that lovely instance of your condescension, which so opportunely relieved me from the perplexity I was in.[3] Every pleasing reflection it has given me since 15 was a further reason for me to thank you again; and I have been sometimes afraid that my omitting it so long might give you hard thoughts of my gratitude. But I sincerely ask pardon for that fear, so injurious both to Aspasia and Selima, with whom I should by no means presume to converse at all had I not so often experienced 20 that candour which was ever as unwilling to observe a fault as willing to excuse it when observed. Do not think, good Aspasia, I am yet so vain as to dare to maintain an intercourse with you but upon a full conviction that you are always ready to forgive me both when I say amiss and when I do not say[4] what your goodness requires. 25

[1] In the obsolete sense of 'prove'.
[2] Having 'collected' Browne's *Human Understanding* (see above, p. 251 n.), Wesley had been transcribing at least one additional fair copy before transmitting it to her. Inside the cover of the 103-page volume in the Methodist Archives he inscribed, 'Mrs. Pendarves', and at the end, 'Xtmass Eve 1730'. This was the copy which he retained, using some of its many blank pages in 1788 for transcribing 'O Gott, du tieffe sonder grund' and other German hymns. Cf. letter of Feb. 13, 1731.
[3] Apparently a letter of which Wesley did not preserve an abstract.
[4] Orig., 'so'.

While I am reflecting on this I can't but often observe with
pleasure the great resemblance between the emotion I then feel
and that with which my heart frequently overflowed in the beginning of my intercourse with our dear Varanese. Yet is there a sort
5 of soft melancholy mixed with it when I perceive that I am making
another avenue for grief, that I am laying open another part of my
soul at which the arrows of fortune[1] may enter. Nay, but here will
I hold; since the Christian name for fortune is Providence, or the
hand of God, should it wound me even in the person of my friend
10 there would be goodness in the severity. Should one to whom I was
united by the tenderest ties, who was as my own soul,[2] be torn from
me, it would be best for me, to me too it would be the stroke of
mercy. Though were it a less good to myself, I ought doubtless not
to grieve because one who deserves so well of me is taken from me to
15 God. Surely if you were called first mine ought not to overflow
because all tears were wiped from your eyes.

That even in this a regard for your happiness ought to take [the]
place of my regard for my own is most certain; but whether I could
do what I ought I have great reason to question. I much doubt
20 whether S[elf-]L[ove] in so trying a circumstance would not be
found too strong for a friendship which I even now find to be less
disinterested than I hitherto imagined. I used to flatter myself that
I had at least the desire to be some way serviceable to Aspasia and
Selima; and that this, unmixed with any meaner motive, was the
25 sole principle of many of my actions. But even with this I perceive
another principle is interwoven, a desire of recommending myself
to their esteem. And if this be a fault, I am much to blame. It is a
fault deeply rooted in my nature. But is it a fault to desire to recommend myself to those who so strongly recommend virtue to me?
30 Ardently to desire their esteem who are so able and willing to make
me in some degree worthy of it? Tell me, Aspasia, tell me, Selima,
if it be a fault that my heart burns within me when I reflect on the
many marks of regard you have already shown your ever obliged
and ever faithful

35   Cy[rus]

Source: Asp, pp. 16–18.

[1] See Shakespeare, *Hamlet*, III. i. 58.
[2] See 1 Sam. 18: 1, 3; 20: 17.

To Mrs. Mary Pendarves

Jan. 11 [1731]

Why will Aspasia let in these unpleasing thoughts, these uneasy fears upon me? From your long silence I can't but apprehend either that you have been out of order, or that I have been so unhappy as to displease you by some indecent or foolish expression. What 5 shelter can I fly to from these apprehensions, unless it were possible to take in a strict sense that strange intimation you have sometimes given of being afraid to converse with me? O Aspasia, if you are afraid you can't come up to the character given you by our dear Varanese, how can I hope to reach that which equal kindness but not 10 equal justice drew? What excuse does your fear leave my presumption? How can I speak if you are silent? I have reasons enough (if any reasons could be enough to keep one so obliged as me from owning it) entirely to decline an intercourse which every step I take shows me unfit for; in which I can no more keep up to the spirit of 15 Aspasia than I can in this or anything answer her expectations, and expectations for which you have too much ground; which considering the many advantages I have long enjoyed, over and above the friendship of our Varanese, though I cannot, I ought to satisfy. I ought to be some way useful to you, as you have been many ways 20 to me. I ought to have turned that charming freedom you indulge me in to yours as well as my own advantage; to have employed it the most generous, friendly way, in endeavouring to correct those failings in Selima and Aspasia (for surely no human creature is wholly spotless) which I have not yet so much as observed. I ought 25 —I know not what. When will these two or three weeks be over, that I may speak what I cannot write? It is in your power to make them move less slow; a line from Aspasia or Selima would make the time roll more swiftly, as it would, I hope, remove the apprehensions of your 30

Cy[rus]

Source: Asp, pp. 18-19.

To the Revd. Samuel Wesley[1]

January [15], 1731

Dear sir

Though some of the *postulata* upon which Archbishop King builds his hypothesis of the origin of evil be such as very few will
5 admit of, yet since the superstructure is regular and well contrived I thought you would not be unwilling to see the scheme of that celebrated work. He divides it into five chapters.

The sum of the first chapter is this. The first notions we have of outward things are our conceptions of motion, matter, and space.
10 Concerning each of these we soon observe that it does not exist of itself, and consequently that there must be some First Cause to which all of them owe their existence. Although we have no faculty for the direct perception of this First Cause, and so can know very little more of him than a blind man of light, yet thus much we know
15 of him by the faculties we have, that he is one, infinite in nature and power, free, intelligent, and omniscient; that consequently he proposes to himself an end in every one of his actions, and that the end of his creating the world was the exercise of his power, and wisdom, and goodness, which he therefore made as perfect as it
20 could be made by infinite goodness, and power, and wisdom.

Chap. II. But if so, how came evil into the world? If the world was made by such an Agent, with such an intention, how is it that either imperfection or natural or moral evils have a place in it? Is not this difficulty best solved by the Manichean supposition, that
25 there is an evil as well as a good principle? By no means; for it is just as repugnant to Infinite Goodness to create what it foresaw would be spoiled by another as to create what would be spoiled by the constitution of its own nature: their supposition therefore leaves the difficulty as it found it. But if it could be proved that to
30 permit evils in the world is consistent with, nay, necessarily results from, infinite goodness, then the difficulty would vanish; and to prove this is the design of the following treatise.

[1] This letter (the date pin-pointed from Wesley's diary) followed up that of Dec. 11, 1730, without any intervening request from his father. Wesley published it in 1780, immediately following that of Dec. 19, 1729 to his father, in which he offered extracts from Ditton's work on the origin of evil, with the note prefixed: '(A little larger answer to this famous question we have in a treatise, *De Origine Mali*, wrote by Dr. King, Archbishop of Dublin, of which I sent my father the following extract.)'

Chap. III. All created beings, as such, are necessarily imperfect; nay, infinitely distant from supreme perfection. Nor can they all be equally perfect, since some must be only parts of others. As to their properties, too, some must be perfecter than others; for suppose any number of the most perfect beings created, infinite goodness 5 would prompt the Creator to add less perfect beings to those, if their existence neither lessened the number nor conveniences of the more perfect. The existence of matter, for instance, neither lessens the number nor the conveniences of pure spirits. Therefore the addition of material beings to spiritual was not contrary to but 10 resulted from infinite goodness.

Chap. IV. As the evils of imperfection necessarily spring from this, that the imperfect things were made out of nothing, so natural evils necessarily spring from their being made out of matter. For matter is totally useless without motion, or even without such a 15 motion as will divide it into parts; but this cannot be done without a contrariety of motions, and from this necessarily flows generation and corruption.

The material part of us being thus liable to corruption, pain is necessary to make us watchful against it, and to warn us of what 20 tends toward it, as is the fear of death likewise, which is of use in many cases that pain does not reach. From these all the passions necessarily spring; nor can these be extinguished while those remain. But if pain and the fear of death were extinguished no animal could long subsist. Since therefore these evils are necessarily joined 25 with more than equivalent goods, the permitting these is not repugnant to, but flows from, infinite goodness. The same observation holds as to hunger, thirst, childhood, age, diseases, wild beasts, and poisons. They are all therefore permitted because each of them is necessarily connected with such a good as outweighs the evil. 30

Chap. V. Touching moral evils (by which I mean, 'inconveniencies arising from the choice of the sufferer'), I propose to show; 1. What is the nature of choice or election. 2. That our happiness consists in the elections or choices we make. 3. What elections are improper to be made. 4. How we come to make such elections; 35 and 5. How our making them is consistent with the divine power and goodness.

1. By liberty I mean an active, self-determining power, which does not choose things because they are pleasing, but is pleased with them because it chooses them. 40

That God is endued with such a power I conclude, (1), because nothing is good or evil, pleasing or displeasing to him, before he chooses it; (2), because his will or choice is the cause of goodness in all created things; (3), because if God had not been endued with
5   such a principle he would never have created anything.

But it is to be observed farther that God sees and chooses whatever is connected with what he chooses in the same instant; and that he likewise chooses whatever is convenient for his creatures in the same moment wherein he chooses to create them.

10   That man partakes of this principle I conclude, (1), because experience shows it; (2), because we observe in ourselves the signs and properties of such a power. We observe we can counteract our appetites, senses, and even our reason if we so choose; which we can no otherwise account for than by admitting such a power in
15   ourselves.

2. The more of this power any being possesses the less subject he is to the impulses of external agents, and the more commodious is his condition. Happiness rises from a due use of our faculties; if therefore this be the noblest of all our faculties, then our chief
20   happiness lies in the due use of this, that is, in our elections. And farther, election is the cause why things please us; he therefore who has an uncontrolled power of electing may please himself always, and if things fall out contrary to what he chooses he may change his choice and suit it to them, and so still be happy. Indeed in this life
25   his natural appetites will sometimes disturb his elections, and so prevent his perfect happiness; yet it is a fair step towards it that he has a power that can at all times find pleasure in itself, however outward things vary.

3. True it is that this power sometimes gives pain, namely when
30   it falls short of what it chooses; which may come to pass if we choose either things impossible to be had, or inconsistent with each other, or such as are out of our power (perhaps because others chose them before us), or lastly, such as necessarily lead us into natural evils.

35   4. And into these foolish choices we may be betrayed either by ignorance, negligence, by indulging the exercise of liberty too far, by obstinacy, or habit; or lastly by the importunity of our natural appetites. Hence it appears how cautious we ought to be in choosing; for though we may alter our choice, yet to make that alteration is
40   painful, the more painful the longer we have persisted in it.

5. There are three ways by which God might have hindered his creatures from thus abusing their liberty. First, by not creating any being free. But had this method been taken, then, (1), the whole universe would have been a mere machine; (2), that would have been wanting which is most pleasing to God of anything in the 5 universe, namely, the free service of his reasonable creatures; (3), his reasonable creatures would have been in a worse state than they are now; for only free agents can be perfectly happy, as without a possibility of choosing wrong there can be no freedom.

The second way by which God might prevent the abuse of 10 liberty is by overruling this power, and constraining us to choose right. But this would be to do and undo, to contradict himself, to take away what he had given.

The third way by which God might have hindered his creatures from making an ill use of liberty is by placing them where they 15 should have no temptation to abuse it. But this too would have been the same in effect as to have given them no liberty at all. I am, dear sir, your affectionate and dutiful son,

John Wesley

Source: *A.M.*, 1780, pp. 607-11, corrected from the errata issued in 1786.

From Mrs. Mary Pendarves[1]

New Bond Street [London], 15 Jan., 1730/31 20

I have but a moment's time, and I cannot employ it better than in assuring Cyrus, though I doubtless appear unworthy of the favour he shows me, that Aspasia has been more unfortunate than ungrateful. The true reason I have not wrote has been my incapacity of doing it. A great weakness I had in my eyes for a considerable time, and the fear of its returning if I strained them too soon, has 25 been the only reason of my silence. I have received all your letters, and am infinitely obliged by them. Selima several times designed making up for my deficiency, but her heart failed, and she said she was ashamed, and talked of her not being able to write well enough, and several things of that sort which I could not agree with her in. We talk of the worth of Cyrus and Araspes whenever 30 we have any private conversation. I desire when you come to town you will let me know what day will be most convenient for you to come to me, a pleasure I depend upon. But do not come without sending, because my brother is in the house with us, and he is frequently engaged with company. It would be a great concern to me and to Selima to have you come at a time when perhaps we may 35

<hr>

[1] Replying to his of Dec. 28, 1730, and Jan. 11, 1731.

either be abroad, or engaged with company that would not be agreeable to you. I hope Araspes is well, though you do [not] mention him in your letter. I am called away. Ought I not to be ashamed to send such a hasty scrawl to Cyrus? If it serves to convince you that I am not quite unworthy of your corre-
5 spondence I shall esteem it one of the best letters I ever wrote. And that you may not think you are the only person who have thought themselves neglected by me, at the same time I received your last I had one from Varanese that wounded my very heart. However, I hope I have regained her favour, and that you will not be less indulgent, to one who knows very well how to value your
10 acquaintance, and is your most faithful friend and humble servant,

Aspasia

I make it my humble request that you will burn every letter I write.[1]

Source: Asp, pp. 20-1.

To Mrs. Mary Pendarves[2]

Westminster, Jan. 27 [1731]

'Tis with a great deal of pleasure, as well as fear, that I take the
15 liberty to acquaint you, we have been in town some hours, and attend your commands as to the time when we may have the happiness of waiting upon you. Tomorrow indeed we are obliged to give to the Westminster Feast. If you are pleased to fix on any day after that, it will be ever owned as a fresh instance of your goodness by
20 your most obliged and obedient servants.

Source: Asp, p. 21.

From Mrs. Mary Pendarves

Jan. 27 [1731]

It is no small pleasure to us, the hope of seeing Cyrus and Araspes on Saturday [Jan. 30] in the afternoon. We shall be at home from five till eight, at which

---

[1] This request was renewed Aug. 26, 1731. Wesley apparently honoured it, but first made the abstracts here presented.

[2] In the course of his letters of Dec. 28 or Jan. 11 Wesley may well have mentioned the likelihood of his going to London, but if so did not preserve this in his abstract (cf. Dec. 11, 1730, to his father). In her reply of Jan. 15 she warned him of the need for making an appointment, which led to this note, written at 1.45 p.m. after their arrival in Dean's Yard at 11 a.m., and delivered by hand, eliciting her speedy reply, though eventually the visit had to be postponed.

hour we are obliged to go abroad to supper. We are sorry to stint your time, but we have been engaged some time, and cannot very well break it off. We join in our humble service to your brother, and are your assured friends and humble servants.

I am in great haste. 5

Source: Asp, p. 22.

From Mrs. Mary Pendarves

Jan. 30 [1731]

It is a vast concern to me and my sister that we are obliged to put off the favour you designed us this afternoon. My sister is so much out of order that she keeps her bed, and I cannot very well leave her bedside. We hope your stay in town will not be short, and if you are not engaged on Monday in the afternoon 10 we hope you and your brother will favour us with your company for an hour or two. If my sister is not well enough to leave her chamber I will send you word. This is a great disappointment to us, but I hope we shall have amends made us. I am, sir, your most humble servant.

Source: Asp, p. 22.

To Mrs. Mary Pendarves

Feb. 4 [1731] 15

I should have been exceedingly pleased could I have read over these papers[1] with Aspasia and Selima, both because I should have hoped to have confirmed or altered my own judgment in several particulars, and because longer experience in things of this nature might perhaps have enabled me to be of some use toward fixing 20 theirs. But 'tis well; I leave you in his hands who shall lead into all truth![2]

Source: Asp, p. 23.

[1] Probably the abstract of Browne's *Human Understanding*, which may have been overlooked when they did in fact visit Aspasia on Monday, Feb. 1.
[2] See John 16: 13.

To Mrs. Mary Pendarves

Feb. 11 [1731]

'Tis as impossible for us to remember as we ought our last obligation to Aspasia and Selima as it is to forget it, and that sure can never be; no, 'not in the land where all things are forgotten'.[1] Even there
5 we hope to remember, and with a more tender regard than we are here capable of, to whom we owe in great measure many changes in ourselves, of which we shall then feel the full advantage; who they were that so nobly assisted us in our great work, in wearing off several stains from our natures; that so strongly recommended, by that
10 irresistible argument, example, whatsoever is honourable or lovely.

There are few (except the harsher passions) of our souls which you did not engage in those late happy moments; but none more than our wonder; our joy itself was not greater than our admiration. That London is the worst place under heaven for preserving a
15 Christian temper anyone will immediately think who observes that there can be none where its professed, irreconcilable enemies, the lust of the eye and the pride of life,[2] are more artfully and forcibly recommended. Yet even here you retain a constant sense what manner of spirit we are to be of. In the utmost affluence of whatever
20 the world can afford to chain down your affections to it, the whole tenor of your words and actions shows you are reserved for sublimer objects.

Who can be a fitter person than one that knows it by experience to tell me the full force of that glorious rule, 'Set your affections on
25 things above, and not on things of the earth'?[3] Is it equivalent to, 'Thou shalt love the Lord thy God with all thy heart, soul, and strength'?[4] But what is it to love God? Is not to love anything the same as habitually to delight in it? Is not then the purport of both these injunctions this, that we delight in the Creator more than his
30 creatures?[5] That we take more pleasure in him than in anything he has made? And rejoice in nothing so much as in serving him? That (to take Mr. Pascal's expression) while the generality of men use God and enjoy the world,[6] we on the contrary only use the world while we enjoy God.

---

[1] Ps. 88: 12 (B.C.P.). [2] 1 John 2: 16. [3] Col. 3: 2.
[4] Mark 12: 30, etc. [5] See Rom. 1: 25.
[6] Blaise Pascal (1623–62), *Pensées*, 'La cupidité use de Dieu et jouit du monde; et

How pleasingly could I spend many hours in talking with you on this important subject! Especially if I could hope to repay thereby one mite of the vast debt I owe you. To recall to your mind any hint, by pursuing of which you might exalt it to a yet firmer temper. But I submit. By thus cutting my time short Providence shows me it has 5 more suitable methods of leading you into all truth, and fixing you in all virtue, than with the weak endeavours of your obliged friend,

C[yrus]

Feb. 12

I have a thousand things to say, would time permit; but, O believe, 10 I can never say half of what I feel! Adieu.

Source: Asp, pp. 23-5.

From Mrs. Mary Pendarves

Feb. 13 [1731]

The few hours that Selima and Aspasia enjoyed the conversation of Cyrus and Araspes are too valuable to be forgot; which I should sooner have endeavoured to convince you of, if I could have found time. And the favour of the book[1] is of 15 so high a nature that we can never be so ungrateful as to look on it without the greatest thankfulness. How happy should we have been to have heard it read by one who so well knows to recommend everything he approves of! I am sensible there must be several things we shall not be able to comprehend in such a treatise; you must therefore give me leave to trouble you with my ignorance, by desiring 20 your explanation of what I may not understand. I hope we shall hear from you soon. I have not time now to enlarge my letter. I must again repeat my acknow-ledgements for the friendship you have shown us in many instances. Selima and Aspasia will always gratefully remember them.

Source: Asp, p. 25.

la charité, au contraire' (ed. H. F. Stewart, London, Routledge and Kegan Paul, 1950, No. 526, pp. 304-5). Wesley read this in *Thoughts on Religion*, the translation by Basil Kennett (1674-1715), which he later abridged for his *Christian Library*, Vol. 23: '[covetousness] employs itself in using God and enjoying the world, [charity] in using the world and enjoying God' (4th edn., London, 1749, p. 123). A few months later (in a sermon on Prov. 11: 30) Wesley wrote about 'the half-Christians who (to speak in the words of an excellent man), "use God, and enjoy the world" '. See also his sermon 'On Riches' (1788), II. 12.

[1] Browne's *Human Understanding*; see letters of Dec. 28, 1730, and Feb. 4, 1731.

To Mrs. Mary Pendarves

Feb. 19 [1731]

Yes, it is better to assure Aspasia now, though it be but in one line, that I am sensible of her strange goodness in thus preventing me a second time, than to put off still what, could it have been
5 avoided, ought not to have been delayed a moment. But what can I do, thus hemmed in as I am with business over and above my own? I am perasuded you would not condemn me, Aspasia, did you know how many days pass over my head in which I have not one poor hour from five to seven but what is engaged long before
10 it comes. Yet never shall any engagement of any kind make me so false both to justice and friendship as to neglect any commands which I may have the pleasure of receiving from Aspasia or Selima. That particular one which your last gives me leave to expect I should earnestly have requested myself had not you mentioned it first. O
15 Aspasia, how gladly should I receive into my soul your ignorance of some points in philosophy, could ignorance of pride, ingratitude, and passion pass at the same time into (I dare hardly say) your friend,

C[yrus]

20 When Aspasia or Selima is the theme, I speak the sense of Araspes in my own. Adieu!

Source: Asp, p. 26.

From Martha Wesley

March 30, 1731

Dear brother

I must confess you were much kinder to me than I deserved in answering
25 my letter so soon, and I intended to ha' followed your example, and ha' writ by the next post, but I knew I could not write to you without thinking, and I was quite sick of thought.[1] You have so often blamed me for complaining that you have long since broke me of it (at least of troubling you with my complaints), yet methinks I'm strongly tempted to trouble you once more, to tell thee all the
30 secrets of my soul, and 'let thee share my most retired distress'. [. . .]

[1] Wesley's diary shows that the letter to which this replies was written on Mar. 4, so that her letter must have been written about Mar. 1.

You know how I liked Mr. Johnson when you was here last. You may remember too that I told you I was not engaged to him by promise, nor am I yet. O that I could think I was not in honour, neither. But when a man presses a woman to marriage, though she may not say she will have him, yet if she does not positively say she will not I think he may reasonably take it for encouragement. 5 [She tells how she has written several letters discouraging him, though she was not averse to marrying him, and did not want to give him pain. Now he has renewed his attractive offers of marriage, though most other people, including John, seem to be trying to match her with Matthew Horbery (*c.* 1707-73), son of the vicar of Haxey and a recent graduate at Lincoln College.] 10

I readily grant all you say of Mr. Horbery to be true! And if I can as you say, 'converse with him without being worse', there is indeed no doubt but I may reap much profit, to say nothing of pleasure, by his conversation. [. . .] Our good people take it for granted that every time I see and talk with Mr. Horbery I love Mr. Johnson so much the less. [. . .] Sister Molly says I am just going after Mrs. 15 Chapone[1] and you, and she has such [. . .] mistaken charity for me as to wish to see me buried alive rather than I should love Mr. Horbery as well as Mrs. Chapone does you! [. . .]

I wish my dear brother would give me his thoughts upon this subject, and tell me what he himself would do if he was in my place. [. . .] 20

You have formerly complained that I did not speak my mind freely enough to you. I think you will never have reason to make that complaint again, since I could not have given you a greater instance of the entire confidence I repose in you than I ha' done by this letter. [. . .] I am, dear brother, your ever faithful friend and sister, 25

Martha Wesley [. . .]

Address: 'To The Revd. Mr John Wesley, Fellow of Lincoln College, Oxon. By way of London'   *End* by JW: 'SP. March 10, 1731 +'   *Source*: MA.

From Mrs. Mary Pendarves

New Bond Street [London], April 4, 1731

In what manner can I make an excuse to Cyrus for being so long without acknowledging the favour of his last letter?[2] By this time he certainly repents of the great indulgence he has shown me. When I consider how every hour of your 30 life is employed, either in your own improvement or bestowing part of your knowledge on those who are happily placed under your care; and that notwithstanding the difficulty it is for you to command any time to yourself you have always remembered me in the most obliging manner, and have studied not only how to entertain but to improve me; when I recollect all this, have I not reason to 35

---

[1] Varanese.
[2] The monthly summary in Wesley's diary for Mar. 1731 shows that he had written to her that month (apparently early in the month) the letter to which she here replies in terms which reveal its challenging contents.

fear the loss of your good opinion? And that you think me unworthy of your
favour and advice? That surrounded by vanity and impertinence, I am fallen
into the snare, and refuse to hear the voice of the charmer, charm he ne'er so
wisely! God forbid my state should be so desperate as to prefer sin and folly to
5 virtue and wisdom! I will sincerely tell you the truth, and trust to your mercy.
All the acquaintance I almost have are now in town. They are continually
soliciting us either to come to them, or they will come to us. My sister being soon to
leave me, all her friends endeavour to give her as much entertainment as they
can; by which means our time is so entirely engrossed that for two months past
10 we have lived in a perpetual hurry, and shall do so for the month to come. I
would not have you imagine we have neglected the book; whatever comes with
your recommendation is of too much value to be neglected. But the subject of it
is too elevated to be read in a hurry; next week I hope we shall have leisure to
read and reflect. I am a little at a loss for some words, not being used to short-
15 hand, but I believe I shall be able to find them out.[1]

Every Sunday evening there is a gentleman in this town has a concert
['consort'] of music. I am invited there tonight, and design to go. I charge you,
on the friendship you have professed for me, tell me your sincere opinion about
it, and all your objections. For if I am in an error by going, you ought to prevent
20 my doing so again.

Dear Varanese I have not heard from a great while. Why are we denied the
happiness and advantage of conversing with such a friend? Araspes may justly
claim our service and esteem. Selima joins with Aspasia in being to Cyrus a
faithful and obliged friend.

25 I have hardly confidence to expect a return to this.

Source: Asp, pp. 27-8.

To Mrs. Mary Pendarves

April 5 [1731]

Aspasia will hardly imagine how often, since I had the pleasure
of returning my thanks for her last favour, I have been angry at this
ill-natured business, which has so long kept me from repeating
30 them. Many a time have I sighed and said to myself, 'No, nothing
ought to keep me from it. I ought not on any account to lose the
only way I now have of enjoying such conversation. This is the voice
of reason, not prejudice. Is there a more improving (as well as
pleasing) employment? When thy heart burns within thee at her
35 words,[2] is it not the warmth of life, of virtue? Do they not inspire
some degree of the purity and softness of that heart from which
they came?' Yet one consideration there is that as often checks my
complaints and bids my soul be still: 'Should I neglect the work

---

[1] Apparently the occasional symbols in Wesley's abbreviated longhand, in which he penned Browne's *Human Understanding* for her.

[2] See Luke 24: 32.

to which Providence so plainly calls me, even in hope of such a
good, by thus striving to be more like, I should be still more unlike
Aspasia.'

The more I observe the dispositions of those poor creatures that
make up the bulk of mankind, the more do I desire to shelter 5
myself from them, under the protection of Varanese and Aspasia and
Selima. The stronger distaste I conceive at those, the more amiable
light these appear in. And this doubtless is one of the uses which
God makes, even of the children of this generation. As they give us
a stronger dislike to vice, which though it appear hateful to 10
abstracted reason, yet

> Thus speaking and thus acting grows tenfold
> More horrid and deform—[1]

so they inspire us with a livelier approbation of virtue, which never
appears more awful-glorious than when it appears, like the great 15
Author of it, 'with clouds and darkness round about it'.[2] Then it is,
when I am tired with the melancholy prospect of them whose eyes
the god of this world hath blinded,[3] whose hearts he hath so bowed
down to earth that their admiration soars not so high as

> The riches of heaven's pavement,[4] 20

that I fly to those whose eyes are opened, whose hearts are enlarged,
who see and love the noblest objects; that I can hardly forbear
crying out aloud, How unlike are these to Selima, Aspasia, Varanese!
That I most earnestly repeat that, my frequent wish:

> O might there be unfeigned 25
> Union of mind, as in us all one soul![5]

Were it possible that my mind should unite with yours, dear
Aspasia, in the single instance of humility, which I can't but particularly observe and admire whenever I consider your behaviour toward
me; I should then dare to hope that he who had wrought in me 'to 30

---

[1] See Milton, *Paradise Lost*, ii. 705-6:
> So speaking and so threatening, grew tenfold
> More dreadful and deform.

[2] See Ps. 97: 2.

[3] 2 Cor. 4: 4.

[4] Milton, *Paradise Lost*, i. 682.

[5] See Milton, *Paradise Lost*, viii. 603-4:
> which declare unfeigned
> Union of mind, or in us both one soul.

think as I ought to think'[1] would in his own time work a farther resemblance to good Aspasia in her most obliged, faithful

C[yrus]

The esteem of Araspes as well as Cyrus must ever attend both
5 Aspasia and Selima.

Source: Asp, pp. 32–4.

To Mrs. Mary Pendarves[2]

April 14 [1731]

I cannot, I will not delay any longer to return my sincerest thanks to dear Aspasia for (I had almost said) the greatest of her favours, as indeed every one seems greater than the preceding. Yet
10 methinks I should not say that you seem to exceed even your former goodness in this, since that expression would imply some room for doubt, which surely there is not here. Not only the justice which you show to the sincerity of my intentions, not only the friendly applause you give me, which, undeserved as it is, is yet exceeding pleasing
15 when I consider it as a mark of that approbation which I must ever have in the highest esteem; but above all that lovely freedom you use with me in a point of the utmost importance, leaves me no room to doubt but I may look upon the last as the greatest of my obligations.
20   Far be it from me to think that any circumstances of life shall ever give the enemy an advantage over Aspasia! Though she walk through the vale of the shadow of death,[3] where sin and vanity are on every side, where vice and folly appear in so fair a light as to deceive, if it were possible, the very elect; where the utmost skill of the world
25 and the prince of it join to tear up humility, the root of Christian virtue; and consideration, which alone (under God) is able to give it any increase; even there her footsteps shall not slide; she shall fear and shall find no evil.[4] He who hath overcome the world[5] and its prince shall give his angels charge over her to keep her in all her

---

[1] Cf. Rom. 12: 3.
[2] Replying to hers of Apr. 4, especially its closing question about attending a Sunday concert.
[3] See Ps. 23: 4.   [4] Ibid.   [5] See John 16: 33.

ways.[1] And far should I be from doubting but they would keep you safe, though you should see cause to withdraw your favour from me, though you should at last perceive some of those numerous faults which were before so strangely hid from you, and so be obliged to choose a fitter object for that friendship, to which I made so unequal 5 returns.

O Aspasia, am I not already betraying myself? Needlessly showing my imperfections? To give way to one thought of losing your friendship, while I have such an evidence of its sincerity before me! I greatly wish I may be able to give a full answer to the question you 10 so obligingly propose, but a direct one I can't give, unless such an one may be deduced from any of the following considerations.

To judge whether any action be lawful on the sabbath or no we are to consider whether it advances the end for which that was ordained. Now the end for which the sabbath was ordained is the[2] 15 attainment of holiness. Whatever therefore tends to advance this end is lawful on this day; whatever does not tend to advance this end is not lawful on this day.

Two things we may infer hence: 1. That works of mercy are lawful on this day, for they directly tend to advance this end, to make 20 us holy as God is holy.[3] 2. That works of necessity are lawful on this day. Of which there are two sorts: first, works which we ought to do but cannot do on another day; second, works that[4] or works the neglect of which would obstruct this end—for whatever can't be omitted without hindering it does indirectly tend to advance it. One 25 of these, to those who can't perform the offices of religion so well without it, is giving themselves some diversion from it. But of this we may observe, that, it being therefore allowed because it tends to advance the end of the day, it is allowable so far, and no farther, as it does tend to it, to our advance in holiness. It is not enough to say 30 this or that diversion does not obstruct this end, for what does so is allowable on no day; but unless it promotes this particular end it is not allowable on this day.

Araspes (whose great esteem, as well as mine, ever attends Aspasia and Selima) was extremely delighted as well as me with a letter 35 we received some time since, acquainting us with a resolution dear

---

[1] Ps. 91: 11; Matt. 4: 6.   [2] Orig., 'O', apparently an error.
[3] See 1 Pet. 1: 15, etc.
[4] Wesley has underlined 'Of which . . . works that' as if for omission—the kind of thing which he did in his drafts of manuscripts, though this is clearly an abstract or a copy made after the original had been sent.

Varanese had lately entered into. Why it is that I am not allowed
a stricter intercourse with such a friend is a question I could never
fully answer but by another, Why is any intercourse with such
a friend as Aspasia or Selima allowed your most obliged

5   Cy[rus]

On Monday we are to set out upon a pretty long journey, which
will keep us out about three weeks.[1] We should be exceedingly
grieved if Selima should be obliged to begin hers before that time,
which would prevent our having that pleasure, the very expectation
10 of which gives us many agreeable moments. Adieu!

Source: Asp, pp. 29–32.

From the Revd. Samuel Wesley, Jun.[2]

[Apr. 28, 1731]

Dear Jack

I can easily allow that you and Charles *do* more business than I, but I can by
no means own that you have more *to do*. Great part of what I should do I often
15 let alone, though I am sorry for it afterwards. I designed to have wrote by Mr.
Bateman, to whom I read part of your last letter concerning the execrable consultation in order to stop the progress of religion by giving it a false name. He
lift up his hands and eyes, and protested he could not have believed such a thing.
He gave Morgan a very good character, and said he should always think himself
20 obliged to him for the pains he took in reclaiming a young pupil of his who was
just got into ill company, and upon the brink of destruction. Who Mr. B. is I
don't well know, for sure it cannot be any man who has any notions of duty
himself. I don't like your being called a club; that name is really calculated to do
mischief. And methinks I would studiously avoid every particularity as far as
25 possible, lest the matter itself should suffer for the manner of doing good. But
the other charge of enthusiasm can weigh with none but such as drink away their
sense, or never had any; for surely activity in social duties and strict attendance
upon the ordained means of grace are the strongest guards imaginable against it.

---

[1] Wesley's diary for Easter Monday, April 19, reads: 'set out on foot for Epworth'.
They paid visits to Stanton both going and returning, so that the absence from Oxford
lasted much longer than anticipated, until May 12; they returned to the Cotswolds ten
days later.

[2] This was apparently a reply to John's missing letter of March 29, in which he seems
to have described the rumblings of persecution beginning against the activities of the
Oxford 'Methodists'. Its contents anticipated those of his letter to the Revd. Joseph
Hoole of May 18, 1731, for which see below, pp. 341–2.

I went to call upon Dr. Terry,[1] in order to desire him to subscribe to Job,[2] but did not meet with him; and in two or three days, *O rem ridiculam et jocosam,*[3] he did me the favour to call upon me; which I was so obliged to him for that I would not then chagrin him with desiring him to part with money. I told him I hoped my two brothers 'have still good characters at Oxford'. He said it now 5 lay out of his way, but he believed so. Quoth I, 'No news is good news', he 'must needs have heard anything remarkable.' He believed again they were studious and sober. When he was got downstairs, without the door to the steps, he turns about and says, 'I think I have heard your brothers are exemplary, and take a great [deal] of pains to instil good principles into young people.' I told him, and 10 you may guess I told him truth, I was very glad to hear such a character of them, especially from him. Mr. Hutchison brings you this. The gentleman who carries it to him has just called upon me, so I don't know how long time I shall have to finish it. I have wrote to my father that I intend to go down to him at Bartholomew-tide (or rather this summer, without naming the time), which I suppose 15 will stop all thoughts of his coming up before I see Epworth at least, and then we may discourse of the matter at large. I have the names of twenty subscribers of yours, but not their titles and dignities, as Revd, and ⟨. . .⟩

End by JW: 'Apr. 28, 1731'   *Source*: Wes Ch, defective, with one half of the sheet missing.

From Ann Granville

Gloucester, 8 May, 1731

I had rather expose my own ignorance in writing than not hear from Cyrus and 20 Araspes, whose letters give so much pleasure and improvement to your friends. Besides, at present I have my mother's commands to warrant my own inclination. She orders me to be very particular in her acknowledgments for the last letter she received from Oxford. We were extremely vexed when we came there to find our agreeable friends had left it. Except that disappointment our journey 25 was as prosperous as we could wish. But my sister was not with us. The weakness we felt at parting we endeavoured to correct by saying, Would not Cyrus blame us for this? The reflection dried our tears, but I must confess sincerely, it did not ease our pain. Is not this wrong in us? Did I (for my sister has more fortitude) make a proper progress in Christianity the things of this world would 30 certainly be more indifferent to me than I find they are. How shall I learn the happiness of being above trifles? Nobody can so well point out the way to me as yourself. But I could not make such a request did I not know how ready you are to do good.

[1] Thomas Terry (*c.* 1678–1735), Regius Professor of Greek, Canon of Christ Church, and also rector of Chalfont St. Giles. In his letter of May 18 Wesley wrote that soon after the 'execrable consultation' at Christ Church it was 'publicly reported that Dr. Terry and the censors were going to blow up the Godly Club'.

[2] Their father's *magnum opus*, long in preparation.

[3] 'A droll and amusing situation'; see Catullus, lvi. 4.

I have not had the pleasure of a letter since I came home from valuable Sappho,[1] but I have heard she is well. My sister and I answered for her dear little girl, but she is in the hands of a person more capable of instructing her. I suppose you have heard from my sister by this time. If not, you must excuse her, because 5 she is at present very much taken with some business in order to a little ramble she goes upon this summer. We were prodigiously obliged to you for the book you favoured us with. The greatest objection I had to London was that I had no time to read it. My sister and I almost quarreled about it when I came away; but she promised to send it me when she had read it. There are some words 10 puzzle us, not understanding shorthand. We must beg of you to explain them, for we can't consent to lose one word.[2]

I am often angry with some of our neighbours, who, impertinently civil, take up more of my time than I am willing to bestow upon them. I am now guilty of the same fault, and write on without considering how many useful good things I 15 may prevent your doing. But I will make no excuses, because I hope you look upon my errors as a friend. Show me you are so by telling me as freely of them as I assure Cyrus and Araspes that I am your most faithful friend and humble servant.

My mother's best wishes attend the good brothers.

Source: Sel[ima Letters], a notebook similar to that in which Wesley transcribed his correspondence with Aspasia, in MA, pp. 1–3.

To Mrs. Mary Pendarves

20   June 2 [1731]

It was not in the power of all the variety of obj[ect]s[3] that occurred to me in my late journeys to lessen the concern I felt at being so long cut off from the conversation of Aspasia.[4] The impression which this had left on my mind was so far from being effaced by any 25 succeeding pleasure that every agreeable entertainment I had recalled it to my thoughts, and made me, as more sensible of my obligations to her, so more desirous again to acknowledge them.

You will easily judge whether the remembrance of Aspasia made that entertainment in particular less agreeable which I enjoyed last 30 week, in the almost uninterrupted conversation of dear Varanese. 'On

[1] For 'Sappho' (Sally Chapone), see p. 286, below.
[2] Cf. p. 274 n.
[3] 'Objections' would seem grammatically more appropriate, though this would not be his normal abbreviation for this word.
[4] In addition to his 'pretty long journey' to Epworth (see Apr. 14), on May 22 he set off for the Cotswolds, not returning until May 31.

this spot she sat', 'Along this path she walked', 'Here she showed
that lovely instance of condescension', were reflections which,
though extremely obvious, yet could not but be equally pleasing,
but give a new degree of beauty to the charming arbour, the fields,
the meadows, and Horrel[1] itself.   5

The happy disappointment we met with here, in having everything succeed beyond our expectations, almost reconciled Araspes
and M[2] to our other disappointment, of a less pleasing nature. And
indeed I, for my part, cannot without the utmost immodesty repine
at any dispensation of Providence while I am so unaccountably   10
indulged both in the friendship of a Varanese, and in calling myself
dear Aspasia's most obliged, faithful

Cy[rus]

Araspes too begs leave to say that he is entirely at Aspasia's
service. Adieu!   15

Source: Asp, pp. 34–5.

To the Revd. Samuel Wesley

[June 11, 1731]

['With respect to their walk' from Epworth to Oxford 'he observes,
that it was not so pleasant to Oxford as from it, though in one respect
more useful.'] For it let us see that four- or five-and-twenty miles
is an easy and safe day's journey in hot weather as well as cold. We   20
have made another discovery, too, which may be of some service,
that it is easy to read as we walk ten or twelve miles, and that it
neither makes us faint nor gives us any other symptom of weariness,
more than the mere walking without reading at all.

Since our return our little company, that used to meet us on   25
a Sunday evening, is shrunk into almost none at all. Mr. Morgan is

---

[1] A plantation of beech-trees cresting a hill south of Stanton, which they visited on
Sunday evening, the 23rd, spending three-quarters of an hour on the Monday morning
'in V's arbour'. Cf. pp. 230, 307.

[2] 'M' here apparently does not stand for 'me' (though this is just possible) but is
Wesley's normal abbreviated nickname for Bob Kirkham, who accompanied the two
brothers on this visit to his own home (cf. Heitzenrater, p. 87).

sick at Holt;[1] Mr. Boyce is at his father's house at Barton;[2] Mr. Kirkham must very shortly leave Oxford to be his uncle's[3] curate, and a young gentleman of Christ Church, who used to make a fourth,[4] either afraid, or ashamed, or both, is returned to the ways
5 of the world, and studiously shuns our company. However, the poor at the Castle have still the gospel preached to them, and some of their temporal wants supplied, our little fund rather increasing than diminishing. Nor have we yet been forced to discharge any of the children which Mr. Morgan left to our care, though I wish they too
10 do not find the want of him—I am sure some of their parents will.

Some, however, give us a better prospect, John Whitelamb[5] in particular. I believe with this you will receive some account from himself, how his time is employed. He reads one English, one Latin, and one Greek book alternately; and never meddles with a new
15 one in any of the languages till he has ended the old one. If he goes on as he has begun I dare take upon me to say that by the time he has been here four or five years there will not be such an one of his standing in Lincoln College, perhaps not in the University of Oxford.

Source: Whitehead, I. 432–3, date confirmed by diary.

To Mrs. Susanna Wesley

20   [June 11, 1731]

The motion and the sun together in our last hundred and fifty miles' walk so throughly carried off all our superfluous humours that we continue perfectly in health, though it is here a very sickly

[1] William Morgan (*c.* 1712–32) of Dublin, who graduated this year, and was the pioneer of the Methodist care for prisoners. He suffered a physical and nervous breakdown which eventually led to his death, attributed by some critics to his ascetic Methodist practices.

[2] John Boyce (1711–76), like Morgan, of Christ Church and graduating this year.

[3] Henry Kirkham, vicar of Stanway.

[4] No such Christ Church man can firmly be identified, though Francis Gore is a possibility (see Green, p. 155).

[5] John Whitelamb (*c.* 1707–69), who had been serving Wesley's father as amanuensis, and living in the rectory as his student. He saved the rector's life in the accident recorded Sept. 5, 1728 (p. 233, above), and the rector sponsored his education at Oxford, welcomed him as curate and husband for his daughter Mary ('Molly'), and eventually resigned the living of Wroot to him.

season. And Mr. Kirkham assures us, on the word of a priest and a physician, that if we will but take the same medicine once or twice a year we shall never need any other to keep us from the gout. When we were with him we touched two or three times upon a nice subject, but did not come to any full conclusion. The point debated was, What is the meaning of being 'righteous overmuch',[1] or by the more common phrase, of being too strict in religion? And what danger there was of any of us falling into that extreme.

All the ways of being too righteous or too strict which we could think of were these: either the carrying some one particular virtue to so great a height as to make it clash with some others; or the laying too much stress on the instituted means of grace, to the neglect of the weightier matters of the law;[2] or the multiplying prudential means upon ourselves so far, and binding ourselves to the observance of them so strictly, as to obstruct the end we aimed at by them, either by hindering our advance in heavenly affections in general, or by retarding our progress in some particular virtue. Our opponents seemed to think my brother and I in some danger of being too strict in this last sense, of laying burdens on ourselves too heavy to be borne, and consequently too heavy to be of any use to us.

It is easy to observe that everyone thinks that rule totally needless which he does not need himself; and as to the Christian spirit itself, almost everyone calls that degree of it which he does not himself aim at, enthusiasm. If therefore we plead for either (not as if we thought the former absolutely needful, neither as if we had attained the latter) it is no great wonder that they who are not for us in practice should be against us. If you who are a less prejudiced judge have perceived us faulty in this matter, too superstitious or enthusiastic, or whatever it is to be called, we earnestly desire to be speedily informed of our error, that we may no longer spend our strength on that which profiteth not. Or whatever there may be on the other hand in which you have observed us to be too remiss, that likewise we desire to know as soon as possible. This is a subject which we would understand with as much accuracy as possible, it being hard to say which is of the worse consequence: the being too strict, the really carrying things too far, the wearying ourselves and spending our strength in burdens that are unnecessary; or the being

---

[1] Eccles. 7: 16.
[2] Matt. 23: 23.

frightened by those terrible words from what, if not directly necessary, would at least be useful.

Source: Whitehead, I. 434–5, date confirmed by diary.

From Mrs. Mary Pendarves[1]

June 16 [1731]

Without the highest vanity, how can I suppose my correspondence of so much
5 consequence as to give Cyrus any pleasure? I have no occasion to think it, but
from your own words. And can I doubt your truth? No carty.[2]

I will not say I envied either Varanese or Cyrus those moments they passed
together, for indeed I did not; but happy should I have been to have shared them
with you. How I please myself with the thoughts that I was not quite forgot at
10 that interview; perhaps I was wished for.

How differently were my hours employed just at that time! Instead of meeting
with a favourite friend, I parted from one, my dearest Selima. I want her every
moment, particularly when I am alone. Her conversation softened every care.
But I own it is ungrateful for me to repine at her absence; my mother can't
15 be happy without her, and I ought to resign her with cheerfulness. My natural
disposition is hasty and impatient under disappointments; but your example and
precepts have already corrected some part of that inexcusable temper, and I
owe you my best thanks for many tranquil hours which I should not have had
without that amendment.

20 The common conversation of the world disgusts me extremely; but I am not
only disgusted at some principles which I find too much encouraged, but really
afflicted. I know men of excellent understanding, learning, humanity, in short
endowed with all the agreeable qualities that can be desired, and not destitute
of good ones: but talk to them of religion and they maintain an opinion that
25 shocks me to hear it. They allow our Saviour to be a great prophet, but divest
him of divinity; admire the Scripture, but call every part that mentions the
Trinity fictitious. I have one friend in particular of this opinion. He is in every
other respect a most amiable man: in all moral duties none can excel him; the
best husband, friend, master, son; charitable without the least ostentation;
30 has a fine understanding, the greatest politeness, without the least tincture of
vanity. What do you say that man's state is with regard to the next world?

Company is come in, and prevents my saying any more; but I shall be glad
to hear soon from you. My service attends Araspes. I am your obliged friend,
Aspasia

Source: Asp, pp. 44–6.

[1] Replying to his of June 2.
[2] i.e., certie, certy, perhaps from certes. See *O.E.D.*

To Ann Granville[1]

[June 17–18, 1731]

May.[2]

In what words can I express my thanks to Selima for the favourable opinion she entertains of me? Of which she has given me so obliging a proof as I extremely desired but knew not how to ask for. 5
Perhaps you don't know the inconvenience you are bringing upon yourself, that your goodness will but embolden me to ask more. Yet thus I can assure [you] it will be: your letters will in one sense never satisfy me. But the oftener you favour me (if you should please to do it again) the more earnestly I shall desire it. You have 10
already effectually convinced me of this, that it may be said with equal justice of every sort of conversation with Aspasia or you, 'It brings to its sweetness no satiety.'[3]

That the tearing asunder of such friends as these should occasion a very sensible pain is surely the effect both of nature and reason, 15
which don't require us to be without passions (No, be it a Roman virtue to be 'without natural affection'[4]), but to proportion them to the occasion. Indeed we are not required by reason to grieve on the severest occasion 'as those without hope';[5] we have a good hope, that severe as it is, it is no less merciful. Nay, more so, since no pain 20
approaches a Christian but to pave the way for more than equal pleasure.

We had so much pleasure in the late hours we spent at Stanton that nothing could [have] added to it but Selima or Aspasia. All things else conspired to complete our happiness; nor was it a small share 25
of it which we owed to Mrs. Astell.[6] Our dear Sappho[7] showed us

---

[1] Ann Granville (*c.* 1708–61), daughter of Mrs. Mary Granville (see above, p. 259), and younger sister of Mrs. Mary Pendarves. She married John Dewes in 1740, and died aged 53, July 16, 1761. Her widower died Aug. 30, 1780, aged 85.

[2] She first wrote to Wesley in a postscript to an unfinished letter of her sister's (Oct. 12, 1730), and then independently (and somewhat timidly) on May 8, 1731, to which this is Wesley's answer. The 'May' possibly indicates the month of receipt, for his diary shows that the letter itself in its final form was written June 17–18.

[3] Cf. Milton, *Paradise Lost*, viii. 216, 'bring to their sweetness no satiety'.
[4] 2 Tim. 3: 3.   [5] Cf. Eph. 2: 12.
[6] Mary Astell (1668–1731), whose *Serious Proposal to Ladies* (1694) for a method of religious retirement was followed by a second part in 1697 proposing a college for women. Although it was published anonymously, her authorship was an open secret. Wesley's diary shows that on May 29 he 'read Mrs. Astell to V[aranese] and M.G.' (apparently

[*Continuation of note 6 and note 7 overleaf.*

her *Proposal to the Ladies*, which gave us several agreeable conversations. Surely her plan of female life must have pleased all the thinking part of her sex, had she not prescribed so much of those two dull things, reading and religion. Reading indeed would be less dull
5 as well as more improving to those who, like her, would use method in it; but then it would not rid them of so much time, because half a dozen books read in course would take up no more of that than one or two read just as they came to hand.

That you propose and attain another end in reading than throwing
10 away a few leisure hours, that one sentence shows wherein you so well express the end for which we live, move, and have our being.[1] How glad should I be could I either teach or be taught by anyone 'to be above trifles'![2] How doubly glad to have Selima for my instructor in indifference to the things of this world! To be indifferent
15 to the world! Why, that is everything! 'Tis to be h[oly]! To be happy! To be renewed after the image wherein we were created![3] To have that mind in us which was also in Christ Jesus![4]

If it be ever in my power to assist anyone in renewing their minds [after] this image, surely the more I conversed with you, the more
20 power I should have, as well as the more inclination to pursue that glorious work. Do not then think, dear Selima, that anything you can say can possibly hinder me from doing good. Every line from so friendly a hand, every word that comes from so good a heart, has a natural tendency to increase both the desire and the power of being
25 useful, in your m[ost] obliged, faithful

Cyrus

June 17
The death of one of the best friends I had in the world, which

Miss Nancy Griffiths of Broadway), and his accounts for that month indicate that he bought two copies (selling them separately in 1732); he read the book carefully June 7-9.
    7 'Sappho' seems to have been an alternative nickname for Sarah Kirkham, Mrs. John Chapone, Wesley's 'Varanese'. In her extant correspondence with Wesley Mrs. Pendarves used his favourite term exclusively, although in the *Autobiography* (I. 15-17) she herself equated 'Sappho' with Sarah Chapone. On the other hand Ann Granville used 'Sappho' exclusively in writing to him (cf. May 8, Aug. 9, Aug. 14, Sept. 29, 1731), and here (as on Aug. 14, 1731) Wesley responds similarly. The diary entries confirm the common identity of the two names. (Cf. note to letter of Aug. 14, 1730.)

    1 Acts 17: 28.
    2 See her letter of May 8: 'How shall I learn the happiness of being above trifles?'
    3 See Col. 3: 10.
    4 See Phil. 2: 5.

happened last week,[1] as it occasioned, will I hope excuse, the delay of this, as well as the defects of it.

Araspes joins with me in sincere thanks to Selima, and begging she would, when it is convenient, present our best respects to good Mrs. G[ranville]. 5

Source: Sel, pp. 3–5.

To Mrs. Mary Pendarves[2]

June 19th [1731]

Is it a proof that I am or that I am not duly sensible of my obligations to dear Aspasia that I so extremely desire to contract more, by more frequently conversing with her? Would it were possible for me, once a month at least, to have the pleasure of seeing your thoughts! 10 You shall not doubt but it would give me improvement too; the same freedom that shines through your last, whenever I admired it, could not but make upon me a lasting as well as pleasing impression.

There was no need of Selima's letter to our Varanese, or of that she was since pleased to favour me with, to make either of us wish 15 both her and Aspasia a share in all our happiest moments. 'Tis but a few days since that I had a little share in your misfortune in parting with a sincere friend. But I shall go to him again, if he does not return to me, though he is gone a longer journey than Selima—I hope, as far as paradise.[3] 20

If Providence has used me as an instrument of doing any good to Aspasia, I had almost said, 'I have my reward';[4] some part of it I have undoubtedly. The thought of having added anything to your ease will make many of my hours the happier. Yet perhaps I ought not to desire you should be easy at the common conversation of the 25 world, which if once it comes to be indifferent to us, will scarce be long before it be agreeable. We are indeed, as to this, in a great strait. Either it displeases—and who would be in pain could it be avoided? Or it pleases, which surely causes, if it does not spring

[1] Dr. John Morley, Rector of Lincoln College, who died June 12, 1731. Wesley's diary for June 15 reads, 'The Rector dead. 8.45, Common Room, talk of the Rector.'
[2] Replying to hers of June 16.
[3] Dr. John Morley; see previous letter.
[4] Cf. Matt. 6: 2, 5, 16.

from, an entire depravation of our affections. Which side shall we
turn to? O that there were a middle way! That we could shun this
unpleasant or fatally pleasing impertinence! But it cannot be. All
we can do is to [be] on our guard when we are engaged in it, and to
5 engage no more in it than is plainly necessary.

Do not be surprised, good Aspasia, when I assure you that I
exceedingly rejoice at your other affliction. I am extremely glad to
find you among those few who are yet concerned for the honour of
their Master, and can't but congratulate you upon your wise choice,
10 'If we suffer with him, we shall also reign with him.'[1] I know there
are in these last days many seduced by fair speeches 'to deny the
Lord that bought them';[2] to affirm that he and the Father are not
one, and that it is robbery to think him equal with God.[3] Indeed
the first reformers of the Christian faith in this point (with whom
15 Dr. Clarke[4] joins) only modestly asserted that the Church was
bought with the blood of Christ, but not of God, i.e. not of 'the God
who is over all',[5] 'who is and was and is to come, the Almighty'.[6]
And it was many hundred years after that Socinus[7] roundly maintained that Christ never purchased any Church at all, nor 'gave his
20 life a ransom for any man, all those phrases being purely metaphysical'.[8] That anyone had any hope of outgoing him I never heard
before; but surely those gentlemen who will prove them to be ficti-
titious have a much better courage than even Socinus's. Yet there
is one step farther for these too—to affirm the same of all the s[aint]s,
25 and then T[inda]l's[9] arguments are ready to their hands.

That sometimes even a good man falls a prey to the cunning
craftiness of these deceivers I can easily believe, having known one
(otherwise) strictly virtuous person who was under that infatuation
several years. That such an one has nothing to hope for from the

---

[1] Cf. 2 Tim. 2: 12. [2] Cf. 2 Pet. 2: 1.

[3] See John 10: 30, Phil. 2: 6.

[4] Dr. Samuel Clarke (1675–1729), whose *Discourse concerning the Being and Attributes
of God* (1705–6) revealed deistic traits, and his *Scripture Doctrine of the Trinity* (1712)
unitarian.

[5] Cf. Rom. 9: 5.

[6] Cf. Rev. 4: 8.

[7] Fausto Paolo Sozzini (1539–1604), whose Latinized name, Faustus Socinus, was
used to describe the form of Unitarianism embodied in the Racovian Catechism (1605).

[8] Wesley is apparently summarizing, not quoting, the lengthy argument in V. viii of
the Racovian Catechism, that the idea of man's redemption by 'ransom' is not to be
taken literally, but symbolically.

[9] Matthew Tindal (1657?–1733), whose *Christianity as Old as the Creation*, a classical
exposition of Deism, appeared in 1730.

terms of the gospel is likewise exceeding plain, seeing exactly equivalent to the words of the Church of England (who did rashly adopt them in her Liturgy), 'This faith, except every man keep whole and undefiled, without doubt he shall perish everlastingly',[1] are those of the very person they thus outrage, 'He that believeth 5 not shall be damned.'[2] Not that we have authority to apply this general sentence to any one particular offender; because, all sin being a voluntary breach of a known law, none but he who seeth the heart,[3] and consequently how far this breach of his law is voluntary in each particular person, can possibly know which infidel shall 10 perish, and which be received to mercy.

Whenever you recommend to that all-sufficient mercy any of those that have erred and are deceived, then especially, dear Aspasia, do not forget your ever obliged

Cyrus 15

The best wishes of Araspes are yours.
Adieu!

Source: Asp, pp. 35-8.

From Kezia Wesley[4]

[July 3, 1731]

Dear brother

I should have writ sooner had not business and indisposition of body prevented 20 me. Indeed, sister Pat's going to London shocked me a little, because it was unexpected, and perhaps may have been the occasion of my ill health the last fortnight. It would not have had so great an effect upon my mind if I had known it before. But 'tis over now:

The past as nothing we esteem;   25
And pain, like pleasure, is but dream.

I should be glad to see Norris's Reflections of the Conduct of Human Understanding, and the book writ by the female author, but I don't expect so great a satisfaction as the seeing either of them except you should have the good fortune for me as to be at Epworth when I am there, which will be the latter end of 30

[1] Cf. B.C.P., Athanasian Creed.   [2] Mark 16: 16.
[3] See 1 Sam. 16: 7.
[4] This letter, apparently in response to John's of June 19 (?), demonstrates the extension of his tutorial responsibilities in a strengthening of what became a lifelong dedication to female education, apparently sparked by the discovery of Sally Chapone's copy of Mary Astell's *Serious Proposal to Ladies* (see pp. 285-6 above).

August, and shall stay a fortnight or three weeks if no unforeseen accident prevent it. I must not expect anything that will give me so much pleasure as the having your company so long, because a disappointment would make me very uneasy.

5　Had your supposition been true, and one of our fine ladies had heard your conference, they would have despised you for a mere ill-bred scholar who could make no better a use of such an opportunity than preaching to young women for the improvement of their minds.

I am entirely of your opinion, that the pursuit of knowledge and virtue will
10　most improve the mind. But how to pursue these is the question. Cut off I am, indeed, from all means which most men, and many women, have of attaining them. I have Nelson's Method of Devotion, and *The Whole Duty of Man*, which is all my stock. As to history and poetry, I have not so much as one book. I could like to read all the books you mentioned if it were in my power to buy 'em.
15　But as it is not at present, nor have I any acquaintance that I can borrow them of, I must make myself easy without 'em if I can. But I had rather you had not told me of them, because it always occasioned me some uneasiness that I had not books and opportunity to improve my mind. Now here I have time, in a morning three or four hours, but want books. At home I had books, and no time, because
20　constant illness made me incapable of study.

I like Nelson's method, the aiming every day at some particular virtue. I wish you would send me the questions you spake of relating to each virtue, and I would read them every day. Perhaps they may be of use to me in learning contentment, for I have been long endeavouring to practise it; yet every temptation
25　is apt to cause me to fall into the same error.

I should be glad if you would say a little to sister Em on the same subject, for she is very likely to have a fit of sickness with grieving for the loss of Miss Emery, who went to Wicom [High Wycombe] last Saturday to live. I can't persuade her to the contrary, because I am so much addicted to the same failing
30　myself. Pray desire brother Charles to bring Prior, the second part, when he comes; or send it, according to promise, for my leaving off snuff till next May; or else I shall think myself at liberty to take, as soon as I please. Pray let me know in your next letter when you design to come down. [. . .] You must not measure the length of your next letter by mine. I am ill, and can't write any
35　more. Your affectionate sister,

> Kezia Wesley

Miss Kitty went to 6 a'clock prayers till she got the fever, and I never miss except sickness prevent me.

> Lincoln, July 3, 1731

Source: Bristol Wesley; cf. Clarke II. 382–4 (no paragraphs in original).

From Mrs. Susanna Wesley

July 12 [1]731

Dear Jacky

I am sorry to put you to the expense of another letter so soon, but I'm so uneasy about poor John Whitelamb that I hope you will excuse it. I presently desired your father to give him one of those guineas you mentioned in yours by 5 Mr. Horbery,[1] and he very readily consented to it, being I believe much pleased with Whitelamb's letter to him. This I hope will be some small relief, though it can bear no proportion to his great necessities. I am glad you have chosen Mr. Isham your rector, for I think he is friendly to you, as the late rector was, and perhaps you may have power to get something for poor starving Johnny, whose 10 deplorable case I have much at heart, and do daily most earnestly recommend to divine providence, for I know what a great temptation it is to want food convenient.

The particulars of your father's fall are as follows. On Friday before Whit Sunday (the 4th of June) he and I, Molly, and young Nanny Brown, were going in 15 our waggon to see the ground we hire of Mrs. Knight at Low Melwood. He sat in a chair at one end of the waggon, I in another at 'tother end, Molly between us, and Nanny behind me. Just before we reached the Close, going down a small hill, the horses took into a gallop. Out flew your father, and his chair. Nanny, seeing the horses run, hung all her weight on my chair, and kept me 20 from keeping him company. She cried out to William to stop the horses, and that her master was killed. The fellow leapt out of the seat and stayed the horses, then ran to Mr. Wesley. But ere he got to him Harry Dixon, who was coming from Ferry, Mrs. Knight's man, and Jack Glew, were providentially met together, and raised his head, upon which he had pitched, and held him backward, 25 by which means he began to respire, for 'tis certain by the blackness in his face that he had never drawn breath from the time of his fall till they helped him up. By this time I was got to him, asked him how he did, and persuaded him to drink a little ale, for we had brought a bottle with us. He looked prodigiously wild, but began to speak, and told me he ailed nothing. I informed him of his fall. He 30 said he knew nothing of any fall, he was as well as ever he was in his life. We bound up his head, which was very much bruised, and helped him into the waggon, and set him at the bottom of it while I supported his head between my hands, and Will led the horses softly home. I sent presently for Mr. Harper, who took a good quantity of blood from him, and then he began to feel pain in several 35 parts, particularly in his side and shoulder. He had a very ill night, but on Saturday morning Mr. Harper came again to him, dressed his head, and gave him something which much abated the pain in his side. We repeated the dose at bedtime, and on Whit Sunday he preached twice, and gave the Sacrament, which was too much for him to do, but nobody could dissuade him from it. On Monday 40 he was ill, slept almost all day. On Tuesday the gout came, but with two or three

---

[1] Euseby Isham was elected Rector of Lincoln College on July 9, so Wesley's letter conveying this information must have been carried to Epworth by Matthew Horbery (see p. 273) between then and the 12th.

nights taking Bateman it went off again, and he has since been better than could
be expected. We thought at first the waggon had gone over him, but it only went
over his gown sleeve, and the nails took a little skin off of his knuckles, but did
him no further hurt.

5   [Of the visit to Epworth of Matthew Wesley, the rector's brother, a London
physician who had helped Suky and Hetty, and on this occasion took Patty to
stay with him for a year or two.]

Before Mr. Wesley went to Scarbro' I informed him of what I knew of Mr.
Morgan's case. When he came back he told me that he had tried the spa at
10 Scarbro', and could assure me that it far excelled all the spas in Europe. [. . .]
Says he, 'If that gentleman you told me of could by any means be gotten thither,
though his age is the most dangerous time in life for his distemper, yet I am of
opinion those waters would cure him.' I thought good to tell you this, that you
might if you please inform Mr. Morgan of it, if 'tis proper.

15 The matter of the tithe stands thus. You know Charles Tate died about Easter.
His sons after his death desired Mr. Wesley to continue them in partnership
this year, which he granted. But afterwards, when the great drought had
consumed most of the flax, they sued for a release, of which I was glad, though he
was nothing pleased; yet however he released them, and now we have it all in
20 our own hands. This has thrown us into more debt for two horses and another
waggon, but still I hope we shall do pretty well, for though line[1] fails, we are
likely to have a large crop of barley, which they say will bear a good price.

This new turn in our affairs will make it very expedient for Emly to come
home, for I cannot manage both house and tithe, and though Molly be a good
25 girl, she is unequal to the work. If Mr. Wesley will but agree with her I shall be
very glad; if not, I doubt he must let his tithe. I am old and infirm, and can't do
as I have done, therefore must have help, or drop the business.

Your father has let Wroot tithe to Will Atkinson this year, and a brave year he
is like to have. But he would not take Canby ground off our hands, so we have
30 burned near twenty acre of it, which if it please God to bless and to send us a
good crop of rapes, we may come to get something by that unfortunate bargain
at last.

Dear Jacky, I can't stay now to talk about Hetty, and Patty; only this, I
hope better of both than some others do.

35 I pray God to bless you. Adieu.

[A note added to Charles Wesley]

Address: 'For The Revd. Mr John Wesley, Fellow of Lincoln, Oxon. By way of
London'   *Postmark*: '12 IY'   *Charges*: ((4)), 'In all 7'   *End* by JW
on p. 1: 'my father's fall'   *Source*: MA; cf. Clarke, I. 75-8, 309-11.

---

[1] i.e. flax.

To Mrs. Mary Pendarves

July 19 [1731]

Is it utterly impossible that I should hear a little oftener from
dear Aspasia? I can't be entirely satisfied till you assure me it is,
that you have too many employments of a noble kind, and too many
more useful and pleasing entertainments, to allow you a vacant 5
hour to throw away upon me so often as once a month. So soon as I
am assured of this I shall cease to importune you about it; but while
I have any hope of success I can't give up a clause the gaining of
which would so much add to my happiness.

I can't help being more desirous now than even at other times of 10
hearing from you, because of an imputation that has lately been
thrown upon me, which I would fain, if it were possible, remove.
I have been charged with being too strict, with carrying things too
far in religion, and laying burdens on myself, if not on others, which
were neither necessary nor possible to be borne. A heavy charge 15
indeed! To be too strict! That is to blaspheme the law of God as
not strict enough. To carry duties too far! Why, what is this but to
change holiness itself into extravagance! To impose unnecessary
burdens! Then am I a hinderer as well as slanderer of the religion
I live to recommend; then have I added to the words of God's Book, 20
and he shall add to me all the plagues that are written in it.

Do not therefore blame me, Aspasia, for using every means to
find whether I am thus guilty or no; and particularly for appealing
to the judgment of one who in this is not likely to be prejudiced in
my favour. Those among whom chiefly your lot is cast are not 25
accused of too much strictness. Whatever other ill weeds may flourish
there, a Court is not a fit soil for this. Give me leave then to lay
freely before you what my sentiments in this point are, and to
conjure you to tell me with the same freedom, which of them you
disapprove of. 30

My present sense is this. I was made to be happy; to be happy I
must love God; in proportion to my love of whom my happiness must
increase. To love God I must be like him, holy as he is holy;[1] which
implies both the being pure from vicious and foolish passions and
the being confirmed in those virtues and rational affections which 35
God comprises in the word charity. In order to root those out of

[1] See 1 Pet. 1: 15, 16.

my soul and plant these in their stead I must use, (1), such means
as are ordered by God, (2), such as are recommended by experience
and reason.

Thus far I believe we are all agreed; but in what follows we are
5 not. For, first, as to the end of my being, I lay it down for a rule that
I can't be too happy or therefore holy, and infer thence that the
more steadily I keep my eye upon the prize of our high calling[1] the
better, and the more of my thoughts and words and actions are
directly pointed at the attainment of it. (2). As to the instituted
10 means, I likewise lay it down for a rule, that as 'none teach like God',[2]
so there are none like them; and consequently that I am to use them
every time I may, and with all the exactness I can. As to prudential
means, I believe this rule holds, of things indifferent in themselves:
whatever hinders the extirpating my vile affections or the transfer-
15 ring my rational ones to proper objects, that to me is not indifferent,
but resolutely to be abstained from, however familiar and pleasing.
Again, of things indifferent in themselves, whatever helps me to
conquer vicious and advance in virtuous affections, that to me is not
indifferent, but to be embraced, be it ever so difficult or painful.
20 These are the points which I am said to carry too far. Whether I do
or no I beg you would not delay to inform me.

Perhaps it may not be long before I have it in my power at once
to return my thanks for that favour (which I shall wait for with some
impatience), and to hear your sentiments more fully on some of these
25 subjects. I extremely desire to see one of my sisters who is lately
come to town;[3] which, with the hopes of waiting upon Aspasia,
makes me greatly wish to spend a few days there. If your journey[4]
begins before I can have that happiness, yet it will be some satisfaction to me to reflect that you are with those who are equally willing
30 as well as far more able to entertain you than your most obliged,
obedient

Cyrus

Araspes joins with me in wishing all happiness to Aspasia. Adieu!

Source: Asp, pp. 38–41.

[1] See Phil. 3: 14.   [2] Cf. Job. 36: 22.
[3] Patty, who had returned from Epworth to stay in London with her uncle Matthew.
See previous letter.
[4] Richard Colley Wesley and his wife, of Dangan (later Lord Mornington), had been
spending some time in London, and Mrs. Pendarves was planning to visit them in
Ireland. (See Delany, I. 255 n., 272, 284–7, and the following letter.)

From Mrs. Mary Pendarves[1]

New Bond Street, July 21, 1731

The frequent interruptions that have happened to my correspondence with Cyrus I cannot place among my little disappointments, for indeed I have been heartily mortified by it; not so much for the loss I have had of an agreeable entertainment as the fear that you should censure me for it, and perhaps (though 5 I believe it would be unwillingly) tax me with ingratitude. As I endeavour in every respect to guide all my words and actions by the rule of truth, even the most minute circumstances of my life, I must tell Cyrus the real cause of my silence, though at the same time I don't think I can excuse (at least to myself) the having so long neglected answering your letters, and fear when I have told 10 you my manner of spending the last two months you may condemn me as much as I do myself. My brother, whose company I am so happy as to enjoy in the house with me, takes up so much of my time in the morning that I with great difficulty find leisure to write to Gloucester. As I am no housekeeper, I seldom dine at home, but either go to my uncle's, or to some particular friend, who will 15 not let me spend one day entirely at home since my sister left me. Besides this, a gentleman and lady that I have a great regard for, who have left England about a week, engrossed so much of my time in going with them to see all the remarkable seats about London, and to shops to assist them in buying of clothes and furniture, that I have lived as much in a hurry as if I was immediately to 20 take a long journey. To add to this, the thoughts I have of following them the next month (for they are gone to Ireland) has furnished me with new materials for employment. This is the true state of my case, and now I have troubled you with this impertinent account, am I guilty or not guilty? Ah, too guilty, I fear! that could not find in all that trifling hurry one moment's leisure to satisfy my mind in 25 a rational way. But I hope you will forgive a fault that has had no ill consequence on your side. Your not hearing from me has done you no wrong: I indeed have suffered by it.

The imputation thrown upon you is a most extraordinary one. But such is the temper of the world; wh[en] they have no vice to feed their spleen with they 30 will condemn the highest virtue. O Cyrus, how noble a defence you make, and how are you adorned with the beauty of holiness! You really are in a state to be envied. But you deserve the happiness you possess, and far be it from me to envy such excellence. I may aspire after some part of it: how ardently do I wish to be as resigned and humble as Cyrus! I am not presumptuous enough 35 (knowing too well I never can attain it) to desire the knowledge and strength of reason that you are endowed with by nature, and that you have carefully cultivated and improved. But I pray to God to give me a humble and contrite spirit, and to let me taste of the crumbs that fall from his table. 'I believe! Lord, help thou my unbelief!' 40

As you say, my lot is fallen among those who cannot be accused of too much strictness in religion; so far from that that they generally make an open profession of having no religion at all. I can't observe my fellow creatures in such

---

[1] Replying to his of July 19.

manifest danger without feeling an inexpressible concern. But God in his good time may make them sensible of their blindness, and call them into a state of salvation.

5 When I am in Dublin, which will be three weeks or a month hence, I doubt my correspondence will meet with more interruptions than it has hitherto. But in the meantime, to make me some amends, I promise to answer your letters as soon as I receive them. I am afraid when you come to town I shall not have the pleasure of seeing you, because I am to go out of town some days before I begin my great journey. I shall think myself very fortunate if I am not, when you come 10 hither. Our friend Varanese is very well, as a letter informed me last post. I have just had time to finish this letter in a hasty manner. Company is come, and will not allow me a longer conversation. I cannot always submit to this sort of life. It encroaches too much. Adieu.

I hope to hear soon, for I am in some doubt and concern about my late silence, 15 and fear this letter is not powerful enough to dissipate those suspicions my past behaviour may have occasioned. Cyrus has no friend in the world that wishes him happiness more sincerely than does his faithful and obliged

Aspasia

Assure Araspes of the same.

Source: Asp, pp. 41-4.

To Mrs. Mary Pendarves[1]

20   July 24 [1731]

You have indeed done me wrong in this, Aspasia, in thinking I could give way to any suspicion to your disadvantage; and yourself, too, in doubting the power of that letter to remove it, if any such there were. Other wrong, I confess, you have done me none, since I must 25 ever acknowledge that delightful means of improvement which it has not been in your power to give me lately a pure effect of your goodness, not justice. I can never pretend any right to that favour, unless this should seem so to generous Aspasia, that I endeavour to esteem it as it deserves, and not to let it be given in vain; and that 30 when I feel something of your spirit transfused i[nto] me, then my heart remembers and blesses you.

I am extremely happy in having your approbation there, where I am most careful to be approved; and though I am sensible how small a part of it I deserve, yet I can't help experiencing

How sweet applause is from an honest tongue.[2]

[1] Replying to hers of July 21.
[2] Richard Steele, *The Funeral: or, Grief A-la-Mode*, V. iv. 100 (*Plays*, ed. S. S. Kenny, Oxford, Clarendon Press, 1971, p. 90).

What is popular fame, laid in the balance with this? Who would not gladly make the exchange? Give me the censure of the many and the praise of the few. What is the evil compared with the good! Evil? It is none at all: it is all good. One that is learning Christ should never think censure an evil. No, it is a gracious gift of a wise 5 Father to his children; it is subservient to the noblest purposes, in particular to the attainment of humility, which in order to holiness is all in all, which whoever thinks he has enough of already, has nothing of yet as he ought to have. By this alone may we judge of the value of censure: God hath so constituted this world that so 10 soon as ever anyone sets himself earnestly to seek a better, censure is at hand to conduct him to it. Nor can the fools cease to count his life madness[1] till they have confirmed him in the wisdom of the just.[2]

May not one reason why God makes even these fools such a means 15 of leading others to wisdom be this, that those whose eyes are opened may the more tenderly pity their blindness? That the contempt and hate which such objects are apt to inspire may melt down into softer passions, and they may be the more unwilling to see those cast away who have (though unknowingly) helped them to their 20 haven?

I do not wonder that Aspasia is thus minded, any more than I did at the temper of dear Varanese when under the sharpest pain an embodied spirit can know. You will easily take knowledge of those words, if you have not heard them before: 'When I was in the greatest 25 of my pains, if my strength would have allowed I would gladly have run out in the streets to warn all I met that they should save themselves from pains sharper than mine.'[3] Something like this methinks 'tis impossible not to feel, even when we read a description of the great place of torment. What would not one do to save a poor wretch 30 from falling into it! How unwilling are we to give over our attempts to help him! How ardent to try every way, while time is! Before the pit shut its mouth upon him![4]

In attaining some share of a better portion, some lot in a fairer heritage, I may aspire to imitate Aspasia; but vainly should hope 35 for the same share in it. You have kept yourself unspotted from the

[1] See Wisd. 5: 4.
[2] Luke 1: 17.
[3] Apparently a quotation from a letter of Varanese.
[4] See Ps. 69: 15.

world;[1] I am sullied with many stains! Your mind is now adorned with many of those dispositions to which mine must probably be yet long a stranger. For though I would fain be nearer you, though I do what I can (Alas! I fear, not always) to overtake you; yet so hard
5 is it to lay aside every weight, these follies do so easily beset me,[2] that I find it will not be—the penitent can't avoid being left behind by the innocent!

True it is that I have all the advantages given me that outward circumstances can afford. I spend day by day many hours in those
10 employments that have a direct tendency to improve me; you can rarely have one wherein to pursue that great work with the full bent of your mind. I have scarce any acquaintance in the world who is not either apt to teach, or willing to learn: you are entangled among several who can plead for themselves little more than that
15 they do no hurt. And would to God even this plea would hold. I much fear it will not. Is it no hurt to rob you of that time for which there is no equivalent but eternity? On the use of every moment of which much more than a world depends? To turn your very sweetness of temper against you? On this very account to encroach upon
20 you with so much cruelty! To force you to stand still so many hours when you are most ardent to press forward? Nay, to strike whole days out of your existence, while he that sitteth in heaven sees that all the kingdoms he hath made are vile compared to the worth of one particle of them! O God, hath thy wisdom prepared a remedy
25 for every evil under the sun? And is there none for this? Must Aspasia ever submit to this insupportable misfortune? Every time a gay wretch wants to trifle away part of that invaluable treasure which thou hast lent him, shall he force away a part of hers too? Tear another star from her crown of glory? Oh! 'tis too much indeed!
30 Surely there is a way to escape! The God whom you serve point it out to you!

In about eight days I hope to be in town. If you leave it before that time, I heartily recommend you to his protection who is able 'to save to the uttermost'.[3] And if I have not the pleasure of seeing
35 you now, I shall the more cheerfully bear my disappointment since you are so good as to assure me that notwithstanding the distance between us you will now and then think of, dear Aspasia, your most sincere friend and most obedient servant,

Cyrus

[1] Jas. 1: 27.　　　　　[2] See Heb. 12: 1.　　　　　[3] Heb. 7: 25.

Though I had almost forgot Araspes, he will never forget what he owes to good Aspasia. Adieu.

Source: Asp, pp. 46–9.

From Mrs. Mary Pendarves[1]

July 29 [1731]

I wish it could have been otherwise, but I doubt I shall not be in town when Cyrus is there. I am now in the country, and shall stay a fortnight longer. To 5 make myself some amends I lay hold of the first opportunity to write; and to convince you that when I have not been regular in my answers to your letters it has been my fault. Though my not being at home is a reason why I have not much time at command, what leisure I have I dedicate to Cyrus. While I read your letters I find myself carried above the world. I view the vanities I left 10 behind with the disdain that is due to them, and wish never to return to them; but as it is my lot to dwell among them as yet, I will at least endeavour to defend myself from their assaults; and with your assistance I hope to baffle and turn aside their sting. But as from every evil we may extract a good, so in this particular I have great consolation, that weak and insignificant as I am, I have some- 15 times found means of maintaining the honour of our great God when I have heard the blasphemer say, 'Where is now their God?' At such an instant, how have I wished for a capacity equal to the mighty cause! For Cyrus's wisdom and words!

There is a young lady, a particular friend of mine, who by all that I can 20 judge of her behaviour omits no duty either to God or man, but is so disconten- ted with herself that she is upon the brink of despair. I believe her in an ill state of health, and that may contribute to her melancholy. I asked her wherein it was that she was most dissatisfied, and promised her great comfort from your advice. She says she has a coldness when she says her prayers (which she con- 25 stantly does twice a day), and wandering thoughts, and that the week before she receives the sacrament she endures such agonies as are not to be expressed. I know no one so able to assist her as you, and I am sure of your endeavour to do it, which will be fresh obligation to your faithful

Aspasia 30

Araspes is very good to me, and I am not ungrateful.

Source: Asp, pp. 50–1.

[1] Replying to his of July 24.

(3 0 0)

To Ann Granville

July [30–1, 1731]

Selima will not believe that any other reason could have kept me so
long from writing but the having so many things which I must do as
scarce give me any time for what I would do. I can by no means
5 think the acknowledging it once[1] a fit return for your last favour,
and have often been upon the point of telling you so, when some
fresh business has seized upon me, and forced me to deny myself
yet longer the pleasure of doing you that justice. And, to say the
truth, I am even now as busy as ever, but not quite so patient, and
10 therefore since there is no end of waiting for this leisure I must
make what I can't find.

I am something the more reconciled to this confinement because,
though it hinders my expressing it so often, yet it never hinders me
from remembering that regard which on so many accounts I owe
15 Selima. Nay, this very circumstance, that I am so confined, often
recalls you to my thoughts, and makes me the more sensible of that
harder trial to which you are frequently exposed. If I am compassed
with business on every side, yet 'tis business of my own. Such especially is that wherein I engage, immediately, for the sake of others,
20 since I know to whom I lend that time and pains, and that what I
so lay out shall be surely paid me again. But Selima, under as great
a multitude of engagements, has not always the same thought to
support her. You often are troubled about many things,[2] few of
which promise even distant pleasure, and are obliged to converse
25 with many persons too wise to learn, though not wise enough to
teach.

O Selima, teach me to submit to such a trial, if ever it should be
my portion. Tell me how you let yourself down to such capacities,
and sustain the insipidness of such conversations, how you do to
30 possess your soul in patience[3] when the floods of impertinence are
round you. I have often wondered how so active a spirit as yours,
that was not made for a common share of glory, but to force its way
through all impediments to the heights of knowledge and virtue,
how such a spirit as this could bear with calmness to have its flight

[1] See June 17-18, pp. 285-7 above.
[2] Luke 10: 41.   [3] See Luke 21: 19.

stopped in the midway by those mere children of earth who will not take pains to be even as the angels of God in heaven;[1] nay, who perhaps would not be angels if they might, since 'tis sure those ancient heirs of salvation[2] are therefore the most happy because they are the most active of all created beings.   5

I have lately had the pleasure of two letters from Aspasia, and hoped for a still greater in waiting upon her next week; but her last informed me she is out of town, and does not return this fortnight, before which time I must leave it. I believe Providence is more careful of me than I am of myself, and knowing that were I to see   10 Aspasia or Selima often I could not possibly act up to the favourable opinion they are pleased to entertain of me, removes me (for my interest, though against my choice) from the opportunities of betraying my weakness.

If I have fewer opportunities too of expressing my gratitude in   15 writing than I could wish, let it not deprive me of the pleasure of sometimes hearing from Selima; yet let me steal a few moments from you. I am sure none of them that converse with you (on how many soever accounts besides you may give them the preference) are more thankful for that favour than your most obliged and most   20 obedient

Cyrus

Source: Sel, pp. 5-7, dated from Wesley's diary.

From Ann Granville[3]

G[loucester], 9 Aug. [1731]

I am ashamed to receive a second letter from Cyrus before I had acknowledged the first. Your readiness to correspond with me shows the extreme desire you   25 have of doing good, and cert[ainly] you succeed in that inclination. I am pleased that you approve of tender sentiments. I confess were I to part with them I should lose much the greatest pleasure of life. I doubt I sometimes carry them too far. You are not yet acquainted with me, I find, or you could not say the obliging things you do. But take care how you commend me. Your praises may   30 be dangerous, and will perhaps raise a vanity I would do everything in my power to suppress. Flattery from any person vexes me, but from Cyrus it would afflict me.

I have never read Mrs. Astell's *Proposal to the Ladies*, but will very soon.

[1] Matt. 22: 30.   [2] Heb. 1: 14.
[3] Replying to his of July 31.

A method in reading is what I want extremely; I am sure I should better understand what I read, and improve more by it. Perhaps in one day I read part of
several books, and by that means have a confusion in my head, which makes me
not able to regulate my thoughts upon any subject. Should I not finish one book
5 before I begin another?

I have been three weeks in Herefordshire, with two sensible, agreeable young
ladies. We passed our time something in the way we did at Stanton; but we had
neither a Sappho nor Cyrus with us. That happiness would have made our hours
quite delightful. The country, I think, is the most rational way of living. One
10 has the leisure for improvement. There are a thousand objects that raise one's
thoughts to goodness which in a town are entirely wanting.

You have no cause to complain that you have not time to bestow upon your
friends, because your goodness of heart is so extensive that all your fellow
creatures are dear to you. To want your assistance is with you a just pretence
15 to have it. I am sure I can upon no other motive demand one moment of you,
whose hours are always employed in things of more importance than answering
such letters as mine are. I have many passions and many weaknesses to correct,
which I hope by your help to do, and shall never scruple to tell you of them,
will you but as freely give me your opinion how I shall conquer those enemies
20 of my peace.

I am sure it was a great concern to Aspasia not to see you when you was in
town. I can answer for her as well as for myself, that we should be much rejoiced
to have an opportunity of improving our acquaintance and friendship with
Cyrus and Araspes. But since we are not yet allowed that advantage, we are
25 very glad to make use of this imperfect way of conversation. I hope another year
to meet you in sweet Horrel with our sweeter Sappho. I had the comfort of
hearing she was well last week, but can't have the joy of seeing her this summer,
which is a great mortification to me. I have another care upon my spirits, my
sister's voyage to Ireland. She makes it late before she goes. The Irish seas are
30 very dangerous. We were never separated so far from each other before. What
accidents may happen before we meet again? You see I am as ignorant in a
method of writing as of reading. If you will instruct me in either it shall be
esteemed a great obligation, and acknowledged with gratitude by

Selima

35 My mother joins with me in best wishes to you and Araspes.

[From Mrs. Granville]¹

My partiality to my dear N[ancy] makes me often overlook her omissions.
But I have really been angry with her today, for saying so little in my behalf to
good Mr. C[yrus]; who I hope will judge favourably of me, and excuse my
Selima, which proceeds really from infirmity. I shall always have a true sense of
40 your worth, which will oblige me to be, as I ought, your sincere humble servant,
M[ary Granville]

Source: Sel, pp. 7–10.

¹ Added to the previous letter after a deep space.

To Mrs. Mary Pendarves[1]

Aug. 12 [1731]

Nothing could have made our journey more prosperous than it was, except the seeing Aspasia. We were successful in every other respect, far beyond our expectations. Indeed, the chief design we went upon was very unlikely, humanly speaking, to succeed at all. But what is likelihood against any undertaking, if he be for it 'whom all things serve'![2]

I am sensible how good you are to me, Aspasia, both in writing so soon, engaged as you were, and in permitting me to hope that when you are less engaged you will again bestow some moments upon me. But this is not the only reason why I shall be heartily glad whenever you are rescued from many of your engagements, whenever it is in your power to burst those chains that hang heavy on your noblest purposes, and to move with a full and free course toward the haven where you would be![3]

I have a good hope that you will continue to disdain all the vanities that surround you, and that those choicest instruments of mischief, 'they that do no harm',[4] will never be able to undermine your resolution, because you take the true method of defence, the not standing barely on the defensive. O may you ever retain this just sense of our state; may you ever remember that we are to resist, not to stand still; that they who would overcome are not barely to repel, but likewise to retort the darts of the enemy! That to be innocent we are to be active; to avoid evil, we must do good; and if it be possible, in that very particular wherein we are solicited to evil. Hath the fool said aloud, 'There is no God'?[5] So much the rather let us prove there is one. Is his Son degraded into an equality with the sons of men? The more zealously let us assert his equality with God. Do any blaspheme his Word? That is our time to show that [by no] other under heaven we obtain salvation.[6] Who indeed is sufficient to prove these things against an artful, practised unbeliever? If even your address be not sufficient of itself, yet he is with you who is

---

[1] Replying to hers of July 29.   [2] Cf. Ps. 119: 91 (B.C.P.).

[3] See Ps. 107: 30 (B.C.P.).

[4] Cf. letter of July 24, 1731, for another example of Wesley's strong criticism of negative virtue, those 'who plead for themselves little more than that they do no hurt'.

[5] Pss. 14: 1; 53: 1.   [6] See Acts 4: 12.

sufficient for all things; who hath often strengthened the weak for
this very thing, 'to still the enemy and the self-avenger'![1]

'Tis a great instance of his never failing them that seek him that
the lady you mention has such a friend as Aspasia. Afflicted as she is,
I can scarce call her unhappy; nay, I am almost tempted to envy
her. Too tender a conscience is a glorious excess! Scarce has anyone
fallen by fearing to fall. Yet it is an excess, and I wish it [may] be in
my power to contribute toward the removing it.

Two things she seems to complain of most, inattention in prayer,
and uneasiness before the sacrament. The latter probably is owing
in good part to the former, which therefore appears to require consideration most.

As to this I would ask first, 'Can you help it?' If not, 'Do you
think God is good?' If he be, he can't be displeased at what you
can't avoid. That would be to be angry at himself, since 'tis his will,
not yours, that you are not more attentive. Next I would ask, 'Do
you expect while upon earth to be "as the angels of God in heaven"?'[2]
If not, you must expect to have a share in that infirmity which no
one quite shakes off till he leaves earth behind him.

As to shaking it off in some degree, if she thinks that worth while,
and is resolved to use any probable means of doing it, I could propose
one or two that seldom fail to be of service to those that regularly
use them. Are you inattentive in prayer? Pray oftener. Do you
address to God twice a day already? Then do so three times. Do you
find yourself very uneasy before sacrament, though you receive it
every month? Your next resolution, with God's leave, should be to
receive it every week.

Your friend's case appears to be this: God, seeing the earnestness
of heart with which she chooses virtue, sees that she is a fit object
for a large measure of his Blessed Spirit. As a preparative for this
he sends this pain (whether the immediate cause of it lie in her
body or mind) to cleanse her from all remaining sinful affections,
and to balance all the temptations that might prevent her pressing
forward to that degree of holiness which becomes them whom God
thus delights to honour. If so, it will continue with her till it has
had its perfect work.

I want to say a great deal more on this subject, but am exceedingly
straitened for time, being to begin a long journey in [a] day or two,
though not so long an one as Aspasia. I was going to say, nor so

[1] Ps. 8: 2.   [2] Matt. 22: 30.

dangerous, but I know no danger that a lover of God can be in till God is no more, or at least has quitted the reins and left chance to govern the world. O yes, there is one danger, and a great one it is, which nothing less than constant care can prevent—the ceasing to love him. But that care will never be wanting in Aspasia. She will 5 continually watch over her affections, and be going on from strength to strength. Every new scene will be to her a new scene of action, of improving herself and others. This reflection greatly softens the thought of the distance that will be shortly between us; especially when I reflect farther that you will still indulge in a share of that 10 improvement, dear Aspasia, your most faithful friend and most obliged servant,

Cyrus

I intend to stay but a fortnight at my father's. If you don't set out till I return, may I not hear from you? 15

You will believe that the gratitude and best wishes of Araspes as well as Cyrus will ever attend Aspasia. Adieu!

Source: Asp, pp. 51-4.

To Ann Granville[1]

Aug. 14 [1731]

I have neither time nor skill to thank Selima as I would for her repeated condescension to me, which nothing can excel but that 20 for which I am so deeply indebted to good Mrs. [Granville]. Both hers and your partiality toward me I can't but observe with wond[er] and gratitude; and hope it will continue to plead in my behalf, and to excuse my many faults and infirmities. And my observing this makes me the less surprised that notwithstanding all my failings 25 you still have so favourable an opinion of me as to think me worth your correspondence.

Perhaps 'tis one of those failings that even when I intend to speak the plain sense of my heart I do it in so unhappy a manner as to make even sincerity look like flattery, a fault I desire as carefully to 30 avoid as stabbing my friend with a smile. For doubtless those words that inspire vanity, if 'they be smooth as oil, yet be very swords'.[2]

[1] Replying to hers of Aug. 9. [2] Cf. Prov. 5: 3-4.

God forbid that mine should ever be such to Selima, or Selima's to me. I trust they will not, but that I shall always be enabled to consider them in the true light, as a picture of what you are, and what I perhaps shall be, if your friendship has its perfect work.

5   What you write with so generous a view as this justly claims the best return I can make, especially when it informs me that there is one particular wherein I may possibly be of some service to Selima. I have indeed spent many thoughts on the necessity of method to a considerable progress either in knowledge or virtue, and am still 10 persuaded that they who have but a day to live are not wise if they waste a moment, and are therefore concerned to take the shortest way to every point they desire to arrive at.

  The method of, or shortest way to, knowledge, seems to be this: (1), to consider what knowledge you desire to attain to; (2), to read 15 no book which does not some way tend to the attainment of that knowledge; (3), to read no book which does tend to the attainment of it unless it be the best in its kind; (4), 'to finish one before you begin another',[1] and lastly, to read them all in such an order that every subsequent book may illustrate and confirm the preceding.

20   The knowledge which you would probably desire to attain to is a knowledge of divinity, philosophy, history, and poetry. If you will be so good as to direct me how I can be of use to you in any of these it will give me a very particular pleasure.

  I am glad you passed your time so agreeably in the country,[2] and 25 doubt not but Sappho would have made it yet more agreeable. Surely you are very just in observing that a country life is in many respects preferable to any other, particularly in its abounding with those beauties of nature that so easily raise our thoughts to the Author of them. Methinks, whenever

30
> About us round we see
> Hill, dale, and shady wood, and sunny plain,
> And liquid lapse of murm'ring stream,[3]

'tis scarce possible to stop that obvious reflection:

> These are thy glorious works, Parent of good.[4]

35 Nor is it hard here, where the busy vanities of a great town do not

---

[1] See her letter of Aug. 9, answered by this.
[2] She had been at Stanton, where they formerly lived. Her sister wrote on Sept. 10, 'I suppose by this time you are returned from Stanton.'
[3] Cf. Milton, *Paradise Lost*, viii. 261–3.
[4] Ibid., v. 153.

flutter about us and break our attention, to fix that reflection so deep upon our souls that it may not pass away, like the objects that occasioned it.

I hope to retain some of the reflections which the smooth turf on which we sat, the trees overshading[1] and surrounding us, the fields and meadows beneath, and the opposite hills, with the setting sun just glimmering over their brows, assisted Aspasia and Selima in inspiring, till I have the happiness of meeting part, at least, of the same company on Horrel again. Perhaps Aspasia may be there, too; though if it should be long before we meet we may trust her with him in whose hands she is. What seems best to him is best both for her and us. 'Tis a cheerful thought that even the winds and seas can only fulfil his word![2] Why is it then that our hearts are troubled for her? Why does tenderness prevail over faith? . . . Because faith is not yet made perfect. Because we yet walk partly by sight. Because we have not yet proved the whole armour of God,[3] and therefore still lie open to this suggestion of the enemy, 'Some things are out of the reach of God's care; in some cases his arm is shortened and cannot save.'[4] Nay, but where is the darkness that covers from his eye? Which is the place where his right hand doth not hold us?[5] As well, therefore, may we be shipwrecked on the dry land as she on the sea, unless he command it. And if he does command any of us to 'arise and go hence',[6] what signifies it where the command finds us? As means can do nothing without his word, so when that is passed they are never wanting:

> Since when obedient nature knows his will
> A fly, a grape-stone, or a hair can kill![7]

Whether it be in my power or no to do anything for Selima that will either make that summons whenever it comes less unpleasing, or in the meantime contribute to your ease and satisfaction, and the conquest of those enemies that too easily beset us all,[8] you will

---

[1] Orig., 'overshad-', whereas the now more familiar alternative would probably have been written 'overshadow-'.

[2] See Ps. 148: 8.

[3] Eph. 6: 11, 13.

[4] Wesley imagining the devil misquoting Scripture; see Isa. 59: 1.

[5] See Ps. 139: 10–11.

[6] Cf. John 14: 31.

[7] Cf. Matthew Prior, 'Ode inscribed to the memory of the Hon. Col. George Villiers', ll. 53–4 (cf. Wesley, *A Collection of Moral and Sacred Poems* (1744), III. 85).

[8] See Heb. 12: 1.

assure yourself of the best endeavours of your most faithful and most obedient

Cyrus

The best service of Araspes as well as Cyrus attends Mrs. [Gran-
5 ville] and Selima. Adieu!

Source: Sel, pp. 10–15.

From Ann Granville[1]

G[loucester], Aug. 24 [1731]

How glad should I be could I communicate the pleasure I am going to enjoy to Cyrus! Tomorrow I go to our dear and valuable Sappho. I shall stay with her a week or ten days, and heartily wish some friends could meet us in our evening
10 walks.

What can I say for your last letter? It gave me a satisfaction beyond any thanks I can return. Cyrus sees more than anyone else can perceive when he finds failings in himself. How then must others, and I particularly, appear to his clear sight? Who come so far, far short of him in wisdom and goodness! No, I
15 don't think you capable of flattery, with a design to deceive; but as it is a word often made use of for complaisance, that way only I applied it to you.

You are willing to think me rather what I should be than what I am, but what I hope I may one day be, if I join my own industry to your friendly advice. How charming is the method you lay down for knowledge! And O, how happy
20 would the attainment of it make me! But so ignorant am I that I hardly can tell what it is I would know. My time has hitherto been passed too much in trifles. I would willingly redeem it, if possible. Divinity is certainly the best and most useful knowledge. It will teach me to be good, to be happy. But what I have read has been in so hasty and confused a manner I can give no good account of it.
25 My future studies shall be directed by you; but I can't understand what is not writ plain, neither can I read with pleasure what is not good language. Does not this show great defect of judgment?

We shall think of you and Milton's hymn when we walk in dear, delightful Horrel hill. Then

30   The hours will fly with down upon their wings.

After what you have said with regard to my dear sister I ought not to be un-easy. Nay, I know 'I should not fear, though the earth were moved, and the waters rage and swell.' And yet so weak I am I cannot help it; my heart is disquieted within me. I have been writing to her this morning the last letter
35 she will receive from me in England. I don't apprehend much danger from her voyage, but to be separated so far asunder, and so many months before there is a possibility of meeting, that it is which gives me anxious thoughts. She is a

[1] Replying to his of Aug. 14.

treasure of inestimable price to me. Indeed no one can know her worth that is
less acquainted with her than I am. I speak not as of a sister, but a friend, and
one quite near to my happiness. Heaven has been very gracious to me, has withheld from me the glittering dangerous temptations of fortune, and made me rich
in worthy, generous friends. O may I never be unthankful for the blessing!   5
Your friendship will greatly help me to support every trial in life. But for
that dreadful one you mention,

> Far be that fatal hour in distant time.

I hope I shall never prove the bitter moment.

I shall be very glad to receive a letter from you while I am at St[anton], and   10
more so because it will be a pleasure to Sappho to hear of you. You may write
to her, and enclose it to me. With what real joy should I do her or you the least
service! It is my misfortune never to be able in any degree to return the kindness
of my friends. Hearty affection, ill expressed, is all I have to give in exchange for
a thousand good offices I daily receive. That Cyrus must accept of for giving me   15
the pleasure and improvement of his correspondence, which I hope in time will
make me as good a Christian as I am now his faithful friend

                                                                          Selima

Araspes has always my good wishes. My mother's attend you both.

Source: Sel, pp. 15–18.

From Mrs. Mary Pendarves

                                                           Aug. 26 [1731]   20

I hope this letter will reach you before I begin my journey, which I intend to
do on Tuesday next. I shall go in five days to Chester, and from thence take
ship for Dublin. The passage is reckoned a bad one, and the time of year subject
to storms. I must desire your prayers for me, particularly at that time. Though
I thank God I have not one anxious thought about my journey or voyage. When   25
I consider the worst thing that can happen will be death, I am not terrified at
the reflection. I hope I am not too presumptuous. Tell me if I am, and teach me
how to fear in a proper way the king of terrors.

The lady for whom you have so kindly given me your advice has been in the
country almost ever since I received your letter. I shall take an opportunity of   30
reading part of it to her, but not all, till I have heard again from you, for a reason
which I will now tell you. A physician ought to know every symptom of a distemper, or how should he know properly to prescribe? You say she should add to
the length of her prayers, or to the frequency of them. But she has tried that
method already, and has reduced herself to death's door by her intense applica-   35
tion to her devotions. To be sincere, I doubt one great cause of her uneasiness is
a pride of heart which she is not sensible of. I have observed instances of it in
trifles; as expecting great civilities and ceremony from her acquaintance, and
thinking that they do not pay her respect enough, and that they neglect her. When

she has had her mind ruffled by any such unkind behaviour, as she calls it, she then falls into a deep melancholy, and from apprehending the loss of her friends' affections she carries those fears farther, almost to despair. She has also a mixture of vanity (which bears a near relation to pride), to appear in as good clothes as any
5 of her companions when she can't so well afford it. If a proper humility could be instilled into her I am apt to think it would dispel all those gloomy thoughts that now perplex her. She would be resigned to all the decrees of Providence when she was once convinced how little we, any of us, deserve the blessings we enjoy. That unfortunate disposition of hers would make me very criminal in her eyes
10 did she know what I have told you of her. But sure the intention with which I do it justifies my discovering those infirmities of my friend that cannot be cured without being known.

When you write to me, which I hope will be soon, direct your letter to my sister at Gloucester, and she will take care to convey it to me. I shall be glad to
15 know from you the definition of pride and vanity, and the difference there is between them. Give me leave to tell you my opinion, and then set me right, if my notion does not agree with yours. The proud man (according to my way of thinking) believes he deserves all honours that can be paid him, and the vain man would be thought to deserve all. I have not time to add a word more. I am
20 to Cyrus and Araspes a faithful friend,

Aspasia

I must insist on your burning all my letters, and pray don't make use of any epithet before my name when you write to me. I have not time to tell my reasons.

Source: Asp, pp. 55-7.

To Ann Granville[1]

Sept. 27 [1731]

25 What can Selima think of my long silence? Will it admit of any favourable interpretation? Can you believe that any business is of such importance as to excuse it in the least degree? That I might not seem utterly inexcusable, I have been several times for throwing everything by; and should have done it had I not been persuaded
30 that you would not condemn me unheard. Every day since my return hither I have been engaged in business of far greater concern than life or death, and business which, as it could not be delayed, so no one else could do it for me. Had it not been for this I should long before now have returned my sincerest thanks to Selima, which
35 are due to her on so many accounts that I know not where to begin.

---

[1] Replying to hers of Aug. 24.

Happy indeed should I have been had it been my lot to meet you once more in that delightful vale! What we could, we did. The places where she was we visited more than once. And though Selima herself was not there, yet there we could find the remembrance of her.[1]

The more I think of you the more convinced I am that here at least I am not guilty of flattery, when I mention the vast advantage you have over me in gratitude as well as humility. The least desire of being serviceable to you is received by you as a real service, and acknowledged in so obliging a manner that at the same time I am quite ashamed of doing so little to deserve it you give me an inexpressible pleasure. How differently turned is my mind! How little moved with the most valuable benefits! In this, too, give me of your spirit, Selima. Let me imitate, as well as admire.

I would fain imitate too that generous ardour which in spite of all the hindrances that surround you so strongly inspires you to burst through all, and redeem time to the noblest purposes. I am afraid of nothing more than of growing old too soon; of having my body worn out before my soul is past childhood. Would it not be terrible to have the wheels of life stand still[2] when we had scarce started [for][3] the goal? Before the work of the day was half done to have the night come, wherein no one can work![4] I shiver at the thought of losing my strength before I have found wisdom! To have my senses fail e'er I have a stock of rational pleasures, my blood cold e'er my heart is warmed with virtue! Strange! To look back on a train of years that have passed 'as an arrow through the air',[5] without leaving any mark behind them, without our being able to trace them in our improvement! How glad am I that this can't be the case of Selima! The hours you have already given to that best of studies, divinity, forbid that, as sufficiently appears by your resolving to pursue it still. That among the multitude of books writ on this subject you prefer those that are clear and elegant is surely right; 'tis doubtless prudent to choose those writers before others who excel in speaking as well as thinking.

Yet as nobly useful as divinity is, 'tis perhaps not advisable to

---

[1] Wesley had visited Stanton with Charles, Sept. 1–14. Ann Granville had been there a week or so earlier (cf. letter of Sept. 29).

[2] See Dryden, *Oedipus*, iv. 1, 'The weary wheels of life at last stand still.'

[3] Orig., 'fr[om]'.

[4] See John 9: 4.

[5] Cf. Wisd. 5: 12.

confine yourself wholly to it; not only for fear it should tire one who has been used to variety of subjects, but chiefly for fear it should make you less useful to those who have the happiness of your acquaintance. For whose sake, therefore, as well as your own, I
5 should fancy you would like to intermix some history and poetry with it.

'Tis incredible what a progress you might [make] in all these in a year or two's time, could you have a fixed hour for each part of your work. Indeed a great part of most days (I sigh while I speak it)
10 is torn from you by your barbarously-civil neighbours.[1] But are not the mornings your own? If they are, why should you not enlarge and improve them as much as possible? O Selima, would it but suit your health as well as it would your inclinations to rise at six, and to give the first hour of the day to your private, and part of the next
15 to your public addresses to God, God is not unrighteous, that he should forget that labour of love;[2] he would repay it in prospering all your following employments. You would then never repent either your giving what time remained of the morning to some lively writer in speculative divinity, or your calling in [for][3] the afternoon
20 or evening (your usual place) an elegant poet or judicious historian.

Were it possible for you to pursue this course it would soon be as agreeable as useful. Your knowledge would swiftly (though insensibly) improve; but not so swiftly as your happiness. You would then find less pain from every accident; even from the absence of
25 Aspasia. A treasure doubtless she is, the value of which nothing can teach so well as experience; every additional degree of intimacy with her must questionless enhance her value. Nor would it be human to be unconcerned at a separation from such a friend. Yet the time may come when that concern, though equally tender, shall not be equally
30 painful to you, when you shall be as much pleased as ever with her presence, and yet not so much displeased at her absence. For there is a way (though it is a way which the world knows not) of dividing friendship from pain. It is called charity, or the love of God. The more acquainted we are with this, the less anxiety shall we receive
35 from the sharpest trial that can befall us. This, while it enlivens every virtuous affection of our souls, adds calmness to their strength.

---

[1] Cf. Selima's letter to him, May 8, 1731: '. . . some of our neighbours, who, impertinently civil, take up more of my time than I am willing to bestow upon them'.
[2] See Heb. 6: 10.
[3] Orig., 'fr[om]'.

At the same time that it swells their stream, this makes it flow
smooth and even.

> Soft peace she brings wherever she arrives;
> She builds our quiet, as she forms our lives;
> Lays the rough paths of peevish nature even,   5
> And opens in each breast a little heaven.[1]

O Selima, never complain that it is not in your power to repay
your friends much more than you receive from them. At least don't
complain with regard to me. Any one of those thousand obliging
things you have said is vastly more than a return for all the little   10
services that it is in my power to do you. I am amazed more and
more, every time I reflect on those strange instances of your condescension, and feel how much I am overpaid, in (what I can never
think of with due esteem and gratitude) the regard you show for
Selima's ever obliged friend and faithful servant,   15

Cyrus

Araspes joins with me in wishing he could make any return to
Mrs. [Granville's] and Selima's goodness.

I beg you to correct what you see wrong in the enclosed, and to
send it when you write. Adieu!   20

Source: Sel, pp. 18–22.

To Mrs. Mary Pendarves[2]

Sept. 28 [1731]

I could not be unmindful of Aspasia, in the stormy weather we
had at the beginning of this month, though I did not receive your
last till near three weeks after, when you too, I hope, had ended
your journey.[3] 'Tis not strange that one who knows how to live   25

---

[1] Cf. Prior, 'Charity', ll. 23–6, and see Wesley, *A Collection of Moral and Sacred Poems* (1744), I. 88.

[2] Replying to her letter of Aug. 26.

[3] On Sept. 10 she wrote to her sister that they were 'weather-bound' for several days, but she apparently reached Dublin on Sept. 17. In a letter of Sept. 26 she wrote: 'I received yours and Sally's joint epistle . . . I suppose you have informed her of my safety, for I have not yet had time to write to her, but will as soon as possible. I desired Cyrus to direct any letter he wrote to me to Glo'ster, but I did not consider that will double the expense, therefore I desire you will send him the direction to me here. I enjoy all the entertainment you had at Stanton, as far as my imagination can reach . . .' (Delany, I. 292.)

should not be afraid to die, since the sting of death is sin.[1] Rather it would have been strange if Aspasia had been afraid, if either her nature or her faith had failed her, as well knowing that where death is the worst of ills, there it is the greatest of blessings.

5   I am very sensible of the confidence you repose in me, in telling me the whole of your friend's illness.[2] The symptoms you mention are these: (1), the expecting great civilities from her acquaintance, with an aptness to think herself neglected by them; (2), a deep sadness upon the apprehension of their unkindness and the supposed
10   loss of their affections, which often carries her to such a length [as][3] to believe that God will forsake her too; (3), a desire to be equally well dressed with her companions, though she has not an equal fortune. The first question is therefore, what disorder it is that is the cause of these effects.

15   One person I knew who had every one of these symptoms: she expected great civilities, and was extremely apt to think her acquaintance neglected her, and showed less respect to her than to other people; the apprehension of whose unkindness joining with ill health sometimes made her deeply melancholy. I have often known
20   her pained at being worse dressed than her companions, and have heard her say more than once that few trials she had met with in her life were harder to be borne.

Is it not likely that it was the same cause that produced the same effects in both these persons? If so, we are not far from finding
25   what it is; for in [the] one I know it was chiefly vanity. Her sense of honour was not under due regulations; she was too fond of being admired, and therefore could ill bear to miss of this, but much worse to be contemned. And from too strong a desire of being approved, and too great an aversion to being despised, which was her original
30   distemper, n[atura]lly proceeded those painful symptoms. She seldom thought she met with respect enough, because she loved it too well; the least shadow of disrespect pained her, because she hated it too much. Hence too she dreaded whatever might expose her to it, and therefore was uneasy when less well dressed than her com-
35   panions. Perhaps her taking their supposed unkindness so deeply might flow from a better fountain. Is too tender a sense of the loss of a friend's affection a necessary proof of vanity? May we not put

---

[1] 1 Cor. 15: 56.
[2] Wesley first wrote 'case', and then underlined it to signify its omission.
[3] Orig., '-', signifying 'and'.

a milder interpretation even upon an aptness to suspect it where there is no real ground of suspicion? This is a weed, but is it not the weed of an excellent soil? For

Such flaws are found in the most noble natures.[1]

It seems probable that this is the disease of yours as well as of my acquaintance, namely, vanity, which you justly distinguish from pride, though indeed they are nearly related, pride regarding (as you well observe) our opinion of ourselves, vanity the opinions of other men concerning us; the former being immoderate self-esteem, the latter immoderate desire of the esteem of others. The proper remedy for either of these distempers you rightly judge to [be] humility. But how to infuse this, God knows: with men it is impossible.[2]

I know none more likely to be an instrument in his hand to perform this work of omnipotence than Aspasia. For you will not depend on your own strength while you insinuate to her the great cause of her melancholy; while you use all your address to make her sensible how apt vanity is to steal in even upon the best tempers. How useful it might be, seeing nothing but the finger of God can cast out this stubborn spirit,[3] to intersperse all our solemn addresses to him with particular petitions against it. O Aspasia, how amiable do you appear while you are employed in such offices as these! Especially in the eyes of him who seeth more clearly than man seeth![4] How just a return are you making to him for the talents he has bestowed upon you! And how generous a use of your power over your friends, while you thus direct it all to their advantage! Watch over me too for good, Aspasia. Though we are far, far divided as to our persons, yet let your thoughts (at least morning and evening) be with your most obliged friend and servant,

Cyrus

Is there need for Aspasia to desire one thing twice of Cyrus or Araspes?[5] I hope both of them are more sensible of their obligations to her. Adieu!

Source: Asp, pp. 57–60.

[1] The source of this quotation has not been identified.
[2] Mark 10: 27.   [3] See Luke 11: 20.
[4] See 1 Sam. 16: 7.
[5] i.e. destroying her letters, which she had requested in that of Jan. 15, 1731, as well as her last of Aug. 26.

From Ann Granville[1]

Why did not Cyrus and Araspes come one week sooner to Stanton, and then I should have seen them? Sappho, dear Sappho and I, in every sweet, delightful walk, wished extremely that we might together once again enjoy the pleasures of
5 friendly conversation in lovely Horrel hill! Why was I denied the satisfaction that would have brought with it a great advantage? 'Tis among the many things my weak reason can't assign a cause for. I believe 'tis best it should be so, but can't help being sorry. For this is the second time this summer I have missed seeing friends whose acquaintance I desire to improve.
10 I suppose you found at your return to Oxford my last letter. I wish you don't repent your encouraging a correspondence that is likely to give you so much trouble. One reason for my writing now is to ask your opinion in regard to a young lady for whom I have a great value, and am much concerned, because she is in a very melancholy way. Nobody's arguments are so plain and strong as
15 yours, therefore your advice would be of service to her. She has conversed with many people without being satisfied. Her case is this. She has always been remarkable for being religious, but is never contented with herself, not thinking she does what is right, being troubled with wandering and (what she terms) wicked thoughts whenever she goes to her private devotions or to church, es-
20 pecially at the sacrament. This she has been afraid of, and in perfect agonies at the time of receiving, for fear she was not well prepared. She says she does not find that pleasure in acts of religion and reading good things which she believes a good Christian ought, but that she does her duty with heaviness, nay sometimes reluctance; therefore she fears 'tis not acceptable. She thought fasting so
25 necessary that she has destroyed her health by it. She has even believed going to sleep was a sin. What pity 'tis, a person with such good inclinations, who desires so earnestly to do what is right, should have so much unhappiness! She is very generous and charitable, has an easy fortune and many friends, who love and value her. But this unfortunate way of thinking corrodes and embitters every-
30 thing. She has some time ago been very much perplexed about the sin of the Holy Ghost. Be so good as to explain what that sin is, and what method she can take to do her duty with cheerfulness. I believe your way of writing will sooner convince her where she is mistaken, and ease her doubts and scruples, than any casuist she has met with. I will not make any excuse for giving you this trouble,
35 because I know to Cyrus a good action rewards itself. My sister (thank God) is safely arrived at Dublin, and now I find how wrong all my fears were.
I reverence and extremely respect the G[odly] and Holy Club, an account of which I had from Sappho. O may success attend every member in their just and regular designs! Sure such examples will turn men to righteousness; among
40 others I hope to reap benefit from them.
I have been much delighted with Mrs. Astell. I wish I had read her books sooner, and I would have endeavoured last winter to have been acquainted

---

[1] Written before she had received Wesley's of Sept. 27.

with her.[1] For alas! among the many I am obliged to converse with how very few give anyone either pleasure or improvement! From you and Araspes I find both, and should be glad could I return either, but 'tis not in my power. I carried the book you favoured us with in town to Stanton. But how was my Sally and I vexed, not to be able to read what we knew was so well worth our study! I 5 won't be so unconscionable as to add any more to this long letter, but that I am to Cyrus and Araspes a most faithful friend,

Selima

My mother's best wishes attend the good brothers. I blush to see how many blots and blunders I have made. After having writ so much it appears ridiculous 10 to say I am in haste, and yet I protest 'tis true.

Source: Sel, pp. 23-5.

To Ann Granville[2]

Oct. 3 [1731]

'Tis in vain for me to think I shall ever be able to tell Selima how much I am obliged to her for her last. Why do you thus add to the obligations that were before too great to admit of any return? I am 15 now entirely reconciled to my late disappointment by the charming manner in which you mention it, and share in the pleasure of those lovely conversations while you tell me I was thought of in them.[3] Nothing could give me a livelier satisfaction unless I should once again meet Selima, and assure her that those are some of the happiest 20 hours of my life when I can give any proof of the value I have for her friendship, and that no employment is more agreeable to me than that which gives me any hopes of improving it.

An account I received some time since from Aspasia (for whose safety you will believe I am sincerely glad) so much resembles yours 25 that I have been in some doubt whether you did not speak of the same person.[4] Whether you did or no, I wish you have not both much too favourable an opinion of me. I am sure I should of myself did I think it in my power 'to heal the broken in heart',[5] to use any words

[1] Mrs. Mary Astell (see above, June 17-18, p. 285 etc.), whose brief obituary had appeared in the *Gent. Mag.* under date May 24, 1731, as 'author of several ingenious pieces, at Chelsea'.

[2] Replying to hers of Sept. 29.

[3] In not meeting her at Stanton. See previous letter.

[4] Cf. Aspasia's letters of July 29 and Aug. 26 with Selima's of Sept. 29.

[5] Cf. Luke 4: 18.

that would cure a wounded spirit or be a medicine for that sickness. Nor indeed have I time to weigh so nice a case throughly. Do not then be surprised, good Selima, if while I dare not wholly decline what you desire, yet I am forced to do it in so imperfect a manner as
5   neither suits the importance of the thing itself nor my obligations to the person that desires it.

One that is generous, charitable, and devout, that has an easy fortune and many sincere friends, is yet unhappy. Something lurking within poisons all these sweets, nor can she taste any of the goods
10   she enjoys. She strives against it, but in vain. She spends her strength, but to no purpose: her enemy still renews his strength, nay, even

> When 'gainst his head her sacred arms she bent,
> Strict watch, and fast severe, and prayer omnipotent.[1]

Still he pursues his prey; still he wounds her with doubts and scrup-
15   les of various sorts, so as to make the very ways of pleasantness uneasy, and the path of life like that which leads to destruction.[2]

And is there no help? Yes—if she can believe; all things are possible to her that believeth.[3] The shield of faith will yet repel all his darts, if she can be taught to use it skilfully, if 'the eyes of her
20   understanding can be enlightened to see what is the hope of our calling',[4] to know that our hope is sincerity, not perfection, not to do well, but to do our best. If God were to mark all that is done amiss, who could abide it?[5] Not the great Apostle himself, who even when he had 'finished his course'[6] on earth, and was ripe for paradise, yet
25   mentions himself as not 'having already attained' that height, not being 'already perfect'.[7]

Perfect, indeed, he was from sin, strictly speaking, which is a voluntary breach of a known law, at least from habits of such sin. As to single acts he 'knew whom he had believed'.[8] He knew who had
30   promised to forgive these, not seven times but seventy times seven.[9] Nay, a thousand times a thousand, if they sincerely desire it, shall all sins be forgiven unto the sons of men.[10] We need except none. No, not the sin against the Holy Ghost, for in truth this phrase is nowhere in the whole Scripture. No, 'the sin against the Holy Ghost' is a
35   term invented by the devil to perplex those whom he cannot destroy. The term used by God is, the blasphemy against the Holy Ghost, a

[1] Samuel Wesley, Jun., *The Battle of the Sexes*, st. xxxvi (*Poems*, 1736, p. 39).
[2] See Prov. 3: 17.   [3] See Mark 9: 23.   [4] Cf. Eph. 1: 18.
[5] See Ps. 130: 3 (B.C.P.).   [6] Cf. 2 Tim. 4: 7.   [7] Cf. Phil. 3: 12.
[8] Cf. 2 Tim. 1: 12.   [9] See Matt. 18: 22.   [10] Mark 3: 28.

phrase that instantly shuts out all thoughts and actions, for blasphemy must be a speech; and what speech this is Christ himself has expressly told us, viz., Mark 3: 22, 29, 30: 'He hath Beelzebub, and by the prince of the devils casteth he out devils.'

Shall he not cast out by the finger of God[1] that anxiety which they have instilled into his servant? Shall he not avenge her that crieth to him day and night, though (for wise reasons) he bear long with her enemies? I trust he shall avenge her speedily.[2] At least, if she cease not to cry unto him to deliver her from her weakness, then let her be assured that it shall not be in vain, for 'God is in the cry, but not in the weakness.'[3]

I do not say that she shall immediately be delivered; nor yet are her good dispositions lost, seeing there is a reward for suffering as well as for acting, and 'Blessed are they that endure temptation.'[4] God has given them a means of improving their good dispositions which is not given to the rest of the world; a means which supplies the want of action, and gives them all the advantage of a busy life without the danger. This is the surest, and it is the shortest way, as to all virtue, so particularly to humility, the distinguishing virtue of Christians, the sole inlet to all virtue.

Neither do I believe that she will ever be wholly freed either from wandering thoughts in prayer, or perhaps from such as would be wicked were they chosen or voluntarily indulged, but which when they are not voluntary are no more voluntary than the panting of the heart or the beating of the arteries. I never heard or read of more than one living person (Mr. De Renty)[5] who had quite shook off this weight, and much doubt whether of the sons of men now alive there be one who is so highly favoured. And perhaps we have scarce another instance of an embodied soul who always did the work of God with cheerfulness. The common lot of humanity seems to be, to be various and fluctuating in all things, more particularly in the

---

[1] Luke 11: 20. [2] See Luke 18: 7-8.

[3] This sentence does not occur in three sturdy seventeenth-century sermons preached on the text, by Ralph Brownrig, Robert Harris, and Arthur Lake, nor does it occur in the commentaries available to Wesley at this time by Burkitt, Gell, Hammond, Henry, Poole, Quesnel, or Whitby.

[4] Cf. Jas. 1: 12.

[5] Wesley had been familiar with the saintly Roman Catholic layman, Gaston Jean Baptiste de Renty (1611-49), for some years. He began 'collecting' Edward Sheldon's English Translation of his life by Saint-Jure in May, 1729, took the work with him for pastoral use in Georgia, and eventually published an abridged version in 1741 (*Bibliog*, No. 43).

things that pertain to God, from whom we are so far estranged by nature. With regard to these even David could sometimes say, 'Why go I so heavily, while the enemy oppresseth me?'[1] His rule it was, therefore, as it is ours, to judge of ourselves, not by what we feel, but
5 by what we do . . .[2]

Source: Sel, pp. 26–9.

To the Revd. Samuel Wesley, Jun.

Lincoln College, Nov. 17, 1731

Dear brother

Considering the other changes that I remember in myself I shall not at all wonder, if the time comes, when we differ as little in our
10 conclusions as we do now in our premisses. In most we seem to agree already, especially as to rising, not keeping much company, and sitting by a fire, which I always do if anyone in the room does, whether at home or abroad. But these are the very things about which others will never agree with me. Had I given up these, or
15 but one of them, rising early,[3] which implies going to bed early (though I never am sleepy now), and keeping so little company, not one man in ten of those that are offended at me as it is would ever open their mouth against any of the other particulars. For the sake of these those are mentioned; the root of the matter lies here.
20 Would I but employ a third of my money, and about half my time, as other folks do, smaller matters would be easily overlooked. But I think *nil tanti est*.[4] As to my hair, I am much more sure that what this enables me to do is according to the Scripture than I am that the length of it is contrary to it.[5]
25   I have often thought of a saying of Dr. Hayward's, when he examined me for priest's orders:[6] 'Do you know what you are about?

---

[1] Ps. 43: 2 (B.C.P.).

[2] This apparently marks the end of Wesley's deliberate extract from this letter, though if so we would have expected an indication of closing salutations. Certainly it ends the extant document devoted to their correspondence, though the correspondence itself continues for several years. The diary records 'wr to Se' on Mon. 4 rather than Sun. 3, and 'end to Sel' on the 7th.

[3] See Mar. 19, 1727 (p. 214).

[4] 'Nothing is of such importance' (cf. letter to John Fletcher, Dec. 15, 1773 (?)).

[5] See letter of May 22, 1727 (p. 222).

[6] Wesley was ordained by John Potter, Bishop of Oxford, Sept. 22, 1728. The ex-

You are bidding defiance to all mankind. He that would live a Christian priest ought to know that, whether his hand be against every man or not, he must expect every man's hand should be against him.' It is not strange that every man's hand who is not a Christian should be against him that endeavours to be so. But is it 5 not hard that even those that are with us should be against us; that a man's enemies (in some degree) should be those of the same household of faith?[1] Yet so it is. From the time that a man sets himself to his business very many, even of those who travel the same road, many of those who are before, as well as behind him, will lay stumb- 10 ling-blocks in his way. One blames him for not going fast enough, another for having made no greater progress, another for going too far—which perhaps, strange as it is, is the more common charge of the two. For this comes from people of all sorts; not only infidels, not only half-Christians, but some of the best of men are very apt to 15 make this reflection: 'He lays unnecessary burdens upon himself; he is too precise; he does what God has nowhere required to be done.' True, he has not required it of those that are perfect; and even as to those who are not, all men are not required to use all means; but every man is required to use those which he finds most 20 useful to himself. And who can tell better than himself whether he finds them so or no? 'Who knoweth the things of a man better than the spirit of a man that is in him?'[2]

This being a point of no common concern I desire to explain myself upon it once for all, and to tell you freely and clearly those 25 general positions on which I ground (I think) all those practices for which (as you would have seen had you read that paper through)[3] I am generally accused of singularity. First, as to the end of my being, I lay it down for a rule that I cannot be too happy, or therefore too holy, and thence infer that the more steadily I keep my eye 30 upon the prize of our high calling[4] the better, and the more of my thoughts, and words, and actions are directly pointed at the attainment of it. Second, as to the instituted means of attaining it I

hortation on this occasion appears to have been delivered by Dr. Thomas Haywood (or Hayward) (1678-1746), the vicar of Charlbury, Oxon., rather than by Dr. George Rye, the Archdeacon of Oxford (with whom Wesley did correspond, 1732-4).

[1] See Matt. 10: 36 ; Gal. 6: 10.
[2] Cf. 1 Cor. 2: 11.
[3] Cf. letter of July 19, 1731, to Aspasia, where he replies to similar charges. No such accusing document appears to be extant.
[4] See Phil. 3: 14.

likewise lay it down for a rule that I am to use them every time I may. Third, as to prudential means I believe this rule holds of things indifferent in themselves: whatever I know to do me hurt, that to me is not indifferent, but resolutely to be abstained from; whatever
5 I know to do me good, that to me is not indifferent, but resolutely to be embraced.

'But', it will be said, 'I am whimsical.' True, and what then? If by 'whimsical' be meant simply *singular*, I own it; if singular without any reason, I deny it with both my hands, and am ready to give
10 a reason to any that asks me of every custom wherein I wilfully differ from the world. I grant, in many single actions I differ unreasonably from others, but not wilfully; no, I shall extremely thank anyone who will teach me to help it. But can I totally help it till I have more breeding, or more prudence, to neither of which I am
15 much disposed naturally? And I greatly fear my acquired stock of either will give me small assistance.

I have but one thing to add, and that is as to my being *formal*. If by that be meant that I am not easy and unaffected enough in my carriage, it is very true; but how shall I help it? I cannot be genteelly
20 behaved by instinct; and if I am to try after it by experience and observation of others, that is not the work of a month, but of years. If by formal be meant that I am serious, this too is very true; but why should I help it? Mirth, I grant, is fit for you; but does it follow that it is fit for me? Are the same tempers, any more than the same
25 words or actions, fit for all circumstances? If you are to 'rejoice evermore'[1] because you have put your enemies to flight, am I to do the same while they continually assault me? You are glad because you are 'passed from death to life'.[2] Well; but let him be afraid who knows not whether he is to live or die. Whether this be my condition
30 or no, who can tell better than myself? Him who can, whoever he be, I allow to be a proper judge whether I do well to be generally as serious as I can.

John Whitelamb wants a gown much, and I am not rich enough to buy him one at present. If you are willing my twenty shillings
35 (that were) should go toward that, I will add ten to them, and let it lie till I have tried my interest with my friends to make up the price of a new one. I am, dear brother, yours and my sister's affectionate brother,

John Wesley

[1] 1 Thess. 5: 16.   [2] John 5: 24, etc.

The Rector[1] is much at your service. I fancy I shall some time or other have much to say to you about him. All are pretty well at Epworth, my sister Molly says.

Address: 'To the Rev. Mr. Wesley, Great Dean's-yard, Westminster'
Source: Priestley, pp. 9–13, collated with Hampson, I. 112–18, which is itself apparently based on the same MS, but much more altered by editing, and lacking the last eleven lines.

From Ann Granville[2]

[Dec. 1, 1731]

It is very unwillingly that I have been so long prevented thanking Cyrus for   5
the last proof of his friendship, though you have reason to be glad of it, for my letters are so trifling that you show the most good nature and humility in the world to suffer my correspondence. I hope in time to be more worthy of it. Nothing will be more conducive to it than the advantage of such an instructor.

I can't help believing my friend is the better for your good and kind advice.   10
She has not mentioned anything upon that subject in her last letters, but says her spirits are more lively, and she enters a little into the diversions of the Bath, which at first she was quite averse to, for I fancy the more satisfied one is with oneself the more cheerfully may one partake of the innocent entertainments of the world. How far, indeed, and what sort of diversions are the most allowable   15
and consistent with one's duty, is what I would fain be satisfied in. Suppose I go every week to an assembly, play at cards two or three hours; if I omit no duty by it, is it a fault? Or would it be in an older person than myself? Though I don't think being young exempts me from any good or religious act.

You see, Cyrus, how freely I expose to you all my errors, all my scruples;   20
and though I expose the weakness of judgment, yet I show how desirous I am to 'reform my will and rectify my thought'. For sure the active principle within is worth improvement. You have confirmed me in the inclination of doing it, have already, and I hope will continue to assist me in it. I shall be extremely thankful for that scheme of books you mention. O that I could make as good a   25
use of them as the person it was made for! What happiness is it to have those we love follow after virtue! And how sensible in affliction to see 'em forsake those paths which can alone make them happy! That is a pain Cyrus has not, and I hope will never know, any otherways than the general benevolence he has for all his fellow creatures makes him grieve when they do amiss.   30

Now give me leave to say that I can't find out the advantage of losing the conversation of particular sensible and virtuous friends. Their words, their

---

[1] Euseby Isham, the newly-elected Rector of Lincoln College.

[2] Apparently a reply to Wesley's letter of Nov. 1, 6, to whose contents it affords some clues along with a probable quotation, although it also touches upon a continuing subject in their earlier correspondence, the pastoral problem dealt with in Wesley's letter of Oct. 3.

example, excite us on to goodness. They blow up and keep alive those sparks of
religion which are too apt (with sorrow I speak it) to grow faint and languid. I
can recollect many instances where they have been of advantage to me. At church
their attention has[1] increased mine. At home they have begun good conversations
5 that I have been the better for. As we were often together we used to assist
each other in bearing a multitude of impertinence that I am now forced to suffer
singly. Now have I not more reason to imagine 'twas rather for their good than
mine that they were removed? Now I fear I show great arrogance to deny anything you say, but I only make this objection in order to be more fully convinced.
10 No one can do it so soon as Cyrus. His arguments are so plain and sensible, and
withal so well expressed, they please the fancy while they inform the understanding, which is what I very seldom have met with before, most instructive things
being dry and tedious, at least to me, who cannot, like my dear Sappho, search
for through all her 'obscure recesses'.
15   I am now reading a book I want your opinion of. 'Tis Mr. Burkitt's Explanation of the New Testament. He calls it Expository Notes with Practical Observations. Sure Cyrus cannot sit without a fire this weather. I hope the good
society prospers; one way I'm sure they do. I often think of them, especially
when the cold makes me shrink. They are those that are 'chosen of peculiar
20 grace'. The influence of it will I hope extend to their weaker brethren.
      The last letter I had from Aspasia she said she was very much concerned she
had not writ to you, and desired me to assure the good brothers of her friendship, and good wishes; as does my mother, who is very much out of order with a
cold. The last time I heard from Sappho she was well. Is not Araspes' hymn
25 quite charming? You have not sent your poetic herd so far, but you can call
'em in whenever you please.
      Cyrus may be certain I shall never forget him in the only way I can show my
gratitude. O that I had reason to think my prayers would be as efficacious as his
with[out] doubt are! What is uttered with so much real piety must be successful
30 for himself and for his friends. There I hope he will always place

                                                            Selima

Gloster 1st Decem[b]er

End by JW: 'M Granville / Dec. 17. 731' and in another place, '1. Dec'
Source: MA.

From the Revd. Samuel Wesley, Jun.[2]

                                                    [Dec. 11, 1731]

Dear Jack
35   Though I have not had time to tell you so much, your last grieved me and
astonished me.
      That I should be a hindrance to your salvation, a stumbling-block in your

---

[1] Orig., 'have'.
[2] Replying to John Wesley's letter of Nov. 17, 1731.

way to heaven, was a concern to me; and it had been much more so had I not opposed only such things as you yourself had made necessary. It is in your power to make everything indifferent a duty or a sin, though not to make any duty or sin indifferent. If you are so minded, I say no more, for your retreat is inaccessible to all but God: the spirit of a man that is in him.   5

But another part amazes me to the last degree. I that am passed from death— I that am free from assaults—To the best of my remembrance I never had the least direct or indirect thought of myself in my last letter. Who am I to be set for a pattern, and much more to set up myself for such! I was out of the question entirely; and you, too, more than you may imagine; for had it not been for fear   10 of your singularity being a disadvantage to other people I should scarce have wrote twice. As to yourself I did and do think sincerity sufficient. My own behaviour, I own, might prejudice me against yours, as to my particular liking; but surely not so far as to make me think you disserving the cause of religion. I fear that opinion is built on a firmer ground than my temper, which by the by   15 is full as grave, not to say melancholy, as yours. I wish I had no more cause to be melancholy.

I agree John Whitelamb shall have the money, on this condition, that he owns he has received that 20s. in part of alleviation of my father's hard bargain with him, for I think 'tis but just when he remembers the one he should not forget   20 the other—'tis on my father's account I consent.

I can't write to Charles tonight. We shall be glad to see you in the Holydays; but we shall be out of town a week, but surely back again by New Year's Day. We join in love to you both. I am, dear Jack, your affectionate friend and brother,   25

S. Wesley

Dec. 11, 1731
    Service to your head.
    N.B. *Ora pro me, fratrem ne desere frater.*[1]

Address: 'To the Reverend Mr. Wesley, Fellow of Lincoln, Oxford'   *Post-marks*: '14 DE', 'EP' (?) within a circle   *Source*: MA.

From the Revd. Samuel Wesley, Jun.

[? Jan. 1, 1732]   30

Dear brother
    Your last letter affected me much. I find by the very way of pronouncing, that you are not *yet* in a consumption, though there is apprehension and danger of your being so. Your life is of benefit and consequence to the world, and I would therefore willingly, for the sake of others, draw your days out to their utmost   35 date. For yourself, indeed, the matter is not much, if you go well whensoever called; as I don't question but you will. As to any faults I have to tell you of, I think you know already all I say and all I think, too, upon that subject. The main

---
[1] 'Pray for me, that brother should not desert brother.'

is what I have often repeated—Your soul is too great for your body: your watching and intention of thought for a long time; your speaking often, and long, when wearied; in short your spirit (though in a better sense than Dryden meant it) o'er-informs its tenement of clay.

Source: A.M., 1778, pp. 129–30, date conjectured from apparent situation, after John's intervening letter of Dec. 17 answering Sam's of Dec. 11.

From Mrs. Susanna Wesley

5   Mon. Feb. 21 [1]731–2

Dear Jacky

I thank God I am much better than I have been, though far from being in health; yet a little respite from much pain I esteem a great mercy. If you had any design to visit our family this spring (which for your own sake I could wish
10 you had not) my health or sickness will be of little consequence; your entertainment would be the same, and I am no company.

I have time enough now, more than I can make a good use of, but yet for many reasons I care not to write to anyone. I never did much good in my life when in the best health and vigour, and therefore I think it would be presump-
15 tion in me to hope to be useful now; 'tis more than I can well do to bear my own infirmity and other sufferings as I ought and would do. All inordinate affection to present things may, by the grace of God, and a close application of our own spirits to the work, be so far conquered as to give us very little or no trouble. [. . .]

I am heartily sorry for Mr. Morgan. 'Tis no wonder that his illness should at
20 last affect his mind; 'tis rather to be admired that it has not done it long ago. [. . .]

The young gentleman you mention seems to me to be in the right concerning the real presence of Christ in the sacrament. I own I never understood by the real presence more than what he has elegantly expressed, 'that the divine nature of Christ is then eminently present to impart (by the operation of his Holy
25 Spirit) the benefits of his death to worthy receivers.' And surely the divine presence of our Lord, thus applying the virtue and merits of the great atonement to each true believer, makes the consecrated bread more than a bare sign of Christ's body, since by his so doing we receive, not only the sign, but with it the thing signified, all the benefits of his Incarnation and Passion! But still, however
30 this divine institution may seem to others, to me 'tis full of mystery. Who can account for the operations of God's Holy Spirit? Or define the manner of his working upon the spirit in man, either when he enlightens the understanding, or excites and confirms the will, and regulates and calms the passions, without impairing man's liberty? Indeed the whole scheme of our redemption by Jesus
35 Christ is beyond all things mysterious. That God! the Mighty God! the God of the spirits of all flesh! the possessor of heaven and earth! who is being itself! and comprehends in his most pure nature absolute perfection and blessedness! that must necessarily be infinitely happy in and of himself! that such a being should in the least degree regard the salvation of sinners! that he himself! the
40 offended, the injured, should propose terms of reconciliation, and admit them

into covenant upon any conditions! is truly wonderful, and astonishing! As
God did not make the world because he needed it, so neither could that be any
reason for his redeeming it. He loved us, because he loved us! And would have
mercy, because he would have mercy! Then the manner of man's redemption,
the way by which he condescends to save us, is altogether incomprehensible! 5
Who can unfold the mystery of the hypostatic union! Or forbear acknowledging
with the Apostle, that 'without controversy, great is the mystery of godliness,
God manifested in the flesh'! That the divine person of the Son of God should
(if it may be permitted so to speak) seem so far to forget his dignity and essential
glory as to submit to a life of poverty, contempt, and innumerable other suf- 10
ferings, for above thirty years, and conclude that life in inexpressible torments!
And all this to heal and save a creature that was at enmity against God, and
desired not to be otherwise. Here is public and benevolent affection in its utmost
exaltation and perfection! And this is the love of Christ, which, as the Apostle
justly observes, passeth knowledge! 15
   I have been led away so far by this vast subject that I have hardly left myself
time or room to add more. The writing anything about my way of education
I am much averse from.[1] It can't (I think) be of service to anyone to know how
I, that have lived such a retired life for so many years (ever since I was with
child of you), used to employ my time and care in bringing up my children. 20
No one can, without renouncing the world in the most literal sense, observe my
method, and there's few (if any) that would entirely devote above twenty years of
the prime of life in hope to save the souls of their children (which they think
may be saved without so much ado); for that was my principal intention, however
unskilfully or unsuccessfully managed. 25
   Dear Jacky, my love and blessing is ever with you. Adieu.

[There follows a letter to Charles Wesley]
Em, Molly, Kez, send their love to ye both.

Address: 'To The Revd Mr John Wesley, Fellow of Lincoln, Oxon' *Postmark*: '25 FE' *Charges*: ((4)), 'In all 7' *End* by JW: 'Feb', with a partly-
erased draft on the cover of the closing paragraph of his reply of Feb. 28, 1732
Source: MA; cf. *M.M.*, 1844, pp. 817–19, including the passages omitted, but
heavily edited.

To Mrs. Susanna Wesley

Linc. Coll. Feb. 28, 1731/2

Dear mother 30
   In the week after Easter I hope to find you a little better recovered;
else our visit will give us small entertainment. Were it not that we

---

[1] Apparently this was a request made to her in Wesley's letter of Jan. 26, to which this
replies, and to whose contents it affords several clues. Wesley's plea led eventually to
her lengthy letter of July 24, 1732, printed in his *Journal*.

desire to have as much as we can of yours and my father's company while we are yet alive together, we should scarce be induced to go a hundred and twenty mile to see Epworth steeple.

A year ago Mr. Morgan was exceeding well pleased with the
5 thoughts of dying shortly. He will not now bear to hear it named, though he can neither sleep, read, stand, nor sit. Yet without hands or feet or head or heart, he is very sure his illness is not at all increased. Surely, now he is a burden to himself, and almost useless to the world, his discharge can't be far off.

10 One consideration is enough to make me assent to his and your judgment concerning the Holy Sacrament, which is, that we can't allow Christ's human nature to be present at it without allowing either con- or trans⟨-su⟩bstantiation. But that his divinity is so united to us then as he never is but to worthy receivers I firmly
15 believe, though the manner of that union is utterly a mystery to me.

That none but worthy receivers should find this effect is not strange to me when I observe how small effect any means of improvement have upon an unprepared mind. Mr. Morgan and my brother were affected as they ought by the observations you made upon that
20 glorious subject.[1] But though my understanding 'approved what was excellent',[2] yet my heart did not feel it! Why was this, but because it was pre-engaged by those affections with which wisdom will not dwell? Because the animal mind cannot relish those truths which are spiritually discerned![3] Yet I have the Writings which the
25 Good Spirit gave to that end! I have many of those which he hath since assisted his servants to give us: I have retirement to apply these to my own soul daily; I have means both of public and private prayer, and above all of partaking in that sacrament once a week. What shall I do to make all these blessings effectual? To gain from
30 them that mind which was also in Christ Jesus?[4] To all who give signs of their not being strangers to it I propose this question as often as I can. And why not to you rather than any, who are now come almost within reach of that 'haven where I would be'?[5] Shall I quite break off my pursuit of all learning but what immediately
35 tends to practice? I once desired to make a fair show in languages and philosophy. But 'tis past. There is a more excellent way,[6] and if I cannot attain to any progress in the one without throwing up all

---

[1] See the lengthy passage in her letter of Feb. 21, 1732, which this answers.
[2] Cf. Phil. 1: 10.   [3] 1 Cor. 2: 14.   [4] Phil. 2: 5.
[5] Cf. Ps. 107: 30 (B.C.P.).   [6] 1 Cor. 12: 1.

thoughts of the other, why, fare it well! Yet a little while, and we shall be equal in all knowledge, if we are in virtue!

'Ever since you was with child of me', you say, 'you have renounced the world.'[1] And what have I been doing all this time? What have I done ever since I was born? Why, I have been plunging myself into it more and more. 'Tis enough. Awake, thou that sleepest.[2] Is there not one Lord, one Spirit, one hope of our calling?[3] One way to attain that hope? Then I am to renounce the world as well as you. That is the very thing I want to do; to draw off my affections from this world, and fix them upon a better world. But how? What is the surest and the shortest way? Is it not to be humble? Surely this is a large step in that way. But the question recurs, How shall I do this? To own the necessity of it is not to be humble. In many things you have interceded for me and prevailed. Who knows but in this too you may be successful? If you can spare me only that little part of Thursday evening which you formerly bestowed upon me in another manner,[4] I doubt not but it would be as useful now for correcting my heart as it was then for the forming my judgment.

When I observe how fast life flies away, and how slow improvement comes, I think one can never be too much afraid of dying before one has learned to live. I mean, even in the course of nature; for were I sure that 'the silver cord should not violently be loosed', that 'the wheel should not be broken at the cistern'[5] till it was quite worn away by its own motion, yet what a time would this give me for what work? A moment, to transact the business of eternity! What are forty years in comparison of this? So that were I sure of what never man yet was sure of, how little would it alter the case! How justly still might I cry out:

> Downward I hasten to my destined place;
> There none obtain thy aid, none sing thy praise!
> Is mercy there, is sweet forgiveness found?
> O save me yet, while on the brink I stand:
> Rebuke these storms, and set me safe on land.
> O make my longings and thy mercy sure!
> Thou art the God of power.[6]

---

[1] See letter of Feb. 21, 1732.   [2] Eph. 5: 14.
[3] See Eph. 4: 4, 5.
[4] In the winter of 1711/12 she began devoting time in the evenings 'to discourse with each child by itself'. See her letter of Feb. 6, 1712, quoted by Wesley in his *Journal* for Aug. 1, 1742.   [5] Cf. Eccles. 12: 6.
[6] An imperfect recollection of st. 2 of Matthew Prior, 'Considerations on part of the eighty-eighth Psalm'.

Dear mother, there is but one cause of uneasiness which I sometimes find in your behaviour towards me. You perform the noblest
offices of love for me, and yet blame the fountain from whence they
flow. You have more than once said you loved me too well, and would
5 strive to love me less. Now this it is I complain of. You d⟨on't⟩
think natural affection evil in itself; far from it. But you s⟨ay you⟩
have but a little time to stay in the world, and therefore should not
have much affection for anything in it. Most true—not any of those
things that perish with the world. But am I one of those? If you think
10 I am 'sick unto death',[1] love me the more, and you will the [more]
fervently pray for me that I may be healed. If you rather incline to
think that there is hope of my recovery, then what if you are to leave
the world in a little time? What if you should die in a year, a month,
a day? Whom God hath joined, can death put asunder?[2] According
15 to your supposition, that unbodied spirits still minister to those who
were their kindred according to the flesh, not a moment! Certainly,
not long. Yet a little while, and if you return not to me, you will
certainly be overtaken by your dutiful and affectionate son,

John Wesley

Address: 'To Mrs Wesley, At Epworth, To be left at ye Post-house in Gainsborough, Lincolnshire. per London'   *No postmark*, because delivered by
hand   *End* by JW: 'my m[othe]r'   *Source*: MA.

From Mrs. Susanna Wesley[3]

20   July 24, 1732

Dear son
    According to your desire I have collected the principal rules I observed in
educating my family; which I now send you as they occurred to my mind. [. . .]
    In order to form the minds of children, the first thing to be done is to conquer
25 their will. To inform their understanding is a work of time, and must proceed
by slow degrees; but the subjecting the will is a thing which must be done at
once—and the sooner the better. For by our neglecting timely correction they
contract a stubbornness which is hardly ever to be conquered, and never without
using that severity which would be as painful to us as to the children. Therefore

[1] 2 Kgs. 20: 1, etc.   [2] See Matt. 19: 6.
[3] In response to his request of Jan. 26, probably renewed in his missing letter of
June 22.

I call those cruel parents who pass for kind and indulgent, who permit their children to contract habits which they know must be afterwards broken.

I insist upon conquering the wills of children betimes, because this is the only foundation for a religious education. When this is thoroughly done, then a child is capable of being governed by the reason of its parent, till its own understanding 5 comes to maturity.

I cannot yet dismiss this subject. As self-will is the root of all sin and misery, so whatever cherishes this in children ensures their after-wretchedness and irreligion; and whatever checks and mortifies it promotes their future happiness and piety. This is still more evident if we consider that religion is nothing else 10 but the doing the will of God, and not our own; and that self-will being the grand impediment to our temporal and eternal happiness, no indulgence of it can be trivial, no denial of it unprofitable. Heaven or hell depends on this alone. So that the parent who studies to subdue it in his children works together with God in the saving of a soul. The parent who indulges it does the devil's work, 15 makes religion impracticable, salvation unattainable, and does all that in him lies to damn his child, soul and body, for ever!

This therefore I cannot but earnestly repeat: break their wills betimes. Begin this great work before they can run alone, before they can speak plain, or perhaps speak at all. Whatever pains it cost, conquer their stubbornness: break 20 the will, if you would not damn the child. I conjure you not to neglect, not to delay this! Therefore, (1), let a child from a year old be taught to fear the rod and to cry softly. In order to this, (2), let him have nothing he cries for, absolutely nothing, great or small; else you undo your own work. (3). At all events, from that age make him do as he is bid, if you whip him ten times running to effect it: 25 let none persuade you it is cruelty to do this; it is cruelty not to do it. Break his will now, and his soul will live, and he will probably bless you to all eternity.

Source: Wesley's sermon, 'On Obedience to Parents', *A.M.*, 1784, pp. 462–4, collated with his *Journal*, Aug. 1, 1742, from which the date and opening sentence only are here presented. Both the well-known lengthy version in the *Journal* and this brief excerpt are based upon the original, but contain Wesley's editorial changes (which have not been pointed out). The last paragraph in this excerpt is not represented in the *Journal* version.

From John Clayton[1]

Oxon. Aug. 1, 1732

Revd. and dear sir

Excuse me from interrupting you from attending to the noble work you have 30 taken in hand, whilst I give you an account of the present state of our affairs in Oxford.

---

[1] John Clayton (1709–73), son of a Manchester bookseller, who proceeded B.A. from Brasenose College on Apr. 16, 1729, and M.A. on June 8, 1732. He was ordained deacon

I cannot but think it an extraordinary piece of providence that when we had lost our best advocate and patron all opposition against us should immediately cease. For know that since you left us nobody has thought it worth while to attack either Mr. Smith[1] or me, or endeavour to remove us from those principles
5 wherein you by the grace of God have fixed us. I have gone every day to Lincoln, big with expectation to hear of some mighty attack made upon Mr. Smith, but I thank God I have always been disappointed, for not one of the Fellows has once so much as tried to shake him, or to convert him from the right way wherein I hope he at present walks. Indeed on Sunday he met with a rub from
10 Mr. Vesey, who refused to read prayers for him in your chapel, for fear of contributing anything to his going to Christ Church. But Mr. Smith had the heart to desire that favour of the Rector which Mr. Vesey had denied him, who immediately promised to read for him, and encouraged him to proceed in the way he was in, and if possible to make further progress in virtue and holiness.
15 He goes out of town tomorrow morning, and so will be entirely out of danger from the Fellows of Lincoln.

We had conversation this morning, whilst we were at breakfast together, concerning the temptations which may possibly arise from strange company and travelling, and Mr. Smith seems to be forearmed against, and determined to
20 oppose them to the utmost of his powers. He joins with me in best respects to your brother and you, and desires you won't forget to send the bands and the poems you promised him.

Poor Mr. Clements is still wavering. He was with me last night two hours, but I doubt to no purpose.
25 My little flock at Brasenose are, God be praised, true to their principles, and I hope to themselves too.

Bocardo, I fear, grows worse upon my hands. They have done nothing but quarrel ever since you left us. And they carried matters so high on Saturday that the bailiffs were sent for, who ordered Tomlyns to be fettered and put in
30 the dungeon, where he lay some hours, and then upon promise of his good behaviour was released again. He has been much better ever since that time,

---

at Chester on Dec. 29, 1732, for the cure of Sacred Trinity Chapel, Salford, where his home became a focal point for the Oxford Methodists. He was very friendly with John Byrom, and was a high churchman sympathetic with the Jacobites. Wesley's letter of Oct. 18, 1732, recounting the history of the Oxford Methodists, describes his first meeting with Clayton on Apr. 20, 1732. His brief immersion in their activities was very influential. He took over the position of chief social worker for the group from William Morgan, who left for Dublin on June 5, and died on Aug. 26. He reinforced Wesley's commitment to the practices of the apostolic church, as in observing the stationary fasts and weekly communion. This letter offers a detailed account of the activities of the Holy Club. It was written while Wesley was in London visiting family and friends, making several new friends important both for himself and the group (including William Wogan, Sir John Philipps, William Law, and James Oglethorpe), and becoming a member of the S.P.C.K. (See Heitzenrater, pp. 160–6, 169–74.)

[1] William Smith (*c*. 1707–65), of Leicester, who proceeded B.A. in 1729 and M.A. in 1732. He was elected a fellow of Lincoln in 1731 in succession to Euseby Isham, upon his becoming Rector. At first very sympathetic to Wesley, he joined in attending weekly communion at Christ Church cathedral, and remained in occasional touch with him after they had both left Oxford.

and I hope will be the better for it all his lifetime. Wisdom has never been to hear me read, notwithstanding his promise. I sent for him yesterday, but he would not come down, and when I had done reading I went upstairs to him and upbraided him with breaking his promise, upon which he very surlily replied that he had thought better of it since he had seen me, and was determined never to come near 5 Blair, lest his indignation should rise at the sight of him.

The Castle is, I thank God, in much better condition. All the felons were acquitted except Salmon, who is referred to be tried at Warwick, to our great disappointment, and the sheep-stealer, who is burnt in the hand, and who I do verily believe is a great penitent. I got Mrs. Topping a copy of her son's indict- 10 ment at the Assizes, which has made her mighty easy ever since; and she is now endeavouring to bring her mind into a due frame for the devout participation of the Holy Communion on Sunday next. Tempro is discharged, and I have appointed Harris to read to the prisoners in his stead. Two of the felons likewise have paid their fees and are gone out, both of them able to read mighty well. 15 There are only two in the gaol who want this accomplishment, John Clanville, who reads but moderately, and the horse-dealer, who cannot read at all. He knows all his letters, and can spell most of the common monosyllables. I hear them both read three times a week, and I believe Salmon hears them so many times a day. 20

One of my college scholars has left me, but the others go on mighty well. The woman, who was a perfect novice, spells tolerably, and so does one of the boys, and the other makes shift to read with spelling every word that is longer than ordinary. The boys can both say their Catechism so far as to the end of the Commandments, and can likewise repeat the morning and evening prayers for 25 children in Ken's *Manual*. Mrs. Trueby has been very ill this last week, so that she has made no great proficiency.

I am to go down at six o'clock to hear the determination of a meeting of St. Thomas's parish concerning separating Bossum and his wife. When I had promised to give a crown towards clothing the woman, and the overseer had 30 determined to take her in upon that condition, the churchwarden would needs have him try to put the man upon me too, to get a crown towards clothing him. But as he is able to work for his living I don't think him a proper object of charity. Nor can I at this time afford to do anything for him, because I am apprehensive that I must be forced to contribute to Salmon's relief, who will want near 35 twenty shillings to subpoena proper witnesses to Warwick at his trial; and I cannot but think it a much greater act of charity to rescue a suffering innocent than to relieve an idle beggar.

I have been twice at the school, viz. on Tuesday and Saturday last, and intend to go again as soon as I have finished this letter. The children go on pretty well 40 except Jervaise's boy, who I find truants till eleven o'clock in a morning. I threatened the boy what we would do to him if ever he truanted any more, and he has promised (as all children do) that he will do so no more; nay, his mother assures me that she will take care for the future that he shall not. I got a shilling for her from our Vice-Principal, and gave her sixpence myself, to preserve the 45 gown that is in pawn from being sold; and the woman who has it has promised not to sell it provided Jervaise will bring her sixpence a week towards redeeming it.

I have obtained leave to go to St. Thomas's workhouse twice a week, and indeed I cannot but hope it will be a noble field of improvement. I'm sure the people stand much in need of instruction, for there is hardly a soul can read in the whole house; and those that can don't understand one word of what they
5 read.

I think I have nothing further to add about our affairs; only I must beg the favour of you, if you can conveniently, to pay Mr. Rivington thirty shillings for my use, and I will repay it when you come to Oxford. Pray don't forget a few Common Prayer Books for the Castle.

10 You cannot imagine the pleasure it is to me to know that you are engaged every morning in prayers for me; I wish for nine o'clock more eagerly than ever I did before; and I think I begin to perceive what is meant by that union of souls which is so much talked of in Père Malebranche and Madame Bourignon, which I never understood before. Good sir, continue your prayers for me, for
15 I feel that I am benefited by them.

I do not envy you the happiness which I know you will have from the conversation of so many pious men as I know you will meet with at London, because I assure myself that I shall have the benefit of it when I have the pleasure to see you again at Oxford.

20 Mr. Hall is not yet come home, so that I am pretty much taken up amongst the poor people and the prisoners, and have not yet had time to consider of any improvements or additions to be made to the list of books for our pupils.

I thank God I have fully conquered my affection for a morning nap, and rise constantly by five o'clock at the furthest, and have the pleasure to see myself
25 imitated by the greatest part of my pupils. I have talked with Mr. Clements, and I hope have made him a proselyte to early rising, though I cannot to constant communion.

Pray God prosper all those designs you have undertaken of doing good at London, and send you a good journey to Oxford. I am, revd. and dear sir,
30 your most affectionate friend and most obliged humble ⟨servant,⟩

J. Clayton

I hope you will not forget to pay my due compliments to Sir John Philipps, Mr. Wogan, and all my other good friends.

Address: '⟨To the Revd. Mr. J. Wesley⟩, to be left with Mr. Rivington, Bookseller in St. Paul's Ch: Yard, London'   *End* by JW: 'Mr Clayton, Aug. 1, 1732'   *Source*: MA, with no paragraphing except for that beginning, 'You cannot imagine . . .'

To Richard Morgan, Sen.[1]

Oct. [19], 1732[2]
Oxon.

Sir

    The occasion of my giving you this trouble is of a very extra-
ordinary nature. On Sunday last I was informed (as no doubt you   5
will be ere long) that my brother and I had killed your son; that the
rigorous fasting which he had imposed upon himself by our advice
had increased his illness and hastened his death. Now though,
considering it in itself, 'it is a very small thing with me to be judged
by man's judgment',[3] yet as the being thought guilty of so mis-   10
chievous an imprudence might make me less able to do the work I
came into the world for I am obliged to clear myself of it, by observing to you, as I have done to others, that your son left off fasting
about a year and an half since, and that it is not yet half a year since
I began to practise it.   15

    I must not let slip this occasion[4] of doing my part toward giving

---

[1] Richard Morgan (*c.* 1679–1742) was born in Barbados, educated at Hart Hall,
Oxford, and the Middle Temple, London, and at this time was the Second
Remembrancer in the Court of Exchequer in Dublin. William Morgan, the pioneer with
Charles Wesley and Robert Kirkham of the Holy Club, was his elder son. In 1731
William Morgan became both physically and mentally ill. On March 15, 1732, his father
wrote telling him that henceforth financial support would be available only for his health
and education, and strongly criticized both 'the ridiculous society' with which he was
associated and his practice of 'entering into poor people's houses, calling their children
together, teaching them their prayers and catechisms, and giving them a shilling at
[his] departure'. On June 5, 1732, William returned to Dublin, where he died on Aug. 26.
(For details see letters of Nov. 22 and Dec. 17, 1733.) On Sept. 5 Richard Morgan wrote
to Charles Wesley, describing his son's last illness, his own change of opinion about the
group's activities, and his readiness to help them in any way he could. His genuine
appreciation of the movement caused him in 1733 to enter his second son, Richard,
under John Wesley's tutorial care at Lincoln College.
    This apologia for the Oxford Methodists was immediately transcribed by Wesley,
who read it to various groups whose sympathetic support he sought to secure. In 1740
he prefixed it to the first extract from his *Journal* (see *Bibliog*, No. 19). Here we reproduce
Charles Wesley's contemporary transcription, which differs at many points from the
version edited by John for publication. (Only the more important of the variants are
noted.)
    [2] Charles Wesley's transcript of this letter is dated Oct. 18, 1732, and all contemporary
editions of JWJ give it as Oct. 18, 1730. John Wesley's diary, however, implies that it
was written Oct. 19–20, 1732, and transcribed Oct. 20–1.
    [3] 1 Cor. 4: 3.   [4] *Journal*, 'opportunity'.

you a juster notion of some other particulars relating both to him
and myself which have been industriously misrepresented to you.

In March last he received a letter from you, which being then not
able to read, he desired me to read to him; several of the expressions
5 whereof I perfectly remember, and shall do till I too am called hence.
I then determined that if God was pleased to take away your son
before me, I would justify him and myself, which I now do with all
plainness and simplicity, as both my character and cause require.

In one practice for which you blamed your son I am only con-
10 cerned as a friend, not as a partner. That therefore I shall consider
first. Your own account of it was in effect this:

> He frequently went into poor people's houses in the villages about Holt, and
> called their children together, and instructed them in their duty to God, their
> neighbour, and themselves. He likewise explained to them the necessity of
15 private as well as public prayer, and provided them with such forms as were
> best suited to their several capacities. And being well apprized how much the
> success of his endeavours depended on their goodwill towards him, to win upon
> their affections he sometimes distributed among them a little of that money
> which he had saved from gaming and the other fashionable expenses of the place.[1]

20 This is the first charge against him, upon which all that I shall
observe is that I will refer it to your own judgment whether it be
fitter to have a place in the catalogue of his faults, or of those virtues
for which he is now numbered among the sons of God.[2]

If all the persons concerned in 'that ridiculous society whose
25 follies you have so often heard repeated'[3] could but give such a
proof of their deserving the glorious title[4] which was once bestowed
upon them, they would be well contented that their lives too should
be counted madness, and their end thought to be without honour.[5]
But the truth is, their title to holiness stands upon much less stable
30 foundations, as you will easily perceive when you know the ground
of this wonderful outcry, which it seems England is not wide enough
to contain.

In November, 1729, at which time I came to reside at Oxford,
your son, my brother, and myself, and one more,[6] agreed to spend
35 three or four evenings in a week together. Our design was to read

---

[1] The original of this undated letter does not appear to be extant.
[2] See Wisd. 5: 5.
[3] Cf. Richard Morgan to Charles Wesley, Sept. 5, 1732, transcribed from CW's copy
in Telford I. 121-2.
[4] Footnote, in JW's hand: 'The Holy Club'.
[5] See Wisd. 5: 4.   [6] Robert Kirkham.

over the classics, which we had before read in private, on common
nights, and on Sunday some book in divinity. In the summer
following Mr. M[organ] told me he had called at the gaol to see a
man that was condemned for killing his wife, and that from the
talk he had with one of the debtors he verily believed that it would 5
do much good if anyone would be at the pains now and then of
speaking with them. This he so frequently repeated that on the 24th
of August, 1730, my brother and I walked down with him to the
Castle. We were so well satisfied with our conversation there that we
agreed to go thither once or twice a week; which we had not done 10
long before he desired me, Aug. 31, to go with him to see a poor
woman in the town who was sick. In this employment, too, when we
came to reflect upon it, we believed that it would be worth while to
spend an hour or two in a week, provided the minister of the parish
in which any such person was were not against it. But that we might 15
not depend wholly on our own judgments, I wrote an account to
my father of our whole design, withal begging that he who had
lived seventy years in the world, and seen as much of it as most
private men have ever done, would advise us whether we had yet
gone too far, and whether we should now stand still or go forward. 20
Part of his answer, dated September 28, 1730,[1] was this:

And now as to your own designs and employments, what can I say less of
them than *valde probo*;[2] and that I have the highest reason to bless God that he has
given me two sons together in Oxford to whom he has given grace and courage to
turn the war against the world and the devil, which is the best way to conquer 25
them. They have but one more enemy to combat with, the flesh, which if they
take care to subdue by fasting and prayer, there will be no more for them to do
but to proceed steadily in the same course, and expect the crown which fadeth
not away. You have reason to bless God, as I do, that you have so fast a friend
as Mr. M[organ], who I see in the most difficult service is ready to break the ice 30
for you. You do not know of how much good that poor wretch who killed his
wife has been the providential occasion. I think I must adopt Mr. M[organ] to
be my son, together with you and your brother Ch[arles]; and when I have such
a ternion to prosecute that war wherein I am now *miles emeritus*,[3] I shall not
be ashamed when they speak with their enemies in the gate. 35
I am afraid lest the main objection you make against your going on in the
business with the prisoners may secretly proceed from flesh and blood. For
who can harm you, if you are followers of that which is so good, and which will
be one of the marks by which the Shepherd of Israel will know his sheep at the
last day?—Though if it were possible for you to suffer a little in the cause you 40
would have a confessor's reward. You own none but such as are out of their

---

[1] The *Journal* dates the letter (probably incorrectly), Sept. 21, 1730.
[2] 'I greatly approve'.   [3] 'a worn-out soldier'.

senses would be prejudiced against your acting in this manner, but say, 'These are they that need a physician.' But what if they will not accept of one who will be welcome to the poor prisoners? Go on then, in God's name, in the path to which your Saviour has directed you, and that track wherein your father has
5 gone before you. For when I was an undergraduate at Oxford I visited those in the Castle there, and reflect on it with great satisfaction to this day. Walk as prudently as you can, though not fearfully, and my heart and prayers are with you.

Your first regular step is to consult with him (if any such there be) who has a
10 jurisdiction over the prisoners, and the next is to obtain the direction and approbation of your bishop. This is Monday morning, at which time I shall never forget you. If it be possible, I should be glad to see you all three here in the fine end of the summer. But if I cannot have that satisfaction, I am sure I can reach you every day, though you were beyond the Indies. Accordingly to him who is
15 everywhere I now heartily commit you, as being your most affectionate and joyful father.

In pursuance of these directions I immediately went to Mr. G[erard],[1] the Bishop of Oxford's chaplain, who was likewise the person that took care of the prisoners, when any were condemned
20 to die (at other times they were left to their own care). I proposed to him our design of serving them as far as we could, and my own intention to preach there once a month if the bishop approved of it. He much commended our design, and said he would answer for the bishop's approbation, to whom he would take the first opportunity
25 of mentioning it. It was not long before he informed me he had done so, and that his lordship[2] not only gave his permission, but was greatly pleased with the undertaking, and hoped it would have the deserved success.

Soon after a gentleman of Merton College, who was one of our
30 little company,[3] which now consisted of five persons, acquainted us that he had been rallied the day before for being a member of the Holy Club; and that it was become a common topic of mirth at his college, where they had found out several of our customs to which we were ourselves utter strangers. Upon this I consulted my father
35 again, in whose answer were these words:

[Dec. 1, 1730]

This day[4] I received both yours, and this evening in our course of reading[5] I

---

[1] Joseph Gerard, rector of St. Martin's (Carfax), Oxford.
[2] John Potter (1674?-1747), Bishop of Oxford, and later Archbishop of Canterbury, who had ordained John Wesley both deacon and priest.
[3] Robert Kirkham.
[4] Dec. 1, 1730, answering John's (and probably one by Charles) dated Nov. 23. Samuel Wesley's letter was reproduced from the holograph in Whitehead, I. 425-7.
[5] Whitehead, 'in the course of our reading'.

thought I found an answer that would be more proper than any I myself could dictate, though since it will not be easily translated I send it in the original. 2 Cor. 7 : 4. Πολλή μοι καύχησις ὑπερ ὑμῶν· πεπλήρωμαι τῇ παρακλήσει· ὑπερπερισσεύμαι τῇ χαρᾷ.[1] What would you be? Would you be angels? I question whether a mortal can arrive to a greater degree of perfection than steadily to 5 do good, and for that very reason patiently and meekly to suffer evil. For my part, on the present view of your actions and designs, my daily prayers are that God would keep you humble, and then I am sure that if you continue to suffer for righteousness' sake, though it be but in a lower degree, the spirit of grace[2] and of glory shall in some good measure rest upon you. Be never weary of well-doing; never 10 look back, for you know the prize and the crown are before you. Though I can scarce think so meanly of you as that you would be discouraged with the crackling of thorns under a pot. Be not high-minded, but fear. Preserve an equal temper of mind under whatever treatment you meet with from a not very just or well-natured world. Bear no more sail than is necessary, but steer steady. The less 15 you value yourselves for these unfashionable duties (as there is no such thing as works of supererogation), the more all good and wise men will value you, if they see your actions are of a piece; or which is infinitely more, he by whom actions and intentions are weighed will both accept, esteem, and reward you.[3]

Upon this encouragement we still continued to sit together as 20 usual; to confirm one another as well as we could in our resolutions to communicate as often as we had an opportunity, which is here once a week; and to do what service we could to our acquaintance, the prisoners, and two or three poor families in the town. But the outcry daily increasing, that we might show what ground there 25 was for it, we proposed to our friends or opponents, as we had opportunity, these or the like questions:

I. Whether it does not concern all men of all conditions to imitate him as much as they can who went about doing good?[4]

Whether all Christians are not concerned in that command, 'While we have 30 time, let us do good to all men'?[5]

Whether we shall not be more happy hereafter the more good we do now?

Whether we can be happy at all hereafter unless we have, according to our power, fed the hungry, clothed the naked, visited those that are sick and in prison, and made all these actions subservient to a higher purpose, even the 35 saving of souls from death?

[1] 'Great is my glorying of you. I am filled with comfort. I am exceeding joyful.'
[2] Whitehead and *Journal*, 'God'.
[3] The letter as reproduced by Whitehead continues:
'I hear my son John has the honour of being styled "the father of the Holy Club". If it be so, I am sure I must be the grandfather of it; and I need not say that I had rather any of my sons should be so dignified and distinguished than to have the title of "His Holiness".'
[4] Acts 10: 38.
[5] Cf. Gal. 6: 10.

Whether it be not our bounden duty always to remember that he did more for us than we can do for him, who assures us, 'Inasmuch as ye have done it to one of the least of these my brethren, ye have done it unto me.'[1]

II. Whether upon these considerations we may not try to do good to our ac-
5 quaintance? Particularly whether we may not try to convince them of the necessity of being Christians?

Whether of the consequent necessity of being scholars?

Whether of the necessity of method and industry in order to either learning or virtue?

10 Whether we may not try to persuade them to confirm and increase their industry by communicating as often as they can?

Whether we may not mention to them the authors whom we conceive to have wrote best on these subjects?

Whether we may not assist them as we are able, from time to time, to form
15 resolutions upon what they read in those authors, and to execute them with steadiness and perseverance?

III. Whether upon the considerations above mentioned we may not try to do good to those that are hungry, naked, or sick? In particular whether if we know any necessitous family, we may not give them a little food, clothes, or physic
20 as they want?

Whether we may not give them, if they can read, a Bible, Common Prayer Book, or *Whole Duty of Man*?

Whether we may not now and then inquire how they have used them, explain what they don't understand, and enforce what they do?

25 Whether we may not enforce upon them more especially the necessity of private prayer, and of frequenting the church and sacrament?

Whether we may not contribute what little we are able toward having their children clothed and taught to read?

Whether we may not take care that they be taught their catechism, and short
30 prayers for morning and evening?

IV. Lastly, whether upon the considerations above mentioned we may not try to do good to those that are in prison? In particular whether we may not release such well-disposed persons as remain in prison for small sums?

Whether we may not lend smaller sums to those that are of any trade, that
35 they may procure themselves tools and materials to work with?

Whether we may not give to them who appear to want it most a little money, or clothes, or physic?

Whether we may not supply as many as are serious enough to read them with a Bible and *Whole Duty of Man*?

40 Whether we may not, as we have opportunity, explain and enforce these upon them especially with respect to public and private prayer and the blessed sacrament?

I do not remember that we met with any person who answered any of these questions in the negative, or who even doubted whether

---

[1] Matt. 25: 35–6, 40.

it were not lawful to apply to this use that time and money which we should else have spent in other diversions. But several we met with who increased our little stock of money for the prisoners and the poor, by subscribing something quarterly to it. So that the more persons we proposed our designs to, the more were we confirmed 5 in the belief of their innocency, and the more determined to pursue them in spite of the ridicule which increased fast upon us during the winter. However, in spring I thought it could not be improper to desire farther instructions from those who were wiser and better than ourselves; and accordingly (on May 18, 1731) I wrote a particu- 10 lar account of all our proceedings to a clergyman of known wisdom and integrity.[1] After having informed him of all the branches of our design as clearly and simply as I could, I next acquainted him with the success it had met with, in the following words:

[May 18, 1731] 15

Almost as soon as we had made our first attempts this way, some of the men of wit in Christ Church entered the lists against us, and between mirth and anger made a pretty many reflections upon the Sacramentarians, as they were pleased to call us. Soon after their allies at Merton changed our title, and did us the honour of styling us, The Holy Club. But most of them being persons of well- 20 known characters, they had not the good fortune to gain any proselytes from the sacrament, till a gentleman eminent for learning, and well esteemed for piety,[2] joining them, told his nephew that if he dared to go to the weekly communion any longer he would immediately turn him out of doors. That argument indeed had no success. The young gentleman communicated the next week. 25 Upon which his uncle, having again tried to convince him that he was in the wrong way, by shaking him by the throat to no purpose, changed his method, and by mildness prevailed upon him to absent from it the Sunday following, as he had done five Sundays in six ever since. This much delighted our gay opponents, who increased their numbers apace, especially when shortly after 30 one of the seniors of the college, having been with the doctor, upon his return from him, sent for two young gentleman severally who had communicated weekly for some time, and was so successful in his exhortations that for the future they proposed to do it only three times a year. About this time there was a meeting (as one who was present at it informed your son) of several of the 35 officers and seniors of the college, wherein it was consulted what would be the speediest way to stop the progress of enthusiasm in it. The result we know not, only it was soon publicly reported that 'Dr. [Terry] and the censors were going

---

[1] Orig., ((as eminent for wisdom and integrity as most private men in the three kingdoms)). Wesley's diary for May 18, 1731, makes it clear that this was the letter then written to the Revd. Joseph Hoole, the vicar of Haxey.

[2] Orig. continues, ((a Doctor in Divinity)). In Wesley's personal copy of his *Works* he filled in the name as 'Terry', i.e. Dr. Thomas Terry, Canon of Christ Church, for whom see above, p. 279.

to blow up the Godly Club'. (This was now our common title, though we were sometimes dignified with that of the Enthusiasts, or the Reforming Club).

Part of the answer I received was as follows:

[May 29?, 1731]

5 Good sir,

A pretty while after the date yours came to my hand. I waived my answer till I had an opportunity of consulting your father, who upon all accounts is a more proper judge of the affair than I am. But I could never find a fit occasion for it. As to my own sense of the matter, I confess I cannot but heartily approve that
10 serious and religious turn of mind that prompts you and your associates to those pious and charitable offices; and can have no notion of that man's religion, or concern for the honour of the university, that opposes you, as far as your design respects the colleges. I should be loath to send a son of mine to any seminary where his conversing with virtuous young men, whose professed
15 design of meeting together at proper times was to assist each other in forming good resolutions, and encouraging one another to execute them with constancy and steadiness, was inconsistent with any received maxims or rules of life among the members. As to the other branch of your design, as the town is divided into parishes, each of which has its proper incumbent, and as there is probably
20 an ecclesiastic who has the spiritual charge of the prisoners, prudence may direct you to consult them. For though I dare not say you would be too officious should you of your own mere motion seek out the persons that want your instructions and charitable contributions, yet should you have the concurrence of their proper pastor your good offices would be more regular, and less liable to censure.

25 Your son was now at Holt. However, we continued to meet at our usual times, though our little affairs went on but heavily without him. But at our return from Lincolnshire in September we had the pleasure of seeing him again, when, though he could not be so active with us as formerly, yet we were exceeding glad to spend what time
30 we could in talking and reading with him. It was a little before this time my brother and I were at London, when going into a bookseller's shop (Mr. Rivington[1] in St. Paul's Church Yard), after some other conversation he asked us whether we lived in town; and upon our answering, 'No, at Oxford': 'Then, gentlemen', said he, 'let me
35 earnestly recommend to your acquaintance a friend I have there, Mr. Clayton of Brazen-nose.' Of this, having small leisure for contract-

[1] Charles Rivington (1688-1742), the leading theological publisher of the day, who took financial responsibility for several of Wesley's early literary ventures, notably his edition of *The Christian's Pattern* (1735; see *Bibliog*, No. 4). Wesley's diary first notes writing to Rivington on Aug. 9, 1731, and from the summer of 1732 they were corresponding three or four times a month until the Wesley brothers left for Georgia, after which the correspondence gradually tailed off, and Rivington seems to have entertained some doubts about the respectability of the Methodists. Clayton wrote to Wesley on Aug. 1, 1732, care of Rivington.

ing new acquaintance, we took no[1] notice for the present. But in the spring (April 20) Mr. Clayton meeting me in the street, and giving Mr. Rivington's service, I desired his company to my room, and there commenced our acquaintance. At the first opportunity I acquainted him with our whole design, which he immediately and 5 heartily closed with; and not long after, Mr. M[organ] having then left Oxford, we fixed two evenings in a week to meet on, partly to talk upon that subject, and partly to read something in practical divinity.

The two points whereunto by the blessing of God and your son's 10 help we had before attained, we still endeavoured to hold fast: I mean, the doing what good we can, and in order thereto communicating as oft as we have an opportunity. To these, by the advice of Mr. Clayton, we have added a third, the observing the fasts of the Church,[2] the general neglect of which we can by no means apprehend to be 15 a lawful excuse for neglecting them. And in the resolution to adhere to these, and all things else which we are convinced God requires at our hands, we trust that we shall persevere, till he calls us too to give an account of our stewardship.[3] As for the names of Methodists, Supererogation men, and so on, with which some of our neighbours 20 are pleased to compliment us, we do not conceive ourselves under any obligation to regard them, much less to take them for arguments. To the law and to the testimony[4] we appeal, whereby we ought to be judged.[5] If by these it can be proved that we are in an error, we will immediately and gladly retract it. If not, we have not so learned 25 Christ as to renounce any part of his service, though men should say all manner of evil against us,[6] with more judgment, and as little truth, as hitherto. We do, indeed, use all the lawful means we know to prevent the good which is in us from being evil spoken of;[7] but if the neglect of known duties be the one condition of securing our 30 reputation, why, fare it well.—We know whom we have believed,[8] and what we thus lay out he will pay us again. Your son already stands before the judgment-seat of him who judges righteous judgment,[9] at the brightness of whose presence the clouds remove.[10] His eyes are open, and he sees clearly whether it was 'blind zeal 35 and a thorough mistake of true religion that hurried him on in the

---

[1] Orig., ((little)), altered in John's hand to 'no', the reading of the *Journal*.
[2] Orig., 'of the Church ((of England and the Church Catholic))'.
[3] See Luke 16: 2.   [4] Isa. 8: 20.   [5] See Acts 25: 10.
[6] See Matt. 5: 11.   [7] See Rom. 14: 16.   [8] See 2 Tim. 1: 12.
[9] See John 7: 24.   [10] See Ps. 18: 12 (B.C.P.).

error of his way',[1] or whether he acted like a faithful and wise servant, who from a just sense that his time was short, made haste to finish his work before his Lord's coming, that when laid in the balance he might not be found wanting.[2]

5   I have now largely and plainly laid before you the real ground of all the strange outcry you have heard; and am not without hope that by this fairer representation of it than you probably ever read before both you and the clergyman you formerly mentioned may have a more favourable opinion of a good cause, though under an ill name.

10   Whether you have or no, I shall ever acknowledge my best services to be due to yourself and your family, both for the generous assistance you have given my father,[3] and for the invaluable advantages your son has (under God) bestowed on, sir, your ever obliged, and most obedient servant,

15   [John Wesley]

Source: Morgan MSS, i.e. CW's transcript, with JW's alterations, pp. 15-35, collated with the printed version prefixed to JWJ (1740).

From Mrs. Susanna Wesley[4]

Oct. 25 [1]732

Dear Jacky

I was very glad to hear ye got safe to Oxford, and should have told you so sooner had I been at liberty from pain of body, and other severer trials not

20   convenient to mention. Let everyone enjoy the present hour. Age, and successive troubles, are sufficient to convince any reasonable man that 'tis a much wiser and safer way to deprecate great afflictions than to pray for them; and that our Lord well knew what was in man when he directed us to pray, 'Lead us not into temptation.'

25   I think heretic Clark, in his exposition on the Lord's Prayer, is more in the right than Castaniza concerning temptations. His words are as follow: 'We are encouraged to glory in tribulation, and to count it all joy when we fall into divers

---

[1] Cf. Morgan's letter of Mar. 15, 1732, to his son William: 'I could not but advise with a wise, pious, and learned clergyman. He told me that he has known the worst of consequences follow from such blind zeal, and plainly satisfied me that it was a thorough mistake of true piety and religion . . . He concluded that . . . as soon as your judgment improved . . . you would see the error of the way you was in . . .'

[2] Cf. Dan. 5: 27.

[3] Richard Morgan subscribed for five copies of Samuel Wesley's volume on Job (see diary, June 21, 1734: 'Sent Mr. Morgan five, from 241 to 245'); cf. letter of Aug. 27, 1734, pp. 393-4 below.

[4] Replying to John's of Sept. 25, to whose contents it offers many clues.

temptations, etc. Nevertheless 'tis carefully to be observed that when the Scripture speaks on this manner concerning rejoicing in temptations, it always considers them under this vein, as being experienced, and already in great measure overcome. For otherwise, as to temptations in general, temptations unexperienced, of which we know the danger but not the success, our Saviour teaches us to 5 pray, Lead us not into temptation. And again, Watch and pray, lest ye enter into temptation. Our nature is frail, our passions strong, our wills biased; and our security, generally speaking, consists much more certainly in avoiding great temptations than in conquering them. Wherefore we ought continually to pray that God would be pleased so to order and direct things in this probation state 10 as not to suffer us to be tempted above what we are able, but that he would with the temptation also make a way to escape, that we may be able to bear it. Our Lord directed his disciples, when they were persecuted in one city, to flee into another. And they who refuse to do it when it is in their power lead themselves into temptation, and tempt God.' 15

I can't tell how you represented your case to Dr. Huntington. I have had occasion to make some observation in consumption, and am pretty certain that several symptoms of that distemper are beginning upon you, and that unless you take more care than you do, you'll put the matter past dispute in a little time. But take your own way. I have already given you up, as I have some before 20 which once were very dear to me. Charles, though I believe not in a consumption, is in a fine state of health for a man of two or three and twenty, that can't eat a full meal but he must presently throw it up again. 'Tis great pity that folks should be no wiser, and that they can't hit the mean in a case where it is so obvious to view that none can mistake it, which do not do it on purpose. 25

I heartily join with your small society in all their pious and charitable actions, which are intended for God's glory; and am glad to hear Mr. Clayton and Mr. Hall has met with desired success. May ye still in such good works go on, and prosper. Though absent in body, I am present with ye in spirit, and daily recommend and commit ye all to divine providence. You do well to wait on the 30 bishop, because 'tis a point of prudence and civility, though (if he be a good man) I can't think it in the power of anyone to prejudice him against you.

Your arguments against horse races do certainly conclude against masquerades, balls, plays, operas, and all such light and vain diversions, which, whether the gay people of the world will own it or no, does strongly confirm and strengthen 35 the lust of the flesh, the lust of the eye, and the pride of life; all which we must renounce, or renounce our God, and hope of eternal salvation. I will not say 'tis impossible for a person to have any sense of religion which frequents those vile assemblies, but I never throughout the course of my long life knew so much as one serious Christian that did. Nor can I see how a lover of God can have any 40 relish for such vain amusements.

The Life of God in the Soul of Man is an excellent good book, and was an acquaintance of mine many years ago; but I have unfortunately lost it. There's many good things in Castaniza, more in Baxter, yet are neither without faults, which I overlook for the sake of their virtues; nor can I say of all the books of 45 divinity I have read which is the best; one is best at one time, one at another, according to the temper and disposition of the mind.

Mr. Horbery is for Oxford soon, by whom if I can I will write to Mr.

Whitelamb, to whom pray give my love and service, and tell him, though I can't show my esteem for him all the ways I would, yet I daily remember him. I must tell ye, Mr. John Wesley, Fellow of Lincoln, and Mr. Charles Wesley, Student of Christ Church, that ye are two scrubby travellers, and sink your
5 characters strangely by eating nothing on the road, ⟨. . .⟩,[1] to save charges. I wonder ye are not ashamed of yourselves. Surely if ye will but give yourselves leave to think a little, ye will return to a better mind.

Your sisters send their love to you and Charles, and I my love and blessing to ye both.

10 [Endorsement in hand of John Wesley: 'Eating on the road: J. Whitelamb: my father: Society' (in abbreviated script).]

Adieu.

Your father is in a very bad state of health; he sleeps little, and eats less. He seems not to have any apprehension of his approaching exit, but I fear he has
15 but a short time to live. 'Tis with much pain and difficulty that he performs divine service on the Lord's day, which sometimes he is forced to contract very much. Everybody observes his decay but himself, and people really seem much concerned both for him and his family.

The two girls, being uneasy in the present situation, do not apprehend the
20 sad consequences which (in all appearance) must attend his death so much as I think they ought to do; for as bad as they think their condition now, I doubt not it will be far worse when his head is laid.

Address: 'To The Revd. Mr Wesley, Fellow of Lincoln College, Oxon'
Postmark: indecipherable, and '30 OC'   *Charges*: ((4)), 'In all 7'   *Source*: Public Library, Melbourne, Australia.

From Richard Morgan, Sen.[2]

Nov. 25th, 1732

Revd sir,
25 Your favour of the 20th past was delayed in its passage, I believe, by contrary winds, or it had not been so long unanswered. I give entire credit to every thing and every fact you relate. It was ill judged of my poor son to take to fasting with[out] regard to his health, which I knew nothing of, or I should have advised him against it. He was inclined to piety and virtue from his infancy. I must own
30 I was much concerned at the strange accounts which were spread here of some extraordinary practices of a religious society which he had engaged in at Oxford, which you may be sure lost nothing in the carriage, lest through his youth and immaturity of judgment he might be hurried into zeals and enthusiastic notions that may prove pernicious. But now indeed that piety and holiness of
35 life which he practised affords me some comfort in the midst of my affliction for

[1] Parts of two lines of writing (about six words), have been clipped from the letter.
[2] A reply to Wesley's letter of Oct. 19, in spite of the anomaly in the dating. Possibly Wesley sent a covering letter dated Oct. 20 before transcribing the whole. See p. 335.

the loss of him, having full assurance of his being for ever happy. The good account you are pleased to give of your own and your friends' conduct in point of duty and religious offices, and the zealous approbation of them by the good old gentleman your father, signified in a manner and style becoming the best of men, reconciles and recommends that method of life to me, and makes me almost 5 wish that I were one amongst you. I am very much obliged to you for the great pains you have been at in transcribing so long and so particular an account of your transactions for my perusal, and shall be always ready to vindicate you from any calumny or aspersion that I shall hear cast upon you; I am much obliged for yours and your brother's great civilities and assistances to my dearest son. 10 I thank your brother Charles for his kind letter which I received, and the author of those lines you sent me, for the regard he has shown to his memory.[1] If ever I can be serviceable to any of you in this kingdom, I beg you will let me know, and I shall with the utmost pleasure and cheerfulness undertake your commands. I am, with respects to your brother, etc., sir, your most obliged, most obedient 15 humble servant,

Richd Morgan

Address: 'To the Revd Mr John Wesley, fellow of Lincoln College in Oxford' *Frank*: 'Hu. Armagh. These', i.e. Hugh Boulter (1672–1742), Archbishop of Armagh   *Postmarks*: 'DUBLIN' and '1 DE'   *Charges*: ((2)) and large scrawled 'FR[EE]'   *End* by J W: 'Mr Morgan, Senr/ Nov. 25, 1732' *Source*: MA; cf. Morgan MSS, pp. 35–7.

To Mrs. Susanna Wesley

[Feb. 15, 1733]

Dear mother

I am glad to hear that my father continues recovering, though it 20 can be but very slowly, considering how his strength is exhausted. 'Tis well if this fine spring does not betray him into a relapse, by tempting him out before his health is confirmed. Of poor Becky[2] my sister Molly says not one word, so I presume she is as she was; and hope I may make the same inference as to you, viz. that you are 25 only half tired to death.

The more I think of the reason you gave me at Epworth for speaking little upon religious subjects, the less it satisfies me. 'We shall all be of your mind when we are of your age.'[3] But who will assure

---

[1] The poem by the Wesleys' elder brother Samuel, 'On the death of Mr. Morgan of Christ Church', which John Wesley appended to the letter in the version published in his *Journal*, and which also appears in Charles Wesley's transcript of the correspondence.

[2] Apparently a maidservant in the Wesley household, Becky Maws.

[3] A quotation from his mother's letter to which he is replying (? Feb. 1), transposed (as so frequently in Wesley's quotations) into indirect speech.

us that we shall ever be of that age? Or suppose we should, is it[1] not better to be of that mind sooner? Is not a right faith of use at thirty as well as at sixty? And are not the actions that flow from a right faith as rewardable now as then? I trust they are; and do therefore 5 earnestly desire that whatever general or particular rules of life your own reflection and experience have suggested to you, I may be tried whether I will conform to them or no. If I do not, the blame lights on me. At this season especially[2] I would not neglect any help, for mortifying the flesh and the lusts thereof, for throwing off the affec- 10 tions of the earthly Adam, and putting on the image of the heavenly.[3]

If I am to be surrounded with the snares of flesh and blood yet many years, will you not give me the best advices to break through them that you can? If I, as well as you, am soon to be laid in the balance, so much the rather assist me, that I may not be found want- 15 ing.[4]

You observed when I was with you that I was very indifferent as [to] the having or not having Epworth living. I was indeed utterly unable to determine either way; and that for this reason: I knew if I could stand my ground here, and approve myself a faithful 20 minister of our blessed Jesus, by honour and dishonour, through evil report and good report, then there was not a place under heaven like this for improvement in every good work. But whether I co⟨uld⟩ stem the torrent which I saw then, but see now much m⟨ore,⟩ rolling down from all sides upon me, that I knew no⟨t. 'Tis⟩ true, 25 there is one who can yet either command the g⟨reat⟩ waterflood that it shall not come nigh me,[5] or mak⟨e a⟩ way for his redeemed to pass through. But then something must be done on my part; and should he give me even that most equitable condition, 'accord- ing to thy faith be it unto thee',[6] yet how shall I fulfil it? Why, he 30 will look to that, too—my father and you helping together in your prayers, that our faith fail us not! I am, dear mother, your dutiful and affectionate son,

John Wesley

Feb. 15, 1732/3 Oxon.

Source: MA.

[1] Orig., 'it is'.   [2] Lent, which began that year on Feb. 7.
[3] See Col. 3: 5; 1 Cor. 15: 45-9.   [4] See Dan. 5: 27.
[5] See Ps. 32: 7 (B.C.P.).   [6] Cf. Matt. 9: 29.

From Richard Morgan, Sen.

Feb. 17, 1732/3

Dear sir

I have your favour of the 3rd instant.[1] You judge right that I never received your brother's letter of the 4th of October, which if I had should not have lain unanswered. I did myself apprehend that he had been so kind as to write, and 5 that it had by some means miscarried, and therefore presumed to write to him to that purpose a post or two ago, before I received your last . . .

If you mean that I have duplicates here of any books my dear son left behind him at Christ Church from a printed catalogue I sent him of a study of books I had bought for him in Dublin, I made a present of that purchase to my daughter's 10 husband, who is a clergyman, so that I have none of those books left, and should be glad to make up a small study of those at Oxford, and some others he has himself, for my only son now living. But if there be duplicates there of any books, one of each sort is at your brother's service.

I assure you, sir, without any dissimulation or flattery, I rejoice sincerely 15 at the recovery of the good old gentleman, your father. And I really am concerned that the scorners of the university continue so malevolent. I could wish they would rather meet you at least halfway in imitation of piety and goodness. I must say that these censures have in a great measure ceased here, and I am comforted by my acquaintance in telling me that I should grieve the less from 20 the assurance we have of my dear son's happiness with God after such a course of piety and godliness that he had engaged in. I pray God to conduct us all to meet together in happiness hereafter. Be assured you shall never want a weak advocate in me to defend you against any calumny that I can hear you or your friends aspersed with. Pray my salutations to your good father when you write 25 to him, and your brother of Christ Church: for I am with great sincerity theirs, and, sir, your very affectionate servant,

Richard Morgan

Source: Morgan MSS, pp. 38–9.

From Richard Morgan, Sen.

[Mar. 10, 1732/3]

Dear sir   30

I am favoured with yours of the 28th past, and am very sorry to find by it that anything has happened to give you any uneasiness. I give you my word and honour that I never read or showed your letter to me of October last to any mortal, but laid it up safe, and have it so still; neither did I communicate to anyone the contents of my letter to my poor son, which you make mention of, 35 so that they must have come to be known by some other means in England. I have indeed taken occasion, to a very few with whom I had some discourse

[1] Probably Morgan had mistaken the date '8' for a '3' in Wesley's letter.

formerly on the subject of those reports then spread abroad of my son and his associates, to vindicate him and them from those aspersions, from the several hints and accounts you were so kind to furnish me with in your epistle, but never produced the letter itself. I am sure that both you and your learned friends in
5 England are much better judges how to manage the pamphlet you mention than I can pretend to be, and am the more at a loss to give any opinion concerning it because I am not able to collect from your letter whether it is intended as a satire or vindication.[1] I am apt to believe that you are so kind as to be under some concern lest if this pamphlet should fall in my way it might give me some
10 trouble. But pray let no such thought disturb you, for you fully satisfied me before in everything: nothing that your adversaries can say or write can alter my good opinion both of you and your actions. I am really sorry that your good designs should be so misrepresented and misconstrued. I hope in time they may meet with due rewards in this world; I am sure they will in the next.
15   . . . I wrote a few lines before to your brother . . . ;[2] and if ever it lies in my power to oblige either him or you I shall most cheerfully do it, for I am, with great sincerity, his, and, dear sir, your very affectionate humble servant,
                                                        Richd Morgan

Mar: 10: 1732/3

Source: Wesley House, Cambridge; cf. Morgan MSS, pp. 39–41, with some minor changes.

To the Revd. Samuel Wesley, Sen.

20   June 13, 1733
The effects of my last journey, I believe, will make me more cautious of staying any time from Oxford for the future,[3] at least till I have no pupils to take care of, which probably will be within a year or two. One of my young gentlemen told me at my return that
25 he was more and more afraid of singularity; another that he had read an excellent piece of Mr. Locke's, which had convinced him of the mischief of regarding authority.[4] Both of them agreed that the observing of Wednesday as a fast was an unnecessary singularity,

---

[1] *The Oxford Methodists: being some account of a society of young gentlemen in that city, so denominated; setting forth their rise, views, and designs. With some occasional remarks on a letter inserted in* Fog's Journal *of December 9th, relating to them. In a letter from a gentleman near Oxford to his friend at London*, London, Roberts, 1733; this was published in February.

[2] See Morgan's letter of Feb. 17, 1733.

[3] Wesley had been at Epworth, and beyond to Manchester, walking both ways, from May 14 to June 9.

[4] John Locke (1632–1704); cf. *An Essay Concerning Human Understanding*, IV. xx. 17, on the error of 'giving up our assent to the common received opinions either of our friends or party, neighbourhood or country'.

the Catholic Church (that is, the majority of it) having long since
repealed by contrary custom the injunction she formerly gave
concerning it. A third, who could not yield to this argument, has
been convinced by a fever and Dr. Frewin.[1] Our seven and twenty
communicants at St. Mary's were on Monday shrunk to five; and
the day before the last of Mr. Clayton's pupils who continued with
us informed me that he did not design to meet us any more.[2]

My ill success, as they call it, seems to be what has frightened
everyone away from a falling house. On Sunday I was considering
the matter a little more nearly; and imagined that all the ill consequences of my singularity were reducible to three: diminution of
fortune, loss of friends, and of reputation. As to my fortune I well
know, though perhaps others do not, that I could not have borne a
larger than I have; and as for that most plausible excuse for desiring
it, 'While I have so little I cannot do the good I would', I ask, Can
you do the good God would have you do? It is enough. Look no
further. For friends, they were either trifling or serious. If triflers,
fare them well; a noble escape. If serious, those who are more serious
are left, whom the others would rather have opposed than forwarded
in the service they have done, and still do us. If it be said, But these
may leave you, too, for they are no firmer than the others were.
First, I doubt that fact; but next, suppose they should, we hope then
they would only teach us a nobler and harder lesson than any they
have done hitherto: 'It is better to trust in the Lord than to put any
confidence in man.'[3] And as for reputation, though it be a glorious
instrument of advancing our Master's service, yet there is a better
than that, a 'clean heart',[4] a single eye, a soul full of God! A fair
exchange, if by the loss of reputation we can purchase the lowest
degree of purity of heart! We beg my mother and you would not
cease to work together with us, that whatever we may lose, we may
gain this; and that having tasted of this good gift,[5] we may count all
things else but dung and dross in comparison of it . . . .[6]

Source: Whitehead, I. 457-8.

[1] Richard Frewin, M.D., (1681?-1761), of Christ Church, Camden professor of
ancient history, who also had an excellent reputation as a physician.
[2] Robert Moreton, of Brasenose College.
[3] Ps. 118: 8.   [4] Ps. 51: 10.
[5] See Heb. 6: 4-5.   [6] See Phil. 3: 8.

From the Revd. John Clayton

July [25], 1733

Revd. and dear sir

I have been thinking upon the two points which you proposed to my consideration in your last,[1] and must acknowledge myself to be utterly unable to form
5 any judgment upon them which will be serviceable to you. My own rule was to
spend an hour every Friday in looking over my diary, and observing the difference between it and the preceding week. [. . .] As to your question about
Saturday, I can only answer it by giving an account how I spend it. I do not
look upon it as a preparation for Sunday, but as a festival itself; and therefore
10 I have continued festival prayers for the three primitive hours and for morning
and evening, from the Apostolical Constitutions, which I think I communicated
to you whilst I was at Oxford. I look upon Friday as my preparation for the
celebration of both the sabbath and the Lord's day. [. . .]

Dr. Deacon gives his humble service to you, and lets you know that the wor-
15 ship and discipline of the Primitive Church have taken up so much of his time
that he has never read the Fathers with a particular view to their moral doctrines,
and therefore cannot furnish you with the testimonies you want out of his
collections. However, if you will give me a month's time, I will try what I can
do for you. [. . .]

20 I was at Dr. Deacon's when your letter came to hand, and we had a deal of
talk about your scheme of avowing yourselves a society, and fixing upon a set of
rules. The Doctor seemed to think you had better let it alone. For to what end
would it serve? It would be no additional tie upon yourselves, and perhaps a
snare for the consciences of those weak brethren that might choose to come among
25 you. Observing the stations and weekly communion are duties which stand
upon a much higher footing than a rule of a society; and they who can set aside
the command of God and the authority of his Church will hardly, I doubt, be
tied by the rules of a private society. As to the mixture, Mr. Colley told me he
would assure me it was constantly used at Christ Church. However, if you have
30 reason to doubt it, I would have you inquire; but I cannot think the want of it
a reason for not communicating. If I could receive where the mixture was used
I would, and therefore I used to prefer the Castle to Christ Church. [. . .]

I am, dear sir, your most affectionate friend and servant, J. Clayton.

Address: To the Revd. Mr. Wesley, Fellow of Lincoln College, Oxon   *Post-*
marks: 'MAN/CHESTER', '27 IY'   *Charges*: ((4)), 'In all 7'   *End*
by JW: 'July 1733' and 'Clat. July 1733'   *Source*: MA.

[1] Probably of July 11, not extant, rather than that of June 27.

To the Revd. John Goole[1]

[July 29, 1733]

Sir

I sent Mr. Boyce word yesterday that I was apt to think you were so far from the desire of revenge, which he had been informed you everywhere showed, that if he could propose any other way of 5 satisfying that desire of clearing your reputation which a Christian ought to have, you would yet desist from your design of publishing your Case . . .[2]

Source: John Goole, *The Contract Violated*, pp. vi–vii, dated from internal evidence and Wesley's diary.

[1] In his diary summaries for 1731 Wesley noted: 'July 29. Mr. B. married Mr. G.'s wife.' This epitomizes a strange emotional and legal tangle which pre-figured Wesley's own relations with Grace Murray nearly twenty years later. Using the Office of Matrimony in the Book of Common Prayer 'Mr. G.' had secretly entered into a 'most binding and sacred engagement' with Margaret Hudson of Eynsham, daughter of the late librarian of the Bodleian, agreeing to defer a public ceremony until she was twenty-one. 'Mr. G.' was the vicar of Eynsham, John Goole, a middle-aged widower. Until the reforms of the Marriage Act of 1754 this constituted a legal marriage. Margaret Hudson was then pushed by her mother into what was technically a bigamous marriage with a much younger and more eligible man, John Boyce, son of Sir John Boyce, three times Mayor of Oxford. Goole sued for restitution, won in the Court of Common Pleas, but lost the final decision two years later in the Court of Arches, when Margaret Hudson was nearing the birth of her second child—a fact which appeared to form a strong though irrelevant argument in her favour. Boyce was one of Wesley's pupils, and for two years Wesley served as a go-between for the contending parties. Goole prepared his vindication, planning to publish it under the title, *The Contract Violated*, and on July 26, 1733, sent the manuscript to Wesley, with the request that he would inform Boyce of Goole's intention to publish.

[2] The preface to Goole's *Contract Violated* continues: 'This letter I answered the Saturday following [Aug. 4], but received no reply till the 18th of August, when I was favoured with a second letter from Mr. Wesley, to which I returned a speedy answer . . . On the 11th of September I called upon him, and told him that I had heard nothing from him since the 18th of August, whereupon he said, "There must have been a fault in the Witney post, for I have sent you a third letter" [which is not noted in Wesley's diary], and then added, "Mr. Boyce waits for and desires to see your proposals." ' For fuller details see Frank Baker, 'John Wesley's First Marriage' (*London Quarterly Review*, Oct., 1967, pp. 305–15).

To Mrs. Susanna Wesley[1]

[Aug. 17, 1733]

The thing that gives offence here is the being singular with regard to time, expense, and company. This is evident beyond exception from the case of Mr. Smith, one of our fellows;[2] who no sooner
5 began to husband his time, to retrench unnecessary expenses, and to avoid his irreligious acquaintance, but he was set upon by not only all these acquaintance but many others, too, as if he had entered into a conspiracy to cut all their throats, though to this day he has not advised any single person, unless in a word or two, and by
10 accident, to act as he did in any of those instances.

It is true, indeed, that 'the devil hates offensive war most, and that whoever tries to rescue more than his own soul from his hands will have more enemies, and meet with greater opposition, than if he was content with "having his own life for a prey"'. That I try
15 to do this is likewise certain; but I cannot say whether I 'rigorously impose any observances on others' till I know what that phrase means. What I do is this. When I am entrusted with a person who is first to understand and practise, and then to teach the law of Christ, I endeavour by an intermixture of reading and conversation
20 to show him what that law is; that is, to renounce all insubordinate love of the world, and to love and obey God with all his strength. When he appears seriously sensible of this I propose to him the means God hath commanded him to use in order to that end; and a week or a month or a year after, as the state of his soul seems to require it,
25 the several prudential means recommended by wise and good men. As to the times, order, measure, and manner, wherein these are to be proposed, I depend upon the Holy Spirit to direct me, in and by my own experience and reflection, joined to the advices of my religious friends here and elsewhere. Only two rules it is my principle to
30 observe in all cases: first, to begin, continue, and end all my advices in the spirit of meekness,[3] as knowing that 'the wrath' or severity 'of man worketh not the righteousness of God';[4] and secondly, to add

---

[1] Wesley's diary for Aug. 16, 1733, noted that at 4 p.m. he received an 'angry letter from my mother', criticizing his rigorous efforts to recapture lost ground with his pupils. In this speedy reply he quotes passages from her letter.

[2] See note, Aug. 1, 1732.

[3] 1 Cor. 4: 21; Gal. 6: 1.   [4] Jas. 1: 20.

to meekness, long-suffering, in pursuance of a rule which I fixed long since—'never to give up anyone till I have tried him at least ten years. How long hath God had pity on thee!'[1]

If the wise and good will believe those falsehoods which the bad invent because I endeavour to save myself and my friends from them, then I shall lose my reputation, even among them, for (though not perhaps good, yet) the best actions I ever did in my life. This is the very case. I try to act as my Lord commands: ill men say all manner of evil of me, and good men believe them. There is a way, and there is but one, of making my peace. God forbid I should ever take it. I have as many pupils as I need, and as many friends. When more are better for me I shall have more. If I have no more pupils after these are gone from me, I shall then be glad of a curacy near you. If I have, I shall take it as a signal that I am to remain here. Whether here or there, my desire is to know and feel that I am nothing, that I have nothing, and that I can do nothing. For whenever I am empty of myself, then know I of a surety that neither friends nor foes, nor any creature, can hinder me from being 'filled with all the fullness of God'.[2] Let not my father's or your prayers be ever slack in behalf of your affectionate son.

Source: Whitehead, I. 459–60.

From the Revd. John Clayton[3]

Manch[ester], Septr. 10, 1733

Revd. and dear sir

[. . .] Dr. Deacon tells me that he had no view in fixing the Psalms for common days, but after reading your letter is convinced of the expediency of serving any of those three ends you mention. The feasts and fasts were the days that he principally regarded; but he would take it as a favour from you, would you communicate to me any improvements you may possibly make in it. He thinks your third rule would be most expedient, namely to put together such Psalms as best explain and illustrate each other. [. . .] His order for reading the Psalter

---

[1] See the opening page of Wesley's diary for 1729–32: 'March 1, 1730/1. Never to give anyone up till either (1), he disclaims my help *totidem verbis* ['in so many words'], or (2), I have tried him ten years. How long has God had pity on thee!'

[2] Eph. 3: 19.

[3] Replying to Wesley's of Aug. 29, to which it offers some clues.

is likely soon to see the light, being to be published with a collection of Primitive
Devotions, both public and private, which is even now in the press.¹
   Poor Miss Potter.² I wonder not that she is fallen; where humility is not the
foundation the superstructure cannot be good. [. . .] Methinks, though, I would
5 not persuade you to leave off reading with her. Who knows whether you may
not again raise her to the eminence from which she is fallen? [. . .]
   As to reading the ancients, I fancy Cotelerii *Bibliotheca Patrum Apostolicorum*
would be the best book to begin with. [. . .] The Apostolic Canons are learnedly
defended by Bishop Beveridge, and they sufficiently vindicate the Constitu-
10 tions. [. . .]
   And now for the last page of your letter. I would answer it, and yet for my
unworthiness I dare not, for my ignorance I cannot. How should I direct my
instructor in the school of Christ, or teach you who am but a babe in religion?
However, I must be free to tell you my sentiments of what you inquire about. On
15 Wednesdays and Fridays I have for some time past used the office for Passion
week out of Spinckes' *Devotions*. [. . .] Refer your last question to Mr. Law.
I dare not give directions for spending that time which I consume in bed, nor
teach you that rise at four, when I indulge myself in sleep till five. Dear sir,
pray for me that I may press forward in the path of perfection, and at length
20 attain the land of everlasting life. Adieu.

J.C.

   [. . .]

Address: 'To the Revd. Mr. Wesley, Fellow of Lincoln Col:, Oxon:'   *Postmarks*: 'MAN/CHESTER', '14/SE'   *Charges*: ((4)), 'In all 7'   *End
by JW*: 'Cl. Sept. 10, 1733 / of the Fathers'   *Source*: MA; cf. Tyerm (OM),
pp. 35-8.

   ¹ *A Compleat Collection of Devotions, both publick and private; taken from the Apostolical Constitutions, the Ancient Liturgies, and the Common Prayer Book of the Church of
England*, London, for the author, 1734. In the Appendix (pp. 72-4) Deacon published
an extract from Wesley's 'Essay upon the Stationary Fasts'.
   ² A Methodist group for Oxford townspeople had been meeting in her home, under
Wesley's oversight, since February, 1733, though by the end of the year it had become
either defunct or quite independent of him. (See Heitzenrater, pp. 212-13, 244, 290,
341.) Wesley had written to her on Aug. 31, 1733, and apparently had informed Clayton
of his disappointment in her. Bishop John Potter had a large family, but rather than being one of his close relations it seems likely that Miss Potter was a member of one of
several old Oxford families of that name; the same was probably true of Sally Potter,
who attended on occasion. She may well have been related to the Revd. Christopher
Potter of Holywell, Oxford, whose son Charles had been one of Wesley's Christ Church
friends, matriculating there on Dec. 9, 1720, and graduating M.A. (like Wesley) in 1727.

From Richard Morgan, Sen.[1]

Dublin, Nov. 22, 1733

Revd. sir

I had the favour of yours, and am very thankful for your care and tenderness about my son, who I am sure will observe your advice and directions in everything. My concern about my only son brings the misfortunes of my other son 5 fresh into my mind, and obliges me now to impart to you, and only to you, what I have hitherto concealed from all men, as far as it could be kept secret.

After he had spent about six weeks with me in Dublin, and the physicians having agreed that the air at Oxford was better for his health than the Irish air, when I was obliged to take a journey with my Lord Primate into his diocese 10

[1] On Sept. 6, 1733, Richard Morgan had written to Charles Wesley: 'Having demonstration of yours and your brother's sincerity and friendship, I desire your consulting together, and to give me your opinion in this nice point. I make no doubt but you have heard from my dear son Will that I have one other, now my only son. It is now three years and a quarter since he left school, having been then fit to enter the university, and at least as good a scholar as his brother was when he went to Oxford. I then purchased an office for him in the law, which diverted me from sending him to the university. I fear he has read but very little of Greek or Latin since, and that he has forgot a great deal of what he had learned at school; but I don't think his parts very bad. He was nineteen years of age last July, and is very lusty of his age, I believe 5 foot 10 inches high. He has been somewhat gay, and gone sometimes to plays and balls, but addicted to no vice. He has often wished rather to have been put forward in his learning than to stick to an office, which if practicable I am now inclined to indulge him in. Then pray be so kind as to give me yours and your brother's opinion, whether in two years he may attain to a tolerable knowledge of the Latin and logic, and what other learning you think proper to qualify him for the study of the law, that he may then commence in the Inns of Court.' In a PS. he added: 'Pray don't delay favouring me with your answer about my son. The more I think of this new scheme, the fonder I am of it, and therefore would lose no more time.' On Oct. 20 he wrote to Charles: 'Yours and your brother's favours of the 14th September I received, and most greatly esteem the candour, generosity, and apparent integrity of both of you. I readily acquiesce under your opinions, and I expect that my son will sail tomorrow to make the best of his way to Oxford. [. . .] I am willing to comply with his desires, and desire he may be entered a Gentleman Commoner of Lincoln under my good friend your brother's tuition. [. . .] He has a bad sight, [. . .] so that he will require a good print and the use of glasses in his private reading. [. . .] I have resolved to pay his tutor ten guineas a year, and I beg that a proper chamber may be provided for him against his coming. I shall write by myself to your brother, to whom this is designed in conjunction with you.' The young man arrived in Oxford on Oct. 30, flouting university statutes by bringing a greyhound with him, causing Wesley to note in his diary, 'Ill prospect'. Wesley found that setting him straight was an unrewarding task, and in reporting a modicum of progress to his father on Nov. 6 also urged that greater strictness might be needed. This is the father's reply to that letter, of which not even a copy has survived, although Charles Wesley reserved pp. 47-8 in his notebook for such a copy. Not until Morgan's letter of Jan. 31, 1734, however, did he make clear to Wesley that his sudden switch to a description of William Morgan's death was intended as a device to secure Wesley's sympathy, so as to relax what he feared might be Wesley's undue restrictions upon his son Richard. (Cf. Heitzenrater, pp. 232-42.)

my dear son was to set out on his journey to England the same day, which he accordingly did. He rode an easy pad, and was to make easy journeys through part of this kingdom to see some relations in the way, and to take shipping at Cork, from which there is a short passage to Bristol, and from thence the journey
5 not great to Oxford.

He travelled twelve miles the first day, attended by that careful servant that was with him at Oxford; the servant observed him to act and talk lightly and incoherently that day. He slept little or none all night, but often cried out that the house was in fire, and used other wild expressions.

10 The second day he grew worse, threw his bridle over the horse's head, and would neither guide him himself nor let the man guide him, whom he charged to stay behind, saying that God would guide him. The horse turned about, went in side roads, and went to a disused quarry filled with water to drink, when my poor child fell off, and had then like to have been lost, the servant not
15 daring to do but as he bid him, whom he often beat and struck. The servant then finding him deprived of all understanding, and outrageous, by great art and management brought him back to Dublin.

Two of our most eminent physicians, and the Surgeon General, were brought to attend him. An express was sent after me, with whom I hastened back to
20 town. He was put into a room [up] two pair of stairs, and the sashes nailed down, yet he found an opportunity to run to one of the windows, tore it down, though nailed, and was more than half out before he could be catched, but was happily saved. He was raging mad, and three men set over him to watch him and hold, and by the direction of the physicians he was threatened with ropes and
25 chains, which were produced to him and rattled.

In his madness he used frequently to say that enthusiasm was his madness, repeated often, 'O religious madness!' that they had hindered him from being now with God—meaning their hindering him from throwing himself out at the window—and named some other persons and things that I shan't mention,
30 but in his greatest rage never cursed or swore, or used any profane expressions. Some have told me since that they looked upon him to be disordered for some time before in his head, but God was pleased to take him to himself in seven days' time, which no doubt the blisterings and severities used by the physicians and surgeon for his recovery precipitated.

35 These are melancholy reflections, which makes me earnestly desire that my surviving son should not go into those over-zealous ways which (as is apprehended) contributed to this great misfortune which finished my other son. I would have him live a sober, virtuous, and religious life, and to go to church and sacraments according to the statutes and customs of his college; but for young
40 people to pretend to be more pure and holy than the rest of mankind is a dangerous experiment. As to charitable subscriptions and contributions, I wholly debar him from making any, because he has not one shilling of his own but what I give him, which I appropriate wholly to his maintenance, education, and moderate and inoffensive recreation and pleasures, and I believe, as a casuist,
45 you will agree with me that it is injustice, and consequently sinful, rather than virtue, to apply my money any other way than as I appropriate it. He must leave me to measure out my own charities, and to distribute them in such manner and proportion as I shall think proper. I hope you will not suspect from anything I

have said that I intend the least reflection or disrespect to you, for if I did not think very well of you, and had not a great opinion of your conduct and abilities, I should not put my only son under your tuition, which I think is the best proof a man can give of his good esteem and opinion of another.

The tragical account given you of my poor deceased son, my son Richard can 5 inform you of as well as I, which I charged him to say nothing of at Oxford, but now he may to you if you think proper to inquire of him about it; and I hope I may be excused for being solicitous to prevent my present son's falling into extremes, which it is *thought* were so prejudicial to my other. I sent a bill of £50 by the last post to Mr. James Huey, merchant in Aldermanbury, London, 10 with directions to transmit the value to you, which I hope is done. I long to have Mr. Lasher paid. As I mentioned in my former letter to you, I shall begrudge no money that is for my son's benefit and advantage, who I would have live as decently as other gents of his station. I am very desirous that he should keep a regular account, that he may attain to a habit of it, knowing the great use and 15 benefit of accounts to all men. I shall depend upon your letting me know when a further supply will be wanting. Pray my respects to your brother, and believe me to be your very affect[ionate] and most humble servant,

Richd Morgan

End by JW: 'Death of Mr. Mo[rgan]!'   *Source*: MA; cf. with Morgan MSS, pp. 49–52.
N.B. There is no paragraphing in either original or transcript.

To Richard Morgan, Sen.[1]

Dec. 17, 1733 20

Sir

The bank-note sent by Mr. Huey was exchanged today; I have paid Mr. Lasher[2] £11. 17s. 6d. of the £50 (and the £9 in my brother's hands), the bursar £24 for caution-money, and 40s., the usual fee for his admission into the common room.[3] Mr. Morgan usually 25 rises about six, and has not yet been wanting in diligence. He seldom goes out of college, unless upon business or to walk for his health,

[1] Answering Richard Morgan's of Nov. 22.
[2] The two brothers were clearing up William Morgan's financial affairs. On Oct. 20 Mr. Lasher's bill (apparently connected with the carriage of his books and other possessions to Dublin) amounted to £20. 7s. 6d., to which was to be added an unknown amount for customs charges. On Oct. 20 Charles Wesley already had £9. 5s. 9d. towards this, and by now more had accrued, so that from the £50 sent by Morgan John Wesley needed to pay only £11. 17s. 6d.; after the college charges also had been met, he still retained a balance of £12. 2s. 6d. for the use of his pupil. (See Morgan's letters of Sept. 6 and Oct. 20 to Charles Wesley, and that of Nov. 22 to John.)
[3] Richard Morgan, Jun., matriculated at Lincoln College on Nov. 23, 1733, aged 19.

which I would willingly persuade him to do every day. He loses no time at taverns or coffee-houses, and avoids as much as possible idle company, which every gentleman here will soon be pestered with if he has not some share of resolution. Some evenings every
5 week he spends in the common room, and others with my brother and me. Of his being admitted into our society (if it deserves so honourable a title) there is no danger. All those gentlemen whom I have the happiness to converse with two or three times a week upon a religious account would oppose me to the utmost should I attempt
10 to introduce among them at those important hours one of whose prudence I had had so short a trial, and who was so little experienced in piety and charity.

Several of the points you mention deserve a fuller consideration than I have leisure to give them. I shall ever own myself extremely
15 obliged for the freedom with which you mention them, and have endeavoured to answer you with the same freedom, which I am persuaded will not be disagreeable to you.

That my dear friend, now with God, was much disordered in his understanding I had often observed long before he left England.
20 That he was likewise sincerely religious all observed; but whoever had seen his behaviour in the successive stages of his illness might as easily have mistaken darkness for light as his madness for his religion. They were not only different, but opposite, too, one counter-acting the other from its beginning. I cannot better describe his
25 religion than in the words of the person who wrote his elegy:

> Mild, sweet, serene, and tender was her mood,
> Nor grave with sternness, nor with lightness free;
> Against example resolutely good,
> Fervent in zeal, and warm in charity!
> 30 Who ne'er forsook her faith for love of peace,
> Nor sought with fire and sword to show her zeal.
> Duteous to rulers, when they most oppress;
> Patient in bearing ill and doing well.[1]

Directly contrary to every article of this was his madness. It was
35 harsh, sour, cloudy, and severe. It was sometimes extravagantly light and sometimes sternly serious. It undermined his best resolutions by an absurd deference to example. It damped the fervour of his zeal, and gradually impaired the warmth of his charity. It had

---

[1] Cf. Samuel Wesley, Jun., *The Battle of the Sexes*, st. 35 (*Poems*, 1736, p. 38), with two minor alterations.

not indeed as yet attacked his duteous regard for his superiors, nor drove him to exterminate sin by fire and sword. For when it had so obscured that clear judgment whereon his holiness stood that his very faith and patience began to be in danger, the God whom he served came to his rescue and snatched him from the evil to come. 5

But though his religion was not the same with his madness, might it not be the cause of it? I answer, No. 'Tis full as reasonable to believe that light is darkness as that it is the cause of it. We may just as well think that mildness and harshness, sweetness and sternness, gentleness and fury, are the same thing, as that the former are the 10 causes of the latter, or have any tendency thereto.

'But he said himself his distemper was religious madness, and who should know better than himself?' Who should know the truth better than one out of his senses? Why, anyone that was in them: especially anyone that had observed the several workings of his 15 soul before the corruptible body pressed it down,[1] when his apprehension was unclouded, his judgment sound, and his reason cool and unimpaired. Then it was that he knew himself and his Master. Then he spoke the words of truth and soberness,[2] and justified by those words the wisdom he loved only not as much as 20 he adorned it by his life.

True it is, God was pleased for the trial both of him and us to visit him with a grievous illness. As his illness increased his reason declined, and consequently his religion built upon it. Till that melancholy effect of his disease I challenge all the fools who counted 25 his preceding life madness to point out one extreme he was in of any sort, or one instance of his zeal which was not according to knowledge.[3] 'Tis easy for any of them to declaim in general against enthusiasm, and carrying things too far, and even to prevail upon an unwary mind, shattered by sickness, to plead guilty to the accusa- 30 tion. But let them come to particulars, and I do hereby undertake to prove that every fact they allege against him is either absolutely false, or that it is agreeable to the strictest rules both of piety and Christian prudence.

His fasting (or abstinence rather, for I do not know that he ever 35 fasted one day) I least of all except, as being firmly persuaded from careful and repeated observations that had he continued it he had been alive to this day. Nor are there wanting as great names for this opinion as any that advised on the contrary; who believe that

[1] See Wisd. 9: 15.   [2] Acts 26: 25.   [3] See Rom. 10: 2.

wine and free diet to one in his circumstances was as sure a recipe as shooting him through the head.

I acknowledge your goodness in having a far better opinion of me than I deserve, or, I trust in God, shall ever desire. I have many 5 things to add when time permits, but one I dare not defer a moment. 'Tis absolutely necessary to guard your surviving son against the least suspicion of my over-great zeal, or strictness. You are fully sensible he is in no danger of either; but if he once fancies I am, that fancy will cut me off from all possibility of doing him any substantial 10 service. Whatever advice I may have occasion to give with regard to his moral conduct, 'Much religion hath made thee mad'¹ will be a sufficient answer to all. For your sake and his I beg to know (what I should otherwise not think it worth while to bestow one thought upon) any overt acts of my enthusiasm which pass current in 15 Ireland either with the gay or the serious part of the world. My brother gladly joins with me in acknowledging all your favours both to him and to, good sir, your obliged and obedient servant,

[John Wesley]

Source: Morgan MSS, pp. 53-7.

From Mrs. Susanna Wesley²

Tuesday, Jan. 1st [1]733/4

20 Dear son

I was highly pleased with receiving a letter from you last Sunday, for I have long wanted to writ to you, but knew not whether you were at London or Oxford. My principal business with you was about Whitelamb, to reprehend your too great caution in not informing me what his moral character is, and 25 about his intrigue at Medley. Had you let me know of the looseness of his principles, and his disreputable practices, I should never have forwarded his going into orders, neither would I have suffered him to renew his addresses to Molly, after such a notorious violation of his promises to her. Indeed when he came hither first he was so full of his new doxy that he could not forbear telling 30 Molly and Kezzy of his amour, which the former informed me of, and I discoursed him about it, and would have convinced him that it was sinful and dishonourable for him to court another woman when he was pre-engaged, [but] he was not much moved with what I could say. So I told him plainly, he should presently renounce one or the other, and that if he did not presently write to 35 Robinson (who is his pimp) and tell him that he would never more have any

---

¹ See Acts 26: 24, 'much learning doth make thee mad'.
² Replying to his of Dec. 19.

conversation with his doll at Medley, I would immediately send Molly away, where he should never see her more; though withal I advised him rather to take his Betty than your sister, for I thought her a much fitter wife for him. Besides, I was extremely unwilling Molly should ever marry at all. But Molly, who was fond of him to the last degree, was of another mind, and persuaded 5 him to write to Robinson, and show me the letter. I did not much approve it, because he seemed to justify those vile practices, which I thought he ought to have condemned; yet to satisfy her importunity I permitted them to go on. Whitelamb wrote to ask your father's leave to marry his daughter, which Mr. Wesley gave him, and on St. Thomas's Day married they were at Epworth, by 10 Mr. Horbery; full sore against my will, but my consent was never asked, and your father, brother Wesley, etc., being for the match. I said nothing against it to them, only laboured what I could to dissuade Molly from it. But the flesh and the devil were too hard for me. I could not prevail. Yet with God nothing is impossible, and though this unequal marriage has to me a terrible aspect, 'tis 15 possible for God to bring good out of this great evil; or otherwise he can take me away from the evil to come. Still, Jacky, I have somewhat more to tell you, but dare not write it, only this. Pray let Robinson (your pupil) know that Whitelamb is married; let him know I was against the match; give my service to him; and tell him from me, I am as good as my word, I daily pray for him, and beg of 20 him, if he have the least regard for his soul, or have yet any remaining sense of religion in his mind, to shake off all acquaintance with the profane and irregular; for it is the free thinker and sensualist, not the despised Methodists, which will be ashamed and confounded when summoned to appear before the face of that Almighty Judge whose Godhead they have blasphemed, and whose offered 25 mercy they have despised and ludicrously rejected. The pleasures of sin are but for a short, uncertain time, but eternity hath no end. Therefore one would think that few arguments might serve to convince a man which has not lost his senses that 'tis of the last importance for us to be very serious in improving the present time, and acquainting ourselves with God while it is called 'Today'; lest being 30 disqualified for his blissful presence our future existence be inexpressibly miserable.

You are entirely in the right in what you say in the second paragraph of your letter. The different degrees of virtue and piety are different states of soul, which must be passed through gradually; and he that cavils at a practical advice 35 plainly shows that he has not gone through those states which were to have been passed before he could apprehend the goodness of the given direction. For in all matters of religion, if there be not an internal sense in the hearer corresponding to that sense in the mind of the speaker, what is said will have no effect. This I have often experienced. Yet sometimes it falls out that while a zealous 40 Christian is discoursing on spiritual subjects the Blessed Spirit of God Incarnate will give such light to the minds of those that hear him as shall dispel their native darkness, and enable them to apprehend those spiritual things of which before they had no discernment. As in the case of St. Peter, who preaching the gospel to Cornelius and his friends, it is said, 'While Peter yet spake these words 45 the Holy Ghost fell on all them which heard the word.'

Mr. Law is a good and a valuable man; yet he is but a man; and therefore no marvel that he could not be so explicit as you could have wished in speaking of

the presence of God. Perhaps his mind was too full of the sense of that Blessed Being readily to hit upon words to express a thing so far above their nature. Who can think, much less speak, on that vast subject—his greatness, his dignity, astonishes us! The purity of his goodness, his redeeming love, confounds and
5 overwhelms us! At the perception of his glory our feeble powers are suspended, and nature faints before the God of nature.

For my part, after many years' search and inquiry, I still continue to pay my devotions to an unknown God. I cannot know him. I dare not say I love him—only this, I have chose him for my only happiness, my all, my only God, in a
10 word, for my God. And when I sound my will, I feel it adheres to its choice, though not so faithfully as it ought. Therefore I desire your prayers, which I need much more than you do mine.

That God is everywhere present, and we always present to him, is certain; but that he should be always present to us is scarce consistent with our mortal
15 state. Some choice souls, 'tis true, have attained such a habitual sense of his presence as admits of few interruptions. But what my dear—Consider, he is so infinitely blessed! So altogether lovely! That every perception of him, every approach (in contemplation) to his supreme glory and blessedness imparts such a vital joy and gladness to the heart as banishes all pain and sense of misery—
20 And were eternity added to this happiness it would be heaven.

I have much to say, but time is expired.

Pray burn this letter, for I would not that any know my thoughts of W[hitelamb] and M[olly], since they are married. She thinks she can reform what is amiss in him. I think myself he grows more serious and regular. My love and
25 blessing to ye both. Wishing ye a Happy New Year. My service to Mr. Hall.

Address: 'To the Revd. Mr. Wesley, Fellow of Lincoln College, Oxon. By way of London'   *Postmark*: '4 IA'   *Charges*: ((4)), 'In all 7'   *End* by JW:
'Jan. 1, 1733/4 my m. +'   *Source*: MA.

From Richard Morgan, Jun. to Richard Morgan, Sen.[1]

[Jan. 14, 1734]

Honoured sir

I received your kind letter of the 22nd of November, which came free. I perused yours to Mr. Wesley very carefully, then sealed it, and delivered it to
30 him. When he had read it over two or three times, he desired me to breakfast

---

[1] The following document is of such importance that we insert it in the text rather than in the footnotes, even though it is written neither to nor by Wesley, but about him. This alone can adequately set the stage for the letter which follows. Wesley's diary for Jan. 14, 1734, contains the passage: '3½ fell up[on] Mo[rgan]'s L[ette]r to h[is] f[ather]; tr[anscribe]d it!'. The exclamation mark reveals how extraordinary Wesley found this conduct in himself, even though he was expected to act as a parent towards his pupil. Nevertheless in his own letter to Morgan's father Wesley states that he 'providentially' saw the open copy of the letter and glanced at it, which led him to read it, though this was contrary to his practice.

with him next morning. His whole discourse turned on the contents of your letter. He said he did not know what to make of it, and was surprised that a father should show so great concern lest his son should not be wicked enough, and went on after that odd manner. He endeavoured to prove that my brother did not weaken his constitution by his great abstinence and strictness in religion; 5 though my brazier's wife, an intimate of Mr. Wesley's, told me she has often heard Dr. Frewin say that while he persisted in that rigid course of life he could be of no service to him.

There is a society of gentlemen, consisting of seven members, whom the world calls Methodists, of which my tutor is president. They imagine they can- 10 not be saved if they do not spend every hour, nay minute, of their lives in the service of God. And to that end they read prayers every day in the common gaol, preach every Sunday, and administer the sacrament once every month. They almost starve themselves to be able to relieve the poor, and buy books for their conversion. They endeavour to reform notorious whores, and allay spirits in 15 haunted houses. They fast two days in the week, which has emaciated them to that degree that they are a frightful sight. One of them had like to have lost his life lately by a decay which was attributed to his great abstinence. They rise every day at five of the clock, and till prayers, which begin at eight, they[a] sing Psalms, and read some piece of divinity. They meet at each others' rooms at six 20 of the clock five nights in the week, and from seven to nine read a piece of some religious book. In short they are so particular that they are become the jest of the whole university.

When I came to college my tutor gave me two rules in writing, which he expected I should follow. The first was to have no company but what he approved 25 of, and the second to read no books but of his choosing. In compliance with the first I have spent every evening of their meeting, from seven to nine, in their company, till I received your letter. From six to seven they read over the petitions of poor people, and relieve their wants, dispose of pious books, and fix the duties of the ensuing day. They told me very solemnly that when I had acquired 30 a pretty good stock of religion they would take me in as an assistant. When we are all met my tutor reads a collect to increase our attention. After that a religious book is read, all the time we are together. They often cry for five minutes for their sins; then lift up their heads and eyes, and return God thanks for the great mercies he has showed them in granting them such repentance, and then 35 laugh immoderately, as if they were mad. The greatest blessing next to that is being laughed at by the world, which they esteem a sufficient proof of the goodness and justness of their actions, for which they also return thanks as aforesaid. Though some of them are remarkable for eating very heartily on Gaudy-days, they stint themselves to twopence meat and a farthing bread and a draught of 40 water when they dine at their own expense; and as for supper they never eat any. There is a text in the Revelations which says that a man had better be very wicked

---

[a] In another copy it was, 'spend in singing Psalms, and reading the Bible, and Nelson's works. They also receive the Holy Sacrament every Sunday. In short they have made themselves so particular that they are the jest, not only of the scholars but of the fellows and the whole university. They meet at each others' rooms at six of the clock five nights in the week; the other two they spend in private.' (This footnote, like the transcript itself, is in CW's hand.)

than lukewarm. This Mr. Wesley explained thus: that there is no medium in religion; that a man that does not engage himself entirely in the practice of religion is in greater fear of damnation than a notorious sinner. When I considered that I was in the middle state I grew very uneasy, and was for several
5 days in a kind of religious madness till I was convinced by a sermon of Dr. Young's, which gives those words a quite different meaning. Mr. Wesley often says that it is madness in any man to leave off reading at the end of the eleventh hour if he can improve himself by the twelfth. This rule he expects his pupils to observe. I have not been an hour idle since I came to college, but when I walk for
10 my health, which he himself advises. He also expects that I should spend an hour every day before prayers in reading Nelson's works, which I have complied with. He has lectured me scarce in anything but books of devotion. He had given me a book of Mr. Nelson to abridge this Christmas. By being his pupil I am stigmatized with the name of a Methodist, the misfortune of which I cannot describe.
15 For what they reckon the greatest happiness, namely of being laughed at, to me is the greatest misery. I am as much laughed at and despised by the whole town as any one of them, and always shall be so while I am his pupil. The whole college makes a jest of me, and the fellows themselves do not show me common civility, so great is their aversion to my tutor. In short, labouring under all these
20 disadvantages, I am grown perfectly melancholy, and have got such a habit of sighing, which I cannot avoid, that it must certainly do me great mischief. Soon after I came to college the rector favoured me with his company, and cautioned me against Mr. Wesley's strict notions of religion, and told me that the character of his society prevented several from entering in the college. You are pleased in
25 both your letters to express a great regard for my welfare, for which I hope you shall find a grateful return in me. And as I myself ought to contribute all in my power thereto, I think it incumbent upon me to inform you that it is my opinion that if I am continued under Mr. Wesley I shall be ruined. For though you should caution him ever so much, he will endeavour to make me as strict
30 as himself; and will say, as he did to part of your letter, that we are not obliged to obey our fathers in anything that contradicts the laws of God. We have but one tutor more in the college, who is reckoned one of the best tutors in the university, and my Lord Lichfield has so great an opinion of him that he will send his eldest son to be taken care of by him. He has what few are in college
35 (except one gentleman commoner and two servitors who are Mr. Wesley's pupils) under his tuition. The character which I presume Mr. Wesley has given of me will, I hope, convince you that I have no view of being idle to occasion this removal. I am so well assured that any prospect I can have of enjoying any part of your fortune depends so much on my good behaviour that I would not
40 propose it if I thought I would not be as diligent under him as Mr. Wesley. Though I have the greatest desire to improve myself, I would choose to return to my office, and forego the advantages of an university education, rather than suffer what I do at present by being his pupil.

transcribed Jan. 14, 1734,

Source: Morgan MSS, pp. 58–63.

To Richard Morgan, Sen.

Jan. 15, 1734[1]

Sir

Going yesterday into your son's room I providentially cast my eyes upon a paper that lay upon the table, and (contrary to my custom) read a line or two of it, which soon determined me to read 5 the rest. It was a copy of his last letter to you; whereby by the signal blessing of God I came to the knowledge of his real sentiments both with regard to myself and to several other points of the highest importance.

In the account he gives of me and those friends which are as my 10 own soul, and who watch over it that I may not be myself a castaway,[2] are some things true; as that we imagine it is our bounden duty to spend our whole lives in the service of him that gave them, or, in other words, 'Whether we eat or drink, or whatever we do, to do all to the glory of God;'[3] that we endeavour (as we are able) 15 to relieve the poor by buying books and other necessaries for them; that some of us read[4] prayers at the prison once a day; that I administer the sacrament once a month, and preach there as often as I am not engaged elsewhere; that we sit together five evenings in a week, and that we observe (in such manner as our health permits) the 20 fasts which the apostles established in the church.[5] Some things are false, but taken up upon trust, so that I hope Mr. Morgan believed them true; as that we almost starve ourselves; that one of us had like lately to have lost his life by too great abstinence; that we endeavour to reform notorious whores, and to lay spirits in haunted houses; 25 that we all rise every day at 5 o'clock, and that I am president of the society, etc. And some things are not only false, but I fear were known so to be when he related them as true (inasmuch as he had then had the repeated demonstration of both his eyes and ears to the contrary);

---

[1] Diary, '6.20 [a.m.] plan[ne]d my L[ette]r to Mr. Mo[rgan]'.

[2] Several passages are struck through in Charles Wesley's copy, probably because, although portions of the letter as dispatched, they were not to be read (or perhaps recopied). There seems little doubt that this document was used as a Methodist apologia, though not so frequently as that of Oct. 18, 1732. The clause 'and who watch . . . castaway' is struck through, though (unlike the others) in pencil. The erased passages (including this one) are omitted from the version of the letter given in Moore I. 198–202.

[3] Cf. 1 Cor. 10: 31.   [4] Orig., 'reads'.

[5] Altered in a later hand to 'the fasts of the church'.

such as that the society consists of seven members (I know no more than four of them);[1] that from five to eight in the morning they sing Psalms and read some pieces of divinity; and that they are emaciated to such a degree that they are a frightful sight. As to the circumstance
5 of the brazier's wife (no intimate of mine) I am in doubt; though she positively denies she ever said so.[2]

As strange as it may appear that one present upon the spot should so far vary from the truth in his relation, I can easily account, not only for his mistake, but for his designed misrepresentation too.
10 The company he is almost daily with, from whom indeed I should soon have divided him had not your letters coming in the article of time tied my hands, abundantly accounts for the former; as his desire to lessen your regard for me, and thereby obviate the force of any future complaint, which he foresaw I might some time have
15 occasion to make to you, does for the latter. And indeed I am not without apprehension that some such occasion may shortly come. I need not describe that apprehension to you. Be pleased to reflect what were the sentiments of your own heart when the ship that took your son from you loosed from shore; and such (allowing for the
20 superior tenderness of a parent) are mine. Such were my father's before he parted from us, when taking him by the hand he said, 'Mr. M[organ], between this and Easter is your trial for life. I even tremble when I consider the danger you are in; and the more because you do not yourself perceive it.'[3] Impute not, sir, this fear
25 either to the error of my youth or to the coldness of his age.[4] Is there not a cause? Is he not surrounded even in this recess with those who are often more pernicious than open libertines? Men who retain something of outward decency, and nothing else; who seriously idle away the whole day, and reputably revel till midnight, and if not
30 drunken themselves, yet encouraging and applauding those that are so. Who have no more of the form than of the power of godliness,[5] and though they do pretty often drop in at public prayers (coming after the most solemn part of them is over), yet expressly

---

[1] i.e. meeting regularly, the two Wesleys, Westley Hall, and Thomas Broughton (see Heitzenrater, p. 238).

[2] The whole section of charges known to be false (from 'And some things') is struck through vertically.

[3] This would be on Jan. 3, 1734, when the Revd. Samuel Wesley, Sen., left Oxford after a week's visit with his sons and their friends.

[4] The four sentences 'Be pleased . . . his age' are struck through.

[5] See 2 Tim. 3: 5.

disown any obligation to attend them. 'Tis true they have not yet laughed your son out of all his diligence, but how long it will be before they have, God knows! They zealously endeavour it at all convenient opportunities. And temporal views are as unable to support him under such an attack as his slender notions of religion are; of which he often says he thinks he shall have enough if he constantly says his prayers at home and in the chapel. As to my advice on this or any other head, they had secured him pretty well before; and your authority added to theirs has supplied him with armour of proof against it. I now beg to know what you would have me do. Shall I sit still and let him swim down the stream? Or shall I plunge in, bound as I am hand and foot, and oppose myself to his company, his inclinations, and his father?

Why, you say, I am to incite him to 'live a sober, virtuous, and religious life'.[1] Nay, but first let us agree what religion is. I take religion to be, not the bare saying over so many prayers morning and evening, in public or in private; not anything superadded now and then to a careless or worldly life; but a constant ruling habit of soul; a renewal of our minds in the image of God;[2] a recovery of the divine likeness; a still-increasing conformity of heart and life to the pattern of our most holy Redeemer. But if this be religion, if this be that way to life which our Blessed Lord hath marked out for us, how can anyone, while he keeps close to this way, be charged with running into extremes? 'Tis true there is no going out of it, either to the right hand or to the left, without running into an extreme; and to prevent this the wisdom of the church has in all ages appointed guides for the unexperienced, lest they should wander into bypaths, and seek death in the error of their life.[3] But while he is in the right way, what fear is there of your son's going too fast in it? I appeal to your own experience. Have you observed any such disposition in him as gives you ground to suspect he will love God too well, or keep himself too unspotted from the world?[4] Or has his past life been such as that you have just reason to apprehend the remainder of it should too much resemble that of our Blessed Master? I will go further. Have you remarked in the various scenes you have gone through, that youth in general is apt to run into the extreme of piety? Is it to this excess that the fervour of their blood and the impetuosity of their passions hurry them? But we may not stop

[1] See letter from Richard Morgan, Sen., Nov. 22, 1733.
[2] See Col. 3: 10.   [3] See Wisd. 1: 12.   [4] Jas. 1: 27.

here. Is there any fear, is there any possibility, that any son of Adam, of whatever age or degree, should too faithfully do the will of his Creator, or too exactly tread in the steps of his Redeemer? Suppose the time now come when you feel within yourself that 'the silver
5 cord of life is loosed, that the dust is returning to the earth as it was, and the spirit unto God who gave it'.[1] The snares of death overtake you.[2] Nothing but pain is on the one hand, eternity on the other. The tears of your friends that surround your bed bear witness with the pangs of your own heart that it has few pulses more to beat
10 before you launch out into the sea without a shore;[3] before the soul shall part from your quivering lips, and stand naked before the judgment-seat of God. Will you then be content with having served God according to the CUSTOM of the place you was in?[4] Will you regret your having been even from your youth 'more pure and holy
15 than the rest of mankind'?[5] Will you complain to the ministering spirits who receive your new-born soul that you have been 'over-zealous'[6] in the love of your Master? Ask not me, a poor, fallible, sinful mortal, never safe either from the snares of ill example or the treachery of my own heart, but ask them: ask HIM who died to make
20 you and me and your son 'zealous of good works',[7] whether you may be excused for your solicitude, your too successful solicitude, to prevent his falling into this 'extreme'![8] How needless has he made that solicitude already! But I spare you—The good God be merciful to us both!
25 Think not, sir, that interest[9] occasions the concern I show. I despise and[10] abhor the thought. From the moment my brother told me, 'Mr. Morgan will be safer with you than me; I have desired he may be sent to you', I determined (though I have never mentioned it to him) to restore to him whatsoever is paid me upon Mr. Morgan's
30 account. It is, with regard to me, an accursed thing; there shall no such cleave unto me.[11] I have sufficient motives, without this, to

---

[1] Cf. Eccles. 12: 6, 7. [2] See 2 Sam. 22: 6.
[3] Cf. Milton, *Paradise Lost*, xi. 750, though the image conveyed there by 'sea without shore' is different—not death but 'depopulation'.
[4] Apparently an allusion to the passage in Morgan's letter of Nov. 22, 1733, about his son's behaving 'according to the statutes and customs of his college'.
[5] Ibid. [6] Ibid.
[7] Titus 2: 14. [8] Letter of Nov. 22, 1733.
[9] Wesley uses the word 'interest' in its early meaning of self-interest, rather than curiosity, which did not develop until much later in the century.
[10] 'despise and' are struck through in pencil.
[11] i.e. devoted to a special purpose; see Josh. 6: 17–18; Deut. 13: 17.

assist your son,[1] so long as he will accept of my assistance. He is the brother of my dear friend, the son of one that was my friend, till great names warped him from his purpose; and what is infinitely more, the creature of my God, and the redeemed and fellow-heir of my Saviour. That neither the cares of the world, not the fair speeches and venerable titles of any who set up their rest therein, may prevent our attaining our better inheritance, is the earnest prayer of, sir, your most obliged and most obedient servant,

[John Wesley]

I beg, if you favour me with another letter, it may not be enclosed in Mr. Morgan's.

Source: Morgan MSS, pp. 63-70.

To Mrs. Susanna Wesley

Jan. [28],[2] 1733/4, Oxon.

Dear mother

As soon as I had informed myself fully of the intrigue at Medley,[3] I determined to inform my sister Molly of the whole, and then leave it wholly with her, either to keep it secret, or to reveal it to whom she pleased. I have a good hope that the measures she has taken will be the means of saving a soul from death.[4] Poor Mr. Robinson[5] seemed concerned, just at the time when I read him what you said; but the time of his laying it to heart is not yet come. I am more and more convinced that few men are satisfied of practical truths by disputing about them, though still there seems to be no doubt but every man may and ought to ask a reason for the advice we give him, and to remonstrate, in an humble and diffident way, if that reason does not appear conclusive. Because the director may possibly be wrong, though not so probably as the directed.

---

[1] Orig., 'him'.
[2] The day of the month ascertained from Wesley's diary.
[3] See her letter of Jan. 1, which this answers.
[4] See Jas. 5: 20.
[5] Apparently Matthew Robinson, one of Wesley's pupils, the son of the vicar of Blyborough, Lincs., who had matriculated, aged 17, Oct. 10, 1730. He became a fellow of Brasenose College, and died in 1745. In her letter of Jan. 1 Susanna Wesley speaks of him as Whitelamb's 'pimp'.

I should be exceeding glad of your advice how to proceed with a gentleman I have now with me.[1] He was remarkable before he came to college for having scarce any knowledge and less sense of religion; and for good nature, idleness, vanity, and insincerity. Since he was 5 here he has seemed well pleased with most things I said; has appeared affected with some religious books we read together; has been very studious of obliging me, tolerably diligent, and full of professions of sincerity. In the meantime he has consorted much with idle and lukewarm people; has joined with them in all their witticisms upon 10 me, and has writ a letter to his father wherein, after relating many things of me which he knew not to be true, he tells him he 'shall be ruined' unless he changes his tutor. As soon as I read it I writ to his father too, and told him some part of the truth. He has answered neither of us yet; but the son suspects I have found him out, and is 15 doubly assiduous in his endeavour to please me. Now what is to be done? May I not hope that God has laid him open to me, in order to amend him? And that if his father heartily joins with me our labour will not be in vain? At least, ought I not, at a convenient season, to let him know that he does not deceive me? And, with all 20 meekness, to tell him the things he has done, and the imprudence of them? Surely, if it be not an advantage to him, it must be a gre⟨at⟩ one to me. He is frequently with my brother, Mr. Hall,[2] and m⟨e⟩. Should we converse then in the simplicity of the gospel; and speak, as we are enabled, with zeal, of the nothingness of things present, 25 the greatness of things future, and the excellency of the love of Christ? Or should we rather soften these glorious truths, and talk morally? 'Tis an important question, and of constant use.

Mr. Hall, bating his idolatry and superstition, is the very picture of Mr. de Renty: he breathes the same spirit in every word and look. 30 Almost every hour we are together I am utterly astonished at his humility, and love to God, and to man for his sake. Every day I am

[1] Richard Morgan; see previous letter.

[2] Westley Hall (c. 1710–76), a native of Salisbury, became a pupil of John Wesley's at Lincoln College on Jan. 26, 1731, though it was over a year before he became closely associated with Methodist activities, just before Clayton joined the group. After Clayton's departure for Manchester in the winter of 1732, Hall remained the only member of the inner circle at Lincoln in addition to the two Wesley brothers, though a few months later there was an influx of new blood. He seemed a model of Christian dedication, a young man of professed piety, approaching Holy Orders. Soon, however, he was courting two of Wesley's sisters, under pressure jilting one to marry the other, and eventually revealing himself as an advocate of polygamy, and doing his best to practise what he preached.

apt to imagine he has finished that course which the wisdom of God hath allotted to man in this period of his being; but every evening he convinces me he has gone such a space since the morning as only experience can make conceivable. Verily this man is (in a sound sense) the great power of God. O may I be a follower of him, as he is 5 of Christ!

Although to perceive God as he is be a blessing which may not be vouchsafed to man not yet made perfect, and although the lively and uninterrupted apprehension of his presence with even embodied spirits be vouchsafed only to a few choice souls,[1] yet is there not an 10 inferior sort of attention to his presence which all Christians ought to aspire after? May not any who sincerely endeavour to obey him hope to advert more and more to those truths: 'He besetteth me behind and before, and layeth his hand upon me!'[2] 'I come to do thy will, O God.'[3] 'I seek not myself, but Christ crucified.'[4] This is 15 that perception of the presence of God which I desire (Alas, how faintly!) to attain to! This ⟨is⟩ that recollection which I study to advance in day by day; this seems to me one stair of 'the ladder to heaven',[5] one degree of Christian simplicity! With regard to this especially, dear mother, I desire your instructions, and your 20 constant prayers for both my brother and your dutiful and affectionate son,

John Wesley

Mr. Hall's service attends you.
Surely you write to me as safely as you could speak. 25
Have a care of my D⟨. . .⟩[6]

Address: 'To Mrs Wesley at Epworth, To be left at the Post=house, In Gainsbro', Lincolnshire, p[er] London' *Postmarks*: 'OXFORD", '29 IA' *Charges*: ((3)), 'In all 7' *End* by JW: 'Acct of Mr. Hall / Rd Morgan' *Source*: The Revd. N. M. Ramm, Oxford.

[1] See the closing section of her letter of Jan. 1.
[2] Cf. Ps. 139: 5. [3] Heb. 10: 7.
[4] Apparently an amalgam of several scriptural texts, notably Matt. 28: 5, John 5: 30–1, 1 Cor. 1: 22–3.
[5] See Gen. 28: 12.
[6] A portion torn from the bottom of the page may have referred, under the generic term of 'devotions', to Wesley's first publication, *A Collection of Forms of Prayer*, which had just appeared (see *Bibliog*, No. 1).

(374)

From Richard Morgan, Sen.

Revd. sir

I am favoured with yours of the 15th, and am very sorry that my last letter has been the occasion of any disquietude to you, which I am sure I never
5 designed. When out of the friendship that had been contracted between us, and the good opinion I had both of your and your brother's sincerity and judgment, I determined chiefly on your advice to send my son to the university, I did not imagine that it would be expected he should join in that strict society which it was known I disliked in my other son; upon this confidence you know I did not
10 offer the least caution against it in my former letters, nor did you in your first letter give any intimation that you expected it, having only expostulated on both sides on the subject of his learning; and thus, preliminaries being, as I thought, happily fixed, I was easy. But afterwards I was greatly surprised and alarmed to find you insist in your letter of the 6th of November that he must keep company
15 with those, and only those, whom you approve of, with other hints tending that way. Then indeed the melancholy end of my other son, and the hazard of my only son being led the same way, made deep impressions on me, and my friends observed me melancholy upon it for some time, my fears and trouble increasing when I saw a letter from Mr. Battely of Christ Church complaining that he had
20 twice invited my son to his chambers, but that he did not come. Then I concluded from the expressions in your letter that he was to be confined to the company of the gentlemen of that society. Yet under all these apprehensions and uneasiness I forebore in my letter to you to make any reflections upon the words of your letter, but urged only, from the tragical experience in my other son, the
25 danger I apprehended of young people's engaging in the same way, and I thought that the dismal account I gave of my poor son (which nothing but my fears about my other son would have made me mention) would rather have met with pity to me than reproaches.

Now I must tell you that I respect and adore both you and every gentleman
30 of that strict religious society that you are engaged in, and doubt not but you will meet with an exalted seat in heaven. I could even wish to be among you, as I formerly hinted to you. Yet I must be of the same opinion still, that it is a dangerous experiment for young people to venture upon, which I think the example I gave you in my last sufficiently proves; and if it were necessary I
35 could give you several other examples how too great a zeal for piety and religion has carried injudicious people into madness. But supposing [it] to be a doubtful case whether it be advisable for a youth to unite in this society or not (as sure it must at least be allowed to be, from the diversity of opinions about it), how must I determine the question? You argue very rationally and piously for it,
40 and five able divines, some of them bishops, men of remarkable learning and piety, of my intimate acquaintance, warn me of the danger of it; then surely from the common rules of prudence and judgment it is plain how I ought to determine.

I agree with you in one thing, that from my son's gaiety, and inclination to
45 pleasures (I cannot say more than, [which] were innocent), I had the less

reason to fear his falling into too strict a course of life; and this I observed to a certain divine, in discoursing with him on that subject, when he heard that you were to be his tutor; but he answered that the danger was the greater, that if such a volatile temper should take a turn that way, he might plunge into deeper extremes than graver persons, and that I did not know what the influence of a 5 tutor might bring to pass. God grant that he does and will continue to do what he has told you, viz. constantly say his prayers at home and in the chapel, and then I will venture to say (though I am no divine), if he also avoids sins of commission, that he may be ranked in the class of good Christians. It is neither my province, nor am I any way equal to you, to manage this point of controversy, 10 therefore I beg we may drop it for the future.

If I have said anything in this or my former letter that is disagreeable to you (for I assure you I would do nothing willingly to disoblige you), I hope you will forgive me, and impute it to my too great anxiety for the welfare of my son, and believe that there is nothing I covet more than his living a good life, and 15 doing his duty both to God and man, which I think is generally the wish of even a wicked parent. And as I am not notoriously so, I hope I am not to be suspected as encouraging my son to depart from the right way.

The enclosed letter, which I have left open for your perusal, shows you how desirous I am that he should obediently submit to your authority and govern- 20 ment, etc.[1] I would never have sent him to the university trusting to the common care of a tutor, after the long habit he had of pleasure and idleness. My dependence on yours or your brother's more than ordinary care of him made me venture upon it, and I hope nothing has happened to create any indifference in you towards him. 25

The former part of your letter I am come now to answer in the last place, and do assure you that I never received the letter you mention, of which you saw the rough draft upon his table, nor anything like it. His last letter that I received was of the 6th of November, and in that, and in every letter that he made any mention of you in, he did it with great respect to you, and expres- 30 sions of your civilities and kindness to him.

[1] pp. 75-6 of the Morgan MSS contain Charles Wesley's further transcription: 'Part of Mr. Morgan's letter to his son, enclosed in the above letter.

"Jan. 31, 1733/4

What, Dick, did you so soon forget our stipulations and conditions on your going to the university as to carry a greyhound with you to Oxford, and to attempt keeping him in your college, contrary to the rules of it? Did not you promise to stick to your studies, and be as subservient to your tutor as if you were a servitor? ... I vowed to you before, and now I vow again, that if you follow an idle, vicious, or extravagant life, you shall never inherit my fortune ... You are now in the hands of a gentleman (it is my happiness, and so you may reckon it, too) that has more honour and conscience than to conceal your faults from me. Your duty to God is always in the first place to be duly attended. Go to bed by times; rise early. Omit no one college duty. Squander not away the morning in tea and chat. Never be seen out of your chamber in studying hours. For the rest I refer to your good tutor, who I am sure will not be wanting in his instructions to you, without engaging you in that society, which I am not for. Banish your dog immediately. *Quid de quoque viro, et cui dicas saepe caveto.* [Horace, *Epistles*, I. xviii. 68, last word being 'videto' in the original—'Beware what you say about anyone, and to whom you say it.'] Always imagine what you do will be known." '

I now conclude with all fervent wishes and desire for his and all our happiness in this and the next world, dear sir, your truly affectionate, most obliged, humble, servant,

Richard Morgan

Source: Morgan MSS, pp. 70–5; paragraphing added.

From the Revd. Samuel Wesley, Jun.[1]

Feb. 7, 1733/4

5

Dear Jack

To the best of my memory your charmer was but little in my thoughts, and my own not at all, in my late letters. I never designed to justify myself; perhaps my laughter is particularly blameable, as my temper is serious, severe, and
10 melancholy.

I have nothing to say against especial seasons or occasions of sorrow. Duty apart, I think him as ridiculous who weeps not at a tragedy as he who does not laugh at a comedy.

Your general arguments stand thus: God is present. All things are serious.
15 Eternity is near (nearer every moment). If I understand the terms, they conclude against *all* laughter. If one contradictory true proves the other false—who can keep off the consequence? Not heaven omnipotent.

Thus ends our notable dispute, or rather we have had none at all. For by your simile of a cordial, and your profession, you are only against excessive
20 laughter, which I was never for; and only for seriousness, which I was never against. There is a time to weep, and a time to laugh. And now methinks each of us may say to the other, as Dick does to Matt:

> That people lived and died I knew
> An hour ago, as well as you.

25 I have had two letters from Charles. [. . .]

We (i.e. father and wife and I) join in love to you and him. Love to Dick [Smyth] too. I am glad he is good. I am, Dear J, your affectionate friend and brother,

S. Wesley

Address: 'To the Revd. Mr. Wesley, Fellow of Lincoln, Oxon'   *Postmarks*: '7 [FE]' and 'WM' within a circle   *Charge*: '7'   *End* by JW: 'Feb. 7. 1734 b Sam'   *Source*: MA.

<hr>

[1] Answering JW's of Jan. 29.

From Mrs. Susanna Wesley

Feb. 14 [1734]¹

Dear son

I cannot well say whether it will answer any good end to let the young gentleman know that you have heard of what he has said against you. I doubt it will make him desperate. I remember a piece of advice which my brother Matthew 5 gave in a parallel case: 'Never let any man know that you have heard what he has said against you. It may be he spake upon some misinformation, or was in a passion, or did it in a weak compliance with the company; perhaps he has changed his mind, and is sorry for having done it, and may continue friendly to you. But if he finds you are acquainted with what he said, he will conclude you 10 cannot forgive him, and upon that supposition will become your enemy.'

Your other question is indeed of great weight, and the resolving it requires a better judgment than mine. But since you desire my opinion, I shall propose what I have to say.

Since God is altogether inaccessible to us but by Jesus Christ, and since none 15 ever was or ever will be saved but by him, is it not absolutely necessary for all people, young and old, to be well grounded in the knowledge and faith of Jesus Christ? By faith I do not mean an assent only to the truths of the gospel concerning him, but such an assent as influences our practice, as makes us heartily and thankfully accept him for our God and Saviour, upon his own conditions. 20 No faith below this can be saving. And since this faith is necessary to salvation, can it be too frequently or too explicitly discoursed on to young people? I think not.

But since the natural pride of man is wont to suggest to him that he is self-sufficient, and has no need of a Saviour, may it not be proper to show (the 25 young especially) that without the great atonement there could be no remission of sin; and that in the present state of human nature no man can qualify himself for heaven without that Holy Spirit which is given by God Incarnate? To convince them of this truth, might it not be needful to inform them that since God is infinitely just, or rather that he is justice itself, it necessarily follows that 30 vindictive justice is an essential property in the divine nature? And if so, one of these two things seems to have been absolutely necessary, either that there must be an adequate satisfaction made to the divine justice for the violation of God's law by mankind; or else that the whole human species should have perished in Adam (which would have afforded too great matter of triumph to the apostate 35 angels)—otherwise how could God have been just to himself? Would not some mention of the necessity of revealed religion be proper here? Since without it all the wit of man could never have found out how human nature was corrupted in its fountain, neither had it been possible for us to have discovered any way or means whereby it might be restored to its primitive purity. Nay, had it been 40 possible for the brightest angels in heaven to have found out such a way to redeem and restore mankind as God hath appointed, yet durst any of them have

---

¹ This letter is clearly a reply to part of that of Jan. 28, 1734, the reference being to Richard Morgan, Jun., and Wesley's problem in dealing with him.

proposed it to the uncreated Godhead?—No. Surely the offended must appoint a way to save the offender, or man must be lost for ever. 'O the depth of the riches of the wisdom, and knowledge, and goodness of God! How unsearchable are his judgments, and his ways past finding out! As the heavens are higher
5 than the earth, so are his thoughts higher than our thoughts, and his ways than our ways!' Here surely you may give free scope to your spirits, here you may freely use your Christian liberty, and discourse without reserve of the excellency of the knowledge and love of Christ, as his Spirit gives you utterance.—What, my son, did the pure and holy person of the Son of God pass by the fallen angels,
10 who were far superior, of greater dignity, and of an higher order in the scale of existence, and choose to unite himself to the human nature; and shall we soften (as you call it) these glorious truths? Rather let us speak boldly, without fear; these truths ought to be frequently inculcated, and pressed home upon the consciences of men. And when once men are affected with a sense of redeeming
15 love, that sense will powerfully convince them of the vanity of the world, and make them esteem the honour, wealth, and pleasures of it as dross, or dung, so that they may win Christ. As for moral subjects, they are necessary to be discoursed on; but then, I humbly conceive, we are to speak of moral virtues as Christians, and not like heathens. And if we could indeed do honour to our
20 Saviour, we should take all fitting occasions to make men observe the excellence and perfection of the moral virtues taught by Christ and his apostles, far surpassing all that was pretended to by the very best of the heathen philosophers. All their morality was defective in principle and direction, was intended only to regulate the outward actions, but never reached the heart, or at the highest it
25 looked no farther than the temporal happiness of mankind. 'But moral virtues evangelized, or improved into Christian duties, have partly a view to promote the good of human society here, but chiefly to qualify the observers of them for a much more blessed and more enduring society hereafter.' I cannot stay to enlarge on this vast subject, nor indeed (considering whom I write to) is it
30 needful. Yet one thing I cannot forbear adding, which may carry some weight with his admirers, and that is, the very wise and just reply which Mr. Locke made to one that desired him to draw up a system of morals. Did the world, says he, want a rule, I confess there could be no work so necessary, nor so commendable. But the gospel contains so perfect a body of ethics that reason may
35 be excused from that enquiry, since she may find man's duty clearer and easier in Revelation than in herself.

That you may continue steadfast in the faith, and increase more and more in the knowledge and love of God, and of his Son, Jesus Christ; that holiness, simplicity, and purity (which are different words signifying the same thing),
40 may recommend you to the favour of God Incarnate; that his Spirit may dwell in you, and keep you still (as now) under a sense of God's blissful presence, is the hearty prayer of, dear son, your affectionate mother, and most faithful friend,

S[usanna] W[esley]

Source: *A.M.*, 1778, pp. 81–4, edited by Wesley, and dated (incorrectly) 'Feb. 14, 1735'.

To Richard Morgan, Sen.

March 15, 1733/4

Sir

A journey which I was obliged to begin very soon after the receipt
of yours was the occasion of my delaying so long to answer it, which
I should otherwise have done immediately.[1] I am satisfied you never   5
designed to give me any uneasiness, either by your last or any of
your preceding letters, and am very sensible that the freedom you
used therein proceeded from a much kinder intention. And should
you ever say anything which I could not approve of I should as soon
as possible mention it to you, as the only sure way either to prevent   10
any misunderstanding between us, or at least to hinder its long
continuance.

As to your son's being a member of our little society, I once more
assure you[2] with all plainness that were you as much for it as you
appear to be against it, I should think it my duty to oppose it to the   15
utmost. I do not conceive him to be anyways qualified for it, and
would as soon advise one of his dispositions to go and convert the
Indies as to minister to his fellow Christians in the manner wherein
my dear friends, by the grace of God, endeavour to do.

I have over and over pressed him to cultivate his acquaintance with   20
Mr. Battely[3] and several other gentlemen of Christ Church, whose
characters I am well acquainted [with], though little or not at all with
their persons. I have seen an answer from Mr. Hulton of Chester to
his letter concerning the greyhound,[4] which I hope we shall very
shortly have an opportunity of returning to him. Mr. Morgan   25

---

[1] Wesley probably received Morgan's letter of Jan. 31 on Monday, Feb. 4, when he
had a lengthy session with his son. They 'talked of Morgan's dog', his pupil was at first
very heated, and then 'quite melted into calmness'. It was a week before he set out on his
lengthy journey, and there were other apparent opportunities after his return, yet he
was indeed very busy with many other things, including urgent literary tasks as well as
Methodist and academic activities. The letters which he did write during this period
probably seemed either more urgent or simpler to deal with, in addition to his hesita-
tions about how long young Morgan's apparent reform would last.

[2] See letter of Dec. 17, 1733.

[3] Samuel Battely, of Horringer, Suffolk, who matriculated at Christ Church on
Dec. 13, 1733, aged 17. See Richard Morgan's letter of Jan. 31, 1734, for Battely's in-
vitations to his son.

[4] The owner of the dog which Morgan had brought into his rooms, contrary to
college regulations; see p. 375 n.

constantly attends public prayers; nor do I know that he omits private, or wilfully runs into any known sins of commission; and, I trust he never will.

Whether a person who goes thus far, who uses public and private prayer, and avoids sins of commission, be a good Christian, is a question which you beg we may drop for the future, because it is not your province to determine it. Alas! sir, you ask what I have no power to grant. When both the glory of my Saviour and the safety of your soul so loudly require me to speak, I may not, I dare not, I cannot be silent! Especially when I consider the reason you give for my being so, viz. that it is not your province to manage this point of controversy. No? Are you not then in covenant with Christ? And is it not your province to know the terms of that covenant? 'This do, and thou shalt live',[1] saith the Lord of life. Is it not your business to understand what this is? Though you are no divine, is it not your concern to be assured what it is to be a Christian? If on this very point depends your title either to life or death eternal, how shall I avoid giving you what light I can therein, without the deepest wound to my own conscience, the basest ingratitude to my friend, and the blackest treachery to my Master?

The question then must be determined some way; and for an infallible determination of it to the law and to the testimony we appeal.[2] At that tribunal we ought to be judged. If the oracles of God are still open to us, by them must every doubt be decided. And should all men contradict them we could only say, 'Let God be true, and every man a liar.'[3] We can never enough reverence those of the episcopal order. They are the angels of the church, the stars in the right hand of God.[4] Only let us remember, he was greater than those who said, 'Though I or an angel from heaven preach any other gospel than that ye have received, let him be accursed.'[5]

Now the gospel we have received does in no wise allow him to be a follower of Christ, to do his duty to God and man, who is constant in public and private prayer and avoids sins of commission. It supposes there are such things as sins of omission, too. Nay, it is notoriously evident that in our Lord's account of his own proceedings at the great day there is no mention of any other: it is for what

---

[1] Luke 10: 28.   [2] Isa. 8: 20.   [3] Rom. 3: 4.
[4] Rev. 1: 20. Wesley alludes to the five divines, including some bishops, whom Morgan had consulted, as mentioned in his letter of Jan. 31.
[5] Cf. Gal. 1: 8.

they have *not done* that the unprofitable servants are condemned to utter darkness.[1] O sir, what would it avail in that day could you confront our Lord with five thousand of his own ambassadors, protesting with one voice against his sentence, and declaring to those on the left hand that he had never said any such thing; that he condemned them for omitting what he had nowhere required them to do; that they were faithful because they were *only* unprofitable servants; that they ought to be ranked in the class of good Christians because they had *only* broken all the positive laws of Christ; that they had done their duty both to God and man, for they had prayed to God, and done neither good nor harm to their neighbours. For God's sake, sir, consider, how would this plea sound? Would it really be received in arrest of judgment? Or would the Judge reply, 'Out of thy own mouth will I judge thee.[2] Thou wicked and slothful servant!'[3] Did I require nothing to be done, as well to be avoided? Was an eternal reward promised to no-work?[4] Were my positive laws no laws at all? Was the pattern I set thee negative only? But thou hast done thy duty to God at least, for thou hast prayed to him. What didst thou pray for? For my Spirit to help thy infirmities?[5] For strength to tread in my steps? For power not only to avoid all sin, but to fulfil all righteousness?[6] Didst thou pray that thy righteousness might exceed that of the scribes and Pharisees?[7] Might not rest in externals, but be an inward vital principle? Didst thou pray for a clean heart? For the renewal of thy mind? For a right spirit, duly conformed to my image?[8] Didst thou pray for a soul continually ardent to do my will on earth, as it is done in heaven?[9] If thou prayedst for anything short of this, or if praying for this thy heart went not along with thy lips, thou prayedst as a fool or a heathen prayed, and thy prayer itself was the greatest of thy abominations. If thou didst pray for this power, which I had promised not to any particular order, but to every one of my disciples earnestly desiring it, why went not thy endeavour along with thy prayer? Because great men, the chief priests and elders, said it need not? Whom then oughtest thou to have believed? Me or them? Behold, I had told

---

[1] Matt. 25, espec. verses 30–3, 41–5.
[2] Luke 19: 22. [3] Matt. 25: 26.
[4] Possibly a word coined by Wesley on the analogy of Bunyan's no-life, no-love, no-sin, no-truth.
[5] See Rom. 8: 26. [6] Matt. 3: 15.
[7] See Matt. 5: 20. [8] See Rom. 8: 29.
[9] See Matt. 6: 10.

thee before, Obey God rather than men.[1] Thy blood be on thy own
head.[2]

Whether divines and bishops will agree to this I know not. But
this I know: it is the plain Word of God. God everywhere declares:
(1), that without doing good as well as avoiding evil, shall no flesh
living be justified.[3] (2). That as good prayers without good works
attending them are no better than a solemn mockery of God, so are
good works themselves without those tempers of heart, from their
subserviency to which they derive their whole value. (3). That those
tempers which alone are acceptable to God, and to procure acceptance for which our Redeemer lived and died, are, (i), Faith, without
which it is still impossible either to please him[4] or to overcome the
world;[5] (ii), Hope, without which we are alienated from the life of
God,[6] and strangers to the covenant of promise,[7] and (iii), Love of
God, and our neighbour for his sake, without which, though we
should give all our goods to feed the poor, yea, and our bodies to
be burned, if we will believe God, 'it profiteth us nothing'.[8]

I need say no more to show with what true respect and sincerity
I am, dear sir, your most obliged and ever obedient servant,

[John Wesley]

Source: Morgan MSS, pp. 76–82.

From Mrs. Susanna Wesley[9]

Sat: March 30th [1]734

Dear son

The young gentleman's father,[10] for aught I can perceive, has a better notion
of religion than many people have, though not the best; for few insist upon the
necessity of private prayer, but if they go to church sometimes, and abstain from
the grossest acts of mortal sin, though they are ignorant of the spirit and power

---

[1] Acts 5: 29.   [2] See Acts 18: 16.
[3] See Ps. 143: 2; Rom. 3: 20.   [4] Heb. 11: 6.
[5] 1 John 5: 4.   [6] Eph. 4: 18.   [7] See Eph. 2: 12.
[8] 1 Cor. 13: 3.
[9] Almost every paragraph of this lengthy letter appears to be a direct response to
John Wesley's missing letter of Mar. 1, whose contents may thus be reconstructed.
Notable exceptions are the fourth, illuminating his family background, and the rhapsody
in the seventh, which (along with similar passages) surely exerted an influence on
Wesley's own literary style.
[10] Richard Morgan. See his letter of Jan. 31, 1734, to Wesley.

of godliness, and have no sense of the love of God and universal benevolence, yet they rest well satisfied of their salvation, and are pleased to think they may enjoy the world as much as they can while they live, and have heaven in reserve when they die. I have met with abundance of these people in my time, and I think it one of the most difficult things imaginable to bring them off from their carnal security, and to convince them that heaven is a state, as well as a place; a state of holiness, begun in this life, though not perfected till we enter upon life eternal; that all sins are so many spiritual diseases, which must be cured by the power of Christ before we can be capable of being happy, even though it were possible for us to be admitted into the kingdom of heaven hereafter. If the young man's father was well apprized of this he would not venture to pronounce his son a good Christian upon such weak grounds as he seems to do. Yet notwithstanding the father's indifference, I can't but conceive good hopes of the son, because he chooses to spend so much of his time with you (for I presume he is not forced to it), and if we may not from thence conclude he is good, I think we may believe he desires to be so. And if that be the case, give him time. We know that the great work of regeneration is not performed at once, but proceeds by slow and often imperceptible degrees, by reason of the strong opposition which corrupt nature makes against it; yet if one grain of divine grace be sown in the heart, though (to use our blessed Lord's simile) it be but as a single grain of mustard seed, it will take root, and bring forth fruit with patience.

Mr. Clayton and Mr. Hall are much wiser than I am, yet with submission to their better judgments I think that though some marks of a visible superiority on your part is convenient to maintain the order of the world, yet severity is not; since experience may convince us that such kind of behaviour towards a man (children are out of the question) may make him a hypocrite, but will never make him a convert. Never trouble yourself to inquire whether he loves you or not: if you can persuade him to love God, he will love you as much as is necessary; if he love not God his love is of no value. But be that as it will, we must refer all things to God, and be as indifferent as we possibly can be in all matters wherein the great enemy, self, is concerned.

If you and your few pious companions have devoted two hours in the evenings to religious reading or conference, there can be no dispute but that you ought to spend the whole time in such exercises which it was set apart for; but if your evenings be not strictly devoted I see no harm in talking sometimes of your secular affairs. But if (as you say) it does your novice no good, and does yourselves harm, the case is plain—you must not prejudice your own souls to do another good; much less ought you to do so when you can do no good at all. Of this ye are better judges than I can be.

'Twas well you paid not for a double letter. I am always afraid of putting you to charge, and that fear prevented me sending you a long scribble indeed a while ago. For a certain person and I had a warm debate on some important points in religion wherein we could not agree.[1] Afterwards he wrote some propositions, which I endeavoured to answer, and this controversy I was minded to have sent you, and to have desired your judgment upon it. But the unreasonable

[1] Probably her husband, though it is just possible that she refers to John Whitelamb, whom Samuel Wesley had recently nominated to the rectory of Wroot, while continuing himself to serve at Epworth.

cost of such a letter then hindered me from sending it, since I have heard him in two sermons contradict every article he before defended, which makes me hope that upon second thoughts his mind is changed; and if so, what was said in private conference ought not to be remembered, and therefore I would not 5 send you the papers at all.

I can't think Mr. Hall does well in refusing an opportunity of doing so much service to religion as he certainly might do if he accepted the living he is about to refuse. Surely never was more need of orthodox, sober divines in our Lord's vineyard than there is now; and why a man of his extraordinary piety and love 10 to souls should decline the service in this critical juncture I can't conceive. But this is none of my business.

You want no direction from me how to employ your time. I thank God for his inspiring you with a resolution of being faithful in improving that important talent committed to your trust. It would be of no service to you to know in any 15 particular what I do, or what method in examination, or anything else, I observe. I am superannuated, and don't now live as I would, but as I can. I can't observe order, or think consistently, as formerly. When I have a lucid interval I aim at improving it, but alas! it is but aiming.

I see nothing in the disposition of your time but what I approve, unless it 20 be that you do not assign enough of it to meditation, which is (I conceive) incomparably the best means to spiritualize our affections, confirm our judgments, and add strength to our pious resolutions of any exercise whatever. If contrition be as 'tis commonly defined, that sorrow for and hatred of sin which proceeds from our love to God, surely the best way to excite this contrition is to meditate 25 frequently on such subjects as may excite, cherish, and increase our love to that blest Being! And what is so proper for this end as deep and serious consideration of that pure, unaccountable love which is demonstrated to us in our redemption by God Incarnate! Verily, the simplicity of divine love is wonderful! It transcends all thought, it passeth our sublimest apprehensions! Perfect love 30 indeed! No mixture of interest! No by-ends or selfish regards. If we be righteous, what give we him? In him we live, and move, and have our being, both in a physical and moral sense; but he can gain nothing by us, nor can we offer him anything that is not already his own. He can lose nothing by losing us, but in our loss of him we lose all good, all happiness, all peace, all pleasure, health, and 35 joy; all that is either good in itself, or can be good for us. And yet this great, this incomprehensible, ineffable, all-glorious God deigns to regard us! Declares he loves us! Expresses the tenderest concern for our happiness! Is unwilling to give us up to the grand enemy of souls, or to leave us to ourselves, but hath commissioned his ambassadors to offer us pardon and salvation upon the most 40 equitable terms imaginable! How long doth he wait to be gracious! How oft doth he call upon us to return and live! By his ministers, his providences; by the still, small voice of his Holy Spirit! By conscience, his vicegerent within us, and by his merciful corrections, and the innumerable blessings we daily enjoy! To contemplate God as he is in himself we cannot; if we aim at doing it we feel 45 nature faints under the least perception of his greatness, and we are presently swallowed up, and lost in the immensity of his glory! For finite, in presence of Infinite, vanishes straight into nothing. But when we consider him under the character of a Saviour we revive, and the greatness of that majesty which before astonished and confounded our weak faculties now enhances the value of his condescension towards us, and melts our tempers into tenderness and love.

But I am got to the end of my paper before I am aware. One word more and I am done. As your course of life is austere, and your diet low, so the passions, as far as they depend on the body, will be low, too. Therefore you must not judge 5 of your interior state by your not feeling great fervours of spirit and extraordinary agitations, as plentiful weeping, etc., but rather by the firm adherence of your will to God. If upon examination you perceive that you still choose him for your only good, that your spirit (to use a Scripture phrase) cleaveth steadfastly to him, follow Mr. Baxter's advice, and you will be easy: 10

Put your souls, with all their sins and dangers, and all their interests, into the hand of Jesus Christ your Saviour; and trust them wholly with him by a resolved faith. It is he that hath purchased them, and therefore loveth them. It is he that is the owner of them by right of redemption. And it is now become his own interest, even for the success and honour of his redemption, to save them. 15

When I begin to write to you I think I don't know how to make an end. I fully purposed when I began to write to be very brief, but I will conclude, though I find I shall be forced to make up such a clumsy letter as I did last time.[1]

Today J[ohn] Brown senior sets forward for London in order to attend your father home. 20

Pray give my love and blessing to Charles. I hope he is well, though I have never heard from him since he left Epworth.

Dear Jacky, God Almighty bless thee!

Source: MA.

From Richard Morgan, Sen.

April 27, 1734

Revd sir 25

I am very much obliged to you for the pains and trouble you have been at in explaining to me the duty of a Christian in your letter of the 15th of March, of which I would not have you suspect me to have been totally ignorant before. I have from my youth conversed pretty much with the clergy of all denominations, and have read some good books, and particularly that excellent book 30 called *The Whole Duty of Man*, and I must have been very stupid not to have learned something from them. Notwithstanding all that has been said, I am still of opinion that a person who attends public and private prayers, and is not observed or known to commit sin, may be ranked in the class of good Christians; for charity, I think, obliges us to believe and presume that that person who behaves 35 in this outward manner does his duty tolerably well in other respects. [. . .]

[1] Apparently a letter (not extant) which similarly occupied almost all the four pages, so that she may have used a makeshift cover or label for the address.

(After talk of business, and intimating as if his son should spend some years at Oxford, he goes on:)

You have hit upon a very just and true answer to the proposal to my contributing to your charities in Oxford. The poverty of this country is too well known:
5 there are to be seen and heard every hour very moving objects and miserable wretches, in all places here, who have much more need to claim the assistance of the neighbouring kingdom than to have anything taken from them. I have received a very obliging letter from your good father, to which I have wrote an answer, but whether to send it enclosed in this, as he desired, or send it away
10 directly to Westminster, I have not yet determined. I am, with great sincerity, dear sir, your truly affectionate obliged and humble servant,

Richard Morgan

Source: Morgan MSS, pp. 82–5.

To the Revd. William Law[1]

[June 26, 1734]

Revd sir

15   I must earnestly beg your immediate advice in a case of the greatest importance. Above two years since I was entrusted with a young gentleman of good sense, an even, generous temper, and pretty good learning.[2] Religion he had heard little of; but Mr. Nelson's *Practice of Devotion*,[3] your two treatises, and Thomas
20 à Kempis, by the blessing of God, awakened him by degrees to a true notion and serious practice of it. In this he continued sensibly improving till last Lent. At the beginning of which I advised him to

---

[1] William Law (1686–1761), whose *A Serious Call to a Devout and Holy Life* (1728) and *A Practical Treatise upon Christian Perfection* (1726) greatly influenced Wesley during his formative years, and of both of which he subsequently published abridged editions. It seems likely that Wesley first read the *Serious Call* in December, 1730 (W.H.S. XXXVII. 78–82, 143–5, 173–7). On July 13, 1732 he wrote to Law, and on July 31 had a lengthy interview with him in his home at Putney. This seems to have led to Wesley's reading of *Christian Perfection*. Their correspondence continued during 1733, interspersed with further personal conferences. Thus it was not out of the blue that Wesley wrote this abrupt appeal to the older and more experienced man.

[2] John Robson, of Sockburn, County Durham, who had matriculated at Lincoln College on May 17, 1732, aged 17, and was apparently Wesley's pupil from the outset. For Wesley's problems with him see Green, pp. 193–4, and Heitzenrater, pp. 273–4.

[3] Robert Nelson (1665–1715), nonjuror, *The Practice of True Devotion* (1698). ('Jackson', found in the text of Moore, Jackson, and Telford, is based on a misreading of the original.)

do as he had done the year before, viz. to obey the order of the
church by using such a sort and measure of abstinence as his health
permitted and his spiritual wants required. He said he did not think
his health would permit [him] to use that abstinence which he did
the year before. And notwithstanding my reply, that his athletic 5
habit could be in no danger by only abstaining from flesh, and using
moderately some less pleasing food, he persisted in his resolution of
not altering his food at all. A little before Easter, perceiving he had
much contracted the times he had till then set apart for religious
reading, I asked him whether he was not himself convinced that he 10
spent too much time in reading secular authors. He answered, he
was convinced any time was too much, and that he should be a better
Christian if he never read them at all. I then pressed him earnestly to
pray for strength, to pray according to that conviction. And he
resolved to try for a week. When that was expired he said his desire 15
of classical reading was not inflamed, but a little abated. Upon
which I begged him to repeat his resolution for a week or two
longer. He said it signified nothing, for he could never part with the
classics entirely. I desired him to read what[1] you say in the *Christian
Perfection* on readin[g] vain authors. He read it, agreed to every word 20
of it, but still in his practice denied it, though appearing in most
other particulars a humble, active, zealous Christian. On Tuesday,
April the [2]3rd,[2] being one of the days the statutes require us to
communicate at St. Mary's, I called upon him just before church,
being to set out for Lincolnshire as soon as the service was over. 25
I asked whether he still halted between two opinions,[3] and after
exhorting him as I could to renounce himself and serve his Master
with simplicity, I left him. He did not communicate that day. On
my return, May 21,[4] I immediately inquired what state he was in,
and found he had never communicated since (which he used to do 30
weekly), that he had left off rising early, visiting the poor, and almost
all religious reading, and entirely given himself up to secular. When
I asked him why he had left off the Holy Eucharist he said, fairly,
because to partake of it implied a fresh promise to renounce himself
entirely, and to please God alone; and he did not design to do so. 35

[1] Orig., 'that'; Moore, Jackson, 'that which'.
[2] See Wesley's monthly summary for that day.
[3] See 1 Kgs. 18: 21.
[4] Wesley visited London for a few days on Apr. 4, and returned to Oxford before
setting off on his much longer journey in May. During the interval he was able to make
several other diary observations about Robson.

I asked whether he was well convinced he ought to do so. He said, 'Yes!' Whether he wished he could design it? He answered, No, he did not desire it.

From time to time, particularly a few days ago, I urged him to tell
5 me upon what he grounded his hope of salvation. He replied, after some pause: 'Christ died for all men', but if none were saved by him without performing the conditions, his death would 'not avail one in a thousand', which was 'inconsistent with the goodness of God'. But this answer, and every part of it, he soon gave up, adding with
10 the utmost seriousness that he cared not whether it was true or no— he was very happy at present, and he desired nothing further.

This morning I again asked him what he thought of his own state. He said he thought nothing about it. I desired to know whether he could, if he considered it ever so little, expect to be saved by the
15 terms of the Christian covenant. He answered he did not consider it at all. Nor did all I could say in the least move him. He assented to all, but was affected with nothing. He grants, with all composure, that he is not in a salvable state, and shows no degree of concern while he owns he can't find mercy.

20 I am now entirely at a loss what step to take. Pray he can't or won't. When I lent him several prayers he returned them unused, saying he does not desire to be otherwise than he is, and why should he pray for it? I do not seem so much as to understand his distemper. It appears to me quite incomprehensible. Much less can I tell what
25 remedies are proper for it. I therefore beseech you, sir, by the mercies of God, that you would not be slack, according to the ability he shall give,[1] to advise and pray for him and, revd. sir, your most obliged servant,

John Wesley

30 Lincoln College, Oxon
June 26, 1734

Source: MA, a contemporary copy, collated with the version in Moore, I. 368–71. The latter shows errors in transcription, some of which are followed by Jackson and Telford, though each seems also to have used the MS copy.

[1] See I Pet. 4: 11.

From Mrs. Mary Pendarves[1]

2d July, 1734

I never began a letter with so much confusion to anybody as I do this to Cyrus. I can't recollect that I ever used anyone so ill (if my being silent may be called ill usage), and at the same time must confess no one deserves it so little. What to do to extenuate my fault I do not know, which has truly been disadvantageous only to myself; did I not find it absolutely necessary to my conduct (in that part of my life which ought to be my greatest concern) to renew this correspondence, I own I am so overcome with shame for what is past that I should not dare to put you in mind of my unworthiness. I give you now an opportunity of showing your forgiveness and generosity—not that you want extraordinary occasions to set those qualities in a proper light. Is it not some degree of grace to own one's faults frankly? But do I not destroy all merit by supposing I have any? When I sat down to write I thought I could have acquitted myself better, but I find it impossible to say anything in my justification. What will avail my saying I have constantly had an esteem for you? You have no reason to suppose that I have so much as barely remembered you. The more I consider the obligations I had to continue my correspondence with one who hath showed so many marks of an unfeigned desire to assist and promote my eternal happiness, the deeper is my concern for having forfeited so great an advantage. I am so sincerely sorry

---

[1] Mary Pendarves went to Ireland in September, 1731, her last-known letter to Wesley being that of Aug. 26, 1731. His diary shows that he wrote to her not only on Sept. 28, 1731 (see above, pp. 313–15), but also on Dec. 15, 1731, Apr. 8, and Aug. 25, 1732. It seems certain, however, that no letter reached him from her during this period, and on Mar. 11, 1732, she confessed to her sister: 'Cyrus by this time has blotted me out of his memory; or if he does remember me it can only be to reproach me. What can I say *for* myself? What can I indeed say *to myself*, that have neglected so extraordinary a correspondent? . . . I can't put myself into better hands for making an excuse for me than yours.' (Delany, I. 343.) (Wesley's correspondence with Selima had apparently remained in better shape, and his diary shows that he received letters from her, as well as writing to her, regularly until Oct. 17, 1732, and probably until his departure for Georgia three years later, though after that only occasionally.) In April, 1733, Aspasia returned from Ireland, and wrote to her sister: 'As for the ridicule Cyrus has been exposed to, I do not at all wonder at it. Religion in its plainest dress suffers daily from the insolence and ignorance of the world; then how should that person escape who dares to appear openly in its cause?' (Ibid., I. 410.) In May she was in London, in July with Lady Weymouth at Longleat House, and from there went to stay with her mother and sister at Gloucester. Wesley wrote three letters to her after her return, on May 7, June 15, and Nov. 16, 1733. It seems almost certain that these letters also were greeted with silence, and that only after Wesley himself had stopped writing did she pluck up sufficient courage to write, perhaps prompted by a reported letter from Wesley to Selima in May, 1734. Wesley's reply (which follows) shows that he did not look for a renewal of their close relationship. His letters dwindled to one a year to Aspasia, until Sept. 17, 1736, and even to Selima he seems to have continued only a year longer, his last recorded one to her being written on June 16, 1737. In 1743 Mary Pendarves married Dr. Patrick Delany (1685?–1768), of whom she saw much while in Ireland. She became a close friend of the Royal Family, and long before her death in 1788 was recognized as a leading and respected figure in social and literary circles.

for the ill impression I have given you of myself that I shall shun you as a
criminal would a judge; and whatever indulgence your goodness may incline
you to show me, I never shall imagine you can have any regard for one that has
so ungratefully neglected your friendship. To tell you my engagements with the
5 world have engrossed me, and occasioned my not writing to you, will be enlarging my condemnation. I must say one thing more, 'that my going to Longleat,
where for some time I was much indisposed, and not very well able to write';
and 'then removing to London to a new unfurnished house put me into a great
hurry'; 'I waited for a leisure hour that I might write to you at large, till shame
10 seized me so violently that I had not courage to write'; but at last have broke
through it, and choose to suffer any reproach rather than lose the advantage of
your friendship, without at least regretting that I have brought this mortification on myself. I would desire my compliments to Araspes, but I fear they can't
be acceptable from one that has behaved herself so ill to Cyrus. Adieu. Your
15 happiness will ever be sincerely desired by

Aspasia.

Source: Asp, pp. 60–2, apparently in the hand of Benjamin Ingham, with fewer
words abbreviated.

To Mrs. Mary Pendarves

[July, 1734]

Alas! Aspasia, are you indeed convinced that I can be of any
service to you? I fear you have not sufficient ground for such a
20 conviction. Experience has shown how far my power is short of my
will. For some time I flattered myself with the pleasing hope, but
I grow more and more ashamed of having indulged it. You need not
the support of so weak a hand. How can I possibly think you do
(though that thought tries now and then still to obtrude itself),[1]
25 since you have so long and resolutely thrust it from you? I dare not
therefore blame you for so doing. Doubtless you acted upon cool
reflection. You declined the trouble of writing, not because it was
a trouble, but because it was a needless one. And if so, what injury
have you done yourself? As for me, you could do me no [injury][2] by
30 your silence. It did indeed deprive me of much pleasure, and of a
pleasure from which I ought to have received much improvement.
But still, as it was one I had no title to but your goodness, to withdraw it was no injustice. I surely thank you for what is past, and

[1] Orig., 'tries ((still)) now & then still to obtrude itself still'.
[2] Orig., 'silence'.

may the God of my salvation return it sevenfold into your bosom. And if ever you should please to add to those thousand obligations any new ones, I trust they shall neither be unrewarded by him nor unworthily received by, Aspasia, [[your obliged and obedient servant]][1]   5

Cyrus

Araspes, too, hopes you will never have reason to tax him with ingratitude. Adieu.

Source: Asp, pp. 62–3 (similar hand and format to previous letters).

From the Revd. John Clayton[2]

Manchester, Aug. 2, 1734

Revd. and dear sir,   10

I have carefully consulted your letter, and consulted Dr. Deacon upon it, and shall give you our thoughts of it with freedom and simplicity. As to the particular case of the gentleman you mention, we could agree with Mr. Law if he had not used that phrase, 'Let him alone.'[3] Indeed I think he is by no means to be let alone. Shall I see my brother fallen into a pit, and not lend him my   15 hand to help him out? As to his classics and philosophy, let him pursue them, for so he will, notwithstanding all you can say to him against it. Therefore let not your advice be thrown away in endeavouring to dissuade him from them, but rather be employed in pointing out the way how studies may be sanctified, and made to turn to account. Indeed I cannot think such books unlawful, but   20 on the contrary esteem them as useful helps, even to the Christian; as they are valuable monuments of antiquity, and authentic records of ancient times, and of the wonderful dealings of God with the sons of men.

As for your pupils in general, we thus far differ from Mr. Law; we agree with him in recommending Norris [and Malebranche];[4] but then it is because we   25

---

[1] This is a somewhat hazardous attempt at deciphering the unfamiliar characters.

[2] This replies to Wesley's of June (30?) and July, letters in which he had posed many searching queries dealing not only with the pastoral problem of how to handle Richard Morgan, Jun., but deep personal concerns affecting his own developing spirituality and churchmanship, fasting, mental prayer, confirmation, absolution, and the Holy Communion as a justifying ordinance. Wesley greatly valued Clayton's advice as a recent Methodist colleague in Oxford, but also as an intimate in Manchester of the non-juring leader, Thomas Deacon.

[3] See Wesley's letter to William Law, June 26, 1734, to which this was apparently Law's reply. Cf. Dec. 24, 1734, when Law gave exactly the same advice to Wesley about Thomas Broughton (p. 413, n.1 below).

[4] Orig., 'Norris Malb: (?)'. The copyist obviously had difficulty in transcribing this, as he did with other passages. It seems likely that Wesley was referring to a work by John Norris, *Reflections upon the Conduct of Human Life: with Reference to Learning and*

think them the best philosophers (where physics are not concerned) as well as
the best Christians. But this as to religion; shall I say I differ from Mr. Law?
Yes, but I believe it is because I am but a babe in Christ, and am not capable to
digest the strong food he administers. For I must own in my present weakness
5 of understanding I can see no other way of giving them a deep sense that they
have but one business to do in life than to be constantly aiming at the *unum
necessarium*;[1] and speaking of it not a *little now and then*, but *frequently* and
fervently. I am sure I want such sort of conversation, and a great deal of it, too.
And as to fasting, communicating, etc., I must say this, that I do not know one
10 instance of a person that took up the practice of them without being first moved
thereto by the advice and exhortations of his friend. And is not fasting a means
of improvement? Are there not some kind of devils not to be cast out but by
fasting and prayer? And then is not the Holy Eucharist the highest means of
grace, and of consequence the likeliest step to improvement? Indeed, I would
15 hope we do not sufficiently understand Mr. Law. He cannot be against these
things in his heart, in however strong language he expresseth himself when he is
combating the but too common notion of their being all that is required of us.
    What is 'too logical' in religion? Is rule and method useful in worldly things
of small importance, and superfluous in the great concerns of religion? True,
20 simplicity of heart is all and in all, but how is this to be attained without prudential helps, and proper regulations? Mental prayer is doubtless a most acceptable
service to God, because it is the most notable instance of our union with him.
Scougal gives it the preference to vocal prayer as well as Mr. Law. So do Poiret
and Madame Bourignon. But why should we put them in competition? Vocal
25 prayer, meditation, hearing the Word, and receiving the Sacrament, are they not
divine institutions? And who then shall say that vocal prayer is proper only for
those who have not attained to the faculty of praying mentally? Fit books for
you and every Christian priest are all the Fathers of the three first centuries,
whereby you may be enabled both to know and profess the faith once delivered
30 to the saints, and to steer your course in the due medium between the monkish
mysticism of the fourth century and the lukewarm indifferency of the present
age. We entirely agree with the seventh observation, as believing that a different
rule is necessary to one that is ripe in the faith from what was useful to him
whilst he was only a babe in Christ.
35   In your last letter you inquire how far the several points in Dr. Deacon's
book[2] are essential. To this the doctor answers that he had nowhere asserted[3]
any of them to be essential, and that he is far from thinking them all of equal
obligation. I believe, though, I could prove that there is no rite or ceremony
prescribed which may not be defended from the writers of the second century.

Knowledge, of which Wesley was on the point of publishing (or perhaps had already pub-
lished) an abridgement—see *Bibliog*, No. 3. Appended was 'A Scheme of Books suited to
the preceding *Reflections*' with the following recommended under 'philosophy': 'Aldrich's
Logic, with Sanderson's first appendix', Keill's *Euclid*, Derham's *Physico-* and *Astro-
Theology*, and the works of the French philosopher, Nicole Malebranche (1638-1715).
(It seems just possible that Clayton wrote, 'Norris's Scheme'.)

    1 'The one thing necessary.'
    2 *A Compleat Collection of Devotions* (1734).
    3 Orig., 'asserted / stated (?)'.

As for the gentleman's case who was confirmed before he was baptized, all that ever I have spoken to about it are of opinion that the confirmation ought to be repeated. For the design of that ordinance, being to complete the Sacrament of Baptism, and confirm to us those privileges we then received, it must suppose baptism to be previous, or otherwise it can be of none effect. 5

What sort of festivals do the Constitutions[1] prefer to fast? I believe none but the greater, none of which can coincide with the Stations except twelve of the fifty days between Easter and Pentecost, which accordingly take [the] place of the fasts.

As for your queries relating to the Holy Eucharist, I believe the two first, 10 relating to its being a means of applying the merits of Christ to the receiver, and of its being the only means, may be fully determined in Johnson's *Unbloody Sacrifice*,[2] in that ch[apter] which proves the Holy Eucharist to be a sacrifice both expiatory and propitiatory. The last query, viz. how this is consistent with authoritative absolution, has made me study the point; the result of which is 15 that I believe the generally received doctrine of absolution is entirely modern and popish; and that the primitive absolution regarded the Ch[urch] censures primarily, and absolution from sin in a secondary sense only, namely as the offender was thereby admitted to the peace of the Church, and of consequence to the participation of the Holy Eucharist, whereby alone remission of sins is to 20 be attained. I think the whole present Church may err—I had almost said that it doth so; it was never thought infallible till the Papists had a turn to serve by thinking it so. Indefectible it is, but I think by no means exempt from error, 'I am with you', etc. [being] confined to the succession, and to a preservation from such error as would destroy the very being of a church. A church may be catholic 25 though not orthodox, may retain all fundamentals, though she be blasted with superstition and error.

J.C.

Address: 'To the Rev. Mr. Wesley, Fellow of Lincoln Col: Oxon.' *Charge*: '4' *End* (by JW?): 'VII. Mr. Clayton / Curious enough' *Source*: MA, a copy in a late hand, probably nineteenth century.

From the Revd. Samuel Wesley, Sen.

Epworth, Aug. 27, Tuesday, 1734

Dear son 30

This is to repeat my thanks for the care you have taken about my Job,[3] for which you deserve the name of his fourth son, who, if Philo does not lie, was

---

[1] The Apostolic Constitutions, one of Deacon's major authorities, which through him and Clayton greatly influenced Wesley's own liturgical thought and practice.

[2] John Johnson (1662-1725), whose *Unbloody Sacrifice* (1714-17) was taken to Georgia by Wesley, and read diligently on the voyage (see diary, Nov. 24-Dec. 24, 1735).

[3] *Dissertationes in Librum Jobi*, then being printed by William Bowyer of London. It was published in 1736, though a few presentation copies appeared in 1735. John Wesley took over from his brother Samuel the task of seeing this through the press,

called Pilias. By the account you give me of the press, they must now have gotten to page 400 or upward. Therefore I desire that you would send me as soon as possible, or cause to be sent, those sheets which have been printed off since I left London, stitched up together, from page 320 (for so far I brought
5 down with me) to the end of what is done, that I may correct that as I have done what I had before, which I doubt will swell my errata into an appendix, for I never yet saw a book of the same bulk printed with, I think, the twentieth part of the faults that are in this, which I think amount to several thousands.

As for us here, we are not idle, but have got the Three Faces of Pentapolis
10 wellnigh finished, and shall have them wrought off by the end of this week. I've likewise just had a letter from Mr. Vertue, that he's going on with Job's Phiz, and that 'twill be ready by that time the work is fit for it. We have received letters per post, as we suppose, from your second Nathanael, though we had not the happiness to see him, and believe he is stepped to give his friends a visit
15 about Cana in Galilee. One thing I've writ you of twice or thrice already, which I think is of moment, but have yet received no answer. 'Tis that relating to Mr. Morgan of Ireland, whether you had sent him any receipts, as he desired. If not, whether I should not send him the whole dozen. For as I wrote you, I have ninety by me to spare, which would not be respited any longer than till the new
20 Proposals are printed, two or three of which I think it would be proper to send along with the receipts. I should be glad to hear whether you have heard from your brother Samuel what receipts he has by him. I believe a good number, though he may have disposed of several of them, as he told me he doubted not to do, amongst his friends in Devonshire.
25 We are all well, except him who may best be spared, who is something better than he has been, and is, with blessing to you and company, your loving father,
Sam. Wesley

All send love.
P.S. Pray do you hear anything of John Lambert, and where he and his family
30 are? For I have not heard a syllable from him since I was in London.

End by JW: 'My F[ather]', 'Au 9 734'   *Source*: MA, the signature only by the rector, the remainder in the hand of the Revd. John Whitelamb, the address half is missing.

especially in view of his brother's removal from London and then of their father's death. He himself translated much or most of the work into Latin, and made other literary contributions. See *Bibliog*, No. 7.

To the Revd. Samuel Wesley, Sen.[1]

[Nov. 15, 1734][2]

[. . . It is now my unalterable resolution not to accept of Epworth living, if I could have it.[3]] . . . The question is not whether I could do more good to others *there* or *here*, but whether I could do more good to myself; seeing wherever I can be most holy myself, there, 5 I am assured, I can most promote holiness in others. But I am equally assured there is no place under heaven so fit for my improvement as Oxford. Therefore . . .

Source: Clarke, I. 339–40; cf. letter of Nov. 20 in reply.

From the Revd. Samuel Wesley, Sen.

Nov. 20, 1734[4]

Your state of the question, and only argument, is: 'The question is not 10 whether I could do more good to others *there* or *here*; but whether I could do more good to myself; seeing wherever I can be most holy myself, there I can

---

[1] On October 11, 1734, a letter from Epworth informed John Wesley of his father's seriously worsening health, and he secured permission to visit him immediately. When he arrived his father was in fact 'mending', but John stayed on to help him in various ways. On October 16 his father urged John to accept the Epworth living, which he proposed to resign in his favour immediately, just as earlier in the year he had resigned that of Wroot in favour of his son-in-law John Whitelamb. John sought advice. The Revd. Joseph Hoole of Haxey seconded the rector's plea. When Wesley returned to Oxford on Nov. 8, however, he was still unconvinced by the arguments in favour of his becoming a parish priest. The renewed Oxford ties, combined with meditation and prayer, resolved any remaining doubts, and on Nov. 15 he informed his father briefly of his decision to stay where he was. (See Heitzenrater, pp. 283–9, and Wesley's diary.) The rector seems to have found it difficult to believe his eyes, began a letter to that effect on Nov. 20, but did not complete and post it until Dec. 4, when he wrote urging his oldest son also to exert pressure upon the reluctant John. Both letters quoted the passage (with minor variations) here reproduced from that to the Revd. Samuel Wesley, Jun.

[2] The specific date comes from Wesley's diary.

[3] See the letter from the rector to the Revd. Samuel Wesley, Dec. 4, 1734:
'. . . I shall throw what I have a mind you should know under three heads . . .
  1. Of our family—where, if I see anything, all *Job* is at stake, for your brother John has at last writ me, "That it is now his unalterable resolution not to accept of Epworth living, if he could have it;" and the reason he gives for it is in these words: "The question is not . . ."' (Clarke, I. 339.) The use of quotation marks for reported speech (familiar throughout Wesley's own writings) implied that the exact words were being reproduced except for such minor alterations as a change from the first to the third person.

[4] Headed in Priestley's version (apparently a fairly accurate reproduction of the

most promote holiness in others. But I can improve myself more at Oxford than
at any other place.'

To this I answer, 1st. It is not dear self, but the glory of God, and the different
degrees of promoting it, which should be our main consideration and direction
5 in the choice of any course of life. Witness St. Paul and Moses.

2. Supposing you could be more holy yourself at Oxford, how does it follow
that you could more promote holiness in others there than elsewhere? Have you
found many instances of it, after so many years' hard pains and labour? Further,
I dare say you are more modest and just than to say, there are no holier men than
10 you at Oxford; and yet it is possible they may not have promoted holiness more
than you have done; as I doubt not but you might have done it much more had
you taken the right method. For there is a particular turn of mind for these
matters: great prudence as well as fervour.

3. I cannot allow austerity, or fasting, considered by themselves, to be proper
15 acts of holiness. Nor am I for a solitary life. God made us for a social life; we
are not to bury our talent, we are to let our light shine before men, and that not
barely through the chinks of a bushel, for fear the wind should blow it out. The
design of lighting it was that it might give light to all that went into the house of
God. And to this academical studies are only preparatory.

document before him), 'Extract of my father's letter, dated Nov. 20, 1734.' This was
written in reply to John's of Nov. 15, 1734. The opening section of the rector's letter
of Dec. 4, to his oldest son Samuel, confirms the general purport of this. After the
opening description of John's letter (see above), he continues: 'Thus stands his argument, the whole of which seems to me to be existical, as his manner is, following that
great man's words too close, as he did the sophists, though not to his honour. [. . .] Yet,
though I am no more fond of this griping and wrangling distemper than I am of Mr.
Harper's boluses and clysters (for age would again have rest), I sat myself down to
try if I could unravel his sophisms, and hardly one of his assertions appeared to me to be
universally true. I think the main of my answer was that he seemed to mistake the end of
academical studies, which were chiefly preparatory, in order to qualify men to instruct
others. He thinks there is no place so fit for his improvement as Oxford [. . .] Besides, be
austerity and mortification either a means of promoting holiness, or in some degree a
part of it, yet why may not a man exercise these in his own house as strictly as in any
college [. . .]? Neither can I understand the meaning or drift of being thus ever learning,
and never coming to a due proficiency in the knowledge and practice of the truth, so as
to be able commendably to instruct others in it.

'Thus far I have written with my own hand in the original, both to you and your
brother, for many days together; but am now so heartily tired that I must, contrary to my
resolution above, get my son Whitelamb to transcribe and finish it. I have done what I
could with such a shattered head and body to satisfy the scruples which your brother has
raised against my proposal, from conscience and duty: but if your way of thinking be
the same with mine, especially after you have read and weighed what follows, you will
be able to convince him in a much clearer and stronger manner. [. . .] I urged to him
among other things the great precariousness of my own health, and sensible decay of my
strength [. . .]; the deplorable state in which I should leave your mother and the family
[. . .]; the loss of near forty years' (I hope honest) labour in this place [. . .]; for I think
I know my successor, who, I am morally satisfied, would be no other than Mr. P., if
your brothers both slight it. [. . .] I hinted at one thing, which I mentioned in my letter
to your brother, whereon I depend more than upon all my own simple reasoning, and
that is, earnest prayer to [God].' (Clarke, I. 340–2.)

4. You are sensible what figures those make who stay in the university till they are superannuated. I cannot think drowsiness promotes holiness. How commonly do they drone away their life, either in a college or in a country parsonage, where they can only give God the snuffs of them, having nothing of life or vigour left to make them useful in the world. 5

5. We are not to fix our eye on one single point of duty, but to take in the complicated view of all the circumstances in every state of life that offers. Thus in the case before us, put all circumstances together: if you are not indifferent whether the labours of an aged father for above forty years in God's vineyard be lost, and the fences of it trodden down and destroyed; if you consider 10 that Mr. M.[1] must in all probability succeed me if you do not, and that the prospect of that mighty Nimrod's coming hither shocks my soul, and is in a fair way of bringing down my grey hairs with sorrow to the grave; if you have any care for our family, which must be dismally shattered as soon as I am dropped; if you reflect on the dear love and longing which this poor people has for you, 15 whereby you will be enabled to do God the more service, and the plenteousness of the harvest, consisting of near two thousand souls, whereas you have not many more scholars in the university; you may perhaps alter your mind, and bend your will to his who has promised, if in all our ways we acknowledge him, he will direct our paths . . . 20

Source: Priestley, pp. 48–50, collated with Hampson, I. 120–4, an independent but much more heavily edited reading of the same extract made from the original, probably by John, but possibly by Samuel. Cf. also versions by Whitehead and Stevenson, which appear to derive from Priestley, though introducing their own variants.

To the Revd. Samuel Wesley, Sen.[2]

Oxon, Dec. 10, 1734

Dear sir

1. The authority of a parent and the call of providence are things of so sacred a nature that a question in which these are any

---

[1] Cf. the letter to Samuel, Dec. 4, where it appears as 'Mr. P.' One transcription must surely be incorrect. A decade earlier there could be no mistaking 'M' and 'P' in the rector's hand, and this seems unlikely even at this time, even though his hand was shaky, though extreme tremulousness or a mishap to the letter might have made the character puzzling—though both Priestley and Hampson interpreted it as 'M'. The passage in the letter of Dec. 4 transcribed by Adam Clarke, however, was in the hand of John Whitelamb, but here again it would be almost impossible under normal conditions to confuse the two characters. 'P' might be John Pennington, Wesley's former curate.

[2] A reply to the rector's challenge of Nov. 20, which had occupied him 'for many days together', so that it was not until Dec. 7 that Wesley entered in his diary, 'Pressing letter from my father to take Epworth'. The son similarly took many days over his reply, planning it during over three hours in the morning of Dec. 10, spending a similar period

way concerned deserves the most serious consideration. I am therefore greatly obliged to you for the pains you have taken to set ours in a clear light; which I now intend to consider more at large, with the utmost attention of which I am capable. And I shall the
5 more cheerfully do it as being assured of your joining with me in earnestly imploring his guidance who will not suffer those that bend their wills to his to seek death in the error of their life.[1]

2. I entirely agree that 'the glory of God, and the different degrees of promoting it, are to be our sole consideration and direction in the
10 choice of any course of life';[2] and consequently that it must wholly turn upon this single point whether I ought to prefer a college life or that of the rector of a parish. I do not say the glory of God is to be my first, or my principal consideration, but my only one; since all that are not implied in this are absolutely of no weight. In presence
15 of this they all vanish away; they are less than the small dust of the balance.[3]

3. And indeed, till all other considerations were set aside I could never come to any clear determination: till my eye was single my whole mind was full of darkness.[4] Every consideration distinct from
20 this threw a shadow over all the objects I had in view, and was such a cloud as no light could penetrate. But so long as I can keep my eye single, and steadily fixed on the glory of God, I have no more doubt of the way wherein I should go than of the shining of the sun at noonday.

25 4. That course of life tends most to the glory of God wherein we can most promote holiness in ourselves and others. I say in ourselves and others, as being fully persuaded that these can never be put asunder. For how is it possible that the good God should make our interest inconsistent with our neighbour's? That he should make our
30 being in one state best for ourselves, and our being in another best for his church? This would be making a strange schism in his body,

---

over the first draft, begun that same afternoon and completed on the 11th. A part of each of the following five days was occupied in transcribing what apparently became a second draft, along with a fair copy, to both of which he put the finishing touches on Dec. 19, after a lapse of two days while he travelled to London, where he posted it to Epworth. Securing a full and accurate text of this epochal document by John is very difficult. For the problems and the attempt at resolving them see 'Sources' below, p. 409.

[1] Wisd. 1: 12. A paragraph on the need for prayer apparently closed the rector's letter: see his companion letter to his son Samuel, dated Dec. 4, quoted in the opening note to that of Nov. 20, p. 396 n., above.

[2] See preceding letter, § 1.

[3] See Isa. 40: 15.   [4] See Matt. 6: 22-3.

such as surely never was from the beginning of the world. And if not, then whatever state is best on either of these accounts is so on the other likewise. If it be best for others, then it is so for us; if for us, then for them.

5. However, when two ways of life are proposed I should choose to begin with that part of the question, Which of these have I rational ground to believe will conduce most to my own improvement? And that, not only because it is every physician's concern to heal himself first,[1] but because it seems we may judge with more ease, and perhaps more certainty, too, in which state we can most promote holiness in ourselves than in which we can most promote it in others.

6. By holiness I mean, not fasting, or bodily austerity, or any other external means of improvement, but that inward temper to which all these are subservient, a renewal of soul in the image of God.[2] I mean a complex habit of lowliness, meekness, purity, faith, hope, and love of God and man. And I therefore believe that in the state wherein I am I can most promote this holiness in myself, because I now enjoy several advantages which are almost peculiar to it.

7. The first of these is daily converse with my friends. I know no other place under heaven where I can have always at hand half a dozen persons nearly of my own judgment, and engaged in the same studies; persons who are awakened into a full and lively conviction that they have only one work to do upon earth; who are in some measure enlightened so as to see, though at a distance, what that one work is, viz., the recovery of that single intention and pure affection which were in Christ Jesus; who, in order to this, have according to their power renounced themselves, and wholly, absolutely, devoted themselves to God; and who suitably thereto deny themselves, and take up their cross daily.[3] To have such a number of such friends constantly watching over my soul, and according to the variety of occasions administering reproof, advice, or exhortation, with all plainness and all gentleness, is a blessing I have not yet found any Christian to enjoy in any other part of the kingdom. And such a blessing it is, so conducive, if faithfully used, to the increase of all holiness, as I defy anyone to know the full value of till he receives his full measure of glory.

8. Another invaluable blessing which I enjoy here in a greater

---

[1] See Luke 4: 23.   [2] See Col. 3: 10.   [3] See Luke 9: 23.

degree than I could anywhere else is retirement. I have not only as much, but as little company as I please; I have no such thing as a trifling visitant except about an hour in a month, when I invite some of the Fellows to breakfast. Unless at that one time no one ever takes
5 it into his head to set foot within my door except he has some business of importance to communicate to me, or I to him. And even then, as soon as he has dispatched his business, he immediately takes his leave.

9. Both these blessings, the continual presence of useful, and
10 uninterrupted freedom from trifling acquaintance, are exceedingly endeared to me, whenever I have spent but one week out of this place. The far greatest part of the conversation I meet with abroad, even among those whom I believe to be real Christians, turns on points that are absolutely wide of my purpose, that no way forward
15 me in the business of life. Now, though they may have time to spare, I have none. 'Tis absolutely necessary for such a one as myself to follow with all possible care and vigilance that excellent advice of Mr. Herbert:

> Still let thy mind be bent, still plotting where,
20 > And when, and how, the business may be done.[1]

And this, I bless God, I can in some measure, so long as I avoid that bane of piety, the company of good sort of men,[2] lukewarm Christians[3] (as they are called), persons that have a great concern for, but no sense of, religion. But these insensibly undermine all my resolu-
25 tions, and quite steal from me the little fervour I have; and I never come from among these 'saints of the world' (as John Valdesso calls them),[4] faint, dissipated, and shorn of all my strength, but I say, 'God deliver me from a half-Christian.'

10. Freedom from care I take to be the next greatest advantage
30 to freedom from useless, and therefore hurtful, company. And this

---

[1] Cf. George Herbert, *The Temple*, 'The Church Porch', ll. 337-8:

> Let thy mind still be bent, still plotting where
> And when and how the business may be done.

[2] Cf. Wesley's introduction to Matt. 25 in his *Explanatory Notes upon the New Testament*: 'But what will become of those who do no harm, honest, inoffensive, "good sort" of people?' Cf. also § 13 below.

[3] See Rev. 3: 16.

[4] See Juan de Valdes (*c.* 1500–41), Consideration 76 of *The Hundred and Ten Considerations*, which Wesley had read in Oct., 1733, in the translation by Nicholas Ferrar (1638). Cf. Sermon, *Scriptural Christianity*, II. 5. (Vol. 1 of this edition, No. 4.)

too I enjoy in greater perfection here than I can ever expect to do anywhere else. I hear of such a thing as 'the cares of the world',[1] and I
read of them, but I know them not. My income is ready for me on so
many stated days, and all I have to do is to count and carry it home.
The grand article of my expense is food, and this too is provided 5
without any care of mine: I have nothing to do but at such an hour
to take and eat what is prepared for me. My laundress, barber, etc.,
are always ready at quarter-day, so I have no trouble on account of
those expenses. And for what I occasionally need I can be supplied
from time to time without any expense of thought. Now to convince 10
me what a help to holiness this is (were not my own experience
abundantly sufficient) I should need no better authority than St.
Paul's: 'I would have you without carefulness. This I speak for your
own profit, that ye may attend upon the Lord without distraction.'[2]
Happy is he that careth only for the things of the Lord, how he may 15
please the Lord.[3] He may be holy both in body and spirit, after the
Apostle's judgment, and I think that he had the Spirit of God.

11. To quicken me in making a thankful and diligent use of all
the other advantages of this place, I have the opportunity of public
prayer twice a day, and of weekly communicating. It would be easy 20
to mention many more, and likewise to show many disadvantages
which a person of greater courage and skill than me could scarce
separate from a country life. But whatever one of experience and
resolution might do, I am very sensible I should not be able to
turn aside one of the thousand temptations that would immediately 25
rush upon me. I could not stand my ground, no, not for one month,
against intemperance in sleeping, eating, and drinking; against
irregularity in study; against a general lukewarmness in my affections and remissness in my actions; against softness and self-
indulgence, directly opposite to that discipline and hardship which 30
become a good soldier of Jesus Christ.[4] And then, when my spirit
was thus dissolved, I should be an easy prey to whatever impertinent
company came in my way. Then would the cares of the world, and
the desires of other things, roll back with a full tide upon me. And it
would be no wonder if, while I preached to others, I myself should 35
be a castaway.[5] I cannot therefore but observe that the question does
not relate barely to [a] higher degree of perfection, but to the very

---

[1] Cf. Mark 4: 19. [2] 1 Cor. 7: 32, 35.
[3] Ibid. [4] 2 Tim. 2: 3
[5] 1 Cor. 9: 27.

essence and being of it: *Agitur de vita et sanguine Turni.*[1] The point
is, whether I shall or shall not work out my salvation,[2] whether I shall
serve Christ or Belial.

12. What still heightens my fear of this untried state is that when
5 I am once entered into it, be the inconveniencies of it found more
or less, *vestigia nulla retrorsum*[3]—when I am there, there I must
stay. If this way of life should ever prove less advantageous I have
almost continual opportunities of quitting it; but whatever difficulties occur in that, whether foreseen or unforeseen, there is no return,
10 any more than from the grave. When I have once launched out into
that unknown sea, there is no recovering my harbour: I must on,
among whatever whirlpools, or rocks, or sands, though all the
waves and storms go over me.[4]

13. Thus much as to myself. But you justly observe that we are
15 not to consider ourselves alone, 'seeing God made us all for a social
life, to which academical studies are only preparatory'.[5] I allow too
that 'he will take an exact account of every talent which he has lent
us, not to bury them, but to employ every mite we have received in
diffusing holiness all around us'.[6] I cannot deny that 'every follower
20 of Christ is, in his proportion, the light of the world; that whoever
is such can no more be concealed than the sun in the midst of heaven;
that being set as a light in a dark place, his shining must be the more
conspicuous; that to this very end was his light given, that it might
shine at least to all that look towards him'; and indeed that 'there is
25 only one way of hiding it, which is to put it out'. Neither can I deny
that 'it is the indispensable duty of every Christian to impart both
light and heat to all who are willing to receive it'. I am obliged likewise, unless I would lie against the truth,[7] to grant that 'there is not
so contemptible an animal upon earth as one that drones away life
30 without ever labouring to promote the glory of God and the good of

[1] Virgil, *Aeneid*, xii. 765, 'They contend about the life and blood of Turnus', paraphrased by Wesley in Vol. 32 of his *Works* (1774), 'Life is at stake'.

[2] See Phil. 2: 12.

[3] See Horace, *Epistles*, I. i. 74–5, translated in Wesley's *Works* (1774), 'There is no
going back'.

[4] See Ps. 42: 9 (B.C.P.).

[5] See Nov. 20, § 3, where the two phrases are separated.

[6] Most of the quotation marks in this section (and elsewhere) are inserted on the
evidence of the *Journal*, though without adopting the almost certainly edited text there.
In Charles Wesley's shorthand copy of the letter (as frequently in John Wesley's own
manuscripts) only an opening quotation mark is inserted (before 'seeing') as an indication that much of the following matter is quoted.

[7] See Jas. 3: 14.

men, and that whether he be young or old, learned or unlearned, in a college or out of it'. Yet granting the superlative degree of contempt to be on all accounts due to a college drone,[1] a wretch that hath received ten talents, and yet employs none; that is not only promised a reward by his gracious Master, but is paid beforehand for his work by his generous founder, and yet works not at all; but allowing all this, and whatever else can be said (for I own it is impossible to say enough) against the drowsy ingratitude, the lazy perjury, of those who are commonly called harmless or good sort of men, a fair proportion of whom I must to our shame confess are to be found in colleges; allowing this, I say, I do not apprehend it will conclude against a college life in general. For the abuse of it does not destroy the use. Though there are some here who are the mere lumber of the creation, it does not follow [that] others may not be of more service to the world in this station than they could in any other.

14. That I in particular could might, it seems, be inferred from what has been proved already, viz., that I could be holier myself here than anywhere else, if I faithfully used the blessings I enjoy. For to prove that the holier any man is himself, the more shall he promote holiness in others,[2] needs no more than this one *postulatum*: 'The help that is done on earth, God doth it himself.'[3] If so, if God be the sole agent in healing souls, and man only the instrument in his hand, there can no doubt be made that the more holy a man is, he will make use of him the more: because he is the more willing to be so used; because the more pure he is, he will be the more fitter instrument for the God of purity; because he will pray more and more earnestly that he may be employed, and that his service may tend to his Master's glory; because all his prayers both for employment and success therein will the more surely pierce the clouds; because the more his heart is enlarged, the wider sphere he may act in without carefulness or distraction; and lastly, because the more he is renewed in the image of God, the more God can renew it in others by him, without destroying him by pride or vanity.

15. But for the proof of every one of these weighty truths experience is worth [a] thousand reasons. I see, I feel them every day. Sometimes I cannot do good to others because I am unwilling to do it; shame or pain is in my way, and I do not desire to serve God at so dear a rate. Sometimes I cannot do the good I desire to do because

---

[1] See Nov. 20, § 4.   [2] See Nov. 20, § 2.
[3] See Ps. 74: 13 (B.C.P.).

I am in other respects too unholy; I know within myself were I fit
to be so employed God would employ me in this work, but my
heart is too unclean for such mighty works to be wrought by my
hands. Sometimes I cannot accomplish the good I am employed
5 in because I do not pray more, and more fervently; and sometimes
when I do pray, and that instantly, because I am not worthy that
my prayer should be heard. Sometimes I dare not attempt to assist
my neighbour because I know the narrowness of my heart, and that
it cannot attend to many things without utter confusion and dissipa-
10 tion of thought. And a thousand times have I been mercifully withheld from success in the things I have attempted, because were one
so vain enabled to gain others he would lose his own soul.

16. From all this I conclude that where I was most holy myself,
there I could most promote holiness in others; and consequently
15 that I could more promote it here than in any place under heaven.
But I have likewise other reasons besides this to think so: and the
first is, the plenteousness of the harvest. Here is indeed a large
scene of various action. Here is room for charity in all its forms.
There is scarce any way of doing good to our fellow creatures for
20 which here is not daily occasion. I can now only touch on the several
heads. Here are poor families to be relieved; here are children to
be educated; here are workhouses wherein both young and old
want and gladly receive the word of exhortation; here are prisons to
be visited, wherein alone is a complication of all human wants; and
25 lastly, here are the schools of the prophets, here are tender minds to
be formed and strengthened, and babes in Christ to be instructed
and perfected in all useful learning. Of these in particular we must
observe, that he who gains only one does thereby as much service
to the world as he could do in a parish in his whole life. For his name
30 is 'legion';[1] in him are contained all those who shall be converted
by him. He is not a single drop of the dew of heaven, but 'a river to
make glad the city of God'.[2]

17. 'But Epworth is yet a larger sphere of action than this; there
I should have the care of two thousand souls.'[3] Two thousand souls!
35 I see not how any man living can take care of an hundred! At least I
could not; I know too well *quid valeant humeri.*[4] Because the weight

---

[1] Mark 5: 9.
[2] See Ps. 46: 4 (B.C.P.).
[3] See Nov. 20, § 5.
[4] Horace, *Art of Poetry*, 40, 'what [my] shoulders can bear'.

that is already upon me is almost more than I can bear. Ought I to increase it tenfold?

> . . . *imponere Pelio Ossam*
> *Scilicet, atque Ossae frondosum involvere Olympum!*[1]

Would this be the way to help either myself or my brethren up to heaven? Nay, the mountains I reared would only crush my own soul, and so make me utterly useless to others.

18. I need but just glance upon several other reasons why I am more likely to be useful here than elsewhere. As, because I have the joint advice of many friends in any difficulty, and their joint encouragement in any danger. Because the good bishop and vice-chancellor are at hand to supply as need is their want of experience. Because we have the eye of multitudes upon us, even without designing it, perform the most substantial office of friendship, apprising us where we have already fallen, and guarding us against falling again. Lastly, because we have here a constant fund (which I believe this year will amount to near eighty pounds) to supply the bodily wants of the poor, and thereby prepare their souls to receive instruction.

19. If it be said that the love of the people of Epworth balances all these advantages here, I ask, 'How long will it last?' Only till I come to tell them plainly that their deeds are evil, and to make a particular application of that general sentence, to say to each, 'Thou art the man!'[2] Alas, sir, do I not know what love they had for you at first? And how have they used you since? Why, just as everyone will be used whose business it is to bring light to them that love darkness.

20. Notwithstanding, therefore, their present prejudice in my favour, I cannot quit my first conclusion, that I am not likely to do that good anywhere, not even at Epworth, which I may do at Oxford. And yet one terrible objection lies in the way: 'Have you found it so in fact? What have you done there in so many years? Nay, have not your very attempts to do good, for want either of a particular turn of mind for the business you engaged in, or of prudence to direct you in the right method of doing it, not only been unsuccessful, but brought such contempt upon you as has in great measure disqualified you for any future success? And are there not men in Oxford who are not only better and holier than you, but who have preserved

---

[1] Virgil, *Georgics*, i. 281–2, paraphrased by Wesley (*Works*, Vol. 32, 1774), 'to heap mountain upon mountain, like the ancient giants, in order to scale heaven'.
[2] 2 Sam. 12: 7.

their reputation, who being universally esteemed, are every way fitter to promote the glory of God in that place?'[1]

21. I am not careful to answer in this matter. It is not my part to say whether or no God has done any good by my hands; whether I have a particular turn of mind for this or no; and whether the want of success in my past attempts[2] was owing to want of prudence, to ignorance of the right method of acting, or to some other cause. But the latter part of this objection, that 'he who is despised can do no good', that 'without reputation a man cannot be useful in the world', being the stronghold of all the unbelieving, the vainglorious, and the cowardly Christians (so called), I will, by the grace of God, see what reason that has thus continually to exalt itself against the knowledge of Christ.

22. With regard to contempt, then (under which term I include all the passions that border upon it, as hatred, envy, etc., and all the fruits that flow from them, such as calumny, reproach, and persecution in any of its forms), my first position, in defiance of worldly wisdom, is this: 'Every true Christian is contemned wherever he lives by all who are not so, and who know him to be such; that is, in effect, by all with whom he converses, since it is impossible for light not to shine.' This position I prove both from the example of our Lord, and from his express assertions. First from his example. If 'the disciple is not above his Master, nor the servant above his Lord',[3] then, as our Master was 'despised and rejected of men',[4] so will every one of his true disciples. But 'the disciple is not above his master, nor the servant above his Lord'. Therefore . . . The consequence will not fail him a hair's breadth.[5] Secondly, from his own express assertions of this consequence. 'If they have called the master of the house Beelzebub, how much more them of his household.'[6] 'Remember' (ye that would fain forget, or evade it) 'the word that I said unto you, the servant is not greater than his Lord. If they have persecuted me, they will also persecute you.'[7] And as for that vain hope that this belongs only to the first followers of Christ,

---

[1] See Nov. 20, § 2.

[2] Charles Wesley's shorthand copy, probably representing John's draft, has 'endeavours', erased and replaced by 'attempts'.

[3] Matt. 10: 24.

[4] Isa. 53: 3.

[5] This is one of the examples where in minutiae (such as the ellipsis) the printed *Journal* agrees with the shorthand copy against all other versions.

[6] Matt. 10: 25 (Wesley's citation in the text).

[7] Cf. John 15: 20.

hear ye him: 'All these things will they do unto you because they know not him that sent me.'[1] And again: 'Because ye are not of the world, therefore the world hateth you.'[2] Both the persons who are hated, the persons who hate them, and the cause of their hating them, are here clearly determined. The *hated* are all that are not of this world, that are born again in the knowledge and love of God; the *haters* are all that are of the world, that know not God so as to love him with all their strength; the *cause of their hatred* is the entire irreconcilable difference between their designs, judgments, and affections—because these know not God, and those are determined to know and pursue nothing besides him; because these esteem and love the world, and those count it dung and dross, and singly desire the love of Christ.

23. My next position is this: 'Till he be thus contemned, no man is in a state of salvation.' And this is no more than a plain inference from the former. For if all that are not of the world are therefore contemned by those that are, then till a man is so contemned he is of the world, that is, out of a state of salvation. Nor is it possible for all the trimmers between God and the world, for all the dodgers in religion, to elude this consequence, which God has established, not man, unless they could prove that a man may be of the world, that is, void both of the knowledge and love of God, and yet be in a state of salvation. I must therefore, with or without the leave of these, keep close to my Saviour's judgment, and maintain that contempt is a part of that cross which every man must bear if he will follow him; that it is the badge of his discipleship, the stamp of his profession, the constant seal of his calling, insomuch that though a man may be despised without being saved, yet he cannot be saved without being despised.

24. I should not spend any more words on this great truth but that it is at present quite voted out of the world. The masters in Israel, learned men, men of renown, seem absolutely to have forgotten it; nay, they censure those who have not forgotten the words of their Lord, as setters forth of strange doctrines.[3] And hence it is commonly asked, 'How can these things be?'[4] How can contempt be necessary to salvation? I answer, As it is a necessary means of purifying souls for heaven; as it is a blessed instrument of cleansing them

---

[1] John 15: 21.
[2] John 15: 19 (Wesley's citation within the text, 'John 16: 20, etc.').
[3] See Acts 17: 18.   [4] John 3: 9.

from pride, which else would turn their very graces into poison;
as it is a glorious antidote against vanity, which would otherwise
pollute and destroy all their labours; as it is an excellent medicine to
heal the anger and impatience of spirit[1] apt to insinuate into their
5 best employments; and, in a word, as it is one of the choicest remedies in the whole magazine of God against self-love and love of the
world, in which whosoever liveth is counted dead before him.

25. And hence (as a full answer to the preceding objection) I
infer one position more, that the being despised is absolutely neces-
10 sary to our doing good in the world. If not to our doing some good
(as God may work by Judas), yet to our doing so much good as we
otherwise should. For since God will employ those instruments most
who are fittest to be employed; since the holier a man is the fitter
instrument he is for the God of holiness; and since contempt is so
15 glorious a means of advancing holiness in him that is exercised
thereby, nay, since no man can be holy at all without it; who can
keep off the consequence, the being contemned is absolutely necessary to a Christian's doing his full measure of good in the world.
[We must know God if we would fully teach others to know him.
20 But if so we do, we must be contemned of those that know him not.][2]
'Where then is the scribe? Where is the wise? Where is the disputer
of this world?'[3] Where is the replier against God, with his sage
maxims, 'He that is despised can do no good in the world; to be
useful a man must be esteemed; to advance the glory of God you
25 must have a fair reputation'? . . . Saith the world so? But what saith
the Scripture? Why, that God hath laughed this heathen wisdom to
scorn![4] It saith that twelve despised followers of a despised Master,
all of whom were of no reputation, who were esteemed as the filth
and offscouring of the world,[5] did more good in it than all the twelve
30 tribes of Israel. It saith that the despised Master of these despised
followers left a standing direction to us and to our children: 'Blessed
are ye' (not accursed with the heavy curse of doing no good, of
being useless in the world), 'when men shall revile you and persecute
you, and shall say all manner of evil against you falsely for my name's

---

[1] The highly compressed shorthand, often with a series of opening consonants strung
into one phraseogram, is frequently difficult to interpret. Here the reading is apparently
'im-sa', and Priestley's text has been followed.

[2] From the *Journal* version, corresponding to an ellipsis indicated in the shorthand
copy.

[3] 1 Cor. 1: 20.   [4] See Ps. 2: 4; 64: 8 (B.C.P.).

[5] See 1 Cor. 4: 13.

sake. Rejoice, and be exceeding glad, for great is your reward in heaven.'[1]

26. These are a part of my reasons for choosing to abide (till I am better informed) in the station wherein God has placed me. As for the flock committed to your care, whom you have so many years 5 diligently fed with the sincere milk of the word,[2] I trust in God your labours shall not be in vain, either to yourself or them. Many of them the great Shepherd[3] has by your hand delivered from the hand of the destroyer, some of whom are already entered into peace, and some remain unto this day.[4] For yourself, I doubt not but when 10 your warfare is accomplished,[5] when you are made perfect through sufferings,[6] you shall come to your grave, not with sorrow,[7] but as a ripe shock of corn,[8] full of years[9] and victories. And he that took care of those poor sheep before you was born will not forget them when you are dead! 15

Ended Dec. 19, 1734

Sources: The original holographs of both drafts and fair copy have disappeared.

(A). Charles Wesley prepared a shorthand copy of what appears to have been both draft (see note 2, p. 406) and reference copy. This is contained in a note-book preserved in MA, which closes with a copy of Wesley's letter of Oct. 10, 1735; it was probably transcribed within a year or so of this date, when Charles was already adept at Byrom's shorthand, and was encouraging John to take it up. Although this document contains some obvious errors, and although the short-hand is occasionally difficult to interpret (see note 1, p. 408), there is no sign that the original text has been edited; it appears to represent John Wesley's contemporary style, and occasionally indicates such minutiae as quotation marks and ellipses, though not underlining, which proves awkward in this medium.

On Jan. 15, 1735, John Wesley began a letter to his brother Samuel and a revised transcript of the letter of Dec. 10-19 to send to him (see diary, Jan. 15, and letter of Feb. 8, 1735). This revised transcript apparently survived until Wesley's death, and formed the basis of (B), the version printed in Priestley's *Letters* (1791), pp. 21-40, which is lightly edited, and also (independently) of (C), the outline and heavily edited quotations given in Hampson's *Wesley* (1791), I. 127-39.

(D). John Wesley himself published the letter in his *Journal* for Mar. 28, 1739, which appeared in 1742. For this he abridged all but sections 1 and 2, omitted section 15, and combined sections 5-6, 14-16, and 24-5, to make three

[1] Matt. 5: 11-12.
[2] 1 Pet. 2: 2; and for the background of this closing section see Nov. 20, § 5.
[3] Heb. 13: 20.   [4] See 1 Cor. 15: 6.
[5] Isa. 40: 2.   [6] Heb. 2: 10.
[7] Cf. Nov. 20 (§ 5), 'bringing down my grey hairs with sorrow to the grave' (Gen. 42: 38, etc.).
[8] See Job 5: 26.   [9] Gen. 25: 8.

from seven, thus reducing the total number of sections from 26 to 22, and altering the numbering of those from 5 onwards. At the same time he tightened the style, softened many phrases, and generally made the document more direct and intelligible to those unfamiliar with the circumstances. Although as always he was more concerned with the impact of the subject-matter than with preserving the original text, in many of the minutiae this version does appear faithfully to represent the original, preserving words and phrases which support Charles Wesley's copy against what appear to be Priestley's editorial changes (see note 5, p. 406), furnishing indications of quotation marks which may possibly have been indicated (possibly by underlinings) in the original (see note 6, p. 402), and retaining two sentences which fit into one of the ellipses indicated in the shorthand (see note 2, p. 408).

The text here presented is based upon Charles Wesley's shorthand copy (A), its occasional errors corrected from Priestley (B), and with some quotation marks, similar minutiae, and the two missing sentences, supplied from the *Journal* (D). It has seemed undesirable to footnote the hundred variants in the Priestley text; the *Journal* version will be found in its own setting.

From the Revd. Samuel Wesley, Jun.

Christmas Day, 1734

Dear Jack

Yesterday I received a letter from my father[1] wherein he tells me you are unalterably resolved not to accept of a certain living if you could get it, and that
5   for this reason:

'The question is not whether I could do more good to others *there* or *here*, but whether I could do more to myself; seeing wherever I can be most holy myself, there I am assured I can most promote holiness in others; but I am equally assured there is no place under heaven so fit for my improvement as Oxford.'
10   After this declaration I believe no one can move your mind but him who made it; much less do I think myself qualified for that purpose. You may perhaps say I have been too passive. I left Oxford, with all its opportunity of good, on a worldly account, at my father's desire. I left my last settlement by the same determination, and should have thought I sinned both times if I had not followed
15   it. You may ask, if I suppose you not to be persuaded, and myself not fit to persuade, why do I write? For a plain reason. It is my duty, if I can, to please

---

[1] This letter received at Tiverton, Devon, on Dec. 24, 1734, was clearly that begun by the rector of Epworth on Dec. 4, informing Samuel of the decision announced by John in his letter of Nov. 15. In that letter of Dec. 4 the rector stated that he had written in his own hand 'for many days together', and was asking John Whitelamb 'to transcribe and finish it'. Thus the date of completion and posting was probably about two weeks later than that of its beginning. Meanwhile, Dec. 10–19, John Wesley had completed his own lengthy apologia for this decision, which also found its way to Tiverton only after another six weeks. It appears that John Wesley's letters of Nov. 15 and Dec. 11 had not mentioned this subject.

and profit my father and mother; and, secondly, to inform and profit you. The event I leave to the Almighty—ὁ Χωρῶν Χωρείτω.[1]

I shall not draw the saw[2] of controversy, and therefore, though I judge every proposition flatly false, except that of your being assured, yet I shall allow every word, and have nevertheless this to say against your conclusions: 5

1. I see your love to yourself, but your love to your neighbour I do not see. This was not the spirit of St. Paul, when he wished himself accursed for his brethren's sake; the lowest sense of which must be thus much, to be deprived of the outward means of grace, and cut off from visible communion. What, would you not lose one degree of glory were it possible to be instrumental in saving   10 several, perhaps very many, from the place of torment?

2. You are not at liberty to resolve against undertaking a cure of souls. You are solemnly engaged to do it before God, and his high priest, and his church. Are you not ordained? Did you not deliberately and openly promise to instruct, to teach, to admonish, to exhort those committed to your charge? Did you   15 equivocate then with so vile a reservation as to purpose in your heart that you would never have any so committed? It is not a college, it is not an university, it is the *order of the Church* according to which you were called. Let Charles, if he is silly enough, vow never to leave Oxford, and therefore avoid orders. Your faith is already plighted to the contrary; you *have 'put your hand to the plough'*, to   20 *that plough.*

I mention no less considerations, but restrain myself, though not a little surprised that you seem to hint, what scarce ever before entered the head of a Christian, that a parish priest cannot attain to the highest perfection possible on this side heaven. I am, etc.,   25

S. Wesley

Source: Priestley, pp. 17–19.

To Mrs. Susanna Wesley

[Jan. 13, 1735]

Dear mother

Give me leave to say once more that our folks do and will, I suppose, to the end of the chapter, mistake the question. Supposing   30 him[3] changed, say they—Right, but that supposition has not proof

---

[1] Freely translated, 'Let him who sees to all events, see to this!'

[2] Orig., 'law'. For the proverbial expression, 'to draw the saw of controversy', see John Wesley's letters of May 22, 1750; Oct. 11, 1764; Sept. 20, 1776; Mar. 25, 1785; Apr. 23, 1789.

[3] The reference here is uncertain, especially as none of Susanna Wesley's letters to John are either extant or recorded during the preceding ten months. It is possible that Suky's husband is intended. The rector wrote to his son Samuel on Dec. 4 that he had little hope about 'Dick Ellison, the wen of my family, and his poor insects that are sucking me to death', adding, 'though I have charity crammed down my throat every

yet—whatever it may have. When it has, then we may come to our other point, whether all this be not providence, i.e. blessing, and whether we are empowered to judge, condemn, and execute an imprudent Christian, as God forbid I should ever use a Turk or
5 deist.

I have had a great deal of conversation lately on the subject of Christian liberty, and should be glad of your thoughts as to several notions of it which good men entertain. I perceive different persons take it in at least six different senses: (1). For liberty from wilful
10 sin, in opposition to the bondage of natural corruption. (2). For liberty as to rites and points of discipline. So Mr. Whiston says, 'Though the stations were constituted by the Apostles, yet the liberty of the Christian law dispenses with them on extraordinary occasions.'¹ (3). For liberty from denying ourselves in little things;
15 for trifles, 'tis ⟨com⟩monly thought, we may indulge in safely, because Christ hath made us free.² This notion, I a little doubt, is not sound. (4). For liberty from fear, or a filial freedom in our intercourse with God. A Christian, says Dr. Knight,³ is free from fear on account of his past sins; for he believes in Christ. And hope
20 frees him from fear of losing his present labour, or of being a cast

day, and sometimes his company at meals, which you will believe as pleasant to me as all my physic' (Clarke, I. 339, 343). It seems more likely, however, that the reference is to Nancy's absent husband, John Lambert, who had deserted her and her children. Lambert's father had been killed in a drunken accident on Jan. 8, and was buried at Wroot on the 11th, John Whitelamb preaching his funeral sermon. Samuel Wesley, senior, wrote a somewhat gruesome report and rebuke to Lambert (apparently in London), calling for his repentance and some restitution to Nancy, closing: 'If you do this thing, and God will have it so, you may have perhaps one squeak more for your life, and this terrible judgment of your father may be turned into a blessing to you, and bring you to a better mind; whereof, though I can have but little hopes, yet I will not quite despair, or cease to pray for you as long as I am, your most unhappy afflicted father.' (MA, no date, in the hand of Martha Wesley, incorrectly ascribed by John Wesley to 1732 and as referring to Richard Ellison.)

¹ Though a similar phrase may occur in one of the voluminous writings of William Whiston (1667–1752), it seems likely that Wesley is summarizing a statement made to him personally by Whiston on Dec. 23, 1734, when he entered in his diary: 'Mr. Whi[ston]'s, on Station[s] and Feast[s]. Clear!' In his *Memoirs* Whiston said that when Wesley was writing 'for the observation of the old Wednesday and Friday stations . . . I gave him my assistance' (2nd edn., 1753, p. 121; cf. p. 438 n.). Whiston subscribed for a copy of the Revd. Samuel Wesley's *Job*.
² Gal. 5: 9.
³ James Knight, D.D. (1672–1735), who was the minister of St. Sepulchre's, London, from 1716 until his death. During his visits to London at this period Wesley both worshipped under Dr. Knight and preached for him, and in his diary noted conversations with him on many subjects, including (Dec. 30, 1734): 'Dr. Kn's, of Xtn Liberty'. Knight also subscribed for a copy of *Job*.

away hereafter. (5). Christian liberty is taken by some for a freedom from restraint as to sleep, or food. So they would say, Your drinking but one glass of wine, or my rising at a fixed hour, was contrary to Christian liberty.[1] Lastly, it is taken for freedom from rules: if by this be meant making our rules yield to extraordinary occasions, well; if the having no prudential rules, this liberty is as yet too high for me; I cannot attain unto it.[2]

We join in begging yours and my father's blessing, and wishing you a Happy Year. I am, dear mother, your dutiful and affectionate son,

John Wesley

Jan. 13, 1734/5

Address: 'To Mrs Wesley at Epworth, To be left at ye Posthouse In Gainsbro, Lincolnshire. per London'   *Seal*: tiny bust, facing left, over pedestal (30) *Postmarks*: 'OXFORD', '14 IA'   *Charges*: ((3)), 'In all 7'   *End* by JW (relating to a bundle of letters, with this on the outside): 'Jan.–Dec.', 'revised Dec. 13, 1751'; *by other hands*: 'J. Wesley / Jany 13, 1734/5', 'Letters from 1735 to 1742'   *Source*: MA.

To the Revd. Samuel Wesley, Jun.[3]

Oxon., Jan 15, 1734/5

Dear brother

Had not my brother Charles desired it might be otherwise, I should have sent you only an extract of the following letter. But if you will be at the pains, you will soon reduce the argument of it to two or three points, which, if to be answered at all, will be easily

---

[1] Thus Wesley met Thomas Broughton at Dr. Knight's on Dec. 22, and noted in his diary: 'I see S[elf] D[enial] all! he wavering! Alas!', and on Dec. 23, 'with Bro[ughton] of S D; he shockt!' On the 24th he discussed this with William Law, who advised, 'Let him alone!'

[2] Ps. 139: 6.

[3] This answers his brother's of Dec. 25, 1734, 'the following letter' being a transcription of his letter to his father of Dec. 10–19, 1734. Wesley's diary for Jan. 15 shows that he wrote the covering letter at 6 a.m., and at 7 a.m. began to 'cor[rect] L[ette]r to f[ather]', while from 10 a.m. to noon he transcribed that letter. The complete document Samuel received within a few days, read it, and drafted a reply, but did not write and date a fair copy for dispatch to John until Feb. 8. After a somewhat slow start this important correspondence then moved along more rapidly. John received Samuel's letter on Feb. 11, writing in his diary, 'Clear as to b[rother] S[am]'s L[ette]r', and replied on Feb. 13. Samuel's answer he received on the 27th.

answered. By it you may observe my present purpose is founded on my present weakness. But it is not indeed probable that my father should live till that weakness is removed.

Your second argument I had no occasion to mention before. To it
5 I answer that I do not, nor ever did, resolve against undertaking a cure of souls. There are four cures belonging to our college, and consistent with a fellowship; I do not know but I may take one of them at Michaelmas. Not that I am clearly assured that I should be false to my engagement were I only to instruct and exhort the
10 pupils committed to my charge. But of that I should think more.

I desire your full thoughts upon the whole, as well as your prayers for, dear brother, your obliged and affectionate brother,

John Wesley

Source: Priestley, pp. 20-1.

From the Revd. Samuel Wesley, Sen.

Epworth, January 21, 1734/5

15 Dear son

About an hour since your λόγος παρακλήσεως[1] of the 13th instant came to hand, and indeed not before I had need of it, being so disturbed with the prospect of all I was to expect from my last that my soul refused comfort, and I had a very little share of common sense left, especially when I considered how extremely
20 weak I was, and found myself grow sensibly weaker every day, by being ground between pain and the forementioned considerations, together with the apprehension that I must soon leave the world, and *Job* unfinished together with it.

However, God helped me so much at last that I hope I did entirely leave both myself and all I had with him, to do just what he pleases with me; and since that
25 I've had a little more rest. My people, I must needs say, have been very kind to me during my long illness, which has brought me now so low that I can't walk half a dozen times about my chamber; but then I'm often refreshed with seeing a great part of Mr. Hale's noble present of books lying in my window, near half of which I've already spread in my parish, some to those who come to see me,
30 and to others I have sent 'em, and that, I bless God, with very good effect, many having read 'em to others, whereby a spirit of Christianity beyond what I have hitherto known seems to be raised amongst 'em; one proof whereof there is in the greater frequency at the sacraments. Nor is Mr. Whitelamb wanting to any part of his duty, though I've not been able to preach or give the sacrament to
35 them myself except one day, and that with his assistance.

So first to the first, and now let's go on to matter of less moment, though I hope not quite frivolous neither.

[1] A word of exhortation, or encouragement; see Acts 13: 15; Heb. 13: 22.

Had I had Mr. Rivington's advice at first, all my plates and cuts I find had been done before this, and that with less expense, and to greater perfection. The agreement you have made with the graver seems to be very reasonable; whether the cuts are to be done in sheets or half-sheets I leave to you and Mr. Rivington; but I would have Leviathan's rival, that is the Whale, as well as the Crocodile: 5 and as for the Elephant, he is so common that he need not be added. I'm glad the Tombs want no more than retouching, and especially that Mr. Garden is not ill-pleased with 'em. Job in Adversity I leave to your direction, as likewise the frontispiece, which Mr. Vertue is doing, who now duns me pretty hard for money for it, and I've writ him lately to send me word what he'll have for the 10 whole, when 'tis finished, and what he desires in part, with a promise to send him some money by the first opportunity I have of doing it; and as soon as ever I hear from him you shall hear from me. As for poor Pentapolis, it must e'en shift as it can, though my heart is pretty much in it, and I've taken no little pains about it. This I must likewise leave with you. But can't you send me a copy of the 15 drafts before they're engraven, that I may weigh 'em as is proper? As for Job's Horse, I can't for my life imagine how I shall get him into my Lord Oxford's stable, I mean get liberty to inscribe it to him, unless you yourself could speak to my Lord Duplin about it, who seems a very well-natured gentleman, and I believe would not be unready to employ his good offices for me. Have you yet 20 found any news of *De Morbo Jobi*,[1] which has been so long incognito? Or is there anything else that you find wanting? I heartily commend you and your brother to God, and am this evening, your somewhat liver[2] father,

Sam Wesley

I have waited for thy SALVATION, O GOD, and MAZAL-TOB is coming.[3] 25

This day in the morning Mr. Whiteley went. God knows whither, though he got his finishing stroke in a draught of double cinnamon water of near a full pint the day before in the morning. But this would not lay conscience to sleep, though it soon did him, as well as his senses, speech, and reason, for 'twas plain that he died in inward horror, and had been so some time before, his body just 30 before his departure turning as black as a coal. However, I have a better account to give you of several young men, the most considerable in my parish, that are lately married, and from whom I hope either I or my successors shall receive comfort, whereof I may write you more at large in my next. Mr. Whiteley is to be buried this night, though I'm afraid no great lamentation will be made 35 over him.

Address: 'To Mr John Wesley, Fellow of Lincoln-College, Oxon, These. per London' *Postmark*: '2[4?]/IA' *Charges*: ((4)), 'In all 7' *End* by JW: '+ m[y] f[ather] Jan. 21, 1734/5 / The last I recd from him' *Source*: MA. All except the signature and the sentence following are in the hand of John Whitelamb.

[1] Job's Disease.
[2] i.e. more lively.
[3] This sentence and the signature are in the rector's own hand. I am grateful to Prof. W. F. Stinespring for pointing out that Mazal-Tob is a post-biblical expression meaning 'good luck'.

From the Revd. Samuel Wesley, Jun.

Feb. 8th, 1734/5, Devon

Dear Jack

Charles was in the right to desire I might have your whole letter. Though you have stated the point so as to take away the question, at least all possibility of
5 differing about it, if it be only this, whether you are to serve Christ or Belial. I see no end of writing now, but merely complying with your desire of having my thoughts upon it, which I here give in short, and I think almost in full, though I pass over strictures on less matters.

1. Your friends, retirement, frequent ordinances, and freedom from care, are
10 great blessings; all except the last you may expect in a *lower degree* elsewhere. Sure all your labours are not come to this, that more is absolutely necessary for you, for the very being of your Christian life, than for the salvation of all the parish priests in England. It is very strange.

2. To the question what good have you done at Oxford you are not careful
15 to answer. How comes it then you are so very careful about the good you might do at Epworth? 'The help that is done on earth, he doth it himself,' is a full solution of that terrible difficulty.

3. The impossibility of return, the certainty of being disliked by them that now cry you up, and the small (comparative) good my father has done, are good
20 prudential reasons; but I think can hardly extend to conscience. You can leave Oxford when you will. Not surely to such advantage. You have a probability of doing good there. Will that good be wholly undone if you leave it? Why should you not leaven another lump?

4. What you say of contempt is nothing to the purpose, for if you will go to
25 Epworth I will answer for it you shall in a competent time be despised as much as your heart can wish. In your doctrine you argue from a particular to a general. 'To be useful a man must be esteemed' is as certain as any proposition in Euclid, and I defy all mankind to produce one instance of directly doing spiritual good without it in the whole Book of God. You join to contempt, hatred and envy; but
30 the first is very hardly consistent, the latter utterly incompatible, with it, since none can possibly envy another but for something he esteems.

5. God, who provided for the flock before, will do it after my father. May he not suffer them to be what they once were, almost heathens? And may not that be prevented by your ministry? It could never enter into my head that you could
35 refuse on any other ground than a general resolution against the cure of souls. I shall give no positive reason for it till my first is answered. *The order of the Church* stakes you down, and the more you struggle, will hold the faster. If there be such a thing as truth I insist upon it you must, when opportunity offers, either perform that promise, or repent of it: *utrum mavis*.[1] I am, dear Jack, yours, etc.
40 As short as this letter is, it has been a full fortnight in transcribing;[2] a fair warning not to take copies.

Source: Priestley, pp. 41-3.

[1] From '*utrum horum mavis accipe*'—'take whichever you prefer'.
[2] He had apparently drafted a reply immediately on receiving John's of Jan. 15,

To the Revd. Samuel Wesley, Jun.

February 13, 1734[/5]

Dear brother

Neither you nor I have any time to spare; so I must be as short as I can.

There are two questions between us, one relating to being good, 5 the other to doing good. With regard to the former:

1. You allow I enjoy more of friends, retirement, freedom from care, and divine ordinances, than I could do elsewhere; and I add, (1), I feel all this to be but just enough; (2), I have always found less than this to be too little for me; and therefore, (3), whatever others 10 do, I could not throw up any part of it without manifest hazard to my salvation. As to the latter:

2. I am not careful to answer 'what good I have done at Oxford', because I cannot think of it without the utmost danger. 'I am careful about what good I may do at Epworth', (1), because I can think of 15 it without any danger at all; (2), because I cannot, as matters now stand, avoid thinking of it without sin.

3. Another can supply my place at Epworth better than at Oxford, and the good done here is of a far more diffusive nature. It is a more extensive benefit to sweeten the fountain than to do the 20 same to particular streams.

4. To the objection, You are despised at Oxford, therefore you can do no good there, I answer: (1) a Christian will be despised anywhere; (2) no one is a Christian till he is despised; (3) his being despised will not hinder his doing good, but much further it, by 25 making him a better Christian. Without contradicting any of these propositions I allow that everyone to whom you do good directly must esteem you, first or last.—N.B. A man may despise you for one thing, hate you for a second, and envy you for a third.

5. God may suffer Epworth to be worse than before. But *I may* 30 *not* attempt to prevent it, with so great hazard to my own soul.

Your last argument is either *ignoratio elenchi*,[1] or implies these two propositions: (1), 'You resolve against any parochial cure of

---

enclosing that of Dec. 10–19, 1734, to their father, and added the date, Feb. 8, only when transcribing a fair copy for posting.

[1] Missing the point ('ignoring the pearl').

souls;' (2), 'The priest who does not undertake the first parochial cure that offers is perjured.' Let us add a third: 'The tutor who, being in orders, never accepts of a parish, is perjured.' And then I deny all three. I am, dear brother, your obliged and affectionate
5 brother,

[John Wesley]

Source: Priestley, pp. 44–6.

To Mrs. Susanna Wesley[1]

Feb. 14, 1735

Dear mother
As the Jews were obliged to adhere even to their ritual law at those
10 very times when it was most inconvenient, but Christians are not, so far we have a liberty which they wanted, extraordinary occasions being a dispensation to us (but not to them) from any external ordinances.
It seems, therefore (to sum up the matter), that this liberty may
15 (with caution) be added to the rest. And so that Christians enjoy:
   1. A liberty from wilful sin, which natural men have not.
   2. A liberty from slavish fears, which awakened sinners have not.
   ⟨3.⟩ A liberty in things of an indifferent nature, which the farther anyone advances in Christianity is enlarged the more, a confirmed
20 Christian being able to use many things to the glory of God which a weak one cannot. This liberty, therefore, infant Christians have not.
   (But may there not be a sort of liberty just opposite to this, which weak Christians have and confirmed ones have not? viz. a liberty to indulge themselves in some particulars wherein they are not yet
25 strong enough to deny themselves? as superfluous clothes, furniture, etc., which when they are stronger, and consequently able, they too will be obliged to renounce?)
   4. A liberty as to external ordinances, to set them aside *pro tempore*, on extraordinary occasions. This the Jews had not.
30   5. A liberty as to rules, (1), to lay aside those prudential rules which we no longer need; (2), to suspend those we do need upon extraordinary occasions, and, (3), to alter those we do not either

---

[1] An answer to an otherwise unknown letter in which she replied to his of Jan. 13 on Christian liberty. Also an answer to the rector's of Jan. 21.

lay aside or suspend continually, as the state of our soul alters. Q[uery]? Whether this liberty does not belong (in some measure, and under due restrictions) to all Christians?

I should be exceeding glad to know: (1), Who those writers are whom you term perfectionists; (2), What those tenets are which 5 distinguish them from other writers, and, (3), What is good therein, and what bad.

I have given order for the payment of six pounds three shillings to my father's engraver for the plates he has done already, and will direct Mr. Bowyer to send the proofs of them with the remainder 10 of the sheets. If they want me, I can give them the meeting at any time. One copy of 'Job's Disease' I have.[1] I will read it over next week, and see if it be perfect. We join in duty to my father and you. I am, dear mother, your dutiful son,

John Wesley 15

Feb. 14, 1734/5, Oxon.

Address: 'To Mrs Wesley at Epworth, To be left at ye Posthouse In Gainsbro', Lincolnshire. per London' *Postmarks*: 'OXFORD', '15/FE' *Charges*: ((3)), 'In all 7' *End* by Mrs. Wesley (notes for an answer): 'The visible order of Providence is to be observed by all, whether strong or weak in the faith, and this can't be done, nor civil government be established and the due subservience of one man to another preserved, without ensigns of authority, and difference in houses, furniture, and apparel, all which are marks of distinction, and as such in obedience to the will of God, and not for vainglory, they ought to be used, and he that breaks his rank and goes out of character, so far as he does so, so far he breaks the external order of the universe and abuses his Christian liberty.' *Source*: MA.

From the Revd. Samuel Wesley, Jun.[2]

[Feb. 22, 1735]

Dear Jack

1. You say you have but just enough. Had ever man on earth more? You have experienced less to be insufficient. Not in the course of priesthood to which you 20 are called. In that way, I am persuaded, though he that gathereth much can have nothing over, yet he that gathereth little can have no lack.

---

[1] See the rector's letter of Jan. 21, p. 415 above. This was to have been a dissertation on Job 2: 7, which was promised in a note on p. 419 of *Job*, but never appeared.

[2] Answering John's of Feb. 13. The date is calculated from that of receipt, Feb. 27, when Wesley noted in his diary: 'L[ette]r fr[om] b.S. alm[os]t conv[ince]d [me] of duty to go to Epw[orth].' On the 28th he wrote asking the Bishop of Oxford if indeed his ordination vows bound him to this duty.

2. There is danger in thinking of the good you have done, but not of what you may. Vainglory lies both ways. But the latter was your duty. So was the former, unless you can compare two things without thinking of one of them.

3. The good at Oxford is more diffusive. It is not *that good* you have promised.
5 You deceive yourself if you imagine you do not here think of *what you have* done. Your want may be better supplied at Epworth; not if my father is right in his successions.

4. 'A Christian will be despised everywhere; no one is a Christian till he is so; it will further his doing good.' If universal propositions, I deny them all.
10 Esteem goes before the good done, as well as follows it. 'A man may both despise and envy.' True; he may have a hot and cold fit of an ague. Contempt in general is no more incompatible with than necessary to benefiting others.

5. See (1) and (3).

6. I said plainly, I thought you had made a general resolution; as to taking
15 the first offer, I supposed an opportunity, a proper one; and declare now my judgment, should you live never so long, in the ordinary course of providence you can never meet another *so proper*. [']An ordained tutor who accepts not a cure is perjured.['] Alter the term into, 'who resolves not to accept', and I will maintain it, unless you can prove either of these two: (1), there is no such
20 obligation at taking orders; (2), this obligation is dispensed with. Both which I utterly deny. I am, dear Jack, yours, etc.

N.B. I forgot the date in the foul copy.

Source: Priestley, pp. 46–8.

From John Potter, Bishop of Oxford[1]

[March 1, 1735]

Revd. sir
25   It doth not seem to me that at your ordination you engaged yourself to undertake the cure of any parish, provided you can as a clergyman better serve God and the Church in your present or some other station; but if I live to see you, I shall be glad to know the grounds of your question and the full effect of it, and may then be able to return you a more particular answer, who am, sir, your
30 affectionate brother,

Jo. Oxford

Old Palace Yard, Westminster,
March 1, 1734/5

Source: Bristol Wesley, 234.

[1] John Potter (1674?–1747), a former Fellow of Lincoln College, and Bishop of Oxford from 1715 to 1737, when he was translated to Canterbury, had ordained John Wesley as deacon on Sept. 19, 1725, and as priest on Sept. 22, 1728. Clearly Wesley's letter to him (noted in his diary for Feb. 28), was as brief and colourless as possible, seeking a reply on general principles.

To the Revd. Samuel Wesley, Jun.[1]

[March 4, 1735]

Dear brother

I had rather dispute (if I must dispute) with you than with any man living, because it may be done with so little expense of time and words. 5

The question is now brought to one point, and the whole of the argument will lie in a single syllogism:

Neither hope of doing greater good, nor fear of any evil, ought to deter you from what you have engaged yourself to do:

But you have engaged yourself to undertake the cure of a parish: 10
Therefore neither that hope nor that fear ought to deter you from it.

The only doubt which remains is whether I have engaged myself or not. You think I did at my ordination, 'before God and his High Priest'. I think I did not. However, I own, I am not the proper judge of the oath I then took, it being certain, and allowed by all: 15 '*Verbis in quae quis jurejurando adigitur, sensum genuinum, ut et obligationi sacramenti modum ac mensuram praestitui a mente, non praestantis, sed exigentis juramentum.*'[2] Therefore it is not I but the High Priest of God before whom I contracted that engagement who is to judge of the nature and extent of it. 20

Accordingly the post after I received yours I referred it entirely to him, proposing this single question to him, Whether I had at my ordination engaged myself to undertake the cure of a parish or no?

His answer runs in these words:

Revd. sir 25
It doth not seem to me that at your ordination you engaged yourself to undertake the cure of any parish, provided you can as a clergyman better serve God and his Church in your present or some other station.[3]

Now that I can, as a clergyman, better serve God and his Church in my present station, I have all reasonable evidence. 30

Oxon, March 4, 1734/5

Source: Drew, a copy in the hand of the Revd. James Hervey; cf. Whitehead, I. 486–7, and Curnock, I. 29–30.

[1] Answering his of Feb. [22?]
[2] Whitehead supplies a translation: 'The true sense of the words of an oath, and the mode and extent of its obligation, are not to be determined by him who takes it, but by him who requires it.' [3] See letter from Potter, Mar. 1, 1735.

From the Revd. Thomas Broughton[1]

[April 15, 1735]

Revd. and dear sir

The same evening I received the favour of yours I waited on Sir John,
promising myself a kind reception. He rejoiced with me indeed to hear that
5 your father was yet alive, but did not close readily with me in attempting what I
hoped he would, which if crowned with success might prove a means of making
our declining friend end his days in peace. What shall we say for so sudden, so
unwished for a change? O put not your trust in princes.—Sir John disowns his
giving me any encouragement to promise you hopes of success. Did I then write
10 you an untruth? If his charge be just I did; but his words were, that 'though he
had solicited the Bishop of London and Sir Robert[2] in behalf of another (not
for Epworth) yet he would be glad to serve Mr. Wesley'. But where lies the
obstacle? Why, my lord of London (who is usually consulted by the Minister of
State on such occasions) spoke some disadvantageous things of you once in the
15 presence of Sir John. But I could not but observe to our friend that the misrepresented strictness of life which gave occasion for those disadvantageous things to
be spoken of you, was so far from being an objection to your being favoured by
a Christian bishop that I humbly hoped it would turn to your good account,
insomuch as over-exactness in behaviour was the sign of a tender and well-
20 disposed mind. But I cannot here help thinking on the case of poor Mr. Rivington, though no hints were given on that score. Yet

[1] John and Charles Wesley (accompanied by Westley Hall) walked to Epworth to be
with their dying father, arriving on Good Friday, Apr. 4, 1735. John took charge both of
the family and of the parish, his older brother being unable to leave Tiverton. In order
to help his father 'end his days in peace' he reversed his earlier decision, and very soon
after his arrival wrote to his Oxford Methodist colleague, Thomas Broughton, now
serving in London, asking him to take the steps which he had already offered to take in
order to secure the Epworth living. Broughton's reply was not as hopeful as both had
expected, although he kept on trying. The rector died on Apr. 25, and on Apr. 30
Charles wrote to Samuel describing his last days, adding: 'We have now got yours of the
21st. My brother had laid aside all hopes (or fears, for I cannot certainly say which) of
succeeding, as Sir J[ohn Philipp]s seemed to decline intermeddling; but by yours we
guess Mr. Oglethorpe has quickened him. A neighbouring clergyman has sent word
that "he has the living", which would be bad news but that another as confidently affirms
he has it. How many more may be sure of it we cannot say, but if Providence pleases a
W[esley] will have it after all, though in the gift of the Crown.' In fact the living went to
the Revd. Samuel Hurst, though John Wesley stayed on as the acting minister for a
further two months. Indeed, more than he then realized, his father's death indeed
constituted the break with Oxford which he had feared and had done so much to avoid,
and never afterwards did he spend more than a week or so there at a time; in 1735, after
leaving Epworth, he had *Job* to care for in London, and at the end of August Georgia
was offered him as a replacement for Epworth. (See Heitzenrater, pp. 308–19, and
Priestley, p. 53.)

Thomas Broughton (1712–77), fellow of Exeter College, Oxford, first undertook
tutoring in London, then became curate of the Tower of London, and from 1743 until
his death was Secretary of the Society for Promoting Christian Knowledge.

[2] Sir Robert Walpole, Prime Minister.

Tros Tyriusve illi nullo discrimine agetur.[1]

Sir John thinks the Bishop of Oxford can be your friend. Yes, I told him, my lord might give you a favourable word, if asked, but I did not think that your interest in his lordship was so prevalent as to make him bestir himself in your behalf. However, if you judge it proper to write to the bishop, I will wait upon 5 him and do the best I can to serve my dear friend. Could your father's book be presented to the Queen soon? It might do good. The thing is not so difficult, I hope, if one could get a hearty friend to espouse you. My interest in The Speaker is not powerful enough, I believe, to bring about so desired a work; yet if there was any other great man to befriend you a serviceable hint might be 10 dropped. I doubt not but our good and loving God will order this and everything else for the great and best good. This is the wish and prayer of, dear sir, yours most sincerely,

T. Broughton

Mr. and Mrs. Rivington join with me in hearty and humble services to all 15 with you, especially your good father. Pray remember us.

London, April 15, 1735.

Pray let me hear from you forthwith. I intend calling at Johnson's Court.

End by JW: 'Brou April 15, 1735'   *Source*: MA.

From George Whitefield[2]

Oxon, May 8th, 1735

Revrd. sr.   20

[1.] Yours I received on Saturday last, just as my cold returned upon me, and in the midst of my evening devotions. But was really something startled to find

[1] Cf. Virgil, *Aeneid*, i. 574, 'Trojan or Tyrian matters little to him'—in orig., 'mihi', 'to me'.

[2] George Whitefield (1714-70) was over eleven years Wesley's junior, and regarded him with some awe. As an impoverished and serious student at Pembroke College, Oxford, from November, 1732, he had admired the 'Methodists' at a distance until 1734, when he diffidently approached Charles Wesley, who befriended him, and introduced him to his older brother and their colleagues. During the spring of 1735 Whitefield was engulfed in physical illness and spiritual distress, inextricably mingled with homesickness, and exacerbated by the stern self-denial and self-examination encouraged by the Wesleys—seven trying weeks which culminated in spiritual release and the experience of 'rejoicing in God his Saviour' (Whitefield, *Journals*, p. 58), three years before the Wesleys themselves passed through a similar experience. During this period he unbosomed himself hesitantly but completely in letters to John Wesley, beginning on April 1, shortly after the two brothers had set out to wait on their dying father. Letters passed rapidly between them, continuing for the two months after Samuel Wesley's death on April 25, when John served as pastor at Epworth, fragmentary clues to several of John's lost replies being preserved in this previously unpublished letter. The moment and the spiritual mechanism of Whitefield's conversion remain unknown, but Wesley's well-intentioned pastoral counsels—however ineffectual they may seem to have proved —form an important element in its background. Whitefield continued to turn to him as his respected father in God (cf. p. 471 below).

your letter in the least favour any design of my leaving Oxford, having not doubted for some time before but that you would send me a positive order not to stir a step upon any solicitations whatsoever. But seeing what you was pleased to write, and reflecting upon some other circumstances that have occurred, I began
5 to think Providence ere long intended (though I even tremble at the mentioning it) that I should see Gloucester [at] last.

[2.] To give you my reasons why I should think so seems to be my next business. Last Tuesday, then, sir, was seve[n]night the doctor came and paid me his last visit, telling me I had nothing to do but to use exercise and eat heartily in order
10 to recover my health. Whilst he was here, in came my kind tutor, and was vastly pressing upon me to go into the country, urging that it was really, as he imagined, my indispensable duty, that change of air was probably the only remedy for my present disorder, and that variety of company, and seeing my friends, might be very effectual towards my recovery. This last part of his advice I replied to by
15 telling him, that as for variety of company, I could not think it would be any means at all, being positive that that company in which I could most improve myself in perfecting my nature was certainly the best for me in any state of health whatsoever. This indeed was some private conversation after the doctor left me, who (if I am not greatly mistaken) advised me positively to go down,
20 and drink milk in a morning; so that whether I am obliged in duty to follow this advice as a prescription under God, or whether this might not proceed from something he had heard of my way of life, and so not to be regarded, give me leave, sir, to leave to your determination.

[3.] As for what my tutor urged, I have found [it] in a great measure true that
25 Oxford air is probably the chief cause of my present illness. For I have frequently been in very fair expectations of recovery, but upon my going out a little something or another has happened that has made me relapse, which I can impute to nothing so much as to those cold winds which blow here in a morning, and which probably were the secondary causes of my present visitation. Last
30 Saturday, I think, sir, was the third time my disorder has returned upon me, and I find no likelihood of its leaving me as yet, the weather still continuing uncertain, so that I am really in great doubt how to act in my present circumstances. But God, I trust, will direct you how to advise me.

[4]. You was pleased to tell me, sir, if Providence makes my 'leaving Oxford
35 unavoidable, the danger, great as it is, will do me no hurt'.[1] As for the danger, sir, alas! I tremble at the thought of it, heartily believing if it is God's will I shall leave Oxford, none but his almighty arm can conduct me through those innumerable difficulties which must necessarily be consequent on my seeing Gloucester. What makes me most solicitous is the want of having that expression
40 in your last explained, viz., 'If Providence makes my leaving Oxford unavoidable', and therefore would beg the favour of you, sir, to inform me whether the reasons here subjoined do in your opinion answer the extent of that expression.

[5.] The same evening I received yours, sir, I was under a great concern, believing I must soon take a journey into the country. Upon that I thought proper
45 to set some time apart before I went to bed, to pray for dir⟨ec⟩tion, which I accordingly did; and afterwards, lying in my bed and finding myself not at all

[1] Apparently part of Wesley's written response of (possibly) May 1 to Whitefield's letter of April 1 or (more probably) a subsequent date, *c*. April 20.

inclinable to sleep, the following thoughts came into my head. 'That if Oxford air was certainly prejudicial to my health it was certainly my duty to go down. That I was here on great expenses, it having cost me, besides my apothecary's bill, which I have not as yet seen, above two guineas in less than a month, and that I knew my friends' circumstances could not support me in this way, and consequently it would be tempting the Lord obstinately to continue here when the country air might probably be an effectual remedy. That I was now a useless member of the society to which I belong, and in all likelihood should still continue so. Add to this that it was very disputable whether my pay, since I cannot serve, would be allowed me or not. And that therefore it was presumption not to follow my friend's advice. Now whether these were only in your opinion, sir, suggestions impressed upon my understanding by the devil in order to delude me, or coming from the Holy Spirit, is a question I trust you will be enabled to resolve.

[6.] Since that, it has occurred to my mind that by my present confinement Providence seems to have shown me he can support me without those means I used to set so great a value on, having not been at public worship except once or twice for a quarter of an hour to communicate ever since Passion week. And then I once narrowly escaped being choked at Mr. Salmon's for going out, as I thought afterwards, too presumptuously, in too cold a morning. All these things very easily come into my mind whilst I am writing, sir, whether from the enemy or not I cannot say. However, I can assure [you] I have prayed heartily ever since the reception of your last for direction, and therefore am fully assured our good and all-gracious God will not let me 'seek death in the error of my life'.

[7.] I have endeavoured, sir, to the utmost of my power, to follow your advice in a former letter, viz., 'to press on, and not to faint'.[1] I have enlarged my morning and evening devotions now, I think, to full two hours. I have frequently renewed my acts of resignation. I have prayed over the Scripture, which is now my entire study almost, every day, and have found it frequently suggested to me that generally there was more than one called in an house. But alas! my understanding is so very deceivable, I could not tell what to think of it. And therefore have been as minute as possible, in order that you by God's assistance may ⟨be⟩ enabled to advise me.

[8.] 'As my day is', you was pleased to tell me, 'so will my strength be.' I should take it as a favour if you would explain that expression a little more fully.

[9.] Before I enumerate to you the symp⟨toms which are against⟩ my continuance at Oxford, give me leave to inform you of one or two more particulars. First, then, ⟨Mr.⟩ Harvy has the last week wrote me a most enlivening letter, exhor⟨ting me⟩ to 'press on and not to faint'; that he reads to the poor, and that their number is somewhat increased; that the clergyman was to deter⟨mine⟩ at his next meeting about his having prayers twice a week. This made me think Providence would equally support me if I did not go without full conviction. He is cured of the disorder in his leg, but sadly afflicted with another disorder, for which he begs our most im⟨portunate pra⟩yers. He tells me the enemy is somewhat repressed in his temptations. But to return. Last Tuesday night, at evening prayer, came Mr. ⟨Sa⟩rney, and disturbed me with the joyful news that he has

---

[1] Almost certainly Wesley's response to the letter of April 1 (for which see W.H.S· X. 17–19), probably written *c*. April 9.

had a frequent conference with the minister of the parish in whose house the Master lodges, particularly the night before, till eleven o'clock! That he had nothing to object against what he said, but that it was contrary to flesh and blood. That he hopes to prevail on him to have sacrament administered once a month,

5 having urged nothing to excuse himself but the fear of a congregation, which he promised to make up out of their own family. And what is still more surprising, the church being very much out of repair, he was put on a project to make a collection of fifteen pounds to new roof it. He has already gotten two guineas, and doubts not of making up the rest. All which made me think that if I was

10 sincere God would equally support me.

[10.] All that seems to be against me is this, that soon after I troubled you, sir, with my last, I received a letter from my mother, with the joyful news, as I thought, of her having resigned me up to God, and left me solely to my own disposal. Upon that I wrote a letter to my brother, who had been before so im-

15 portunate with me to come down, desiring the same favour of him and my other friends to this. I have as yet received no answer. This I thought had put a full stop to all further temptations to leave Oxford. But soon after came your letter, which made me quite change my opinion.

[11.] My illness still continues, sir, and my cold not at all, in all appearance, the

20 better. Indeed I am freed of the doctor, but am still confined to my room, which has made me think that Providence intends to prepare me by this visitation to go out in the world. But all future things belong to God. Into his all-gracious arms I blindly throw myself, not doubting but that he will still guide me as well as he has hitherto done. To sum up all this tedious scribble in one general question, I

25 beg, sir, you would be pleased to inform me as soon as opportunity will permit whether, supposing my illness continues, or if I do recover, if my friends repeat their solicitations, I should dare venture down, without laying any projects how to act, but merely to go down because God will have me; and in doing this you will greatly oblige, reverend sir, your troublesome but sincerely humble

30 servant,

George Whitefield

Mr. Smith came home, I think on Monday. Pray, sir, my hearty love to your brother. And let me beg all your prayers, dear sir.

Address: 'To / The Revrd Mr. John Westley at Epworth / (to be sent from Gainsborough post offi⟨ce⟩)'   *Postmarks*: 'OXFORD'', '9 MA'   *End* by JW: 'Mr Whitefield / May 5 [*sic*], 1735', and the outline of his reply (see p. 427) *Source*: Wesley House, Cambridge.

To George Whitefield[1]

[Epworth, May 13?, 1735]

[[1. Prov[idence] intends [that you will] sooner see Gloucester.[2]

4. New milk or whey in a morning now.[3]

5. Oxford air in a morning.[4] Therefore, w[alk] not in a morning.

6. Gloucester air worse.[5]   2. Money and c[omfort] nothing at all.[6]   1. If P[rovidence] makes it unav[oidable].[7]

3. Ill health, nothing else.

7. Means.[8] He can help without. Will not. Case.

8. As thy day, so thy strength.[9] Sarn[ey][10] and Harvey,[11] therefore if health.

9. 2. Friends' solicitations nothing.[12]]]

Source: Added by JW at the head of Whitefield's letter of May 8, beneath the date.

[1] This endorsement on Whitefield's letter of May 8, 1735, clearly comprises the abbreviated draft outline of Wesley's reply, numbered and renumbered to display the probable arrangement of the paragraphs, though the substance of the argument is in most cases deducible only from the letter to which it responds.

[2] Cf. May 8, § 1, etc. Whitefield does not appear to have been able to return home to Gloucester since coming to Oxford two and a half years earlier.

[3] Ibid., § 2.

[4] Ibid., § 3.

[5] Ibid., § 5.

[6] Ibid.

[7] Ibid., §§ 4, 5.

[8] Ibid., §§ 6–7.

[9] Ibid., § 8.

[10] John Sarney, an Oxford mercer whose home was a major focal point for Wesley's sympathizers among the townsmen. Charles Wesley lodged with him in 1737, and when John Wesley stayed with him on Feb. 17, 1738, he described Sarney as 'the only one now remaining here of many who at our embarking for America were used to "take sweet counsel together", and rejoice in "bearing the reproach of Christ"' (JWJ). Within a few months, however, he also was 'estranged by the offence of the cross' (CWJ, Sept. 28, 1738). He became prominent in the official life of the city, a freeman in 1740, a chamberlain in 1741, and junior bailiff in 1744 (Green, *Wesley*, p. 280). Whitefield had described his religious zeal in the letter of May 8, § 9.

[11] i.e. James Hervey, the Oxford Methodist; cf. May 8, § 9 (where 'Harvy' is a phonetic spelling apparently followed by Wesley), and the note on p. 581.

[12] Cf. May 8, § 11.

To a Roman Catholic Priest

[May, 1735?][1]

Sir

I return you thanks both for the favour of your letter, and for your recommending my father's *Proposals* to the Sorbonne.

5　I have neither time nor inclination for controversy with any; but least of all with the Romanists. And that both because I can't trust any of their quotations without consulting every sentence they quote in the originals; and because the originals themselves can very hardly be trusted in any of the points controverted between them

10　and us. I am no stranger to their skill in *mending* those authors who did not at first speak home to their purpose; as also in *purging* them from[2] those passages which contradicted their emendations. And as they have not wanted opportunity to do this, so doubtless they have carefully used it with regard to a point that so nearly concerned

15　them as the supremacy of the Bishop of Rome. I am not therefore surprised if the works of St. Cyprian[3] (as they are called) do strenu-

---

[1] It has proved impossible to discover the name of the recipient of this important letter, which seems to be Wesley's earliest written challenge to the teachings of the Church of Rome. Even the dating is only a rough approximation. He introduced it in his *Journal* for Aug. 27, 1739, thus: '. . . I will here add my serious judgment concerning the Church of Rome, wrote some time since to a priest of that communion'. The few internal clues are not conclusive. Printed *Proposals* for his father's *Job* were issued in 1730, 1731, 1733, and 1734, when John Wesley himself began to promote the work with great zeal. He was most active between the departure of his brother Samuel for Tiverton in the spring of 1734 and his presentation of a specially bound copy to Queen Caroline on Oct. 12, 1735. The printed list of subscribers contains no mention of the Sorbonne, nor of any address in Paris; from the lack of the appropriate title it seems highly unlikely that either of the only two subscribers with French names, 'Mr. Fraigneau' and 'George Lewis Tiessier, M.D.', was a priest. In default of any explicit clues in his extant diary either to the Sorbonne or a Roman Catholic priest, or to the *Canons and Decrees* of the Council of Trent, the most likely date would seem to be at some time when no diary is available, as from Apr. 23 to Sept. 6, 1734 (though monthly summaries for this period are extant), or Mar. 1 to Oct. 16, 1735. The suggested date, however, remains purely conjectural, and may well prove incorrect. The phrase, 'my father's *Proposals*', might indeed be slightly more appropriate for a date when Samuel Wesley was still alive.　　　[2] i.e. 'of'.

[3] Bishop of Carthage, died A.D. 258. His works consist mainly of short treatises and letters. In his *Journal* for Jan. 9, 1738, Wesley wrote: 'The great mercy of God just now [threw] me upon reading St. Cyprian's *Works*', though he does not state that this was for the first time; indeed this was apparently one of the items which he had taken with him to Georgia, and was now carrying back. In later years Wesley kept copies of Cyprian's Latin works in his various studies, prescribed them for others' study, and frequently quoted them. In his sermon on 'The Mystery of Iniquity' (No. 61, § 25) he cited Cyprian as 'in every respect an unexceptionable witness' in his 'abundance of letters' to 'the state of religion in his time'.

ously maintain it; but I am, that they have not been better *corrected*
—for they still contain passages that absolutely overthrow it. What
gross negligence was it to leave his Seventy-fourth Epistle (to
Pompeianus) out of the *Index Expurgatorius*, wherein Pope Cyprian
so flatly charges Pope Stephen[1] with 'pride and obstinacy, and with
being a defender of the cause of heretics, and that against Christians
and the very church of God'![2] He that can reconcile this with his
believing Stephen the infallible head of the church may reconcile
the Gospel with the Alcoran.

Yet I can by no means approve the scurrility and contempt with
which the Romanists have often been treated. I dare not rail at or
despise any man, much less those who profess to believe in the same
Master. But I pity them much, having the same assurance that Jesus
is the Christ and that no Romanist can expect to be saved according
to the terms of his covenant. For thus saith our Lord: 'Whosoever
shall break one of the least of these commandments, and shall teach
men so, he shall be called the least in the kingdom of heaven.'[3]
And, 'If any man shall add unto these things, God shall add unto
him the plagues that are written in this book.'[4] But all Romanists,
as such, do both. *Ergo* . . .

The minor I prove, not from Protestant authors, [n]or even from
particular writers of their own communion, but from the public,
authentic records of the Church of Rome. Such are *The Canons and
Decrees of the Council of Trent*.[5] And the edition I use was printed
at Cologne,[6] and approved by authority.

And first, all Romanists, as such, do break and teach men to
break one (and not the least) of those commandments, the words of
which, concerning images, are these: לֹא תִשְׁתַּחֲוֶה לָהֶם.[7] Now שׁתח
(as every smatterer in Hebrew knows) is *incurvare se—procumbere,
honoris exhibendi causa*[8] (and is accordingly rendered by the Seventy

---

[1] Stephen I (died A.D. 257), Pope from 254, who became involved with Cyprian in a
bitter dispute over the validity of baptism by heretics, which Cyprian himself would not
recognize. Using the parallel title of 'Pope' for Cyprian is apparently Wesley's own ecclesiastical satire.

[2] This is not in fact a single quotation, but a composite derived from §§ 1, 7, 8. See
Ante-Nicene Fathers, V. 386–90, where Epistle 74 (in some editions) is numbered as 73.

[3] Cf. Matt. 5: 19.   [4] Rev. 22: 18.

[5] Wesley is translating into English the title of the Latin work which he used, *Canones
et Decreta Concilii Tridenti*.

[6] In the British Library are thirteen editions of the *Canones et Decreta* published at
Cologne between 1564 and 1722.

[7] Exod. 20: 5.

[8] 'To bow down before anyone, in token of honouring him' (Wesley's note).

in this very place by a Greek word of the very same import, προσ-
κυνεῖν). But the Council of Trent (and consequently all Romanists as such, all who allow the authority of that Council) teaches
that it is *legitimus imaginum usus . . . eis honorem exhibere, procumbendo*
5 *coram eis.*[1]

Secondly, all Romanists, as such, do add to those things which are
written in the Book of life. For in the Bull of Pius IV, subjoined to
those *Canons and Decrees*,[2] I find all the additions following: (1),
seven sacraments; (2), transubstantiation; (3), communion in one
10 kind only; (4), purgatory, and praying for the dead therein; (5),
praying to saints; (6), veneration of relics; (7), worship of images;
(8), indulgences; (9), the priority and universality of the Roman
Church; (10), the supremacy of the Bishop of Rome. All these
things, therefore, do the Romanists add to those which are written
15 in the Book of life. I am . . .

[John Wesley]

Source: JWJ, Aug. 27, 1739 (first published 1742).

From Emilia Wesley

[Aug. 13, 1735]

Dear brother
I doubt not but you think long before this that I have laid aside all regard
20 for you, that your last letter[3] has extinguished the great love I had for many
years bore you, and, in short, that my friendship is as much in the wane as your
own has visibly been ever since I left Lincoln. [. . .] However, I can assure you
no resentment or ill-nature, but abundance of business [. . .] has prevented my
answering yours. [. . .]
25 And now what can I answer? [. . .] To lay open the state of my soul to you,
or any of our clergy, is what I have no manner of inclination to at present, and
believe I never shall. Nor shall I put my conscience under the direction of mortal
man, frail as myself. To my own Master I stand or fall. Nay, I shall not scruple

---

[1] 'i.e. the proper use of images is to honour them, by bowing down before them.
(Session 25, paragraph 2).' (Wesley's note).

[2] The greatest achievement of Pope Pius IV (1499–1565) was bringing to a successful
conclusion the Council of Trent (1545–63). His summary of its doctrinal decisions, the
Bull 'super forma juramenti professionis fidei', or the Tridentine Creed, was appended
to the *Canones et Decreta*, and he imposed it on all holders of ecclesiastical office.

[3] For some years they had written three or four weeks after receiving a letter from the
other. John's letter to her, therefore, had probably been written in May or early June—
surely after their father's death, even though it harked back to what he considered her
indiscretions of early 1734 (see Feb. 7, 1734).

to say that all such desires in you or any other ecclesiastic seems to me to look very much like church tyranny, and assuming to yourselves a dominion over your fellow-servants which never was designed you by God. [. . .]

You tax me with making the world my God, the being negligent of duties public and private, the setting up my rest here, seeking for happiness in this life, etc.—all this heavy charge after living three days together. Whether I omitted family prayer must be known to all; whether I neglected private devotion can only be known to the Almighty and myself. Therefore 'tis criminal in you to suppose that there was such neglect. Whether I hold the necessity of frequent communion equally with you was a secret to our family, but now I own I do not hold it necessary to salvation, nor a means of Christian perfection. Don't mistake; I only think communicating every Sunday, or very frequently, lessens our veneration for that sacred ordinance, and consequently our profiting by it. You seem to assert we ought to fix all our thoughts, hopes, desires, on God alone; here again I differ. That God ought to have the preference in our practical judgment, that whenever duty comes in competition with our worldly interest or pleasure, this world should ever give place to the other, is my firm belief; but sure that wise and good Being who formed us and gave us these bodies with their several desires and tendencies never designed to take away our liberty so far as to deny all subordinate love to the creature. [. . .] And herein you yourself speak as one that is guilty. Had you not lost your dear Mrs. C[hapo]n[e], where had your love been fixed? On heaven, I hope, principally, but a large share too had been hers; you would not have been so spiritualized, something of this lower world would have had its part of your heart, wise as you are. But being deprived of her, there went all hope of worldly happiness. And now the mind, which is an active principle, losing its aim here, has fixed on its Maker; for happiness will ever be the end that all rational beings will aim at, and when disappointed of one thing will soon fix on another. I hope we both shall place our affections chiefly there where true joys are to be found. Thus far in reply to yours. Now give me leave to expostulate with the friend.

Full well you know that even from our childhood you have been selected from all our numerous family for my intimate companion, my counsellor in difficulties, the dear partner of my joys and griefs. To you alone my heart lay open at all times, nor am I conscious of ever concealing my sentiments from your knowledge these many years, except in one only instance, which has happened lately. Say, where slept your friendship, dear brother, when you could censure me so hardly for no offence? If I have since I came to Gainsbro' swerved from that strictness which I practised for many years at licentious Lincoln, [. . .] you can have no right to censure for secret faults. [. . .] Yet whatever faults I have been guilty of in respect of God, to you I have been blameless, except loving you ⟨too⟩ well has been one. [. . .] I am ⟨your affectionate⟩ sister, Emilia Wesley.

Address: 'To the Revd Mr John Wesley, Fellow of Lincoln Coll. Oxford. by way of London' *Postmark*: '13 AV' *Charges*: ((4)), 'In all 7' *End* by JW: 'S. Em. Aug. 13. 1735 / S[he] angry' *Source*: MA; cf. Stev, pp. 270–2.

From James Edward Oglethorpe[1]

Old Palace Yard, West[minste]r,
Sepr. 9th, 1735

Sir

I received yours, and the chief point you say to be considered is whether any
5 other can do the business God has required of you. I suppose that is in England.
Surely there are more persons capable of doing the offices required by the
Church in England than there are capable of undergoing all that is necessary
for propagating the gospel in new countries. I believe it is right to consider
where a man can be most useful, and the best guide says, Matt. 10, 'Whoever
10 shall not receive you nor hear your words, depart out of that house or city, and
shake off the dust of your feet.' Again Cap. 13th, v. 57 and 58. Consider whether
you can be so useful where people are in the situation described Matt. 13, v. 15,
as you can be where the heathen is desirous to receive the Word. Read Matt. 18,
v. 12-19th, v. 29. I should have said more, but the post is just going. I am,
15 sir, your most humble servant,

James Oglethorpe

[1] James Edward Oglethorpe (1696–1785) obtained a commission in the British army
in 1710, and saw military service in Europe for a few years before returning to oversee
his family estate and (from 1722) to serve as Member of Parliament for Haslemere.
His attention was drawn to the terrible conditions in debtors' prisons, which he publicly
exposed. This in turn led to his securing a charter to settle the colony of Georgia in
America, partly as an outlet for social misfits, partly as an opportunity for developing
new territory both as a market and as a buffer zone against the encroachments of the
Spanish in the south. The Georgia Trust, of which he was the chairman, set up offices in
Old Palace Yard, Westminster, where they received subscriptions, and met regularly to
administer the affairs of the new colony. In 1732 Oglethorpe escorted the first 114
settlers to Georgia, and during 1734–5 was recruiting a further contingent, as well as
reinforcements and perhaps a replacement for its spiritual leadership, the first minister,
the Revd. Samuel Quincy, having fallen below expectations. On Dec. 7, 1734, the
Revd. Samuel Wesley, Sen., had recommended the services of his son-in-law, the
Revd. John Whitelamb, at the same time regretting that he himself was too old for the
task (Clarke, I. 337–9; cf. S.P.C.K. Minutes, Vol. 16, p. 48; for Whitelamb's letter
to Wesley of Dec. 5, 1734, in which he offered himself for this task, see George
F. Jones, *Henry Newman's Salzburger Letter-books*, Univ. of Georgia Press, Athens,
Georgia, 1966, pp. 515–17). On Aug. 27, 1735, says John Wesley, 'Mr. Burton met
me in Ludgate Street, [London], and first mentioned Georgia to me', so that he 'had
a conference or two with Mr. Oglethorpe upon that subject' before returning to
Oxford. This project he then talked over with William Law, with his friends in
Manchester, and his mother (Heitzenrater, pp. 316–18). He wrote (possibly on Sept.
5) informing Oglethorpe that he was prepared to consider an appointment, though some
uncertainty still remained. This is Oglethorpe's reply to that letter.

[From the Revd. John Clayton][1]

[[Dear sir

I made bold to open your letter, that I might have an opportunity of writing a line in it, as judging there were no secrets between Mr. Oglethorpe and you. I have been these two evenings at Dr. Deacon's, who is getting forward with the catechism with all possible expedition. He would have you buy Whiston's 5 catechesis (?) to take along with you, and I will write the other out as soon as it is done, and send it after you. Be sure remember to dip when you baptize, if it can be possibly done, according to the church's direction. Adieu, dear sir, J(ohn) C(layton).]]

Source: Bristol Wesley, 210.

From Richard Morgan, Jun.[2]

[Sept. 25, 1735] 10

Dear sir

I hope this will find you and the rest of our friends well. This morning the rector sent for me. He told me he had heard I had returned to my former strict way of life, and that he must acquaint my father with it. I desired he would come to particulars, that where I was wrong I would be glad to be set right. He said 15 I looked thin, and feared I would hurt myself by rigorous fasting. I told him I dined in the hall on Wednesdays, and that I ate bread and butter on Friday mornings. He was pretty well satisfied with this account. He advised me to eat something else instead of tea after fasting, which I promised to do. His next charge was, not sitting in the common room. I said I intended to sit there three 20 nights every week, which he thought was sufficient. I unguardedly told him that if it were agreeable to him I would dine in the hall even on Fridays. He very much approved of this proposal, and said I might observe any other day as a fast instead of it. I believe, if I would go into the hall on fast days all my other activities would be less taken notice of, and I should put it out of the rector's 25 or Mr. Hutchin's power to make any complaints of me to my father. If I could be sure of not injuring religion by my example I believe I might comply with the rector herein, for you are very sensible I might notwithstanding observe the same degree of abstinence even on those days. I depend on the advice of my friends in this affair, and hope God will sanctify it to me. The Gospel tells us 30 that the children of God must suffer persecution from the world, but the rector

[1] Beneath Oglethorpe's signature on the foregoing letter is this from the Revd. John Clayton, written in Byrom's shorthand. The address sheet is missing, but Clayton apparently wrote from Manchester (to which Oglethorpe's reply was sent), probably on Sept. 11.

[2] This young man had become one of the Oxford Methodists whom he had previously despised. See letters of Nov. 22, Dec. 17, 1733, and Jan. 14, 15, 28, 31, and Mar 15, 1734. For Wesley's reply see Sept. 30, 1735. On Nov. 27, 1735, Morgan wrote expressing a wish to follow Wesley to Georgia, and describing his Methodist activities in Oxford.

says we must endeavour to have our persons in esteem, and those things wherein we differ from the world, we must do them privately. We must take care our good be not evil spoken of. Though the Church enjoins fasting, yet because the bishops, the pillars of the Church, do not observe it, it loses its force. When he
5 finds his blood hot, he says, he fasts, but unknown to anybody. He thinks it's a relative duty, and not confined to any particular time. He looks upon it only as a remedy against unchastity, and if we are not troubled with this passion, I suppose, not obligatory. He advised me to read such books as were genteel accomplishments. I have, through God's assistance, in some degree seen my own weakness
10 by the effects of this anti-Christian doctrine, for it has quite discomposed me, though I was enabled to see the fallacy of it. I see nothing so well qualified to destroy my soul, to make me eternally miserable, as the conversation of temporizing Christians, which I hope God will by your advice and other means prevent, as I am sure he will if I am faithful to him. When I desire your advice
15 in this affair I only desire you to prevent my eternal damnation, for it is in the greatest danger from this most subtle, deceitful, and dangerous of all enemies. O that I could express to you the dangers I foresee from this enemy. [. . .] You cannot sufficiently arm me against the rector. I suspect him of insincerity to you. I believe, and Mr. Horne is of the same opinion, that my going to Ireland depends
20 on my going into the hall on fast days. The rector said as much as if you frightened others from religion by your example, and that you might have done a great deal of good if you had been less strict. [. . .] On the contents of this letter depends my eternal salvation. O lay this to your heart, and make my case your own! Do not think you can spend your time better than in answering this letter. I hope
25 you will not forget to pray to God to enable me to follow you wherever it is his will, and never to omit putting me in mind of Christ when you write to me. Pray in your letter to me exhort us to sup together every night, yet to leave the world, and to be together as much as possible. Mr. Robson is in a dangerous way. He is convinced of the necessity of being a Christian, but cannot leave the
30 world. Mr. Carter, I fear, is not steady. Mr. Hervey is gone. Mr. Broughton is not yet returned. If he go to Georgia, it is best . . .

End by JW: 'Mr. Morgan, Sept. 25, 1735. ⊣' *Source*: Bristol Wesley, 214, apparently incomplete, with four full pages, but no address or closing section corresponding to the closing section of Wesley's reply of Sept. 30. Cf. Tyerm (OM), pp. 21–3, which itself is not a complete transcript.

From the Revd. John Burton[1]

Eton College, 7 ber 28, 1735

Dear sir
This day, being obliged to attend at our altar upon the celebration of the
35 sacrament, I left town without seeing you when I knew not where to find. You

---

[1] John Burton (1696–1771), scholar of Corpus Christi College, Oxford, and from 1733 fellow of Eton College (where he spent much of his time), had been friendly with John

may imagine that some circumstances or other would continually suggest fresh matter to my thoughts; give me leave to say what occurs to me on this occasion.

The motive to your pious undertaking is the desire of doing good to the souls of others, and in consequence of that to your own. You will readily improve the first opportunity offered to attain this end. Now a very considerable one is 5 offered before you come to Georgia, I mean while you [are] a-shipboard. There you have a numerous family under your care, and confined to attendance; your private as well as public address to them will then most probably have the best effect on their minds while they see the wonders of [the] Lord in the deep; thus will they come better disposed for religious habits from such impressions. It 10 may be perhaps more convenient for you four[1] to be all together, but it would be much better for the people if some one of you should be in the other ship.[2] You may perhaps alternately attend in the other vessels as they go in company. Pray labour this first point; 'tis a most useful exercise of the clergyman's abilities, and most beneficial to the people. 15

Under the influence of Mr. Oglethorpe giving weight to your endeavours, much may be effected under the present circumstances. The apostolical manner of preaching from house to house will through God's grace be effectual to turn many to righteousness. You come to a people, some ignorant, and most disposed to licentiousness. Your good offices will be required at Savannah town at first, 20 which is but a few miles distant from the Indians. The magistrate will authorize your access to every family, and the younger will be under obligation to receive instructions. I consider you all at first for some time as joint labourers in the

Wesley for a decade, Wesley's first recorded letter to him being dated May 2, 1726. From 1731 he was also vicar of Buckland, Berks., where Wesley occasionally preached for him (Green, pp. 73, 98, 103, 136 n.). He was a careful theological and classical scholar, and in 1752 was awarded the D.D. Burton was a very active founding trustee of the colony of Georgia, and was helping to underwrite the cost of a catechist there (Egmont, *Diary*, II. 32). Having recruited Wesley for the project on Aug. 28, 1735, on Sept. 8 he wrote to him: 'Your short conference with Mr. Oglethorpe has raised the hopes of many good persons that you and yours would join in an undertaking which cannot be better executed than by such instruments.' He urged that Wesley should speedily inform Oglethorpe or him of his decision, as Oglethorpe planned to embark on Oct. 5. (Wesley had already written to Oglethorpe, though not yet with a firm decision—see preceding letter.) On Sept. 18 Burton welcomed Wesley's acceptance: 'It was with no small pleasure that I heard your resolution on the point under consideration . . . We enjoy your readiness to undertake the work. When it is known that good men are thus employed, the pious and charitable will be more encouraged to promote this work. You have too much steadiness of mind to be disturbed by light scoffs of idle and profane . . . You are desired by Mr. Oglethorpe to come hither [London] as soon as you can.' He offered to escort Wesley from Mapledurham, near Reading, a wealthy living which he had just secured. He added: 'Let me put a matter to be considered by your brother Charles. Would it not be more advisable that he were in orders? This would easily be obtained.'

[1] John and Charles Wesley, Matthew Salmon, and Westley Hall, though the latter two backed out at the last minute, and were replaced by Benjamin Ingham and Charles Delamotte. The eventual four were originally assigned to the large cabin, with fourteen other people, but preferring privacy secured two small cabins near the forecastle (Heitzenrater, pp. 322–8; Clarke, II. 176).

[2] The *Simmonds*, Capt. Cornish (on which the Wesleys sailed), and the *London Merchant*, Capt. Thomas, with the royal sloop *Hawk* as escort.

same place; you will soon be dispersed to your several stations and employments in the same work; and you'll find abundant room for the exercise of patience and prudence, as well as piety. The generality of the people are babes in the progress of their Christian life, to be fed with milk instead of strong meat. The
5 wise householder will bring out of his stores food proportioned to the necessities of his family. The circumstances of their present Christian pilgrimage will furnish the most affecting subjects of discourse, and what arises *pro re nata*[1] will have greater influence than a laboured discourse on a subject in which men think themselves not so immediately concerned. Thus the 107th Psalm, the history
10 of the patriarch's sojourning, Ezra and Nehemiah, etc., furnish matter suited to their apprehension and circumstances; and it is to be observed that historical narratives gain attention more than other sorts of discourses, and insensibly convey with them the good moral which often miscarries under other sorts of conveyance. Of this kind was our Saviour's preaching in parables to the people.
15   One end for which we were associated was the conversion of negro slaves. As yet nothing has been attempted in this way. But a door is opened, and not far from home. The Purrysburgers have purchased slaves; they act under our influence, and Mr. Oglethorpe will think it advisable to begin there. You see the harvest is truly great—καὶ τίς ἱκανός ἐστι πρὸς ταῦτα;[2] this is a point among
20 others to be kept in view.
    With regard to your behaviour and manner of address, that must be determined according to the different circumstances of persons, etc.; but you will always in the use of means consider the great end, and therefore your applications will of course vary. You will keep in view the pattern of the gospel preacher,
25 St. Paul, who became all things to all men, that he might gain some. Here is a nice trial of Christian prudence. Accordingly in every case you would distinguish between what is essential and what is merely circumstantial to Christianity, between what is indispensable and what is variable, between what is of divine and what is of human authority. I mention this because men are apt to deceive
30 themselves in such cases, and we see the traditions and ordinances of men frequently insisted on with more rigour than the commandments of God, to which they are subordinate; singularities of less importance are often espoused with more zeal than the weighty matters of God's law. As in all points we love ourselves, so especially in our hypotheses. Where a man has as it were a property
35 in a notion, he is most industrious to improve it, and that in proportion to the labour of thought he has bestowed upon it; and as its value rises in imagination we are in proportion more unwilling to give it up, and dwell upon it more pertinaciously than upon considerations of general necessity and use. This is a flattering mistake against which we should guard ourselves. Now as you are
40 placed among people of various persuasions in religious matter[s] [this will prove] the great difficulty in your behaviour.
    The trustees have been careful to provide all manner of stores for the temporal necessities and conveniences of our people. I could wish that the like care had been taken to supply the spiritual householder, that he might be furnished with
45 proper tools for every good work. I hope still, by the liberality of pious persons, you will be enabled to procure all books of more immediate use. I presume you

---

[1] 'to meet some special circumstances'.
[2] 'And who is sufficient for these things?' (2 Cor. 2: 16.)

have Gastrell's Institutes, Concordance, and lesser instruments of knowledge—these you should have severally.

I am now on the road toward Shermanbury in Sussex, whither I was called about ten days ago on account of my mother's indisposition. I ventured to postpone that visit hitherto. I hope to see you at Gravesend if possible. I write in 5 haste what occurs to my thoughts. At a leisure hour you may hear from me again. *Disce, docendus adhuc quae censet amiculus.*[1] May God prosper your endeavours for the propagation of his gospel! *Ita vovet*[2] your sincere friend,

John Burton

Address: 'The Reverd Mr John Wesley'   *End* by JW: 'Mr Burton / Sept. 28, 1738' and (in a large hand, on the address portion of the cover, as if the title for a bundle of such letters) 'VI Advice Concerng Georgia'   *Source*: MA.

To Richard Morgan, Jun.[3]

[Sept. 30, 1735] 10

Dear sir

The dining in the hall on Friday seems to me utterly unjustifiable. It is giving offence in the worst sense, giving men occasion to think that innocent which is grossly sinful. The plausible pretences for throwing off the very form of godliness[4] that must be esteemed if 15 we will do good, that we must keep those things private wherein we differ from the world, and so on, you will find fully examined in *Nicodemus*.[5] The bishops can no more dispense with the law, the reason of which still subsists, than you or I can. Fasting is not a means of chastity only, but of deadness to pleasure, and heavenly-mindedness, 20 and consequently necessary (in such measure as agrees with health) to all persons in all times of life. Had I been less strict, as 'tis called, I should have not only not done more good than I have (that is, God by me), but[6] I never should have done any at all, nor indeed desired to do any. Till a man gives offence he will do no 25 good, and the more offence he gives by adhering to the gospel of

---

[1] 'Listen to the views of a humble friend, who still needs teaching himself.' (Horace, *Epistles*, I. xvii. 3.)   [2] 'So wishes'.

[3] Answering that of Sept. 25.   [4] See 2 Tim. 3: 5.

[5] *Nicodemus; or, a Treatise against the Fear of Man* (1701), by August Hermann Francke (1663–1727), Pietist leader of Halle. An English translation by A. W. Boehm had been published, which Wesley began to read on Nov. 19, 1733, and was soon urging upon his pupils and colleagues. He began abridging it in Georgia, Dec. 7, 1736, and in 1739 published this abridgement, which passed through seven separate editions (see *Bibliog*, No. 15).   [6] Orig., 'that'.

Christ the more good he will do;[1] and the more good he does the more offence he will give. As to lukewarm company, I can only advise you, first, to keep out of it—as much as you can; second, when you cannot, to pray before, after, and during your stay in it, fervently
5 and without ceasing.[2] But this you can't do. I know it. But God can make you able to do it. And in him you must put your trust.

I am not satisfied (as I have told the rector[3] for this twelvemonth past) that the Wednesday fast is strictly obligatory; though I believe it very ancient, if not apostolical.[4] He never saw what I writ upon it.[5]
10 Dr. Tilly's sermons on free will are the best I ever saw.[6] His text is, 'Work out your [own] salvation with fear and trembling.'[7] May you all assist one another so to do, and be not ashamed of the gospel of Christ.[8] Παρακαλεῖτε ἀλλήλους, etc.[9] Bear ye one another's burdens.[10] I charge Mr. Robson in the name of the Lord Jesus that he
15 no longer halt between two opinions. If the Lord be God, serve him,[11] love him with all your heart, serve him with all your strength;[12] and pray for us that faith and utterance may be given us, that we may speak boldly as we ought to speak.[13]

Sept. 30, 1735

Source: MA, in Colman MSS, (Wesley's diary, Feb. 13–Aug. 31, 1737), copied (apparently contemporaneously) in a hand similar to those of both Benjamin Ingham and Charles Delamotte, yet probably that of neither.

[1] See letter of Dec. 10, 1734, § 25.   [2] 1 Thess. 5: 17.
[3] Orig., '(as I have been told the rector . . .)'; query add 'by'. The Rector of Lincoln College was the Revd. Euseby Isham.
[4] Cf. letter of June 13, 1733.
[5] 'Essay upon the Stationary Fasts', part of which was published in the Appendix (pp. 72–4) of Thomas Deacon, *A Compleat Collection of Devotions* (1734); cf. his consulting William Whiston on this, p. 412 n., above.
[6] William Tilly, D.D., whose *Sixteen Sermons* (1712) Wesley purchased in June, 1732, and began to 'collect' in July, 1732. Four of these abridgements are extant, bearing evidence that Wesley himself preached from them, so that they have sometimes been mistakenly published as his original manuscripts. The abridgements of the two sermons on free will were first used by Wesley on Aug. 14 and Oct. 1, 1732, in the Castle prison at Oxford. (See Charles A. Rogers, 'John Wesley and William Tilly', W.H.S. XXXV. 137–41 (June, 1966).)
[7] Phil. 2: 12.   [8] Rom. 1: 16.
[9] 'Comfort one another' (1 Thess. 5: 11).
[10] Gal. 6: 2.   [11] See 1 Kgs. 18: 21.
[12] See Mark 12: 30, etc.   [13] See Eph. 6: 19–20.

To the Revd. John Burton[1]

To Mr. Burton   Oct. 10, 1735

Dear sir

I have been hitherto unwilling to mention the grounds of my design of embarking for Georgia, for two reasons; one, because they were such as I know few men would judge to be of any weight, the other because I was afraid of making favourable judges think of me above what they ought to think. And what a snare this must be to my own soul I know by dear-bought experience.

But on farther reflection I am convinced that I ought to speak the truth with all boldness, even though it should appear foolishness to the world, as it has done from the beginning; and that whatever danger there is in doing the will of God, he will support me under it. In his name, therefore, and trusting in his defence, I shall plainly declare the thing as it is.

My chief motive, to which all the rest are subordinate, is the hope of saving my own soul. I hope to learn the true sense of the gospel of Christ by preaching it to the heathens. They have no comments to construe away the text, no vain philoso phyto corrupt it, no luxurious, sensual, covetous, ambitious expounders to soften its unpleasing truths, to reconcile earthly-mindedness and faith, the Spirit of Christ and the spirit of the world. They have no party, no interest to serve, and are therefore fit to receive the gospel in its simplicity. They are as little children, humble, willing to learn, and eager to do the will of God. And consequently they shall know of every doctrine I preach, whether it be of God. From[2] these, therefore, I hope to learn the purity of that faith which was once delivered to the saints,[3] the genuine sense and full extent of those laws which none can understand who mind earthly things.

A right faith will, I trust, by the mercy of God, open the way for a right practice, especially when most of those temptations are removed which here so easily beset me. Toward mortifying the lust of the flesh,[4] the desire of sensual pleasures, it will be no small thing

---

[1] Cf. letter from Burton to Wesley, Sept. 28, 1735. This of Oct. 10 may be in reply to a subsequent letter from Burton, otherwise unknown, with an exhortation referring to 1 John 2: 16, or may be independent of any approach by him.

[2] Orig., 'From', altered by editor to 'By'.   [3] Jude 3.

[4] 1 John 2: 16, 'lust' changed by the editor here and in all subsequent occurrences to 'desire'.

to be able, without fear of giving offence, to live on water and the fruits of the earth. This simplicity of food will, I trust, be a blessed means both of preventing my seeking that happiness in meats and drinks which God designed should be found only in[1] faith and love
5 and joy in the Holy Ghost;[2] and will assist me, especially where I see no woman but those which are almost of a different species from me, to attain such a purity of thought as suits a candidate for that state wherein they neither marry nor are given in marriage, but are as the angels of God in heaven.[3]

10 Neither is it a small thing to be delivered from so many occasions as now surround me of indulging the lust of the eye.[4] They here compass me in on every side. But an Indian hut affords no food for curiosity, no gratification of the desire of grand, or new, or pretty things; though indeed the cedars which God hath planted[5] round it
15 may so gratify the eye as to better the heart by lifting it to him whose name alone is excellent, and his praise above heaven and earth.[6]

If by the pride of life[7] you[8] understand the pomp and show of the world, that has no place in the wilds of America; if pride in general, this, alas, has a place everywhere. Yet there are uncommon
20 helps against it, not only by the deep humility of the poor heathens, fully sensible of their want of an instructor, but that happy contempt which cannot fail to attend all who sincerely endeavour to instruct them, and which, continually increasing, will surely make them in the end as the filth and offscouring of the world.[9] Add to this that
25 nothing so convinces us of our own impotence as a zealous attempt to convert our neighbour; nor, indeed, till he does all he can for God, will any man feel that he can himself do nothing.

Further, a sin which easily besets me is unfaithfulness to God in the use of speech. I know that this is a talent entrusted to me by my
30 Lord, to be used as all other, only for his glory. I know that all conversation which is not seasoned with salt,[10] and designed at least to minister grace to the hearers, is expressly forbid by the Apostle as corrupt communication, and as grieving the Holy Spirit of God.[11]

Yet I am almost continually betrayed into it by the example of
35 others, striking in with my own bad heart. But I hope, from the moment I leave the English shore under the acknowledged character

---

[1] Orig. 'its'; editor emends similarly to 'in'.
[2] Rom. 14: 17.   [3] Matt. 22: 30.
[4] 1 John 2: 16.   [5] See Ps. 104: 16.
[6] Ps. 148: 12 (B.C.P.).   [7] 1 John 2: 16.   [8] Editor, 'we'.
[9] See 1 Cor. 4: 13.   [10] Col. 4: 6.   [11] Eph. 4: 29–30.

of a teacher sent from God,[1] there shall no word be heard from my lips but what properly flows from that character. As my tongue is a devoted thing, I hope from the first hour of this new era to use it only as such, that all who hear me may know of a truth the words I speak are not mine, but his that sent me.[2]

The same faithfulness I hope to show through his grace in dispensing the rest of my Master's goods, if it please him to send me to those who, like his first followers, had all things in common.[3] What a guard is here against that root of evil, the love of money,[4] and all the vile attractions that spring from it! One in this glorious state, and perhaps none but he, may see the height and depth of that privilege of the first Christians, as poor, yet making many rich, as having nothing, yet possessing all things.[5]

I then hope to know what it is to love my neighbour as myself, and to feel the powers of that second motive to visit the heathens, even the desire to impart to them what I have received,[6] a saving knowledge of the gospel of Christ. But this I dare not think on yet. It is not for me, who have been a grievous sinner from my youth up, and am yet laden with foolish and hurtful lusts,[7] to expect God should work so great things by my hands. But I am assured, if I be once converted[8] myself, he will then employ me both to strengthen my brethren and to preach his name to the Gentiles, that the very ends of the earth may see the salvation of our God.

But you will perhaps ask, Can't you save your own soul in England as well as in Georgia? I answer, No, neither can I hope to attain the same degree of holiness here which I may there; neither, if I stay here knowing this, can I reasonably hope to attain any degree of holiness at all. For whoever, when two ways of life are proposed, prefers that which he is convinced in his own mind is less pleasing to God, and less conducive to the perfection of his soul, has no reason from the gospel of Christ to hope that he shall ever please God at all, or receive from him that grace whereby alone he can attain any degree of Christian perfection.

To the other motive, the hope of doing more good in America, it is commonly objected that there are heathens enough, in practice if not theory, at home. Why then should you go to those in America?[9]

---

[1] See John 3: 2. [2] See John 14: 24. [3] See Acts 2: 44.
[4] See 1 Tim. 6: 10. [5] 2 Cor. 6: 10.
[6] See 1 Cor. 15: 3. [7] 1 Tim. 6: 9.
[8] Editor, 'fully converted'.
[9] Orig., 'India', apparently altered to 'America' by Wesley.

Why, for a very plain reason. Because these heathens at home[1] have Moses and the prophets,[2] and those have not. Because these who *have* the gospel trample upon it, and those who have it not earnestly call for it; therefore seeing these judge themselves unworthy of
5 eternal life, lo, I turn to the Gentiles.[3]

If you object further the losses I must sustain in leaving my native country I ask, Loss of what? Of anything I desire to keep? No: I shall still have food to eat and raiment to put on,[4] enough of such food as I choose to eat, and such raiment as I desire to put on; and
10 if any man have a desire of other things, or of more food than he can eat, or more raiment than he need put on, let him know that the greatest blessing which can possibly befall him is to be cut off from all occasions of gratifying those desires, which, unless speedily rooted out, will drown his soul in everlasting perdition.

15 But what shall we say to the loss of parents, brethren, sisters, nay, of the friends which are as my own soul,[5] of those who have so often lifted up my hands that hung down, and strengthened my feeble knees,[6] by whom God hath often enlightened my understanding and warmed and enlarged my heart? What shall we say? Why,
20 that if you add the loss of life to the rest, so much the greater is the gain. For though the grass withereth, and the flower fadeth, the word of our God shall stand for ever.[7] Say, that when human instruments are removed he, the Lord, will answer us by his own self, and the general answer which he hath already given us to all questions
25 of this nature is, Verily I say unto you, there is no man that hath left father or mother or lands for my sake but shall receive an hundredfold now in this time, with persecutions, and in the world to come eternal life.[8]

Source: MA, in Colman MSS (Wesley's diary, Oct. 15, 1739–Aug. 4, 1741), copied on the opening leaves in the same hand as that of the copy of the letter of Sept. 30, 1735, to Richard Morgan. There are some later editorial alterations, two of which may possibly (one probably) be in Wesley's hand.

[1] 'at home' added above the line, possibly by Wesley.
[2] Luke 16: 29.   [3] See Acts 13: 46.   [4] See Gen. 28: 20.
[5] 1 Sam. 18: 1, etc.   [6] See Heb. 12: 12.
[7] Isa. 40: 8.   [8] See Mark 10: 29–30.

From Henry Newman[1]

To the Reverend Mr. Wesley,   Bartlet's Buildings
   going to Georgia   13 Oct. 1735

Revd. sir

I hope you received the packet of books in due time by the Society's messenger, a list of which is enclosed, by which you will see the Society desire you would 5
spare what you can to supply the present wants of Messrs. Bolzius and Gronau, and in return I am sure you will be welcome to receive any out of their or Mr. Quincy's store which you may happen to want.

I hope you long since received the Society's circular letter for this year, but my clerk having omitted to enter it in the index for that purpose I have herewith 10 covered a copy of it, for fear it has been forgot.

I heartily wish you and your fellow travellers, with Mr. Oglethorpe, a prosperous voyage, and that it may please God to bless you with health and success in the high errand you have undertaken for his glory, of which it will be a great pleasure to the Society to be as frequently informed as opportunities offer, by, 15 Revd. sir, your most obedient humble [servant,

Henry Newman]

Source: S.P.C.K., Misc. Letters, CN2/1, p. 57, a draft.

---

[1] The Society for Promoting Christian Knowledge, especially through its publication of devotional and pastoral literature, furnished a valuable support for beleaguered piety in Wesley's day. The Society was especially active in assisting overseas missions, and in particular took the Salzburg refugees in Georgia under its wing. Wesley had been elected a corresponding member on Aug. 3, 1732, requested his first packet of books on Jan. 1, 1733, and during the following months had made ten further requests. On Sept. 23, 1735, he again wrote, 'desiring a packet of books, he being to go to Savannah in Georgia', and was himself present at the meeting when this request was approved. On this occasion there was no charge: 'Ordered the books gratis, to the value of £13. 14s. -d.' The Secretary, Henry Newman (1670–1743), sent this personal greeting. Newman was a New Englander, son of a Congregational minister, educated at Harvard, a pious bachelor who was the general factotum of the Society from 1708 until his death. (See W. K. Lowther Clarke, *Eighteenth Century Piety*, London, S.P.C.K., 1944, espec. pp. 30–8, and L. W. Cowie, *Henry Newman*, London, S.P.C.K., 1956.)

To the Revd. Samuel Wesley, Jun.

Gravesend, on board the *Simmonds*, Oct. 15, 1735[1]

Dear brother

I presented *Job* to the Queen on Sunday, and had many good words and smiles.[2] Out of what is due to me on that account I beg
5 you would first pay yourself what I owe you, and if I live till spring I can then direct what I would have done with the remainder.

The uncertainty of my having another opportunity to tell you my thoughts in this life obliges me to tell you what I have often thought of, and that in as few and plain words as I can. Elegance of style is
10 not to be weighed against purity of heart, purity both from the lusts of the flesh, the lusts of the eye, and the pride of life.[3] Therefore whatever has any tendency to impair that purity is not to be tolerated, much less recommended, for the sake of that elegance. But of this sort (I speak not from the reason of the thing only, nor from my
15 single experience) are the most of the classics usually read in great schools, many of them tending to inflame the lusts of the flesh (besides Ovid, Virgil's *Aeneid*, and Terence's *Eunuch*), and more, to feed the lust of the eye, and the pride of life. I beseech you, therefore, by the mercies of God, who would have us holy as he is holy,[4] that
20 you banish all such poison from your school, that you introduce in their place such Christian authors as will work together with you in building up your flock in the knowledge and love of God. For assure yourself, dear brother, you are even now called to the converting of heathens as well as I.

25 So many souls are committed to your charge by God, to be prepared for a happy eternity. You are to instruct them, not only in the beggarly elements of Greek and Latin, but much more, in the gospel. You are to labour with all your might to convince them that Christianity is not a negation, or an external thing, but a new heart,
30 a mind conformed to that of Christ,[5] 'faith working by love'.[6]

---

[1] Wesley had embarked for Georgia on the *Simmonds* on Tuesday, Oct. 14, along with his brother Charles, Benjamin Ingham, and Charles Delamotte. They had been accompanied to Gravesend by John Burton, Richard Morgan, and James Hutton. The ship was delayed for want of a wind until the 21st, and then was becalmed off the Isle of Wight until Dec. 1.

[2] For *Job* see letters of Aug. 27, 1734, and Jan. 21, 1735.

[3] See 1 John 2: 16, and cf. letter of Oct. 10 to John Burton.

[4] See 1 Pet. 1: 15, 16.   [5] See Rom. 8: 29.   [6] See Gal. 5: 6.

We recommend you and yours to God. Pray for us. I am, your affectionate brother and servant in Christ,

John Wesley

Address: 'To the Rev. Mr. Wesley, at Tiverton, Devon'   *Source*: Priestley, pp. 56–7.

From James Vernon[1]

London, 18th Novbr, 1735

Mr. Wesley

The enclosed is copy of a letter from your mother, which I transmit to you, not out of vanity, but to give you an undoubted testimony of my regard to what you recommend to me. I shall continue my care of what relates to your mother's interest in her husband's books, and flatter myself it will not be without success. I am convinced it is a work agreeable to God to be serviceable to a person endued with so much piety and worth, and who like Hannah has lent a loan unto the Lord; and to use no disguises to you, I have an interest in making you my debtor, that you may as opportunity offers repay it to my son, who goes to Georgia with Captain Gascoigne, by seasoning his mind with the principles of true Christianity. Wishing you all success in your undertakings I remain, your most obedient humble servant,

Ja: Vernon

Address: 'For The Reverd Mr John Wesley in Georgia'   *Source*: MA, with Wesley's label pasted on: 'VIII. Lrs recd in Georgia from Engld'.

From Mrs. Susanna Wesley

Gainsborough, Nov. 27, 1735

[Dear son]

. . . God is being itself! The I AM! And therefore must necessarily be the supreme good! He is so infinitely blessed that every perception of his blissful presence imparts a vital gladness to the heart. Every degree of approach toward him is in the same proportion a degree of happiness. And I often think that were

---

[1] A Commissioner of Excise, and one of the original and most active Georgia trustees. Wesley had written to him on Oct. 18, 1735.

he always present to our minds as we are present to him, there could be no pain or sense of misery. I have long since chose him for my only good! My all! My pleasure, my happiness in this world, as well as in the world to come! And although I have not been so faithful to his grace as I ought to have been, yet
5 I feel my spirit adheres to its choice, and aims daily at cleaving steadfastly unto God. Yet one thing often troubles me, that notwithstanding I know, *while* we are present with the body we are absent from the Lord, notwithstanding I have no taste, no relish left for anything the world calls pleasure, yet I do not long to go home, as in reason I ought to do. This often shocks me; and as I constantly
10 pray (almost without ceasing) for thee, my son, so I beg you likewise to pray for me, that God would make me better, and take me at the best. Your loving mother,
Susanna Wesley

Source: A.M., 1778, pp. 84-5.

To Sir John Philipps[1]

On board the *Simmonds*
[Jan. 20, 1736]

15 Honoured sir
Your prayers have not been in vain, for God hath greatly prospered us, ever since we set out from London. We have wanted no manner of thing that is good. Plenty of temporal conveniences has been added to higher blessings, even of those which we least
20 expected. In the midst of the sick, our health has been preserved. When the strong men fainted, and the experienced in this way of life fell down, I was no more affected than if I had been on land, nor ever prevented for one hour from reading, writing, or pursuing any other employment.
25 While we were in Cowes' Road[2] there were several storms, in one

---

[1] Sir John Philipps, fourth baronet (1666?-1737), of Picton Castle, county Pembroke, was a leading figure in philanthropy and piety, a member of all the major societies organized by the Church of England, and the most influential member of the S.P.C.K. from a month after its foundation until his death. Sir Robert Walpole had married his niece, and he was linked in some way with most of the ruling families. Even the Wesleys were distantly related to him, Wesley's great-great-grandfather, Sir Francis Annesley (1585-1660) having married Dorothy, daughter of an earlier Sir John Philipps, Bart., of Picton Castle. His eldest son, Sir Erasmus Philipps, also one of Wesley's correspondents, and active in the S.P.C.K., succeeded his father in the baronetcy, but died in 1743, and was succeeded by his brother, another Sir John Philipps (1701-64).
[2] Nov. 2-20, 1735.

of which two ships were cast away on the back of the island,[1] as we should probably have been had it not pleased God to detain us in that safe station. By this means too we had many opportunities of instructing and exhorting the poor passengers, most of whom at their embarking knew little more of Christianity than the name. But God has so assisted our little endeavours in catechizing the children, explaining the Scriptures, and applying them in private conversation, that we have reason to hope a great part of them are throughly awakened, and determined to pursue the prize of their high calling![2]

We can't be sufficiently thankful to God for Mr. Oglethorpe's presence with us. There are few, if any, societies in England more carefully regulated than this is. The very sailors have for some time behaved in a modest, regular manner. The knowing that they are continually under the eye of one who has both power and will to punish every offender keeps even those who, it is to be feared, have no higher principle, from openly offending against God or their neighbour. So that we have an appearance at least of Christianity from one end of the ship to the other. And those few who do not love it rarely show their dislike, unless in a corner, among their intimates. May the good God show them too in this their day the things that make for their peace![3]

We have had but one storm since we were at sea, and that lasted but a few hours. One unaccustomed to the sea would have imagined the ship would have been swallowed up every moment. A single wave covered it over, burst into the cabin where we were, with a noise and shock almost like that of a cannon, and after having steeped one or two of us from head to foot, passed through into the great cabin, from whence we at last emptied it out of the windows. This too I hope was not a little blessing; the fright which it occasioned in several persons having made them more susceptible of useful impressions.

May he who hath helped us, and poured his benefits upon us, continue to have you and yours under his protection! May he prosper all the designs of your Society[4] for his glory, and strengthen your hands against all the power of the enemy! He shall repay the kindness you have shown us for his sake, especially by making

---

[1] The Isle of Wight.
[2] See Phil. 3: 14.
[3] See Luke 19: 42.
[4] The S.P.C.K., to whose office the letter was addressed.

mention of us in your prayers; whereof none stands more in need than, honoured sir, your most obliged and obedient servant,

John Wesley

Jan. 20, 1735/6[1]

Address: 'To Sr John Philipps Bart. In Bartlet's Buildings Holborn'   *End* (by Sir John Philipps?): 'Revnd. Mr John Wesley, dated Janry 20th, 1735–6 Recd the 16th. of March following.'[2]   *Source*: Ocean Grove Camp Meeting Association, Ocean Grove, New Jersey, U.S.A. A contemporary copy, with a few minor variants, printed in W.H.S. XII. 3, and in Telford, is now owned by Frank Baker.

To Johann Martin Bolzius and Israel Christian Gronau[3]

[Mar. 13, 1736]

5

Gratias ago Optimo Maximo bonorum omnium Datori[4] quod mihi tandem copiam dederit, amicitiam vestram petendi, et dextram societatis. Et par quidem est ut primus petam, quippe cui maxime opus est, tum vestris precibus tum consilio. Liceat tamen mihi,

10 qualiscunque sim, vos hortari, nequis vestrum ab afflictionibus istis nostris concutiatur, ad quas, vocati sumus. Liceat et obsecrare, ut ejus opera uti nunquam gravemini, si qua in re vobis adjumento esse poterit, qui est, milites Dei fideles, servus vester in Christo,

[Johannes Wesley]

15 Mart. 13, 1736, Savannae.[5]

¹ Wesley's diary records no letter written on this day, but the entry for Jan. 23 shows that one to 'Sir John' occupied three hours in the morning.
² This letter was apparently one of two answered on behalf of Sir John by Henry Newman on June 16, 1736.
³ Johann Martin Bolzius (1703–65) and Israel Christian Gronau (who died 1745 in Georgia) were the two Lutheran pastors in spiritual charge of a group of Protestant refugees from Salzburg, led by Commissary Philipp von Reck, who had sailed in the *London Merchant*, companion ship to the *Simmonds*, in order to settle in Ebenezer, 20–30 miles north-west of Savannah. They had been active as teachers under August Hermann Francke in the Orphan House at Halle, and had been ordained in Germany specifically for their American mission. Henry Newman, Secretary of the S.P.C.K., had asked Wesley in his letter of Oct. 13, 1735: 'Spare what you can to supply the present wants of Messrs. Bolzius and Gronau.'
⁴ Orig., 'Datoru[m]'.
⁵ This may be translated (with acknowledgements to Professors Francis Newton and harles R. Young):
   'I give thanks to the Greatest and the Best, the Giver of all good gifts, because now

Address: 'To Mr. Boltzius & Gronau' *Source*: Bristol Wesley, Morley MSS, folio 198ᵛ, a draft, with many alterations, on blank page of that of Oct. 9, 1735, from the Revd. Thomas Broughton to Wesley.

To Count Zinzendorf[1]

[March 15, 1736]

Comiti de Zinzendorf
Johannes Wesley
Salutem in Christo Sempiternam[2]

Graviora tua negotia literis meis interpellare non auderem, nisi te crederem illius esse discipulum, qui linum ardens non extingui 5

at last he has given me the opportunity of seeking your friendship and the right hand of fellowship. And indeed it is fitting that I should be the first to seek it, inasmuch as I have the greatest need both of your prayers and your advice. Allow me, however, whatever kind of person I am, to exhort you that none of you be alarmed by these sufferings of ours, to which we are called. Let me implore you also, faithful soldiers of God, that you should never be reluctant to make use of the help (if in any way he can help you) of him who is your servant in Christ,

Savannah, Mar. 13, 1736.   [John Wesley]

[1] Count Nikolaus Ludwig von Zinzendorf (1700-60), who had been educated at Francke's school at Halle and the Lutheran university of Wittenberg, and in 1722 welcomed exiles from Moravia to settle at Herrnhut on his Berthelsdorf estate, so that he became their patron and leader, and from 1737 their bishop. Wesley was led to initiate their correspondence because of the tremendous respect which he had acquired for the Moravians who had accompanied him to Georgia in the *Simmonds*. For the Count's reply see Oct. 23, 1736.

[2] The letter may be translated thus:

'John Wesley to Count Zinzendorf, eternal well-being in Christ.

'I would not dare to interrupt your more weighty affairs with a letter of mine unless I believed you to be a disciple of him who would not quench the smoking flax nor break a bruised reed (Isa. 42: 3). But since I am quite convinced of this, I earnestly implore you that in your prayers and those of the church that sojourns with you I may be commended to God, to be instructed in true poverty of spirit, in gentleness, in faith, and in the love of God and my neighbour. And whenever you have a moment's leisure, do not disdain to offer to God this brief prayer, which I have frequently heard offered by your brethren (would they were mine also!) at Savannah:

A patient, a victorious mind,
That, life and all things cast behind,
Springs forth, obedient to thy call,
A heart that no desire can move,
But still t'adore and praise and love,
Give me, my Lord, my life, my all.

Savannah, March 15, 1736 (Old Style).'

vult neque calamum quassatum confringi. Id vero quum persuasum habeam, maximopere te obtestor, ut et tuis et ecclesiae tecum peregrinantis precibus Deo commender, in vera spiritus paupertate, mansuetudine fide, ac amore Dei proximique erudiendus. Et si
5 quando tibi paululum otii suppetat, breve illud votum Deo offerre ne dedigneris, quod a fratribus tuis (utinam et meis) Savannensibus saepius oblatum audivi.

> Einen Helden muth
> Der da Gut und Blut
10 Gern um deinet willen lasse
> Und des fleisches lüste hasse
> Gieb ihm, Höchstes Gut,
> Durch dein theures Blut![1]

Savannae, Mart. 15. V.S. 1736[2]

Address: 'Comiti de Zinzendorf'   *Source*: Herrnhut.

To Mrs. Susanna Wesley

15   Savannah, March 18, 1736

Dear mother
    I doubt not but you are already informed of the many blessings which God gave us in our passage, as my brother Wesley must before now have received a particular account of the circumstances
20 of our voyage, which he would not fail to transmit to you by the first opportunity.[3]

---

[1] This is stanza 13 of Freylinghausen's hymn, 'Wer ist wohl, wie du, Jesu süsze ruh?', which we have reproduced in the very free translation of John Wesley in his *Collection of Psalms and Hymns* (Charleston, 1737), p. 39. A much more literal translation is that in the Moravian *A Collection of Hymns for the Children of God in all ages*, London, 1754, p. 377:

> Give me courage good,
> That my wealth and blood
> I may lose for thee with gladness,
> And hate flesh's lustful madness.
> Grant me this, my God!
> Through thy precious blood.

[2] Wesley's diary notes this letter as written Mar. 13, 1736.
[3] Wesley had written to his elder brother Samuel on Jan. 21–2 and again on Feb. 1, 1736, while he was still on board the *Simmonds*, letters which would probably remain with the ship's captain for return to England.

We are likely to stay here some months. The place is pleasant beyond imagination, and by all I can learn exceeding healthful, even in summer for those that are not intemperate. It has pleased God that I have not had a moment's illness of any kind since I set my foot upon the continent. Nor do I know any more than one of 5 my seven hundred parishioners who is sick at this time. Many of them indeed are, I believe, very angry already. For a gentleman, no longer ago than last night, made a ball; but public prayers happening to begin about the same time the church was full, and the ballroom so empty that the entertainment could not go forward. 10

I should be heartily glad if any poor and religious men or women of Epworth or Wroot would come over to me. And so would Mr. Oglethorpe, too; he would give them land enough, and provisions gratis, till they could live on the produce of it. I was fully determined to have wrote to my dear Emmy today; but time will not permit. O 15 hope ye still in God, for ye shall yet give him thanks who is the help of your countenance, and your God![1] Renounce the world. Deny yourselves. Bear your cross with Christ, and reign with him![2]

My brother Harper[3] too has a constant place in our prayers. May the good God give him the same zeal for holiness which he has 20 given to a young gentleman of Rotterdam who was with me last night![4] Pray for us, and especially for, dear mother, your dutiful and affectionate son,

John Wesley

Source: Modern typescript copy, on the basis of minutiae apparently from original, at Drew. Cf. Whitehead, II. 13–14.

[1] See Ps. 43: 5.
[2] See 2 Tim. 2: 12.
[3] Whitehead, 'Hooper'. Wesley had married his sister Emilia to Robert Harper, the apothecary who had treated his father, shortly before leaving for Georgia. (See p. 590, l. 24 below.)
[4] Peter Appee (also spelt Apie, Appy), a young Dutch adventurer who later confessed to Charles Wesley (with whom he was associated more than with John) that 'his only principle was an insatiable thirst of glory', who believed that both the Wesleys were hypocrites, but who at this time was enjoying playing the new role for him of a devout Christian. In fact he proved to be lazy, vain, a thief, a liar, and a coward, and Charles Wesley shook him off after they had reached London in December, 1736, resolving never again to be so gullible in accepting what people said about themselves. (See CWJ, I. 36–40, 52–3, 59–65.)

To the Revd. Charles Wesley[1]

Savannah, March 22, 1736

Dear brother

How different are the ways wherein we are led! Yet, I hope, toward the same end. I have hitherto no opposition at all. All is smooth
5 and fair and promising. Many seem to be awakened. All are full of respect and commendation. We can't see any cloud gathering. But this calm cannot last; storms must come hither, too. And let them come, when we are ready to meet them.

'Tis strange so many of our friends should still trust in God.
10 I hope, indeed, whoever turns to the world, Mr. Tackner[2] and Betty, with Mr. Hird's family,[3] and Mr. Burk,[4] will zealously aim at the prize of their high calling.[5] These especially I exhort, by the mercies of God, that they be not weary of well-doing,[6] but that they labour more and more to be meek and lowly, and daily to advance in the
15 knowledge and love of God.

---

[1] Charles Wesley, ordained for just such a purpose, was given spiritual charge of the fifty families in the new British outpost, Fort Frederica, on St. Simon's Island, about seventy miles due south of Savannah, approached by intracoastal waterway. He was also serving as Oglethorpe's secretary, and had arrived at Fort Frederica with Oglethorpe on Mar. 9, 1736. Nearly all the settlers there had sailed out with the Wesleys on the *Simmonds*, who were thus personally familiar with them already.

[2] Ambrose Tackner (also spelt Tuckner), a locksmith, aged 30, who had been baptized by John Wesley, having previously undergone only lay baptism. He was Wesley's first tutor in German aboard the *Simmonds*. Martha Tackner, aged 40, was apparently his wife, though she travelled in a separate cabin, with her two children, Elizabeth Hazle, aged 18, and her son John, aged 12. At the communion on Nov. 23, 1735, on board the *Simmonds*, Wesley listed the communicants as the Hird family (whom he had also baptized), 'Mr. Tackner and Betty', as well as Burk and West. Betty therefore seems to have been either Tackner's daughter or his niece.

N.B. The most valuable source of information for the passengers on the *Simmonds* is a pastoral list prepared by Wesley (at Bristol Wesley), printed (with many inaccuracies) in '*Simmonds* list'; and for the early Georgia settlers in general, Coulter & Saye.

[3] Thomas Hird, a dyer, aged 42, who in 1739 became Constable of Frederica; his wife Grace, aged 39; their son Mark, aged 21, who served as a lay leader in Frederica for Wesley; and their daughter Phebe, aged 17. The family were Quakers, and Wesley had baptized the four of them on Nov. 16, 1735, and had noted their presence at communion on Nov. 23. The Hirds had two other children on the ship, Frances, aged 13, and John, aged 12.

[4] Although Burk does not appear in Coulter & Saye, the *Simmonds* list shows 'Thomas Burk, 33'—another of Wesley's communicants on Nov. 23.

[5] See Phil. 3: 14.

[6] See Gal. 6: 9; 2 Thess. 3: 13.

I hope too Mr. Weston,[1] Mr. Moore,[2] Mr. Allen,[3] and Mr. White,[4] as well as Mr. Ward and his wife,[5] continue in the same wise resolutions. I must not forget Mr. Reed[6] and Mr. Daubry,[7] both of whom I left fully determined to shake off every weight,[8] and with all their might to pursue the one thing needful.[9]

Conciones omnes meas jamnunc habes, praeter istas quas misi. Aliquae in pyxide sunt (de qua ne verbum scribis), una cum Bibliis in quarto. Liber de Disciplina quam celerrime potes, remittendus est. Quanta est concordia fratrum—tui, volo, et fratris B[enjamin]i![10]

You are not, I think, at liberty στρέφεσθαι εἰς τὸ ἔθνη, ἕως οἱ

---

[1] Willes ('William' in the *Simmonds* list) Weston, a tanner, aged 20.

[2] Probably William Moore, aged 39, a tanner, who was unmarried; 'he built a large house and set up a good mill for grinding bark'. Another possibility is Francis Moore (with his wife Mary), who was the storekeeper, and also the Recorder of Frederica. Later he published an account of the voyage.

[3] William Allen, a baker, aged 32, who came over in the *Simmonds* with his wife Elizabeth, also aged 32; with them in the cabin was the Hirds' young daughter, Frances. He was appointed tithingman for Frederica.

[4] Richard White, hatter, aged 39, who shared a cabin with William Weston. He was appointed deputy bailiff of Frederica.

[5] Benjamin Ward, aged 28, and his wife Margaret, aged 21, neither being listed in Coulter & Saye.

[6] Will Reed (or Reid), whose hut Charles Wesley shared, and whom John Wesley persuaded to read evening prayers at Frederica during their absence. He was one of the servants of Dr. Patrick Tailfer, who published the satirical *A True and Historical Narrative of the Colony of Georgia* (1741).

[7] Apparently Elisha Dobree (or Daubray), who came from Carolina in 1734, bought a lot in Savannah, and then settled in Frederica, where he was clerk of the stores. His wife was not prepared to bring their three children over from England.

[8] See Heb. 12: 1.

[9] One of Wesley's favourite phrases, from Luke 10: 42.

[10] No postal service was available to them in Georgia, so they were at the mercy of whatever personal messenger was available. They therefore used Latin, Greek, and shorthand to disguise the more confidential passages in their letters. (See following letter.) The Latin of this paragraph may be translated thus:

'You now have all my sermons, besides those which I have sent. Some are in the box (of which you write not a word), along with the quarto Bible. The Book of Discipline must be returned as soon as possible. How great is the harmony of brethren! I mean of thee and brother Benjamin.' [i.e. Ingham]

Charles Wesley had been copying out his brother's file of sermons for his own use. (Some, indeed, exist only in these copies by Charles, and have been assumed to be his own original sermons.)

'The Book of Discipline' may refer to the first book of that title drawn up by John Knox and his fellow-reformers at Edinburgh in 1568, an adaptation of the Genevan polity to the Scots Kirk, which was followed in 1578 by a second Book of Discipline, issued by stricter Presbyterians and endorsed by the General Assembly in 1581. Neither received complete civil recognition. It is less likely that Wesley intended a book which he is known from his diary to have used, Nathaniel Marshall, *The Penitential Discipline of the Primitive Church* (1714).

συμφυλέται σου, ἀπωθοῦσι σε.¹ If that period comes soon, so much the better. Only in the mean while reprove and exhort with all authority, even though all men should despise thee.² Ἀποβήσεταί σοι εἰς μαρτύριον.³

5   I conjure you, spare no time or address or pains to learn the true cause τῆς πάλαι ὀδύνης τῆς φίλης μου.⁴ I much doubt you are [in] the right. Μὴ γένοιτο, ἵνα οὕτω πάλιν ἁμαρτάνῃ. Γρηγόρει, Φυλάσσου, ὡς μάλιστα δύνῃ. Γράφε μοι, πῶς με δεῃ γράφειν, πρὸς αὐτήν.⁵

    If Mr. Ingham were here, I would try to see you. But omit no
10 opportunity of writing. Κινδυνεύω πᾶσαν ὥραν· δύω ἤ τρεῖς εἰσι γυναῖκες, νεώτεραι, ἀστεῖαι, φοβούμεναι τὸν Θεόν. Προσεύχου, ἵνα μήτινα αὐτῶν γινώσκω κατὰ σάρκα.⁶

    Let us be strong and very courageous;⁷ for the Lord our God is with us.⁸ And there is no counsel or might against him!⁹ Adieu!¹⁰

Address: 'To ye Revd Mr Wesley, with a Box of Books & Papers'   *End* by
JW: 'JW, March 22', and later 'To C'   *Source*: Garrett.

From the Revd. Charles Wesley¹¹

15   Frederica, March 27th [1736]

Dear brother
    I received your letter and box. My last to you was opened, the contents being publicly proclaimed by those who were so ungenerous as to intercept it. I have

----

¹ 'to turn to the Gentiles [Acts 13: 46], till your own countrymen shall cast you out'.
² See Titus 2: 15.
³ 'This will be your opportunity to testify' (Luke 21: 13).
⁴ 'of my friend's earlier distress'.
⁵ 'God forbid that she should again miss the mark, in like manner. Watch over her, take care of her as much as possible. Write me how I ought to write to her.' The last pronoun makes it clear that a woman is intended. This must surely be either Beata, wife of the surgeon, Thomas Hawkins, or Anne, wife of John Welch the carpenter. On the *Simmonds* both women had revealed themselves as dissemblers and supposedly innocent mischief-makers, and now both confessed to Charles Wesley that Oglethorpe had committed adultery with them, and then told Oglethorpe that Wesley was maliciously spreading this false story, whilst himself guilty of sexual misconduct with them. (See CWJ, Mar. 1-24, Apr. 14-24, 1736, in Telford's edn., 1910.)
⁶ 'I am in danger every hour [see 1 Cor. 15: 30]. There are two or three God-fearing, refined young women. Pray that I know none of them after the flesh.'
⁷ See Josh. 1: 7.   ⁸ See 2 Chron. 32: 8.   ⁹ See Prov. 21: 30.
¹⁰ At the left margin there is another 'Adieu' in shorthand outline.
¹¹ Answering John's of Mar. 22. Probably delivered personally by Benjamin Ingham, whom on the evening of Mar. 27 (a Saturday), Charles persuaded to go to Savannah to fetch his brother John, though he did not set off until the following day.

not yet complained to Mr. Oglethorpe . . . Though I trust I shall never either write or speak what I will not justify both to God and man, yet I would not have the secrets of my soul revealed to everyone. For their sakes, therefore, as well as my own, I shall write no more, and desire you will not. Nor will you have occasion, as you visit us so soon. I hope your coming may be of use to many. 5

Mr. Oglethorpe gave me an exceeding necessary piece of advice for you: 'Beware of hypocrites, in particular of log-house converts.' They consider you as favoured by Mr. Oglethorpe, and will therefore put on the form of religion, to please—not God, but you. To this I shall only add, Give no temporal encouragement whatsoever to any seeming converts, else they will follow you for 10 the sake of the loaves. Convince them thus that it can never be worth their while to be hypocrites. Stay till you are in disgrace, in persecution, by the heathen, by your own countrymen; till you are accounted the offscouring of all things (as you must infallibly be, if God is true) and then see who will follow you—I.

God, you believe, has much work to do in America. I believe so, too, and 15 begin to enter into the designs which he has over *me*. I see why he has brought me hither, and hope ere long to say with Ignatius, 'It is now that I *begin* to be a disciple of Christ.' God direct you to pray for me. Adieu.

Source: Whitehead, I. 122–3.

To the Revd. Charles Wesley[1]

[April 21, 1736]

[Dear brother] 20

. . . I still extremely pity poor Mrs. Hawkins. But what can I do more till God show me who it is that continually exasperates her against me? Then I may perhaps be of some service to her. There is surely someone who does not play us fair. But I marvel not at the matter. He that is higher than the highest regardeth; and there is 25 that is mightier than they.[2] Yet a little while and God will declare

---

[1] In response to Charles Wesley's appeal, delivered by Ingham, John Wesley tried immediately to leave for Frederica, but was delayed both in setting off and during the actual voyage by contrary winds, so that he did not arrive until Apr. 10. Charles was ill with dysentery, but improved with his brother's arrival. Through many interviews during his week's stay, especially with Mrs. Hawkins, much more strong-willed than Mrs. Welch, Wesley attempted to unravel the complex and dangerous situation, leaving a little more contented, but disillusioned. On arriving in Savannah on Apr. 20 he noted (somewhat optimistically) in his *Journal:* 'O blessed place, where, having but one end in view, dissembling and fraud are not, but each of us can pour out his heart without fear into his brother's bosom!' The following day he wrote to Charles, to Hawkins, and to Oglethorpe.

[2] See Eccles. 5: 8 (for the last phrase see Num. 14: 12).

who is sincere. Tarry thou the Lord's leisure, and be strong, and he shall comfort thy heart.[1]

Source: Whitehead, II. 16–17.

To James Edward Oglethorpe

[April 21, 1736]

[Dear sir]

5   I found Mr. Quincy[2] here last night, who, hearing you was not certain as to the time of your return hither, resolved to make use of the first opportunity of waiting upon you at Frederica. I have not only heard more than I usually do of what the people here say concerning his behaviour among them, but have purposely asked several
10   questions about it. And if they were (as I suppose) answered sincerely, his carriage has not been such as I believed it was, but in the general more than inoffensive. All I have spoke to inform me that they judge him to be a good-natured, friendly, peaceful, sober, just man, and that they have no complaint against him, either relating to

---

[1] See Ps. 31: 27 (B.C.P.).

[2] The Revd. Samuel Quincy, formerly a Presbyterian minister of New England, who had conformed to the Established Church and married an English wife. He embarked for Georgia in 1733, as the first minister there. Unfortunately he did not keep in touch with the Trustees, and while absenting himself for six months from the Colony left an unauthorized layman in charge. Other complaints were made, so that when he resigned, ostensibly because his wife refused to come out, the Trustees expressed relief. He stayed on in Georgia for a further three months, however, becoming friendly with the Wesleys, especially after John Wesley had thus fulfilled his commission of inquiry from Oglethorpe. He may well have been the messenger who carried this letter to Frederica, and at the beginning of May he served as Charles Wesley's messenger from Frederica to Savannah (see May 1 below). Charles recommended him to John as a suitable messenger to England, whither he was going in order to vindicate himself against the widespread criticism which (rightly or wrongly) would have led to his dismissal had he not resigned —a fact which was pointed out at his interview with the Trustees on Oct. 20, 1736. In spite of his wife's objections he was already seeking further pastoral employment in South Carolina, where the Revd. Alexander Garden befriended him, terming the charges against him 'frivolous and groundless'. After a lengthy delay, perhaps partly caused through opposition, partly ill health, from 1742 to 1749 he did serve three parishes there before retiring to his native Boston. (See Weis, p. 91; Coulter & Saye, p. 42; Egmont, *Diary* and *Journal*, and E. L. Pennington, in *Georgia Historical Quarterly*, II. 157–65.)

Oglethorpe's letter quoting this paragraph thus points out the occasion: 'I not having time to stay at Savannah desired Mr. Wesley to inquire concerning Mr. Quincy's behaviour there; and this is a copy of a paragraph by him sent to me in his letter.'

his private life or to the execution of his office as a clergyman, except his absence from them (in New England, I apprehend), which they believe was chiefly owing to his ill state of health . . .[1]

Savannah never was so dear to me as now. I believe, knowing by whom I send, I may write as well as speak freely. I found so little either of the form or power of religion at Frederica that I am sincerely glad I am removed from it. Surely never was any place, no, not London itself, freer from one vice, I mean hypocrisy:

O curvae in terris animae, et coelestium inanes![2]

Jesus, Master, have mercy upon them[3] . . . There is none of those who did run well whom I pity more than Mrs. Hawkins. Her treating me in such a manner would indeed have little affected me had my own interests only been concerned. I have been used to be betrayed, scorned, and insulted by those I had most laboured to serve. But when I reflect on her condition my heart bleeds for her. Yet with Thee nothing is impossible![4]

With regard to one who ought to be dearer to me than her I cannot but say that the more I think of it the more convinced I am that no one, without a virtual renouncing of the faith, can abstain from the public as well as the private worship of God. All the prayers usually read morning and evening at Frederica and here, put together, do not last seven minutes. These cannot be termed long prayers. No Christian assembly ever used shorter. Neither have they any repetitions in them at all.[5] If I did not speak thus plainly to you,

[1] The following paragraph in Oglethorpe's letter to the Trustees also contained quotation marks in the left margins, but these have been struck through, apparently as an indication that the passage is in Oglethorpe's own words (the letter is in the hand of an amanuensis): 'With respect to his marrying an Englishman to an Indian woman unbaptized, he was advised to do so by most of the people then in Savannah (and by what I found in conversing with them) the generality of the people thought they had done a very pretty thing in getting an intermarriage.'

[2] Persius, *Satires*, ii. 61, 'O souls bowed down to earth, and void of all heavenly thoughts!'

[3] See Luke 17: 13.

[4] See Luke 1: 37.

[5] Probably this criticism was directed against Oglethorpe himself. Cf. his remark (recorded in CWJ, Apr. 16), 'My religion does not, like the Pharisees, consist in long prayers.' That the letter is not complete is revealed by Oglethorpe's reaction, as given by CWJ, Apr. 24: 'Mr. Wesley, you know what has passed between us. I took some pains to satisfy your brother about the reports concerning me, but in vain. He here renews his suspicions in writing. I did desire to convince him, because I had an esteem for him; and he is just so considerable to me as my esteem makes him.'

which I fear no one else in England or America will do, I should by
no means be worthy to call myself, sir, yours, etc.,

John Wesley

Sources: (*a*) para. 1, quoted in letter from Oglethorpe to the Georgia Trustees,
Apr. 24, 1736, from Frederica (P.R.O., CO5/638/387-8); (*b*) the remainder,
Whitehead, II. 17-18.

From the Revd. Samuel Wesley, Jun.[1]

[April 29, 1736]

5 Dear brother

Natural affection made me rejoice to see your hand, a quality I shall never
think it my duty to get rid of while I can read St. Paul. My time is never worth
a Journal, so if I were not to write till I could answer you in kind, our correspondence would be as much at an end as our conversation. You must therefore
10 be content with such letters as I can write. My present will consist partly of
remarks on your diary, which perhaps you may have some regard to, and partly
of news, which I believe you will not.

I am glad my brother Hall's not going gave you more conveniencies on shipboard; though that is not the only reason why I rejoice at his stay. You know my
15 opinion already as to the first adult you baptized, so I need not repeat it. The
character of the Moravians is truly amiable.

Your next step grieves me, and would astonish me if I had not left wondering
for some time. You and Charles are trying how a vegetable diet will agree with
you. For what? You cannot imagine you have the same call to it that Daniel
20 had to refuse the king's provision. It cannot be religion, for abstaining from
meats is a doctrine of devils, and well may it be called so peculiarly in the present
case—since 'tis arrogant and sullen dashing back again to God his own grant
after the flood. It cannot be policy, in my humble opinion, unless you had not
a sufficient stock on board. Otherwise 'tis quite contrary to common sense to
25 weaken your strength and spirits (as vegetable food comparatively must do) at
the very time when your work is increasing. I dare say you will find work enough
in the colony, without going into the desert to seek more.

Forty out of eighty on board a ship I take to be a very num'rous and glorious
congregation. The length and danger of your voyage seems to be very providen-
30 tial, for the benefit of many; several you mention in your letter may have cause
to rejoice for it. You have had leisure to learn German, which is perfectly right.
I hope you will endeavour to learn modern Hebrew, too, and dispute with the
Jews in their own tongue—not forgetting the Highlanders. Your harvest is great,
and I doubt not but your success will be so, too.

35 Mr. Oglethorpe's giving up his cabin to the sick gentlewoman, and his for-
giving his servant, was no more than I could have expected of him; 'twas done

---

[1] Apparently in answer to John's of Feb. 1, 1736.

like himself. I know of no other part of yours that requires any remark, except perhaps that of my brother Charles's preaching in Cowes—I hope by the behaviour of those poor people he is fully convinced that he needed not have gone to Georgia in order to do good by his ministry.

What strange turns have I seen in the compass of this last year! My father's death left my mother as you know. She has been arrested for thirty pounds, as perhaps you remember, for 'tis some months ago, and I never retain dates. I have since paid the money, and cleared the matter. Another has sprung up. Mrs. Knight threatened the same usage. It seems you engaged for one year's rent, but as my mother scorned taking any advantage of that wonderful engagement— So I have sent fifteen pounds, and that peril too is past. Mr. Hutchinson and Mr. Vernon have sent my mother ten guineas apiece, I think. *Job* is now published, but without an index. I should, I believe, have attempted the making one myself, for I look upon that book as the most sacred legacy, next my mother, that my father left me. But I had a peremptory letter from my cousin Richardson, with this direct declaration: If your two brothers had not time to make one, should you attempt in your state of health such a work, I'll positively burn the copies rather than you shall hazard your life. So there was an end of that design. I cannot but say, as it is not my own fault, I am not very sorry that he was so kindly positive. Mr. Horne, who though a good man is not much given to—the carnal means of heeding—sent no word to poor Kezy about your order. She was frighted out of her wits, and wrote to my uncle Matt. He sent her ten guineas, there being almost half a year owing for, which I think you ought to repay. My mother has met with abundance of troubles, which my distance has hindered me from preventing so much as I would have done.

I hear from Oxford that there was no inventory of yours or Charles's goods; not from Mr. Horne, for I can't get a word from him. Dick Smith has sent me a catalogue of Charles's books. I wish with all my heart that some good editions of the classics that Dick had parted with had been amongst them. I am getting collections for a classic library; however you may approve of the other books, I am sure you will like the first that has been given me, the Polyglot Bible.

I know not whether it is worthwhile to tell you of an accidental good I have been the occasion of, yet I'll do it, since perhaps it may please you. I sheltered a bankrupt merchant in my house till he had got his creditors to sign his liberty. I gave him the liberty of my books, the event of which has been that he has turned from the dissenters and come with his whole family to church.

I know you have neither time nor inclination to tell me much of your designs and proceedings, and therefore am not at all surprised when I hear casually from others what I might naturally have expected to have had from yourself. I heartily wish you may have done one thing that is concealed only by your taciturnity—or the infection of it among your friends: that you may have provided for my mother's subsistence, if I should die. If you have done so (I mean in a human way, and according to second causes) 'tis well, I will never reproach you with not letting me know it, nor will any unkindness ever disturb me, after you have robbed me of Charles. 'Tis true it might have made my death a little more comfortable, which you had no reason to think was far off, my wife's health and my own being so precarious when you went. If you have not taken any care for her, if surviving me, 'tis a guilty, a very guilty omission, which I would not willingly have been stained with—no, not to convert a continent. Without a particular revelation 'tis neither better nor worse than dashing one of God's daughters against the other, and breaking the second table in honour of the first. I don't blame you, upon the whole, for not taking my sister Ellison along with

5 you, but I should have commended you exceedingly had you taken three or four of her children, who in all human probability in a few years may want conversion as much even as those poor people you are going among. Poor families will be sending over perpetually, and they are worse than double orphans. Time was when I could take some care of them, but 'tis past. Any ship would take care of

10 them in their passage, for the sake of Mr. Oglethorpe. I hope you have privately made some sort of allowance to them, or—I should say, and—to sister Lambert. I shall take Jacky as soon as I can fairly dispose of Sam. Bentham, but he and Jack Ellison at once are as many as I can well dispense with.

I find I have with my news mixed advice, and therefore I will give you one

15 piece of counsel more. You know that a church where there are only presbyters is *res unius aetatis*.[1] Aim therefore with all your strength at getting bishops on your side the sea. If Mr. O[glethorpe], to whom I have mentioned it, would but once have that point at heart, I should not fear the success, though I foresee great difficulties. If this letter should ever come safe to you, and I hear of its

20 arrival, I may then perhaps speak more largely. I pray God preserve you in body and soul, and prosper your endeavours for his glory. I am, dear Jack, your affectionate friend and brother,

Salisbury, Apr. 29,   S. Wesley
    1736

Address: 'To the Revd Mr John Wesley']   *End* by JW: 'April 29, 1736/
b[rother] S[amuel]'   *Source*: MA.

From the Revd. Charles Wesley

25   [May 1, 1736]

Dear brother
    The trial is at last over, but has left me as a man in whom is no strength. I am fully satisfied of Mr. [Oglethorpe]'s innocency, and he of mine; nor can I say which has been traduced most. (God forgive the same wicked instruments of

30 all!) He gave me, when going lately εἰς πύλας θανάτου,[2] an infallible demonstration of his affection and of his virtue. I will, God willing, never forget him for it. To be so obliged by one who had all reason to think me his worst enemy is far more painful to me than the ingratitude of those who had all reason to think me their best friend. I am heartily weary of my fellow-creatures. [. . .] My increasing

35 abhorrence not of the persons but of the false-heartedness of this people cleaves

---

[1] A legal term, 'an affair of one generation only'.
[2] 'into the gates of death' (cf. Job 38: 17). Oglethorpe was going into battle against the Spaniards, and expected death (see CWJ, Apr. 24, 1736).

so fast to me that I shall never shake it off. Yet while I am constrained to dwell with Mesech I shall labour to make full proof of my ministry. When a way is made me to escape, escape I shall, for my life, and not look behind. [. . .]

I send your papers by Mr. Quincy, and look for all the large sermon paper you can spare, that I may not come unfurnished. [. . .] The Spaniard's seven sail are 5 gone, the *Hawk* arrived, the guns mounted, and sowing-time begun. Mr. [Oglethorpe] will desire our friend B[enjamin Ingham] to supply my place here for a little while. A wooden house will be ready against his coming. Send me half a dozen cups and saucers, or basins or *quid capax*,[1] with a teapot. You will, for I can't, answer Mr. Regnier's, to whom my respects. Patrick's *Christian* 10 *Sacrifice* is not forthcoming, any more than the coat. I, and therefore you, have money to buy another.

I thank B. I[ngham] for his last—but I am beyond the reach of advice or consolation. *Verba sicut mortuo*.[2] When you write to England (which you may now do by Mr. Q[uincy]), make my excuse; for I cannot, I will not, write to any. 15 My love to my namesake and brother Benjamin, who may set forward when he pleases. Adieu.

Frederica, May 1, 1736

What would I give to be under no necessity of ever writing another letter!

I send you Wake; and Lawrence, whom I mean ⟨to⟩ read over again with you. 20

Address: 'To The Revd. Mr. Wesly at Savanna'   *End* by JW: 'C[harles]. Frederica. May 1, 17⟨36⟩'[3]   *Source*: MA.

To the Revd. John Burton

[May 10, 1736]

Dear sir

From all the information I have yet been able to procure, I believe Mr. Quincy[4] has been much wronged. I find none here who will to my face affirm anything which they have whispered to others 25 against his behaviour in general. As to the particular parts of it which were liable to exception, he desires to answer for himself. I should be very glad if both Dr. Hale[s][5] and you could have leisure

---

[1] 'whatever is suitable'.

[2] 'Like words to a dead man.'

[3] The letter was over a week in reaching him. His diary and summary for May 10 both read, 'Letter from Charles. Oglethorpe innocent!'

[4] See p. 456 n., above.

[5] Stephen Hales (1677–1761), Fellow of Corpus Christi College, Cambridge, created D.D. of Oxford in 1733, a country clergyman best known for his scientific works, his chief writings being *Statical Essays* (1733), two volumes both of which Wesley knew. He was also a member of the Common Council of the Georgia Trust, and one of those

to converse with him fully and freely on that subject. I doubt not then but you would be enabled to discover (what only guilt dreads) the plain truth.

Mr. Oglethorpe told me before he left the ship, he was afraid if
5 I once got to Savannah I should not soon leave it—it was so pleasant a place. If the time of my stay here was to be determined by the pleasantness of the place, that would be a miserable reason for prolonging it one day. But I doubt whether another reason be not of weight enough to keep me here some months longer than I in-
10 tended. My answer in England to that objection against leaving it, viz. 'Darkness, alas! and heathens are at home',[1] viz. that 'these heathens will not hear', fails me now. For hitherto those I am among have shown great willingness. The question therefore which I desire Dr. Hale[s] and you deeply to consider, and to send your thoughts
15 upon, is whether I ought to go forward to publish the gospel to other nations, till those here who desire it are fully instructed therein.

Even this work is indeed far too great for me, and [I] am often ready to cry out, 'I wonder that any pastor in the church should be
20 saved!'[2] So many souls, for every one of whom we must give account! If any one of whom perish for want of our assisting him in public, in private, in every possible way, his blood will be required at our hands![3] May God enable us to watch and strive, and pray without

who saw the *Simmonds* passengers off from Gravesend in October, 1735. He took a warm personal interest in the Wesleys.

[1] Cf. letter to Burton, Oct. 10, 1735: '. . . it is commonly objected that there are heathens enough, in practice if not theory, at home. Why then should you go to those in America? Why, for a very plain reason. Because these heathens at home have Moses and the prophets, and those have not. Because these who *have* the gospel trample upon it . . .' Although the quotation itself may have been used by Burton, it seems more probable that it occurred in an otherwise unknown letter from Wesley's brother Samuel, who had strong reservations about the Georgia mission (see his letter of Apr. 29, para. 5). It comes from an eleven-line poem by Samuel referring to the frustrated scheme of Dr. George Berkeley, the philosopher, to found a college in the West Indies to educate natives:

> To distant climes th'Apostle need not roam;
> Darkness, alas! and heathens are at home.

(These verses were not published in any edition of Samuel Wesley's *Poems*, from 1736 to 1862, but may be found in Wesley's *A.M.*, 1780, p. 564.)

[2] See Chrysostom, *On the Epistle to the Hebrews*, Homily xxxiv. 1 (on Heb. 13: 17): '*Miror an fieri possit ut aliquis ex rectoribus sit salvus*'—'I marvel that any leader ['rector'] in the church should be saved.' Cf. *A Farther Appeal*, Pt. II, II. 34 (11. 247 of this edition).

[3] See Ezek. 3: 18.

ceasing[1] for them as well as ourselves. Neither do you, I hope, cease to pray for your obliged and affectionate brother in Christ,

John Wesley

Savannah, May 10,
1736   5

Address: 'To the Revd. Mr. Burton, Fellow of Eaton Colledge, near Windsor'
Source: Egmont Papers; a contemporary copy.

From Henry Newman

London, 16 June, 1736

Revd. sir

I wrote to you the beginning of this month by the *Two Brothers,* Capt. Thomson, to whom I delivered ten large and small packets for Georgia. But yesterday the Society had the pleasure of seeing a letter from you of the 23rd of March to   10
Sir John Philipps,[2] signifying your want of Bibles and Common Prayer Books, whereupon I was ordered to provide immediately a box of

40 Bibles, Minion
40 New Testaments, Long Primer, and
40 Common Prayer Books, Minion.   15

These are all packed up in one box directed to yourself by the *Two Brothers,* which I hope may go safe, if I can be so happy as to ship these before the ship falls down.

Writing is very troublesome to Sir John Philipps, and therefore he hopes you will excuse his not answering this and a former letter which he received, with   20
his and the good wishes of the Society that the blessing of God may always attend your labours for his glory, wherein joins, revd. sir, your most humble servant,

H. N[ewman]

Address: 'To the Revd. Mr. John Wesley, at Savannah, in Georgia'   *Source*:
S.P.C.K., Misc. Letters, CN2/2, p. 40, a draft.

[1] 1 Thess. 5: 17.
[2] See Appendix, Mar. 23, 1736.

To *The Gentleman's Magazine*

[July 20, 1736]

Monday, July 20, 1736,[1] five of the Chickasaw Indian warriors came to us with Mr. Andrews,[2] their interpreter, four of them head men of the nation, two chiefs, Postubee and Mingomawtaw.[3] The
5 substance of our conference was as follows:

Q [uestion]. Do you believe there is One above, who is over all?

Postubee answered, We believe there are four beloved things above: the clouds, the sun, the clear sky, and he that lives in the clear sky.

10 Q. Do you believe there is but One that lives in the clear sky?

A. We believe there are two with him, three in all.

Q. Do you think he made the sun, and the other beloved things?

A. We cannot tell. Who hath seen?

Q. Do you think he made you?

15 A. We think he made all men at first out of the ground.

Q. Do you believe he loves you?

A. I don't know. I cannot see him.

Q. But has he not often saved your life?

A. Yes, he has. For I have had many bullets gone on this side
20 and that side, but he would not let them hurt me. And these young men have had many bullets that went into them, but still they are alive.

Q. Then he can save you from your enemies now?

A. Yes; but who knows if he will have mercy? We have so many
25 enemies now all round about us that I think of nothing but death. And if I am to die, I shall die, and I will die like a man. But if he

---

[1] Wesley's diary shows that this conference, apparently the first real testing of his original purpose in coming to America, began with the coming of Mr. Andrews on Monday, July 19, 1736, and continued on Tuesday, July 20, the 'Chickasaws' last audience' beginning at 5.0 p.m., though from 10.0 a.m until noon that day he had 'writ conference'. Probably the manuscript was carried by Charles Wesley, who (accompanied by John as far as Charleston) within a few days left Savannah for England.

[2] Probably the Revd. William Andrews (b. 1671), who served in Virginia for two years, and then settled in Albany, New York, where he was a missionary to the Mohawk Indians (1712–19), translating a primer and prayers for them. Like Wesley he had been educated at Lincoln College, Oxford. (See C. F. Pascoe, *History of the S.P.G.*, London, S.P.G., 1901, pp. 70–1, 800, 855, and Weis, *Colonial Clergy of Virginia*, p. 2.)

[3] The *Journal* account describes them as Paustoobee and Mingo Mattaw.

will have me live, I shall live, though I have ever so many enemies. He can destroy them all.

Q. How do you know that?

A. From what he has done. When our enemies came against us before, then the beloved clouds came for us; and often much rain, and sometimes hail has come upon them, and that in a very hot day. And I saw when many French and Choctaws and other Indians came against one of our towns. And the beloved ground made a noise under them, and the beloved ones in the air behind them; and they were afraid, and all went away, and left their meat and drink, and guns. I tell no lie. These saw it too.

Q. Have you ever heard such noises at other times?

A. Yes, often; before and after almost every battle. (Here Mr. Andrews said he had often heard them himself, and so had all the traders.)

Q. What sort of noises were they?

A. Like the noise of drums, and guns, and shoutings.

Q. Have you heard any such lately?

A. Yes; four days after our last battle with the French.

Q. Then you heard nothing before it?

A. The night before I dreamed I heard many drums beating up there, and many trumpets there, with much stamping of feet and shouting. Till then I thought we should all die; but then I believed the beloved ones were come to help us. And the next day I heard about an hundred guns go off before the battle began (as did I, said Mr. Andrews), and I said, When the sun is there, the beloved ones will come to take our part, and we shall conquer our enemies; and we did so.

Q. Do you think and talk of the beloved ones?

A. We think of them always, wherever we are; we talk of them, and to them, abroad, at home, in peace, in war, before and after we fight, and indeed whenever or wherever we meet together.

Q. Where do you think your souls go after death?

A. We believe the souls of bad men walk up and down the place where they died, or where their bodies lie; for we have often heard cries and noises near the place where any prisoners have been burnt.

Q. Where do the souls of white men go after death?

A. We can't tell. We have not seen.

Q. Do you believe the souls of good men go up?

A. I do, but I told you the talk of the nation. (Here Mr. Andrews said, You know what they said at the burial of Miss Bovey,[1] that they knew what you was doing. You was speaking to the beloved ones above, to take up the spirit of the young woman.)

5 Q. We have a Book which tells us many things of the beloved ones above, which you don't know. Would you be glad to know?

A. Our enemies are all about us; we have no time now but to fight. If ever we be at peace we should be glad to know.

Q. Do you ever expect to know what the white men know?— Andrews said, he told Mr. Oglethorpe they believe the time will
10 come when the red and white men will be one.—(N.B. There seems to be an universal tradition among the Americans that the whites are to come to teach their natives knowledge.)

Q. What do the French teach you?

A. The French black kings (i.e. their priests) never go out. We
15 see you walk about. We like that. That is good.

Q. How came your nation by the knowledge they have?

A. As soon as the ground was sound and fit to stand upon, it came to us, and has been with us ever since. But we are young men. If our old men were here, they could tell you more of these things.
20 There are only a few whom the beloved one chooses from children, and is in them, and takes care of them, and teaches them, and they know these things. And our old men practise, therefore they know. But I do not practise, therefore I know little.

Source. Gent. Mag., 1737, pp. 318–19 (May), headed: 'From Georgia. Extract of the Rev. Mr. John Wesley's Journal, Minister of Savannah; containing a Conference had with some of the Chickasaw Indians, showing what a deep and habitual sense of a divine Providence is imprinted on the minds of those ignorant heathens, and how excellently they are prepared to receive the Gospel.' JWJ as eventually published contains dozens of variants large and small.

[1] Rebecca Bovey, betrothed to Peter Appee, died suddenly on July 10, 1736, and was buried on July 12.

To Archibald Hutcheson[1]

[July 23, 1736]

[Sir]

By what I have seen during my short stay here I am convinced that I have long been under a great mistake in thinking no circumstances could make it the duty of a Christian priest to do anything else but preach the gospel. On the contrary, I am now satisfied that there is a possible case wherein a part of his time ought to be employed in what *less* directly conduces to the glory of God, and peace and good will among men. And such a case, I believe, is that which now occurs, there being several things which cannot so effectually be done without me; and which, though not directly belonging to my ministry, yet are by consequence of the highest concern to the success of it. It is from this conviction that I have taken some pains to inquire into the great controversy now subsisting between Carolina and Georgia, and in examining and weighing the letters wrote and the arguments urged on both sides of the question. And I cannot but think that the whole affair might be clearly stated in few words. A Charter was passed a few years since establishing the bounds of this province, and empowering the Trustees therein named to prepare laws, which when ratified by the King in Council, should be of force within those bounds. Those Trustees have prepared a law, which has been so ratified, for the regulation of the Indian trade, requiring that none should trade with the Indians who are within this province till he is so licensed as therein specified. Notwithstanding this law the governing part of Carolina have asserted both in conversation, in writing, and in the public newspapers, that it is

---

[1] Archibald Hutcheson (1661–1740) (also spelt Hutchison, Hutchenson, and Hutchinson), M.P. for Hastings, 1715–22, during which period he made a name for himself by over twenty publications on the national debt, the use of public funds, and the South Sea Company. Although he did not become a member of the Georgia Trust, he was one of Oglethorpe's friends and supporters in the enterprise, and served with him on the General Court of St. George's Hospital. At his death in 1740 he was Treasurer of the Middle Temple, which he had entered Oct. 13, 1680, becoming a Bencher in 1726. Hutcheson requested that after his death his young widow should put herself under the spiritual direction of William Law, which she did, to become an influential figure in his King's Cliffe community, dying in 1781. Hutcheson was a personal friend of the Wesley family, subscribing to the rector's *Job*, and helping to support his widow. (See p. 469 n., below.) John Wesley's diary notes a letter to him on Oct. 18, 1735, one on Jan. 22, 1736, and another on May 27, 1737, in addition to this on the problem of the stormy trade relations between South Carolina and Georgia.

lawful for anyone not so licensed to trade with the Creek, Cherokee, or Chickasaw Indians; they have passed an ordinance not only asserting the same, but enacting that men and money shall be raised to support such traders, and in fact they have themselves licensed
5 and sent up such traders both to the Creek and Chickasaw Indians.[1]

This is the plain matter of fact. Now as to matter of right. When twenty more reams of paper have been spent upon it I cannot but think it must come to this short issue at last: (1). Are the Creeks, Cherokees, and Chickasaws within the bounds of Georgia or not?
10 (2). Is an act of the King in Council, in pursuance of an Act of Parliament, of any force within these bounds, or not? That all other inquiries are absolutely foreign to the question a very little consideration will show. As to the former of these, the Georgian Charter, compared with any map of these parts which I have ever
15 seen, determines it; the latter I never heard made a question of but in the neighbourhood of Carolina.

Mr. Johnson's brother[2] has been with us some days. I have been twice in company with him at Mr. Oglethorpe's; and I hope there are in Carolina—though the present proceeding would almost make
20 one doubt it—many such gentlemen as he seems to be, men of good nature, good manners, and understanding. I hope God will repay you sevenfold for the kindness you have shown to my poor mother, and in her to, sir, your most obliged, most obedient servant,

John Wesley

Source: Whitehead, II. 18–20, as 'to Mr. Hutcheson', the name and spelling supported by Wesley's diary.

[1] For the South Carolina point of view, claiming trading privileges with the Indians because they could not justly be bound by the laws of Georgia, which were intended only for its own settlers and Indians, see the lengthy document of Aug. 6, 1736, addressed to the Board of Trade in London by the Lieutenant-Governor of South Carolina, Col. Thomas Broughton (*State Papers: Col*, 1736, No. 376, pp. 261–9).

[2] Probably a brother of Robert Johnson, the former Governor of South Carolina, who had died May 3, 1735, and had been succeeded by his brother-in-law, Thomas Broughton. Clearly Broughton himself is not intended, however, for Wesley's diary specifically states 'vis[ited] Jo[hn]son' (July 15) and 'Mr. Jo[hn]son' (July 22). No other brother appears to have been present at the Governor's funeral (see *South Carolina Gazette*, May 10, 1735), nor does the *Dict. of American Biography* list any other children of Sir Nathanial Johnson, himself a former Governor of South Carolina, as well as a former M.P. for Newcastle, England, knighted in 1680. Just as there was a daughter who married Broughton, however, there may well have been a brother who came out to visit his nieces and nephews after their father's death, and other members of his family.

To James Vernon[1]

[July 23, 1736]

[Sir]

. . . As short a time as I have for writing, I could not pardon myself if I did not spend some part of it in acknowledging the continuance of your goodness to my mother; which indeed neither she nor [5] I can ever lose the sense of.

The behaviour of the people of Carolina finds much conversation for this place. I dare not say whether they want honesty or logic most. It is plain a very little of the latter, added to the former, would show how utterly foreign to the point in question all their voluminous [10] defences are. Here is an Act of the King in Council, passed in pursuance of an Act of Parliament, forbidding unlicensed persons to trade with the Indians in Georgia. Nothing therefore can justify them in daily sending unlicensed traders to the Creek, Cherokee, and Chickasaw Indians but the proving, either that this Act is of no [15] force, or that those Indians are not in Georgia. Why then are these questions so little considered by them, and others so largely discussed? I fear for a very plain, though not a very honest reason: that is, to puzzle the cause. I sincerely wish you all happiness in time and in eternity, and am, sir, . . . [20]

[John Wesley]

Source: Whitehead, II. 20–1, as written 'at the same time . . . to Mr. Vernon on the same subject' to that of July 23 to Hutcheson; confirmed by Wesley's diary.

[1] See letter of Nov. 18, 1735, from Vernon, and letter of Apr. 29, 1736, from Samuel Wesley: 'Mr. Hutchinson [i.e. Archibald Hutcheson] and Mr. Vernon have sent my mother ten guineas apiece, I think.' The letter clearly follows the same general pattern as that of the same date to Hutcheson.

To James Edward Oglethorpe[1]

Aug. 23 [1736]

Sir

I choose to write rather than speak, that I may not say too much.[2]
I find 'tis utterly impossible anything should be kept secret unless
5 both parties[3] are resolved[4] upon it. What fell out yesterday is already
known to every family in Frederica; but to many it has been represented in such a light that 'tis easy to know whence the representation c[ame]. Now, sir, what can I do more? Though I have given
my reputation to G[od], I must not absolutely neglect it. The treat-
10 ment I have met with was not barely an assault; you know one part
of it was felony. I can't see what I can do but desire an open hearing
in the pres[ence] of all my countrymen of this place. If you[5] (to
whom I can gladly entrust my life and my all in this world [?])
are excepted against as partial, let a jury be empanelled, and upon
15 a full inquiry[6] determine what such breaches of the laws deserve.
I am, sir, your obliged and most obedient servant,

[John Wesley]

Source: MA, MS Journal, Aug. 20–Sept. 8, [1736], draft, with alterations, the
letter being a distinct document confined to the larger part of one page only,
unnumbered, between folios 154 and 155, in abbreviated longhand, here extended silently except in cases of some uncertainty.

[1] After seeing Charles off to England, John Wesley visited Frederica again, delivering
letters from South Carolina to Oglethorpe, and hoping to break down the strong prejudice which now focused upon him instead of upon his brother, only to find bitter
animosity. On Sunday, Aug. 22, he recorded in his MS Journal: 'Mrs. Hawkins sent me
by her maid a note, wherein she desired to speak with me upon an affair of importance.
I paused a little, and asked the servant whether she knew what her mistress wanted.
She said, "No;" upon which I replied, "If a parishioner desires my company, I must
go; but, be sure, stay you within." ' Mrs. Hawkins made a murderous attack upon him
with both a loaded pistol and a pair of scissors, but Wesley just managed to hold her
off until help came. He then told Oglethorpe what had happened. Oglethorpe summoned
Mrs. Hawkins and her husband, who promised 'better behaviour for the future'. The
community remained in a turmoil, however, Wesley being generally vilified, though
he was reluctant to expose Mrs. Hawkins publicly. In this dilemma he wrote the following morning to Oglethorpe.
[2] Orig., 'say ((more than is proper))'.
[3] Orig., 'kept secret ((wh[en] one of the)) parties'.
[4] Orig., 'are ((agre)) resolved'.
[5] Orig., 'If you ((are not excep))'.
[6] Orig., 'a full ((hearing of the cause))'.

To the Revd. George Whitefield and the Oxford Methodists[1]

[Savannah, Sept. 10, 1736]

[Sept. 8. W(ed): Mr. Von Reck and his brother came to town. [. . .] The next morning I desired them to make use of our house,

[1] For Whitefield's important correspondence with Wesley culminating in his 'conversion' see the letters of May 8 and 13(?), 1735. The two continued to correspond frequently and intimately throughout that summer and after the Wesleys had embarked for Georgia in the autumn. In Apr. 1736 Whitefield wrote from Gloucester to Wesley in Savannah: 'My friends here are for drawing me into orders.' That letter also mentioned his own readiness to follow the other members of the group to Georgia. A letter of Sept. 2, 1736, told of his changed status—he had been ordained deacon on June 20, and had accepted Sir John Philipps's offer of £30 per annum to stay in Oxford and 'superintend the affairs of the Methodists'. From this he was drawn away on Aug. 4 for two months to supply for Thomas Broughton as the minister of the Tower of London. While there a letter from his colleagues in Georgia made him 'long to go abroad for God, too'—provided his body were strong enough for the voyage. In mid-December letters poured in rapidly. From the returned Charles Wesley came a message, said Whitefield, 'wherein he informed me that he had come over to procure labourers, but added, "I dare not prevent [i.e. act in advance of] God's nomination." ' (*Journals*, p. 79). Whitefield continued: 'In a few days after this came another letter from Mr. John Wesley, wherein were these words: "Only Delamotte is with me, till God shall stir up the hearts of some of his servants, who, putting their lives in their hands, shall come over and help us, where the harvest is so great, and the labourers so few. What if thou art the man, Mr. Whitefield?" ' (Probably written in late August from Frederica. Charles Wesley had left for England on July 26, and shortly afterward Benjamin Ingham went to live among the Indians at old Yamacraw, four miles NW. of Savannah, on Pipe Makers Creek, even though his schoolhouse-cum-dwelling-house on the ancient mound near by called Irene would not be quite ready until 'a few days' after he reported on Sept. 15 to Sir John Philipps (P.R.O., CO5/638/196–7). While John Wesley was in Frederica, however, pastoral charge of Savannah was left in the hands of the Revd. Edward Dyson, not Ingham.)
'In another letter', continued Whitefield, 'were these words: "Do you ask me what you shall have? Food to eat, and raiment to put on; a house to lay your head in, such as your Lord had not; and a crown of glory that fadeth not away." Upon reading this my heart leaped within me, and, as it were, echoed to the call.' Within two or three weeks all was settled, and on New Year's Day, 1736, he went to Gloucester to see his bishop and to take leave of his mother, even though a year passed by before he actually set sail for Georgia. This second quotation clearly reflects the document here presented, which is a fragment of John Wesley's manuscript journal, bearing signs of much revision by him both in the course of writing and subsequently. As this unfinished fragment dealt with Sept. 8–10, it seems highly likely that it was incorporated into a journal-letter written to Whitefield (according to Wesley's diary) on Sept. 10 (misdated '11'), from 9.0 a.m. to 10.0 a.m., which Whitefield (on the evidence of a phrase such as 'any of you') was expected to lend or read to others of the few available Oxford Methodists.

while they stayed. On Friday we began our morning prayers at a quarter past five, an hour we hope to adhere to all the winter. [. . .]

[I had often observed that I scarce ever visited any persons in health or sickness but they attended public prayer for some time 5 after. This increased my desire of seeing not only those who were sick, but all my parish, as soon as possible at their own houses. Accordingly, I had long since begun to visit them in order from house to house. But I could not go on two days, the sick increasing so fast as to require all the time I have to spare (which is from one in the 10 afternoon till five). Nor is even that enough to see them all (as I would do) daily. So that even in this town (not to mention Frederica and all the smaller settlements), here are above five hundred sheep that are (almost) without a shepherd. He that is unjust must be unjust still.[1] Here is none to search out and lay hold on the *mollia* 15 *tempora fandi*,[2] and to persuade him to save his soul alive.[3] He that is a babe in Christ[4] may be so still. Here is none to attend the workings of grace upon his spirit, to feed him by degrees with food convenient for him, and gently lead him till he can follow the Lamb wherever he goeth.[5] Does any err from the right way? Here is none 20 to recall him: he may go on to seek death in the error of his life.[6] Is any wavering? Here is none to confirm him. Is any falling? There is none to lift him up. What a single man can do is not seen or felt. Where are ye, who are very zealous for the Lord of hosts? Who will rise up with me against the wicked? Who will take God's part 25 against the evildoers?[7] Whose spirit is moved within to prepare himself for publishing glad tidings to those on whom the Sun of Righteousness never yet arose,[8] by labouring first for those his countrymen, who are else without hope, as well as without God in the world?[9] Do you ask what you shall have? Why, all you desire: food 30 to eat, raiment to put on,[10] a place where to lay your head (such as your Lord had not),[11] and[12] a crown of life that fadeth not away![13] Do you seek means of building up[14] yourselves in the knowledge and

---

[1] See Rev. 22: 11.
[2] 'favourable occasions for speaking'; cf. Virgil, *Aeneid*, iv. 293-4, *mollissima fandi / tempora*.
[3] Ezek. 18: 27.   [4] See 1 Cor. 3: 1.   [5] Rev. 14: 4.
[6] See Wisd. 1: 12.   [7] Ps. 94: 16 (B.C.P.).   [8] See Mal. 4: 2.
[9] See Eph. 2: 12.   [10] See Gen. 28: 20.
[11] See Matt. 8: 20; Luke 9: 58.
[12] Orig., 'and ((salvation for)) a crown'.
[13] See Jas. 1: 12; 1 Pet. 5: 4; Rev. 2: 10. (N.B. Whitefield's *Journal*, like Peter, has 'crown of glory'.)   [14] Orig., 'means of ((advancing))'.

love of God?[1] I call the God whom we serve to witness, I know of no place under heaven where there are more, or perhaps so many, as in this place. Does your heart burn within you[2] to turn many others to righteousness? Behold, the whole land, thousands of thousands, are before you! I will resign to any of you all or any part of my charge. Choose what seemeth good in your own eyes. Here are within these walls children of all ages and dispositions. Who will bring them up in the nurture and admonition of the Lord,[3] till they are meet to be preachers of righteousness?[4] Here are adults from the farthest parts[5] of Europe and Asia, and the inmost kingdoms of Africa.[6] Add to these the known and unknown natives of this vast continent, and you will indeed have a great multitude which no man can [number][7]. . .]

Source: MA, pp. 158–60 of a fragment of a manuscript journal by John Wesley, Aug. 20–Sept. 10, 1736, with rectos only inscribed, and numbered 148–60. (Cf. *W.M.M.*, 1844, pp. 921–2, which dates it Sept. 8, 1737, and introduces a few variant readings, apparently in error.)

To James Vernon

[Sept. 11, 1736]

Sir

You have a just claim to my repeated acknowledgments, not only for the continuance of your regard to my mother, but for your strengthening my hands, and encouraging me not to look back from the work wherein I am engaged. I know that if it shall please our great God to give it his blessing, the god of this world[8] will oppose in vain; and that therefore the whole depends on our approving our hearts before him, and placing all our confidence in his power and mercy.

Mr. Ingham has made some progress in the Creek language. But the[9] short conversation I had with the chiefs of the Chickasaws

[1] B.C.P., blessing in Communion and Ordinal.   [2] See Luke 24: 32.
[3] Eph. 6: 4.   [4] See 2 Pet. 2: 5.
[5] Orig., 'adults from ((every country e))'.
[6] Orig., 'Africk', as normally with Wesley.
[7] See Rev. 7: 9. The verso of the page is blank, so that the continuation, with 'number' and probably other matter, would be on the missing sheet numbered '161', and possibly others.
[8] 2 Cor. 4: 4.   [9] Georgia copy, 'But a'.

(which my brother, I presume, has informed you of) moves me to desire rather to learn their language, if God shall give me opportunity. The generality of that despised and almost unheard-of nation, if one may judge from the accounts given either by their own country-
5   men or strangers, are not only humble and teachable (qualities scarce to be found among any other of the Indian nations), but have so firm a reliance on Providence, and so settled a habit of looking up to a Superior Being in all the occurrences of life, that they appear the most likely of all the Americans to receive and rejoice in the glorious
10 gospel of Christ.[1]

    What will become of this poor people, a few of whom now see the light, and bless God for it, when I am called from among them, I know not. Nor indeed what will become of them while I am here; for the work is too weighty for me. A parish of above two hundred
15 miles in length laughs at the labour of one man. Savannah alone would give constant employment for five or six to instruct, rebuke, and exhort as need requires. Neither durst I advise any single person to take charge of Frederica, or indeed to exercise his ministry there at all unless he was an experienced soldier of Jesus Christ,[2] that
20 could rejoice in reproaches, persecutions, distresses, for Christ's sake. I bless God for what little of them I have met with there, and doubt not but they were sent for my soul's health. My heart's desire for this place is, not that it may be a famous or a rich, but that it may be a religious colony, and then I am sure it cannot fail of the
25 blessing of God, which includes all real goods, temporal and eternal. I am, sir, your much obliged and obedient servant,

[John Wesley]

Savannah, 11th Septr. 1736

Source: Copy, in contemporary hand, in P.R.O., CO5/638/141, headed in the same hand: 'A Copy of the Revd. Mr. John Wesley's Letter to Mr. Vernon.' With this has been collated another contemporary copy from the Egmont Papers, with some minor variants, including the omission of the subscribed date and a different superscript: 'Copy of a Letter from the Revd. Mr. John Wesley to Mr. Vernon dated Savannah the 11th of September 1736.'

[1] 2 Cor. 4: 4.   [2] 2 Tim. 2: 3.

From Henry Newman

London, 22d Sepr. 1736

Revd Sr

The Revd. Mr. Archdeacon Rye of Islip having lately sent a benefaction of three guineas to the Society, to [be] laid out in Bibles and sent to you and your brother to be disposed of in Georgia, that sum has been laid out in purchasing 5 twenty Bibles, Minion, which are packed up in a box directed to you at Savannah, and sent to the Georgia Office to be forwarded by the first opportunity. In the same box are packed up a few of the Society's books lately imported into their store, of which they desire your acceptance by, revd sr, your most humble servant,   10

H. N.

Address: 'To the Revd Mr Wesley at Savannah in Georgia'   *Source*: S.P.C.K., Misc. Letters, CN2/2, p. 58, a draft.

To Ann Granville[1]

Savannah, 24th Sept., 1736

The mutual affection, and indeed the many other amiable qualities of those two sisters, one of whom is lately gone to a happier place,[2] would not have suffered me to be unmindful of your friend 15

[1] Wesley's diary for Sept. 17, 1736, noted: 'wr[it] to Asp[asia], to Sel[ima]', and on Sept. 24 he wrote to his friend Charles Rivington, presumably enclosing the previously prepared letters to Mrs. Pendarves, and a double letter to Ann Granville and her mother (on the evidence of the address to the mother on the verso of the half-sheet to the daughter). At the same time he apparently added the current date. For Rivington as his London agent for forwarding or gathering together such letters—an enormous economy—see paragraph three.

[2] Margaret Bovey and her dead sister, Rebecca. It is very difficult to ascertain Margaret Bovey's English background, or even to be sure of her marital status. On July 1, 1736, Wesley's *Journal* spoke about 'the younger of the Miss Boveys', but Egmont's Diary refers to her as 'the widow Bovey' (May 5, 1735; Oct. 19, 1737). Wesley, however, was closer to them, and more probably correct. Musgrave notes the death of Charles Bovey, of Stow, Cambridge, Nov. 29, 1728, and of Catherine, widow of William Bovey, of Flaxley, Gloucestershire, in 1726, aged 56. This wealthy philanthropic lady had no children, but it is tempting to believe that as her husband had been lord of the manor of Flaxley, less than thirty miles from the Granvilles' former home at Buckland, and as both families moved in 'county' circles, some relationship of the future emigrants to Georgia with Catherine Bovey (1670–1726), may well have brought them into touch with the Granvilles. Although the name does not occur in Mary Granville's *Correspondence*, it is clear that they did indeed know each other, and from the reference to St. James's Palace it also seems that the Boveys must have moved at least occasionally in Court

and you, had I had nothing else to remind me of you. I am persuaded that heavy affliction will prove the greatest blessing to the survivor which she ever yet received. She is now very cheerful, as well as deeply serious. She sees the *folly* of placing one's happiness in *any*
5 *creature*, and is fully determined to give her whole heart to him from whom death cannot part her.

I often think how different her way of life is at Savannah from what it was *at St. James's*, and yet the wise, polite, gay world counts her removal thence *a misfortune*. I should not be at all grieved if *you*
10 were fallen into the *same misfortune, far removed from the pride of life, and hid in some obscure recess*[1] where you were scarcely seen or heard of, unless by a few plain Christians, and by God and his angels.

Mr. Rivington will send your letter, if you should ever have leisure to favour with a few lines, your sincere friend and most obedient
15 servant.

Do you still watch and strive and pray, that your heart may be right before God? Can you 'deny yourself', as well as 'take up your cross'?[2] Adieu.

Address: 'To Mrs. Ann Granville, in Gloster'   *Postmark*: 'the English post-mark, 7th December' (i.e. London bishop mark, '7 DE')   *Seal*: 'The seal of this letter was a cross'   *Source*: Delany, I. 580–1, unsigned.

From the Revd. Charles Wesley[3]

[Oct. 1–6, 1736]

20   [[To my brother
[[Dear brother
[[I take advantage of the deepest seriousness and best temper I have known since the fatal hour I left Oxford to lay open my very heart, as I call God to

circles. The younger sister (or possibly sister-in-law), Rebecca, died on July 10, 1736. Margaret married James Burnside on March 12, 1737, but she also died within a few years. Wesley continued to correspond with them after he left Georgia.

[1] It is possible that the italicizing denotes in part a quotation from someone's letter (perhaps Ann Granville's) referring to the Bovey sisters.
[2] Matt. 10: 24.
[3] Leaving Savannah on Monday, July 26, 1736, Charles Wesley was escorted by John to Charleston, South Carolina, where he boarded a vessel for England, and after various adventures, made more hazardous by their drunken captain, Indivine, landed at Boston, Massachusetts, on Friday, Sept. 24. Here they remained, re-embarkation repeatedly delayed, until Monday, Oct. 25. Although Charles was ill, sometimes desperately ill, throughout this period and much of the voyage, he nevertheless came into friendly

witness that what I now write comes from it. You know what has passed in
Georgia. The spiritual man is himself discerned by none; therefore, and therefore only, I cannot understand—. But this much I know, though Mr. L[awley]
has glorious qualities, he is subject to the great infirmity of vindictiveness. The
prejudices he has imbibed with regard to me are eternal. He cannot possibly   5
look upon me as he has done, and I would not that he should. God is my witness
that I choose his disesteem before his praise. 'Tis infinitely safer. But at the
same time I own I would not increase his present prejudices. The continual
abuse about my embezzling the public stores, my betraying his secrets, etc.,
etc., 'like drops of eating water on the marble' have left an impression which I 10
am content should be indelible. For hereby Providence saves me from his
esteem and favour, a blessing for which I daily pour out my soul in thanksgiving!
The snare is broken, and I am delivered by the only expedient that could have
saved me.

[[I acknowledge Mr. ——'s tenderness for my reputation; but it needed not. 15
He was not more mistaken either about my fear of the Spaniards, or my hopes
from the traders. 'Tis a small thing with me to be judged of man's judgment.
Setting Christianity out of the question, after having been so thought of by him,
the opinion of others cannot much affect me; the bitterness of contempt is past.
But when I further consider that this is the unavoidable persecution of all 20
Christians, who must bear the reproach of Christ, and suffer this persecution,
I willingly submit to it; and should look upon myself as reprobate was I not to
expect that[1] treatment from (?) which his kindness would contrive to save me.

[[I can't yet shake off my weakness with regard to him, and am ashamed to
own I would not have him think me a hypocrite. I ardently desire, what apparently 25
he can't but grant, that he would not think of me at all, and to see his face
no more, till we stand together before that Being who alone can disentangle
truth from falsehood. Then, and not till then, will he know whether and how far
I have been charged unjustly.

[[I sometime think how to dispose of the remainder of a wretched life. I can 30
either live at Oxford or with my brother; who before I left England had provided
for me without my asking. He will labour all he can to settle me, but I trust
God will not suffer me to set up my rest there. I am offered, if I will fix here,]]
£100 [[a year sterling; but this is too public. Here is noise and commendation
by women. Mr. Price has likewise made provision for a minister at]] Hopkinton[[, 35

contact with many Boston clergy, preached for them, and was offered at least two church
livings; he called on the Governor, visited Harvard, and enjoyed the immense contrast
with the primitive living conditions in Georgia. At leisure he sought to find God's
purposes for his life. His manuscript journal for Oct. 1 contains this entry: 'Wrote to my
brother concerning my return to Georgia, which I found myself inclined to refer wholly
to God.' This surely refers to this letter, written almost completely in protective shorthand, here imperfectly transcribed. On Oct. 5 he added two paragraphs in Latin, and on
Oct. 6 a sentence in longhand, three in Greek, and another long passage in shorthand,
with insertions in Latin and Greek. The letter was then folded and addressed to his
brother for delivery by messenger. It contains exhortations that John also should learn
Byrom's shorthand, and must have been translated for John by the one whom Charles
refers to at the end as 'my namesake', Charles Delamotte (for whom see p. 494 n.).

[1] Orig., 't-th' or 'the that', apparently in error.

a country town of about]] forty [[families]] twenty [[miles distant. To the house
and glebe of]] three hundred [[acres he will get the Society's]] £50, [[and presses
me much to accept it: . . . But Georgia alone can give me the solitude I sigh
after. I cannot look for a long life there, but neither do I count that a blessing.
5 Pray ask Mr. ——, who knows me better than I do myself, these]] two [[questions:

    1. [[Whether he thinks me fit to be trusted with the care of souls?

    2. [[Whether I could have a small village remote from any town, where I may
hide myself from all business and all company?

10 [[I need not article for[1] the necessaries of life; these I know he will never
suffer me to want. His immediate answer to this may much assist me in the
temptation I am entering upon.

    [[This much, if you think proper, you may transcribe]] verbatim [[and show
to Mr. ——.]]

15 Oct. 5

Taedet me populi huiusce φιλοξένου, ita me urbanitate sua divexant et perse-
quuntur. Non patiuntur esse solum. E rure veniunt invisentes clerici; me
revertentis in rus trahunt. Cogor hanc Angliam contemplari, etiam antiqua
amoeniorem; et nequeo non exclamare, 'O fortunata regio, nec muscas alens,
20 nec crocodilos, nec delatores!' Sub fine huius Hebdomadis navem certissime
conscendimus, duplicato sumptu patriam empturi. Carolinensium nemo viatica
suppeditavit; et hic itidem 'Nil nisi cum pretio.' Pessime me habet quod cogor
moram hanc emere, magnumque pretium digressionis solvere. Sed hoc de meo;
qua propter silentium tibi impono perpetuum.
25 Morbus meus, aere hoc saluberrimo semel fugatus, iterum rediit. Suadent
amici omnes ut medicum consulam. Sed 'Funera non possum tam pretiosa pati.'[2]

Oct. 6

If you are as desirous as I am of a correspondence, you must set upon Byrom's
shorthand immediately. I leave my Journal and other papers with Mr. Price,
30 which he will send you if I fall short of England. Ἐκεῖνα γράφω σοι μόνῳ—
ἀνάρρητα εἰς τοὺς αἰῶνας. Οὐδαμῶς ἐπιτρέπω ἑρμηνεῦσι χρῆσ-⟨. . .⟩
Ἢ αὐτὸς μαθών[3] βραχιγραφίαν ἀνάγνωθι; ἡ ἐμοῦ κ⟨. . .⟩θέντος, εἰς πῦρ

---

[1] 'stipulate', an obsolete usage.

[2] 'I am wearied with these hospitable people, they so pursue me and pull me about
with their civilities. They won't let me be alone. Clergy come in on visits from the
country, and drag me back with them when they return. I am constrained to view this
England as more pleasant even than the old, and cannot help but exclaim: "O happy
country, that sustains neither flies, nor crocodiles, nor informers!" About the end of this
week we shall certainly go on board the ship, having to pay our passage a second time.
No Carolinian had made provisions for the journey, and here too "everything has its
price". I take it very badly to be compelled to purchase this delay, and then to pay a
great price for my departure. But this is on my own account; wherefore I impose on you
a perpetual silence.

'My illness, once put to flight by this most health-giving air, has again returned. All
my friends urge me to see a physician, but "I cannot afford so expensive a funeral." '

[3] Orig., 'μαθείς'.

ἔμβαλε. Πιστεύω σε οὔπω καταχ⟨...⟩θαι ταύτῃ τῇ πεποιθήσει μου.¹ [[I am *amazed* you yourself did not propose b⟨eginning⟩ shorthand before our parting, when you know 'tis our only way of conversing, *like* the (*nibbles*)² of the two friends, and when *poor Charles Delamotte* does it *for this* very *reason*. Should I finish my course before I reach England, perhaps your natural affection for me, added to your inclination for knowing the particulars of a strangely miserable life, may determine you—when I shall be no longer interested in wishing it. Your intercourse with me would be then cut off, but for your own sake I desire it now, and assure you, you are much concerned in knowing my history. The colour of your following life depends upon it: your going to the heathen, or continuance in Georgia, or return to England.

[[I have just heard what is enough to make me run mad. The officers appointed by the Judge of the Admiralty to examine]] Indivine's [[ship, have declared by oath that 'she might have proceeded on the voyage, and there was no necessity of putting in here.'–So that next we go on board with Captain]] Corney. [[I expect a constant account both of Oglethorpe's proceedings and yours. My namesake will transcribe your journal, as everything else, in shorthand. Send me that part of your journal which you supplied in Charleston, a conversation had, I think, with Oglethorpe.]]

Μηδενὶ πίστευε εἰ μὴ Χριστιανῷ.³ [[I have been so befouled, abused, and discredited that I can hardly believe, or expect to be believed by, anyone. My love to my only two unw⟨avering⟩ friends in Georgia, Benjamin and Charles.⁴]]

Address: 'To The Revd. Mr Wesly in Sav[ann]a'   *End* by JW: 'C. Oct. 5. 1736', and (at left top of address panel) 'IV.'   *Source*: MA.

From Count Zinzendorf⁵

[Oct. 23, 1736]

Viro in Jesu Christo, amore mihi crucifixo
Perdilecto
Salutem dicit
Nicolaus Ludovicus Zinzendorfius
Fratrum Moravorum minister.

¹ The defective Greek may be roughly translated thus: 'These things I write to thee alone—proclaimed to the ages. I would by no means allow [journeymen (?)] to [use (?)] it. Either you yourself must learn to read shorthand, or when I am [dead (?)] throw it in the fire. I trust that you [will] never [misuse] this confidence of mine.'
² The exact transcription of Wesley's shorthand (if correctly written—and he does make errors) seems to be 'needles', but allowing for two minor errors it might be 'nibbles', which in an obsolete sense might be a means of communication, 'to fidget or play with the fingers' (*O.E.D.*).
³ 'Trust no one if not a Christian.'
⁴ i.e. Ingham and Delamotte.
⁵ Replying to Wesley's overture of Mar. 15, 1736.

Perjucundae mihi fuerunt literae tuae, venerabilis Westley. Itane ad gentes abis remotissimas et Christi ignaras? Itane relicta patria amoenissima, cultissima, moratissima barbaros adis, anthropophagos maledictioni cuidam quasi obnoxios? Vale sis Angliae, salve Georgiae et incultas fove terras, iam labora, felicissimas
5 aliquando relinque. Ignotum ferme amas me, mihimet ipsi parumper clarum, quid aliis? Amo te, immo veneror ex Spangenbergii olim, ex Davidis Nitschmanni, ex tua nunc ipsius relatione. Benedictus sis Domino Deo nostro per Benedictum. Aliquam TIBI mei rationem reddam, antequam in via pergamus ambo, indulgens anime, Deo chare. Accipe hic adiectam cum epistola ad Tomo
10 Chichi, regem nobis vicinum, quam lingua ipsi familiari vestitam, ad manus, si fieri potest, porriges.

Dicam Deo meo, Christo cum Patre et Spiritu, Vero Deo, dicam Homini, misellorum animum probe intelligenti, experto, in pectore quondam gerenti, dicam cordicitus, einen Heldenmuth, gib dem Westley ein, durch dein Blut
15 allein. Bene nunc habe, amice nove, cum Ecclesia J.C. mea et Hernhuthanae, sorore intima, res omnes Jesu feliciter age et prima occasione ad quaestiunculas responde familiariter, animo simplici, non enim sunt ad theologorum morem examinis factae, sed apum.

I. An Immanuelem, Messiam Eundem, omni modo cogitabili, cum Patre
20 credis et Spiritu: (1), ad ductum baptismi in nomine Patris, Filii, et Spiritus Sancti, sine discrimine nuncupati; (2), ad probatissimum illud Trinitatis vestigium: Faciamus hominem in effigie nostrum? Homo divinus spiritum habet integrum, habet animam et corpus. Homo mortuus non nisi animam viventem in corpore, quod post animae evasionem cadaver audit, et tamen homines non
25 sunt. Homo divinus corde gaudens, vita et machina, sed homo unus, ineffabilis res, tamen vera. Argumenta non probationis loco adiecta, sed illustrationis, ut mens mea eo clarior evadat.

II. An Messiam, Jesum, ex virgine natum (vere eundem ipsum Immanuelem, sed κενοῦντα ἑαυτόν) hominem credis purem putum ab infantia usque ad resur-
30 rectionem; adeo hominem, ut finiat imperare, 1 Cor. 15, sicut incepit in utero matris obtemperare, Ebr. 2, et reddat regnum Patri, quod accepit, ad dextram scandendo; adeo hominem ut spiritu, anima, et corpore homines Dei reliquos praeeat, non excedat? Passiones ipsius veras fuisse in spiritu, anima, et corpore, obsequium eius Adami restitutioni vergens, iisdem tentationibus fuisse obnoxium,
35 et deficiendi omnes omnimode adfuisse possibilitates, illas, queis constrictus cedidit primus parens? Attamen hunc ipsum Jesum, hominem, cum per omnes aetates profectuum, miseriarum, dolorum, luctuum, et victoriarum, requiei et gloriae grassatus fuerit circulos, et ultimum deitatis humanae attigerit culmen (usque quo reliquos fratrum extollere et poterat et voluerat) atque adeo humanis
40 exemtus rebus, regnum Patri tradiderit, et ita Deitas sola regnum repetierit, non cessaturum; sed Verbum carne exutum per aeternitates aeternitatum sine fine mansurum Deum, cum Patre et Spiritu essentialiter inseparabilem, nisi Deitas moriatur, quod cogitatu horrendum, factu impossibile. Aeterna hic Deitas Jesu Christi scopus est, cum Patris et Spiritus Dei unitate perfecte eadem;
45 reliqua cum modum attingant non presse teneo, cum modalitas rerum divinarum, aeternarum immense nos fugiat, et ultra probabilitatem, quae clare exscriptis non prostant, extendi posse dubitem.

III. Sanguis Jesu Christi in Passione effusus, lytrum est recuperationis humanae vitae, in eodem sensu, quo mille thaleri lytrum esse possunt Algerensis captivi, mortis poenam laturi, et cum longe distem a curiosa inquisitione huius mysterii, mysterium ipsum penitus adoro.

IV. Sacramentum sive mysterium communionis Christianorum corpus et sanguinem Christi, crucis non gloriae obiecta, incomprehensibiliter sed vere 5 manducanda, et cum spiritus, animae, et corporis essentia miscenda porrigit; apud irregenitos nullum est, sed illos tamen ob audaciam judicio reddit obnoxios, cum, quid rei subsit, cognoverint; cum ignoraverint, reliquum ignorantiae vel culpae gradum non excedit. Regenitos et fratres illa Paulli manet comminatio I Cor. II, quapropter fideles ad sacram synaxim omnes admittere incivile est; 10 illos tantum admittendos credo, qui et in genere Christi bella gerunt improbe, et in specie communionis tempore, sive distractionem sive aliam certaminis sacri intermissionem passi sunt nullam; sin minus arcendi sunt, ne illotis mysterium manibus arripiant: moestos[1] lugentes, pusillanimes his non adscribo, sed cura et judicio pastorum relinquo. 15

V. Baptismus eodem, quo circumcisio, jure ad infantes pertinet. Aetate profectiores fidem quam credimus, amplexi sint opus est antequam, vel abluantur, vel immergantur, fidem dantes cruci et morti J.C. aeternum non intermissuram.

VI. Sententiarum et doctrinarum in unum compilatio religionem facit sive 20 civitatem religiosam; cordium in Jesum coalitio, ecclesiam. Ecclesia est triplex: *spiritualis*, invisibilis, ubi idem sentitur; *animalis*, ubi idem et sentitur et statuitur, haec partim visibilis, partim invisibilis; *corporalis*, ubi idem et sentitur et creditur et videtur, haec est visibilis et exigua.

Ministri Domini in republica religiosa praecones sunt, in *invisibili* vel apostoli, 25 vel evangelistae, in mixta *animali et rationali* doctores; in *corporali* seu locali et visibili membra, pro viribus et χαρισμάσι collocanda. Ecclesia Reformata religio est; ad invisibilem in omni terrarum orbe properant animi, mixta est, quae vel Presbyterio, vel episcopatui, vel alii favet ritui, visibilis est, e.g. coetus in Georgia fratrum. 30

d[atae]: 23 Oct. 1736[2]

---

[1] Orig., 'moesti'.

[2] The following is a rough translation of what Professor Newton considers far poorer Latin than Wesley's:

To a man esteemed in Jesus Christ, crucified in love for me, Nicholas Ludwig Zinzendorf, Minister of the Moravian Brethren, sends greetings.

Your letter, venerable Wesley, was very pleasing to me. So you go to the most remote nations, who know not Christ; so, having abandoned your most pleasant homeland, so refined, so moral, you approach the heathen, those cannibals who are as it were subject to some curse. Say goodbye, if you will, to England and welcome to Georgia; cherish the uncultivated fields, work now in them, leaving behind the richest. You love me dearly, though unknown; me who am but known for a little while to my own self—how to others? I love you, nay rather I honour you, first because of the account given by Spangenberg and David Nitschmann, and now by you yourself. May you be blessed by our Lord God through the Blessed One. I will give you some account of myself before we both continue on our journey, dear soul, precious to God. Please accept it added along with the letter to Tomo Chichi, the neighbouring king to us. If possible, share its contents with him in a tongue familiar to him.

Let me say to my God, to Christ, with the Father and the Spirit, let me say to the

Source: Herrnhut. The Moravian Archives at Herrnhut possess this document in three forms: (1), an incomplete draft in the hand of Zinzendorf; (2) a copy

Man, to the wise Man who fathoms the soul of the unfortunates, and once bore it in his breast, let me say from the heart: Inspire in Wesley a heroic spirit, through thy blood alone. May you think well, my new friend, of my Church of Jesus Christ and of its dear sister the church at Herrnhut. Consider all things favourably in Jesus, and answer these little questions as soon as possible, in a friendly manner, in a frank spirit; for they are not prepared in the manner of a swarm of theologians, but of a swarm of bees.

I. Whether you believe Immanuel, the Messiah, to be the same in every conceivable way as the Father and the Spirit: (1) for the administration of baptism in the name of the Father, of the Son, and of the Holy Spirit, without a distinction as to who is named; (2) for that most established trace of the Trinity, 'Let us make man in *our* image'? The divine man, to be sure, has a whole spirit, he has soul and flesh. A man who is dead has only a soul divine in the body which after the departure of the soul is called a corpse— and yet they are not men. The divine man, rejoicing in a heart, life, and bodily frame, is a simple man—an unutterable thing, yet true. Arguments, not proving, but illustrating this, are here added, so that my mind, being clearer, may deal with it.

[One of several footnotes added to the MS appears at this point: 'The arguments he omits, and errs in the peculiar individual concept.']

II. Whether you believe the Messiah [to be] Jesus, born of a virgin (truly himself the very Immanuel, but emptying himself), to be a perfectly pure man, from infancy to resurrection; so much a man that he should put an end to all authority, 1 Cor. 15[: 24], just as in his mother's womb he began to be obedient, Heb. 2[: 14–18], and should give back the kingdom to the Father, which he received on ascending to his right hand; so much a man that in spirit, soul, and body, he might be first among the remaining men of God, not that he might transcend them absolutely? [Do you believe] that there were true passions in his spirit, soul, and body, his obedience tending toward the restitution of Adam; that he was liable to the same temptations, and that all sorts of possibilities of failing were open to him, those by which the first parent was overcome and fell? And yet [do you believe] that this same Jesus, as a man, in all his different ages, traversed the orbits of the successes, miseries, afflictions, sorrows, and victories, rest, and glory, and reached the highest summit of human deity (to the end that he thus both could and would lift up the rest of his brethren); and so much exempt from human things [that] he delivered up the kingdom to the Father, and so deity alone reclaimed the kingdom, a kingdom that shall have no end; but that the Word, stripped of the flesh, will remain as God throughout all eternity, essentially inseparable from the Father and the Spirit, unless God were to die—which is dreadful to contemplate, and in fact impossible? Here the essential point is the eternal deity of Jesus Christ; in every way the same with the unity of the Father and the Spirit. I do not hold other matters so firmly, when they approach the outer limits [of our knowledge], since the modality of divine and eternal things far exceeds our grasp, and I doubt that the things which are not clear from Scripture can be extended beyond probability.

III. The blood of Jesus Christ, poured out in his Passion, is the sacrificial offering for the restoration of human life in the same sense in which a thousand thalers might be the ransom for an Algerian captive under sentence of death; and I am so far from entering any idle investigation into this mystery that inwardly I reverence the very mystery itself.

IV. The sacrament, or the mystery of the communion of Christians, offers the body and blood of Christ, the objects not of glory but of the cross, to be eaten incomprehensibly, yet truly, and to be mixed with the essence of spirit, soul, and body. It is of no effect among the unregenerate, it makes them subject to judgment for their boldness, since they knew the underlying reality; even though they might be ignorant, what

by an unknown amanuensis, seemingly closer to the original, and including the Greek; (3) a copy by another amanuensis, with the Greek transliterated, the introduction of normal scribal abbreviations, and the addition at the end of 'descript.', which apparently implies 'descriptio', or transcript. Here (2) is reproduced, without noting the variants introduced both by Zinzendorf and his amanuenses. For both checking the Latin manuscripts and for immeasurably improving my translation of the text I am greatly indebted to Professor Francis Newton.

From the Revd. Charles Wesley

[Oct. 15–25, 1736]
Friday   Boston

Dear brother

If I ever see England, it will be by that time this reaches you.—My poor friend here has not yet convinced me of your hypocrisy, but I take for granted   5
you have still a disinterested concern for my happiness. I should be glad for your sake to give a satisfactory account of myself, but that you must never expect from me. They have dragged me at last to a physician, whose prescriptions I have followed hitherto without effect; but he cannot answer for their success unless I could stay a few days on shore, which is impracticable.—'Tis fine talking while   10
we have youth and health on our side, but sickness would spoil your marooning

ignorance or guilt remained in them did not go beyond a certain degree; and that warning of Paul's in 1 Cor. 11[: 29] applies to the regenerate and brethren, wherefore it is unreasonable to admit all the faithful to the holy gathering. I believe that those only should be admitted who are generally indomitable soldiers of Christ, and who specifically on that occasion of communion are neither distracted nor interrupted in their holy struggle; otherwise they are to be held back, lest they lay hold of the mystery with unclean hands. I do not include among them the afflicted, the mourners, the faint-hearted, but leave these to the care and judgment of their pastors.

V. Baptism pertains to infants, by that same law as did circumcision. Those more advanced in years must have embraced the faith which we believe before they may be either sprinkled or immersed, making a pledge that will never be revoked to the cross and death of Jesus Christ.

VI. The gathering together of judgments and doctrines into one compilation makes religion or the religious community; the gathering of hearts in Jesus Christ makes the Church. The Church is threefold: *spiritual* and invisible, where the same thing is felt; *animate*, where the same thing is felt and determined—and this is partly visible, partly invisible; *corporeal*, where the same thing is both felt and believed and seen—this is visible and narrowly limited. The ministers of the Lord in the religious commonwealth are heralds; in the invisible commonwealth they are either apostles or evangelists; in the mixed animate and reasoning commonwealth they are called doctors; in the corporeal or local and visible commonwealth they are called members, to be placed according to their strength and spiritual gifts. The Reformed Church is a religion. The invisible church is that to which in every region of the earth souls hasten; but the mixed is that which prefers either the Presbyterian form or the Episcopalian form or some other form; the visible one is like the assembly of the [Moravian] brethren in Georgia.

Oct. 23, 1736

as well as mine. I am now glad of a warm bed; but must quickly betake myself to my board again וְגַם זֹת לְטוֹבָה.[1]

Though I am apt to believe I shall at length arrive in E[ngland] to deliver what I am entrusted with, yet do I not expect or wish for a long life. How strong
5 must that principle of self-preservation be which can make such a wretch as me willing to live at all!—Or rather, unwilling to die; for I know no greater pleasure in life than in considering it cannot last for ever!

> The temptations past
> No more shall vex me; every grief I feel
10 Shortens the destined number; every pulse
> Beats a sharp moment of the pain away,
> And the last stroke will come. By swift degrees
> Time sweeps me off, and I shall soon arrive
> At life's sweet period: O celestial point
15 That ends this mortal story!

Today completes my three weeks' unnecessary stay at Boston. Tomorrow the ship falls down. I am just now much worse than ever, but nothing less than death shall hinder my embarking. Mr. O[glethorpe], I know, will gladly excuse my writing. I should write to my two other Georgia friends, would pain permit.
20 Don't forget poor Laserre.

Oct. 18. A blast attends all that belongs to me. The ship that carries *me must* meet with endless delays. 'Tis well if it sails this week.—I have lived so long in honours and indulgences that I have almost forgot whereunto I am called, being strongly urged to set up my rest here. But I will lean no longer upon men.
25 When I again put myself in the power of any of my own merciless species, by either expecting their kindness or desiring their esteem—Ἀνελθέτω![2] Φρεδερείκη

I must mention an unhappy man to you, Mr. John Chechley, and *valeat quantu valere potest*.[3] By the strictest inquiry of friends and enemies I find he has been throughout his life persecuted, only not to death, by the spirit of presby-
30 tery. It has reduced him and his family to the last extremity. He has excellent natural parts, much solid learning, and true primitive piety; is acquainted with the power, and therefore holds fast the form, of godliness. Obstinate as was my father in good, and like him, not to be borne down by evil: κάλος στρατιώτης; ἄοκνος θεοδρόμος; ἄκμων τυπτόμενος.[4] Mr. O[glethorpe] himself does not bet-
35 ter understand nor is more beloved by the Indians than he. He is activity itself, made for *abstinence* and hardships. But for his family he had *taken a walk* ere now to see Mr. O. He has studied America as much as most men in it. I carry recommendations of him to the Bishop of London, who was formerly frightened by his pretended Jacobitism from admitting him into Holy Orders, to which he has
40 for above these twenty years devoted himself.—He understands surveying and fortification, on which and a thousand other accounts I thought he might be of great use in Georgia, but could not venture proposing it him without first obtaining Mr. O's directions.—Should I die in the passage, you are at liberty to

---

[1] 'This also is for the best.'
[2] 'Let Frederica come up!' i.e. as a warning.
[3] 'Let him pass for what he's worth.'
[4] 'a good soldier' (2 Tim. 2: 3); 'a resolute messenger of God'; 'a beaten anvil'.

give him anything that was mine. My sole heir and executor at Tiverton, I am sure, will consent to it.

Appy, like an errant gentleman as he is, has drawn me into monstrous expenses for ship stores, etc. So that what with my three weeks' stay at Charleston, my month's stay here, and my double passage, from courtier I am turned philoso- 5 pher. But this I absolutely forbid your mentioning to Mr;—except in the above case of my death.—Then add to the burden my 'life laid down in his service', and let him judge on whose side is the balance!

Oct. 21. I am worried on all sides by my friends' solicitations to defer my winter's voyage till I have recovered a little strength. So far I agree with them 10 and the physicians, that to go in my condition is running upon certain death. If my pains have any intermission, the walking up or down stairs, or the speaking three sentences, brings them back again. Mr.——, I am apt to think, would allow me to wait a fortnight for the next ship, but then if I recover my stay will be thought unnecessary. I *must die* to prove myself sick; and I can do no more at sea. 15 I am therefore determined to be carried on board tomorrow morning, and leave the event to God.

Oct. 25. The ship fell down as was expected, but Providence sent a contrary wind that hindered my following till now. Since the 21st I have tried the virtue of vomits, purges, bleeding, and opiates. I am at present something better, on 20 board the Hannah, Captain Corney, in the stateroom, which they have forced upon me. I have not strength for more. Adieu!

Address: 'To The Revd. Mr Wesley at Savannah in Georgia'   *End* by JW: 'C. Oct. 25. 1736', and on address panel, 'Boston, Oct. 21, &c'   *Source*: MA.

To Harman Verelst[1]

[Nov. 10, 1736]

Sir

I return you thanks for your favour. The good I have found here 25 has indeed been beyond my expectation. The contrary behaviour of many was no more than I looked for, being convinced several years before I left England that in every city or country under heaven the majority of the people are not the wisest or the best part. But we have an advantage here which is not frequent in other places, that 30 is, a magistracy not only regular in their own conduct, but desirous

---

[1] Harman Verelst was appointed accomptant or treasurer to the Georgia Office at the fifth meeting of the Trustees, Aug. 5, 1732. He also served as secretary of Dr. Bray's Associates, in which capacity mainly he sent books to Wesley. His work in both offices was at first voluntary, for he also held a position at the Custom House, but from 1736 he received (like Martyn, the Secretary) £150 a year (see Trevor R. Reese, *Georgia Historical Quarterly*, XXXIX. 348-52).

and watchful to suppress, as far as in them lies, whatever is openly ill in the conduct of others.

I am obliged to you for the hint you give as [to] the regulating that too-prevailing neglect in the case of administering public oaths. Without doubt it should be done with all possible solemnity. For surely no hurry of business can excuse any want of reverence towards the God to whom all our business should be consecrated, since it is for his sake that we ought to undertake everything, as well as to perform everything as in his sight. I am, dear sir, your most humble servant,

10 Nov. 1736   John Wesley
Savannah

Pray when you send me any books, send a letter of advice. I have received no books from you since I came hither.

Address: 'To Mr Verelst At the Georgia Office'   *Source*: P.R.O., CO5/639/330–1, apparently the same as that listed in Wesley's diary as written Nov. 11.

To the Earl of Egmont[1]

[Nov. 12, 1736]

My Lord

I return your lordship thanks for the account of Carolina which you favoured me with some time since. I looked it over soon after I received it. Many things are true in it, and many false. I am not at present likely to have much acquaintance with that province, more than what depends upon the relations of others. But if I have sufficient evidence of anything worth notice concerning it, I shall not fail to set it down, as your lordship desires.

Savannah is already much too large for my care. I wish we had fewer men, so we had more Christians, in it. And yet there are more who desire and endeavour to be Christians than I ever found in any town of the same size in England. May the good God, who hath so wonderfully prospered your undertakings hitherto, give to you and

[1] John Perceval or Percival (1683–1748), a vigorous supporter of Oglethorpe's project from the outset, appointed the first President of the Trustees. His diary, journal, and other voluminous papers furnish a rich source of information about the venture. He was created Earl of Egmont in 1733.

all who join with you in this glorious work a constant care to advance
(whatever else be advanced or hindered) the knowledge and love of
him and of his Christ! I am, my lord, your lordship's most obedient
servant,

John Wesley 5

Savannah
Novr. 12, 1736

Source: Egmont Papers, Vol. 14202, p. 217, a contemporary copy. Cf. Egmont
Diary, II. 333 (Jan. 22, 1737): 'I passed the evening at home, and received a
letter from Mr. John Wesley, our minister at Savannah, acknowledging the
receipt of my collection of tracts concerning Georgia, and acquainting me that
the people of Savannah are too numerous for his care, that he could wish they
were better Christians, though for their number he finds more willing and
desirous to be good than in any other town he knows of.' Wesley's diary, Nov.
12, 'Writ to L[ord] Perciv[a]l'.

To the Revd. Samuel Wesley, Jun.

Savannah, Nov. 23d, 1736

'Οι Θεοῦ μεμνημένοι, καὶ τῆς ἐπισκοπῆς, καὶ παντὸς ἔργου ἀγαθοῦ
μνησθήσονται.¹   10
O pray write (and if it may be) speak, that they may remember him
again, who did run well, but are now hindered.²
I think the rock on which I had the nearest made shipwreck of
the faith was in the writings of the mystics, under which term I
comprehend all, and only those, who slight any of the means of 15
grace.
I have drawn up a short scheme of their doctrines, partly from
conversations I have had, and letters, and partly from their most
approved writers, such as Tauler,³ Molinos,⁴ and the author of

¹ 'Those who remember God will remember both spiritual oversight and all good
works.' This may be a quotation from one of the Fathers, but no source has been traced.
² See Gal. 5: 7.
³ Johann Tauler (*c.* 1300–61), German Dominican mystic, a favourite of Luther.
Wesley read his *Life* on Mar. 4, 1736 (see diary).
⁴ Miguel de Molinos (*c.* 1640–97), Spanish mystic, whose *Spiritual Guide*, urging
Christians to absolute quiescence in order to enjoy God, brought him to death at the
hands of the Inquisition. Wesley was acquainted with *The Spiritual Guide* in Feb., 1735
(probably recommended, as were others, by William Law), and published an abridgement of it in his *Christian Library*, Vol. 38 (1754).

Theologia Germanica.[1] I beg your thoughts upon it, as soon as you can conveniently; and that you would give me them as particularly, fully, and strongly as your time will permit. They may be of consequence not only to all this province but to nations of Christians
5 yet unborn.[2]

All means are not necessary for all men; therefore each person must use such means, and such only, as he finds necessary for him. But since we can never attain our end by being wedded to the same means, therefore we must not obstinately cleave unto anything, lest it become a hindrance, not a help.

10 Observe further, when the end is attained the means cease. Now all the other things enjoined are means to love; and love is attained by them who are in the inferior way, who are utterly divested of free will, of self-love, and self-activity, and are entered into the passive state. These deified men, in whom the superior will has extinguished the inferior, enjoy such a contemplation as is not only
15 above faith, but above sight, such as is entirely free from images, thoughts, and discourse, and never interrupted by sins of infirmity, or voluntary distractions. They have absolutely renounced their reason and understanding; else they could not be guided by a divine light. They seek no clear or particular knowledge of anything, but only an obscure general knowledge, which is far better. They
20 know it is mercenary to look for a reward from God, and inconcistent with perfect love.

Having thus attained the end, the means must cease. Hope is swallowed up in love. Sight, or something more than sight, takes [the] place of faith. All particular virtues they possess in the essence (being wholly given up to the
25 divine will), and therefore need not the distinct exercise of them. They work likewise all good works essentially, not accidentally, and use all outward means only as they are moved thereto, and then to obey superiors, or to avoid giving offence, but not as necessary or helpful to them.

Public prayer, or[3] any forms, they need not, for they pray without ceasing.[4]
30 Sensible[5] devotion in any prayer they despise, it being a great hindrance to perfection. The Scripture they need not read, for it is only his letter with whom they converse face to face. And if they do read it now and then, as for expounders living or dead, reason, philosophy (which only puffs up, and vainly tries to bind God by logical definitions and divisions), as for knowledge of tongues or
35 ancient customs, they need none of them, any more than the apostles did, for they have the same Spirit. Neither do they need the Lord's Supper (for they never cease to *remember* Christ in the most acceptable manner), any more than fasting, since by constant temperance they keep a continual fast.

[1] An anonymous German mystical treatise of the late fourteenth century, whose first printed edition (1518) was supervised by Luther. William Law gave Wesley a copy in 1732.
[2] Although various themes in this summary may be traced to Tauler's *Sermons*, the *Theologia Germanica*, and *The Spiritual Guide* of Molinos, there are no close quotations. Paragraphs 4, 5, and 7 seem to derive almost wholly from those mystics with whom Wesley had been in touch personally. Because he had already repudiated mysticism (see *Journal*, May 24, 1743, § 8) his approach is understandably negative and critical.
[3] Orig., 'on'.   [4] 1 Thess. 5: 17.   [5] i.e. 'which can be felt'.

You that are to advise them that have not yet attained perfection, press them to nothing, not to self-denial, constant private prayer, reading the Scriptures, fasting, communicating. If they love heathen poets, let them take their full swing in them. Speak but little to them (in the mean time) of eternity. If they are affected at any time with what you say, say no more; let them apply it, not you. 5 You may advise them to some religious books, but stop there; let them use them as they please, and form their own reflections upon them without your inter-meddling. If one who was religious falls off, let him alone. Either a man is converted to God, or not: if he is not, his own will must guide him, in spite of all you can do; if he is, he is so guided by the Spirit of God as not to need your 10 direction.

You that are yourselves imperfect, know love is your end. All things else are but means. Choose such means as lead you most to love; those alone are neces-sary for you. The means that others need are nothing to you. Different men are led in different ways. And be sure be not wedded to any means. When anything 15 helps you no longer, lay it aside. For you can never attain your end by cleaving obstinately to the same means. You must be changing them continually. Conver-sation, meditation, forms of prayer, prudential rules, fixed return of public or private prayer, are helps to some; but you must judge for yourself. Perhaps fasting may help you for a time, and perhaps the Holy Communion. But you 20 will be taught by the Holy Spirit, and by experience, how soon, how often, and how long, it is good for you to take it. Perhaps too you may need the Holy Scripture. But if you can renounce yourself without reading, it is better than all the reading in the world. And whenever you read it, trouble yourself about no helps: the Holy Ghost will lead you into all truth.[1] 25

As to doing good, take care of yourself first. When you are converted, then strengthen your brethren. Beware of (what is incident to all beginners) an eager desire to set others a good example. Beware of an earnestness to make others feel what you feel yourself. Let your light shine as nothing to you. Beware of a zeal to do great things for God. Be charitable first; then do works of charity: 30 do them when you are not dissipated thereby, or in danger of losing your soul by pride and vanity. Indeed, till then you can do no good to men's souls; and with-out that, all done to their bodies is nothing. The command of doing good con-cerns not you yet. Above all take care never to dispute about any of these points. Disputing can do no [good. Is a][2] man wicked? Cast not pearls before swine.[3] 35 Is he imperfect? He that disputes any advice is not yet ripe for it. Is he good? All good men agree in judgment, they differ only in words, which all are in their own nature ambiguous.

May God deliver you and yours from all error, and all unholiness. My prayers will never, I trust, be wanting for you. I am, dear 40 brother, my sister's and your most affectionate brother,

John Wesley

---

[1] See John 16: 13.

[2] Priestley's note preceding a blank space—which may have represented anything from a few words to a whole line—reads, 'The folding of this letter makes this illegible.'

[3] See Matt. 7: 6.

Pray remember me to Philly.[1]

Address: 'To Mr. Wesley, Tiverton'   *Source*: Priestley, pp. 58–63.

To Sophia Christiana Hopkey[2]

Feb. 6 [1737]

I find, Miss Sophy, I can't take fire into my bosom, and not be burnt.[3] I am therefore retiring for a while, to desire the direction of
5 God. Join with me, my friend, in fervent prayer that he would show me what is best to be done.

Source: MA, JW. MSS. III. 5, Account of Sophy Hopkey, § 43 (p. 25).

[1] Samuel Wesley's only child to survive, aged about 9 at this time, four other children having been buried at Westminster. Later she married an apothecary of Barnstaple named Earle.

[2] Sophia Christiana Hopkey, niece to Martha, wife of Thomas Causton, the store-keeper and chief magistrate of Savannah, had emigrated from England with her aunt in 1733 when the latter rejoined her husband, one of the pioneers of 1732. Although on coming out Wesley himself had 'determined to have no intimacy with any woman', and although at first he was put off by Sophy's somewhat affected ways, her piety coupled with her distress over an emotional entanglement with a rascal named Tom Mellichamp caused him to pay her special attention. In July, 1736, he kissed her—the first of many occasions, encouraged as he was by the matchmaking enthusiasm of the Caustons. In his manuscript journal for Nov. 1, 1736 (her eighteenth birthday) he made a flattering summary of her character: guileless and direct; having a calm spirit, yet 'active, diligent, indefatigable'; a gentlewoman with the toughness of a pioneer; neat and plain in dress; serious, adaptable, and extremely intelligent; teachable, meek, gentle, reticent; attuned and resigned to God's will. He realized that he was becoming infatua-ted; on Nov. 10 he told her of his resolve to break off the physical aspects of their relation-ship, innocent though they were. On Nov. 20 he broke his resolution, 'kissed her once or twice', 'resolved again, and relapsed again several times during the five or six weeks following'. For months he was on the brink of proposing marriage, and felt that on Feb. 3, 1737 he had 'a very narrow escape' when she said it was probably better for clergymen not to marry, and that she too was resolved 'never to marry'. The Moravian Johann Töltschig saw no harm in his marrying her. Benjamin Ingham suspected that she was a hypocrite adroitly angling for marriage, and advised Wesley to go to Irene to think it over among the Indians for a few days. This he did, first sending her this letter.
  As a result of this turning-point he tapered off his relationship with her, telling her on Feb. 14, 'I am resolved, Miss Sophy, if I marry at all, not to do it till I have been among the Indians.' She decided to reduce the frequency and intimacy of her visits to him, and on the 19th became 'sharp, fretful, and disputatious'. On Mar. 4 he agreed with Charles Delamotte that it might be God's will to settle the issue by lot. On three slips of paper he wrote, 'Marry', 'Think not of it this year', and on the third, 'Think of it no more'. Charles Delamotte drew the third, and happily Wesley exclaimed, 'Thy will be done!'

[3] See Prov. 6: 27.

[To Richard Morgan, Jun.][1]

[Savannah, Feb. 16, 1737]

Dear sir

Mr. Ingham has left Savannah for some months, and lives at a house built for him a few miles off, near the Indian town. So that I have now no fellow-labourer but Mr. Delamotte, who has taken 5 the charge of between thirty and forty children. There is therefore great need that God should put it into the hearts of some to come over to us and labour with us in his harvest. But I should not desire any to come unless on the same views and conditions with us: without any temporal wages other than food and raiment, the plain 10 conveniencies of life. And for one or more in whom was this mind there would be full employment in the Province, either in assisting Mr. Delamotte or me while we were present here, or in supplying our places when abroad, or in visiting the poor people in the smaller settlements as well as at Frederica, all of whom are as sheep 15 without a shepherd.[2]

By these labours of love might any that desired it be trained up for the harder task of preaching the gospel to the heathen. The difficulties he must then encounter God only knows; probably martyrdom would conclude them. But those we have hitherto met 20 with have been small, and only terrible at a distance. Persecution, you know, is the portion of every follower of Christ, wherever his lot is cast. But it has hitherto extended no farther than words with regard to us (unless in one or two inconsiderable instances). Yet 'tis sure every man ought, if he would come hither, be willing and 25

---

[1] Wesley's diary shows that on Feb. 15, 1737, he wrote 'to the rector (of Lincoln College, Euseby Isham), and on the 16th to 'Mr. Burton' (of Eton), 'Hutchings', and to 'Moⁿ', surely Richard Morgan, who had been registered at the Middle Temple on Mar. 28, 1734, but had returned to Lincoln College, to become the leader of the Oxford Methodists. (See his letter to Wesley, Sept. 25, 1735, and Wesley's reply of Sept. 30, pp. 433-4, 437-8 above.) On Sept. 3, 1736, James Hutton informed Charles Wesley, 'Mr. Morgan is obliged by his father's orders to study physic at Leyden; at that place the name of Wesley stinks as well as at Oxford', but by 1737 he had returned to Dublin, to assist his father, and in 1740 was called to the Bar. His final interlude at Oxford, therefore, could only have been brief. Thomas Jackson, followed by Telford, identified the recipient as John Hutchings of Pembroke College, but he was far less mature than Morgan, while Richard Hutchins, Fellow of Lincoln College, (quite apart from Wesley's spelling of the name) was unsympathetic, and a priest, as well as older than would seem appropriate from the tone of the letter.

[2] See Matt. 9: 36, etc.

ready to embrace (if God should see them good), the severer kinds of it. He ought to be determined, not only to leave parents, sisters, friends, houses, and lands,[1] for his Master's sake, but to take up his cross,[2] too; cheerfully submit to the fatigue and danger of (it may 5 be) a long voyage, and patiently to endure the continual contradiction of sinners,[3] and all the inconveniencies which it often occasions.

Would anyone have a trial of himself, how he can bear this? If he has felt what reproach is, and can bear that for but a few weeks as he ought, I shall believe he need fear nothing. Other trials will after- 10 wards be no heavier than that little one was at first. So that he may then have a well-grounded hope that he will be enabled to do all things through Christ strengthening him.[4]

May the God of peace[5] himself direct you to all things conducive to his glory, whether it be by fitter instruments, or even by your 15 friend and servant in Christ,

John Wesley

Address: 'To Mr. —— in L[incol]n C[ollege], Oxon'   *Source*: *Gent. Mag.*, VII. 575 (Sept., 1737), headed, 'Extract of a letter from the Rev. Mr. Wesley, dated at Savanna[h], in Georgia, Feb. 16, 1736/7.'

To James Edward Oglethorpe[6]

[Savannah, Feb. 24, 1737]

Sir

You apprehended strong opposition before you went hence; and 20 unless we are misinformed, you have found it. Yesterday morning I read a letter from London wherein it was asserted that Sir Robert

---

[1] See Matt. 19: 29.   [2] Matt. 16: 24, etc.   [3] Heb. 12: 3.
[4] See Phil. 4: 13.   [5] See Rom. 15: 33, etc.
[6] Oglethorpe had sailed for England on Nov. 23, 1736, and arrived in London on Jan. 6, being warmly thanked by the Trustees for his report before their Council on Jan. 12. On Feb. 6 he had a stormy private session with Sir Robert Walpole, when the Prime Minister complained that the Trustees were at odds with each other and with the Government, and Georgia a failure, while Oglethorpe urged that Walpole himself must decide whether he was ready to ensure the colony's success by putting more money into its settlement, and especially into its defence against the Spaniards. He claimed 'that this colony was a national affair, and he did not pretend to be a Don Quixote for it' (Egmont *Journal*, pp. 223, 225, 231–3). Oglethorpe made his point strongly, but much more 'warm discourse' with Sir Robert, and many months of political bickering, were still needed to establish the national importance of Georgia.

had turned against you; that the Parliament was resolved to make a severe scrutiny into all that has been transacted here; that the cry of the nation ran the same way; and that even the Trustees were so far from acknowledging the service that you have done that they had protested your bills, and charged you with misapplying the 5 monies you had received, and with gross mismanagement of the power wherewith you was entrusted.

Whether these things are so or no, I know not; for it is ill depending on a single evidence. But this I know, that if your scheme was drawn (which I shall not easily believe) from that first-born of hell, 10 Nicholas Machiavel,[1] as sure as there is a God that governs the earth, he will confound both it and you. If on the contrary (as I shall hope, till strong proof appear) your heart was right before God,[2] that it was your real design to promote the glory of God, by promoting peace and love among men; let not your heart be troubled;[3] the 15 God whom you serve is able to deliver you.[4] Perhaps in some things you have shown you are but a man; perhaps I myself may have a little to complain of; but Oh! what a train of benefits have I received to lay in the balance against it! I bless God that you was born. I acknowledge his exceeding mercy in casting me into your hands. I 20 own your generous kindness all the time we were at sea. I am indebted to you for a thousand favours here. Why then, the least I can say is, Though all men should revile you, yet, if God shall strengthen me, will not I.[5] Yea, were it not for the poor creatures whom you have as yet but half redeemed from their complicated misery, I 25 could almost wish that you were forsaken of all, that you might clearly see the difference between men of honour and those who are in the very lowest rank, the followers of Christ Jesus.

O where is the God of Elijah?[6] Stir up thy strength, and come and help him![7] If the desire of his heart be to thy name,[8] let all his 30 enemies flee before him![9] Art thou not he who hast made him a father to the fatherless,[10] a mighty deliverer to the oppressed! Hast thou not given him to be feet to the lame, hands to the helpless,

---

[1] Niccolo Machiavelli (1469–1527), whose works (especially *The Prince*) he had read on the boat from Frederica less than a month earlier, commenting that 'should a prince form himself by this book, so calmly recommending hypocrisy, treachery, lying, robbery, oppression, adultery, whoredom, and murder of all kinds, Domitian or Nero would be an angel of light compared to that man' (JWJ, Jan. 26).

[2] See Ps. 78: 37. [3] John 14: 1, 27. [4] See Dan. 3: 17.
[5] See Mark 14: 29. [6] See 2 Kgs. 10: 15.
[7] See Ps. 80: 2 (B.C.P.). [8] See Isa. 26: 8.
[9] See Ps. 68: 1. [10] Ps. 68: 5.

eyes to the blind![1] Hath he ever withheld his bread from the hungry,[2] or hid his soul from his own flesh?[3] Then, whatever thou withholdest from him, O thou Lover of men, satisfy his soul with thy likeness; renew his heart in the whole image of thy Christ;[4] purge his spirit

5 from self-will, pride, vanity, and fill it with faith and love, gentleness and long-suffering. Let no guile ever be found in his mouth,[5] no injustice in his hands![6] And among all your labours of love[7] it becomes me earnestly to entreat him, that he will not forget those you have gone through for, sir, your obliged and obedient servant,

10   John Wesley

Source: Whitehead, II. 25–7, date confirmed by Wesley's diary.

To Dr. Bray's Associates[8]

[Savannah, Feb. 26, 1737]

. . . Our general method is this. A young gentleman who came with me[9] teaches between thirty and forty children to read, write, and cast accounts. Before school in the morning, and after school in

15 the afternoon, he catechizes the lowest class, and endeavours to fix something of what was said in their understandings as well as their

---

[1] See Job 29: 15.   [2] See Job 22: 7.   [3] See Isa. 58: 7.
[4] See Col. 3: 10.   [5] See 1 Pet. 2: 22; Rev. 14: 5.
[6] See Job 16: 17.   [7] 1 Thess. 1: 3.

[8] Thomas Bray (1656–1730), educated at Oxford (D.D., 1666), through an involvement in overseas missions was directed to the need of impoverished clergy (from whose ranks most missionaries came) for books. In 1701 he founded the S.P.G., and his own special auxiliary labours in sponsoring parochial libraries both in England and America were perpetuated by the formation in 1723 of 'Dr. Bray's Associates for founding clerical libraries and supporting negro schools'. Both the Earl of Egmont and James Oglethorpe were among the Associates, whose books Wesley had been using for some months (e.g. several of Dr. Bray's own writings, read Nov. 20–6, 1736), and to whom he had already written on Feb. 15, 1737. The first part of this letter probably referred to the Savannah library, and the reason for the extract here given he explains in his preamble.

[9] Charles Delamotte (*c.* 1715–96), son of Thomas Delamotte, sugar merchant of Blendon Hall, Bexley, who apparently came out to Georgia as his father's business agent, but speedily teamed up with the Wesleys and Ingham, served as schoolmaster without remuneration, and also assisted Wesley in various pastoral duties. After the original three ministers had all left, Delamotte continued to maintain Wesley's gatherings for spiritual fellowship until Whitefield's arrival, though in June, 1738, he also returned to England, to manage a branch of the Delamotte sugarboiling business in Hull. Cf. Wesley's letter of Aug. 26 (?), 1736, 'Only Mr. Delamotte is with me' (p. 471 n. above), and Delamotte's letter to Wesley, Feb. 23, 1738 (pp. 529–31 below).

memories. In the evening he instructs the larger children. On Saturday, in the afternoon, I catechize them all. The same I do on Sunday before the evening service. And in the church, immediately after the Second Lesson, a select number of them having repeated the Catechism and been examined in some part of it, I endeavour ₅ to explain at large and to enforce that part, both on them and the congregation.

Some time after the evening service as many of my parishioners as desire it meet at my house (as they do also on Wednesday evening) and spend about an hour in prayer, singing, and mutual exhortation. ₁₀ A smaller number (mostly those who design to communicate the next day) meet here on Saturday evening; and a few of these come to me on the other evenings, and pass half an hour in the same employment.

Source: JWJ, Feb. 26, 1737, introduced thus: 'By Mr. Ingham [who was leaving for England to secure more recruits for Georgia] I writ to Dr. Bray's Associates, who had sent a parochial library to Savannah. It is expected of the ministers who receive these to send an account to their benefactors of the method they use in catechizing the children and instructing the youth of their respective parishes.'

From Henry Newman

London, 2 March, 1736/7 ₁₅

Revd. sir

I received your letter of the 7th of September last by Mr. Von Reck, who with his brother arrived here in December, and after a short indisposition, having recovered their health, returned to their friends in Germany in January.

The Society desire your acceptance of a small packet sent in the Missionaries ₂₀ Parcel B G No. 4 by this ship.[1] I shall be glad to hear of any success you and Mr. Ingham have in your conferences with the Indians, and to understand that they are more tractable to instruction in Christianity than they used to be in New England. Mr. Oglethorpe is well, and will I hope be able to see you again this summer, to perfect [the] establishment he has taken so much pains to encourage. ₂₅

I have not yet seen your brother since his return, though I should be glad of it, which I attribute to the death of your and his good friend, Sir John Philipps, the beginning of January last,[2] and presume he has never been this way since.

[1] 'B G No. 4' will surely mean the fourth parcel to the Salzburgers Bolzius and Gronau.

[2] Sir John died Jan. 5, 1737, aged 76, and was succeeded by his son, Sir Erasmus Philipps (*c.* 1700–43).

Mr. Quincy is in the country, somewhere in Suffolk, and I hear enjoys his health much better than he did in Georgia.

May you never want it, for the good use you make of it, is the wish of the Society as well as, revd. sir, yours,

5   H. N[ewman]

Address: 'To the Revd. Mr. John Wesley at Savannah in Georgia'   *Source*: S.P.C.K., Misc. Letters, CN2/3, pp. 18–19, a draft.

To the Georgia Trustees[1]

[March 4, 1737]

Gentlemen

When the account of the mission expenses, commencing March 1, 1736, and brought down to the end of November, was delivered
10 to me, I was much surprised to find it amount to (in Carolina currency)[2]   666 – 17 – 00½
which reduced to sterling is   090 – 02 – 04.
A day or two since I received a second account, brought down to March 1, 1737, which being added to the former the total expense of
15 the year was   Currency   726 – 07 – 03½
                                        Sterling   098 – 08 – 01½.
But upon reading over both I observed, as you will be pleased to do: (1), that of the sum above-mentioned 191 – 19 – 06½ was paid

---

[1] Wesley's subsistence as a missionary came from the S.P.G. via the Georgia Trustees, and he was naturally disturbed to note that the official accounts for his first year's work apparently showed a financial deficit, and especially that a warning had been issued against overspending in the future. He wrote a careful analysis of the accounts, showing that in fact he had lived well within his expected income, and reacted somewhat stiffly against the supposed warning. When the Trustees received this letter, on June 15, 1737, the Minutes recorded: 'All present were surprised at this, and we ordered Mr. Martyn our Secretary to write this very night to him, that we knew of no one body [who] had accused him of doing anything amiss, and therefore that he should acquaint the Trustees who he had such intelligence from.' (Egmont *Journal*, pp. 283–4). It seems possible that Thomas Causton may have misinterpreted some communication from the Trustees, and exceeded his duty in passing on this misinterpretation. Martyn did write a reassuring letter that night, as did the Revd. John Burton, who was present at the Council—see their letters below.

[2] On July 24, 1735, the Trustees had issued 4,000 £1 sola bills of exchange, though these were not popular with South Carolina merchants, so that the rate went to £8 (sola) for £1 sterling. Wesley reckons in the more easily negotiable South Carolina currency, which in 1734 was £6.40 for £1 sterling, but by this time had crept higher still. (See W. E. Heath, 'The Early Colonial Money System of Georgia', *Georgia Historical Quarterly*, XIX. 145–60.)

Mr. Quincy, partly for a bed, hangings, and furniture, partly for making a cellar, building a hut, and improvements by him made in and about the house; (2), that 86 – 06 – 09 has been since expended at several times for necessary repair of the cellar (which was fallen in), the house, and the fences round it and the garden, a great part of which fell down, being quite decayed; (3), that

98 – 10 – 09

was expended in three journeys to Frederica, twice by water and once by land; whither not my own pleasure but the desire of some of that desolate people, and the need of all, called me; (4), that

26 – 01 – 09

was expended at several times in clothing for Mr. Ingham. These particulars together amounting to 402 – 18 – 09, the expense of Mr. Ingham's food for two or three months, and of mine and Mr. Delamotte's subsistence from March 1, 1736, to March 1, 1737, amounts to Currency 323 – 08 – 06½
Sterling 044 – 04 – 04.

I thought, gentlemen, before I left England, that from the little knowledge you had of my manner of conversation, you would not easily have believed me capable of embezzling yours, any more than my own goods. But since it is otherwise, since you have sent orders to limit my expenses to the Society's £50 a year; be it so. I accept it, and (during my stay here) desire to have neither less nor more. One thing farther I desire. That whenever I am accused to you, on this or any other head (and it is necessary that offences should come),[1] you would allow me the justice due to a common criminal, the knowing my accuser (which I must insist upon before God and man), and the being heard before I am condemned.

I can't but acknowledge the readiness of the magistrates here, Mr. Causton[2] in particular, in assisting me, so far as pertains to their office, both to repress open vice and immorality, and to promote the glory of God by establishing peace and mutual goodwill among men. And I trust their labour hath not been quite in vain. Many ill practices seem to lose ground daily, and a general face of decency and order prevails, beyond what I have seen anywhere else in America.

[1] See Matt. 18: 7.
[2] On Sept. 13, 1735, Thomas Causton was made first bailiff (or magistrate), Henry Parker second bailiff, and John Dearn third bailiff. Causton was also the keeper of the public stores, and in that capacity handled much of the Trustees' finances. In 1739 he was turned out of both offices for abusing his trust.

Gentlemen, my prayer to God for you is that you may with one heart and one mind glorify God our Saviour in all things, that neither open nor covert opposition may ever be able to disjoin your hearts or weaken your hands; but that you may calmly and steadily 5 pursue his work, even though men should therefore cast out your names as evil.[1] And the God of glory shall accept your service, and reward every one of you sevenfold into his bosom![2] I am, gentlemen, your most obedient servant,

John Wesley

10 Savannah,
March 4, 1737

Source: P.R.O., CO5/639/207–8, no address (verso of p. 208 blank).

To Sophy Hopkey[3]

[March 10, 1737]

M[iss] S[ophy]
Will you see me or not?

Source: MA, JW. IV. 2, p. 17 (Wesley, MS Journal, March 1736–Sept. 12, 1737, para. 35).

From the Revd. George Whitefield

15   London, March 17, 1737

Reverend sir
Though I have had thoughts of going to Georgia for above these seven months, yet I never resolved till I received your kind letter.[4]

---

[1] See Luke 6: 22.   [2] See Ps. 79: 13 (B.C.P.)

[3] On Wednesday, March 9, 1737, Wesley was devastated at Sophy Hopkey's announced intention of marrying William Williamson, 'the bastard son of Mr. Taylor of Bridewell', a young man who 'was wild when in England . . ., being bred an attorney' (Egmont *Diary*, III. 65). This she did to get away from the Caustons, confessing to Wesley, 'I have no particular inclination for Mr. Williamson.' The following day Wesley asked to see her again, to which Williamson objected, so that Wesley 'desired a piece of paper, and writ these words' (i.e. the note above), whereupon she 'immediately came down', and assured him that she was 'fully determined' to go on with the marriage. On this he delivered an exhortation to the two of them, 'and went home easy and satisfied'.

[4] Whitefield apparently refers to Wesley's letter of Sept. 10, 1736, which, arriving in December, marked the turning-point in his career, rather than to some unnoted

I am now in London. My intention in coming hither was to wait on the Trustees and the bishop; and both, I believe, will approve of my going. We are not likely to sail till July. Your brother intends returning with me; and I hope God will sanctify our voyage. I hear of no one yet like minded, though there is some hope, I believe, of your seeing Mr. Hall. God direct him for the best! 5

Next week or the week after I go to Bath, in order to preach a public sermon for the poor Americans. God has inclined the hearts of his people to give me above £200 already in private charities, and more, I hope, will still be collected.

Innumerable are the blessings our God has poured on me since I saw you last, and remarkably has he set his blessed seal to my ministry in England; which 10 encourages me to hope he will likewise do so in Georgia.

I suppose your brother has informed you, reverend sir, how matters stand at Oxon, and therefore I need only add that I believe there will be a remnant of pious students left in the university, who will take root downwards, and bear fruit upwards. 15

I could say a great deal more, and would also write dear Mr. Ingham, but I knew not that the ship was to sail tomorrow, and the Trustees have engaged me to dine with them; so I must beg leave to subscribe myself, with earnest prayers for your success in every undertaking, reverend sir, your dutiful son and servant, 20

George Whitefield

P.S. I salute dear Mr. Ingham and Mr. Delamotte, whom I desire to love in the bowels of Jesus Christ.

Address: 'To the Rev. Mr. John Wesley, minister at Savannah' *Source*: Tyerm (*Wd*), I. 75.

To William Wogan[1]

28 March, 1737. Savannah

Dear sir 25

The more particularly you will at any time express your thoughts, the greater obligation you will lay upon me. I hope no difference of

hypothetical letter which he may well have written in Dec. or Jan. There was certainly sufficient time for Wesley's letter of Feb. 16 to have arrived, though only just.

[1] William Wogan (1678–1758), educated at Westminster School and Trinity College, Cambridge, a devout London layman who published several works, at least one of which Wesley read at Oxford, his *Right Use of Lent* (1732). His most important was *An Essay on the Proper Lessons of the Church of England* (4 vols., 1753). He was a good friend of John Clayton and Thomas Broughton, and sympathetic to the Oxford Methodists in general. Wesley knew him personally at least from the summer of 1732; they visited each other, and corresponded fairly frequently. Although Wesley met Wogan after his return from Georgia (see diary, Sept. 21, Nov. 2, 1738), they parted company, apparently because Wogan was strongly opposed to the separatist tendencies of the Methodist societies.

opinion, especially as to smaller points, will ever occasion any coldness between us. I can almost engage it will not cause any on my
part; neither do I apprehend it will on yours.

I entirely agree with you that religion is love and peace and joy
5 in the Holy Ghost;[1] that as it is the happiest, so it is the cheerfullest
thing in the world; that [it] is utterly inconsistent with moroseness,
sourness, severity, and indeed with whatever is not according to the
softness, sweetness, and gentleness of Christ Jesus. I believe it is
equally contrary to all preciseness,[2] stiffness, affectation, and un-
10 necessary singularity. And these[3] I call unnecessary which do not
either directly or indirectly affect their progress in holiness who use
them. I allow too that prudence, as well as zeal, is of the utmost
importance in the Christian life. But I do not yet see any possible
case wherein trifling conversation can be an instance of it. In the
15 following Scriptures I take all such to be flatly forbidden: 'Verily,
verily, I say unto you, Every idle word ('tis ἀργός, not πονηρός,
wicked, because idle) that men speak, they shall give an account
thereof at the Day of Judgment';[4] 'Neither foolish talking, nor
jesting (ἐυτραπελία, literally, wit, witty conversation, facetiousness),
20 which are not convenient' (or befitting our calling);[5] 'Let no corrupt
communication proceed out of your mouth.'[6] But what conversation
is corrupt? The opposite will tell us—that which is not 'good, to
the use of edifying, fit to minister grace to the hearers'.[7] Lastly,
'Let your conversation be always in grace' (πάντοτε ἐν χάριτι),
25 steeped (as it were) therein, throughly impregnated thereby: not
sprinkled only, but 'seasoned (ἠρτυμένος) with this salt'[8]—which
meat can by no means be said to be till every particle of it has lost
its freshness, and contracted this new flavour.

That I shall be laughed at for this I know: so was my *Master*. But
30 that I shall catch the flavour of men,[9] I know not. If I do any, it is
not my strength or prudence: 'No man cometh to him, except the
Father draw him.'[10] But this I am determined, never to 'catch them
by guile'[11]—an imputation St. Paul expresses a strong abhorrence of,
as anyone may observe from the manner wherein he clears himself
35 of that crime, which some, it seems, had accused him of to the
Corinthians.

---

[1] See Rom. 14: 17.   [2] In the obsolescent sense of puritanical severity.
[3] Gatliff, *Pulpit*, 'all these'; Marriott, 'those'.   [4] See Matt. 12: 36.
[5] Eph. 5: 4.   [6] Eph. 4: 29.   [7] Ibid.
[8] See Col. 4: 6.   [9] *Pulpit*, 'fewer men'.
[10] See John 6: 44.   [11] See 2 Cor. 12: 16.

Not that I am for a stern, austere manner of conversing neither.
No. Let all the cheerfulness of faith be there; all the joyfulness of
hope, all the amiable sweetness, the winning easiness of love.[1] If we
must have art, *Hic mihi erunt artes*.[2] So soon as God shall adorn[3]
my soul with them, and without any other than these, with the power 5
of the Holy Ghost preventing, accompanying, and following me,[4]
I know that I (that is, the grace of God which is in me)[5] shall save
both myself and those that hear me![6]

Dear sir, continue your prayers for your obliged and very affectionate servant in Christ Jesus, 10

John Wesley

Address: 'To William Wogan, Esqr. in Spring Gardens, London' *End*:
'Savannah, 28 Mar. 1737, from Mr. Wesley, ab[ou]t Conversation. R[eceive]d
14 June.' *Sources*: (A), James Gatliff, Life of Wogan, in Wogan, *An Essay
on the Proper Lessons . . . of the Church of England*, 3rd edn., London, Ogles, etc.,
1818, 4 vols, I. xxxviii–xl, apparently revised for publication; (B), *The Pulpit*,
Dec. 20, 1827, pp. 302–3, similarly revised for publication; (C), transcript
addressed, 'Rev. Henry Moore, w[i]t[h] Thos. Marriott's Respts', n.d., but
probably about the same time as Marriott's transcript of the letter of Oct. 7,
1749, for Moore, viz. Aug. 29, 1828, an edited selection; (D), a transcript in a
volume in MA entitled 'Copies of Original Letters and other Documents collected from Different Sources. By James Everett. Volume I', p. 253. This contains
a marginal note: 'The letter from which this was copied was in the handwriting
of Mr. Wesley, and was offered to Mr. Ambrey, a Bookseller, in Manchester, for
sale. It had on the back of it, apparently in the hand of Mr. Wogan, "Savannah
. . . 14 June" [as given above]. J. Everett, July 26, 1833.' Each of these four seems
to be independent of the others, and to be based upon the actual holograph, but
C omits the opening paragraph, A, B, and C display editorial changes, and in the
reproduction of minutiae D is certainly closer to the holograph. Less reliable
secondary printed versions also occur: (E), in the *W.M.M.*, 1842 (based on B);
(F), in the *Wesley Banner*, 1852 (based on C); and (G), in Telford, based on C
and F. (Cf. Intro., p. 125 n.)

[1] *Pulpit* italicizes faith, hope, love—probably an editorial alteration.
[2] 'These shall be my arts'; cf. Virgil, *Aeneid*, vi. 852, 'hae tibi erunt artes'.
[3] In the holograph, as deliberately presented by Everett, Wesley had first written
'bless', struck it through, and added above the line, 'adorn', indicating the alteration by
a caret.
[4] See Thomas Ken, *The Practice of Divine Love, being an Exposition of the Church
Catechism* (1685), which Wesley abridged for his *Christian Library*, Vol. 25 (1753),
p. 302: 'O let thy grace . . . ever prevent, accompany, and follow me.'
[5] See 1 Cor. 15: 10.
[6] See 1 Tim. 4: 16.

To Mrs. Mary Chapman[1]

[Savannah, March 29, 1737]

True friendship is doubtless stronger than death, else yours could never have subsisted still, in spite of all opposition, and even after thousands of miles are interposed between us.

5 In the last proof you gave of it there are a few things which I think it lies on me to mention. As to the rest, my brother is the proper person to clear them up, as I suppose he has done long ago.

You seem to apprehend that I believe religion to be inconsistent with cheerfulness, and with a sociable friendly temper. So far from 10 it that I am convinced, as true religion or holiness cannot be without cheerfulness, so steady cheerfulness, on the other hand, cannot be without holiness or true religion. And I am equally convinced that religion has nothing sour, austere, unsociable, unfriendly in it, but on the contrary implies the most winning sweetness, the most 15 amiable softness and gentleness. Are you for having as much cheerfulness as you can? So am I. Do you endeavour to keep alive your taste for all the truly innocent pleasures of life? So do I likewise. Do you refuse no pleasure but what is a hindrance to some greater good, or has a tendency to some evil? It is my very rule; and I know no 20 other by which a sincere, reasonable Christian can be guided. In particular I pursue this rule in eating, which I seldom do without much pleasure. And this I know is the will of God concerning me: that I should enjoy every pleasure that leads to my taking pleasure in him, and in such a measure as most leads to it. I know that, as to 25 every action which is naturally pleasing, it is his will that it should be so; therefore in taking that pleasure, so far as it tends to this end (of taking pleasure in God), I do his will. Though therefore that

[1] Probably the mother of the Revd. Walter Chapman (1711-91), Wesley's colleague in Pembroke College, Oxford, who became a well-known evangelical clergyman in his family home of Bath. (The 'William' Chapman described by Tyerman, Curnock, and others, is the same person, who usually signed himself simply 'W. Chapman'.) The father of this Oxford Methodist was another Walter Chapman (1669-1729), Mayor of Bath in 1726, who had married Mary Morgan, Walter being their third son. Mrs. Chapman seems to have been a friend of Wesley's brother Samuel, but she may well have been linked with Richard Morgan of Dublin: James Hervey wrote to Chapman on June 12, 1736, 'If Mr. Morgan is at Bath, pray present my thanks and love to him.' (Tyerm (*OM*) pp. 208-9.) Chapman's mother died in 1741, aged 71, and he himself does not appear to have married his first wife (Susanna Dingley) until about 1744. (Ruth Young, *Mrs. Chapman's Portrait*, Bath, Gregory, 1926, pp. 37-8.)

pleasure be in some sense distinct from the love of God, yet is the taking of it by no means distinct from his will. No; you say yourself, 'It is his will I should take it.' And here indeed is the hinge of the question, which I had once occasion to state in a letter to you, and more largely in a sermon on the love of God.[1] If you will read over those, I believe you will find you differ from Mr. Law[2] and me in words only. You say the pleasures you plead for are distinct from the love of God, as the cause from the effect. Why, then, they tend to it; and those which are only thus distinct from it no one excepts against. The whole of what he affirms, and that not on the authority of men but from the words and example of God incarnate, is, There is one thing needful,[3] to do the will of God. And his will is our sanctification, our renewal in the image of God, in faith and love, in all holiness and happiness. On this we are to fix our single eye, at all times, and in all places—for so did our Lord. This one thing we are to do—for so did our fellow-servant Paul; after his example, 'whether we eat or drink, or whatsoever we do, we are to do all to the glory of God'.[4] In other words, we are to do nothing but what directly or indirectly leads to our holiness, which is his glory; and to do every such thing with this design, and in such a measure as may most promote it.

I am not mad, my dear friend, for asserting these to be the words of truth and soberness; neither are any of those, either in England or here, who have hitherto attempted to follow me. I am, and must be, an example to my flock; not indeed in my prudential rules, but in some measure (if giving God the glory I may dare to say so) in my spirit, and life, and conversation. Yet all of them are, in your sense of the word, unlearned, and most of them of low understanding; and still not one of them has been as yet entangled in any case of conscience which was not solved. And as to the nice distinctions you speak of, it is you, my friend, it is the wise, the learned, the disputers of this world,[5] who are lost in them, and bewildered more and more, the more they strive to extricate themselves. We have no need of

---

[1] For the reconstructed text of this sermon, on 1 Cor. 13: 3, first preached in Savannah on Feb. 20, 1737, see Vol. 4, Sermon 149, in this edn. A part of the two-and-a-half hours which Wesley spent on the letter may well have been used in preparing at least a partial transcript.

[2] Mrs. Chapman had apparently been studying one or both of Wesley's favourite works by William Law, his *Practical Treatise on Christian Perfection* (see espec. chapters 3–5), and *A Serious Call to a Devout and Holy Life* (see espec. chapter 4).

[3] See Luke 10: 42.   [4] Cf. 1 Cor. 10: 31.

[5] See 1 Cor. 1: 20.

nice distinctions, for I exhort all—Dispute with none. I feed my brethren in Christ, as he giveth me power, with the pure unmixed milk of his Word.[1] And those who are as little children receive it, not as the word of man, but as the Word of God. Some grow thereby,
5   and advance apace in peace and holiness. They grieve, 'tis true, for those who did run well, but are now turned back; and they fear for themselves, lest they also be tempted. Yet through the mercy of God they despair not, but have still a good hope that they shall endure to the end. Not that this hope has any resemblance to enthusiasm,
10 which is a hope to attain the end without the means. This they know is impossible, and therefore ground their hope on a constant, careful use of all the means. And if they keep in this way, with lowliness, patience, and meekness of resignation, they cannot carry the principle of pressing toward perfection too far. O may you, and I, carry it
15 far enough! Be fervent in spirit![2] Rejoice evermore! Pray without ceasing! In everything give thanks![3] Do everything in the name of the Lord Jesus.[4] Abound more and more[5] in all holiness, and in zeal for every good word and work![6]

Source: Whitehead, II. 31-4, the date confirmed by Wesley's diary.

To the Georgia Trustees

[March 31, 1737]

20 Gentlemen

Robert Hows,[7] a freeholder of this place, has officiated here as parish clerk, not only ever since I came, but as I am informed for above two years before. He constantly attends both the morning and evening service (a little before sunrise and after sunset) on other

---

[1] See 1 Pet. 2: 2.   [2] Rom. 12: 11.   [3] 1 Thess. 5: 16-18.
[4] Col. 3: 17.   [5] 1 Thess. 4: 1.   [6] 2 Thess. 2: 17.

[7] Wesley's *Journal* for Mar. 24, 1737, describes how 'a fire broke out in the house of Mr. Robert Hows, and in an hour burnt it to the ground. A collection was made for him the next day; and the generality of the people showed a surprising willingness to give a little out of their little for the relief of a necessity greater than their own.' Wesley himself went a step farther, making this appeal to the Trustees. Hows, a sawyer, was one of the 1733 settlers, coming over at the same time as the tailor, Robert Gilbert, whose daughter he had married. Within a few months his wife died, and some time later his daughter Mary also. The Gilberts were Wesley's loyal supporters, known as 'Methodists', and Hows one of his most trusted lay leaders. For the success of Wesley's appeal see the letter of Benjamin Martyn, June 15, 1737.

days as well as Sundays, and is in the whole of his behaviour a sober, industrious man. But sickness in his family had reduced him to straitness of circumstances even before the 24th instant, on which (while he was employed in the public work) his house was burnt to the ground, and all that was in it (except two saws) consumed. 5

I therefore, gentlemen, take the liberty to recommend him to your favour and assistance. As to the manner of which (whether by way of salary or otherwise) you are the proper judges. I recommend you and all your labours to him in whose steps you tread, the great Helper of the friendless, and am, gentlemen, your most obedient 10 servant,

John Wesley

Savannah, 31 March, 1737

Address: 'To The Honourable the Trustees For establishing the Colony of Georgia' *Source*: P.R.O., CO5/639/241–2.

From the Revd. George Whitefield

Gloucester, April 15th, 1737

Revrd sir 15

I hope you received my last by Captain Diamond. Mrs. Hutton writes me word a ship sails in a fortnight; what hinders that I should not embrace this opportunity of sending you a line? You see, reverend sir, where I am. Providence led me hither, but God gave me such great success when I was here last that the clergymen combined to use me as I deserve, viz. to thrust me out of their syna- 20 gogues. O that I may humbly rejoice in being made in the least degree conform- able to my great Exemplar Jesus Christ. Licence was granted to preach at Bath in order for a public collection for the Americans, but the late news which has been spread abroad, that the Spaniards have or will take Georgia, I fear will make that design impracticable. You cannot do better, reverend sir, than send an 25 exact account of the civil as well as religious affairs of the country you now are placed in, for most I apply to for charity inquire chiefly about the former; but I hope to see you before I receive a letter. You talk of Mr. Oglethorpe going about June or July. Your brother and I, God willing, go with him too. Methinks I long for the time to come. What business have I now in England? 30 But God's time is the best. I hope likewise a second Delamotte will come with us, one who seems to be wonderfully stirred up to leave all and follow Christ. He is to be schoolmaster at Frederica. Surely there ⟨w⟩ill some good come out of Georgia. Many excellent texts have been powerfully applied to my heart, and amidst the late news I found in myself not the least inclination to draw back. The good 35 Lord keep me steadfast and unmovable unto the end. I have had about a week of your brother's company, though with little conversation, through the hurry

of business. I hope next time we meet it will be better. He is somewhere in Gloucestershire at present, I believe, but where I cannot exactly tell. *Floret Oxoniae Evangelium.*[1] Friends are numerous and ⟨zealo⟩us for the most part. Nor is Gloucester without many disciples of Christ, though alas too many of the
5　outward stamp. I have several things to say, but cannot write them now. May God strengthen my resolution, and give me a good voyage. I doubt not but your company, instructions, and communications, will afford great satisfaction to, reverend sir, your obedient and very humble servant,

GW

10　P.S. It's to be doubted whether Mr. H[a]ll will not come with us. The collection, I believe, will still be made in Bath.

Address: 'To The Revrd. Mr. Wesly at Savannah to be left at Mr. Hutton's in College street, Westminster'　　*Source*: MA, in abbreviated longhand with symbols apparently based on Wesley's earlier system.

To Harman Verelst

Savannah [June 10, 1737]

Sir

I have received the four boxes of which you was so kind as to
15　give me advice,[2] as well as the bundle fro⟨m⟩ Mr. Causton.

I can't imagine how you can support yourself under such a weight of business as lies upon you. May he who alone is able, so support you that in the greatest hurry of temporal things you may never forget that there are things eternal. I am, sir, your most humble
20　servant,

John Wesley

10 June, 1737.

Address: 'To Mr. Verelst At the Georgia Office Westminster'　　*Source*: P.R.O., CO5/639/297.

---

[1] 'May the Gospel of Oxford flourish!'

[2] Verelst sent a letter on Mar. 23 'to Thomas Causton, by *Peter and James*, Capt. George Dymond', with many advices, including 'four boxes and a parcel for Mr. Wesley'. In the same letter Causton was instructed to 'pay John Wesley and Mr. Ingham £50 apiece as missionaries' (P.R.O., CO5/667/9-12). Doubtless a separate brief advice was sent to Wesley, in accordance with his request of Nov. 1, 1736. On June 6 Wesley's diary recorded: 'Recd. letters from England!!!'

From Benjamin Martyn[1]

Georgia Office, June 15, 1737

Sir

The Revd. Mr. Burton has this day laid before the Trustees a letter from you to them dated Savannah, March 4th, 1737, wherein you express a concern that they should receive an accusation of your embezzling any part of their goods, and 5 likewise a desire to know the name of your accuser.

The Trustees have ordered me to assure you that they are very much surprised at any apprehension you have of such accusation being brought before them. No complaint of any kind has been laid before them relating to you. They have never as a board, nor any of them privately, heard of one, nor have they the 10 least suspicion of any ground for one. They would not (if they had received any), form a judgment of you without acquainting you with the accusation, and the name of your accuser. At the same time they believe you'll think it reasonable to let them know who has informed you that any such accusation has been brought before them, and that for the future you will only regard what may be sent to 15 you from them, and that you will not believe nor listen to any private informations, or any insinuations that must make you uneasy, and may lead you to distrust the justice of the Trustees, and the regard they have for you.

The Trustees are very sensible of the great importance of the work you are engaged in, and they hope God will prosper the undertaking and support you 20 in it, for they have much at heart, not only the success of the colony in general, but the promotion of piety amongst the people, as well as the conversion of the Indians. They are very glad to find that Mr. Causton has seconded your endeavours to suppress vice and immorality, and that a reformation gains ground, as you observe it does. I am, sir, your most obedient servant, 25

Benj. Martyn, Secretary

P.S. The Trustees will take into consideration your application to them in favour of Robert Hows, and have a regard to it.[2]

End by JW: 'The Trustees L[ette]r, / June 17 [*sic*], 1737, / fully acquitting me'
Source: MA (no address).

[1] Benjamin Martyn (1699–1763) was appointed Secretary to the Georgia Trustees at their third council, on Aug. 3, 1732, and on the same occasion the Trustees ordered the publication of his *Reasons for establishing the Colony of Georgia* (1733). Egmont spelled his name 'Martin', but he is not to be confused with Benjamin Martin (1704–82), the compiler of many volumes on scientific and educational subjects. Martyn also was a man of many parts, however, chiefly responsible for erecting the monument to Shakespeare in Westminster Abbey, and collaborating with Alexander Pope in a tragedy, *Timoleon*, staged at Drury Lane. In 1741 he published *An Impartial Enquiry into the State and Utility of the Province of Georgia*.

[2] The postscript is in reply to Wesley's letter of Mar. 31, 1737. At the Common Council of July 6, 1737, reports the Earl of Egmont, 'We ordered that the house of one Hows, who officiates at Savannah as Parish Clerk, being burnt down, the same in consideration of his services should be rebuilt at the Trustees' charge, out of the money appropriated for religious uses.' (Egmont *Diary*, II. 418.)

From the Revd. John Burton[1]

Georgia Office, June 15th [1737]

Dear sir

I communicated your letter to the board this morning. We are surprised at your apprehensions of being charged with the very imputation of having embez-
5 zled any public or private monies. I cannot learn any ground for even suspicion of anything of this kind. We never heard of any accusation, but on the contrary are persuaded both of your frugality and honesty. We beg you not to give weight to reports or private insinuations. The Trustees have a high esteem of your good services, and on all occasions will give further encouragement; and would not
10 have the express mention of the fifty pounds, in lieu of the same sum formerly advanced by the Society for Propagation, so understood as not to admit of enlargement upon proper occasions. I am ordered by all the members present to acquaint you of this, and to give you assurance of their approbation of your conduct, and readiness to assist you. The Vice-Provost of Eton has given you
15 ten pounds, for your private use and doing works of charity; I have desired Mr. Oglethorpe to convey this to you in a private way. Mr. Whitefield will shortly, and by the next convenient opportunity, go over to Georgia. There are three hundred acres granted to the church in Frederica. Be not discouraged by many hasty insinuations; but hope the best while many labour for the best.
20 In good time matters will bear a better face. God strengthen your hands, and give efficacy to your honest endeavours. In a former letter I spoke my mind at large to you concerning many particulars. I am in much haste at present, your affectionate friend,

J. Burton

25   P.S. My lord Egmont gives his respects and kind wishes, and begs you not to be discouraged.

Source: Whitehead, II. 35–6.

[1] In response to Wesley's of Mar. 4, 1737; see also preceding letter.

To James Hutton[1]

[June 16, 1737]

Dear sir

I think our Lord is beginning to lift up his standard against the flood[2] of iniquity which hath long covered the earth. Even in this place it hath pleased him, in some measure, to stir up his might and 5
come and help us.[3] There is a strange *motus animorum*,[4] as it seems, continually increasing. Those 'who fear the Lord speak often together',[5] and many of them are not ashamed of the gospel of Christ[6] in the midst of an adulterous and sinful generation.[7] The enemy hath great wrath,[8] and rageth much. May it be a sign that his time 10
is short![9] One or two, whom he has long seemed to lead captive at his will, are just now recovering out of his snare,[10] and declare openly, without fear or shame, that they will not serve him, but the Living God. Likewise 'out of the mouth of babes and sucklings is he perfecting praise'.[11] Not only young men and maidens praise the name of 15
the Lord,[12] but children too (in years, though in seriousness and

[1] James Hutton (1715–95), was the son of the Revd. John Hutton (1676–1750), a non-juror who had resigned his living, and whose wife was the former Elizabeth Ayscough, second cousin to Sir Isaac Newton. The Huttons boarded scholars at Westminster School, and lived in a house adjoining that of the Revd. Samuel Wesley, Jun., in Dean's Yard, Westminster. Like Charles Wesley, James Hutton was himself educated at Westminster, and through his brothers John Wesley had become friendly with the Huttons. His first recorded letter to the Revd. John Hutton is dated Dec. 17, 1731, his last, Jan. 23, 1734. The elder Hutton's place in the family as Wesley's chief correspondent was taken in part by Mrs. Hutton, to whom his first recorded letter was dated Sept. 8, 1736, but much more by James, who wrote to Wesley on his twenty-first birthday, Sept. 3, 1736. James Hutton had been converted under a sermon on 'One thing is needful' (Luke 10: 42), preached by John Wesley at the Huttons' while he was staying there on the eve of his departure for Georgia in October, 1735. He saw the party off when they embarked at Gravesend, but was dissuaded by his parents from accompanying them. He followed their progress with keen interest, however, and the Huttons' home became one of the clearing-houses for letters to Georgia (see Whitefield's letter of Apr. 15, 1737). He and his sister (who had been converted on the same occasion) persuaded their parents to open the house for regular meetings of a religious society, and then James opened another in his own bookshop. On the Wesleys' return to England he eagerly co-operated in their religious activities, and published many of their early works. When they split with the Moravians, however, he parted company with them, and became the main English leader of that movement.

[2] See Isa. 59: 19.   [3] See Ps. 80: 2 (B.C.P.).
[4] 'moving of spirits', Virgil, *Georgics*, iv. 86.   [5] See Mal. 3: 16.
[6] Rom. 1: 16.   [7] See Mark 8: 38.   [8] See Rev. 12: 12.
[9] Ibid.   [10] See 2 Tim. 2: 26.
[11] See Matt. 21: 16.   [12] See Ps. 148: 12 (B.C.P.).

understanding, men) are not terrified from bearing the reproach of Christ.[1] Indeed the little share of persecution which as yet falls to me plainly shows I have no strength. Who then will rise up with me against the ungodly?[2] You, I trust, for one, when the time is come. Till then, strive mightily with God, you and all your father's house, that I may not, when I have preached to others, be myself a castaway![3]

June 16, 1737. Savannah.

Address: 'To Mr James Hutton, At Mr Innys',[4] In S. Paul's Church Yard, London'   *Source*: MorA.

From Baron Philipp Georg Friedrich von Reck[5]

Windhausen, the
$$\frac{28 \text{ June}}{9 \text{ July}} \ 1737$$

Dear reverend sir

I am with my brother so much penetrated with a true thankfulness for all the goodness you bestowed upon us in Savannah, that we never cease to pray to God (who said that whosoever shall give to drink unto one of these little ones a cup of water only in the name of a disciple, verily he shall in no wise lose his reward) to fulfil this promise, having received so a great many benefits from you and my dear Delamotte, though we are the most unworthy servants of our Saviour, and to fortify you with Spirit in the work of the Lord.

---

[1] See Heb. 11: 26; 13: 13.   [2] See Ps. 94: 16 (B.C.P.).

[3] 1 Cor. 9: 27.

[4] Hutton was apprenticed to Innys for his career as a bookseller and publisher.

[5] Von Reck was the nephew of Baron von Reck, English-Hanoverian envoy at Ratisbon, and brother of Ernst Ludwig von Reck, who planned to settle in Georgia. Philipp von Reck was a truly devout young man, who had absorbed the piety both of Halle and of Herrnhut, and fruitlessly hoped to reconcile the wrangling Salzburgers and Moravians. In March, 1734, he brought the first party of Salzburger refugees to Georgia, approving the site earlier chosen for their settlement, Ebenezer. By May 12, 1734, a chapel was completed; May 13 was a day of thanksgiving; on May 14 von Reck left to seek support for the new settlement, both in the other American colonies and back in Germany. His enthusiasm led to a second party being sent out in October, under John Vat. Meanwhile conditions deteriorated in Ebenezer. Both Bolzius and Vat complained about the poor soil and the flooding, and as early as February, 1735, suggested a new site on higher land. In March, 1736, Oglethorpe returned, along with Wesley in the *Simmonds* and von Reck and the third party of Salzburgers in the *London Merchant*. Von Reck agreed that the change of site was advisable, but urged that much more land was needed. Nor did he trust Vat, an older man. On Mar. 16, 1736, Oglethorpe asked Wesley to investigate the situation and report to him; eventually Vat was recalled by the Trustees. On Oct. 15, 1736, von Reck also returned to Germany with his brother, both of them disillusioned and ill. He settled at Halle, among his chief interests the theological lectures there.

You know we went away very weak and sick. We recovered a little at sea, and arrived after a great many tempestuous weather, and dangers through the Bristol Channel into the English, and so further at London safe and very well received by the Honourable Trustees, and Society.[1] All false imputations were dispersed, and it pleased God to set everything in the most favourable light. 5 We escaped a great storm in the North Sea, and recovered from a great many ⟨sickn⟩esses who befell us in our native country. I received some instructions to engage more people for Georgia, and to return to England and Georgia in this month, but finding none at present I don't know if the Honourable Trustees intend to dispose of me any further.   10

I saw a short extract of your Journal translated into the German tongue, and I have begun to translate Mr. Law's books. If it should please God to open you a door amongst the Indians and heathen Christians I heartily desire you to write me the great works of God in Georgia, that we may assist you in Germany with our prayers and fortunes. Your letters will come to my hands by the way of Mr. 15 Newman.

Pray how go the Salzburgers on in their spiritual and temporal welfare? How the good Herrenhutiens? Mr. Ingham, Mr. Delamotte, and Mr. Doelsche find here my hearty salutations from me and my brother [. . .], dear reverend sir, your humble servant,   20

Pray to send the enclosed to Mr. Bolzius.   P v Reck

Address: 'To The Reverend Mr John Wesely at Savannah'   *End* by JW:
'Mr Von Reck / Jan. 28, 737. / Thank[ing] m[e].'   *Source*: MA.

To Thomas Causton[2]

[July 5, 1737]

Sir

To this hour you have shown yourself my friend. I ever have and ever shall acknowledge it. And it is my earnest desire that he who 25 hath hitherto given me this blessing would continue it still.

---

[1] i.e. the S.P.C.K., who sponsored the Salzburgers, and whose secretary, Henry Newman, was to be his agent for forwarding letters.

[2] On Mar. 12 Sophy Hopkey had married William Williamson (see above, p. 498 n.). The more Wesley thought about it, the more it seemed that she had deliberately lied to him on several occasions, and was therefore unfit to be admitted to Holy Communion without prior repentance. Whether successfully or not, he tried to set aside all elements of personal resentment and professional diplomacy, and wrestled with the matter for several months as a question of ecclesiastical discipline. Twice he confronted Sophy herself about her conduct, on May 16 and on July 3, after communion; he asked the advice of several whom he trusted as committed Christians, Mr. and Mrs. Brownfield, Charles Delamotte, and Mr. Burnside, who replied, 'While things appear to you as they do now, you can't admit to the Holy Communion. The consequences of rejecting her you know; but be they what they will, that doesn't alter your duty.' Mrs. Causton protested

But this cannot be unless you will allow me one request, which is not so easy an one as it appears: 'Don't condemn me for doing, in the execution of my office, what I think it my duty to do.'

If you can prevail upon yourself to allow me this, even when I
5 act without respect of persons, I am persuaded there will never be, at least not long, any misunderstanding between us. For even those who seek it shall, I trust, find no occasion against me, except it be concerning the law of God . . .

Source: MA, Wesley, MS Journal, J.W. IV. 2, p. 27.

To Sophy Williamson[1]

[July 5, 1737]

10 If the sincerity of friendship is best to be known from the painful offices, then there could not be a stronger proof of mine than that I gave you on Sunday,[2] except this which I am going to give you now, and which you may perhaps equally misinterpret.

Sophy's complete innocence. In this letter Wesley put Thomas Causton on his guard about what seemed almost inevitable. The following day Causton came to Wesley with witnesses to complain about the letter, saying, 'How could you possibly entertain such a thought of me as that I should oppose you in executing any part of your office?' To which Wesley replied, 'Sir, what if I should think it the duty of my office to repel one of your family from the Holy Communion?' Causton replied, 'If you repel me or my wife, I shall require a legal reason. But I shall trouble myself about none else.' A month later, on Sunday, Aug. 7, when Sophy Williamson presented herself for communion, Wesley felt impelled to whisper to her, 'I can't administer the Holy Communion to you before I have spoken with you.'

[1] In one of his manuscript journals Wesley wrote: 'Sunday, July 3, [1737]. Immediately after the Holy Communion I reproved Mrs. Williamson for her insincerity and other faults. She absolutely denied that she was in any fault, and was very angry at me for thinking so. The next day Mrs. Causton said, She was much grieved, and desired me to write and tell her what I disliked. I did so on Tuesday. The effect was not what I expected. However, "I have delivered my own soul." ' Sophy Williamson suffered a miscarriage on July 11. After no attempt at an interview with Wesley she presented herself for communion on Aug. 7, when she was repelled. She vented her anger to Mrs. Burnside (the former Miss Bovey, who had been her companion when the two were married at Purrysburg). Mrs. Burnside told her: 'You was much to blame, after receiving that letter from Mr. Wesley, to offer yourself at the table before you had cleared yourself to him. But you may easily put an end to this by going to Mr. Wesley now, and clearing yourself of what you are charged with.' She replied, 'No, I will not show such a meanness of spirit as to speak to him about it myself, but somebody else shall.' The following day a warrant was issued for Wesley's arrest for defamation of character, the beginnings of his worst public trials and eventual departure from Georgia four months later.

[2] The rebuke after communion.

Would you know what I dislike in your past or present behaviour? You have always heard my thoughts as freely as you asked them. Nay, much more freely. You know it well. And so you shall do, as long as I can speak or write.

In your present behaviour I dislike, (1), your neglect of half the public service, which no man living can oblige you to;[1] (2), your neglect of fasting, which you once knew to be a help to the mind, without any prejudice to the body; (3), your neglect of almost half the opportunities of communicating which you have lately had.[2]

But these things are small in comparison of what I dislike in your past behaviour. For, (1), you told me over and over, you had entirely conquered your inclination for Mr. Mellichamp. Yet at that very time, you had not conquered it. (2). You told me frequently, you had no design to marry Mr. Williamson. Yet at that very time you spoke, you had that design. (3). In order to conceal both these things from me, you went through a course of deliberate dissimulation. O how fallen! How changed! Surely there was a time when in Miss Sophy's lips there was no guile![3]

Own these facts, and own your fault, and you will be in my thoughts as if they had never been. If you are otherwise minded, I shall still be your friend, though I can't expect you should be mine.

Address: 'To Mrs. Williamson, July 5th'   *Source*: MA, Wesley, MS Journal, J.W. IV. 2, pp. 27–8, prefaced thus: 'An hour or two after [writing the preceding letter] I sent the following note to Mrs. Williamson, which I wrote in the most mild and friendly manner I could . . .'

From Henry Newman

London, 19 July, 1737

Revd. sir

I cannot forward the enclosed from Sir Erasmus Philipps without thanking you for your letter to the Society of the 30th March last, and letting you know their concern for the difficulties you meet with.

Mr. Oglethorpe being appointed to General of His Majesty's Forces in South

---

[1] Apparently the availing herself of one only out of the two main public services which Wesley conducted each Sunday.

[2] 'Looking over the register, I found she had absented from it [communion], five times in April and May only; in this month, June, four times more, viz. the 11th, 12th, 24th, and 29th.' (MA, J.W. IV. 2, p. 25.)

[3] John 1: 47.

Carolina and Georgia is preparing to return thither, by whom I expect orders
of the Society to trouble you with a fuller answer. This takes its chance by the
way of Charlestown, with desires that you may be assured that I am, revd. sir,
your most humble servant,

5   [Henry Newman]

Address: 'To the Revd. Mr. John Wesley at Savannah in Georgia'   *Source*:
S.P.C.K., Misc. Letters, CN2/3, p. 51, a draft.

To Dr. David Humphreys[1]

[July 22, 1737]

. . . Where is the seed sown, the *sanguis martyrum*?[2] Do we hear of
any who have sealed the faith with their blood in all this vast
continent? Or do we read of any church flourishing in any age or
10 nation without the seed first sown there? Give me leave, sir, to speak
my thoughts freely. When God shall put it into the hearts of some of
his servants, whom he hath already delivered from earthly hopes
and fears, to join hand in hand in this labour of love; when out of
these he shall have chosen one or more to magnify him in the sight
15 of the heathen by dying, not with a stoical or Indian indifference,
but blessing and praying for their murderers, and praising God in
the midst of the flame, with joy unspeakable and full of glory;[3]
then the rest, 'waxing bold by their sufferings',[4] shall go forth in the

  [1] David Humphreys (1689–1740), who proceeded D.D. by royal mandate in 1728,
after education at Trinity College, Cambridge. He was secretary to the S.P.G. from
1716 until his death. Wesley's MS Journal shows that on July 12 he read Humphrey's
Historical Account of the Society (published 1730), noting: '(1). That nine out of ten of
the missionaries sent into America have died before the end of the fourth year. (2). That
out of that vast number not above two (or three at most) are mentioned who were not
"well spoken of by all men". If these then were the disciples of Christ, the scandal of the
cross is ceased!' He continued, 'Concerning the conversion of the heathen I could not
but say in my letter to Dr. Humphreys—', which led him into the extract presented.
(The original draft read 'ask', which was then altered to 'add', and later to 'say'.)
That the date of the letter was July 22 rather than July 12 (that of the reading) is shown
by the entries in Wesley's diary.
  [2] See Tertullian, *Apologeticus*, L. 13, 'Plures efficimur, quotiens metimur a vobis;
semen est sanguis christianorum'—'We multiply whenever we are mown down by you;
the blood of Christians is seed.' (Loeb, 226–7.) The more familiar phrase which substituted *martyrum* for *christianorum* was already long familiar in Wesley's day, so that
'The blood of the martyrs is the seed of the church' became almost proverbial. Cf.
Wesley's sermon, 'The Mystery of Iniquity', No. 61, § 26.
  [3] 1 Pet. 1: 18.   [4] See Phil. 1: 14.

name of the Lord God, and by the power of his might cast down every high thing that exalteth itself against the[1] faith of Christ. Then shall ye see Satan, the grand ruler of this New World, as lightning fall from heaven![2] Then even these lands shall be full of the knowledge of the Lord, as the waters cover the seas.[3]

Source: MA, Wesley, MS Journal, J.W. III. 4, pp. 31–2.

To Dr. Timothy Cutler[4]

[July 23, 1737]

. . . How to attain to the being crucified with Christ[5] I find not, being in a condition which I neither desired nor expected in America—in ease and honour and abundance. A strange school for him who has but one business, γυμνάζειν ἑαυτὸν πρὸς εὐσέβειαν.[6]

Source: MA, Wesley, MS Journals, J.W. III. 4, p. 33, and J.W. IV. 1, p. 25.

---

[1] See 2 Cor. 10: 5.
[2] See Luke 10: 18.
[3] Isa. 11: 9.
[4] Timothy Cutler (1684–1765), after education at Harvard was elected the first President of Yale, 1719–22, where he publicly disavowed presbyterian ordination. In 1723 he proceeded S.T.D. at Oxford, and in that same year became the first rector of Christ Church, Boston, where he remained until his death. Charles Wesley preached for him on Sept. 26, 1736, and assisted him in administering the Lord's Supper on Oct. 3, as well as being with him on other occasions and accompanying his son to England (gladly accepting his proffered cabin). The first letter to him noted in John Wesley's diary was for Feb. 15, 1737, the next being this of which he gives an extract, and to which Cutler replied on Oct. 22 (q.v.).
In his journal Wesley introduced the letter thus: 'Sa[turday, July] 23. The strange esteem which Mr. C[auston] seemed to show for us, by which means we had nothing without but ease and plenty, occasioned my expressing myself thus in a letter to a friend.' (J.W. III. 4, the opening abridged in J.W. IV. 1 to 'Reflecting on the state wherein we ourselves were', i.e. as opposed to the martyrs lauded in his preceding letter to Dr. Humphreys.)
[5] Gal. 2: 20.
[6] 'to train himself in godliness'; see 1 Tim. 4: 7.

To the Society for the Propagation of the Gospel

[July 23–6, 1737]

[[The Committee also read a letter from the Revd. Mr. Westley, dated Savannah, July 26th, 1737; in which he gives an account of his services among the inhabitants there; and says his first design
5 was to receive nothing of any man but food to eat and raiment to put on, and those in kind only, that he might avoid as far as in him lay worldly desires and worldly cares, but being afterwards convinced by his friends that he ought to consider the necessities of his flock, as well as his own, he thankfully accepted that bounty of the Society
10 which he needed not for his own personal subsistence.

[[Agreed by the Committee that this abstract be laid before the Society.]]

Source: S.P.G., Minutes of the Standing Committee, July 17, 1738; cf. S.P.G. Journal, July 21, 1738. An abstract, the original not preserved. Wesley's diary for July 23 notes that from 8 until 10 a.m. he 'writ to the Society for propagating the gospel', and on Tuesday, July 26, 7 until 8 a.m., 'tr[anscribed] L[ette]r'— presumably that of July 23, a fair copy for dispatch.

From Thomas Causton[1]

Savannah, Aug. 10, 1737

Sir

I have heard of a difference between you and Mr. William Williamson touching
15 matters which (I am informed by the magistrates) you say are ecclesiastical.

---

[1] On Aug. 7 Wesley repelled Sophy Williamson from communion, and was arrested on Aug. 8. (See pp. 512–13 above.) The same manuscript in which Wesley preserved this letter introduced it thus: 'The next day Mr. Jones (who had before told Mr. Coates in the fullness of his heart, "Mr. Causton is at the bottom of all this; but he will be seen in it as little as possible") brought me the following letter from him.' Wesley continued:
'63. On this letter I must observe,
'First, that I was surprised at the civility of it, till Mr. Causton informed me he had sent it to the Trustees, and that he wrote it with that design.
'Secondly, that I never received from Mr. Causton any proposal of accommodation before or besides this.
'Thirdly, that there is gross prevarication in the very first words of it, "I have heard of a difference—"
'Fourthly, that the same artful disingenuity runs through the whole, particularly in talking of "the bad effects of my behaviour"; whereas my behaviour this whole week

As there is no ecclesiastical court in this Province,

To preserve the character of Mrs. Sophia Williamson my niece, who has received her education by my means;

To prevent the bad effects your behaviour in this case may have on the minds of ill-disposed people, who doubtless will be glad to embrace such an opportunity 5 as this appears to be;

To prevent all manner of misunderstanding whatever, and for the sake of yourself, religion, and justice, I desire that you would meet me at four of the clock in the courthouse, and in the presence of all Christians (who think it proper to be there) make known the reasons why you refused the Sacrament of the 10 Lord's Supper to my said niece, to the intent that the differences may be rightly understood, and if not accommodated, a case may be agreed upon to be laid before the Trustees.

As this, sir, is sincerely offered upon the principles of a Christian in a private capacity, and with a just regard to the friendship which has, till this affair, 15 subsisted between us, I hope I need not doubt your concurrence, and am, sir, your humble servant,

T. Causton

P.S. If the time fixed does not suit you, be pleased to appoint your own.

Source: MA, Wesley, MS Journal, J.W. IV. 2, § 62, pp. 34-5. Cf. brief summaries in MS Journals, J.W. III. 4 and J.W. IV. 1.

To Thomas Causton

[Aug. 10, 1737] 20

Sir

I apprehend many ill consequences that may arise from a public conversation on this subject.

[[I cannot assent to this on several accounts. As, (1), because 'all the people' are not proper judges of ecclesiastical matters'; (2,) 25 because I am unwilling to expose her; and (3), because I foresee that you yourself would probably be insulted by the people.]]

Why may not a case be agreed on in a more private manner, to be laid before the Trustees?[1] I am, sir, your humble servant,

John Wesley 30

was to sit still, to be quiet, and mind my own business, speaking to few persons at all, to fewer upon this affair, and enlarging upon it to none.

'Lastly, that the whole and sole crime which is here charged upon me, as causing a breach in that friendship between Mr. Causton and me, which himself here testifies "subsisted till this affair", is "the refusing the Sacrament of the Lord's Supper to Mr. Causton's niece".'

[1] In J.W. IV. 2, § 64, Wesley comments on the use made of this sentence: 'Before

Source: MA, Wesley, MS Journal, J.W. IV. 2, § 64, p. 36, beginning, 'My short answer was:'. Within this has been inserted the central paragraph, reconstructed from an account in indirect speech in J.W. III. 4, pp. 41–2. Cf. J.W. IV. 1 (p. 28), a summary of the opening and closing points given in J.W. IV. 2.

To Mrs. Sophia Williamson[1]

[Aug. 11, 1737]

At Mr. Causton's request I write once more. The rules whereby I proceed are these:

So many as intend to be partakers of the Holy Communion shall signify their
5 names to the curate at least some time the day before.

This you did not do.

And if any of those . . . have done any wrong to his neighbours by word or deed, so that the congregation be thereby offended, the curate . . . shall advertise him that in any wise he presume not to come to the Lord's table until he hath
10 openly declared himself to have truly repented.[2]

If you offer yourself at the Lord's table on Sunday, I will advertise you (as I have done more than once) wherein you 'have done wrong'; and when you have 'openly declared yourself to have truly repented', I will administer to you the Mysteries of God.

15   John Wesley

Aug. 11, 1737.

Address: 'To Mrs. Sophia Williamson'   *Source*: MA, Wesley, MS Journal, J.W. IV. 2, § 68, pp. 41–2.

this I was accused of refusing a private conference—"a plain proof", says Mr. Causton, "of his spite and malice". Now I was accused of desiring a private conference—"a plain proof", says the same Mr. Causton, "of his guilt" . . .'

[1] Thomas Causton had urged Wesley to write to Sophy, stating his reasons for repelling her. At first Wesley refused, fearing the uses to which such a letter might be put, but finally agreed. After quoting the letter Wesley continued: 'Mr. Delamotte carrying this, Mrs. Williamson insisted she had done nothing amiss. Mr. Causton said, "I am the person that am injured. I am ill used. The affront is offered to me, and I will espouse the cause of my niece. It will be the worst thing Mr. Wesley ever did in his life, to fix upon my family. She shall not offer herself on Sunday. She shall never communicate with him more. Neither will I, as long as I live; nor shall any of my family." After many other sharp words he added, "But I have made his character public to all the world. I have sent it to England already, and will publish it in every newspaper in England and America." '

[2] The quotations are, of course, from the opening rubrics of Holy Communion in the Book of Common Prayer, rubrics which Wesley made a habit of enforcing on all.

To the Savannah Magistrates[1]

[Sept.] 8, 1737

Gentlemen

If you are not apprised that Mr. Dyson[2] intends this day publicly
to perform several ecclesiastical offices in Savannah, and (as he says)
by your authority, I do now apprise you thereof, and am, gentlemen,   5
your humble servant,

John Wesley

Address: 'To the Magistrates of the town of Savannah'   *Source*: MA,
Wesley, Journal, J.W. III. 4, p. 65; also J.W. IV. 1, p. 39.

[From the Revd. Alexander Garden][3]

[Sept., 1737]

I am much concerned at some reports and papers concerning you from
Georgia. The papers contain some affidavits made against you by one Mrs.   10
Williamson; and a parcel of stuff called presentments of you by the grand jury,

---

[1] Wesley's MS Journal for Sept., 1737, reads: 'Wedn. 7. Mr. Dyson, Chaplain to
the Company of soldiers at Frederica, called at a house where I was and said that he
had now authority from the magistrates to perform ecclesiastical offices at Savannah,
and should begin so to do the next day, by reading prayers, preaching, and administering
the sacrament. On Th. the 8th, at nine, the first bell was accordingly rung, upon which I
wrote and sent by Mr. Delamotte the following note . . . [as given above, incorrectly
dated 'Aug. 8' in both accounts of the incident]. Mr. Delamotte delivered it to Mr.
Recorder. However at 10 the bell rung again, and Mr. Dyson entered upon his office, by
reading prayers and preaching in the church to Mrs. Causton (Mr. Causton being walked
out of town), Mr. Williamson, Mrs. Williamson, and eight or ten more. He told the
congregation he should do so every Thursday; that he had intended likewise to administer
the Lord's Supper, but some of his communicants were indisposed; and that he would
administer baptism also, to as many as he was desired.' (J.W. III. 4, pp. 65–6; similar,
with some verbal changes, in J.W. IV. 1, pp. 39–40.) It will be noted that Causton and
his fellow-magistrates were thus seeking to provide supplementary pastoral service, not
to replace Wesley.

[2] A Church of England minister, the Revd. Edward Dyson (Wesley spells the name
'Dison'), who seems to have been both drunken and disreputable; he was in Christ
Church parish (Berkeley), South Carolina, Feb.–July, 1730, and also filled in as an
army chaplain at Port Royal and at Frederica. In 1736 he had supplied for Wesley in
Savannah, but unsatisfactorily.

[3] Alexander Garden (*c.* 1685–1756), a Scotsman who emigrated to Charleston, South
Carolina, in 1719, to become rector of St. Philip's Church. From 1726 to 1748 he was
also the ranking clergyman in the south, as Commissary to the Bishop of London. A
majority of the grand jury (mainly men depending upon Causton for their livelihood)

for matters chiefly of your mere office as a clergyman. Has our Sovereign Lord
the King given the temporal courts in Georgia ecclesiastical jurisdiction?
If he has not, then sure I am that, whatever your failings in your office may be,
a grand jury's presentments of them, being repugnant to the fundamental laws
5 and constitution of England, is a plain 'breach of his peace', and an open insult
on 'his crown and dignity'; for which they themselves ought to be presented,
if they have not incurred a *premunire*. The presentments, a sad pack of nonsense,
I have seen; but not the affidavits. They were both designed to have been
published in our *Gazette*, but our friends here have hitherto prevented it . . .
10 I shall be glad to have some light from yourself into these matters, and wherewith to oppose the reports industriously spread here to your disadvantage.
Meantime I remain your most obedient humble servant,

A. Garden[1]

Source: Whitehead, II. 43.

From Henry Newman

London, 10 Oct. 1737

15 Revd. sir
I received your favour of the 11th of June last, by which the Society were
glad to hear of your welfare, notwithstanding the discouragement you meet
with on the part of the heathen in your neighbourhood and the province you are
engaged in.
20 I shall acquaint Mr. Archdeacon Rye of your thankful acceptances of his
benefaction.
As to the circumstances of good Sir John Philipps' death which you inquire
after, [Newman here gives a brief conventional statement, crosses this through,
and goes into much greater detail].
25 He had dined the 5th January last with some of his dear friends, who were
always welcome to his table, and they had left him about half an hour when, his
sons being gone out, his servants below stairs hearing a noise in the dining-room,
they immediately run up to see what was the matter, and found him fallen from
his chair, with his head against one of the legs of the table, upon which he seems
30 to have expired in a moment, without fetching one breath, or given one groan.
For though a surgeon and apothecary were immediately sent for, they could not
get one drop of blood from several veins which I saw opened in his arm, temples,
and among the jugular veins.
This was just such an exit as I believe Sir John himself would have chose, who
found two presentments 'true bills' on Aug. 23, and a further eight on Aug. 31, but
a minority forwarded the reasons for their dissent to the Trustees. When Wesley eventually left for England he carried with him a letter from Garden to the bishop, presenting
a sympathetic outline of the events which had forced Wesley's resignation, and describing the presentments as 'all either impertinent, false, or frivolous'. (Dec. 22, 1737; see
South Carolina Historical Magazine, Oct., 1977.)

1 Orig., 'S. Garden'.

had the happiness of an habitual preparation for death. To leave the world without the anxieties of a lingering sickness, and the agonies that usually attend the separation of soul and body, is a privilege every good man is not to expect.

May it please God to fit us for our departure from this frail state, though it should happen to be in a manner as sudden (resembling a translation) as the 5 instance I have given, and that you may be instrumental in bringing many to salvation by Jesus Christ, is the sincere wish of, reverend sir, yours,

[Henry Newman]

Sir Erasmus Philipps is gone to Montpellier for his health. All your friends of the Society are well. Your brother will inform you of Mr. Oglethorpe's 10 preparations, and when he intends to set out for Georgia, with a regiment which the King has given him.

Address: 'To the Revd. Mr. John Wesley at Savannah in Georgia'   *Source*: S.P.C.K., Misc. Letters, CN2/3, pp. 76–7, a draft.

From the Revd. Benjamin Ingham

Oct. 19, 1737

Dear brother

By your silence one would suspect that you was offended at my last letter. 15 Am I your enemy because I tell you the truth? But perhaps I was too severe. Forgive me, then. However, I am sure that by soaring too high in your own imaginations you have had a great downfall in your spiritual progress. Be lowly, therefore, in your own eyes; humble yourself before the Lord, and he will lift you up. I do assure you it is out of pure love, and with concern, that I write. 20 I earnestly wish your soul's welfare. O pray for mine also. The Lord preserve you.

Could not you, think you, live upon the income of your fellowship? If you can, do. The Trustees are indeed very willing to support you, and they take it ill that anybody should say you have been too expensive. But the Bishop of London 25 (as I have heard) and some others have been offended at your expenses. Not indeed altogether without reason, because you declared at your leaving England that you should want scarce anything.

I just give you these hints. Pray for direction, and then act as you judge best.

Charles is so reserved I know little about him. He neither writes to me, nor 30 comes to see me. What he intends is best known to himself. Mr. Hutton's family go on exceeding well. Your friend Mr. Wogan (I heard) either has or is about publishing a book to prove that everyone baptized with water is regenerate. All friends at Oxford go on well. Mr. Kinchin, Mr. Hutchins, Mr. Washington, Bell, Sarney, Hervey, Watson, are all zealous. Mr. Atkinson labours under severe 35 trials in Westmoreland, but is steady and sincere, and an excellent Christian. Dick Smith is weak, yet not utterly gone. Mr. Robson and Grieves are but indifferent. The latter is married to a widow, and teaches school at Northampton. Mr. Thompson of Queen's has declared his resolution of following Christ.

He writ me this ode, which he enclosed in a sermon on the new birth which I
lent him to read, referring to the words of the text, 'If any man be in Christ,
he is a new creature. [. . .]' (2 Cor. 5 : 17). [1][. . .]
    Remember me to Wm. Wallis, Mark Hird, and the family Davison, Mrs.
5 Gilbert, Mears, Mr. Campbell, Mr. and Mrs. Burnside, Mr. and Mrs. Williamson. Yours in Christ,

                                                              B. Ingham

Ossett, Octr. 19, 1737

Address: 'To The Revd. Mr John Wesley at Savannah in Georgia'   *End* by
JW: 'b[rother] Ingham / Oct. 19, 1737'   *Source*: MA.

From Dr. Timothy Cutler

                                                      [Oct. 22, 1737]

10 Revd. sir
    It is now some time ago that I had the pleasure of your letter dated July 23.
Therein you hint your answer to my first letter, but nothing of my acknowledging
the receipt of it, so that I fear my second letter (by whom sent I forget) hath
totally miscarried.
15   I am sorry, sir, for the clouds hanging over your mind respecting your undertaking and situation, but hope God will give an happy increase to that good seed
you have planted and watered according to his will. The best of men, in all
ages, have failed in the success of their labour; and there will ever be found too
many enemies to the cross of Christ. For earth will not be heaven. This reminds
20 us of that happy place, where we shall not see and be grieved for transgressors;
and where, for our well-meant labours, our judgment is with the Lord, and our
reward with our God. And you well know, sir, that under the saddest appearances
we may have some share in the consolations which God gave Elijah; and may
trust in him that there is some wickedness we repress or prevent, some goodness
25 by our means (weak and unworthy as we are) beginning, preserved, or increasing
in the hearts of men; at present perhaps like a grain of mustard seed, that in
God's time may put forth, spread, and flourish; and that if the world seems not
the better for us, it might be worse without us. Our low opinion of ourselves is a
preparative to these successes; and so the modest and great Apostle found it.
30   No doubt, sir, you have temptations where you are, nor is there any retreat
from them. They hint to us the care we must take, and the promises we must
apply to; and blessed is the man that endureth temptations.
    I rejoice in the good character which, I believe, you well bestow on Mr.
Whitefield, coming to you, and desire you would tender to him my compliments
35 and best wishes, as also to your reverend and worthy brother. But I question
not but his labours will better be joined with than supersede yours; and even his,
and all our sufficiency and efficiency, is of God.

    [1] Five four-line stanzas, beginning, 'I strung my Lyre;—When Love appear'd', and
signed at the end, 'Wm. Thompson'.

It is the least we can do to pray for one another; and if God will hear me (a great sinner!), it will strengthen your interest in him. I commend myself to a share in your prayers for his pardon, acceptance, and assistance; and beg that my family, particularly a dear son, now curate to the Dean of Bocking in Essex, may not be forgotten by you. I am, reverend sir, your most affectionate, humble 5 servant,

Tim.*θ* Cutler

Boston, 8br. 22, 1737

End by JW: '1737 Oct. 22 / Dr. Cutler'   *Source*: MA.

[From Mrs. Elizabeth Fallowfield][1]

[Dec. 27, 1737]

Sir   10

How shall I return you sufficient thanks for your good advice, or enough regret the loss of such a friend, since I need never hope to see you here again. No, you have met with too much ingratitude from a thoughtless, wicked people, who knew not the value of that blessing heaven had lent them. May it still continue to preserve you from all attempts their malice can invent, and guard 15 you from all danger of the sea. Let not the remembrance of their baseness make you forget those few that still retain a grateful sense of your care and kindness amongst us. Should heaven once more grant me the happiness of seeing your return, methinks I should ask no more ((in)) this world could give. So great is the happiness of a friend on whom one may depend, and from whose advice if 20 carefully observed cannot fail of giving peace and rest to the distressed and afflicted mind. May Almighty God aid and strengthen me to pursue those methods you direct, and earnestly endeavour to decline the bad effects of too careless an example. O may the Almighty Power change his heart,[2] and make me happy in him. Cease not to pray for me, that divine Providence may preserve and 25 defend me from all sin, and if not happy here, yet hereafter. May heaven grant

[1] John Fallowfield was a freeholder of Savannah who had arrived in 1734, in 1735 married and was made 'Collector' by the Trustees, and in 1739 a bailiff. He became the leader of the 'clamorous malcontents' who petitioned the Trustees for more self-government by the settlers, was discharged from office by the Trustees in 1741, and in 1742 with his family left Georgia. His wife Elizabeth seems to have been the person described by Wesley in his *Journal* for May 25, 1737, as 'a convert to the Church of Rome' who was convinced she should return to the Church of England (cf. his diary for May 25, 28; June 3, 16; July 1, 25; Aug. 26, 1737). Although the only tangible evidence linking this letter to her is a statement on the nineteenth-century transcript of this document at Drew University, and the defective original carries no proof about either writer or recipient, it seems quite clear that this is indeed an example of the admiration of those loyal supporters whose affectionate letters followed Wesley to England after his troubled departure from Savannah on Dec. 2, 1737.

[2] Apparently her husband is intended, as in the 'too careless an example' of the preceding sentence.

you health and success in all your undertakings is [the] earnest desires and constant prayers of, sir, your obliged, humble ⟨. . .⟩

Savannah, Dec[e]mb[er] 27

Sir, let me hear from you when you can conveniently.[1]

Source: MA, on three-quarters of a sheet, one quarter separated from the remainder, and the other quarter (containing the signature, probably Wesley's endorsement, and possibly the address, missing). Very poor writing and spelling, and no punctuation.

From the Revd. Charles Wesley[2]

5   College Street, [London]
                                                            Janu. 2, 1737/8

Dear brother

From my soul I congratulate you upon your late glorious treatment; nor do I less envy you. 'Tis now that you begin to be a disciple of Christ. I have just
10 read over the returned papers without any emotion but that of joy. Had I even resolved to have set up my rest here, your present trial would have broke my resolution, and forced me back to America, to partake with you in your sufferings for the gospel. Such you may most assuredly reckon what you now labour under (I should rather say, what you now rejoice and glory in). For it is not the
15 mixture of infirmity that can prevent God's accepting them as endured for his sake. If you have the testimony of a good conscience, your sufferings are interpretatively his, and human wisdom can never dispute you out of it. We know that worldly, and even partially good men, the strangers as well as the enemies to the cross of Christ, observing some failings in God's children, ascribe the whole of
20 their persecutions to those only. The scandal of the cross with them is ceased, the reproach of Christ no longer subsists, the contrariety betwixt his light and the darkness, betwixt his Spirit and the spirit of the world, is at an end; and our conformity to our persecuted Master is all resolved into *want of prudence*. In vain do we press them with the plain words of Scripture: 'All that will live
25 godly in Christ Jesus *shall suffer persecution*;'—'The disciple is not above his master;'—'If they have persecuted me, they *will also persecute you*;'—and a thousand others. Experience only can convince them that the sense of these Scriptures is literal and eternal. But this I need not tell you. You *know* the absolute impossibility of being inwardly conformed to Christ without this
30 outward conformity, this badge of discipleship, these marks of Christ. You marvel not, as if some new thing had happened unto you, but rejoice in tribulation, as knowing that hereunto you are called, and can only be made perfect through these sufferings.

These are the trials that must fit you for the heathen; and you shall suffer

---

[1] Wesley's diary shows that he wrote to her on June 28, 1740, though he may well have written to her earlier.

[2] Replying to a letter probably written about Oct. 7 (cf. MS Journal).

greater things than these! When your name is cast out as evil, and[1] when you cannot live among them, but are driven out from your own countrymen, *then* is your time for turning to the Gentiles.

That time may still be at a great distance. As yet the bridle is in their mouths, and all the arrows they shoot out are bitter words. But stay till those words are credited and seconded by actions; lest he that letteth, letteth no longer, but the whole storm burst upon you, and the fiery trial commences;—and then will be shown how you have learned Christ, and whether you are chosen to teach him to the heathen.

You remember the case of *Athanasius contra mundum*.[2] The charge brought against *him* was worth bringing: treason, adultery, and murder, at once. I wonder no more is said against *you*. The devil himself could not wish for fitter instruments than those he actuates and inspires in Georgia. Whatever he will suggest, they will both say and swear to. But things are not yet ripe on your part. You have but begun the lesson of meekness and gentleness and love, and God in ⟨his⟩ pity of your weakness has sent you a fellow-labourer and fellow-sufferer.[3] He comes συζῆν καὶ συναοθανεῖν;[4] and here are many more who long to be partakers with you in the sufferings of the gospel. I too would be of the number, and shall follow, in sure and certain expectation of your treatment. The fiery furnace, I trust, shall purify me, and if emptied of myself I would defy the world and the devil to hurt me. We would then join in turning the war against them, and make them fear us.

You have as great reason to depend upon the Trustees' justice as you can have upon any men. As to all the other charges, they judge it wholly impertinent in the wise accusers to bring them. The affidavit being concerning a fact, you must answer to it, and then pray for reparation. We will pursue this matter to the utmost, in the name of God and the spirit of meekness. Meantime your comfort is that noble passage in Kempis, which I have just opened upon:

Pro amore Dei dabis omnia libenter subire, labores scilicet et dolores, tentationes, vexationes, anxietates, necessitates, infirmitates, injurias, oblocutiones, reprehensiones, humiliationes, confusiones, correctiones, et despectiones.

Hac juvant ad virtutem; haec probant Christi tyronem; haec fabricant coelestem coronam.

Ego reddam mercedem aeternam pro brevi labore, et infinitam gloriam pro transitoria confusione.[5]

---

[1] The clause, 'it is not fit for such a fellow to live' at this point is underlined, apparently for exclusion rather than emphasis.

[2] 'Athanasius against the world', a proverbial phrase arising from the titles of several of his writings, especially those attacking the Arians.

[3] George Whitefield, whom the group was seeing off on his first voyage to America.

[4] 'to live and die'; see 2 Cor. 7: 3.

[5] *De Imitatio Christi*, III. xxxv. 2, translated in John Wesley's edition, *The Christian's Pattern* (1735), based on Dr. John Worthington's of 1677:

'Thou oughtest for the love of God willingly to undergo all things, even labours, griefs, temptations, vexations, anxieties, necessities, infirmities, injuries, detractions, reproaches, humblings, shame, corrections, and contempts.

'These help to virtue; these try a young soldier of Christ; these make the heavenly crown.

'I will give an everlasting reward for a short labour, and infinite glory for transitory shame.'

Gravesend, Jan. 3

I am here with G. Whitefield, my brothers Hall and Hutton, and a long etc. of zealous friends. God has poured out his Spirit upon them, so that the whole nation is in an uproar. Tell dearest Charles[1] we dined in our way at ⟨Blen⟩don,
5 where we found his sisters, brother Will, and mother, exceedingly zealous for the Lord of Hosts. Will has raised a party for God at Cambridge. They are already stigmatized for *Methodists*. We see all about us in an amazing ferment. Surely Christianity is once more lifting up its head. O that I might feel its renovating spirit, and be thereby qualified to diffuse it among others! I trust you pray
10 without ceasing for me. I long to break loose, to be devoted to God, to be in Christ a new creature! Brethren, pray for us,

Charles Wesley, Westley Hall, George Whitefield, James Hutton, Isaac Burton, John Hutchings, John Bray, John Doble, Jephthah Harris, James Habersham.[2]

[From James Hutton][3]

Jan. 3, 1737[/38]

15 Dear sir

I have now opened a shop, and am entering myself into a new world; you will suit your prayers accordingly. I too bear part in the reproach of Christ, I hope, as I do not sell plays, and as the London and Oxon Methodists come to my house and sing Psalms audibly, against the peace and quiet of the neighbourhood.
20 I am stigmatized as mad, Presbyterian, fanatic, but I bless God I mind not the foolish words of simple men. I pray they may be converted. I am just at Temple Bar, amidst the fiery darts of the devil. Your brother has been of great help to me. So has Mr. Hall, and Mr. Whitefield. My kindest love attends Charles Delamotte. I rejoice in what God has done for his family. I congratulate you on your
25 sufferings, and almost wish you the glorious red crown of martyrdom. I must conclude, your servant,

James Hutton

Address: 'To The Revd. Mr J. Wesley, Minister of Savannah, per Whitacre,[4] Captn Whiting, Q.D.S.'   *End* by JW: 'C. Jan. 2, 1737/8 / ad. by coming', and 'rev[iewe]d Dec. 13, 1751'. In another hand, referring to a bundle, of which this was apparently the first, 'those [*sic*] Letters have been looked over but not read'.   *Source*: MA, with many indications of revision for publication in the *A.M.* Supp., 1797, pp. 11–13, which also omitted two paragraphs.

[1] Charles Delamotte.
[2] All the signatures were added personally, in one column.
[3] Added to Whitefield's letter.
[4] i.e. the *Whitaker*, on which Whitefield sailed to Georgia.

From the Revd. John Gambold[1]

Janu. 27, 1737–8

Dear sir

The point you mention has long been a difficulty to me; of which I could find no end but that general solution of all doubts, and cure of all anxieties, resignation to eternal Providence. [. . .]   5

But to come to the point. That regeneration is the beginning of a life which is not fully enjoyed but in another world we all know. But how much of it may be enjoyed at present? What degrees of it does the experience of mankind encourage us to expect? And by what symptoms shall we know it? Let us consult our observation as to the gradual progress of a religious life. [. . .] It seems to be the   10 order of Providence now, that none should have much holiness, that all may have a little.

Dear sir, I have given no particular answer to your questions, but I have said something hastily; perhaps very wrong, but I know to whom. Miss Wesley gives her love, and would have written, but she is somewhat indisposed. Your   15 affectionate brother and servant,

JG

Source: MA, a very long letter, with no address sheet.

To the Revd. George Whitefield[2]

[Feb. 1, 1738]

. . . When I saw God, by the wind which was carrying you out, brought me in, I asked counsel of God. His answer you have   20 enclosed.

[1] John Gambold (1711–71), an Oxford Methodist ordained in 1733 to become vicar of Stanton Harcourt, Oxon., where Kezia Wesley was a member of his household for two years. In 1742 he resigned his living to become a Moravian, of whose community he was consecrated a bishop in 1754.

[2] As noted from the previous letter, Whitefield had been waiting for some weeks to set sail from Deal harbour. Wesley disembarked in the same harbour on Feb. 1, discovering that the vessel apparently leaving was the *Whitaker*, with Whitefield aboard. He drew lots as to what he should do, possibly to try to reach the *Whitaker* by means of a rowing-boat, or wait around in the hope of the vessel's not managing to get away, or to move on to London immediately. Apparently the last lot was the one drawn, and 'after reading prayers and explaining a portion of Scripture to a large company at the inn, [he] left Deal, and came in the evening to Faversham'. The *Whitaker* did not get away until the following day, so that Whitefield came ashore that night, read Wesley's letter, and replied to it in such a way as to make it clear that he took the 'return to London' to refer to him rather than Wesley—which indeed may well have been the case, though it seems strange for Wesley to be drawing a lot about someone else's conduct, even though that

[Whitefield's comment: 'This was a piece of paper, in which were written these words, "Let him return to London." ']

Source: George Whitefield, *A Letter to the Reverend Mr. John Wesley, in answer to his Sermon, entituled*, Free-Grace, London, Strahan, 1741, p. 7.

From the Revd. George Whitefield

Downs, Feb. 1, 1738

Rev. and dear sir

5   I received the news of your arrival (blessed be God) with the utmost composure, and sent a servant immediately on shore to wait on you, but found you was gone. Since that your kind letter has reached me. But I think many reasons may be urged against my coming to London. For, first, I cannot be hid if I came there, and the enemies of the Lord will think I am turning back, and so

10   blaspheme that Holy Name wherewith I am called. Secondly, I cannot leave the flock committed to my care on shipboard; and perhaps while I am at London the ship may sail. Thirdly, I see no cause for not going forwards to Georgia. Your coming rather confirms (as far as I can hitherto see) than disannuls my call. It is not fit the Colony should be left without a shepherd. And though they

15   are a stiff-necked and rebellious people, yet as God hath given me the affections of all where I have been yet, why should I despair of finding his divine presence in a foreign land? For these reasons, reverend and dear sir, I should rather think it more advisable for you either to come to Deal immediately, or send me an account of things as you shall judge most proper . . .

20   Whether I am right or not God only knows. However, this is my comfort, to the best of my knowledge I simply desire to do the divine will. And therefore I spread your letter before the Lord in prayer, and asked for direction, but as yet find no inclination in myself, or intimation from Providence, to follow you to London. I rather dread it, and reflect on the prophet who went back contrary to

25   the divine command at the solicitations of the other prophet, and was slain by a lion in the way. God forbid I should compare you to a false prophet; but you know it is no uncommon thing for our blessed Master to try us even by servants of his own. O, dear sir, I should rejoice to see you if God shall think fit. If you commend me to God and the Word of his grace, and pray that I may be always

might seem the natural implication of 'him'. When Whitefield published this small extract in his *Letter* of 1741 he was clearly annoyed at what had happened, though this did not show in his letter at the time: 'The morning [before] I sailed from Deal to Gibraltar you arrived from Georgia. Instead of giving me an opportunity to converse with you, though the ship was not far off the shore, you drew a lot, and immediately set forwards to London. You left a letter behind you, in which were words to this effect . . . [as quoted above]. When I received this, I was somewhat surprised. Here was a good man telling me he had cast a lot, and that God would have me return to London. On the other hand, I knew my call was to Georgia . . . I betook myself with a friend to prayer . . . I wrote you word, that I could not return to London.'

ready, *nudus nudum [Christum] sequi*,[1] and follow the Captain of my salvation, though it be through a sea of blood.

I throw myself blindfold into the hands of God. His strength will be made perfect in my weakness. And, I trust, I shall be made more than conqueror through him that made me. 5

Reverend sir, I rejoice that you are once more come to your native shore; and am, I trust, sincerely, rev. sir, your most affectionate son and servant,

George Whitefield

P.S. Pray salute all in my name.

Address: 'To the Rev. John Wesley in London'   *Source*: *A.M.* Supp., 1797, pp. 16–17.

From Charles Delamotte

Savannah, Febry. 23d, 1737[/8] 10

Oh! my dear brother, how greatly do I long after you in the bowels of Jesus Christ! What God hath done for us in your absence I trust will be a comfort to you and all the brethren.

For six weeks we went on in the spirit of slumber, and even poor William had left off most of the means of grace. But hath God forgotten to be gracious? No! 15 for when things were desperate, then the Almighty laid to his hand, and let the enemy loose upon us, who with scorpions hath united us together, and against all opposition do now join with one heart and one voice in morning and evening prayers. Some who were hirelings are gone out from amongst us (Mrs. Cross, Mrs. Ann, Mr. Grant), and others who never have had any sense of their duty 20 are become zealous advocates for the Lord God of Hosts.

Oh! If you did but know how much one or more of you were wanted[2] here, I am sure you would not delay coming one minute. Let not then a soldier of Jesus Christ tarry to provide gold or silver or scrip for their journey, for the disciple must be as his Master, and the servant as his Lord. 25

Mr. Causton still continues the same man, only more angry than before. I went one day to him about the children, and immediately he sent for the other magistrates, who after treating me with some scurrilous language, in form they forbade me ever to have any more prayers at my house, etc., adding that my teaching the children was a scandalous thing, who out of pretence of doing good 30 I only made it a cloak to inquire into everybody's private affairs, and that he would write to the Trustees and have me removed. This, I bless God, quickened me much, and I resolved, through Christ strengthening me, to persevere with all my might, being strongly possessed at the same time that unless I watched over my own wicked heart very narrowly I should be puffed up, and fall through 35 pride.

[1] 'Naked to follow a naked Christ', the ideal of St. Francis of Assisi; cf. Wesley's letter of July 2, 1739, p. 664 below.
[2] Orig., 'wanting'.

I have not obeyed Mr. Causton's authority in this, which has made him publicly declare he would put out all his strength to break the neck of our meeting together, and accordingly took all opportunities of speaking separately to each member, first by fair promises, saying, if they would not meet here they
5 should want for nothing; and if this had no effect he then threatened to present me for a public annuisance, and to show them no favour; but blessed be God, all to no purpose. In particular poor Mr. How[s], whom he told, I believe, Mr. How[s], you have a good design in going there, not being acquainted with their bad designs; but I would not advise you to run yourself into any danger, for
10 you are a principal man, and many other things to the same effect, which he summed up, saying, It signifies nothing parlaying; all I mean is this, that if you don't set the Psalm they will break up by degrees; upon which Mr. How[s] told him he knew we had no bad intention, but a good one, and while he had health and opportunity he must do what he thought was his duty, let the con-
15 sequence be what it would. This so enraged Mr. Causton that it made him ready to kick Mr. How[s] out of doors.

About a fortnight ago there went a great cry through the streets, 'News concerning the saints', that now there was a proof of the horrid proceedings of that monster Wesley and his crew—Mr. Campbell had committed adultery with Mrs.
20 Mears, and had made confession, and received absolution from you. 'What need have we of further proof of his being a Roman priest, and all his followers Roman Catholics?' This made Mr. Causton consider after his usual way that here something might be made out, and accordingly sent for Mrs. Cross and Mrs. Ann, who presently made a second Sophy's affidavit of two sheets of paper
25 full of the horridest lies and nonsense that ever were put together. 'First, that all present were sworn with the Bible ⟨. . .⟩ Secresy,[1] that both parties acknowledged they had laid together several times at Highgate, at the Cowpen, and at his house, and then goes on to describe the manner she put her legs and his manner of acting very obscenely, and after they had done they greeted each
30 other with a holy kiss, and sang a Psalm. It speaks then particularly of the posture we all sat in at the time of confession, Mr. B—— upon the stairs, hanging down his head, Mrs. Gilbert clapping her daughter upon the back and saying, Speak up, Betty, never fear, when it is out there is an end of it, etc., and much more nonsense of the same import. Now human means are not to be despised,
35 therefore being met together we all judged it necessary to send the enclosed certificate, that if you should be charged with Mrs. Ann's affidavit you might have something to prove it false.

Yesterday I was presented to the Grand Jury by Mr. Causton for a breaker of the law, and raising parties; but agreeable to our present weakness the whole
40 jury made a jest of it, and said it was nothing but spite and malice against Mr. Wesley. This usage must not be expected always, else would the cross of Christ cease, which is the only support we have to keep life in us. O pray mightily for us all, but more especially for me, that the new cloth of the glorious

---

[1] It is barely possible that 'Bible' (with no period) at the foot of p. 1 should be followed by 'Secresy' (possibly an error for 'Secondly') at the head of p. 2, but almost certain that on the missing half-sheet the address was on p. 4, and the continuation of the letter from 'Bible' on p. 3—a missing passage roughly equal in length to the opening six paragraphs.

gospel may not be put into the old garment of [a] wicked unregenerate heart, that being truly mortified to all the pleasures of sense I may be very zealous to every good word and work, from your dutiful son in Christ,

Chas Delamotte

P.S. I am poor and in debt, and my not knowing at one meal where I shall get 5 the next is a great help to thankfulness.

End by JW: 'CD, Feb. 23, 1737' *Source*: MA.

From the Revd. Walter Chapman[1]

Bath, Feb. 27th, 1737/8

My dear friend
So I take the liberty of calling you, though your silence to my last letter gives me too much reason to suspect the justice of my claim to that endearing appella- 10 tion. If I should be so happy as to conjecture wrong, and a hurry of business, and variety of engagements have hindered me as yet from that pleasure, snatch the first opportunity after the receipt of this of writing to your friend.

I should be glad to know how you have left affairs at Georgia? When you propose returning? And what was the cause of your sudden and unexpected 15 coming? I ask this last because I have heard variety of reasons assigned for it. Why is Charles so obstinately silent? Something extraordinary surely must be in the way to make him act so contrary to his nature.

God, I humbly trust, blesses my endeavours in his service greatly, and that I may every day grow a fitter instrument to be thus employed your prayers are 20 earnestly requested by, dear sir, your affectionate friend in Christ,

W: Chapman

My love and service to Charles, Mr. Broughton, and all other friends.

End by JW: 'Mr. Chapman, Feb. 27' *Source*: Bristol Wesley, p. 218.

---

[1] See p. 502 n. above.

To Lady Cox[1]

March 7, 1737/8, Oxon

Madam

Some days since I was shown several Queries which had been sent to Bath,[2] and an answer to them intended to have been sent likewise. 5 But I could not approve of that answer, it seeming to me to savour too much of the wisdom of the world, which they will never know how to be enough afraid of who have seen what havoc it makes even among the children of God. I will therefore answer them myself, with all simplicity, and without any regard to the judgment of the

---

[1] Lady Cox, or Cocks, was the widow of Sir Richard Cox, second Baronet of Dumbleton, Gloucestershire. She was his second wife, born Mary, daughter of William Bethel, Esq., of Swinton, Yorkshire. They had no children. On his death in 1726 he was succeeded by his brother, the Revd. Sir Robert Cocks, D.D., rector of Bladon cum Woodstock and Rollright, Oxon., who died in 1736 and was succeeded by his son, another Sir Robert Cocks. This fourth baronet died without issue in 1765, when the baronetcy became extinct.

Lady Mary Cox lived in Queen Square, Bath, with her sister Bridget Bethel, and was one of Whitefield's earliest converts there. Both contributed generously to his Georgia Orphan House. She was also friendly with the Countess of Huntingdon. Mrs. Mary Pendarves wrote thus candidly of her to Ann Granville on Dec. 22, 1738: 'I am sorry for my Lady Cox, and lament the want of judgment in a woman of such excellent virtues; but a warm heart, with excess of good nature, will lead people into error without a *proper resolution* and very *discerning judgment* to keep the balance even.' She does not seem to have moved within Wesley's orbit much, though the Oxford Methodist Walter Chapman conveyed greetings from her in a PS. to his letter to Wesley on Sept. 3, 1736: 'My Lady Cocks and sisters are now in Oxford, and they desire their best services to you, etc., and wish you good luck in the name of the Lord.' Wesley also visited her in Bath on at least one occasion (diary, July 11, 1739).

[2] The following is on a page prefixed to the letter itself, the name of the recipient (possibly unknown to Wesley at the time), being supplied later, apparently in the hand of Thomas Marriott, who prepared the document for No. XVIII of his 'Wesley Papers' in *W.M.M.*, 1846, pp. 1088–90:

'Queries sent to Mrs [Bethel?] at Bath.

1st. Do not the Methodists in writing and speaking use canting language?

'2ndly. Do they not frequently talk of extraordinary notices and directions to determine their actions, etc?

'3rdly. Do they not imagine all or some of them have certain divine impulses, like the divine inspiration of the apostles?

'4thly. Do they not impose on themselves and others certain duties and works at certain times and after certain manners? As, to fast, abstain from meats, rise at midnight, etc., otherwise than is appointed in Scripture? Or without such appointment?

'5thly. Do they not form themselves into a sect, distinguish themselves from other Christians? Have not some of them set up conventicles, etc.?

'6thly. Do they not require voluntary poverty in their members?

'7thly. Do they not despise marriage?'

world, as knowing that if my words do not appear foolishness to the world it is because there is nothing of the wisdom of God in them.

A plain account of the beginning of the sect inquired after was printed two or three years since.[1] To which need only be added that though some time after Mr. M[organ]'s death my brother and I were left alone, yet this loss was overbalanced the following year by our acquaintance with Mr. Clayton. With him several of his pupils, and afterward some of mine, joined together in the labour of love,[2] to whom were soon added Mr. Broughton, Ingham, Whitefield, Hervey, whose zeal stirred up many others not to be ashamed of their Master or his words, even in the midst of a crooked and perverse generation.[3]

But in the beginning of the year 1735 it pleased God to break us in pieces again, and to scatter us not only throughout England, but almost to the ends of the earth. My brother and I were first called into the country, and then sent with Mr. Ingham into America. Neither were we suffered to be long together there, one, before his return home, being driven to New England,[4] another being called into Pennsylvania,[5] and I only remaining in Georgia. Meanwhile Mr. Broughton, Whitefield, Hervey, and the rest of our friends, were dispersed each a several[6] way. So that at my return to Oxon this month[7] I found not one of those who had formerly joined with me, and only three gentlemen who trod in their steps, building up one another in the faith.

To anyone who asketh me concerning myself or these whom I rejoice to call my brethren, what our principles are, I answer clearly, We have no principles but those revealed in the Word of God. In the interpretation whereof we always judge the most literal sense to be the best, unless where the literal sense of one contradicts some other Scripture.

If it be asked whether they do not 'imagine themselves to have certain divine impulses, like the divine inspiration of the apostles', they answer: (1) There never was a good man[8] without a divine

---

[1] *The Oxford Methodists*, 1733.   [2] 1 Thess. 1: 3, etc.
[3] Phil. 2: 15.   [4] Charles Wesley.   [5] Benjamin Ingham.
[6] Unlike its use in the previous paragraph (line 7), Wesley here has in mind the word's primary meaning of separate or distinct, which was gradually becoming obsolescent.
[7] In fact Wesley had visited Oxford for a few hours on Feb. 17, along with Peter Böhler, but returned for over a week on Mar. 4 because of the reported illness there of his brother Charles.
[8] Orig., 'a ((Christian))'.

impulse; and let those who will not believe this on St. Paul's[1] assertion go to the heathen Cicero for the same information.[2] Yet, (2), they learn from the oracles of God that 'the inspiration of the Holy Spirit'[3] which every Christian is to expect is different in kind
5 as well as degree from the inspiration of the apostles. It does not enable him[4] to speak new tongues, or to work outward miracles; therefore it is different in kind. Neither does it give him the same measure of holiness;[5] therefore it is different in degree. But, (3), they believe the change wrought by it in the heart to be equivalent to
10 all outward miracles, as implying the selfsame power which gave eyes to the blind, feet to the lame, and life to the dead.

   The language wherein they talk of these mighty works is that of the Spirit whereby they are wrought. They call, for instance, a person thus changed, 'regenerated',[6] 'born again',[7] 'a new creature';[8] and
15 in all other cases endeavour to express spiritual things in spiritual words, as being assured there are none like them, quick and powerful,[9] full of light and life.[10] Yet they are not ignorant that to the world which knoweth not, neither can know, the hidden meaning of those expressions, they ever from the beginning did appear cant and
20 jargon, and will do so to the end.

   If it be asked whether they do not 'talk of extraordinary notices and directions to determine their actions' they say, Yes, they do. As to extraordinary directions, they do not doubt but in extraordinary cases, too difficult to be determined by reason, as perhaps depending
25 on many future contingencies, and yet too important to be left undetermined, God will if applied to by fervent prayer 'give a perfect lot'.[11] And to extraordinary notices . . .[12]

---

   [1] Orig., 'S. Paul's'.

   [2] e.g. Wesley's quotation in his sermon, 'The End of Christ's Coming' (No. 62, 1781), § 3: 'Cicero . . . once stumbled upon that strange truth, *Nemo unquam vir magnus sine afflatu divine fuit*, "There never was any great man who was not divinely inspired." ' (See Cicero, *De Natura Deorum*, ii. 66.)

   [3] B.C.P., Communion, first collect.   [4] Orig., 'them'.

   [5] Orig., 'neither does it ((enable)) him ((to work outward miracles))'—which seems to imply a slip in transcription (duplicating a passage already transcribed) rather than the revision of a draft, as do the other alterations.

   [6] See Titus 3: 5, 1 Pet. 1: 3.   [7] John 3: 3.
   [8] 2 Cor. 5: 17.   [9] Heb. 4: 12.   [10] John 8: 12.

   [11] 1 Sam. 14: 41. Wesley's practice of directing issues in this way, especially during his early years, drew much criticism, as by Whitefield upon Wesley's decision to leave Deal (see p. 527 n.), and especially later about his sermon, *Free Grace*, with the lot, 'Preach and print'.

   [12] This surviving fragment of the letter deals only with the first three of the seven queries.

Address: 'To the Lady Cox at Bath'   *Source*: Morgan MSS, pp. 86–90, apparently a reference copy revised from a rough draft, which in its turn was transcribed for dispatch to Lady Cox.

From the Revd. James Hervey

Stoke Abbey, March 21, 1738

Rev. and honoured sir

How agreeably surprising was the news which a letter of Mr. Chapman's lately brought me. I am at a loss to say whether it was more unexpected or more grateful. It assured me that Mr. Wesley was arrived in England; had visited 5 Oxon; and was coming to Bath. And shall I not hasten a congratulatory address to welcome the friend of my studies, the friend of my soul, the friend of all my valuable and eternal interests? To do it cannot be deemed impertinency; but not to do it would justly bring upon me the imputation of ingratitude.

I hope, sir, your health is not impaired by your travels. [. . .] 10

I believe you had the pleasure of finding some of the Oxonians grown considerably in grace. They have made haste, since your departure, to improve their talents; and to edify their neighbours, as though they were earnestly and resolvedly desirous to enjoy their company in a better world.

You cannot but have heard, and, hearing, you cannot but rejoice at the 15 successful zeal of our friend Whitefield. All London, and the whole nation ring of μεγαλεῖα τοῦ θεοῦ[1] done by his ministry. But, alas! it will damp your rising satisfaction to receive an account of useless, worthless Hervey's having run a round of sin and vanity. [. . .] Send a line, and accompany it with a prayer, to warm my frozen and benumbed soul. [. . .] 20

I am retired from the scene of action into a worthy and wealthy gentleman's family. Mr. Chapman will inform you how much he deserves your prayers, and the prayers of all who are mighty with God and prevail.

Dear sir, if other business, if other charitable employments, will allow you leisure, pray favour me with a letter. To none will it be more acceptable, by 25 none is it more needed, than by your most obliged humble servant,

James Hervey

Source: Tyerm (*OM*), p. 215.

To James Hutton

March 26, 1738. Oxon.

Enclosed I send the key of my brother's bureau.[2] In one of the drawers are all my papers. Among them are several relating to 30

[1] 'The wonderful works of God' (Acts 2: 11).
[2] Apparently in the Huttons' home.

Capt. Watson.[1] Out of these pray take John Coates'[2] affidavit, and the certificates of Elisha Foster,[3] Thomas Salter,[4] and a third signed by about forty persons concerning Mr. Watson's sound understanding (not that signed by me). These, and no more, when you have taken attested copies of them, deliver as soon as possible to Mrs. Watson. Lose not an hour. Mr. Campbell[5] will tell you where she lives, whom I wish you would bring acquainted with Mr. Fox.[6] Dear Jemmy, Adieu.

[Added in the hand of Charles Wesley:]

Let me know by next post whether you can and will receive the money, and inquire when Mr. O[glethorpe] goes. I cannot write to him till I hear from you.—I dare not trust myself to say any more.

CW

Sunday night

Address: The address sheet is badly torn, leaving only the smallest fragments of three lines of the address: '⟨To Mr. James⟩ Hutton / ⟨In Dean's Ya⟩rd ⟨Westminster . . .⟩tely [?]'   *Seal*: Wreathed head (21)   *Source*: MorA./

[1] Joseph Watson, partner of John Musgrove, the Indian interpreter and trader in Savannah, mismanaged their affairs, was a quarrelsome person, and was eventually convicted of killing an Indian, but was declared insane, and recommended for mercy. On Nov. 6, 1737, 'being fully satisfied of his integrity as well as understanding', Wesley admitted him to communion. His wife Sarah sought redress in England for his three years' incarceration, and even petitioned the King on his behalf; Wesley was clearly trying to help her. (For a brief account of the protracted and complex story see Sarah B. Gober Temple and Kenneth Coleman, *Georgia Journeys*, Athens, Georgia, Univ. of Georgia Press, 1961, pp. 81–9.)

[2] John Coates, a turner, and a constable, who left Savannah with Wesley on Dec. 3, 1737.

[3] Elisha Foster, a tythingman of Savannah, 1736.

[4] Thomas Salter, bricklayer of Savannah, and a tythingman in 1739.

[5] James Campbell, barber, who left Savannah with Wesley on Dec. 3, 1737, supposedly to avoid his debts, but who returned, and in Jan., 1741, 'was employed to read prayers for want of a minister'.

[6] Mr. Fox and his wife were leaders of the Methodist society in the city of Oxford, to whom many references occur both in Wesley's letters and in his diary (see espec. Nov. 16, 24, 1738, pp. 580, 588–9 below). A search through the parish registers available in the Bodleian Library, Oxford, makes it almost certain that they are to be identified with Thomas and Elizabeth Fox, who had five children baptized 1727–40, four at All Saints and one at St. Mary the Virgin, at least three of these dying in infancy.

To James Hutton

Oxon. April 28, 1738

My dear friend

This thing I do: I still follow after, if haply I may attain faith. I preach it to all, that at length I may feel it.[1] Only may I never be content with any other portion!   5

I left two little books (which I want as well as my shoes) at your house—A. M[ari]a Schurman[2] and Corbet.[3] If my brother is gone[4] you will buy the leathern bags for Mr. Kinchin.[5] I think he says they cost but half a guinea. But if it be more, it will be repaid with thanks. The shop at Charing Cross is the place.   10

Stephen Kinchin got hither a day before me. I will send you word before I begin another journey. Commend me to all our friends. Adieu!

Pray give our Brother Böhler the enclosed, to be delivered with his own hand.[6]   15

---

[1] On Mar. 4, 1738, Peter Böhler had urged upon John Wesley, now a strenuous spiritual seeker: 'Preach faith *till* you have it, and then, *because* you have it, you *will* preach faith' (see *Journal*).

[2] Anna Maria van Schurman (1607–78), a learned and pious Dutch woman. In 1733 Wesley had read a Latin work by her translated into English, *The Learned Maid: or, Whether a Maid may be a Scholar* (1659), and doubtless this 64-page volume was the one for which he asked.

[3] Apparently a posthumous devotional work by the Puritan John Corbet (1620–80), *Self-Employed in Secret* (1681), which went through several editions. The second part of this (pp. 35–53) was 'Thoughts upon Painful Afflictions', which probably had been printed separately as a small tract, though no example is listed in the catalogue of the British Library.

[4] Charles Wesley returned to London on Apr. 28, when his diary reads: 'No sooner was I got to James Hutton's, having removed my things thither from his father's, than the pain in my side returned, and with that my fever.' On May 11 he was 'just going to remove to old Mr. Hutton's when God sent Mr. Bray to me, a poor ignorant mechanic', at whose house in Little Britain the sick man remained for several weeks.

[5] The Revd. Charles Kinchin (1711–41), fellow and then Dean of Corpus Christi College, an Oxford Methodist who became rector of Dummer, and was served by other Oxford Methodists as curates or preachers—Hervey, Whitefield, Broughton, Gambold, Hutchings. His brother Stephen matriculated at Trinity College, Oxford, on Mar. 23, 1738, aged 16.

[6] Peter Böhler (1712–75) had been ordained on Dec. 15, 1737, by Zinzendorf, to be the Moravian pastor in Savannah, Georgia, and to undertake missionary work among the slaves in Purrysburg, South Carolina. He arrived in London en route to America a few days before Wesley's return from Savannah, and on Feb. 7, 1738, they met. Wesley procured lodgings for Böhler, and Böhler instructed Wesley and his brother Charles in Moravian piety, which culminated for both of them in a personal experience of saving

[To the Revd. Charles Wesley][1]

April 28, 1738
Oxon.

Dear brother

If this reaches you at London, I wish you would pay Mrs. Hutton
5 (with many thanks) what she has paid for my letters and washing.
And buy for Mr. Kinchin a pair of leathern bags, as like yours as
possible. I wanted much to have seen you before I set out, and
therefore stayed to the utmost extent of my time. My sister[2] is much
better. Could not you bring with you a few of Mr. Corbet's *Thoughts*?
10 If so, call at the little hut where the coach usually stops to let the
passengers walk, on the brow of Stokenchurch Hill, and give one to
the old man.[3] I promised him a little book when I called there in my
last walk to town. Adieu!

Address: 'To Mr James Hutton, Bookseller, Near Temple-bar, London'
Seal: Cross in oval frame (17)   *Postmark*: '29 AP'   *Charges*: ((3)), '6
WC'   *Source*: MorA.

From the Revd. John Clayton

Salford, May 1, 1738

15 Revd. and dear sir

I would have writ to you before had I known where a letter might have found
you, to express the great uneasiness that myself, as well as all your Lancashire
friends, labour under on your account. Indeed we are greatly afraid for you, and
doubt that you are running yourself into difficulties beyond your strength to
20 bear. We all see and rejoice at your sincerity and zeal, and pray fervently for

faith, for Charles on May 21, and for John on May 24, 1738. A few days earlier Böhler
had left London for America, but not before he and John Wesley had founded a new
religious society in Fetter Lane, London, on May 1, 1738. The meaning of the sentence
is that (if Charles Wesley had left), Hutton was to tear off the annexed half-sheet containing the letter to Charles, and ask Böhler to deliver it personally. In fact Charles's
presence made this unnecessary.

[1] On p. 3 of the preceding letter to Hutton.
[2] i.e. Kezia, who had come to stay with Charles in Oxford on Feb. 28. A week or two
later she also was ill, and Charles summoned Dr. Fruin to help her (see CWJ).
[3] Wesley's diary for 11.15–11.30 a.m. on Apr. 27, 1738, reads, 'at the Hut; religious
talk'. On Oct. 10, 1738, he similarly stopped for a conversation there. The hut was
about 18 miles from Oxford on the London road.

your perseverance therein. But we think ourselves likewise obliged to beseech Almighty God to give you a right judgment in all things, that so your zeal may be tempered by prudence, and you may have the light of the gospel as well as the heat. What I feared would be the case is actually come to pass: few or none were edified by Mr. Wesley's preaching, because they were offended with his manner. 5 And your using no notes, and so very much action, has with the generality established your reputation for self-sufficiency and ostentation. ⟨Even⟩ to the most serious it is matter of grief, because they fear that ⟨such pro⟩digious singularities set you upon such an eminence as makes such a behaviour necessary as the spirit of an apostle alone can produce. And who is sufficient for these things? 10 I remember in the holy life of Bernard Gilpin, preaching extempore is called tempting God; at least it is tempting the world to censoriousness, and yourself to think more highly of yourself than you ought to think. Mr. Byrom says of you that if he were in your place he would constantly preach by book; he would have you cut off your hair, which he thinks contributes much to the distinguish- 15 ing appearance you make, and to curb your action and vehement emphasis, th⟨at⟩ so there might not be so remarkable a singularity in your person and behaviour; and all this he thinks a sacrifice you ought to make of self-will for the sake of your brethren's weakness. And that you would gain more progress in the spiritual life by such a submission upon principle than you can possibly do by 20 any outward thing.

We feared much that you was the author of 'The Oxford Methodists', prefixed to Mr. Whitefield's sermons, but Mr. Kinchin has relieved ⟨us.⟩

It is the opinion of Dr. Deacon, Dr. Byrom, and his brother Josiah, as well as myself, that you had better forbear publishing, at least for a time, till your 25 difficulties are blown over. Because it does not appear that you are necessarily called to it, and therefore the doing it would be like running into temptations which you have power to avoid. Dr. Byrom has the same fears about the Poems as the Methodists, and doubts you are too sanguine and hasty about them. O my brother, that you had a director! One to whom you might submit the conduct 30 of your soul! For I cannot but think, however mean his attainments were, provided he had more age and experience than yourself, you would find your spiritual account in abiding by his counsels. Did it serve no other end, it would save you from the danger of self-will, which is not to be avoided while you are your own director. And I believe there is nothing where self-will proves stronger, 35 and is attended with worse consequences, than where it is engaged upon spiritual matters. God Almighty direct you for the best, and raise up a proper instrument for the promoting his glory and your welfare.

⟨I respectfully (?)⟩ must request you to send me a copy of all your Statutes relating to the constitution and power of your Visitor, and the obedience you are 40 bound to pay him. But this not on your own account, but for the sake of the Fellows of our collegiate church, to whom it may possibly prove of the greatest service. Why did you not write in shorthand? Have you forgot it? I hope your brother is well recovered. God be with you all. Cease not to pray fervently for your most affectionate brother, friend, and servant, 45

J. Clayton

My sisters pay their respects to you and your brother.

Address: 'To the Revd. Mr. Wesley, Fellow of Lincoln College, Oxon.'
Postmarks: 'MAN/CHESTER', and an indecipherable Bishop mark
Charges: '4', 'In all 7'   *End* by JW: 'Mr Clayton! / 1738. Mystical. / No. 8';
also a list on flap of address page: 'Mr Law / Walker / Remarks on ((Theolo[gic]a
Mystica)) / Molinos / Temo d'Enfant / Mr Gambold / ((Chev[alie]r Ramsay)) /
((S Wesley's Lr)) / Thts on Mysticism / de Origine Mali / ((Predestination)) /
Perfection' [N.B. Here and later words enclosed within ((. . .)) are struck
through.]   *Source*: MA.

To the Revd. William Law[1]

May 14, 1738

Revd. sir

It is in obedience to what I think the call of God that I[2] take upon
me to speak to you of whom I have often desired[3] to learn the first
5 elements of the gospel of Christ.

If you are born of God you will approve the design,[4] though it
may be weakly executed.[5] If not, I shall grieve for you, not for
myself. For as I seek not praise from men, so neither regard I the
contempt, either of you or of any other.

10   For two years (more especially) [I] have been preaching after the
model of your two practical treatises. And all that heard have allowed
that this law is great, wonderful, and holy. But no sooner did they
attempt to follow it than they found it was too high for man, and

---

[1] We have seen above (p. 386 n.) the great influence upon Wesley of Law's devotional
works, *A Practical Treatise upon Christian Perfection* (1726) and *A Serious Call to a
Devout and Holy Life* (1728). He continued to value these works, but the emphasis of
Peter Böhler upon faith almost to the exclusion of good works led Wesley to a temporary
revulsion, even though Böhler 's teaching had not yet issued in his own personal assurance of salvation. In his spiritual turmoil he did not approach his former mentor personally, probably because he knew that Law had now become a disciple of Behmen's
mystical teachings, which had first been evident in his answer to Hoadly's *Plain Account
. . . of the Sacrament*. Instead he wrote a strongly critical letter, whose note of asperity
may partly derive from, as it certainly illustrates, the criticisms of John Clayton and
his friends (see preceding letter).

[2] In the original, a draft which exercised Wesley's mind considerably, he first wrote,
'that I who have the sentence of death in my own soul', struck this through, altered it to,
'who am myself a miserable sinner', and then erased that also. The major alterations are
noted, the erasures within double parentheses.

[3] Orig., ((rejoiced)).

[4] Wesley first wrote 'the', altered it to 'my', and changed this back again to 'the'.

[5] Wesley first wrote, 'though [changed to 'while'] you pity the imperfect [changed
to 'weak'] manner wherein it is executed', and erased this for the final draft.

that by doing the works of this law should no flesh living be justified.[1]

To remedy this I exhorted them, and stirred up myself, to pray earnestly for the grace of God, and to use[2] all the other means[3] of obtaining that grace which the all-wise God had appointed. But still both they and I were only more[4] convinced that this was a law whereby a man could not live, the law in our members continually warring against it, and bringing us into deeper captivity to the law of sin.[5]

Under this heavy yoke I might have groaned till death had not an holy man to whom God lately directed me,[6] upon my complaining thereof, answered at once: 'Believe, and thou shalt be saved. Believe in the Lord Jesus with all thy heart, and nothing shall be impossible to thee. This faith, indeed, as well as the salvation it brings, is the free gift of God. But seek, and thou shalt find. Strip thyself naked of[7] thy own works, and thy own righteousness, and fly[8] to him. For[9] everyone that cometh to him he will in no wise cast out.'

Now, sir, suffer me to ask, How you will answer it to our common Lord, that[10] you never gave me this advice? Did you never read the manner wherein Peter, John, and Paul answered those who cried out, What must we do to be saved?[11] Or are you wiser than they? Why did I scarce ever hear you name the name of Christ? Never, so as to ground anything upon faith in his blood?[12] Who is this that is laying another foundation?[13] If you say you advised other things as preparatory to this, what is this but laying a foundation below the foundation? Is not Christ, then, the first, as well as the last?[14] If you say you advised them because you knew I had faith already, verily, you knew nothing of me, you discerned not my spirit at all. I know that I had not faith.[15] Unless the faith of a devil, the faith of a Judas, that speculative, notional, airy shadow which lives in the head, not the heart. But what is this to the living,[16] justifying faith in the blood

[1] See Gal. 2: 16.
[2] Orig., ((to be zealous of)).
[3] Orig., 'all those means'.
[4] Orig., 'more and more'.
[5] See Rom.7: 23.
[6] Orig., '((guided)) me'.
[7] Orig., 'Cast away'.
[8] Orig., 'and ((go naked))'.
[9] Orig., ((And)).
[10] Orig., 'to ask ((you, in the)) How . . . Lord, ((why))'.
[11] Orig., '((Did you never read the Acts of or Epistles of S.)) Peter, Paul, and John?'.
[12] Rom. 3: 25.
[13] See 1 Cor. 3: 11.
[14] Orig., 'Is not ((faith in)) Christ the first, ((then)) as well as the last?'.
[15] Orig., 'I know that ((to this hour)) I ha((ve not faith)).'
[16] Orig., 'the ((true,)) living, ((savi[ng]))'.

of Jesus? The faith that cleanseth from all sin,[1] that gives us to have free access to the Father,[2] to rejoice in hope of the glory of God,[3] to have the love of God shed abroad in our hearts by the Holy Ghost which dwelleth in us;[4] and the Spirit itself bearing witness with
5 our spirit, that we are the children of God.[5]

I beseech you, sir, by the mercies of God, to consider deeply and impartially whether the true reason of your never pressing this upon me was not this, that you had it not yourself? Whether that man of God were not in the right who gave this account:[6] 'I began to speak
10 to him of faith in Christ. He was silent, then began to speak of mystical matters. I spoke of faith in Christ again. He was silent, then spoke of mystical matters again. I saw his state at once.' And a very dangerous one in his judgment, whom I know to have the Spirit of God.[7]

15 Once more, sir, let me beg you to consider whether your extreme roughness, I might say, sourness, of behaviour, at least on many occasions, can possibly[8] be the fruits of a living faith in Christ.[9] If not, the God of peace and love fill up what is yet wanting in you! I am, revd. sir, your obliged servant,

20   John Wesley

May 14, 1738

Post-Wesley endorsements: in ink, at beginning: '14th May, 1738'; in pencil, at beginning, 'Vol. 1, page 358', and 'Recd from Mr. Moor/ Octr. 17/ 1836 RH'
Source: MA, a draft, on four duodecimo pages.

[1] See 1 John 1:7.   [2] See Eph. 2:18.   [3] Rom. 5:2.
[4] See Rom 5:5.   [5] See Rom. 8:16.
[6] Orig., 'this account ((of a late interview he had with you))'.
[7] Although no specific evidence is available from Wesley, Law, or Böhler, it seems ikely that the 'man of God' here (as undoubtedly 'an holy man' in para. 5) was Peter Böhler.
[8] Orig., '((can possi[bly]—and whether your rash and absolutely false judgment of that faithful child of God, George Whitefield)), can possibly'.
[9] That Wesley eventually added another charge is shown by the closing paragraph of Law's reply of May 19: 'Your last paragraph, concerning my sour, rough behaviour, and obscurity of conversation on the most important subjects, as inconsistent with Scripture and the fruits of a living faith in Christ . . .'

From the Revd. William Law

May 19, 1738

Revnd. sir

Yours I received yesterday. As you have written that letter in obedience to a divine call, and in conjunction with another extraordinary good young man whom you know to have the Spirit of God, so I assure you that considering your 5 letter in that view I neither desire nor dare to make the smallest defence of myself. If a messenger from God should represent me as a monster of iniquity that had corrupted all that had conversed with me, etc., I should lay my hand upon my mouth, and with my eyes shut submit myself to the divine justice. And as you lay claim to this character, as a messenger sent from God to lay 10 my sins before my face, and have not executed this message till a divine man highly favoured of God had passed sentence upon me; so I assure you that I have not the least inclination to distrust or question your mission, nor the smallest repugnance to own, receive, reverence, and submit myself to you both in these exalted characters. May God vouchsafe his favours to you both, and his 15 mercies to me, according to his own good pleasure.

This is the whole of my answer to your letter considered in that light in which you represent it, as written in obedience to a divine call, and the message of it rectified by a person whom you know to have the Spirit of God.

But now, upon supposition that you had here only acted by that ordinary 20 light which is common to good and sober minds, I should remark upon your letter as follows. How you may have been two years preaching the doctrine of the two practical discourses, or how you may have tired yourself and your hearers to no purpose, is what I cannot say much to. But if you are not more exact in what you say of this matter than in what you say of the conversation I have had with 25 you, there is great mistakes in it.

A holy man, you say, taught you thus: 'Believe, and thou shalt be saved. Believe in the Lord Jesus with all thy heart, and nothing shall be impossible to thee—Strip thyself naked of thy own works, and thy own righteousness, and fly to·him. For everyone that cometh to him he will in no wise cast out.' 30

I am to suppose that till this time of your lately meeting with this holy man from Germany you had not been taught this doctrine, and that for want of it you might have groaned under a certain heavy yoke to your death. Did you not above two years ago give a new translation of Thomas à Kempis? Will you call Thomas to account, and to answer it to God, as you do me, for not teaching you 35 that doctrine? Or will you say that you took upon you to restore the true sense of that divine writer, and to instruct others how they might best profit by reading him, before you had so much as a literal knowledge of the most plain, open, and repeated doctrine contained in his book? You can't but remember what value I always expressed for Kempis, and how much I recommended it to your medita- 40 tion.

You have had a great many conversations with me, and I dare say that you never was with me for half an hour without my being large upon that very doctrine which you make me totally silent and ignorant of.

As an undeniable proof of this you must remember that the second time I saw 45

you, and when your brother was with you, I put into your hands the little book of the German Theology,[1] and said all that I could in recommendation of the doctrine contained in it. If that book does not plainly lead you to Jesus Christ, I am content to know as little of Christianity as you are pleased to believe; or if you
5 are for stripping yourself naked of your own works, or your own righteousness, further than that book directs, I had rather you was taught that doctrine by anyone else than by me.

Above a year ago I published a book against the *Plain Account of the Sacraments*, etc. You may perhaps be too much prejudiced against me to read it, but
10 as you have made yourself a judge of the state of my heart, and of my knowledge in Christ, you ought to have seen that book, to help you to make a right judgment of my sentiments. What I have there written I judged to be well-timed after my former discourses; governed through all that I have written and done by these two common, fundamental, unchangeable maxims of our Lord, 'Without me ye
15 can do nothing'; 'If any man will come after me, or be my disciple, let him take up his cross and follow me.' If you are for separating the doctrine of the cross from following Christ, or faith in him, you have numbers and names enough on your side, but not me. The conversation I have had with you is past and gone, and you have it in your power to represent it as you please; but the facts I
20 have appealed to must continue facts, and prove all that which I appeal to them for.

You say, 'Why did I scarce ever hear you name the name of Christ? Never, so as to ground anything upon faith in his blood.' This I leave untouched, and bear it as if you had called me a Mahometan.
25 You go on, 'If you say you advised other things as preparatory to this, if you advised them because you knew I had faith already, verily you knew nothing of me, you discerned not my spirit at all. I know that I had not faith, unless the faith of a devil, the faith of Judas, that speculative, notional, airy shadow, which lives in the head, and not in the heart.'
30 Did you never hear anything of this from me? How far I may have discerned your spirit, or the spirit of others that have conversed with me, may perhaps be more a secret to you than you imagine, but I claim nothing on that head.

But granting you to be right in the account of your own faith, how am I chargeable with it? Have either I or any of my writings any tendency to fill your
35 head full of airy shadows?[2]

Here I am to suppose that after you had been some time meditating upon an author that of all others leads us the most directly to a real, living faith in Jesus Christ, after you had judged yourself such a master of his sentiments and doctrines as to be able to publish them to the world, with directions and in-
40 structions concerning such experimental divinity, that years after you had done this you had only the faith of a devil, or Judas, an empty notion only, in your head; and that you was in this state through ignorance that there was any better to be sought after, and that you was in this ignorance because in my conversation I never directed or called you to this true faith.
45 But, sir, as Kempis and I have both of us had your acquaintance and

---

[1] *Theologia Germanica.* See letter of Nov. 23, 1736.
[2] Orig., 'tendency to bring the spirit of the devil or Judas into you, only fill your head'.

conversation, so pray let the fault be divided betwixt us, and I shall be content to have it said that I left you in as much ignorance of this faith as he did, or that you learnt no more of it by conversing with me than with him.

If you had only this faith till some weeks ago, let me advise you not to be too hasty in believing that because you have changed your language or 5 expressions you have changed your faith. The head can as easily amuse itself with a 'living and justifying faith in the blood of Jesus' as with any other notion; and the heart which you suppose to be a place of security, as being the seat of self-love, is more deceitful than the head.

I must now transcribe a long passage in your letter, because not a word of it 10 ought to be omitted. It is thus: 'I beseech you, sir, by the mercies of God, to consider deeply and impartially whether the true reason of your never calling me to this was not that you had it not in yourself? Whether that man of God was not in the right who gave this account: "I began to speak to him of faith in Christ. He was silent. Then he began to speak of mystical matters. I spoke of 15 faith in Christ again. He was silent. Then he spoke of mystical matters again. I SAW HIS STATE AT ONCE." And a very dangerous one, in his judgment, whom I know to have the Spirit of God.'

This man of God, whom I can willingly believe to be as divine as you represent him to be, and whose conversation, short as it was, left a good impression 20 upon my mind, was accidentally presented to me in Somerset Gardens, as the acquaintance of an author I was inquiring after, and whose book was then in my hands. I was not half an hour with him in that public place, nor had any intention at that time of saying anything to him but upon the matter above mentioned. In discourse of that kind he took occasion, as he says, to speak of faith in 25 Christ. I was silent, except in approbation of what he said. But that I then began to speak of mystical matters is as false as anything that can be said of me. For I spoke not one single word of any doctrine of religion, either mystical or not. Or if I had spoke of mystical matters, would that have been a receding from the subject he was upon? Is not faith in Jesus Christ the very sum and substance 30 of what is meant by mystical religion? He said very little to me on faith, but for aught I know there might be what he calls a first and second time in what he said to me. But that I a second time began to speak to him of mystical matters is a second great falsity.[1] I leave you now to judge of his *seeing my dangerous state at once.* 35

As this falsity lies amongst us three, I suppose you will not think it proper that either of you should have any share in it, it being fitter to be ascribed to that state you have provided for me. I am content that you should do with it according to your pleasure.

Your last paragraph, concerning my sour, rough behaviour, and obscurity of 40 conversation on the most important subjects, as inconsistent with Scripture and the fruits of a living faith in Christ, I leave in its full force. Whatever you can say of me of that kind without hurting yourself will be always well received by me. I am your real friend and well-wisher,

W. Law 45

---

[1] A passage added here is struck through by Law: 'For as I said before, not one syllable came from me concerning any doctrine of religion.'

May 19, 1738

I have not yet received Bartholomaeus a Martyribus, which I long ago lent to Mr. Horn[e] and you.

End by JW: 'Mr Law'   *End* by others: 'These papers to be kept perfectly clean and returned to Mr. Pawson', in hand not recognized. Editorial erasures of several passages, minor revisions, and the following comment, are added in the hand of John Pawson, probably for the letter's publication in the *A.M.*, 1797, pp. 149–52, where it appears as a link between this and the preceding letter of May 14 which prompted it: 'How far Mr. Wesley is to be justified in writing the above letter to Mr. Law, and whether he formed a right judgment of the state of his mind, will appear from Mr. Law's answer. It seems as if he did not understand Mr. Wesley at all.' Also added is a title, 'To the Rev. Mr. John Wesley', with 'Mr.' struck through, though this may have been the original address, in a hand other than Law's.   *Source*: MA.

To the Revd. William Law

May 20, 1738

5 Revd. sir

I sincerely thank you for a favour I did not expect, and presume to trouble you once more.

How I have preached all my life, how qualified or unqualified I was to correct a translation of Kempis, and translate a preface to it;[1]
10 whether I have now, or how long I have had, a living faith;[2] whether I am for separating the doctrine of the cross from it;[3] what your state or sentiments are,[4] and whether Peter Böhler spoke truth[5] in what he said when two beside[6] me were present; are circumstances on which the main question does not turn, which is this[7] and no
15 other: whether you ever advised me, or directed me to books that did advise, to seek first[8] a living faith in the blood of Christ.[9]

---

[1] Orig., ((his book)). Wesley is careful to rephrase Law's statement about 'a new translation', for he had in fact revised and re-issued Worthington's edition of 1677.

[2] Orig., 'Whether I have now a living faith ((or no, and how long I have)), and ((whether I have had it a longer or shorter time)).

[3] Orig., ((faith in Christ)).

[4] Orig., 'What your state', and 'What state you are in, ['and', struck through] or Principles are'—all erased except (apparently in error), 'or Prin-'. The final revision, from 'whether I am' to 'sentiments are', Wesley wrote on the adjoining page (4).

[5] Orig., 'truth ((or no))'.

[6] Orig., 'two ((others)) beside'.

[7] Orig., 'is ((simply)) this'.   [8] Orig., 'seek ((after))'.

[9] Orig. continues, ((as that whereby alone I could be justified?)).

You appeal to three facts to prove you did: (1), that you put into my hands *Theologia Germanica*; (2), that you published an answer to the *Plain Account of the Sacrament*;[1] and (3), that you are governed through all you have writ and done by these two fundamental maxims of our Lord, 'Without me ye can do nothing,' and, 'If any man will come after me, let him take up his cross and follow me.'

The facts I allow, but not the consequence. In *Theologia Germanica* I remember[2] something of Christ our pattern, but nothing express of Christ our atonement.[3] Your answer to the *Plain Account*[4] I believe to be an excellent book, but not to affect the question.[5] Those two maxims may imply but do not express that third, 'He is our propitiation, through faith in his blood.'[6]

'But how are you chargeable with my not having had this faith?' If, as you intimate, you discerned my spirit, thus:

(1). You did not tell me plainly I had it not. (2). You never once advised me to seek or pray for it. (3). You gave me advices proper only[7] for one who had it already,[8] and (4), advices[9] which led me farther from it the closer I adhered to them. (5). You recommended books to me which had no tendency to plant[10] this faith, but a direct one to destroy good works.

However, 'Let the fault[11] be divided between you and Kempis.' No; if I understood Kempis wrong, it was your part, who discerned my spirit,[12] under that mistake, to have explained him, and set me right.

---

[1] *A Demonstration of the Gross and Fundamental Errors of a late Book, called,* 'A Plain Account of the Nature and End of the Sacrament of the Lord's Supper' . . .; *wherein also the nature and extent of the redemption of all mankind by Jesus Christ is stated and explained* . . . (1737). The *Plain Account* was published anonymously in 1735 by Benjamin Hoadly, at that time Bishop of Winchester.

[2] Orig., ((find)).

[3] Orig. continues, ((Therefore that author I charge with [earlier 'for' erased] laying An)).

[4] Orig., 'ye ((book you lately published))'.

[5] Orig., 'present point'.

[6] See Rom. 3: 25. (Wesley had originally begun his quotation with the correct first word of the verse in the A.V.)

[7] Orig., 'You advise((d me to exercises which were only)) proper'.

[8] Orig. continues: ((I have them by me, written down at that time.)).

[9] Orig., '4. ((You gave me other)) advices'.

[10] Orig., ((establish)).

[11] Orig., 'The fault ((must))'.

[12] Orig., 'who discerned ((that error in)) my spirit, ((to who))'.

I ask pardon, sir, if I had said anything disrespectful![1] I am, revd. sir, your most obedient servant,

[John Wesley]

Source: MA, a draft, on four duodecimo pages, heavily revised by Wesley, upon which was based the version in *A.M.*, 1797, pp. 152–3. [N.B. The 'facsimile' of this document in Telford's *Wesley*, p. xiii, has been redrawn, and contains several inaccuracies.]

From the Revd. William Law

[May 22(?), 1738]

5   Sir

Without the smallest degree of disregard either to you or your letter, I had not sent you an answer to it had it not been for the part of it where you say there were two persons present with Mr. Böhler and myself. There were two persons present, but only one witness, for we spoke only in Latin, and they

10   both declared to me they understood not Latin.

I mentioned not your qualification for translating Kempis with the least intention to reproach either your design or performance, but only to show you that it deeply engaged your attention to those very truths which you suppose you were a stranger to through my conversation.

15   If you remember the *Theologia Germanica* so imperfectly as only to remember 'something of Christ our pattern, but nothing express of Christ our atonement', it is no wonder that you can remember so little of my conversations with you. I put that author into your hands, not because he is fit for the first learners of the rudiments of Christianity, who are to be prepared for baptism, but because

20   you were a *clergyman*, that had made profession of divinity, had read as you said with much approbation and benefit the two practical discourses, and many other good books; and because you seemed to me to be of a very inquisitive nature, and much inclined to meditation. In this view nothing could be more reasonable for you than that book, which most deeply, excellently, and fully contains the

25   whole system of Christian faith and practice, and is an excellent guide against all mistakes both in faith and works. What that book has not taught you I am content that you should not have learnt from me.

You say the two maxims I mention may imply, but do not express, 'He is our propitiation, through faith in his blood.' Is not this, therefore, a mere contest

30   about words and expressions? When I refer you to these two maxims or texts of Scripture, will you confine me to them alone? Does not my quoting them necessarily refer to every part of Scripture of the same import? When Christ says, 'Without me ye can do nothing;' when the Apostle says, 'There is no other

---

[1] Orig., 'anything ((inconsistent with the obligations I owe you, and the respect I bear to your character))'; 'disrespectful' added below.

name given under heaven by which we can be saved;' when he says 'We are sanctified through faith in his blood', and 'through faith in him', is there anything here but a difference of words, or one and the same thing imperfectly and only in part expressed?

I mentioned not the answer to the *Plain Account*, etc., as a proof of the manner 5 of my conversation with you, but of my faith in Christ as the atonement for us by his blood, at this time; which is what you directly questioned and called upon me for.

You number up all the parts of my letter, which are only speaking to the same parts in yours, as things entirely beside the point. If they are not to the point 10 in mine, how came they to have a place in yours, which was written under *divine direction*? Why did you give me occasion to speak of things that needed nothing to be said of them? Had you said but one thing, I would have spoke to nothing else. In your first letter I was blamed for not calling you to such a faith in Christ as strips us naked of our own works, our own righteousness; for not teaching 15 you this doctrine, 'Believe in the Lord Jesus Christ with all thy heart, and nothing shall be impossible to thee.' This is the faith in Christ which all mystical spiritual books are full of. What you have heard from me on this head of faith, in our former conversations, would make a volume; but because I appealed to a text of Scripture, 'Without me ye can do nothing,' you have quitted this 20 faith; and now you say this, and no other, is the question, 'whether I ever advised you to seek first a living faith in the blood of Christ'.

But, sir, this is not the main question of your first letter; had you had only this question to have proposed you would not have written to me at all. But if I tell you that you conceived a dislike to me, and wanted to let me know that a 25 man of God had shown you the poverty and misery of my state; if I tell you that this was the main intent of your letter, you know that I tell you the truth . . . But this matter, it seems, now is of no importance.

I was a stranger to him,[1] received him friendly, listened to him humbly, consented to his instructing me. I said not one single syllable of any doctrine 30 of religion, mystical or not. We presently parted, in all appearance friendly. He passes a sentence of condemnation upon me as in a poor miserable state, which lay open to his eyes. This *man of God* told nothing of this to *myself*, but goes away to another man of God, and invents and tells things as false as if he had charged me with picking his pocket; and, what is well to be observed, 35 this judgment passed upon me is founded upon those very things which are thus false and wholly his own invention. This other man of God confirms this sentence, as spoken by one that he knew had the Spirit of God, and in obedience to a divine call is obliged to let me know . . .

Who made me your teacher? Or can make me answerable for any defects in 40 your knowledge? You sought my acquaintance, you came to me as you pleased, and on what occasion you pleased, and to say to me what you pleased. If it was my business to put this question to you, if you have a right to charge me with guilt for the neglect of it, may you not much more reasonably accuse them who are authoritatively charged with you? Did *the Church* in which you are educated 45 put this question to you? Did the bishop that *ordained* you either deacon or

---

[1] Walton's note, 'Peter Böhler'.

priest do this for you? Did the bishop that sent you a missionary into Georgia require this of you? Pray, sir, be at peace with me.

[W. Law]

Source: [Christopher Walton], *Notes and Materials for an adequate Biography of . . . William Law*, Printed for Private Circulation, London, 1854, pp. 94–5. Walton states: 'This letter is copied from the original rough draft in the author's own handwriting, in which the passages of his opponent's letter are omitted.' The italicizing may have been inserted by Walton himself.

[To the Revd. John Gambold?][1]

[May 24, 1738]

5   O why is it that so great, so wise, so holy a God, will use such an instrument as me! Lord, 'Let the dead bury their dead!'[2] But wilt thou send the dead to raise the dead? Yea, thou sendest whom thou *wilt* send,[3] and showest mercy by whom thou *wilt* show mercy![4] Amen! Be it then according to thy will![5] If thou speak the word, 10 Judas shall cast out devils.

I feel what you say (though not enough), for I am under the same condemnation.[6] I see that the whole law of God is holy and just and good.[7] I know every thought, every temper of my soul ought to bear God's image and superscription.[8] But how am I fallen from 15 the glory of God! I feel that 'I am sold under sin'.[9] I know that I too deserve nothing but wrath, being full of all abominations; and having no good thing in me to atone for them, or to remove the wrath of God. All my works, my righteousness, my prayers, need an atonement for themselves. So that my mouth is stopped, I have 20 nothing to plead. God is holy; I am unholy. God is a consuming fire;[10] I am altogether a sinner, meet to be consumed.

Yet I hear a voice (and is it not the voice of God?) saying, 'Believe, and thou shalt be saved,'[11] 'He that believeth is passed from death unto life.'[12] 'God so loved the world that he gave his only

---

[1] John Gambold was passing through similar experiences to both the Wesley brothers at about the same time, and was in correspondence with both of them. (Cf. Tyerm (*OM*), pp. 165–72, the letter given as Jan. 23, 1738–9 being in fact dated June 23, 1738. See also above, letter of Jan. 27, 1738.)

[2] Luke 9: 60.	[3] See Exod. 4: 13.	[4] See Exod. 33: 19.
[5] See Luke 1: 38.	[6] Luke 23: 40.	[7] See Rom. 7: 12.
[8] Matt. 22: 20, etc.	[9] Rom. 7: 14.	[10] Heb. 12: 29.
[11] Acts 16: 31.		[12] See John 5: 24.

begotten Son, that whosoever believeth on him should not perish, but have everlasting life.'[1]

O let no one deceive us by vain words, as if we had already attained this faith! By its fruits we shall know.[2] Do we already feel 'peace with God',[3] and 'joy in the Holy Ghost'?[4] Does his 'Spirit bear witness with our spirit, that we are the children of God'?[5] Alas, with *mine* he does not. Nor, I fear, with yours. O thou Saviour of men, save us from trusting in anything but *thee*! Draw us after thee! Let us be emptied of ourselves, and then fill us with all peace and joy in believing;[6] and let nothing separate us from thy love,[7] in time or in eternity! . . .

Source: JWJ, May 24, 1738, introduced thus: 'Monday, Tuesday, and Wednesday I had continual sorrow and heaviness in my heart; something of which I described, in the broken manner I was able, in the following letter to a friend.'

To Mrs. Susanna Wesley[8]

Amsterdam, June 19, O.S., 1738

Dear Mother

I stayed at Stanton Harcourt[9] till Sunday (the 11th instant) in the afternoon. Thence returning to Oxford, I learned that Mr. Ingham was expected to set out on Monday or Tuesday. Therefore I left Oxford on Monday morning, and in the evening met with him and Mr. Töltschig, who were to embark the next morning. On Tuesday (the 13th) we took ship and fell down to Gravesend, many of our

---

[1] John 3: 16.   [2] See Matt. 7: 20, etc.   [3] Rom. 5: 1.
[4] Rom. 14: 17.   [5] See Rom. 8: 16.
[6] See Rom. 15: 13.   [7] See Rom. 8: 35.

[8] Wesley's contacts with the Moravians on board the *Simmonds* and in Georgia had awakened a great admiration for their spirituality, and a desire to see their headquarters on Zinzendorf's estate. Böhler's influence had reinforced this desire. For the visit he joined with others, including his old Oxford and Georgia friend, Benjamin Ingham, and a Moravian leader whom he had met in Georgia, Johann Töltschig (1703–64) (usually, as here, spelt 'Telchig' by Wesley). After a farewell visit to his mother, at the time living with the Revd. Westley Hall and Wesley's sister Martha, in Salisbury, he made his way back to Oxford, and thence to London for embarkation.

[9] Not to be confused with Stanton, Glos., the home of the Kirkhams. The Revd. John Gambold was vicar of Stanton Harcourt in Oxfordshire, and Wesley's youngest sister Kezia seems to have been keeping house for him.

acquaintance bearing us company thither, two of whom were determined to go on with us, whithersoever it should please God to call us.[1] We set sail from Gravesend on Wednesday, lost sight of England about four in the afternoon, and before seven the next morning saw
5 the coast of Holland. About eight we entered the Maas,[2] and sailing by Brielle,[3] between ten and eleven came to Rotterdam.

Never did common fame more grossly vary from the truth than in the English accounts of Holland. They tell us of a dirty, slovenly, unpolished people, without good nature, good manners, or common
10 decency; whereas the very first thing that must strike everyone that has eyes, and that before he has gone a hundred yards from Rotterdam Haven, is that this is the cleanest place he ever saw in his life, there being scarce a speck of dirt to be seen either on the doors or steps of any of the houses, or on the stones of the street. And all the
15 natives he meets, whether men, women, or children, are of a piece with the place they live in, being so nicely clean from head to foot, both in their persons and clothes, as I have seen very few in my life, even of the gentry in England. There is likewise a remarkable mildness and lovingness in their behaviour. All you meet on the road
20 salute you. Everyone is ready to show the way, or to answer any questions, without anything of the English surliness. And the carriage as well as dress of all the women we have yet seen is exactly modest, and altogether natural and unaffected.

On Thursday in the afternoon we left Rotterdam. The road we
25 travelled in for several miles was a continued arbour, and as clean (excepting a very little dust) as a gentleman's parlour, or indeed his table, need be. We lay that night at Gouda[4] (being eight in all, five English and three Germans). On Friday morning (after having seen the great church there, famous for its painted glass) we set out
30 again, and were surprised more and more at the pleasantness of the road. Walnut trees shaded it for many miles, and the little houses stood so thick on either side that it seemed like walking through a train of villages. The hedges were exactly cut all along, and all the houses neat almost to an extreme. In the afternoon we came to
35 IJsselstein,[5] where we were received with open arms by the Baron

---

[1] Altogether there were eight in the party, the other three Englishmen being John Browne, John Holmes, and probably Richard Viney.
[2] Orig., 'Mase'.
[3] Orig., 'Brill'.
[4] Orig., 'Goudart'.
[5] Orig., 'Yssel-stein'.

Watteville,[1] and the church which is in his house.[2] There are about twenty (beside children) in that little community, and their number increases daily, who are of one heart and one soul, and have all things in common.[3] Saturday the 17th (my birthday) was their monthly thanksgiving-day. From about two in the afternoon till nine at night the time was spent in prayer, praise, and such other exercises as became those who were 'all filled with the Holy Ghost'.[4] Many strangers were present, with some of whom we set out in the *track-skuyt*[5] early in the morning, and went by Utrecht through a country which is, as it were, all one garden, to Amsterdam, about thirty miles from IJsselstein.

A physician, who had lived some years at Herrnhut,[6] carried us to his lodgings, where we design to stay one or two days.[7] Both he and the master of the house are full of faith and love. O may our Lord give us more and more of their spirit. From hence (if God permit) we shall go by Frankfort, where Count Zinzendorf now is, to Herrnhut. Dear mother, pray earnestly for me, that all things may work together for my good,[8] and that by all God would build me in the faith which is in Christ Jesus![9] I am, your affectionate and dutiful son,

John Wesley

James Hutton can send any letter to me, if it be writ before the middle of July, O.S. Else I shall probably be on my journey home.

Address: 'To Mrs: Westley Senr:', possibly in the hand of James Hutton, though larger and more elaborate than usual for him   *End* by CW: 'B. from Amsterdam, Jun 19, 1738', and (later) 'B's Romantic Account of Holland' *Source*: MA.

---

[1] Baron Frederic de Watteville (1700–77), from Montmirail, Neuchâtel, Switzerland, educated at Halle, where he and Zinzendorf, together with two others, dedicated themselves in a covenant relationship with Christ and each other. He shared with Zinzendorf the early responsibilities at Herrnhut, and in 1746 was made a bishop of the Unitas Fratrum. In the same year his adopted son Johann married Zinzendorf's daughter, and in 1747 he also was made a bishop of the church.

[2] See Rom. 16: 5.

[3] See Acts 4: 32.

[4] Acts 4: 31.

[5] Anglicized form of *trekschuit*, a canal- or river-boat drawn by horses.

[6] Orig., 'Hernhuth', as usual with Wesley.

[7] In his *Journal* Wesley states that he was entertained by Mr. Decknatel, a Mennonite minister, with whom lodged Dr. Barkhausen, a Russian physician.

[8] See Rom. 8: 28.

[9] 2 Tim. 3: 15.

(554)

To the Revd. Charles Wesley

Cologne,[1] June 28, O.S., 1738

Dear brother

You will send my mother, wherever she is, her letter,[2] by the first opportunity.

5 By the conversation I have had with the brethren that journey with us, as well as with those at IJsselstein and at Amsterdam, I find the judgment of their Church is: (1), that we ought to distinguish carefully both in thinking and speaking between faith (absolutely speaking), which is one thing, justifying or saving faith, which is
10 a second thing (and ought to be called, not faith, absolutely, but always justifying or saving faith), the assurance of faith, where⟨by⟩ we know and feel that we are justified, and the being born again, which they say is a fourth thing, and often distant in time (as well as in the notion of it) from all the rest; (2), that a man may have, and
15 frequently has, justifying faith before he has the assurance that he is justified.

My dear brother, pray (you and all the brethren) for us, that all things may work together for our good,[3] and that we may be more and more rooted in faith, joyful through hope, and grounded in
20 charity! Adieu!

Address: 'A Monsieur / Monsieur Charles Wesley, Chez Monsieur Jaques Hutton, Proche Temple-bar, Londres à l'Angleterre'[4]   *Postmarks*: '44' (?), 'IY 7'   *Charge*: '10'   *End* by CW: 'Colen, B, June 28, 38' and 'June 1738, B from Colen'   *Source*: MA, part of a double letter with that of the same date to Mrs. Susanna Wesley.

[1] Wesley uniformly spells this, 'Colen'.
[2] This was part of a double letter sent to Charles, the other half to be separated and forwarded to their mother. (See Intro., pp. 64–8.)
[3] See Rom. 8: 28.
[4] 'To Mr. / Mr. Charles Wesley, At the home of Mr. James Hutton, Near Temple Bar, London, England.'

To Mrs. Susanna Wesley

Cologne, June 28, O.S., 1738

Dear mother

We left Amsterdam on Thursday evening last, and coming to
Utrecht in the morning, walked thence through a most pleasant and
fruitful country to Buren,[1] a walled town belonging to the Prince of 5
Orange. Hence on Saturday we went, partly by land, partly by
water, to Nijmegen,[2] the last town in Holland, strongly fortified
with a triple wall and ditch. And having walked three or four hours
through a double row of trees, which ran (mostly) through large
cornfields, we took up our lodging an hour short of Kleve.[3] Sunday 10
the 25th we made a short journey after our morning service, and
lying by the middle ⟨p⟩art of the day, in the evening came to a
convenient lodging, only that, after the manner of the Lutherans,
they were fiddling, singing, and dancing in the next room till we
went to bed. The next day we found by the crosses everywhere set 15
up we were got out of the Lutheran Electorate, as well as by the
convents, many of which were in every city, and some in the country
we passed through. Yesterday evening we came hither. It is the
ugliest, dirtiest town I ever yet saw. There is neither form nor
comeliness[4] belonging to it. The great church itself is mere heaps 20
upon heaps, a vast, misshaped or rather no-shaped building, with
no regularity or proportion within or without: many of the stones
broken, the windows dusty and full of cobwebs, and the pavement
less clean than that of many English stables. This afternoon we are
to set out by water for Mainz,[5] forty-eight hours from hence, and 25
eight hours only distant from Frankfort, where Count Zinzendorf
now is.

God has been pleased greatly to bless us hitherto, continuing us
all in health and cheerfulness and love to one another, which, with
all other good gifts, we trust he will confirm and increase in us day 30
by day. Before you receive this I hope you will be placed, according
to your desire, where you may serve God without distraction from
outward cares, till he takes you to himself.

O pray for me, that he would sanctify all I meet with to me, and

---

[1] Orig., 'Beurn'.   [2] Orig., 'Nimwegen'.   [3] Orig., 'Cleves'.
[4] Isa. 53: 2.   [5] Orig., 'Mentz'.

give me fully to believe the Son of his love, and to have a right judgment in all things![1] I am, dear mother, your most affectionate son,

John Wesley

Source: MA, part of a double letter addressed to Charles Wesley—see previous letter.

To Mrs. Susanna Wesley

[July 6, 1738]

5

Dear mother

Soon after I had finished my last to you we left Cologne, in the passage-boat, and travelled slowly four days upon the Rhine, through a double range of rocks and mountains, diversified with more
10 variety than ever painter could imagine. Some were smooth, as if polished by art; some rough, abrupt, and ragged, as if torn by a fresh earthquake. Some again were quite bare, others clothed with grass, others with trees, corn, or vines. On Sunday in the evening we came to Mainz, and on Monday, before noon, to Frankfort,
15 where the father of Peter Böhler (lately with me at London and Oxon) received us with all kindness.[2] About one o'clock on Tuesday we came safe to Marienborn,[3] a small village, seven hours from Frankfort, where Count Zinzendorf has hired for three years (till one is built a few miles off on his own land, which is already begun),
20 a large house, and tolerably convenient, which lodges the greatest part of the small congregation here.

The Count received us in a manner I was quite unacquainted with, and therefore know not how to express. I believe his behaviour was not unlike that of his Master (if we may compare human with
25 divine) when he took the little children in his arms and blessed them. We should have been much amazed at him, but that we saw ourselves encompassed with a cloud of those who were all followers of him, as he is of Christ. Eighty-eight of them praise God with one heart and one mouth at Marienborn. Another little company at
30 Ronneburg,[4] an hour off, another at Büdingen, an hour from thence,

---

[1] B.C.P., Collect for Whitsunday.
[2] Johann Konrad Böhler, a brewer, and a burgher of the city.
[3] Orig., 'Marienbourn'.   [4] Orig., 'Runnenburg'.

and yet another at Frankfort. I now understand those words of poor
Julian, 'See how these Christians love one another!'[1] Yea, how they
love all who have the faintest desire to love the Lord Jesus Christ
in sincerity![2] O may he sanctify to us their holy conversation, that
we may be partakers of the spirit which is in them, of their faith
unfeigned,[3] and meekness, wisdom, and love which never faileth![4]
Dear mother, forget not often to desire this for your dutiful and
affectionate son,

John Wesley

Utph[5]

July 6, O.S., 1738

End by CW: 'B. Utph / July 6, 1738 / Commendation of Germany'   *Source*:
Emory, part of a double letter, the other half (with the address) dated July
7, to Charles Wesley.

To the Revd. Charles Wesley

Utph, July 7, O.S., 1738

Dear brother

I am now with the Count, at his uncle's, the Count of Solms, five
or six hours from Marienborn, and have stole an hour to let you
know that hitherto God hath been very merciful to us in all things.
The spirit of the brethren is beyond our highest expectations.
Young and old, they breathe nothing but faith and love, at all times
and in all places. I do not therefore concern myself with smaller
points, that touch not the essence of Christianity, but endeavour
(God being my helper)[6] to grow up in these, after the glorious
examples set before me; having already seen with my own eyes more
than one hundred witnesses of that everlasting truth, 'Everyone that
believeth hath peace with God, and is freed from sin, and is in
Christ a new creature.'[7]

[1] See Tertullian, *Apologeticus*, 39: 'See, they say, how they love one another; how
they are ready even to die for one another.' Julian the Apostate (in Epistle 49) did
ascribe the success of the Christians mainly to their charity, but did not use the exact
phrase, though Wesley similarly credits him with it in his sermon, 'The Cure of Evil-
speaking' (No. 49), III. 5. See also letter of July 7 to Samuel Wesley.
[2] Eph. 6: 24.   [3] 1 Tim. 1: 5.   [4] See 1 Cor. 13: 8.
[5] The home of the Count of Solms, Zinzendorf's uncle, where Wesley stayed overnight.   [6] B.C.P., Baptism of Adults, Question 4.
[7] A composite of Rom. 1: 16; 5: 1; 6: 7; 2 Cor. 5: 17.

See therefore, my brethren, that none of you receive the grace of God in vain![1] But be ye also living witnesses of the exceeding great and precious promises,[2] which are made unto every one of us through the blood of Jesus! Adieu!

Address: 'A Monsieur/ Monsieur Charles Wesley/ Chez Monsr Hutton, Marchand Libraire / Proche Temple-bar/ à Londres / Angleterre'[3]   *End* by CW: 'B. Utlp [*sic*], July 7, 1738' and (later) 'B. from Utph, Panegyric on Germans'
Source: MA, part of a double letter, the other half dated July 6, to their mother.

To the Revd. Samuel Wesley, Jun.

5   Marienborn, near Frankfort, July 7, O.S., 1738

Dear brother

God has given me at length the desire of my heart. I am with a church whose conversation is in heaven,[4] in whom is the mind that was in Christ,[5] and who so walks as he walked.[6] As they have all one
10 Lord and one faith, so they are all partakers of one spirit, the spirit of meekness and love, which uniformly and continually animates all their conversation. O how high and holy a thing Christianity is! And how widely distant from that—I know not what—which is so called, though it neither purifies the heart, or renews the life after
15 the image of our blessed Redeemer.

I grieve to think how that holy name by which we are called must be blasphemed among the heathen while they see discontented Christians, passionate Christians, resentful Christians, earthly-minded Christians. Yea (to come to what we are apt to count small things),
20 while they see Christians judging one another, ridiculing one another, speaking evil one of another, increasing instead of bearing one another's burdens.[7] How bitterly would Julian have applied to these, 'See, how these Christians love one another!'[8] I know I myself, I doubt *you* sometimes, and my sister often, have been under this
25 condemnation. O may God grant we may never more think to do him service by breaking those commands which are the very life of

---

[1] See 2 Cor. 6: 1.   [2] 2 Pet. 1: 4.
[3] 'To Mr. / Mr. Charles Wesley, At the home of Mr. Hutton, bookseller, Near Temple Bar, London, England.'
[4] See Phil. 3: 20.   [5] See Phil. 2: 5.
[6] See 1 John 2: 6.   [7] See Gal. 6: 2.
[8] Cf. letter of July 6, 1738, to their mother.

his religion! But may we utterly put away all anger, and wrath, and malice, and bitterness, and evil-speaking.[1]

I was much concerned when my brother Charles once incidentally mentioned a passage that occurred at Tiverton: 'Upon my offering to read', said he, 'a chapter in the *Serious Call*, my sister said, "Who 5 do you read that to? Not to these young ladies, I presume; and your brother and I do not want it." ' Yes, my sister, I must tell you in the spirit of love, and before God, who searcheth the heart, you do want it; you want it exceedingly. I know no one soul that wants to read, and consider deeply, so much the chapter of 'Universal love', and 10 that of 'Intercession'.[2] The character of Susurrus there is your own.[3] I should be false to God and you did I not tell you so. O may it be so no longer, but may you love your neighbour as yourself, both in word and tongue, and in deed and truth.

I believe in a week Mr. Ingham and I shall set out for Herrnhut, 15 about 350 miles from hence. O pray for us, that God would sanctify to us all those precious opportunities, that we may be continually built up more and more in the spirit of power, and love, and of a sound mind.[4] I am, dear brother, your most affectionate friend and brother, 20

John Wesley

Address: 'To the Rev. Mr. Wesley, at Tiverton, Devon'   *Source*: Priestley, pp. 80-2.

[1] See Col. 3: 8 and Eph. 4: 31.
[2] See chapters 20 and 21 of William Law, *A Serious Call to a Devout and Holy Life*.
[3] See chapter 21: 'Susurrus is a pious, temperate, good man, remarkable for abundance of excellent qualities . . . Yet Susurrus had a prodigious failing along with these great virtues. He had a mighty inclination to hear and discover all the defects and infirmities of all about him . . . If you would but whisper anything gently, though it was ever so bad in itself, Susurrus was ready to receive it . . . Susurrus had such a tender, compassionate manner of relating things the most prejudicial to his neighbour that he even seemed, both to himself and others, to be exercising a Christian charity at the same time that he was indulging a whispering, evil-speaking temper . . .'
[4] 2 Tim. 1: 7.

(560)

To the Revd. Charles Wesley

Herrnhut, Aug. 4, O.S., 1738

Dear brother
Thus far God hath greatly helped us in all things. An account of
the people here you must not expect till we come face to face, when
5 I hope we shall part no more. O that after I have proved all things[1]
I may be enabled throughly δοκιμάζειν τὰ διαφέροντα,[2] and calling
no man master, in faith, practice, and discipline, to hold fast that
which is good![3]

Salute our brethren in London and Oxford by name, and exhort
10 them all, in the name of the Lord Jesus, that they love and study
the oracles of God more and more; that they work out their salvation
with fear and trembling,[4] never imagining they have already attained,
or are already perfect;[5] never deceiving themselves, as if they had
now less need than before to be serious, watchful, lowly-minded;
15 and that above all things they use great plainness of speech, both
with each other and towards all men: μὴ ἐν δόλῳ πανουργίας, μηδὲ
δολοῦντες τὸν λόγον τοῦ Θεοῦ, ἀλλὰ φανερώσει τῆς ἀληθείας πρὸς
πάντας ἀνθρώπους.[6]

My dearest brother and friend, I commend you to the grace of
20 God, to be more and more renewed in the image of his Son![7] Pray
ye all for me continually! Adieu.

Address: 'To the Rev. Mr. Charles Wesley, At Mr. Hutton's, Booksellers, Near
Temple Bar, London, England'   *Source*: MA, a photograph of the original,
inscribed on the mount, 'Owner, Rev. Wellesley-Wesley'; present whereabouts
of holograph unknown. The address is given in Telford, I. 253, who describes
his source as 'Book Room Collection'. (The photograph shows that the half-
sheet is mounted only loosely, so that the address would be visible on the verso.)
Formed a double letter with the following.

[1] See 1 Thess. 5: 21.
[2] 'to approve what is excellent', Phil. 1: 10.
[3] 1 Thess. 5: 21.
[4] See Phil. 2: 12.
[5] See Phil. 3: 12.
[6] 2 Cor. 4: 2, slightly misquoted: 'not in the guile of craftiness, nor adulterating the
Word of God, but by manifestation of the truth to all men'.
[7] See Rom. 8: 29.

To James Hutton, etc.

Herrnhut, Aug. 4, O.S., 1738

My dear brother

I hope you and those with you stand fast in the grace of our Lord Jesus Christ, and are in no wise shaken from your purpose, of declaring his goodness to the children of men. Ye are a few of those 5 whom he hath chosen to be witnesses of the merits of his death and the power of his resurrection.[1] And ye cannot too largely or too boldly declare the things he hath done for your own souls. If ye have indeed found mercy through his blood you must 'use great plainness of speech';[2] not as Moses, and the Judaizing Christians still among 10 us, who put a veil over their face,[3] to the intent that the glory of the Lord should not shine, which ought to shine in the eyes of all men. Many indeed will blaspheme, even though Paul speak, and speak only the words of truth and soberness.[4] But ought Paul therefore to forbear speaking? 'We have not so learned Christ.'[5] Many also 'will 15 persecute and revile you, and say all manner of evil of you, for his name's sake.'[6] Why, then ye are heirs of the blessing.[7] Then the Spirit of God, the Spirit of glory, shall rest upon you.[8] Then rejoice and be exceeding glad,[9] that ye are partakers of the reproach of Christ.[10] 'And when Christ, which is your life, shall appear, ye shall 20 also appear with him in glory.'[11]

We are here compassed about with a cloud of witnesses[12] that the Ancient of days[13] waxeth not old;[14] that his arm is not shortened,[15] but still worketh mightily in[16] and for those that believe. All of these are living proofs that Christianity, as its Author, is the same yester- 25 day, today, and for ever;[17] that the same gifts are still given unto men, the same holiness and happiness, the same freedom from sin, the same peace and joy in the Holy Ghost.[18] These likewise bear witness with one accord that there is but one way under heaven given to men of attaining to a fellowship in these great and precious 30 promises,[19] namely, faith in him who loved us and gave himself for

[1] Phil. 3: 10.
[2] 2 Cor. 3: 12.
[3] See 2 Cor. 3: 13.
[4] Acts 26: 25.
[5] Eph. 4: 20.
[6] See Matt. 5: 11.
[7] See 1 Pet. 3: 7, 9.
[8] See 1 Pet. 4: 14.
[9] Matt. 5: 12.
[10] Heb. 11: 26.
[11] See Col. 3: 4.
[12] See Heb. 12: 1.
[13] Dan. 7: 9, 22.
[14] Luke 12: 33.
[15] See Isa. 59: 1.
[16] See Col. 1: 29.
[17] Heb. 13: 8.
[18] Rom. 14: 17.
[19] See 2 Pet. 1: 4.

us,[1] and 'bare our sins in his own body upon the tree'.[2] And also
that 'whosoever seeketh this, findeth',[3] so he seek it humbly,
earnestly, and perseveringly, absolutely renouncing all his own
righteousness, as well as his own works, and coming to Christ as
5 poor, miserable, and naked!

My dear friends, be lowly, be serious, be watchful. Let not any
pretence to mental make you slack in vocal prayer. Be good stewards
of the manifold grace of God.[4] And the God of peace and love be
with you, even unto the end!

10 Be not forgetful of praying much for your weak brother in Christ,
John Wesley

To James Hutton, etc.

Source: MorA, originally part of a double letter with that of the same date to
Charles Wesley.

To the Revd. Arthur Bedford[5]

To Mr. Art. Bedford   Sept. 28, 1738
Revd. sir

15 1. A few days ago I met with a sermon of yours, said to be written
against me. It is entitled, *The Doctrine of Assurance*. When I first
read of the three propositions there laid down—(1), that an assurance
of salvation is not of the essence of faith;(2), that a true believer may
wait long before he hath it; and (3), that after he hath it, it may be

---

[1] See Gal. 2: 20.   [2] See Eph. 5: 2.
[3] See Matt. 7: 8, etc.   [4] 1 Pet. 4: 10.

[5] Arthur Bedford (1668–1745) was a versatile clergyman who wrote widely on a
variety of subjects: the immorality of the stage, church music, chronology, mathematics,
and theology. After a long career in the Bristol area, in 1724 he became chaplain of the
Haberdashers' Hospital at Hoxton, London, where he was buried. On Aug. 13, 1738,
he preached a sermon in St. Lawrence Jewry which he published as *The Doctrine of
Assurance: or the case of a weak and doubting conscience*. The Appendix (pp. 19–39) constituted an attack on 'those who have of late asserted that they who are not assured of
their salvation by a revelation from the Holy Ghost are in a state of damnation' (p. 19).
Neither Wesley nor the Methodists are mentioned by name, however, though 'Moravia'
appears once (p. 34). As yet, in fact, Wesley had referred to assurance in preaching, but
not in print. His diary shows that he began to answer the pamphlet on Sept. 25, though
the letter does not appear to have been sent until Sept. 28. On Oct. 6 he followed this up
with a visit to Bedford at Hoxton, 'to tell him, between me and him alone, of the injury
he had done both to God and his brother by preaching and printing that very weak
sermon on assurance' (*Journal*).

weakened and intermitted by many distempers, sins, temptations, and desertions—I thought there was[1] nothing herein but what I both believed and preached. But in going on I was convinced of the contrary, and saw clearly that by this one phrase, 'assurance of salvation', we meant entirely[2] different things, you understanding thereby 'an assurance[3] that we shall persevere[4] in a state of salvation', whereas I mean no more[5] by that term than 'an assurance that we are in such a state'.

2. How easily then might a short question have prevented this whole dispute,[6] and saved you the trouble of a mere *ignoratio elenchi*[7] for almost forty pages together! As to the assurance you speak of, neither my brother nor I, nor any of our friends that I know of,[8] hold it, no, nor the Moravian Church, whose present judgment I have had better opportunity to know than the author of what is called your catechism.[9] I dare not affirm so much of *this* assurance as that 'it is given to very few', for I believe it is given to none at all. I find it not in the Book of God. Yea, I take it to be utterly contrary thereto, as implying the impossibility of falling from grace;[10] from asserting which fatal doctrine I trust the God whom I serve will always deliver me.

3. That assurance of which alone I speak I should not choose to call an assurance of salvation, but rather (with the Scriptures),[11] the assurance of faith.[12] And even this, I believe, is not of the essence of faith, but a distinct gift of the Holy Ghost, whereby God shines upon his own work, and shows us that[13] we are justified through faith in Christ. If anyone chooses to transpose the words, and to term this, instead of 'the assurance of faith', 'the faith of assurance', I should not contend with him for a phrase, though I think the scriptural words are always the best, and in this case particularly, because

---

[1] Orig., ((saw)). [2] Orig., ((absolutely)).
[3] Orig., 'an ((infallible)) assurance'. [4] Orig. adds, '((to the end))'.
[5] Orig., 'whereas I ((do not, nor ever did)), mean ((any)) more'.
[6] Orig., ((controversy)). [7] 'missing the real point'.
[8] Orig. adds, 'friends ((unless Presbyterians)) hold'.
[9] Orig. continues '((which I never saw)), and ((as it is called))' (later replaced by the superscript, 'of what is called').
[10] Orig. here continues: '((An opinion which su))rely, ((if any other, deserves to be ranked among the doctrines of devils.))'. This is replaced above the line by the clause as it follows in the text.
[11] Orig., '((as)) the Scriptures ((do))'.
[12] See Heb. 10: 22 and § 4 below. The orig. continues: 'faith; ((since the Greek word, plerophory, is scarce understood))'.
[13] Orig., 'and ((witnesses together with our spirit)) that'.

otherwise we may seem to make two faiths, whereas St. Paul knew but of one.

4. This πληροφορία πίστεως,[1] however we translate it,[2] I believe is neither more nor less than hope; or a conviction, wrought in us
5 by the Holy Ghost, that we have a measure[3] of the true faith in Christ,[4] and that as he is already made justification unto us, so *if* we continue[5] to watch and strive and pray, he will gradually become 'our sanctification here, and our full redemption hereafter'.[6] This assurance, I believe, is given[7] to some in a smaller, to others in a
10 larger degree; to some also sooner, to others later, according to the counsels of his will.[8] But since it is promised to all, I cannot doubt but it will be given to all that diligently seek it.[9] I cannot doubt but all 'who truly believe in Christ Jesus, and endeavour to walk in all good conscience before him', will in due time 'be assured that they are in
15 a state of grace, and may persevere therein unto salvation',[10] by the Holy Spirit enabling them to discern in themselves those graces to which the promises of life are made, and 'bearing witness with their spirits that they are the children of God'.[11]

5. Now I beseech you, sir, to consider calmly whether it be I or
20 you who hath broken the royal law of charity. Being informed that I and some of my friends were in a fault,[12] you did not go and tell[13] your brother of it,[14] between you and him alone; you did not tell it[15] to the elders of the church only; but at one step to[16] all the world. You brand us at once with 'spiritual pride, enthusiasm, false doc-
25 trine, heresy, uncharitableness';[17] with 'crude,[18] indigested notions,

---

[1] 'full assurance of faith', Heb. 10: 22.
[2] Orig., '((it be)) translated'.
[3] Orig., '((some)) measure'.
[4] Orig. continues, '((that hereby we are accepted of God through him))'.
[5] Orig., 'continue ((watchful))'.
[6] As in many instances in the letter, only the closing quotation mark is given. The source of the quotation is not known; it does not come from Bedford's pamphlet. Cf. 1 Cor. 1: 30.
[7] Orig., 'I ((have known)) given'.
[8] See Eph. 1: 11.   [9] See Heb. 11: 6.
[10] See Bedford, *Doctrine of Assurance*, 2nd edn., London, 1739, p. 35.
[11] See Rom. 8: 16.
[12] Orig. continues, '((which fault in truth was not committed at all))'.
[13] Orig., 'go ((or send, to)) tell'.
[14] Orig., 'brother of ((his fault of his fau))'.
[15] Orig., 'you ((was not content with telling)) it'.
[16] Orig., 'step ((published it)) to'.
[17] See Bedford, op. cit., p. 35.
[18] Orig., 'with ((advancing)), [and superscript ((teaching))] crude'.

of dismal consequences',[1] because we would fain set ourselves up to be the heads of a party'.[2] You declare that we 'serve not the Lord Jesus Christ, but by fair speeches deceive the hearts of the simple';[3] that we have 'swerved from faith and a good conscience, and turned aside unto vain jangling; desiring to be teachers of the law, under- standing neither what we say nor whereof we affirm'.[4] You say 'we consent not to the words of our Lord Jesus Christ, nor to the doctrine which is according to godliness; but that we are proud, knowing nothing, but doting about questions and strifes of words'.[5] In short, that 'we are men of corrupt minds, and destitute of the truth'.[6]

6. O, sir, how could you possibly be induced to pass such a sentence, even in your heart, till you had done us the common heathen justice of hearing us answer for ourselves? How then was you induced to declare[7] it to all mankind! Especially when those you were to declare hateful to God[8] and man were those of whom you had once hoped better things, even things that accompany salvation! Yea, whom you had received as sincere, though weak brethren, and strengthened their hands in God![9] What evidence, less than hearing them with your own ears pronounce the words laid to their charge, could constrain you so to judge of them? Much more,[10] so to speak of them, since your words cannot be recalled, but must remain a stumbling-block to the weak,[11] a grief to the lovers of peace and union, and a triumph to the enemy!

7. It is not I, or my brother or our friends, who cause or foment divisions and offences! With us, glory be to God, is no anger or clamour or bitterness or evil-speaking![12] We avoid as we would avoid the fire of hell all envy, strife, railings, evil surmisings,[13] and follow after lowliness, meekness, and love,[14] with all that[15] seek the

---

[1] See Bedford, op. cit., p. 35.　　　　　　　　　　　　　　　　　　[2] Ibid.
[3] Rom. 16: 17–18, quoted Bedford, op. cit., p. 37.
[4] 1 Tim. 1: 5–7, quoted Bedford, op. cit., p. 36.
[5] 1 Tim. 6: 3–5, quoted Bedford, op. cit., pp. 36, 37.
[6] 1 Tim. 6: 5, quoted ibid.
[7] Orig.: '((How then could you be prevailed on, not only thus to condemn us unheard, much more)) to declare'.
[8] Orig., 'haters of God'.
[9] Probably a reference to the fact that Bedford was an active member of the Georgia Trust and of Dr. Bray's Associates, and thus sponsored Wesley's mission to Georgia.
[10] Orig., ((What motive)).　　　　　　　　　　　　　　[11] See 1 Cor. 8: 9.
[12] See Eph. 4: 31.　　　　　　　　　　　　　　　　　[13] See 1 Tim. 6: 4.
[14] Orig., 'meekness, lowliness, and love'; see Eph. 4: 2.
[15] Orig., '((those)) that'.

Lord Jesus Christ in sincerity.[1] And with this end it is that I have
written now, hoping that if in anything I *do* err from the truth, you
will restore me in the spirit of meekness,[2] that I may again give God
thanks on your behalf,[3] and have a fresh instance of your readiness
5 to support the weak and comfort the feeble-minded.[4] To do which,
after the ability which God giveth,[5] is also the desire of, revd. sir,
your obedient servant,

J[ohn] W[esley]

Source: MorA, a draft on 5 pp. duodecimo, probably kept as a reference copy,
and then lent at some time to James Hutton, and not returned.

To the Moravians[6]

September [27–8], 1738

10 My dear brethren

I cannot but rejoice in your steadfast faith, in your love to our
blessed Redeemer, your deadness to the world; your meekness,
temperance, chastity, and love of one another. I greatly approve of
your conferences and bands; of your method of instructing children;
15 and in general of your great care of the souls committed to your
charge.

But of some other things I stand in doubt, which I will mention in
love and meekness. And I wish that, in order to remove those doubts,
you would on each of those heads, first, plainly answer whether the
20 fact be as I suppose, and if so, secondly, consider whether it be right.

Do you not wholly neglect joint fasting?

Is not the Count all in all? Are not the rest mere shadows? Calling
him 'Rabbi'?[7] Almost implicitly both believing and obeying him?

---

[1] Eph. 6: 24.   [2] See Gal. 6: 1.   [3] See 1 Cor. 1: 4.
[4] See 1 Thess. 5: 14.   [5] See 1 Pet. 4: 11.
[6] Wesley arrived in London after his visit to the Moravians in Germany on Saturday,
Sept. 16, 1738. Speedily he began the account of Herrnhut which later formed the
nucleus of the second extract from his *Journal*. On Sept. 27 he 'writ letter' in the afternoon, and apparently continued the same letter on the morning of the 28th. This is
probably that thus introduced in his *Journal* two years later, when his relations with the
Moravians had become very strained: 'In September, 1738, soon after my return to
England, I began the following letter to the Moravian Church. But being fearful of
trusting my own judgment, I determined to wait yet a little longer, and so laid it by
unfinished.' Some of these criticisms were incorporated in his lengthy letter to the
Moravians dated Aug. 8, 1740.
[7] See Matt. 23: 7, 8.

Is there not something of levity in your behaviour? Are you, in general, serious enough?

Are you zealous and watchful to redeem time? Do you not sometimes fall into trifling conversation?

Do you not magnify your own church too much? Do you believe 5 any who are not of it to be in gospel liberty?

Are you not straitened in your love? Do you love your enemies, and wicked men, as yourselves?

Do you not mix *human* wisdom with *divine*? Joining worldly prudence to heavenly? 10

Do you not use cunning, guile, or dissimulation in many cases?

Are you not of a close, dark, reserved temper and behaviour?

Is not the spirit of secrecy the spirit of your community?

Have you that childlike openness, frankness, and plainness of speech so manifest to all in the apostles and first Christians? 15

Source: JWJ, Sept. 3, 1741; cf. *An Answer to the Rev. Mr. Church's Remarks* (1745), I.5, for a much abbreviated version of this letter.

From William Delamotte[1]

October 10, 1738

Dear sir

I thank God for your coming to Blendon; though I myself had not so much of your company, I can trace your footsteps and reap the benefit of it in the blessed effect it has had on others. O may God continue to set his seal to your ministry 20 wherever you go! Mr. Piers, I believe, has felt great comfort, and is pressing for the full assurance of faith. God grant he may feel his desire accomplished! And may we all so increase in grace as to become helpers of your joy.

Can a man properly be said to be born of God till he has an assurance of faith? St. John makes the test of our new birth *our* victory over the world and 25 sin; if so, I fear, I am still unregenerate, for sin works powerfully in me, and seems to be frequently proclaiming its conquests over me. And yet my soul is often in a sweet peace, nay, sometimes overwhelmed with joy, and always

[1] William Delamotte was the brother of Wesley's Georgia companion, Charles, but died in February, 1743. It seems that it was through this family's influence that the vicar of Bexley, the Revd. Henry Piers, was drawn within the Methodist orbit. It is just possible that Delamotte was the 'friend' to whom Wesley sent an extract on Oct. 9 of the *Faithful Narrative* of Jonathan Edwards, as far as it related to 'weak faith', to which the reply (received Oct. 14), led to self-searching about his own spiritual state, and a lengthy meditation thereon in his *Journal*. It is more likely, however, that his correspondent in this instance was a more long-standing friend such as the Revd. John Gambold.

pants for closer union, a fuller manifestation of the Son of God. How is this consistent with the true justifying faith? I could be glad of your opinion and advice. I would have spoke to you at Mr. Bray's, but my mouth was held in that I could not speak. Therefore I should be glad if you would supply the want
5 of that, with a line or two, and you will very much oblige, your sincere friend in Christ,

William De Lamotte

God has increased my audience last night to upwards of eighty. O may he increase them in number, and knowledge, and the love of his holy name. Con-
10 tinue your prayers for us. Adieu!

Source: *A.M.* Supp., 1797, p. 20.

To Dr. Johannes de Koker[1]

[Oct. 13, 1738]

I have delayed writing till now, in hopes I might have had an opportunity of transcribing the papers you desired before I wrote. But I find I cannot have time for this yet; it having pleased God to
15 give me full employment of another nature. His blessed Spirit has wrought so powerfully both in London and Oxford that there is a general awakening, and multitudes are crying out, What must we do to be saved?[2] So that till our gracious Master sendeth more labourers into his harvest,[3] all my time is much too little for them.
20 May our blessed Lord repay sevenfold into your bosoms[4] the kindness showed to us for his name's sake! That you may be found in him, not having your own righteousness, which is of the law, but that which is through the faith of Christ, the righteousness which is of God by faith,[5] is the earnest prayer of, dear sir, your unworthy
25 brother in Christ,

[John Wesley]

Source: Whitehead, II. 87–8; date confirmed by Wesley's diary.

[1] Dr. Johannes de Koker, a physician of Rotterdam, had delivered his medical dissertation in 1719 on *De morbo epidemico* ('On epidemic disease'), and was probably considerably older than Wesley. He welcomed Wesley and his companions to Holland on June 15, 1738, and gave them the hospitality of his home on their return eleven weeks later. He was a cordial correspondent of Wesley's for over a decade. Although Koker himself wrote in Latin, it appears that he could read English, and translated some of Wesley's writings into Dutch.

[2] See Acts 16: 30.　　　　　　　　　　　　　　[3] See Matt. 9: 38.
[4] See Ps. 79: 12.　　　　　　　　　　　　　　　[5] See Phil. 3: 9.

To the Revd. Benjamin Ingham[1]

[Oct. 13, 1738]

O my dear brother, God hath been wonderfully gracious to us ever since our return to England. Though there are many adversaries, yet a great door and effectual is opened;[2] and we continue, through evil report and good report, to preach the gospel of Christ to all people, and earnestly to contend for the faith once delivered to the saints.[3] Indeed, he hath given unto us many of our fiercest opposers, who now receive with meekness the engrafted word.[4] One of the bitterest of them could have no rest in his spirit till on Saturday the 30th of September, O.S., he was compelled to send for me, who knew him not so much as by face, and to tell me the secrets of his heart.[5] He owned with many tears that in spite of all his endeavours he was still carnal, sold under sin;[6] that he continually did the thing he would not,[7] and was thereby convinced of the entire corruption of his whole nature; that the very night before, after the most solemn resolutions to the contrary, he had been guilty of gross drunkenness, and had no hope of escaping, having neither spirit nor strength left in him. We fell on our knees, and besought our Lord to bring this sinner unto God, who through his blood justifieth the ungodly.[8] He arose, and his countenance was no longer sad, for he knew, and testified aloud, that he was passed from death unto life,[9] and felt in himself that he was healed of his plague.[10] And from that hour to this he hath had peace and joy in believing,[11] and sin hath no more dominion over him.[12]

---

[1] It seems clear that Ingham remained behind when Wesley left Germany, but Wesley's letter of Nov. 16 was addressed to him at Hutton's in London. Wesley had last visited Oxford in the spring of 1738, and now in October he passed on to his former Oxford colleague his observations on what he had recently found, especially about the batch of younger men who had now reached the canonical age of 22, and thus had recently been ordained: Thomas Combes, John Robson, and John Hutchings. He wrote also about their own contemporaries, Christopher Wells, Charles Kinchin, John Gambold, and George Stonehouse, as well as a young clergyman, John Sparkes, educated in Cambridge, but now serving in London alongside their colleague Thomas Broughton.

[2] See 1 Cor. 16: 9.   [3] See Jude 3.   [4] Jas. 1: 21.

[5] Mr. Jennings (see Wesley's diary), who seems to have left little mark on either Methodist or Moravian history (cf. letter to Edmonds, Apr. 9, 1739).

[6] Rom. 7: 14.   [7] See Rom. 7: 19.   [8] Rom. 4: 5.

[9] See 1 John 3: 14.   [10] See Mark 5: 29.

[11] Rom. 15: 13.   [12] See Rom. 6: 9, 14.

Mr. Stonehouse[1] hath at length determined to know nothing but Jesus Christ, and him crucified;[2] and to preach unto all remission of sins[3] through faith in his blood.[4] Mr. Sparkes[5] also is a teacher of sound doctrine. Mr. Hutchin[g]s[6] is strong in the faith, and mightily
5 convinces gainsayers,[7] so that no man hitherto hath been able to stand before him. Mr. Kinchin, Gambold, and Wells[8] have not yet received comfort, but are patiently waiting for it. Mr. Robson,[9] who is now a minister of Christ also, is full of faith, and peace, and love. So is Mr. Coombs,[10] a little child, who was called to minister in

[1] George Stonehouse (1714–93), an Oxford Methodist, of Pembroke College, vicar of Islington from 1738, opened his pulpit and his churchyard to the Wesleys and White-field, but in 1739 was compelled to desist, by threat of disciplinary action under Canons 47–54, although he remained friendly with the Wesleys, and St. Mary's, Islington, became an evangelical stronghold.

[2] 1 Cor. 2: 2.   [3] See Luke 24: 47.   [4] Rom. 3: 25.

[5] John Sparkes (c. 1713–47), of Peterborough, educated at St. John's College, Cambridge, and ordained deacon on Feb. 16 and priest on Apr. 16, 1738. He seems to have been assisting the Revd. Thomas Broughton in London, and on July 10 had persuaded Charles Wesley to preach in Newgate prison to ten malefactors condemned to death. Charles had been trying to bring Sparkes to a personal faith, and on June 8, 1738, 'had the satisfaction of hearing Mr. Sparkes confess himself convinced now that he is under the law, not under grace', and on Oct. 27 that he was 'fully persuaded his sins [were] forgiven'. Later Sparkes became rector of Newton Bromswold, Northants.

[6] John Hutchings (to be distinguished from Richard Hutchins, though sometimes, as here, the Wesleys omitted the 'g' in his name) matriculated at Pembroke College on May 30, 1734, aged 18, graduating and entering Holy Orders in 1738, and serving for much of his time during the following year or two as Kinchin's curate at Dummer. In 1741 he joined the Moravians.

[7] See Titus 1:9.

[8] Christopher Wells, a fellow of Jesus College, just two or three years younger than Wesley, whom Charles Wesley described on Sept. 29, 1737, as 'on the brink of the new birth', and whose experience had been deepened on Aug. 31, 1738, when Charles told of the conversion of Mrs. Platt, who, when asked by Charles Kinchin, 'Have you forgive-ness of sins?' replied confidently, 'I am perfectly assured I have.' After Wells returned as a clergyman to Cardiff he invited Charles Wesley to preach in his churches there, although in 1744, when John Wesley preached on 'Scriptural Christianity' before the university assembled at St. Mary's, Wells tried to dissociate himself from the Method-ists.

[9] Charles Wesley records that on July 21, 1738, John Robson (for whom cf. p. 386n. above) theoretically 'received the strange doctrine of faith', and on July 22 'was quite overpowered, and even compelled to believe, till at last he was filled with strength and confidence'. In the summer of 1740 Robson went on a brief preaching tour with Charles Wesley, but three years later (in Oxford) Charles referred to him as 'poor, languid, dead Mr. Robson', 'denying both justification and sanctification' (CWJ, I. 123, 139, 244, 319, 334).

[10] Thomas Coombs, the son of William Coombs, an Oxford tradesman, who matricu-lated at Brasenose College on Dec. 17, 1733, aged 17, and therefore came of canonical age for ordination in 1738, having graduated the previous year. It may well have been during the week following his ordination that he walked from London to Oxford with Charles Wesley, who tried to introduce him to personal faith to such good effect that

holy things two or three weeks ago. Indeed, I trust our Lord will let us see, and that shortly, a multitude of priests that believe. My brother and I are partly here,[1] and partly in London, till Mr. Whitefield, or some other, is sent to release us from hence.

Pray for us continually, my dear brother, that we may make full 5 proof of our ministry;[2] and may ourselves stand fast in the grace of our Lord Jesus; and as soon as you can, send word of what he is doing by and for you.

Address: 'To Mr. Ingham, at Hernhuth'   *Source*: Whitehead, II. 88–9, date confirmed by Wesley's diary.

To the Church at Herrnhut[3]

[Oct. 14–20, 1738]

To the Church of God which is in Herrnhut, John Wesley, an 10 unworthy presbyter of the Church of God in England, wisheth all grace and peace in our Lord Jesus Christ, October 14.

Glory be to God, even the Father of our Lord Jesus Christ, for his unspeakable gift![4] For giving me to be an eye-witness of your faith, and love, and holy conversation in Christ Jesus. I have borne 15 testimony thereof with all plainness of speech in many parts of

they 'sang and shouted all the way to Oxford'. After communicating on the following day (Sept. 28) Coombs told Charles that 'his warmth had returned through *professing* his faith'. (Wesley spells the name 'Combes'.)

[1] i.e. in Oxford.
[2] See 2 Tim. 4: 5.
[3] Wesley's diary for Oct. 14, 1738, records: 'writ to Ct. Z[inzendorf], to H[errn]-H[ut]'. The purpose of both letters was to respond to his experiences among the German Moravians, and to describe the conditions to which he had returned. The original of the letter to Zinzendorf is preserved in the Moravian Archives at Herrnhut, dated at the end, 'October 30, 1738', which would seem to mark the occasion when it was finally dispatched *via* personal messenger to Zinzendorf in Amsterdam. The letter to the Herrnhut congregation seems to have disappeared, but in the Archives there is a German translation of this letter, dated at the end, 'London, October 20, 1738'. This follows the same basic text as that presented by Whitehead, which was doubtless derived from Wesley's English draft, retained as a reference copy. It seems fairly certain that the actual letter sent to the congregation, like that to Zinzendorf, was in English. The German translation implies that Wesley made a few alterations in the letter finally sent—a fairly common practice with him. I am very grateful to Mrs. Ruth S. Phelps for pointing out the major variants, noted below.
[4] See 2 Cor. 9: 15.

Germany, and thanks have been given to God by many on your behalf.[1]

We are endeavouring here also, by the grace which is given us, to be followers of you, as ye are of Christ.[2] Fourteen were added to us since our return, so that we have now eight bands of men, consisting of fifty-six persons, all of whom seek for salvation only in the blood of Christ.[3] As yet we have only two small bands of women, the one of three, the other of five persons. But here are many others who only wait till we have leisure to instruct them how they may most effectually build up one another in the faith and love of him who gave himself for them.[4]

Though my brother and I are not permitted to preach in most of the churches in London, yet thanks be to God there are others left, wherein we have liberty to speak the truth as it is in Jesus.[5] Likewise every evening, and on set evenings in the week at two several places, we publish the word of reconciliation,[6] sometimes to three or four hundred[7] persons met together to hear it. We begin and end all our meetings with singing and prayer; and we know that our Lord heareth our prayer, having more than once or twice—and this was not done in a corner[8]—received our petitions in that very hour.

Nor hath he left himself without other witnesses of his grace and truth. Ten ministers I know now in England who lay the right foundation, 'The blood of Christ cleanseth us from all sin.'[9] Over and above whom I have found one Anabaptist, and one if not two of the teachers among the Presbyterians here, who, I hope, love the Lord Jesus Christ in sincerity,[10] and teach the way of God in truth.[11]

O cease not, ye that are highly favoured, to beseech our Lord that

---

[1] The German translation presupposes an English original which reads: 'I have heard and seen the clearest testimony of this in many parts of Germany, Holland, and England, and your love has awakened and quickened many souls, who thank God on your behalf.'

[2] See 1 Cor. 11: 1.

[3] Wesley was apparently describing the society founded in Fetter Lane, London, on May 1, 1738, by Peter Böhler and him, which eventually split into Moravian and Methodist contingents. His visit to Herrnhut had convinced him in particular of the value of subdividing such religious societies into 'bands', small homogeneous groups of people of the same sex and marital status—a modification of the Moravian 'choirs'.

[4] See Gal. 2: 20.   [5] Eph. 4: 21.   [6] 2 Cor. 5: 19.

[7] The German translation implies that in the final letter Wesley wrote: 'sometimes to twenty or thirty, sometimes fifty of sixty, sometimes to three or four hundred'.

[8] Acts 26: 26. This interpolation was apparently omitted from the letter as sent to Herrnhut.

[9] See 1 John 1: 7.   [10] See Eph. 6: 24.

[11] See Matt. 22: 16; Mark 12: 14.

he would be with us even to the end; to remove that which is
displeasing in his sight, to support that which is weak among us,
to give us the whole mind that was in him,[1] and teach us to walk
even as he walked![2] And may the very God of peace fill up what is
wanting in your faith, and build you up more and more in all lowliness 5
of mind, in all plainness of speech, in all zeal and watchfulness, that
he may present you to himself a glorious Church, not having spot
or wrinkle, or any such thing,[3] but that ye may be holy and un-
blameable[4] in the day of his appearing . . .

London, October 20, 1738[5]   10

Sources: Whitehead, II. 91-2, from the draft, collated with the German translation of the letter as sent, at Herrnhut.

To Count Zinzendorf[6]

[Oct. 14-30, 1738]

May our gracious Lord, who counteth whatsoever is done unto the
least of his followers as done to himself,[7] return sevenfold unto you
and the countess and all the brethren the many kindnesses you did
unto us! It would have been a great satisfaction to me if I could have 15
spent more time with the Christians that love one another.[8] But that
could not be now, my Master having called me to work in another
part of his vineyard. Nor did I return hither at all before the time.
For though a great door and effectual had been opened,[9] the adversary had laid so many stumbling-blocks before it that the weak were 20
daily turned out of the way.[10] Numberless misunderstandings had
arisen, by reason of which the way of truth was much blasphemed.
And hence had sprung anger, clamour, bitterness, evil-speaking,
envyings, strifes, railings, evil surmisings,[11] whereby the enemy had

---

[1] See Phil. 2: 5.   [2] See 1 John 2: 6.
[3] See Eph. 5: 27.   [4] See Col. 1: 22.
[5] This date is in the German translation only, which omits 'Oct. 14' at the beginning,
apparently because it was not in the letter as sent.
[6] See introductory note to previous letter.
[7] See Matt. 25: 40. The draft has 'brethren', not 'followers'.
[8] See letters of July 6, 7, 1738.
[9] 1 Cor. 16: 9.   [10] See Heb. 12: 13.   [11] See 1 Tim. 6: 4.

gained such an advantage over the little flock that of the rest durst no man join himself unto them.[1]

But it has now pleased our blessed Master to remove in great measure these rocks of offence.[2] The word of the Lord runs and is glorified,[3] and his work goes on and prospers. Great multitudes are everywhere awakened, and cry out, What must we do to be saved?[4] Many of them see that there is only one name under heaven whereby they can be saved,[5] and more and more of those that seek it find salvation in his name. Their faith hath made them whole.[6] And these are of one heart and one soul.[7] They all love one another, and are knit together in one body and one spirit, as in one faith and one hope of their calling.[8]

The love and zeal of our brethren in Holland and Germany, particularly at Herrnhut, hath stirred up many among us, who will not be comforted till they also partake of the great and precious promises.[9] I hope, if God permit, to see them at least once more, were it only to give them that fruit of my love, the speaking freely on a few things which I did not approve, perhaps because I did not understand them.[10] May our merciful Lord give you a right judgment in all things![11] And make you to abound more and more,[12] in all lowliness and meekness,[13] in all simplicity and godly sincerity,[14] in all watchfulness and seriousness; in a word, in all faith and love, particularly to those that are without, till ye are merciful as your Father which is in heaven is merciful![15]

I desire your constant and earnest prayers that he would vouchsafe a portion of the same spirit to your much obliged and very affectionate, but unworthy, brother in Christ,

John Wesley

London, October 30,
1738

Address: 'To Count Zinzendorf, at Amsterdam'   *Source*: Herrnhut; cf.

---

[1] Acts 5: 13. Wesley refers to some internal dissensions within the various religious societies in London which he visited, and in general to the misunderstanding and rejection of his evangelical teaching, as exemplified in the Revd. Arthur Bedford's sermon (see Sept. 28 above).

[2] Rom. 9: 33, etc.   [3] See 2 Thess. 3: 1.   [4] See Acts 16: 30.
[5] See Acts 4: 12.   [6] See Matt. 9: 22, etc.   [7] Acts 4: 32.
[8] See Eph. 4: 4–5.   [9] 1 Pet. 1: 4.
[10] See the draft letter of Sept. 27–8 (pp. 566–7).
[11] B.C.P., Collect for Whit Sunday.   [12] 1 Thess. 4: 1.
[13] Eph. 4: 2.   [14] 2 Cor. 1: 12.   [15] See Matt. 16: 17; Luke 6: 36.

Whitehead, II. 90–1, clearly based on the draft-reference copy, with a dozen verbal differences in addition to the omission of the sentence, 'Their faith hath made them whole' and the closing salutation. In this draft the address is given as 'To Count Zinzendorf, at Marienborn'—where on Oct. 14 Wesley apparently expected him to be.

To the Revd. Samuel Wesley, Jun.[1]

London, October 30, 1738

Dear brother

That you will always receive kindly what is so intended I doubt not. Therefore I again recommend the character of Susurrus, both to you and my sister,[2] as (whether real or feigned) striking at the 5
root of a fault of which both she and you were (I think) more guilty than any other two persons[3] I have known in my life. O may God deliver both you and me from all bitterness and evil-speaking, as well as from all false doctrine, heresy, and schism.

With regard to my own character, and my doctrine likewise, I 10
shall answer you very plainly.[4] By a Christian I mean one who so believes in Christ as that sin hath no more dominion over him. And in this obvious sense of the word I was not a Christian till May 24 last past.[5] For till then sin had the dominion over me,[6] although I fought with it continually;[7] but since[8] then, from that time to this, 15
it hath not.[9] Such is the free grace of God in Christ.[10] What sins they were which till then reigned over me, and from which by the grace of God I am now free, I am ready to declare on the house-top, if it may be for the glory of God.

[1] The first half of this letter is available both in Wesley's holograph draft and in the version printed by Dr. Joseph Priestley from the letter as dispatched, which therefore remains the preferred source for actual content, though the manuscript is a more reliable guide to Wesley's stylistic usages.

[2] See letter of July 7, 1738 (p. 559).

[3] Draft, 'you and she were more guilty than (I think) any two persons'.

[4] The draft adds, '((As to the first))'—a reminder that Wesley was answering points in his brother's letter written a week or so earlier.

[5] i.e. the occasion when his heart was 'strangely warmed'.

[6] See Rom. 6: 14.   [7] Draft, '((daily))'.

[8] Priestley, 'surely', apparently a misreading of 'since', which appears in the draft.

[9] Draft, erased, 'daily; but had not the victory. And since then'. This was then altered to, 'But from that time to this I have had the victory, through Christ which strengtheneth me'. This also was later changed to, 'But since then', apparently with 'from that time to this' rescued from the erased text for the fair copy.

[10] This sentence is not represented in the draft.

If you ask by what means I am made free (though not perfect,
neither infallibly sure of my perseverance), I answer, by faith in
Christ; but such a sort or degree[1] of faith as I had not till that day.
My desire[2] of this faith I knew long before, though not so clearly
5 till Sunday, Jan. 8 last, when being in the midst of the great deep
I wrote a few lines in the bitterness of my soul, some[3] of which
I have transcribed;[4] and may the good God[5] sanctify them both to
you and me:

By the most infallible of all proofs, inward feelings, I am convinced,[6]
10   1. Of unbelief, having no such faith in Christ as will prevent my heart's
being[7] troubled, which it could not be if I believed in God, and rightly believed
also in him.[8]
   2. Of pride throughout my life past, inasmuch as I thought I had what I
find I have not.[9]
15 Lord, save, or I perish![10] Save me,
   1. By such a faith in thee and in thy Christ as implies trust, confidence,
peace, in life and in death.
   2. By such humility as may fill my heart, from this hour for ever, with a
piercing uninterrupted sense, *Nihil est quod hactenus feci,*[11] having evidently
20 built without a foundation.
   3. By such a recollection as may[12] cry to thee every moment, but more
especially when all is calm (if it should so please thee), 'Give me faith, or I die!
Give me a lowly spirit. Otherwise, *Mihi non sit suave vivere.*'[13]
   Amen! Come, Lord Jesus![14]
25   Υἱὲ Δαυίδ, ἐλέησον με.[15]

Some measure of this faith, which bringeth salvation, or victory
over sin, and which implies peace and trust in God through Christ,[16]
I now enjoy by his free mercy, though in very deed it is in me but
as a grain of mustard seed;[17] for the πληροφορία πίστεως[18]—'the seal

---

[1] Draft, 'degree or sort'.   [2] Draft, 'want'.
[3] Draft, ((a few of)).
[4] For another transcription see *Journal*, Jan. 8, 1738.
[5] Draft adds, '((whom we serve))'.   [6] Draft continues, 'this day'.
[7] Draft, 'my heart from being'.   [8] i.e. in Christ; see John 14: 1.
[9] Priestley, 'had not', probably in error. The *Journal* here adds two more points, 'gross
irrecollection', and 'levity, or luxuriancy of spirit'.
[10] See Matt. 8: 25.
[11] 'What I have done hitherto is nothing' (*Imitatio Christi,* I. xix. 1).
[12] Priestley, 'that I may'; the draft agrees with the *Journal*.
[13] 'Let life be a burden to me.' Cf. Terence, *Heauton Timorumenos* ('The Self-
Tormentor'), 482, *Tibi autem porro ut non sit suave vivere*—'how it will embitter all your
future life' (Loeb).
[14] Rev. 22: 20.
[15] 'Son of David, pity me!' (Mark 10: 48, etc.). The draft fragment ends here.
[16] Priestley adds 'which', surely in error.   [17] Matt. 17: 20.
[18] 'full assurance of faith' (Heb. 10: 22).

of the Spirit',[1] 'the love of God shed abroad in my heart',[2] and producing joy in the Holy Ghost,[3] 'joy which no man taketh away',[4] 'joy unspeakable, and full of glory'[5]—this witness of the Spirit I have not, but I patiently wait for it. I know many who have already received it, more than one or two in the very hour we were praying for it. And having seen and spoken with a cloud of witnesses[6] abroad, as well as in my own country, I cannot doubt but that believers who wait and pray for it will find these Scriptures fulfilled in themselves. My hope is that they will be fulfilled in me. I build on Christ, the rock of ages,[7] on his sure mercies, described in his Word, and on his promises, all which I know are yea and amen.[8] Those who have not yet received joy in the Holy Ghost, the love of God, and the *plerophory* of faith[9] (any or all of which I take to be the witness of the Spirit with our spirit that we are the sons of God[10]), I believe to be Christians in that imperfect sense wherein I call myself such; and I exhort them to pray that God would give them also 'to rejoice in hope of the glory of God',[11] and to feel his love 'shed abroad in their hearts by the Holy Ghost which is given unto them'.[12]

On men I build not, neither on Matilda Chipman's[13] word, whom I have not talked with five minutes in my life; nor on anything peculiar in the weak, well-meant relation of William Hervey,[14] who yet is a serious humble-acting Christian. But have you been believing on these? Yes, I find them, more or less, in almost every letter you have written on the subject. Yet were all that has been said on 'visions, dreams, and balls of fire', to be fairly proposed in

---

[1] Cf. Eph. 1: 13; 4: 30.   [2] Cf. Rom. 5: 5.   [3] Rom. 14: 17.
[4] Cf. John 16: 22.   [5] 1 Pet. 1: 8.   [6] Heb. 12: 1.
[7] Isa. 26: 4 (margin).   [8] See 2 Cor. 1: 20.
[9] Heb. 10: 22, transliterating the Greek πληροφορία, 'full assurance'.
[10] See Rom. 8: 16.   [11] Rom. 5: 2.   [12] See Rom. 5: 5.
[13] Apparently the woman who appears several times in the correspondence (highly critical of John Wesley's extravagant claims and anecdotes) between his brother Samuel and Mrs. Hutton; she dreamed that 'a ball of fire fell upon her, and burst, and fired her soul' (see Mrs. Hutton to Samuel Wesley, June 6, 1738, in Priestley, p. 70). Cf. his reply of June 17: 'When the ball of fire fired the woman's soul (an odd sort of fire, that), what reference had it to my two brothers?' (ibid., p. 73).
[14] This seems to be another anecdote of John Wesley's, thus retailed by Mrs. Hutton to Samuel Wesley: 'Another young man, when he was in St. Dunstan's Church, just as he was going to receive the sacrament, had God the Father come to him, but did not stay with him, but God the Son did stay, who came with him, holding his cross in his hands' (Priestley, p. 70). William Hervey was the younger brother of the Oxford Methodist, James Hervey, and working in London at the time. He wrote an account of his conversion, which John Wesley annotated (ibid., p. 76).

syllogisms, I believe it would not prove a jot more on one than on the other side of the question.

O brother, would to God you would leave disputing concerning the things which you know not (if indeed you know them not), and beg of God to fill up what is yet wanting in you. Why should not you also seek till you receive that 'peace of God which passeth all understanding'?[1] 'Who shall hinder you',[2] notwithstanding the 'manifold temptations',[3] from 'rejoicing with joy unspeakable, by reason of glory'?[4] Amen, Lord Jesus! May you, and all who are near of kin to you (if you have it not already) feel his love shed abroad in your hearts, by his Spirit which dwelleth in you,[5] and be sealed with the Holy Spirit of promise, which is the earnest of your inheritance.[6] I am, yours and my sister's most affectionate brother,

John Wesley

Address: 'To the Rev. Mr. Wesley, at Tiverton, Devon'   *Source*: Priestley, pp. 83–7; cf. for the first 12 paras. (of which the first three are numbered), Wesley's MS draft, in Bristol Wesley, 146.

From the Revd. Samuel Wesley, Jun.

Tiverton, Devon, November 15, 1738

Dear Jack

The charge of evil-speaking is carried as high as it can go, so that my wife understands my being included now, as well as I did at first. Your bitterness is much better than Mr. Law's, though did Susurrus[7] fit me even as exactly as you can suppose, that would by no means excuse his having drawn it, no more than his fault or yours could justify mine. To convince you I may sometimes pray against it, I will apply to the same magazine that furnished me against false doctrine: 'From envy, hatred, and malice, and all uncharitableness, Good Lord deliver me.'

I have many remarks to make on your letter, but do not care to fight in the dark, or run my head against a stone wall. You need fear no controversy with me, unless you hold it worth while to remove these three doubts:

1. Whether you will own, or disown in terms, the necessity of a sensible information from God of pardon? If you disown it, the matter is over as to you; if you own it, then—

2. Whether you will not think me distracted to oppose you, with the most infallible of all proofs, inward feeling in yourself, and positive evidence in your friends, while I myself produce neither?

[1] Phil. 4: 7.   [2] Cf. Gal. 5: 7.   [3] 1 Pet. 1: 6.
[4] Cf. 1 Pet. 1: 8.   [5] See Rom. 5: 5.   [6] See Eph. 1: 13–14.
[7] See Wesley's letter of Oct. 30 to his brother Samuel, which this answers, and of Nov. 30, which answers this.

3. Whether you will release me from the horns of your dilemma, that I must either talk without knowledge, like a fool, or against it, like a knave? I conceive neither part strikes. For a man may reasonably argue against what he never felt, and may honestly deny what he has felt to be necessary to others.

You build nothing on tales, but I do. I see what is manifestly built upon them; if you disclaim it, and warn poor shallow pates of their folly and danger, so much the better. They are counted signs or tokens, means or conveyances, proofs or evidences of the sensible information, etc., calculated to turn fools into madmen, and put them without a jest into the condition of Oliver's porter.

When I hear visions, etc., reproved, discouraged, and ceased among the new brotherhood, I shall then say no more of them; but till then I will use my utmost strength that God shall give me to expose these bad branches of a bad root, and thus—[1]

Such doctrine as encourages and abets spiritual fireballs, apparitions of the Father, etc., etc., is delusive and dangerous. But the sensible necessary information, etc., is such; *ergo,*—I mention not this to enter into any dispute with you, for you seem to disapprove them, though not expressly disclaim, but to convince you I am not out of my way, though encountering of windmills. I will do my best to make folks wiser.

I will borrow from our Litany, a prayer you will join in: 'That it may please thee to strengthen such as do stand, to comfort and help the weak-hearted, to raise up them that fall, and finally to beat down Satan under our feet. We beseech thee to hear us, good Lord.'

My wife joins with love. We are all pretty well. I am, dear Jack, your sincere and affectionate friend and brother,

Samuel Wesley

Address: 'To the Rev. Mr. John Wesley'   *Source*: Priestley, pp. 88–90.

To Benjamin Ingham and James Hutton[2]

[Nov. 16, 1738]

My dear brethren, Ingham and Hutton

Be ye strong in the Lord, and in the power of his might![3] There begins to be a little revival of his power here also. The few gownsmen who meet love one another, and press forward toward the prize of our high calling.[4] But I fear they do not all build on the true

[1] The closing hyphen may indicate a mutilation in the holograph in front of Priestley, but more probably implies Samuel Wesley's hint: 'If you wish me to stop criticizing, mend your ways!'

[2] Both John and Charles Wesley had left the promising work in London for a month's visit to Oxford, arriving Nov. 11.

[3] Eph. 6: 10.   [4] See Phil. 3: 14.

foundation; for some seem still to be establishing their own right-eousness,[1] as the joint cause (at least) with that of our Lord of their acceptance with God. Charles Kinchin stands clear of this charge, and is full of love for souls and of prayer. But neither (I fear) does he
5 speak the truth as it is in Jesus.[2] He (as our brother Hutchings) mightily insists both in conversation and preaching that no one can be justified without knowing it, and that none is born again, or has saving faith, till he has the full assurance of faith,[3] continual joy in the Holy Ghost,[4] and the immediate witness of the Spirit with his
10 spirit.[5] O when will our Lord give us to be of one mind and one soul,[6] to speak and think the same thing![7]

This evening I begin reading to a little company in St. Clements, and on Tuesday evening (if God will) to one in St. Giles. But what meant Mr. Fox by talking of leaving Oxford? Ye have need to send
15 ten men full of faith to us, rather than to take one from us. Besides, Mrs. Fox is the very life and spirit (under God) of all the women here that seek our Lord. And if the adversary designed to blast at once all hopes of a harvest for God among them, he could not take a more probable way than now, at this critical time, to remove her
20 from them. 'But he can't live at Oxford.' No, nor anywhere else, as he is now burdened with debt. But let his debts be paid, and then see what he can do. If that be not enough, we will pay his house-rent for a year or two. But at all hazards let them not go hence while our Lord's work in this place so loudly calls upon them to stay. Speak,
25 my brethren, of this immediately.

I have four- or five-and-thirty other letters to write, so can say no more. Send us word how our Master works in London. I am dead and cold. O pray much for your affectionate, heavy brother in Christ,

30   John Wesley

Linc. Coll. Nov. 16, 1738

Hymn-books,[8] bound and unbound, and Prayers,[9] should be sent immediately, and two Intercessional Offices.[10]

---

[1] See Rom. 10: 3.   [2] See Eph. 4: 21.   [3] Heb. 10: 22.
[4] Rom. 14: 17.   [5] See Rom. 8: 16.
[6] See Acts 4: 32.   [7] See 1 Cor. 1: 10.
[8] *A Collection of Psalms and Hymns*, printed by William Bowyer for Wesley, May 24, 1738, and sold by Hutton (see *Bibliog*, No. 9).
[9] *A Collection of Forms of Prayer for Every Day in the Week*, first published by Wesley in 1733, and reprinted by John Lewis for Hutton in 1738 (see *Bibliog*, No. 1).
[10] Possibly an ephemeral pamphlet published by Hutton from a Moravian prototype:

Address: 'To Mr James Hutton, Bookseller, Near Temple-bar, London'
Seal: Crucifixion and 'Der ist mein' (5)   *Postmarks*: 'OXFORD', '17 NO'
Charge: '3'   *Source*: MorA.

To the Revd. James Hervey[1]

[Nov. 21, 1738]

My dear friend

Surely the report is true which was spread here some time since, that you was at the point of death. Otherwise how is it possible that month after month should pass without our receiving one line from 5 you? Can it be that you should forget those who have so often walked with you to the house of God as friends? Can you ⟨die⟩, without having a tender concern for their welfare? Without ever asking what God hath done for their souls? For many of them he hath done marvellous things.[2] With his own right hand and with 10 his holy arm hath he gotten himself the victory.[3] He hath delivered them from the spirit of fear, and given them that of power, and love, and a sound mind.[4] And in truth Dr. Knight's citation from Isaiah seems to be in good measure fulfilled: 'When iniquity hath overspread the land as a flood, the Spirit of the Lord shall lift up his 15 standard against it.'[5] The standard is surely lifted up, and many

the Moravian practice of regular Intercession Days was transplanted to Wesley's societies (see letter of May 28, 1739, etc.).

[1] The Revd. James Hervey (1714–58), a student at Lincoln College, Oxford, from 1731, from 1733 onwards came strongly under Wesley's influence. On leaving Oxford in 1736 he conducted 'little catechetical lectures' among his father's parishioners in Northamptonshire, was ordained on Sept. 19, 1736, and began to serve as curate to the Revd. Charles Kinchin at Dummer (Tyerm (*OM*), pp. 208–13). When he wrote his letter welcoming John Wesley back from Georgia (Mar. 21, 1738; see p. 535 above), it was from Stoke Abbey in Devon, where he remained the private chaplain of Paul Orchard for over two years. Having been ordained as priest in 1739, in 1740 he served as curate at Bideford for three years. In 1743 he returned to his native area, to become his father's curate for a time at Weston Favell, succeeding him in 1752. His invalidism proved the occasion for developing his strong literary gifts, and his *Meditations among the Tombs* (1746), *Contemplations on the Starry Heavens* (1747), and similar works were extremely popular in their day, though they prove somewhat over-ornate for modern taste.

[2] Ps. 98: 1.   [3] Ibid.   [4] See 2 Tim. 1: 7.

[5] On Dr. James Knight see p. 412 n. above. For *A Sermon preached to the Societies for Reformation of Manners, at St. Mary-le-Bow, on Monday, January the 15th, 1732* (London, Downing, 1733), he took as his text Isa. 59: 19. He opened with the A.V. translation, 'When the Enemy shall come in like a Flood . . .', but made it clear in the

flow in unto it. There is a general shaking of the dry bones, and not
a few of them stand up and live.[1]

O my friend, what is our Lord doing where you are? Who is risen
up with you against the evil-doers?[2] Is your own soul very zealous
5 for the Lord of hosts?[3] Does your heart burn within you for his
glory?[4] Do you know by experience what that meaneth, 'The
kingdom of God is righteousness and peace and joy in the Holy
Ghost'?[5] If you are able, let me have joy on your behalf, by your
immediately sending word of your welfare to, my dear friend, your
10 very weak, but affectionate, brother

John Wesley

Linc. Coll. 21 Nov. 1738

Address: 'To The Revd Mr Hervey, At Paul Orchard's Esq,[6] At Stoke-Abby,
near Biddiford, Devon'   *Postmark*: 'OXFORD'   *Charge*: '4'   *Source*:
Lincoln College, Oxford.

To Dr. John de Koker

[Nov. 22, 1738]

My desire and prayer to God is that the glorious gospel of his Son
15 may run and be glorified[7] among you as it doth among us, and much
more abundantly! I should rejoice to hear what our Lord hath done
for you also. Is the number of believers multiplied?[8] Do they love
one another? Are they all of one heart and one soul?[9] Do they build
up one another in the knowledge and love of our Lord Jesus Christ?
20 May he multiply your little flock a thousandfold, how many soever
you be! May he fill you with all peace and joy in believing[10] May he
preserve you in all lowliness of spirit! And may he enable you to use
great plainness of speech,[11] both toward each other and toward all
men, and by manifestation of the truth to commend yourselves to
25 every man's conscience in the sight of God![12]

Even to this hour I have not had one day's leisure to transcribe

sermon itself that the enemy was 'iniquity' in its many forms, for which he prescribed
spiritual and social reformation.

[1] See Ezek. 37: 2, 7, 10.	[2] See Ps. 94: 16.	[3] See 2 Kgs. 19: 31, etc.
[4] See Luke 24: 32.	[5] Rom. 14: 17.	[6] See note, p. 609.
[7] 2 Thess. 3: 1 (margin).	[8] See Acts 6: 1, 7.	[9] Acts 4: 32.
[10] See Rom. 15: 13.	[11] 2 Cor. 3: 12.	[12] See 2 Cor. 4: 2.

for you the papers I brought from Herrnhut.¹ The harvest here also is so plenteous, and the labourers so few,² and it increases upon us daily.³ Verily the Spirit of the Lord hath lift up his standard against the iniquity which had overspread our land as a flood!⁴ O pray ye for us, that he would send more labourers into his harvest!⁵ And that he would enable us whom he hath already sent to approve ourselves faithful ministers of the New Covenant, by honour and dishonour, by evil report and good report!⁶ In particular let all the brethren and sisters who are with you pray that God would warm with his love the cold heart of, dear sir, your much obliged and very affectionate brother in Christ,

J. Wesley

Address: 'To Dr. Koker, at Rotterdam'   *Source*: Whitehead, II. 93-4; date confirmed by Wesley's diary.

To Richard Viney⁷

[Nov. 22, 1738]

. . . After a long sleep, there seems now to be a great awakening in this place also. The Spirit of the Lord hath already shaken the dry bones, and some of them stand up and live.⁸ But I am still dead and

---

¹ See letter of Oct. 13, p. 568.
² See Matt. 9: 37.   ³ See Acts 16: 5.
⁴ See Isa. 59: 19, and previous letters.
⁵ See Matt. 9: 38.   ⁶ See 2 Cor. 6: 4, 8.
⁷ Richard Viney was an Englishman who had thrown in his lot with the Moravians. He spoke German, and had visited Germany in 1736, so that he was able to interpret for Peter Böhler in London. He may well have accompanied Wesley to Germany, or perhaps went out earlier; certainly he seems to have remained later. This letter is addressed to him at the Moravian community in IJsselstein, where Wesley had visited Baron Frederic de Watteville, and on May 25, 1739 he wrote his published *Letter from an English Brother of the Moravian Persuasion in Holland to the Methodists in England*, dated from Herrndyke, at IJsselstein. By 1740 he had returned to England, was one of the founding members of the Moravian continuation of the Fetter Lane society, in 1742 superintended the Moravian boarding school at Broad Oaks, Essex, and in 1743 went to labour in the Moravian societies in Lancashire, but was excommunicated later that year by Spangenberg. During 1744, therefore, he transferred his allegiance to Methodism, plying his trade as a tailor and staymaker, and also working for Wesley in various capacities, including that of bookbinder. His diary for that year is a mine of information on early Methodism, though his later career is obscure. (Benham, pp. 140-2; W.H.S., XV. 184-5.)
⁸ Ezek. 37: 2, 7, 10; cf. letter of Nov. 21.

cold, having peace indeed, but no love or joy in the Holy Ghost.¹
O pray for me, that I may see and feel myself a sinner, and have a
full interest in the Lamb of God that taketh away the sins of the
world!² . . .

Address: 'To Mr. Viney, at Ysselstein'   *Source*: Whitehead, II. 94.

To Isaac Lelong³

5   Oxford, November 22d [–Dec. 31] 1738

Do not think, my dear brother, that I have forgotten you! I cannot
forget you, because I love you. Though I can't yet love anyone as I
ought, because I can't love our blessed Lord, *as I ought*.⁴ My heart
is cold and senseless. It is indeed a heart of stone. O when will he
10 take it out of the midst of me, and give me a heart of flesh?⁵ Pray
for me, and let all your household pray for me, yea, and all the
brethren also, that our God would give me a broken heart, and a
loving heart, a heart wherein his Spirit may delight to dwell.

May our good Lord repay you all a thousandfold, and especially
15 our brother Decknatel,⁶ for the love you showed to us. How does his
gospel prosper at Amsterdam? Are believers multiplied? And is his
grace mighty among them?⁷ Is their name yet cast out as evil⁸ (for
that must be next)? And do men despitefully use you and persecute

¹ See Rom. 14: 17. Cf. his somewhat despondent meditation in the *Journal*, under
the date Oct. 14, 1738.
² See John 1: 29.
³ Isaac Lelong was one of the Moravian friends whom Wesley had made on his visit
to Amsterdam earlier in the year, apparently at the home of the Revd. John Decknatel
and his wife Elizabeth—for whom see W. C. Reichel, *A Register of Members of the
Moravian Church . . . between 1727 and 1754*, Nazareth, Pennsylvania, 1873, p. 327.
Lelong himself does not appear to have been a member in Amsterdam in 1744, when
that section of this list was compiled.
    For the temporary experience of 'desertion' expressed in this letter see also that preced-
ing, to Richard Viney, and the meditation in Wesley's *Journal* for Oct. 14, 1738. Cf.
Wesley, *A Second Letter to the Author of the Enthusiasm of the Methodists*, etc., § 25
(Vol. II, p. 402 of this edition).
⁴ The closing italicized phrase is found in the draft only, probably omitted in error
(as a duplication) by the amanuensis, and not noticed by Wesley.
⁵ See Ezek. 11: 19; 36: 26. This sentence is not present in Whitehead's version of the
draft.
⁶ 'and . . . Decknatel', absent from Whitehead.
⁷ Draft, 'among you'.
⁸ See Luke 6: 22.

you?[1] I want you to say a great deal to me of it. But above all I want you to pray a great deal for your poor weak brother,

John Wesley

P.S. Pray write soon. I should be glad to write to and hear from you at least once a month. Grace be with you all. Amen.[2]

I thank you much for your letter. I wish to hear from you often. Will you send my letters to our dear brethren? You see how long they have been delayed.

Dec. 31, 1738

Address: 'To Mr. Isaac Lelong, at Amsterdam'   *Sources*: Herrnhut, all in the hand of an amanuensis except the signature, the second postscript, and the address; Whitehead, II. 94–5, clearly from the draft, preserved as a reference copy, from which some variations have been made in the letter as dispatched, both by Wesley and by his amanuensis.

From James Hutton[3]

Novr. 23, 1738

Dear friend

At a general meeting of the bands the matters of greatest importance I send you account of.

Some persons had been ensnared, and many more were likely to be, by the too familiar intercourse at societies with young women. One of our brethren's

---

[1] Matt. 5: 44.

[2] All the preceding (except the signature) is in the hand of Wesley's amanuensis. Neither first nor second postscript is given by Whitehead.

[3] Religious societies in London had a long history already, to which Wesley and Böhler added on May 1, 1738, when they formed that in Fetter Lane. Unlike most, it was open not only to members of the Church of England but to others, at least as visitors, and through the advocacy of Böhler it was subdivided 'into several bands, or little societies'. The same was true of a similar society founded later that same month by James Hutton. When Wesley returned from Herrnhut he strove to reform these and as many other of the older religious societies as would agree to various measures for improving their spiritual efficacy, especially that of incorporating bands as small confessional groups within their organization. When he moved on to Oxford to reform the societies there along similar lines, Ingham and Hutton were left in charge of the London societies. Speedily Hutton, though a layman, became the key administrator, especially as Ingham seemed eager to evangelize his native Yorkshire. The important correspondence between Wesley and Hutton on the administration of these London societies during late 1738, 1739, and 1740 is known chiefly from the letters preserved by Hutton, now in the Moravian Archives, while for over twenty of Wesley's thus extant Wesley retained only three of Hutton's: this of Nov. 23 (answering Wesley's of Nov. 16, and itself answered on Nov. 26), and those of Mar. 4 and July 1, 1740).

hearts is in very great confusion on this account, insomuch that he meets not with his band, and our brother Shaw has escaped with the skin of his teeth; and my own heart has, indeed, escaped, but it was owing to a secret passion which I had for *another*, which I found not out till yesterday. The devil would
5 make havoc of us altogether. Some people also, the present archbishop especially some time since, took offence at the promiscuous meeting of persons of both sexes, and themselves pointed out the regulations we are come to on that head, viz. that the women, married and unmarried, meet by themselves, excepting only the husbands of any of them with their wives and the ministers or he that
10 expounds. I seem to see that this will produce a speedy settling of some female bands, a thing we much wanted.

A register or writer was appointed—Jas. Hutton!

Also Mr. Broughton advised us to be cautious whom we admit, so then— every person to be admitted at our Friday society is to give in his name on a
15 Friday, which the *bands* are to consider, whether he or she be proper to be admitted. This may for a time keep off that which *must* come—*false brethren*.

Also we appointed Novr. 24 a day of solemn fasting and prayer, to beg of God to be with us on Monday next, when we shall first (it having been found that the want of a president at every meeting has been the cause, or seemed to be, of
20 confusion) cast a lot to see whether it will be good for us to have a president for the *year*, whose business is to preside in our meetings, and only to see to the execution of what shall be determined by the whole society. We are unanimous almost that such an office will be of use, but as a doubt may arise we will cast a lot about it. Then the names of all the bands, with as many blanks as bands, will
25 be shaken together, out of whom one will be taken for that office, as it shall happen. N.B. Now if a blank be drawn, it seems as if the person to be presid⟨ent⟩ was not yet admitted into the bands, so that the choice will be put off another month or longer, as shall be judged proper. The first lot will determine whether there shall be such an officer.

30 Then out of the rest of the lots will be chosen two persons monitors, whose business will be to tell everyone what faults are observed in him, concealing his informer. And no defence of himself to be allowed, only put to his own heart, no farther notice being taken of anything unless the person persist in his misbehaviour. These are to meet with the leaders of the bands.

35 That leaders and other officers wait and serve at love-feasts.

That they that speak stand up, and no one speak till he be sat down.

That one person keep the door, another snuff the candles and place the people in their seats, every night, this office to go through all the bands. I and Hartlie[1] are the two first.

40 My beloved brother, God is with us. He also is with you. May he strengthen your hands in God, and may Charles Delamotte and your brother also feel the divine influence. May your hearts burn with love to your Saviour and mine while you speak of the wonderful things *he* hath done for us all. May ye all be of one heart and soul, without jealousies, evil-surmisings, or evil-speaking, a fault
45 or set of faults too easily admitted into religious people. May ye all speak the same thing. May you and I be preserved from the creatures! May your societies

---

[1] Barnard Hartley.

increase! I have not been able to get a quarter of an hour with brother Fox since I saw yours to me. He owes me a little money, and I fancy fears to come near me. He need not. I am very glad to hear of the daily offence taken at you and your brother. Walk simply with God, and I will engage you shall not want it; walk in darkness, and you may chance to stumble upon it, and that would do 5 you no good. I will send Mr. Wells's money with a parcel of books directed to some of you speedily.

My love to Mr. Sarney, Graves, Combes, Washington, Watson, Evans, and whoever is among you that feareth the Lord, Mrs. Cleminger, Mrs. Fox, Mrs. Ford, to C. W[esley] and C. Delamotte. Your dear brother, 10

Jas Hutton, Reg[iste]r

B. Ingham works har⟨d⟩ for him and me.

[added in the hand of Ingham] My spirit is with you. Grace be with you all. B.I.

Address: 'To The Revd John Wesley, A.M., Fellow of Lincoln College, Oxford'
Postmark: '23 NO'   *Charge*: '3'   *End* by JW: 'Js Hut. Nov. 23, 1738 + / J Gamb[old']s Money of Mr. Rock'   *Source*: MA.

To James Hutton and Mr. Fox

[Nov. 24, 1738] 15

Dear Jemmy

First, let us get trifles out of the way. My brother left behind him almost all the things I wanted, which I desire may be sent without fail, by the very next carrier, viz.:

A gown, cassock, and sash. 20

The papers which my brother put into the little box which has the key in it.

My eight cups, teapot, sugar-basin, and slop-basin.

Have you paid Mrs. Turner[1] for the tea and sugar bought when brother Richter[2] was with us? 25

The three New Testaments, second hymn-book,[3] Italian Gram-

---

[1] The sister of John Bray (see letter from Wm. Holland to F. W. Neisser, Jan. 21, 1744, in MorA), who appears to have been nursing Charles Wesley in her brother's home at the time of CW's conversion on May 21, 1738, there are several references to her in CWJ.

[2] Abraham Ehrenfried Richter (*c.* 1689–1740), a prosperous merchant who threw in his lot with Zinzendorf in 1734, and undertook evangelistic missions in Western Germany and in London, and died while on a mission to slaves in Algeria. He was one of the little group for whom John Wesley found lodgings on their arrival in London with Peter Böhler on Feb. 7, 1738.

[3] *A Collection of Psalms and Hymns* (1738), the second volume by Wesley thus entitled (see *Bibliog*, Nos. 8 and 9).

mar, ⟨and⟩ Dictionary (from your father's), German Dictionary, and the little ⟨engr⟩aved German book, and Newcomb's Psalms.[1]

Many here would buy hymn-books, and the Sermon on faith.[2] [added by Charles Wesley] Send them therefore with the rest.

5 I do very exceedingly disapprove of the excluding women when we meet to pray, sing, and read the Scriptures. I wish it might not be done before we have talked together, at least unless you *first* fix a night for them to come by themselves, which I firmly believe will give more offence.

10 Send us word how the Word of God prospers among you.

And how the fierceness of men turns to his praise,[3] that we may rejoice together.

You will show Mr. Fox what is on the other side. Are not your own flocks and herds enough, but must you have our little ewe lamb 15 also?[4]

[To Mr. Fox][5]

Nov. 24, Oxon.

Dear Mr. Fox

Mrs. Badger earnestly desires you would procure her a trumpet to help her deafness. Mrs. Ford[6] would not have any of the tea Mrs. 20 Cleminger[7] brought, because it is very bad.

Charles Kinchin, Charles Delamotte, Mrs. Ford, Mrs. Hall,[8] Mrs. Fox, and my brother, desire me to speak their judgment (as well as mine) concerning your removal to London.

The reason for it, you say, is this: you can't maintain your family 25 at Oxford. To this we answer, 'You have not tried what you can do

---

[1] Thomas Newcombe (1682?-1765), clergyman poet, whose major work was a Miltonic poem in twelve books, *The Last Judgment* (1723). Among his many works was *Sacred Hymns, or, An Attempt to discover and revive the original Spirit, Elevation, and Beauty . . . of some of the Select Psalms* (1736).

[2] Wesley, *A Sermon on Salvation by Faith* (1738); see *Sermons*, No. 1, and *Bibliog*, No. 10.

[3] Ps. 76: 10 (B.C.P.).   [4] 2 Sam. 12: 3.

[5] Added on the verso of the half-sheet containing the previous letter.

[6] Apparently one of the leaders of the Oxford society, meetings being held in her home; see diary, Oct. 11, 1738, onwards.

[7] Who 'appeared in the pangs of the new birth', Aug. 29, 1738 (CWJ), and received peace on Mar. 12, 1739 (letter of Mar. 16, 1739).

[8] 'Who had been in despair several years', and 'received a witness that she was a child of God' on Dec. 10, 1738 (see JWJ).

when you are clear in the world (which Mr. F[ree?] promises), and you live in your house rent free. (For that we will take ca⟨re.)⟩ If you desire only food and raiment for yourself and family, you have all reason at least to make the experiment for a while whether Providence will not give you these at Oxford, when you have these helps 5 which you had not before.

The reason against her[1] going hence is as evident as it is weighty: we have no one here like-minded. She is the very life (under God) of all her companions here, nor could the enemy devise so likely a means of destroying the work which is just beginning among them 10 as the taking her away from their head. Which, then, is dearest to you, the interest of Christ, or your own? O consider the question deeply, and the good God direct your heart! Pray for your affectionate brother,

J. Wesley 15

Source: MorA, a double letter with the address half missing.

From Mrs. Emilia Harper[2]

[Nov. 24, 1738]

Dear brother

Yours I received, and thank you for remembering me, though your letter afforded me small consolation. For God's sake tell me how a distressed woman who expects daily to have the very bed taken from under her for rent can con- 20 sider the state of the churches in Germany. I am ready to give up the ghost with grief. How is it possible in such extremity to think of anybody's concerns but my own, till this storm be blown over some way, or my head laid low in Gainsborough churchyard? We owe at Christmas two years' rent for this house, and as it was my hard hap to marry a tradesman without a trade, the burden of the 25 day has laid on me from the beginning. Yet still I hoped for better, and when Mr. Harper went to Derbyshire, last Martinmas was twelvemonth, I helped him with all my summer profits, in hopes if his business was good for anything he would pay me with interest. But vain were my hopes. He just can after a very poor manner maintain himself, and sometimes—once in six months, perhaps— 30 he will give me 10s, and thinks himself very kind to me, too. I have sold many of my clothes for bread. Is not that calamity? I want many of the common necessaries of life, and am almost always sick. If this be not a state of affliction, there is no such thing in the world. Not but yet I have a bed to lie on, but Christmas will soon be here, and if Bob Harper will do nothing for to raise half a 35

---

[1] Mrs. Fox. Cf. pp. 536 n., 580.
[2] Replying to Wesley's of Nov. 4, to whose contents it offers clues.

year's rent I cannot get it myself, though I could help somewhat towards it.
And 'tis a cold time of year to be turned out of doors. Sam and Charles (God
bless 'em) kept me safe at midsummer. My comfort is, this is the last year I
have to turn over in this house, and some way perhaps (though unknown to
5 me) God may bring me out of my troubles. Now that you may not think me
a reprobate because I feel my afflictions, I assure you that I habitually trust in
God and submit to his providences. Nay, further, I always have a secret hope
that I shall not be quite brokenhearted, but shall still live to see happier days.
Pray write soon. Remember the natural affection you have always shown to your
10 Emme, and forsake her not in the day of her distress. Love to your sister in
trouble is more pleasing in the sight of God and man than preaching to a thousand where you have no business. If you had come to me, instead of going to
Germany, and laid out *your money* in travelling hither instead of visiting Count
Zinzendorf you would have been, I dare say, as acceptable to our common
15 Master. Where is honest Charles? Pray give my love to him, and abundance of
thanks for midsummer. I have but an unfortunate life to lose, and am commanded by our Saviour not to fear them who can only kill the body. I know
all things are possible with God, and he can even now preserve this weak sick
creature, and restore me to a state of comfort, but since in all human appearance
20 my time draws near its end, my health is not only decayed, but destroyed, and
the storm just ready to fall on me will in all likelihood take the small remains of
life I have left. Hear and remember *these*, which may prove my dying words.
You seem to love me from your infancy. I am sure of my side (for I know not
seemings) I loved you tenderly. You married me to this man, and as soon as
25 sorrow took hold of *me you left me to it*. Had you the same, nay, a quarter of the
love to me I have for you, long since you would have been with me. It was in
your power. You who could go to Germany, could you not reach Gainsborough?
Yes, *certainly*, and had my soul been lost through self-murder *my damnation*
would have justly laid at your door. I can write no more, but am, dear brother,
30 while I live, your affectionate sister, and real friend,

Emilia Harper

Nov 24
1738

Address: 'To The Revd. Mr. John Wesley, Fellow of Lincoln Colledge, Oxford.
By way of London'   *Postmark*: '27 NO'   *Charges*: ((4)), 'In all 7'
End by JW: 'S. Em. Nov. 24. 1738   *Source*: MA.

To James Hutton

Oxon, Nov. 26, 1738

35 My dear friend
    If the time for the women's meeting apart be fixed *before* they are
excluded from the general meeting I have no more to say on that
head.

I gave our brother Shaw[1] the names of six female bands settled already. Why do you speak of the settling 'some'[2] as a thing still to be begun? Have you suffered those to fall in pieces again? Or has no thought at all been taken about them?

Doubtless too much caution cannot be used in the admission of strangers.

What is proposed as to casting lots concerning a president seems liable to no exception. But you seem to design him (if there should be one) just nothing to do. Would not that ⟨require⟩ more particular consideration?

I have thought much (my brother is out of town with Mr. Wells) of the monitors,[3] and am very much afraid that design is not right. And that for several reasons. First, it seems needless. Every man in my band is my monitor, and I his. Else I know no use of our being in band. And if anything particular occur, why should not the leaders (as was agreed before) delegate a monitor *pro tempore*? Secondly, I doubt it would be hurtful, and indeed many ways: by lessening the care of every member for every other, when so great a part of his care was transferred to another; by lessening mutual freedom, and making it in one instance unnecessary; by setting aside the commandment of God, 'Thou shalt in any wise reprove thy brother';[4] by depriving thee (i.e. everyone beside the monitors) of the improvement and reward of so doing. Thirdly, I have seen it has produced these effects. Sin (as they esteemed it) was suffered in me at Savannah, first seven months, afterwards five months, without one breath of reproof—notwithstanding the command of God, notwithstanding earnest, continual entreaty on one side, and solemn, repeated promises on the other. And how could this be? Why, there were stated monitors to reprove. Others therefore judged reproof to be a thing quite out of their way. But I fell not under the care of the monitors. Therefore I might have gone unreproved to this hour had not John[5] reproved me, for which (as he could not deny) he was

---

[1] Almost certainly John Shaw, one of the founding members of the Fetter Lane society as constituted by Wesley and Böhler, May 1, 1738 (see Benham, p. 33).

[2] See Hutton's letter of Nov. 23 (which this answers), 'some female bands'.

[3] Wesley had seen the eleven monitors in operation at Herrnhut, and noted that some were secretly appointed to check the behaviour of everyone without warning, including 'the rulers of the church' (see JWJ, Aug. 10, 1738, 'the present discipline of the Church at Herrnhut'). It was such a scheme of which Hutton had written to Wesley in his letter of Nov. 23. [4] See Lev. 19: 17.

[5] Johann Martin Bolzius, to whom Wesley had refused the Lord's Supper at Savannah on July 17, 1737, because he was not episcopally ordained (see JWJ, Sept. 30, 1749).

roundly reproved himself. Lastly, a general monitor commissioned by God to reprove every one of his brethren you have, so long as you have any priest or deacon among you. Therefore methinks this point might be reconsidered.

5 'They that speak, stand up,' I don't understand. If I do understand it, I doubt of the propriety of it.

Is the book and letter sent to Mr. Rock?[1] I believe the letter mentions money to be received of him, and sent hither as soon as may be.

10 Nothing is done here yet. We are only beginning to begin. All the Scriptures direct me to think of suffering. I fear not that, but my own heart.

Be not in haste, my dear brethren.[2] Determine few things at a time, and those with the deepest deliberation. You know we are 15 blind children. And if it is our Father who leads us by the hand, he leads gently.

We all remember you, and much desire to be remembered by you all. Let my dear brother Ingham and you pray very much for your affectionate brother,

20 J. Wesley

Address: 'To Mr J. Hutton, Bookseller, Without Temple-bar, London'
Postmarks: 'OXFORD', '27 NO'   *Charge*: '3'   *Source*: MorA.

To James Hutton[3]

27 Nov. 1738

Your scrip, Jemmy, comes next. As to the point of the women, we are agreed. As to the monitors, I have one more doubt. I believe

[1] This obscure reference is made only slightly less obscure by Wesley's reminder to himself that he must write about the subject to Hutton, added as an endorsement to Hutton's letter of Nov. 23: 'J. Gamb[old]'s Money of Mr. Rock'. It seems clear that a book and a letter (possibly from Gambold) were to be sent to Rock, who was himself owing money to Gambold. Rock's identity also is uncertain, though probably intended is the Revd. Richard Roche, vicar of Locking, Somerset, who graduated from St. Edmund Hall, Oxford, in 1729, having matriculated at Hart Hall in 1726 as Rock, from Catcott, Somerset.

[2] Most of Wesley's letters to Hutton were at the same time pastoral letters to the society in London.

[3] It seems probable that Hutton's 'scrip' to which Wesley was turning was a letter dated Nov. 25 in answer to Wesley's of Nov. 24, just received, and the answer returned,

bishops, priests, and deacons to be of divine appointment (though I think our brethren in Germany do not). Therefore I am tender of the first approach towards 'pastors appointed by the congregation'.[1] And if we should begin with appointing fixed persons to execute *pro officio*,[2] I doubt it would not end there. My dear brother, this may seem of little weight to some of our brethren, especially when urged by one so weak as me; and they may think it deserves no other answer than, 'He hath not the Spirit.'[3] But our brother Bray[4] hath. I refer you to him and all the brotherhood, or such a number of them as you judge proper.

My brother, suffer me to speak a little more. If as a fool, then as a fool bear with me.[5] I believe you don't think I am (whatever I was) bigoted either to the ancient church or the Church of England. But have a care of bending the bow too much the other way.[6] The national church to which we belong may doubtless claim some, though not an implicit, obedience from us. And the primitive church may thus far at least be reverenced, as faithfully delivering down for two or three hundred years the discipline which they received from the apostles, and th⟨e apostles⟩ from Christ. And I doubt, w⟨hether . . .⟩ were among them who w⟨ere . . .⟩[7]

Address: 'To My Dear Brother, James Hutton'   *Source*: MorA.

by personal messenger from London. The letter of Nov. 24 had dealt with the question of excluding women from meetings, to which he referred again on Nov. 26. Wesley then reverted to the question of the monitors; this was in effect a postscript to the letter of Nov. 26, which Hutton had not yet received.

[1] It is possible that in his presumptive letter of Nov. 25 Hutton had used this phrase, but more likely that Wesley was himself introducing it as a summary of the congregational polity which he saw as a dangerous tendency of the monitor scheme.

[2] 'In the place of that office'.

[3] See Rom. 8: 9.

[4] John Bray, a brazier of Little Britain, London, one of the foundation members of the Fetter Lane society. He was very helpful to Charles Wesley, who was lodging in his home at the time of his conversion on May 21, 1738, and John Wesley regularly corresponded with him throughout 1738 and 1739.

[5] See 2 Cor. 11: 16.

[6] For this proverbial expression, in a similar context, see Wesley's memorandum of Jan. 25, 1738, § 5, 'Nor was it long before I bent the bow too far the other way: (1), by making antiquity a co-ordinate (rather than subordinate) rule with Scripture . . .' (see *Journal*, notes at that date). Cf. Sermon 20, *The Lord our Righteousness*, II. 20, 'Is this not bending the bow too much the other way?'

[7] The letter is torn, so that over half of two lines is missing.

To the Revd. Samuel Wesley, Jun.[1]

[Nov. 30, 1738]

. . . I believe every Christian who has not yet received it ought to pray for 'the witness of God's Spirit with his spirit, that he is a child of God'![2] In being a child of God the pardon of his sins is
5 included; therefore I believe the Spirit of God will witness this also. That this witness is from God, the very terms imply; and this witness, I believe, is necessary for my salvation. How far invincible ignorance may excuse others I know not.

But this, you say, is delusive and dangerous, 'because it encourages
10 and abets idle visions and dreams'.[3] It 'encourages'—true, accidentally, but not essentially. And that it does this accidentally, or that weak minds may pervert it to an ill use, is no reasonable objection against it; for so they may pervert every truth in the oracles of God, more especially that dangerous doctrine of Joel, cited by St. Peter:
15 'It shall come to pass in the last days, saith God, I will pour out of my spirit upon all flesh; and your sons and your daughters shall prophesy, and your young men shall see visions, and your old men shall dream dreams.'[4] Such visions, indeed, as you mention are given up. Does it follow that visions and dreams in general are bad
20 branches of a bad root? God forbid! This would prove more than you desire . . .

Source: Whitehead, II. 108-9, date confirmed by Wesley's diary.

To James Hutton

[Dec. 1, 1738]

Dear Jemmy

The box I have received from the carrier, and the parcel by the
25 coach, and (which is best of all) two letters by the post.[5] Our brother Ingham should stir us up as often as he[6] can. I can but just say 'us', gownsmen. For Charles Kinchin went today, and there is none

[1] This incomplete letter replies to that of Nov. 15, and is answered by that of Dec. 13, which offers clues to the missing contents. See also Samuel Wesley's letter of Dec. 9, 1738, to Mrs. Hutton (MorA), which surely thus refers to this same letter: 'He owns a sensible (or as he chooses to word it, a clear) information from God of pardon necessary to salvation, except in case of invincible ignorance. He says visions, dreams, etc., are given up . . . He complained in a former letter [i.e. Oct. 30, 1738] that I had more or less about them in every one of mine . . .' [2] See Rom. 8: 16.
[3] The actual phrase, 'delusive and dangerous' (like some others below) does occur in Priestley's version of the letter of Nov. 15, but the words quoted are in part a paraphrase. [4] Acts 2: 17; cf. Joel 2: 28. [5] See letter of Nov. 21. [6] Orig., 'we'.

besides that joins with my brother and me cordially. Indeed you should write to Mr. Hutchings. How can any who truly desire the enlargement of our Lord's kingdom approve of his and Mr. Kinchin's both being shut up in a little village, when there is so loud a call for both (if it could be) at Oxford? 5

The case of the monitors is past; so let it rest.[1] Only I cannot approve of that circumstance (which you may probably think the most necessary of all), the forbidding the person reproved to answer. First, because I doubt it may be a snare to many weak consciences, who may think (as I do in several cases) that it is their duty to 10 answer. Secondly, because it naturally tends to beget or increase, even in the strong, that mystical silence which is the very bane of brotherly love. For my own part, I never should be willing to reprove anyone without hearing him answer for himself; nor do I find any Scripture that forbids it, either directly or by clear inference 15 —Though it may have ill effects. The impatience of hearing it seems to be a very unchristian temper.

Indeed, my brother, you have no need to multiply forms of any kind. The standing up at speaking[2] is a ceremony used neither at Herrnhut nor among any of the Brethren elsewhere. At mealtimes 20 especially it appears quite contrary to common sense, and is surely likely to be attended with more ill consequences than it is supposed proper to remove.

Are we members of the Church of England? First then let us observe her laws, and then the by-laws of our own society. First 25 secure the observance of the Friday fast. Then I will fast with you, if you please, every day in the week. Only let us except Sundays and the solemn festivals, to fast on which is contrary (to say no more) to the laws of our own Church.

Thanks be to God in Christ, I have no more anger than joy. But 30 we are all young men—though I hope few of you are so young in spiritual, experimental knowledge as ⟨your po⟩or brother,

J. Wesley

Dec. 1, 1738. Oxon.

Could not you purchase for me half a dozen Bath-metal tea- 35 spoons?[3]

---

[1] See letters of Nov. 23, 26, 27.
[2] See letters of Nov. 23, 26.
[3] Added vertically from foot to head on p. (2), the second half of the letter being on p. (4), vertically, from head to foot, and the address on p. (3).

I am to thank somebody (I suppose my brother James) for some very good tea.[1]

Address: 'To Mr. J. Hutton, Bookseller, Near Temple-bar, London'   *Post-marks*: 'OXFORD', '4 DE'   *Charge*: '3'   *Source*: MorA.

From the Revd. James Hervey[2]

Stoke Abbey, Dec. 1, 1738

Most dear and Revd. sir

5   Whom I love and honour in the Lord. Indeed it is not through any forgetful-ness of your favours, or unconcernedness for your welfare, that you have not heard from me, but through the miscarriage of my letter. Immediately on the news of your first arrival in England I made haste to salute you, and wondered why your answer was so long in coming. But wondered more when I heard that
10 you had left the nation a second time, without being so condescending as to own me, or so kind as to vouchsafe me a single line. But now, sir, that I am assured under your own hand that you have escaped the perils of the sea, the perils of foreign countries, the perils of those that oppose the truth; are restored in safety to your native country, are re-settled at Oxon, and both have been
15 doing, and still are doing, spiritual and everlasting good to men—I may truly say, 'My heart rejoiceth, even mine.' O that I could give you a comfortable account of myself, and of my zeal for God! Alas! I must confess with shame and sorrow, 'My zeal has been to sit still!' I am not strong in body, and lamentably weak in spirit; sometimes my bodily disorders clog the willing mind, and are a
20 grievous weight upon its wheels; at other times the mind is oppressed with sloth, and thereby rendered listless and indisposed for labouring in the Lord. Pray for me, dearest sir, and engage all my friends to cry mightily to heaven in my behalf, if so be this dry rod may bud and blossom, this barren tree may bring forth much fruit.

25 I live in the family of a worthy gentleman, who is a hearty well-wisher to the cause of pure and undefiled religion; who desires no greater happiness than to love the Lord Jesus Christ in sincerity; who would be glad of a place for himself and household in your prayers. Dear sir, will you permit me to inform you what is said, though I verily believe slanderously said, of you? 'Tis reported that the
30 dearest friends I have in the world are setters forth of strange doctrines, that are contrary to Scripture and repugnant to the Articles of our Church. This cannot but give me uneasiness, and I should be glad to have my fears removed by yourself.[3] 'Tis said that you inculcate faith without laying any stress upon good works; that you endeavour to dissuade honest tradesmen from following

---

[1] Added at the top right corner of p. (1), over which the date 'Dec. 1, 1738' has later been added by a hand other than Wesley's.

[2] Answering Wesley's of Nov. 21, 1738.

[3] Wesley's reply of Mar. 20, 1739, implies that at this point his extract for the *A.M.* omits one of Hervey's questions, which was probably in this form: 'How far do you believe that privilege of the children of God, the not committing sin, to extend?'

their occupations, and persuade them to turn preachers. Now these calumnies I wish you would give me power to confute, who am, dear sir, your ever obliged and grateful friend,

J. Hervey

Source: *A.M.*, 1778, pp. 132–3.

To Charles Delamotte[1]

[Dec. 2, 1738] 5

. . . In this you are better than you was at Savannah. You know that you was then quite wrong. But you are not yet right. You know that you was then blind. But you do not yet see.

I doubt not but God will bring you to the right foundation. But I have no hope for you on your present foundation. It is as different 10 from the true as the right hand from the left. You have all to begin anew.

I have observed all your words and actions, and I see you are of the same spirit still. You have a simplicity, but it is a simplicity of your own. It is not the simplicity of Christ. You think you do not 15 trust in your own works. But you do trust in your own works, and your own righteousness. You do not yet believe in, or build on, the rock Christ.

Your present freedom from sin is only a temporary suspension of, not a deliverance from, it. And your peace is not a true peace. If 20 death were to approach, you would find all your fears return.

But I am forbid to say any more. My heart sinks in me like a stone . . .

Source: MA, Wesley, MS diary, Colman XVII, fragments for 1738–9, occupying one page between the pages devoted to Nov. 27 and Nov. 28, 1738, in abbreviated longhand.

[1] In his *Journal* for Nov. 23, 1738, Wesley notes that at Oxford he met Charles Delamotte (the name given as 'C.D.' only), who stayed with him until Nov. 27, and adds this document, with the preface: 'His last conversation with me was as follows.' This, of course, is not a conversation, but a monologue. The *Journal* was not published until four years later (see *Bibliog*, No. 21), and possibly Wesley did not quite know what to do with this unusual feature of a document inserted between two pages of his diary, as it was probably both a summary of the points made by Wesley in their conversations, but also in staccato sentences an outline of a letter which Wesley's diary shows him to have written to Delamotte five days later.

Delamotte had left Savannah on June 2, 1738; he settled in Hull, moved in the 1770s to Barrow-on-Humber, and was buried in Aylesby, Lincs., on Apr. 14, 1796, aged 82.

From the Revd. Samuel Wesley, Jun.[1]

[Dec. 13, 1738]

Dear Jack

You own abundantly enough to clear Mrs. Hutton from any misrepresentation as to you, and me from misunderstanding her. I was but too right in my judgment.

1. You was not a Christian before May 24, but are so now, in a sense of the word you call obvious; which was so far from it that it astonished all who heard you then, and which I deny to be so much as *true*.

2. You hold the witness of the Spirit as containing a clear information of adoption, whereof pardon is a part, to be absolutely necessary to your salvation and that of others, unless excused by invincible ignorance. Enough! Enough! yet,

3. You apply Joel amazingly, though you give up *such* visions as I speak of; yet not allowing me to call *such* bad branches of a bad root. That I may not be guilty any more of putting them more or less into every letter, I'll discuss their matter fully by itself once for all, desiring you in the meantime to say what other Scripture dreams or visions you would insist on, whether all between Genesis and Revelation? I am afraid Ahab's lying spirits may be but too pertinent.

That you were not a Christian before May, in your sense, anyone may allow; but have you ever since continued sinless? Sin has not the dominion? Do you never, then, fall? Or do you mean no more than that you are free from presumptuous sins? If the former, I deny it; if the latter, who disputes?

Your misapplication of the witness of the Spirit is so thoroughly cleared by Bishop Bull that I shall not hold a candle to the sun. What portion of love, joy, etc., God may please to bestow on Christians is in his hand, not ours. Those texts you quote no more prove them generally necessary in what you call your imperfect state than rejoic[ing] in the Lord always contradicts. Blessed are they that mourn. There is a time to weep, and a time to laugh, till that day comes when all tears shall be wiped from our eyes—which I take it will hardly be before death; to which happiness God of his infinite mercy, through Christ, bring us all.

We join in love. As your last letter is dated from Oxford, I write thither, though you may be gone by this time. I am, Dear J[ack], your affectionate, sincere friend and brother,

S. Wesley

Dec. 13, 1738

I had much more to say, but it will keep if ever it should be proper.

Address: 'To the Revd. Mr. John Wesley, Fellow of Lincoln, Oxford. by + post'
Postmark: 'TIVER/TON'   *Charge*: '4'   *End* by JW: 'b S. Dec. 13, 1738 / Ansd this and the next and Visions to [them?]'; on p. (3), 'You make no more of infant baptism than they do; but require as full a change as though there had been no such thing.' (Both endorsements in abbreviated longhand.)
Source: MA.

[1] Replying to that of Nov. 30, and itself apparently answered by that of Feb. 3, 1739.

From the Revd. Samuel Wesley, Jun.[1]

[Jan. 24, 1739]

Dear Jack

Charles tells me you reckon I am a letter in your debt. In value it may be,
but 'tis not in number, for I had no answer to my last. I cannot say it positively
either desired or deserved one, and perhaps you may stay for my letter about 5
dreams, which has lai⟨d⟩ by me a good while, to save postage, but at last I
believe I shall b⟨e⟩ provoked to send it anyway, rather than raise expectation
so long for a trifle, or what you may think so. I have heard something since
I wrote which I look upon myself as obliged to tell you.

1. A place is taken, I am told from the news, for Mr. Whitefield to expound in 10
publicly. I hope it is with the bishop's approbation and consent at least, and not
done in ⟨fo⟩rce of the Act of Toleration only.

2. You have permitted and enc⟨our⟩aged an Anabapt⟨ist⟩ t⟨eac⟩her in one
of our pulpits, being presen⟨t⟩ yourself both a⟨t Morning Prayers⟩ and the
sermon. 15

3. You have spoke in build⟨ings not consecrated,⟩ not using the Liturgy,
and pray⟨ing extempory⟩ . . . but said you would do so no m⟨ore . . .⟩[2]
We join in love . . .

Janry. 24, 1738/9

Tiverton, Devon 20

Source: MA, a badly mutilated letter, mounted in a folio volume.

To the Revd. Samuel Wesley, Jun.[3]

[Feb. 3, 1739]

. . . I think Bishop Bull's sermon on the witness of the Spirit[4]
(against the witness of the Spirit it should rather be entitled) is full

[1] From the evidence of his diary (admittedly inconclusive), John Wesley does not
appear to have replied immediately to his brother's letter of Dec. 13, and this letter
supports such a conclusion, as does his endorsement of the Dec. 13 letter. Thus it seems
likely that the letter noted in the diary as written to Samuel Wesley on Feb. 3, 1739,
in fact answered that of Dec. 13 and this of Jan. 24, although unfortunately the extract
from that reply preserved by Whitehead refers only to the letter of Dec. 13.

[2] The beginnings of eight lines follow.

[3] See note to previous letter, which this apparently answers, as well as that of Dec.
13. For other elements in the letter see Wesley's endorsement on the letter of Dec. 13,
and the presumed reply to this, Mar. 26, 1739.

[4] George Bull (1634–1710), Bishop of St. David's, whose sermons and discourses
were published posthumously in 1713, the work here intended being entitled, 'The
Testimony of the Spirit of God in the Faithful' (III. 879–914). Wesley followed up

of gross perversions of Scripture, and manifest contradictions both to Scripture and experience. I find more persons day by day who experience a clear evidence of their being in a state of salvation. But I never said this continues equally clear in all as long as they
5 continue in a state of salvation. Some indeed have testified—and the whole tenor of their life made their testimony unexceptionable— that from that hour they have felt no agonies at all, no anxious fears, no sense of dereliction. Others have.

But I much fear we begin our dispute at the wrong end. I fear
10 you *dissent* from the fundamental Articles of the Church of England. I know Bishop Bull does. I doubt you do not hold justification by faith alone. If not, neither do you hold what our Articles teach concerning the extent and guilt of original sin; neither do you feel yourself a lost sinner; and if we begin not here, we are building on
15 the sand. O may the God of love, if my sister or you are otherwise minded, reveal even this unto you . . .

Source: Whitehead, II. 109–10. Whitehead says: 'A part of this letter I have not been able to find', so that he dates it only 'in the beginning of the present year, 1739'. He adds: 'Mr. Wesley's papers have been separated, and parts of them selected several times, I believe for the magazines, and for his other publications; for some years also they have been so much exposed to various persons that probably some have been lost . . .'

From the Revd. George Whitefield[1]

Steeple Ashton, Wilts., Feb. 13, 1739

Honoured sir

Your prayer is heard! This morning I visited your mother, whose prejudices
20 are entirely removed, and she only longs to be with you in your societies in London. Arguments from Tiverton, I believe, will now have but little weight. We parted with prayer. Brother Hall rejoiced in spirit, and so, methinks, will you and brother Charles. Honoured sir, how shall I express my gratitude to you for past favours? I pray for you without ceasing. But that is not enough; I
25 want to give you more substantial proofs. Believe me, I am ready to follow you to prison and to death. Today I was thinking, suppose my honoured friend was

this charge against Bull in his Latin sermon on Isa. 1:21; see letter of Oct. 27, 1739, to Samuel Wesley, and *Sermons*, Vol. 4 in this edition.

[1] Having returned from his first visit to America, Whitefield began touring the West Country. In his *Journal* he told how after leaving Salisbury on Feb. 13 he visited 'an old disciple, my brother Wesley's mother', staying with her son-in-law, the Revd. Westley Hall. That evening he reached Steeple Ashton (called 'Stapleashwin' in both *Journal* and letter), held a service in his lodgings, and 'wrote some letters'.

laid in a dungeon for preaching Christ. O how would I visit him! How would I kiss his chain, and continue with him till midnight singing Psalms! Perhaps our friends may think none of these things shall befall us. But I know not but they may be nigh, even at the door. As for my own part, I expect to suffer in the flesh. I believe I shall be exalted; I know I must be first humbled. I am assured 5 you will not be ashamed of me when I am a prisoner. I only suspect myself. But God's grace will be sufficient for me. Let us, then, honoured sir, (if such a one as I may give a word of exhortation) follow our Master without the camp, bearing his reproach. Let us cheerfully suffer the loss of all things, and lay down our lives for his sake. I pray continually that as your day is, so may your strength 10 be. I pray that you may not only have peace, but joy in the Holy Ghost, and be filled with all the fullness of God. I know you pray for, honoured sir, your affectionate son in the faith,

George Whitefield

Address: 'To the Rev. John Wesley, in London'   *Source*: *A.M.*, Supp., 1797, p. 18.

To the Revd. George Whitefield and William Seward

[Feb. 26, 1739] 15

My dear brother

One or two letters (since the receipt of yours)[1] I have had from my mother. Let us praise God on her behalf. Our Lord's hand is not shortened among us. Yesterday I preached at St. Katherine's[2] and at Islington, where the church was almost as hot as some of the 20 society rooms use to be. I think I never was so much strengthened before. The fields, after service, were white with people praising God. About three hundred were present at Mr. Sims's;[3] thence I went to Mr. Bell's,[4] then to Fetter Lane, and at nine to Mr. Bray's,

[1] i.e. Whitefield's of Feb. 13, telling of his visit to Wesley's mother.

[2] This was St. Katherine's near the Tower, where the incumbent (1738–46) was the Hon. John Berkeley.

[3] Peter Sims (born 1716), a butcher in Paved Alley, Leadenhall Street. In a large building close to his home, the Minories society met from the summer of 1738 onwards. Charles Wesley frequently expounded there, and on Sunday, Feb. 18, 1739, 'expounded at Sims's to two several companies'.

[4] Probably Richard Bell, a watch-case maker of Vine Court, Bishopsgate Street, in 1742, when he was one of the leaders of the married men of the Moravian society in Fetter Lane. In 1740 he had become one of the strong proponents of those who advocated 'stillness' in religion, thus precipitating a split in the original society. (The Moravian records also note a William Bell, the registrar of the society from 1744 onwards.)

where also we only wanted more room. Today I expound in Skinner's[1] at four, at Mrs. West's[2] at six, and to a large company of poor sinners in Gravel Lane (Bishopsgate) at eight. The society at Mr. Crouch's[3] does not meet till eight;[4] so that I expound before I go to him near St. James's Square, where one young woman has been lately filled with the Holy Ghost, and overflows with joy and love. On Wednesday at six we have a noble company of women, not adorned with gold or costly apparel, but with a meek and quiet spirit,[5] and good works. I cannot say so much of those who come to Mrs. Sims's[6] on Thursday. But they attend to the Word, so that I hope it will show them what it is that becometh women professing godliness.[7] At the Savoy on Thursday evening we have usually two or three hundred, most of them (at least) throughly awakened. Mr. Abbot's[8] parlour is more than filled on Friday, as is Mr. Parker's[9] room twice over, where I think I have commonly had more power given me than at any other place. A week or two ago a note was given me there, as near as I remember in these words: 'Your prayers are desired for a child that is lunatic and sore vexed day and night, that our Lord would heal him, as he did those in the days of his flesh, and that he would give his parents faith and patience till his time is come.'[10] You will hear more of this.

On Saturday sennight a middle-aged, well dressed woman at Beech Lane (where I expound, usually to five or six hundred,

---

[1] Whitefield's version of the letter gives 'the Minories', i.e. the wide street running north from the Tower of London.

[2] Mrs. West frequently appears in Wesley's diary from Apr. 23, 1738, onwards. In 1741 one of her sons married Esther Hopson—who is also often mentioned. It was probably her daughter whom Wesley described in a journal fragment for Feb. 23-6, 1756, as the possessed child of 'R—— West, a serious woman, the wife of Joseph West, a weaver, living in Hunt Street, Spitalfields (both of whom I had known for many years)'.

[3] 'Crouch's Society' (as Charles Wesley called it on Apr. 22, 1739) met on Tuesday evenings at the home of Mr. and Mrs. Crouch, at least from Feb. 1739 to June 1740, and John Wesley frequently had meals in their home, especially supper after the society meeting at Long Lane from 1740 onwards.

[4] This was on Tuesday, Feb. 27.

[5] See 1 Pet. 3: 3-4.

[6] The wife of Peter Sims mentioned above, formerly Hannah Howarth.

[7] 1 Tim. 2: 10.

[8] Possibly the same Mr. Abbot who in 1747 leased a large Baptist meeting-house in White's Alley, near Little Moorfields, to Peter Böhler (Benham, p. 197).

[9] Mr. Parker's society was in Wapping, where he also on occasion gave Wesley hospitality for the night. Possibly he was the John Parker who in June 1745 was a member of band 15 at the Foundery, London.

[10] See JWJ, Feb. 9, 1739; cf. Appendix, Feb. 9, 1739.

before I go to Mr. Exall's[1] Society) was seized, as it appeared to several about her, with little less than the agonies of death. We prayed that God, who had brought her to the birth, would ⟨give⟩ strength to bring forth,[2] and 'that he would work speedily, t⟨hat⟩ many might see it and fear, and put their trust in the Lord'.[3] Five days she travailed and groaned, being in bondage. On Thursday evening our Lord got himself the victory.[4] And from that moment she has been full of joy and love, which she openly declared at the same place on Saturday last. So that thanksgivings also were given to God by many on her account. It is to be observed, her friends have accounted her mad for these three years, and accordingly bled, blistered her, and what not. Come and let us praise the Lord, and magnify his name together![5]

London, Feb. 26

Address: 'To The Revd. Mr. Whitefield, At Mrs. Grevil's, In the Wine-Street, Bristol'   *Postmark:* '27/[FE]'   *Charge:* '4'   *End* by Whitefield on address panel: 'Answered March 3rd'   *Source:* Wes Ch; cf. Whitefield, *Journals,* Mar. 1, 1739: 'Amongst my other letters by this day's post, I received the following one from the Rev. Mr. John Wesley.' The text is then given, dated 'Feb. 20, 1739', with several omissions, the use of initials only for most names, and some minor alterations in the substance of the letter. The original holograph is an intact double letter, with the letter to Whitefield on pp. 1–2, the address on p. 4, and the following letter to Seward on p. 3.

[To William Seward][6]

London, Feb. 26, 1738/9

My dear brother Seward

Many of us joined together last night in prayer that the Word of God might have free course, and be glorified among you.[7] Persecution here seems to be at a stand, or rather, to decrease; doubtless

[1] William Exall, of Islington, one of the founding members of the Fetter Lane society in 1738, who does not appear to have joined the Moravians.
[2] See 2 Kgs. 19: 3. [3] See Pss. 31: 2, and 40: 4 (B.C.P.).
[4] See Ps. 98: 2 (B.C.P.). [5] Ps. 34: 3 (B.C.P.).
[6] William Seward (1704–42), a gentleman of Badsey, near Evesham, Worcestershire. Converted by means of Charles Wesley, he strongly supported the Georgia project, accompanied Whitefield there, was considering settling in the colony, and died as a result of a blow received while touring South Wales to raise support for Whitefield's Orphan House in Savannah, and at the same time to proclaim the gospel. This was on Oct. 22, 1740, though the tombstone (erected much later) mistakenly reads 1742.
[7] See 2 Thess. 3: 1.

because of our present weakness, lest those who have not yet root in themselves in time of temptation should fall away.[1] I have had a second confer⟨ence⟩ (a little before[2] Mr. Venn's[3] death) with Mr. Berriman.[4] ⟨We⟩ did not enter into the merits of the cause, ⟨but⟩ he
5 spoke largely in commendation of the serv⟨ice⟩ of our Church, and of the necessity of church un⟨ity⟩, in all which we were fully agreed. His whole behaviour was mild and friendly. At parting I told him there was no other thing he desired which I would not gladly comply with, only I could not cease to publish the gospel of Christ,
10 a dispensation of the gospel being committed to me.[5]

Pray for us, my dear brother, especially for your poor, weak brother,

John Wesley

From the Revd. George Whitefield[6]

Bristol, March 3, 1739

15 Honoured sir

I rejoice sincerely in your indefatigable zeal, and great success in the gospel of our dear Redeemer. Does not God by this cry out to those that have ears to hear, 'This is the way; walk in it'? Just now I am come from Bath, and was much refreshed by the sight of Mr. Thomson, Griffith Jones, etc. God greatly
20 blessed my conversation to them. Lady C[ox] is as yet self-righteous. But what I said staggered her. She will henceforward, I believe, pray for deliverance. I wrote to her this morning. Another young gentleman from Bath intends joining our friends at the university. Brave news brother Kinchin sends from thence.

---

[1] See Luke 8: 13.   [2] Orig., ((since)).

[3] The Revd. Richard Venn (1691–1739), rector of St. Antholin's, Watling Street, London (1725–39), where he was buried Feb. 20 after dying on Feb. 16. (The date given for his death in *D.N.B.*—1740—is an error.)

[4] The Revd. John Berriman (1691–1768), lecturer of St. Mary Aldermanbury and St. Thomas Apostle, and rector of Newtimber, Sussex, a popular London preacher. On Dec. 21, 1738, Charles Wesley had been refused the pulpit of St. Antholin's by Venn's orders, who had 'forbidden any Methodist to preach'—though in the event the clerk relented, and let him preach. Whitefield had similarly been refused early in Jan., 1739, and had a long conference with Venn on Jan. 26. This was followed up by a conference lasting four hours on Jan. 29, at which those present included John Wesley, Whitefield, Venn, and Berriman. Venn and Berriman objected to the Methodist organization of societies not controlled by the parish clergy, the use of extempore prayer in what they insisted was undoubtedly public worship, and of course Methodist teaching upon the new birth. After Whitefield had left London, and Venn had died, Wesley engaged in a second conference with Berriman alone, on Feb. 14 (see diary), which he thus reports (somewhat strangely) to Seward rather than to Whitefield, though it was clear that Whitefield had access to the letter, as it formed an integral part of that to himself.

[5] 1 Cor. 9: 17.   [6] Apparently replying to Wesley's of Feb. 26.

How secretly, in spite of all opposition, is the kingdom of Jesus Christ carried on! Here is a child of nine years old filled with the love of God, and very desirous of receiving the sacrament! Brother Brown knows him. How would you advise me to act? I think I would not advise brother Brown to come here till you do. He will be a great help to you in this city, because he knows our friends. There 5 is a glorious door opened among the colliers. You must come and water what God has enabled me to plant.

Since I begun this I hear you are gone to Oxon. Honoured sir, I heartily pray God to bless your endeavours, and make you stronger and stronger. Opposition here is not so great as it has been. I am now cast out, blessed be 10 God. May I not now hope that I begin to be a disciple of Christ? Honoured sir, I love you more than words can express, and am, honoured sir, your dutiful son and servant,

George Whitefield

Source: *A.M.* Supp., 1797, pp. 18-19.

[To the Revd. George Whitefield[1]]

[March 16, 1739] 15

My dear brother

On Thursday (the 8th instant) we breakfasted at Mr. Score's,[2] who is patiently waiting for the salvation of God. Thence we went to Mrs. Compton's,[3] who has set her face as a flint, and knows she shall not be ashamed.[4] After we had spent some time in prayer Mr. 20 Washington[5] came, with Mr. Gibbes,[6] and read several passages out

[1] This letter, like those of Feb. 26 and Mar. 3, is not closely related to any other, because its primary function was to keep a colleague up to date on what was happening. Wesley's diary shows that he had also written a letter to Whitefield on Mar. 8, which would be a similar journal-letter, leaving off where this takes up.

[2] Mr. Score was for a time a member of the growing Methodist society in the city of Oxford, in whose house groups met for fellowship.

[3] Mrs. Compton, though hospitable to Wesley personally, was a strong opponent of Methodism in Oxford until Mar. 6, when after dinner in her home Wesley turned from arguing with her to prayer (see JWJ and diary). Immediately she became one of his strongest advocates, and her home became a regular meeting-place for the society.

[4] See Isa. 50: 7.

[5] Henry Washington, of Queen's College, Oxford, came from Penrith to matriculate in 1733, aged 16, and became a member of the Oxford Methodist group. After graduating in 1737 he was now in residence for his M.A. Although during the summer of 1738 he rejected the possibility of a personal knowledge of salvation, and of that salvation being based upon the imputed righteousness of Christ, yet he and his friend Robert Watson remained in frequent and friendly touch with the Wesleys until December, 1738. They, along with Gibbes, another Queen's man, were now the Wesleys' opponents.

[6] (Orig., 'Gibs'.) Francis Gibbes, from Huish, Wiltshire, the son of a clergyman, who matriculated at Queen's College, Oxford, on Nov. 18, 1736, aged 19, graduated in 1740, and eventually became rector of Belton in Leicestershire.

of Bishop Patrick's *Parable of the Pilgrim*,[1] to prove that we were all under a delusion, and that we were to be justified by faith and works. Charles Metcalf[2] withstood him to the face,[3] and declared the simple truth of the gospel. When they were gone we again be-
5 sought our Lord that he would maintain his own cause.[4] Meeting with Mr. Gibbes soon after, he was almost persuaded to seek salvation only in the blood of Jesus. Meanwhile Mr. Washington and Watson[5] were going about to all parts and confirming the unfaithful. At four we met them (without design), and withstood them again. From
10 five to six we were confirming the brethren. At six I expounded at Mrs. Ford's, as I designed to do at Mrs. Compton's at seven. But Mr. Washington was got thither before me, and [was] just beginning to read Bishop Bull against the witness of the Spirit.[6] He told me he was authorized by the minister of the parish so to do. I advised all
15 that valued their souls to go away. And perceiving it to be the less evil of the two, that they who remained might not be perverted I entered directly into the controversy, touching both the cause and the fruits of justification. In the midst of the dispute James Mears's wife[7] began to be in pain. I prayed with her a little when Mr.
20 W[ashington] was gone, and then (having comforted the rest as I was enabled) went down to sister Thomas's.[8] In the way Mrs. Mears's pains so increased that she could not avoid crying out aloud in the

---

[1] Simon Patrick (1626–1707), Bishop of Chichester (1689) and Ely (1691), one or two of whose writings Wesley had read at Oxford, and whose *Christian Sacrifice* he used in his pastoral work in Georgia, and abridged for his *Christian Library*. The *Parable of the Pilgrim* (1664) was constructed along the lines of Bunyan's *Pilgrim's Progress*, and went through several editions, including an 1839 abridgement.

[2] Charles Metcalf, one of Wesley's London supporters, who had apparently accompanied him to Oxford. With his friend James Hutton, Metcalf became one of the leading English Moravian leaders, though in 1759 Zinzendorf characterized him as 'a good man, but a busybody' (Benham, p. 361).

[3] See Gal. 2: 11.

[4] See Ps. 74: 23 (B.C.P.).

[5] Robert Watson, another of the Methodist group at Queen's College, like his friend Washington from the north. Watson was an older man (matriculated Mar. 18, 1730, aged 18), and completed his M.A. on Feb. 26, 1739. He was at first a little more sympathetic to Charles Wesley's 'enthusiasm' than Washington. Like most of these men, he became a clergyman. (He is to be distinguished from George Watson of Christ Church, another Oxford Methodist, who had graduated M.A. in 1732.)

[6] See Feb. 3, 1739.

[7] The home in St. Ebbe's of James Mears and his wife seems to have become the meeting-place for a Methodist society from about October, 1738, and in October, 1769, Wesley preached to a huge crowd in James Mears's garden.

[8] Nothing is known of sister Thomas, unless she is to be identified with the Bristol Methodist, Margaret Thomas, who died in Oct. 1740.

street. With much difficulty we got her to Mrs. Shrieve's[1] (where also Mr. Washington had been before us). We made our request known to God, and he heard us, and sent her deliverance in the same hour. There was great power among us, and her husband also was set at liberty. Soon after I felt such a damp strike into my soul (and so did Mrs. Compton and several others) as I do not remember to have ever found before. I believed the enemy was near us. We immediately cried to our Lord to stir up his power and come and help us.[2] Presently Mrs. Shrieve fell into a strange agony both of body and mind. Her teeth gnashed together, her knees smote each other, and her whole body trembled exceedingly. We prayed on, and within an hour the storm ceased. She now enjoys a sweet calm, having remission of sins, and knowing that her Redeemer liveth.[3]

At my return to Mrs. Fox's I found our dear brother Kinchin just come from Dummer. We rejoiced and gave thanks, and prayed, and took sweet counsel together,[4] the result of which was that instead of setting out for London (as I designed) on Friday, [we agreed that] I should set for Dummer, there being no person to supply that church on Sunday. On Friday, accordingly, I set out, and came in the evening to Reading, where I found a young man (Cennick[5] by name), strong in the faith of our Lord Jesus. He had begun a society there the week before, but the minister of the parish had now wellnigh overturned it. Several of the members of it spent the evening with us, and it pleased God to strengthen and comfort them.

In the morning our brother Cennick rode with me, whom I found willing to suffer, yea, to die, for his Lord. We came to Dummer in the afternoon. Miss Molly[6] was very weak in body, but strong in the

---

[1] Mrs. Shrieve is not otherwise known.

[2] See Ps. 80: 2.

[3] See Job 19: 25.   [4] Ps. 55: 14.

[5] Orig., 'Senwick'—a clue to the pronunciation. John Cennick (1718–55) was a native of Reading, whose grandparents had been Quakers, but whose parents were loyal church people. He experienced a religious transformation on Sept. 6, 1737, and sought out the Methodists in Oxford in late 1738. In 1739 Wesley employed him to teach in his Kingswood school, but he also preached occasionally, and helped administer the society there. Within two years, however, he broke with Wesley, joined Whitefield, and then threw in his lot with the Moravians, for whom in 1745 he became a pioneer preacher in Ireland.

[6] Miss Molly Kinchin, sister of the Revd. Charles Kinchin, the Oxford Methodist incumbent of Dummer. On May 2, 1738, Kinchin wrote to John Wesley: 'My sister is much mended in health. She has received much benefit from you, under God, as to her spiritual concerns.'

Lord and in the power of his might.[1] Surely her light ought not thus to be hid under a bushel.[2] She has forgiveness, but not the witness of the Spirit, perhaps for the conviction of our dear brother Hutchings, who seemed to think them inseparable. On Sunday
5 morning we had a large and attentive congregation. In the evening the room at Basingstoke was full, and my mouth was opened.

We expected much opposition, but found none at all. On Monday, Mrs. Cleminger being in pain and fear, we prayed, and our Lord gave her peace. About noon we spent an hour or two in conference
10 and prayer with Miss Molly, and then set out in a glorious storm. But even I had a calm within. We had appointed the little society at Reading to meet us in the evening. But the enemy was too vigilant. Almost as soon as we were out of town the minister sent or went to each of the members, and began[3] arguing and threatening, [and]
15 utterly confounded them, so that they were all scattered abroad. Mr. Cennick's own sister did not dare to see us, but was gone out on purpose to avoid it. I trust, however, our God will gather them together again, and that the gates of hell shall not prevail against them.[4]

20 About one in the afternoon on Tuesday I came to Oxford again, and from Mr. Fox's (where all were in peace) I went to Mrs. Compton's. I found the minister of the parish had been there before me, to whom she had plainly declared the thing as it was, that she 'never had a true faith in Christ till two in the afternoon' on the Tuesday
25 preceding. After some other warm and sharp expressions he told her, upon that word he 'must repel' her 'from the Holy Communion'. Finding she was not convinced of her error, even by that argument, he left her, calmly rejoicing in God her Saviour.[5]

At six in the evening we were at Mr. Fox's society, about seven
30 at Mrs. Compton's. The power of our Lord was present at both, and all our hearts were knit together in love.[6] The next day we had an opportunity to confirm most, if not all, the souls which had been shaken. In the afternoon I preached at the Castle. We afterwards joined together in prayer, having now Charles Graves[7] added to us,

---

[1] See Eph. 6: 10.   [2] See Matt. 5: 15, etc.
[3] Orig., 'being'.   [4] See Matt. 16: 18.
[5] See Luke 1: 47.   [6] Col. 2: 2.
[7] Charles Caspar Graves, or Greaves (*c.* 1717–87), was now an undergraduate at Magdalen College, Oxford, from Mickleton, Gloucestershire. For a few years he served the Methodist societies as a clergyman, but from 1759 until his death was the rector of Tissington, Derbyshire.

who is rooted and grounded in the faith.[1] We then went to Mr.
Gibbes's room, where were Mr. Washington and Watson. Here an
hour was spent in conference and prayer, but without any disputing.
At four in the morning I left Oxford. God hath indeed planted and
watered. O may he give the increase![2] . . .   5

Source: MA, a reference copy by an amanuensis, with Wesley's endorsement on
p. (1), 'To G Wd, March 16', and along the fold of p. (4), 'to GW, March 16,
1739'. The date and recipient are confirmed by Wesley's diary.

To the Revd. James Hervey

[March 20, 1739]

My dear brother
    I am not certain whether I have answered your letter.[3] But I am
afraid I have not. The fears you had are, I hope, partly removed by
means of Mr. Orchard's[4] conversations with our brother White-   10
field. But whether it be so or no, it is easy to answer the questions
you proposed, for him as well as myself. If honest tradesmen were to
undertake dishonest occupations (that of pawnbroking, for instance),
those we should dissuade them from following; but not from following honest ones. Preachers of righteousness[5] they must be (in a sense,   15
and in their own sphere), if they are truly honest, and that both by
words and actions. But not public preachers (which is quite another
thing) until they are 'called thereto, as was Aaron'.[6]
    How far I believe that privilege of the children of God, the not

[1] See Eph. 3: 17.   [2] See 1 Cor. 3: 6.
[3] Of Dec. 1, 1738; see pp. 596-7 above. For Hervey's friendly reply to this see
Apr. 4, 1739.
[4] Paul Orchard (*c.* 1682-1740), son of Charles Orchard of Kilkhampton, Cornwall,
matriculated at Exeter College, Oxford, Dec. 10, 1699, aged 17, became a student of the
Inner Temple in 1700, and served as M.P. for different constituencies, 1711-15. It was
in his home at the ancient Stoke Abbey (later called Hartland Abbey) in Devon that
Hervey lived from 1738 to 1740 as a private chaplain. Orchard visited the Revd. Samuel
Wesley at Tiverton, Devon, in order to enlist his influence in restraining John Wesley's
'dangerous and extravagant tenets', and followed this up by a letter on May 7, 1739,
written by Hervey on his behalf. (See Priestley, pp. 98-100, where 'T. Hervey' should
surely be 'J. Hervey'.) By his third wife, Rebecca, daughter of Charles Smith of Isles-
worth, Middlesex, came his only son, another Paul Orchard (1739-1812), for whom
Hervey served as godfather, and to whom in 1747 he dedicated his *Contemplations on the
Night*.
[5] See 2 Pet. 2: 5.   [6] See Heb. 5: 4.

committing sin, to extend, you have probably seen in my printed *Sermon on Salvation by Faith*. That salvation, of which I believe deliverance from sin to be the greatest branch, the Scripture teaches is only by or through faith; and the Church of England expressly
5 teaches the same thing, viz. that the cause of our salvation is, only the righteousness and blood of Christ; and the condition of it, only faith, faith without works, faith exclusive of all works whatsoever (in which I was mistaken),[1] but necessarily productive of all holiness and good works if we continue rooted and grounded therein.
10   My dear brother, this is that faith (largely described in our Articles and Homilies) which by your account of yourself I perceive you want. You want a living faith in Christ. (Is not that a hard saying?)[2] Ask and receive this, and sin shall no more have dominion over you,[3] and you shall have sweet peace in the blood of Jesus, and
15 shall rejoice with joy unspeakable and full of glory![4] Amen! Lord Jesus!
     Write to and pray for, your most affectionate brother,

                                                          J. Wesley

London, March 20,
20   1738/9

Address: 'To the Revd. Mr. Hervey, At Paul Orchard's Esq. at Stoke-Abby, near Biddiford, Devon'   *Postmark*: '24 MR'   *Charge*: '4'   *End*, presumably by Hervey, with a line of shorthand above the closing courtesies
Source: Lincoln College, Oxford.

To the Revd. George Whitefield[5]

March 20, 1739

My dear brother
     Would you have me speak to you freely? Without any softening or reserve at all? I know you would. And may our loving Saviour

---

[1] Before his contacts with the Moravians Wesley had in some measure looked to his own efforts for salvation, albeit believing that these efforts were made possible only by the grace of God (see letters of July 19, 1731; Aug. 17, 1733, and Dec. 10, 1734, §§ 1–6). Such efforts were what he rejected when he proclaimed that until May 24, 1738, he was not a Christian (see letter of Oct. 30, 1738), although he later modified this to a statement that previously he had had the faith of a servant, who lives under the law, but not that of a son, who lives under grace.

[2] John 6: 60.   [3] See Rom. 6: 14.   [4] 1 Pet. 1: 8.

[5] Wesley's charge against Whitefield does not seem to be mainly that of divisiveness,

speak to your heart, so my labour shall not be in vain. I do not commend you with regard to our brothers S[eward] and C[ennick]. But let me speak tenderly. For I am but a little child.[1] I know our Lord has brought good out of their going to you; good to you, and good to them; very much good. And may he increase it a thousand- 5 fold, how much soever it be! But is everything good, my brother, out of which he brings good? I think that does not follow. O my brother, is it well for you or me to give the least hint of setting up our will[2] or judgment against that of our whole society? Was it well for you once to mention a desire which they had all solemnly declared 10 they thought unreasonable? Was not this abundant cause to drop any design which was not manifestly grounded on a clear command of our Lord? If our brother R[oberts?] or P[arker?] desired anything, and our other brethren disapproved of it, I cannot but think he ought immediately to let it drop. How much more ought you or 15 I! They are upon a level with the rest of their brethren. But I trust you and I are not; we are the servants of all. Thus far have I spoken with fear and much trembling,[3] and with many tears. O may our Lord speak the rest; for what shall such an one as I say to a beloved servant of my Lord? O pray that I may see myself a worm and no 20 man.[4] I wish to be your brother in Jesus Christ,

John Wesley

Source: *A.M.* Supp., 1797, pp. 19–20; cf. two extracts in Whitefield's letter of Mar. 22, 1739, to Jas. Hutton (MorA).

From the Revd. George Whitefield[5]

Bristol, March 22nd, 1738/9

Honoured sir

I rejoice at the success God has given you at Oxford and elsewhere. And 25 immediately kneeled down and prayed that you may go on from conquering to conquering. I propose, God willing, to write to Washington, etc. Turn them, O Lord, and they shall be turned!

I thank you most heartily for your kind rebuke. I can only say it was too tender. I beseech you, by the mercies of God in Christ Jesus, whenever you see 30 me do wrong, rebuke me sharply. I have still a word or two to offer in defence of

but lack of democracy in drawing some Methodists into allegiance to himself and his teaching. Whitefield's meek reply (echoed in his letter to Hutton) was written Mar. 22–3, and indicates that the unavailable opening of Wesley's letter dealt with his continued work at Oxford, and the opposition of Washington, Watson, and Gibbes.

[1] See 1 Kgs. 3: 7.   [2] Whitefield, Mar. 24, 'our own will'.   [3] 1 Cor. 2: 3.
[4] Ps. 22: 6.   [5] Answering Wesley's of Mar. 20, to whose opening it offers clues.

my behaviour, but shall defer it till I come to town. If I have offended, I
humbly ask pardon, and desire the brethren to pray that I may be such as God
would have me to be.

   If the brethren after prayer for direction think proper, I wish you would be
5 here the latter end of next week. Brother Hutchin[g]s sets out tomorrow for
Dummer. Mr. Chapman brings an horse to London which you may ride.
I go away, God willing, next Monday seven[n]ight. If you was here before my
departure, it might be best. Many are ripe for bands. I leave that entirely to
you—I am but a novice; you are acquainted with the great things of God.
10 Come, I beseech you, come quickly. I have promised not to leave this pe⟨ople⟩
till you or somebody came to supply my place. I am ⟨re⟩signed as to brother
Hutton's coming hither. The good Lord direct him.

   Desire the brethren's advice in the following case. Joseph[1] is arrived. Because
he would not submit to a lot whether he should go with me to England or
15 not, I said he never should return if he went. On board he behaved well, exceeding well. William Wallace did not so, which made me think that had he
submitted to a lot it would have been appointed him to go with me. What shall I
do? Shall I keep to my vow that he should not return, or shall I break it? I am
indifferent. I will do as the brethren shall direct.

20   Great comfort and joy in the Holy Ghost does God of his free grace give me.
I find myself strengthened in the inner man day by day. I feel an intenseness
of love, and long that all should be partakers of it also. I hope I grow in grace.
To free grace be all the glory.

   God will fight for our dear brother Charles. ⟨I thank⟩ him for his letter.
25 Blessed be God that y⟨ou⟩ both are not so brief as usual. God will bring light
out of darkness. All these things are not against but for us.

   Be pleased to bring the account of my temptations with you, and though
unworthy permit me to subscribe myself, honoured sir, your dutiful son and
servant,

30   GW

March 23rd, 1738/9

Honoured sir
   I beseech you come next week. It is advertised in this day's journal. I pray
for a blessing on your journey in our meetings. The people expect you much.
35 Though you come after, I *heartily* wish that you may be preferred before me.
Even so, Lord Jesus. Amen. Amen.

   Our brethren are here together. They advise that you should go through
Basingstoke, and call at Dummer, and there take the horse brother Hutchin[g]s
rides thither. Whosoever you shall appoint may ride brother Chapman's. The
40 Lord direct us all in all things.

Address: 'To The Revrd. Mr. John Wesly, at Mr. John Bray's a Brazier in little
Britain in Aldersgate, London'   *Postmarks*: 'B/ris/tol' (i.e. 'ris' 'tol' within
loops of 'B'), '26 MR'   *Charge*: '4'   *End*: 'Mr. Whitfield' in contemporary
hand, not Wesley's   *Source*: MA.

   [1] Apparently Joseph Doble ('J.D.') in Whitefield's *Journal*, though Whitefield's
printed expenses have 'John', possibly from 'Jo.'

From the Revd. Samuel Wesley, Jun.[1]

26th March, 1739

Dear Jack

I might as well have wrote immediately after your last as now, for any new information that I expected from my mother; and I might as well let it alone for any effect it will have, farther than showing you, I neither despise you on the one 5 hand nor am angry with you on the other.

I am sorry Georgia lies should pursue Whitefield. I like not any lies, but that epithet does not mend them. I shall never understand that matter now, since I am persuaded you will hardly ever see me face to face in this world, though somewhat nearer than Count Zinzendorf. 10

I am glad you encouraged no sectary to preach in our Church. The matter of any discourse or prayer after it was not objected against, but there being any such exhortation at all; but you will do it no more, and it is past.

Charles has at last told me in plain terms—he believes no more of dreams and visions than I do. Had you said so I believe I should hardly have spent any time 15 upon them, though I find others credit them, whatever you may do. You quoted Joel, gave a good character of him that saw the Father, and said assurance so given might be. This was either defending them, or else to no purpose that I can see. It was otherwise unnecessary puzzling the cause.

You make two degrees or kinds of assurance. That neither of them are 20 necessary to a state of salvation I prove thus:

1. Because multitudes are saved without either. These are of three sorts: (1). All infants baptized who die before actual sin. (2). All persons of a melancholy and gloomy constitution, who without a miracle cannot be changed. (3). All penitents who live a good life after their recovery, and yet never attain to 25 their first state.

2. The lowest assurance is an impression[2] from God, who is infallible, that heaven shall be actually enjoyed by the person to whom it is made. How is this consistent with fears of miscarriage, with deep sorrow, and going on the way weeping? How can any doubt after such a certificate? If they can, then here is an 30 assurance whereby the person who has it is not sure.

3. If this be essential to a state of salvation, 'tis utterly impossible any should fall from that state finally, since how can anything be more fixed than what Truth and Power has said he will perform? Unless you will say of the matter here (as I observed of the person) that there may be assurance wherein the thing 35 itself is not certain.

We join in love; we are pretty well in health. I shall take up no more of your time than to tell you, I am, your affectionate friend and brother,

S. Wesley

Mar. 26, 1739 40
Tiverton, Devon

Source: Queen's College, Melbourne, Australia; cf. W.H.S. XII, 103–4.

[1] Apparently a reply to the imperfect letter of Feb. 3, 1739, and itself answered by John on Apr. 4, 1739.

[2] Annotation over the line, possibly by John Wesley, 'No'.

[To the Revd. John Clayton?][1]

[Mar. 28, 1739?]

Dear sir

The best return I can make for the kind freedom you use is to use the same to you. O may the God whom we serve sanctify it to us
5 both, and teach us the whole truth as it is in Jesus.[2]

You say you cannot reconcile some parts of my behaviour with the character I have long supported. No, nor ever will. Therefore I have disclaimed that character on every possible occasion. I told all in our ship, all at Savannah, all at Frederica, and that over and over,
10 in express terms, 'I am not a Christian; I only follow after, if haply I may attain it.'[3] When they urged my works and self-denial, I answered short, 'Though I give all my goods to feed the poor, and my body to be burned, I am nothing.'[4] For I have not charity. I do not love God with all my heart. If they added, 'Nay, but you could
15 not preach as you do if you was not a Christian', I again confronted them with St. Paul: 'Though I speak with the tongue of men and

---

[1] This important letter, Wesley's apologia for his controversial stand, 'I look upon all the world as my parish', has previously been thought to be that written to the Revd. James Hervey on Mar. 20, as recorded in Wesley's diary. The discovery of the actual letter to Hervey refutes that claim. We are therefore left with a letter published by Wesley in June 1739 as written 'some time since' to an unknown 'friend'. That it was written to Hervey on some other occasion is rendered highly unlikely by its opening salutation, 'Dear sir', more formal than the 'My dear brother' by which he addressed both Whitefield and Hervey. The 'friend' to whom it was written, however, was strongly critical of the breaches of ecclesiastical propriety into which Wesley had recently been drawn. His former Oxford Methodist colleague, the Revd. John Clayton, admirably meets these criteria, and on May 1, 1738, had written a critical letter, in association with Dr. Deacon and Dr. Byrom of Manchester, Non-jurors (see above, pp. 538–9). The opening salutation, however, cannot be checked, for of the 26 letters to Clayton recorded in Wesley's diary none survives except possibly this, the last. (The evidence of Wesley's correspondents' salutations to him is an untrustworthy guide to his own salutations in reply, but for what it is worth Clayton's of May 1, 1738, was 'Revd. and dear sir'.)

Wesley's diary shows that Wesley wrote to Clayton on Mar. 21, 1739, spending a good part of the morning, and two-and-a-half hours in the afternoon, on this, and the following day apparently wrote a letter of introduction for a Mr. Brown to take to Clayton. Then on Mar. 24 Wesley again wrote to Clayton for an hour, and on Mar. 28 'transcribed to Clayton'. Dismissing the letter of Mar. 22, the other entries may all refer to this letter, carefully drafted on Mar. 21, revised on Mar. 24, and transcribed for dispatch (possibly with more revisions) on Mar. 28. Both date and recipient, however, remain matters of speculation.

[2] See Eph. 4: 21.
[3] See Phil. 3: 12.
[4] See 1 Cor. 13: 3.

angels, and have not charity, I am nothing.'[1] Most earnestly, therefore, both in public and private, did I inculcate this: 'Be not shaken,
however I may fall; for the foundation standeth sure.'[2]

If you ask on what principle, then, I acted, it was this: a desire
to be a Christian, and a conviction that whatever I judge conducive
thereto, that I am bound to do; wherever I judge I can best answer
this end, thither it is my duty to go. On this principle I set out for
America; on this I visited the Moravian Church; and on the same
am I ready now (God being my helper)[3] to go to Abyssinia or China,
or whithersoever it shall please God by this conviction to call me.

As to your advice that I should settle in college, I have no business there, having now no office and no pupils. And whether the
other branch of your proposal be expedient for me, viz. to 'accept
of a cure of souls', it will be time enough to consider when one is
offered me.

But in the meantime, you think, I ought to sit still; because otherwise I should invade another's office if I interfered with other people's
business and intermeddled with souls that did not belong to me. You
accordingly ask, how is it that I assemble Christians who are none
of my charge to sing psalms and pray and hear the Scriptures
expounded; and think it hard to justify doing this in other men's
parishes, upon catholic principles.

Permit me to speak plainly. If by *catholic* principles you mean
any other than *scriptural*, they weigh nothing with *me*. I allow no
other rule, whether of faith or practice, than the Holy Scriptures.
But on scriptural principles I do not think it hard to justify whatever I do. God in Scripture commands me, according to my power,
to instruct the ignorant, reform the wicked, confirm the virtuous.
Man forbids me to do this in another's parish; that is, in effect, to
do it at all; seeing I have now no parish of my own, nor probably
ever shall. Whom then shall I hear? God or man? 'If it be just to
obey man rather than God, judge you.'[4] 'A dispensation of the
gospel is committed to me, and woe is me if I preach not the gospel.'[5]
But where shall I preach it upon the principles you mention? Why,
not in Europe, Asia, Africa, or America; not in any of the Christian
parts, at least, of the habitable earth. For all these are, after a sort,
divided into parishes. If it be said, 'Go back then to the heathens

---

[1] See 1 Cor. 13: 1–2.   [2] See 2 Tim. 2: 19.
[3] B.C.P., Adult Baptism, response to Question 4.
[4] See Acts 5: 29.   [5] See 1 Cor. 9: 16–19.

from whence you came', nay, but neither could I now (on your principles) preach to them; for all the heathens in Georgia belong to the parish either of Savannah or Frederica.

Suffer me now to tell you *my* principles in this matter. I look upon
5 *all the world* as *my parish*;[1] thus far I mean, that in whatever part of it I am, I judge it meet, right, and my bounden duty[2] to declare unto all that are willing to hear the glad tidings of salvation. This is the work which I know God has called me to. And sure I am that his blessing attends it. Great encouragement have I therefore to be
10 faithful in fulfilling the work he hath given me to do. His servant I am, and as such am employed (glory be to him) day and night in his service. I am employed according to the plain direction of his Word, 'As I have opportunity, doing good unto all men'.[3] And his providence clearly concurs with his Word, which has disengaged me
15 from all things else that I might singly attend on this very thing, 'and go about doing good'.[4]

If you ask, 'How can this be? How can one do good of whom men "say all manner of evil"?'[5] I will put you in mind (though you once knew this, yea, and much established me in that great truth), the
20 more evil men say of me for my Lord's sake, the more good will he do by me. That it is 'for his sake'[6] I know and he knoweth, and the event agreeth thereto; for he mightily confirms the words I speak, by the Holy Ghost given unto those that hear them. O my friend, my heart is moved toward you. I fear you have herein made ship-
25 wreck of the faith.[7] I fear, 'Satan, transformed into an angel of light'[8] hath assaulted you, and prevailed also. I fear that offspring of hell, *worldly or mystic prudence*, has drawn you away from the simplicity of the gospel. How else could you ever conceive that the being reviled and 'hated of all men',[9] should make us less fit for our
30 Master's service? How else could you ever think of 'saving yourself and them that hear you'[10] without being 'the filth and offscouring of the world'?[11] To this hour is this Scripture true. And I therein rejoice, yea, and *will* rejoice.[12] Blessed be God, I enjoy the reproach of Christ![13] O may you also be vile, exceeding vile for his sake! God

---

[1] Cf. Whitefield, letter of Nov. 10, 1739 (written at sea), 'The whole world is now my parish.'
[2] B.C.P., Communion, exhortation 3.
[3] See Gal. 6: 10.   [4] Cf. Acts 10: 38.   [5] Matt. 5: 11.
[6] Ibid.   [7] See 1 Tim. 1: 19.   [8] 2 Cor. 11: 14.
[9] Matt. 10: 22, etc.   [10] Cf. 1 Tim. 4: 16.   [11] Cf. 1 Cor. 4: 13.
[12] Phil. 1: 18.   [13] Heb. 11: 26.

forbid that you should ever be other than *generally* scandalous. I had almost said, *universally*. If any man tell you there is a new way of following Christ, 'he is a liar, and the truth is not in him'.[1] I am, etc. . . .

Source: JWJ, June 11, 1739, introduced thus: 'Yet during this whole time I had many thoughts concerning the *unusual manner* of my ministering among them. But after frequently laying it before the Lord, and calmly weighing whatever objections I heard against it, I could not but adhere to what I had some time since wrote to a friend, who had freely spoken his sentiments concerning it. An extract of that letter I here subjoin . . .'

From John Cennick[2]

March 29, 1739

Dear brother

Forever blessed be the Lord my strength! Because he is not slack in his promise, as some men count slackness, for when all fled from me, and I was left alone, yet was I not alone, for the Spirit of my God was powerful upon me! And my dear Saviour excited me to courage! By mere providence I did not receive yours till this morning, and I dare say you will praise God with me when I relate my reason. On Saturday last the 29th instant, as I conceive it might be past six in the evening, I was inclined to walk, thinking to divert my soul in solemn solitude. (It was after I had borne the slanders of an incensed people, and the slight carriage of my intimate friends; I can't say but I was entirely composed, though just before a gentlewoman had sent to me to know if I had altered my principles, and if not, to forbear to hold friendship with her son. This then I weighed, whether the love I bore to him, which was extremely [great], or the love of a crucified Saviour, was most to be desired; and immediately answered in these words, Pray give my service to Mrs. Pidgeon, and when I see the way I have taken displeases my Redeemer, then I will readily decline it, and be again fond of my dear company, but till then I am glad to lose a friend, knowing 'tis for my Master's sake.) I had scarce been walking an hour ere I thought on the troubles I was brought out of, the cares I had so lately overcome, when heaven descended into my calm breast, and filled me with unutterable joy, and such peace that neither the world could give or take away. My soul abode in this transporting enjoyment till near eight of the clock. All this while I had sweet communion with God and his Christ. I triumphed mightily over all the glory of the world, all the reproaches of Christ I esteemed riches, and all the shame I was to share I trampled on and despised! I looked for Satan to disturb me, but he was gone! for the old man to allure me, but that was silent! Within was love and peace, without thankful adoration, amazement, and rejoicing! I beheld the beauty of the Trinity, shining on my soul as the sun in his

---

[1] 1 John 2: 4.   [2] Answering Wesley's of Mar. 21, 1739.

strength! The Lamb of God embraced me as a son of his love! And the Holy
Spirit moved prolific on my spirit, as it did once on the confused waters in the
creation! My barren bosom flamed as the altar when the bright rays of the Sun
of righteousness shined upon me. My soul was ravished into angelic harmony,
5 and my heart danced for joy, for lo! I saw the day of peace dawn, the eyelids of
the morning were opened, and the promised Star of Jesse arose in his glory!
O for some angel's tongue to tell the beauties that sparkled in his light! But it
sufficeth that we believe hereafter we shall all receive of his fullness, and be
eternal partakers in boundless felicity. And now I was interrupted with the
10 coming of Mr. Pidgeon and Mrs. Mortimer, both inspired with sparks of in-
fernal rage, and it pleased God to give me power not only to silence their perverse
disputes, but they went away all serene and peaceable, and thanked me for my
good company. So may God calm the fury of every opposer, and show his truth
and salvation to every enemy that hath [done] evil in his sanctuary.
15   Now had I received your letter before I had declared the goodness of the Lord
to them of mine acquaintance, then perhaps they had readily concluded it to be
mere delusion, because you mentioned intercession for my concerns on Saturday; and because of your encouraging me to fight manfully on Christ['s]
banner. My sister is greatly reclaimed, and begs me to give her sincere love to
20 you. Mrs. Newbery is the only person that comes to the society, and [it] is her
alone that is not shaken, who also desires to be remembered. Mr. Boody is
indifferently silent, but ready to hear our reproach, and to join in despising.
I have much to write, but am obliged to defer. All I at present shall say is that
I believe many if not all will return to our society, being generally inclined. I
25 think to be in Oxford next Monday in business, God willing. Pray remember
me in love to all the friends of Christ. The grace of our Lord Jesus Christ be
with your spirit.

Jno: Cunnick

Pray be so good when you write to mention your care for Mrs. Willmot, and
30 entreat God for her conversion. I heartily wish it may please God to send hither
our dear brother W[h]it[e]field, for many have told me should he come they
would hear him, though all opposed him. God's will be done in earth, as it is in
heaven. Amen.

Address: 'To The Revd. John Westley, att Mr. Huttons, Bookseller, near Temple
Bar, London'   *Postmark*: '. . . AD . . .' (fraction of 'Reading', in a circle);
'30 MR'   *Charge*: '3'   *Source*: MorA.

To James Hutton and the
Fetter Lane Society[1]

Bristol, April 2, 1739

My dear brethren (and sisters too),

The first person I met with on the road hither was one that was inquiring the road to Basingstoke. We had much conversation together till evening. He was a Somersetshire man, returning home, very angry at the wickedness of London, and particularly of the infidels there. He held out pretty well to Basingstoke, but during the expounding there (at which between twenty and thirty were present) his countenance fell, and I trust he is gone down to his house saying, 'God be merciful to me a sinner!'[2]

I stayed an hour or two at Dummer in the morning with our brother Hutchings, who is strong in faith, but very weak in body; as most probably he will continue to be, so long as he hides his light under a bushel.[3] In the afternoon a poor woman at Newbury and her husband were much amazed at hearing of a salvation so far beyond all they had thought of or heard preached. The woman hopes she shall follow after, till she attains it. My horse tired in the evening, so that I was obliged to walk behind him, till a tradesman who overtook me lent me one of his, on which I came with him to Marlborough,[4] and put up at the same inn. As I was preparing to alight here, my watch fell out of my pocket, with the glass downward, which flew out to some distance, but broke not. After supper I preached the gospel to our little company, one of whom (a gentleman) greatly withstood my saying, till I told him he was wise in his own eyes,[5] and had not 'a heart right before God'.[6] Upon which he silently withdrew, and the rest calmly attended to the things that were spoken.

In the morning I prayed to him that 'saveth both man and beast',[7]

---

[1] Whitefield had pleaded that Wesley should take over the evangelistic work which he had begun in Bristol (see letter of Mar. 22–3), favourable lots had been drawn about the wisdom of Wesley's thus leaving the London society, companions for the venture were similarly chosen by lot, and Wesley had set off from London on Mar. 29 and arrived in Bristol on Saturday evening, Mar. 31. He kept his London friends informed of the work in Bristol.

[2] Luke 18: 13.   [3] See Matt. 5: 15, etc.

[4] Orig., 'Marlborow', though 'Marlborough' later in the letter.

[5] See Prov. 3: 7, etc.   [6] See Ps. 78: 37.   [7] Cf. Ps. 36: 7 (B.C.P.).

and set out, though my horse was so tired he could scarce go a foot-pace. At Calne[1] (twelve miles from Marlborough), I stopped. Many persons came into the room while I was at breakfast, one of whom I found to be a man of note in the place, who talked in so obscene
5 and profane a manner as I never remember to have heard anyone do, no, not in the streets of London. Before I went I plainly set before him the things he had done. They all stood looking at one another, but answered nothing.

At seven, by the blessing of God, I came hither. At eight our
10 dear brother Whitefield expounded in Weavers' Hall[2] to about a thousand souls. On Sunday morning to six or seven thousand at the Bowling Green; at noon to much the same number at Hanham Mount;[3] and at five to I believe thirty thousand from a little mount on Rose Green. At one today he left Bristol. I am straitened for
15 time. Pray ye, my dear brethren, that some portion of his spirit may be given to your poor, weak brother,

John Wesley

Dear Jemmy
None of my things are come. I want my gown and cassock every
20 day. O how is God manifested in our brother Whitefield! I have seen none like him, no, not in Herrnhut!

We are all got safe to Bristol, praised be God for it.[4]

Address: 'To Mr. James Hutton, Bookseller, Near Temple-bar, London'
Seal: very large, design uncertain (fragments only)   *Postmarks*: 'B/ris/tol',
'4 AP'   *Charge*: '4'   *End* by Hutton: 'Ap. 2, 1739'   *Source*: MorA.

[1] Orig., 'Cane'.
[2] In Temple Street, near Temple Church, belonging to the Weavers' Guild. White-field's preaching enlarged the old religious society meeting there. Wesley took over this work, and in 1751 leased the building for Methodist purposes; later during his lifetime it became a synagogue.
[3] Orig., 'Hannam Mount', as usual with Wesley.
[4] This sentence is written in the hand of John Purdy, who died in 1759. Wesley wrote to his son, Victory, on Feb. 17, 1784: 'Your father was one of our first society which met at Fetter Lane, and one of the first that found peace with God. When it was thought best that I should go to Bristol, we spent a considerable time in prayer, and then cast lots who should accompany me thither. The lot fell upon him; and he was with me day and night till he judged it proper to marry'—which was in 1746. Their allotted companion was 'brother Easy'.

From the Revd. George Whitefield[1]

April 3rd, 1739

Honoured sir

Yesterday I began to play the madman in Gloucestershire, by preaching on a table in Thornbury street. Today I have exhorted twice, and by and by shall begin a third time—nothing like doing good by the way. I suppose you have 5 heard of my proceedings in Kingswood. Be pleased to go thither, and forward the good work as much as possible. I desire you would open any letters that come directed for me, ⟨and⟩ (if you judge me worthy) send me a line to Gloucester. I wish you all the success imaginable in your ministry, and I pray God my dear Bristol friends may grow in grace under it. Parting from them has struck 10 a little damp upon my joy. God will quickly revisit, honoured sir, your unworthy son and servant,

GW

My hearty love to the brethren.

Address: 'To The Revrd. Mr. John Wesly, at Mrs. Grevil's in Wine-street, Bristol'   *Sealed*, and delivered by personal messenger   *End* by JW, 'G Wh, April 3, 1739'   *Source*: MA.

To James Hutton[2]

[April 4, 1739]

In his letter to me, brother Seward desires you would print a new 15 edition of the Extract of the Homilies,[3] and send 1000 hither on his account immediately.

---

[1] On Sunday, Apr. 1, Whitefield introduced John Wesley to 'this strange way of preaching in the fields', and on Monday, Apr. 2, took his leave of Bristol, where Wesley took over this ministry, thus described in his *Journal* for that day: 'At four in the afternoon I submitted to "be more vile", and proclaimed in the highways the glad tidings of salvation.'

[2] George Whitefield and his companion William Seward left Bristol for Wales on Monday, April 2, via Kingswood, where he laid a stone for the future schoolhouse there. Here Seward began a letter to Hutton, noting, 'Br. Westley begins preaching this evening in the open air at the glasshouses where the poor man was pelted, and is to go to Newgate tomorrow, and to Rose Green, Hanham, etc.' Finishing the letter later in the day, he seems to have enclosed it with a letter to Wesley, for Wesley to forward together with his own message.

[3] *The Doctrine of Salvation, Faith, and Good Works. Extracted from the Homilies of the Church of England.* Wesley had published this in Oxford in 1738, and clearly Seward's letter of Apr. 2 had offered to subsidize another edition, which probably appeared the following month; cf. JW's letter of May 8 to Hutton, and *Bibliog*, No. 11.

Where is my gown, etc.?
The lion begins to roar. Adieu!

April 4

Source: A postscript added by JW to the letter by Wm. Seward to Hutton
Apr. 2, 1739, addressed by Seward, 'To Mr. James Hutton, Bookseller at
Temple Bar, London', charged '4', and postmarked 'B/ris/tol' and in London,
'6 AP' (MorA).

To the Revd. Samuel Wesley, Jun.[1]

Bristol, April 4, 1739[2]

5 Dear brother
    I rejoice greatly at the temper with which you now write, and
trust there is not only mildness, but love also in your heart. If so,
you shall know of this doctrine, whether it be of God.[3] Though
perhaps not by my ministry.
10   To this hour you have pursued an *ignoratio elenchi*.[4] Your
'assurance' and mine are as different as light and darkness. I mean
an assurance that I am *now* in a state of salvation, you an assurance
that I shall *persevere* therein. The very definition of the term cuts
off your second and third observation. As to the first I would take
15 notice: (1). No kind of assurance (that I know), or of faith, or
repentance, [is] essential to their salvation who die infants. (2). I
believe God is ready to give all true penitents who fly to his free
grace in Christ a fuller sense of pardon than they had before they
fell. I know this to be true of several; whether these are exempt
20 cases I know not. (3). Persons that were of a melancholy and gloomy
constitution, even to some degree of madness, I have known in
a moment (let it be called a miracle, I quarrel not) [brought] into
a state of firm, lasting peace and joy.
    My dear brother, the whole question turns chiefly, if not wholly,
25 on matter of fact. You deny that God does now work these effects,
at least that he works them in such a manner. I affirm both, because
I have heard those facts with my ears, and seen them with my eyes.
I have seen (as far as it can be seen) very many persons changed in

---

[1] Answering that of Mar. 26.   [2] Orig., '1738'.
[3] John 17: 17.   [4] 'missing the point'.

a moment from the spirit of horror, fear, and despair, to the spirit
of hope, joy, peace; and from sinful desires, till then reigning over
them, to a pure desire of doing the will of God. These are matters
of fact, whereof I have been, and almost daily am, [an] eye- or ear-
witness. What, upon the same evidence (as to the suddenness and   5
reality of the change) [do] I believe, or know, touching visions and
dreams [?] This I know: several persons in whom this great change
from the power of Satan unto God[1] was wrought either in sleep, or
during a strong representation to the eye of their minds of Christ,
either on the cross or in glory. This is the fact. Let any judge of it as   10
they please. But that such a change was then wrought appears (not
from their shedding tears only, or sighing, or singing psalms, as
your poor correspondent did by the woman of Oxford, but) from
the whole tenor of their life, till then[2] [well known for their evil ways,
but whose virtues] were not remarked; from that time holy, just,   15
and good.

Saw you him that was a lion till then, and is now a lamb; him that
was a drunkard, but now exemplarily sober; the whoremonger that
was, who now abhors the very lusts of the flesh? These are my living
arguments for what I assert, that God now, as aforetime, gives   20
remission of sins and the gift of the Holy Ghost,[3] which may be
called 'visions'. If it be not so, I am found a false witness; but,
however, I do and will testify the things I have both seen and heard.

I do not now expect to see your face in the flesh. Not that I believe
God will discharge you yet, but I believe I have nearly finished my   25
course. O may I be found in him, not having my own righteousness:[4]

> When I thy promised Christ have seen,
>   And clasped him in my soul's embrace,
> Possessed of thy salvation then,
>   Then may I, Lord, depart in peace.[5]   30

The great blessing of God be upon you and yours. I am, dear
brother, your ever affectionate and obliged brother,

John Wesley

I expect to stay here some time, perhaps as long as I am in the
body.   35

Address: 'The Rev. Mr. Wesley, Tiverton, Devon'   *Source*: Priestley,
pp. 64–7.

---

[1] Acts 26: 18.   [2] Whitehead notes: 'The MS is here injured by folding.'
[3] See Acts 2: 38.   [4] Phil. 3: 9.
[5] John and Charles Wesley, *Hymns and Sacred Poems*, 1739, p. 74.

From the Revd. James Hervey[1]

Revd. and dear sir

Yesterday I returned from St. Gennys, the parish of worthy Mr. Thomson, where I have been about six weeks, dispensing, according to my slight know-
5 ledge and weak capacities, the Word of God among them. O that my frailties and imperfections may be pardoned, and my poor service be acceptable to our Creator, profitable to our fellow-creatures!

I take this first opportunity of acknowledging the receipt of your last, which awaited me at the Abbey. I heartily thank you, good sir, and beg leave to com-
10 mend you. Commend you for clearing up and vindicating your doctrine from the objections raised against it. I think the preachers of the gospel are to stop the mouths of the gainsayers, as well as to warn them that are unruly, support the weak, comfort the feeble-minded. Your printed sermon I have not had the pleasure and advantage of reading, therefore am still in the dark with regard
15 to your opinion concerning the regenerate's not committing sin. But I presume you understand that text to be meant of habitual sin; that those who are children of God cannot sin of malicious wickedness, cannot be reconciled to the love of sin, nor continue in a course of sin. That they cannot knowingly and con- tentedly admit of any iniquity to dwell undisturbedly within them, as filth and
20 sediments do at the bottom of a standing water; but like the working sea are always emptying and discharging themselves of whatever filth they have con- tracted, or iniquity they have committed. So that though sin and wicked in- clinations, tempers, passions, be in them, yet not as their delight, but great unhappiness, not as the friends they caress but as the enemies they abhor; which
25 are always hated, and as constantly fought against as felt.

For your plain dealing I both commend you and thank you. Faithful are the wounds of a friend, as health to the soul; and a soothing silence while I am in the way to destruction is the worst of cruelties. That I want a living faith in Christ is undoubtedly a hard saying, but I cannot, I dare not, say it is a false one.
30 No, dear and faithful sir, I submit to the charge, I plead guilty, and promise to practice your advice. To ask that I may receive. O that I had a spirit of prayer and supplication! that I could pour out strong cries to him that is able to save, to give me faith among the true believers, and holiness among them that are sanctified! You know my wants (while others, wretchedly mistaken, believe me
35 rich). You are acquainted with my misery, therefore I hope, I beg, you will pray, and more abundantly pray for, dear and honoured sir, your loving, grateful, though very unworthy, humble servant,

J. Hervey

I hope to hear from you soon.

Address: 'To The Revd. Mr. John Wesley, at Mr. James Hutton's, at the Bible & Sun, next the Rose Tavern, Temple Bar, London' *Postmarks*: One in- distinguishable, and '9 AP' *Charge*: '4' *End* (all by Charles Wesley):

[1] Answering Wesley's of Mar. 20.

'Hervey /Apr. 4 /'39.', 'Ann Gestine [?]/ S. Rickard/ B Sharp', and in a later, bolder hand, 'April 4, 1739/ Jam[e]s Hervey to my B./ simple, kindly, honest.' *Source*: MA.

To James Hutton and the Fetter Lane Society

[Bristol, April 9, 1739]

My dear brethren

On Sunday evening the first instant I began to expound at Nicholas Street society,[1] our Lord's Sermon on the Mount. The room, passage, and staircase were filled with attentive hearers. On Monday I talked with several in private, to try what manner of spirit they were of.[2] And at four in the afternoon went to a brickyard adjoining to the city, where I had an opportunity of preaching the gospel of the kingdom (from a little eminence) to three or four thousand people. The Scripture on which I spoke was this: 'The spirit of the Lord is upon me, because he hath anointed me to preach the gospel to the poor, he hath sent me to heal the broken-hearted, to preach deliverance to the captives, and recovering of sight to the blind, to set at liberty them that are bruised, to preach the acceptable year of the Lord.'[3] At seven I began expounding the Acts of the Apostles to the society in Baldwin Street.[4] We had more company than the room would hold, and the power of our Lord was with us.

On Tuesday the third I began preaching at Newgate[5] (as I continued to do every morning) on the Gospel of St. John. Many Presbyterians and Anabaptists came to hear. Afterwards I transcribed some of the rules of our society[6] for the use of our (future) brethren

[1] In Nicholas Street and Baldwin Street met two of the religious societies originally established by the Church of England, after the pattern of Dr. Josiah Woodward's societies in London. These and similar meeting-places became so crowded in response to Whitefield's and then Wesley's preaching that within a few months Wesley erected the 'New Room' in the Horsefair, in which these two societies henceforth met jointly, becoming known as the 'United Societies', and eventually 'The United Society'.

[2] See Luke 9: 55.   [3] Luke 4: 18-19.   [4] See note 1.

[5] i.e. the chapel in the city gaol, like that of London named 'Newgate'. This was situated at the eastern end of Narrow Wine Street, and the keeper was Whitefield's convert, Abel Dagge (see Wesley's letter of Jan. 1, 1761, to the *London Chronicle*).

[6] Rules for the Fetter Lane society had gradually accumulated, and were much elaborated after Wesley's return from Herrnhut. These were codified by him on Dec. 25, 1738, as *Rules of the Band Societies*, though they were not printed until five years later

here. In the evening I expounded on, 'Blessed are those that mourn',[1] at Nicholas Street society. I hope God spake to the hearts of many there.

The next day the audience increased at Newgate. At four in the afternoon I offered the free grace of God from those words, 'I will heal their backsliding, I will love them freely',[2] to about fifteen hundred, in a plain near Baptist Mills, a sort of suburb or village not far from Bristol, where many, if not most, of the inhabitants are Papists. O may they effectually lay hold on the one Mediator between God and man, Christ Jesus!

About seven in the evening three women who desire only to know Jesus Christ, and him crucified[3] (Mrs. Norman,[4] Mrs. Grevil,[5] and Mrs. Panou[6]) agreed to meet together once a week; to confess their faults to one another, and pray one for another, that they may be healed.[7] And Mrs. Panou desired she might propose their design to her two sisters, and offer them the liberty of joining with them. At eight Samuel Wathen, surgeon,[8] Richard Cross,

as an addendum to the *General Rules* (see *Bibliog*, No. 81). From the mention of 'future brethren' it is clear that Wesley expected the Bristol societies soon to be organized along similar lines to those in London.

[1] See Matt. 5: 4.   [2] Hos. 14: 4.
[3] 1 Cor. 2: 2.

[4] Mrs. John Norman (1695–1779), who lived on St. Philip's Plain, her husband owning a brickyard and apparently the land on which Wesley preached his first sermon in the open air on Apr. 2. (For the specific use of Norman's brickyard see Wesley's diary, Apr. 23, 1739.) He died in 1744, leaving her with one daughter, Constant, who married James Ireland, another prominent Bristol Methodist. She was genteel, talented, and deeply spiritual (see *A.M.*, 1789, pp. 240–5, and W.H.S., II. 5–6).

[5] Whitefield's sister Elizabeth, who had married Mr. C. Grevil, a grocer of Wine Street, Bristol. She seems to have been a widow, and her mother lived with her. Whitefield lodged with them, as did the Wesleys from time to time, especially until the building of the New Room in the Horsefair—witness the letter of Apr. 3, 1739. At first she was a stalwart of the society, which occasionally met in her home, but her allegiance became somewhat spasmodic. (The name was sometimes spelt 'Greville', as in Samuel Wesley's letter of Apr. 16, 1739.)

[6] Mrs. J. Panou has not been further identified. Deschamps Panou, a boy of ten admitted to membership, was surely her son (see Apr. 26). Her two sisters (who later joined the band) were Esther Deschamps and Mary-Anne Page (see letter of Apr. 16).

[7] See Jas. 5: 16.

[8] According to Cennick, Samuel Wathen was apprenticed to a surgeon in Corn Street (apparently William Thornhill, see p. 637 n., below), and a leading member of the Baldwin Street society, whose reading to the colliers on Hanham Mount furnished the first occasion for Cennick's preaching (W.H.S., VI. 107). He is probably to be identified with Samuel Wathen who later secured academic qualifications, receiving his M.D. at Aberdeen in 1752, and being admitted a Licentiate of the College of Physicians in 1756. He had settled in London, treated Charles Wesley there in 1750, and operated on John Wesley's hydrocele in 1774. He died in 1787.

upholsterer,[1] Charles Bonner, distiller,[2] and Thomas Westall, carpenter,[3] met and agreed to do the same; who also desired they might make the offer of joining with them to three or four of their acquaintance. If this work be not of God, let it come to naught: if it be, who shall overthrow it?[4]

On Thursday, at five in the evening, I began the Epistle to the Romans at a society in Castle Street, where after the expounding a poor man gave glory to God by openly confessing the things he had done. About eight a young woman of Nicholas Street society sunk down as one dead. We prayed for her, and she soon revived, and went home strengthened and comforted both in body and in spirit.

A Presbyterian minister was with us at Newgate on Friday and Saturday. On Friday evening we were at a society without Lawford's Gate,[5] where the yard being full as well as the house, I expounded part of the first chapter of the First Epistle of St. John at the window. On Saturday evening Weavers' Hall was quite full. A soldier was present at the preaching on Monday, two at the expounding on several of the following days, and five or six this evening. I declared to them all that they were damned sinners, but that 'the gospel was the power of God unto salvation to everyone that believeth'.[6]

Beginning at seven (an hour earlier than usual) at the Bowling Green (which is in the heart of the city) yesterday morning there were not, I believe, above a thousand or twelve hundred persons present. And the day being very cold and stormy (beside that much rain had fallen in the night) many who designed it were hindered from going to Hanham Mount, which is at least four miles distant

[1] Richard Cross was apparently an apprentice upholsterer, made a freeman of Bristol in 1740. In the 1741 membership list of the Bristol society he is named among the married men.

[2] Charles Bonner's occupation of distiller makes him an unlikely prospect for a founding member of a Methodist band, and little more is known about him, though he may have been the father of Samuel Bonner, the senior partner in the printing firm of Bonner and Middleton, who from 1774 issued their own *Bristol Journal*, and the following year published Wesley's *A Calm Address to our American Colonies*.

[3] Thomas Westell or Westall (*c*. 1719-94), who appeared on the membership list for Jan. 1, 1741, among the unmarried men—he finished his apprenticeship to Luke Wilmot, joiner, that year, and was admitted a freeman—became one of Wesley's first three lay itinerant preachers, the only one who remained loyal to the end, when he was buried in Portland Chapel, Bristol.

[4] See Acts 5: 38-9.

[5] Orig., 'La-fore Gate'.

[6] See Rom. 1: 16.

from the town. Between ten and eleven I began preaching the gospel there in a meadow, on the top of the hill. Five or six hundred people from Bristol (of whom several were Quakers) were there, and (I imagine) about a thousand of the colliers. I called to them, in the words of Isaiah, 'Ho, everyone that thirsteth, come ye to the waters, and he that hath no money. Come ye, buy and eat, yea, come buy wine and milk without money and without price.'[1]

On Rose Green (which is a plain upon the top of a high hill) are several small hills where the old coal-pits were. On the edge of one of these I stood in the afternoon, and cried in the name of my Master, 'If any man thirst, let him come unto me and drink. He that believeth on me (as the Scriptures have said), out of his belly shall flow rivers of living water.'[2] About five thousand were present, many of whom received the Word gladly, and all with deep attention.

From thence we went to the society in Baldwin Street, whose room containing but a small part of the company we opened the doors and windows, by which means all that was spoken of the true Christian life, described in the end of the second chapter of the Acts, was heard clearly by those in the next room, and on the leads, and in the court below, and in the opposite house, and the passage under it. Several of the soldiers and of the rich were there, and verily the power of the Lord was present to heal them.[3]

My dear brethren, who among you writes first to strengthen our hands in God? Where is our brother Bray and Fish,[4] and whosoever else finds his heart moved to send unto us the word of exhortation? You should no more be wanting in your instructions to, than your prayers for, your affectionate, but weak, brother,

John Wesley

Bristol, April 9, 1739

Address: 'To Mr James Hutton, Bookseller, near Temple-bar, London'
Seal: Crucifixion and 'Der ist mein' (5)   *Postmarks*: 'B/ris/tol', '13 [?] AP'
Charge: '4'   *End* by Hutton: 'Ap. 9, 1739'   *Source*: MorA.

[1] Isa. 55: 1.

[2] See John 7: 37–8.

[3] Luke 5: 17.

[4] With Bray he was one of the original members of the London Fetter Lane society, visited Newgate with Bray and Charles Wesley on July 17, 1738, and eventually went over to the Moravians. Surviving letters from both men to Wesley show Fish to have been much more polished than Bray.

To James Hutton,[1] John Edmonds,
The Revd. Charles Wesley

Bristol, April 9, 1739

Dear Jemmy

I want nothing of this world. Pray give the guinea to my brother Charles, for my sister Kezzy. God will reward our brother Thomas[2] better than with my thanks. I am, you may believe, much straitened 5 for time. Therefore I can write but little. And neither of our brethren here has the pen of a ready writer. Why does not Charles Metcalf[3] come? I wish you would send me those two letters wrote to me at Oxford by brother Bray, and those two by our brother Fish in November and December last.[4] They are in my great box at 10 Mr. Bray's. Can't you get from our brother Shaw[5] and send me 'the Herrnhut Experiences and Transcript of B[rother] Hopson's Letters'?[6] They would be very useful here. Don't neglect, or delay. Adieu!

What is the matter with our sisters? My brother Charles complains of them. 15

G. Whitefield will be tonight at Mr. Harris, Junr, bookseller in Gloucester.[7]

---

[1] The preceding letter is that noted in Wesley's diary for Apr. 9 as 'writ to Fetterlane' at 6.30 a.m. At one o'clock he 'writ to J. H, Edmu[nd]s, to Ch[arles]'. The first was his regular weekly journal-epistle, the latter a series of three personal messages on one sheet.

[2] Thomas Wilson, of whom nothing is known (see annexed letter to Charles Wesley).

[3] Orig., 'Medcalf'; see p. 606 n. above.

[4] The holographs of those by John Bray of Nov. 18 and Dec. 5, 1738, and of William Fish of Nov. 25, are preserved in the Methodist Archives, and another of Dec. 5, 1738, to Fish was available to Henry Moore. Clearly Wesley sought to use them as spiritual challenges for his Bristol hearers, just as he published a conflation of Fish's two letters in his *Journal* for Dec. 5, 1738.

[5] John Shaw was one of the original members of the Fetter Lane society, who was removed on June 13, 1739, because he rejected the Church of England (CWJ).

[6] Although Wesley punctuates this as if one manuscript only was involved, it seems likely that he intended two, both of which seem to have disappeared.

[7] Added below date on p. (1).

[To John Edmonds][1]

Dear brother Edmonds,

I thank you much for yours. O write as often and as much as you can. For I want stirring up; or rather, I want to be made alive. When shall I hear the voice of the Son of man and live![2] Surely there never
5 was such a deceiver of the people[3] as I am. They reverence me as a saint, and I am a poor sinner; or, in truth, a rich sinner. Else I should not be thus poor long. Go and exhort our brother Jennings[4] to count relations, friends, and all things but dung that he may win Christ.[5] Adieu, my dear brother! Adieu!

[To Charles Wesley]

10 Dear brother Charles

Against next post I will consider your verses. The clergy here *gladiatorio animo ad nos affectant viam.*[6] But the people of all sorts receive the Word gladly. Hitherto I have so full employment here that I think there can be no doubt whether I should return already
15 or no. You will hear more from time to time, and judge accordingly. But whenever it seems expedient I should return, a lot will put it out of doubt. The God of peace fill you with all peace and joy in believing![7] Adieu!

Bristol, April 9, 1739

20 I forgot. I must subscribe to the Kingswood Colliers' School-house.[8] So I will take the money of Mr. Wilson.

[1] Orig., 'Edmunds', i.e. John Edmonds (1710–1803), whose own letter to Wesley of Oct. 8, 1739, is signed 'Edmonds', the spelling Wesley himself used later. He was a founding member of the Fetter Lane society, and became a Moravian. On Feb. 22, 1781, the society celebrated the 51st wedding anniversary of him and his wife Mary, when he, along with Hutton and John West, were the oldest surviving male members of the congregation (Benham, pp. 90, 537–8).
[2] See John 5: 25.   [3] See John 7: 12.
[4] See letter of Oct. 13, 1738.   [5] See Phil. 3: 8.
[6] Cf. Terence, *Phormio*, 964, 'hunt us down like gladiators'.
[7] See Rom. 15: 13.
[8] Whitefield had not only begun preaching in Bristol itself, but in Kingswood, three or four miles to the west, where the colliers lived in the most squalid conditions among the comparatively new coal-pits. On Apr. 2 Whitefield had laid the foundation-stone of a school for them, and Wesley was implementing this project.

Address: 'To Mr. James Hutton, Bookseller, near Temple-bar, London'
Seal: Crucifixion, and 'Der ist mein' *Postmarks*: 'B/ris/tol', '11 AP'
Charge: '4' *End* by Hutton: 'Ap. 9, 1739' *Source*: MorA.

To James Hutton and the
Fetter Lane Society

Bristol, April 16,
1739

My dear brother

Sunday, April 8, about eight in the evening, Mr. Wathen and his
brethren met, and received several persons into their little society.[1] 5
After prayer their leaders were chose, and the bands fixed by lot,
in the order following:

I. Band, Richard Leg (haberdasher), leader; Thos. Mitchell,
Chs. Bonner, Willm. Wynne, Richd Cross.

II. Band, Jo. Palmer, leader; James Lewis, John Davis, James 10
Smith, Willm. Waters.

III. Band, Henry Crawley (barber), leader; Thos. Harding,
John Wiggins, Samuel Wathen, Thomas Westall.

It was farther agreed that a few other persons then mentioned
might be admitted into the society. 15

Monday, April 9. At two in the afternoon Mrs. Panou and Mrs.
Grevil met, together with Esther Deschamps and Mary-Anne Page
(Mrs. Panou's sisters), whom they then received as sisters, and
Esther Deschamps was by lot chose leader of the band, which stood
as follows: 20

Esther Deschamps, J. Panou, M. Page, Eliz. Davis (then proposed
and admitted), and Eliz. Grevil.

At five in the evening Anne Williams, Mary Reynolds, Eliz. Ryan,
Esther Highnam, Frances Wilds, and Rachel England met together,
and agreed to meet every Sunday; Anne Williams was chose their 25
leader.

The Assizes prevented my preaching at Newgate this week,
except only on Monday and Tuesday. On Monday at four I preached
to three or four thousand people at the brickyard, on 'I came, not

[1] i.e. the Baldwin Street society.

to call the righteous, but sinners to repentance.'[1] On Tuesday, about one, having sent our brethren Easy and Purdy before, I set out for Bath. Soon after I came in the person who rented the ground where many people were met sent me word I should not preach on his
5 ground; if I did he would arrest me. Presently after a good woman sent to tell me I was welcome to preach on hers. Thither we went at five. It is a meadow, on the side of the hill close to the town, so that they could see us from Lady Cox's in the Square plainly. Here I offered God's free grace to about two thousand souls. At eight in
10 the evening I preached remission of sins to many casual hearers, from some steps at the end of a house in Gracious Street. Griffith Jones[2] was one of them, who afterwards refreshed us with his company about an hour at our inn.

On Wednesday Morning Mr. Chapman[3] stayed with us awhile,
15 to whom we spake the truth in love. At ten I preached in the meadow again, to, I judge, about twenty-five hundred. At four I offered Jesus Christ, as our wisdom and righteousness, sanctification, and redemption,[4] to above three thousand. At seven all the women in band met together, and having received Mary Cutler into fellowship
20 with them, spent the evening in conference and prayer.

At eight the bands of men [met] at the society-room in Baldwin Street, and received into fellowship with them William Lewis, James Robins, Kenelm Chandler, Anthony Williams, and Thomas Robins. The remainder of the evening was spent in singing, confer-
25 ence, and prayer.

Thursday, 12. We went to pitch on a proper place upon Rose Green to raise a little place for me to stand on in preaching. At the societies in the evening there was great power, and many were convinced of sin. But I believe more on Friday evening at both the
30 societies.

On Saturday I waited on one of the clergy of this city who had sent me word I was welcome to preach in his church—if I would tell nobody of it; but he had altered his mind, and told me now he could not let me preach.[5] At four I began preaching on the steps

---

[1] Mark 2: 17, etc.

[2] The Revd. Griffith Jones (1683–1761), rector of Llanddowror, and founder of the Welsh Charity School movement. The Phillips of Picton Castle were the patrons of Llanddowror, and Jones married Margaret, daughter of Sir Erasmus Phillips.

[3] The Revd. Walter Chapman, former Oxford Methodist.

[4] See 1 Cor. 1: 30.

[5] The Revd. John Gibb, vicar of St. Mary Redcliffe, 1701–44.

at the door of the poorhouse. Four or five hundred of the richer sort were within, and I believe fifteen hundred or two thousand without. About an hour and half I spent with them in prayer, and in explaining and applying those words, 'When they had nothing to pay, he frankly forgave them both.'[1]

Weavers' Hall was quite filled in the evening, and many, I trust, were cut off from their confidence in the flesh. On Sunday morning I applied the Parable of the Pharisee and the Publican[2] to six or seven thousand attentive hearers in the Bowling Green. It rained till I began preaching on Hanham Mount. Therefore I stood near the door of the house (in which we put the women). Three thousand (at least) were content to stand without. I preached at Newgate after dinner to a crowded audience. Between four and five we went (notwithstanding the rain) to Rose Green. It rained hard at Bristol, but not a drop fell on us, while I preached from the fullness which was given me to about five thousand souls, 'Jesus Christ, our wisdom, righteousness, sanctification, and redemption.'[3]

At six, being with the Lawford's[4] Gate society, I did not go up into the room, but stood on a table below, by which means not only all in the room and shop, but those in the yard and entries could hear, to whom I declared that 'The blood of Jesus Christ cleanseth us from all sin.'[5]

I am still dead and cold, unless while I am speaking. Write often to, and pray much for, my dear brethren, your poor brother,

John Wesley

Having a desire to receive a holy woman of deep experience into the female bands, we doubted what to do, because she is a Dissenter. The answer we received from Scripture was Gal. 3, verse 8.[6] This seemed clear. However, having determined to cast lots, we did so; and our direction was, 'Refer it to the bands (at London), to be decided by lot.'

Address: 'To Mr. James Hutton, Bookseller, Near Temple-bar, London'
Seal: Crucifixion and 'Der ist mein' (5)   *Postmarks*: 'B/ris/tol', '1[?] AP'
Charge: '4'   *End* by Hutton: 'Bristol, Ap. 16, 1739'   *Source*: MorA.

[1] Luke 7: 42.   [2] Luke 18: 9–14.   [3] 1 Cor. 1: 30.
[4] Orig., 'Lafore'.   [5] 1 John 1: 7.
[6] 'And the Scripture, foreseeing that God would justify the heathen through faith, preached before the gospel unto Abraham, saying, In thee shall all nations be blessed.'

From the Revd. Samuel Wesley, Jun.[1]

[April 16, 1739]

Dear Jack

I heartily pray God we may meet each other with joy in the next life; and beg him to forgive either of us as far as guilty, for our not meeting in this. I ack-
5 nowledge his justice in making my friends stand afar off and hiding my acquaintance out of my sight!

I find brevity has made me obscure. I argue against assurance (in your or any sense) as part of the gospel covenant. Because many are saved without it. You own you cannot deny exempt cases, which is giving up the dispute. *Your*
10 *assurance*, being a clear impression of God upon the soul, I say must be perpetual, must be irreversible, else 'tis not assurance from God Infallible and Omnipotent.

Your seeing persons reformed is nothing to this. Dear ⟨broth⟩er, do you dream I deny the grace of God? But to ⟨suppo⟩se the means whereby they are so [in][2]
15 this sense is [in] my opinion as very *petitio principii*[3] as ever was. You quarrel not at the word miracle, nor is there any reason you should, since you are so well acquainted with the thing. If I was as I have been, I should desire some of the plainest. You say the cross is strongly represented to the eye of the mind. Do those words signify in plain English, 'the fancy'? Inward eyes, ears, and feelings,
20 are nothing to other people; I am heartily sorry such alloy should be found among so much piety. The little reflection on my poor correspondent at Oxford is quite groundless. I don't remember he says singing (add rolling, etc.) was the only sign of her new birth; 'tis brought as a fruit of it. May we judge the tree by the fruit? Such visions I think may fairly be concluded fallacious—only for
25 being attended with so ridiculous an effect.

My mother tells me she fears a formal schism is already begun among you, though you and Charles are ignorant of it. For God's sake take care of that, and banish extemporary expositions and extemporary prayers. I have got your abridgment of Halyburton, and have sent for Watts. If it please God to allow
30 me life and strength I shall by his help demonstrate that the Scot as little deserv⟨es⟩ preference to all Christians but our Saviour as the ⟨book⟩ to all writings but those you mention. There are ⟨two⟩ flagrant falsehoods in the very first chapter. But your eyes are so fixed upon one point that you overlook everything else. You overshoot, but Whitefield raves.
35 I entreat you to let me know what reasons you have to think you shall not live long. I received yours dated 4th on Saturday the 14th. The post will reach me much sooner, and I shall want much to know what ails you. I should be very angry with you, if you cared for it, should you have broken your iron constitution already; as I was with the glorious Pascal for losing his health and living
40 almost twenty years in pain.

---

[1] Answering that of Apr. 4, which did not arrive until the 14th.
[2] Orig., 'is'.
[3] 'begging the question'.

My wife joins in love. We are all in tolerable health. I am, dear Jack, your sincere and affectionate friend and brother,

S. Wesley

Apr. 16, 1739
Tiverton, Devon

⟨*Τὸ* λ⟩*οιπὸν, ἀδελφώ, προσεύχεσθον περί ἡμῶν. κ.τ.λ.*[1]

Address: 'To the Revd. Mr. John Wesley at Mrs. Grevilles in Wine Street, Bristol'   *Charge*: '3' (but no postmarks)   *End* by JW: 'April 16, bS. [answered] May 9, 1739.' and at a later date, '⟨Gre⟩at Piety, tho mistaken! / I think ys was ye last I recd fr him.'   *Source*: MA.

To James Hutton and the Fetter Lane Society

[Apr. 21–6, 1739]

My dear brother

On Sunday evening the 15th the women had their first love-feast.

On Monday about three thousand were at the brickyard. In the evening the brother of the person who owns it told me his brother did not care I should be there any more, and desired me to look out for some other place. There was much power at the society this night.

Tue. 17. At three in the afternoon eleven unmarried women met at Mrs. Grevil's, and desired three others might be admitted among them. They were then divided into three bands.[2]

The same day we were with the two prisoners who are under sentence of death, the younger of whom seemed much awakened. At five I was at a society where I had not been before.[3] The upper room in which we were was propped beneath, but the weight of people made the floor give way, so that in the beginning of the expounding the post which propped it fell down with much noise. However, we stayed together till seven. I then went to Baldwin

---

[1] 'Finally, brothers, pray both of you for us.' (Cf. 2 Thess. 3: 1.) 'κ[αί] τ[ὰ] λ[οιπά]', i.e. 'all the rest', or 'etc.'.

[2] The following was included in the original letter, then struck through (surely because it was duplicated later): ((Of one which Lucretia Smith (this morning baptized, having been a Quaker) was this morning [the preceding two words separately erased] ['by lot' added over the line] chose leader.))

[3] Back Lane, where John Haydon lived, joining Old Market Street at its eastern end (near Lawford's Gate) with Jacob's Lane (later Jacob Street).

Street society, where it was much impressed upon me to claim the
promise of the Father for some that heard it, if the doctrine was of
God. A young woman (named Cornish) was the first who felt that
our prayer was heard, being, after a short agony, fully set at liberty.[1]
5 The next was another young woman (Eliz. Holder). The third was
one Jane Worlock.[2] The last (a stranger in Bristol), John Ellis, was
so filled with the Holy Ghost that he scarce knew whether he was in
the body or out of the body;[3] he is now gone home to declare the
marvellous works of the Lord. Behold how he giveth us above what
10 we can ask or think![4] When Miss Cornish began to be in pain, we
asked God to give us a living witness that signs and wonders were
now wrought by the name of his Holy Child Jesus.[5] We asked for
one—and he hath given us four!

Wed. 18. About twenty-five hundred were present at Baptist
15 Mills. At six the female bands met, and admitted Lucretia Smith
(late a Quaker, who was baptized the day before), Rebecca Morgan
(deeply mourning), Eliz. Holder, Hannah Cornish, Jane Worlock,
and Mary Cutler. Lucretia Smith was by lot chose leader. At seven,
all the female bands being met together, Rebecca Morgan received
20 the promise of the Father.

At eight the men met, and received into fellowship with them
Richard Hereford (leader), William Farnell, John Goslin, Joseph
Ellis, Capel Giles, Thomas Oldfield, and John Purdy.

Likewise William Lewis was by lot added to the first, Kenelm
25 Chandler to the second, and James Robins to the third band.

Then the married band was filled up, as follows: John Brooks (a
soldier), leader, John Williams, Thomas Arnot (a soldier), William
Davis, Anthony Williams, and Thomas Robins. But Thomas
Robins has since declined meeting.

30 Two boys were also admitted: Thomas Davis, aged fourteen,
and Deschamps Panou, aged ten, both of whom 'have found the
Saviour in their hearts'.

Thur. 19, Mr. Gr[iffith] Jones called in his return to Wales, and
went with us to Castle Street society, where two were deeply con-
35 vinced of sin. At seven several in Nicholas Street received much

---

[1] On June 2 Wesley entered in his diary, 'religious talk to Miss Cornish; she in love
with me'—a constant peril with the pious young women to whom he ministered.

[2] In his *Journal* for May 2 Wesley describes how Jenny Worlock's faith was rekindled
after a relapse.

[3] See 2 Cor. 12: 2.   [4] See Eph. 3: 20.

[5] See Acts 4: 27, 30.

comfort. On Good Friday,[1] at five in the evening, Mr. Wathen's mistress[2] received remission of sins. As at seven did Samuel Goodson and Anne Holton, who had long been in heaviness. On Easter Eve the rain obliged me to preach in the poorhouse (not at the door, as usual). While we were afterwards in prayers at Weavers' Hall a 5 young man was seized with a violent trembling, and in a few minutes sunk down on the ground. We prayed on, and he was soon raised up again. On Easter Day was a thorough rain, so that we could not stand in the Bowling Green, nor in the open air at Hanham Mount. All I could do was to preach at Newgate, at eight in the morning 10 and two in the afternoon, and to as many as the house would hold at Hanham at eleven in the forenoon. In the afternoon we likewise gathered at a house near Rose Green as many of the neighbours as we could together, after which we had a large company at Nicholas Street, where many were wounded, and many comforted. 15

Every day this week I have been out of town, which prevented my writing sooner. Pray ye much that after I have preached to others I may not myself be a castaway.[3] I am, my dear brethren, your ever affectionate brother,

John Wesley 20

Bristol, April 26, 1739

Address: 'To Mr. James Hutton, Bookseller, Near Temple-bar, London' *Postmarks*: 'B/ris/tol', '30 AP'   *Charge*: '4'   *End* by Hutton: 'Bristol, Ap. 26, 1739'   *Source*: MorA.

To James Hutton and the
Fetter Lane Society

Bristol, April 30
1739

My dear brethren

Monday the 23rd about twenty-four of us walked to Pensford, a 25 little town five or six miles off, where a society is begun, five of whose

---

[1] Apr. 20.

[2] Wesley's diary shows that this was almost certainly Mrs. Thornhill of Baldwin Street society, whose husband William was a member of the staff of Bristol Infirmary from 1735 to 1765. Rebecca (later Scudamore) was their daughter. He must surely have been the surgeon in Corn Street to whom Cennick stated that Samuel Wathen was apprenticed (see above, p. 626 n.).   [3] See 1 Cor. 9: 27.

members were with us at Baldwin Street the Tuesday before. We sent to the minister to desire the use of the church, and after waiting some time and receiving no answer, being neither able to get into the church nor the churchyard, we began singing praise to God in the
5 street. Many people gathered about us, with whom we removed to the market-place, where from the top of a wall I called to them, in the name of our Master, 'If any man thirst, let him come unto me and drink.'[1] At four in the afternoon we met about four thousand people in another brickyard, a little nearer the city. To these I
10 declared, 'The hour is coming, and now is, when the dead shall hear the voice of the Son of man, and they that hear shall live.'[2]

The rain on Tuesday morning made them not expect me at Bath, so that we had not above a thousand or twelve hundred in the meadow. After preaching we read over the rules, and fixed two bands,
15 one of men and one of women. The men are Joseph Feachem (a man full of the Holy Ghost),[3] Mr. Bush, Mr. Cotton, and Mr. Richards (of Oxford).[4] The women are Rebecca Thomas (one of Lady Cox's servants), Sarah Bush, Grace Bond, Mary Spenser (mourning, and refusing to be comforted),[5] and Margaret Dolling. Their
20 general meeting is on Tuesday, their particular meeting on Monday evening at five o'clock.

A greyheaded old man, one Dibble, a silversmith, at eleven gladly received me into his house, where I preached on the righteousness of the scribes and Pharisees,[6] at the window of an upper room, to
25 those in the yard and street, as well as the house. At four in the afternoon I met the colliers by appointment, at a place about the middle of Kingswood called Two Mile Hill. After preaching to two or three thousand we went to the stone our brother Whitefield

---

[1] John 7: 37.   [2] John 5: 25.
[3] Acts 6: 3.

[4] Probably Thomas Richards (1717–98), the son of the Revd. Thomas Richards, vicar of Verwig and Cardigan, Wales. He matriculated at Trinity College, Oxford, in 1734, though there is no record of his graduating. On a journey with him in 1741 John Nelson spoke of him as a collegian, and Richard Viney's diary for Mar. 8, 1744, referring to 'a young student' preaching in Yorkshire, seemed to have in mind the 'Mr. Richards' named on Mar. 12. Wesley listed Richards as the second of his lay itinerant preachers to be enrolled, after Thomas Maxfield. In 1748 he taught languages (poorly) at Kingswood School for a time, and in 1749 married the housekeeper there, Mary Davey. In 1759 he left the Methodists, was ordained through the influence of the Countess of Huntingdon, and became curate of St. Sepulchre's, London, for over thirty years, dying there in 1798.

[5] See Jer. 31: 15.
[6] Matt. 5: 20.

laid.[1] I think it cannot be better placed. 'Tis just in the middle of the wood, two mile every way from either church or school. I wish he would write to me, positively and decisively, that 'for this reason' he would 'have the first school there or as near it as possible'. In the evening, at Baldwin Street, John Bush received remission 5 of sins.

I was in some doubt how to proceed. Our dear brethren, before I left London, and our brother Whitefield here, and our brother Chapman since, had conjured me to enter into no disputes, least of all concerning predestination, because this people was so deeply 10 prejudiced for it. The same was my own inclination. But this evening I received a long letter (almost a month after date) charging me roundly with 'resisting and perverting the truth as it is in Jesus' by preaching against God's decree of predestination. I had not done so yet, but I questioned whether I ought not now to declare the 15 whole counsel of God.[2] Especially since that letter had been long handed about in Bristol before it was sealed and brought to me, together with another, wherein also the writer exhorts his friends to avoid me as a false teacher. However, I thought it best to walk gently, and so said nothing this day. 20

Wed. 25.[3] I dined at Frenchay,[4] about four miles from Bristol, at Anthony Purver's,[5] a Quaker, one of much experience in the ways of God. I believe about four thousand people were present at Baptist Mills, to whom (as God enabled me) I expounded that Scripture, 'Ye have not received the spirit of bondage again unto 25 fear, but ye have received the spirit of adoption, whereby we cry, Abba, Father.'[6] At seven, the female bands meeting, four new members were proposed. One was accepted, and the rest postponed, of whom one has now shown what spirit she was of by turning a most bitter opposer. At eight, the men meeting, several new 30 members were proposed, some of whom were postponed, and eight admitted upon trial.

Thursday, 26. Preaching at Newgate on those words, 'He that believeth hath everlasting life',[7] I was led, I know not how, to

---

[1] On Apr. 2 (see p. 630 above).
[2] See Acts 20: 27.
[3] Orig., 'Wedn. 24', followed by 'Thursday, 25', and 'Friday, 26'.
[4] Orig., 'French-Hay'.
[5] Anthony Purver (1702–77), a self-educated farmer's son, who translated the whole Bible, the work being published in 1764 by Dr. John Fothergill.
[6] Rom. 8: 15. [7] See John 3: 36; 6: 47.

speak strongly and explicitly of predestination, and then to pray that
if I spake not the truth of God he would stay his hand, and work no
more among us; if this was his truth, he would 'not delay to confirm
it by signs following'.[1] Immediately the power of God fell upon us.
One, and another, and another, sunk to the earth. You might see
them dropping on all sides as thunderstruck. One cried out aloud.
I went and prayed over her, and she received joy in the Holy Ghost.[2]
A second falling into the same agony, we turned to her, and received
for her also the promise of the Father. In the evening I made the
same appeal to God, and almost before we called, he answered.
A young woman was seized with such pangs as I never saw before.
And in a quarter of an hour she had a new song in her mouth,
a thanksgiving unto our God.[3]

   This day, I being desirous to speak little, but our brother Purdy
pressing me to speak and spare not, we made four lots, and desired
our Lord to show what he would have me to do. The answer was,
'Preach and print.'[4] Let him see to the event.

   At midnight we were waked with a cry of fire. It was two doo⟨rs
off,⟩ and being soon discovered was soon extinguished.

   Friday, 27. All Newgate was in an uproar again, and two wome⟨n⟩
received the spirit of adoption,[5] to the utter astonishment of all, and
the entire conviction of some who before doubted.

   At four on Saturday five and twenty hundred (I suppose) were
at the poorhouse. My spirit was enlarged to pray for the rich that
were there especially, that our Lord would show them, they were
poor sinners. At night many were convinced of sin, and one received
remission of sins at Weavers' Hall.

   On Sunday morning (being so directed again by lot) I declared
openly for the first h[our] against 'the horrible decree',[6] before about
four thousand persons at the Bowling Green. I then went to Clifton[7]
(a little mile off) and thence to a little plain near Hanham Mount,
being desired by some of the neighbours to remove thither. About

---

   [1] See Mark 16: 20.
   [2] Rom. 14: 17.   [3] See Ps. 40: 3 (B.C.P.).
   [4] On Apr. 25 Wesley's diary recorded, 'writ upon predestination', and at noon on
Apr. 26, 'appealed to God concerning predestination'. The result was the preaching
and publication of his sermon, *Free Grace* (see *Sermons*, Vol. 4, and *Bibliog*, No. 14).
   [5] See Rom. 8: 15.
   [6] See Calvin, *Institutes*, III. xxxiii. 7, *Decretum quidem horribile fateor*—'The decree
[i.e. of predestination of some to eternal death], I admit, is dreadful'.
   [7] The curate of Clifton, the Revd. John Hodges (1698-1739), was dying, and Wesley
had been asked to supply his pulpit (see letter of May 28, 1739).

three thousand or thirty-five hundred were present. Thence I went to Clifton again. The church was more than full at the prayers and sermon, as was the churchyard at the burial that followed. From Clifton we went straight to Rose Green, where were upwards of seven thousand, and thence to the society at Gloucester Lane, where also were many that have this world's goods. Two very fine young women, who came in a chariot, stood close to the table on which I was, and patiently heard me expound on 'the desire of the flesh, the desire of the eye, and the pride of life'.[1] And one or two were seized with strong pangs, which, I hope, has before now ended in true comfort. Thence we went to our love-feast in Baldwin Street, where the spirit of love was present with us.

Praise ye the Lord, who reneweth my bodily strength. May I feel in my soul that he is my strength and my salvation![2] Your affectionate brother,

J. Wesley[3]

Address: 'To Mr. Js. Hutton, Bookseller, Near Temple-bar, London'   *Seal*: Crucifixion and 'Der Ist Mein' (fragment only)   *Postmarks*: 'B/ris/tol', '2 MA'   *Charge*: '4'   *End* by Hutton: 'Bristol, Ap. 30, 1739'   *Source*: MorA.

To James Hutton and the Fetter Lane Society

May 7, 1739,[4] Bristol

My dear brethren

We understood on Monday that the Keeper of Newgate was much offended at the cries of the people on whom the power of God came; and so was a physician, who wishes well to the cause of God, but feared there might be some fraud or delusion in the case. Today one who had been his patient and his acquaintance for many years was seized in the same manner. At first he would hardly believe his own eyes and ears; but when her pangs redoubled, so that all her bones shook, he knew not what to think, and when she revived in a moment and sang praise, he owned it was the finger of God.[5]

[1] 1 John 2: 16.   [2] See Exod. 15: 2, etc.
[3] The salutation and signature are in Purdy's hand.
[4] Orig., '1738'.   [5] Luke 11: 20.

Another that sat close to Mr. Dagge,[1] a middle-aged woman, was seized at the same time. Many observed, the tears trickled down his cheeks, and I trust he will be no more offended.

Tue. May 1. I went to the colliers in the middle of Kingswood, and prayed with them (several being in tears), in a place formerly a cockpit, near which it was agreed to build the schoolhouse, being close to the place where the stone was laid by our brother Whitefield. Many were offended at Baldwin Street in the evening, for the power of God came mightily upon us.[2] Many who were in heaviness received the comforts of the Holy One, and ten persons remission of sins. A Quaker who stood by was very angry at them, and was biting his lips and knitting his brows when the Spirit of God came upon him also, so that he fell down as one dead. We prayed over him, and he soon lifted up his head with joy, and joined with us in thanksgiving.

Wed. 2. Another mourner received comfort at Newgate. We afterwards went to a neighbouring house, to read a letter wrote against me, as a false teacher, for opposing predestination. A rigid asserter of it was present, when a young woman came in (who had received remission of sins) all in tears, and in deep anguish of spirit. She said she had been in torment all night by reasoning, and verily believed the devil had possession of her again. In the midst of our prayers she cried out, 'He is gone, he is gone! I again rejoice in God my Saviour.' Just as we rose from giving thanks another young woman reeled four or five steps, and then dropped down. We prayed with her. She is now in deep poverty of spirit, groaning day and night for a new heart.

I did not mention that one John Haydon,[3] a weaver, was quite enraged at what had occurred in Baldwin's Street, and had laboured above measure to convince all his acquaintance that it was all a delusion of the devil. We were now going home, when one met us and informed us that John Haydon was fallen raving mad. It seems he had sat down with an intention to dine, but had a mind first to end the sermon on *Salvation by Faith*. At the last page he suddenly changed colour, fell off his chair, and began screaming terribly, and beating himself against the ground. I came to him between one and

---

[1] Abel Dagge, the Keeper, a convert of Whitefield's.

[2] See Judg. 14: 6; 15: 14.

[3] John Haydon of Back Lane, Bristol, whose story, told at length in JWJ (though with his name disguised by the use of initials) offered a focal point for the sceptical anger of the critics of revival phenomena.

two, and found him on the ground, the room being full of people,
whom his wife would have kept away; but he cried out, 'No; let
them all come. Let all the world see the just judgment of God!'
Two or three were holding him as well as they could. He immediately
fixed his eyes upon me, and stretching out his arm, said, 'Ay, this is 5
he I said was a deceiver of the people. But God has overtaken me.
I said it was a delusion; but this is no delusion.' Then he roared
aloud, 'O thou devil! Thou cursed devil! Yea, thou legion of devils,
thou canst not stay in me. Christ will cast thee out. I know his work
is begun. Tear me to pieces if thou wilt; but thou canst not hurt 10
me.' He then beat himself again, against the ground, and with violent sweats and heavings of the breast strained as it were to vomit
(which, with many other symptoms I have since observed in others
at or near the time of their deliverance, much inclines me to think
the evil spirit actually dwells in everyone till he receives the Holy 15
Ghost). After we had ⟨been⟩ praying about half an hour he was set
at liberty.

⟨From⟩ him I went to Baptist Mills, where about two thousand
persons stayed, notwithstanding several showers. I testified to them
the holiness and happiness of true believers, from those words of 20
St. Peter, 'Him hath God exalted . . . to give unto Israel repentance
and remission of sins. And we are his witnesses of these things, and
so is the Holy Ghost, whom God hath given to them that believe
him.'[1] Returning to John Haydon, we found his body quite worn out,
and his voice lost, but his soul was in peace; rejoicing in hope of 25
the glory of God,[2] and full of love and the Holy Ghost.[3]

The female bands meeting at seven, and a young woman complaining of blasphemous thought, and an inability to pray, we began
praying for her. During which another young woman (Miss Cutler)[4]
fell into a strong agony, and received power in a few minutes to cry 30
out, 'My Lord and my God.'[5] The next day I visited Anthony
Purver[6] (a Quaker) at Frenchay, with whom was a Dutchman,
lately arrived from Ireland,[7] who, I verily think, is full of the Spirit,

---

[1] See Acts 5: 31–2. [2] Rom. 5: 2. [3] See Acts 6: 5.
[4] On Wednesday, Apr. 11, Mary Cutler met with the female bands, and on the 18th
was apparently admitted as a member (see pp. 632, 636 above, and JWJ).
[5] John 20: 28.
[6] See previous letter.
[7] Probably Gharret van Hassen (1695–1765), who in 1737 settled in Dublin, and as
John Garret gave Irish Methodism influential support, especially through his daughter,
Mrs. Dorothea King (see *Journal* of Friends Historical Society, III. 86).

and breathes nothing but Jesus Christ. On Friday evening, at Gloucester Lane society, a woman received remission of sins.

Sat. 5. Six Quakers, three from Ireland, one from the north, and two from Frenchay, met six of us by appointment. We prayed together, and our hearts were much enlarged towards one another. At four (being forbid to preach any more at the poorhouse), I preached at the Bowling Green to about two thousand, on those words (at the request of an unknown friend), 'Be still, and know that I am God.'[1]

Sunday the 6th. I preached in the Bowling Green to about seven thousand, on Matt. 18:3; on Hanham Mount to about three thousand on Gal. 3:22 (after a young woman had received remission of sins); at Clifton to a church-full, and many hundred in the church-yard, on Christ our wisdom, righteousness, sanctification, and redemption;[2] and at Rose Green to about five thousand, on 'The Scripture hath concluded all under sin, etc.'[3]

O my dear, dear brethren, pray that when I have preached to others I may not myself be a castaway![4]

JW[5]

Address: 'To Mr. J. Hutton, Bookseller, Near Temple-bar, London'   *Post-marks*: 'B/ris/tol', '11 MA'   *Charge*: '4'   *End* by Hutton: 'Bristol, May 7, 1739'   *Source*: MorA.

To James Hutton

May 8, 1739

Dear Jemmy

You seem to forget what I told you: (1), that being unwilling to speak against predestination we appealed to God, and I was by lot commanded to preach and print[6] against it; (2), that the very first time I preached against it explicitly the power of God so fell on those that heard as we have never known before, either in Bristol, or London, or elsewhere. Yet generally I speak on faith, remission of sins, and the gift of the Holy Ghost.

Our brother Seward promised to give us five hundred or a

---

[1] Ps. 46: 10.
[3] Gal. 3: 22.
[5] The initials are in Purdy's hand.

[2] See 1 Cor. 1: 30.
[4] See 1 Cor. 9: 27.
[6] See p. 640 above.

thousand Homilies[1] to give away. These are better than all our sermons put together. Adieu!

[Added by John Purdy]

Brother Hutton, you are desired to send our brother Wesley six of Dr. James Knight's sermons,[2] vicar of St. Sepulchre's, as soon as 5 you can.

It would be better to send our brother Wesley['s] sermons on faith.[3] They are the best to lay the foundation.

Address: 'To my D[ea]r Brother Hutton'   *Seal*: a circular smear of wax, scraped   *End* by Hutton: 'Bristol, 1st. Sermon on Predestination'   *Source*: MorA.

To the Revd. Samuel Wesley, Jun.[4]

Bristol, May 10, 1739

Dear brother   10

The having abundance of work upon my hands is only *a* cause of my not writing sooner. *The* cause was rather my unwillingness to continue an unprofitable dispute.

The gospel promises to you and me, and our children, and all that are afar off, even as many of those whom the Lord our God shall 15 call,[5] as are not disobedient unto the heavenly vision,[6] 'the witness of God's spirit with their spirit that they are the children of God';[7] that they are *now*, at this hour, all accepted in the beloved;[8] but it witnesses *not, that they shall be*. It is an assurance of *present* salvation only. Therefore, not necessarily perpetual, neither irreversible. 20

I am one of many witnesses of this matter of fact, that God does now make good this his promise daily, very frequently during a representation (how made I know not, but not to the outward eye)

---

[1] Wesley's *Doctrine of Salvation*, etc.; see p. 621 n. above.
[2] See p. 581 n. above.
[3] *A Sermon on Salvation by Faith* (1738), and *Free Grace* (1739).
[4] Answering his brother's of Apr. 16. From the evidence of Wesley's diary it was actually begun on May 9.
[5] See Acts 2: 39.   [6] Acts 26: 19.
[7] See Rom. 8: 16.   [8] Eph. 1: 6.

of Christ either hanging on the cross, or standing on the right hand
of God. And this I know to be of God, because from that hour
the person so affected is a new creature, both as to his inward
tempers and outward life. Old things are passed away, and all things
5 become new.[1]

A very late instance of this I will give you. While we were praying
at a society here on Tuesday 1st instant, the power of God (so I call
it) came so mightily among us that one, and another, and another
fell down as thunderstruck. In that hour many that were in deep
10 anguish of spirit were all filled with peace and joy. Ten persons till
then in sin, doubt, and fear, found such a change that sin had no
more dominion over them; and instead of the spirit of fear they
are now filled with that of love, and joy, and a sound mind.[2] A
Quaker who stood by was very angry at them, and was biting his
15 lips and knitting his brows when the Spirit of God came upon him
also, so that he fell down as one dead. We prayed over him, and he
soon lifted up his head with joy, and joined with us in thanksgiving.[3]

A bystander, one John Haydon, was quite enraged at this, and
being unable to deny something supernatural in it, laboured beyond
20 measure to convince all his acquaintance that it was a delusion of
the devil.[4] I was met in the street the next day by one who informed
me that John Haydon was fallen raving mad. It seems he had sat
down to dinner, but wanted first to make an end of a sermon he was
reading. At the last page he suddenly changed colour, fell off his
25 chair, and began screaming terribly, and beating himself against the
ground. I found him on the floor, the room being full of people,
whom his wife would have kept away; but he cried out, 'No; let
them all come; let all the world see the just judgment of God.' Two
or three were holding him as well as they could. He immediately
30 fixed his eyes on me, and said, 'Ay, this is he I said deceived the
people; but God hath overtaken me. I said it was a delusion of the
devil; but this is no delusion.' Then he roared aloud, 'O thou devil!
Thou cursed devil! Yea, thou legion of devils! Thou canst not stay
in me. Christ will cast thee out. I know his work is begun. Tear me
35 to pieces, if thou wilt. But thou canst not hurt me.' He then beat
himself again, and groaning again, with violent sweats, and heaving

---

[1] See 2 Cor. 5: 17.   [2] 2 Tim. 1: 7.

[3] This incident took place on May 1, but the second sentence appears to come
from the letter of Apr. 30 (see pp. 640, 642). The conflation may have been a not unusual
error by Wesley, or Priestley's in reproducing this letter.

[4] See letter of May 7 (pp. 642–3 above), to which some details are added.

of the breast. We prayed with him, and God put a new song in his mouth.[1] The words were, which he pronounced with a clear, strong voice: 'This is the Lord's doing, and it is marvellous in our eyes. This is the day which the Lord hath made: we will rejoice and be glad in it.[2] Blessed be the Lord God of Israel, from this time forth for evermore.'[3] I called again an hour after. We found his body quite worn out, and his voice lost. But his soul was full of joy and love, rejoicing in hope of the glory of God.[4]

I am now in as good health (thanks be to God) as I ever was since I remember, and I believe shall be so as long as I live; for I do not expect to have a lingering death. The reasons that induce me to think I shall not live long old are such as you would not apprehend to be of any weight. I am under no concern on this head. Let my Master see to it.

O may the God of love be with you and my sister more and more! I am, dear brother, your ever affectionate brother,

John Wesley

Address: 'To the Rev. Mr. Wesley, at Tiverton, Devon'   *Source*: Priestley, pp. 101–4.

To James Hutton and the Fetter Lane Society

[May 14, 1739]

My dear brethren

On Monday the 7th instant about twelve of us met at six in the morning at our room in Baldwin Street. Others came after, some of whom were employed till six in the evening in intercession, prayer, and thanksgiving.

About eight I was preparing to go to Pensford (the minister having sent me word I was welcome to preach in either of his churches), when a messenger brought me the following note:

Sir

Our minister, being informed you are beside yourself, does not care you should preach in any of his churches.[5]

[1] See Ps. 40: 3.   [2] Ps. 118: 23–4 (B.C.P.).
[3] See Ps. 113: 2.   [4] Rom. 5: 2.
[5] Wesley's *Journal* for May 7 reproduced the same letter, but reading, 'having been informed'.

We found, however, a very convenient place on Priestdown, near Publow, half a mile from Pensford, where was an attentive, serious congregation. But many of them appeared not a little amazed at hearing that strange doctrine, that 'Christ is made of God unto us
5 wisdom, and righteousness, and sanctification, and redemption.'[1]

About four thousand were afterwards at the brickyard, whom I exhorted to 'become as little children'.[2] After preaching at Newgate the next morning I set out for Bath. We were turned out of the ground where I used to preach. But God opened the heart of
10 a Quaker (one Richard Merchant)[3] to offer me his ground, where I preached 'Christ our wisdom'[4] to a thousand or fifteen hundred people. Afterwards he called me aside and said, 'My friend, deal freely with me. I have much money, and it may be thou hast little. Tell me what thou wilt have.' I accepted his love, after expounding
15 at Mr. Dibble's[5] window, to many in the house and many out of it. O pray ye for the soul of Richard Merchant!

On Wednesday [the] 9th, after the service at Newgate, we took possession of the ground where the room is to be built.[6] We have also articled to pay the workmen about 160 pounds as soon as it is
20 finished. As to the money, God will see to that. At four I was much enlarged at Baptist Mills in recommending the childlike temper. The company was about two thousand or twenty-five hundred, our usual congregation there. It was this evening agreed at our society that the leaders of the bands meet together at 5.30[7] every Wednesday
25 evening. The next day several curious persons being at Nicholas Street, and a fine lady among the rest, I was desired, in a note given me, to pray for her; and she was 'almost persuaded to be a Christian'.[8]

Fri. 11. As we were going to the second society in the evening we
30 were desired to call upon a young woman who was in the agonies

---

[1] See 1 Cor. 1: 30.   [2] Matt. 18: 3.

[3] For Richard Merchant (or Marchant, *c.* 1666–1739) see *Journal* of Friends' Historical Society, VIII. 82. It was probably on Richard Merchant's field (where later the Circus was built) that Wesley had his well-known encounter with Beau Nash, after which the fashionable ladies flocked into Merchant's parlour in hope of being presented to Wesley (see letter of June 7). On July 17 Merchant also refused his land to Wesley.

[4] From 1 Cor. 1: 30, as at Priestdown on the previous day.

[5] The old silversmith, who appears frequently in Wesley's diary as the central figure in early Bath Methodism (see p. 638).

[6] The New Room in the Horsefair, which became the headquarters of Bristol Methodism.

[7] Orig., '5 ½', as Wesley normally expressed points of time in his diary.

[8] Cf. Acts 26: 28.

of despair. With much difficulty we brought her to the society, where almost as soon as we began praying for her the enemy was cast out, and she was filled with peace and joy in believing.[1]

Sat. 12. Mr. Labbé,[2] who had been often in doubt, chiefly from the objections his wife made, was quite astonished at Newgate; for God overtook her there, so that she knew she was accepted in the Beloved.[3] Thence we went and laid the first stone of our house, with the voice of praise and thanksgiving. Three or four thousand were present at the Bowling Green this afternoon; and at Weavers' Hall in the evening, in answer to our prayers that our Lord would then show whether 'he was willing that all men should be saved',[4] three persons immediately sunk down, and in a short time were raised up and set at liberty.

Sunday, 13th. About six thousand were at the Bowling Green, where I explained the beginning of the thirteenth of the First Corinthians. At Hanham I ended my sermon on 'The Scripture hath concluded all under sin', etc.,[5] to about four thousand, our usual congregation. The church at Clifton was much too small for us in the afternoon; but those who were without could hear as well as they within. About six thousand were at Rose Green, where I was desired by a young woman to go into her chariot, whom I found quite awakened, and longing for Christ, after having been for some years the finest, gayest thing in Bristol.[6] She came with me to

---

[1] See Rom. 15: 13.

[2] A surgeon in Castle Street, Bristol, friendly to the Methodists, who frequently appears in the journals and correspondence of both John and Charles Wesley, and also of Howell Harris. On May 15, 1739 Wesley 'christened Sara Labbé', i.e. Mrs. Labbé (see letter of May 28). Mr. and Mrs. Labbé seem to have been raised as Baptists, and on Sept. 24, 1740, he threatened to separate from the Wesleys because they taught universal redemption and perfection, which to him were 'doctrines of devils' (see letter from Charles Wesley, Sept. 27, 1740).

[3] Eph. 1: 6.   [4] See 1 Tim. 2: 4.   [5] Gal. 3: 22.

[6] The diary shows that this was Miss S. Burdock (whom on May 29 he names 'Sally', on June 25, 'Suky'). She was in frequent touch with him during this summer, and from June 4 to Oct. 22 at least eighteen letters passed between them, in one of which she confided in a postscript, 'I believe I love you as well as I do my papa.' She asked Wesley to keep their correspondence secret, for fear of her parents, and eventually asked for the return of her letters, in case he was 'taken away suddenly' and they fell into the wrong hands. Wesley seems to have returned them on Aug. 11, after getting John Purdy and John Cennick to make transcripts for him. (These are still extant, though none of the originals, or copies of his own letters have survived.) Her father did find out that she was consorting with the Methodists, and in her letter of June 23 she told Wesley that he had forbidden her to converse any more with Mrs. Thornhill, at whose home she had occasionally met Wesley, as also at Mrs. Norman's. On July 13, 1744, Wesley's sister Hetty wrote to him, sending greetings from 'Mrs. Burdock and Miss'.

Gloucester Lane society, where God overtook her three or four weeks ago. Here a young woman, after strong pangs, received the gift of the Holy Ghost.

My dear brethren, pray much for, and write, all of you, to, your
5 weak, but loving, brother,

John Wesley

Dear Jemmy

Send me fifty more *Hymns* immediately.[1] I give the Homilies, and sell the Sermons on *Free Grace*. Is that right?[2] Adieu!
10   B[rother] W[esley's] things is left at the Inn by Hobburn bridge.[3]

Address: 'To Mr. James Hutton, Bookseller, Nigh Temple Bar, London' (in the hand of John Purdy)   *Postmarks*: '[CHIPP?]/ENHAM', '16 MA'   *Charge*: '4'   *Source*: MorA.

To James Hutton and the
Fetter Lane Society

Bristol, 28 May, 1739

My dear brethren
On Sunday the 13th I began expounding the thirteenth of the First of Corinthians at the Bowling Green. About six thousand were
15 present. More than half that number were at Hanham Mount, to whom I explained 'the promise by faith of Jesus Christ',[4] as I did to about six thousand at Rose Green, after I came from Clifton, where it pleased our good God to give me a strong mouth in speaking on those words, 'He that drinketh of this water shall thirst again.
20 But whoso drinketh of the water that I shall give him shall never thirst; but the water which I shall give him shall be in him a well of water, springing up into everlasting life.'[5]
Monday, 14. About five thousand were at the brickyard, whom I

---

[1] *Hymns and Sacred Poems*, which had been published in London in March (see *Bibliog*, No. 13). Cf. below, p. 656 n., for the use of the volume in Bristol.
[2] Seward had underwritten the Homilies, but the others had to be paid for out of the sales (cf. May 8 above).
[3] This is added on the flap in Purdy's hand.
[4] Gal. 3: 22.   [5] John 4: 13-14.

exhorted to be 'as little children'.[1] Three mourners were comforted this evening, as was one the night before.

Mrs. Labbé (educated as an Anabaptist) was baptized the next day, and filled with the Holy Ghost. At three in the afternoon I preached at Two Mile Hill, on those words of Isaiah (upon which the book opened), . . .[2] Afterwards we went to look out a proper place for the school, and at last pitched on one between the London and Bath Road. Soon after five I began expounding at the Back Lane, on the righteousness of the scribes and Pharisees;[3] but the house being too small, I stood in a little garden at one end of the lane, so that all who were in the lane, or at the windows, or on the adjoining walls (about a thousand), could hear well. The power of God fell on several of those that heard, one or two of whom were soon comforted, as were three others at the society in Baldwin Street. About ten, two that had before been comforted, but were in heaviness again, came to Mrs. Grevil.[4] We prayed, and they were again filled with peace and joy in believing.[5]

Wed. 16. The rain prevented many from coming to Baptist Mills, but twelve or fifteen hundred stayed. While I was taking occasion from those words of Isaiah, chapter 53rd, 5th and 6th verses, to call poor sinners to Christ, a young man began beating his breast, and strongly crying out for mercy. During our prayer God put a new song in his mouth.[6] Some mocked, and others believed. Particularly a maid-servant of Baptist Mills, who went home full of anguish, and is now full of peace and joy in the Holy Ghost.

The portion of Scripture which came (in turn) to be explained today at Newgate was the former part of the 7th of St. John. The words I was led chiefly to insist on were, 'The world cannot hate you. But me it hateth, because I testify of it that its deeds are evil!'[7] And, 'There was murmuring concerning him among the multitude. For some said, "He is a good man." Others said, "Nay, but he deceiveth the people."'[8] When I was going out a message was delivered me, that the sheriffs had ordered, I 'should preach there for the future but once a week'.

---

[1] Matt. 18: 3.

[2] Wesley left a line blank, obviously intending to insert the text, only to find that he had not recorded it in his diary.

[3] See Matt. 5: 20.

[4] On this and some other occasions Wesley spells her name 'Grevile'.

[5] See Rom. 15: 13. [6] See Ps. 40: 3. [7] See John 7: 7.

[8] See John 7: 12.

I called on Thursday at the house of one who said [I] had driven his daughter mad, and indeed as such they used her, confining her, and obliging her to take physic. He would not suffer me to come in.[1] But we went to prayers for him, and in two days God turned his
5 heart, so that he has now set her at liberty.

On Friday I began preaching in a large, convenient room, which held near as many as the chapel at Newgate; which I did for three days.[2] And then the Mayor and Aldermen (to whom the tenant was in debt) sent and put a padlock on the door.

10 We had a sweet day in Baldwin Street on Saturday. In the afternoon about two thousand were at the Bowling Green. I wish you would constantly send me extracts of all your foreign letters, to be read on our intercession-day.[3] At Weavers' Hall a young woman first, and then a boy (about fourteen years old), were deeply bruised,
15 and afterwards comforted.

At the Bowling Green on Sunday we had about seven thousand. To two thousand at Hanham I explained the same Scripture (1 Cor. 13). Seeing at Clifton church many of the great and rich, my heart was enlarged and my mouth opened toward them. My
20 Testament opened on those words, 'I came not to call the righteous, but sinners to repentance.'[4] The power of the Lord was indeed present to heal them!

His 'sending forth lightning with the rain'[5] did not hinder about fifteen hundred poor sinners from staying with me at Rose Gree⟨n.⟩
25 Our Scripture was, 'It is the glorious God that maketh the thunder⟨.⟩ The voice of the Lord is mighty in operation; the voice of the Lord is a glorious voice!'[6] In the evening God spake to the hearts of ⟨them⟩ that were sore vexed, and there ensued a sweet calm.

Monday, 21. The minister of Clifton died. O what has God done
30 by adding those four weeks to his life![7] In the afternoon, as I was enforcing those words, 'Be still, and know that I am God!'[8] he began

---

[1] Wesley's diary reads, 'at Mr. Godly's, in talk, religious, to Miss Rachel at the window'; on the 11th he had recorded, 'Gloucester Lane, Miss Godly!'.

[2] Diary, 'preached at the Dial'.

[3] The Moravians observed intercession days for their foreign work, when letters of missionaries were read, and examples of such collections of letters are extant in the Moravian Archives, London, including one group for 1740.

[4] Luke 5: 32.   [5] See Ps. 135: 7 (B.C.P.).

[6] Ps. 29: 3–4 (B.C.P.).

[7] Wesley had been supplying the Clifton pulpit for the Revd. John Hodges for three weeks, but the comment remains obscure.

[8] Ps. 46: 10.

to make bare his arm, in the eyes of twenty-five hundred witnesses.
One and another and another were struck to the earth, and in less
than an hour seven knew the Lord, and gave thanks. I was interrupted in my speaking on the same subject at Nicholas Street by
the cries of one that was cut to the heart. I then recapitulated what 5
God had done among us already in proof of his free love to all men.
Another dropped down, close to one who was a rigid asserter of the
opposite doctrine. While he stood astonished at her cries and groans,
a little boy standing by was seized in the same manner. A young man
who was near smiled at this, and sunk down as one dead, but soon 10
began to roar out, and beat himself against the ground, so that six
men could scarce hold him.[1] I never saw anyone (except John
Haydon) so torn by the evil one. Before he was delivered many others
began to cry out, so that all the room (and indeed all the street) was
in an uproar. And it was near ten before the Spirit of life set some 15
of them free from the law of sin and death.[2]

A Presbyterian (who a little before was much offended) took me
home with him to supper.[3] Whence I was called in haste to a woman
who had run out of the society for fear she should expose herself.
But the power of God went with her, so that she continued in the 20
same agony till we prayed, and she found rest in Christ. We then
besought our Lord [for] one that was sick in the same house, and her
soul was straightway healed. About twelve we were importuned to
visit one more. She had only one struggle after we came, and then
was comforted. I think twenty-nine, in all, were accepted in the 25
Beloved this day.

Brethren, pray for [me]. Adieu!

Address: 'To Mr. James Hutton, Book-seller Nigh Temple Barr, London'
(in the hand of John Purdy)   *Postmarks*: 'B/ris/tol', '30 MA'   *Charge*: '4'
End by Hutton: 'Bristol, May 28, 1739'   *Source*: MorA.

[1] The *Journal* adds: 'His name was Thomas Maxfield', i.e. the first layman whom
Wesley accepted as a full-time itinerant preacher.
[2] Rom. 8: 2.
[3] Diary, 'Mr. Page'.

To James Hutton and the
Fetter Lane Society

Bristol, June 4, 1739

My dear brethren

Tuesday 22nd, about a thousand were present at Bath, and several fine, gay things among them, whom I exhorted in St. Paul's words, 'Awake, thou that sleepest, and arise from the dead, and Christ shall give thee light!'[1] The next morning I was sent for to the young woman whose relations had confined her as mad.[2] They now agreed she should go where she would, and seem themselves 'not far from the kingdom of God'.[3]

I preached to about two thousand on Wednesday at Baptist Mills, on 'Hear what the unjust judge saith'.[4] In the evening the female bands admitted seven women on trial, and ten children. And Elizabeth Cutler, and six other women, having been on trial their month, were by lot fixed in their several bands.

At eight we received into our society (after the month's trial), Jonathan Reeves[5] and six others, who at the love-feast on the 27th instant were by lot fixed in their bands. We then received upon trial John Haydon and eight other men, and Thomas Hamilton (aged fourteen) with four other children.

Thur. 24. We breakfasted at Richard Champion's,[6] where were eight or nine other Quakers. We had a mild conference on justification by faith alone, concluded with prayer, and both met and parted in love. At three I preached again on Priestdown near Publow, to a larger congregation than before, on 'The chastisement of our peace was upon him, and by his stripes we are healed.'[7]

On Friday I preached (the first time) at the Fishponds, on the edge

---

[1] Eph. 5: 14.

[2] Rachel Godly; see previous letter. The diary reads, '8.45 at Mrs. Godly's, religious talk, tea, 10.30'.

[3] Mark 12: 34.   [4] Luke 18: 6.

[5] Jonathan Reeves became one of Wesley's itinerant preachers, was ordained as a clergyman of the Church of England, and served as the first chaplain of the Magdalen Hospital, London (1758–64), and for the last eighteen years before his death in 1787 was lecturer of the parish of West Ham, in which he succeeded the notorious Dr. William Dodd upon his resignation. He was also joint lecturer in Whitechapel.

[6] Richard Champion, a Bristol merchant, probably the uncle of Richard Champion (1743–91), a leading figure in Bristol china manufacture.

[7] See Isa. 53: 5.

of Kingswood, about two mile from Bristol, on the same words, to about a thousand souls. The next morning one came to us in deep despair. We prayed together an hour, and he went away in peace. About two thousand (as is usual on Saturdays) were at the Bowling Green. To whom, and to about six thousand on Sunday morning, I farther explained the great law of love.[1] To about twenty-five hundred at Hanham I preached on Isaiah 53: 5-6; at Rose Green to upwards of ten thousand on 'Ye know not what manner of spirit ye are of; for the Son of man is not come to destroy men's lives, but to save them.'[2] At the society in the evening, at Gloucester Lane, eleven were cut to the heart, and soon after comforted.

Monday 28, I began preaching in the morning at Weavers' Hall, where two persons received remission of sins; as did seven in the afternoon at the brickyard, before several thousand witnesses, and ⟨ten⟩ at Baldwin Street in the evening, of whom two were children.

On Tuesday in the afternoon I preached at Two Mile Hill, to about a thousand of the colliers; and at five expounded to about the same number in the Back Lane, at John Haydon's door. The next morning a young woman (late a Quaker) was baptized, and filled with the Holy Ghost. In the afternoon I (unknowingly) fell in with a famous infidel, a champion of the unfaithful in these parts.[3] He was shocked, desired I would pray for him, and promised to pray earnestly himself that God would show him the right way to serve him.

We went from him to Baptist Mills. Two or three thousand were present, on whom I enforced those words, on which my Testament opened, 'And all the people which heard him, and the publicans, justified God . . . But the Pharisees and lawyers rejected the counsel of God against themselves.'[4]

On Holy Thursday, many of us went to Kings Weston Hill, four or five miles from Bristol. As we were sitting on the grass two gentlemen went by, and by way of jest sent up many persons to us from the neighbouring villages, to whom therefore I took occasion to speak on those words, 'Thou hast ascended up on high, thou hast led captivity captive', etc.[5] In the evening, our landlady in Baldwin Street not permitting us to meet there any more, we had our second society at Weavers' Hall; where I preached the next morning also.

---

[1] ? Luke 10: 27, etc.   [2] Luke 9: 55-6.

[3] Wesley's diary mentions Whitehead (possibly the John Whitehead who had been converted on Friday morning) and Mr. Pitts, the most probable person. The suggestion that the infidel was Dr. William Oliver (1695-1764) of Bath seems unlikely.

[4] Luke 7: 29-30.   [5] Ps. 68: 18.

In the afternoon I was at a new brickyard, where were twelve or fifteen hundred. The rain was so violent on Saturday that our congregation in the Bowling Green consisted of only nine hundred or a thousand. But in the morning we had about seven thousand,
5 to whom I described (in concluding the subject) a truly charitable man.

At Hanham were about three thousand, to whom I explained those words, 'That every mouth may be stopped, and all the world guilty before God.'[1] The same I again insisted on at Rose Green,
10 to (I believe) eight or nine thousand. We could not meet in the evening at Nicholas Street. But we made shift to do so in the shell of our schoolroom, without and within which (I suppose) about two thousand or twenty-five hundred were present. We had a glorious beginning. The Scripture that came in turn to be read was, 'Marvel
15 not if the world hate you.'[2] We sung, 'Arm of the Lord, awake, awake.'[3] 'And God, even our own God, gave us his blessing!'[4]

Farewell in the Lord, my dear brethren; and love one another!

Address: 'To Mr Hutton, Bookseller, Near Temple-bar, London'   *Postmarks*: 'B/ris/tol', '6 IV'   *Charge*: '4'   *End* by Hutton: 'Bristol, June 4, 1739'   *Source*: MorA.

To James Hutton and the Fetter Lane Society

Bristol, June 7, 1739

My dear brethren
20   After I came from preaching at Weavers' Hall on Monday, many came to advise me, in great sincerity, not to go to the brickyard in the afternoon, because of some terrible things that were to be done there if I did. This report brought many thither of what they call the better sort, so that it added a thousand, at least, to the usual
25 audience. On whom I enforced (as not my choice, but the providence of God, directed me) those words of Isaiah, 'Fear thou not,

---

[1] See Rom. 3: 19.   [2] 1 John 3: 13.
[3] See John and Charles Wesley, *Hymns and Sacred Poems* (1739), pp. 222–3, based upon Isa. 51: 9. This volume had been published in March, and on May 14 Wesley asked Hutton for 'fifty more *Hymns* immediately'.
[4] See Ps. 67: 6 (B.C.P.).

for I am with thee: be not dismayed, for I am thy God: I will strengthen thee, yea, I will help thee; yea, I will uphold thee with the right hand of my righteousness.'[1] My nose began bleeding[2] in the midst of the sermon, but presently stopped, so that I went on without interruption, and the power of God fell on all, so that the scoffers stood looking one on another, but none opened his mouth.

All Bath on Tuesday was big with expectation of what a great man[3] was to do to me there, and I was much entreated not to preach, 'because no one knew what might happen'. By this report also I gained (I believe) a thousand new hearers of the rich and great of this world. I told them plainly, 'The Scripture had concluded them all under sin',[4] high and low, rich and poor, one with another. They appeared not a little surprised, and sinking apace into seriousness, when their champion appeared, and having forced his way through the people, asked by what authority I did these things. I answered, 'By the authority of Jesus my Master, conveyed to me by the (now) Archbishop of Canterbury.'[5] He said it was contrary to the Act of Parliament; there was an Act of Parliament against conventicles. I replied, 'The conventicles there mentioned were seditious meetings', but there was no such here. He said, Yes, it was—for I frighted people out of their wits. I asked if he had ever heard me preach; if not, how he could judge of what he never heard. He said, 'By common report', for he knew my character. I then asked, 'Pray, sir, are you a justice of peace, or the mayor of this city?' Answer: No, I am not. Question: 'Why then, sir, pray by what authority do you ask me these things?' (Here he paused a little, and I went on), 'Give me leave, sir, to ask, Is not your name Nash?' Answer: Sir, my name is Nash. W[esley]: Why then, sir, I trust common report is no good evidence of truth. (Here the laugh turned full against him, so that he looked about and could scarce recover. Then a bystander said), 'Sir, let an old woman answer him.' Then turning to Mr. Nash she said, 'Sir, if you ask what we come here for, we come for the food of our souls. You care for your body. We care for our souls.' He replied not one word, but turned and walked away.

---

[1] Isa. 41: 10.

[2] For Wesley's nose-bleeding cf. letter of Sept. 23, 1723.

[3] Richard ('Beau') Nash (1674–1761), the master of ceremonies and nicknamed 'the King of Bath'.   [4] See Gal. 3: 22.

[5] Wesley had been ordained both deacon and priest by John Potter when he was Bishop of Oxford, whence he had been translated to Canterbury in 1737.

We immediately began praying for him, and then for all the despisers. As we returned, they hollowed and hissed us along the streets, but when any of them asked, Which is he? and I answered, 'I am he', they were immediately silent. Ten or twelve fine ladies
5 followed me into the passage of Richard Merchant's house. I turned back to them, and told them, I supposed what they wanted was to look at me, which they were very welcome to do. Perceiving them then to be more serious, I added, 'I do not expect the rich of this world to hear me. For I speak plain truth, a thing you know little
10 of, and do not desire to know.' A few words more passed between us, and I hope not in vain.

Wed. 6. Two men and one woman were baptized. About twenty-five hundred were at Baptist Mills, to whom I explained the ninth of St. John. In the evening, after our meeting in Baldwin Street,
15 I went (in obedience to God's command by lot) to the house of Mrs. Cooper, the supposed prophetess.[1] Her agitations were nothing near so violent as those of Mary Plewit are.[2] She prayed awhile (as under the hand of God) and then spoke to me for above half an hour. What spirit she spoke by I know not. The words were good. Some
20 of them were these: 'Thou art yet in darkness. But yet a little while, and I will rend the veil, and thou shalt see the King in his beauty.' I felt no power while she spoke. Appearances are against her. But I judge nothing before the time.

On Thursday, after exhorting the little society at Pensford (who
25 stand as a rock, continually battered, but not shaken), I went to Priestdown, where we had a larger company than before. I preached on, 'What must I do to be saved?'[3] It rained hard, but none went away except one young woman, who came again in a few minutes. In the midst of the prayer two men (who came for that purpose)
30 began singing a ballad. After a few mild words (for I saw none that

---

[1] When the revocation of the Edict of Nantes in 1685 removed the concessions made to French Protestants they sought refuge in many parts of Europe, and many Huguenot communities developed in England. The fanatical Camisards who revolted against Louis XIV during the first decade of the eighteenth century similarly came over, bringing with them many emotional excesses, so that the 'French Prophets' were shunned by most religious people. Bristol was one of their strongholds, and Mrs. Cooper one of their representatives, none of whom attracted more than sporadic attention. Wesley warned the Methodists against them, even though the revival phenomena evinced among his own followers this year were very similar to the practices of the French Prophets (cf. letter of July 2, 1739).

[2] A French Prophetess whom Wesley visited in London on Jan. 28, 1739 (see JWJ).

[3] Acts 16: 30.

were angry) we began singing a Psalm, which utterly put them to
silence. We then prayed for them, and they were quite confounded.
I offered them books, but they could not read. I trust this will be
a day much to be remembered by them, for the loving-kindness of
the Lord.   5

My brethren, be meek and lowly; be wise, but not prudent. Stir
up the gift that is in you,[1] by keeping close together. Love one
another, and be ye thankful you are much on the heart, as well as
in the prayers, of your affectionate brother in Christ,

John Wesley 10

Jemmy Hutton, if I have not fifty more *Hymns* next Friday, I will
not thank you.

Where are the twelve Haliburtons,[2] and the Nalson's *Sermons*,[3]
which Mr. Seward writes me word he ordered you to send me, with
twenty *Hymns*, on his account?   15

June 10, 1739   O Jemmy, Jemmy!

Address: 'To Mr. Hutton, Bookseller Near Temple-bar, London'   *Postmarks*:
'B/ris/tol', '15 IV'   *Charge*: '4'   *End* by Hutton: 'Bristol, June 7, 1739'
Source: MorA.

---

[1] See 2 Tim. 1: 6.

[2] In the Spring of 1739 Wesley had published *An Abstract of the Life and Death of
the Reverend Learned and Pious Mr. Tho. Halyburton* (1674-1712), with a recommenda-
tory epistle by George Whitefield (see *Bibliog*, No. 12). Wesley greatly admired the
piety of this Presbyterian divine.

[3] *Twenty Sermons on Several Subjects*, by the Revd. Valentine Nalson (1641-1724),
Prebendary of York. The first edition appeared in 1724, Wesley read it in 1734,
frequently commended the volume, and made extracts in later years for his *A.M.*

To the Revd. Charles Wesley[1]

Bristol, June 23,[2] 1739

Dear brother

My answer to them which trouble me is this:

God commands me to do good unto all men,[3] to instruct the ignorant, reform
5 the wicked, confirm the virtuous.

Man commands me not to do this in another's parish; that is, in effect, not
to do it at all.

If it be just to obey man rather than God,[4] judge ye.

'But' (say they) 'it is just that you "submit yourself to every ordinance of
10 man, for the Lord's sake".'[5]

True—to every ordinance of man which is not contrary to the command
of God.

But if any man (bishop, or other) ordain that I shall not do what God
commands me to do, to submit to that ordinance would be to obey man rather
15 than God.

And to do this I have both an ordinary call and an extraordinary.

My ordinary call is my ordination by the bishop: 'Take thou
authority to preach the Word of God.'

My extraordinary call is witnessed by the works God doth by my
20 ministry, which prove[6] that he is with me of a truth in this exercise
of my office.

Perhaps this might be better expressed in another way.[7] God bears
witness in an *extraordinary manner* that my *thus exercising* my
ordinary call is well-pleasing in his sight.[8]

---

[1] Charles Wesley also had begun to preach in the open air, on May 29, 1739, in a
farmer's field, and had been present on June 14 while John Wesley preached on Blackheath for Whitefield during a visit to London. A basic ecclesiastical problem about
field-preaching, of course, was that it implied preaching in another man's parish, for in
effect every acre was a part of some parish (cf. pp. 615–16 above). The strong scruples that
Charles Wesley retained were clearly discussed during John Wesley's visit, which led to
John Wesley sending this brief apologia. Meantime matters had been brought to a
head by Whitefield's urging Charles to follow his brother's example in London. Charles
took the plunge before the letter arrived, preaching on Sunday, June 24, to about ten
thousand hearers in Moorfields. He added the comment, 'My load was gone, and all my
doubts and scruples'.

[2] Wesley first wrote '24', then superimposed '3' over the '4'.

[3] See Gal. 6: 10.
[4] See Acts 5: 29.
[5] Cf. 1 Pet. 2: 13.
[6] Orig., 'evidence'.
[7] Orig., 'manner'.

[8] Heb. 13: 21. For the possible influence of Richard Hooker's *Laws of Ecclesiastical
Polity* on this view see Frank Baker, *John Wesley and the Church of England* (London,
Epworth Press, 1970), p. 64.

But what if a bishop forbids this? I do not say as St. Cyprian, *Populus a scelerato antistite separare se debet.*[1]

But I say, God being my helper,[2] I will obey him still. And if I suffer for it, his will be done . . .

Address: 'To [the remainder of the sheet is missing]'   *Postmarks*: 'B/ris/tol', '25 IV'   *End* by CW: 'B.'s Apology, June 1739' and 'J.W., Jun. 25, 1739'
Source: MA, imperfect, lacking half of pp. 3–4, comprising close of letter and major portion of the address.

From the Revd. George Whitefield[3]

London, June 25th, 1739   5

Honoured sir

I wrote my last before I saw your kind letter. I thank you for it, and hereafter shall, by the divine assistance, observe your caution.

I suspend my judging of brother Wathen's and Cennick's behaviour till I am better acquainted with the circumstances of their proceeding. I think there's a   10 great difference between them and Howell Harris. He has offered himself thrice for Holy Orders. Him therefore and our friends at Cambridge I shall encourage. Others I cannot countenance in acting in so public a manner. The consequences of beginning to teach too soon will be exceeding bad. Brother Ingham is of my opinion.   15

I cannot think it right in you, honoured sir, to give so much encouragement to those convulsions which people have been thrown into under your ministry.

[1] See Cyprian, *Epistola*, LXVII. 3, 'plebs . . . a peccatore praeposito separare se debet', which translates into roughly the same English—'a people ought to separate itself from a sinful overseer'. (Clearly Wesley was correctly remembering the sentiment, and translating it back into his own Latin. Strangely enough, in his letter of June 20, 1755, he retained the same word, 'antistite' instead of 'praeposito', suggesting that here it meant, not bishop, but 'the minister of a parish'.)

[2] B.C.P., Adult Baptism, Answer 4.

[3] From the evidence of his diary Wesley furnished summaries of his Bristol ministry not only to Hutton and the members of the Fetter Lane society, but to Whitefield who had originally urged him to take over this work. Letters to him are noted on Apr. 18, May 5 and 16, June 3, 20, and 23, none of which are extant. From the Gloucester area Whitefield had moved to London on Apr. 25, beginning a successful open-air ministry there, making preaching excursions into neighbouring towns, and preparing for his return to Georgia. When John Wesley visited London June 11–19 Whitefield introduced him to his preaching arena at Blackheath. This letter apparently answers Wesley's of June 23. To a letter from Charles, Whitefield had replied on June 22: 'God knows I do not want to make a party. I wish you both may increase, though I *decrease*. I am not touched at present with the *least tincture of envy*. If your brother will be but silent about the doctrine of election and final perseverance, there never will be a division between us. The very thought of it shocks my soul . . .' This was enclosed in a letter to James Hutton, which ended: 'God willing, I will send a line to my *yet honoured friend and father, Mr. JW*—.' (MorA)

Was I to do so, how many would cry out every night? I think it is tempting God to require such signs. That there is something of God in it I doubt not. But the devil, I believe, does interpose. I think it will encourage the French Prophets, take people from the written Word, and make them depend on
5 visions, convulsions, etc., more than on the promises and precepts of the gospel. Honoured sir, how could you tell that some who came to you 'were in a good measure sanctified'?[1] What fruits could be produced in one night's time? By their fruits, says our Lord, shall you know them.

I hear, honoured sir, you are about to print a sermon against predestination.
10 It shocks me to think of it. What will be the consequence but controversy? If people ask me my opinion, what shall I do? I have a critical part to act. God enable me to behave aright. Silence on both sides will be best. It is noised abroad already that there is a division between you and me. Oh! my heart within me is grieved! Providence tomorrow calls me to Gloucester. If you will be pleased
15 to come next week to London, I think God willing to stay a few days at Bristol. Your brother Charles goes to Oxon. I believe we shall be excommunicated soon. May the Lord enable us to stand fast in the faith. and stir up your heart to watch over the soul of, honoured sir, your dutiful son and servant,

                                                                        GW

20   God willing, I intend answering brother Wathen's letter in person. It gave me satisfaction. I would have brother Mi[t]chel[l] sell my *Journals*. My hearty love to him and all.

Address: 'To the Revnd. Mr. John Wesly, at Mrs. Grevil's a Grocer in Wine-street, Bristoll'   *Postmarks*: '26 IV' and an indistinguishable one-line name, probably nine letters   *Charge*: '4'   *End* by JW: 'GWh. June 26. 1739 / ad 27'   *Source*: MA.

To James Hutton and the
Fetter Lane Society

                                                                [July 2, 1739]

Dear brethren
25   I left London[2] about six on Monday morning, and on Tuesday evening at seven preached (as I had appointed, if God should permit) to about five thousand people in the Bowling Green at Bristol, whose hearty affection moved me much. My subject was the same

    [1] Orig., 'justified'. In the extant letters Wesley does speak of people receiving 'remis-sion of sins', 'the gift of the Holy Ghost', or 'the Spirit of adoption', but there seems to be no instance of this phrase, which is probably quoted from the missing letter of June 23.
    [2] Wesley had come to London on June 11, and left on Monday the 18th.

as at Kennington.[1] About nine that faithful soldier of Christ, Howell Harris,[2] called upon me. He said he had been much tempted not to do it at all; that many had told him I was an Arminian, a free-willer, and so on; so that he could hardly force himself to come to the Bowling Green. But he added, 'I had not been long there 5 before my spirit was knit to you, as it was to dear Mr. Whitefield, and before you had done I was so overpowered with joy and love that ⟨I coul⟩d scarce stand, and with much difficulty got home.'

It is incredible what advantage Satan had gained here by my absence of only eight days. Disputes had crept in, and the love of 10 many was waxed cold,[3] so that all our society was falling in pieces. I preached on Wednesday at Newgate at eleven, and at four at Baptist Mills, on those words, 'Simon, Simon, behold Satan hath desired to have you, that he may sift you as wheat.'[4] At seven I met the women bands at Elizabeth Davis's[5] house (Mrs. Grevil having 15 forbidden them hers). I found disputes had hurt them also, so that many were resolved to quit the society. Finding it necessary to speak to them apart, I fixed times to meet each band singly, which I did on the days of the following week; and all of them were (I hope) stablished in the faith. At eight I met our brethren in Baldwin 20 Street, where instead of disputing we prayed together; the Spirit of the Holy One was with us. All divisions were healed, all misunderstandings vanished away, and we all felt our hearts drawn together, and sweetly united in the bowels of Jesus Christ.[6]

Thur. 21. I talked an hour or two with a young man of Gloucester 25 who was deeply prejudiced against my dear brother Whitefield and me.[7] He went away of another mind. In the afternoon I preached at Publow, as usual, without any disturbance, on Isa. 45:22. In the evening I was at the schoolroom, and had a large and attentive audience, though the [room] was uncovered, and it rained hard. 30

[1] He had preached at Kennington Common, London, on Sunday evening, June 17, on Isa. 45: 22, 'Look unto me, and be ye saved, all the ends of the earth.'
[2] Howell Harris (1714–73), a Welsh schoolmaster who within a few months of his conversion in 1735 begàn to preach and found societies in Wales. With the Revd. Daniel Rowland (1713–90) he was the founder of Welsh Calvinistic Methodism. Although on doctrinal grounds he was more attracted to Whitefield, Harris sought to avoid theological rivalries, and continued to maintain friendly relations with the Wesleys.
[3] See Matt. 24: 12.
[4] Luke 22: 31.
[5] In his letter of Apr. 16 Wesley noted her admission, as also that of John Davis (possibly her husband) on the previous day. His *Journal* of Jan. 3, 1741, speaks of her burial.
[6] Phil. 1: 8.   [7] Diary, 'Mr. Bailis'.

Afterward I met with Molly Deacon's band, whose openness and childlike simplicity pleased me much; where also I spoke with a young man who was fully determined, 'naked to follow a naked Master',[1] having been turned out-of-doors by his friends the night
5 before for coming to the societies.

Friday 22. I writ to a society just begun at Wells, which I hope to visit when God permits. At nine I called on Mr. Whitehead,[2] whom G. Whitefield baptized at Gloucester. 'You did run well. Who hath bewitched you?'[3] 'Woe unto the prophets, saith the
10 Lord, which prophesy in my name, and I have not sent them.'[4] At Weavers' Hall I endeavoured to point them out, and exhorted all to cleave to the law and the testimony.[5]

In the afternoon I preached at Fishponds on the same words as at Publow, but had no life or spirit in me. I came back to the band on
15 trial, whose behaviour (especially Mrs. Thornhill) a little revived and comforted me, but when I left them to go to Gloucester Lane society I was more dead and cold than ever, and much in doubt whether God would not now lay me aside, and send more faithful labourers into his harvest. When I came thither, my soul being
20 grieved for my brother Whitehead, I began in much weakness to exhort them to try the spirits, whether they were of God.[6] I told them they must not judge of the spirits either by common report or by appearances, or by their own feelings, no, nor by any dreams, visions, or revelations made to their souls, or outward effects upon
25 their bodies. All these, I warned them, were of a doubtful nature in themselves, which might be of God, or of the devil; and were not either to be simply condemned or relied on, but to be tried by the law and the testimony. While I was speaking a woman dropped down before me, and presently a second and third; and one after another
30 five others. All the outward symptoms were as violent as those at London the Friday before. Upon prayer five of them were comforted; one continued in pain an hour longer; and one for two or three days.

---

[1] The ideal of St. Francis of Assissi, *nudi nudum Christum sequi*; cf. Wesley, *Journal*, Mar. 7, 1736, and the letter from Whitefield to Wesley, Feb. 1, 1738 (p. 529 above).

[2] Thomas Whitehead, 'a professed Quaker, about sixty years of age, who was convinced of the necessity of being born of water, as well as the Spirit', whom Whitefield recorded baptizing in St. Mary de Crypt, Gloucester, on Apr. 17, 1739. Wesley's *Journal* states that he 'did run well', 'till he was hindered by some of those called French Prophets'.

[3] See Gal. 5: 7.   [4] See Jer. 14: 14, etc.
[5] Isa. 8: 20.   [6] See 1 John 4: 1.

Sat. 23. I spoke severally with those which had been so troubled the night before, some of whom I found were only awakened; others had peace in the blood of Christ. At four I preached to about two thousand at the Bowling Green on, 'Do all to the glory of God;'[1] at seven in the morning to four or five thousand, and at ten to about three thousand, at Hanham. As I was riding afterwards to Rose Green in a smooth, plain road, my horse pitched upon his head, and rolled over and over. I received no other hurt than a little bruise on the side I fell, which made me lame for two or three days. For the present I felt nothing, but preached there on the same words to six or seven thousand people, and in the evening explained the twelfth of the Acts to twelve or fifteen hundred at the New Room. On Saturday evening Ann Allen (a young woman) was seized with the pangs at Weavers' Hall. They did not continue long before the snare was broken, and her soul delivered. Sarah Murray[2] (aged thirteen) and four or five other persons (some of whom had felt the power of God before) were as deeply convinced on Sunday evening, and with most of the same symptoms groaned for deliverance. At Weavers' Hall, on Monday 25, a young woman named Mary Pritchard was cut to the heart, and soon after comforted, as was Mary Greenwood at four in the afternoon. At Gloucester Lane in the evening one Mary Conway, who as she was sitting at work at ten in the morn⟨ing⟩ was suddenly seized with strong trembling and bitter agonies of soul, in which ⟨she⟩ had continued all the afternoon, was restored to peace, as were four or five others, ⟨who⟩ were there cut to the heart.

On Tue. 26 I preached the first time under the sycamore tree, near the school at Kingswood, during a violent rain, on those words of Isaiah, 'As the rain cometh down from heaven, and returneth not thither, but watereth the earth, and maketh it bring forth and bud . . ., so shall my word be that goeth out of my mouth; it shall not return unto me void, but it shall accomplish that which I please, and it shall prosper in the thing whereto I sent it.'[3]

After expounding to some hundreds in the Back Lane, I went as usual to the schoolroom, where the pains of hell came about three persons, who soon after saw the light of heaven. At Baptist Mills

[1] 1 Cor. 10: 31.
[2] In his *Journal* for Sept. 19, 1739, Charles Wesley tells how he 'hastened to pray by Sally Murray, who lay a-dying, and triumphing over death'.
[3] Isa. 55: 10–11.

on Wednesday I explained to two thousand or twenty-five hundred, 'All things are lawful for me, but all things edify not.'[1] At seven the women's[2] bands met, and agreed to defer admitting any new members till the next month, and to wait a little longer before they excluded

5 those who had for some time excluded themselves,[3] if haply they might return. At Baldwin Street William Farnell and Richard Hereford were excluded the society, as being not only unwilling to attend it, but utterly incapable (as yet) of improving by it. I was afterward much enlarged in praying for Mrs. G[revil]. O that she

10 could again feel herself a lost sinner! I went on Thursday in the afternoon to preach on the south edge of Kingswood, near a sort of a village called The Cupolas, but the people not having notice but few came, so that having used some prayer with them I promised to come again the next day, and then preached on, 'Believe, and

15 thou shalt be saved.'[4]

Sat. 30. Ann Williams (Anthony Williams's wife) was the thirteenth time tapped for the dropsy. She desires to be dissolved and to be with Christ,[5] but gives herself up to him for life or for death.

To about twelve hundred in the Bowling Green I showed that

20 many lawful things edify not.[6] At Weavers' Hall Kitty Deschamps, about fourteen, Prudence Woodward, and five more, roared for the very disquietness of their heart,[7] and all, upon prayer, were relieved, and sang praise unto our God, and unto the Lamb that liveth for ever and ever.[8] Yours in Christ,

25   John Wesley

Bristol, July 2, 1739

Address: 'To Mr. James Hutton, Book-seller near Temple Barr, London'
Postmarks: 'B/ris/tol', '6 IY'   *Charge*: '4'   *End* by Hutton: 'Bristol, July 2, 1739'   *Source*: MorA, completely in the hand of John Purdy.

[1] See 1 Cor. 10: 23.
[2] Orig., 'woman', probably Purdy's error—of which there are several.
[3] Orig., 'had for some time had for some excluded themselves'.
[4] Acts 16: 31.   [5] See Phil. 1: 23.
[6] See 1 Cor. 10: 23, and Wed., June 27.
[7] See Ps. 38: 8 (B.C.P.).   [8] Rev. 4: 9.

From the Revd. George Whitefield

Gloucester, July 2nd, 1739

Honoured sir

I confess my spirit has been of late sharpened on account of some of your proceedings: my heart has been quite broken within me. I have been grieved from my soul, knowing what dilemma I am reduced to. How shall I tell the 5 Dissenters I do not approve of their doctrines without wronging my own soul? How shall I tell them I do without contradicting my honoured friend, whom I desire to love as my own soul? Lord, for thy infinite mercy's sake direct me so to act as neither to injure myself nor friend. Is it true, honoured sir, that brother Stock is excluded the society because he holds predestination? If so, is it right? 10 Would Jesus Christ have done so? Is this to act with a catholic spirit? Is it true, honoured sir, that the house at Kingswood is intended hereafter for the brethren to dwell in as at Herrnhut? Is this answering the primitive design of that building? Can I beg money for a thing I count unnecessary? Did the Moravians live together till they were obliged by persecution? Does the scheme 15 at Islington succeed? As for brother Cennick's expounding, I know not what to say. Brother Wathen I think no way qualified for any such thing. Dear honoured sir, if you have any regard to the peace of the Church, keep in your sermon on predestination. But you have cast a lot. Oh! my heart in the midst of my body is like melted wax. The Lord direct us all! Honoured sir, indeed I wish you all the 20 success you can wish for. May you increase though I decrease! I would willingly wash your feet. God is with us mightily. I have just now wrote to the bishop. O wrestle, wrestle, honoured sir, in prayer, that not the least alienation of affections may be between you and, honoured sir, your obedient son and servant in Christ, 25

GW

Address: 'To The Revrd. Mr. John Wesly, at Mrs. Grevil's a Grocer, in Wine-street, Bristoll' *Postmark*: 'GLOCES/TER' *Charge*: '3' *End* by JW: 'July 2, 1739 G Wh./ a[nswere]d 3d', and separately, 'July, Aug., Sept., Oct./ 1739' *Source*: MA.

To James Hutton[1]

[Bristol, July 9, 1739]

The Islington Rules do not seem to want either alteration or addition yet. Pray don't you think of Holland any more than marriage

---

[1] William Seward, who served as Whitefield's business manager on his evangelistic tour of 1739, remained in almost daily correspondence with James Hutton in London—as did Whitefield himself, and also Wesley. Seward's letters reported on the progress of the work, frequently gave the text of reports to be inserted in the *Daily Advertiser*, and

without the full consent of the bands. Two or four Scougal's Works,[1] and four *Christian's S[acred] Sc[riptur]e Nucleus*,[2] may be sent with my clasps and Greek Testament (left at Mrs. West's),[3] my diaries (fetched by C[harles] W[esley] from brother Agutter's),[4] and other
5 books. Adieu, my brother, and be not in haste.

Source: MorA, near the end of a letter from Wm. Seward to Hutton, dated Bristol, July 9, 1739, to which Seward adds the postscript: 'Br. Westly not having filled the paper I must, and tell you that I heard this day from Wales, where the gentlemen continue their resolution of prosecuting their malice against our brother Howell Harris . . . W. S.'

From the Revd. George Whitefield[5]

London, July 23, 1739

Honoured sir

I thank you for your kind reproof. Henceforward I will beg of God to keep the door of my lips, that I offend no more with my tongue. I would not willingly
10 have one unprofitable word proceed out of my mouth. I am often with persons that commend me; I take it as my cross. I look upon them only as people talking in their sleep. I generally find those that so praise me to my face are but mere novices in the spiritual life. However, God always gives me thorns in the flesh. May I by them be taught true humility and poverty of spirit. I love you more for
15 reproving me. I abhor nothing more in Christians than reservedness. Matters go on well here. People are more and more hungry, and God gives me greater power. Forty pounds were collected yesterday for the colliers.

also ordered books from Hutton. Apparently Hutton had sent some message to Wesley in a recent letter to Seward, who invited Wesley to add a note to his own reply.
[1] Henry Scougal (1650–78), whose *The Life of God in the Soul of Man* (1677) was reprinted in 1726 by Patrick Cockburn along with 'nine other discourses' by Scougal. Wesley met this volume in 1732, became tremendously enthusiastic about it, read it to others both in England and Georgia, and in 1744 published his own abridgement (*Bibliog*, No. 93).
[2] No such title seems to appear in *BL Catalogue*, *National Union Catalog*, Darling, etc.
[3] Wesley had briefly visited London from Bristol, June 13–17, and spent much time at Mrs. West's, for whom see p. 602n. above.
[4] Jonathan Agutter (1689–1762), who in 1733 was admitted one of the poor brothers in the Charterhouse Hospital, where Wesley frequently visited him. He died a Moravian.
[5] There seems little doubt that some of Whitefield's criticisms in his letter of July 2 had been based on unfounded hearsay, and that Wesley's answering letter of July 19 (to which this replies) made this point.

Your brother Charles may be expected the middle of next week. Ralph
Erskine has sent you a letter: pray keep up a constant correspondence with him,
and, honoured sir, your unworthy son and servant in Christ,

GW

Source: *A.M.*, Supp., 1797, p. 21.

To Dr. Henry Stebbing[1]

[July 25, 1739] 5

Reverend sir

1. You charge me (for I am called a 'Methodist', and consequently
included within your charge) with 'vain and confident boastings, rash,
uncharitable censures, damning all who do not *feel* what I *feel*';[2] 'not
allowing men to be in a salvable state unless they have experienced   10
some *sudden* operation, which may be distinguished as the hand of
God upon them, overpowering as it were the soul';[3] with 'denying
men the use of God's creatures, which he hath appointed to be
received with thanksgiving, and encouraging abstinence, prayer, and
other religious exercises, to the neglect of the duties of our station'.[4]   15
O sir, can you prove this charge upon me? The Lord shall judge in
that day.

[1] The Revd. Henry Stebbing, D.D. (1687–1763), preacher to the Society of Gray's
Inn from 1731 and Chaplain in Ordinary to the King from 1732, gained a reputation as
the champion of Church of England orthodoxy, writing many treatises, and challenging
both Hoadly and Warburton, both Whitefield and Wesley. In the summer of 1739 he
published *A Caution against Religious Delusion. A Sermon on the New Birth: occasioned
by the pretensions of the Methodists*, which passed through six editions that year. Wesley's
Journal for July 31 noted: 'Having *A Caution against Religious Delusion* put into my hands
about this time, I thought it my duty to write to the author of it, which I accordingly
did, in the following terms.' This was a private letter of protest, and the *Journal* in
which it appeared was not published until over three years later, in Oct., 1742. The letter
was probably drafted on July 25, when Wesley's diary from 9.30 until 11.0 a.m. recorded,
'Writ to Dr. Stebbing', and a fair copy may well have been prepared the following day,
during two periods noted simply as 'letter'.
[2] Stebbing, *Caution*, 3rd edn., London, Gyles, 1739, p. 14. Wesley has added the
emphasis upon 'feel'.
[3] Ibid., cf. p. 8: 'But they will have it to be a *sensible* operation; an operation which
may be *felt* and *distinguished* as the hand of God upon them; *overpowering*, as it were,
the soul. And unless men are able to give account of their having at some time or other
experienced some such sudden change within themselves, they will not allow him to be
regenerate, nor therefore in a sa[l]vable state.' It seems likely that the emphasized 'sudden'
in Wesley's rough quotation was intended as the word which Stebbing continually
italicized—*sensible*.
[4] Ibid., cf. p. 14.

2. I do indeed go out into the highways and hedges to call poor sinners to Christ. But not 'in a tumultuous manner',[1] not 'to the disturbance of the public peace' or 'the prejudice of families'.[2] Neither herein do I break any law which I know, much less 'set at
5 naught all rule and authority'.[3] Nor can I be said to 'intrude into the labours'[4] of those who do not labour at all, but suffer thousands of those for whom Christ died to 'perish for lack of knowledge'.[5]

3. They perish for want of knowing that *we* as well as the heathens are 'alienated from the life of God';[6] that *every one of us*, by the
10 corruption of our inmost nature, 'is very far gone from original righteousness', so far that 'every person born into the world deserveth God's wrath and damnation';[7] that we have by nature no power either to help ourselves, or even to call upon God to help us, all our tempers and works, in our natural state, being only evil continually.
15 So that *our* coming to Christ, as well as *theirs*, 'must infer a great and mighty change'.[8] It must infer, not only an *outward change*, from stealing, lying, and all corrupt communication; but a thorough *change of heart*, an *inward* renewal in the spirit of our mind. Accordingly 'the old man' implies infinitely more than outward 'evil con-
20 versation',[9] even 'an evil heart of unbelief',[10] corrupted by pride and a thousand deceitful lusts. Of consequence the 'new man' must imply infinitely more than *outward* 'good conversation',[11] even '*a good heart*',[12] 'which after God is created in righteousness and true holiness';[13] a heart full of that faith which, working by love,[14] produces
25 all holiness of conversation.

4. The change from the former of these states to the latter is what I call 'the new birth'. But, you say, I am 'not content with this plain and easy notion of it, but fill myself and others with fanatical conceits'[15] about it. Alas, sir, how can you prove this? And if you
30 cannot prove it, what amends can you make, either to God or to me or to the world, for publicly asserting a gross falsehood?

---

[1] Cf. Stebbing, *Caution*, etc., p. 14, 'gathering tumultuous assemblies'.
[2] Ibid.   [3] Ibid.
[4] Cf. ibid., 'intruding into other men's labours'.
[5] Cf. Hos. 4: 6.   [6] Eph. 4: 18.
[7] Cf. B.C.P., Thirty-nine Articles, Article 9, 'Of Original or Birth Sin'.
[8] Stebbing, op. cit., p. 3.
[9] Ibid., p. 4, citing Eph. 4: 22–9.   [10] Heb. 3: 12.
[11] Jas. 3: 13, etc.
[12] Cf. Luke 8: 15; 1 Tim. 1: 5.
[13] Eph. 4: 24; cf. Stebbing, op. cit., p. 4.   [14] See Gal. 5: 6.
[15] Cf. Stebbing, op. cit., p. 7.

5. Perhaps you say you 'can prove this of Mr. Whitefield'.[1] What then? This is nothing to me. I am not accountable for *his* words. The *Journal* you quote I never saw till it was in print. But indeed you wrong him as much as me. First, where you represent him as judging the notions of the Quakers *in general* (concerning being led by the Spirit) to be right and good; whereas he speaks only of those *particular men* with whom he was then conversing.[2] And again where you say he 'supposes a person believing in Christ' to be without any 'saving knowledge' of him.[3] He *supposes* no such thing. 'To believe in Christ' was the very thing he 'supposed' wanting; as understanding that term 'believing' to imply, not only an assent to the Articles of our Creed, but also, 'a true trust and confidence of the mercy of God through our Lord Jesus Christ'.[4]

6. Now this it is certain a man may want, although he can truly say, 'I am chaste, I am sober, I am just in all my dealings, I help my neighbour, and use the ordinances of God'.[5] 'And however' such a man 'may have behaved in these respects, he is not to think well of his own state till he experiences something within himself which he has not yet experienced', but 'which he may be beforehand assured he shall',[6] if the promises of God are true. That 'something' is a living faith: 'a sure trust and confidence in God, that by the merits of Christ his sins are forgiven, and he reconciled to the favour of God'.[7] And from this will spring many other things which till then he experienced not, as the love of God shed abroad in his heart,[8] that peace of God which passeth all understanding,[9] and joy in the Holy Ghost,[10] joy, though not *unfelt*, yet *unspeakable* and full of glory.[11]

7. These are some of those *inward* 'fruits of the Spirit'[12] which

---

[1] Stebbing does not in fact say this in so many words, but in three lengthy footnotes he quotes Whitefield's *Journal* (pp. 16, 19, 21), and refers to Whitefield by name, though he never so mentions Wesley.

[2] Stebbing, op. cit., p. 19.

[3] Ibid., p. 16.

[4] Homilies, On the Passion, Pt. II.

[5] Cf. Stebbing, op. cit., pp. 15–16: 'Am I sober, am I chaste; am I just and charitable to my neighbour; do I serve God in the use of his ordinances?'

[6] Cf. ibid., p. 16, introduced by Stebbing with 'But', with the last quoted clause beginning 'and which', and continuing, 'this will lead him to cast off all hope in God, and to give himself up to despair'—Wesley affirms what Stebbing rejects.

[7] Homilies, Of Salvation, Pt. III—Wesley's favourite definition.

[8] See Rom. 5: 5.

[9] Phil. 4: 7.

[10] Rom. 14: 17.

[11] 1 Pet. 1: 8.

[12] Stebbing, op. cit., p. 12; cf. Gal. 5: 22.

must be *felt*, wheresoever they are. And without these I cannot learn
from Holy Writ that any man is 'born of the Spirit'.[1] I beseech you,
sir, by the mercies of God, that if as yet you 'know nothing of such
inward feelings',[2] if you do not 'feel in yourself these mighty workings
5 of the Spirit of Christ',[3] at least you would not contradict and blaspheme. When the Holy Ghost hath fervently kindled *your* love
towards God, you will know these to be very *sensible* operations. As
you 'hear the wind, and feel it, too', while it 'strikes upon your
bodily organs',[4] you will know you are under the guidance of God's
10 Spirit the same way, namely, by *feeling it in your soul*;[5] by the present
peace and joy and love which you feel within, as well as by its
outward and more distant effects. I am, etc.

Source: JWJ, July 31, 1739.

To James Hutton

[Bristol, Aug. 3, 1739]

I had opportunity to talk largely with our brother[6] concerning
15 the outward signs which had here attended the work of God. But
there was little need of disputing, for God answered for himself. He
had been told these things were owing to my encouraging them,
and that if they were not encouraged no such thing would ever be.
But the next day, no sooner had he himself begun to call all sinners
20 to be in Christ than four were seized before him in a moment. One
of them dropped down and lay without motion. A second trembled
exceedingly. The third was in strong convulsions, but made no noise,
unless by groans. The fourth, equally convulsed, called upon God
with strong cries and tears also. From this time, I hope, we shall all
25 suffer God to carry on his own work his own way. Thursday, July

---

[1] John 3: 6, 8.
[2] Stebbing, op. cit., p. 11.
[3] Cf. Thirty-nine Articles, Article 17, 'Of Predestination and Election': '. . . such as
feel in themselves the working of the Spirit of Christ'.
[4] Stebbing, op. cit., p. 12.   [5] Ibid.
[6] Note added by amanuensis: 'meaning Mr. Whitefield'. Whitefield arrived in
Bristol from London on July 6, 1739, and Wesley's *Journal* for July 7-12 is very
similar in content to this first extract.

the 12th, after dinner, I went to a person[1] much troubled with lowness of spirits, as they term it. Many such I have seen before, but I can by no means believe it to be a bodily distemper. They wanted something, they knew not what, and were therefore uneasy. The plain case was, they wanted God, they wanted Christ, they 5 wanted faith; and God convinced them of this want in a way which [they] themselves no more understood at first than their physician did. Nor did any physic avail till the Great Physician came; for in spite of all natural means, he who made them for himself would not suffer them to rest till their soul rested in him . . .[2] 10

Source: MorA, item (1) on a foolscap sheet containing three extracts from Wesley's letters of Aug. 3, 15, and 24, all to James Hutton, in an unidentified hand with very erratic spelling and punctuation. It is headed, 'Extract from a letter from Mr. John Wesley, directed for Mr. James Hutton, Bookseller, near Temple Bar, from Bristol, August the 3rd, concerning persons falling into fits at their being new born.'

To The Revd. James Hervey[3]

[Aug. 8, 1739]

Dear sir

Why is it that I have never had a line from you since I wrote to you from London? Have you quite forgotten me? Or have the idle stories which you once despised at length prevailed over you? If so, 15 if thy brother offend thee, what is to be done? 'Tell him of his fault, between thee and him alone.' God is able to do whatsoever pleaseth him. How knowest thou, O man, but thou mayst gain thy brother?[4]

But what are you doing yourself? Sleeping on, ⟨and⟩ taking your rest?[5] I cannot understand this. Our Lord calls aloud for labourers 20 in his vineyard. And you sit still. His people perish by thousands

---

[1] JWJ, 'a gentleman', probably the 'Mr. Cutler' noted in the diary.

[2] See Augustine, *Confessions*, i. 1, translated by Wesley, 'Thou hast made us for thyself; and our heart cannot rest, till it resteth in thee' (see his 1789 sermon on Mark 12: 32, 'There is one God', § 9).

[3] It seems that Hervey's letter of Apr. 4, 1739 (see above, pp. 624–5), had been answered by Wesley 'from London', which must mean between June 13–17, though such a letter is not mentioned in his diary, no more than is this, except for a note, 'writ'.

[4] See Matt. 18: 15 for the four preceding sentences.

[5] See Matt. 26: 45; Mark 14: 41.

for lack of knowledge. ⟨An⟩d the servant of the Lord hideth himself
in a cave.[1] Come forth, my brother, come forth![2] Work for our Lord,
and he will renew your strength. O that he would send you into this
part of his harvest! Either with or without your preaching, here is
5 work enough! Come, and let us again take sweet counsel together![3]
Let me have joy over you once more. Think if there be no way for
your once more seeing, my dear friend, your affectionate brother,

John Wesley

Bristol,
10 Aug. 8, 1739

End: 'Mr. Westley's Letr to Mr. Harvey'   *Source*: The Revd. Walter
J. Joyce, Shaftesbury, England.

To James Hutton

[Aug. 13, 1739]

Thursday, July 26, in the evening at the society several were
deeply convinced of sin, but none was delivered: the children came
to the birth, but there was not strength to bring forth.[4] The same
15 thing was observed many times before. Many were the conjectures
concerning the reason of it. Indeed, I fear we have grieved the
Spirit of God by questioning his work, and that therefore he is
withdrawn from us[5] for a season; but surely he will return, and
abundantly pardon.[6]
20 Monday the 30th I had much conversation with a good and
friendly man[7] concerning those outward signs of the inward work of
God. I found my mind much weak[en]ed thereby, and thrown upon
reasonings which profited nothing. At eight two persons were in
strong pain, but though we cried to God there was no answer, neither
25 did he deliver them at all.
The 31st, etc., I was enabled to speak strongly to them on those

---

[1] See 1 Kgs. 19: 9.   [2] John 11: 43.   [3] See Ps. 55: 14.
[4] See 2 Kgs. 19: 3.   [5] See Hos. 5: 6.   [6] See Isa. 55: 7.
[7] This may have been the well-known Baptist minister, Joseph Stennett (1692–
1758), on a visit west from his congregation in Little Wild Street, London. (Until 1737
he had ministered in Exeter.) Wesley's diary reads: '10.00 at home, Mr. Stennet,
religious talk, 11.00'.

words, Ask, and ye shall receive,[1] and to claim the promise in prayer for those that mourned, one of whom was filled with joy and peace in believing,[2] as was also this day a young woman who had been a strenuous opposer of this work of God, and particularly zealous against those who cried out, saying she was sure they might help it if they would. But on Monday night at the society, in the midst of her zeal, she was struck in a moment, and fell to the ground trembling and roaring for the disquietness of her heart.[3] She continued in pain twelve or fourteen hours, and then was set at liberty, but her master immediately forbid her his house, saying he would have none with him who had received the Holy Ghost . . .

Address: ['Mr. James Hutton, Bookseller, near Temple Bar, London']
Source: MorA, item (2) in document described p. 673. Begins, 'From a second letter, postmark August the 15, from J.W. to Ja:Hutton. These letters are wrote by way of journals giving an account from day to day what happens.' Wesley's diary shows that he 'writ' on Monday morning, Aug. 13, but was travelling on the 14th. The dated postmark would be added in London.

From Ebenezer Blackwell[4]

London, 14 August, 1739

Dear sir

Mr. Seward, when I supped with him and Mr. Whitefield last Sunday night, said he would send me the money they collected that evening on Blackheath for Kingswood School. By the newspaper of this day it mentions that there was collected £16.1.6, but I had sent me only £15.11, so that there is half a guinea difference. What is the reason I don't know till I hear from Mr. Seward, but however for the £15.11 I have sent our shop note, which Mr. Burrows or any other gentleman that remits money to London will give you cash for. I thought it was the best way to send it, because as I have seen g[oo]d handwriting (though I have not the pleasure of your acquaintance), before I should pay it I should know that it got safe to you.

It would be needless for me to pretend to give an account of all our friends, because I suppose the Captain and Mr. Mitchell before this have acquainted you of everything, as they and I parted from Mr. Whitefield and Mr. Seward at the same time. This I can say, that there is a great number of our friends who earnestly wish for somebody to supply the place of our dear brother Whitefield; for my part I desire to trust to the Lord, who is not only able, but will certainly in his due time send us more of his true ministers; but at present for all-wise ends he may suffer us to grapple a little by ourselves, and have after this great

---

[1] John 16: 24.   [2] Rom. 15: 13.   [3] See Ps. 38: 8.
[4] For Blackwell see Wesley's reply to this letter, Aug. 23, 1739.

plenty, as it were a dearth of religion in order to purge us and try us, that we know how to prize and value them that preach the truth as it is in Jesus. O that we had more thankful hearts for the mercies we daily receive, and made a more conscientious use of our closets, to look up to the Almighty for directions
5 in all affairs, not in the least resting or relying on anything that we can do, but solely trusting in the merits, death, and suffering of our dear Lord Jesus for life and salvation. Then might we expect the blessing of God in this world, and our souls' everlasting salvation in the next. I should be glad when you have a leisure minute to have a line or two, and beg you will present my kind love and
10 service to Mrs. Grevil, and tell her that I thought I should have heard from her before now. I am, dear sir (with earnest prayers to the Almighty for continued success in your labours, and that all who name the name of Jesus may depart from evil), your weak but affectionate servant in Christ,

Eb Blackwell

15   Pray give my kind respects to the Capt., Mr. Mitchell, etc.

Address: 'To The Revd. Mr. Jno Wesly'   *End* by JW: 'Mr Blackwell /
Aug. 14, 1739 / a[nswere]d 22'   *Source*: MA.

From the Revd. Charles Wesley

Bengeworth and Evesham,
Aug. 20, 1739

Dear brother
    We left the brethren at Oxford much edified, and two gownsmen, besides C.
20 Graves, throughly awakened. On Saturday afternoon God brought us hither. Mr. Seward being from home there was no admittance for us, his wife being an opposer, and having refused to see G. Whitefield before me.
    At seven Mr. Seward found us at our inn, and carried us home. I expounded at eight in the schoolroom, which contains two hundred, and held out the pro-
25 mises from John 16, I will send the Comforter, etc.
    On Sunday morning I preached from George Whitefield's pulpit, the wall, 'Repent ye, and believe the gospel.' The notice being short we had only a few hundreds, but such as those described in the Morning Lesson, 'These were more noble than those of Thessalonica, in that they received the word with all
30 readiness of mind.' In the evening I showed to near two thousand their Saviour in the Good Samaritan. Many, I am persuaded, found themselves stripped and wounded and half-dead; and are therefore ready for the oil and wine.
    Once more God strengthened me at nine to open the new covenant at the school-house, which was crowded with deeply attentive sinners . . .

Source: MA (Charles Wesley, MS journal, Aug. 16–20, 1739).

From the Revd. James Hervey

[Aug. 21, 1739]

Dear and honoured sir

Your letter from London[1] occasioned a speedy answer and a thankful acknowledgment. I suppose my epistle miscarried, otherwise you would not have taxed me with forgetfulness of a friend whom I am infinitely obliged to, and whom I dearly esteem. 5

You ask what I am doing in my present situation. I answer, The same that Basil and Nazianzen did in the wilderness: studying the Scriptures, furnishing my mind with saving knowledge, and fitting a poor deacon for the service of Christ's Church. With this farther difference between my inconsiderable self 10 and those excellent persons, that they retired in the vigour of health, I under the infirmities of a crazy constitution; which I hope to have repaired by enjoying the most comfortable conveniences of life, and a respite from labour. At present, had I the strongest inclination, I have no manner of ability to bestir myself in the way you propose. I be a thundering Boanerges?—I lift up my voice to 15 the whole world, and make the canopy of the skies ring? Never, dear sir, never could you have made choice of so improper a person, so vastly unequal to the task.

Besides, I freely own I cannot approve of itinerant preaching. I think it is repugnant to the apostolical as well as English constitution. I find Timothy 20 settled at Ephesus, Titus stationed at Crete, and other of our Captain's commanders assigned to their particular posts. These labourers (and industrious labourers they were) did not think it necessary or expedient to travel from this county to that, with words of exhortation in their mouths, but chose to lay out their pastoral vigilance upon the flock consigned to their care. Thus would I 25 humbly advise my dear Mr. Wesley to act. Be content to imitate those primitive and only not inspired preachers. Fix in some parish, visit carefully your people, let every individual be the object of your compassionate zeal, in a word be a living Ouranius.[2] O what good might this do to the cause of Christianity! How might neighbouring ministers follow the unexceptionable example, and from 30 inveighing against my good friend, as they now unanimously do, honour him and tread in his steps!

Straitness of time obliges me to put an end to my letter; but no difference of opinion, no long-continued absence, nothing, I trust, in time or through eternity, shall be able to put an end to my respectful and honourable regard, my 35 most affectionate and grateful esteem for dear Mr. Wesley; whom I love, and whose I am, with the greatest sincerity,

J. Hervey

August 21, 1739

Source: Lincoln College, Oxford.

[1] Of Aug. 4.

[2] A character in Law's *Serious Call*, chapter 21: 'Ouranius is a holy priest, full of the spirit of the gospel, watching, labouring, and praying for a poor *country village* . . .' When Wesley reprinted his own abridgement of *A Serious Call* in his *Works* (Vol. 5, 1771), he placed an asterisk before this passage to emphasize its importance.

To James Hutton

[August 22, 1739]

August the 6th, breakfasted with some persons who were much offended at people's falling into those fits (as they called them), being sure they might help it if they would. A child of ten years old
5 came on a message while we were at breakfast, and in a few minutes began to cry out, 'My heart, my heart!' and fell to the ground trembling and sweating exceedingly. One of her aunts went to her to hinder her from beating herself and tearing her hair, but three or four could scarce restrain her. After calling upon God above two
10 hours, with strong cries, and tears, and all possible expressions of the strongest agonies of soul, that horrible dread was in a good measure taken away, and she found some rest. The eighth, the child which had been ill on Monday was in as strong an agony as before, to the conviction of many who doubted. But others still mocked on,
15 nor indeed would these [believe] though one rose from the dead.[1] August 11, two were seized with strong pangs at Weavers' Hall, but were not as yet set at liberty. Sunday, four were wounded in the evening, but not healed. Our time is in thy hand, O Lord. Four were[2] seized the next evening in Gloucester Lane, one of whom was on
20 the point of leaving our society; but she hath now better learned Christ.

Address: ['Mr. James Hutton, Bookseller, near Temple Bar, London']
Source: MorA, item (3) in document described p. 673, with prefixed note, 'August 24 postmark'. (The dated postmark was added in London, so that the letter was probably written and posted in Bristol two days earlier.)

To Ebenezer Blackwell[3]

[Aug. 23, 1739]

Dear sir
     I have not had half an hour's leisure to write since I received yours
25 of the 14th instant, in which the note for £15.11s. was enclosed.

---

[1] See Luke 16: 31.   [2] Orig. of amanuensis, 'was'.
[3] Ebenezer Blackwell (1711–82), trained in banking by Thomas Martin of Martin's

The Captain's[1] journey to London, as he owns it was the happiest, so I believe was the most useful one he ever had. His resolution was a little shaken here; but he appears more settled than before. Satan hath desired indeed to have us, that he may sift us as wheat. But our Lord hath prayed for us, so that the faith of few has failed.[2] Far the greater part of those who have been tempted has come as gold out of the fire.

It seems to me a plain proof that the power of God is greatly with this people, because they are tempted in a manner scarce common to men; no sooner do any of them begin to taste of true liberty but they are buffeted both within and without. The messengers of Satan close them in on every side. Many are already turned out of doors by their parents or masters; many more expect it every day. But they count all these things dung and dross that they may win Christ.[3] O let us, if his name be called upon us, be thus minded! I am, dear sir, your affectionate friend and servant in Christ,

John Wesley

Bristol, Aug. 23, 1739

Address: 'To Mr. Blackwell At Mr. Martin's, Banker, In Lombard Street, London'   *End* by Blackwell: 'Mr John Westley Dated Bristol 23d Augst, 1739'   *Source*: MA.

Bank, London, of which he became a partner in 1746. He was distantly related to Whitefield, and was assisting him by dealing with the money collected for the colliers' school at Kingswood at Whitefield's farewell gathering on Blackheath. Wesley was supervising the erection of the school, and in arranging to transfer the money to him Blackwell wrote on Aug. 14 (see above, pp. 675-6), a letter which led to a lasting correspondence and friendship which was important to them both, even though the spiritual ardour displayed in Blackwell's first letter cooled considerably during later years. Blackwell's home, The Limes, Lewisham, became one of Wesley's favourite retreats for his literary activities.

[1] Capt. James Whitefield, older brother of George, and a Bristol merchant, who died suddenly in 1766. He had apparently come to London to share in his brother's farewell gatherings (see p. 675 above).

[2] See Luke 22: 31-2.

[3] See Phil. 3: 8.

To the Revd. Ralph Erskine[1]

Bristol, Aug. 24, 1739

Reverend and dear sir

Many souls hath our blessed Lord here turned from darkness
unto light, and from the power of Satan unto God.[2] A great and
5 effectual door is indeed opened among us,[3] and the many adversaries
cannot shut it. But what a little surprised us at first was the outward
manner wherein *most* of these were affected, who are cut to the heart
by the sword of the Spirit.[4] Some of them drop down as dead,
having no strength nor appearance of life left in them. Some burst
10 out into strong cries and tears, some exceedingly tremble and quake;
from some great drops of sweat fall to the ground, others struggle
as in the agonies of death, so that four or five strong men can hardly
restrain a weak woman or a child from hurting themselves or others.
Of these many are in that hour filled with peace and joy; others
15 continue days or weeks in heaviness, so that sometimes their bodies
almost sink under the weight of the wounded spirit.

I should be glad to know whether any outward appearances like
these have been among you, and how the work of the Lord prospers
in your hands. It would be a comfort to our little flock, in whose
20 prayers you and your fellow-labourers are not forgotten. O may you
see Satan as lightning fall from heaven![5] We have (forty or fifty of
us) been this day calling together upon our God, that he would
please to hasten his kingdom. I commend you and your dear brother
(both after the flesh and after the spirit) to his protection, and am,

---

[1] Clearly disturbed by the mounting criticism of the revival phenomena which were
attending his Bristol ministry, even from close colleagues such as Whitefield, Wesley
sought the counsel of other evangelical leaders. On the advice of Whitefield he wrote to
Ralph Erskine (1685–1752), who in 1736 had joined his brother Ebenezer (1680–1754)
in seceding from the Church of Scotland to form an 'Associate Presbytery'. Both were
fervent evangelists, and Ralph was also a poet. The evidence of Whitefield's letter of
July 23 shows that Wesley and Erskine exchanged letters in June–July, and in his
Journal for June 30, 1739, Wesley printed an extract of what appeared to be Erskine's
reply to his first letter. In fact it was that of Sept. 28, sent in reply to this of Aug. 24,
which is apparently Wesley's second to Erskine. Their correspondence turned to
different subjects. On June 26, 1740, Wesley wrote that the tracts sent by Erskine had
convinced him that every congregation 'had an indisputable right to choose its own
pastor'. Eventually, however, Calvinism came between them: Erskine wrote his last
letter on Jan. 31, 1741, and Wesley on Nov. 30, 1742.

[2] Acts 26: 8.   [3] See 1 Cor. 16: 9.
[4] Eph. 6: 17.   [5] Luke 10: 18.

reverend and dear sir, your affectionate brother, and servant in Christ,

John Wesley

Source: Ralph Erskine, *Fraud and Fals[e]hood Discovered*, Edinburgh, 1743, pp. 5–6.

From the Revd. Samuel Wesley, Jun.[1]

[Sept. 3, 1739]

Dear Jack   5

It has pleased God to visit me with sickness, else I should not have been so backward in writing. Pray to him for us, that he would 'give us patience under our sufferings, and a happy issue out of all our afflictions; granting us in this world knowledge of his truth, and in the world to come life everlasting'.

It is good news that you have built a charity-school, and better still that you   10 have a second almost up, as I find by yours that Mr. Wigginton brought me. I wish you could build not only a school, but a church, too, for the colliers, if there is not any place at present for worship where they can meet; and I should rejoice heartily to have it endowed, though Mr. Whitefield were to be the minister of it, provided the bishop fully joined.   15

Your distinction between the discipline and doctrine of the church is, I think, not quite pertinent. For surely episcopacy is matter of doctrine, too; but granting it otherwise, you know there is no fear of being cast out of our synagogue for any tenets whatsoever. Did not Clarke die preferred? Were not Collins and Coward free from anathema? Are not Chubb and Gordon now   20 caressed? My knowledge of this makes me suspect Whitefield, as if he designed to provoke persecution by his bodings of it. He has already personally disobliged the bishops of Gloucester and London, and doubtless will do as much by all the rest if they fall not down before his whimsies, and should offer to stand in his way. Now if he, by his madness, should lay himself open to the small   25 remains of discipline amongst us, as by marrying without licence, or any other way, and get excommunicated for his pains, I am very apprehensive you would still stick to him as your dear brother, and so, though the church would not excommunicate you, you would excommunicate the church. Then I suppose you would enlarge your censure, which now takes in only most of the inferior   30 clergy; but you have taught me to have the worse opinion of no man on that account, till you have proved your charge against Bishop Bull. At present I am inclined to think that the being blamed with him is glory.

You yourself doubted at first, and inquired, and examined, about the ecstasies; the matter is not therefore so plain as motion to a man walking. But   35 I have my own reason, as well as your own authority, against the exceeding clearness of divine interposition there. Your followers fall into agonies. I confess

[1] Probably in reply to John's letter of June 26 (noted in his diary), to whose contents it affords some clues.

it. They are freed from them after you have prayed over them. Granted·
They say it is God's doing. I own they say so. Dear brother, where is your
ocular demonstration? Where, indeed, is the rational proof? Their living well
afterwards may be a probable and sufficient argument that they believe them-
5 selves; but it goes no farther.

I must ask a few more questions. Did these agitations ever begin during the
use of any collects of the Church? Or during the preaching of any sermon that
had before been preached within consecrated walls without that effect, or during
the inculcating any other doctrine besides that of your new birth? Are the main
10 body of these agents, or patients, good sort of people beforehand, or loose and
immoral?

My wife joins in love to you, and Charles, if he is with you, or indeed wherever
he is. For you know best his notions, and he is likely to hear from you before
me. Phill is very well, my wife indifferent, and I on the mending hand in spite
15 of foul weather. I am, dear Jack, your sincere and affectionate friend and
brother,

Samuel Wesley

Tiverton, Sept. 3, 1739

Address: 'To Mr. John Wesley'   *Source*: Priestley, 105–8.

From the Revd. Joshua Read[1]

Bradford, 7br. 11th[2] [1739]

20 Honrd sir

Yours I received not till after you preached at Burryfield, and that day I
was under a very great disorder of body, and the day being wet could not attend
your ministry.[3]

---

[1] The Revd. Joshua Read (who died an old man, *c.* 1745–6)—not Dr. Josiah Read,
as in *Victoria County History of England, Wiltshire*, VII. 33—was the minister of the
Grove Meeting House at Bradford-on-Avon, Wilts., whose Presbyterian congregation
was at this very time being split by doctrinal controversy, so that Read's junior colleague,
a Unitarian, took over, while Read himself built a new Independent Chapel on Morgan's
Hill—the 'very trying dispensations of Providence' mentioned in the letter. Wesley had
first met Read on one of the occasions when he preached in the open air at Bath, probably
on June 5, when he had his encounter with Beau Nash. Read had warmly thanked
Wesley, so that when Wesley was refused the parish church at Bradford on July 17 he
went to see Read, only to find him less friendly, especially as he had been informed that
at Oxford Wesley was taken to be 'a little crack-brained'. Wesley therefore preached
on the hill overlooking the town at a place 'called Bear Field, or Bury Field'. He preached
there on several subsequent occasions, including July 31, Aug. 14, and Aug. 28. On Aug.
23, according to his diary, Wesley wrote to Read, and this is Read's reply, showing that
this was another of those letters seeking advice about the physical phenomena occurring
among his Bristol adherents. The closing set of questions Wesley answered in some
detail in his extant letter of Oct. 27, 1739.

[2] The date might possibly be '17th'—the second numeral is smeared.

[3] The paragraph was apparently added after the completion of the letter and the
postscript.

As you began your last letter to me thus, 'I am neither a Calvinist or an Arminian', so I shall begin mine, assuring you that I am neither a 'bigot or a sceptic in religion'. You write that you contend for the faith once delivered to the saints with earnestness, which I desire alway to do; and what if I prove from what you have wrote to me, and from what I have heard from you, that you are a 5 Calvinist, though you will not own the name? For—

First: one great doctrine you have strenuously asserted is man's lost and undone estate by nature; (2), you frequently inculcate the necessity of the 'new birth'; (3), this you describe from Acts 26 : 18; (4), you assert God alone to be Author thereof, from Phil. 2 : 13. All which doctrinal truths Mr. Calvin earn- 10 estly contends for, and nothing in his writings is contrary thereunto. I heartily agree with you, that I do not count a man converted to God because he is converted from wrong opinions, as you write many of the Quakers and Papists have been by your ministry. As some resist the truth, so many hold the truth, in unrighteousness. O that you and I may daily experience that Christ hath 15 set up his kingdom, and doth sway his righteous and gracious sceptre by his Word and Spirit, in our souls. If the kingdom of God is not within us, we may preach to others, and be castaways ourselves! O that we were more conformed to the Dñ [? dominion] and life of our Saviour! I ascribe all the success of my ministry to free and sovereign grace, by which grace I am what I am. 20

I cannot pass over in silence (as you have done) the 17th Article of the Church of England, which we both solemnly have subscribed, and by our subscription professed before all the world our belief of. [. . .]

It is a strange, and even a surprising account you give of some under your ministry, and as I seem to conclude from what you wrote, that yourself was a 25 stranger thereto till you came to Bristol.

I shall pass by the outrages of the Anabaptists at Münster in Germany; as also the unaccountable agitations both of mind and body in the Quakers at their first appearances in this land, and sometimes (as I have heard) to this very day in some of their assemblies; and I have thought these people the more admire you 30 on the account of what you have related, and many are witnesses to.

As to the French Prophets, their rise, progress, and fall, you perhaps know as much as I can tell you.

[On John Mason (1646?–94), millenarian, known to 'my honour'd pastor, Mr. Chandler of Bedford'] 35

That which I have further to add is concerning Mr. Davis, a minister in Rothwell, Northants, whom I know and have heard. He was a man of good learning and a ready utterance. At his first coming into the county he was for some time at my father's house, and told my mother at his departure that he was going to preach the gospel at Rothwell, which my mother thought he 40 spoke with an air of too much self-confident boasting. I think about two years after he, with his wife, were again at our house, and by that time many were in very strange fits, and being asked concerning them his wife thus expressed herself, that she could wish her soul in their souls' stead who had these fits. Their antic gestures and unbecoming behaviour while Mr. Davis was preaching 45 would take up much time particularly to relate. When they were in these fits while Mr. D[avis] was preaching he would thus express himself, 'Regard them not, 'twill be well enough with them, etc.' The observation I then made (being well acquainted with the relation—from first to last) was, Some of these appeared afterwards to be real Christians, but many others not so.

I shall now briefly give you some observations on the whole, and propose a few queries, to which I shall desire your answers.

5　First, then, I observe that much of nature was to be seen in such fits. Daily experience proves that a moving discourse hath a natural tendency to raise the affections, . . . and women more generally are sooner and easier affected than men, from some causes you and I can account for.

Secondly, I observe there is sometimes a diabolical agency in raising or
10　promoting such fits, and as you have mentioned this I need not insist on it, as otherwise I could do. And in the French Prophets I have thought that Satan had a principal hand in their agitations.

Thirdly, I observe that 'tis the work of the Holy Spirit to convince of sin. And the convictions of the Spirit are either common or special. Many come under
15　a common work who never prove sincere converts, and yet God's ordinary way of working true grace in the souls of his elect is first by bringing 'em under a spirit of bondage by the law before he lovingly reveals his Christ and his covenant to their souls by the spirit of adoption. Thus the law is a schoolmaster to bring us to Christ, who is the end of the law for righteousness to everyone that
20　believeth.

The queries I would propose are these three:

First, how was it with them before they had these fits upon them? Were they before this persons of ignorance or knowledge? Were they of sober lives, or vicious and profane?

25　Secondly, how is it with them under those fits? Can they, after the fit is over, tell you what most affected 'em in hearing the word? Was it any particular doctrine you was upon, or come they upon any when you are treating on different and various subjects?

Thirdly, how is it with 'em after the fit is over? Are they subject to these fits
30　only while they are hearing of you, or is it afterwards as well as then?

And finally, what can their conversations witness for them?

I shall rejoice might the evidences of a sound conversion appear in an humble and close walking with God. Some remarkable instances I can give you of some while they have been hearing of me. But having already enlarged, I shall instance
35　only in one. While I was preaching at Basingstoke, Hants, (where I often preached) a young woman was hearing of me, and fell into a fit, and was immediately carried away. I think 'twas about the middle of the sermon; the text was in 20 John, 2nd verse. I do not remember she made any disturbance in the congregation. When I had done the exercise, I went to her house, knowing her to
40　have a godly character. I told her I was sorry she should be so taken while she was hearing of me. Her answer was either in these words, or in words to this effect, That she was never better in all her life, and that the opportunity was a good opportunity to her.

And now, dear sir, I commend you to God; and pray you may be greatly
45　owned of him in bringing in and building up, desiring your prayers for me, who lately have met with very trying dispensations of Providence, and who continually stand in need of the supplies of the Spirit of Christ. And so remain an unworthy labourer in the Lord's vineyard,　　　　　　　　　　　Joshua Read

P.S. Not one link of that glorious chain, Rom. 8 : 30, shall or can ever be broken, either by men or devils. The Lord enlighten such who are ignorant of his truth, and convince such who are opposers of it. I find the godly in all ages have not questioned the truth of God's electing love, though under darkness and temptation they have at times been under many doubts and fears as to their 5 interest therein, in which they have been supported by fresh applications by faith to the blood of the covenant.

Source: MA, four pages, no address, '1739' added in another hand after the date; down the margin of p. (1) JW has written: 'Write to Mr. Harris of Mr. Stevens'.

To the Revd. Charles Wesley[1]

Islington, Sept. 21, 1739

My dear brother

A Scotch gentleman who was present here gave us a plain account 10 of Mr. Erskine[2] and his Associates, the substance of which was this. Some years since Mr. Ebenezer Erskine, preaching before the Assembly, reproved them for several faults with all simplicity. This was so resented by many that in a following Assembly he was required to make an open recantation, and persisting in the charge 15 the Assembly determined that he, with three other ministers who spoke in his behalf, should be deprived, and their livings declared vacant. Four messengers were sent for this purpose; but they returned *re infecta*,[3] fearing the people, lest they should stone them. In another Assembly directions were[4] given to neighbouring 20 ministers [to procure] informations concerning the doctrine and behaviour of Mr. Erskine's and their adherents. Out of these informations an indictment was formed, to which they were summoned to answer in the next Assembly.

Here it was debated whether they should be suffered to come in, 25

[1] Throughout September Charles Wesley took his brother's place in Bristol, while John spent the month in London, returning to Bristol on Oct. 1 by way of Oxford. Something like this pattern of alternation remained normal for much of their subsequent ministries.

[2] See Wesley's letter to Ralph Erskine, Aug. 23, 1739. It seems at least possible that the 'Scotch gentleman' was Adam Gib (1714-88), who as an undergraduate at Edinburgh University had followed the controversy, and threw in his lot with the Erskines. On Sunday, Sept. 9, Wesley spent an hour with 'b[rother] Gibs'. It is more likely, however, that this was Francis Gibbes, for whom see Mar. 16, 1739, above.

[3] 'Without accomplishing their task'.

[4] Orig. (by amanuensis), 'was'.

and carried by a small majority that they should. The Moderator then spoke to this effect:

'My reverend brethren, ye are summoned to answer an indictment charging you with erroneous doctrine and irregular practices. But if 5 ye will submit to the Kirk, and testify your amendment, we will receive you with open arms.'

Mr. Erskine answered for himself and brethren (they were now increased to eight) to this purpose:

'Moderator, both you and those that are with you have erred from 10 the faith. And your practices are irregular, too. And you have no discipline. Therefore you are no Kirk. We are the Kirk, and we alone, who continue in her faith and discipline. And if ye will submit to us, and testify your amendment, we will receive you with open arms.'

15 None answered a word; so after a short time they withdrew. The Moderator then asked, 'My reverend brethren, what shall we do?' One replied, 'Moderator, I must answer you in our proverb: "You have put the cat into the kirn (i.e. churn); and ye must get her out again how you can."'

20 Again silence ensued, after which the Moderator asked, 'Shall these men be excommunicated, or only deposed?' Answer was made, The question is not right. Let it be asked, 'Shall they be deposed or not.' This was accordingly done, and it was carried by five votes 'that they should not be deposed'. Having received help from God, 25 they continue to this day, declaring to all that their congregation is the Kirk of Scotland; that they (the ministers, now ten in all) are the proper presbytery, and there is no other, those commonly so called having made shipwreck both of the faith and discipline once delivered to the saints.

30 Friday, Sept. 14. I expounded again at Islington; but the house being too small for the company I stood in the garden, and showed them how vainly they trusted to baptism for salvation unless they were holy of heart, without which their circumcision was actually become uncircumcision.[1] Afterwards I went to Fetter Lane, where 35 [I] brought down the high looks of the proud by an exposition of those words, 'All things are lawful for me; but all things edify not'.[2]

Sat. Sept. 15. I expounded those words on which the book opened, at Lady H[ume]'s,[3] 'The cares of this world, and the deceitfulness

---

[1] See Rom. 2: 25.　　　　　　　　　　　　　　[2] See 1 Cor. 10: 23.
[3] Of several possibilities, including Lady Grisell Hume (1665–1746), Scots poetess,

of riches, and the desires of other things, chokes the word, and it becometh unfruitful.'[1] At Fetter Lane I was directed to those words, 'I will pray the Father, and he shall give you another Comforter, that he may abide with you forever.'[2] Many were cut to the heart both here and at Mr. Exall's,[3] where I enforced those words of our Lord, 'Except ye be born again, ye cannot see the kingdom of God.'[4]

Sunday 16, I preached at Moorfields to about ten thousand, and at Kennington Common to between twenty and thirty thousand, on those words, 'We desire to hear of thee[5] what thou thinkest, for as concerning this sect, we know it is everywhere spoken against.'[6] At both places I described in very plain words the difference between true, old Christianity, commonly called by the new name of Methodism, and the Christianity now generally taught. Thence I went to Lambeth, where I found our congregation considerably increased, and exhorted them to cry mightily to our Lord, that he might [say] unto them, as unto the sick of the palsy, 'Be of good cheer. Thy sins are forgiven thee.'[7] From our love-feast at Fetter Lane I went to Islington House. Sufficient for this day was the labour thereof.[8]

Pray my love to brother Mitchell, and let the leaden cistern be gone about. On Monday sennight I intend, God willing, to set out. Tuesday I hope to spend at Oxford. On Wednesday night let Jo[hn] Ellis[9] meet me at Gloucester. Then I will lay out the three or four following days as we shall agree, if God permit. I heartily thank our bro[thers] Westell, Oldfield, Cross, Haydon, and Wynne, and our sisters Deffel, Shafto, Oldfield, Thomas, Stephens, Mrs. Thomas,

the most likely seems to be Elizabeth (formerly Pettis), who in 1737 married Alexander Hume (1708–60), the second son of the 2nd Earl of Marchmont, Sir Alexander Hume (1675–1740). Both Alexander and his older twin brother Hugh (1708–94), who succeeded to the earldom, added their mother's name, Campbell, and both were M.P.s for Berwickshire in 1739; Alexander's wife died without issue in 1770, Hugh's had four children to look after, and died in 1747. Still another possibility is Lady Mary Hume, daughter of Sir Gustavus Hume of Castle Hume, Ireland.

[1] See Mark 4: 19. [2] John 4: 16.
[3] William Exall; see Feb. 26, 1739.
[4] See John 3: 3.
[5] Orig., 'ye'.
[6] Acts 28: 22.
[7] See Matt. 9: 2.
[8] See Matt. 6: 34 (pages 1 and 4, which end here, are completely in the hand of Wesley's amanuensis, John Purdy).
[9] This may well be the same John Ellis, 'a stranger in Bristol' (possibly from Gloucester), who on Apr. 17, 1739, was filled with the Holy Ghost (see p. 636 above).

and Mrs. Deschamps. I wish any would write by Wednesday's post.
Pray for us. Adieu!
   Sat. night. Mrs. Exall's. [i.e. Sept. 22.]

Address: 'To The Revd. Mr. Wesley, At Mrs. Grevile, Bristol'   *Postmark*:
'22 SE'   *Charge*: '3'   *End* by CW: 'B. Sept. 1739 / the Erskines before
the Kirk'   *Source*: MA. (Most of the letter is in the hand of John Purdy.)

From the Revd. Ralph Erskine[1]

Dunfermline, Sept. 28, 1739

5 Revd. and dear sir
       I desire to bless the Lord for the good and great news your letter bears about
   the Lord's turning many souls from darkness to light, and from the power of
   Satan unto God, and that such a great and effectual door is opened among you
   as the many adversaries cannot shut. May he that hath the keys of the house of
10 David, that openeth and no man shutteth, and shutteth and no man openeth,
   set the door of faith more and more open among you, till his house be filled,
   and till he gather together the outcasts of Israel, and may that prayer for
   adversaries be heard, 'Fill their faces with shame, that they may seek thy name,
   O Lord.'
15   As to the outward manner you speak of, wherein most of these were affected
   who were cut to the heart by the sword of the Spirit, no wonder that they were at
   first surprising to you, since they are indeed so very rare that have been thus
   pricked and wounded. Yet some of the instances you give seem to be exemplified
   in the outward manner wherein Paul and the gaoler were at first affected, as also
20 Peter's hearers, Acts two. The last instance you give, of some struggling as in
   the agonies of death, and in such a manner as four or five strong men can hardly
   restrain a weak woman or a child from hurting themselves or others, this is to me
   somewhat more inexplicable, if it do not resemble the child spoke of Mark 9 : 26
   and Luke 9 : 42, of whom it is said that 'when he was yet coming the devil
25 threw him down and tare him'. Or what influence sudden and sharp awakenings
   may have upon sudden bodily convulsions I pretend not to explain. But I
   make no question, Satan, so far as he gets power, may exert himself on such
   occasions, partly to mar and *hinder* the beginning of the good work in the persons
   that are touched with the sharp arrows of conviction, the enemy being unwilling
30 to quit his old possession; and partly also to prevent the success of the gospel on
   others, while he seeks thus to disparage the work of God, and bring it under
   contempt and reproach, as if it tended to lead people only to madness and distraction. And in the meantime a holy sovereign God may permit it for hardening
   a wicked generation, justly leaving them to stumble, and for trying the faith
35 and constancy of his own children, whom he has called effectually. However,
   the merciful issue of these conflicts, in the conversion of these persons thus
   affected, is the main thing. When they are brought, by the saving arm of God,

[1] See Wesley's letter of Aug. 24, 1739, which this answers.

to receive Jesus Christ, to have joy and peace in believing, and then to walk in him, and give evidence that the work is a saving work at length, whether more quickly or gradually accomplished, there is great matter of praise.

As to the work of God among us, an account whereof you seem to desiderate, though we cannot deny but we sensibly feel now and then some remarkable 5 breathings of the Spirit of God in praying and preaching, and frequently hear of savoury impressions made by the Word upon the hearts of people, and of some good fruits following; and though any instances of his powerful presence this way seem at this juncture to relate more to the carrying on of the good work where begun than to the remarkable conversion of others; yet we want 10 not instances of his power and pity this way, though not appearing outwardly in such sudden and visible effects as these you mention. All the outward appearances of people's being affected among us, in time of preaching, and especially at sacramental occasions, in time of communicating, or other such solemn seasons, may be reduced to these two sorts. One is, hearing with a 15 close, silent attention, with gravity and greediness, discovered by fixed looks, weeping eyes, joyful or sorrowful like countenances, evidencing tenderness in hearing. Another sort is, when the Word is so affecting to the congregation as to make them lift up their voice and weep aloud, some more depressedly, others more highly, and at times the whole multitude in a flood of tears, all as it 20 were crying out at once, till their voice be ready to drown out the minister's, so as he can scarcely be heard for the weeping noise that surrounds him. And though we judge that the more solid and judicious of the auditory are seldom so noisy as others, though perhaps as much and more affected inwardly, yet of these that are thus outwardly affected we conceive some to be under a more 25 common, and others under a special gracious influence of the Spirit of God, which we can know only by the fruits and effects that follow. The common influence, like a land flood, dries up, we hear of no change wrought; the other appears afterward in the fruits of righteousness and the tract of a holy conversation. 30

As to the impression the Word makes upon these whom we take afterward to be true converts, the degrees and duration of a law work or conviction are various, and the saving issue comes to be known also at sundry times and in divers manners. Some have been more quickly touched and turned to the Lord and his ways, others have been many weeks, yea, many months, if not years, 35 under much heaviness, bondage, grievous terrors, and horrible temptations; some relieved very gradually, with a word now and a word then impressed upon them, and some outpouring of the Spirit upon them now and then, and further degrees of illumination and divine teaching, till by little and little they have come to more establishment in the faith, and till they be brought off from 40 all confidence not only in their own works and duties in point of justification before God, but also from all confidence in and dependence upon their best frames, tears, enlargements, influences, and attainments, to a solid life of faith upon the grounds that are unchangeable, viz. the promise of God, the righteousness of Christ, the grace and fullness that is in him, etc. 45

May the Lord strengthen you to go on in his work, and in praying for the coming of his kingdom with you and us. I hope you shall not be forgotten among us in our joint applications to the throne of grace. Pray let me hear at your leisure hours more and more of what the Lord is doing among you. I am, reverend and very dear sir, your affectionate brother and servant in Christ,

Ralph Erskine

Source: Ralph Erskine, *Fraud and Fals[e]hood Discovered*, Edinburgh, 1743, pp. 6–9; cf. JWJ, June 30, 1739, an undated, abridged, and edited version; cf. also Donald Fraser, *Life and Diary of the Revd. Ralph Erskine*, Edinburgh, 1834, pp. 291–7, where pp. 294–7 (over half the letter) are an extension of the paragraph beginning, 'As to the impression . . .'—which seems very peculiar in view of Erskine's strong criticism of 'Mr. Webster's false copy' of his letter. (See pp. 9–32. Alexander Webster, *Divine Influence the true Spring of the extraordinary Work at Cambuslang and other places in the West of Scotland*, 2nd edn., Edinburgh, 1742, pp. 62–3, had reprinted Erskine's letter from the heavily edited text in Wesley's *Journal*, which had just appeared. In *Fraud and Falshood* Erskine unfairly chastised Webster for the alterations. Webster retaliated on Mar. 15, 1743, with a *Letter* pointing out his source, and claiming that Erskine in fact knew this in advance.)

From the Revd. Charles Kinchin[1]

Dummer, Oct. 9, 1739

5 My dear brother

I write this to inform you that I am just upon setting out for Oxford, and thence probably for London, in order to print my sermon upon the Necessity and Marks of the New Birth. I have revised and enlarged it, have made a preface and a dedication to the Vice-Chancellor, Dr. Mather, [and] the Heads of Houses,
10 with their societies. Mr. Hutchings has perused the whole. I shall leave him at Dummer in the meanwhile. I asked the Vice-Chancellor for liberty of the University Press. His answer was that he could by no means consent to it. I have wrote him a letter, to desire him to peruse the discourse before he absolutely refuses the Press. I write this to desire your prayers and the prayers of your
15 friends around you, that God would bless my journey and the design of publishing the discourse. The Vice-Chancellor has wrote me no answer. I propose therefore to wait upon him at Oxford, to know whether he received my letter, and to desire Mr. Gambold and Mr. Wells to peruse my sermon. If I had any opportunity I could be glad you might have a sight of it, too. My dear brother,
20 I was not at Oxford when you directed a letter to me at Mr. Fox's the latter end of July. But I have had the letter since, and will you not hear me patiently if I fairly represent the matter concerning Mr. Fox again unto you? I think it my duty, my brother, for I hope upon reconsidering the thing it will appear to you as well as to me, etc., that you are not clear of your engagement to him. This is a
25 paragraph of your letter to me: 'When I was at Oxford I set upon recovering the Castle stock, and collecting the arrears of subscriptions, out of which I engaged

---

[1] This reply to Wesley's letter of July 28, 1739, about the support of Mr. Fox, the ex-prisoner of Oxford, also quotes an important paragraph from that missing letter.

to pay Mr. Fox's rent. When I was called away, I supposed you would have
supplied my place. While I am here, I can't solicit contributions at Oxford.
Ten shillings I will gladly contribute myself. I shall rejoice to hear you have
fixed him in some business.' Now, my brother, is there not more of evasion than
simplicity in this paragraph? Here you allow you engaged to pay Mr. Fox's 5
rent. Therefore ought you not to stand to your engagement? To dissolve it you
say, 'When I was called away, I supposed you would have supplied my place.'
How so, my brother? Who is most concerned to fulfil your engagements? You
or I? If the care of my parish would have allowed me to have resided in Oxford,
after I had resigned my fellowship, yet why should you imagine that I would 10
of course take upon me your engagement to pay Mr. Fox's rent, without your
giving me any intimation of what you had done, or of what you would have me
do in your stead? I knew nothing of what you had engaged till Mr. Fox told
me, which occasioned my writing to you upon the subject. And he said nothing
as I know of as to your promising it out of the Castle stock. You say, 'While 15
I am here, I can't solicit contributions at Oxford.' Nor more can I, while I am
here, by word of mouth speak to you *at* Bristol. You say, 'I shall rejoice to
hear you have fixed him in some business.' Mr. Fox is in debt. His debts should
be paid first. The best business he and we can think of is to buy and sell fowl
and pigs (which he can keep in his yard), and cheeses. There will be need of 20
about £30. Mr. Hutchings wrote this very day to Mr. Ingham to ask charity
for him. I am to write to Lady Cocks, Mr. Stonehouse, etc. We propose he shall
have the money we can raise by way of loan, which we may withdraw upon mismanagement, and to make him accountable for everything. You know how much
you was for his staying at Oxford, when there was a motion for his settling at 25
London. If you shall rejoice to hear him fixed in some business, lend a helping
hand, my dear brother, and do as we do upon the occasion; then it is likely, with
God's blessing, you may see him fixed in some business soon. We all join in
love to you and all friends around you. We constantly pray for you, and desire
your prayers. If you write within a week, direct to Mr. Fox's. Your unworthy 30
brother,

C. Kinchin

Address: 'To The Revd Mr John Wesley at Mrs Grevil's, Grocer, in Wine-
Street, Bristol' *Postmarks*: One illegible, and '12 OC' *Charges*: ((3)),
'In all 7' *End* by JW: 'C Kinchin / Oct. 9, 1739 / a[nswer]d Dec. 17'; also
(struck through), 'Mr. Godfr[ey], Exeter'[1] *Source*: MA.

[1] On this day, Dec. 17, 1739, Wesley wrote to a Quaker, Lawford Godfrey of Exeter,
who replied Dec. 25 (see Appendix).

To the Revd. James Hervey[1]

[Oct. 25, 1739]

My dear brother

I did not receive yours till a few days since, having been at London for some time.

5   Though Basil[2] and Nazianzen[3] were good men, I know a better, Jesus of Nazareth. And were I now to prepare myself for the service of his church, I would do it by following his example, 'going about doing good',[4] temporal or spiritual, as of the small 'ability which God giveth'.[5]

10   After his example, as well as by his commission, which man cannot take away, 'while I have time I do good unto all men',[6] knowing the night cometh, when no man can work.[7] The manner wherein I do this (as confidently as it has been asserted), is contrary to no law that I know, either of church or state. Though if it were, I would

15 still act as I do; for I am to obey God rather than man.[8] A dispensation of the gospel is committed to me, and woe is me if I preach not the gospel.[9]

'But you would have me preach it in a parish.'[10] What parish, my brother? I have none at all. Nor I believe ever shall. Must I there-

20 fore bury my talent in the earth? Then am I a wicked, unprofitable servant.[11]

The constitution of the apostolical church is as much for our preaching everywhere as the example of the apostles. The travels of Timothy are recorded in the Acts. Nor do I believe either *he or*

25 *Titus or any Christian minister was confined to any one place till the love of Christians waxed cold.*[12]

---

[1] Replying to Hervey's letter of Aug. 21.

[2] St. Basil the Great (*c.* 330–79), whose example (with that of 'Nazianzen') Hervey had written that he was following in his rural seclusion. Basil settled as a hermit near Caesarea, from which he and 'Nazianzen' would go on preaching missions together, until 370, when Basil was persuaded to follow Eusebius as Bishop of Caesarea.

[3] St. Gregory of Nazianzus (329–89), with Basil one of the 'Cappadocian fathers', with whom he had studied at the University of Athens. In 381 he was appointed Bishop of Constantinople, but resigned the following year to continue the life of a Christian recluse.

[4] See Acts 10: 38.   [5] 1 Pet. 4: 11.   [6] See Gal. 6: 10.
[7] John 9: 4.   [8] See Acts 5: 29.   [9] 1 Cor. 9: 16–17.
[10] This is one of many hundreds of examples of Wesley's use of quotation marks to show that he is echoing his source's sentiments, if not his exact words.
[11] See Matt. 25: 25, 26, 30.   [12] See Matt. 24: 12.

But indeed I could not serve (as they term it) a cure now. I have tried, and know it is impracticable to observe the laws of the English Church in any parish in England. I observed them in my parish of Savannah, till I was obliged to fly for my life. Mr. Stonehouse is now persecuted on every side for observing them; and the good bishop, 5 instead of defending his presbyter, is at the head of his persecutors.

Set the matter in another light, and it comes to a short issue. I everywhere see God's people perishing for lack of knowledge. I have power (through God) to save their souls from death. Shall I use it, or shall I let them perish—'because they are not of my parish'? 10

My dear brother, may our good God lead you into all truth! To hear often from you would be a pleasure to, your ever affectionate friend and brother,

J. Wesley

Bristol, Oct. 25, 1739 15

Address: 'To The Revd. Mr. Hervey At Paul Orchard's, Esq. At Stoke-abby, near Biddiford' *Postmark*: 'B/ris/tol' *Charge*: '4' *Source*: Lincoln College, Oxford.

To the Revd. Samuel Wesley, Jun.[1]

[Oct. 27, 1739]

Dear brother

For teaching erroneous doctrine I grant there is no fear anyone should now be presented. For the world will love its own, and will tolerate everything—but the gospel of Christ. 20

In a few days my brother and I are to go to Oxford to do exercise for our degrees.[2] Then, if God enables me, I will prove my charge

---

[1] Replying to his brother's letter of Sept. 3. Samuel Wesley's health had been declining, and on Nov. 6 he died suddenly.

[2] This is puzzling. Both John and Charles Wesley would seem to have had their fill of academic exercises, both for their bachelors' and masters' degrees; John had graduated M.A. on Feb. 14, 1726/7, and Charles on Mar. 12, 1732/3. Yet the evidence of this letter implies that both were toying with the idea of going on to their B.D. at Oxford, which necessitated an additional five years of disputations, university sermons, fees, and (possibly) residence. This is confirmed by the entry in CWJ for Nov. 2, 1739: 'Received a summons from Oxford, to respond in Divinity Disputations; which, with other concurrent providences, is a plain call to that place.' It appears that the sudden death of their elder brother made them drop the idea, at least for the time being. In 1741 John

against Bishop Bull, either in my Latin sermon,[1] or Supposition Speech.[2]

You ask four questions concerning those who have been taken ill here. I answer: (1), some have been so affected in the church, while
5 I was preaching *within consecrated walls*; (2), most of these were cut to the heart while I was inculcating the general doctrine that Christ died to save sinners; (3), many of them were gross sinners, whoremongers, drunkards, common swearers, till that hour, but not afterwards. And many of them were people of unblemished characters,
10 and as touching the outward law of God, blameless.

I still think it a full proof that this was God's work that 'in that hour they felt the love of God shed abroad in their hearts, and they were filled with inward righteousness, and peace and joy unspeakable and full of glory; and that the reality of this inward change appeared
15 by their holiness in all manner of conversation.'[3]

O my brother, who hath bewitched you,[4] that for fear of I know not what distant consequences you cannot rejoice at, nor so much as acknowledge, the great power of God? How is it that you can't praise God for saving so many souls from death, and covering such a
20 multitude of sins,[5] unless he will begin this work within 'consecrated

at least returned to the project, but little came of it except a scathing but unused Latin sermon (see JWJ, June 18, 1741).

[1] A Latin sermon preached in St. Mary's was one of the exercises prescribed for a B.D. candidate. A gap in Wesley's diary prevents our discovering whether Wesley did anything about this during his foreshortened visit to Oxford *en route* to Tiverton on Nov. 13–15, but probably he did not. On June 22, 1741, however, he 'writ plan of Latin sermon' (on Isa. 1: 21), and completed the manuscript in English on June 24, and in Latin on June 27. (Both manuscripts are extant, and are included in this edition, Vol. 4.) This sermon does incorporate passages from Bishop Bull's *Harmonia Apostolica* which deny justification by faith alone by stating that good works are essential, thus following up Wesley's letter to his brother of Feb. 3, 1739 (see p. 599 above); Wesley also challenges the university in general for its disregard of many of its own statutes. On July 3, 1741, he began a sermon on Acts 26: 28 ('The Almost Christian', No. 2, in Vol. 1), which he preached in St. Mary's on July 25, one of the triennial calls upon him to preach before the University at a regular service, rather than the Latin exercise. (He may indeed have pondered preaching the startling Isaiah sermon on both occasions, but his diary shows no use of it by Aug. 8, 1741, after which the diary is missing; nor are there any letters to illuminate that period.)

[2] The disputations were introduced by a 'supposition speech' setting forth a summary of the position taken by the 'respondent' on the question to be debated.

[3] Although this passage contains two major scriptural quotations (Rom. 5: 5 and 1 Pet. 1: 8), it is probably a quotation from one of Wesley's own letters to his brother Samuel, which has disappeared, though the general sentiments appear in several letters to him during the preceding months.

[4] Gal. 3: 1.   [5] See 1 Pet. 4: 8.

walls'? Why should he not fill heaven and earth? You cannot, indeed
you cannot, confine the Most High within temples made with hands.[1]
I do not despise them, any more than you. But I rejoice to find that
God is everywhere. I love the rites and ceremonies of the Church.
But I see, well-pleased, that our great Lord can work without them. 5
And howsoever and wheresoever a sinner is converted from the
error of his ways,[2] nay, and by whomsoever, I therein rejoice, yea,
and will rejoice!

I rejoice that our God is mighty to save![3] And I know that notwithstanding the inveterate (and humanly speaking unconquerable) 10
prejudices which both my sister and you have to me, he is able to
make us of one heart and of one mind.[4] What would you think of
our new faith (as you term it) if God should send two or three that
believe in his name (I lightly touch upon it, because the thing is
not yet clear to me) and the prayer of faith should save the sick,[5] and 15
your health be restored from that hour?[6]

May the God of our fathers rest with you and yours. I am, dear
brother, your ever affectionate brother,

John Wesley

Oct. 27, 1739   20
Bristol

Source: Lambeth Palace Library, London.

To the Revd. Joshua Read[7]

[Oct. 27, 1739]

Dear sir

Hurry of business prevented my writing sooner. Is Mr. Davis[8]
now alive?   25

I believe nature might have a part in those fits, as well as Satan,
raging before he is cast out; but that the Holy Spirit, deeply convincing them of sin, is the chief agent in most of those who are seized
with them.

---

[1] See Acts 7: 48; 17: 24.   [2] See Jas. 5: 20.   [3] Isa. 63: 1.
[4] See Acts 4: 32.   [5] Jas. 5: 15.   [6] See Matt. 9: 22.
[7] Replying to Read's of Sept. 11, which see for a note on Read and his links with
Wesley.
[8] A Nonconformist minister at Rothwell, Northants, members of whose congregation,
said Read, were subject to 'very strange fits' during his ministry.

To your questions I answer:

1. Some of these persons were very ignorant before that time; some were (what the world calls) very knowing. Again, some of them were grossly vicious and profane; others, as touching the righteous-
5 ness of the law, blameless.[1]

2. Some of them can afterwards give a distinct account of the words that affected them. These have usually been some single sentence, often taken from the Holy Scripture, which suddenly pierced their soul like a dart, so that they lost all command of
10 themselves in that moment. The subjects were various, but always bordering upon the love of Christ to lost sinners.

3. The fit commonly ends as suddenly as it begins. Either they see Christ by the eye of faith; or a scriptural promise is applied to their soul as they are filled with peace and joy, they know not how.
15 And at that instant strength is often restored to their bodies, as well as comfort given to their souls. Some are thus affected only once, and that while they are hearing the Word; others, many times, chiefly in hearing; but sometimes in their own houses.

4. We have reason to hope, most of those who have been seized
20 but ONCE are indeed new creatures. Of some that were ill many times I stand in doubt, lest they should draw back into perdition.[2]

I should be glad of your farther thoughts on this head, as likewise of your advice how to proceed with those who after they have believed are again in darkness. What do you think are the surest signs where-
25 by to distinguish desertion from the law-work? The darkness following faith from that preceding it?

I commend you, dear sir, to our good God, and desire your constant prayers for, your weak, but affectionate brother,

John Wesley

30 Bristol,
Oct. 27, 1739

Address: 'To the Revd. Mr Read at Bradford'   *Postmark*: 'B/ris/tol'
Charge, etc.: '3', and 'per Nolls' or 'Wolls'—probably 'Noll's', i.e. by 'Oliver's' postbag, rather than the name of a place   *Source*: Sevenoaks Methodist Church, England.

[1] See Phil. 3: 6.   [2] See Heb. 10: 39.

From Thomas Andrews[1]

[Oct. 29?, 1739]

Reverend sir

As I wrote the *Rules* and *Considerations* (in No. 25 of *Country Common-Sense*) with an eye to *Mr. Whitefield, yourself,* and your *opposers,* from a sincere desire to do some service to Christianity, according to the *imperfect* notions I had 5 at that time of the real merits of the cause, I at the same time resolved to take any opportunity that should offer for my *better* information.

On this principle it was that I made one of your audience, October 23, at Bradford. And because I thought I could form the best judgment of you and your doctrines from your sermon, I resolved to hear that first; which was the 10 reason that, although by accident I was at the same house, and walked two miles with you to the place you preached at, I spoke little or nothing to you. I must confess, sir, that the discourse you made that day, wherein you pressed your hearers in the closest manner, and with the authority of a true minister of the gospel, not to stop at faith ONLY, but to add to it all *virtues,* and to show forth 15 their *faith* by every kind of *good works,*[2] convinced me of the great wrong done you by a public report, common in people's mouths, that you preach *faith* without *works.* For that is the only ground of *prejudice* which any true Christian can have, and is the sense in which your adversaries would take your words when they censure them. For that we are *justified* by faith ONLY is the doctrine 20 of Jesus Christ, the doctrine of the apostles, and the doctrine of the Church of England. I am ashamed that, after having lived twenty-nine years since my baptism into this faith, I should speak of it in the lame, unfaithful, I may say, *false* manner I have done in the paper above mentioned! What mere *darkness* is man, when truth hideth her face from him! 25

Man is by nature a *sinner,* the child of the devil, under God's *wrath,* in a

---

[1] Thomas Andrews (1710–39) of Seend, Wiltshire, though a young man, was 'remarkable above his years both for piety, sense, and learning' (JWJ, Mar. 12, 1749). He was the reputed author of a series of essays entitled *Country Common-Sense*, by 'a Gentleman of Wiltshire' (J. de L. Mann, *The Cloth Industry in the West of England from 1640 to 1880*, Oxford, Clarendon Press, 1971, pp. 109-10). Part III was advertised in *The Gloucester Journal* for Aug. 14, 1739, the last of its eight essays being therein described as: 'XXV. A Discourse on *Enthusiasm*. Rules to be observed by its *Opposers*, with several Considerations proper to discover a *Spirit of Delusion*, and to keep *well-meaning Christians* from it.' This Wesley read while in Wiltshire, and in his *Journal* for July 31, 1739, reprinted Andrews' irenic rules, as 'published about this time' (*Country Common-Sense*, London, Hitch, 1739, pp. 161-2). Wesley announced that he would preach at Bearfield, Bradford-on-Avon (see p. 682 n. above) on Tuesday, Oct. 23, at 11 a.m. Seend was about seven miles to the east, but Andrews apparently happened to be in the hamlet of Turleigh, two miles west of Bradford, where Wesley arrived at 9.45 a.m.—possibly invited by the Longs to the recently rebuilt manor house (see Wesley's diary and V.C.H., Wiltshire, VII. 21). Andrews observed Wesley closely, but cautiously made no overtures. Unfortunately he died of smallpox shortly afterwards, but not before his reports of this and Wesley's sermon a few days later so enthused his father that the Revd. Thomas Andrews also eventually sought an acquaintance with Wesley (JWJ, Mar. 12, 1749).   [2] From Rom. 8:15 (see Wesley's diary).

state of *damnation*. The Son of God took pity on this our misery. He made himself man, he made himself sin for us; that is, he hath borne the *punishment* of our sin, the chastisement of *our* peace was upon him, and by his stripes we are healed. To receive this boundless mercy, this inestimable benefit, we must have
5 faith in our Benefactor, and through him in God. [. . .] But then true faith is not a lifeless principle, as your adversaries seem to understand it. They and you mean quite another thing by *faith*. They mean a bare believing that Jesus is the Christ. You mean a living, growing, purifying principle, which is the root both of inward and outward holiness; both of *purity* and *good works*, without which
10 no man can have faith, at least no other than a dead faith.

This, sir, you explained in your sermon at Bradford, Sunday, October 28,[1] to near ten thousand people, who all stood to hear you, with awful silence and great attention. I have since reflected how much good the clergy might do if, instead of *shunning*, they would come to hear and converse with you; and in
15 their churches and parishes would farther enforce those *catholic doctrines* which you preach, and which I am glad to see have such a surprising *good effect* on great numbers of souls.

I think, indeed, too many clergymen are culpable in that they don't inform themselves better of Mr.Wh[itefiel]d, yourself, and your doctrines, from your
20 own mouths. I am persuaded if they did this with a Christian spirit the differences between you would soon be at an end. Nay, I think those whose *flocks* resort so much to hear you ought to do it out of their *pastoral duty* to them; that if you preach *good doctrine* they may edify them on the impression so visibly made by your sermons, or, if *evil*, they may reclaim them from error.
25 I shall conclude this letter with putting you in mind, in all your sermons, writings, and practice, *nakedly* to follow the *naked* Jesus: I mean, to preach the *pure doctrines* of the gospel without respect of persons or things. Many *preachers*, many *reformers*, many *missionaries*, have fallen by not observing this; by not having continually in mind, 'Whosoever shall break the least of these command-
30 ments, and teach men so, he shall be called the least in the kingdom of heaven.'[. . .]

Source: JWJ, Nov. 1, 1739, thus introduced: 'About this time I received a letter from the author of those reflections which I mentioned July 31; an extract of which I have subjoined.'

From the Revd. George Whitefield[2]

Wrote at sea, dated at Philadelphia, Nov. 8, 1739

Honoured and dear sir
God has been pleased to send us a comfortable passage. The orphan-house accounts come right, within ten pounds. I have had great assurances given me
35 that it will be a Pietas Georgiensis, equally remarkable with the Pietas Hallensis.
I am almost persuaded that what was to be done by Dean Berkeley elsewhere,[3]

---

[1] From Acts 20: 26–7 (ibid.).
[2] After long delays, on Aug. 13 Whitefield embarked on the *Elizabeth*, which arrived at Philadelphia on Nov. 2.
[3] See above, p. 462 n.

God's mighty hand will bring to pass in Georgia. I shall continue there above six months. If Mr. Hutchings would come to supply my place, I would keep the parsonage of Savannah. Otherwise, I will resign all but the orphan-house. God has been pleased to send me great inward trials; but uncommon enlargements have followed afterwards. I have read Guyse and Doddridge on the Evangelists, 5 and wrote to both. The former I think excellent, the latter, ingenious, elaborate. but too superficial. Neal's Lives of the Puritans have been of use. I think they held the truth as it is in Jesus. The Quakers have set us an example of patient, resolute suffering, as the best means to weary our enemies. I want the lives of Luther and Calvin, to get some short account of the history of the Reformation. 10

At my return I trust I shall open my mouth and speak boldly, as I ought to speak. The account of my infant years was wrote by the will of God. Pray let it be published, without any material diminution or addition. He that hideth his sins shall not prosper. My Letter to the Religious Societies I give for the schools at Bristol. The Lord prosper the work of your hands upon you. I have wrote to 15 the Bishop of Gloucester, and have delivered my soul by meekly telling him of his faults. God has made my pen the pen of a ready writer. I long to hear how affairs go on in England. Are you yet the Lord's prisoner? If they make any laws whatsoever, I trust notwithstanding I shall preach with all boldness. O, dear sir, pray publicly, as well as in private, for your unworthy, loving servant, 20
GW

Source: *A.M.*, 1778, pp. 178–9. Wesley added his own comment at the end: 'I recommend this letter (which, I presume, is not published in the late collection)[1] to the consideration of Mr. Rowland Hill. It seems Mr. Whitefield was just now warping towards Calvinism, which all the Oxford Methodists utterly abhorred.

[To James Hutton (?)][2]

[Nov. 14 (?), 1739]

. . . Sunday, Nov. 11. I preached at eight, to five or six thousand, on the spirit of bondage and the spirit of adoption;[3] and at five in the evening to seven or eight thousand, in the place which had been the 25

[1] *The Works of the Reverend George Whitefield*, . . . *With a Select Collection of Letters*, London, 6 vols., 1771–2 (this letter not being included).
[2] On Oct. 24, 1739, Hutton returned from a visit to Germany, and Wesley spent two hours with him on Nov. 9, and the whole morning on Nov. 10, along with Spangenberg and Molther. Unfortunately Wesley's diary is missing from Nov. 11 to Apr. 12, 1740, so that is is extremely difficult to follow his activities. It seems quite certain, however, that either during his two days at Oxford (Nov. 13–14) or during his brief stay in Bristol (Nov. 16–19), he resumed his correspondence with Hutton, who remained his most trusted colleague in London in the absence of his brother Charles.
[3] See Rom. 8: 15.

King's Foundery for cannon.[1] O hasten thou the time, when nation shall not rise up against nation, neither shall they know war any more . . .[2]

[Monday, Nov. 12, at High Wycombe.] Here we unexpectedly found Mr. Robson and Gambold, with whom, after much prayer and consultation, we agreed: (1), to meet yearly at London, if God permit, on the eve of Ascension Day;[3] (2), to fix then the business to be done the ensuing year: where, when, and by whom; (3), to meet quarterly there, as many as can: viz. on the second Tuesday in July, October, and January; (4), to send a monthly account to one another of what God hath done in each of our stations; (5), to inquire whether Mr. Hall, Sympson,[4] Rogers,[5] Ingham, Hutchins,[6] Kinchin, Stonehouse, Cennick, Oxlee,[7] and Brown,[8] will join with us herein; (6), to consider whether there be any others of our spiritual friends who are able and willing so to do . . .

Source: Whitehead, II. 125–6, from a source or sources which he does not describe, but most probably a journal-letter to James Hutton, no longer extant—the fate of several similar letters to him (see p. 673, *source*, above).

[1] Messrs. Ball and Watkins had pleaded with him 'once and again' to preach here (see *Earnest Appeal*, in this edn., ll. 84–5). On this occasion (from the numbers hearing him) he apparently spoke in the area adjoining the building, but after his return to London on Dec. 19 Wesley began to meet a group of his followers on Thursday evenings in the patched-up premises, and in January asked Hutton to begin negotiations for securing a permanent lease of the derelict building (see below, Jan. 25, 1740).

[2] See Mic. 4: 3.   [3] In 1740, Wednesday, May 14.

[4] John Sympson of Gainsborough, Lincs., who was admitted to Lincoln College, Oxford, in 1728, where in 1730 Wesley became his tutor. After his graduation in 1731 Wesley's diary continued to note letters to him, as 'Sympson' from 1733–8, but from 1739–40 as 'Simpson'. After ordination he seems to have served in Leicestershire, but for a time at least he was associated with the Moravians. He is almost certainly to be identified with the Revd. John Sympson reported by the *Gent. Mag.* for 1756 as becoming vicar of 'Brinksey', Lancs. (? Friskney or Grimsby, Lincs.), and probably with the Revd. John Simpson whose death the same magazine reported at Stone Hall, near Stoney Middleton, Derbyshire, Apr. 5, 1784.

[5] The Revd. Jacob Rogers, of Gildersome, Yorks., educated at Trinity College, Cambridge, ordained deacon at Lincoln in 1737, to become curate of St. Paul's, Bedford, where his evangelical preaching sparked a revival, until he was dismissed for preaching against drunken clergy, and began field-preaching, collaborating with Whitefield. Eventually he became the mainstay of the Moravian work in Bedford.

[6] Apparently the Revd. John Hutchings, rather than Richard Hutchins.

[7] William Oxlee, one of the early members of the Fetter Lane society, who became a leading London Moravian. Like the other two named at the end of this list, he was a layman. (The majority of those named became Moravians at some time.)

[8] Almost certainly John Browne, a London woollen-draper, one of the founding members of the Fetter Lane society, who had accompanied Wesley to Herrnhut. He threw in his lot with the Moravians, and later became one of their pastors.

To Thomas Price[1]

[Dec. 6, 1739]

My dear brother

Our sincere thanks attend you for your seasonable assistance. I have writ to our dear brother Howell Harris,[2] and sent him a short account of the design which we are carrying on in Kingswood also; which perhaps may be agreeable to them who are with you, too, for which reason I have sent you a copy[3] of it, vizt:[4]

Few persons have lived long in the West of England who have not heard of the colliers of Kingswood, a people famous from the beginning hitherto for neither fearing God nor regarding man;[5] so ignorant of the things of God that they could only be compared to the beasts that perish;[6] and therefore utterly without desire of instruction, as well as without the means of it.

To this people Mr. Whitefield last spring began to preach the gospel of Christ, and as there were thousands of them who went to no place of public worship, he went out into their own wilderness, to seek and to save that which was lost.[7] When he was called away others went into the highways and hedges, to compel them to come in.[8]

---

[1] Thomas Price (1712–83), of Watford, a prominent Methodist layman and exhorter, at whose home assembled the formative Methodist Association of Jan. 5–6, 1743, with Whitefield presiding, and among those present Joseph Humphreys and John Cennick, in addition to the Revd. Daniel Rowlands, Howell Harris, and other leaders of Welsh Methodism. Watford was a village on the south side of Caerphilly, about six miles north of Cardiff. Both John and Charles Wesley held services in Price's home during 1740, and John Wesley may well have met him during his visit to Cardiff in October, 1739.

[2] For Howell Harris see letter of July 2, 1739, p. 663 n.

[3] This seems to have been one of the instances where Wesley made multiple copies of a letter in order to solicit support—in part by employing an amanuensis (see Intro., p. 39). At least three copies are known to have been prepared:

(1) That to 'Mr. D', published in Wesley's *Journal* for Nov. 27, 1739, thus introduced: 'I writ Mr. D. (according to his request) a short account of what had been done in Kingswood, and of our present undertaking there.' Doubtless this was opened and closed with personal greetings and messages.

(2) That to Howell Harris, probably written about Dec. 1, 1739, and alluded to in the present letter.

(3) This to Thomas Price, the only holograph extant. In many details this differs from (1). Some variations may be due to hasty copying by Purdy, but it seems that Wesley revised his prototype, and there are considerable alterations in the fourth paragraph: completely new is the passage, 'It is proposed . . . may not be hindered.'

[4] This copy of the body of the letter is in the hand of John Purdy, as is the endorsement.

[5] See Luke 18: 2.

[6] See Ps. 49: 12, 20.

[7] Luke 19: 10.

[8] See Luke 14: 23.

And by the grace of God their labour was not in vain. The scene was entirely changed. Kingswood does not now, as a year ago, resound with cursing and blasphemy. It is no longer the seat of drunkenness, uncleanness, and all idle diversions that lead thereto.
5 It is no longer filled with wars, fightings, with clamour and bitterness, with strife and envying.[1] Peace and love are now there; the people (in general) are become mild, gentle, and easy to be entreated;[2] they do not cry, neither strive, and hardly is their voice heard in the streets;[3] or indeed in their own wood, unless when they are at their
10 usual evening diversions—singing Psalms unto God their Saviour. That their children also might know the things that make for their peace,[4] it was proposed some months since to build a school in Kingswood. And after many difficulties the foundation of it was laid in June last, in the middle of the wood, on a place called Two
15 Mile Hill, between the London and Bath roads, about three measured miles from Bristol. A large room was begun there for a school, having four small rooms at each end for the schoolmasters, and hereafter (if it should please God) some poor children, to lodge in it. Two persons are ready to teach, so soon as the house is fit to
20 receive them, the shell of which is nearly finished. It is proposed, in the usual hours of the day, to teach (chiefly the poorer) children to read, write, and cast accounts; but more especially (by God's assistance), 'to know God, and Jesus Christ whom he hath sent'.[5] The elder people, being not so proper to be mixed with children
25 (we expect scholars of all ages, some of them grey-headed), will be taught in the inner rooms, either early in the morning or late at night, so as their work may not be hindered.

It is true, although the masters will not take any pay (for the love of Christ constrains them,[6] as they have freely received, freely to
30 give),[7] yet this undertaking is attended with great expense. But let him that feedeth the young ravens[8] see to that. If he puts it into your heart or the hearts of any of your friends to assist us in bringing this work to perfection, in this world look for no recompense; but it shall be remembered in that day when our Lord shall say unto you,
35 Inasmuch as ye did it unto the least of these my brethren, ye did it unto me.[9]

---

[1] See Eph. 4: 28; Rom. 13: 13.   [2] Jas. 3: 17.
[3] See 2 Cor. 5: 14.   [4] See Luke 14: 12.   [5] John 17: 13.
[6] See 2 Cor. 5: 14.   [7] See Matt. 10: 8.   [8] Ps. 147: 9 (B.C.P.).
[9] See Matt. 25: 40. The portion copied by Purdy ends here.

My love and service attends all our brethren at Cardiff, especially Mr. Glascott.[1] I am (in hast[e]), my dear brother, yours affectionately,

John Wesley

Dec. 6, 1739, Bristol

Address: 'For Mr. Thomas Price, at Cardiff, Wales' ['Thomas' is altered by John Purdy to 'Nath[anae]ll'. Only 'Mr. Thomas Price' is in Wesley's own hand] *End*: 'Mr. Price, We ale [all] oppened the Letter, being Directed for Arthur Price, Cardiff,[2] but it appears to Us ale the Letter is for you, Which we Desire to be Excus'd for the opening it'; (? by Price) 'Mr. John Wesley Letter, Bristoll Dec. 6, 1739' *Source*: MA; cf. letter of Oct. 27, 1739, in Wesley's *Journal* for that date.

[1] Thomas Glascott had entertained Wesley during his first visit to Cardiff on Oct. 18–19, and accompanied him to Newport the following morning. His son Cradock (1743–1831) was one of Wesley's correspondents in 1764, before his ordination the following year, after which he was associated for a time with Lady Huntingdon, and from 1781 to 1831 was vicar of Hatherleigh, Devon.

[2] Apparently there *was* a Nathanael Price in Cardiff at this time (W.H.S. XXIX. 119), which would explain the local assumption that because of the address it was intended for him—though any misreading of the very clear 'Nathll' as 'Arthur' is very difficult to understand. Clearly there was a succession of errors, beginning with Purdy's supplying of 'Cardiff' as the address instead of 'Caerphilly' (or Watford itself). It seems clear, however, that Wesley did intend the letter to go to Thomas Price of Watford, whom it probably reached eventually via the Methodist Society in Cardiff.

APPENDIX

Wesley's Correspondence

In this appendix is attempted a complete listing of the letters known to
have been written or received by John Wesley, whether or not the text is
extant. Not included, however, are letters which are merely inferred from
the existence of a presumed reply, or the frequent entry in his diary, 'writ
letters'. Similarly, references to letters from or to unnamed correspondents
are not usually included, such as the thousands recorded in Wesley's
later diaries. For inclusion in this list there must be something specific,
at least a clue to the correspondent or an indication of the letter, and
usually both. The appendix will be continued in the succeeding volumes,
and each instalment will list the known correspondence only for the years
covered by that volume.

Because of the evidence available in Wesley's early diaries the entries
in this first volume are much more numerous in proportion to the actual
known texts than will be the case in later volumes. These diaries frequently note the writing of letters, and occasionally their receipt. The
receipt of letters is mentioned also in Wesley's financial accounts (1731–3),
together with the amounts which he paid for them. Not only are there
gaps (some very large), but Wesley frequently omitted from those diaries
details about letters which do survive and which are in themselves complete. The extant diaries cover 1725–7, 1729–41, and 1782–91—but not
fully. Discrepancies occur between the dating of the holographs and the
references to them in the diaries, the accounts, and in other letters,
sometimes because Wesley himself misdated entries and did not discover
his error. In many instances he began to write a letter on one day, but
completed and dated it on another. In view of such problems multiple
dates will sometimes be assigned, in an attempt to combine information
from different sources, though the date given in the holograph remains
of primary importance.

The columns in the tables below list in order the date, the writer, the
recipient, and details of the source—which in the case of many consists
simply of the numbers of the pages where they are printed in this volume.
Incorporated in the appendix, however, are many letters from John
Wesley himself (and from his correspondents) which are not included in
the main text because the details available are comparatively few, though
possibly important: abstracts, extracts, quotations, references to the
contents or purpose. (In the index to Wesley's correspondents these

entries are noted within parentheses.) Where manuscripts exist of in-letters which are not printed here, an attempt is made to assist the reader by noting at least one printed version, the most authentic known. Similarly, when only printed sources are available, the primary source is listed, and usually that alone. Thus a printed extract published by Wesley in his *Arminian Magazine* takes precedence over reprints in works by Adam Clarke, Tyerman, and Stevenson, unless it is ascertained that they used the holograph rather than the printed extract.

Dates before 1752 are given Old Style, except that they are arranged in the New Style manner, i.e. those from 1 Jan. to 24 Mar. are listed as 1727 rather than 1726/7. To assist the reader in ascertaining the days of the week, this is noted in square brackets after the first date in each month.

When two or more letters are listed for the same date they are arranged in the order in which it is known or assumed that Wesley dealt with them, though out-letters always precede in-letters except where a letter was received and answered on the same day, when the in-letter comes first.

For the sake of brevity in this table many abbreviations are here used which do not occur in the main text. These are explained in the following glossary and list of abbreviated names. The abbreviations used for the sources, manuscript and printed, will be found on pp. xvi–xix above.

GLOSSARY

abstr[act]	Some indication of the contents of the letter.
acc[ounts]	Wesley's financial records, indicating amounts paid for letters received.
addr[ess, -essed]	
ans[wer, -wered]	
corr[ected]	
dia[ry]	
end[orsed]	By the recipient unless otherwise stated.
extr[act]	The quotation of two or more continuous sentences.
min[utes]	
orig[inal]	
quot[ation]	The quotation of a single phrase or sentence.
rec[eived]	Indicates the date when the letter was received, and that the date given refers to its receipt rather than to its presumed writing and dispatch.
ref[erence]	Some record of a letter's having been written by or to, or received by, an individual; may also imply some note about its contents.

sum[maries]	Summaries added to Wesley's diaries, sometimes at the foot of a page, sometimes at the end of a volume to cover each month in that volume, listing the more important events (only occasionally noted here, especially to indicate that according to the monthly summary more letters were written to a named individual than appears from the diary itself).
transcr[ibed]	The preparation either of a fair copy for dispatch or of a reference copy, occasionally carried out long after the composition of the letter.

NAMES ABBREVIATED
(based mainly on Wesley's diary entries)

Aspasia	Mary Granville, later Mrs Pendarves, then Mrs Delany.
Athenais	Betty Kirkham, later Mrs Wilson.
CW	Charles Wesley, JW's younger brother.
Emly W	Emilia (also 'Em', 'Emme') Wesley, JW's older sister, even after she married Robert Harper in 1735.
Hetty W	Mehetabel Wesley, JW's older sister, even after she married William Wright on 13 Oct. 1725.
JW	John Wesley.
Kezzy W	Kezia Wesley, JW's younger sister.
Matthew W	Matthew Wesley, JW's uncle in London.
Molly W	Mary Wesley, JW's older sister, even after she had married the Revd John Whitelamb on 21 Dec. 1733.
Nancy W	Anne Wesley, JW's older sister, even after she had married John Lambert in 1725.
Patty W	Martha Wesley, JW's older sister, even after she married the Revd Westley Hall on 13 (or 18) Sept. 1735.
Sam W, Sen	The Revd Samuel Wesley, rector of Epworth, JW's father.
Sam W, Jun	The Revd Samuel Wesley, JW's elder brother.
Selima	Ann Granville.
Serena	Susy Boyse (?).
Suky W	Susanna Wesley, JW's older sister, even after she had married Richard Ellison, probably in 1719.
Mrs Sus W	Mrs Susanna Wesley, JW's mother.
Varanese	Sarah ('Sally') Kirkham, who married the Revd John Chapone on 28 Dec. 1725.

Note: no attempt has been made to identify many of the people noted in JW's diary, nor to check his spelling of their names. Wesley's normal diary abbreviations have usually been extended without comment: 'bS' to Sam W, Jun, 'M' to Bob Kirkham, '*m*f' to Sam W, Sen, '*m*m' to Mrs Sus W, 'NG' to Nancy Griffiths, 'sP' to Patty W, etc. The titles 'Mr', 'Mrs', 'Rev', here recorded without square brackets, are present in the originals.

WESLEY'S CORRESPONDENCE

Date	Writer	Recipient	Source
1717			
Sept 10 [WE]	Nancy W	JW	MA; cf. Stev, 323
1721			
Nov 3 [FR]	JW	Ambrose Eyre	143
1723			
July 7 [MO]	Suky W	JW	ref, LB
Sept	Mrs Sus W	JW	ans, Sept 23
Sept 23 [TU]	JW	Mrs Sus W	144–5
1724			
?	Suky W	JW	ref, LB
Jan	CW	JW	ref, LB
Apr 21 [TU]	Mr C	JW	ref, LB
May?	Sam W, Jun	JW	ref, June 17
June 17 [WE]	JW	Sam W, Jun	146–8
Aug 19 [WE]	Mrs Sus W	JW	148
Aug 26?	JW	Mrs Sus W	ref, 149
Sept 1 [MO]	H H[ammond]	JW	ref, LB
Sept 7	Sam W, Sen	JW	ref, LB
Sept 10	Mrs Sus W	JW	149
Sept 10	Patty W	JW	Clarke II. 312; *WMM*, 1845, 779
Oct 20 [TU]	H H[ammond]	JW	ref, LB
Nov 1 [SU]	JW	Mrs Sus W	149–52
Nov 19	CW	JW	ref, LB
Nov 24	Mrs Sus W	JW	152–3
Nov 24	Emly W	JW	ref, LB
Dec 18 [FR]	JW	Mrs Sus W	153–6
Dec 18	Emly W	JW	ref, LB
Dec 21	Mr Wood	JW	ref, LB
1725			
?	F H[ammond]	JW	ref, LB
Jan 5 [TU]	Sam W, Sen	JW	156
Jan 5	Mrs Sus W	JW	157
Jan 12?	JW	Sam W, Sen	ans, Jan 26
Jan 26	Sam W, Sen	JW	157–9
Feb 11 [TH]	Emly W	JW	ref, LB
Feb	JW	Sam W, Sen	ref, Mar 17
Feb 23	Mrs Sus W	JW	159–60
Feb 26	Emly W	JW	ref, LB
Mar 7 [SU]	JW	Emly W	ref, Apr 7
Mar 7	Hetty W	JW	MA; cf. Stev, 358–9, as Martha; ref, LB, as 1725/6
Mar 17	Sam W, Sen	JW	160–1

Date	Writer	Recipient	Source
1725			
Apr 4 [SU]	Sam W, Jun	JW	ref, LB
Apr 7	Emly W	JW	161
May 2 [SU]	H H[ammond]	JW	ref, LB
May 10	Sam W, Sen	JW	161-2
May 12	W	JW	ref, LB
May 13	R Griffiths	JW	ref, LB
May 20	R Griffiths	JW	ref, LB
May 21	Patty W	JW	ref, LB
May 28	JW	Mrs Sus W	162-3
May	Molly W	JW	ref, LB
June 7 [MO]	CW	JW	ref, LB
June 8	Mrs Sus W	JW	163-7
June 13	W	JW	ref, LB
June 17	JW	Varanese	ref, dia
June 18	JW	Mrs Sus W	167-70
June 23	JW	Varanese	ref, dia
June 27	JW	Varanese	ref, dia
June 27	JW	Nancy Griffiths	ref, dia
July 1 [Th]	JW	Varanese	ref, dia
July 2	JW	Sam W, Sen	ref, dia
July 3	Emly W	JW	ref, LB
July 6	[R Griffiths]	JW	ref, LB
July 7	JW	CW	ref, dia
July 7	JW	Sam W, Jun	ref, dia
July 8	JW	Varanese	ref, dia
July 8	Sam W, Jun	JW	ref, LB
July 14	Sam W, Sen	JW	170-1
July 14	Patty W	JW	ref, LB
July 16	JW	Mrs Sus W	ref, dia
July 17	JW	Mr T[ooker]	ref, dia
July 21	JW	Sam W, Sen	ref, dia
July 21	Mrs Sus W	JW	172-3
July 22	JW	Varanese	ref, dia
July 23	Sam W, Jun	JW	ref, LB
July 27	Sam W, Jun	JW	ref, LB
July 28	JW	Hetty W	ref, dia
July 29	JW	Mrs Sus W	173-6
Aug 2 [MO]	Sam W, Sen	JW	176-7
Aug 2	Mrs Sus W	JW	ref, LB
Aug 4	JW	Mrs Sus W	quots, 183
Aug 10 ?	JW	Hetty W	refs, 177
Aug 11	JW	Sam W, Sen	ref, dia (as '10')
Aug 11	JW	Mrs Sus W	ref, dia (as '10')
Aug 12	Sam W, Sen	JW	177
Aug 13	JW	Nancy W	ref, dia
Aug 13	JW	Emly W	ref, dia
Aug 18	JW	Sam W, Sen	ref, dia
Aug 18	Mrs Sus W	JW	178-80
Aug 23-4	JW	Mrs Sus W	dia; ref, 183-4
Aug 25	JW	Mrs Sus W	ref, dia (? same as last)
Aug 27	Sam W, Sen	JW	180-1

Date	Writer	Recipient	Source
1725			
Sept 1 [WE]	Sam W, Sen	JW	181
Sept 7	Sam W, Sen	JW	182
Sept 8	JW	Sam W, Sen	ref, dia
Sept 8	JW	Mr Tooker	ref, dia
Sept 15	JW	Mr T[ooker]	ref, dia
Sept 15	JW	M[iss] [F] T[ooker]	ref, dia
Sept 16	JW	Nancy Griffiths	ref, dia
Sept 16	JW	Varanese	ref, dia
Sept 20	JW	Sam W, Sen	ref, dia; ans, 182
Sept 22	JW	Sam W, Jun	ref, dia
Sept 22	JW	Nancy Griffiths	ref, dia
Sept 23	JW	Varanese	ref, dia
Sept 28	Nancy Griffiths	JW	ref, LB
Sept	[Rd Reynolds,] Bp of Lincoln	JW	ref, LB
Sept	F H[ammond]	JW	ref, LB
Oct 5 [TU]	Sam W, Jun	JW	ref, LB
Oct 13–14	JW	Mrs Sus W	ref, dia; ans. 184–5
Oct 19	Sam W, Sen	JW	182–3
Oct 19	Nancy Griffiths	JW	ref, LB
Oct 21	JW	Nancy Griffiths	ref, dia
Oct 26	Nancy Griffiths	JW	ref, LB
Nov 3 [WE]	JW	Mrs Sus W	ref, dia
Nov 3	JW	Nancy Griffiths	ref, dia
Nov 3	JW	M[iss] [F] T[ooker]	ref, dia
Nov 4	JW	Varanese	ref, dia
Nov 10	JW	Nancy Griffiths	ref, dia
Nov 10	Mrs Sus W	JW	183–5
Nov 11	JW	Varanese	ref, dia
Nov 17	JW	Mrs Sus W	ref, dia
Nov 17	JW	Nancy Griffiths	ref, dia
Nov 22–3	JW	Mrs Sus W	186–9; cf. dia ('24')
Nov 22	Nancy Griffiths	JW	ref, LB
Nov 25	JW	Varanese	ref, dia
Nov 30	Sam W, Sen	JW	189
Nov 30	Mr Griffiths	JW	ref, LB
Dec 2 [TH]	JW	Mr Griffiths	ref, dia ('1')
Dec 2	JW	Nancy Griffiths	ref, dia ('1')
Dec 6	Nancy Griffiths	JW	ref, LB
Dec 6	R Griffiths	JW	ref, LB
Dec 7	Mrs Sus W	JW	189–90
Dec 9	JW	Nancy Griffiths	ref, dia ('8')
Dec 9	JW	Varanese	ref, dia ('8')
Dec 10	JW	Nancy Griffiths	ref, dia ('9')
Dec 18	JW	Mr Vaughan	ref, dia
Dec 20	JW	Emly W	ref, dia
?	Mr [Rd] Woodeson	JW	ref, LB
1726			
Jan 18 [TU]	JW	Smith	ref, dia

Date	Writer	Recipient	Source
1726			
Jan 18	JW	Nancy Griffiths	ref, dia
Jan 18	JW	R Griffiths	ref, dia
Jan 20	JW	Athenais	ref, dia
Jan 24	JW	Athenais	ref, dia
Jan 25	Nancy Griffiths	JW	ref, LB
Jan 26	JW	R Griffiths	ref, dia
Jan 26	JW	Nancy Griffiths	ref, dia
Jan 27	JW	Varanese	ref, dia
Feb 1 [TU]	Nancy Griffiths	JW	ref, LB
Feb 2	Mrs Sus W	JW	ref, LB
Feb 3	JW	Nancy Griffiths	ref, dia
Feb 4	JW	Sam W, Sen	ref, dia
Feb 10	JW	Nancy Griffiths	ref, dia
Feb 10	JW	Mr Smith	ref, dia
Feb 15	JW	Mr Wilmot	ref, dia
Feb 15	Nancy Griffiths	JW	ref, LB
Feb 17	JW	Nancy Griffiths	ref, dia
Feb 17	JW	Sam W, Jun	ref, dia
Feb 17	Mrs Sus W	JW	ref, LB
Feb 21	CW	JW	ref, LB
Feb 22	Nancy Griffiths	JW	ref, LB
Feb 24	JW	Nancy Griffiths	ref, dia: 'Wr. to Na; did not send it'
Feb 25	JW	Varanese	ref, dia
Feb 28	JW	Varanese	ref, dia
Mar 1 [TU]	JW	Varanese	ref, dia
Mar 1	Emly W	JW	ref, LB
Mar 2	JW	Nancy Griffiths	ref, dia
Mar 7	JW	Emly W	ref, dia
Mar 8	Nancy Griffiths	JW	ref, LB
Mar 9	JW	Sam W, Sen	ref, dia
Mar 9	JW	Mr Tott[enham]	ref, dia
Mar 12	Sam W, Jun	JW	ref, LB
Mar 14	JW	Sam W, Jun	ref, dia
Mar 17	JW	Dr [J] Morley	ref, dia: 'wr. an Ep[istle] to Dr. Morley' (? in verse)
Mar 18	JW	Sam W, Sen	ref, dia; see 167, 169
Mar 19	Sam W, Jun	JW	ref, LB
Mar 19	CW	JW	ref, LB
Mar 20	Patty W	JW	MA; ref, LB, '1725/6'; cf. Stev, 359–60, as Sept. 1725
[Mar 21]	JW	Sam W, Jun	190–3
Mar 21	Sam W, Sen	JW	193
Mar 22	Sam W, Jun	JW	ref, LB
Mar 25?	JW	Sam W, Sen	ref, 169
Mar 30	Mrs Sus W	JW	193–4; cf. dia, Apr 5 below
Mar	Mr Smith	JW	ref, LB
Mar	Mr Smith	JW	ref, LB
Apr 1 [FR]	Sam W, Sen	JW	194–5; cf. dia, Apr 5 below
Apr 3	Mrs Sus W	JW	ref, LB

Date	Writer	Recipient	Source
1726			
Apr 4	JW	Sam W, Jun	195–8; cf. dia
Apr 5			dia: 'recd a Letter from my F/2 and M/1 dated March [30]/1 and Apr. 1/2'
Apr 6	JW	Sam W, Sen	ref, dia
Apr 6	JW	Mrs Sus W	ref, dia
Apr 9	Mrs Sus W	JW	198
Apr 12	JW	Mrs Sus W	ref, dia; see 174
Apr 13	Mr Wood	JW	ref, LB
Apr 16	Mrs Sus W	JW	198
Apr 17	Sam W, Sen	JW	198–9
Apr 19	Sam W, Jun	JW	ref, LB
May 2 [MO]	JW	Nancy Griffiths	ref, dia
May 2	JW	Mr [J] Burton	ref, dia
May 13	Mr Tottenham	JW	ref, LB
May 17	JW	F Hammond	ref, dia
May 26	JW	Mr Bailiff	ref, dia
May 26	JW	CW	ref, dia
June 4 [SA]	Sam W, Jun	JW	ref, dia; rec. June 9
June 10	JW	Sam W, Jun	ref, dia
June 28	JW	Nancy Griffiths	ref, dia
June	Hetty W	JW	ref, LB
July 1 [FR]	JW	Hetty W	ref, dia
July 21	JW	Mr Tottenham	ref, dia
July 21	Sam W, Jun	JW	ref, LB
July 21	Nancy Griffiths	JW	refs, LB, dia; rec. Aug. 3
July 29	JW	Sam W, Jun	ref, dia
Aug 4 [TH]	JW	Nancy Griffiths	ref, dia
Aug 6	Sam W, Jun	JW	ref, LB
Aug 16	Sam W, Jun	JW	ref, dia; rec. Aug. 19
Aug 22	Nancy Griffiths	JW	ref, LB
Aug 23	JW	Mr Ward	ref, dia
Sept 1 [TH]	Varanese	JW	ref, dia, rec two
Sept 2	JW	Varanese	ref, dia
Sept 6	JW	Mr C	ref, dia
Sept 26	JW	H H[ammond]	ref, dia
Sept 28	Mrs Sus W	JW	199
Sept 30	JW	Mrs Sus W	ref, dia
Oct 3 [MO]	JW	Mrs Sus W	ref, dia; see 199
Oct 3	JW	Sam W, Jun	ref, dia
Oct 5	Mr Tooker	JW	ref, LB
Oct 6	Nancy Griffiths	JW	ref, LB
Oct 9	Emly W	JW	ref, LB
Oct 12	Mrs Sus W	JW	199–200; cf. dia, Oct. 20
Oct 20	JW	Mrs Sus W	ref, dia: 'Answered m[y] M lett[er] dated Oct. 12'
Oct 20–1, 24	JW	Athenais	ref, dia; transcr Oct. 27
Nov 1 [TU]	JW	Athenais	ref, dia ('2'); transcr (3)
Nov 3	JW	Mr T[ooker]	ref, dia
Nov 3	Sam W, Jun	JW	refs, LB, dia; rec. Nov. 6
Nov 6	JW	Sam W, Jun	ref, dia

Date	Writer	Recipient	Source
1726			
Nov 9	JW	Sam W, Sen	ref, dia
Nov 9	JW	Emly W	ref, dia
Nov.10	JW	Athenais	ref, dia
Nov 11	JW	Nancy W	ref, dia
Nov 17	JW	Nancy Griffiths	ref, dia
Nov 19	Athenais	JW	ref, LB
Nov 24	JW	Sam W, Jun	ref, dia
Nov 29	Mrs Sus W	JW	200
Nov 29	Athenais	JW	ref, dia (rec. Dec. 1)
Dec 1 [TH]	JW	R Griffiths	ref, dia
Dec 1	JW	Mr T[ooker]	ref, dia
Dec 1	JW	Athenais	ref, dia
Dec 3	JW	[Athenais] ['ב']	ref, dia
Dec 3	Sam W, Jun	JW	ref, dia (rec. Dec. 5)
Dec 5	JW	Mrs Sus W	ref, dia
Dec 5	Athenais	JW	refs LB, dia (rec. Dec. 9)
Dec 5–6	JW	Sam W, Jun	201–5
Dec 6	Nancy Griffiths	JW	ref, dia (rec. Dec. 10)
Dec 8	Sam W, Jun	JW	ref, LB
Dec 10	Sam W, Jun	JW	205–6
Dec 11	JW	Nancy Griffiths	ref, dia
Dec 11	JW	Mr Tooker	ref, dia
Dec 14	Emly W	JW	ref, LB
Dec 22	CW	JW	ref, dia (rec. Dec. 24)
Dec 26	JW	[Sam W. Jun: 'my brother']	ref, dia
Dec 26	JW	Mr [Rd] Hutch[ins]	ref, dia
Dec 26	JW	Mr Lushington	ref, dia
Dec 27	JW	Nancy Griffiths	ref, dia
1727			
Jan 2 [MO]	CW	JW	ref, LB; dia, Jan. 9; 'recd 2 letters from Br. Ch.'
Jan 5	Nancy Griffiths	JW	ref, LB
Jan 6	CW	JW	ref, LB: cf. dia, as Jan. 2
Jan 11	Mr [Rd] Hutchins	JW	ref, LB
Jan 11	Sam W, Jun	JW	ref, LB; cf. dia, rec Jan. 20
Jan 19	Mr Griffiths	JW	ref, dia (date rec)
Jan 19	JW	Mr Griffiths	ref, dia
Jan 20	JW	Sam W, Jun	ref, dia
Jan 20	JW	Sam W, Sen	ref, dia
Jan 20	Molly W	JW	MA; ref, LB; cf. Stev, 290 as 1726
Jan 22–3	JW	Nancy Griffiths	ref, dia
Jan 23	JW	Athenais	ref, dia
Jan 24	JW	Mrs Sus W	208–9
Jan 24	JW	Patty W	ref, dia
Jan 25	JW	Molly W	ref, dia (? ans Jan. 20, Molly)
Jan 26	Mr Griffiths	JW	ref, dia (rec)
Jan 29	Athenais ['Z']	JW	refs, LB, dia (rec. Feb. 2)

Date	Writer	Recipient	Source
1727			
Jan 30	Nancy Griffiths	JW	ref, LB
Jan 31	Mrs Sus W	JW	209–11
Feb 1 [WE]	Mr Leybourne	JW	ref, LB
Feb 2	JW	Mr Tooker	ref, dia
Feb 2	JW	Mr Griffiths	ref, dia
Feb 3, 8	JW	Athenais	refs, dia
Feb 4	Bob Kirkham	JW	ref, LB
Feb 6	Mr Thorold	JW	ref, LB
Feb 7	JW	Mr Leybourne	ref, dia
Feb 7	Patty W	JW	MA; cf. Stev, 361–2
Feb 8	JW	Bob Kirkham	ref, dia; refs, Feb. 20
Feb 9	JW	Sam W, Jun	ref, dia
Feb 9	Mr Griffiths	JW	ref, dia (rec)
Feb 9	JW	Mr Griffiths	ref, dia
Feb 10	JW	Nancy Griffiths	ref, dia
Feb 10	JW	Mrs Sus W	ref, dia; see 190
Feb 13	JW	Patty W	ref, dia
Feb 15	Mr Leybourne	JW	ref, LB
Feb 15	Mrs Sus W	JW	? rec, dia: 'read my mother's letters'
Feb 17	Emly W	JW	ref, LB
Feb 20	Bob Kirkham	JW	MA; ref, LB; cf. Tyerm (JW), as Feb 2
Mar 8 [WE]	Nancy Griffiths	JW	MA; ref, LB, as 1726; cf. W.H.S. 32. 127–8
Mar 11 ?	Emly W	JW	ref, 214–15
Mar 14	Mrs Sus W	JW	211–12
Mar 19	JW	Mrs Sus W	212–15
Mar 27	Emly W	JW	ref, dia (rec)
Mar 29	Bob Kirkham	JW	ref, dia (rec)
Mar 29	JW	Bob Kirkham	ref, dia
Apr 4 [TH]?	JW	Mrs Sus W	refs, ans, 215–16
Apr 7	JW	Mrs Sus W	refs, ans, 217
Apr 10	[from home]	JW	ref, dia (rec)
Apr 10	[from Reading]	JW	ref, dia (rec)
Apr 22	Mrs Sus W	JW	215–16
Apr 26	Sam W, Jun	JW	ref, LB; cf. acc (rec. Apr. 26)
May 8 [MO]	JW	Mrs Sus W	refs, ans, 218
May 14	Mrs Sus W	JW	217–18
May 15	Sam W, Jun	JW and CW	218–20
May 20	Patty W	JW	ref, dia (rec)
[May 22]	JW	Sam W, Jun	220–3
June 2 [FR]	Mr Tottenham	JW	ref, dia (rec); cf. acc
June 6	Sam W, Sen	JW	223
June 8	Bob Kirkham ['M']	JW	ref, acc (rec. two letters)
June 8	Nancy Griffiths	JW	ref, acc (rec)
June 9	Sam W, Jun	JW	ref, acc (rec)
June 14	JW	Sam W, Sen	refs 223, 224, 225
June 15	JW	Mrs Sus W	ref, 210
June 21	Sam W, Sen	JW and CW	223–4

Date	Writer	Recipient	Source
1727			
June 23	Sam W, Jun	JW	ref, acc (rec)
June 24?	Bob Kirkham	JW	acc (rec)
June 24?	JW	Bob Kirkham	acc
June 24	Nancy Griffiths	JW	acc (rec)
June 25	JW and CW	Sam W, Sen	ref, ans, 225–6
June 26	Sam W, Sen	JW	224–5
July 5 [WE]	Sam W, Sen	JW and CW	225–6
July 5	Mrs Sus W	JW	226–7
July 15	JW	Sam W, Sen	refs, 227
July 15	JW	Mrs Sus W	210–11
July 18	Sam W, Sen	JW and CW	227
July 26	Sam W, Sen	JW	228
July 26	Mrs Sus W	JW	228–9
July	Nancy Griffiths	JW	acc (rec)
July	Nancy Griffiths	JW	acc (rec)
Nov 18 [SA]	Sam W, Jun	JW	Bristol Wesley; cf. Clarke II. 165–6
Dec 28 [TH]	Lewis Fenton	JW	Whitehead I. 414
1728			
Jan 6 [SA]	Sam W, Jun	JW	MA; cf. extrs Stev, 282, 305, as '1727'
Jan 6	CW	JW	acc (rec)
Jan 10	Henry Sherman	JW	MA; cf. W.H.S. 32. 126; *end* 'Mr. Sherman / My tutor'
Jan 17	JW	CW	refs, quots, 213–15
Jan 20	CW	JW	229–31
Jan 20	Bob Kirkham	JW	231–2
Feb 9 [FR]	Sam W, Sen	JW	acc (rec): 'for a letter for [*sic*] my father'
July ?	JW	Mrs Sus W	refs, 232
Aug 12 [MO]	Mrs Sus W	JW	232
Aug [23]	Sam W, Sen	JW	ref, 232
Sept [1 ?]	JW	Mrs Sus W	refs. 232
Sept 5 [TH]	Sam W, Sen	JW	232–3
Sept	Mrs Sus W	JW	233
Sept 19	Wm Wright	JW	Bristol Wesley; cf. Stev, 309
Dec	JW	CW	ref, 235
1729			
Jan 5 [SU], and 22	CW	JW	233–6
Jan 18	JW	CW	refs, 235–6
[Apr 30]	JW	CW	ref, 237
May 5 [MO]	CW	JW	237–9
May 8	JW	Kezzy W	dia
May 19	JW	Sam W, Jun	dia
May 19	JW	CW	dia
June 16 [MO]	Mr Kirkham	JW	dia (transcr)
June 23	JW	Sam W, Sen	dia
June 24	JW	Emly W	dia
June 24	JW	Kezzy W	dia; refs, July 12

Date	Writer	Recipient	Source
1729			
July 6 [SU]	JW	Sam W, Sen	dia
July 6	JW	Mrs Sus W	dia
July 6	JW	Sam W, Jun	dia
July 10	JW	Nancy Griffiths	dia
July 12	Kezzy W	JW	*WMM*, 1845, 779–80
July 21	JW	Mr [E] Isham	dia
July 21	JW	[Matt?] Robinson	dia
July 21	JW	Archbald	dia
July 28	JW	Kezzy W	dia
Aug 1 [FR]	JW	Sam W, Jun	dia, sum
Aug 1	JW	Mrs Sam W, Jun	dia, sum
Aug 1	JW	Emly W	dia
Aug 6	JW	Mrs Sus W	dia; ref, 239
Aug 6	JW	Sam W, Jun	dia
Aug 11	Mrs Sus W	JW	239–40
Aug 14	JW	Sam W, Sen	dia
Aug 15	JW	Sam W, Jun	dia
Aug	JW	Mr [Rd] Hutchins	sum
Aug	JW	Mr [E] Isham	sum
Sept 3 [TH]	JW	Miss B Taylor	dia, sum: 'writ a note to . . .'
Sept [18]	JW	Varanese	sum
Sept 25	JW	Athenais	dia
[Sept?]	CW	JW	Wesley House, Cambridge; cf. W.H.S., 2. 222–3
Oct 6 [MO]	JW	Sam W, Jun	dia
Oct 6	JW	Kezzy W	dia
Oct 6	JW	Mr [E] Isham	dia
Oct 7	JW	Mr [Rd] Hutchins	dia
Oct 21	Dr [J] Morley	JW	240
Oct 25	JW	Mrs Sus W	dia
Oct 27	JW	Dr [J] Morley	dia
Oct 27	JW	Mr [M?] Robinson	dia
[Nov 1?] [SA]	Patty W	JW	W.M.C. (draft?)
Nov 3–4	JW	Sam W, Jun	dia
Nov 4	JW	Mr Tottenham	dia
Nov 18	JW	Sam W, Sen	dia
Nov 24	JW	Sam W, Sen	dia
Nov 24	JW	Mrs Sus W	dia
Nov 24	JW	Molly W	dia
Dec 5–6	JW	Patty W	dia; quots, 242–3
Dec 12 [FR]	JW	Mr [E] Isham	dia
Dec 13	JW	Nancy Griffiths	dia
Dec 14	JW	Sam W, Jun	dia
Dec 19	JW	Sam W, Sen	240–2
Dec 20	Mrs Sus W	JW	dia: 'h[ear]d from my mother'

Date	Writer	Recipient	Source
1729			
Dec 20–1	JW	Mrs Sus W	dia
Dec 22–3	JW	Emly W	dia
Dec 25	JW	Mr [E] Isham	dia
Dec 27	JW	Sam W, Jun	dia
Dec 28–9	JW	Kezzy W	dia; refs in Jan. 26, 1730
Dec 30	JW	Nancy Griffiths	dia
Dec 31	Emly W	JW	MA; cf. Stev, 265–7
1730			
Jan 5–7	JW	Emly W	dia; refs, Feb. 9
Jan 10 [SA]	Patty W	JW	242–3
Jan 23	JW	Sam W, Jun	dia
Jan 23–4	JW	Cox	dia
Jan 24–6	JW	Varanese	dia
Jan 24	JW	Mr [E] Isham	dia
Jan 26	Kezzy W	JW	MA; cf. Clarke, II. 376–9, and Stev, 416–18, including a passage re CW not seeing her letters to JW
Jan 26	JW	Mr Lewis	dia
Jan 26, 30	JW	Mrs Sus W	dia
Jan 26	JW	Molly W	dia
Jan 27	Sam W, Sen	JW and CW	Bristol Wesley, addr to JW, but his half missing; cf. Stev, 130
Jan 28	JW	Sam W, Sen	dia
Jan 30	JW	Patty W	(dia
Jan	JW	Nancy Griffiths	sum
Feb 1–2	JW	Sam W, Sen	dia
Feb 2 [MO]	JW	Sam W, Jun	dia
Feb 2	JW	Mr Lewis	dia
Feb 5	Varanese	JW	dia (rec)
Feb 5–7	JW	Varanese	dia
Feb 7	JW	H H[ammond]	dia
Feb 9	Emly W	JW	MA: 'I thank you for the trouble you gave yourself of inquiring after L[eybourne]. He shifts place so quick that 'tis hard to find him, but not impossible.'
Feb 10	Kezzy W	JW	dia (rec)
Feb 10, 16	JW	Kezzy W	dia
Feb 11	JW	Sam W, Jun	dia
Feb 12, 16–18	JW	Emly W	dia
Feb 24	JW	H H[ammond]	dia
Feb 25	JW	Sam W, Sen	dia
Feb 28	JW	Mrs Sus W	244–6
Feb 28	JW	Cox	dia
Mar 10 [TU]	Patty W	JW and CW	Bristol Wesley; cf. Clarke II. 324–5
Mar 11	JW	Patty W	dia
Mar 16	JW	Mrs Sus W	dia

Date	Writer	Recipient	Source
1730			
Mar 16	JW	Molly W	dia
Mar 16	JW	Nancy W	dia
Mar 16	JW	Sam W, Jun	dia
Mar 17–18	JW	Varanese	dia
Mar 30	JW	H H[ammond]	dia
Apr 6 [MO]	JW	CW	dia
Apr 7	JW	Mr Canby	dia, sum (for his father)
Apr 9	JW	Sam W, Jun	dia
Apr 20	JW	CW	dia
May 8 [FR]	JW	Kezzy W	dia
May 9	JW	Sam W, Jun	dia
May 11	JW	Mrs Sus W	dia
May 20	JW	Sam W, Sen	dia
May 21	JW	Emly W	dia
May 26	JW	Burman	dia
June 8 [MO]	JW	Sam W, Jun	dia
June 8	JW	Patty W	dia
June 9	JW	Athenais	dia
June 20	JW	Mrs Sus W	dia
June 22	JW	Suky W	dia
July 13 [MO]	JW	Bob Kirkham	dia
July 13	JW	CW	dia
Aug 13–14	JW	Aspasia	246–8; dia, 13, 'Beg[an] Lr to Mrs P[endarves]'; 14, 'end Lr'
Aug 14 [FR]	JW	Sam W, Jun	dia
Aug 15	JW	Emly W	dia
Aug 15	JW	Kezzy W	dia
Aug 19	JW	Mrs Sus W	dia
Aug 19	JW	Patty W	dia
Aug 20	JW	Nancy Griffiths	dia
Aug 20	JW	Mr Tooker	dia
Aug 21	JW	Varanese	dia; ? ref, 248
Aug 24	JW	Varanese	dia
Aug 26	JW	Sam W, Jun	dia
Aug 26	JW	Mr [E] Isham	dia
Aug [26]	Varanese	JW	refs, 248
Aug 27	JW	Athenais	dia
Aug 28	Aspasia	JW	248
Aug 29	JW	Varanese	dia
Sept 7 [MO]	JW	Sam W, Jun	dia; on the eternity of hell torments; see reply, Sept 19
Sept 9	JW	Varanese	dia
Sept 9	[Varanese]	JW	248–9
Sept 10	JW	Nancy Griffiths	dia
Sept 12	JW	Aspasia	249–50
Sept 14	JW	Sam W, Sen	dia; refs, quot, Sept. 28
Sept 14	JW	Emly W	dia; quot, Oct. 15
Sept 19	Sam W, Jun	JW	AM, 1778, 127–9 (on the eternity of hell torments)

Date	Writer	Recipient	Source
1730			
Sept 22	JW	Sam W, Jun	dia
Sept 25	JW	Bob Kirkham	dia
Sept 28	Sam W, Sen	JW	quot, 337–8
Oct 3 [SA]	JW	Aspasia	250–1
Oct 12	JW	Varanese	dia
Oct 12	JW	Patty W	dia
Oct 12	Aspasia	JW	251–2
Oct 12	Selima	JW	252
Oct 13	JW	Sam W, Sen	dia
Oct 15	Emly W	JW	MA; bro. Sam not so friendly to her as 'Jack'; in spite of 'your own words, "Should I only tell him £40 would be of service to me, he would immediately lend me *that* or *more* to do me a kindness."'
Oct 16	JW	Mrs Sus W	dia
Oct 19	JW	Sam W, Jun	dia
Oct 19	JW	Kezzy W	dia; refs, Oct. 28
Oct 24	JW	[Thomas?] Cox	dia
Oct 24–5	JW	Aspasia	252–3
Oct 26	Aspasia	JW	253–4
Oct 28	JW	Varanese	dia
Oct 28	Kezzy W	JW	MA: 'I suppose one of the company you have so lately been engaged with is the wonderful bright lady you spoke of in your last letter. I shall be glad to know what they are, and where they come from, and whether you think I shall ever have the satisfaction of seeing 'em or no. 'Tis impossible to express how much you obliged me in writing so kind a letter before I had answered your last.' 'Miss Kitty gives her service, thanks for the verses.' Kezzy ill 'since you left Lincoln'. Postmark, 'Boston'.
Oct 29	JW	Sam W, Jun	dia
Oct 30	JW	[Rd] Woodeson	dia
Oct 30	JW	Mrs Sus W	dia
Oct 30	JW	Molly W	dia
Oct 30	JW	John Whitelamb	dia
Oct 30	JW	Emly W	dia

Date	Writer	Recipient	Source
Oct ? 1730	Kezzy W	JW	Sotheby's, Dec. 20, 1948, 'giving him family news, and referring to Mr. Johnson's attentions to her sister'.
Nov 3 [TU]	JW	Aspasia	254
Nov 9	JW	Kezzy W	dia
Nov 17	JW	Hetty W	dia
Nov 19	Aspasia	JW	255; dia, rec. 21
Nov 20	JW	Mrs Granville	dia
Nov 23	JW	Sam W, Sen	dia
Nov 24-5	JW	Aspasia	255-7
Dec 1 [FR]	Sam W, Sen	JW	Whitehead I. 425-7; cf. 338-9 above
Dec 3	JW	Mr Leak[e]	dia, sum ('2')
Dec 3	JW	Mr Sanson	dia, sum ('2')
Dec 4	JW	Patty W	dia
Dec 4	JW	Molly W	dia
Dec [8?]	JW	Mr [E] Isham	ref, Hutchins, Dec. 14
Dec [8?]	JW	Rd Hutchins	ref, Hutchins, Dec. 14: Wesley in Gloucestershire, his misfortunes; Fanny [Tooker] sends her service
Dec 11	JW	Sam W, Sen	257-9
Dec 12	JW	Mrs Granville	259-61
Dec 14	Rd Hutchins	JW	Bristol Wesley; refs to JW's of Dec. 8
Dec 25	JW	Sam W, Jun	dia
Dec 28	JW	Aspasia	261-2
1731			
Jan 11 [MO]	JW	Aspasia	263
Jan 12	JW	Mr Walker	dia
Jan 15	JW	Sam W, Sen	264-7
Jan 15	Aspasia	JW	267-8
Jan 20	JW	Hayward	dia
Jan 21	JW	Varanese	dia
Jan 27	JW	Aspasia	268
Jan 27	Aspasia	JW	268-9
Jan 30	Aspasia	JW	269
Feb 4 [MO]	JW	Aspasia	269
Feb 5	Wm Morgan	JW	MA; cf. Curnock, VIII. 259
Feb 6-17	Sam W, Sen	JW	MA; cf. Clarke, II. 418-20; ans to Dec. 11 and Jan. 15; 'P.S. Feb. 17, 1730/31. I desire you'd translate Job's Wife into Latin, which I believe your bro. will send you from Westminster; for though you have business he must have more, now the book is in the press.'

Date	Writer	Recipient	Source
1731			
Feb 10	JW	Mr [J] Burton	dia
Feb 10, Mar 14	Emly W	JW	MA; P.S., Mar. 14: 'Miss Kitty [Hargreaves] sends her service to her man, and wants his attendance.'
Feb 11–12	JW	Aspasia	270–1
Feb 12	JW	Sam W, Jun	dia
Feb 13	Aspasia	JW	271
Feb 15	[Mr J] Burton	JW	acc (rec)
Feb 18	JW	Varanese	dia
Feb 19	JW	Aspasia	272
Feb 22	JW	Sam W, Sen	dia
Feb 26	JW	Bob Kirkham	dia
Mar [1?]	Patty W	JW	refs, 272
Mar 4 [TH]	JW	Patty W	dia, refs, 272
Mar 6	JW	Varanese	dia
Mar 8	JW	Cox	dia
Mar 8	JW	Jos Goldsworth	dia
Mar 10	JW	Mrs Sus W	dia
Mar [12?]	JW	Aspasia	sum; see 274–6
Mar 13	JW	Varanese	dia
Mar 22	JW	Emly W	dia
Mar 26	JW	Varanese	dia
Mar 26	JW	Nancy Griffiths	dia
Mar 29	JW	Mr [J] Burton	dia
Mar 29	JW	Sam W, Jun	dia; refs, 278
Mar 30	Patty W	JW	272–3
Mar 31–Apr 1	JW	Mrs Granville	dia
Apr 1 [TH]	JW	Varanese	dia
Apr 4	Aspasia	JW	273–4
Apr 5	JW	Aspasia	274–6
Apr 14	JW	Aspasia	276–8
Apr 28	Sam W, Jun	JW	278–9
May 8 [SA]	Selima	JW	279–80
May 18	JW	Mr [Jos] Hoole	341–2
May 19–20	JW	Mrs Granville	dia
May 20	JW	Emly W	dia
[May 29?]	Jos Hoole	JW	quot, 342
June 2 [WE]	JW	Mr [J] Burton	dia
June 2	JW	Aspasia	280–1
June [3?]	JW	Patty W	sum
June 5	JW	Varanese	dia
June 9	JW	Kezzy W	dia
June 10	JW	Sam W, Jun	dia
June 11	JW	Mr [J] Burton	dia
June 11	JW	R[d] Westley	dia
June 11	JW	Sam W, Sen	281–2
June 11	JW	Mrs Sus W	282–4
[June 15?]	Sam W, Jun	JW	*AM* 1778, 129

Date	Writer	Recipient	Source
1731			
June 16	JW	R[d] Westley	dia
June 16	JW	Sam W, Jun	dia
June 16	Aspasia	JW	284
June 17–18	JW	Selima	285–7
June [19?]	JW	Kezzy W	sum; refs, 289–90
June 19	JW	Aspasia	287–9
June 24	JW	Sam W, Jun	dia
June 24	JW	Patty W	dia
June 26	JW	Varanese	dia
June 26	Emly W	JW	Drew, *end*: 'She will stay with Mrs. Taylor at my desire.'
June 28	JW	Sam W, Sen	dia
June 28	JW	Molly W	dia
June [28?]	JW	Mrs Sus W	sum
June 30	JW	Emly W	dia
July 1 [TH]	JW	Kezzy W	dia
July 1	JW	Nancy Griffiths	dia
July 3	Kezzy W	JW	289–90
July [10?]	JW	Mrs Sus W	refs, 291
July 12	Mrs Sus W	JW	291–2
July 19	JW	Aspasia	293–4
July 20	JW	Hetty W	dia
July 20	JW	Patty W	dia
July 20	JW	Sam W, Jun	dia
July 21	JW	[Wm] Morgan	dia
July 21	Aspasia	JW	295–6
July 24	JW	Aspasia	296–9
July 24	JW	Mr Coxeter	dia
July 29	Aspasia	JW	299
July 30–1	JW	Selima	300–1
Aug 9 [MO]	JW	Sam W, Jun	dia
Aug 9	JW	Mr [C] Rivington	dia
Aug 9	Selima	JW	301–2
Aug 9	[Mrs Granville]	JW	302
Aug 12	JW	Aspasia	303–5
Aug 14	JW	Selima	305–8
Aug 15	JW	Sam W, Jun	dia
Aug 24	Selima	JW	308–9
Aug 26	Aspasia	JW	309–10
Aug 30	JW	[J] Boyce	dia
Sept 6 [MO]	JW	Sam W, Jun	dia
Sept 15	Hetty W	JW	MA; cf. Stev, 311
Sept 20	JW	Sam W, Sen	dia
Sept 20	JW	Mrs Sus W	dia
Sept 21–2	JW	Sam W, Jun	dia
Sept 21	JW	Nancy Griffiths	dia
Sept 22	JW	Patty W	dia
Sept 22	JW	J Lambert	dia
Sept 22	JW	Nancy W [=Lambert]	dia

Date	Writer	Recipient	Source
1731			
		[. . Lambert]	
Sept 27	JW	Selima	310–13
Sept 27	JW	Smith	dia
Sept 28	JW	Aspasia	313–15
Sept 29	Selima	JW	316–17
Sept 30	JW	Varanese	dia
Sept 30	JW	Nancy Griffiths	dia
Oct 1 [FR]	JW	Patty W	dia
Oct 1	JW	Sam W, Jun	dia
Oct 3–4, 7	JW	Selima	317–20
Oct 7	JW	Nancy Griffiths	dia
Oct 13	JW	Nancy Griffiths	dia
Oct 20	JW	Mrs Sus W	dia
Oct 20	JW	Molly W	dia
Oct 21	JW	Emly W	dia
Oct 21	JW	Nancy Griffiths	dia
Oct 22	JW	Patty W	dia
Oct 22	JW	Goodwin	dia
Nov 1 [MO], 6	JW	Selima	dia; quot?, refs, 323
[Nov 8?]	Molly W	JW	ref, 323
Nov 16	JW	Mr [J] Burton	dia
Nov 16	JW	Smith	dia
Nov 17	JW	Patty W	dia
Nov 17	JW	Sam W, Jun	320–3
Nov 19	JW	Varanese	dia
Nov 24	JW	Mr Trollop	dia
Nov 28	Emly W	JW	Bristol Wesley, 176
Dec 1 [WE]	Selima	JW	323–4
Dec 3	JW	Patty W	dia
Dec 4	JW	Goodwin	dia
Dec 6	JW	Molly W	dia
Dec 7	JW	Kezzy W	dia
Dec 8	JW	Bob Kirkham	dia
Dec 8	JW	Emly W	dia
Dec 9	JW	Mr [J] Bu[rto]n	dia
Dec 10	JW	Selima	dia
Dec 11	Sam W, Jun	JW	324–5
Dec 15–16	JW	Aspasia	dia
Dec 17	JW	Mr [John] Hutton	dia
Dec 17	JW	Green	dia
Dec 17	JW	Sam W, Jun	dia; refs, 325
1732			
[Jan 1?]	Sam W, Jun	JW	325–6
Jan 8 [SA]	JW	[J] Boyce	dia
Jan 10	JW	Sam W, Sen	dia
Jan 19	JW	Mr [J] Bu[rto]n	dia
Jan 20	JW	Mr [J] Goole	dia
Jan 20	Kezzy W	JW	MA; cf. Stev, 419–20 (as 1731)
Jan 20	[Molly W]	JW	added to last

Date	Writer	Recipient	Source
1732			
Jan 22	JW	Mr [J] Goole	dia
Jan 24	JW	Bob Kirkham	dia
Jan 24	JW	Patty W	dia
Jan 25	JW	Burman	dia
Jan 26	JW	Mrs Sus W	dia; refs, quot, 326-7
Jan 26	JW	Kezzy W	dia
Jan 26, 29	JW	Selima	dia
Jan 29	JW	Mr Richmond	dia, sum
Jan	JW	Molly W	sum
Jan	JW	Bulman	sum
Jan	JW	Mr Richmond	sum ('Mr Richmd 2')
Feb 5 [SA]	JW	Mr Bu[rma]n	dia, sum
Feb 9	JW	Kezzy W	dia
Feb 10	JW	Sam W, Jun	dia
Feb 21	Mrs Sus W	JW and CW	326-7
Feb 23	JW	Burman	dia
Feb 23	JW	Emly W	dia
Feb 24	JW	Patty W	dia
Feb 28	JW	Mrs Sus W	327-30
Feb 29	JW	Mr Iliffe	dia
Feb	JW	Cox	sum
Mar 2 [TH]	JW	Mr Iliffe	dia
Mar 13	JW	Mr Iliffe	dia
Mar 17	JW	Bob Kirkham	dia
Mar 17	JW	Sam W, Jun	dia
Mar 18	JW	Mr Bu[rma]n	dia
Mar 23, 27	JW	Patty W	dia
Mar 26	JW	Mr Trollop	dia
Mar 27	JW	Dr [Geo] Rye	dia
Mar 30	JW	Sam W, Jun	dia
Mar	JW	Mr Iliffe	sum ('Mr Iliffe 3')
Apr 3 [MO]	JW	Mr Burman	dia
Apr 4, 6	JW	Selima	dia
Apr 8	JW	Selima	dia
Apr 8	JW	Sam W, Jun	dia
Apr 8	JW	Aspasia	dia
Apr 10	JW	Mrs Sus W	dia
Apr 10	JW	Sam W, Sen	dia
Apr 10	JW	Mr Burman	dia
May 22 [MO]	JW	Sam W, Jun	dia
May 22	JW	Mr Barnard	dia
May 24-5	JW	Selima	dia
May 26	JW	Sam W, Sen	dia
May 26-7	JW	Varanese	dia
May 31	JW	Patty W	dia
June 2 [FR]	JW	Sam W, Jun	dia
June 2	JW	Mr Wood	dia
June 4	JW	Patty W	dia
June 8	JW	Mr Wood	dia
June 8	JW	Mr [C] Rivington	dia

Date	Writer	Recipient	Source
1732			
June [11?]	Selima	JW	dia (read June 14)
June 14	JW	Patty W	dia
June [15?]	Selima	JW	sum
June 17	JW	Kezzy W	dia
June 19	JW	Hetty W	dia
June 21	JW	Sam W, Sen	dia
June 21	JW	Molly W	dia
June 21	JW	Sam W, Jun	dia
June 22	JW	Mrs Sus W	dia; ans, 330-1
June 22	JW	Emly W	dia
June 23-4, 27	JW	Selima	dia
June 27	JW	Mr Bishop	dia
June 29	JW	Mr Iliffe	dia
June 29	JW	Cox	dia
June 30	JW	Varanese	dia
July 3 [MO]	JW	Mr Bishop	dia
July 5	JW	Varanese	dia
July 7	JW	Mr Bishop	dia
July 12	JW	Patty W	dia
July 12	JW	Robert Boyse	dia
July 12	Mr [Wm] Wogan	JW	dia (date read)
July 12-13	JW	Wm Law	dia
July 15	JW	Sir John Philipps	dia
July 15	JW	Mr [C] Rivington	dia
July 23	JW	Mr [C] Rivington	dia
July 23	JW	Sam W, Jun	dia
July 23	Selima	JW	dia (date read)
July 24	Mrs Sus W	JW	330-1
Aug 1 [TU]	John Clayton	JW	331-4
Aug 3	JW	Patty W	dia
Aug 7	JW	Kezzy W	dia
Aug 7	JW	Sam W, Jun	dia
Aug 8	JW	[C] Rivington	dia
Aug 8	JW	Sir John Philipps	dia
Aug 9	JW	Mrs Sus W	dia
Aug 11	JW	Patty W	dia
Aug 11	JW	Hetty W	dia
Aug 14	JW	Mr Sheldon	dia
Aug 16	Matthew W	JW	dia (date read)
Aug 17	JW	Patty W	dia
Aug 17	JW	Hetty W	dia
Aug 18	JW	Wm Law	dia
Aug 23	JW	Sir John Philipps	dia
Aug 24	JW	Davies	dia
Aug 24	JW	Dr [Geo] Rye	dia
Aug 24	JW	Mr [C] Rivington	dia
Aug 25	JW	Aspasia	dia
Aug 25	JW	Blair	dia

Date	Writer	Recipient	Source
1732			
Aug 25	JW	Selima	dia
Sept 4–5	John Clayton	JW	MA; cf. Curnock, VIII. 278–81
Sept 5 [TU]	JW	Westley Hall	dia
Sept 9	JW	Patty W	dia
Sept 25	JW	Mrs Sus W	dia; refs, 344–5
Sept 25, 27	JW	Sam W, Jun	dia
Sept 28	JW	Kezzy W	dia
Sept 28–9	JW	Emly W	dia
Oct 7 [SA]	JW	Mr Guy	dia
Oct 18–19	JW	Mr Sheldon	dia
Oct 19–21	JW	Rd Morgan, Sen	335–44
Oct 20	JW	Sir John Philipps	dia
Oct 25	Mrs Sus W	JW	344–6
Oct 26	JW	Patty W	dia
Oct 26	JW	Sam W, Jun	dia
Oct 27	Selima	JW	dia (date read)
Nov 6 [MO]	JW	Mr [Jos] Hoole	dia
Nov 6	JW	Sir John Philipps	dia
Nov 8	Patty W	JW	dia (date read)
Nov 9	JW	Sam W, Jun	dia
Nov 9	JW	Mr [C] Rivington	dia
Nov 9	JW	Patty W	dia
Nov 10	JW	Emly W	dia
Nov 10	JW	Mrs Sus W	dia
Nov 11	JW	Kezzy W	dia
Nov 15	JW	Sam W, Sen	dia
Nov 16	JW	Mr Leake	dia
Nov 18	JW	Mrs Brooks	dia
Nov 22	JW	Selima	dia (transcr, 24; corr, 26)
Nov 25	Rd Morgan, Sen	JW	346–7
Nov 28	JW	Sir John Philipps	dia
Nov 28	JW	Patty W	dia
Dec 8 [FR]	JW	John Clayton	dia
Dec 8	Wm Law	JW	dia (date read)
Dec 11	JW	Selima	dia
Dec 20	JW	Mr Green	dia
Dec 23	JW	Mrs Brooks	dia
Dec 23	JW	Sam W, Sen	dia
Dec 23	JW	Mrs Townsend	dia
Dec 25	JW	Patty W	dia
Dec 29	JW	Patty W	dia
Dec 30	JW	Goodwin	dia
Dec	JW	Mr Leake	sum
[1732?]	J Romley	[JW?]	Bristol Wesley (in Greek)
1733			
Jan 1 [MO]	JW	[Hen] Newman	SPCK, abstr: 'John Wesley at Oxon, 1st January. Desiring a Packet of books

Date	Writer	Recipient	Source
1733			
			on the terms of the Society, and also a list of the books dispersed by the Society.' — 'Ordered the books desired.'
Jan 1	JW	Mr [C] Rivington	dia
Jan 2	JW	Patty W	dia
Jan 3	JW	S[mith]	dia ('S'), sum
Jan 8	JW	Selima	dia
Jan 8	JW	Sam W, Jun	dia
Jan 15	JW	Westley Hall	dia
Jan 16	JW	Sam W, Jun	dia
Jan 23	JW	Sam W, Jun	dia
Jan 23	JW	CW	dia
Jan	JW	Emly W	sum
Feb [1 ?]	Mrs Sus W	JW	refs, quot, 347
Feb 7 [WE]	JW	Mr Guy	dia
Feb 7	JW	Sam W, Sen	dia
Feb 8	JW	Rd Morgan, Sen	dia; cf. 349, asking if CW's letter of Oct. 4 rec, if any books from Wm Morgan's library available for CW
Feb 13	JW	Sam W, Jun	dia
Feb 15	JW	Mrs Sus W	347-8
Feb 15	JW	Molly W	dia
Feb 17	Rd Morgan, Sen	JW	349
Feb 20	JW	Sam W, Jun	dia
Feb 21	JW	Mr [C] Rivington	dia
Feb 21	JW	Sympson	dia
Feb 23	JW	Serena	dia, sum
Feb 26	JW	Congreve	dia
Feb 28	JW	Rd Morgan, Sen	dia; ref, 349-50
Mar 2 [FR]	JW	[C] Rivington	dia
Mar 3	JW	Serena	dia
Mar 3	JW	Varanese	dia
Mar 10	JW	[Matt] Salmon	dia
Mar 10	Rd Morgan, Sen	JW	349-50
Mar 18	JW	F Hammond	dia
Mar 19	JW	Mr [C] Rivington	dia
Mar 26	Kezzy W	JW	MA
Mar	JW	Patty W	sum
Apr 12 [TH]	JW	[Rev Mr] Laserre	dia
Apr 16	JW	Sam W, Jun	dia
Apr 16	JW	Kezzy W	dia
Apr 18	JW	Molly W	dia
Apr 19	JW (for Blair)	Mr Prince	dia, sum
Apr 19	Varanese	JW	dia (date read)

Date	Writer	Recipient	Source
1733			
Apr 21	JW	Mrs Townsend	dia
Apr 21	JW	Mr [C] Rivington	dia
Apr 23	JW	Mr [C] Rivington	dia
Apr 24	JW	Sam W, Jun	dia
May 2 [WE]	JW	Mr [C] Rivington	dia
May 3	JW	Clements	dia
May 3	JW	Mr Guy	dia
May 3	JW	Sympson	dia
May 4	JW	John Clayton	dia
May 4	JW	Bulman	dia
May 5	JW	Varanese	dia
May 7	JW	Aspasia	dia
May 12	JW	Goodwin	dia
June 11 [MO]	JW	John Clayton	dia
June 11	JW	Bob Kirkham	dia
June 13	JW	Sam W, Sen	350-1
June 13	JW	Mr [Jos] Hoole	dia
June 13	JW	Sam W, Jun	dia
June 15	JW	Emly W	dia
June 15	JW	Aspasia	dia
June 15	JW	Mr [C] Rivington	dia
June 15	JW	Serena	dia
June 21	Sam W, Jun	JW	Clarke, II. 174
June 25	JW	Sam W, Jun	dia
June 27	JW	John Clayton	dia
June 27	JW	Mr [Wm] Wogan	dia
July 7 [SA]	Mr [Wm] Wogan	JW	dia: 'read Mr. Wogan's Letter to me (agst D)'; ditto, July 8, 9
July 9	JW	Mr [Jos] Hoole	dia, 'abt D at Xt C'
July 9-10	JW	Sir John Philipps	dia
July 11	JW	John Clayton	dia; refs, 352
July 18	JW	Serena	dia
July 18	JW	Varanese	dia
July 20	JW	Mr [C] Rivington	dia
July 20	JW	Waddilov[e]	dia
July 25	JW	Mr [Wm] Wogan	dia
July 25	JW	[J] Boyce	dia
July 25	JW	Mr [J] Goole	dia
July [25]	John Clayton	JW	352
July 28	Mrs Sus W	JW	dia (date read)
July 29	JW	Mr [J] Goole	353
Aug 1 [WE]	JW	Mrs Sus W	dia
Aug 1	JW	[J] Boyce	dia
Aug 1	JW	Kezzy W	dia
Aug 3	JW	John Clayton	dia

Date	Writer	Recipient	Source
1733			
Aug 4	JW	[J] Boyce	dia
Aug 4	John Goole	JW	ref; see 353 n
Aug 9	JW	Varanese	dia
Aug 10	JW	Selima	dia
Aug 15	JW	Varanese	dia
Aug 15	Emly W	JW	dia (rec)
Aug 16	Mrs Sus W	JW	dia (rec 'Angry Letter from my mother'); quots, 354
Aug 17	JW	Mrs Sus W	354–5
Aug 18	JW	[J] Boyce	dia
Aug 18	JW	Mr [J] Goole	dia; cf. 353 n
[Aug 21 ?]	John Goole	JW	ref, 353 n
Aug 22	JW	Emly W	dia; see Sept. 4
Aug 24	JW	Mr [Jos] Hoole	dia
Aug 24	JW	Mr [C] Rivington	dia
Aug 29	JW	John Clayton	dia; refs, 355
Aug 29	JW	Mr [Wm] Wogan	dia
Aug 31	JW	[Miss Potter], 'MP'	dia
Sept 3 [MO]	JW	Patty W	dia
Sept 3	JW	Mrs Sus W	dia
Sept 4	JW	Mr [C] Rivington	dia
Sept 4	JW	Bulman	dia
Sept 4	Emly W	JW	MA; answers Aug. 22; distressed that he concealed his lack of money when with her in Lincoln. 'I know not the ladies you mention.'
Sept 7	JW	Serena	dia
Sept 8	JW	Varanese	dia
Sept 10	John Clayton	JW	355–6
Sept 12	JW	[J] Boyce	dia
Sept 14	JW (with CW)	Rd Morgan, Sen	dia; refs, 357 n
Sept 14	JW	Sam W, Jun	dia
Sept 17	JW	Sam W, Jun	dia
Sept 18	JW	Patty W	dia
Sept 25	SPCK	JW	SPCK, abstr, 'in answer to his of [blank] that the packet desired was sent 28 Aug, value 4s. 2d.'
Oct 8 [MO]	JW	Mrs Sus W	dia
Oct 8	JW	Emly W	dia
Oct 8	JW	Kezzy W	dia
Oct 8	JW	Molly W	dia
Oct 16	JW	Sam W, Jun	dia
Oct 17	JW	[Hen] Newman	dia; SPCK, abstr, 'Acknowledging the receipt of H N's of last month, as also a

Date	Writer	Recipient	Source
1733			
			packet of books for which he hopes in a short time to pay'.
Oct 24	JW	Greive	dia
Oct 26	JW	Mr [Wm] Wogan	dia
Oct 26	JW	Mr [C] Rivington	dia
Oct 27	Rd Morgan, Sen	[JW or CW]	dia (date read)
Nov 1 [TH]	Emly W	JW	dia, rec 'kind letter from S[ister] E[mly]'
Nov 5	JW	Sam W, Jun	dia
Nov 5	JW	Sam W, Sen	dia
Nov 6	JW	Rd Morgan, Sen	dia; refs 357–9, 374
Nov 8	JW	John Whitelamb	dia
Nov 8	JW	Molly W	dia
Nov 8	JW	Emly W	dia
Nov 10	Mr Robinson	JW	dia (rec)
Nov 10	Mr [Wm] Wogan	JW	dia (rec)
Nov 16	JW	Aspasia	dia
Nov 16	JW	Selima	dia
Nov 16	JW	Mr [C] Rivington	dia
Nov 16	JW	[Hen] Newman	SPCK, abstr, 'desiring a package of books on the terms of the Society; that Mr. Smith a gentleman of his college sets out for London on Monday next, who will bring the money for 'em.'
Nov 19	JW	Mr [C] Rivington	dia
Nov 19	JW	Patty W	dia
Nov 19	JW	Mr Black	dia; sum, 'Mr Black's F[athe]r'
Nov 21	JW	John Clayton	dia
Nov 22	Rd Morgan, Sen	JW	357–9
Nov 29	SPCK	JW	SPCK, abstr, 'in answer to his of 16 Novr. that the books desired were sent 21 Novr. to Mr. Rivington's in St. Paul's Church Yard, value £5. 10s. 8½d.'
Dec 7 [FR]	JW	[Jas] Huey	dia
Dec 10	JW	Mr [Wm] Wogan	dia
Dec 14	JW	[Jas] Huey	dia
Dec 14	JW	Sam W, Jun	dia
Dec 14	JW	Jo[seph] Bentham	dia
Dec 14	JW	Rd Morgan, Sen	359–62
Dec 19	JW	Sam W, Sen	dia

Date	Writer	Recipient	Source
1733			
Dec 19	JW	Mrs Sus W	dia; refs, 362–4
Dec 19	JW	Mr Coxeter	dia
Dec 21	JW	Mr Harris	dia
Dec 21	JW	John Clayton	dia
Dec 24	JW	Wm Law	dia
Dec 24	JW	Jo[seph] Bentham	dia
Dec 26	JW	Molly W	dia
Dec 26	JW	Kezzy W	dia; ref, Jan. 18, 1734
Dec 28	JW	Mr Greenway	dia
Dec	JW	Mr [Jas] Huey	sum
1734			
Jan 1 [TU]	Mrs Sus W	JW	362–4
Jan 7	JW	Jo[seph] Bentham	dia
Jan 14	Rd Morgan, Jun	Rd Morgan, Sen	364–6
Jan 15	JW	Rd Morgan, Sen	367–71
Jan 17	JW	Varanese	dia
Jan 18	Kezzy W	JW	MA; on marriage of Molly W and Whitelamb; JW advising Kezzy to break off acquaintance with un-named suitor
Jan 23	JW	Mr Stanley, Sen	dia [? linked with Sir John Stanley, Aspasia's uncle by marriage]
Jan 23	JW	John Whitelamb	dia
Jan 23	JW	Molly W	dia
Jan 23	JW	Jo[seph] Bentham	dia
Jan 23	JW	Mr [John] Hutton	dia
Jan 23	JW	Smith	dia
Jan 24	JW	Patty W	dia
Jan 26	Chapman	JW	dia (rec), sum
Jan 28	JW	Mrs Sus W	371–3
Jan 29	JW	Sam W, Jun	dia; refs, 376
Jan 30	JW	Selima	dia
Jan 31	Rd Morgan, Sen	JW	374–6
Feb 6 [WE]	Wm Smith	JW	MA; end by JW, 'Prof-[ession] of fr[ien]dship'; cf. Tyerm (OM), 27 n
Feb 7	Sam W, Jun	JW	376
Feb 7	Emly W	JW	MA; informing JW she has broken with Quaker suitor for whom she had been keeping house; end by JW, 'Adieu to Dr. Hu.'; see Stev, 269–70 (as 1733)
Feb 8	JW	Selima	dia

Date	Writer	Recipient	Source
1734			
Feb 8	JW	[John Potter,] Bishop of Oxford	dia
Feb 9	JW	John Clayton	dia
Feb 14	Mrs Sus W	JW	377-8
Feb 16	JW	John Greives	dia
Feb 16	JW	[Hen] Newman	dia; SPCK abstr, 'desiring a packet of books on the terms of the Society'— 'Ordered the books'
Feb 25	JW	Sam W, Jun	dia
Feb 26	JW	Selima	dia
Feb 27	JW	Congreve	dia
Feb 27	JW	Smith	dia
Feb 28	JW	Emly W	dia
Feb 28	JW	Kezzy W	dia
Feb 28	JW	Sam W, Sen	dia
Mar 1 [FR]	JW	Mrs Sus W	dia; refs, 382-5
Mar 3	Sam W, Jun	JW	dia (rec)
Mar 4	JW	Sam W, Jun	dia
Mar 5	JW	Mr Greenway	dia
Mar 14	JW	Mr [Th] Hall, Jun	dia
Mar 15	JW	Rd Morgan, Sen	379-82
Mar 16	Walker	JW	dia (rec)
Mar 16	Molly W	JW	dia (rec)
Mar 18	JW	Mr [C] Rivington	dia
Mar 18	JW	Sam W, Jun	dia
Mar 21	JW	Sam W, Jun	dia
Mar 25	JW	John Clayton	dia
Mar 29	JW	Rd Morgan, Sen	dia
Mar 29	JW	Molly W	dia
Mar 30	Mrs Sus W	JW	382-5
Apr 1 [MO]	JW	Bob Kirkham	dia
Apr 1	JW	Rd Westley	dia
Apr 7	JW	Mr [Hen] Newman	dia; SPCK abstr, 'desiring a packet of books on the terms of the Society'— 'Ordered the books. Answd. the 25th April, 1734. Value . . . £1. 1s. 4d.'
Apr 9	Prideaux Selby	JW	F. Baker, end JW, 'Selby, Apr. 9, 1734—New birth'
Apr 10	JW	John Clayton	dia
Apr 14	JW	[Jas] Huey	dia
Apr 16	JW	Sam W, Jun	dia
Apr 18	JW	CW	dia
Apr 18	JW	Smith	dia
Apr 18	JW	Ward	dia
Apr 19	JW	Mr [Th] Hall	dia

Date	Writer	Recipient	Source
1734			
Apr [19]	Geo Stonehouse	JW	Bristol Wesley, 216; dia (rec 20); sum
Apr 25	Hen Newman	JW	SPCK; see Apr. 7
Apr 26	JW	Hen Newman	SPCK, abstr, 'desiring a Packet of books on the Society's terms'—'Ordered the books, 24 May, 1734. Mr. Rivington paid G. Smith for Mr. Wesley's last Packets, £7. 7s. 8d., being all that was due from Mr. Wesley for packets.'
Apr 27	Rd Morgan, Sen	JW	385-6
May	JW	Sam W, Jun	sum
May	JW	Bowyer	sum
May	JW	Mr Woods	sum
May	JW	Sam W, Sen	sum
May	JW	Patty W	sum
May	JW	Kezzy W	sum
May	JW	Mr Tooker	sum
May	JW	[Prid] Selby	sum
May	JW	Rd Morgan, Sen	sum
May	JW	Serena	sum
May	JW	Selima	sum
May	JW	Congreve	sum
June	JW	Bowyer	sum
June	JW	Mrs Hall	sum
June	JW	Mr [C] Rivington	sum
June	JW	Sam W, Sen	sum
June	JW	Sam W, Sen	sum
June	JW	Patty W	sum
June	JW	Mrs Sus W	sum
June	JW	Emly W	sum
June 16 [SU]	Kezzy W	JW	MA; cf. extr, Moore I. 87, etc.
June	JW	Kezzy W	sum
June	JW	Sam W, Jun	sum
June 19	JW	Hen Newman	SPCK, abstr, 'desiring a packet of books on the Society's terms'—'Ordered the books'
June	JW	Mr Greenway	sum
June	JW	Smith	sum
June 22	Patty W	JW	MA; end by JW, 'Acct. of A[unt] Nancy', i.e. Ann Annesley, who had just died at Hackney
June	JW	Patty W	sum
June	JW	Rd Morgan, Sen	sum

Date	Writer	Recipient	Source
1734			
June 26	JW	Wm Law	386–8
June [30?]	JW	John Clayton	sum; refs, 391–3
July 2 [FR]	Aspasia	JW	389–90
July 3	Kezzy W	JW	MA; cf. Stev, 267, 282–3 (as 1731)
July	JW	Mr [Wm] Wogan	sum
July	JW	Mr [C] Rivington	sum
July	JW	Mr [C] Rivington	sum
July	JW	Kezzy W	sum
July	JW	Sam W, Jun	sum
July	JW	Aspasia	390–1
July 22	JW	Hen Newman	SPCK, abstr, 'desiring a packet of books on the Society's Terms'—'Ordered the books'
July	JW	Sam W, Sen	sum
July 27	Ben Ingham	JW	Bristol Wesley, 196; cf. *Wes. Ban.*, 1852, 125–6, and Tyerm (*OM*), 57–8
July 29	JW	Hen Newman	SPCK, abstr, 'desiring a packet of books on the Society's terms'—'Ordered the books'
July	JW	Dr [Geo] Rye	sum
July	JW	John Clayton	sum; refs, 391–3
Aug 2 [FR]	John Clayton	JW	391–3
Aug	JW	Mr [C] Rivington	sum
Aug	JW	Mr [C] Rivington	sum
Aug 6	JW	Hen Newman	SPCK, abstr, 'desiring a packet of books on the Society's terms'—'Ordered the books. Answed. the 21st Sepr. 1734. Value, £1. 9. 2.'
Aug 6	Hen Newman	JW	SPCK, abstr, 'J. Wesley at Lincoln College 6 Augt. in answer to his of the 19th June acquainting him that his packets were left 25 June and 29 July at Mr. Rivington's in St. Paul's Churchyard.'
Aug	JW	Sam W, Sen	sum
Aug	JW	Mr Collins	sum (for T. Wayte)
Aug	JW	Mr Collins	sum (for T. Wayte)
Aug	JW	Sam W, Jun	sum
Aug 14	Kezzy W	JW	MA; outlining her life at the

Date	Writer	Recipient	Source
1734			
			Boyces', Barnswell
Aug	JW	Kezzy W	sum
Aug	JW	Emly W	sum
Aug	JW	Ben Ingham	sum (Ingham rec Aug. 18)
Aug	JW	John Whitelamb	sum
Aug	JW	Mrs Sus W	sum
Aug	JW	Aspasia	sum
Aug	JW	Wm Law	sum
Aug 27	Sam W, Sen	JW	393-4
Sept 16 [MO]	JW	Bowyer	dia
Sept 16	JW	Sam W, Sen	dia, sum
Sept 17	JW	Nancy Griffiths	dia, sum
Sept 17	JW	Mrs Sus W	dia, sum
Sept 18	JW	Kezzy W	dia, sum: ? ref to this or Nov. 11 in Hall MS: 'I immediately sent her word that the neutrality my mother had advised me to was at an end.'
Sept 18	JW	Patty W	dia, sum
Sept 18	JW	Westley Hall	dia, sum; ? ref to this or Nov. 11 in Hall MS: 'At the same time I writ to Sarum that I must see him just then; and if he could not come to me, I would to him. He came without delay . . .'
Sept 19	JW	John Clayton	dia, sum
Sept 19	JW	Emly W	dia, sum
Sept 19	JW	Serena	dia, sum
Sept 21	Hen Newman	JW	ref, Aug 6, and SPCK abstr: 'that his packet was left the 17 August at Mr. Rivington's in St. Paul's Ch:yard, value 1.9.2.'
Sept 27	JW	Smith	dia, sum
Oct 11 [FR]	Patty W	JW	dia (rec)
Oct 11	JW	Hen Newman	SPCK, abstr, 'desiring a packet of books on the Society's terms'—'Ordered the Books. Answered the 7th November, 1734. Value £ 4. - . 6¾ Box and 1 . 6 porter ——— 4 . 2 . -¾'
Oct 14	JW	Thos Broughton	dia
Oct 26	JW	Dr Corudder	dia
Oct 29	JW	Thos Broughton	dia
Nov 7 [TH]	Hen Newman	JW	SPCK, abstr, 'Acquainting

Date	Writer	Recipient	Source
1734			
			him that his packet was sent the 21st October to Mr. Rivington's in St. Paul's Churchyard.
			Value £ 4. -s. 6¾
			Box and 1 . 6
			porter, etc.
			4. 2 . -¾'
Nov 9	John Clayton	JW	MA, end by JW, 'of Clemens Alexan[drinu]s'; 'please inform me particularly of your method of meditating'
Nov 11	JW	Westley Hall	dia
Nov 11	JW	Sympson	dia
Nov 11	JW	Mr [C] Rivington	dia
Nov 11	JW	Mrs Sus W	dia
Nov 11	JW	Kezzy W	dia
Nov 12	JW	Burman	dia
Nov 13	JW	Patty W	dia
Nov 13	JW	Emly W	dia
Nov 13	JW	Rd Morgan, Sen	dia
Nov 14	JW	Hen Newman	dia; SPCK, abstr, 'signifying that he received the papers relating to the Saltzburgers and is surprised the university has never been applied to on their account; that there is a collection now making there for Don Louis de las Torres.'
Nov 14	JW	Mr Ralfs	dia
Nov 15	JW	Sam W, Sen	395
Nov 15	JW	Sam W, Jun	dia
Nov 15	JW	Mr Iliffe	dia
Nov 15	JW	Selima	dia
Nov 20	Sam W, Sen	JW	395-7
Nov 20	Thos Broughton	JW	MA
Nov 25	JW	Burman	dia
Nov 25	JW	Sympson	dia
Nov 26	JW	Thos Broughton	dia
Nov 26	JW	Mr [C] Rivington	dia
Nov 26	JW	John Clayton	dia
Nov 27	JW	Aspasia	dia
Nov 27	JW	Mr Iliffe	dia
Nov 27	JW	John Whitelamb	dia
Nov 30	Ben Ingham	JW	MA; cf. Tyerm (OM), 59-60
Dec 4 [WE]	Sam W, Sen	Sam W, Jun	395-6 n.

Date	Writer	Recipient	Source
1734			
Dec 9	JW	Mr [C] Rivington	dia
Dec 10	JW	Mr [C] Rivington	dia
Dec 10	JW	Emly W	dia
Dec 10–19	JW	Sam W, Sen	397–410
Dec 10	Congreve	JW	dia (rec)
Dec 11	JW	Westley Hall	dia
Dec 11	JW	Sam W, Jun	dia
Dec 11	JW	Kezzy W	dia
Dec 14	Patty W	JW	dia (rec)
Dec 15	JW	Mr [C] Rivington	dia
Dec 25	Sam W, Jun	JW	410–11
1735			
Jan 4 [SA]	JW	Mr [C] Rivington	dia
Jan 10	JW	[Westley] H[all]	dia
Jan 10	JW	Rd Morgan, Sen	dia
Jan 10	JW	Sympson	dia
Jan 10	JW	Kezzy W	dia
Jan 10	JW	Patty W	dia
Jan 11	JW	Smith	dia
Jan 11	JW	Mr Stanley, Sen	dia
Jan 11	JW	John Clayton	dia
Jan 11	JW	Mr [C] Rivington	dia
Jan 13	JW	Sam W, Sen	dia; refs, 414–15
Jan 13	JW	Mrs Sus W	411–13
Jan 13	JW	John Whitelamb	dia
Jan 14	JW	Aspasia	dia
Jan 14	JW	Sir John Philipps	dia
Jan 15	JW	Sam W, Jun	413–14
Jan 20	JW	Aunt Dyer	dia
Jan 20	JW	Mrs Rivington	dia
Jan 21	Sam W, Sen	JW	414–15
Jan 23	JW	Mr [C] Rivington	dia
Jan 24	JW	Ben Ingham	dia
Jan 27	JW	[Matt] Salmon	dia
Jan 28	JW	Sam W, Sen	dia (? = transcr, Dec. 10, 1734)
Jan 28	Mr Jo Iliffe	JW	dia, rec 'letter from 2 Iliffe's!'
Jan 28	Mr G Iliffe	JW	dia; cf. Jan. 31
Jan 29	JW	Mr Bulman, Sen	dia
Jan 30	JW	John Clayton	dia
Jan 31	JW	G Iliffe	dia
Jan 31	JW	Jo Iliffe	dia
Jan 31	JW	Mr [C] Rivington	dia

Date	Writer	Recipient	Source
1735			
[Feb 1?]	Mrs Sus W	JW	ans, 418–19
Feb 5 [WE]	JW	Mr Woods	dia
Feb 5	JW	Mr Cole	dia
Feb 5	JW	Greive	dia
Feb 8	Sam W, Jun	JW	416
Feb 10	JW	[Westley] H[all]	dia
Feb 13	JW	Sam W, Jun	417–18
Feb 14	JW	Patty W	dia
Feb 14	JW	Mrs Sus W	418–19
Feb 14	JW	Sam W, Sen	419 (end of letter to JW's mother)
Feb 22	JW	Dr Jones	dia
Feb [22?]	Sam W, Jun	JW	419–20
Feb 25	JW	Mr Macl[　]	dia
Feb 27	Ben Ingham, at Ossett	JW	Tyerm (*OM*), 57–8, on his rule of life: 'I have methodized my time according to the following scheme. Suppose I rise at five or sooner, I spend till six in devotion—repeating a hymn, and chanting a psalm, then praying and reading the Holy Scriptures. At six, Christian treatises. At seven we breakfast. I then get a lesson out of the New Testament, then a Collect, and most of the Common Prayer. Then forty-two poor children come to me to read . . . I propose to observe the three ancient hours of prayer when at home . . . I shall readily submit to your better directions.'
Feb 28	JW	Bp John Potter	dia; ref, 420
Mar 1 [SA]	Bp John Potter	JW	420
Mar 4	JW	Sam W, Jun	421
Mar 29	Emly W	JW	Hall MS, rec: 'That day I received a letter from my eldest sister informing me that my father's illness increased, so that if I desired to see him alive, I must set out without delay.'
Apr 1 [TU]	Whitefield	JW	MA; cf. W.H.S., X. 17–19, and 424 n, 425 n above

Date	Writer	Recipient	Source
1735			
Apr [7?]	JW	Thos Broughton	refs, 422–3
Apr [9?]	JW	Whitefield	ref, quot, 425
Apr 15	Thos Broughton	JW	422–3
Apr [20?]	Whitefield	JW	ref, 424 n.
Apr 30	CW	Sam W, Jun	Priestley, 51–5; cf. 422 n.
[May 1?]	JW	Whitefield	ref, quots, 423–4
May 8 [TH]	Whitefield	JW	423–6
May [13?]	JW	Whitefield	427
[May?]	JW	Roman Catholic	428–30
June 11 [WE]	Whitefield	JW	MA; cf. *AM*, 1798, 439–40
June 17	Ben Ingham	JW	MA; cf. Tyerm (*OM*), 61–3
[June?]	JW	Emly W	refs, 430–1
July 11 [FR]	Whitefield	JW	F. Baker, copy
Aug 2 [SA]	Mr [C] Rivington	JW	Hall MS, rec: 'On Sat, Aug. 2, Mr. Rivington sent me word that my father's book must stand till I came to town.'
Aug 13	Emly W	JW	430–1
Aug [16?]	JW	Hen Newman	SPCK (rec Aug 19), abstr: 'J Wesley at Lincoln College, Oxford, August, desiring a packet of books on the Society's terms.' 'Ordered the books. Answered the 28 Aug, 1735. Value 2. 1. 6 Box, Porter, 6. 6 etc. 2. 8. -'
Aug 28	Hen Newman	JW	ref, Aug. [16?]
[Sept 1?]	JW	Ben Ingham	extr, Tyerm (*OM*), 64
[Sept 4?]	Ben Ingham	JW	extr, Tyerm (*OM*), 64
[Sept 4?]	JW	Oglethorpe	ref, 432
Sept 8 [MO]	John Burton	JW	MA; quot, 435 n.; cf. Curnock, VIII. 285
Sept 9	Oglethorpe	JW	432
Sept [11?]	John Clayton	JW	433
Sept [15]	Westley Hall	JW	Hall MS, ref: 'I received a letter from him a day or two after my return to college (which was on Monday, Sept. 15), subscribed, "Your affectionate brother, W.H."'
Sept 18	John Burton	JW	MA; quot, 435 n.; cf. Curnock, VIII. 286
Sept 23	JW	Hen Newman	443 n
Sept 25	Rd Morgan, Jun	JW	433–4
Sept 28	John Burton	JW	434–7
Sept 30	JW	Rd Morgan, Jun	437–8
Oct 9 [TH]	Thos Broughton	JW	Bristol Wesley, 198

Date	Writer	Recipient	Source
1735			
Oct 10	JW	John Burton	439–42
Oct 13	Hen Newman	JW	443
Oct 15	JW	Sam W, Jun	444–5
Oct 17	JW	rector [E Isham]	dia
Oct 17	JW	Mr [Rd] Hutchins	dia
Oct 17	JW	Emly W	dia
Oct 18	JW	Varanese	dia
Oct 18	JW	Miss Sally Andrews	dia
Oct 18	JW	Emly W	dia
Oct 18	JW	[Matt] Salmon	dia
Oct 18	JW	John Clayton	dia
Oct 18	JW	Kezzy W	dia
Oct 18	JW	Mr [Jas] Vernon	dia
Oct 18	JW	Mr [A] Hutcheson	dia
Oct 18	JW	Mrs Sus W	dia
Oct 18	JW	[C] Rivington	dia
Nov 1 [SA]	JW	Mrs Sus W	dia
Nov 1	JW	Mr [Jas] Vernon	dia
Nov 14	JW	[C] Rivington	dia
Nov 17	JW	[John] Clayton	dia
Nov 17	JW	[Matt] Salmon	dia
Nov 18	JW	Mrs Sus W	dia
Nov 18	Jas Vernon	JW	445
Nov 19–20	JW	Mr [Jas] Vernon	dia
Nov 21, 24	JW	Mr T Delamotte	dia
Nov 27	Rd Morgan, Jun	JW	MA; cf. Curnock, VIII. 264–5, and 433 n
Nov 27	Thos Broughton	JW	*AM*, 1797 (Supp), 4–5, Tyerm (*OM*), 335
Nov 27	Mrs Sus W	JW	445–6
1736			
Jan 20 [TU]	JW	Sir John Philipps	446–8
Jan 21–3	JW	Sam W, Jun	dia
Jan 22	JW	Mr [Jas] Vernon	dia
Jan 22	JW	Mr [A] Hutcheson	dia
Feb 1 [SU]	JW	Sam W, Jun, 'etc'	dia; refs, 458–60
Feb 29	'received letters from Oxon'	JW	dia
Mar 13 [SA]	JW	Zinzendorf	dia; cf. 449–50
Mar 13	JW	Bolzius & Gronau	448–9
Mar 14	JW	Varanese	dia
Mar 14	JW	Mrs Skinner	dia
Mar 15	JW	Zinzendorf	449–50
Mar 16	Oglethorpe	JW	MA, PRO, orig & copy, both in hand of CW: 'I

Date	Writer	Recipient	Source
1736			
			must desire you to examine the complaints made by Mr. Von Reck and Mr. Bolzius against Mr. Vat, and Mr. Vat against Mr. Von Reck, and to make a true state of the case, that I may judge concerning them.'
Mar 17	JW	[C] Rivington	dia
Mar 17	JW	Jas Vernon	dia
Mar 17	JW	Nancy W	dia
Mar 17	JW	[Matt] Salm[on]	dia
Mar 17	JW	Ilif[fe]	dia
Mar 18	JW	Mrs Sus W	450–1
Mar 18	JW	Sam W, Jun	dia
Mar 18	JW	Kezzy W	dia
Mar 18	JW	Nancy W[?]	dia—'S L[amber]t'
Mar 18	JW	Mr [John] Burton	dia
Mar 18	JW	Mr Brown	dia
Mar 19	JW	[Wm] Wogan	dia
Mar 19	JW	R Wood	dia
Mar 19	JW	Mr [Wm] Wogan	dia [probably same letter as the other to 'Wogan', same date]
Mar 19	JW	[John] Clayton	dia
Mar 20	JW	Horne	dia
Mar 20	JW	[Thos] Broughton	dia
Mar 20	JW	[Rd] Morgan [Jun]	dia
Mar 20	JW	Sally A[ndrew]s	dia
Mar 20	JW	M[rs] Musg[rove]	dia [who came in afternoon]
Mar 21	JW	Oglethorpe	dia
Mar 21–2	JW	CW	452–4
Mar 22	JW	Mr Sarney	dia
Mar 22	JW	rector [E Isham]	dia
Mar 23	JW	Sir J Philipps	dia; refs, 463; cf. SPCK, Min, June 15: '1. Upon reading a letter from the Reverd. Mr. Wesley at Savannah in Georgia, 23 of March last to Sr John Philipps, signifying the want of Bibles and Common prayer books among the poor there, 2. Agreed that it be recommended to the next Standing Committee to

Date	Writer	Recipient	Source
1736			
			send Mr. Wesley a packet of the undermentioned books by the Two Brothers, Capt. Thomson, Commander, bound to Georgia, viz. 40 Bibles minion 40 New Testaments long primer 40 Common prayer books minion.'
Mar 24	JW	Von Reck	dia
Mar 27	CW	JW	454-5
Mar 29	JW	Mr E[rasmu]s Philipps	dia 'on business'
Mar 29	JW	Mr [Thos] Hawkins	dia
Mar 31	JW	Bolzius	dia
Mar 31	JW	Von Reck	dia
Apr 21 [WE]	JW	CW	455-6
Apr 21	JW	Mr [Thos] Hawkins	dia
Apr 21	JW	Oglethorpe	456-8
Apr	Whitefield	JW	*AM* 1798, 357-9
Apr 29	Sam W, Jun	JW	458-60
May 1 [SA]	JW	Oglethorpe	dia
May 1	CW	JW	460-1 (rec May 10)
May 7	JW	Oglethorpe	dia
May 10-13	JW	Oglethorpe	dia
May 10	JW	Mr [John] Burton	461-3
May 11	JW	CW	dia
May 24	Sir John Thorold	JW	MA; see *AM* 1797 (Supp), 5-7; *Wes. Ban.*, 1849, 272-3
June 7 [SA]	JW	CW	dia
June 8-12	Hen Newman	JW	SPCK; see Jones, *Newman*, 194-5 (Wesley's difficulties with Indians compared with those of John Eliot)
June 9	JW	CW	dia
June 9	JW	Oglethorpe	dia
June 16	JW	Mrs [T] Hawkins	dia (5 hours)
June 16	Hen Newman	JW	463
June 24	JW	Mrs [T] Hawkins	dia (on boat)
June 24	JW	Mr Colwell	dia (on boat)
June 24	JW	Mrs Colwell	dia (on boat)
June 26	Spangenberg	JW	dia (date read, Savannah)
July 3 [SA]	JW	[Edmund Gibson,] Bp of	dia (i.e. by Oglethorpe: 'he writ a Lr for me to the Bp

Date	Writer	Recipient	Source
1736			
		London	of L.'
July 4	JW	[C] Rivington	dia
July 5	Mrs [T] Hawkins	JW	dia (date read)
July 5-6	JW	Mrs [T] Hawkins	dia (transcr July 6)
July 12	JW	Mr [Pet] Appee	dia
July 12	JW	Mr Colwell	dia
July 13	JW	'wrote [letters] for the parish'	dia
July 14	JW	Mrs [T] Hawkins	dia (transcr July 15)
July 20	JW	*Gent's Mag*	464-6
July 21	JW	Mrs [T] Hawkins	dia
July 23	JW	A Hutcheson	467-8
July 23	JW	Mr [Jas] Vernon	469
Aug 19 [TH]	JW	T Moore	dia
Aug 22	Mrs [T] Hawkins	JW	ref, 470 n
Aug 23	JW	Oglethorpe	470
Aug [26?]	JW	Whitefield	see 471 n
Sept 2 [TH]	Jas Hervey	JW	*AM* 1778, 130-2
Sept 2	Whitefield	JW	MA; see *AM*, Supp, 1797, 8-10
Sept 3	W[alter] Chapman	JW	MA; see *AM*, Supp, 1797, 10-11; Tyerm (*OM*), 362-3
['Sept 7, 1756'	JW	'Madam'	Wes. Chap. In hand of Whitefield, prob. Jan-June, 1740; date, and spurious 'J Wesley' signature added later]
Sept 7	JW	Mr Hird	dia
Sept 7	JW	Miss Sophy [Hopkey]	dia, ref in MS Journal
Sept 7	JW	Hen Newman	SPCK, abstr, Dec. 7: 'John Wesley at Savannah in Georgia, 7 Septr., that his Bro's return to England has thrown all the care of his flock upon him; that the heat is nothing there to what he expected, and that the country is very fruitful, but not without industry.'
Sept 8	JW	Oglethorpe	dia
Sept 8	JW	CW	dia
Sept 8	JW	Mrs Hutton	dia
Sept 8	JW	Hen Newman	dia (see Sept 7; surely same)
Sept 8	JW	Bro [Wm] Wright	dia

Date	Writer	Recipient	Source
1736			
Sept 9	JW	Sam W, Jun	dia
Sept 10	JW	Patty W	dia
Sept 10	JW	Whitefield	471-3
Sept 10	JW	John Clayton	dia
Sept 11	JW	Jas Vernon	473-4
Sept 11	JW	Sir John Thorold	dia
Sept 15	JW	Emly W	dia
Sept 15	JW	Mr [C] Rivington	dia
Sept 16	JW	Kezzy W	dia
Sept 16	JW	Mrs Sus W	dia
Sept 16	JW	S Ellison	dia (= Suky W)
Sept 16	JW	Nancy W	dia
Sept 16	JW	Serena	dia
Sept 16	JW	Jas Hervey	dia
Sept 17	JW	J Burton	dia
Sept 17	JW	Aspasia	dia
Sept 17	JW	Selima	dia (surely same as Sept. 24)
Sept 22	Hen Newman	JW	475
Sept 23	JW	Sophy Hopkey	dia, MS Journal, ref
Sept 24	JW	[C] Rivington	dia
Sept 24	JW	Mr Laserre of Charlestown	dia
Sept 24	JW	[Selima] Ann Granville	475-6
Oct 1-6	CW	JW	476-9
Oct 20 [MO]	JW	Georgia Trustees	dia
Oct 23	Zinzendorf	JW	479-83
Oct 15-25	CW	JW	483-5
Nov 2 [TU]	JW	Georgia Trustees	dia
Nov 10	JW	H Verelst	485-6
Nov 11	JW	Mr Reinier	dia
Nov 11	JW	CW	dia
Nov 12	JW	Earl of Egmont	486-7
Nov 12, 15	JW	Oglethorpe	dia; revised 15
Nov 13	JW	Sam W, Jun	dia
Nov 21	JW	Sir John Philipps	dia
Nov 23	JW	Sam W, Jun	487-90
Nov 30	CW	JW	dia (date read 'letters')
Dec 1 [WE]	Watkins	JW	dia (date read)
Dec 2	JW	CW	dia
Dec 2	JW	Rev Laserre	dia
Dec 2	JW	[Sam] Eveleigh of Charleston	dia
Dec 2	JW	Watk[ins]	dia
Dec 13	JW	Mr Butler	dia
Dec 26	Spangeberg	JW	dia (date read)

Date	Writer	Recipient	Source
1737			
Jan 10 [MO]	JW	Mr Citenby(?)	dia
Feb 6 [SU]	JW	Sophy Hopkey	490
Feb 15	JW	Georgia Trustees	dia
Feb 15	JW	Dr Bray's Assoc	dia
Feb 15	JW	rector [E Isham]	dia
Feb 15	JW	Dr T Cutler	dia
Feb 16	JW	Mr [John] Burton	dia
Feb 16	JW	Rd Mo[rga]n [Jun]	491–2
Feb 16	JW	Whitefield	dia
Feb 18	JW	[Walter] Chapman	dia
Feb 18	JW	Horne	dia
Feb 18	JW	Jas Hervey	dia
Feb 18	JW	Sarney	dia
Feb 18	JW	Mr Jones (Beaufort)	dia
Feb 19	JW	Sam W, Jun	dia
Feb 21	JW	Mr [Wm] Horton	dia
Feb 21	JW	Mr Hird (Frederica)	dia
Feb 24	JW	Oglethorpe	492–4
Feb 24	JW	CW	dia (transcr Feb. 25)
Feb 26	JW	Dr Bray's Assoc	494–5
Mar 2 [WE]	Hen Newman	JW	495–6
Mar 3	JW	[Rev] Laserre	dia
Mar 3	JW	[Edmund Gibson] Bp of London	dia
Mar 4	JW	Georgia Trustees	496–8
Mar 6	JW	[Mark] Hird	dia
Mar 6	JW	Mrs Weston of Frederica	dia
Mar 6	JW	Mrs Robinson of Frederica	dia
Mar 6	JW	Mr [T] Causton	dia
Mar 10	JW	Sophy Hopkey	498
Mar 15	JW	Mr Kimberley(?)	dia (as 21, 'cimrelr'?)
Mar 15	JW	[Edmund Gibson] Bp of London	dia
Mar 15	JW	Miss B—	dia (?Bovey, i.e. same as Mar 16, Burnside—her married name)
Mar 16	JW	Mrs Burnside	dia
Mar 17	Whitefield	JW	498–9
Mar 21	JW	Mr Kimberley(?)	dia (as 15)

Date	Writer	Recipient	Source
1737			
Mar 28	JW	Mrs Hutton	dia
Mar 28	JW	Jas Hutton	dia
Mar 28	JW	Mr Macquin	dia
Mar 28	JW	Bailey	dia
Mar 28	JW	Wm Wogan	499–501
Mar 28	JW	Sam W, Jun	dia (re love affair); see July 19(?)
Mar 29	JW	Mrs Chapman	502–4
Mar 30	JW	SPCK: 'our society'	dia; SPCK abstr, June 14: 'John Wesley at Savannah in Georgia, 30 March, that he is much concerned to hear of the death of good Sir John Philipps, and giving some account of his present affairs there'; ref July 19
Mar 30	JW	Sir Er Philipps	dia
Mar 31	JW	Georgia Trustees	504–5
Apr 1 [FR]	JW	Mr [Wm] Horton of Frederica	dia
Apr 1	JW	Mr Hird (Frederica)	dia
Apr 1	JW	Mr Weston (Frederica)	dia
Apr 15	Whitefield	JW	505–6
Apr 17	JW	CW	dia
Apr 17	JW	Mrs Sus W	dia
Apr 18	JW	Mr Gu—	dia
Apr 18	JW	Mrs Laceby	dia
May 2 [MO]	JW	CW	dia
May 2	JW	Mr Laserre	dia
May 2	JW	Mrs Laserre	dia
May 2	JW	Miss Molly [?Laserre]	dia
May 7	JW	Mr Laserre	dia
May 7	JW	Mark Hird	dia
May 7	JW	Mrs Dalton	dia
May(?)	JW	H Verelst	ref, 506 n.
May 27	JW	[Mark] Hird	dia
May 27	JW	Mr G Hutchins	dia
June 6 [MO]	'Letters from England!!!'	JW	dia
June 7	JW	Kezzy W	dia; abstr. MS Journal, M.A, J.W. III. 4, p. 26: 'I writ to my S. Kezzy & made her an offer of living with me here. But upon reflection I was in doubt whether I had done well,

Date	Writer	Recipient	Source
1737			
			considering the slippery ground on which I stand. However, I leave the whole matter in God's hand: let him order for us what is best!'
June 7	JW	Mr Butler	dia
June 10	JW	Mr Hird	dia
June 10	JW	Mark Hird	dia
June 10–11	JW	Mr Hen Newman	dia; SPCK abstr, Sept. 6: 'John Wesley at Savannah in Georgia, 11 June. Thanks to Mr. Archdeacon Rye for his benefaction and the Society for their tracts; desiring to be favoured with an account of Sr. John's death and the sickness that occasioned it. That the heathen there are as yet inaccessible to 'em, being the most corrupted of all the heathens upon the continent.' Ref, Oct. 10
June 10	JW	H Verelst	506
June 10	JW	Mr [Wm] Horton	dia
June 10	JW	CW	dia
June 12	JW	Mr Burns[ide]	dia
June 12	JW	Mr Bailey	dia
June 13	JW	Mrs Skinn[er]	dia
June 13	JW	Mrs B[radley]	dia [Mrs. Eliz. Bradley had just died; this might have been a relative]
June 13	JW	Mr B[radley]	dia [see previous entry]
June 13	JW	Mrs W—	dia
June 14	JW	[John] Clayton	dia
June 14	JW	CW	dia
June 14	JW	Mr [Westley] Hall	dia
June 15	Georgia Trustees, per Ben Martyn	JW	507
June 15	John Burton	JW	508
June 16	JW	Jas Hutton	509–10
June 16	JW	Selima	dia
June 28	Von Reck	JW	510–11
July 2 [SA]	JW	Mr Baker	dia
July 5	JW	Thos Causton	511–12
July 5	JW	Sophy Williamson	512–13

Date	Writer	Recipient	Source
1737			
July 8	JW	Mr [Alex] Garden	dia
July 8	JW	Mr [?Bravex Hack]	dia
July 19	Hen Newman	JW	513–14
July 19(?)	Sam W, Jun	JW	Whitehead, II. 30, quot: 'I am sorry you are disappointed in one match, because you are very unlikely to find another.' ? answer to Mar. 28
July 22	JW	Dr D Humphreys	514–15
July 23	JW	Dr T Cutler	515
July 23	JW	SPG	516
Aug 10 [WE]	Thos Causton	JW	516–17
Aug 10	JW	Thos Causton	517–18
Aug 11	JW	Sophy Williamson	518
Aug 16	JW	Georgia Trustees	dia
Aug 16	JW	John Burton	dia
Aug 23	JW	Mr Hird	dia
Aug 30	Zinzendorf	JW	dia (date read)
[Sept] 8 [TH]	JW	Savannah Magistrates	519
[Sept?]	Alex Garden	JW	519–20
[Oct 7?]	JW	CW	refs, 524–6
Oct 10 [MO]	Hen Newman	JW	520–1
Oct 19	Ben Ingham	JW	521–2
Oct 22	Dr T Cutler	JW	522–3
Dec 14 [WE]	H Verelst	JW	PRO, Calendar 630: 'to John Wesley at Savannah, enclosing copy of letter lately received from William Williamson at Savannah and an affidavit made by his wife. The Trustees hope that you will be able to justify yourself, having in the meantime suspended their judgment until they receive your answer, that they may consider the complaint and answer at the same time.'
Dec 27	[Mrs Fallowfield?]	JW	523–4
1738			
Jan 2 [MO	CW	JW	524–6
Jan 2	Westley Hall, Whitefield, Jas Hutton,	JW	ref, 526

Date	Writer	Recipient	Source
1738			
	Isaac Burton, John Hutchings, John Bray, John Doble, Jepthah Harris, Jas Habersham		
Jan 3	Jas Hutton	JW	526
Jan 27	John Gambold	JW	527
Feb 1 [WE]	JW	Whitefield	527–8
Feb 1	Whitefield	JW	528–9
Feb 6	John Hutchings	JW	Drew
Feb [13?]	JW	Wm Delamotte	ref, Feb. 18
Feb 18	Wm Delamotte	JW	Bristol Wesley, 208
Feb 23	Chas Delamotte	JW	529–31
Feb 27	Walter Chapman	JW	531
Mar [3?]	JW	Sam W, Jun	Sam. W, Jun. to Jas. Hutton, Mar. 18, 1737/8 (MorA): 'If you hear any tidings of my brothers let me know, for 'tis almost a fortnight since I had a line or two from Jack, that Charles had been like to die at Oxford, and not one word since.'
Mar 7 [TU	JW	Lady Cox	532–5
Mar 21	Jas Hervey	JW	535
Mar 26	JW	Jas Hutton	535–6
Apr 18 [TU]	Westley Hall	JW	Sam. W., Jun. to Jas. Hutton, Apr. 26, 1738 (MorA): 'Dear Jem, Not knowing how to direct to my brother Jack I must desire you to communicate the following note to him, which I received by post yesterday: "Unless you remit me according to my proposals twenty pounds before the end of next month, you will oblige me to prefer a Bill in Chancery against you, without further notice from yours, etc. W.H. Sarum, 18 April, 1738."'
Apr 20	JW	Chas Kinchin	dia
Apr 20	JW	Chas Delamotte	dia
Apr 20	JW	Mrs Prince	dia
Apr 20	JW	Molly Kinchin	dia
Apr 21	JW	Mr Brown	dia

Date	Writer	Recipient	Source
1738			
Apr 22	JW	Chas Kinchin	dia
Apr 22	Sarah Hurst	JW	MA (copy)
Apr 28	JW	'Hugh Brian, etc'	dia
Apr 28	JW	Jas Hutton	537
Apr 28	JW	CW	538
Apr 28	JW	P Böhler	(enclosed in Hutton's)
Apr 30	JW	Mr Salwey	dia
Apr 30	JW	Jas [?Chas] Kinchin	dia
May 1 [MO]	John Clayton	JW	538–40
May 2	Chas Kinchin	JW	*AM*, 1778, 176; Tyerm (*OM*), 368; quot, 607 n.
May 8	J H[utchings]	JW	MA
May 8	P Böhler	JW	JWJ, May 10, 1738
May 10	Miss M[olly] Kinchin	JW	*AM*, 1778, 177–8
May 13	Kezzy W	JW	MA
May 14	JW	Wm Law	540–2
May 16	Jas Burnside	JW	MA
May 19	Wm Law	JW	543–6
May 20	JW	Wm Law	546–8
May [22?]	Wm Law	JW	548–50
May 24	JW	[John Gambold?]	550–1
[May–June?]	JW	Whitefield	Whitefield, *Letter to Wesley*, re sailing from Deal, Feb. 1–2, 1738: 'We sailed immediately. Some months after I received a letter from you at Georgia, wherein you wrote words to this effect: "Though God never before gave me a wrong lot, yet perhaps he suffered me to have such a lot at that time, to try what was in your heart." . . . It is plain you had a wrong lot given you here, and justly, because you tempted God in drawing one.' See pp. 527–8 above.
June 6 [TU]	from Oxford	JW	rec; JWJ, June 6: '. . . in the evening I received a letter from Oxford which threw me into much perplexity. It was asserted therein that no doubting could consist with the least degree of true faith; that whoever at any time felt any doubt or

Date	Writer	Recipient	Source
1738			
			fear was not *weak in faith*, but had *no faith* at all; and that none hath any faith till the law of the Spirit of life has made him *wholly* free from the law of sin and death.'
June 19	JW	Mrs Sus W	551–3
June 28	JW	CW	554
June 28	JW	Mrs Sus W	555–6
July 6 [TH]	JW	Mrs Sus W	556–7
July 7	JW	CW	557–8
July 7	JW	Sam W, Jun	558–9
Aug 4 [FR]	JW	CW	560
Aug 4	JW	Jas Hutton	561–2
Aug 25	Jas Burnside	JW	MA
Sept 18 [MO]	JW	Mr Fox	dia
Sept 25–8	JW	Rev A Bedford	562–6
Sept 27–8	JW	The Moravians	566–7
Oct 10 [TU]	Wm Delamotte	JW	567–8
Oct 11	JW	[John Gambold?]	ref, 567 n.
Oct 12	JW	Sam W, Jun	dia
Oct 12	JW	Mrs Sus W	dia
Oct 12	JW	Chas Kinchin	dia
Oct 13	JW	Dr Koker	568
Oct 13	JW	Ben Ingham	569–71
Oct 14	JW	Allicock	dia
Oct 14	[John Gambold?]	JW	rec reply; cf. JWJ, Oct. 12–13
Oct 14–20	JW	Church at Herrnhut	571–3
Oct [21?]	Sam W, Jun	JW	reply, 575–8
Oct 14–[30]	JW	Zinzendorf	573–4
Oct 30	JW	Sam W, Jun	575–8
Nov 4 [SA]	JW	Emly W	dia; reply, 589–90
Nov 15	Sam W, Jun	JW	578–9
Nov 16	JW	Ingham & Hutton	579–81
Nov 18	John Bray	JW	MA
Nov 21	JW	Jas Hervey	581–2
Nov 22	JW	Dr Koker	582–3
Nov 22	JW	Rd Viney	583–4
Nov 22	JW	Is Le Long	584–5
Nov 22	JW	Moscheros	dia
Nov 22	JW	Töltschig	dia
Nov 23	JW	R Aldwor[th]	dia
Nov 23	Jas Hutton	JW	585–7
Nov 24	JW	Jas Hutton	587–8
Nov 24	JW	Mr Fox	588–9
Nov 24	JW	Ben Ingham	dia (address sheet of 587–9)

Date	Writer	Recipient	Source
1738			
Nov 24	Emly W	JW	589–90
Nov 25	Wm Fish	JW	MA; cf. JWJ, Dec. 5, 1738
Nov 25	JW	Jas Hutton	590–2
Nov 27	JW	Wm Fish	dia
Nov 27	JW	Summers	dia
Nov 27	JW	J[ephthah] Harris	dia
Nov 27	JW	Jas Hutton	592–3
Nov [29?]	Jas Hutton	JW	refs, 594–5
Nov 30	JW	Sam W, Jun	594
Dec 1 [FR]	JW	[John] Hutchi[ngs]	dia
Dec 1	JW	Wats[on]	dia
Dec 1	JW	Mrs Sus W	dia
Dec 1	JW	Jas Hutton	594–6
Dec 1	Jas Hervey	JW	596–7
Dec 2	JW	Emly W	dia
Dec 2	JW	Chas D[elamotte]	597
Dec 3	JW	[Geo] Stonehouse	dia
Dec 3	JW	Sympson	dia
Dec 3	JW	Marschall (Jena)	dia
Dec 4	JW	Gottschalck	dia
Dec 5	John Bray	JW	MA
Dec 5	Wm Fish	JW	Moore I. 109–10
Dec 12	Zinzendorf	JW	Herrnhut Archives (draft)
Dec 13	Sam W, Jun	JW	598
Dec 14	JW	Mr Griffin	dia (Georgia)
Dec 14	JW	Mrs Griffin	dia (Georgia)
Dec 14	JW	Mrs Vanderplank	dia (Georgia)
Dec 15	JW	[Mark] Hird	dia (Georgia)
Dec 15	JW	Mr Tolly	dia (Georgia)
Dec 16	JW	Jo[hn] Lindal	dia
Dec 16	JW	Mr [Jas] Burns[ide]	dia (Georgia)
Dec 18	JW	[Jas] Habersham	dia (Georgia)
Dec 18	JW	Mr [Alex] Garden	dia (Charleston)
Dec 19	JW	Kezzy W	dia
[Dec?]	[Wm Delamotte?]	JW	JWJ, Dec. 5, 1738
1739			
Jan 6 [SA]	JW	Kezzy W	dia
Jan 11	B[etty] H[opson]	JW	dia, rec
Jan 20	JW	Kezzy W	dia
Jan 24	Sam W, Jun	JW	599
Feb 3 [SA]	JW	Mrs Sus W	dia
Feb 3	JW	Mr Fox	dia
Feb 3	JW	Sam W, Jun	599–600
Feb 5	JW	Mr [Rd] Hutchins	dia

Date	Writer	Recipient	Source
1739			
Feb 5	JW	Sallie's mother [Mrs Andrews?]	dia
Feb 9	A follower	JW	JWJ, Feb. 9: 'Sir, Your prayers are desired for a child that is lunatic, and sore vexed day and night, that our Lord would be pleased to heal him, as he did those in the day of his flesh, and that he would give his parents faith and patience till his time is come.' Cf. p. 602 above.
Feb 12	JW	Mr Hook[er]	dia
Feb 13	A follower	JW	JWJ, Feb. 13: 'Sir, I return you hearty thanks for your prayers on Friday for my tortured son. He grows worse and worse; I hope, the nearer deliverance . . .'
Feb 13	Whitefield	JW	600–1
Feb 15	JW	Mr Barn[ard]	dia
Feb [15?]	Mrs Sus W	JW	ref, 601
Feb 20	JW	[Rd] Morgan [Jun]	dia
Feb 20	JW	Mr Wragg	dia
Feb 22	JW	H Hatfield	dia
Feb 22	JW	Mr Simpson	dia
Feb 22	JW	Emly W	dia
Feb 22	JW	Mr [Rd] Hutchins	dia
Feb 22	JW	Ridley	dia
Feb 23	JW	Dr Webster	dia
Feb [23?]	Mrs Sus W	JW	ref, 601
Feb 26	JW	Whitefield	601–3
Feb 26	JW	Mr [Wm] Seward	603–4
Feb 27	JW	Rd Viney	dia
Mar 3 [SA]	Whitefield	JW	604–5
Mar 8	JW	Whitefield	dia; cf. Seward to Hutton, Bristol, Mar. 10, 1738/9 (MorA): 'Our dear brother [Whitefield] has just received Brother John Westly's letter from Oxon. We all greatly rejoice, but he has not time to answer it this post.'
Mar 16	JW	Mrs Fox	dia
Mar 16	JW	Perkins	dia
Mar 16	JW	Patty Thurston	dia

Date	Writer	Recipient	Source
1739			
Mar 16	JW	Chas Kinchin	dia
Mar 16	JW	Emly W	dia
Mar 16	JW	Miss Simpson	dia
Mar 16	JW	Westley Hall	dia
Mar 16	JW	Whitefield	605-9
Mar 20	JW	Jas Hervey	609-10
Mar 20	JW	Whitefield	610-11; cf. refs, 611-12
Mar 20	JW	Seward	dia
Mar 20	JW	Ben Ingham	dia
Mar 20	JW	Hen Newman	SPCK abstr, Mar. 20: 'John Wesley at London, 20 March, desiring a Packet of Books on the Society's Terms'; 'ordered the books'.
Mar 21	JW	John Cennick	dia; refs, 618
Mar 21	JW	John Clayton	dia
Mar 22	JW	Dr P Doddridge	dia
Mar 22	JW	John Clayton	dia
Mar 22-3	Whitefield	JW	611-12
Mar [23?]	Seward	JW	JWJ, Mar. 15 onwards: 'I received . . . a letter from Mr. Whitefield, and another from Mr. Seward, entreating me in the most pressing manner to come to Bristol without delay.'
Mar 26	Sam W, Jun	JW	613
Mar 27	JW	Chas Kinchin	dia
Mar 27	JW	Seward	dia
Mar 28	JW	[John] Clayton	614-17
Mar 29	John Cennick	JW	617-18
Apr 2 [MO]	JW	Jas Hutton, etc	619-20
Apr 3	Whitefield	JW	621
Apr 4	JW	Jas Hutton	621-2
Apr 4	JW	CW	dia
Apr 4	JW	Emly W	dia
Apr 4	JW	Simpson	dia
Apr 4	JW	Westley Hall	dia
Apr 4	JW	Mrs Vaughan	dia
Apr 4	JW	Sam W, Jun	622-3
Apr 4	Jas Hervey	JW	624-5
Apr 5	JW	Esther Hopson	dia
Apr 9	JW	Jas Hutton, etc	625-8
Apr 9	JW	Jas Hutton	629-31
Apr 9	JW	John Edmonds	630
Apr 9	JW	CW	630
Apr 13	Wm Oxlee	JW	MA, 'a[nswere]d 27'
Apr 14	JW	Mr [Josiah] Tucker	dia
Apr 16	JW	Jas Hutton, etc	631-3

Date	Writer	Recipient	Source
1739			
Apr 16	Sam W, Jun	JW	634-5
Apr 18	JW	Whitefield	dia
Apr 18	JW	Seward	dia
Apr 18	JW	Mitchell	dia
Apr 19-20	JW	Mr [Josiah] Tucker	dia 'writ answer to Mr. Tucker's Queries'
Apr 21	JW	CW	dia
Apr 21-6	JW	Jas Hutton, etc	635-7 (dia, Apr. 21)
Apr 21	JW	[J] West	dia
Apr 21	JW	Mrs Storer	dia
Apr 24	a critic	JW	rec, quot, 639
Apr 27	JW	John Bray	dia
Apr 27	JW	Nowers	dia
Apr 27	JW	G Chapman	dia
Apr 27	JW	[Hen] Newman	dia
Apr 27	JW	Waldron	dia
Apr 27	JW	Parker	dia
Apr 27	JW	[Wm] Oxlee	dia (docket to Apr. 13)
Apr 30	JW	Jas Hutton, etc	637-41
Apr 30	JW	[J] Edmonds	dia
Apr 30	JW	[John] Hodges	dia
May 1 [TU]	JW	Mrs Fox	dia
May 1	JW	[Mrs?] Compton	dia
May 1	JW	Jas Mears	dia
May 1	JW	Sarah Hurst	dia
May 1	JW	Mrs Robinson	dia
May 1	JW	Mills	dia
May 1	JW	Bro Thompson	dia
May 5	JW	CW	dia
May 5	JW	Jas Hutton	dia [cf. May 7, 8]
May 5	JW	Whitefield	dia
May 5	JW	Seward	dia
May 5	JW	[J] Hutchin[g]s	dia
May 7	JW	Jas Hutton, etc	641-4
May 7	Churchwarden (Pensford)	JW	647
May 8	JW	Mrs Sus W	dia
May 8	JW	Bowes	dia
May 8	JW	Nowers	dia
May 8	JW	Jas Hutton	644-5
May 8	JW	Mr Fox	dia
May 8	JW	Chas Graves	dia
May 9	JW	CW	dia
May 9-10	JW	Sam W, Jun	645-7
May 11	John Bray	JW	MA, 'a[nswere]d June 2'
May 14	JW	Jas Hutton, etc	647-50
May 16	JW	Whitefield	dia
May 23	JW	Seward	dia
May 24	JW	Bro Sone	dia
May 24	JW	Exall	dia
May 24	JW	Parker	dia

Date	Writer	Recipient	Source
1739			
May 24	JW	P Sims	dia
May 24	JW	Mrs Grevil	dia
May 24	JW	Chas D[elamotte]	dia
May 25	Wm Seward	JW	ref, 659
May 28	JW	Jas Hutton, etc	650–3
June 2 [SA]	JW	[John] Bray	dia (docket to May 11)
June 2	JW	[J] Edmonds	dia
June 2	JW	Easy	dia
June 2	JW	J Chambers	dia
June 2	JW	Wm Seward	dia
June 2	JW	[Chas] Metcalf	dia
June 2	JW	Esther Hopson	dia
June 2	JW	[Wm] Oxlee	dia
June 2	JW	Clapham	dia
June 2	JW	Mrs Thacker	dia
June 2	JW	Holland	dia
June 2	JW	Chas Graves	dia
June 2	JW	Betty Hughes	dia
June 2	JW	Jas Mears	dia
June 3	JW	Whitefield	dia
June 3	JW	Jas Hutton	dia (see June 4)
June 4	JW	Jas Hutton, etc	654–6
June 4	Miss S Burdock	JW	MA
June 5	JW	Miss [S] Burdock	dia
June 6	JW	Mrs Fox	dia
June 6	JW	Sarah Hurst	dia
June 6	JW	Bro Gibbs	dia
June 6	JW	Shaw	dia
June 6	JW	Clark	dia
June [6?]	[Miss] S Burdock	JW	MA (copy)
June 7	JW	Sam W, Jun	dia
June 7	JW	Miss [S] Burdock	dia
June 7–10	JW	Jas Hutton, etc	656–9
June 8	JW	Bro Hodges	dia
June 8	JW	Gould	dia
June [8?]	[J Edmonds?]	JW	JWJ, June 11: 'I received a pressing letter from London (as I had several others before) to come thither as soon as possible, our brethren in Fetter Lane being in great confusion for want of my presence and advice.'
June 9	JW	Dr [E] Isham	dia
June 9	JW	[Miss] S Burdock	dia
June [11?]	Miss [S] Burdock	JW	MA (copy)

Date	Writer	Recipient	Source
1739			
June 11	JW	Miss [S] Burdock	dia
June 14	JW	Bro [J] Purdy	dia
June [16?]	JW	Jas Hervey	ref, 673 n.
June 20	JW	Whitefield	dia (?refs, June 25)
June 22	JW	Society at Wells	dia
June 22	Whitefield	CW	quot, 661 n.
June 23	JW	CW	660-1
June 23	JW	Whitefield	dia; refs, 661 n.
June 23	[Miss] S Burdock	JW	MA (copy)
June 25	JW	Bro Ellis	dia
June 25	JW	Ben Ingham	dia
June 25	JW	Mr Abbott	dia
June 25	JW	CW	dia
June 25	JW	Bro Parker	dia
June 25	Whitefield	JW	661-2
June 25	Wm Delamotte	JW	MA
June 25	F Okely	JW	MA (double letter with last)
June 26	JW	Sam W, Jun	dia; refs, 681-2
June 27	JW	Whitefield	dia (docketed to June 25)
June 29	JW	Whitefield	dia
July 2 [MO]	JW	Jas Hutton, etc	662-6
July 2	Whitefield	JW	667
July 3	JW	Dr [E] Isham, etc	dia
July 3	JW	Whitefield	docket on Whitefield's, July 2
July 3	JW	Jas Hutton	dia (cf. July 2 above)
July 3	JW	Mrs Storer	dia
July 4	JW	Mr De-berdt	dia
July 8	JW	Miss [S] Burdock	dia
July 9	JW	Mr Davidson	dia
July 9	JW	Mr [J] Oulton	dia
July 9	JW	Jas Hutton	667-8; cf. dia
July 12	JW	Miss [S] Burdock	dia
July 13	John Oulton	JW	*AM*, 1797 (Supp), 25-6
July 19	JW	Whitefield	dia; refs, 668
July 21	JW	[J] Edmonds	dia
July 21	JW	Mr De-berdt	dia
July 21	JW	Patty W	dia
July 23	JW	Mr De-berdt	dia
July 23	Whitefield	JW	668-9
July 25	JW	Dr H Stebbing	669-72
July 27	JW	Patty W	dia
July 28	JW	Mr [J] Oulton	dia
July 28	JW	[T] Richards	dia
July 28	JW	Cartwright	dia, 'of E[ve]sham'
July 28	JW	Mr [Rd] Hutchins	dia

Date	Writer	Recipient	Source
1739			
July 28	JW	Chas Kinchin	dia; quot, 690–1
July 28	JW	Whitefield	dia
July 28	JW	Seward	dia
July 30	JW	Miss [S] Burdock	dia
Aug 3 [FR]	JW	Jas Hutton	672–3
Aug 6	JW	Miss [S] B[urdock]	dia
Aug 8	JW	Jas Hervey	673–4
Aug 8	JW	Severs (Wells)	JWJ, Aug. 8: 'Having frequently been invited to Wells, particularly by Mr [Severs], who begged me to make his house my home, on Thursday the 9th I went thither, and wrote him word the night before.'
Aug 9	Miss [S] Burdock	JW	MA (copy)
Aug 11	JW	Mr Griffiths	dia
Aug [11?]	Miss [S] Burdock	JW	MA (copy)
Aug 11	JW	Miss [S] Burdock	dia
Aug [13]	JW	Jas Hutton	674–5
Aug 14	Eben Blackwell	JW	675–6
Aug 16	JW	[Wm Jefferies], Mayor of Bristol	dia
Aug 20	CW	JW	676
Aug 21	JW	Patty W	dia
Aug 21	JW	Miss [S] Burdock	dia
Aug 21	Jas Hervey	JW	677
Aug [22?]	JW	Jas Hutton	678
Aug 23	JW	Ben Ingham	dia
Aug 23	JW	Eben Blackwell	678–9
Aug 23	JW	Darracote [? Revd Risdon Darracott]	dia
Aug 23	JW	[Revd Joshua] Read	dia, quot, 683
Aug 24	JW	Revd Ralph Erskine	680–1
Aug 25	JW	Mr Davidson	dia
Aug 25	CW	JW	CWJ, Aug. 25
Aug 26	CW	JW	CWJ, Aug. 26
Sept 3 [MO]	Sam W, Jun	JW	681–2
Sept 10	John Cennick	JW	*AM*, 1797 (Supp), 26–8
Sept 11	Revd Joshua Read	JW	682–5
Sept 12	John Cennick	JW	*AM*, 1778, 179–81

Date	Writer	Recipient	Source
1739			
Sept 14	Ben Ingham	JW	*AM*, 1778, 181-2
Sept 21-2	JW	CW	685-8
Sept 24	JW	Sew[ard]	dia
Sept 25	JW	CW	dia
Sept 25	JW	John Cennick	dia
Sept 28	Revd Ralph Erskine	JW	688-90
Sept 29	JW	Bedd[er]	dia
Sept 29	JW	Ben Seward, etc	dia
Oct 8 [MO]	John Edmonds	JW	MA, 'a[nswere]d 10'
Oct 9	Chas Kinchin	JW	690-1
Oct 10	JW	John Edmonds	docket to Oct. 8
Oct 11	JW	[Miss S Burdock]	dia
Oct 13	JW	Bro [Rt] Harper	dia
Oct 13	JW	John Bray	dia
Oct 13	JW	Mr Rutter	dia
Oct 13	JW	Nancy W	dia
Oct 14	JW	Patty W	dia
Oct 15	JW	[Wm] Fish	dia
Oct 22	JW	J Edmonds	dia
Oct 22	JW	Miss [S] Burdock	dia
Oct 23	JW	John Bray	dia
Oct 23	JW	Mrs Sus W	dia
Oct 23	JW	Spangenberg	dia
Oct 25	JW	Jas Hervey	692-3
Oct 25	JW	Mrs Dutton	dia
Oct 27	JW	Sam W, Jun	693-5
Oct 27	JW	Revd Joshua Read	695-6
Oct 27	JW	Mills	dia
Oct 27	JW	Woods	dia
Oct 27	JW	[Wm] Oxlee	dia
Oct [29?]	[Thos Andrews]	JW	697-8
Oct 30	JW	Capt Whitefield	dia
Nov 6 [TU]	JW	Capt Whitefield	dia
Nov 6	JW	Nancy W	dia
Nov 8	Whitefield	JW	698-9
Nov [14?]	JW	Jas Hutton	699-700
Nov 27	JW	Mr D[unscombe?]	JWJ, Nov. 27
Dec [1?] [SA]	JW	Howell Harris	ref, 701 n.
Dec 6	JW	Thos Price	701-3
Dec [11-12?]	London Meths	JW	JWJ, Dec. 13: 'During my short stay here [Oxford] I received several unpleasing accounts of the state of things in London, a part of which I have subjoined.'
Dec 14	London Meth	JW	JWJ, Dec. [17-18]: 'We long to see you; nay, even

Date	Writer	Recipient	Source
1739			
			those would be glad to see you who will not be directed by you. I believe, indeed, things would be much better if you would come to town.
			'This day I was told, by one that does not belong to the bands, that the society would be divided. I believe brother Hutton, Clarke, Edmonds, and Bray are determined to go on according to Mr. Molther's directions, and to *raise a church*.'
Dec 14	Mrs MacCune	JW	MA, end, 'Ans[wered] by going'
Dec 17	JW	Chas Kinchin	end, 691
Dec 17	JW	Lawford Godfrey	end, Dec. 25; see 691
Dec 25	Lawford Godfrey	JW	*AM*, 1797 (Supp), 21–5

INDEX TO WESLEY'S CORRESPONDENTS

This index notes both the letters published in the main text and (within parentheses) those represented by the quotation or description of specific passages either in other letters or in the Appendix. The references are given in the chronological order of their writing, which does not always coincide with the numerical order of the pages.

Andrews, Thomas: *from*—697–8
'Aspasia': *see* Pendarves, Mrs. Mary

Bedford, Revd. Arthur: *to*—562–6
Blackwell, Ebenezer: *to*—678–9; *from*—675–6
Bolzius, Revd. J. M., and Revd. I. C. Gronau: *to*—448–9
Bray, John: *from*—(526)
Bray, Dr. Thomas, associates of: *to*—494–5
Broughton, Revd. Thomas: *to*—(422–3); *from*—422–3
Burton, Isaac: *from*—(526)
Burton, Revd. John: *to*—439–42, 461–3; *from*—(435*n*, two), 434–7, 508

Causton, Thomas: *to*—511–12, 517–18; *from*—516–17
Cennick, John: *to*—(618); *from*—617–18
Chapman, Mrs.: *to*—502–4
Chapman, Revd. Walter: *from*—531
Chapone, Mrs. Sarah ('Varanese'): *to*—(248); *from*—248
Clayton, Revd. John: *to*—(352), (355), (391–3, two), 614–17; *from*—331–4, 352, 355–6, 391–3, (736), 433, 538–40
Cox, Lady Mary: *to*—532–5
critic, a: *from*—(639)
Cutler, Dr. Timothy: *to*—515; *from*—522–3

Delamotte, Charles: *to*—597; *from*—529–31
Delamotte, William: *from*—567–8
Doble, John: *from*—(526)

Edmonds, John: *to*—630; *from*—(756)
Egmont, John Perceval, Earl of: *to*—486–7
Erskine, Revd. Ralph: *to*—680–1; *from*—688–90

Eyre, Ambrose: *to*—143

[Fallowfield, Mrs.?]: *from*—523–4
followers: *from*—(753, two)
Fox, Mr.: *to*—588–9

Gambold, Revd. John: *to*—550–1, (567*n*); *from*—527
Garden, Revd. Alexander: *from*—519–20
Gentleman's Magazine: *to*—464–6
Georgia Trustees: *to*—496–8, 504–5; *see also* Martyn, Benjamin; Verelst, Harman
Gibson, Edmund, Bishop of London: *to*—(742)
Godfrey, Langford: *to*—(691*n*)
Goole, Revd. John: *to*—353, (353*n*); *from*—(353*n*)
Granville, Ann ('Selima'): *to*—285–7, 300–1, 305–8, 310–13, 317–20, (323), 475–6; *from*—252, 279–80, 301–2, 308–9, 316–17, 323–4
Granville, Mrs. Mary: *to*—259–61; *from*—302
Gronau, Revd. I. C.: *see* Bolzius, J. M.

Habersham, James: *from*—(526)
Hall, Revd. Westley: *to*—(735); *from*—(739), (526), (749); cf. Wesley, Martha (Mrs. Westley Hall)
Harper, Mrs. Robert: *see* Wesley, Emilia
Harris, Howell: *to*—(701*n*)
Harris, Jephthah: *from*—(526)
Hawkins, Mrs. Thomas (Beata): *from*—(470*n*)
Herrnhut, Church at: *to*—571–3; *see also* Le Long, Isaac; Moravians, the; Zinzendorf, Count N. L. von
Hervey, Revd. James: *to*—581–2, 609–10, 673–4, 692–3; *from*—535, 596–7, 624–5, 677
Hoole, Revd. Joseph: *to*—341–2, (728); *from*—(342)

Hopkey, Sophia (Mrs. William Williamson): *to*—490, 498, 512-13, 518
Humphreys, Dr. David: *to*—514-5
Hutcheson, Archibald: *to*—467-8
Hutchings, Revd. John: *from*—(526)
Hutchings, Revd. Richard: *to*—(720)
Hutton, James: *to*—509-10, 535-6, 537,
561-2, 579-81 (and Ingham), 587-8,
590-2, 592-3, 594-6, 619-20, 621-2,
625-8, 629-31, 631-3, 635-7, 637-41,
641-4, 644-5, 647-50, 650-3, 654-6,
656-9, 662-6, 667-8, 672-3, 674-5,
678, 699-700; *from*—(526), 585-7,
(594-5)

Ingham, Revd. Benjamin: *to*—569-71,
579-81 (and Hutton); *from*—(734),
521-2

Kinchin, Revd. Charles: *to*—(690-1);
from—(607n), 690-1
Kirkham, Robert: *from*—231-2
Koker, Dr. Johannes de: *to*-568, 582-3

Lambert, Mrs. John: *see* Wesley, Anne
Law, Revd. William: *to*—386-8, 540-2,
546-8; *from*—543-6, 548-50
Le Long, Isaac: *to*—584-5
London Methodists: *from*—(759)
London Methodist, a: *from*—(759-60)

Martyn, Benjamin: *from*—507
Moravians, the: *to*—566-7; *see also*
Herrnhut, Church at, etc.
Morgan, Richard, Sen.: *to*—335-44, (349),
(349-50), (357n), (357-9, 374), 359-62,
367-71, 379-82; *from*—346-7, 349,
349-50, 357-9, 374-6, 385-6
Morgan, Richard, Jun.: *to*—437-8, 491-2;
from—433-4, 433n); *from, to* Richard
Morgan, Sen., 364-6
Morley, Dr. John: *to*—(711); *from*—240

Newman, Henry: *to*—(726-7), (729-30),
(730), (732, two), (733, two), (734, two),
(735), (736), (739), (443n), (743), (746),
(747), (754); *from*—(729), (730), (734),
(735), (735-6), 443, (742), 463, 475,
495-6, 513-14, 520-1

Oglethorpe, James E.: *to*—(432), 456-8,
470, 492-4; *from*—432, (740-1)

Pendarves, Mrs. Mary ('Aspasia'): *to*—
246-8, 249-50, 250-1, 252-3, 254,
255-7, 261-2, 263, 268, 269, 270-1,
272, (274-6), 274-6, 276-8, 280-1,
287-9, 293-4, 296-9, 303-5, 313-15,
390-1; *from*—248, 251-2, 253-4, 255,
267-8, 268-9, 269, 271, 273-4, 284,
295-6, 299, 309-10, 389-90
Pensford churchwarden: *from*—(647)
Perceval, John: *see* Egmont Earl of
Philipps, Sir John: *to*—446-8, (463,
741-2)
Potter, John, Bishop of Oxford: *to*—(420);
from—420
Price, Thomas: *to*—701-3
Purdy, John (scribe for JW):—645

Read, Revd. Joshua: *to*—(683), 695-6;
from—682-5
Rivington, Charles: *from*—(739)
Roman Catholic priest: *to*—428-30

Savannah magistrates: *to*—519; *see also*
Causton, Thomas
Selby, Revd. Prideaux: *from*—(732)
'Selima': *see* Granville, Ann
Severs, Mr.: *to*—(758)
Seward, William: *to*—603-4; *from*—
(754), (659)
Smith, William: *from*—(731)
S.P.C.K.: *see* Newman, Henry (secretary)
S.P.G.: *to*—516; *see also* Humphreys, Dr.
David
Stebbing, Dr. Henry: *to*—669-72

Tucker, Revd. Josiah: *to*—(755) [? a
letter]

'Varanese': *see* Chapone, Mrs. Sarah
Verelst, Harman: *to*—485-6, (506n), 506;
from—(748)
Vernon, James: *to*—469, 473-4; *from*—445
Viney, Richard: *to*—583-4
Von Reck, Baron P. G. F.: *from*—510-11

Wesley, Charles: *to*—(229-31), (235),
(235-6), (237), 452-4, 455-6, (524-6),
538, 554, 557-8, 560, 630, 660-1, 685-8;
from—229-31, 233-6, 237-9, 454-5,
460-1, 476-9, 483-5, 524-6, 676; *from,
to* Samuel Wesley, Jun., (422n)
Wesley, Emilia (Mrs. Robert Harper):
to—(161), (729), (430-1); *from*—161,
(214-15), (717), (719), (721), (729),
(730), (731), (738), 430-1, 589-90

Wesley, Kezia: *to*—(717), (289-90, two), (731), (735), (746-7); *from*—(717), (719), (719-20), 289-90, (731), (734-5)
Wesley, Martha ('Patty', Mrs. Westley Hall); *to*—(242-3), (272); *from*—242-3, 272-3, (733)
Wesley, Mary ('Molly', Mrs. John White-lamb): *from*—(323)
Wesley, Mehetabel ('Hetty', Mrs. William Wright): *to*—(177)
Wesley, Revd. Samuel, Sen.: *to*—(157-9), (160), (182), (194-5), (223, 224, 225), (225-6), (232), 240-2, 257-9, 264-7, 281-2, 350-1, 395, 397-410, (414-15), 419; *from*—156, 157-9, 160-1, 161-2, 170-1, 176-7, 177, 180-1, 181, 182, 182-3, 189, 193, 194-5, 198-9, 223, 223-4, 224-5, 225-6, 227, 228, 232-3, (337-8), (338-9), (720), 393-4, 395-7, 414-15; *from, to* Revd. Samuel Wesley, Jun., (395-6n)
Wesley, Revd. Samuel, Jun.: *to*—146-8, 190-3, 195-8, 201-5, 220-3, (718), (278), 320-3, (325), (376), 413-14, 417-18, 421, 444-5, (458-60), 487-90, (742), (749), 558-9, 575-8, 594, 599-600, 622-3, 645-7, (681-2), 693-5; *from*—(146), 205-6, 218-20, (718), 278-9, 324-5, 325-6, 376, 410-11, 416, 419-20, 458-60, (744), (575-8), 578-9, 598, 599, 613, 634-5, 681-2

Wesley, Mrs. Susanna: *to*—144-5, (149), 149-52, 153-6, (159), 162-4, 167-70, 173-6, (183), (183-4), (184-5), 186-9, (199), 208-9, (211-12), 212-15, (215-16), (217), (218), (227), (228-9), (232), (239), 244-6, 282-4, (291), (326-7), 327-30, (330-1), (344-5), 347-8, 354-5, (362-4), 371-3, (382-5), 411-13, 418-19, 450-1, 551-3, 555-6, 556-7; *from*—(144-5), 148, 149, 152-3, 157, 159-60, 164-7, 172-3, 178-80, 183-5, 189-90, 193-4, 198 (two), 199, 199-200, 200, 209-11, 211-12, 215-16, 217-18, 226-7, 228-9, 232, 233, 239-40, 291-2, 326-7, 330-1, 344-6, (347), (354), 362-4, 377-8, 382-5, (418-19), 445-6, (601, two)
Whitefield, Revd. George: *to*—(425), (423-4), 427, (471n), 471-3, 527-8, (750), 601-3, (753), 605-9, 610-11, (661n), (668); *from*—(424n), 423-6, 498-9, 505-6, (526), 528-9, 600-1, 604-5, 611-12, (754), 621, 661-2, 667, 668-9, 698-9; *from, to* CW, (661n)
Williamson, Mrs. William: *see* Hopkey, Sophia
Wogan, William: *to*—499-501; *from*—(728)

Zinzendorf, Count N. L. von: *to*—449-50, 573-4; *from*—479-83

CPSIA information can be obtained at www.ICGtesting.com
Printed in the USA
LVOW07*2301270115

424617LV00002B/4/P

9 780687 462162